ISC Exams 2026

AF819935

All in One®

Physics

Class 11

- Simplified Theory
- In-Text & Chapter Exercises
- Exam Pattern Questions
- Sample Papers

Author
Keshav Mohan (M.Sc.)

arihant
SUCCESS AND NOTHING LESS

arihant
SUCCESS AND NOTHING LESS

ARIHANT PRAKASHAN
(School Division Series)

卐 ADMINISTRATIVE & PRODUCTION OFFICES

Regd. Office

'Ramchhaya' 4577/15, Agarwal Road, Darya Ganj, New Delhi -110002
Tele: 011- 47630600, 43518550; Fax: 011- 23280316

卐 *Head Office*

Kalindi, TP Nagar, Meerut (UP) - 250002, Tel: 0121-7156203, 7156204

卐 SALES & SUPPORT OFFICES

Agra, Ahmedabad, Bengaluru, Bareilly, Chennai, Delhi, Guwahati, Hyderabad, Jaipur, Jhansi, Kolkata, Lucknow, Nagpur & Pune.

PO No : *TXT-XX-XXXXXXX-X-XX*

Published By Arihant Publications (India) Ltd.

For further information about the books published by Arihant, log on to www.arihantbooks.com or e-mail at info@arihantbooks.com

Follow us on

卐 PRICE ₹ 590.00

PRODUCTION TEAM

Publishing Managers
Mahendra Singh Rawat &
Keshav Mohan

Cover Designer
Salman Shaikh

Inner Designer
Ankit Tyagi

Project Head
Yojna Sharma

Page Layouting
Subash Chaprana

Proof Reader
Mansi

Index *cum* Study Planner

		Studied	Revised	Exam ready
1. Units and Measurement	***1-30***			
System of Units		☐	☐	☐
Significant Figure		☐	☐	☐
Dimensional of a Physical Quantity		☐	☐	☐
2. Motion in a Straight Line	***31-69***			
General Introduction of Motion		☐	☐	☐
Uniformly Accelerated Motion		☐	☐	☐
3. Motion in a Plane	***70-108***			
Scalar and Vectors		☐	☐	☐
Projectile Motion		☐	☐	☐
4. Laws of Motion	***109-153***			
Newton's Laws of Motion		☐	☐	☐
Friction and Circular Motion		☐	☐	☐
5. Work, Energy and Power	***154-194***			
Work		☐	☐	☐
Energy		☐	☐	☐
Power and Collisions		☐	☐	☐
6. System of Particles and Rotational Motion	***195-231***			
Centre of Mass and Rotational Inertia		☐	☐	☐
Moment of Inertia		☐	☐	☐
7. Gravitation	***232-266***			
Theory of Planetary Motion		☐	☐	☐
Acceleration due to Gravity and Gravitational Potential Energy		☐	☐	☐
Escape Velocity, Geostationary and Solar Satellites		☐	☐	☐
8. Mechanical Properties of Solids	***267-290***			
Elastic and Plastic Behaviour of Solids		☐	☐	☐
Modules of Elasticity or Elastic Modulus		☐	☐	☐

			Studied	Revised	Exam ready

9. Mechanical Properties of Fluids *291-335*
- Hydrostatics
- Hydrodynamics
- Surface Tension and Surface Energy

10. Thermal Properties of Matter *336-370*
- Temperature and Its Measurement
- Calorimetry
- Heat Transfer

11. Thermodynamics *371-401*
- Heat and First Law of Thermodynamics
- Heat Engine and Second Law of Thermodynamics

12. Kinetic Theory of Gases *402-429*
- Kinetic Interpretation of Behaviour of Gases
- Motion of Gas Molecules

13. Oscillations *430-462*
- Simple Harmonic Motion
- Force and Energy in SHM and System Executing SHM

14. Waves *463-502*
- Waves and Their Properties
- Superposition of Waves and Beats
- Stationary or Standing Wave

Sample Question Papers (1-3) *505-528*

One Book- Endless Features

to Help you Succeed

In this Chapter

At the start of each chapter, all the topics of the chapter have been listed, so that students may know what they are going to study.

CHAPTER
06
Work, Energy and Power

In daily life, we generally use the terms work, energy and power. Work is any activity involving mental or physical effort.
Whereas, energy is our capacity to do work. The word power is also used in everyday life with different shades of meaning. In this chapter, we will study these terms from the vision of science.

- Work
- Energy
- Power and Collision

Example 2 A coolie is holding a bag by applying a force of 15 N. He moves forward and covers the horizontal distance of 8 m and then he climbs up and covers the vertical distance of 10 m. What will be the work done by him?

Sol. Given, $F = 15\,\text{N}, s_1 = 8\,\text{m}$ and $s_2 = 10\,\text{m}$

As coolie is walking horizontally, therefore, the angle between the bag and distance covered is 90°.

$\therefore$ Work done to cover the distance of 8 m.

$$W_1 = Fs_1 \cos\theta = 15 \times 8 \cos 90^\circ = 0\,\text{J}$$

When the coolie climb.

Thus, $\theta = 0^\circ$

The work done, $W_2 = Fs_2 \cos\theta = 15 \times 10 \times \cos 0^\circ = 150\,\text{J}$

The net work done by him

$$W = W_1 + W_2 = 0 + 150 = 150\,\text{J}$$

Complete Theory in Each Chapter

Each chapter has Complete, Easy to Understand and Simplified theory covering latest syllabus and latest NCERT Textbook. Theory is developed in such a way that it is Suitable for all typer of learners.

Solved Examples

To explain the application of concept, Solved Examples have been given in between the theory. These examples have been solved in Step-by-Step manner, so that students can learn the problem solving process completely.

TOPIC
01 **Work**

Work is said to be done by a force, when the body is displaced actua through some distance in the direction of the applied force. Thus, w done on a body only if the following two conditions are satisfied:

(i) A force acts on the body.

(ii) The point of application of the force moves in the direction of force.

e.g. Work is done when an engine pulls a train, a man goes up a hil pulls a cart, etc.

Topic Practice 1

Multiple Choice Questions

(1 Mark)

1. 1 kilowatt hour (kWh) = ...*A*... joule. Here, *A* refers to
 (a) 4×10^2 (b) 3.6×10^6 (c) 4×10^4 (d) 3.6×10^5

2. The earth, moving around the sun in a circular orbit, is acted upon by a force and hence work done on the earth by the force is
 (a) zero (b) + ve
 (c) – ve (d) None of these

Topical Exercises

To make students understand the chapter in a smooth part-by-part manner, Topical Exercises have been given in each chapter. These Exercises help students to assess the understanding of related concepts at regular interval.

One Book- Endless Features
to Help you Succeed

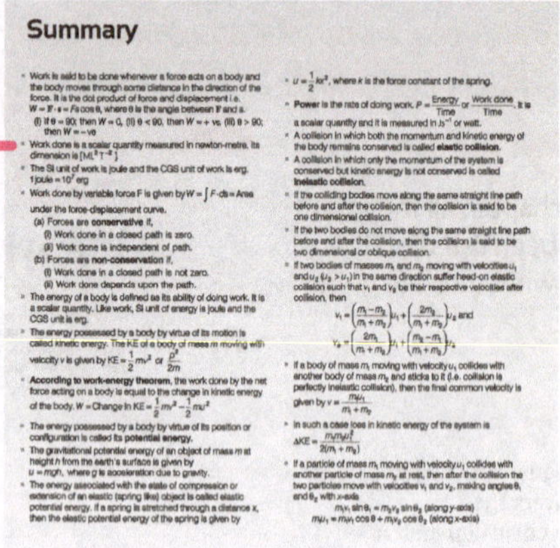

Summary

- Work is said to be done whenever a force acts on a body and the body moves through some distance in the direction of the force. It is the dot product of force and displacement i.e. $W = \mathbf{F} \cdot \mathbf{s} = Fs\cos\theta$, where θ is the angle between $\mathbf{F}$ and $\mathbf{s}$.
  (i) If $\theta = 90$; then $W = 0$, (ii) $\theta < 90$, then $W = +$ ve, (iii) $\theta > 90$; then $W = -$ve
- Work done is a scalar quantity measured in newton-metre. Its dimension is $[ML^2T^{-2}]$
- The SI unit of work is joule and the CGS unit of work is erg. 1 joule $= 10^7$ erg
- Work done by variable force F is given by $W = \int F \cdot ds =$ Area under the force-displacement curve.
  (a) Forces are **conservative** if,
    (i) Work done in a closed path is zero.
    (ii) Work done is independent of path.
  (b) Forces are **non-conservation** if,
    (i) Work done in a closed path is not zero.
    (ii) Work done depends upon the path.
- The energy of a body is defined as its ability of doing work. It is a scalar quantity. Like work, SI unit of energy is joule and the CGS unit is erg.
- The energy possessed by a body by virtue of its motion is called kinetic energy. The KE of a body of mass m moving with velocity v is given by $KE = \frac{1}{2}mv^2$ or $\frac{p^2}{2m}$
- **According to work-energy theorem**, the work done by the net force acting on a body is equal to the change in kinetic energy of the body. $W =$ Change in $KE = \frac{1}{2}mv^2 - \frac{1}{2}mu^2$
- The energy possessed by a body by virtue of its position or configuration is called its **potential energy**.
- The gravitational potential energy of an object of mass m at height h from the earth's surface is given by $U = mgh$, where g is acceleration due to gravity.
- The energy associated with the state of compression or extension of an elastic (spring like) object is called elastic potential energy. If a spring is stretched through a distance x, then the elastic potential energy of the spring is given by
- $U = \frac{1}{2}kx^2$, where k is the force constant of the spring.
- **Power** is the rate of doing work. $P = \frac{\text{Energy}}{\text{Time}}$ or $\frac{\text{Work done}}{\text{Time}}$. It is a scalar quantity and it is measured in Js^{-1} or watt.
- A collision in which both the momentum and kinetic energy of the body remains conserved is called **elastic collision.**
- A collision in which only the momentum of the system is conserved but kinetic energy is not conserved is called **inelastic collision.**
- If the colliding bodies move along the same straight line path before and after the collision, then the collision is said to be one dimensional collision.
- If the two bodies do not move along the same straight line path before and after the collision, then the collision is said to be two dimensional or oblique collision.
- If two bodies of masses m_1 and m_2 moving with velocities u_1 and u_2 ($u_2 > u_1$) in the same direction suffer head-on elastic collision such that v_1 and v_2 be their respective velocities after collision, then

$$v_1 = \left(\frac{m_1 - m_2}{m_1 + m_2}\right)u_1 + \left(\frac{2m_2}{m_1 + m_2}\right)u_2 \text{ and}$$
$$v_2 = \left(\frac{2m_1}{m_1 + m_2}\right)u_1 + \left(\frac{m_2 - m_1}{m_1 + m_2}\right)u_2$$

- If a body of mass m_1 moving with velocity u_1 collides with another body of mass m_2 and sticks to it (i.e. collision is perfectly inelastic collision), then the final common velocity is given by $v = \frac{m_1u_1}{m_1 + m_2}$
- In such a case loss in kinetic energy of the system is $\Delta KE = \frac{m_1m_2u_1^2}{2(m_1 + m_2)}$
- If a particle of mass m_1 moving with velocity u_1 collides with another particle of mass m_2 at rest, then after the collision the two particles move with velocities v_1 and v_2, making angles θ_1 and θ_2 with x-axis

$$m_1v_1\sin\theta_1 = m_2v_2\sin\theta_2 \text{ (along y-axis)}$$
$$m_1u_1 = m_1v_1\cos\theta + m_2v_2\cos\theta_2 \text{ (along x-axis)}$$

Chapter Summary

Summary of chapter given at the end helps to revise the chapter quickly at the time of examination or routine school tests.

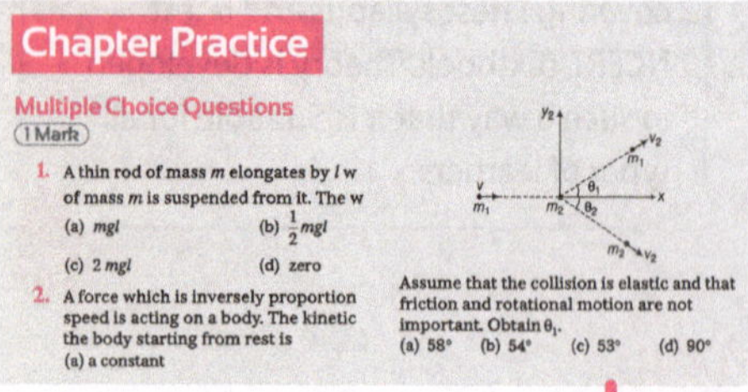

Chapter Practice

Multiple Choice Questions

(1 Mark)

1. A thin rod of mass m elongates by l w of mass m is suspended from it. The w
   (a) mgl (b) $\frac{1}{2}mgl$
   (c) $2\,mgl$ (d) zero
2. A force which is inversely proportion speed is acting on a body. The kinetic the body starting from rest is
   (a) a constant

Assume that the collision is elastic and that friction and rotational motion are not important. Obtain θ_1.
(a) 58° (b) 54° (c) 53° (d) 90°

Chapter Practice

The students can check their understanding of the chapter through Chapter Practice given at the end of each chapter.

Sample Question Papers

To make students practice of examination in real sense, there are 3 Sample Question Papers at the end. All these Sample Questions Papers are exactly prepared on the latest syllabus & pattern of examination.

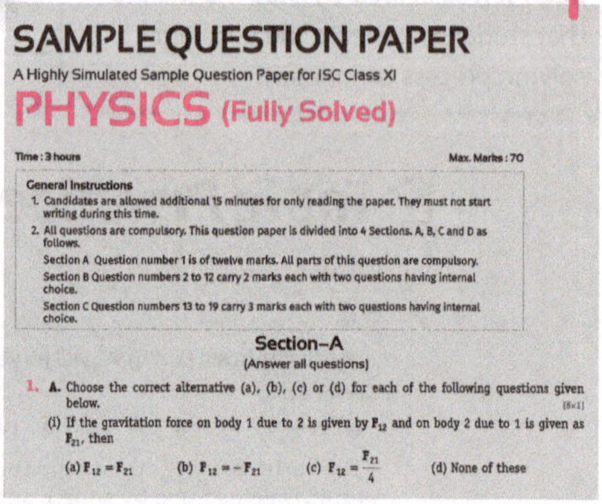

SAMPLE QUESTION PAPER

A Highly Simulated Sample Question Paper for ISC Class XI

PHYSICS (Fully Solved)

Time : 3 hours

Max. Marks : 70

General Instructions

1. Candidates are allowed additional 15 minutes for only reading the paper. They must not start writing during this time.
2. All questions are compulsory. This question paper is divided into 4 Sections. A, B, C and D as follows.
   Section A Question number 1 is of twelve marks. All parts of this question are compulsory.
   Section B Question numbers 2 to 12 carry 2 marks each with two questions having internal choice.
   Section C Question numbers 13 to 19 carry 3 marks each with two questions having internal choice.

Section–A

(Answer all questions)

1. **A.** Choose the correct alternative (a), (b), (c) or (d) for each of the following questions given below. [8×1]
   (i) If the gravitation force on body 1 due to 2 is given by $\mathbf{F}_{12}$ and on body 2 due to 1 is given as $\mathbf{F}_{21}$, then
   (a) $\mathbf{F}_{12} = \mathbf{F}_{21}$ (b) $\mathbf{F}_{12} = -\mathbf{F}_{21}$ (c) $\mathbf{F}_{12} = \frac{\mathbf{F}_{21}}{4}$ (d) None of these

Latest Course Structure

There will be two papers in the subject.

PAPER I Theory	70 marks
PAPER II Practical	15 marks
Project Work	10 marks
Practical File	5 marks

PAPER 1 THEORY 70 Marks

SN	Units	Total Weightage
1.	Physical World and Measurement	23 Marks
2.	Kinematics	
3.	Laws of Motion	
4.	Work, Energy and Power	17 Marks
5.	Motion of System of Particles and Rigid Body	
6.	Gravitation	
7.	Properties of Bulk Matter	20 Marks
8.	Heat and Thermodynamics	
9.	Behaviour of Perfect Gases and Kinetic Theory of Gases	
10.	Oscillations and Waves	10 Marks
	Total	**70 Marks**

Note

(i) Unless otherwise specified, only SI Units are to be used while teaching and learning, as well as for answering questions.

(ii) All physical quantities to be defined as and when they are introduced along with their units and dimensions.

(iii) Numerical problems are included from all topics except where they are specifically excluded or where only qualitative treatment is required.

1. PHYSICAL WORLD AND MEASUREMENT

Units and Measurements Measurement : need for measurement; units of measurement; systems of units : fundamental and derived units in SI; errors in significant figures.

Dimensional formulae of physical quantities and constants, dimensional analysis and its applications.

(a) *Importance of measurement in scientific studies; physics is a science of measurement. Unit as a reference standard of measurement; essential properties. Systems of units; CGS, FPS, MKS, MKSA and SI; the seven base units of SI selected by the general conference of weights and measures in 1971 and their definitions, list of fundamental, supplementary and derived physical quantities; their units and symbols (strictly as per rule); sub units and multiple units using prefixes for powers of 10 (from atto for 10^{-18} to tera for 10^{12}); other common units such as fermi, angstrom (now outdated), light year, astronomical unit and parsec. A new unit of mass used in atomic physics is unified atomic mass unit with symbol* u *(not amu); rules for writing the names of units and their symbols in SI (upper case/lower case). Derived units (with correct symbols); special names wherever applicable; expression in terms of base units (e.g.* $N = \text{kg m}/\text{s}^2$*).*

(b) *Significant figures; their significance; rules for counting the number of significant figures; rules for (a) addition and subtraction, (b) multiplication and division; 'rounding off' the uncertain digits; order of magnitude as statement of magnitudes in powers of 10; examples from magnitudes of common physical quantities–size, mass, time, etc.*

(c) *Dimensions of physical quantities; dimensional formula; express derived units in terms of base units (*$N = \text{kg} - \text{m s}^{-2}$*); use symbol [ ] for dimensions of or base unit of; e.g.: dimensional formula of force in terms of fundamental quantities written as* $[F] = [\text{MLT}^{-2}]$*. Principle of homogeneity of dimensions. Expressions in terms of SI base units and dimensional formula may be obtained for all physical quantities as and when new physical quantities are introduced.*

(d) *Use of dimensional analysis to (i) check the dimensional correctness of a formula/equation; (ii) to obtain the dimensional formula of any derived physical quantity including constants; (iii) to convert units from one system to another; limitations of dimensional analysis.*

2. KINEMATICS

(i) **Motion in a Straight Line** Frame of references, Motion in a straight line (one dimension) : Elementary concepts of differentiation and integration for describing motion, uniform and non-uniform motion, instantaneous velocity

and uniformly accelerated motion, velocity-time and position-time graphs. Relations for uniformly accelerated motion (graphical treatment).

Frame of reference, concept of point mass, rest and motion; distance and displacement, average speed and average velocity, uniform velocity, instantaneous speed and instantaneous velocity, acceleration, instantaneous acceleration, s-t, v-t and a-t graphs for uniform acceleration and conclusions drawn from these graphs; kinematic equations of motion for objects in uniformly accelerated rectilinear motion derived using graphical, calculus or analytical method, motion of an object under gravity, (one dimensional motion).

Differentiation as rate of change; examples from physics–speed, acceleration, velocity gradient, etc. Formulae for differentiation of simple functions: x^n, $\sin x$, $\cos x$, e^x and $\ln x$. Simple ideas about integration–mainly. $\int x^n \cdot dx$. Both definite and indefinite

integrals to be mentioned (elementary calculus not to be evaluated).

(ii) **Motion in a Plane** Scalar and vector quantities with examples. Position and displacement vectors, general vectors and their notations; equality of vectors, addition and subtraction of vectors, unit vector; resolution of a vector in a plane, rectangular components, scalar and vector product of two vectors. Projectile motion and uniform circular motion.

(a) *General vectors and notation, position and displacement vector. Vectors explained using displacement as a prototype–along a straight line (one dimensional), on a plane surface (two dimensional) and in an open space not confined to a line or a plane (three dimensional); symbol and representation; a scalar quantity, its representation and unit, equality of vectors. Unit vectors denoted by $\hat{i}, \hat{j}, \hat{k}$ orthogonal unit vectors along x, y and z axes respectively. Examples of one dimensional vector $\vec{v}_1 = a\hat{i}$ or $b\hat{j}$ or $c\hat{k}$ where a, b, c are scalar quantities or numbers; $\vec{v}_2 = a\hat{i} + b\hat{j}$ is a two dimensional or planar vector, $\vec{v}_3 = a\hat{i} + b\hat{j} + c\hat{k}$ is a three dimensional or space vector. Concept of null vector and co-planar vectors.*

(b) ***Addition**: use displacement as an example; obtain triangle law of addition; graphical and analytical treatment; discuss commutative and associative properties of vector addition (Proof not required). Parallelogram Law; sum and difference; derive expressions for magnitude and direction from parallelogram law; special cases : subtraction as special case of addition with direction reversed; use of triangle law for subtraction also; if $\vec{a} + \vec{b} = \vec{c}$; $\vec{c} - \vec{a} = \vec{b}$; In a parallelogram, if one diagonal is the sum, the other diagonal is the difference; addition and subtraction with vectors expressed in terms of unit vectors $\hat{i}, \hat{j}, \hat{k}$; multiplication of a vector by a real number.*

(c) *Use triangle law of addition to express a vector in terms of its components. If $\vec{a} + \vec{b} = \vec{c}$ is an addition fact, $\vec{c} = \vec{a} + \vec{b}$ is a resolution; $\vec{a}$ and $\vec{b}$ are components of $\vec{c}$. Rectangular components, relation between components, resultant and angle between them. Dot (or scalar) product of vectors $\vec{a} \cdot \vec{b} = ab\cos\theta$; example $W = \vec{F} \cdot \vec{s} = Fs\cos\theta$. Special case of $\theta = 0°$, $90°$ and $180°$. Vector (or cross) product $\vec{a} \times \vec{b} = [ab\sin\theta]\,\hat{n}$; example : torque $\vec{\tau} = \vec{r} \times \vec{F}$; Special cases using unit vectors $\hat{i}, \hat{j}, \hat{k}$ for $\vec{a} \cdot \vec{b}$ and $\vec{a} \times \vec{b}$.*

(d) *Various terms related to projectile motion; obtain equations of trajectory, time of flight, maximum height, horizontal range, instantaneous velocity, [projectile motion on an inclined plane not included]. Examples of projectile motion.*

(e) *Examples of uniform circular motion : details to be covered in unit 3 (d).*

3. LAWS OF MOTION

General concept of force, inertia, Newton's first law of motion; momentum and Newton's second law of motion; impulse; Newton's third law of motion.

Law of conservation of linear momentum and its applications.

Equilibrium of concurrent forces. Friction: Static and kinetic friction, laws of friction, rolling friction, lubrication.

Dynamics of uniform circular motion : Centripetal force, examples of circular motion (vehicle on a level circular road, vehicle on a banked road).

(i) Newton's first law : Statement and explanation; concept of inertia, mass, force; law of inertia; mathematically, if $\Sigma F = 0$, $a = 0$.

Newton's second law : $\vec{p} = m\vec{v}$; $\vec{F} \propto \frac{d\vec{p}}{dt}$; $\vec{F} = k\frac{d\vec{p}}{dt}$. Define unit of force so that $k = 1$; $\vec{F} = \frac{d\vec{p}}{dt}$; a vector equation. For classical physics with v not large and mass m remaining constant, obtain $\vec{F} = m\,\vec{a}$. For $v \to c$, m is not constant. Then $m = m_0 / \sqrt{1 - v^2/c^2}$ Note that $F = ma$ is the special case for classical mechanics.It is a vector equation. $\vec{a} \| \vec{F}$. Also, this can be resolved into three scalar equations $F_x = ma_x$ etc. Application to numerical problems; introduce tension force, normal reaction force. If $a = 0$ (body in equilibrium), $F = 0$. Statement, derivation and explanation of principle of conservation of linear momentum. Impulse of a force : $F\Delta t = \Delta p$.

Newton's third law: Obtain it using Law of Conservation of linear momentum. Proof of Newton's second law as real law. Systematic solution of problems in mechanics; isolate a part of a system, identify all forces acting on it; draw a free body diagram representing the part as a point and representing all forces by line segments, solve for resultant force which is equal to $m\vec{a}$. Simple problems on "Connected bodies" (not involving two pulleys).

(ii) Force diagrams; resultant or net force from triangle law of forces, parallelogram law or resolution of forces. Apply net force $\Sigma\vec{F} = m\,\vec{a}$.

Again for equilibrium $a = 0$ and $\Sigma F = 0$. Conditions of equilibrium of a rigid body under three coplanar forces. Discuss ladder problem.

(iii) Friction; classical view and modern view of friction, static friction a self-adjusting force; limiting value; kinetic friction or sliding friction; rolling friction, examples.

Laws of friction : Two laws of static friction; (similar) two laws of kinetic friction; coefficient of friction $\mu_s = f_s(max) / N$ and $\mu_k = f_k / N$; graphs. Friction as a non-conservative force; motion under friction, net force in Newton's second law is calculated including f_k. Motion along a rough inclined plane–both up and down. Pulling and pushing of a roller. Angle of friction and angle of repose. Lubrication, use of bearings, streamlining, etc.

(iv) Angular displacement (θ), angular velocity (ω), angular acceleration (α) and their relations. Concept of centripetal acceleration; obtain an expression for this acceleration using $\Delta\vec{v}$. Magnitude and direction of $\vec{a}$ same as that of $\Delta\vec{v}$; Centripetal acceleration; the cause of this acceleration is a force–also called centripetal force; the name only indicates its direction, it is not a new type of force, motion in a vertical circle; banking of road and railway track (conical pendulum is excluded).

4. WORK, POWER AND ENERGY

Work done by a constant force and a variable force; kinetic energy, work-energy theorem, power.

Potential energy, potential energy of a spring, conservative forces: Conservative and non-conservative forces. Concept of collision: elastic and inelastic collisions in one and two dimensions.

(i) Work done $W = \vec{F}\cdot\vec{s} = Fs\cos\theta$. If F is variable $dW = \vec{F}\cdot d\vec{s}$ and $W = \int dW = \int \vec{F}\cdot d\vec{s}$, for $\vec{F} \| d\vec{s}$ $\vec{F}\cdot d\vec{s} = Fds$ therefore, $W = \int F\,ds$ is the area under the F-s graph or if F can be expressed in terms of s, $\int F\,ds$ can be evaluated. Example, work done in stretching a spring $W = \int Fdx = \int kxdx = \frac{1}{2}kx^2$. This is also the potential energy stored in the stretched spring $U = 1/2\,kx^2$.

Kinetic energy and its expression, Work-Energy theorem $E = W$. Law of conservation of energy; oscillating spring. $U + K = E = K_{max} = U_{max}$ (for $U = 0$ and $K = 0$ respectively); graph different forms of energy and their transformations. $E = mc^2$ (no derivation). Power $P = W/t$; $P = \vec{F}\cdot\vec{v}$.

(ii) Collision in one dimension; derivation of velocity equation for general case of $m_1 \neq m_2$ and $u_1 \neq u_2 = 0$; Special cases for $m_1 = m_2 = m$; $m_1 >> m_2$ or $m_1 << m_2$. Oblique collisions i.e. collision in two dimensions.

5. MOTION OF SYSTEM OF PARTICLES AND RIGID BODY

Idea of centre of mass : centre of mass of a two-particle system, momentum conservation and centre of mass motion. Centre of mass of a rigid body; centre of mass of a uniform rod.

Moment of a force, torque, angular momentum, laws of conservation of angular momentum and its applications.

Equilibrium of rigid bodies, rigid body rotation and equations of rotational motion, comparative study of linear and rotational motions.

Moment of inertia, radius of gyration, moments of inertia for simple geometrical objects (no derivation).

(i) Definition of centre of mass (CM), centre of mass (CM) for a two particle system $m_1x_1 + m_2x_2 = Mx_{cm}$; differentiating, get the equation for v_{cm} and a_{cm}; general equation for N particles - many particles system; [need not go into more details]; centre of gravity, principle of moment, discuss ladder problem, concept of a rigid body; kinetic energy of a rigid body rotating about a fixed axis in terms of that of the particles of the body; hence, define moment of inertia and radius of gyration; physical significance of moment of inertia; unit and dimension; depends on mass and axis of rotation; it is rotational inertia; equations of rotational motions.

Applications: only expression for the moment of inertia, I (about the symmetry axis) of : (i) a ring; (ii) a solid and a hollow cylinder, (iii) a thin rod (iv) a solid and a hollow sphere, (v) a disc–only formulae (no derivations required).

(a) Definition of torque (vector); $\vec{\tau} = \vec{r} \times \vec{F}$ and angular momentum $\vec{L} = \vec{r} \times \vec{p}$ for a particle (no derivations); differentiate to obtain $d\vec{L}/dt = \vec{\tau}$; similar to Newton's second law of motion (linear); hence $\tau = I\alpha$ and $L = I\omega$ (only scalar equation); law of conservation of angular momentum; simple applications. Comparison of linear and rotational motions.

6. GRAVITATION

Kepler's laws of planetary motion, universal law of gravitation. Acceleration due to gravity (g) and its variation with altitude, latitude and depth.

Gravitational potential and gravitational potential energy, escape velocity, orbital velocity of a satellite.

(i) Newton's law of universal gravitation; Statement; unit and dimensional formula of universal gravitational constant, G [Cavendish experiment not required]; gravitational acceleration on surface of the earth (g), weight of a body $w = mg$ from $F = ma$.

(ii) Relation between g and G. Derive the expression for variation of g above and below the surface of the earth; graph; mention variation of g with latitude and rotation, (without derivation).

(iii) Gravitational field, intensity of gravitational field and potential at a point in earth's gravitational field. $V_p = W_{\infty p}/m$. Derive expression (by integration) for the gravitational potential difference $\Delta V = V_B - V_A = G\cdot M(1/r_A - 1/r_B)$; here $V_p = V(r) = -GM/r$; negative sign for attractive force field; define gravitational potential energy of a mass m in the earth's field; expression for gravitational potential energy $U(r) = W_{\infty p} = m\cdot V(r) = -G\,M\,m/r$; show that $\Delta U = mgh$, for $h << R$. Relation between intensity and acceleration due to gravity.

(iv) Derive expression for the escape velocity of earth using energy consideration; v_e depends on mass of the earth; for moon v_e is less as mass of moon is less; consequence-no atmosphere on the moon.

(v) Satellites (both natural (moon) and artificial) in uniform circular motion around the earth; Derive the expression for orbital velocity and time period; note the centripetal acceleration is caused (or centripetal force is provided) by the force of gravity exerted by the earth on the satellite; the acceleration of the satellite is the acceleration due to gravity[$g' = g(R/R+h)^2$; $F'_G = mg'$].

(vi) Kepler's laws of planetary motion: Explain the three laws using diagrams. Proof of third law (for circular orbits only).

7. PROPERTIES OF BULK MATTER

(i) **Mechanical Properties of Solids :** Elasticity in solids, stress-strain relationship, Hooke's law, Young's modulus,bulk modulus, shear modulus of rigidity, Poisson's ratio; elastic energy. work strain energy.

(ii) **Mechanical Properties of Fluids :** Pressure due to a fluid column; Pascal's law and its applications (hydraulic lift and hydraulic brakes), effect of gravity on fluid pressure.

Viscosity, Stokes' law, terminal velocity, streamline and turbulent flow, critical velocity, Bernoulli's theorem and its simple applications.

Surface energy and surface tension, angle of contact, excess of pressure across a curved surface, application of surface tension ideas to drops, bubbles and capillary rise.

(a) Pressure in a fluid, Pascal's law and its applications.

(b) General characteristics of fluid flow; equation of continuity $v_1a_1 = v_2a_2$; conditions; applications like use of nozzle at the end of a hose; Bernoulli's principle (theorem); assumptions–incompressible liquid, streamline (steady) flow, non-viscous and irrotational liquid–ideal liquid; derivation of equation; applications of Bernoulli's theorem atomizer, dynamic uplift, Magnus effect etc.

(c) *Streamline and turbulent flow-examples; streamlines do not intersect (like electric and magnetic lines of force); tubes of flow; number of streamlines per unit area α velocity of flow (from equation of continuity $v_1a_1 = v_2a_2$); critical velocity; Poiseuille's formula with numericals.*

(d) *Viscous drag; Newton's formula for viscosity, co-efficient of viscosity and its units.*

Flow of fluids (liquids and gases), laminar flow, internal friction between layers of fluid, between fluid and the solid with which the fluid is in relative motion; examples; viscous drag is a force of friction; mobile and viscous liquids.

Velocity gradient dv / dx (space rate of change of velocity); viscous drag $F = \eta A(dv/dx)$; coefficient of viscocity $\eta = \frac{F}{A}\left(\frac{dv}{dx}\right)$ depends on the nature of the liquid and its temperature; units: N-s/m² and dyne-s/cm² = poise.1 poise = 0.1 N-s/m².

(e) *Stoke's law, motion of a sphere falling through a fluid, hollow rigid sphere rising to the surface of a liquid, parachute, obtain the expression of terminal velocity; forces acting; viscous drag, a force proportional to velocity; Stoke's law; v-t graph.*

(f) *Surface tension (molecular theory), drops and bubbles, angle of contact, work done in stretching a surface and surface energy, capillary rise, measurement of surface tension by capillary (uniform bore) rise method. Excess pressure across a curved surface, application of surface tension for drops and bubbles.*

8. HEAT AND THERMODYNAMICS

(i) **Thermal Properties of Matter :** Heat, temperature, thermal expansion; thermal expansion of solids, liquids and gases, anomalous expansion of water; specific heat capacity, c_P-c_V calorimetry; change of state, specific latent heat capacity.

Heat transfer-conduction, convection and radiation, thermal conductivity, qualitative ideas of blackbody radiation, Wein's displacement law .

(a) *Temperature and heat, measurement of temperature (scales and inter conversion). Ideal gas equation and absolute temperature, thermal expansion in solids, liquids and gases.*

Specific heat capacity, calorimetry, change of state, latent heat capacity, steady state and temperature gradient. Thermal conductivity; co-efficient of thermal conductivity, Use of good and poor conductors, Searle's experiment, (Lee's Disc method is not required). Convection with examples.

(b) *Black body is now called ideal or cavity radiator and black body radiation is cavity radiation; Stefan's law is now known as Stefan Boltzmann law as Boltzmann derived it theoretically. There is multiplicity of technical terms related to thermal radiation–radiant intensity $I(T)$ for total radiant power (energy radiated/second) per unit area of the surface, in W/m², $I(T) = \sigma T^4$; dimension and SI unit of σ. For practical radiators $I = \epsilon \cdot \sigma T^4$; where ϵ (dimension less) is called emissivity of the surface material; $\epsilon = 1$ for ideal radiators. The spectral radiancy $R(\lambda) \cdot I(T) = \int_0^{\alpha} R(\lambda)\, d\lambda$. Graph of $R(\lambda)$ versus λ for different temperatures. Area under the graph is $I(T)$. The λ corresponding to maximum value or R is called λ_{max}; decreases with increase in temperature.*

Wien's displacement law; Stefan's law and Newton's law of cooling. [Deductions from Stefan's law not necessary].

(ii) **Thermodynamics** Thermal equilibrium and definition of temperature (zeroth law of thermodynamics), heat, work and internal energy. First law of thermodynamics, isothermal and adiabatic processes.

Second law of thermodynamics : reversible and irreversible processes.

(a) *Thermal equilibrium and zeroth law of thermodynamics : Self explanatory.*

(b) *First law of thermodynamics:*

Concept of heat (Q) as the energy that is transferred (due to temperature difference only) and not stored; the energy that is stored in a body or system as potential and kinetic energy is called internal energy (U). Internal energy is a state property (only elementary ideas) whereas, heat is not; first law is a statement of conservation of energy, when, in general, heat (Q) is transferred to a body (system), internal energy (U) of the system changes and some work W is done by the system; then $Q = \Delta U + W$; also $W = \int pdV$ for working substance–an ideal gas; explain the meaning of symbols (with examples) and sign convention carefully (as used in physics : $Q > 0$ when added to a system, $\Delta U > 0$ when U increases or temperature rises and $W > 0$ when work is done by the system). Special cases for $Q = 0$ (adiabatic), $\Delta U = 0$ (isothermal) and $W = 0$ (isochoric).

(c) *Isothermal and adiabatic changes in a perfect gas described in terms of p-V graph; pV = constant (isothermal) and pV^{γ} = constant (adiabatic); joule and calorie relation (derivation of pV^{γ} = constant not required).*

Note that 1 cal = 4.186 J exactly and J (so-called mechanical equivalent of heat) should not be used in equations. In equations, it is understood that each term as well as the LHS and RHS are in the same units; it could be all joules or all calories.

(d) *Derive an expression for work done in isothermal and adiabatic processes; principal and molar heat capacities; C_p and C_V; relation between C_p and C_V ($C_p - C_V = R$). Work done as area bounded by p-V graph.*

(e) *Second law of thermodynamics, Carnot's cycle. Some practical applications.*

Only one statement each in terms of Kelvin's impossible steam engine and Clausius' impossible refrigerator. Brief explanation of the law. Reversible and irreversible processes, Carnot's cycle–describe realisation from source and sink of infinite thermal capacity, thermal insulation, etc. Explain using p-V graph (isothermal process and adiabatic process) expression and numericals (without derivation) for efficiency $\eta = 1 - T_2 / T_1$.

9. BEHAVIOUR OF PERFECT GASES AND KINETIC THEORY OF GASES

(i) **Kinetic Theory** Equation of state of a perfect gas, work done in compressing a gas. Kinetic theory of gases–assumptions, concept of pressure. Kinetic interpretation of temperature; rms speed of gas molecules; degrees of freedom, law of equipartition of energy (statement only) and applications to specific heat capacities of gases; concept of mean free path, Avogadro's number.

(a) *Kinetic Theory of gases; derive $p = 1/3\rho\overline{c^2}$ from the assumptions and applying Newton's laws of motion. The average thermal velocity (rms value) $c_{rms} = \sqrt{3p/\rho}$; calculations for air, hydrogen and their comparison with common speeds. Effect of temperature and pressure on rms speed of gas molecules.*

[Note that $pV = nRT$ the ideal gas equation cannot be derived from kinetic theory of ideal gas. Hence, neither can other gas laws; $pV = nRT$ is an experimental result. Comparing this with $p = 1/3\rho\overline{c^2}$, from kinetic theory of gases, a kinetic interpretation of temperature can be obtained as explained in the next sub unit].

(b) *From kinetic theory for an ideal gas (obeying all the assumptions especially no intermolecular attraction and negligibly small size of molecules, we get $p = (1/3)\rho\overline{c^2}$ or $pV = (1/3)M\overline{c^2}$. (No further, as temperature is not a concept of kinetic theory). From experimentally obtained gas laws, we have the ideal gas equation (obeyed by some gases at low pressure and high temperature) $pV = RT$ for one mole. Combining these two results (assuming they can be combined), $RT = (1/3)M\overline{c^2} = (2/3)\cdot 1/2M\overline{c^2} = (2/3)K$; Hence, kinetic energy of 1 mole of an ideal gas $K = (3/2)RT$. Average K for 1 molecule $= K/N = (3/2)RT/N = (3/2)kT$, where k is Boltzmann's constant. So, temperature T can be interpreted as a measure of the average kinetic energy of the molecule of a gas.*

(c) *Degrees of freedom and calculation of specific heat capacities for all types of gases. Concept of the law of equipartition of energy (derivation not required). Concept of mean free path and Avogadro's number N_A.*

10. OSCILLATIONS AND WAVES

(i) **Oscillations** Periodic motion, time period, frequency, displacement as a function of time, periodic functions and their Application.

Simple harmonic motion (SHM) and its equation; phase; oscillations of a spring, restoring force and force constant; energy in SHM. Kinetic and potential energies; simple pendulum and derivation of expression for its time period.

Simple harmonic motion. Periodic motion, time period T and frequency f, $f = 1/T$; uniform circular motion and its projection on a diameter defined SHM; displacement, amplitude, phase and epoch, velocity, acceleration, time period; characteristics of SHM; Relation between linear simple harmonic motion and uniform circular motion. Differential equation of SHM. $d^2y/dt^2 + \omega^2 y = 0$ from the nature of force acting $F = -ky$; solution $y = A\sin(\omega t + \phi_0)$ where $\omega^2 = k/m$; obtain expressions for velocity, acceleration, time period T and frequency f. Graphical representation of displacement, velocity and acceleration. Examples, simple pendulum, a mass m attached to a spring of spring constant k. Derivation of time period of simple harmonic motion of a simple pendulum, mass on a spring (horizontal and vertical oscillations) Kinetic and potential energies at a point in simple harmonic motion. Total energy $E = U + K$ (potential + kinetic) is conserved. Draw graphs of U, K and E versus y.

(ii) **Waves** Wave motion, transverse and longitudinal waves, speed of travelling wave displacement relation for a progressive wave, principle of superposition of waves, reflection of waves, standing waves in strings and organ pipes, fundamental mode and harmonics, beats.

(a) *Transverse and longitudinal waves : characteristics of a harmonic wave; graphical representation of a harmonic wave. Distinction between transverse and longitudinal waves; examples; displacement, amplitude, time period, frequency, wavelength, derive $v = f\lambda$; graph of displacement with time/position, label time period/wavelength and amplitude, equation of a progressive harmonic (sinusoidal) wave, $y = A\sin(kx \pm \omega t)$ where k is a propagation factor and equivalent equations.*

(b) *Production and propagation of sound as a wave motion; mechanical wave requires a medium; general formula for speed of sound (no derivation). Newton's formula for speed of sound in air; experimental value; Laplace's correction; variation of speed v with changes in pressure, density,humidity and temperature. Speed of sound in liquids and solids–brief introduction only. Concept of supersonic and ultrasonic waves.*

(c) *Principle of superposition of waves; interference (simple ideas only); dependence of combined wave form, on the relative phase of the interfering waves; qualitative only–illustrate with wave representations. Beats (qualitative explanation only); number of beats produced per second = difference in the frequencies of the interfering waves. Standing waves or stationary waves; formation by two identical progressive waves travelling in opposite directions (e.g.,: along a string, in an air column-incident and reflected waves); obtain $y = y_1 + y_2 = [2y_m \sin(kx)]\cos(\omega t)$ using equations of the travelling waves; variation of the amplitude $A = 2y_m \sin(kx)$ with location (x) of the particle; nodes and antinodes; compare standing waves with progressive waves.*

(d) *Laws of vibrations of a stretched string. Obtain equation for fundamental frequency $f_0 = (1/2l)\sqrt{T/m}$;*

(e) *Modes of vibration of strings and air columns (closed and open pipes); standing waves with nodes and antinodes; also in resonance with the periodic force exerted usually by a tuning fork; sketches of various modes of vibration; obtain expressions for fundamental frequency and various harmonics and overtones; mutual relations.*

CHAPTER 01

Units and Measurement

One of the important aspect of science is observation of world around us. To observe with accuracy we need to measure different physical quantities involved in that event. In quest to understand the world around us scientists seek to find relationship among physical quantities that can be measured.

- System of Units
- Significant Figures
- Dimensions of a Physical Quantity

TOPIC 01 System of Units

Need for Measurement

All engineering phenomena deal with definite and measured quantities, and so depend on the making of the **measurement**. We must be clear and precise in making these measurements. To make a measurement, magnitude of the physical quantity (unknown) is compared with a standardized part of that quantity called unit. e.g. Weighing a material compares it with a standard weight of one kilogram. The result of the comparison is expressed in terms of multiples of the known quantity, i.e. so many kilograms.

Units of Measurement

The measurement of physical quantity is the process of comparing this quantity with a standard amount of the physical quantity of the same kind, called its unit. Hence, to express the measurement of a physical quantity, we need to know two things

(i) The unit in which the quantity is measured.

(ii) The numerical value or the magnitude of the quantity(n), i.e. the number of times that unit (u) is contained in the given physical quantity.

or physical quantity, $\boxed{Q = nu}$

where, n denotes the magnitude of physical quantity in terms of chosen unit.

Physical Quantities

All those quantities which can be measured directly or indirectly and in terms of which the laws of physics can be expressed are called physical quantities. Physical quantities are classified as

(i) Fundamental Quantities

Those physical quantities which are independent of other physical quantities and are not defined in terms of other physical quantities, are called fundamental quantities or base quantities. e.g. Mass, length, time, temperature, luminous intensity, electric current and the amount of substance, etc.

(ii) Derived Quantities

Those quantities which can be derived from the fundamental quantities are called derived quantities. e.g. Velocity, acceleration and linear momentum, etc.

Physical Unit

The standard amount of a physical quantity chosen to measure the physical quantity of the same kind is called a physical unit. The physical unit can be classified as

Fundamental Units

The physical units which can neither be derived from one another, nor they can be further resolved into more simpler units are called fundamental units. The units of fundamental quantities, i.e. length, mass and time are called fundamental units or base units.

Derived Units

The units of measurement of all other physical quantities which can be obtained from fundamental units are called derived units.

e.g. $$\text{Speed} = \frac{\text{Distance}}{\text{Time}}$$

$$\therefore \quad \text{Unit of speed} = \frac{\text{Unit of distance}}{\text{Unit of time}}$$

$$= \frac{\text{m}}{\text{s}} = \text{ms}^{-1}$$

Unit of speed (i.e. ms^{-1}) is a derived unit.

The International System of Units

A system of units is the complete set of units, both fundamental and derived for all kinds of physical quantities.

The common systems of units used in mechanics are given below

(i) **FPS System** It is the British engineering system of units, which uses foot as the unit of length, pound as the unit of mass and second as the unit of time.

(ii) **CGS System** It is based on Gaussian system of units, which uses centimetre, gram and second for length, mass and time, respectively.

(iii) **MKS System** It uses metre, kilogram and second as the fundamental units of length, mass and time, respectively.

(iv) **International System of Units** (SI Units) The system of units, which is accepted internationally for measurement is the System Deinternational Units (French for International System of Units) abbreviated as SI.

The SI, with standard scheme of symbols, units and abbreviations, was developed and recommended by **General Conference on Weights and Measures** in 1971 for international usage in scientific, technical, industrial and commercial work.

This system of units makes revolutionary changes in the MKS system and is known as **rationalised MKS system.** It is helpful to obtain all the physical quantities in Physics.

SI units have several advantages over other systems.

(i) SI is **rational,** i.e. it gives one unit for one physical quantity, e.g. for energy of any type i.e. mechanical or heat or electrical, there is only one unit, joule (J). But in MKS system unit for mechanical energy is joule.

(ii) It is a **coherent** system, that is all derived units, can be obtained simply by multiplying or dividing the fundamental units, without introducing any numerical factor.

(iii) SI is **metric** system, i.e. multiples and sub-multiples of units are obtained when unit is multiplied by powers of 10. e.g. $1\,\text{km} = 1 \times 10^3\,\text{m}$

In SI system, there are seven base units and two supplementary units as listed below

SI base quantities and units

Base quantity	SI units		
	Name	Symbol	Definition
Length	Metre	m	The metre is the length of the path travelled by light in vacuum during a time interval of 1/299,792,458 of a second. (1983)
Mass	Kilogram	kg	The kilogram is equal to the mass of the international prototype of the kilogram (a platinum-iridium alloy cylinder) kept at international Bureau of Weights and Measures at Sevres, near Paris, France. (1889)
Time	Second	s	The second is the duration of 9,192,631,770 periods of the radiation corresponding to the transition between the two hyperfine levels of the ground state of the cesium-133 atom. (1967)
Electric current	Ampere	A	The ampere is that constant current which, if maintained in two straight parallel conductors of infinite length, of negligible circular cross-section, and placed 1 m apart in vacuum, would produce a force between these conductors equal to 2×10^{-7} N/m of length. (1948)
Thermodynamic temperature	Kelvin	K	The kelvin is the fraction 1/273.16 of the thermodynamic temperature of the triple point of water. (1967)
Amount of substance	Mole	mol	The mole is the amount of substance of a system which contains as many elementary entities as there are atoms in 0.012 kg of carbon-12. (1971)
Luminous intensity	Candela	cd	The candela is the luminous intensity in a given direction of a source that emits monochromatic radiation of frequency 540×10^{12} Hz and that has a radiant intensity in that direction of 1/683 watt per steradian. (1979)

Supplementary quantities and their SI units

Supplementary quantity	SI units		
	Name	Symbol	Definition
Plane angle	Radian	rad	One radian is the angle subtended at the centre of a circle by an arc equal in length to the radius of the circle. i.e. $d\theta = \frac{ds}{r}$ 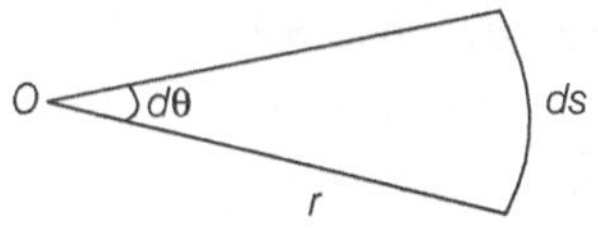
Solid angle	Steradian	sr	One steradian is the solid angle subtended at the centre of a sphere, by that surface of the sphere, which is equal in area, to the square of radius of the sphere. i.e. $d\Omega = \frac{dA}{r^2}$ 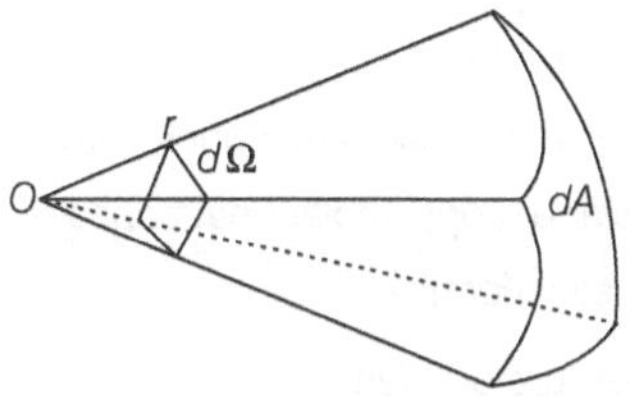

Note

- The FPS system is not a metric system. This system is not in much use these days.
- The drawback of CGS system is that many of the derived units on this system are inconveniently small.
- The advantages of MKS system is that some of the derived units are of convenient size.

SI derived units with special names

Physical Quantity	SI unit		
	Name	Symbol	Expression in terms of SI base units
Frequency	Hertz	Hz	s^{-1}
Force	Newton	N	$kg\ m\ s^{-2}$
Pressure, stress	Pascal	Pa	$kg\ m^{-1}s^{-2}$
Energy, work, quantity of heat	Joule	J	$kg\ m^2 s^{-2}$
Power, radiant flux	Watt	W	$kg\ m^2\ s^{-3}$
Quantity of electricity, electric charge	Coulomb	C	As
Electric potential, potential difference, electromotive force	Volt	V	$kg\ m^2\ s^{-3}\ A^{-1}$
Capacitance	Farad	F	$A^2\ s^4\ kg^{-1}\ m^{-2}$
Electric resistance	Ohm	Ω	$kg\ m^2\ s^{-3} A^{-2}$
Conductance	Siemens	S	$m^{-2}\ kg^{-1} s^3\ A^2$
Magnetic flux	Weber	Wb	$kg\ m^2 s^{-2}\ A^{-1}$
Magnetic field, magnetic flux density, magnetic induction	Tesla	T	$kg\ s^{-2}\ A^{-1}$
Inductance	Henry	H	$kg\ m^2 s^{-2} A^{-2}$
Magnetic moment	Joule per tesla	JT^{-1}	$m^2\ A$
Dipole moment	Coulomb metre	C m	s A m
Dynamic viscosity	Poiseuille	Pl or $N\ s\ m^{-2}$	$m^{-1}\ kg\ s^{-1}$
Torque, couple, moment of force	Newton metre	N m	$m^2\ kg\ s^{-2}$
Surface tension	Newton per metre	N/m	$kg\ s^{-2}$
Heat capacity, entropy	Joule per kelvin	J/K	$m^2\ kg\ s^{-2}\ K^{-1}$
Specific heat capacity, specific entropy	Joule per kilogram kelvin	J/kg K	$m^2\ s^{-2}\ K^{-1}$
Specific energy, latent heat	Joule per kilogram	J/kg	$m^2\ s^{-2}$
Thermal conductivity	Watt per metre kelvin	$W\ m^{-1}\ K^{-1}$	$m\ kg\ s^{-3}\ K^{-1}$
Electric field strength	Volt per metre	V/m	$m\ kg\ s^{-3}\ A^{-1}$
Electric charge density	Coulomb per cubic metre	C/m^3	$m^{-3}\ A\ s$
Permittivity	Farad per metre	F/m	$m^{-3}\ kg^{-1}\ s^4\ A^2$
Permeability	Henry per metre	H/m	$m\ kg\ s^{-2}\ A^{-2}$
Angular momentum, Planck constant	Joule second	J s	$kg\ m^2\ s^{-1}$
Molar entropy, molar heat capacity	Joule per mole kelvin	J/mol K	$m^2\ kg\ s^{-2}\ K^{-1}\ mol^{-1}$
Elastic moduli	Newton per square metre	N/m^2	$kg\ m^{-1}\ s^{-2}$
Pressure gradient	Pascal per metre	Pa/m	$kg\ m^{-2}\ s^{-2}$
Pressure energy	Pascal cubic metre	$Pa\ m^3$ or N m	$kg\ m^2\ s^{-2}$
Impulse	Newton second	N s	$kg\ ms^{-1}$
Angular impulse	Newton metre second	N m s	$kg\ m^2\ s^{-1}$
Specific resistance	Ohm metre	Ω m	$kg\ m^3\ s^{-3}\ A^{-2}$
Surface energy	Joule per square metre	J/m^2	$kg\ s^{-2}$

Rules for Writing SI Units in Symbols

(i) Small letters are used for symbols of units.
(ii) Symbols are not followed by a full stop.
(iii) The initial letter of a symbol is capital only when the unit is named after a scientist.
(iv) The full name of a unit always begins with a small letter even if it has been named after a scientist.
(v) Symbols do not take plural form.

Prefixes of Powers of 10

When the magnitudes of the physical quantities are very large or very small, it is convenient to express them in the multiples or submultiples of the SI units.

The various prefixes used for powers of 10 are listed below in table

Prefixes for Powers of Ten

Multiple	Prefix	Symbol	Sub-multiple	Prefix	Symbol
10^1	deca	da	10^{-1}	deci	d
10^2	hecto	h	10^{-2}	centi	c
10^3	kilo	k	10^{-3}	milli	m
10^6	mega	M	10^{-6}	micro	μ
10^9	giga	G	10^{-9}	nano	n
10^{12}	tera	T	10^{-12}	pico	p
10^{15}	peta	P	10^{-15}	femto	f
10^{18}	exa	E	10^{-18}	atto	a

Note

CGS, MKS and SI Systems of Units CGS, MKS and SI are metric or decimal systems of units. This is because the multiples and sub-multiples of the base units are obtained by multiplying base unit with powers of 10.

Some Important Practical Units

For Length/Distance

(i) **Astronomical Unit** It is the mean distance of the earth from the sun. 1 AU $= 1.496\times 10^{11}$ m.

(ii) **Light year** It is the distance travelled by light in vacuum in one year. 1 ly $= 9.46\times 10^{15}$ m

(iii) **Parallactic second** It is the distance at which an arc of length 1 astronomical unit subtends an angle of 1 second of arc.
1 parsec $= 3.084\times 10^{16}$ m $= 3.26$ ly

(iv) **Micron or micrometer,** $1\ \mu\text{m} = 10^{-6}$ m

(v) **Nanometer,** $1\ \text{nm} = 10^{-9}$ m

(vi) **Angstrom unit,** $1\ \text{Å} = 10^{-10}$ m

(vii) **Fermi** This unit is used for measuring nuclear sizes
$1\ \text{fm} = 10^{-15}$ m

Example 1 How many parsec are there in one metre?

Sol. Given, 1 parsec $= 3.084\times 10^{16}$ m

or 3.084×10^{16} m = 1 parsec

$$\therefore\quad 1\text{m} = \frac{1}{3.084\times 10^{16}}\ \text{parsec}$$
$$= 3.25\times 10^{-17}\ \text{parsec}$$

Example 2 Deduce relations between astronomical unit, light year and parsec. Arrange them in decreasing order of their magnitudes.

Sol. We know that, 1 AU $= 1.5\times 10^{11}$ m

1 ly $= 9.46\times 10^{15}$ m

1 parsec $= 3.08\times 10^{16}$ m

$$\therefore\quad \frac{1\ \text{ly}}{1\ \text{AU}} = \frac{9.46\times 10^{15}}{1.5\times 10^{11}} = 6.3\times 10^4$$

$$1\ \text{ly} = 6.3\times 10^4\ \text{AU} \quad ...(\text{i})$$

Conversion of light year into parsec

$$\text{i.e.}\quad \frac{1\ \text{parsec}}{1\ \text{ly}} = \frac{3.08\times 10^{16}}{9.46\times 10^{15}} = 3.26$$

$$\therefore\quad 1\ \text{parsec} = 3.26\ \text{ly} \quad ...(\text{ii})$$

Comparing results from Eqs. (i) and (ii), we get

1 parsec > 1 ly > 1 AU

For Mass

(i) Pound, 1 lb = 0.4536 kg
(ii) Slug, 1 Slug = 14.59 kg
(iii) Quintal, 1 q = 100 kg
(iv) Tonne or Metric ton, 1 t = 1000 kg
(v) Atomic mass unit (it is defined as the 1/12th of the mass of one ${}^{12}_{6}\text{C}$ atom) 1 amu $= 1.66\times 10^{-27}$ kg

For Time

(i) **Solar day** It is the time taken by the earth to complete one rotation about its own axis w.r.t. the sun.

(ii) **Sidereal year** It is the time taken by the earth to complete one rotation about its own axis w.r.t. a distant star.

(iii) **Solar year** It is the time taken by the earth to complete one revolution around the sun in its orbit.
1 solar year = 365.25 average solar days
= 366.25 sedrial days

(iv) **Tropical year** The year in which there is total solar eclipse is called **tropical year.**

(v) **Leap year** The year which is divisible by 4 and in which the month of February has 29 days is called a **leap year.**

(vi) **Lunar month** It is the time taken by the moon to complete one revolution around the earth in its orbit.

1 lunar month = 27.3 days

(*vii*) **Shake** It is the smallest practical unit of time.

$$1 \text{ shake} = 10^{-8} \text{ s}$$

Example 3 Which type of phenomena can be used as a measure of time? Give three examples.

Sol. A phenomena which repeats itself at regular intervals can be used as a measure of time.

Some examples are given below

(i) oscillation of a pendulum

(ii) rotation of earth around its axis

(iii) revolution of earth around the sun

For Areas

(i) Barn, 1 barn $= 10^{-28}$ m^2

(ii) Acre, 1 acre $= 4047$ m^2

(iii) Hectare, 1 hectare $= 10^4$ m^2

For Other Quantities

(i) Litre (for volume), $1 \text{ L} = 10^3 \text{ cc} = 10^{-3} \text{m}^3$

Where, cc represents cubic centimetre, i.e. cm^3.

(ii) Gallon (for volume),

In USA, 1 gallon = 3.7854 L

In UK, 1 gallon = 4.546 L

(iii) Pascal (for pressure), $1 \text{ Pa} = 1 \text{ Nm}^{-2}$

Pressure exerted by earth's, atmosphere.

$1 \text{ atm} = 1.01 \times 10^5 \text{ Pa}$

(iv) Bar (for pressure),

$1 \text{ bar} = 1 \text{ atm} = 1.01 \times 10^5 \text{ Pa} = 760 \text{ mm of Hg}$

(v) Torr (for pressure),

1 torr = 1 mm of Hg column = 133.3 Pa

(vi) Electron volt, $1 \text{ eV} = 1.6 \times 10^{-19} \text{ J}$

(vii) Erg (for energy/work), $1 \text{erg} = 10^{-7} \text{ J}$

(viii) Kilowatt hour (for energy), $1 \text{ kWh} = 3.6 \times 10^6 \text{ J}$

(ix) Horse power (for power), 1 HP = 746 W

(x) Dioptre (for power of a lens), $1 \text{ D} = 1 \text{m}^{-1}$

(xi) Degree (for angle), $1° = \frac{\pi}{180}$ rad

Topic Practice 1

Multiple Choice Questions

1 Mark

1. The fundamental units are also called as

(a) Base units

(b) derived units

(c) system of units

(d) international system of units

2. The combination of the base units are known as

(a) system of units

(b) derived units

(c) base units

(d) international system of units

3. The units of permeability of vacuum (μ_0) is

(a) $\frac{N}{A}$ (b) $\frac{N}{A^2}$ (c) NA (d) $\frac{J}{A^2}$

4. Which of the following pairs of physical quantities may be represented in the same unit.

(a) Heat and temperature

(b) Temperature and mole

(c) Heat and work

(d) Specific heat and heat

5. The difference in the lengths of a mean solar day and a sidereal day is about

(a) 1 min (b) 4 min

(c) 15 min (d) 56 min

6. $\frac{\text{Watt}}{\text{Kelvin}}$ is the unit of

(a) Stefan's constant

(b) Wien's constant

(c) Cooling's constant

(d) Thermal conductance

7. Which of the following relation is wrong?

(a) 1 Ampere × 1 Ohm = 1 Volt

(b) 1 Watt × Sec = 1 Joule

(c) 1 Newton per Coulomb = Volt per meter

(d) 1 Coulomb × 1 Volt = 1 Watt

8. Curie is a unit of

(a) Energy of γ-rays (b) Half-life

(c) Radioactivity (d) Intensity of γ-rays

9. The damping force on an oscillator is directly proportional to the velocity. The unit of the constant of proportionality is

(a) kg ms^{-1} (b) kg ms^{-2}

(c) kg s^{-1} (d) kg s

Very Short Answer Type Questions

1 Mark

10. If N_1 and u_1 are numeric value and unit of a physical quantity in one system of units and its respective values in other system are N_2 and u_2, then give relation between them.

11. Is it possible to have length and velocity both as fundamental quantities? Why?

12. How many astronomical units make one metre?

13. How many light years make 1 parsec?

14. Which of these is largest : astronomical unit, light year and parsec?

15. Which unit is used to measure size of a nucleus?

16. What is the difference between nm, mN and Nm?

17. How many amu make 1 kg?

Short Answer Type I Questions

2 Marks

18. Why SI system is called rational?

19. What are the disadvantage of measuring length in FPS system.

20. Does AU and Å represent the same unit of length?

21. Find the value of one light year in giga metre.

22. If the velocity of light is taken as the unit of velocity and year as the unit of time, what must be the unit of length? What is it called?

23. How many metric tons are there in teragram?

24. What is common between bar and torr?

Short Answer Type II Questions

3 Marks

25. Why length, mass and time are chosen as base quantities in mechanics?

26. Distinguish between fundamental and derived units.

27. What are the advantages of SI unit?

28. Express the average distance of earth from the sun in (i) light year (ii) parsec.

29. Why has second been defined in terms of periods of radiations from cesium-133?

Numerical Problems

30. Express an acceleration of 10 m/s^2 in km/h^2. **[2 M]**

31. The mass of a proton is 1.67×10^{-27} kg. How many protons would make 1 g? **[2 M]**

32. The radius of atom is of the order of 2 Å and radius of a nucleus is of the order of fermi. How many magnitudes higher is the volume of atom as compared to the volume of nucleus? **[3 M]**

33. The unit of length convenient on the atomic scale is known as an angstrom and is denoted by Å.
$1\ \text{Å} = 10^{-10}$ m. The size of the hydrogen atom is about 0.5 Å. What is the total atomic volume in m^3 of a mole of hydrogen atoms? **NCERT [3 M]**

Hints & Solutions

1. (*a*) The fundamental units are also called as base units.

2. (*b*) The physical quantities which are expressed in terms of fundamental or base units are called derived units.

3. (*b*) Force per unit length between two current carrying wires is, $\frac{dF}{dL} = \frac{\mu_0}{4\pi} \times \frac{2I_1 I_2}{r} \Rightarrow$ unit of $\mu_0 = \frac{N}{A^2}$

4. (*c*) Heat and work have same unit as joule (J) in SI system.

5. (*b*) Difference in length of a day $= \frac{24 \times 60}{365} \simeq 4$ min
i.e. sidereal day is 4 min smaller than the solar day.

6. (*d*) Thermal resistance $(R) = \frac{L}{KA}$
$$= \frac{\text{(Meter)}}{(\text{Watt meter}^{-1}\ \text{Kelvin}^{-1})\ (\text{meter})^2} = \frac{\text{Kelvin}}{\text{Watt}}$$
Thermal conductance $= \frac{1}{R} = \frac{\text{Watt}}{\text{Kelvin}}$

7. (*d*) 1 Coulomb × 1 Volt
$$= \text{Charge} \times \frac{\text{work}}{\text{charge}} = \text{work} = 1\ \text{joule}$$

8. (*c*) curie $= \frac{\text{disintegration}}{\text{sec}}$ = unit of radioactivity

9. (*c*) Given, damping force ∝ velocity
$$F \propto v \Rightarrow F = kv \Rightarrow k = \frac{F}{v}$$
$$\text{unit of } k = \frac{\text{Unit of } F}{\text{Unit of } v} = \frac{\text{kg-ms}^{-2}}{\text{ms}^{-1}} = \text{kg s}^{-1}$$

10. $N_1 u_1 = N_2 u_2$

11. No, since length is fundamental quantity and velocity is the derived quantity.

12. 1 m = 6.67×10^{-12} AU

13. 3.26 light years make 1 parsec.

14. Parsec is larger than light year which in turn is larger than an astronomical unit.

15. The size of nucleus is measured in fermi.
1 fermi = 10^{-15} m

16. nm stands for nanometer, 1 nm = 10^{-9} m, mN stands for milli-newton, 1 mN = 10^{-3} N, N-m stands for newton-metre.

17. 1 amu = 1.66×10^{-27} kg

$\therefore$ 1 kg = $\frac{1}{1.66\times10^{-27}}$ amu = 0.6×10^{27} amu

18. Refer to text on page 02 (The international system of units).

19. Refer to text on page 03 (Note).

20. No, AU and Å represent two different units of length. [1]

1 AU = 1 astronomical unit = 1.496×10^{11} m [1/2]

1 Å = 1 angstrom = 10^{-10} m [1/2]

21. We know that, 1 ly = 9.46×10^{15} m [1/2]

Also, 1 Gm = 10^9 m [1/2]

$\therefore$ 1 ly = $\frac{9.46\times10^{15}}{10^9}$ = 9.46×10^6 Gm [1]

22. Unit of length = Unit of velocity × Unit of time

= $3\times10^8\ \text{ms}^{-1}\times1$ year [1]

= $3\times10^8\ \text{ms}^{-1}\times365\times24\times60\times60$ s

= 9.45×10^{15} m = 1 light year [1]

23. In 1 teragram = 10^{12} g [1/2]

In 1 metric ton = 10^3kg = $10^3\times10^3 = 10^6$ g [1/2]

$\therefore$ Number of metric tons are in teragram

$= \frac{10^{12}\text{ g}}{10^6\text{ g}} = 10^6$ [1]

24. Both bar and torr are the units of pressure. [1/2]

1 bar = 1 atmospheric pressure = 760 mm of Hg column = 10^5N/m^2 [1]

1 torr = 1 mm of Hg column

$\therefore$ 1 bar = 760 torr [1/2]

25. In mechanics, length, mass and time are chosen as the base quantities because

(i) there is nothing simpler to length, mass and time. [1]

(ii) all other quantities in mechanics can be expressed in terms of length, mass and time. [1]

(iii) length, mass and time cannot be derived from one another. [1]

26. Refer to text on page 02 (Fundamental and derived units).

27. Refer to text on page 02 (SI units have several advantages over other systems).

28. Average distance of earth from the sun is (r)

i.e. $r = 1\text{ AU} = 1.496\times10^{11}$ m [1]

$= \frac{1.496\times10^{11}}{9.46\times10^{15}}$ light year

$= 1.58\times10^{-5}$ light year [1/2]

Also, $r = \frac{1.496\times10^{11}}{3.08\times10^{16}}$ parsec [1/2]

$= 4.86\times10^{-6}$ parsec [1]

29. Second has been defined in terms of periods of radiation, because

(i) this period is accurately defined. [1]

(ii) this period is not affected by change of physical conditions like temperature, pressure and volume etc. [1]

(iii) the unit is easily reproducible in any good laboratory. [1]

30. Acceleration = $\frac{10\text{ m}}{(1\text{s})^2} = \frac{10\times10^{-3}\text{ km}}{\left[\frac{1}{60\times60}\text{ h}\right]^2}$ [1]

$= (3600)^2\times10^{-2}\text{ km/h}^2$

$= 1.29\times10^5\text{ km/h}^2$ [1]

31. Number of protons = $\frac{\text{Total mass}}{\text{Mass of each proton}}$ [1]

$= \frac{10^{-3}}{1.67\times10^{-27}}$ [1/2]

$= 5.99\times10^{23}$ [1/2]

32. R_A i.e. radius of atom is 2 Å = 2×10^{-10} m [1]

R_N i.e. radius of nucleus is 1 fermi = 10^{-15} m [1/2]

$$\frac{V_A}{V_N} = \frac{\frac{4}{3}\pi R_A^3}{\frac{4}{3}\pi R_N^3} = \left[\frac{R_A}{R_N}\right]^3 = \left[\frac{2\times10^{-10}}{10^{-15}}\right]^3 = 8\times10^{15}$$ [1½]

33. Radius of a hydrogen atom (r) = 0.5 Å = 0.5×10^{-10} m

Volume of each hydrogen atom $(V) = \frac{4}{3}\pi r^3$ [1]

$= \frac{4}{3}\times3.14\times(0.5\times10^{-10})^3 = 5.234\times10^{-31}\text{m}^3$ [1/2]

Number of atoms in 1 mole of hydrogen = Avogadro's number (N)

$= 6.023\times10^{23}$ [1/2]

$\therefore$ Atomic volume of 1 mole of hydrogen atoms (V') = Volume of a hydrogen atom × Number of atoms

$V' = V\times N$ [1/2]

$= 5.236\times10^{-31}\times6.023\times10^{23}\text{m}^3$

$= 3152\times10^{-7}$ m [1/2]

TOPIC 02

Significant Figures

Significant Figures

Normally, the reported result of measurement is a number that includes all digits in the number that are known reliably plus first digit that is uncertain. The digits that are known reliably plus the first uncertain digit are known as **significant digits** or **significant figures.**

e.g. When a measured distance is reported to be 374.5 m, it has four significant figures 3, 7, 4 and 5. The figures 3, 7, 4 are certain and reliable, while the digit 5 is uncertain. Clearly, the digits beyond the significant digits reported in any result are superfluous.

The rules for determining the number of significant figures are

***Rule* 1** All non-zero digits are significant.

e.g. $x = 1234$ has four significant figures.

***Rule* 2** All the zeros between two non-zero digits are significant, no matter where, the decimal point is, if at all.

e.g. $x = 1007$ has four significant figures and $x = 10.07$ also contains four significant figures.

***Rule* 3** If the number is less than one, the zero(s) on the right of decimal point and to the left of first non-zero digit are not significant.

e.g. In $\underline{0}.\underline{0}\underline{0}5704$, the underlined zeros are not significant. The zero between 7 and 4 is significant. The number of significant figures is 4.

***Rule* 4** In a number without a decimal point, the terminal or trailing zeros are not significant.

e.g. $x = 3210$ has three significant figures, the trailing zeros are not significant.

***Rule* 5** The trailing zero(s) in a number with a decimal point are significant.

e.g. 3.500 has four significant figures.

***Rule* 6** The multiplying or dividing factors, which are neither rounded numbers nor numbers representing measured values are exact. They have infinite number of significant digits as per the condition.

e.g. In radius, $r = \frac{d}{2}$ and circumference, $s = 2\pi r$, the factors 2 is an exact number. It can be written as 2.0, 2.00 and 2.000, etc. as required.

***Rule* 7** The number of significant figures does not depend on the system of units. So, 16.4 cm, 0.164 m and 0.000164 km, all have three significant figures.

Ambiguity in Significant Figures

There can be some confusion regarding the trailing zeros. Suppose a measured length is reported as $x = 4.700$ m. Clearly, the zeros are meant to convey the precision of measurement and are therefore, significant. If we can rewrite the same length as $x = 0.004700$ km; $x = 470.0$ cm and $x = 4700$ mm.

As per rule 4, we would errorneously conclude that $x = 4700$ mm has two significant digits. While $x = 0.004700$ km has four significant digits and a mere change of units cannot change the number of significant figures (Rule 7).

To remove such ambiguities in determining the number of significant figures, the best way is to report every measurement in scientific notation (in the power of 10).

In this notation, every number can be expressed as $a \times 10^b$ where, a is the number between 1 to 10 and b is any positive or negative exponent (or power) of 10.

Then, the number can be expressed approximately as 10^b in which exponent (or power) b of 10 is called **order of magnitude** of the quantity.

$$x = 4.700 \text{ m} = 4.700 \times 10^{-3} \text{ km}$$

In this case, the number of significant digit is 4, as the power of 10 is irrelevant to the determination of significant figures.

Example 1 Write down the number of significant figure in the following.

(i) 0.072 (ii) 12.000 (iii) 0.060
(iv) 3.08×10^{11} (v) 1.2340 (vi) 0.04

Sol. (i) Two (ii) Five
(iii) Two (iv) Three
(v) Five (vi) One

Rounding Off

The result of computation with approximate numbers, which contain more than one uncertain digit, should be rounded off. While rounding off measurements, we use the following rules by convention:

Rule 1 If the digit to be dropped is less than 5, then the preceding digit is left unchanged.

e.g. $x = 7.82$ is rounded off to 7.8.

Rule 2 If the digit to be dropped is more than 5, then the preceding digit is raised by one.

e.g. $x = 6.87$ is rounded off to 6.9.

Rule 3 If the digit to be dropped is 5 followed by digits other than zero, then the preceding digit is raised by one. e.g. $x = 16.351$ is rounded off to 16.4.

Rule 4 If the digit to be dropped is 5 or 5 followed by zeros, then the preceding digit is left unchanged, if it is even. e.g. $x = 3.250$ becomes 3.2 on rounding off.

Rule 5 If the digit to be dropped is 5 or 5 followed by zeros, then the preceding digits is raised by one, if it is odd. e.g. $x = 3.750$ is rounded off to 3.8.

Example 2 Round off the following number as indicated

(i) 18.35 upto 3 digits = 18.4

(ii) 143.45 upto 4 digits = 143.4

(iii) 189.67 upto 3 digits = 190

(iv) 321.1355 upto 5 digits = 321.14

(v) 31.325×10^{-5} upto 4 digits $= 31.32 \times 10^{-5}$

(vi) 101.55×10^{6} upto 4 digits $= 101.6 \times 10^{6}$

Rules for Arithmetical Operations with Significant Figures

The following rules for arithmetic operations with significant figures that make final result more consistent with the precision of the measured values.

Addition and Subtraction

In both, addition and subtraction, the final result should retain as **many decimal places** as are there in the number with the **least decimal** places. e.g. The sum of three measurement of length 2.1 m, 1.78 m and 2.046 m is 5.926 m, which is rounded off to 5.9 m (upto smallest number of decimal places in the three measurements).

Similarly, if $x = 12.587$ m, and $y = 12.5$ m, then $(x - y)$ is $12.587 - 12.5 = 0.087$ m, which is rounded off to 0.1 m, upto smallest number of decimal places in y.

Multiplication and Division

In multiplication or division, the final result should retain as many significant figures, as are there in the original number with the least significant figures.

e.g. The speed of light is 3.00×10^{8} m/s and one year has 3.1557×10^{7} s, then light year is given by

$$= 3.00 \times 10^{8} \times 3.155 \times 10^{7}$$
$$= 9.4685 \times 10^{15} \text{ m}$$
$$= 9.5 \times 10^{15} \text{ m}$$

[Rounded off upto 2 significant figures]

Example 3 Each side of a cube is measured to be 7.203 m. What are the total surface area and the volume of the cube to appropriate significant figures? **[NCERT]**

Sol. Given, Side of the cube = 7.203 m

$$\text{Total surface area} = 6 \times (\text{side})^2 = 6 \times (7.203)^2$$
$$= 311.299254 \text{ m}^2 = 311.3 \text{ m}^2$$

[Rounded off to 4 significant figures]

$$\text{Volume} = (\text{side})^3 = (7.203)^3$$
$$= 373.714754 \text{ m}^3$$
$$= 373.7 \text{ m}^3.$$

[Rounded off to 4 significant figures]

Example 4 5.74 g of a substance occupies 1.2 cm^3. Express its density keeping significant figures in view. **[NCERT]**

Sol. $$\text{Density} = \frac{\text{Mass}}{\text{Volume}} = \frac{5.74 \text{ g}}{1.2 \text{ cm}^3} = 4.783 \text{ g cm}^{-3}$$

$= 4.8$ g cm $^{-3}$ [Rounded off upto 2 significant figures]

Rules for Determining Uncertainty in the Results of Arithmetic Calculations

Rule 1 Suppose, we use a metre scale to measure length and breadth of a thin rectangular sheets as 15.4 cm and 10.2 cm, respectively.

Each measurement has three significant figures and a precision upto first place of decimal. Therefore,

we can write length $(l) = (15.4 \pm 0.1)$ cm

$$= 15.4 \pm \left(\frac{0.1}{15.4} \times 100\right) = 15.4 \text{ cm} \pm 0.6\%$$

Similarly, breadth $(b) = (10.2 \pm 0.1)$ cm

$$= 10.2 \pm \left(\frac{0.1 \times 100}{10.2}\right)\%$$

$$= 10.2 \text{ cm} \pm 1\%$$

Thus, the error of the product i.e. area of thin sheetis $(15.4 \times 10.2) \pm (0.6 + 1.0)\text{ cm}^2$

$$= 157.08 \text{ cm}^2 \pm 1.6\%$$

$$= 157.08 \text{ cm}^2 \pm \left(\frac{1.6}{100} \times 157.08\right)\text{cm}^2$$

$$= (157.08 \pm 2.51)\text{ cm}^2.$$

As per rule, the final value of area can contain only three significant figures and error can contain only one significant figures, we can write the final result as $A = (157 \pm 3)\text{ cm}^2$

***Rule* 2** If a set of experimental data is specified to n significant figures, a result obtained by combining the data will also be valid to n significant figures.

e.g. $x = 13.7$ m and $y = 8.08$ m, both have three significant figures.

Now, $x - y = 13.7 - 8.08 = 5.62$ m

So, the final result should retain as many decimal places as, there is the number with least decimal places. Therefore, rounding off to one place of a decimal, we get $x - y = 5.6$ cm

***Rule* 3** The relative error of a value of number specified to n significant figures depends not only on n, but also on the number itself.

e.g. $m_1 = (1.04 \pm 0.01)$ kg

and $m_2 = (9.24 \pm 0.01)$ kg

Relative error in 1.04 kg is

$$\pm\left(\frac{0.01}{1.04}\right) \times 100 = \pm 1\%$$

Similarly, the relative error in 9.24 kg is

$$\pm\left(\frac{0.01}{9.24}\right) \times 100 = \pm 0.1\%$$

Thus, the relative error depends on the number itself.

***Rule* 4** In a multi-step computation, the intermediate results should be calculated to one more significant figure in every measurement, then the number of digits in the least precise measurement.

e.g. $x = 9.58$ has three significant digits. Now, reciprocal of x is $\frac{1}{x} = \frac{1}{9.58} = 0.104$, rounded off to three significant digits. When we take reciprocal of 0.104, we get 9.62, rounded off to three significant digits.

However, if we calculate $\frac{1}{x} = \frac{1}{9.58} = 0.1044$, rounded off to four significant figures, then $\frac{1}{0.1044} = 9.58$, rounded off to three significant digits.

Thus, retaining one more extra digits in intermediate steps of complex calculations would avoid additional errors in the process of roundingoff the numbers.

Example 5 Solve the following and express the result to an appropriate number of significant figures.

(i) Add 6.2g, 4.33g and 17.456g

(ii) Subtract 63.54 kg from 187.2 kg

(iii) $75.5 \times 125.2 \times 0.51$

(iv) $\frac{2.13 \times 24.78}{458.2}$

Sol. (i) $6.2\text{ g} + 4.33\text{ g} + 17.456\text{ g} = 27.986 = 28.0$ g

[rounded off to first decimal place]

(ii) $187.2\text{kg} - 63.54\text{kg} = 123.66\text{kg} = 123.7\text{kg}$

[rounded off to first decimal place]

(iii) $75.5 \times 125.2 \times 0.51 = 4820.826 = 4800$

[rounded off upto two significant figures]

(iv) $\frac{2.13 \times 24.78}{458.2} = 0.115193 = 0.115$

[rounded off to three significant figures]

Example 6 The length, breadth and height of a rectangular block of wood were measured to be

$l = 12.13 \pm 0.02$ cm,

$b = 8.16 \pm 0.01$ cm

and $h = 3.46 \pm 0.01$ cm

Determine the percentage error in the volume of the block.

Sol. Volume of block, $V = lbh$

The percentage error in the volume is given by

$$\frac{\Delta V}{V} \times 100 = \left(\frac{\Delta l}{l} + \frac{\Delta b}{b} + \frac{\Delta h}{h}\right) \times 100$$

$$= \left(\frac{0.02}{12.13} + \frac{0.01}{8.16} + \frac{0.01}{3.46}\right) \times 100$$

$$= \frac{200}{1213} + \frac{100}{816} + \frac{100}{346}$$

$$= 0.1649 + 0.1225 + 0.2890$$

$= 0.58\%$ [rounded off to two significant figures]

Topic Practice 2

Multiple Choice Question

1 Mark

1. If 3.8×10^{-6} is added to 4.2×10^{-5} giving due regard to significant figures, then the result will be

(a) 4.58×10^{-5} (b) 4.6×10^{-5}
(c) 45×10^{-5} (d) None of these

Very Short Answer Type Questions

1 Mark

2. If all measurements in an experiment are taken upto same number of significant figures, then which measurement is responsible for maximum error?

3. In a number without decimal, what is the significance of zeros on the right of non-zero digits?

Numerical Problems

4. Round off to four significant figures
(i) 36.879 (ii) 1.0084 **[1 M]**

5. Solve with due regard to significant figures $\sqrt{6.5 - 6.32}$ **[1 M]**

6. A jeweller put a diamond weighing 5.42 g in a box weighing 1.2 kg. Find the total weight of the box and the diamond to correct number of significant figures. **[2 M]**

7. The mass of a box measured by a grocer's balance is 2.3 kg. Two gold pieces of masses 20.15 g and 20.17 g are added to the box. What is (i) the total mass of the box (ii) the difference in the mass of the pieces to correct significant figures? **NCERT [3 M]**

8. State the number of significant figures in the following **[3 M]**

(i) 0.007 m^2 (ii) 2.64×10^{24} kg
(iii) 0.2370 g/cm^3 (iv) 6.320 J
(v) 6.032 N/m^2 (vi) 0.0006032 m^2

9. Write down the number of significant figures in the following
(i) 5238 N
(ii) 4200 kg
(iii) 34.000 m
(iv) 0.02340 N/m **[3 M]**

10. The length, breadth and thickness of a rectangular sheet of metal are 4.234 m, 1.005 m and 2.01 cm, respectively. Give the area and volume of the sheet to correct significant figures. **[3 M]**

Hints & Solutions

1. (*b*) By adding 3.8×10^{-6} and 42×10^{-6}, we get
$= 45.8 \times 10^{-6} = 4.58 \times 10^{-5}$
As least number of significant figures in given values are 2, so we round off the result to 4.6×10^{-5}.

2. The maximum error will be due to
(i) measurement which is least accurate.
(ii) measurement of the quantity which has maximum power in the formula.

3. All such zeros are not significant. e.g. $x = 678000$ has only three significant figures.

4. (i) 36.88 (ii) 1.008

5. $\sqrt{6.5 - 6.32} = \sqrt{0.18} = 0.4242$, upto two decimal place $= 0.42$ (having 2 significant figures).

6. Weight of diamond = 5.42 g = 0.00542 kg **[1]**
Total weight = 1.2 + 0.00542
= 1.20542 kg = 1.2 kg **[1/2 + 1/2]**

7. Given, mass of the box $(m) = 2.3$ kg
Mass of first gold piece $(m_1) = 20.15 \text{ g} = 0.02015$ kg **[1/2]**
Mass of second gold piece $(m_2) = 20.17 \text{ g} = 0.02017$ kg
(i) Total mass of the box $(M) = m + m_1 + m_2$
$= 2.3 + 0.02015 + 0.02017 = 2.34032$ kg **[1]**
As the mass of the box has least decimal place i.e. one decimal place, therefore, total mass of the box can have only one decimal place. Rounding off the total mass of the box up to one decimal place, we get
Total mass of the box $(M) = 2.3$ kg **[1/2]**
(ii) Difference in masses of gold pieces $(\Delta m) = m_2 - m_1$
$= 20.17 - 20.15 = 0.02$ g
(The masses of two gold pieces has two decimal places, therefore, it is correct up to two places of decimal.) **[1]**

8. The number of significant figures in the given quantities are given below.

(i) In 0.007, the number of significant figures is 1 because in a number less than 1, the zero's on the right of the decimal point but to the left of the first non-zero digit are not significant. [1/2]

(ii) In 2.64×10^{24}, the number of significant figures is 3 because all non-zero digits are significant, power of 10 are not taken in significant figure. [1/2]

(iii) In 0.2370, the number of significant figures is 4, as all non-zero digits left to decimal and trailing zero are significant. [1/2]

(iv) In 6.320, the number of significant figures is 4 (reason is same as in part 'iii'). [1/2]

(v) In 6.032, the number of significant figures is 4 (reason is same as in part 'iii'). [1/2]

(vi) In 0.0006032, the number of significant figures is 4 (reason is same as in part 'i'). [1/2]

9. (i) 5238 N has four significant digits. [1/2]

(ii) 4200 kg $= 4.200 \times 10^3$ kg has four significant figures [1/2]

(iii) 34.000 m has five significant digits. [1]

(iv) 0.02340 N/m has four significant digits. [1]

10. Given, length $(l) = 4.234$ m

Breadth $(b) = 1.005$ m

Thickness $(t) = 2.01$ cm $= 0.0201$ m [1/2]

$$\text{Area of sheet } (A) = 2(l \times b + b \times t + t \times l)$$
$$= 2[(4.234 \times 1.005) + (1.005 \times 0.0201) + (0.0201 \times 4.234)]$$
$$= 2 \times 4.3604739 = 8.7209478 \text{ m}^2$$ [1]

As, thickness has least number of significant figures 3, therefore, rounding off area up to three significant figures, we get

Area of sheet $(A) = 8.72 \text{ m}^2$

$$\text{Volume of sheet } (V) = l \times b \times t = 4.234 \times 1.005 \times 0.0201$$
$$= 0.0855289$$ [1]

Rounding off up to three significant figures, we get

Volume of the sheet $= 0.0855 \text{ m}^3$ [1/2]

TOPIC 03 Dimensions of a Physical Quantity

The dimensions of a physical quantity are the powers (or exponents) to which the units of base quantities are raised to represent a derived unit of that quantity. There are seven base quantities: length [L], mass [M], time [T], electric current [A], thermodynamic temperature [K], luminous intensity [Cd] and amount of substances [mol].

e.g. The volume occupied by an object is expressed as the product of length. So, its dimension is given by

$$V = [\text{L}] \times [\text{L}] \times [\text{L}] = [\text{L}^3]$$

As there is no mass and time in volume, so the dimension of volume is expressed as

$$V = [\text{M}^0\text{L}^3\text{T}^0]$$

Similarly, for force, it is the product of mass and acceleration. It can be expressed as

$$F = \text{mass} \times \text{acceleration}$$
$$= \text{mass} \times \frac{\text{length}}{(\text{time})^2}$$

$\therefore$ The dimension of force is given by

$$F = [\text{M}] \times \frac{[\text{L}]}{[\text{T}]^2} = [\text{MLT}^{-2}]$$

Dimensional Formulae and Dimensional Equations

The expression which shows how and which of the fundamental quantities represent the dimension of the physical quantity is called the **dimensional formula** of the given physical quantity.

e.g. Some of the dimensional formulae are as given below

$$\text{Acceleration} = [\text{M}^0\text{L}^1\text{T}^{-2}]$$
$$\text{Mass density} = [\text{ML}^{-3}\text{T}^0]$$
$$\text{Volume} = [\text{M}^0\text{L}^3\text{T}^0]$$

The equation obtained by equating a physical quantity with its dimensional formula is called the **dimensional equation** of the given physical quantity.

e.g. Some of the dimensional equations are as given below

$$\text{Linear momentum} = \text{mass} \times \text{velocity} = [\text{M}^1\text{L}^1\text{T}^{-1}]$$
$$\text{Impulse} = \text{Force} \times \text{time} = [\text{M}^1\text{L}^1\text{T}^{-1}]$$
$$\text{Moment of Inertia} = \text{mass} \times \text{radius of gyration} = [\text{M}^1\text{L}^2\text{T}^0]$$

Example 1 Find out the dimensions of universal gravitational constant used in Newton's law of gravitation.

Sol. According to Newton's law of gravitation, the force F, between two masses m_1 and m_2 separated by distance r can be given as

$$F = G\frac{m_1 m_2}{r^2}$$

Where, G = universal gravitational constant

$$G = \frac{Fr^2}{m_1 m_2}$$

$$G = \frac{\text{Newton} \times (\text{metre})^2}{(\text{kg})^2}$$

$$G = \frac{(\text{mass} \times \text{acceleration}) \times (\text{metre})^2}{(\text{mass})^2}$$

$$= \frac{1}{\text{mass}}\left(\frac{\text{Change in velocity}}{\text{Time}}\right) \times (\text{Length})^2$$

$$G = \frac{(\text{Length})^2}{\text{Mass} \times \text{Time}} \times \frac{\text{Distance}}{\text{Time}}$$

$$G = \frac{[L]^2}{[M] \times [T]} \times \frac{[L]}{[T]} = [M^{-1} L^3 T^{-2}]$$

Dimensional Formula of Some of the Important Mechanical Quantities

Physical quantity	Relation with other quantities	Dimensional formula	SI unit
Area	length × breadth	$L \times L = L^2 = [M^0 L^2 T^0]$	m^2
Volume	length × breadth × height	$L \times L \times L = L^3 = [M^0 L^3 T^0]$	m^3
Density	$\frac{\text{mass}}{\text{volume}}$	$\frac{M}{L^3} = [M^1 L^{-3} T^0]$	$kg\ m^{-3}$
Specific gravity	$\frac{\text{density of body}}{\text{density of water at 4°C}}$	$\frac{M/L^3}{M/L^3} = 1 = [M^0 L^0 T^0] \rightarrow$ no dimensions	No units
Speed or velocity	$\frac{\text{distance or displacement}}{\text{time}}$	$\frac{L}{T} = LT^{-1} = [M^0 L^1 T^{-1}]$	ms^{-1}
Linear momentum	mass × velocity	$M \times LT^{-1} = [M^1 L^1 T^{-1}]$	$kg\ ms^{-1}$
Acceleration	$\frac{\text{change in velocity}}{\text{time taken}}$	$\frac{L/T}{T} = LT^{-2} = [M^0 L^1 T^{-2}]$	ms^{-2}
Acceleration due to gravity (g)	$\frac{\text{change in velocity}}{\text{time taken}}$	$\frac{L/T}{T} = LT^{-2} = [M^0 L^1 T^{-2}]$	ms^{-2}
Force	mass × acceleration	$M \times LT^{-2} = [M L T^{-2}]$	N (newton)
Impulse	force × time	$M LT^{-2} \times T = [M^1 L^1 T^{-1}]$	Ns
Pressure	force/area	$\frac{MLT^{-2}}{L^2} = [M^1 L^{-1} T^{-2}]$	Nm^{-2}
Universal constant of gravitation (G)	From Newton's law of gravitation. $F = \frac{Gm_1m_2}{r^2}$ or $G = \frac{Fr^2}{m_1 m_2}$, where F is force between masses m_1, m_2 at a distance r	$G = \frac{[MLT^{-2}]\ L^2}{MM} = [M^{-1} L^3 T^{-2}]$	$Nm^2\ kg^{-2}$
Work	force × distance	$M LT^{-2} \times L = [M^1 L^2 T^{-2}]$	J (joule)
Energy (All types)	work	$[M^1 L^2 T^{-2}]$	J (joule)
Moment of force	force × distance	$M LT^{-2} \times L = [M^1 L^2 T^{-2}]$	N-m
Power	$\frac{\text{work}}{\text{time}}$	$\frac{M L^2 T^{-2}}{T} = [M^1 L^2 T^{-3}]$	W (watt)
Surface tension	$\frac{\text{force}}{\text{length}}$	$\frac{M L T^{-2}}{L} = [M^1 L^0 T^{-2}]$	Nm^{-1}
Surface energy	Energy of free surface	$[M^1 L^2 T^{-2}]$	J

Physical quantity	Relation with other quantities	Dimensional formula	SI unit
Force constant	$\frac{\text{force}}{\text{displacement}}$	$\frac{MLT^{-2}}{L} = [M^1 L^0 T^{-2}]$	Nm^{-1}
Thrust	force	$[M^1 L^1 T^{-2}]$	N (newton)
Tension	force	$[M^1 L^1 T^{-2}]$	N (newton)
Stress, Pressure	$\frac{\text{force}}{\text{area}}$	$\frac{MLT^{-2}}{L^2} = [M^1 L^{-1} T^{-2}]$	Nm^{-2}
Strain	$\frac{\text{change in dimension}}{\text{original dimension}}$	$\frac{L}{L} = [M^0 L^0 T^0]$	No units
Coefficient of elasticity	$\frac{\text{stress}}{\text{strain}}$	$\frac{M^1 L^{-1} T^{-2}}{1} = [M^1 L^{-1} T^{-2}]$	Nm^{-2}
Radius of gyration (K)	distance	$L = [M^0 L^1 T^0]$	m
Moment of inertia (I)	mass (radius of gyration)^2	$ML^2 = [M^1 L^2 T^0]$	kg m^2
Angle (θ) or Angular displacement (θ)	$\frac{\text{length } (l)}{\text{radius}(r)}$	$\frac{L}{L} = 1 = [M^0 L^0 T^0]$	radian
Angular velocity (ω)	$\frac{\text{angle}(\theta)}{\text{time}(t)}$	$\frac{1}{T} = T^{-1} = [M^0 L^0 T^{-1}]$	rad s^{-1}
Angular acceleration (α)	$\frac{\text{change in angular velocity}}{\text{time taken}}$	$\frac{1/T}{T} = T^{-2} = [M^0 L^0 T^{-2}]$	rad s^{-2}
Angular momentum	$I\omega$	$[ML^2][T^{-1}] = [M^1 L^2 T^{-1}]$	kg m^2 s^{-1}
Torque	$I\alpha$	$[ML^2][T^{-2}] = [M^1 L^2 T^{-2}]$	N-m
Wavelength (λ)	length of one wave, i.e., distance	$L = [M^0 L^1 T^0]$	m
Frequency (ν)	number of vibrations/sec	$\frac{1}{T} = T^{-1} = [M^0 L^0 T^{-1}]$	s^{-1} or Hz (hertz)
Angular frequency (ω)	$2\pi \times$ frequency	$T^{-1} = [M^0 L^0 T^{-1}]$	radian/sec
Velocity of light in vacuum (c)	$\frac{\text{distance travelled}}{\text{time taken}}$	$\frac{L}{T} = [M^0 L^1 T^{-1}]$	ms^{-1}
Velocity gradient	$\frac{\text{velocity}}{\text{distance}}$	$\frac{LT^{-1}}{L} = T^{-1} = [M^0 L^0 T^{-1}]$	s^{-1}
Rate of flow	$\frac{\text{volume}}{\text{time}}$	$\frac{L^3}{T} = L^3T^{-1} = [M^0 L^3 T^{-1}]$	m^3s^{-1}
Planck's constant (h)	$\frac{\text{energy } (E)}{\text{frequency } (\nu)}$	$\frac{ML^2T^{-2}}{T^{-1}} = [M^1 L^2 T^{-1}]$	J-s
Linear mass density (m)	$\frac{\text{mass}}{\text{length}}$	$\frac{M}{L} = [M^1 L^{-1} T^0]$	kg m^{-1}
Distance travelled in nth second	$\frac{\text{distance}}{\text{time}}$	$\frac{L}{T} = [M^0 L^1 T^{-1}]$	ms^{-1}
Avogadro's number (N)	Number of atoms/ molecules in one gram atom/mole	$[M^0 L^0 T^0]$	$mole^{-1}$
Magnetic dipole moment (M)	$M = IA$	$AL^2 = [M^0 L^2 T^0 A^1]$	Am^2
Pole strength (m)	$m = \frac{M}{2l}$	$\frac{AL^2}{L} = AL = [M^0 L^1 T^0 A^1]$	Am

Physical quantity	Relation with other quantities	Dimensional formula	SI unit
Magnetic permeability of free space (μ_0)	From Coulomb's law in magnetism, $F = \frac{\mu_0}{4\pi}\frac{m_1 m_2}{r^2}$, where m_1, m_2 are strengths of two poles; $[\mu_0] = \frac{4\pi[F][r^2]}{m_1 m_2}$	$\frac{[MLT^{-2}][L^2]}{[AL]^2} = [M^1 L^1 T^{-2} A^{-2}]$	Hm^{-1}
Resistance (R)	$\frac{\text{potential difference}}{\text{current}}$	$\frac{ML^2T^{-3}A^{-1}}{A} = [M^1 L^2 T^{-3} A^{-2}]$	Ω (ohm)
Capacitance (C)	$\frac{\text{charge}}{\text{potential difference}}$	$\frac{AT}{M L^2 T^{-3} A^{-1}} = [M^{-1} L^{-2} T^4 A^2]$	F (farad)
Surface density of charge	$\sigma = \frac{\text{charge}}{\text{area}}$	$\frac{AT}{L^2} = [M^0 L^{-2} T^1 A^1]$	Cm^{-1}
Electric dipole moment (p)	$q(2a)$	$AT(L) = [M^0 L^1 T^1 A^1]$	Cm
Specific Resistance or resistivity (ρ)	$\frac{RA}{l}$	$\frac{[ML^2T^{-3}A^{-2}][L^2]}{L} = [M^1 L^3 T^{-3} A^{-2}]$	ohm-m
Conductance (G)	$\frac{1}{R}$	$\frac{1}{[ML^2T^{-3}A^{-2}]} = [M^{-1} L^{-2} T^3 A^2]$	ohm^{-1}
Conductivity (σ)	$\frac{1}{\rho}$	$\frac{1}{[M^1L^3T^{-3}A^{-2}]} = [M^{-1} L^{-3} T^3 A^2]$	$(ohm\text{-}m)^{-1}$
Electric flux	Electric field × area	$[M^1L^1T^{-3}A^{-1}][L^2] = [M^1 L^3 T^{-3} A^{-1}]$	$Nm^2 C^{-1}$
Faraday constant	Avogadro number × elementary charge	$\frac{1}{mol} \times AT = [M^0 L^0 T^1 A^1 mol^{-1}]$	C

Example 2 Derive the dimensions formula of physical quantities.

(i) Tension (ii) Velocity gradient

(iii) Linear mass density (iv) Impulse

Sol. (i) Tension = force = mass × acceleration

$[M] \times [LT^{-2}] = [MLT^{-2}]$

(ii) Velocity gradient $= \frac{\text{Velocity}}{\text{Distance}} = \frac{[LT^{-1}]}{[L]} = [T^{-1}]$

(iii) Linear mass density $= \frac{\text{Mass}}{\text{Length}} = \frac{[M]}{[L]} = [ML^{-1}]$

(iv) Impulse = force × time $= [MLT^{-2}] \times [T] = [MLT^{-1}]$

Dimensional Analysis and Its Applications

The dimensional analysis helps us in deducing the relations among different physical quantities and checking the accuracy, derivation and dimensional consistency or its homogeneity of various numerical expressions.

Its applications are as given below

1. Checking the dimensional consistency of equations
2. Conversion of one system of units into another
3. Deducing relation among the physical quantities

1. Checking the Dimensional Consistency of Equations

The magnitudes of physical quantities may be added together or subtracted from one another only if they have the same dimensions.

Thus, mass cannot be added to velocity or an electric current cannot be subtracted from time. We use the principle of homogeneity of dimensions to check the consistency and correctness of an equation.

Principle of Homogeneity of Dimension

This **principle** states that a physical quantity equation will be dimensionally correct, if the dimensions of all the terms occurring on both sides of the equation are same.

e.g. Let us check the dimensional consistency of the equation of motion as

$$s = ut + \frac{1}{2}at^2$$

Dimensions of different terms are

$$[s] = [L]$$

$$[ut] = [LT^{-1}][T] = [L]$$

$$\left[\frac{1}{2}at^2\right] = [LT^{-2}][T^2] = [L]$$

As all the terms on both sides of the equations have the same dimensions, so the given equation is dimensionally correct.

Example 3 Check whether the given equation is dimensionally correct $\frac{1}{2}mv^2 = mgh$. **NCERT**

Sol. The dimensions of LHS $= [M]\,[LT^{-1}]^2 = [ML^2T^{-2}]$

The dimensions of RHS $= [M]\,[LT^{-2}][L] = [ML^2T^{-2}]$

The dimensions of LHS and RHS are same and hence the consistency is verified.

Example 4 Check the dimensional consistency of the following equations.

(i) de-Broglie wavelength, $\lambda = \frac{h}{mv}$

(ii) Escape velocity, $v = \sqrt{\frac{2GM}{R}}$

Sol. (i) Given, $\lambda = \frac{h}{mv}$

LHS as wavelength is a distance $\lambda = [L]$

Also RHS, $\frac{h}{mv} = \frac{\text{Planck's constant}}{\text{Mass} \times \text{Velocity}} = \frac{[ML^2T^{-1}]}{[M] \times [LT^{-1}]} = [L]$

$\therefore$ LHS = RHS

Hence, the given equation is dimensionally correct.

(ii) Here, $v = \sqrt{\frac{2GM}{R}}$

LHS $v = [LT^{-1}]$ RHS $= \left[\frac{2GM}{R}\right]^{1/2}$

$$G = [M^{-1}L^3T^{-2}],\ R = [L],\ M = [M]$$

$$= \left[\frac{M^{-1}L^3T^{-2}M}{L}\right]^{1/2} = [L^2T^{-2}]^{1/2} = [LT^{-1}]$$

$\therefore$ Dimensions of LHS = Dimensions of RHS

Hence, the equation is dimensionally correct.

2. Conversion of One System of Units into Another

As we know numerical value is inversely proportional to the size of the unit but the magnitude of the physical quantity remains the same, whatever be the system of its measurement.

i.e. $$n_1u_1 = n_2u_2 \Rightarrow n_2 = \frac{n_1u_1}{u_2} \quad \ldots\text{(i)}$$

Where, u_1 and u_2 are two units of measurement of the quantity and n_1 and n_2 are their respective numerical values. If M_1, L_1 and T_1 are the fundamental units of mass, length and time in one system and while for other system, M_2, L_2 and T_2 are the fundamental units of mass, length and time then $u_1 = [M_1^aL_1^bT_1^c]$ and $u_2 = [M_2^aL_2^bT_2^c]$

From Eq. (i) $n_2 = \frac{n_1[M_1^aL_1^bT_1^c]}{[M_2^aL_2^bT_2^c]}$

$$= n_1\left[\frac{M_1}{M_2}\right]^a\left[\frac{L_1}{L_2}\right]^b\left[\frac{T_1}{T_2}\right]^c$$

Example 5 A calorie is a unit of heat or energy and it equals about 4.2 J, where $1\text{ J} = 1\text{ kg-m}^2/\text{s}^2$. Suppose we employ a system of units in which the unit of mass equals α kg, the unit of length is β m, the unit of time is γ s. Show that a calorie has a magnitude $4.2\,\alpha^{-1}\beta^{-2}\gamma^2$ in terms of new units. **NCERT**

Sol. The dimensional formula of energy $= [ML^2T^{-2}]$

Let M_1, L_1, T_1 and M_2, L_2, T_2 are the units of mass, length and time in given two systems.

$$\therefore \quad M_1 = 1\text{ kg},\ M_2 = \alpha\text{ kg}$$
$$L_1 = 1\text{ m},\ L_2 = \beta\text{ m}$$
$$T_1 = 1\text{ s},\ T_2 = \gamma\text{ s}$$

For any physical quantity, the product of its magnitude and unit is always constant.

$$n_1u_1 = n_2u_2$$

or $$n_2 = n_1\frac{u_1}{u_2} = 4.2 \times \frac{[M_1L_1^2T_1^{-2}]}{[M_2L_2^2T_2^{-2}]}$$

$$= 4.2\left[\frac{M_1}{M_2}\right] \times \left[\frac{L_1}{L_2}\right]^2 \times \left[\frac{T_1}{T_2}\right]^{-2}$$

$$= 4.2\left[\frac{1}{\alpha}\text{kg}\right] \times \left[\frac{1}{\beta}\text{m}\right]^2 \times \left[\frac{1}{\gamma}\text{s}\right]^{-2}$$

$$n_2 = 4.2\alpha^{-1}\beta^{-2}\gamma^2 \text{ new unit}$$

$$\therefore \quad 1\text{ cal} = 4.2\alpha^{-1}\beta^{-2}\gamma^2 \text{ new unit}$$

Example 6 Find the value of 60J per min on a system that has 100 g, 100 cm and 1 min as the base units.

Sol. Given, $P = \frac{60 \text{ joule}}{1 \text{min}} = \frac{60 \text{ joule}}{60 \text{ s}}$

$= 1 \text{ watt}$

which is the SI unit of power

Dimensional formula of power is $[ML^2T^{-3}]$.

$\therefore \; a = 1, b = 2$ and $c = -3$

SI	New System
$n_1 = 1$	$n_2 = ?$
$M_1 = 1 \text{ kg} = 1000 \text{ g}$	$M_2 = 100 \text{ g}$
$L_1 = 1 \text{ m} = 100 \text{ cm}$	$L_2 = 100 \text{ cm}$
$T_1 = 1 \text{ s}$	$T_2 = 1 \text{ min} = 60 \text{ s}$

$$n_2 = n_1 \left[\frac{M_1}{M_2}\right]^a \left[\frac{L_1}{L_2}\right]^b \left[\frac{T_1}{T_2}\right]^c$$

$$= 1\left[\frac{1000}{100}\right]^{-1} \left[\frac{100}{100}\right]^{2} \left[\frac{1}{60}\right]^{-3}$$

$$= 2.16 \times 10^4$$

$\therefore \; 60 \text{ J min}^{-1} = 2.16 \times 10^4$ new units of power.

3. Deducing Relation among the Physical Quantities

The method of dimensions is used to deduce the relation among the physical quantities. We should know the dependence of the physical quantity on other quantities. We explain the process in following example

Example 7 Consider a simple pendulum, having a bob attached to a string, that oscillates under the action of the force of gravity. Suppose that the period of oscillation of the simple pendulum depends on

(i) mass m of the bob,

(ii) length l of the pendulum and

(iii) acceleration due to gravity g at the place.

Derive the expression for its time period using method of dimensions. **NCERT**

Sol. Let us assume that $T \propto m^a l^b g^c$ or $T = k m^a l^b g^c$ ...(i)

where, k is a dimensionless constant.

The dimensions of various quantities are

$$[T] = \text{T}, [m] = \text{M}, \quad [l] = \text{L}, [g] = \text{LT}^{-2}$$

Substituting these dimensions in Eq. (i), we get

$$\text{T} = [\text{M}]^a [\text{L}]^b [\text{LT}^{-2}]^c$$

or $\quad \text{M}^0\text{L}^0\text{T}^1 = \text{M}^a \text{L}^{b+c} \text{T}^{-2c}$

Equating the exponents of M, L and T on both sides, we get

$$a = 0, \; b + c = 0, \; -2c = 1$$

On solving, $a = 0, \quad b = \frac{1}{2}, \quad c = -\frac{1}{2}$

$$\therefore \qquad T = k m^0 l^{1/2} g^{-1/2} = k\sqrt{\frac{l}{g}}$$

From experiments, $k = 2\pi$

Therefore, $\qquad T = 2\pi\sqrt{\frac{l}{g}}.$

So, dimensional analysis is very useful in deducing relations among the interdependent physical quantities. It can only test the dimensional validity but not the exact relationship between physical quantities in any given equation.

Limitations of Dimensional Analysis

(i) It does not give any information whether a physical quantity is a scalar or a vector.

(ii) It gives no information about the dimensionless constant in the formula e.g. 1, 2, 3 ... π etc.

(iii) We cannot drive the formula containing the trigonometrical function logarithmic function, exponential function which have no dimensions.

(iv) If a quantity depends on more than three factors, having dimensions, the formula cannot be derived. This is because, equating the powers of M, L and T on either side of the dimensional equation, we can obtain three equations from which we can compute only three unknown dimensions.

Example 8 A body of mass m hung at one end of the spring executes SHM. Prove that the relation $T = 2\pi m/k$ is incorrect, where k is the force constant of the spring. Also, derive the correct relation.

Sol. It is given that $T = \frac{2\pi m}{k}$

LHS, $\qquad T = [\text{T}]$

RHS, $\qquad \frac{2\pi m}{k} = \frac{[\text{M}]}{[\text{MT}^{-2}]} = [\text{T}^2]$

$$\left[\because k = \frac{\text{Force}}{\text{Length}} = \frac{[\text{MLT}^{-2}]}{[\text{L}]} = [\text{MT}^{-2}]\right]$$

$\therefore \qquad$ LHS $\neq$ RHS

Hence, the relation is incorrect.

To find the correct relation, suppose $T = k m^a k^b$, then

$$[\text{T}]^1 = [\text{M}]^a [\text{MT}^{-2}]^b = \text{M}^{a+b}\text{T}^{-2b}$$

$\therefore \qquad a + b = 0, \; -2b = 1$

On solving, we get $b = \frac{-1}{2}, a = \frac{1}{2}$

$\therefore \quad T = km^{1/2}k^{-1/2}$

Hence, $\quad T = k\sqrt{\frac{m}{k}}$

Example 9 The frequency 'v' of vibration of stretched string depends upon

(i) its length l,

(ii) its mass per unit length 'm' and

(iii) the tension T in the string

Obtain dimensionally an expression for frequency v.

Sol. Let the frequency of vibration of the string be given by

$$v = Kl^a m^b T^c \quad \text{...(i)}$$

where K = a dimensionless constant

Dimensions of the various quantities are

$$v = [T^{-1}], l = [L]$$

Tension or force = $[MLT^{-2}]$

and $\quad m = \frac{\text{mass}}{\text{length}} = [ML^{-1}]$

Substituting these dimensions in equation (i), we get

$$[T^{-1}] = [L]^a [ML^{-1}]^b [MLT^{-2}]^c$$

or $\quad [M^0L^0T^{-1}] = [M^{b+c}L^{a-b+c}T^{-2c}]$

Equating the powers of M, L and T, we get

$$b + c = 0, a - b + c = 0 \text{ and } -2c = -1$$

on solving, $\quad a = -1, b = -\frac{1}{2} \text{ and } c = \frac{1}{2}$

$\therefore \quad (v) = Kl^{-1}m^{-1/2}T^{1/2} \text{ or } (v) = \frac{K}{l}\sqrt{\frac{T}{m}}$

Example 10 The time of oscillation T of a small drop of a liquid under surface tension (whose dimensions are those of force per unit length) depends upon the density d, the radius r and the surface tension σ. Derive dimensionally the relationship $T \propto \sqrt{dr^3/\sigma}$.

Sol. Let the time of oscillation of a small drop of a liquid is given by

$$T \propto d^a r^b d^c$$

$$T = kd^a r^b \sigma^c \quad \text{...(i)}$$

where, K = a dimensionless constant

Dimension of the various quantities are

$$\sigma = [MT^{-2}], \; d = [ML^{-3}], \; r = [L]$$

Substituting these dimensions in eq^n (i), we get,

i.e. $\quad [M^0L^0T^1] = k[ML^{-3}]^a[L]^b[MT^{-2}]^c$

$$= [M^{a+c}\,L^{-3a+b}T^{-2c}]$$

Equating the powers of M, L and T, we get,

$$a + c = 0, -2c = 1, \; -3a + b = 0$$

We get, $c = -1/2, a = 1/2$ and $b = 3/2$

$$T \propto d^{1/2}r^{3/2}\sigma^{-1/2} \quad \text{i.e. } T \propto \sqrt{\frac{dr^3}{\sigma}}$$

Topic Practice 3

Multiple Choice Questions

1 Mark

1. The dimensional formula for impulse is
(a) MLT^{-2} (b) $[MLT^{-1}]$ (c) $[ML^{-2}T^{-1}]$ (d) $[M^2L^2T^{-1}]$

2. If force F is applied on a body and it moves with the velocity v then the power will be
(a) Fv^2 (b) Fv (c) F/v^2 (d) F/v

3. Velocity of a particle depends upon t as $v = A + Bt + Ct^2$. If velocity is in ms^{-1}, the unit of B will be
(a) ms^{-1} (b) ms^{-2} (c) ms (d) m^2/s

4. Which of the following sets have different dimensions?
(a) Dipole moment, electric field and electric flux
(b) Pressure, Young's modulus, stress
(c) Heat, work and energy
(d) Emf, potential difference and potential

5. A system has basic dimensions as density D, velocity v, and area A. The dimensional representation of force in this system is
(a) Av^2D (b) A^2vD (c) AvD^2 (d) AvD

Very Short Answer Type Questions

1 Mark

6. Give an example of a physical quantity which has a unit but no dimension.

7. Give an example of a constant with unit and a constant without any unit.

8. Write the dimensional equation of molar gas constant R.

9. Write the dimensional formula of wavelength and frequency of a wave.

10. Obtain the dimensional formula for coefficient of viscosity.

11. What is the dimensional formula for torque?

12. Write three pairs of physical quantities, which have same dimensional formula.

13. Express one joule in terms of fundamental unit.

14. Are all constants dimensionless?

15. Name some physical quantities which are dimensionless.

16. Is Avogadro's number a dimensionless quantity?

17. If $x = a + bt + ct^2$, where x is in metres and t is second, what is the dimensional formula of c?

18. What are the dimensions of a and b in the relation : $F = a + bx$, where F is force and (x) is distance?

Short Answer Type I Questions

2 Marks

19. Find the dimensional formulae of (i) Kinetic energy and (ii) Pressure.

20. State dimensional formulae for stress, strain and Young's modulus.

21. Using the relation $E = h\nu$, obtain the dimensions of Planck's constant.

22. Magnitude of force F experienced by a certain object moving with speed v is given by $F = kv^2$, where k is constant. Find the dimensions of k.

23. The rotational kinetic energy of a body is given by $E = \frac{1}{2}I\omega^2$, where ω is the angular velocity of the body. Use the equation to obtain dimensional formula for moment of inertia I. Also, write SI unit of energy.

24. Distinguish between dimensional variables and dimensional constants. Give example too.

25. A book with many printing errors contains four different formulae for the displacement y of a particle undergoing a certain periodic motion **NCERT**

(i) $y = a\sin\frac{2\pi t}{T}$ (ii) $y = a\sin vt$

(iii) $y = \left(\frac{a}{T}\right)\sin\left(\frac{t}{a}\right)$

(iv) $y = \left(\frac{a}{\sqrt{2}}\right)\left(\sin\frac{2\pi t}{T} + \cos\frac{2\pi t}{T}\right)$

(where, a = maximum displacement of the particle, v = speed of the particle, T = time period of motion). Rule out the wrong formulae on dimensional grounds.

26. A famous relation in Physics relates 'moving mass' m to the 'rest mass' m_0 of a particle in terms of its speed v and speed of light c. (This relation first arose as a consequence of special relativity due to Albert Einstein). A boy recalls the relation almost correctly but forgets where to put the constant c. He writes $m = \frac{m_0}{(1 - v^2)^{1/2}}$.

Guess, where to put the missing c? **NCERT**

27. If $x = a + bt + ct^2$, where x is in metre and t in second, what are the units of a, b and c?

28. A man walking briskly in rain with speed v must slant his umbrella forward making an angle θ with the vertical. A student derives the following relation between θ and v : $\tan\theta = v$ and checks that the relation has a correct limit as $v \to 0$, $\theta \to 0$, as expected. (We are assuming there is no strong wind and that the rain falls vertically for a stationary man). Do you think this relation can be correct? If not, guess the correct relation. **NCERT**

29. Check the correctness of the relation $v^2 - u^2 = 2as$ by method of dimensions. The symbol have their usual meaning.

30. The speed of sound in a solid is given by the formula

$$v = \sqrt{E/\rho}$$

where, E is coefficient of elasticity and ρ is density of given solid. Check the relation by method of dimensional analysis.

31. If force F, length L and time T are taken as fundamental units then what will be the dimensions of mass?

Short Answer Type II Questions

3 Marks

32. Give uses and limitations of dimensional analysis.

33. Distinguish between unit and dimension of some physical quantity.

34. In the relation $p = (a/b)e^{-(az/\theta)}$, b is the pressure, Z is the distance, and θ is the temperature. What is the dimensional formula of p?

35. The SI unit of energy is $J = kgm^2s^{-2}$, that of speed v is ms^{-1} and acceleration a is ms^{-2}. Which of the formulae for kinetic energy (K) given below can you rule out on the basis of

dimensional arguments (m stands for the mass of the body)?

(i) $K = m^2v^3$ (ii) $K = (1/2)mv^2$

(iii) $K = ma$ (iv) $K = (3/16)mv^2$

(v) $K = \left(\frac{1}{2}\right)mv^2 + ma$

NCERT

36. How will you convert a physical quantity from one unit system to another by method of dimensions?

37. The wavelength λ associated with a moving particle depends upon its mass m, its velocity v and Planck's constant h. Show dimensional relation between them.

Long Answer Type Questions

5 Marks

38. The orbital velocity v of a satellite may depend on its mass m, distance r from the centre of earth and acceleration due to gravity g. Obtain an expression for orbital velocity.

39. A large fluid star oscillates in shape under the influence of its own gravitational field. Using dimensional analysis, find the expression for period of oscillation (T) in terms of radius of star (R). Mean density of fluid (ρ) and universal gravitational constant (G).

40. Find an expression for viscous force F acting on a tiny steel ball of radius r moving in a viscous liquid of viscosity η with a constant speed v by the method of dimensional analysis.

Numerical Problems

41. Find the value of 60 W on a system having 100 g, 20 cm and 1 min as the fundamental units. **[3 M]**

42. The value of G in CGS system is 6.67×10^{-8} dyne cm^2g^{-2}. Calculate its value in SI units. **[3 M]**

43. In CGS system, the value of Stefan's constant is $\sigma = 5.67 \times 10^{-5}$ $ergs^{-1}\ cm^{-2}K^{-4}$. Find its value in SI units. ($1\ J = 10^7$ erg). **[3 M]**

44. If unit of force is 1 kN, unit of length 1 km and unit of time is 100 s, what will be the unit of mass? **[3 M]**

45. The density of mercury is 13.6 gcm^{-3} in CGS system. Find its value in SI units. **[3 M]**

46. If unit of force, energy and velocity are 20 N, 200 J and 5 ms^{-1}, find units of length, mass and time. **[3 M]**

Hints & Solutions

1. (*b*) Impulse = Force × Time

$$= [MLT^{-2}] \times [T] = [MLT^{-1}]$$

2. (*b*) Power $= \frac{\text{Work}}{\text{Time}} = \frac{\text{Force} \times \text{distance}}{\text{Time}}$

$$= \text{Force} \times \text{Velocity} = Fv$$

3. (*b*) $ms^{-1} = B \times s \Rightarrow B = ms^{-2}$

4. (*a*) Heat, work and energy are same thing, so they have same dimensions.

Emf, potential difference and potential have the same dimensions.

Pressure $= \frac{\text{Force}}{\text{Area}}$, Stress $= \frac{\text{Force}}{\text{Area}}$

$$Y = \frac{\text{Stress}}{\text{Strain}} = \frac{\text{Force / Area}}{\text{Dimensionless}} = \text{Force / Area}$$

So, they have same dimensions.

5. (*a*) Force = Mass × Acceleration

$$= \text{Density} \times \text{Area} \times \text{length} \times \frac{\text{Velocity}}{\text{Time}}$$

$$= \text{Density} \times \text{Area} \times (\text{Velocity})^2 = [Av^2D]$$

6. Angle or solid angle.

7. Constant with unit is gravitational constant G. Constant without any unit is Reynold number (Re).

8. Molar gas constant $[R] = [ML^2T^{-2}K^{-1}mol^{-1}]$

9. Wavelength $[\lambda] = [L]$

Frequency $[\nu] = [T^{-1}]$

10. Coefficient of viscosity $(\eta) = \frac{Fdx}{A \cdot dv}$

$$= \frac{[MLT^{-2}]\,[L]}{[L^2]\,[LT^{-1}]} = [M^1L^{-1}T^{-1}]$$

11. Torque $= [ML^2T^{-2}]$

12. (i) Work and energy (ii) Energy and torque
(iii) Pressure and stress

13. Energy $= [ML^2T^{-2}]$

Hence, 1 Joule $= 1\ kg \times 1\ m^2 \times 1\ s^{-2} = 1 kgm^2s^{-2}$

14. No

15. Solid angle, relative density, strain, Reynold's number and Poisson's ratio.

16. No, it has dimensions. In fact, its dimensional formula is $[mol^{-1}]$.

17. Here, $x = [L]$

$t = [T]$; $x = ct^2$

$$[L] = c \times [T^2]$$

$$\Rightarrow \quad \frac{[L]}{[T^2]} = c \Rightarrow c = [LT^{-2}]$$

18. $[a] = [F] = [MLT^{-2}]$

$$[b] = \left[\frac{F}{x}\right] = \left[\frac{MLT^{-2}}{L}\right] = [MT^{-2}]$$

19. (i) $KE = \frac{1}{2}mv^2$, i.e. dimensional formula of KE is $[ML^2T^{-2}]$ [1]

(ii) $\text{Pressure} = \frac{\text{Force}}{\text{Area}} = \frac{[MLT^{-2}]}{[L^2]} = [ML^{-1}T^{-2}]$ [1]

20. Strain is dimensionless quantity.
Dimensional formula for stress is $[ML^{-1}T^{-2}]$ [1]

Young's modulus has same dimensional formula as stress, i.e. $[ML^{-1}T^{-2}]$. [1]

21. We know that dimensional formula of energy E of photon is $[M^1L^2T^{-2}]$ and dimensional formula of frequency ν is $[T^{-1}]$

$$[h] = \frac{[E]}{[\nu]} = \frac{[M^1L^2T^{-2}]}{[T^{-1}]} = [M^1L^2T^{-1}]$$ [2]

22. Since, $\quad F = kv^2$.

Hence, $\quad [k] = \frac{[F]}{[v^2]} = \frac{[MLT^{-2}]}{[LT^{-1}]^2} = [M^1L^{-1}]$ [2]

23. The given relation is $E = \frac{1}{2}I\omega^2$ [1]

$$I = \frac{[E]}{[\omega^2]} = \frac{[ML^2T^{-2}]}{[T^{-1}]^2}\left[\frac{ML^2T^{-2}}{T^{-2}}\right] = [ML^2]$$

SI unit of energy is joule. [1]

24. Dimensional variables are those quantities which have dimensions and whose numerical value may change. Speed, velocity, acceleration, etc. are dimensional variables. [1]

Dimensional constants are quantities having dimensions but having a constant value, e.g. gravitation constant (G), Planck's constant (H), Stefan's constant (σ), etc. [1]

25. According to the principle of homogeneity of dimensions, if the dimensions of each term adding or subtracting in a given relation are same then it is correct, if not then it is wrong. The dimension of LHS of each relation is [L], therefore, the dimension of RHS should be [L] and the argument of the trigonometrical function i.e. angle should be dimensionless.

(i) As $\frac{2\pi t}{T}$ is dimensionless, therefore, dimension of RHS = [L]. This formula is correct. [1/2]

(ii) Dimension of RHS = $[L]\sin[LT^{-1}][T] = [L]\sin[L]$

As angle is not dimensionless here. Therefore, this formula is wrong. [1/2]

(iii) Dimension of RHS $= \frac{[L]}{[T]}\sin\frac{[T]}{[L]} = [LT^{-1}]\sin[TL^{-1}]$

As angle is not dimensionless here, therefore this formula is wrong. [1/2]

(iv) Dimension of RHS $= [L]\left[\sin\frac{[T]}{[T]} + \cos\frac{[T]}{[T]}\right]$

$= [L]$

As angle is dimensionless and dimension of RHS is equal to the dimension of LHS, therefore, this formula is correct. [1/2]

26. The relation is written by the boy

$$m = \frac{m_0}{(1 - v^2)^{1/2}}$$ [1/2]

According to the principle of homogeneity of dimensions, the dimensions on either side of a relation must be same i.e., the powers of M, L, T on either side of a relation must be same.
Dimension of m is equal to the dimension of m_0, therefore, the denominator $(1 - v^2)^{1/2}$ should be dimensionless. In denominator 1 is dimensionless but factor v^2 is not dimensionless.
To make it dimensionless, we have to divide it by the same physical quantity with same power, therefore, it should be v^2/c^2, to become dimensionless. [1]

Hence, the correct relation should be $m = \frac{m_0}{(1 - v^2/c^2)^{1/2}}$ [1/2]

27. As $x = a + bt + ct^2$, where x is in metre and t in second. Hence, in accordance with the principle of homogeneity of dimensions, we have [1]

Unit of $a = x$ = metre

Unit of b = unit of $\frac{x}{t}$ = m/s and [1/2]

Unit of c = unit of $\frac{x}{t^2}$ = m/(s)^2 [1/2]

28. Relation derived by the man, $\tan\theta = v$

The left hand side of the relation is dimensionless as it is a trigonometrical function.

The dimension of right hand of the relation = $[LT^{-1}]$ [1]

The dimension of LHS is not equal to the dimension of RHS. Therefore, this relation is not correct.

To be dimensionless, the RHS should be v/u.
Hence, the correct relation becomes $\tan\theta = v/u$ [1]

29. The relation is given as $v^2 - u^2 = 2as$

On LHS Dimension of $v^2 = [L^2T^{-2}]$ [1]

and $\quad u^2 = [LT^{-1}]^2 = [L^2T^{-2}]$

RHS $2as = [LT^{-2}][L] = [L^2T^{-2}]$

As dimensions of both terms on LHS are equal to the dimensions of RHS, the relation is dimensionally correct. [1]

30. In the given relation dimensions of LHS terms v are $[LT^{-1}]$.

Dimensional formula for E and ρ are $[ML^{-1}T^{-2}]$ and $[ML^{-3}]$. [1]

$$\text{Dimensions of RHS} = \sqrt{\frac{ML^{-1}T^{-2}}{ML^{-3}}} = \sqrt{L^2T^{-2}} = [LT^{-1}]$$

As dimensions of LHS and RHS of the equation are same. Hence the equation is dimensionally correct. **[1]**

31. Suppose dimensions of mass M be $[F^aL^bT^c]$. Then, we have

$$[M] = [MLT^{-2}]^a[L]^b[T]^c \quad [1/2]$$
$$= M^aL^{a+b}T^{-2a+c}$$
$$a = 1, a+b = 0, -2a+c = 0 \quad [1/2]$$
$$a = 1,\ b = -1,\ c = 2 \quad [1/2]$$

Hence, dimensions of mass M are $[F^1L^{-1}T^2]$ [1/2]

32. Refer to text on pages 16 and 18 (Dimensional analysis and its applications and limitations of dimensional analysis).

33. Refer to text on pages 14 to 16 (Table).

34. Since, $e^{-(aZ/\theta)}$ is dimensionless, we have $aZ/\theta = 1$

or $$a = \frac{\theta}{Z} = \frac{K}{L} = [L^{-1}K] \quad [1]$$

We find that a/b = dimensions of p and $b = [ML^{-1}T^{-2}]$.

Therefore, dimensional formula of p is obtained as [1/2]

$$p = \frac{a}{[ML^{-1}T^{-2}]} = \frac{[L^{-1}K]}{[ML^{-1}T^{-2}]} = [M^{-1}L^0T^2K] \quad [1 + ½]$$

35. As SI unit of energy, $J = kgm^2s^{-2}$,

So, $[\text{energy}] = [ML^2T^{-2}]$

(i) $[m^2v^2] = [M^2][LT^{-1}]^2 = [M^2L^2T^{-2}]$ [1/2]

(ii) $[1/2m^2v^2] = [M][LT^{-1}]^2 = [ML^2T^{-2}]$ [1/2]

(iii) $[ma] = [M][LT^{-2}] = [MLT^{-2}]$ [1/2]

(iv) $[3/16mv^2] = [M][LT^{-1}]^2 = [ML^2T^{-2}]$ [1/2]

(v) The quantities $(1/2)mv^2$ and ma have different dimensions and hence, cannot be added. [1/2]
Since, the kinetic energy K has the dimensions of $[ML^2T^{-2}]$, formulae (i), (iii) and (v) are clearly ruled out.
Dimensional analysis cannot tell which of the two, (ii) or (iv), is the correct formula. From the actual definition of kinetic energy, only (ii) is the correct formula for kinetic energy. [1/2]

36. If a given quantity is measured in two different unit system, then $Q = n_1u_1 = n_2u_2$ [1]

Let the dimensional formula of the quantity be $[M^aL^bT^c]$, then we have $n_1[M_1^aL_1^bT_1^c] = n_2[M_2^aL_2^bT_2^c]$ [1]

Here M_1, L_1, T_1 are the fundamental unit of mass, length and time in first unit system and M_2, L_2, T_2 in the second unit system.

Hence, $$n_2 = n_1\left[\frac{M_1}{M_2}\right]^a\left[\frac{L_1}{L_2}\right]^b\left[\frac{T_1}{T_2}\right]^c$$

This relation helps us to convert a physical quantity from one unit system to another. [1]

37. Suppose wavelength λ associated with a moving particle depends upon (i) its mass (m), (ii) its velocity (v) and (iii) Planck's constant (h) [1/2]

$$\lambda = km^av^bh^c$$

where, k is a dimensionless constant.

Writing dimensions of various terms, we get

$$[M^0L^1T^0] = [M]^a[LT^{-1}]^b[ML^2T^{-1}]^c \quad [1]$$
$$= M^{a+c}L^{b+2c}T^{-b-c} \quad [1/2]$$

Comparing power of M, L and T on two sides of equation, we have

$$a+c = 0, b+2c = 1, -b-c = 0 \quad [1/2]$$

We get $a = -1, b = -1, c = +1$

Hence, the relation becomes $\lambda = \dfrac{kh}{mv}$ [1/2]

38. Suppose orbital velocity of satellite be given by the relation $v = km^ar^bg^c$ [1]

where, k is a dimensionless constant and a, b, c are unknown powers.

Writing dimensions on two sides of equation, we have

$$[M^0L^1T^{-1}] = [M]^a[L]^b[LT^{-2}]^c = [M^aL^{b+c}T^{-2c}] \quad [1]$$

Applying principle of homogeneity of dimensional equation, we find that

$$a = 0 \Rightarrow b+c = 1 \Rightarrow -2c = -1 \quad [1]$$

On solving these equations, we find that

$$a = 0, b = +\frac{1}{2} \text{ and } c = +\frac{1}{2} \quad [1]$$
$$v = kr^{1/2}g^{1/2} \Rightarrow v = k\sqrt{rg} \quad [1]$$

39. Suppose period of oscillation T depends on radius of star R, mean density of fluid ρ and universal gravitational constant (G) as

$T = kR^a\rho^bG^c$, where k is a dimensionless constant [1]

$$[M^0L^0T^1] = [L]^a[ML^{-3}]^b[M^{-1}L^3T^{-2}]^c \quad [1/2]$$
$$= M^{b-c}L^{a-3b+3c}T^{-2c} \quad [1/2]$$

Comparing powers of M, L and T, we have

$$b - c = 0 \quad [1]$$
$$a - 3b + 3c = 0 \text{ and } -2c = 1$$

On simplifying these equations, we get [1]

$$c = -1/2, b = -1/2, a = 0$$

Thus, we have $T = k\rho^{-1/2}G^{-1/2} = \dfrac{k}{\sqrt{\rho G}}$ [1]

40. It is given that viscous force F depends on (i) radius r of steel ball, (ii) coefficient of viscosity η of viscous liquid (iii) Speed v of the ball

i.e., $F = kr^a\eta^bv^c$, where k is dimensionless constant [1]

Dimensional formula of force

$$F = [MLT^{-2}], r = [L] \quad [1/2]$$

$\eta = [M^1L^{-1}T^{-1}]$ and $v = [LT^{-1}]$,

we have

$[MLT^{-2}] = [L]^a [M^1L^{-1}T^{-1}]^b [LT^{-1}]^c$ [1/2]

$= [M^b L^{a-b+c} T^{-b-c}]$

Comparing powers of M, L and T on either side of equation, we get

$$b = 1$$ [1]

$$a - b + c = 1$$

$$-b - c = -2$$

On solving, these above equations, we get [1]

$$a = 1,\ b = 1 \text{ and } c = 1$$ [1/2]

Hence, the relation becomes

$$F = kr\eta v$$ [1/2]

41. $n_1 = 60$ W, power is $[M^1L^2T^{-3}]$ [1/2]

In first system, $M_1 = 1$ kg, $L_1 = 1$ m, and $T_1 = 1$s [1/2]

In second system, $M_2 = 100$ g, $L_2 = 20$ cm, and $T_2 = 1$ min $= 60$ s

So, $n_2 = n_1\left[\frac{M_1}{M_2}\right]^1\left[\frac{L_1}{L_2}\right]^2\left[\frac{T_1}{T_2}\right]^{-3}$ [1]

$= 60\left[\frac{1000\text{ g}}{100\text{ g}}\right]\left[\frac{100\text{ cm}}{20\text{ cm}}\right]^2\left[\frac{1\text{ s}}{60\text{ s}}\right]^{-3}$ [1/2]

$= 60 \times \frac{1000}{100} \times \frac{100}{20} \times \frac{100}{20} \times 60 \times 60 \times 60$

$= 3.24 \times 10^9$ units [1/2]

42. As, $F = G\frac{m_1 m_2}{r^2}$

$\Rightarrow G = \frac{Fr^2}{m_1 m_2}$

$[G] = \frac{[MLT^{-2}][L^2]}{[M^2]} = [M^{-1}L^3T^{-2}]$ [1]

Using principle of homogeneity,

$$n_2 = n_1\left[\frac{M_1}{M_2}\right]^a\left[\frac{L_1}{L_2}\right]^b\left[\frac{T_1}{T_2}\right]^c$$

$= 6.67 \times 10^{-8}\left[\frac{1\text{g}}{1\text{kg}}\right]^{-1}\left[\frac{1\text{cm}}{1\text{m}}\right]^3\left[\frac{1}{1}\right]^{-2}$ [1]

$= 6.67 \times 10^{-8}\left[\frac{1}{1000}\right]^{-1}\left[\frac{1}{100}\right]^3[1]^{-2}$

$= 6.67 \times 10^{-8} \times 10^3 \times 10^{-6}$

$= 6.67 \times 10^{-11}$ N - m^2 kg^{-2} [1]

43. In CGS system, $\sigma = 5.67 \times 10^{-5}$ ergs^{-1} cm^{-2} K^{-4}

In SI system, 1 erg $= 10^{-7}$J, 1 cm $= 10^{-2}$ m, then

$\sigma = 5.67 \times 10^{-5} [10^{-7}][10^{-2}]^{-2}$ Js^{-1} m^{-2} K^{-4}

$= 5.67 \times 10^{-8}$ Js^{-1} m^{-2} K^{-4} [2]

Thus, in SI system, value of Stefan's constant,

$\sigma = 5.67 \times 10^{-8}$ Js^{-1} m^{-2} k^{-4} [1]

44. Force, $[F] = [MLT^{-2}]$

Length, $[L] = [L]$

Time, $[T] = [T]$ [1]

$\Rightarrow$ Mass, $[M] = \frac{[MLT^{-2}][T^2]}{[L]} = \frac{FT^2}{L}$ [1]

$= \frac{1 \times 10^3 \text{N} \times (100)^2 \text{s}^2}{1 \times 10^3 \text{m}}$

$= 10^4 \frac{\text{kg - ms}^{-2}\text{s}^2}{\text{m}} = 10^4$ kg [1]

45. [Density] $= [M^1L^{-3}]$

Using principle of homogeneity,

$$n_2 = n_1\left[\frac{M_1}{M_2}\right]\left[\frac{L_1}{L_2}\right]^{-3}$$

$= 13.6\left[\frac{1\text{g}}{1\text{kg}}\right]\left[\frac{1\text{cm}}{1\text{m}}\right]^{-3}$ [2]

$= 13.6\left[\frac{1}{1000}\right]\left[\frac{1}{100}\right]^{-3}$

$= 13.6 \times 10^3$ kgm^{-3} [1]

46. Force, $[F] = [MLT^{-2}] = 20$N ...(i)

Energy, $[E] = [ML^2T^{-2}] = 200$ J ...(ii)

Velocity, $[v] = [LT^{-1}] = 5$ ms^{-1} ...(iii) [1]

Dividing Eq. (ii) by Eq. (i), we get

$$\frac{[ML^2T^{-2}]}{[MLT^{-2}]} = \frac{200}{20}$$

$\Rightarrow$ $[L] = 10$ m [1]

Putting the value of [L] in Eq. (iii), we get

$$[T] = \frac{10}{5} = 2\text{ s}$$

Putting the value of [L] and [T] in Eq. (i), we get

$$[M] = \frac{20 \times 2 \times 2}{10} = 8\text{ kg}$$ [1]

SUMMARY

- All the quantities in terms of which laws of physics are described and whose measurement is necessary, are called physical quantities.
- **Types of physical quantities**
  - (i) **Fundamental quantities** The physical quantities which can be treated as independent of other physical quantities and are not usually defined in terms of other physical quantities are called fundamental quantities. e.g. mass, length , time etc.
  - (ii) **Derived quantities** Those physical quantities which are derived from fundamental quantities are called derived quantities. e.g. velocity, acceleration, force etc.
- **Unit** The standard amount of a physical quantity chosen to measure the physical quantity of the same kind is called a physical unit.
- **Types of physical units**
  - (i) **Fundamental units** The physical units which can neither be derived from one another, nor they can be further resolved into more simpler units are called fundamental units. e.g. kg, metre, second, etc.
  - (ii) **Derived units** All other units which can be expressed in terms of fundamental units are called derived units
    e.g. m/s, m/s^2, etc.
- **Rules for finding significant figures**
- The dimensions of a physical quantity are powers (or exponents) to which the base quantities are raised to represent the quantity.
- The expression which shows how and which of the base quantities represent the dimensions of a physical quantity is called the dimensional formula.
- The equation which expresses a physical quantity in terms of the fundamental units of mass, length and time is called dimensional equation.
- If the dimensions of left hand side of an equation are equal to the dimensions of right hand side of the equation, then the equation is dimensionally correct. This is known as homogeneity principle. Mathematically [LHS] = [RHS]

Chapter Practice

Multiple Choice Questions

1 Mark

1 The dimensions of a/b in the equation $p = \frac{a - t^2}{bx}$ when p is pressure, x is distance and t is time, are
(a) $[M^2LT^{-3}]$ (b) $[MT^{-2}]$
(c) $[LT^{-3}]$ (d) $[ML^3T^{-1}]$

2 When 1 m, 1 kg and 1 min are taken as the fundamental units, the magnitude of the force is 36 units. What will be the value of this force in CGS system?
(a) 10^5 dyne (b) 10^3 dyne
(c) 10^8 dyne (d) 10^4 dyne

3 Which of the following has neither units nor dimensions?
(a) Angle
(b) Energy
(c) Relative density
(d) Relative velocity

4 The solid angle subtended by the periphery of an area 1 cm^2 at a point situated symmetrically at a distance of 5 cm from the area is
(a) 2×10^{-2} steradian
(b) 4×10^{-2} steradian
(c) 6×10^{-2} steradian
(d) 8×10^{-2} steradian

5 Young's modulus of steel is 1.9×10^{11} Nm^{-2}. When expressed in CGS units of dyne cm^{-2}, it will be equal to ($1N = 10^5$ dyne, $1 \ m^2 = 10^4 cm^2$)
(a) 1.9×10^{10} (b) 1.9×10^{11}
(c) 1.9×10^{12} (d) 1.9×10^{13}

6 If momentum p, area A and time T are taken to be fundamental quantities, then energy has the dimensional formula
(a) $pA^{-1}T^1$ (b) p^2AT
(c) $pA^{-1/2}T$ (d) $pA^{1/2}T^{-1}$

7 In the expression $P = El^2 m^{-5} G^{-2}$, where E, m, l and G denote energy, mass, angular momentum and gravitational constant, respectively. The dimensions of P are
(a) $[MLT^0]$ (b) $[M^2 LT^{-1}]$
(c) $[M^0 L^0 T^0]$ (d) $[M^0 LT^{-2}]$

Assertion and Reason

Directions (Q. Nos. 8-12) *In the following questions, two statements are given- one labelled Assertion (A) and the other labelled Reason (R). Select the correct answer to these questions from the codes (a), (b), (c) and (d) as given below*
(a) Both Assertion and Reason are true and Reason is the correct explanation of Assertion.
(b) Both Assertion and Reason are true but Reason is not the correct explanation of Assertion.
(c) Assertion is true but Reason is false.
(d) Assertion is false but Reason is true.

8. **Assertion (A)** The unit based for measuring nuclear cross-section is barn.
Reason (R) 1 barn $= 10^{-14} m^2$.

9. **Assertion (A)** Pressure has the dimensions of energy density.
Reason (R) Energy density $= \frac{\text{Energy}}{\text{Volume}}$

10. **Assertion (A)** The method of dimensions analysis cannot validate the exact relationship between physical quantities in any equation.
Reason (R) It does not distinguish between the physical quantities having same dimensions.

11. **Assertion (A)** Let us consider an equation
$$(1/2)\, mv^2 = mgh$$
where, m is the mass of the body, v is velocity, g is the acceleration due to gravity and h is the height.
Reason (R) Equation is dimensionally correct.

12. **Assertion (A)** Force cannot be added to pressure.
Reason (R) Both force and pressure has different dimensions.

Short Answer Type I Question

2 Marks

13 If p represents radiation pressure, c represents the speed of light and q represents the radiation energy per unit area per unit time.

Calculate the non-zero integers x, y and z such that $p^x q^y c^z$ is dimensionless.

Short Answer Type II Questions

3 Marks

14 If velocity of sound in air v depends on the modulus of elasticity E and density ρ.

Find expression of v.

15 Check the relation $s = ut + \frac{1}{2}at^2$ by method of dimension.

16 If the time period (T) of vibration of a liquid drop depends on surface tension (s), radius (r) of the drop, and density (ρ) of the liquid. Derive an expression for T using dimensional analysis.

17 The depth x to which a bullet penetrates a human body depends upon (i) coefficient of elasticity η and (ii) kinetic energy E_k. By the method of dimensions, show that $x \propto \left[\frac{E_k}{\eta}\right]^{1/3}$

18 Rule out or accept the following formula for kinetic energy on the basis of dimensional arguments.

(i) $K = \frac{3}{16}mv^2$ (ii) $K = \frac{1}{2}mv^2 + ma$

Case Based Questions

Directions (Q. No. 19) *These questions are case study based questions. Read the following paragraph and answer the questions.*

19. All quantities in mechanics are represented in terms of base units of length, mass and time. Additional base unit of temperature (kelvin) is used in heat and thermodynamics. In magnetism and electricity, the additional base unit of electric current is ampere.

(i) Find the dimension of universal gravitational constant.

(ii) What is the dimension of the coefficient of thermal conductivity?

(iii) Derive the dimension of resistance.

(iv) Given, force $= \frac{\alpha}{\text{Density} + \beta^3}$.

What are the dimensions of α, β?

(v) Which quantity has unit but no dimension?

Numerical Problems

20 How many protons would make 1 kg? (Mass of proton $= 1.67 \times 10^{-27}$ kg) **[1 M]**

21 Wavelength of a laser light is 6463 Å. Express it in nm and micron. **[1 M]**

22 Find the value of 1 J of energy in CGS system of units. **[1 M]**

23 Find the value of the following upto the appropriate significant figures in the following.

(i) $3.27 + 33.5472$ (ii) $53.312 - 53.3$

(iii) 2.02×23 (iv) 3.908×5.5 **[2 M]**

24 If unit of force, velocity and energy are 100 dyne, 10 cm/s and 400 ergs, respectively. What will be the unit of mass, length and time? **[2 M]**

25 How many significant figures are there in the following results for quantities measured in the laboratory?

(i) 3.0120 (ii) 123.0 km

(iii) 0.006235 s (iv) 0.23×10^{-3}

(v) 100.007 g (vi) 143000 km **[3 M]**

Answers

1 (b) Given, $p = \frac{a - t^2}{bx}$ or $pbx = a - t^2$

By the law of homogeneity of dimensional equation,

Dimensions of a = Dimensions of t^2

Hence, $a = [T^2]$

Dimensions of b = Dimensions of $\frac{t^2}{px}$

Pressure, $p = [ML^{-1} T^{-2}]$

$$b = \frac{t^2}{px} = \frac{[T^2]}{[ML^{-1} T^{-2}][L]} = [M^{-1}T^4]$$

So, dimensions of $\frac{a}{b}$ is $\frac{[T^2]}{[M^{-1} T^4]} = [MT^{-2}]$

2 (b) As, dimensional formula of force $= [MLT^{-2}]$

$n_1 = 36$, $M_1 = 1$ kg, $L_1 = 1$ m, $T_1 = 1$ min $= 60$ s

$n_2 = ?, M_2 = 1\,g, L_2 = 1\,cm, T_2 = 1\,s$

So, conversion of 36 units into CGS system

i.e., $n_2 = n_1 \left[\frac{M_1}{M_2}\right]^a \left[\frac{L_1}{L_2}\right]^b \left[\frac{T_1}{T_2}\right]^c$

$n_2 = n_1 \left[\frac{1\,kg}{1g}\right]^1 \left[\frac{1\,m}{1\,cm}\right]^1 \left[\frac{1\,min}{1\,s}\right]^{-2}$

$= 36\left[\frac{1000\,g}{1\,g}\right]\left[\frac{100\,cm}{1\,cm}\right]^1\left[\frac{60\,s}{1\,s}\right]^{-2}$

$= 10^3$ dyne

3 (c) Relative density has pure digits as it is the ratio of two densities. It does not have any dimensions.

4 (b) Solid angle, $d\Omega = \frac{dA}{r^2} = \frac{1\,cm^2}{(5\,cm)^2}$

$= 0.04$ steradian $= 4\times10^{-2}$ steradian

5 (c) Given, Young's modulus

$Y = 1.9\times10^{11}\ Nm^{-2}$, $1N = 10^5$ dyne

Hence, $Y = 1.9\times10^{11}\times10^5$ dyne/m^2

We know that, 1m = 100 cm

$\therefore\ Y = 1.9\times10^{11}\times10^5\ \text{dyne}/(100)^2\ \text{cm}^2$

$= 1.9\times10^{16-4}$ dyne/cm^2

$Y = 1.9\times10^{12}$ dyne/cm^2

6 (d) Given, fundamental quantities are momentum p, area A and time T.

We can write energy E as

$E \propto p^a A^b T^c \Rightarrow E = kp^a A^b T^c$

where, k is dimensionless constant of proportionality.

Dimensions of

$E = [ML^2T^{-2}]$

and $p = [MLT^{-1}]$

$A = [L^2],\ T = [T]$

$E = kp^a A^b T^c$

Putting all the dimensions, we get

$[ML^2T^{-2}] = [MLT^{-1}]^a[L^2]^b[T]^c = [M^a L^{2b+a} T^{-a+c}]$

By principle of homogeneity of dimensions,

$a = 1,\ 2b + a = 2$

$\Rightarrow\ 2b + 1 = 2$

$\Rightarrow\ b = 1/2, -a + c = -2$

$\Rightarrow\ c = -2 + a = -2 + 1 = -1$

Hence, $E = [pA^{1/2}T^{-1}]$

7 (c) The given expression is $P = El^2m^{-5}G^{-2}$

Dimensions of energy, $E = [ML^2T^{-2}]$

Angular momentum, $l = [ML^2T^{-1}]$

Mass, $m = [M]$

Gravitation constant, $G = [M^{-1}\ L^3\ T^{-2}]$

Substituting dimensions of each term in the given expression,

$P = [ML^2T^{-2}]\times[ML^2T^{-1}]^2\times[M]^{-5}\times[M^{-1}L^3T^{-2}]^{-2}$

$= [M^{1+2-5+2}L^{2+4-6}T^{-2-2+4}] = [M^0L^0T^0]$

Therefore, P is a dimensionless quantity.

8 (c) Barn is used in nuclear Physics for expressing the cross-sectional area of nuclei and nuclear reaction. It is defined as 10^{-28} m^2 and it is used to measure the probability of interaction between the particles.

9 (a) Pressure $= \frac{\text{Force}}{\text{Area}} = \frac{\text{Force}\times\text{Distance}}{\text{Area}\times\text{Distance}}$

$= \frac{\text{Energy}}{\text{Volume}} = \frac{[ML^2T^{-2}]}{[L^3]}$

$= [ML^{-1}\ T^{-2}]$ = Energy density

10 (a) Dimensional analysis is very useful in deducing relations among the interdependent physical quantities. However, dimensionless constants cannot be obtained by this method. The method of dimensions can only test the dimensional validity but not the exact relationship between physical quantities in any equation. It does not distinguish between the physical quantities having same dimensions.

11 (a) The dimensions of LHS are

$[M]\ [LT^{-1}]^2 = [M]\ [L^2\ T^{-2}] = [ML^2T^{-2}]$

The dimensions of RHS are

$[M]\ [LT^{-2}]\ [L] = [M]\ [L^2\ T^{-2}] = [ML^2T^{-2}]$

The dimensions of LHS and RHS are the same and hence the equation is dimensionally correct.

12 Addition and subtraction can be done between quantities having same dimension.

13 Radiation pressure $(p) = ML^{-1}T^{-2}$

Speed of light $(c) = LT^{-1}$

Radiation energy per unit area per unit time (q)

$= \frac{[ML^2T^{-2}]}{[L^2][T]} = [ML^0T^{-3}]$

Then, $p^x q^y c^z = [M^0L^0T^0]$

$\Rightarrow\ [ML^{-1}T^{-2}]^x\ [ML^0T^{-3}]^y\ [LT^{-1}]^z = [M^0L^0T^0]$

$\Rightarrow\ [M^{x+y}][L^{z-x}][T^{-2x-3y-z}] = [M^0L^0T^0]$ [1]

Equating power, we get

$x + y = 0 \Rightarrow x = -y$

$z - x = 0$

$\Rightarrow\ x = z$

and $-2x - 3y - z = 0$

$\Rightarrow\ -2z + 3z - z = 0$

$\Rightarrow\ z = 0 \Rightarrow x = 0 \Rightarrow y = 0$ [1]

14 Given $v \propto E^a\rho^b$

Using dimensional analysis method,

$v = [LT^{-1}]$

$$E = [ML^{-1}T^{-2}]$$
$$\rho = [ML^{-3}]$$
$$\Rightarrow \quad [LT^{-1}] = [ML^{-1}T^{-2}]^a\,[ML^{-3}]^b$$
$$[LT^{-1}] = [M^{a+b}][L^{-a-3b}][T^{-2a}] \quad [1½]$$

Equating powers, we get

$$a + b = 0$$
$$\Rightarrow \quad a = -b$$
$$\Rightarrow \quad -a - 3b = 1$$
$$\Rightarrow \quad -2b = 1$$
$$\Rightarrow \quad b = -\frac{1}{2}$$
$$\Rightarrow \quad -2a = -1$$
$$\Rightarrow \quad a = \frac{1}{2}$$
$$\Rightarrow \quad V = KE^{1/2}\rho^{-1/2} \Rightarrow V = K\sqrt{\frac{E}{\rho}}$$

where, K is constant of proportionality. [1½]

15 $s = ut + \frac{1}{2}at^2$

Magnitude of physical quantities may be added together or subtracted from one another only if they have the same dimension. [1]

$$\therefore \quad s = [L]$$
$$ut = [LT^{-1}]\,[T] = [L]$$
$$\frac{1}{2}at^2 = [LT^{-2}][T^2] = [L] \quad [1]$$

As all terms have same dimension of length on both side of the equation, so the given equation is dimensionally correct. [1]

16 Solve as example 10 on page 19.

17 Let $x \propto \eta^a E_k^b$

$$x = k\eta^a E_k^b$$

where, k is a dimensionless constant.

Dimension of quantities are

$$x = [L]$$
$$\eta = [ML^{-1}T^{-2}]$$
$$E_k = [ML^2T^{-2}]$$
$$\Rightarrow \quad [L] = [ML^{-1}T^{-2}]^a\,[ML^2T^{-2}]^b$$
$$[L] = [M^{a+b}]\,[L^{-a+2b}]\,[T^{-2a-2b}] \quad [1½]$$

Equating powers, we get

$$a + b = 0 \Rightarrow a = -b$$
$$-a + 2b = 1 \Rightarrow b = \frac{1}{3}$$
$$-2a - 2b = 0 \Rightarrow a = -\frac{1}{3}$$

$$\therefore \quad x \propto \eta^{-1/3}E_k^{1/3} \quad \text{or} \quad x \propto \left[\frac{E_k}{\eta}\right]^{1/3} \quad [1½]$$

18 (i) $k = \frac{3}{16}mv^2 = \text{kg}(\text{ms}^{-1})^2 = \text{kgm}^2\text{s}^{-2}$ [1]

(ii) $k = \frac{1}{3}mv^2 + ma = \text{kg}(\text{ms}^{-1})^2 + \text{kg ms}^{-2}$

$= \text{kg m}^2\text{s}^{-2} + \text{kg ms}^{-2}$

Thus using dimensional argument case (i) is correct for kinetic energy $[ML^2T^{-2}]$

But in Case (ii), the quantities having different dimensions can not be added. So, it is wrong. [2]

19 (i) Universal gravitational constant,

$$G_1 = \frac{Fr^2}{m_1 m_2} = \frac{[M\,L\,T^{-2}]\,[L^2]}{[M]\,[M]} = [M^{-1}L^3T^{-2}]$$

(ii) As we know that, rate of heat flow,

$$\frac{\Delta Q}{\Delta t} = KA\frac{dT}{dx}$$

$\Rightarrow$ Coefficient of thermal conductivity,

$$K = \frac{\Delta Q}{\Delta t} \times \frac{dx}{AdT}$$
$$= \frac{[ML^2\,T^{-2}]\,[L]}{[TL^2\,K]} = [M\,L\,T^{-3}K^{-1}]$$

(iii) Resistance, $R = \frac{V}{I}$

$$\Rightarrow \quad V = \frac{W}{Q} = \frac{[ML^2T^{-2}]}{[AT]} = [ML^2T^{-3}A^{-1}]$$

(iv) Dimensions of β^3 = Dimensions of density = $[ML^{-3}]$

$$\beta = [M^{1/3}\,L^{-1}]$$

Also, α = Force × Density = $[MLT^{-2}]\,[ML^{-3}]$

$$= [M^2L^{-2}T^{-2}]$$

(v) Angle has unit of radian but has no dimensions because $\theta = \frac{l}{r}$.

20 Number of protons $= \frac{1}{1.67 \times 10^{-27}}$

$= 5.99 \times 10^{26}$

21 $\lambda = 6463\text{Å} = 6463 \times 10^{-10}$ m

$= 646.3 \times 10^{-9}\,\text{m} = 646.3\,\text{nm}$

$= 0.6463 \times 10^{-6}\,\text{m} = 0.6463\,\mu\text{m}$

22 $1\,\text{J} = 1\,\text{kg m}^2\text{s}^{-2}$

In CGS system, $n_2 = n_1\left[\frac{1\text{kg}}{1\text{g}}\right]\left[\frac{1\text{m}^2}{1\text{cm}^2}\right]\left[\frac{1\text{s}^{-2}}{1\text{s}^{-2}}\right]$

$= 1\left[\frac{10^3\text{g}}{1\text{g}}\right]\left[\frac{10^4\,\text{cm}^2}{1\text{cm}^2}\right]\left[\frac{1\text{s}^{-2}}{1\text{s}^{-2}}\right]$

$= 10^7$ CGS units

23 (i) $3.27 + 33.5472 = 36.8172 \simeq 36.82$ [1/2]

(ii) $53.312 - 53.3 = 0.012 \simeq 0$ [1/2]

(iii) $2.02 \times 23 = 46.46 \simeq 46$ [1/2]

(iv) $3.908 \times 5.5 = 21.494 \simeq 21$ [1/2]

24 Force $= MLT^{-2} = 100$ dyne

$$= 100 \text{ g cm s}^{-2} \quad \text{... (i)}$$

$$\text{Velocity} = LT^{-1} = 10 \text{ cm s}^{-1} \quad \text{... (ii)}$$

$$\text{Energy} = ML^2T^{-2} = 400 \text{ ergs}$$

$$= 400 \text{ g cm}^2 \text{ s}^{-2} \quad \text{... (iii)}$$ [1/2]

Divide Eq. (iii) by Eq. (i), we get

$$\frac{ML^2T^{-2}}{MLT^{-2}} = \frac{400}{100} \text{ cm} \Rightarrow L = 4 \text{ cm}$$ [1/2]

Divide Eq. (iii) by Eq. (ii)

$$\frac{ML^2T^{-2}}{LT^{-1}} = \frac{400}{10} = 40 \text{ g cm s}^{-1}$$

$$MLT^{-1} = 40 \text{ g cm s}^{-1} \quad \text{...(iv)}$$ [1/2]

Divide Eq. (i) by Eq. (iv), we get

$$\frac{MLT^{-2}}{MLT^{-1}} = \frac{100}{40} \text{s}^{-1}$$

$$\Rightarrow \quad T = \frac{4}{10} = 0.4 \text{ s} \quad \text{...(iv)}$$

Put value of T and L into Eq. (iv), we get

$$M(4)(0.4)^{-1} = 40 \Rightarrow M = 4 \text{ g}$$ [1/2]

25 (i) 3.0120 has 5 significant figures. [1/2]

(ii) 123.0 km has 4 significant figures. [1/2]

(iii) 0.006235 s has 4 significant figures. [1/2]

(iv) 0.23×10^{-3} has 2 significant figures. [1/2]

(v) 100.007 g has 6 significant figures. [1/2]

(vi) 143000 km has 6 significant figures. [1/2]

CHAPTER

02

Motion in a Straight Line

Motion in a straight line is also called rectilinear motion. It involves no change in direction so its study is relatively simple. Under this head, we will study motion of object either along X-axis or along Y-axis.

- General Introduction of Motion
- Uniformly Accelerated Motion

TOPIC 01 General Introduction of Motion

Mechanics is a branch of physics that deals with physical energy and forces; and their effects on objects.

There are three branches of mechanics that examine the motion of an object such as

Statics It is a branch of mechanics in which we study the objects at rest. In statics, time factor does not play any role.

Kinematics It describes the motion of objects without looking at the cause of the motion. Here, time factor plays an important role.

Dynamics It relates the motion of objects to the forces which cause them. The time factor also plays an important role.

Frame of Reference

We choose a rectangular coordinate system of three mutually perpendicular axes as x, y and z. The point of intersection of these three axes is called **origin** (O) and considered as the **reference point**.

The x, y, z-coordinates describe the position of the object w.r.t. the coordinate system. To measure time, we need a clock. This coordinate system alongwith a clock constitutes a **frame of reference**.

So, the frame of reference is a coordinate system with a clock w.r.t. which, an observer can describe the position, displacement, acceleration of an object.

Frame of reference are of two types

(i) **Inertial frame of reference** These are the frame of reference in which, Newton's first law of motion is applicable.

(ii) **Non-inertial frame of reference** These are the frame of reference in which, Newton's first law of motion is not applicable.

Point Object (Point Mass)

An object is considered as point object if the size of the object is much smaller than the distance it moves in a reasonable duration of time. e.g.

(i) A train under a journey of several hundred kilometres can be regarded as a point object.

(ii) Earth can be regarded as a point object for studying its motion around the sun. As the diameter (size) of earth is very small as compared to the distance between the sun and the earth.

The following example helps us to decide about a point object.

Example 1 In which of the following examples of motion, can the body be considered approximately a point object? **NCERT**

(i) A railway carriage moving without jerks between two stations.

(ii) A monkey sitting on the top of a man cycling smoothly on a circular track.

(iii) A spinning cricket ball that turns sharply on hitting the ground.

Sol. Any object can be considered as a point object if the distance travelled by it is very large in comparison to its dimensions.

(i) A railway carriage is moving without jerks between two stations, it means stations are at large distance, therefore railway carriage can be taken as a point object.

(ii) Man along with monkey is cycling smoothly which indicates that the distance travelled by the man is very large, therefore monkey can be taken as a point object.

(iii) The distance travelled by the ball is not so large therefore, spinning cricket ball cannot be taken as a point object.

Rest

If the position of an object does not change w.r.t. its surrounding with the passage of time, it is said to be at **rest**. e.g. Book lying on the table, a person sitting on a chair, etc.

Motion

If the position of an object is continuously changing w.r.t. its surrounding, then it is said to be in the **state of motion**. Thus, motion can be defined as a change in position of an object with time.

Types of Motion

On the basis of the nature of path followed, motion is classified as

(i) **Rectilinear Motion** The motion in which a particle moves along a straight line is called **rectilinear motion.**

e.g. Motion of a sliding body on an inclined plane.

(ii) **Circular Motion** The motion in which a particle moves in a circular path is called **circular motion.**

e.g. A string whirled in a circular loop.

(iii) **Oscillatory Motion** The motion in which a particle moves to and fro about a given point is known as **oscillatory motion.**

e.g. Simple pendulum

On the basis of the number of coordinates required to define the motion, motion is classified as

(i) **One-dimensional Motion** The motion of an object is considered as 1-D if only one coordinate is needed to specify the position of the object.

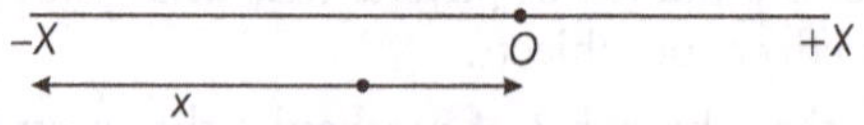

Motion in 1-D

In 1-D motion, the object moves along a straight line. In this type of motion, there are only two directions (backward and forward, upward and downward) in which an object moves and these directions are specified by + and – signs.

e.g. A boy running on a straight road, etc.

(ii) **Two-dimensional Motion** The motion of an object is considered as 2-D if two coordinates are needed to specify the position of the object. In 2-D motion, the object moves in a plane.

e.g. A satellite revolving around the earth, etc.

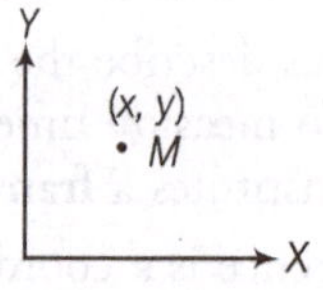

Motion in 2-D

(iii) **Three-dimensional Motion** The motion of an object is considered as 3-D if all the three coordinates are needed to specify the position of the object. This type of motion takes place in three-dimensional space.

e.g. Butterfly flying in garden, the motion of water molecules, etc.

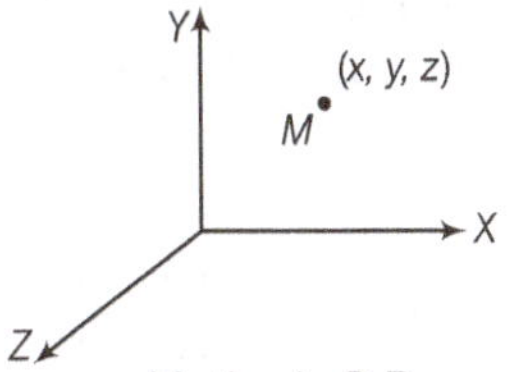

Motion in 3-D

Note

- **Scalars** If only the magnitude is required to specify a physical quantity, that physical quantity is known as **scalar quantity** or **scalars.** e.g. Mass, length, time, speed, etc.
- **Vectors** If magnitude as well as direction both are required to specify a physical quantity, that physical quantity is known as **vector quantity** or **vectors.** e.g. Displacement, velocity, acceleration, etc.

Some Definition Relating to Motion

1. Position

It is defined as the point where an object is situated. Position can be determined by the coordinate axis that is, marked in units of length and that has positive and negative directions.

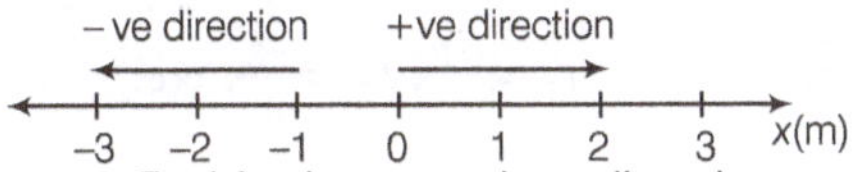

Position in +ve and –ve direction

e.g. If an object is situated at – 1 m, then minus sign indicates that the position has negative direction but if the object is at 0 m position then it will be said to be at rest.

2. Path Length/Distance

The length of the path covered by an object in a given time-interval, is known as its **path length** or **distance travelled.** Its SI unit is metre.

Example 2 A scooter is moving along a straight line *AB* covers a distance of 360 m in 24 s and returns back from *B to C* and coveres 240 m in 18 s. Find the total path length travelled by the scooter.

Sol. From the above question, we draw the following figure.

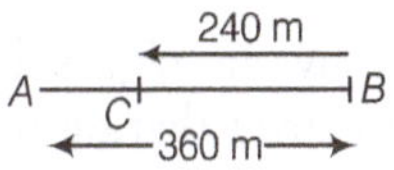

Total path length $= AB + BC = 360 + 240$

$= 600$ m

3. Displacement

The change in position of an object in a particular direction is termed as **displacement,** i.e. the difference between the final and initial positions of the object. It is denoted by Δx. Mathematically, it is represented by

$$\text{Displacement, } \Delta x = x_2 - x_1$$

where, x_1 and x_2 are the initial and final position of the object, respectively.

Cases

(i) If $x_2 > x_1$, then displacement is positive.

(ii) If $x_1 > x_2$, then displacement is negative.

(iii) If $x_1 = x_2$, then displacement is zero.

Displacement is a **vector quantity** as it possesses both, the magnitude and direction.

Note

- The magnitude of displacement may or may not be equal to the path length traversed by an object.
- The magnitude of the displacement for a course of motion may be zero but the corresponding path length will never be zero.

Example 3 A boy starts moving from –20 m towards $+x$-axis as shown in figure. He turns at time instant t_2 and starts moving towards $-x$-axis. At time t_3, he reached at –50 m as shown in the figure.

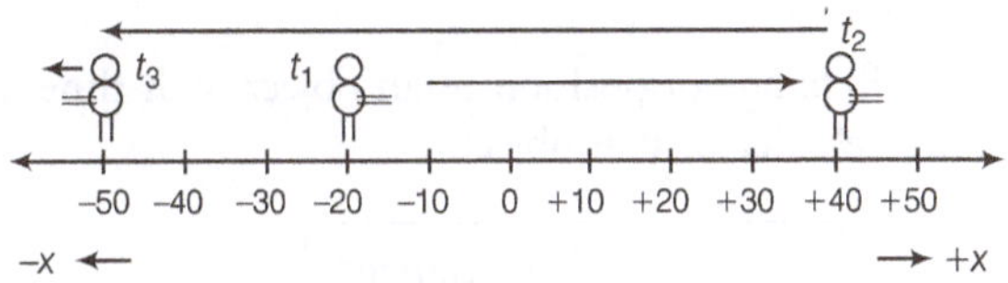

Sol. (i) For t_1 to t_2,

Distance covered $= 20 + 40 = 60$ m

Displacement $= 40 - (-20)$

$= +60$ m (towards + x-axis)

(ii) For t_1 to t_3,

Distance covered $= 60 + 90 = 150$ m

Displacement $= -50 - (-20)$

$= -30$ m (towards – x-axis)

4. Speed

The distance covered by an object divided by the time taken by the object to cover that distance is called the **speed** of that object.

$$\text{Speed} = \frac{\text{Distance travelled}}{\text{Time taken}}$$

Speed is a **scalar quantity.** The speed of the object for a given interval of time is always positive.

Unit of speed The unit of speed in MKS (SI) is m/s and in CGS as cm/s.

Dimensional formula $[M^0LT^{-1}]$

Uniform Speed If an object is moving with a uniform speed, it means that it covers equal distance in equal interval of time.

Variable or Non-Uniform Speed If an object is moving with a non-uniform speed, it means that it covers equal distances in unequal intervals of time or unequal distances in equal intervals of time.

Example 4 A train 100 m long is moving with a speed of 60 km/h. In what time shall it cross a bridge of 1 km long?

Sol. Given length of the train, $s_1 = 100$ m

Length of the bridge, $s_2 = 1 \text{ km} = 1000 \text{ m}, t = ?$

Total length, $s = 100 + 1000 = 1100$ m

Speed of train, $s = 60 \text{ km/h} = 60 \times \frac{5}{18} = \frac{50}{3}$ m/s

$$\therefore \quad t = \frac{\text{Distance}}{\text{Speed}} = \frac{1100}{\frac{50}{3}} = 66 \text{ s}$$

5. Velocity

The rate of change of position of an object with time is called the **velocity** of that object.

i.e.
$$\text{Velocity} = \frac{\text{Displacement}}{\text{Time}}$$

Velocity is a **vector** quantity.

Unit of velocity The unit of velocity is cms^{-1} in CGS and ms^{-1} in MKS or SI.

Dimensional formula The dimensional formula of velocity is $[M^0LT^{-1}]$.

Uniform Velocity An object is said to possess uniform velocity, if it covers equal displacement in equal interval of time.

Non-uniform Velocity If an object is moving with a non-uniform velocity, then it will have unequal displacements in equal interval of time.

Note The velocity of an object can be positive, zero and negative according to its displacement is positive, zero and negative.

Example 5 During a hard sneeze, your eyes might shut for 0.5 s. If you are driving a car at 90 km/h during such a sneeze, how far does the car move during that time?

Sol. Given, $t = 0.5$ s

$$\text{Velocity } (v) = 90 \text{ km/h} = \frac{90 \times 1000}{60 \times 60} = 25 \text{ m/s}$$

We know that, $v = \frac{\Delta x}{\Delta t}$

$$\therefore \quad \Delta x = v\Delta t = (25 \text{ m/s})(0.5 \text{ s}) = 12.5 \text{ m} \approx 13 \text{ m}$$

6. Average Speed

Average speed of an object is defined as the total distance travelled by the object divided by the total time taken.

$$\text{Average speed, } v_{av} = \frac{\text{Total distance travelled}}{\text{Total time taken}}$$

Let us consider the average speed in **two cases** as given below

(i) If a particle covers distances $s_1, s_2, \ldots, s_n$, with speeds $v_1, v_2, \ldots, v_n$, then

$$\text{Average speed, } v_{av} = \frac{s_1 + s_2 + \ldots}{\left(\frac{s_1}{v_1} + \frac{s_2}{v_2} + \frac{s_3}{v_3} + \ldots\right)}$$

where, $t_1 = \frac{s_1}{v_1}, t_2 = \frac{s_2}{v_2}$, etc.

(ii) If a particle moves with speeds v_1, v_2, v_3, for the time intervals t_1, t_2, t_3, then

$$\text{Average speed} = \frac{\text{Total distance covered}}{\text{Total time taken}}$$

$$= \frac{v_1t_1 + v_2t_2 + v_3t_3 + \ldots}{t_1 + t_2 + t_3 + \ldots}$$

Example 6 A car covers the first half of the distance between two places at a speed of 40 km/h and second half at 60 km/h. Calculate the average speed of the car.

Sol. Speed in first half, $v_1 = 40$ km/h

Speed in second half, $v_2 = 60$ km/h

Let the total distance covered is x km.

Distance covered in first half, $s_1 = \frac{x}{2}$

Distance covered in second half, $s_2 = \frac{x}{2}$

Time taken in first half = t_1 and second half = t_2

We need to clarify all the variables by figure.

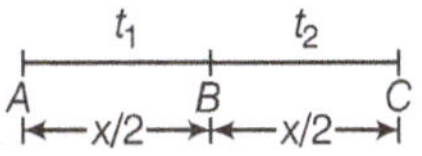

Total time taken by the body to travel first half and second half.

$$t_1 = \frac{x/2}{40} = \frac{x}{80}\text{ h} \quad \text{and} \quad t_2 = \frac{x/2}{60} = \frac{x}{120}\text{ h}$$

$$\text{Average speed, } v_{av} = \frac{s_1 + s_2}{t_1 + t_2} = \frac{\frac{x}{2} + \frac{x}{2}}{\frac{x}{80} + \frac{x}{120}}$$

$$v_{av} = \frac{\frac{1}{2} + \frac{1}{2}}{\frac{1}{80} + \frac{1}{120}} = \frac{80 \times 120}{(120 + 80)} = 48 \text{ km/h}$$

The average speed of car is 48 km/h.

7. Average Velocity

Average velocity of a body is defined as the change in position or displacement (Δx) divided by the time interval (Δt) in which that displacement occurs.

Suppose a body is moving along the path PR. At time t_1, suppose the body is at P and its position w.r.t. origin O is given by vector x_1 and at time instant t_2 the body is at position x_2.

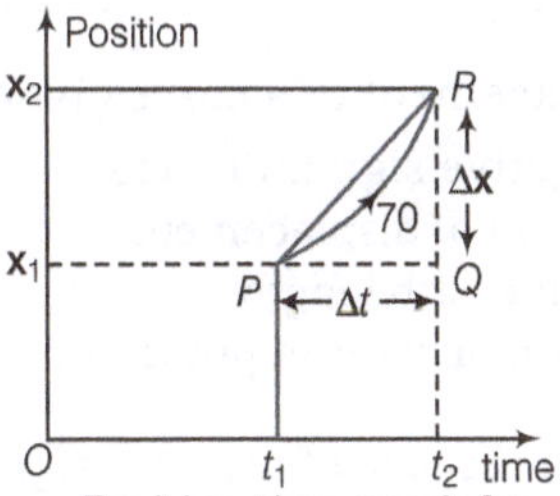

Position-time graph for displacement

Thus, displacement of the body, $\Delta x = x_2 - x_1$

The total time taken for displacement **x** is, $\Delta t = t_2 - t_1$

$\therefore$ Average velocity of the body is given by

$$\mathbf{v}_{av} = \frac{\Delta x}{\Delta t} = \frac{x_2 - x_1}{t_2 - t_1} = \text{slope of line } PR = \frac{RQ}{QP}$$

Example 7 A car is moving along a straight line, say OP in the given figure. It moves from O to P in 18 s and returns from P to Q in 6.0 s. What are the average velocity and average speed of the car in going (i) from O to P ? and (ii) from O to P and back to Q? **NCERT**

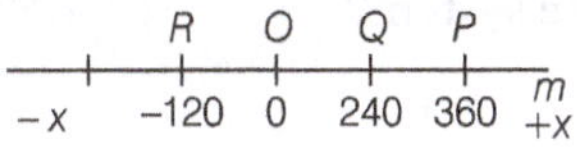

Sol. (i) From O to P

$$\text{Average velocity} = \frac{\text{Displacement}}{\text{Time interval}}$$

$$\mathbf{v}_{av} = \frac{+360\text{m}}{18\text{s}} = +20\text{ms}^{-1}$$

$$\text{Average speed} = \frac{\text{Path length}}{\text{Time interval}}$$

$$= \frac{360\text{m}}{18\text{s}} = 20\text{ms}^{-1}$$

Thus, in this case, the average speed is equal to the magnitude of the average velocity.

(ii) From O to P and back to Q

$$\text{Average velocity} = \frac{\text{Displacement}}{\text{Time interval}} = \frac{+240\text{ m}}{(18+6.0)\text{ s}}$$

$$= +10\text{ms}^{-1}$$

$$\text{Average speed} = \frac{\text{Path length}}{\text{Time interval}} = \frac{OP + PQ}{\Delta t}$$

$$= \frac{360+120}{24} = 20\text{m/s}$$

Example 8 A body travels from A to B at 40 m/s and from B to A at 60m/s. Calculate the average velocity.

Sol. Total time taken by the body to travel from A to B and then from B to A,

$$t_1 + t_2 = \frac{AB}{40} + \frac{BA}{60} = AB\left(\frac{1}{40} + \frac{1}{60}\right) = \frac{AB}{24}\text{s}$$

As the body comes back to its initial position A, its net displacement is zero.

$$\therefore \text{ Average velocity} = \frac{\text{Displacement}}{\text{Time}} = \frac{0}{AB/24} = 0$$

8. Instantaneous Speed

Speed at an instant is defined as the limit of the average speed as the time interval (Δt) becomes infinitesimally small or approaches to zero.

Mathematically, instantaneous speed at any instant of time (t) is expressed as

$$\boxed{\text{Instantaneous speed, } s_i = \lim_{\Delta t \to 0} \frac{\Delta s}{\Delta t} \text{ or } s_i = \frac{ds}{dt}}$$

[ds is the distance covered in time dt]

where, $\frac{ds}{dt}$ is the differential coefficient of s w.r.t. t.

Example 9 If the average speed of the particle is $[2t^2\hat{i} + 3t\hat{j}]$, then find out the instantaneous speed of the particle.

Sol. Given, position of the particle

$$s = [2t^2\hat{i} + 3t\hat{j}]$$

$$s_i = \frac{ds}{dt} = \frac{d}{dt}[2t^2\hat{i} + 3t\hat{j}]$$

Instantaneous speed of the particle is

$$s_i = 4t\,\hat{i} + 3\hat{j}$$

9. Instantaneous Velocity

Instantaneous velocity at an instant is defined as the limit of average velocity as the time interval (Δt) becomes infinitesimally small or approaches to zero.

Mathematically, instantaneous velocity at instant of time (t) is given by

$$v_i = \lim_{\Delta t \to 0} \frac{\Delta x}{\Delta t} \quad \text{or} \quad v_i = \frac{dx}{dt}$$

where, dx is displacement for time dt.

Note

$\lim_{\Delta t \to 0} \frac{\Delta x}{\Delta t}$ is called **differential coefficient** of displacement x w.r.t. time t, i.e. $\frac{dx}{dt}$.

Example 10 The displacement (in metre) of a particle moving along x-axis is given by $x = 18t + 15t^2$. Find the instantaneous velocity at $t = 0$ and $t = 2$s.

Sol. Given, Displacement,

$$x = 18t + 15t^2$$

Instantaneous velocity,

$$v_i = \frac{dx}{dt} = 18 + 30t$$

Instantaneous velocity at

$t = 0$, $v = 18 + 30 \times 0 = 18$ m/s

$t = 2$s, $v = 18 + 30 \times 2 = 78$ m/s

Topic Practice 1

Multiple Choice Questions

1 Mark

1. Which of the following statements is true for a car moving on the road?
   (a) With respect to the frame of reference attached to the ground, the car is at rest
   (b) With respect to the frame of reference attached to the person sitting in the car, the car is at rest
   (c) With respect to the frame of reference attached to the person outside the car, the car is at rest
   (d) None of the above

2. The x-t graph representing an object at rest is

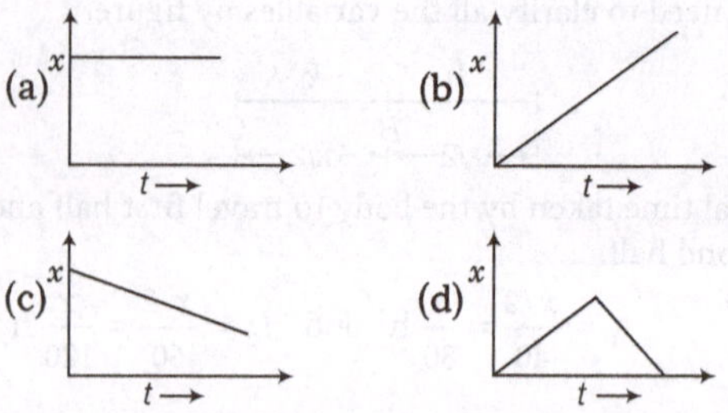

3. The coordinates of object with respect to a frame of reference at $t = 0$ are $(-1, 0, 3)$. If $t = 5$ s, its coordinates are $(-1, 0, 4)$, then the object is in
   (a) motion along Z-axis
   (b) motion along X-axis
   (c) motion along Y-axis
   (d) rest position between $t = 0$ s and $t = 5$ s

4. The position-time graph for a uniform motion is represented as

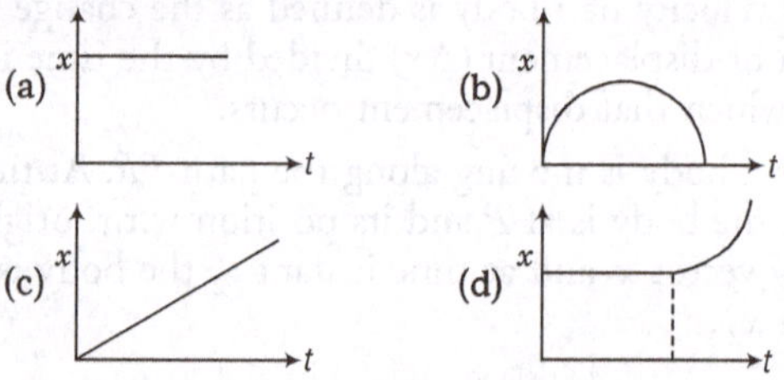

5. The displacement of a car is given as -240 m. Here, negative sign indicates
   (a) direction of displacement
   (b) negative path length
   (c) position of car is at point whose coordinate is -120
   (d) no significance of negative sign

6. A cyclist moving on a circular track of radius 40 m completes half a revolution in 40 s. Its average velocity is
   (a) zero (b) 2 ms^{-1}
   (c) 4π ms^{-1} (d) 8π ms^{-1}

Very Short Answer Type Questions

1 Mark

7. Can a tumbling beaker that has slipped off the edge of a table considered as a point object? **NCERT**

8. Does the displacement of an object depend on the choice of the position of origin of the coordinate system?

9. For which condition, the distance and the magnitude of displacement of an object have the same values?

10. Position-time graph could have negative slope. Is it true or false?

11. The displacement-time graph of a particle is parallel to time-axis, what is the velocity of the particle ?

12. Here is a distance-time graph, observe it and comment.

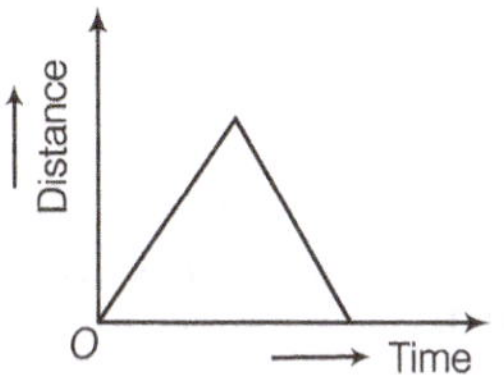

13. Which speed is measured by speedometer of your scooter?

14. Speed of a particle cannot be negative. Why?

15. With zero speed a particle may have non-zero velocity. Is the statement true or false, explain? NCERT

16. Is it possible that a body could have constant speed but varying velocity?

17. For which condition, the magnitude of average velocity is equal to the average speed for a particular motion?

18. For which condition, the average velocity will be equal to the instantaneous velocity?

19. Is it possible to have negative value in speed and displacement?

Short Answer Type I Questions

(2 Marks)

20. From the given examples, find if the motion is one or two or three-dimensional.
   (i) A kite flying in the sky
   (ii) A cricket ball hit by a player
   (iii) Moon revolving around the earth and
   (iv) The motion of a stone in a circle

21. For what condition, an object could be considered as a point object? Describe in brief.

22. Explain how an object could have zero average velocity but non-zero average speed?

23. If the displacement of a body is zero, is distance necessarily zero? Answer with one example.

24. The data regarding the motion of two different objects P and Q are given in the following table. Examine them carefully and state whether the motion of the objects are uniform or non-uniform.

Time	Distance travelled by object P (in m)	Distance travelled by object Q (in m)
9:30 am	10	12
9:45 am	20	19
10:00 am	30	23
10:15 am	40	35
10:30 am	50	37
10.45 am	60	41
11:00 am	70	44

25. A body travels with a velocity v_1 for time t_1 and with a velocity v_2 for time t_2, find the average velocity of the body for the total time.

Short Answer Type II Questions

(3 Marks)

26. A person travels along a straight road for the first half with a velocity v_1 and the second half with velocity v_2. What is the mean velocity of the person?

27. Explain clearly with examples, the distinction between
   (i) magnitude of displacement (sometimes called distance) over an interval of time and the total length of the path covered by a particle over the same interval.
   (ii) magnitude of average velocity over an interval of time and the average speed over the same interval. [Average speed of a particle over an interval of time is defined as the total path length divided by the time interval]. Show in both (a) and (b) that the second quantity is either greater than or equal to first. When is the equality sign true? [For simplicity, consider one-dimensional motion only] NCERT

28. The instantaneous speed is always equal to the magnitude of instantaneous velocity. Why? NCERT

Numerical Problems

29. The displacement-time graph for two particles X and Y are straight lines making angles of 30° and 60° with the time axis. What is the ratio of the velocities of Y and X?

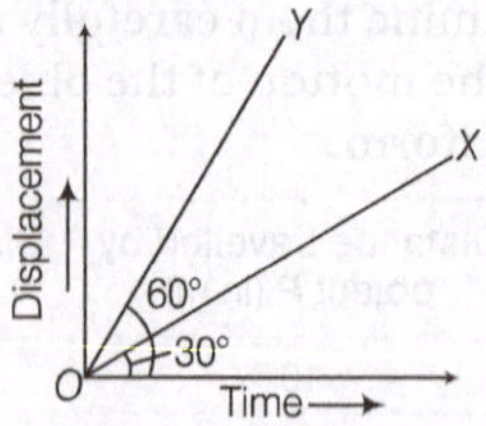

[1 M]

30. The position coordinate of a moving particle is given by $x = 6 + 18t + 9t^2$, where x is in metres and t in seconds. What is the velocity at $t = 2$s? **[1 M]**

31. The position x of a body is given by $x = A\sin(\omega t)$. Find the time at which the displacement is maximum. **[2 M]**

32. A woman starts from her home at 9:00 am walks with a speed of 5 km/h on straight road up to her office 2.5 km away, stays at the office up to 5.00 pm and returns home by an auto with a speed of 25 km/h. Choose suitable scales and plot the x-t graph of her motion. **NCERT [2 M]**

33. A body is moving in a straight line along x-axis. Its distance from the origin is given by the equation $x = at^2 - bt^3$, where x is in metre and t is in second. Find
(i) the average speed of the body in the interval $t = 0$ and $t = 2$s and
(ii) its instantaneous speed at $t = 2$s. **[3 M]**

34. The position of an object moving along x-axis is given by $x = a + bt^2$, where $a = 8.5$ m, $b = 2.5$ m and t is measured in seconds. What is its velocity at $t = 0$ s and $t = 2.0$ s? What is the average velocity between $t = 0$ s and $t = 4.0$ s? **NCERT [3 M]**

35. A man walks on a straight road from his home to a market 2.5 km away with a speed of 5 km/h. Finding the market closed, he instantly turns and walks back with a speed of 7.5 km/h. What is the (i) magnitude of average velocity and (ii) average speed of the man, over the interval of time (a) 0 to 30 min (b) 0 to 50 min (c) 0 to 40 min? **NCERT [3 M]**

36. A drunkard walking in a narrow lane takes 5 steps forward and 3 steps backward, followed again 5 steps forward and 3 steps backward, and so on. Each step is 1 m long and requires 1 s. Determine how long the drunkard takes to fall in a pit 13 m away from the start. **NCERT [2 M]**

37. For the motion shown in the figure, find the displacement of car between the time intervals t_1 and t_3.

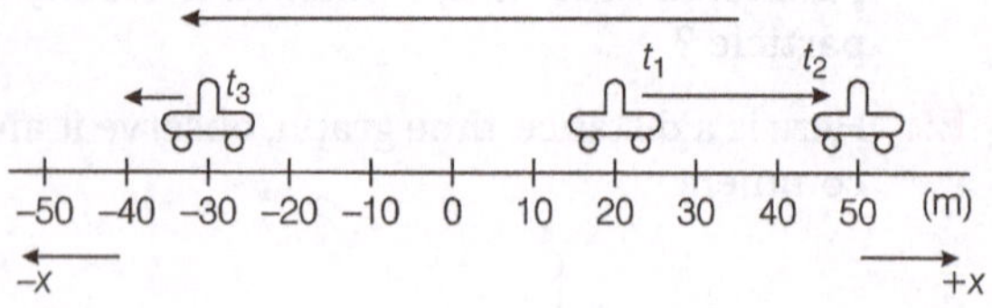

[2 M]

38. The position of an object is given by $x = 2t^2 + 3t$. Find out that its motion is uniform and non-uniform. **[2 M]**

Hints & Solutions

1. (*b*) For a car in motion, if we describe this event w.r.t. a frame of reference attached to the person sitting inside the car, the car will appear to be at rest as the person inside the car (observer) is also moving with same velocity and in the same direction as car.

2. (*a*) For an object at rest, position coordinate must not change.

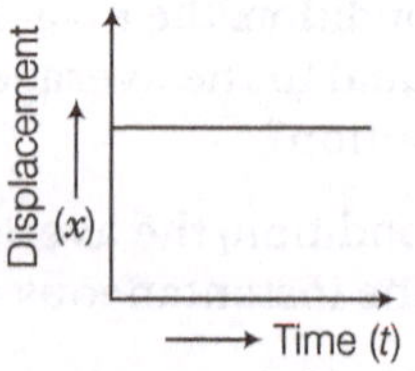

3. (*a*) Given, at $t = 0$ s, position of an object is $(-1, 0, 3)$ and at $t = 5$ s, its coordinate is $(-1, 0, 4)$. So, there is no change in x and y-coordinates while z-coordinate changes from 3 to 4. So, the object is in motion along Z-axis.

4. (*c*) If an object moving along the straight line covers equal distances in equal intervals of time, it is said to be in uniform motion along a straight line.

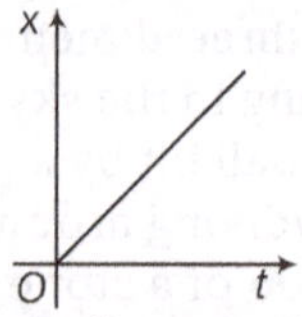

5. (*a*) The displacement of a car is given as −240 m. Here, negative sign indicates the direction of displacement.

6. (*b*) Average velocity $= \dfrac{\text{Displacement}}{\text{Time taken}}$

$$= \frac{2R}{t} = \frac{2 \times 40}{40} = 2\,\text{ms}^{-1}$$

7. No, because the size of the beaker is not negligible as compared to the height of the table.
8. No, the displacement of the object does not depend on the choice of the position of the origin.
9. The distance and the magnitude of displacement of an object have the same values, when the body is moving along a straight line path in a fixed direction.
10. It is true because if the velocity of the object is negative, then slope of v-t graph is negative.
11. The velocity of the particle is zero because the slope of x-t graph is zero.
12. The distance-time graph is not correct because for a moving body distance cannot decrease, it will always increase.
13. Instantaneous speed of the scooter is measured by the speedometer.
14. Speed is the distance travelled in unit time and distance cannot be negative.
15. False, because velocity is the speed of body in a given condition.

    When speed is zero, the magnitude of velocity of body is zero. Thus, velocity is zero.
16. Yes, a body could have constant speed but varying velocity if only the direction of motion changes.
17. When a particle is moving along a straight line with the fixed direction.
18. When a body moves with a uniform velocity, then

$$v_{av} = v_{inst}$$

19. Displacement can have negative value when the difference between final and initial positions of the object is negative. But speed can never be negative because speed = distance/time and distance cannot be negative.
20. (i) A flying kite in the sky comes under **three**-dimensional motion.

    (ii) A cricket ball hit by a player comes under **two**-dimensional motion.

    (iii) Moon revolving around the sun-earth comes under **two**-dimensional motion.

    (iv) The motion of the stone in circular motion comes under **two**-dimensional motion. [½ × 4]
21. An object could be considered as a point object if it covers a distance much larger than its own size.

    e.g. If a bus of 5 m in size move 100 km, then the bus can be considered as a point object. [2]
22. Average velocity, $v_{av} = \dfrac{\text{Net displacement}}{\text{Total time taken}}$

    and average speed, $s_{av} = \dfrac{\text{Total distance travelled}}{\text{Total time taken}}$ [1]

    If an object moves along a straight line starting from origin and then returns back to origin.

$$\text{Average velocity} = 0$$

and $\text{Average speed} = \dfrac{2s}{t}$ [1]

23. No, because the distance covered by an object is the path length of the path covered by the object. The displacement of an object is given by the change in position between the initial position and final position. [1/2]

    e.g. A boy starts from his home and moves towards market along a straight path. Then, he returns to home from the same path. Here, displacement is zero but distance is non-zero. [1½]
24. We can see that the object P covers a distance of 10 m in every 15 min. In other words, it covers equal distance in equal intervals of time. So, the motion of object P is uniform. [1]

    On the other hand, the object Q covers 7 m from 9:30 am to 9:45 am, 4 m from 9:45 am to 10:00 am and so on. In other words, it covers unequal distances in equal intervals of time. So, the motion of object Q is non-uniform. [1]
25. Displacement travelled in time

$$(t_1 + t_2) = s_1 + s_2 = v_1 t_1 + v_2 t_2 \quad [1]$$

$$\therefore \text{ Average velocity} = \frac{\text{Net displacement}}{\text{Total time taken}} = \frac{v_1 t_1 + v_2 t_2}{(t_1 + t_2)} \quad [1]$$

26. Time taken by person to travel first half

$$t_1 = \frac{(d/2)}{v_1} = \frac{d}{2v_1}$$

Time taken by person to travel second half

$$t_2 = \frac{d/2}{v_2} = \frac{d}{2v_2} \quad [1]$$

$$\because \text{ Total time} = t_1 + t_2 = \frac{d}{2}\left[\frac{1}{v_1} + \frac{1}{v_2}\right] = \frac{d(v_1 + v_2)}{2v_1 v_2} \quad [1]$$

$\therefore$ Mean velocity or average velocity

$$= \frac{d}{t_1 + t_2} = \frac{2v_1 v_2}{(v_1 + v_2)} \quad [1]$$

27. (i) Magnitude of displacement of a particle in motion for a given time is the shortest distance between the initial and final position of the particle in that time, whereas the total length of the path covered by particle is the length of actual path traversed by the particle in the given time. [1]

    (ii) Let us consider an example

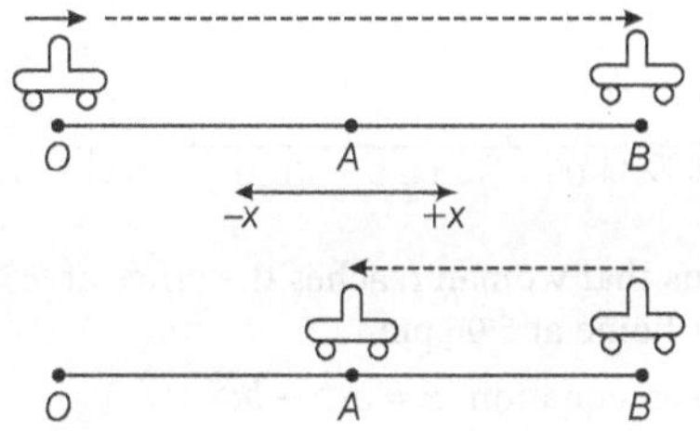

A car starts from O and moves along positive x-axis. The car stops at B and starts moving towards negative x-axis. Finally, the car reaches at A.

For the motion from O to B.

So, |Displacement| = Distance covered

|Average velocity| = Average speed [1]

For the motion from $O \rightarrow B \rightarrow A$

So, |Displacement| < Distance covered

|Average velocity| < Average speed [1]

28. Instantaneous speed (v_{ins}) of the particle at an instant is the first derivative of the distance with respect to time at that instant of time i.e. $v_{ins} = \frac{dx}{dt}$. [1]

Since, in instantaneous speed, we take only a small interval of time (dt) during which direction of motion of a body is not supposed to change, hence there is no difference between total path length and magnitude of displacement for small interval of time dt.

Hence, instantaneous speed is always equal to magnitude of instantaneous velocity. [2]

29. Slope of displacement-time graph = velocity of the object. Hence, ratio of two velocities

$$\frac{v_Y}{v_X} = \frac{\tan 60°}{\tan 30°} = \frac{\sqrt{3}}{1/\sqrt{3}} = 3:1$$

30. Given, $x = 6 + 18t + 9t^2$

$$v_t = \frac{dx}{dt} = 18 + 18t$$

At $t = 2$, $v_2 = 18 + 18 \times 2 = 54$ m/s

31. The value of position x will be maximum, when the value of $\sin(\omega t)$ is maximum, for this

$$\sin(\omega t) = 1 = \sin \pi/2 \quad [1]$$

or $\omega t = \frac{\pi}{2} \Rightarrow t = \left(\frac{\pi}{2\omega}\right)$ [1]

32. Time taken in reaching the office $= \frac{\text{distance}}{\text{speed}} = \frac{2.5}{5} = 0.5$ h

Time taken in returning from office $= \frac{2.5}{25} = 0.1$ h $= 6$ min [1]

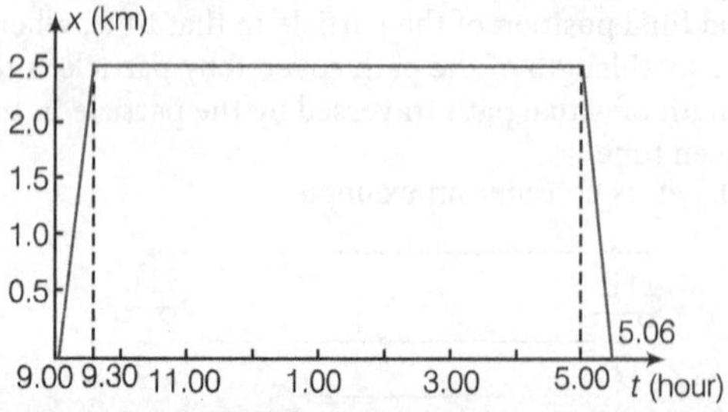

It means that woman reaches the office at 9:30 am and returns home at 5:06 pm. [1]

33. The given equation $x = at^2 - bt^3$

(i) If $t = 0$, $x_0 = 0$

If $t = 2s$, $x_2 = 4a - 8b$

$\because \Delta x = x_2 - x_0 = 4a - 8b - 0 = 4a - 8b$ [1/2]

$\therefore$ Average speed in the given interval of time,

$$v_{av} = \frac{\Delta x}{\Delta t} = \frac{4a - 8b}{2} = 2a - 4b \quad [1]$$

(ii) Instantaneous speed

$$v = \frac{dx}{dt} = \frac{d}{dt}(at^2 - bt^3) = 2at - 3bt^2 \quad [1]$$

At $t = 2s$, $v = 4a - 12b$ m/s [1/2]

34. We know that, $v = \frac{dx}{dt}$ [1]

On differentiating w.r.t. t, we get

$$v = \frac{d}{dt}(a + bt^2) = 2bt = 5t \text{ m/s} \quad [\because b = 2.5 \text{ m}]$$ [1]

At $t = 0, v = 0$, $t = 2$s and $v = 10$ m/s

$$\text{Average velocity} = \frac{x(4) - x(2)}{4 \quad 2} = \frac{a + 16b - a - 4b}{2}$$

$$= 6 \times b = 6 \times 2.5 = 15 \text{ m/s} \quad [1]$$

35. Time taken by man to go from his home to market

$$t_1 = \frac{\text{Distance}}{\text{Speed}} = \frac{2.5}{5} = \frac{1}{2} \text{ h}$$

Time taken by man to go from market to his home

$$t_2 = \frac{2.5}{7.5} = \frac{1}{3} \text{h}$$

$\therefore$ Total time taken, $t_1 + t_2 = \frac{1}{2} + \frac{1}{3} = \frac{5}{6}$ h $= 50$ min

(i) **0 to 30 min**

(*a*) Average velocity $= \frac{\text{Displacement}}{\text{Time}} = \frac{2.5}{1/2} = 5$ km/h

(*b*) Average speed $= \frac{\text{Distance}}{\text{Time}} = \frac{2.5}{1/2} = 5$ km/h [1]

(ii) **0 to 50 min**

Total distance travelled = 2.5 + 2.5 = 5 km

Total displacement = 2.5 − 2.5 = 0

(a) Average velocity $= \frac{\text{Displacement}}{\text{Time}} = 0$

(b) Average speed $= \frac{\text{Distance}}{\text{Time}} = \frac{5}{5/6} = 6$ km/h [1]

(iii) **0 to 40 min**

Distance moved in 30 min (from home to market) = 2.5 km.

Distance moved in 10 min (from market to home) with speed 7.5 km/h $= 7.5 \times \frac{10}{60} = 1.25$ km

So, displacement = 2.5 − 1.25 = 1.25 km

Distance travelled = 2.5 + 1.25 = 3.75 km

(*a*) Average velocity $= \frac{1.25}{(40/60)}$

$= 1.875$ km/h

(*b*) Average speed $= \frac{3.75}{(40/60)} = 5.625$ km/h [1]

36. The effective distance travelled by drunkard in 8 steps $= 5 - 3 = 2$ m

Therefore, he takes 32 steps to move 8 m. [1]

Now, he will have to cover 5 m more to reach the pit, for which he has to take only 5 forward steps.

Therefore, he will have to take $= 32 + 5 = 37$ steps to move 13 m. Thus, he will fall into the pit after taking 37 steps i.e. after 37 s from the start. [1]

37. A car moving towards $+x$-axis. At time t_1 it is at +20 m.

It turns at +50 m and starts moving towards $-x$-axis. At time t_3, it reached at -30 m. [1]

The displacement of car in the interval $(t_3 - t_1) = \Delta t$ is $-30-(+20) = -50$ m (negative sign shows the direction of displacement is towards $-x$-axis). [1]

38. As given, $x = 2t^2 + 3t$

By differentiating x w.r.t. t, we get

Velocity, $$v = \frac{dx}{dt} = \frac{d}{dt}(2t^2 + 3t)$$ [1]

$$v = (4t + 3)$$

As velocity is time dependent, it means that motion is non-uniform. [1]

TOPIC 02 Uniformly Accelerated Motion

Acceleration

The existence of acceleration was given by Galileo in his different thoughts. **Acceleration of a body can be expressed as the rate of change of velocity with time.** By acceleration, we can understand that how fast or slow the velocity of an object is changing. Acceleration is a **vector quantity.**

$$\text{Acceleration} = \frac{\text{Change in velocity}}{\text{Time taken}}$$

Its SI unit is metre per second square (m/s^2) and CGS is cm/s^2. The dimensional formula is $[M^0L^1T^{-2}]$.

Average Acceleration

The average acceleration over a time interval is defined as **the change in velocity divided by the time interval.**

Suppose that at any time (t_1) a body has velocity $(\mathbf{v}_1)$. At a later time (t_2), it has velocity $(\mathbf{v}_2)$. Thus,

$$\text{Average acceleration, } \mathbf{a}_{av} = \frac{\Delta \mathbf{v}}{\Delta t} = \frac{\mathbf{v}_2 - \mathbf{v}_1}{t_2 - t_1}$$

The slope of velocity-time graph gives acceleration.

Instantaneous Acceleration

It is defined as the acceleration of a body at a certain instant or the limiting value of average acceleration when time interval becomes very small or tends to zero.

So, $$\text{Instantaneous acceleration, } \mathbf{a}_{inst} = \lim_{\Delta t \to 0} \frac{\Delta \mathbf{v}}{\Delta t} = \frac{d\mathbf{v}}{dt}$$

where $\frac{dv}{dt}$ is the differential coefficient of v w.r.t. t.

Uniform Acceleration

If an object is moving with uniform acceleration, it means that the change in velocity is equal for equal intervals of time.

Non-uniform Acceleration

If an object has variable or non-uniform acceleration, it means that the change in velocity is unequal in equal intervals of time.

Elementary Concept of Integration for Describing Motion

We know that, $v = \frac{ds}{dt}$, $a = \frac{dv}{dt}$

If the displacement is given and we have to find the velocity and acceleration, then we use differentiation. If the acceleration is given and we have to find the velocity and displacement, then we use integration.

If velocity is a function of displacement, $v = f(x)$, for average of v from $x = x_1$ to $x = x_2 \Rightarrow \bar{v} = \dfrac{\int_{x_1}^{x_2} v\, dt}{\int_{x_1}^{x_2} dt}$

As it is in definite limits, so called definite integral.

The above procedure can be applied to find the average value of any quantity like velocity, acceleration, force, etc.

Formula of integration

$$\int x^n \cdot dx = \frac{x^{n+1}}{n+1} + C \quad (C \text{ is integration constant})$$

Example 1 Starting from a stationary position, a bus attains a velocity of 6 m/s in 30 s. Then, the driver of the bus applies a brake such that the velocity of the bus comes down to 4 m/s in the next 5 s. Calculate the acceleration of the bus in both the cases.

Sol. Case I Initial velocity of the bus, $u = 0$

Final velocity, $v = 6$ m/s; Time taken, $t = 30$ s

$$\therefore \text{Acceleration} = \frac{\text{Change in velocity}}{\text{Time taken}} = \frac{\text{Final velocity} - \text{Initial velocity}}{\text{Time taken}}$$

$$= \frac{v-u}{t} = \frac{6-0}{30} = 0.2 \text{ m/s}^2$$

Case II Initial velocity, $u = 6$ m/s

Final velocity, $v = 4$ m/s

$$\therefore \text{Acceleration} = \frac{v-u}{t} = \frac{4-6}{5} = -0.4 \text{ m/s}^2$$

Thus, the acceleration in both the cases are 0.2 m/s^2 and -0.4 m/s^2

Example 2 The velocity of a particle is given by $v = 2t^2 - 3t + 10$ m/s. Find the instantaneous acceleration at $t = 5$ s.

Sol. Given, $v = 2t^2 - 3t + 10$ m/s

$$a_{in} = \frac{dv}{dt} = 4t - 3 \text{ m/s}^2$$

If $t = 5$, $a_{in} = 5 \times 4 - 3 = 17$ m/s^2

Example 3 A particle is moving in a straight line. Its displacement at any instant t is given by $x = 10t + 15t^3$, where x is in metres and t is in seconds. Find

(i) the average acceleration in the interval $t = 0$ to $t = 2$ s

(ii) instantaneous acceleration at $t = 2$ s.

Sol. Given equation, $x = 10t + 15t^3$

and the variables are

(i) $t = 0$ to $t = 2$s (ii) $t = 2$ s

$$\text{Velocity of particle, } \mathbf{v} = \frac{dx}{dt}$$

$$\mathbf{v} = \frac{d}{dt}(10t + 15t^3) = 10 + 45t^2$$

At $t = 0$, $\mathbf{v}_0 = 10 + 45(0) = 10$ m/s,

At $t = 2$ s, $\mathbf{v}_2 = 10 + 45 \times (2)^2 = 10 + 180 = 190$ m/s

$$\Delta\mathbf{v} = \mathbf{v}_2 - \mathbf{v}_0 = 190 - 10 = 180 \text{ m/s}$$

$$\Delta t = 2 - 0 = 2 \text{ s}$$

$$\therefore \quad \mathbf{a}_{av} = \frac{\Delta \mathbf{v}}{\Delta t} = \frac{180}{2} = 90 \text{ m/s}^2$$

$$\mathbf{a} = \frac{d}{dt}(10 + 45t^2) = 90t$$

At $t = 2$ s, $\mathbf{a} = 90 \times 2 = 180$ m/s^2

The instantaneous acceleration of a particle at 2s is 180 m/s^2.

Example 4 The displacement x of a particle varies with time t as $x = 4t^2 - 15t + 25$.

(i) Find the position, velocity and acceleration of the particle at $t = 0$.

(ii) Can we call the motion of the particle as one with uniform acceleration?

Sol. (i) Given position, $x = 4t^2 - 15t + 25$

$$\text{Velocity, } v = \frac{dx}{dt} = \frac{d}{dt}(4t^2 - 15t + 25) = 8t - 15$$

$$\text{Acceleration, } a = \frac{dv}{dt} = \frac{d}{dt}(8t - 15) = 8 \text{ m/s}^2$$

At time $t = 0$, we have

$$x = 4t^2 - 15t + 25 = 4(0) - 15(0) + 25 = 25 \text{ m}$$

$$v = 8t - 15 = 8(0) - 15 = -15 \text{ m/s and } a = 8 \text{ m/s}^2$$

(ii) Yes, the particle has a uniform acceleration because it does not depend on time t.

Position-Time Graphs for Positive, Negative and Zero Acceleration

(i) **Positive Acceleration** When distance covered by a moving object goes on increasing with time, the object is said to have positive acceleration.

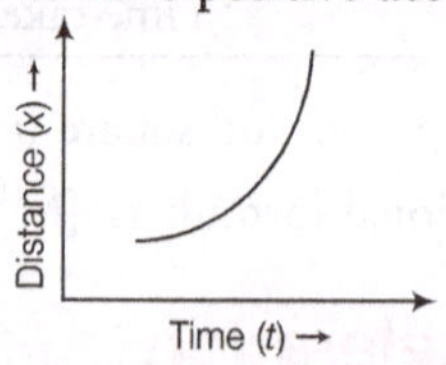

(ii) **Negative Acceleration** When distance covered by a moving object goes on decreasing with time, the object is said to have negative acceleration.

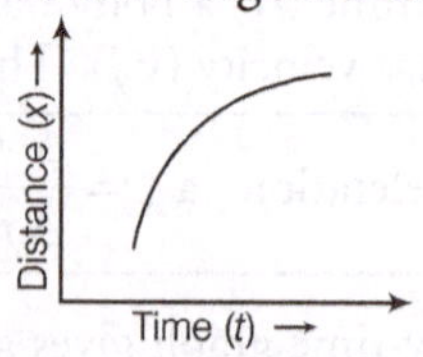

(iii) **Zero Acceleration** When the moving object covers equal distance in equal time, the object is said to have zero acceleration.

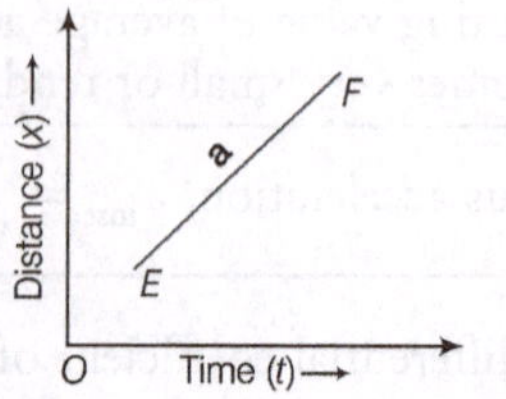

Displacement-Time Graph (s-t graph)

A graph showing time along X-axis and displacement along Y-axis is known as displacement-time graph.

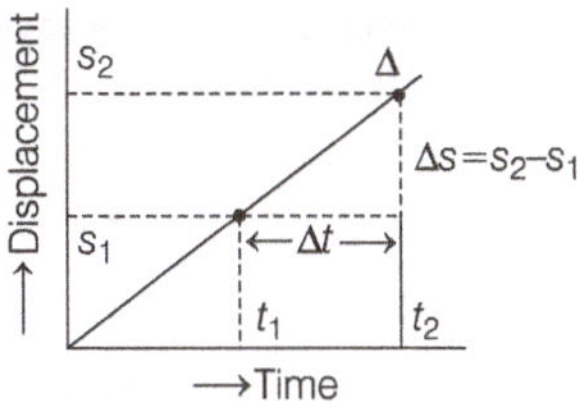

If the graph represents a straight line that means the object is moving with a uniform velocity, i.e. its average velocity and instantaneous velocity are the same. From this graph, we can determine following facts about the motion of object.

(i) **Determination of velocity from time-displacement graph**

$$v = \text{slope of the graph} = \frac{s_2 - s_1}{t_2 - t_1} = \frac{AB}{BC}$$

(ii) **Comparison of two or more velocities**

By comparing the slopes of the s-t graphs.

Greater the slope of the displacement-time graphs of two objects A and B, greater will be the velocity of the object. e.g. Velocity of object A is more than velocity of object-B.

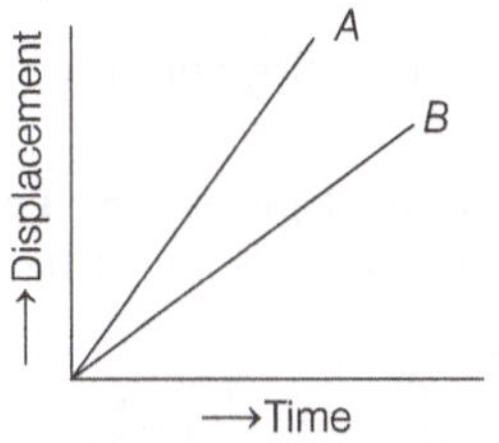

Note If the displacement-time graph is a straight line parallel to X-axis, i.e. the slope is zero, it means that the velocity of the object is zero (object is in the position of rest).

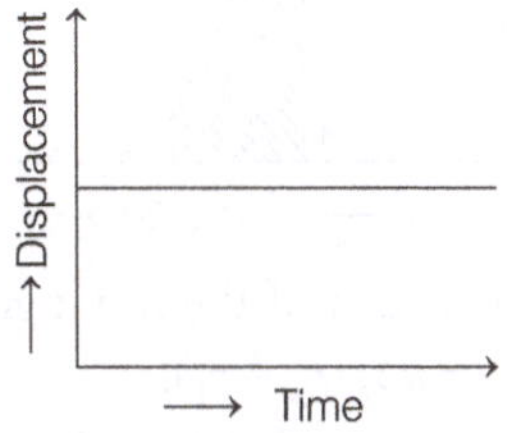

(iii) **Determination of negative acceleration**

If the line makes an angle greater than 90° with the X-axis (slope of the line is negative), i.e. the object is moving in reverse direction.

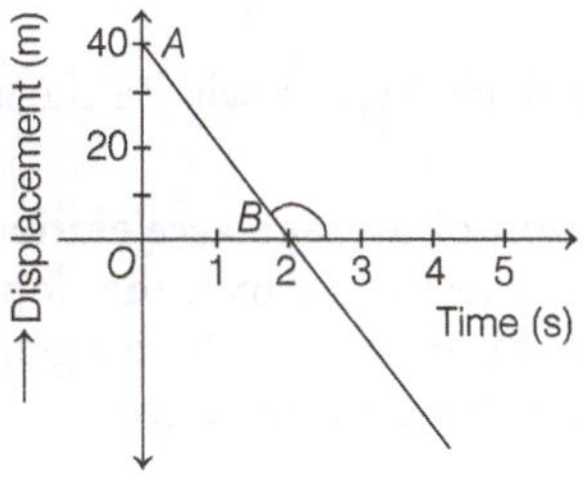

$$\text{Slope } v = \frac{AO}{OB} = \frac{0-40}{2-0} = 20\,\text{ms}^{-1} = -\text{ve}$$

Negative sign implies that the object is returning.

(iv) **If the displacement-time graph of a moving object has several lines of different slopes,** then the object has variable velocity.

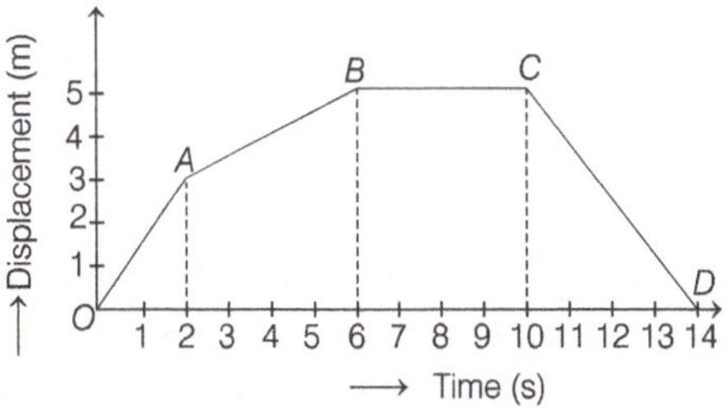

In this graph, we can say the velocity of objects is changing rapidly.

(v) **If the displacement-time graph of an object is a continuous curve,** i.e velocity of the object is continuously changing, we can find the average velocity of the object by the slope of the tangent at that point.

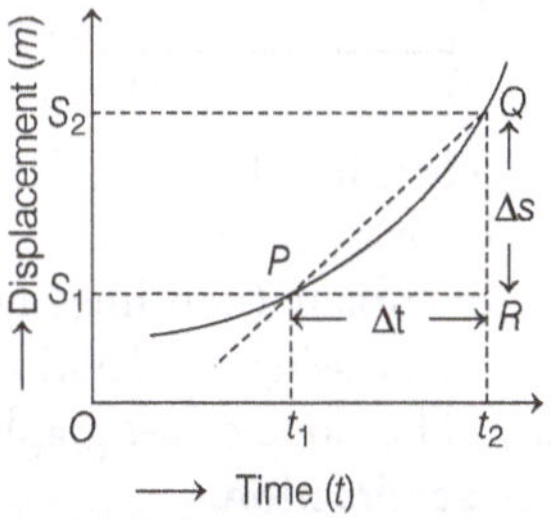

As the time interval Δt is infinitesimally small ($\Delta t \to 0$), then the point Q will be infinitesimally close to point P. In this limit, PQ being tangent at the point P, the slope of the tangent at the point P.

$$\lim_{\Delta t \to 0} \to \frac{\Delta s}{\Delta t} = \frac{ds}{dt}$$

ds/dt is the instantaneous velocity of the object at time t. Hence, instantaneous velocity of the object at time t is obtained from the slope of the tangent drawn at a point (t, s) on s-t graph ($\Delta t \to 0$).

Velocity-Time (v-t) Graphs for an Accelerated Motion

(i) **Zero Acceleration** In case of zero acceleration, the velocity of the object does not change with time.

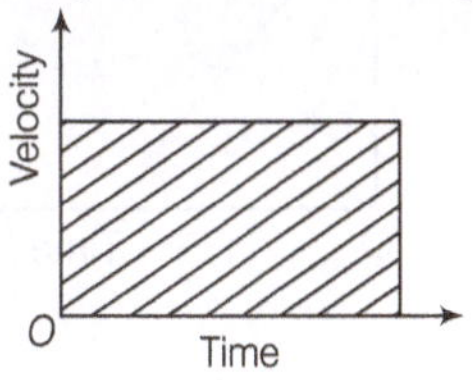

(ii) **Positive Acceleration**

(a) If the object is moving with positive acceleration having zero initial velocity, then **the velocity-time graph is a straight line starting from origin.**

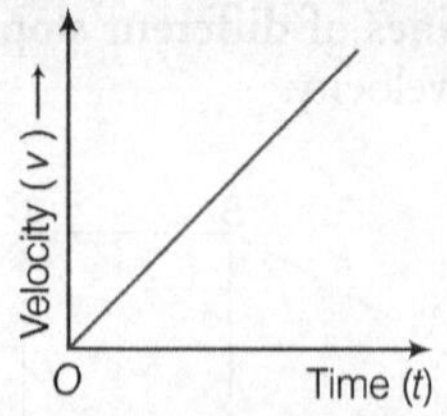

In case of positive acceleration, the velocity of the object goes on increasing with time.

(b) If the object is moving with positive acceleration having some initial velocity, then **the velocity-time graph is a straight line starting from *P*.**

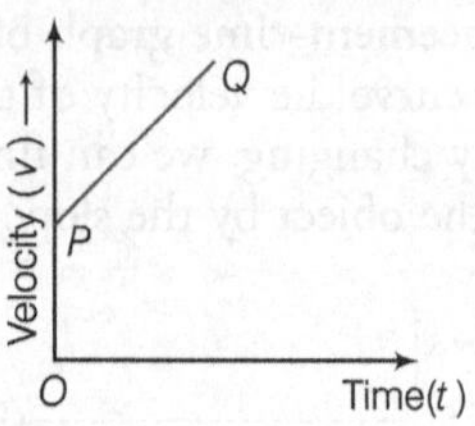

(iii) **Increasing Acceleration** In case of increasing acceleration, the velocity of the object goes on increasing exponentially (non-linearly). If the object is moving with increasing acceleration having zero initial velocity. The slope of *v-t* graph gives the **instantaneous acceleration.**

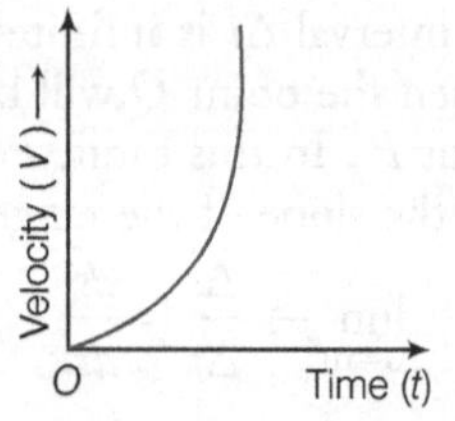

(iv) **Negative Acceleration**

(a) In case of negative acceleration, the velocity of the object decreases linearly with time. If the object is moving with negative acceleration, has some positive initial velocity, then velocity-time graph is a straight-line having negative slope.

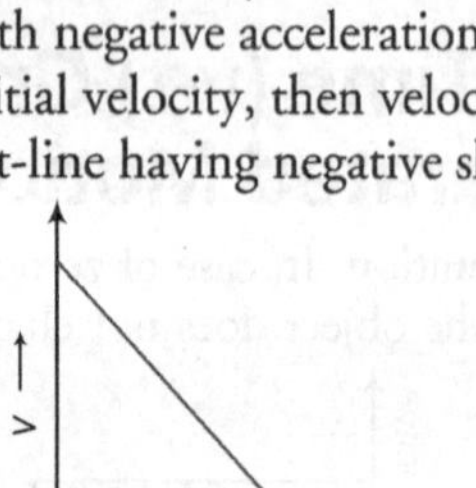

(b) If the object is moving with negative acceleration, have some negative initial velocity, then **the velocity-time graph is a straight line starting from point *P* having negative slope and negative velocity.**

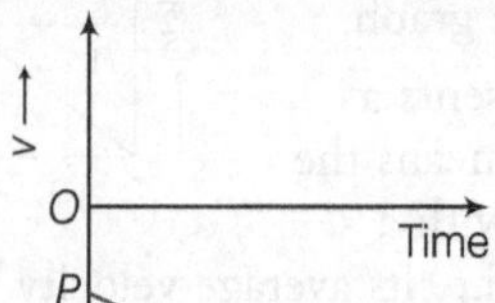

(c) If the object moving with negative acceleration has some positive initial velocity, then **the slope of velocity-time graph will remain constant for uniform acceleration.**

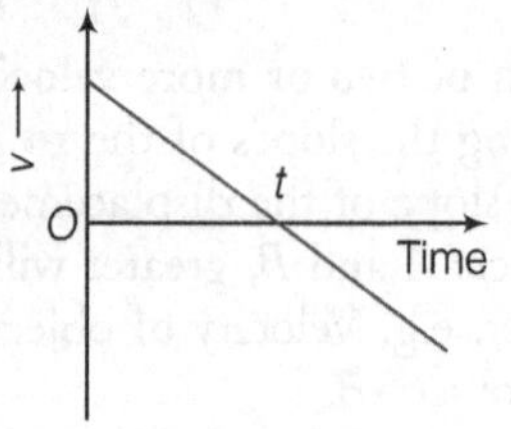

From the velocity time (*v-t*) graph, the following quantities can be determined

(i) **Determination of displacement** The area enclosed between the *v-t* graph whatever be the shape of the graph.

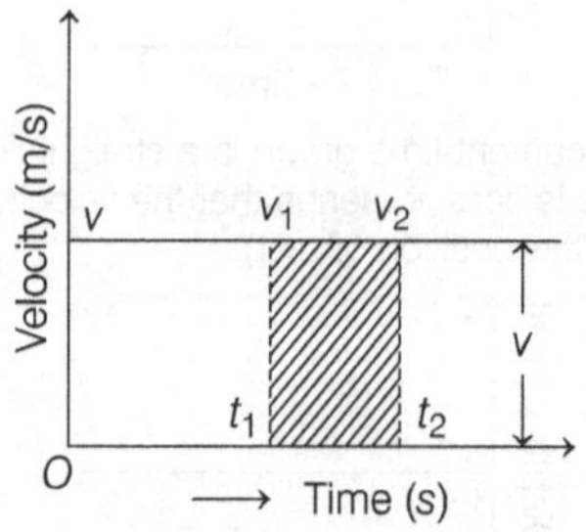

Displacement = Area of the rectangle

$$= v \times (t_2 - t_1).$$

(ii) **Determination of acceleration** Slope of time-velocity graph of an object is equal to the acceleration of that object.

i.e. $$a = \frac{v_2 - v_1}{t_2 - t_1}$$

Greater the slope, greater will be the acceleration of the object.

(iii) **Determination of average acceleration** If the *v-t* graph of an object is a curve, the slope of the line joining any two points on the *v-t* graph is the average acceleration of the object.

If the time interval is made infinitesimally small ($\Delta t \to 0$), then PQ will be tangent at the point P.

Slope of tangent at point P,

$$\lim_{\Delta t \to 0} \frac{\Delta v}{\Delta t} = \frac{dv}{dt} = \text{instantaneous acceleration}$$

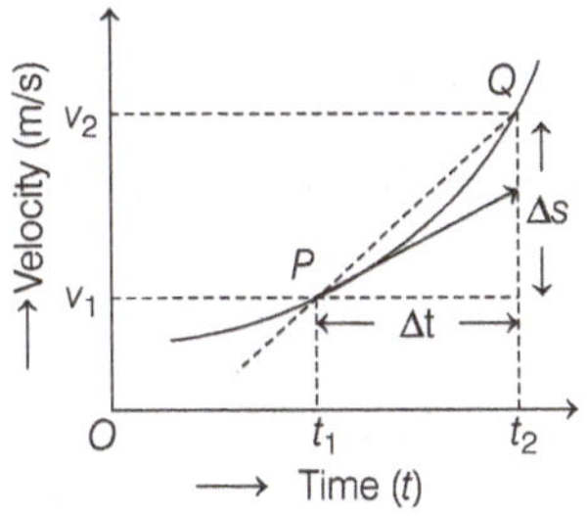

Acceleration-Time Graph

For a body moving with constant acceleration, the acceleration-time graph is a straight line AB, parallel to the time-axis.

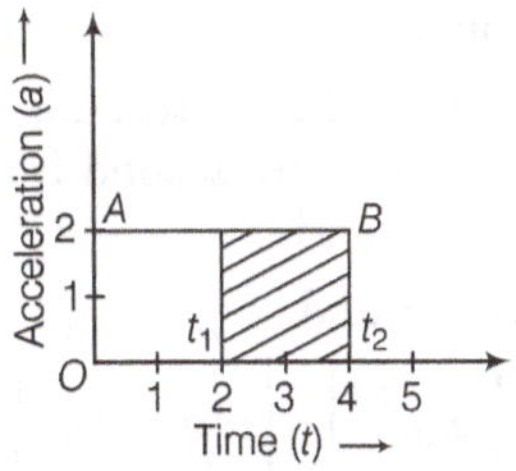

From the above graph, if acceleration of the object is a, we can determine velocity by the area of the graph.

Hence, velocity = area of the rectangle = length × breadth

$$= 2 \times (4-2) = 4\,\text{ms}^{-1}$$

Thus, velocity of the object increases by 4 ms^{-1} between 2nd and 4th seconds.

When the acceleration of a body increases uniformly with time, its a-t graph is a straight line OA inclined to the time-axis.

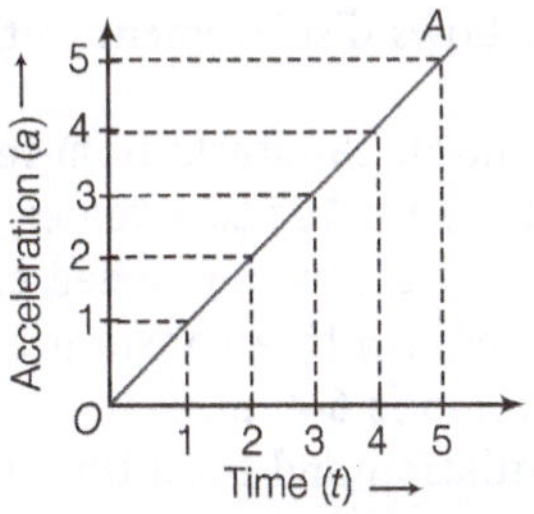

Example 5 With the help of above velocity-time graph, find the

(i) displacement in first three seconds and

(ii) acceleration for the above graph.

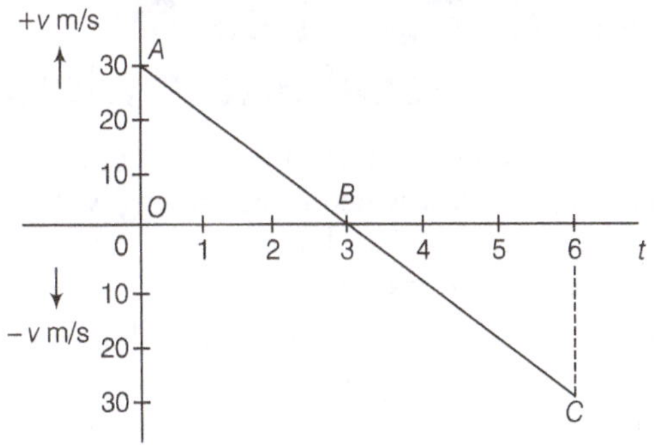

Sol. (i) Displacement in first three seconds = Area of ΔOAB

$$= \frac{1}{2}(OB) \times (OA) = \frac{1}{2}(3) \times (+30) = +45\,\text{m}$$

(ii) Acceleration = Slope of v-t graph

As, v-t graph is a straight line. So, consider the slope of line AB.

$$\therefore \quad \text{Slope of line } AB = \frac{y_2 - y_1}{x_2 - x_1} = \frac{0-30}{3} = -10\,\text{m/s}^2$$

So, the acceleration is negative.

Example 6 The velocity-time graph of a particle in one-dimensional motion is shown in figure. Which of the following formulae are correct for describing the motion of the particle over the time interval t_1 to t_2?

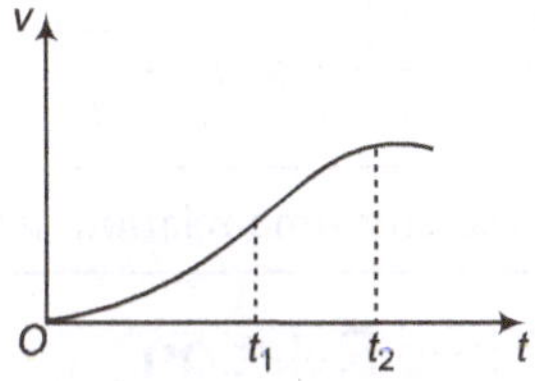

(i) $x(t_2) = x(t_1) + v(t_1)(t_2 - t_1) + \frac{1}{2} a (t_2 - t_1)^2$

(ii) $v(t_2) = v(t_1) + a(t_2 - t_1)$

(iii) $v_{av} = \left[\frac{x(t_2) - x(t_1)}{(t_2 - t_1)}\right]$

(iv) $a_{av} = \frac{[v(t_2) - v(t_1)]}{(t_2 - t_1)}$

(v) $x(t_2) = x(t_1) + v_{av}(t_2 - t_1) + \frac{1}{2} a_{av}(t_2 - t_1)^2$

(vi) $x(t_2) - x(t_1)$ = Area under v-t curve bounded by the t-axis and the dotted line shown. **NCERT**

Sol. The slope of the given graph over the time interval t_1 to t_2 is not constant and is not uniform. It means acceleration is not constant or uniform, therefore relations (*i*), (*ii*) and (*v*) are not correct which is uniform accelerated motion, but relations (*iii*), (*iv*) and (*vi*) are correct, because these relations are true for both uniform or non-uniform accelerated motion.

Kinematic Equations for Uniformly Accelerated Motion

If the change in velocity of an object in each unit of time is constant, then object is said to be moving with constant acceleration and such a motion is called **uniformly accelerated motion.**

If an object moves along a straight line with a constant acceleration a. Let u be the initial velocity at $t = 0$ and v be the final velocity of the object after time (t).

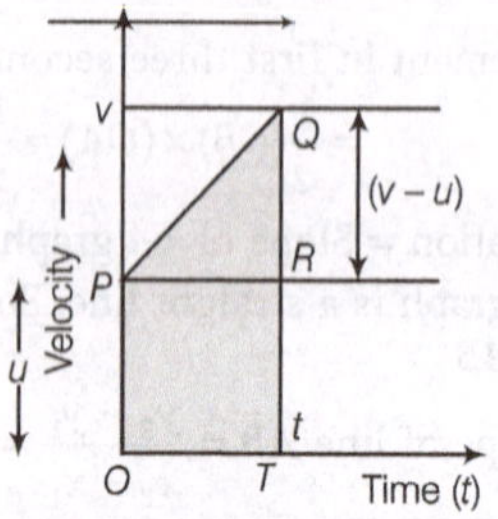

(i) Velocity-Time Relation

The slope of velocity-time graph gives the acceleration of the object.

$\therefore \quad a = \text{Slope of } PQ$

$$a = \frac{QR}{PR} = \frac{v-u}{t} \Rightarrow a = \frac{v-u}{t} \Rightarrow v - u = at$$

Velocity-time relation, $v = u + at$

(ii) Position-Time Relation

The area under the velocity-time graph gives the displacement. Displacement of an object in time interval t is given by

$$x = \text{Area of } \Delta PQR + \text{Area of rectangle } OPRT$$

$$= \frac{1}{2} QR \times PR + OP \times PR = \frac{1}{2}(v-u)t + ut$$

$$= \frac{1}{2}(at)t + ut \qquad [\because v - u = at]$$

$$= \frac{1}{2}at^2 + ut = \frac{1}{2}at^2 + ut$$

Position-time relation $x = ut + \frac{1}{2}at^2$

(iii) Position-Velocity Relation

Again the displacement in time interval (t) is given by

$$x = \text{area of trapezium } OPQT.$$

$$= \frac{1}{2}(OP + QT) \times OT$$

$$x = \frac{1}{2}(u + v) \times t \qquad \text{...(i)}$$

From $v - u = at$,

$$t = \frac{v-u}{a} \qquad \text{...(ii)}$$

On substituting the value of t in Eq. (i), we get

$$x = \frac{1}{2}(u+v) \times \frac{(v-u)}{a}$$

$$\Rightarrow \quad v^2 - u^2 = 2ax$$

$\Rightarrow$ **Position-velocity relation, $v^2 = u^2 + 2ax$**

Displacement of the Particle in *n*th Second

Let an object is moving with initial velocity u under constant acceleration a.

To find the displacement in nth second, we subtract the position of particle at $(n-1)$th second from the position of the particle at nth second.

Displacement in nth second $= s_n - s_{n-1}$

$$s\,(n\text{th}) = \left[un + \frac{1}{2}a(n^2)\right] - \left[u(n-1) + \frac{1}{2}a(n-1)^2\right]$$

$$= un + \frac{1}{2}an^2 - un + u - \frac{1}{2}a(n-1)^2$$

$$= u + \frac{a}{2}[n^2 - (n-1)^2]$$

$$= u + \frac{a}{2}(n^2 - n^2 - 1 + 2n)$$

Displacement in the nth second, $s(n\text{th}) = u + \frac{a}{2}(2n-1)$

Above expression shows displacement in the nth second.

Example 7 A motor car starts from rest and accelerates uniformly for 10s to a velocity of 20 m/s. After that car runs at a constant speed and is finally brought to rest in 40m with a constant aceleration. Total distance covered is 640 m. Find the value of acceleration, retardation and total time taken.

Sol. Let x_1, x_2 and x_3 be distances covered in three parts of the motion.

For first part of the motion, we have

$$u = 0,\ t = 10\text{s},\ v = 20 \text{ m/s}$$

As $\qquad v = u + at$

$\therefore \quad 20 = 0 + a \times 10$

Acceleration, $a = 2\ \text{m/s}^2$

Distance, $x_1 = ut + \frac{1}{2}at^2 = 0 \times 10 + \frac{1}{2} \times 2 \times (10)^2 = 100\ \text{m}$

For second part of the motion, we have

$$x_1 = 100\text{m},\ x_3 = 40\text{m}$$

As $\quad x_1 + x_2 + x_3 = 640$

$\therefore \quad 100 + x_2 + 40 = 640 \quad \text{or} \quad x_2 = 500\text{m}$

This distance is covered with a uniform speed of 20 m/s.

$\therefore$ Time taken $= \frac{500}{20} = 25\ \text{s}$

For third part of the motion, we have

$$u = 20\ \text{m/s},\ v = 0,\ x = x_3 = 40\text{m}$$

As $\quad v^2 - u^2 = 2ax$

$\therefore \quad (0)^2 - (20)^2 = 2 \times a \times 40$

or $\quad a = -\frac{400}{80} = -5\text{m/s}^2$

$\therefore$ Retardation $= 5\text{m/s}^2$

Time taken, $t = \frac{v-u}{a} = \frac{0-20}{-5} = 4\text{s}$

Total time taken $= 10 + 25 + 4 = 39$ s

Equations of Motion by Calculus Method

(i) From the definition of average acceleration,

$$a = \frac{dv}{dt} \Rightarrow dv = a\,dt$$

Integrating both sides and taking the limit for velocity u to v and for time 0 to t.

$$\int_u^v dv = \int_0^t a\,dt = a\int_0^t dt = a[t]_0^t$$

[$\because$ a is constant]

$$v - u = at$$

$$\boxed{v = u + at}$$

(ii) Now, from the definition of velocity, $v = \frac{dx}{dt}$

$\Rightarrow \quad dx = v\,dt$

Integrating both sides and taking the limit for displacement x_0 to x and for time 0 to t.

$$\int_{x_0}^x dx = \int_0^t v\,dt = \int_0^t (u + at)dt = v_0[t]_0^t + a\left[\frac{t^2}{2}\right]_0^t$$

$$x - x_0 = ut + \frac{1}{2}at^2$$

$$\boxed{x = x_0 + ut + \frac{1}{2}at^2}$$

(iii) Now, we can write

$$a = \frac{dv}{dt} = \frac{dv}{dx}\frac{dx}{dt} = v\frac{dv}{dx} \quad \text{or} \quad v\,dv = a\,dx$$

Integrating both sides and taking the limit for velocity u to v and for displacement x_0 to x.

$$\int_u^v v\,dv = \int_{x_0}^x a\,dx\,; \quad \frac{v^2 - u^2}{2} = a(x - x_0)$$

$$v^2 = u^2 + 2a(x - x_0)$$

This method is also be used for motion with non-uniform acceleration.

Non-uniformly Accelerated Motion

When acceleration of particle is not constant or acceleration is a function of time, then following relations hold for one-dimensional motion.

(i) $v = \frac{ds}{dt}$ (ii) $a = \frac{dv}{dt} = \frac{dv}{dx} \times \frac{dx}{dt} = v\frac{dv}{dx}$

(iii) $ds = v\,dt$ and (iv) $dv = a\,dt$ or $vdv = adx$

Example 8 Two particles move along x-axis. The position of particle 1 is given by $x = 6.00t^2 + 3.00t + 2.00$ (in metre and in seconds); acceleration of particle 2 is given by $a = -8.00\,t$ (in m/s^2 and seconds) and at $t = 0$, its velocity is 20 m/s. When the velocities of the particles match, find their velocities.

Sol. List all informations about particle 1 and particle 2.

For particle 1,

$$x_1 = 6.00\,t^2 + 3.00\,t + 2.00$$

For particle 2,

$$a_2 = -8.00\,t,\ \text{m/s}^2$$

$$v_2 = 20\ \text{m/s at}\ t = 0\ \text{s}$$

We know that, $v(t) = \frac{dx}{dt}$

$$v(t) = 12\,t + 3 + 0$$

$$v(t) = 12\,t + 3$$

For particle 2,

We know that, $\int a(t)dt = v(t)$

$\Rightarrow \quad v(t) = \int -8.00t\,dt = -8\int t\,dt = \frac{-8\,t^2}{2} + C$

$$v(t) = -4\,t^2 + C$$

If $v(t) = 20$ m/s and $t = 0$s, then

$$20\text{m/s} = -4\,(0)^2 + C$$

$\Rightarrow \quad 20 = 0 + C \Rightarrow C = 20$

So, $\quad v_2(t) = -4t^2 + 20$

Since the particles' velocities have to match, you have to set the two equations equal to each other

$$v_1(t) = v_2(t)$$
$$12t + 3 = -4t^2 + 20$$
$$4t^2 + 12t - 17 = 0$$

Since, you could not factor out, you probably know to use the quadratic formula

$$= \frac{-b \pm \sqrt{b^2 - 4ac}}{2a} = \frac{-12 \pm \sqrt{(12)^2 - 4(4)(-17)}}{2(4)}$$
$$= \frac{-12 \pm \sqrt{144 + 272}}{8}$$
$$t = \frac{-12 \pm \sqrt{416}}{8} = \frac{-12 \pm 20.3}{8}$$
$$t = -4.04 \text{ s}$$

or $t = 1.04$ s

As time cannot be negative, hence $t = 1.04$ s.

Finding the velocities of different particles.

$$v(t_1) = 12(1.04) + 3 = 15.48 \text{ m/s}$$
$$v(t_2) = -4(1.04)^2 + 20 = 15.67 \text{ m/s}$$

Equations of Motion for the Motion of an Object under Gravity

When an object is thrown upwards or fall towards the earth, then its motion is called **motion under gravity** because in these conditions (upward or downward), the acceleration of the body is equal to the acceleration due to gravity.

In case of motion under gravity, the equations of motion are given below

$$v = u + (\pm g)t \quad \text{...(i)}$$
$$h = ut + \frac{1}{2}(\pm g)t^2 \quad \text{...(ii)}$$
$$v^2 = u^2 + 2(\pm g)h \quad \text{...(iii)}$$

In case of upward motion, acceleration due to gravity (g) is taken as **positive** and for downward motion, g is taken as **negative**.

Equations of Motion Along a Smooth Inclined Plane

Let us consider an object O sliding down a smooth inclined plane AB. The acceleration of O is less than g if the object fall freely downwards. In fact, the acceleration of the object O sliding down the plane is $g \sin\theta$.

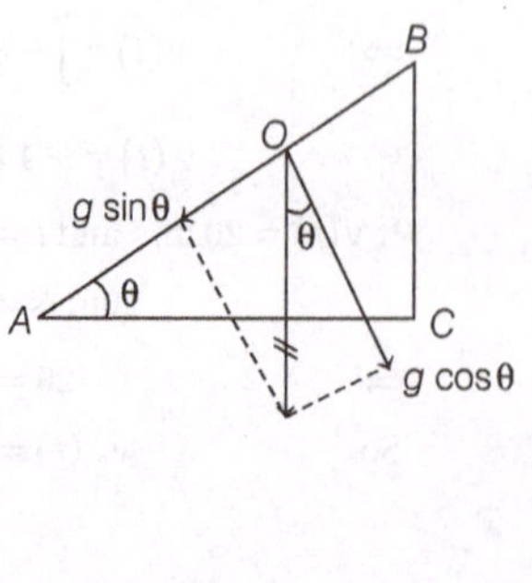

Hence, the equations for a body sliding down a smooth inclined plane are

(i) $v = u + (g\sin\theta)t$

(ii) $s = ut + \frac{1}{2}(g\sin\theta)t^2$

(iii) $v^2 = u^2 + 2(g\sin\theta)s$

Further, if the body is moving up along an inclined plane, then its acceleration will be $(-g\sin\theta)$ and the equation of kinematics will be

(i) $v = u - (g\sin\theta)t$

(ii) $s = ut - \frac{1}{2}(g\sin\theta)t^2$

(iii) $v^2 = u^2 - 2(g\sin\theta)s$

Feeling Weightlessness

There is a misconception that in free fall, no force acted on us since we are not able to feel our weight. Actually we feel our weight due to the reaction we get from earth. As in free fall, we are not pushing anything, so we are not getting any reaction (Newton's third law) and feeling weightlessness.

Example 9 A ball is thrown vertically upwards with a velocity of 20 m/s from the top of a multi storey building. The height of the point from where the ball is thrown 25 m from the ground.

(i) How high will the ball rise?

(ii) How long will it be before the ball hits the ground? Take $g = 10 \text{ m/s}^2$ **NCERT**

Sol. (i) Consider vertical upward motion of ball upto highest point, we have

$$u = 20 \text{ m/s}, v = 0,$$
$$a = -10 \text{ m/s}^2, t = t_1,$$
$$x = ? \text{ (say)}$$

Using theorem,

$$v^2 = u^2 + 2ax$$
$$x = \frac{v^2 - u^2}{2a} = \frac{0 - (20)^2}{2 \times (-10)} = 20 \text{m}$$

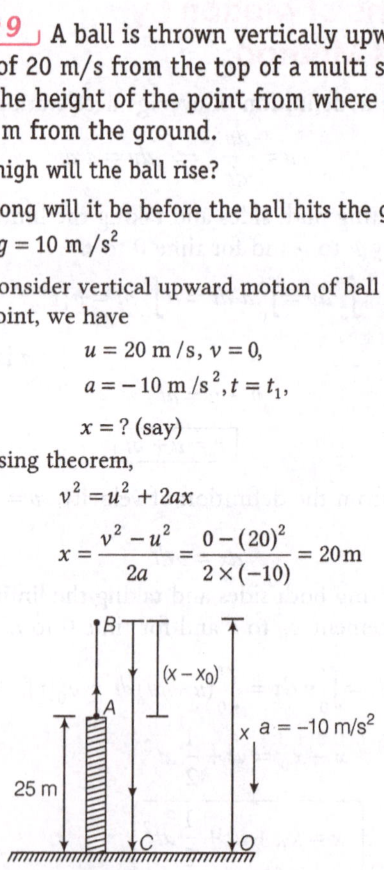

(ii) As shown in figure, we have upward motion A to B in time (t_1) and downward motion (B to C) in time (t_2). Velocity at B is zero

$\therefore$ $$v = u - gt$$
$$0 = 20 - 10\,t_1 \Rightarrow t_1 = 2\text{s}$$

From the top, the ball falls freely under acceleration due to gravity.

$\therefore$ $$x = x_0 + ut + \frac{1}{2}gt_2^2$$
$$x = 0,\ x_0 = 45\ \text{m}, u = 0 \quad \text{and} \quad g = 10\ \text{m/s}^2$$
$$0 = 45 + 0 + \frac{1}{2}(-10)\,t_2^2 = 45 - 5t_2^{\,2}$$
$$t_2^{\,2} = 9 \Rightarrow t_2 = 3\text{s}$$

$\therefore$ Total time taken by the ball to hit the ground
$$t = t_1 + t_2 = 2 + 3 = 5\ \text{s}$$

Alternate method

In this method we shall consider net displacement
= Final position − Initial position
= 25m.

Using the formula, $x = ut + \frac{1}{2}gt^2$

$\Rightarrow$ $$-25 = +20t - \frac{1}{2}gt^2 = +20t - 5t^2$$
$\Rightarrow$ $$t^2 - 4t - 5 = 0$$
$$(t-5)(t+1) = 0 \Rightarrow t = 5\ \text{s}$$

Stopping Distance for a Vehicle

When brakes are applied to a moving vehicle, the distance it travels before coming to halt is called **stopping distance.**

It is also an important factor for road safety. Its value depends upon the speed at which the vehicle is running and the efficiency of the braking system.

Let the distance travelled by the vehicle before it stops be d_s.

Using the equation of motion,
$$v^2 = u^2 + 2\,ax$$

If $v = 0$ and $x = d_s$, then

$$\text{Stopping distance,}\quad d_s = \frac{-u^2}{2a}$$

Thus, the stopping distance is proportional to the square of the initial velocity. If we double the initial velocity, its stopping distance increase by a factor of 4 for same deceleration.

Example 10 A car moving with a speed of 50 km/h can be stopped by brakes after covering 6 m. What will be the minimum stopping distance, if the same car is moving at a speed of 100 km/h?

Sol. **In first case,**
$$u = 50\ \text{km/h} = 50 \times \frac{5}{18} = \frac{125}{9}\ \text{m/s},\ v = 0,\ x = 6\ \text{m}$$

Using the relation, $v^2 - u^2 = 2ax$
$$0 - \left(\frac{125}{9}\right)^2 = 2a \times 6$$
$\Rightarrow$ $$a = \frac{-125 \times 125}{81 \times 2 \times 6} = -16.07\ \text{m/s}^2 \simeq 16\ \text{m/s}$$

In second case,
$$u = 100\ \text{km/h} = 100 \times \frac{5}{18} = \frac{250}{9}\ \text{m/s}$$
$$v = 0,\ a = -16\ \text{m/s}^2 \text{and } x = ?$$

Using the relation, $v^2 - u^2 = 2ax$
$$0 - \left(\frac{250}{9}\right)^2 = 2 \times (-16)\,x$$
$\Rightarrow$ $$x = \frac{250 \times 250}{81 \times 2 \times 16} = 24.1\ \text{m}$$

Topic Practice 2

Multiple Choice Questions

(1 Mark)

1. A car is moving with a velocity of 30 ms^{-1}. On applying the brakes, the velocity decreases to 15 ms^{-1} in 2 s. The acceleration of the car is
(a) $+7.5\ \text{ms}^{-2}$
(b) $-7.7\ \text{ms}^{-2}$
(c) $-7.5\ \text{ms}^{-2}$
(d) $+15\ \text{ms}^{-2}$

2. A car is moving with an initial velocity $2\,v_0$. It increases its velocity to $4\,v_0$ in t seconds. The relation which describes the distance covered in t second (considering uniformly accelerated motion) is
(a) $x = 3\,v_0 t$
(b) $x = 2v_0 t$
(c) $x = v_0 t$
(d) $x = v_0 t/2$

3. An object starts from rest and moves with uniform acceleration a. The final velocity of the particle in terms of the distance x covered by it is given as
(a) $\sqrt{2ax}$ (b) $2ax$
(c) $\sqrt{\frac{ax}{2}}$ (d) $\sqrt{ax}$

4. The velocity of a particle is given by the expression

$$v(x) = 3x^2 - 4x$$

where, x is distance covered by the particle. The expression for acceleration is
(a) $(3x^2 - 4x)(6x - 4)$ (b) $6(3x^2 - 4x)$
(c) $(6x - 4)^2$ (d) $(3x^2 - 4x)6x$

5. A particle is situated at $x = \pm 3$ units at $t = 0$. It starts moving from rest with a constant acceleration of $4\,ms^{-2}$. The position of the particle at $t = 3$ s is
(a) $x = \pm 21$ units (b) $x = +18$ units
(c) $x = -21$ units (d) None of these

6. The slope of the straight line connecting the points corresponding to (v_2, t_2) and (v_1, t_1) on a plot of velocity *versus* time gives
(a) average velocity
(b) average acceleration
(c) instantaneous velocity
(d) None of the above

7. A particle of unit mass undergoes one-dimensional motion such that its velocity varies according to $v(x) = \beta x^{-2n}$, where β and n are constants and x is the position of the particle. The acceleration of the particle as a function of x is given by
(a) $-2n\beta^2 x^{-2n-1}$ (b) $-2n\beta^2 x^{-4n-1}$
(c) $-2\beta^2 x^{-2n+1}$ (d) $-2n\beta^2 e^{-4n+1}$

8. The slope of the tangent to the (v-t) curve gives the value of
(a) instantaneous acceleration
(b) instantaneous velocity
(c) average acceleration
(d) None of the above

9. The motion of a particle along a straight line is described by equation

$$x = 8 + 12t - t^3$$

where, x is in metre and t in sec. The retardation of the particle when its velocity becomes zero, is
(a) $24\,ms^{-2}$ (b) zero
(c) $6\,ms^{-2}$ (d) $12\,ms^{-2}$

Very Short Answer Type Questions

(1 Mark)

10. When a body accelerates by βt, what is the velocity after time t, when it starts from rest?

11. Give an example of uniformly accelerated linear motion.

12. Constant acceleration means that x-t graph will have constant slope? Yes/No

13. Draw v-t graph for non-uniform accelerated motion.

14. Consider that the acceleration of a moving body varies with time. What does the area under acceleration-time graph for any time interval represent ?

15. A car starts accelerating from rest for sometime, maintains the velocity for sometime and then comes to rest with uniform deceleration. Draw v-t graph.

16. Write an expression for distance covered in nth second for a uniformly accelerated motion.

17. Find the acceleration and velocity of a ball at the instant it reaches its highest point if it was thrown up with velocity v.

Short Answer Type I Questions

(2 Marks)

18. The displacement of a particle is given by at^2. What is dependency of acceleration on time?

19. Define uniform and non-uniform acceleration.

20. What is zero acceleration? Show graphically.

21. Which of the following is true for displacement?
(i) It cannot be zero.
(ii) Its magnitude is greater than the distance travelled by the object.

22. How displacement-time graph can be used to find the velocity of object?

23. What are uses of a velocity-time graph?

24. Find acceleration from v-t graph for initial velocity u and final velocity v.

Short Answer Type II Questions

(3 Marks)

25. The displacement s of a particle which is moving along a straight line at any time t is given by $s = t^3 - 6t^2 + 3t + 4$. Calculate the velocity when the acceleration is zero.

26. Suggest a suitable physical situation for each of the following graph. **NCERT**

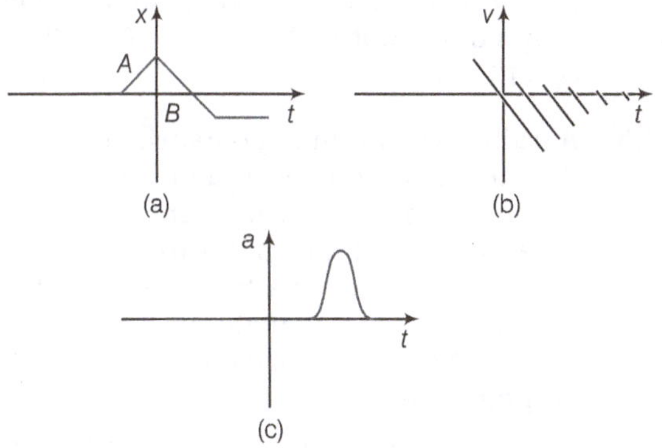

27. Figure shows the x-t plot of a particle in one-dimensional motion. Three different equal intervals of time are shown. In which interval the average speed is greatest and in which it is the least? Give the sign of average speed for each interval. **NCERT**

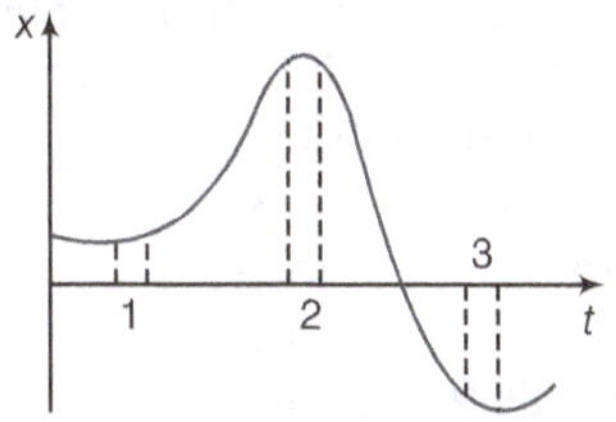

28. Figure gives a speed-time graph of a particle in one-dimensional motion. Three different equal intervals of time are shown. In which interval is the average acceleration greatest in magnitude? In which interval is the average speed greatest? Choosing the positive direction as the constant direction of motion, give the signs of u and a in the three intervals. What are the accelerations at the points A, B, C and D? **NCERT**

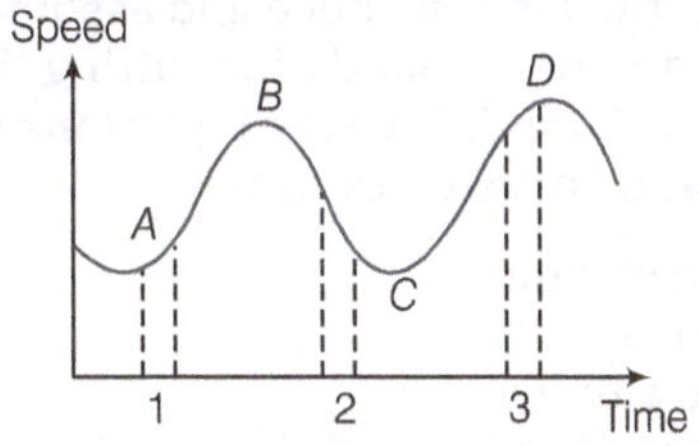

29. Figure shows x-t plot of one-dimensional motion of a particle. Is it correct to say from the graph that the particle moves in a straight line for $t < 0$ and on a parabolic path for $t > 0$? If not, suggest a suitable physical context for this graph. **NCERT**

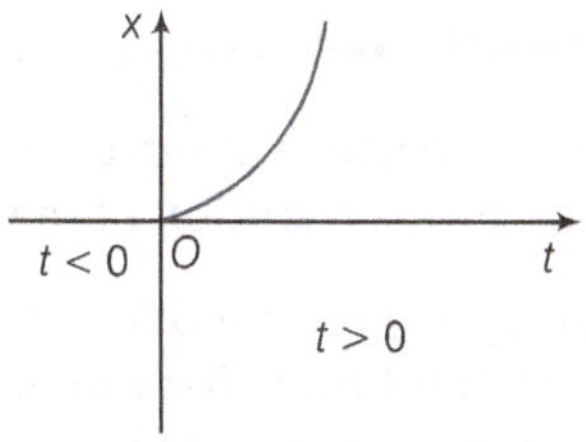

30. Read each statement below carefully and state with reasons and examples if it is true or false.

A particle in 1-D motion

(i) with zero speed at an instant may have non-zero acceleration at that instant.

(ii) with zero speed may have non-zero velocity.

(iii) with constant speed must have zero acceleration.

(iv) with positive value of acceleration must be speeding up. **NCERT**

31. (i) Its not possible to stop a car instantaneously by applying brakes. Justify.

(ii) What is the ratio of the distance travelled by a ball falling freely from rest in the first, second and third seconds of its fall?

32. A car experiences constant acceleration for 20 s after starting from rest. If it travels a distance d_1 in first 10 s and distance d_2 in next 10 s, find the relation between d_1 and d_2.

Long Answer Type Questions

5 Marks

33. Discuss the motion of an object under free fall. Neglect air resistance. **NCERT**

34. Explain v-t graph for positive and negative acceleration for different situation.

35. Define uniform accelerated motions. Derive kinematic equations for uniform accelerated motion in a straight line.

36. (i) A car accelerates from rest at a constant rate X for sometime after which it retards at constant rate Y to come to rest. If the total time is T seconds, calculate the maximum velocity reached and the total distance travelled in terms of X, Y and T.

(ii) Show that instantaneous acceleration is the limiting value of average acceleration.

Numerical Problems

37. If position of a particle at instant t is given by $x = 2t^3$, find the acceleration of the particle. [1 M]

38. A bus starting from rest moves with a uniform acceleration of 0.1 m/s^2 for 2 min.
Find (i) the speed acquired and (ii) the distance travelled. [2 M]

39. Points P, Q and R are in a vertical line such that $PQ = QR$. A ball at P is allowed to fall freely. What is the ratio of the times of descent through PQ and QR? [2 M]

40. Two trains A and B of length 400 m each are moving on two parallel tracks with a uniform speed of 72 km h^{-1} in the same direction with A ahead of B. The driver of B decides to overtake A and accelerates by 1 ms^{-2}. If after 50 s, the guard of B just brushes past the driver of A, what was the original distance between them? NCERT [3 M]

41. A jet plane beginning its take off moves down the runway at a constant acceleration of 4.00 m/s^2.
(i) Find the position and velocity of the plane 5.00 s after it begins to move.
(ii) If a speed of 70.0 m/s is required for the plane to leave the ground, how long a runway is required? [3 M]

42. A car starting from rest, accelerates at the rate f through a distance s, then continues at constant speed for sometime t and then decelerate at the rate $f/2$ to come to rest. If the total distance is 5s, then prove that $s = \frac{1}{2} ft^2$. [3 M]

43. A player throws a ball upwards with an initial speed of 29.4 ms^{-1}.
(i) What is the direction of acceleration during the upward motion of the ball?
(ii) What are the velocity and acceleration of the ball at the highest point of its motion?
(iii) Choose $x = 0$ and $t = 0$ be the location and time at its highest point, vertically downward direction to be the positive direction of x-axis and give the signs of position, velocity and acceleration of the ball during its upward and downward motion.
(iv) To what height does the ball rise and after how long does the ball return to the player's hands? (Take $g = 9.8 \text{ ms}^{-2}$ and neglect air resistance) NCERT [3 M]

44. A ball is dropped from a height of 90 m on a floor. At each collision with the floor, the ball loses one tenth of its speed. Plot the speed-time graph of its motion between $t = 0$ to 12s. ($g = 10 \text{ ms}^{-2}$) NCERT [3 M]

45. A train takes 4 min to go between stations 2.25 km apart starting and finishing at rest. The acceleration is uniform for the first 40s and the deceleration is uniform for the last 20s. Assuming the velocity to be constant for the remaining time, calculate the maximum speed, acceleration and retardation, use only the graphical method. [5 M]

46. A train passes a station A at 40 kmh^{-1} and maintains its speed for 7 km and is then uniformly retarded, stopping at B which is 8.5 km from A. A second train starts from A at the instant the first train passes and being accelerated some part of the journey and uniformly retarded for the rest, stops at B at the same times as the first train. Calculate the maximum speed of the second train, use only the graphical method. [5 M]

47. Two stones are thrown up simultaneously from the edge of a cliff 200 m high with initial speeds of 15 ms^{-1} and 30 ms^{-1}. Verify that the graph shown in figure, correctly represents the time variation of the relative position of the second stone with respect to the first.

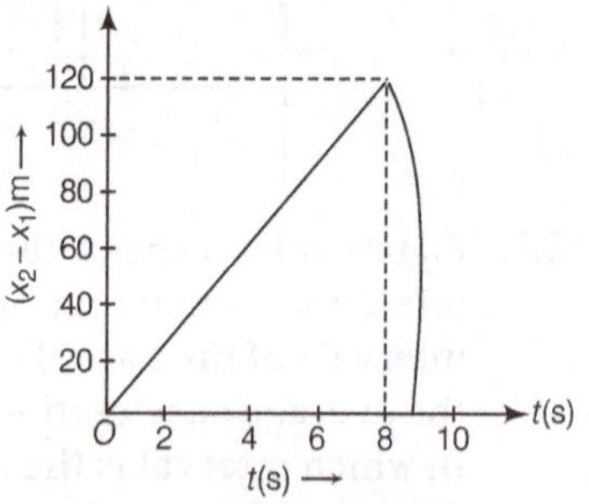

Neglect the air resistance and assume that the stones do not rebound after hitting the ground. Take $g = 10 \text{ ms}^{-2}$. Give the equations for the linear and curved part of the plot. NCERT [5 M]

48. The speed-time graph of a particle moving along a fixed direction is shown below in figure. Obtain the distance travelled by the particle between (i) $t = 0$ s to 10 s (ii) $t = 2$ s to 6 s.

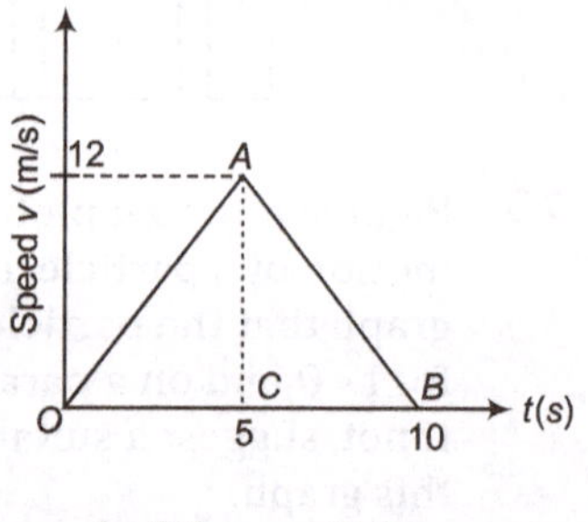

What is the average speed of the particle over the intervals in (i) and (ii)? NCERT [5 M]

49. A motor car moving at a speed of 72 km/h cannot come to a stop is less than 3.0 s while for a truck time interval is 5.0 s. On a highway, the car is behind the truck both moving at 72 km/h. The truck gives a signal that it is going to stop at emergency. At what distance the car should be from the truck so that it does not bumb onto (collide with) the truck? Human response time is 0.5 s. **NCERT Exemplar [5 M]**

50. It is a common observation that rain clouds can be at about a kilometre altitude above the ground.

(i) If a rain drop falls from such a height freely under gravity, what will be its speed? Also, calculate in km/h ($g = 10\ \text{m/s}^2$).

(ii) A typical rain drop is about 4 mm diameter. Momentum is mass × speed in magnitude. Estimate its momentum when it hits ground.

(iii) Estimate time required to flatten the drop.

(iv) Rate of change of momentum is force. Estimate how much force such a drop would exert on you?

(v) Estimate the order of magnitude of force on umbrella. Typical lateral separation between two rain drops is 5 cm.

(Assume that umbrella is circular and has a diameter of 1 m and cloth is not pierced through it.) **NCERT Exemplar [5 M]**

51. A ball is thrown upward with an initial velocity of 100 m/s. After how much time will it return? Draw velocity-time graph for the ball and find from the graph.

(i) Maximum height attained by ball and

(ii) Height of the ball after 15 s. Take $g = 10\ \text{ms}^{-2}$

[5 M]

52. Figure gives the x-t plot of a particle executing one-dimensional simple harmonic motion. Give the signs of position, velocity and acceleration variables of the particles at $t = 0.3$ s, 1.2 s, – 1.2 s.

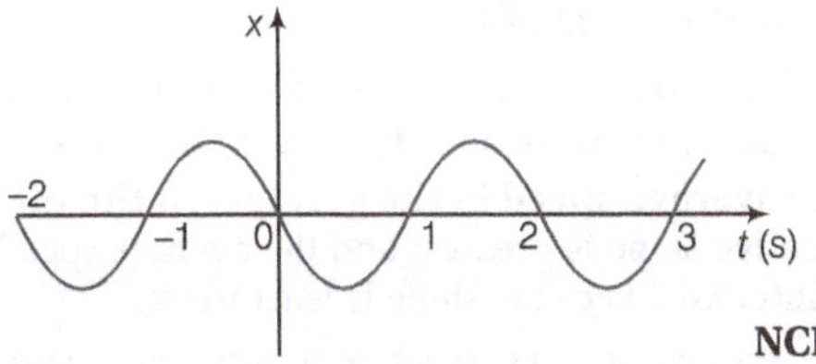

NCERT [3 M]

53. A three wheeler starts from rest, accelerates uniformly with $1\ \text{ms}^{-2}$ on a straight road for 10 s, and then moves with uniform velocity. Plot a graph between the distance covered by the vehicle during the nth second ($n = 1, 2, 3, \ldots$) *versus* n. What do you expect the plot to be during accelerated motion a straight line or a parabola? **NCERT [5 M]**

Hints & Solutions

1. (c) Here, $v = 15\ \text{ms}^{-1}$, $v_0 = 30\ \text{ms}^{-1}$ and $t = 2$ s

Using relation, $v = v_0 + at$

$\Rightarrow \quad 15 = 30 + a \times 2$

or Acceleration of the car $a = \dfrac{(15-30)\ \text{ms}^{-1}}{2\ \text{s}} = -\dfrac{15}{2}\ \text{ms}^{-2}$

$= -7.5\ \text{ms}^{-2}$

2. (a) Initial velocity $= 2v_0$

Final velocity, $v = 4v_0$

For constant acceleration,

$\because$ Average distance covered,

$$x = \frac{v + v_0}{2} t = \left(\frac{4v_0 + 2v_0}{2}\right) t = 3v_0 t$$

Using relation is $x = 3v_0 t$

3. (a) Given, $\quad v_0 = 0$

Using relation, $v^2 = v_0^2 + 2ax$

$v^2 = 2ax$

$\therefore \quad v = \sqrt{2ax}$

4. (a) Here, $v(x) = 3x^2 - 4x$

$$a = v\frac{dv}{dx} = (3x^2 - 4x) \times \frac{dv}{dx}$$

$$= (3x^2 - 4x) \times (6x - 4)$$

5. (a) Given, $\quad x_0 = 3$ units, $a = 4\ \text{ms}^{-2}$, $t = 3$ s

$\Rightarrow \quad v_0 = 0$

Using relation, $x = x_0 + v_0 t + \frac{1}{2}at^2$

$$= 3 + \frac{1}{2} \times 4 \times (3)^2 = +21 \text{ units}$$

6. (b) Average acceleration is also defined as the average change of velocity per unit time.

7. (b) Given, $v = \beta x^{-2n}$

$$a = \frac{dv}{dt} = \frac{dx}{dt} \cdot \frac{dv}{dx}$$

$$\Rightarrow \quad a = v\frac{dv}{dx} = (\beta x^{-2n})(-2n\beta x^{-2n-1})$$

$$\Rightarrow \quad a = -2n\beta^2 x^{-4n-1}$$

8. (c) On a plot of velocity *versus* time, the average acceleration is the slope of the straight line connecting the points corresponding to (v_2, t_2) and (v_1, t_1).

9. (*d*) Given, $x = 8 + 12t - t^3$

We know $v = \frac{dx}{dt}$

and acceleration $a = \frac{dv}{dt}$

So, $v = 12 - 3t^2$ and $a = -6t$

At $t = 2\text{ s}$

$v = 0$ and $a = -6 \times 2$

$a = 12\text{ ms}^{-2}$

So, retardation of the particle $= 12\text{ ms}^{-2}$.

10. Given, acceleration $a = \beta t$

It can be written as $\int dv = \int \beta t dt$

On integrating, we get $v = \frac{\beta t^2}{2} + C = \frac{\beta t^2}{2}$ $[\because C = 0]$

11. Motion of a body under gravity.

12. Acceleration means that velocity is non-uniform. So, *x-t* graph will be curved.

13. Here, acceleration is increasing.

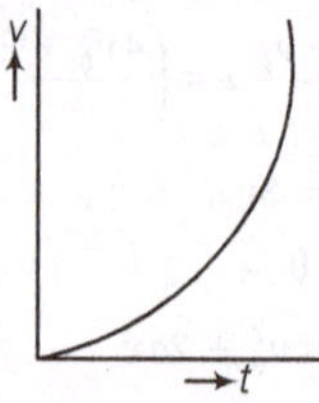

14. The area under acceleration-time graph for any time interval represents the change of velocity of the body during that time interval.

15.

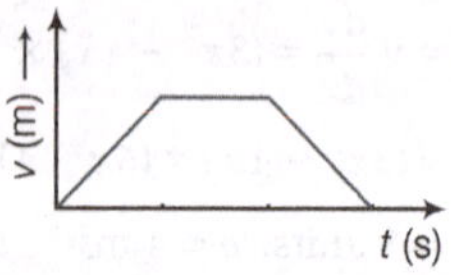

16. If a is the uniform acceleration, then

$$s_n = s_{(n\text{ th})} = u + \frac{1}{2} a(2n-1)$$

where, s_n is the distance covered in nth second, u is the initial velocity.

17. Acceleration is 9.8 m/s^2 (downwards) and velocity is zero at the highest point.

18. Let x be the displacement.

Then, $x = at^2$

$\therefore$ Velocity of the object, $v = \frac{dx}{dt} = 2at$ [1/2]

Acceleration of the object, $a = \frac{dv}{dt} = 2a$ [1/2]

It means that a is constant. [1]

19. Refer to text on page 41 (Uniform and non-uniform acceleration).

20. Refer to text on page 43 (Note).

21. Both these statements are not true, because

(i) Its magnitude can be zero. [1]

(ii) Its magnitude is either less than or equal to the distance travelled by the object. [1]

22. Refer to text on page 43 (Displacement-time graph (i)).

23. From a velocity-time graph, we can find out

(i) The velocity of a body at any instant. [1/2]

(ii) The acceleration of the body and [1/2]

(iii) The net displacement of the body in a given time-interval. [1]

24. Refer to text on page 46 (Velocity-time relation).

25. As given, $s = t^3 - 6t^2 + 3t + 4$

Hence, $v = \frac{ds}{dt} = 3t^2 - 12t + 3$ ...(i)

Differentiating it again w.r.t. t, we have

$\frac{dv}{dt}$ = acceleration $= \frac{d}{dt}(3t^2 - 12t + 3) = 6t - 12$ [1½]

When acceleration is zero, then

$t = 2\text{ s}$

Putting the value in Eq. (i), we get

$v = 3 \times (2)^3 - 12 \times 2 + 3 = -9\text{ m/s}$ [1½]

26. (i) In Fig. (a), the *x-t* graph shows that initially x is zero i.e. at rest, then it increases with time, attains a constant value and again reduces to zero with time, then it increases in opposite direction till it again attains a constant value i.e. comes to rest.

The similar physical situation arises when a ball resting on a smooth floor is kicked which rebounds from a wall with reduced speed. It then moves to the opposite wall which stops it. [1]

(ii) In Fig. (b), the velocity changes sign again and again with passage of time and every time some speed is lost. The similar physical situation arises when a ball is thrown up with some velocity, returns back and falls freely. On striking the ground, it rebounds with reduced speed each time it strikes against the ground. [1]

(iii) In Fig. (c), initially the body moves with uniform velocity. Its acceleration increases for a short duration and then falls to zero and thereafter the body moves with a constant velocity. The similar physical situation arises when a cricket ball moving with a uniform speed is hit with a bat for a very short interval of time. [1]

27. We know that average speed in a small interval of time is equal to the slope of *x-t* graph in that interval of time. **The average speed is the greatest in the interval 3 because** slope is greatest and the average speed is least in interval 2 because slope is least there. [1½]

The average speed is positive in intervals 1 and 2 because slope of *x-t* is positive there and **average speed is negative in interval** 3 because the slope of *x-t* is negative. [1½]

28. We know that average acceleration in a small interval of time is equal to slope of velocity-time graph in that interval. As the slope of velocity-time graph is maximum in interval 2 as compared to other intervals 1 and 3, hence the magnitude of average acceleration is greatest in interval 2. The **average speed is greatest in interval 3** for obvious reasons. [1]

In interval 1, the slope of velocity-time graph is positive, hence **acceleration *a* is positive**. The speed u is positive in this interval due to obvious reasons. [1/2]

In interval 2, the slope of velocity-time graph is negative, hence **acceleration *a* is negative**. The speed u is positive in this interval due to obvious reasons. [1/2]

In interval 3, the velocity-time graph is parallel to time axis, therefore **acceleration *a* is zero** in this interval but **v is positive** due to obvious reasons.

At points A, B, C and D, the velocity-time graph is parallel to time axis. Therefore, acceleration a **is zero at all the four points**. [1]

29. No, because the x-t graph does not represent the trajectory of the path followed by a particle. From the graph, it is noted that at $t = 0$, $x = 0$. [2]

Context The above graph can represent the motion of a body falling freely from a tower under gravity. [1]

30. (i) True, when a body is thrown vertically upwards in the space, then at the highest point, the body has zero speed but has downward acceleration equal to the acceleration due to gravity. [1/2]

(ii) False, because velocity is the speed of body in a given direction. When speed is zero, the magnitude of velocity of body is zero, hence velocity is zero. **[1/2]**

(iii) True, when a particle is moving along a straight line with a constant speed, its velocity remains constant with time. Therefore, acceleration (i.e. change in velocity/time) is zero. [1]

(iv) False, if the initial velocity of a body is negative, then even in the case of positive acceleration, the body speeds down. A body speeds up when the acceleration acts in the direction of motion. [1]

31. (i) As brakes of the cars are not so perfect, which can stop the car instantaneously because if the car is to stop instantaneously, its velocity is to be zero within an extremely small time interval. To achieve that, the car needs infinite acceleration which is not possible. [1½]

(ii) According to the question,

$$u = 0, \; a = g$$

Using relation, $h_1 = u + \frac{1}{2} g(2n-1)$

$$\Rightarrow \quad h_1 = \frac{g}{2}(2.1-1) = \frac{g}{2}$$

$$\Rightarrow \quad h_2 = \frac{g}{2}(2.2-1) = \frac{3g}{2}$$

$$\Rightarrow \quad h_3 = \frac{g}{2}(2.3-1) = \frac{5g}{2}$$

Hence, $h_1 : h_2 : h_3 = 1:3:5$ [1½]

32. As, $u - 0$, $t = 10$s

Distance covered $= d_1$

$$\therefore \; d_1 = 0 \times 10 + \frac{1}{2} \times a \times (10)^2 = 50a \quad ...(i)$$

Again, $(d_1 + d_2) = 0 \times 20 + \frac{1}{2} \times a \times (20)^2 = 200a$ [1]

Hence, $d_2 = (d_1 + d_2) - d_1$

$$= 200a - 50a = 150a$$ [1]

$$\therefore \quad \frac{d_2}{d_1} = \frac{150a}{50a} = 3 \Rightarrow d_2 = 3d_1$$ [1]

33. An object released near the surface of the earth is accelerated downward under the influence of the force of gravity. The magnitude of acceleration due to gravity is represented by g. If air resistance is neglected, the object is said to be in **free fall**. If the height through which the object falls is small as compared to the earth's radius, g can be taken constant, equal to 9.8 ms^{-2}. Free fall is thus a case of motion with uniform acceleration. [1]

We assume that the motion is in y-direction, more correctly in $(-y)$ direction because we choose upward direction as positive. Since, the acceleration due to gravity is always downward, it is in the negative direction and we have

$$a = -g = -9.8 \text{m s}^{-2}$$ [1]

The object is released from rest at $y = 0$. Therefore, $u = 0$ and the equations of motion become

$$v = 0 - gt = -9.8t \text{ ms}^{-1}$$

$$h = 0 - 1/2gt^2 = -4.9t^2 \text{ m}$$

$$v^2 = 0 - 2gh = -19.6h\text{m}^2\text{s}^{-2}$$ [1]

These equations give the velocity and the distance travelled as a function of time and also the variation of velocity with distance.

The variation of acceleration, velocity and distance with time have been plotted in Fig. (a), (b) and (c).

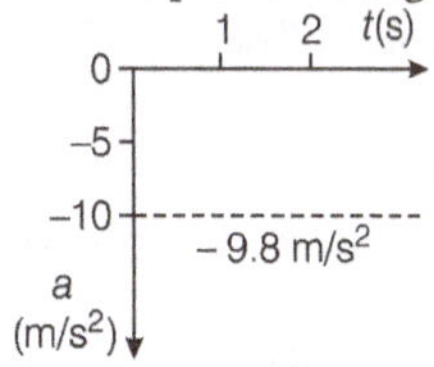

(a) Variation of acceleration with time

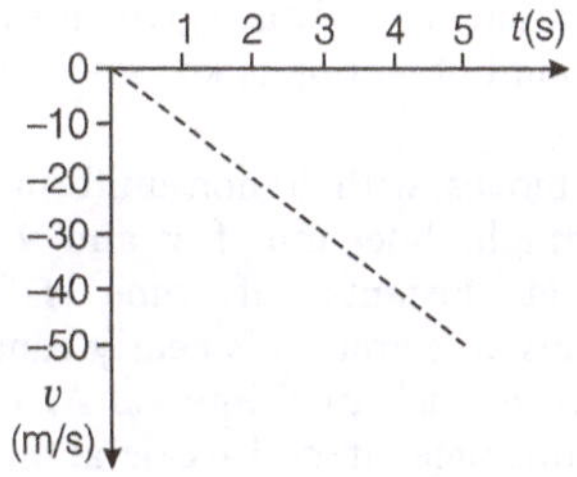

(b) Variation of velocity with time

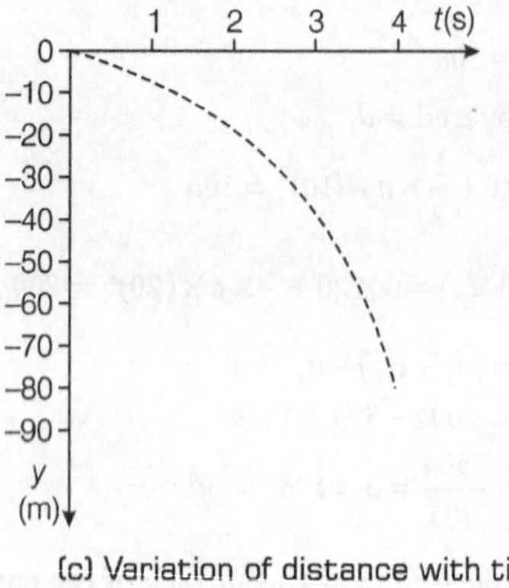

(c) Variation of distance with time

Note Here, magnitude of displacement and distance is equal. [2]

34. Refer to text on page 44 (*v-t* graph (ii) positive acceleration and (iv) negative acceleration).

35. Refer to text on page 46 (Kinematic equations for uniformly accelerated motion).

36. (i) If the car has uniform acceleration for time t_1 and uniform retardation for time t_2, then total time,

$$T = t_1 + t_2 \quad ...(i)$$

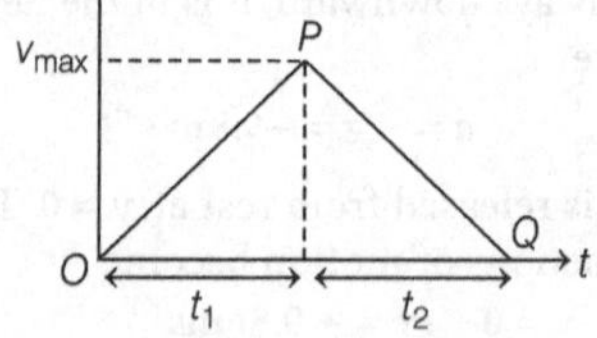

[1]

Maximum velocity of the car = v_{max}

So, from *v-t* graph,

Slope, $X = \frac{v_{max}}{t_1}$

$Y = \frac{v_{max}}{t_2}$

Thus, $\frac{1}{X} + \frac{1}{Y} = \frac{t_1 + t_2}{v_{max}} = \frac{T}{v_{max}}$

or $v_{max} = \frac{XYT}{(X+Y)}$ [1]

Area under *v-t* graph gives the distance travelled in a given time.

So, $s = \frac{1}{2}(v_{max}) \times T = \frac{XYT^2}{2(X+Y)}$ [1]

(ii) The acceleration of a body at a given instant of time or at a given point of motion is known as instantaneous acceleration.

If a body moves with a non-uniform acceleration along a straight line and if $\mathbf{v}$ and $\mathbf{v} + \Delta\mathbf{v}$ be the velocities at instants of time t and $t + \Delta t$, instantaneous acceleration is nearly equal to average acceleration in small time interval Δt when $\Delta t \to 0$, because in this time interval acceleration of the object is considered to be uniform considering time interval Δt as small as possible

$$\mathbf{a} = \lim_{\Delta t \to 0}\left(\frac{\Delta \mathbf{v}}{\Delta t}\right)$$

Thus, instantaneous acceleration of an object at a given instant of time is the limiting value of average acceleration in small time interval around the given instant. [2]

37. Given, $x = 2t^3$,

velocity, $v = \frac{dx}{dt} = \frac{d(2t^3)}{dt} = 6t^2$ [1/2]

$\therefore$ Acceleration, $a = \frac{dv}{dt} = \frac{d(6t^2)}{dt} = 12t$ [1/2]

38. $u = 0, a = 0.1 \text{ m/s}^2$ and $t = 2 \text{ min} = 120 \text{ s}$

(i) $v = u + at = 0 + 0.1 \times 120 = 12 \text{ m/s}$ [1]

(ii) $s = ut + \frac{1}{2}at^2 = 0 + \frac{1}{2} \times 0.1 \times (120)^2$

$= \frac{1}{2} \times 01 \times 120 \times 120 = 720 \text{ m}$ [1]

39. Let t_1 and t_2 be the times of descent through *PQ* and *QR*, respectively.

Let $PQ = QR = h$

Then, $h = \frac{1}{2}g t_1^2$ and $2h = \frac{1}{2}g(t_1 + t_2)^2$ [1]

By dividing, we get

$\frac{1}{2} = \frac{t_1^2}{(t_1 + t_2)^2}$ or $\frac{1}{\sqrt{2}} = \frac{t_1}{t_1 + t_2}$

Hence, $t_1 : t_2 = 1 : (\sqrt{2} - 1)$ [1]

40. For a train *A*, $u = 72 \text{ kmh}^{-1} = \frac{72 \times 1000}{60 \times 60} = 20 \text{ ms}^{-1}$

$t = 50 \text{ s}, a = 0, x = x_A$

As, $x = ut + \frac{1}{2}at^2$

$\therefore x_A = 20 \times 50 + \frac{1}{2} \times 0 \times 50^2 = 1000 \text{ m}$ [1]

For train *B*, $u = 72 \text{ km/h} = 20 \text{ ms}^{-1}$,

$a = 1 \text{ m/s}^2, t = 50 \text{s}, x = x_B$

As, $x = ut + \frac{1}{2}at^2$

$\therefore \quad x_B = 20 \times 50 + \frac{1}{2} \times 1 \times 50^2$

$= 2250 \text{ m}$ [1]

Taking the guard of the train *B* in the last compartment of the train *B*, it follows that original distance between the two trains = length of train *A* + length of train *B*.

$= 800 \text{ m}$

or original distance between the two trains is given by

$= x_B - x_A$

$= 2250 - 1000 = 1250 \text{ m}$

or original distance between the two trains

$= 1250 - 800 = 450 \text{ m}$ [1]

41. Because the acceleration is constant, we can apply the equations of motion derived above.

(i) We take the origin of the x-axis to be the initial position of the plane, so that $x_0 = 0$.

It is useful to begin by listing all the data given in the problem.

$$a = 4.00 \text{ m/s}^2, \; v = 0, \; x = 0$$ [1]

The problem may be stated in terms of the symbols as follows

Find x and v at $t = 5.00$ s

When x and u are zero, these two equations reduce

to $\quad v = at$ and $x = \frac{1}{2}at^2$

At $t = 5.00$ s

$$v = (4.00 \text{ m/s}^2)(5.00\text{s}) = 20.0 \text{ m/s}$$

$$x = \frac{1}{2}(4.00 \text{ m/s}^2)(5.00\text{s})^2$$

$$x = 50.0 \text{ m}$$ [1]

(ii) The problem here may be stated as

Find x when $v = 70.0$ m/s

It contains the single unknown x, as well as a and v, which are known with $u = 0$, $v_x^2 = 2a_x x$

Solving for x, we obtain

$$x = \frac{v^2}{2a} = \frac{(70.00 \text{ m/s})^2}{2(4.00 \text{ m/s}^2)} = 613 \text{ m}$$ [1]

42. For accelerated motion,

$$u = 0, a = f, s = s$$

As $\quad v^2 - u^2 = 2as,$

$\therefore \quad v_1^2 - 0^2 = 2fs \Rightarrow v_1 = \sqrt{2fs},$

Distance travelled, $s_2 = v_1 t = t\sqrt{2fs}$ [1½]

For decelerated motion,

$$u = \sqrt{2fs}, a = -f/2, v = 0$$

As $\quad v^2 - u^2 = 2as,$

$\therefore \quad 0^2 - (\sqrt{2fs})^2 = 2 \times (-f/2)\, s_3$

Distance travelled, $s_3 = 2s$

Given, $\quad s + s_2 + s_3 = 5s$

$\Rightarrow \quad s + t\sqrt{2fs} + 2s = 5s$

$\Rightarrow \quad t\sqrt{2fs} = 2s$

$\Rightarrow \quad s = \frac{1}{2}ft^2$ [1½]

43. (i) Since, the ball is moving under the effect of gravity, the direction of acceleration due to gravity is always vertically downwards. [1/2]

(ii) At the highest point, the velocity of the ball becomes zero and acceleration is equal to the acceleration due to gravity = 9.8 ms^{-2} in vertically downward direction. [1/2]

(iii) When the highest point is chosen as the location for $x = 0$ and $t = 0$ and vertically downward direction to be the positive direction of x-axis and upward direction as negative direction of x-axis.

During upward motion, sign of position is negative, sign of velocity is negative and sign of acceleration is positive. During downward motion, sign of position is positive, sign of velocity is positive and sign of acceleration is also positive. [1]

(iv) Let t be the time taken by the ball to reach the highest point where height from ground be s.

Taking vertical upward motion of the ball, we have $u = -29.4$ ms^{-1}, $a = 9.8$ ms^{-2}, $v = 0$, $s = S$, $t = ?$

As, $\quad v^2 - u^2 = 2as$

$\therefore \quad 0 - (-29.4)^2 = 2 \times 9.8 \times S$

or $\quad S = \frac{-(29.4)^2}{2 \times 9.8} = -44.1$ m

Here, negative sign shows that the distance is covered in upward direction.

As, $\quad v = u + at$

$\therefore \quad 0 = -29.4 + 9.8 \times t$

or $\quad t = \frac{29.4}{9.8} = 3$s

It means time of ascent = 3 s

When an object moves under the effect of gravity alone, the time of ascent is always equal to the time of descent.

Therefore, total time after which the ball returns to the player's hand $= 3 + 3 = 6$s. [1]

44. Taking vertical downward motion of ball from a height 90 m, we have

$$u = 0, a = 10 \text{ m/s}^2, s = 90 \text{ m}, t = ?; u = ?$$

$$t = \sqrt{\frac{2s}{a}} = \sqrt{\frac{2 \times 90}{10}} = 3\sqrt{2} \text{ s} = 4.24 \text{ s}$$ [1/2]

$$u = \sqrt{2as} = \sqrt{2 \times 10 \times 90} = 30\sqrt{2} \text{ m/s}$$

Rebound velocity of ball,

$$u' = \frac{9}{10}u = \frac{9}{10} \times 30\sqrt{2} = 27\sqrt{2} \text{ m/s}$$

Time to reach the highest point is

$$t' = \frac{u'}{a} = \frac{27\sqrt{2}}{10} = 2.7\sqrt{2} = 3.81 \text{ s}$$ [1/2]

Total time $= t + t' = 4.24 + 3.81$

$= 8.05$s

The ball will take further 3.81 s to fall back to floor, where its velocity before striking the floor $= 27\sqrt{2}$ m/s

Velocity of ball after striking the floor

$$= \frac{9}{10} \times 27\sqrt{2} = 24.3\sqrt{2} \text{ m/s}$$ [1/2]

Total time elapsed before upward motion of ball

$= 8.05 + 3.81 = 11.86$s [1/2]

Thus, the speed-time graph of this motion is shown in the figure.

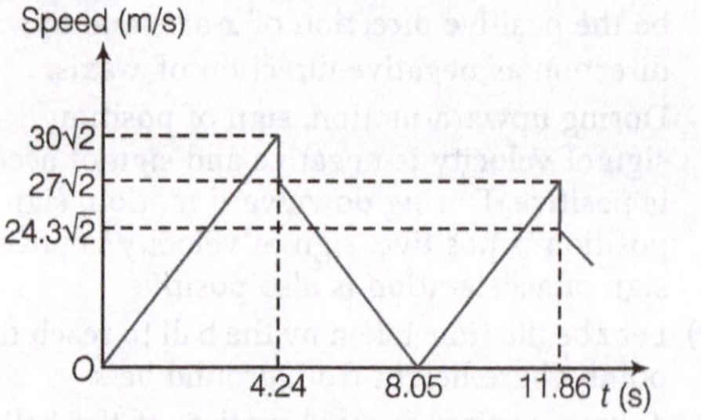

[1]

45. The velocity-time graph of the train's motion is shown in the following figure

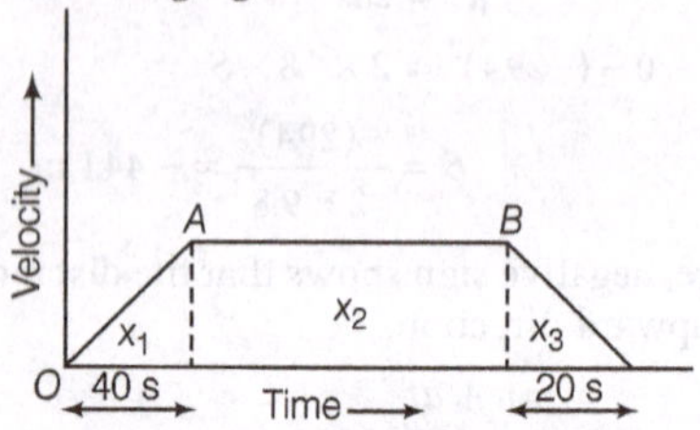

[1]

Let v represents the maximum speed of the train if x_1 be the distance covered during the first 40 s, then

$$\frac{v}{2} \times 40 = x_1 \text{ or } x_1 = 20\,v$$ [1]

Since total time is 4 min, i.e. 240 s therefore, the time corresponding to velocity-time graph AB is $(240 - 40 - 20)$ s i.e. 180 s. If x_2 be the distance covered during this time, then $x_2 = 180\,v$. [1]

If x_3 be the distance covered during the last 20 s, then

$$x_3 = \frac{v}{2} \times 20 = 10\,v$$

Now, $x_1 + x_2 + x_3 = 20\,v + 180\,v + 10\,v$

or $2250 = 210\,v$

or $v = \frac{225}{21}\,\text{ms}^{-1} = 10.7\,\text{ms}^{-1}$ [1]

Acceleration $= \frac{v}{40} = \frac{10.7}{40}\,\text{ms}^{-2} = 0.2675\,\text{ms}^{-2}$

Retardation $= \frac{v}{20} = \frac{10.7}{20}\,\text{m s}^{-2} = 0.535\,\text{ms}^{-2}$ [1]

46. Area $AEFG = AE \times AG \Rightarrow 7 = 40 \times AG$ or $AG = \frac{7}{40}$ h [1]

Area FGB gives the distance covered under retardation, it is $(8.5 - 7)$ km $= 1.5$ km

Area of $\Delta FGB = \frac{1}{2}\,GB \times FG \Rightarrow GB = \frac{2 \times 1.5}{40}\,\text{h} = \frac{3}{40}\,\text{h}$ [1]

Total time $= \left(\frac{7}{40} + \frac{3}{40}\right)\text{h} = \frac{1}{4}\,\text{h}$ [1/2]

Area of $\Delta ACB = \frac{1}{2}\,AB \times CD$

$$8.5 = \frac{1}{2} \times \frac{1}{4} \times v$$

$$v = 8.5 \times 8\,\text{kmh}^{-1} = 68\,\text{kmh}^{-1}$$ [1½]

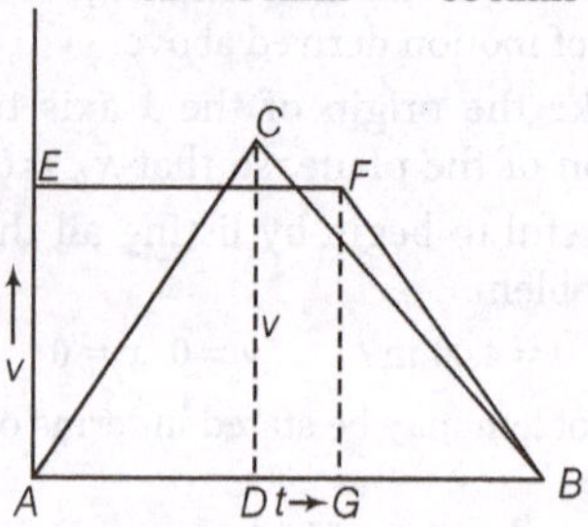

[1]

47. Taking vertical upward motion of the first stone for time t, we have

$$x_0 = 200\text{ m}, u = 15\text{ m/s},$$
$$a = -10\,\text{m/s}^2, t = t, x = x_1$$

As, $x = x_0 + ut + \frac{1}{2}at^2$

$\therefore$ $x_1 = 200 + 15t + \frac{1}{2}(-10)\,t^2$ [1]

or $x_1 = 200 + 15t - 5t^2$ ...(i)

Taking vertical upward motion of the second stone for time t, we have

$$x_0 = 200\text{ m}, u = 30\text{ ms}^{-1},$$
$$a = -10\text{ ms}^{-2}, t = t, x = x_2$$

Then, $x_2 = 200 + 30\,t - \frac{1}{2} \times 10\,t^2$

$= 200 + 30\,t - 5\,t^2$ ...(ii) [1]

When the first stone hits the ground, $x_1 = 0$, from Eq (i).

So, $t^2 - 3t - 40 = 0$

or $(t - 8)(t + 5) = 0$

$\therefore$ Either $t = 8$ s or -5 s

Since, $t = 0$ corresponds to the instant, when the stone was projected. Hence, negative time has no meaning in this case. So, $t = 8$ s. [1]

When the second stone hits the ground, $x_2 = 0$, from Eq (ii).

So, $0 = 200 + 30\,t - 5\,t^2$ or $t^2 - 6\,t - 40 = 0$

or $(t - 10)(t + 4) = 0$

Therefore, either $t = 10$ s, or $t = -4$ s

Since, $t = -4$ s is meaningless, so $t = 10$ s. [1]

Relative position of second stone w.r.t. first is

$$= x_2 - x_1 = 15\,t$$ ...(iii)

Since, $(x_2 - x_1)$ and t are linearly related, therefore, the graph is a straight line till $t = 8$ s.

For maximum separation, $t = 8$ s, so maximum separation $= 15 \times 8 = 120$ m

After 8 s only, second stone would be in motion for 2 s, so the graph is in accordance with the quadratic equation, $x_2 = 200 + 30\,t - 5\,t^2$ for the interval of time 8 s to 10 s. [1]

48. (i) Distance travelled by the particle between time interval $t = 0$ s to $t = 10$ s

$$= \text{Area of triangle } OAB$$
$$= \frac{1}{2} \times \text{Base} \times \text{Height}$$
$$= \frac{1}{2} \times OB \times AC$$
$$= \frac{1}{2} \times 10 \times 12 = 60 \text{ m}$$

Average speed of the particle for this time interval

$$= \frac{\text{Total distance travelled}}{\text{Total time taken}} = \frac{60}{10} = 6 \text{ m/s}$$ [1½]

(ii) From the part OA of the given graph (in accelerated motion)

When $t = 0, u = 0$

$t = 5$ s, $v = 12$ m/s

Using equation of motion,

$$v = u + at$$
$$12 = 0 + a \times 5$$

or $$a = \frac{12}{5} \text{ m/s}^2 = 2.4 \text{ m/s}^2$$

Speed of the particle at the end of $t = 2$ s

$$v' = u + at = 0 + 2.4 \times 2 = 4.8 \text{ m/s}$$

Now, distance travelled in accelerated motion from $t = 2$ s to $t = 5$ s i.e. in 3 s, for which initial speed is $u = v' = 4.8$ m/s

Using equation of motion,

$$s_1 = ut + \frac{1}{2}at^2$$
$$= 4.8 \times 3 + \frac{1}{2} \times 2.4 \times (3)^2 = 14.4 + 10.8$$
$$s_1 = 25.2 \text{ m}$$ [1½]

From the part AB of the given graph (retarded motion)

Initial speed at $t = 5$ s, $u = 12$ m/s

Time taken, $t = (10 - 5) = 5$ s

Final speed at $t = 10$ s, $v = 0$

Using equation, $v = u + at$

$$0 = 12 + a \times 5$$

or $$a = -\frac{12}{5} = -2.4 \text{ m/s}^2$$

Now, distance travelled by the particle in retarded motion from $t = 5$ s to $t = 6$ s i.e. in 1 s,

$$s_2 = ut + \frac{1}{2}at^2$$
$$= 12 \times 1 + \frac{1}{2}(-2.4) \times 1 \times 1$$
$$= 12 - 1.2 = 10.8 \text{ m}$$ [1]

∴ Total distance travelled by the particle from $t = 2$ s to $t = 6$ s

$$s = s_1 + s_2$$
$$= 25.2 + 10.8 = 36.0 \text{ m}$$

Average speed of the particle for this time interval

$$= \frac{\text{Total distance travelled}}{\text{Total time taken}}$$
$$= \frac{36}{(6-2)} = \frac{36}{4} = 9 \text{ m/s}$$ [1]

49. Given, speed of the car as well as truck = 72 km/h

$$= 72 \times \frac{5}{18} \text{ m/s} = 20 \text{ m/s}$$

Retarded motion for truck

$$v = u + a_t t$$
$$0 = 20 + a_t \times 5$$

or $$a_t = -4 \text{ m/s}^2$$

Retarded motion for the car

$$v = u + a_c t$$
$$0 = 20 + a_c \times 3$$

or $$a_c = -\frac{20}{3} \text{ m/s}^2$$ [1½]

Let car be at a distance x from truck, when truck gives the signal and t be the time taken to cover this distance.

As human response time is 0.5 s, therefore time of retarded motion of car is $(t - 0.5)$ s.

Velocity of car after time t,

$$v_c = u - at$$
$$= 20 - \left(\frac{20}{3}\right)(t - 0.5)$$

Velocity of truck after time t,

$$v_t = 20 - 4t$$

To avoid the car bump onto the truck, $v_c = v_t$

$$20 - \frac{20}{3}(t - 0.5) = 20 - 4t$$

or $$4t = \frac{20}{3}(t - 0.5)$$

or $$t = \frac{5}{3}(t - 0.5)$$

or $$3t = 5t - 2.5$$

or $$t = \frac{2.5}{2} = \frac{5}{4} \text{ s}$$ [1½]

Distance travelled by the truck in time t,

$$s_t = u_t t + \frac{1}{2}a_t t^2$$
$$= 20 \times \frac{5}{4} + \frac{1}{2} \times (-4) \times \left(\frac{5}{4}\right)^2$$
$$s_t = 25 - 3.125 = 21.875 \text{ m}$$ [1]

Distance travelled by the car in time t

= Distance travelled by the car in 0.5 s (without retardation) + Distance travelled by car in $(t - 0.5)$ s (with retardation)

$$s_c = (20 \times 0.5) + 20\left(\frac{5}{4} - 0.5\right) - \frac{1}{2}\left(\frac{20}{3}\right)\left(\frac{5}{4} - 0.5\right)^2$$

$= 23.125$ m

$\therefore s_c - s_t = 23.125 - 21.875$

$= 1.250$ m

Therefore, to avoid the bumb onto the truck, the car must maintain a distance from the truck more than 1.250 m. [1]

50. Here, height $(h) = 1$ km $= 1000$ m, $g = 10$ m/s^2

(i) Velocity attained by the rain drop in freely falling through a height h.

$$v = \sqrt{2gh} = \sqrt{2 \times 10 \times 1000}$$

$$= 100\sqrt{2} \text{ m/s}$$

$$= 100\sqrt{2} \times \frac{60 \times 60}{1000} \text{ km/h}$$

$$= 360\sqrt{2} \text{ km/h} \approx 510 \text{ km/h}$$ [1]

(ii) Diameter of the drop $(d) = 2r = 4$ mm

$\therefore$ Radius of the drop $(r) = 2$ mm $= 2 \times 10^{-3}$ m

Mass of a rain drop $(m) = V \times \rho$

$$= \frac{4}{3}\pi r^3 \rho = \frac{4}{3} \times \frac{22}{7} \times (2 \times 10^{-3})^3 \times 10^3$$

[$\because$ density of water $= 10^3$ kg/m^3]

$\approx 3.4 \times 10^{-5}$ kg

Momentum of the rain drop $(p) = mv$

$= 3.4 \times 10^{-5} \times 100\sqrt{2}$

$\approx 4.7 \times 10^{-3}$ kg-m/s [1]

(iii) Time required to flatten the drop

= time taken by the drop to travel the distance equal to the diameter of the drop near the ground

$$t = \frac{d}{v} = \frac{4 \times 10^{-3}}{100\sqrt{2}}$$

$= 0.028 \times 10^{-3}$ s $= 2.8 \times 10^{-5}$ s [1]

(iv) Force exerted by a rain drop

$$F = \frac{\text{Change in momentum}}{\text{Time}}$$

$$= \frac{p - 0}{t}$$

$$= \frac{4.7 \times 10^{-3}}{2.8 \times 10^{-5}} \approx 168 \text{ N}$$ [1]

(v) Radius of the umbrella $(R) = \frac{1}{2}$ m

$\therefore$ Area of the umbrella $(A) = \pi R^2$

$$= \frac{22}{7} \times \left(\frac{1}{2}\right)^2 = \frac{22}{28} = \frac{11}{14} \approx 0.8 \text{ m}^2$$

Number of drops striking the umbrella simultaneously with average separation of 5 cm or 5×10^{-2} m

$$= \frac{0.8}{(5 \times 10^{-2})^2} = 320$$

$\therefore$ Net force exerted on umbrella

$= 320 \times 168 = 53760$ N [1]

51. Here, $u = 100$ ms^{-1},

$g = -10$ ms^{-2}

At highest point, $v = 0$

As $v = u + gt$

$\Rightarrow 0 = 100 - 10 \times t$

$\therefore$ Time taken to reach highest point

$$t = \frac{100}{10} = 10 \text{ s}$$

The ball will return to the ground at

$t = 20$ s.

Velocities of the ball at different instants of time will be as follows.

At $t = 0$, $v = 100 - 10 \times 0 = 100$ ms^{-1}

At $t = 5$ s, $v = 100 - 10 \times 5 = 50$ ms^{-1}

At $t = 10$ s, $v = 100 - 10 \times 10 = 0$

At $t = 15$ s, $v = 100 - 10 \times 15 = -50$ ms^{-1}

At $t = 20$ s, $v = 100 - 10 \times 20 = -100$ ms^{-1} [2]

The velocity time-graph will be as shown in figure.

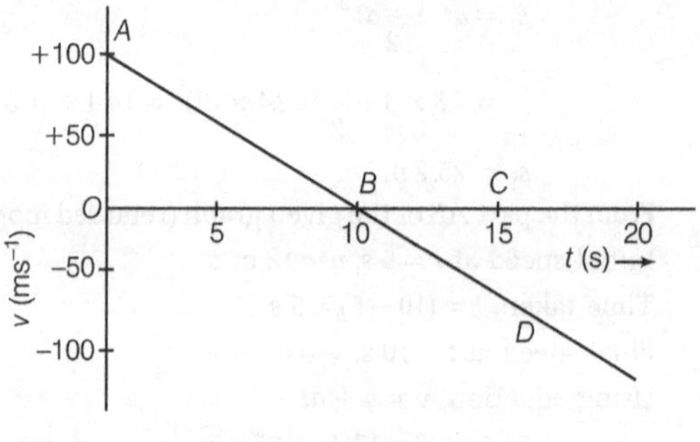

[1]

(i) Maximum height attained by ball

= Area of ΔAOB

$= \frac{1}{2} \times 10\text{s} \times 100$ ms^{-1}

$= 500$ m [1]

(ii) Height attained after 15 s

= Area of ΔAOB + Area of ΔBCD

$= 500 + \frac{1}{2}(15 - 10) \times (-50)$

$= 500 - 125 = 375$ m [1]

52. In the SHM, acceleration $a = -\omega^2 x$, where ω (i.e. angular frequency) is constant.

(i) At time $t = 0.3$ s, x is negative, the slope of x-t plot is negative, hence **position and velocity are negative**. Since $a = -\omega^2 x$, hence acceleration is positive. **[1]**

(ii) At time $t = 1.2$s, x is positive, the slope of x-t plot is also positive, hence position and velocity are positive. Since $a = -\omega^2 x$, hence **acceleration is negative**. **[1]**

(iii) At $t = -1.2$s, x is negative, the slope of x-t plot is also negative. But since both x and t are negative here, hence **velocity is positive**. Finally, acceleration ***a* is also positive**. [1]

53. Here, $u = 0$, $a = 1\text{ ms}^{-2}$ [1]

Distance covered in nth second is

$$D_n = u + \frac{a}{2}(2n-1)$$

$$D_n = 0 + \frac{1}{2}(2n-1) = 0.5\,(2n-1) \quad \text{...(i)}$$

[1]

Putting $n = 1, 2, 3, \ldots$, we can find the value of D_n. The various values of n and corresponding values of D_n are shown below

n	1	2	3	4	5	6	7	8	9	10
D_n	0.5	1.5	2.5	3.5	4.5	5.5	6.5	7.5	8.5	9.5

[2]

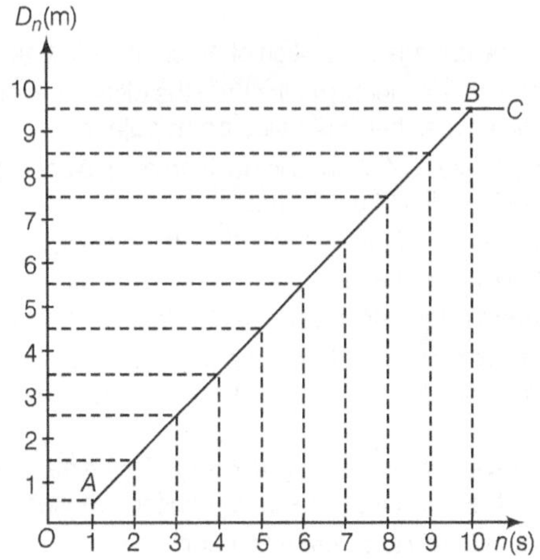

On plotting a graph between D_n and n, we get a straight line AB as shown in figure. From Eq. (i), $D_n \propto n$ so the graph is a straight line. After 10 s, the graph is a straight line BC parallel to time axis. [1]

SUMMARY

- **Motion** is the change in position of an object with time.
- If the object size is much smaller than the distance it moves in a reasonable time, then it is called **point object**.
- **Velocity** is the rate of change in position or displacement of an object with time. It's SI unit is m/s.
- **Speed** is the ratio of the path length or the distance covered by an object to the time taken.
- **Acceleration** is the rate of change of velocity with time.
- If a body travels equal distance in equal interval of time along a straight line, then the body is said to be in uniform motion in a straight line.
- If a body travels equal distance in unequal intervals of time or *vice-versa*, then it is said to be in non-uniform motion.
- For a non-uniformly accelerated motion,
  $$v = \frac{ds}{dt}, \quad a = \frac{dv}{dt}$$
- **Instantaneous speed** is the limit of the average speed as the time interval becomes infinitesimally small or approaches to zero. It is given by $s_{in} = \lim_{\Delta t \to 0} \frac{\Delta s}{\Delta t} = \frac{ds}{dt}$
- **Average acceleration** is the ratio of change in velocity of the object to the time interval. It is given by,
  $$a_{av} = \frac{\Delta v}{\Delta t} = \frac{v_2 - v_1}{t_2 - t_1}$$
- **Instantanous acceleration** is the acceleration of a body at a certain instant or the limiting value of average acceleration when time interval tends to zero. It is given by
  $$a_n = \lim_{\Delta t \to 0} \frac{\Delta v}{\Delta t} = \frac{dv}{dt}$$
- **Kinematics equations for uniformly accelerated motion** (Symbols have their usual meaning)
  1. $v = u + at$
  2. $x = x_0 + ut + \frac{1}{2}at^2$
  3. $v^2 = u^2 + 2ax$
- Displacement of a particle in the nth second is given by
  $$s_n = u + \frac{a}{2}(2n - 1)$$
- Equation of motion under gravity is given by (Symbols have their usual meaning)
  1. $v = u + (\pm g)t$ +
  2. $h = ut + \frac{1}{2}(\pm g)t^2$
  3. $v^2 = u^2 + 2(\pm g)h$
- **Stopping distance** for a vehicle is given as
  $$d_s = \frac{-u^2}{2a}$$

Chapter Practice

Multiple Choice Questions

(1 Mark)

1 The distance travelled by a particle is proportional to the square of time, then the particle travels with

(a) uniform acceleration (b) uniform velocity
(c) uniform speed (d) None of these

2 Which of the following graph represents the uniform motion?

(a)
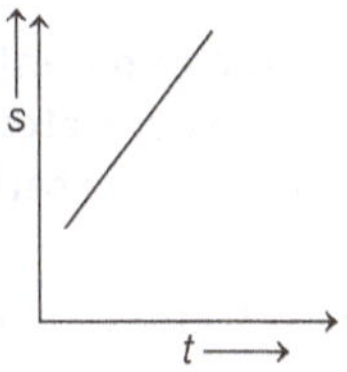

(b)
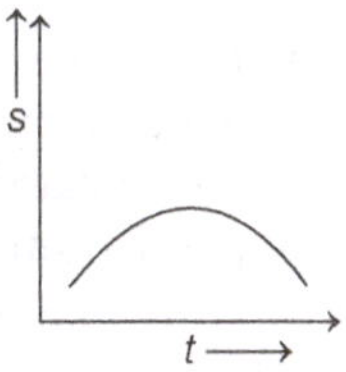

(c)
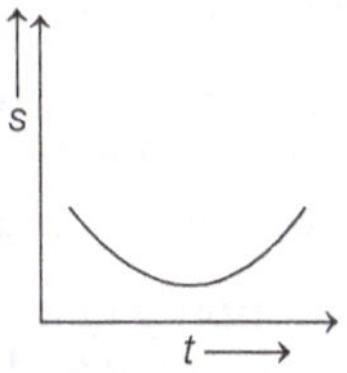

(d) None of these

3 An object is moving in positive direction till time t_1 and then turns back with same negative acceleration. The velocity-time graph which best describes the situation is

(a)
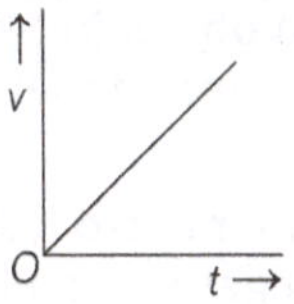

(b)
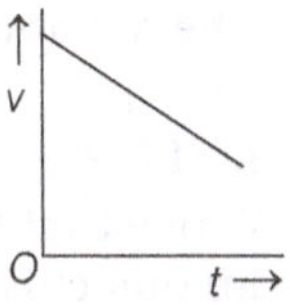

(c)
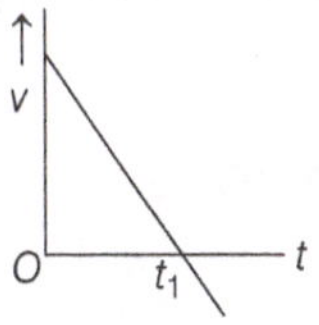

(d)
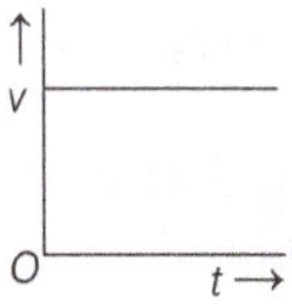

4 The x-t equation is given as $x = 2t + 1$. The corresponding v-t graph is

(a) a straight line passing through origin
(b) a straight line not passing through origin
(c) a parabola
(d) None of the above

5 A 100m long train crosses a man travelling at 5 kmh^{-1}, in opposite direction in 7.2 s. Then, the velocity of train is

(a) 40 m/s
(b) 25 m/s
(c) 20 m/s
(d) 45 m/s

Assertion and Reason

Directions (Q. Nos. 6-10) *In the following questions, two statements are given- one labelled Assertion (A) and the other labelled Reason (R). Select the correct answer to these questions from the codes (a), (b), (c) and (d) as given below*

(a) Both Assertion and Reason are true and Reason is the correct explanation of Assertion.
(b) Both Assertion and Reason are true but Reason is not the correct explanation of Assertion.
(c) Assertion is true but Reason is false.
(d) Assertion is false but Reason is true.

6 **Assertion** (A) A body may be accelerated even when it is moving uniformly.

Reason (R) When direction of motion of the body is changing, then body may have acceleration.

7 **Assertion (A)** Displacement of a body may be zero when distance travelled by it is not zero.

Reason (R) The displacement is the longest distance between initial and final position.

8 **Assertion (A)** For uniform motion, velocity is the same as the average velocity at all instants.

Reason (R) In uniform motion along a straight line, the object covers equal distances in equal intervals of time.

9 **Assertion** (A) Displacement of a body is vector sum of the area under velocity-time graph.

Reason (R) Displacement is a vector quantity.

10 **Assertion (A)** A positive acceleration of a body can be associated with a slowing down of the body.

Reason (R) Acceleration is a vector quantity.

Very Short Answer Type Questions

1 Mark

11 What do you understand by positive and negative acceleration?

12 Draw x-t graph for positive acceleration.

13 Can earth be regarded as a point object when it describes its yearly journey around the sun?

14 Write the expression for distance covered in nth second by a uniformly accelerated body.

15 Why does a parachute descend slowly?

16 What does speedometer record: the average speed or the instantaneous speed?

17 Why the speed of an object can never be negative?

18 Draw displacement-time graph for a uniformly accelerated motion. What is its shape?

Short Answer Type I Questions

2 Marks

19 If the displacement-time graph of a particle is parallel to (i) displacement axis and (ii) the time axis. What will be the velocity of the particle?

20 Write two uses of v-t graph.

21 Two bodies of different masses m_1 and m_2 are dropped from two different heights a and b. What is the ratio of time taken by the two bodies to drop through these distances?

22 The speed-time graph for a car is shown in figure below

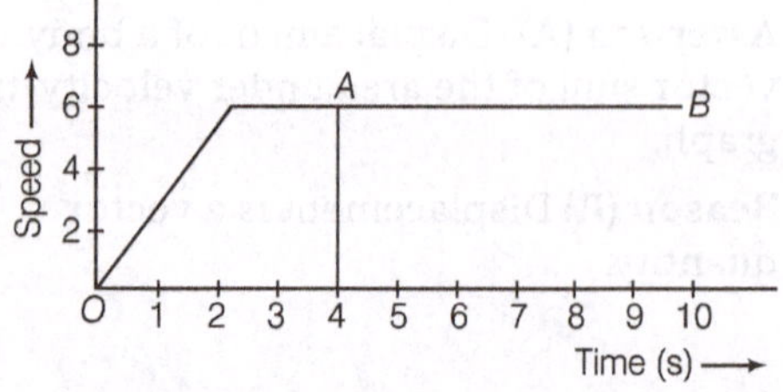

(i) Find how far does the car travel in the first 4s. Shade the area on the graph that represents the distance travelled by the car during the period.

(ii) Which part of the graph represents uniform motion of the car?

23 What is uniform and non-uniform velocity?

24 What are the uses of displacement-time graph?

25 Determine the displacement from v-t graph.

26 Write relations for non-uniformly accelerated motion.

Short Answer Type II Questions

3 Marks

27 A car accelerates from rest at a constant rate α for some time, after which it decelerates at a constant rate β to come to rest. If t is total time elapsed, then calculate

(i) the maximum velocity attained by the car.

(ii) the total distance travelled by the car.

28 Discuss the motion of an object under free fall and draw (i) acceleration-time (ii) velocity-time and (iii) position-time graph for this motion.

29 Derive an expression for stopping distance of a vehicle in terms of initial velocity u and deceleration a.

30 Establish the relation $x(t) = ut + 1/2at^2$ by calculus method.

31 The distance covered by an object between timings t_1 and t_2 is given by area under the v-t graph between t_1 and t_2.

Prove that the above statement also holds when an object is moving with negative acceleration has velocities positive at time t_1 and negative at t_2.

Long Answer Type Questions

5 Marks

32 Derive the three equations of motion by calculus method. Express the conditions under which they can be used.

33 How displacement-time graph is used to find

(i) comparision of velocities?

(ii) instantaneous velocity?

(iii) negative acceleration?

34 Use velocity-time graph to find
(i) displacement
(ii) acceleration
(iii) average acceleration

Case Based Questions

Directions (Q. No. 35) *These questions are case study based questions. Read the following paragraph and answer the questions.*

35 When an object moves along a straight line with uniform acceleration, it is possible to related its velocity, acceleration. During motion and the distance covered by it in a certain time interval by a set of equations known as the equations of motion. For convenience, a set of three such equations are given below

(I) $v = u + at$

(II) $s = ut = \frac{1}{2}at^2$

(III) $2as = v^2 - u^2$

where, u is the initial velocity of the object which moves with uniform acceleration a for time t, v is the final velocity and s is the distance travelled by the object in time t.

(i) An object takes 4s in falling from the top of the tower to the ground. If acceleration during fall is constant and equal to 9.8 ms^{-2}, find the height of the tower.

(ii) An object of mass 1 kg is relased from the top of a tower of height 125 m. What time will it take to strike the ground? (Take, $g = 10 \text{ m/s}^2$)

(iii) An object is made to fall form the top of a tower of height 78.4 m. Find the distance travelled by it in the Ist second.

(iv) Under what condition is the relation $s = ut$ correct?

(v) What happens to kinematic equations under time reversal?

Numerical Problems

36 If the velocity of a particle is given by $v = \sqrt{180 - 16x}$ m/s, what will be its acceleration? **[1 M]**

37 A body moving with a uniform acceleration describes 12 m in 3rd s of its motion and 20 m in the 5ths. Find the velocity after 10 s. **[2 M]**

38 A car moving with a speed of 50 km/h can be stopped by brakes after at least 6 m. What will be the minimum stopping distance, if the same car is moving at a speed of 100km/h? **[2 M]**

39 A train moves from one station to another in 4 h time. Its speed during the motion is shown in graph. Determine the maximum acceleration during the journey. Also, calculate the distance covered during the time interval from 1.5 h to 2 h.

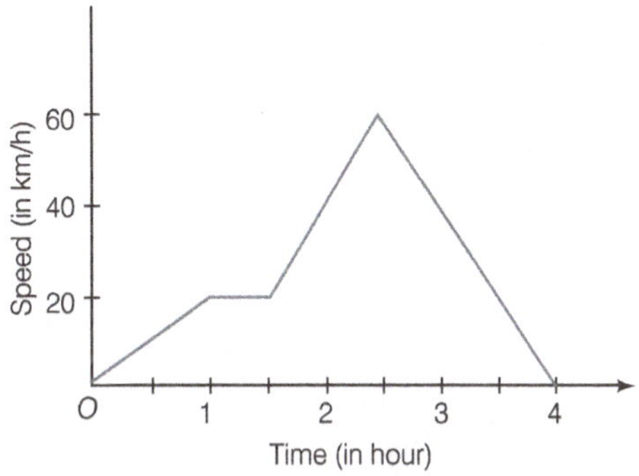

[3 M]

40 A ball is dropped from a height of 100 m on a floor. At each collision with floor, the ball loses one-tenth of its speed. Plot the speed-time graph of its motion between $t = 0$ s and $t = 12$ s. **[5 M]**

41 The velocity-time graph of a particle moving along a straight line as shown in figure by curve $OABCD$. Calculate the distance covered by the particle between (i) $t = 0$ to 18 s (ii) $t = 2$ s to $t = 12$ s and the maximum value of acceleration during this interval.

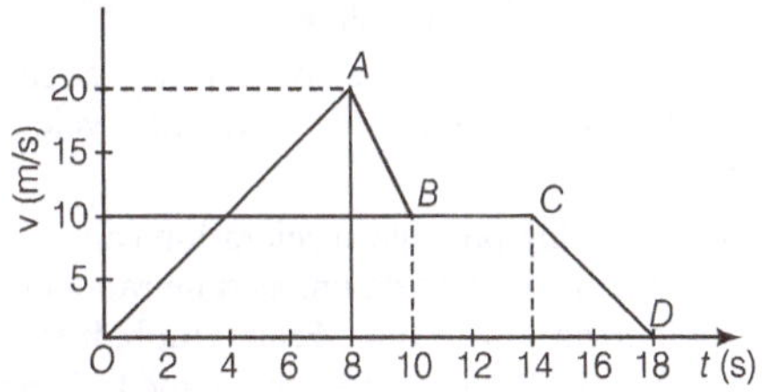

[5 M]

Answers

1 (*a*) $s \propto t^2$ (given)

$\therefore \; s = kt^2$

acceleration, $a = \frac{d^2s}{dt^2} = 2k$ (constant)

It means the particle travels with uniform acceleration.

2 (*d*) Uniform motion means uniform velocity or constant slope of *s-t* graph.

3 (*c*) Here, we observe that the object is moving in positive direction till time $t = o$ to $t = t_1$ and at $t = t_1$, we find that the velocity becomes negative, i.e. the object changes its direction at $t = t_1$ and continues in negative direction hence forth.

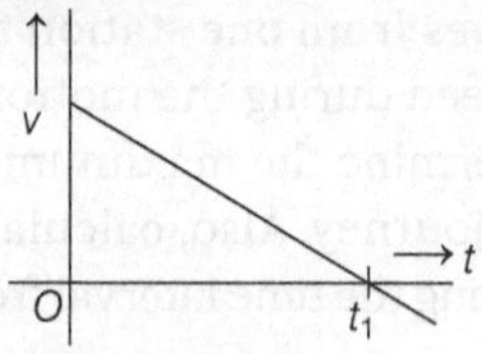

4 (*b*) $v = \frac{dx}{dt} = 2\ \text{ms}^{-1}$ = constant

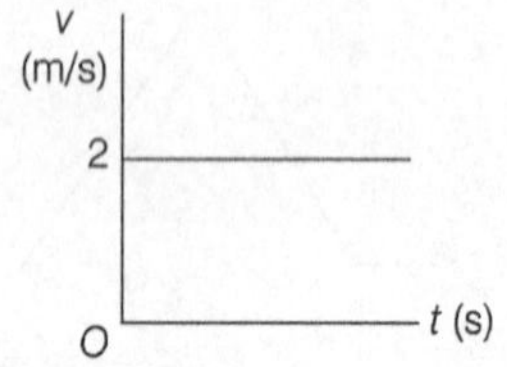

5 (*d*) Velocity $= \frac{\text{Distance}}{\text{Time}}$

$$(v+5)\frac{5}{18} = \frac{100}{7.2} \Rightarrow v + 5 = 50 \text{ or } v = 45 \text{ m/s}$$

6 (*a*) In uniform circular motion, there is acceleration of constant magnitude.

7 (*c*) The displacement is the shortest distance between initial and final position.

When final position of a body coincides with its initial position, displacement is zero but the distance travelled is not zero.

8 (*b*)

9 (*a*) According to definition,

displacement = velocity × time

Since, displacement is an vector quantity, so its value is equal to the vector sum of the area under velocity-time graph.

10 (*b*) A body having positive acceleration can be associated with slowing down, as time rate of change of velocity increases with time. From graph, it is clear that slope with time axis decreases but velocity increases with time.

11 Refer to text on page 44 (Positive and negative acceleration).

12 Refer to text on page 44 (Positive acceleration).

13 Yes, because during its motion around the sun, diameter or size of earth is very small as compared to the distance between the sun and the earth.

14 $\mathbf{s}_{nth} = \mathbf{u} + \frac{1}{2}\mathbf{a}\,(2n-1)$

where, $\mathbf{s}_{nth}$ = distance travel in *n*th second

and $\mathbf{a}$ = acceleration

15 Due to air resistance exerted downward motion in a parachute, the net downward acceleration is reduced, so it descend slowly.

16 A speedometer records the instantaneous speed.

17 Speed is a scalar quantity, which is given as

$$\text{Speed} = \frac{\text{Total distance travelled}}{\text{Total time taken}}$$

∵ Total distance can never be negative and hence the speed also.

18 It is parabolic in shape as shown below.

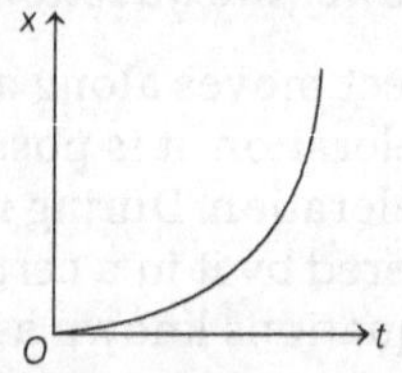

19 (i) If the displacement-time graph of a particle is parallel to displacement-axis, then velocity is infinite which is practically not possible. [1]

(ii) If the displacement-time graph is a straight line parallel to time-axis, the slope is zero, it means that the velocity of the object is zero (object is in the position of rest).

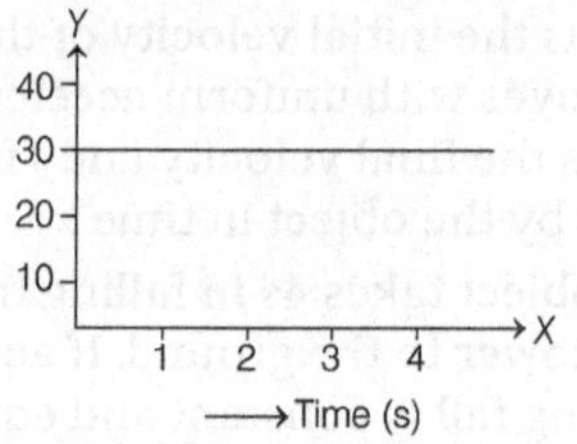

[1]

20 Two uses of *v*-*t* graph are as follows: (i) used to determine displacement by calculating area (ii) used to determine acceleration by calculating slope of the graph. The greater slope will be the greater acceleration. [2]

21 Given, masses m_1 and m_2 and heights *a* and *b*.

As we know, $s = ut + \frac{1}{2}gt^2$

So, $s_1 = a = 0 + \frac{gt_1^2}{2}$ and $s_2 = b = 0 + \frac{gt_2^2}{2}$ [1]

Hence, the ratio of time

$$\frac{\frac{gt_1^2}{2}}{\frac{gt_2^2}{2}} = \frac{a}{b} \Rightarrow \frac{t_1}{t_2} = \sqrt{\frac{a}{b}}$$

So, $t_1 : t_2 = \sqrt{a} : \sqrt{b}$ [1]

22 (i) Distance travelled by car in first 4s is area of trapezoid

$$= \frac{2+4}{2} \times 6 = 18\text{m}$$ [1]

(ii) The straight line parallel to *X*-axis (time-axis) represent the uniform motion of car. [1]

23 Refer to text on page 34 (Velocity).

24 Refer to text on page 43 (Displacement-time graph).

25 Refer to text on page 44 (Determination of displacement from v-t graph).

26 Refer to text on page 47 (Non-uniformly accelerated motion).

27 Given, starting acceleration = α, v = final velocity = 0, retarding acceleration = β and total time of journey = t

As we known, $v = u + at \Rightarrow v_{max} = \alpha t_1$

and $0 = v_{max} - \beta t_2 \Rightarrow v_{max} = \beta t_2$

$$t_1 + t_2 = \frac{v_{max}}{\alpha} + \frac{v_{max}}{\beta} = v_{max}\left[\frac{\alpha+\beta}{\alpha\beta}\right]$$

$$\Rightarrow \quad v_{max} = \frac{\alpha\beta t}{\alpha+\beta} \quad \text{...(i) } [\because t_1 + t_2 = t(\text{given})]$$ [1]

Also, $v^2 - u^2 = 2as$

$$v^2_{max} = 2\alpha s_1$$

and $v^2_{max} = 2\beta s_2$

$$\Rightarrow \quad s_1 + s_2 = \frac{v^2_{max}}{2}\left[\frac{1}{\alpha} + \frac{1}{\beta}\right]$$ [1]

From Eq. (i), we get

$$s = \frac{t^2}{2} \cdot \frac{\alpha\beta}{\alpha+\beta} \quad [\because s_1 + s_2 = s]$$ [1]

28 Refer to example 10 on page 49.

29 Refer to text on page 49 (Stopping distance for a vehicle).

30 Refer to text on page 47 (Equations of motion by calculus method (ii)).

31 The velocity-time graph is as shown below. Let v_1 be the velocity at time t_1 and $-v_2$ be the velocity at time t_2.

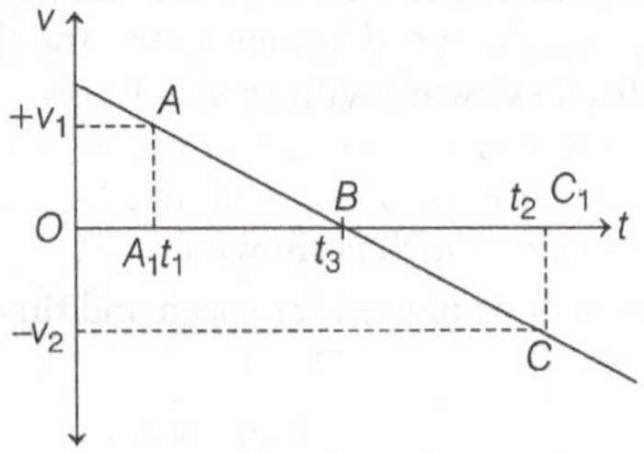

Area under graph between time t_1 and t_2

$$= \text{Area } \Delta\, AA_1B + \text{Area } \Delta CC_1B$$

$$= \frac{1}{2}v_1(t_3 - t_1) + \frac{1}{2}(-v_2)(t_2 - t_3)$$

$$= \frac{1}{2}v_1(t_3 - t_1) - \frac{1}{2}v_2(t_2 - t_3) \quad \text{...(i)}$$ [1]

Acceleration for time t_1 to t_3 is

$$a = \text{slope of } AB = \frac{0 - v_1}{t_3 - t_1}$$

$$\Rightarrow \quad t_3 - t_1 = -\frac{v_1}{a} \quad \text{...(ii)}$$

Acceleration for time t_3 to t_2 is

$$a = \text{slope of } BC = \frac{-v_2 - 0}{t_2 - t_3}$$

$$\Rightarrow \quad t_2 - t_3 = -\frac{v_2}{a} \quad \text{...(iii)}$$ [1]

Put values from Eqs. (ii) and (iii) in Eq. (i), we get

Area under v-t graph (for t_1 and t_2)

$$= \frac{1}{2}v_1\left(\frac{-v_1}{a}\right) - \frac{1}{2}v_2\left(\frac{-v_2}{a}\right)$$

$$= -\frac{1}{2}\frac{v_1^2}{a} + \frac{1}{2}\frac{v_2^2}{a} = \frac{1}{2a}(v_2^2 - v_1^2)$$

$$= \frac{2as}{2a} = s \quad [\because v^2 - u^2 = 2as]$$

= Distance covered by the object between time t_1 and t_2. [1]

32 Refer to text on page 47 (Equations of motion by calculus method).

33 Refer to text on page 43 (Displacement-time graph).

34 Refer to text on pages 43 and 44 (Velocity-time graphs for accelerated motion).

35 (i) $\because$ Object is falling from the top of the tower.

$\therefore$ $u = 0$

$g = 9.8$ m/s

$t = 4$s

$\because$ According to Newton's second equation of motion,

$$s = ut + \frac{1}{2}at^2 = 0 \times 4 + \frac{1}{2} \times 9.8 \times (4)^2$$

$$= 4.9 \times 16 = 78.4 \text{ m}$$

(ii) Given, mass, $m = 1$kg

Initial velocity, $u = 0$ m/s

Height, $h = 125$m

According to Newton's second equation of motion,

$$125 = 0 \times t + \frac{1}{2} \times 10 \times t^2$$

$$\Rightarrow \quad 125 = 5t^2$$

$$\Rightarrow \quad t^2 = 25$$

$$\Rightarrow \quad t = 5\text{s}$$

(iii) Initial velocity of the object will be zero as it was initially at rest.

$u = 0$

$g = 9.8$ m/s^2

From second equation of motion,

$$h = ut + \frac{1}{2}gt^2$$

$$\Rightarrow \quad h = 0(t) + \frac{1}{2} \times gt^2$$

$$\Rightarrow \quad h = 0 \times (1) + \frac{1}{2} \times 9.8 \times (1)^2$$

$$\Rightarrow \quad h = \frac{1}{2} \times 9.8 = 4.9 \text{ m}$$

(iv) The given relation is valid only when the particle moves with uniform velocity and along a straight line

(v) The kinematic equations of motion do not change in the form under time reversal.

36 The velocity of a particle is given by

$$\frac{dx}{dt} = v = \sqrt{180-16x}$$

$$\Rightarrow \quad a = \frac{dv}{dt} = \frac{1}{2}(180-16x)^{-1/2}(-16)\frac{dx}{dt}$$

$$\Rightarrow \quad a = -8 \times \frac{\sqrt{180-16x}}{\sqrt{180-16x}} = -8\ \text{m/s}^2$$

37 $s_{3rd} = 12\text{m}, s_{5th} = 20\text{m}$

$$s_{3rd} = u + \frac{a}{2}(2\times3-1) = 12$$

$$u + \frac{5}{2}a = 12 \quad \text{...(i)}$$

$$s_{5th} = u + \frac{a}{2}(2\times5-1) = 20\ \text{m}$$

$$u + \frac{9}{2}a = 20 \quad \text{...(ii)}$$ [1]

Subtracting Eq. (i) from Eq. (ii), we get

$$u + \frac{9}{2}a - u - \frac{5}{2}a = 20-12$$

$$2a = 8 \Rightarrow a = 4\text{m/s}^2$$

From Eq. (i), $u + \frac{5}{2}\times 4 = 12$

$$u = 12-10 = 2\text{m/s}$$

$$v = u + at = 2 + 4\times10 = 2+40 = 42\ \text{m/s}$$ [1]

38 Given that, $u_1 = 50\ \text{km/h} = \frac{125}{9}\ \text{m/s}, s = 6\ \text{m}$

and $u_2 = 100\ \text{km/h} = \frac{250}{9}\ \text{m/s}$

As we know, $v^2 - u^2 = 2as$

$$\left(\frac{125}{9}\right)^2 = 2a \times 6$$

$$a = \frac{1}{12}\left[\frac{125}{9}\right]^2$$

and $$\left(\frac{250}{9}\right)^2 = 2a \times s_2$$

$$s_2 = \left(\frac{250}{9}\right)^2 \frac{1}{2a} = \left(\frac{250}{9}\right)^2 \times \left(\frac{9}{125}\right)^2 \times \frac{12}{2} = 24\text{m}$$

where, s_2 is stopping distance. [2]

39 From the graph, the acceleration between time 1.5h to 2.5h

$$\alpha_1 = \frac{v_2 - v_1}{t_2 - t_1} = \frac{60-20}{2.5-1.5} = 40\ \text{km/h}^2$$

The retardation between time 2.5h to 4 h

$$\alpha_2 = \frac{0-60}{4-2.5} = -\frac{60}{1.5} = -40\ \text{km/h}^2$$

So, the maximum acceleration is 40km/h^2. [1½]

Distance covered during the time interval from 1.5h to 2h is the area of trapezoid,

$$D = \frac{40+20}{2} \times 0.5 = 15\text{km}$$

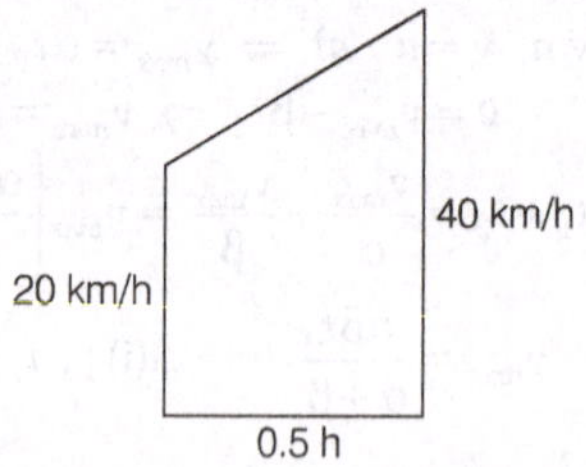

[1½]

40 The time taken to cover a height of 100m is $x = ut + \frac{1}{2}gt^2$

$$\Rightarrow \quad 100 = 0\times t + \frac{1}{2}9.8\,t^2 \Rightarrow t = \sqrt{\frac{2\times100}{9.8}} \simeq 4.5\text{s}$$

Speed, $v = u + gt = 0 + 9.8\times4.5 \simeq 44\ \text{ms}^{-1}$ [1]

For time $t = 0$ to $t = 4.5$s, $v = 9.8t \Rightarrow v \propto t$ this is shown by *OA*. At first collision, the speed lost by ball

$$= \frac{1}{10}\times 44 = 4.4\ \text{ms}^{-1}$$

Thus, speed becomes,

$$v = 44 - 4.4 = 39.6\ \text{ms}^{-1}$$ [1]

The time acquired to get maximum height in upward motion is given by

$$v = u - gt = 39.6 - 9.8t \Rightarrow t = +\frac{39.6}{9.8} \simeq 4\text{s}$$ [1]

Thus, total time = 4.5 + 4 = 8.5s. This is shown by *BC*. At highest point the speed becomes zero and the ball again accelerates downward with speed 39.6ms^{-1}. The time taken in this is also same as that of previous to get maximum height as 4s. So, total time becomes 8.5s + 4s = 12.5s which is shown by *CD*. [1]

The graph can be plotted for speed and time as shown below.

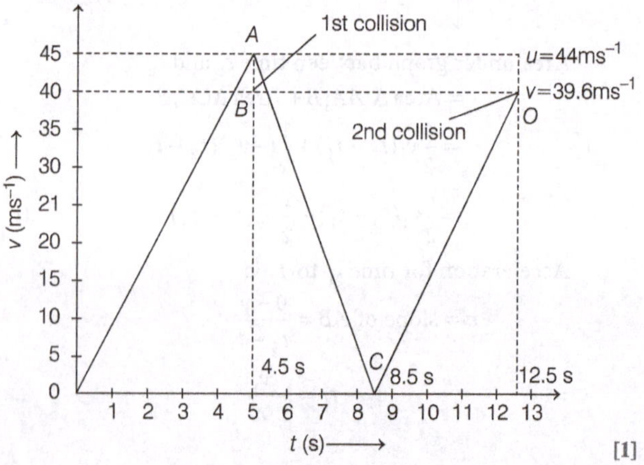

[1]

41 The graph can be represented as

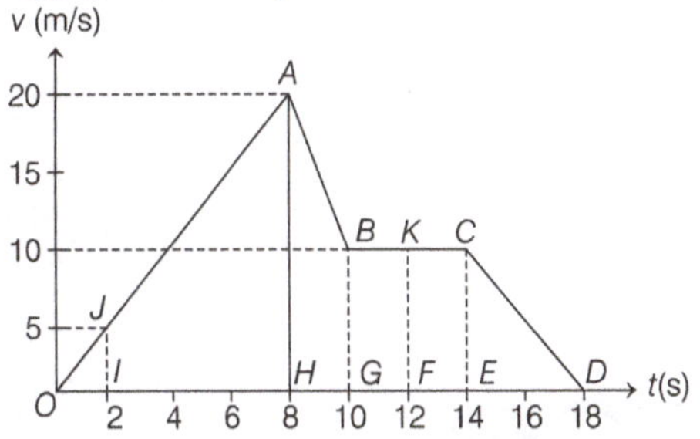

[1]

(i) Distance covered between $t = 0$ to 18 s

$= \text{Area } OAH + \text{Area } ABGH + \text{Area } BCEG + \text{Area } CDE$

$= \frac{1}{2} \times 8 \times 20 + \frac{1}{2} \times (20 + 10) \times 2 + 4 \times 10 + \frac{1}{2} \times 4 \times 10$

$= 80 + 30 + 40 + 20 = 170 \text{ m}$ [2]

(ii) Distance covered between $t = 2$ to 12 s

$= \text{Area } JAHI + \text{Area } ABGH + \text{Area } BKFG$

$= \frac{1}{2} \times (5 + 20) \times 6 + \frac{1}{2} \times (20 + 10) \times 2 + 2 \times 10$

$= 75 + 30 + 20 = 125 \text{ m}$

As, acceleration $a = \frac{\Delta v}{\Delta t}$, which is maximum when change in velocity is maximum for minimum time interval. From graph it is seen during AB part,

$$\therefore \quad a_{\text{max}} = \frac{v_B - v_A}{t_B - t_A} = \frac{10 - 20}{10 - 8}$$

$$= \frac{-10}{2} = -5.0 \text{ ms}^{-2}$$

[2]

CHAPTER

03

Motion in a Plane

Earlier, we have studied the motion of an object along a straight line. In this chapter, we will study the motion of an object in two dimensions (in plane) and in three dimensions (in space). As a simple case of motion in a plane, we shall discuss motion with constant acceleration and treat it in details as projectile and circular motion.

- Scalars and Vectors
- Projectile Motion

TOPIC 01 Scalars and Vectors

In order to describe the motion of an object to be in two-dimensional and in three-dimensional, we need to understand the concept of vectors first. Many quantities that have both magnitude and direction need a special mathematical language i.e. the language of vectors to describe such quantities. On the basis of magnitude and direction, all the physical quantities are classified into two groups as scalars and vectors.

Scalar Quantities

These are the physical quantities which have only magnitude but no direction. It is specified completely by a single number, alongwith the proper unit. e.g. Temperature, mass, length, time, work, etc.

Vector Quantities

These are the physical quantities which have both magnitudes and directions and obey the triangle/parallelogram laws of addition and subtraction. e.g. Displacement, acceleration, velocity, momentum, force, etc. A vector is represented by a **bold face** type or by **an arrow** placed over a letter

i.e. $\mathbf{F}, \mathbf{a}, \mathbf{b}$ or $\vec{F}, \vec{a}, \vec{b}$

Note The magnitude of a vector is often called its absolute value, indicated by $|\mathbf{v}| = v$.

e.g. Suppose a body has a velocity 40 m/s due East. If 1 cm is chosen to represent a velocity of 10 m/s, a line *OP* of 4 cm in length and drawn towards East with arrowhead at *P* will completely represent the velocity of the body.

The point P is called **head** or **terminal point** and point O is called **tail** or **initial point** of the vector **OP**.

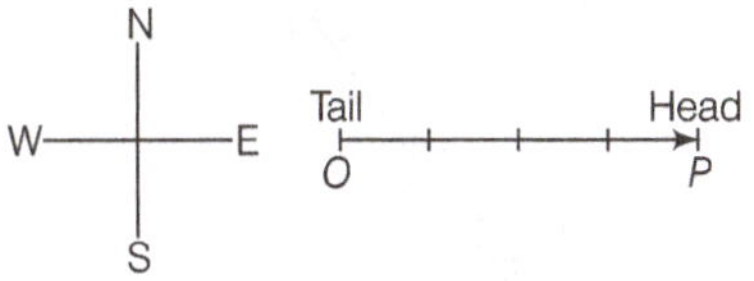

Representation of vector OP

The length of the line gives the magnitude and the arrowhead gives the direction.

Important Definitions Related to Vectors

(i) Modulus of a Vector

The magnitude of a vector is called **modulus** of that vector. For a vector **A**, it is represented by $|\mathbf{A}|$ or A.

(ii) Unit Vector

A vector having magnitude equal to unity but having a specific direction is called a **unit vector.** A unit vector of A is written as $\hat{A}$ and read as A cap. It is expressed as

$$\hat{\mathbf{A}} = \frac{\mathbf{A}}{|\mathbf{A}|} = \frac{\mathbf{A}}{A} = \frac{\text{Vector}}{\text{Magnitude of the vector}}$$

$$\boxed{\mathbf{A} = |\mathbf{A}|\hat{\mathbf{A}}}$$

Hence, any vector can be expressed as the magnitude times the unit vector along its own direction.

In cartesian coordinates, $\hat{\mathbf{i}}, \hat{\mathbf{j}}$ and $\hat{\mathbf{k}}$ are the unit vectors along X-axis, Y-axis and Z-axis.

The magnitude of a unit vector is unity and has no unit or dimensions.

(iii) Null Vector

A vector with magnitude zero and having an arbitrary direction is called a **null vector.**

This vector is also known as **zero vector** and denoted by 0 (zero). e.g. The velocity vector of a stationary object, the acceleration vector of an object moving with uniform velocity.

(iv) Equal Vectors

Two vectors are said to be equal if they have equal magnitude and same direction.

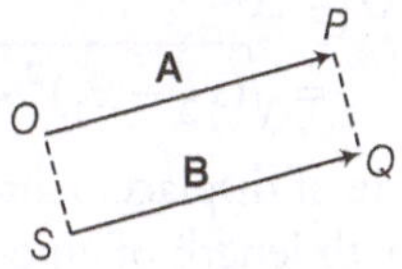

A and **B** are equal vectors

Consider two vectors **A** and **B** which are represented by two equal parallel lines having the same magnitude and drawn in same direction.

Thus, $\mathbf{OP} = \mathbf{SQ}$

or $\mathbf{A} = \mathbf{B}$

Vectors do not have fixed locations. When we displace a vector parallel to itself, then the vector does not change, such vectors are known as **free vectors.**

e.g. The velocity vector of a particle moving along a straight line is a free vector.

(v) Negative Vector

Two vectors are said to be the negative of each other if their magnitudes are equal but directions are opposite.

The negative vector of **A** is represented as $-\mathbf{A}$.

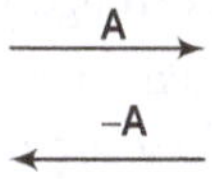

Negative vector

(vi) Collinear Vectors

The two or more vectors are said to be collinear, when they act along the same lines or parallel lines. e.g. Tug of war.

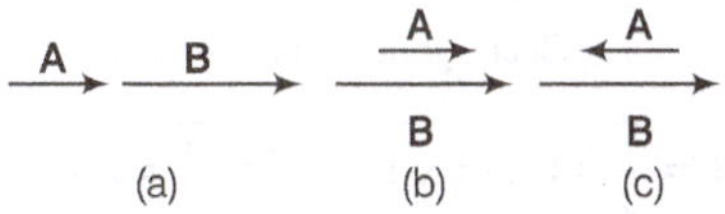

Collinear vectors

If **A** and **B** are two collinear vectors, then they can be represented along a line in the same direction [Fig. a] or along the parallel lines in same direction [Fig. b] or along parallel lines in opposite direction [Fig. c]. Two collinear vectors having the same directions are called **like parallel vectors.** In this case, the angle between those two vectors will be zero. Similarly, the two collinear vectors having the opposite directions are called **anti-parallel vectors.** In this case, the angle between those two vectors will be 180°.

(vii) Coplanar Vectors

The vectors lying in the same plane are called **coplanar vectors.** Three vectors **A, B** and **C** are lying in the same plane of paper as shown in figure, hence they are coplanar vectors.

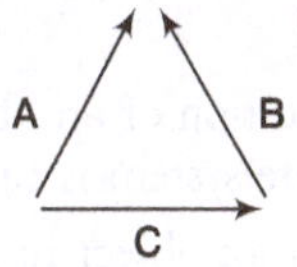

Coplanar vectors

(viii) Co-initial Vectors

The vectors which have the same initial point are called co-initial vectors.

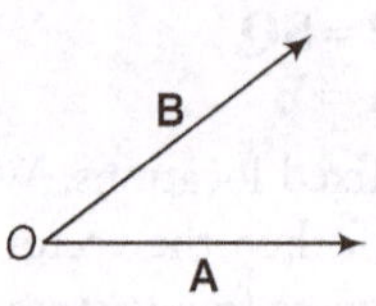

Co-initial vectors

Two vectors **A** and **B** have been drawn from the common initial point *O*. Therefore, **A** and **B** are called **co-initial vectors.**

(ix) Orthogonal Unit Vectors

If two or three unit vectors are perpendicular to each other, they are known as **orthogonal unit vectors.**

The unit vectors along *x*-axis, *y*-axis and *z*-axis are denoted by $\hat{\mathbf{i}}, \hat{\mathbf{j}}$ and $\hat{\mathbf{k}}$. These are orthogonal unit vectors.

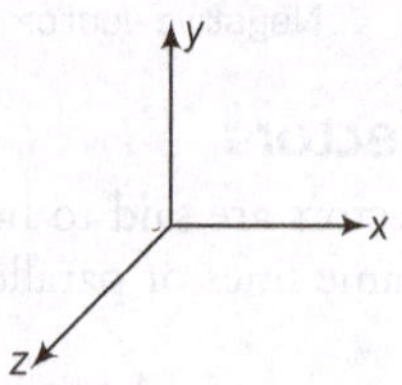

Orthogonal unit vectors

$$\hat{\mathbf{i}} = \frac{\mathbf{x}}{x} \Rightarrow \mathbf{x} = x\,\hat{\mathbf{i}}\ ;\quad \hat{\mathbf{j}} = \frac{\mathbf{y}}{y} \Rightarrow \mathbf{y} = y\,\hat{\mathbf{j}}$$

$$\hat{\mathbf{k}} = \frac{\mathbf{z}}{z} \Rightarrow \mathbf{z} = z\,\hat{\mathbf{k}}$$

(x) Localised Vectors

Those vectors whose initial point is fixed are known as **localised vectors.** e.g. Position vector of a particle (initial point lies at the origin).

(xi) Non-localised Vectors

Those vectors whose initial point is not fixed are known as **non-localised vectors.** e.g. Velocity vector of a particle moving along a straight line.

Position and Displacement Vectors

Position Vector

A vector which gives position of an object with reference to the origin of a coordinate system is called **position vector.**

Consider the motion of an object in *xy*-plane with origin at *O*. Suppose an object is at point *A* at any instant *t*.

Then, OA is the position vector of the object at point *A*.
i.e. $\mathbf{OA} = \mathbf{r}$

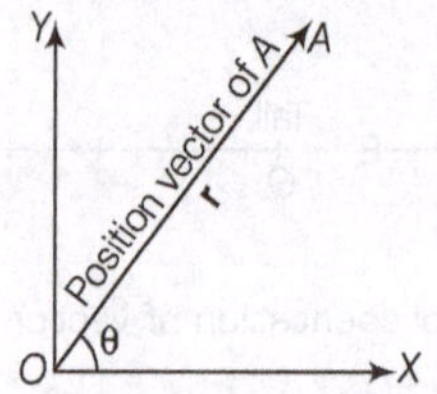

Position vector representation

The position vector provides two informations such as

(i) It tells us about the minimum distance of an object from the origin *O*.

(ii) It tells us about the direction of the object w.r.t. *X* and *Y*-axis.

Displacement Vector

The vector which tells how much and in which direction an object has changed its position in a given interval of time is called **displacement vector.**

Consider an object moving in the *xy*-plane. Suppose it is at point *A* at any instant *t* and at point *B* at any later instant *t′*. Then, vector **AB** is the displacement vector of the object in time *t* to *t′*.

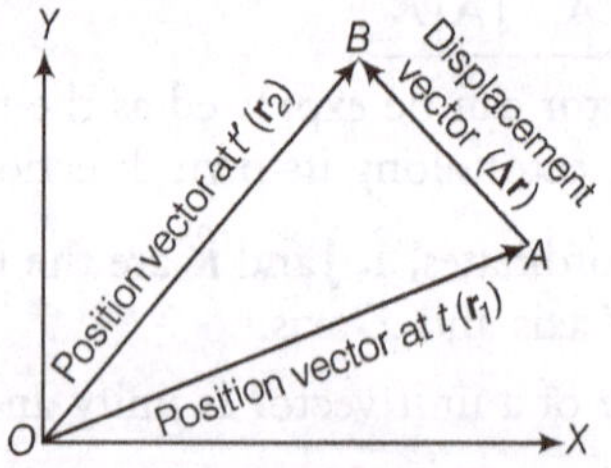

Displacement vector representation

If the coordinates of points *A* and *B* are (x_1, y_1) and (x_2, y_2), then the position vector of the object at point *A*, $\mathbf{r}_1 = x_1\hat{\mathbf{i}} + y_1\hat{\mathbf{j}}$ and the position vector of the object at point *B*, $\mathbf{r}_2 = x_2\hat{\mathbf{i}} + y_2\hat{\mathbf{j}}$

∴ The displacement vector for *AB* can be given as

$$\Delta r = \mathbf{r}_2 - \mathbf{r}_1$$

Displacement vector, $\Delta r = (x_2 - x_1)\,\hat{\mathbf{i}} + (y_2 - y_1)\hat{\mathbf{j}}$

(i) Magnitude of the displacement vector is given by

$$|\Delta \mathbf{r}| = \Delta r$$
$$= \sqrt{(x_2 - x_1)^2 + (y_2 - y_1)^2}$$

The magnitude of displacement is either less or equal to the path length of an object between two points.

(ii) Magnitude of vectors for three-dimension is given by

$$\Delta \mathbf{r} = \sqrt{(x_2 - x_1)^2 + (y_2 - y_1)^2 + (z_2 - z_1)^2}$$

Resultant Vector

The resultant vector of two or more vectors is defined as the single vector which produces the same effect as two or more vectors (given vectors) combinedly produces.

There are two cases

Case I **When two vectors are acting in the same direction.**

Consider the vectors **A** and **B** are acting in the same direction as shown below

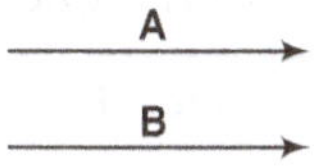

Then, the resultant of these two vectors is given by a vector having direction as same as that of **A** or **B** and the magnitude of the resultant vector will be equal to the sum of respective vectors i.e. $(A + B)$.

Thus, Resultant vector, $\mathbf{R} = \mathbf{A} + \mathbf{B}$

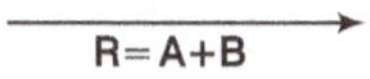

Case II **When two vectors are acting in mutually opposite directions.**

Consider the vectors **A** and **B** are acting in mutually opposite direction as shown below.

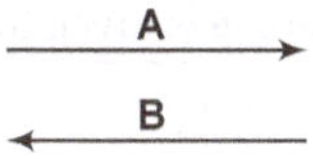

Then, the resultant of these two vectors is given by a vector having direction same as that of vector with larger magnitude. The magnitude of the resultant vector will be equal to $|A - B|$.

Thus, Resultant vector, $\mathbf{R} = \mathbf{A} - \mathbf{B}$

(i) If **B** > **A**, then direction of **R** is along **B**.

(ii) If **A** > **B**, then direction of **R** is along **A**.

Conditions for Zero Resultant Vector

If three vectors acting on a point object at the same time are represented in magnitude and direction by the three sides of a triangle taken in the same order, their resultant is zero. The object is said to be in equilibrium.

Consider the three vectors **A**, **B** and **C** acting on an object at the same time represented by **OP**, **PQ** and **QO**, respectively.

Then, $$\frac{A}{\sin\alpha} = \frac{B}{\sin\beta} = \frac{C}{\sin\gamma}$$

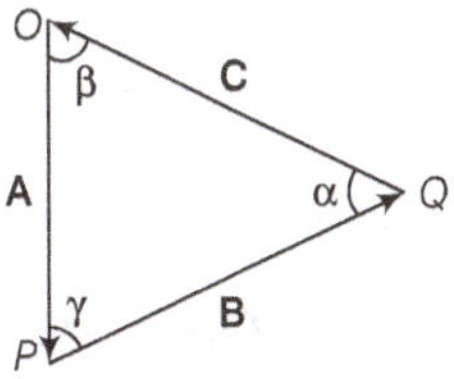

Vectors **A**, **B** and **C** acting along **OP**, **PQ** and **QO** respectively

Similarly, if number of vectors acting on an object at the same time are represented in magnitude and direction by the various sides of a closed polygon taken in the same order, their resultant vector is zero and the object will be in equilibrium.

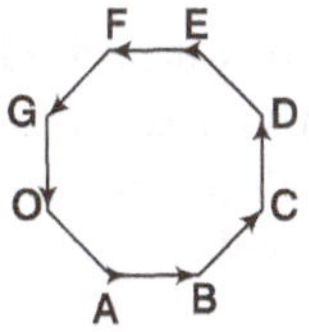

Vectors represented by a closed polygon

Resultant vector, $\mathbf{R} = \mathbf{OA} + \mathbf{AB} + \mathbf{BC} + \mathbf{CD} + \mathbf{DE} + \mathbf{EF} + \mathbf{FG} + \mathbf{GO} = 0$

Addition of Vectors (Graphical Method)

Two vectors can be added if both of them are of same nature e.g. A displacement vector cannot be added to a force but can be added to displacement vector only.

Graphical method of addition of vectors helps us in visualising the vectors and the resultant vectors.

This method contains following laws

1. Triangle Law of Vector Addition

This law states that **if two vectors can be represented both in magnitude and direction by the two sides of a triangle taken in the same order**, then their resultant is represented completely, both in magnitude and direction, by the third side of the triangle taken in the opposite order.

Consider two vectors **A** and **B** that lie in a plane as shown in Fig. (a). Draw a vector **OM** equal and parallel to vector **A** as shown in Fig. (b). From head of **OM**, draw a vector **MN** equal and parallel to vector **B**.

Then, the resultant vector is given by **ON** which joins the tail of **A** and head of **B**.

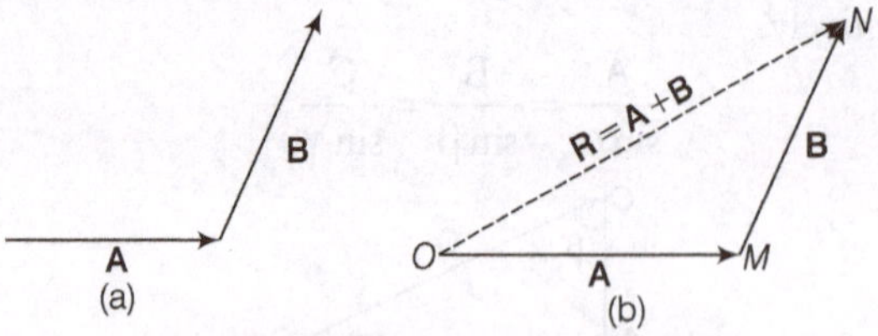

Triangle law of vector addition

The resultant of **A** and **B** is **ON = OM + MN**

or Resultant vector, **R = A + B**

Example 1 A boy travels 10 m due to North and then 7 m due to East. Find the displacement and direction of the body.

Sol. Let the boy start moving from point *O* as shown in figure.

where, **OA** = 10 m, due North

AB = 7 m, due East

According to triangle law of vector addition, **OB** is the resultant displacement.

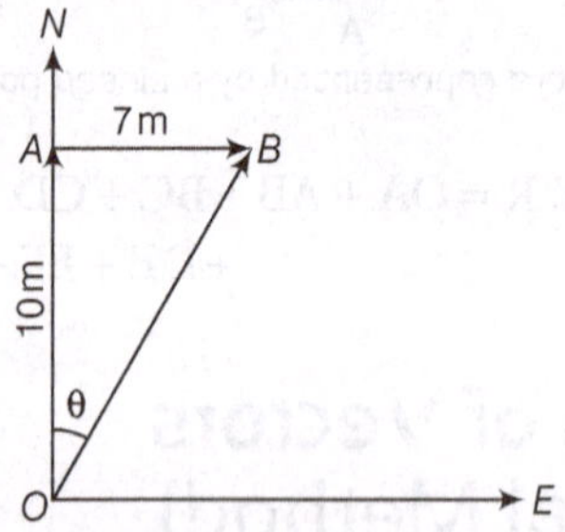

The magnitude of the resultant displacement,

$$|\mathbf{OB}| = OB = \sqrt{(OA)^2 + (AB)^2} = \sqrt{(10)^2 + (7)^2}$$

$$= \sqrt{100 + 49} = 12.21 \text{ m}$$

Since, the resultant displacement makes an angle θ with the North direction. Then,

$$\theta = \tan^{-1}\left(\frac{AB}{OA}\right) = \tan^{-1}\left(\frac{7}{10}\right) = 35^\circ$$

2. Parallelogram Law of Vector Addition

This law states that **if two vectors acting on a particle at the same time are represented in magnitude and direction by two adjacent sides of a parallelogram drawn from a point,** then their resultant vector is represented in magnitude and direction both by the diagonal of the parallelogram drawn from the same point.

Consider two vectors **A** and **B** that lie in a plane as shown in Fig. (a). From a common point *O*, draw a vector **OP** equal and parallel to **A** and vector **OR** equal and parallel to **B**. Complete the parallelogram **OPQR** as shown in Fig. (b). Then, the resultant vector is given by **OQ**.

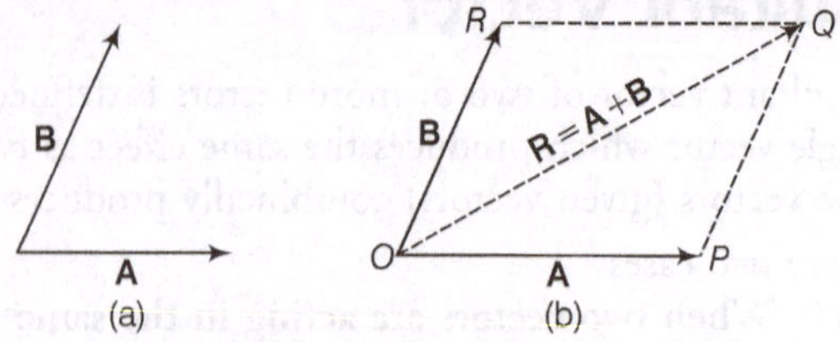

Parallelogram law of vector addition

According to parallelogram law of vector addition,

OQ = OP + OR

or Resultant vector, **R = A + B**

Example 2 A body is simultaneously given two velocities of 30 m/s due East and 40 m/s due North, respectively. Find the resultant velocity.

Sol. Let the body be starting from point *O* as shown.

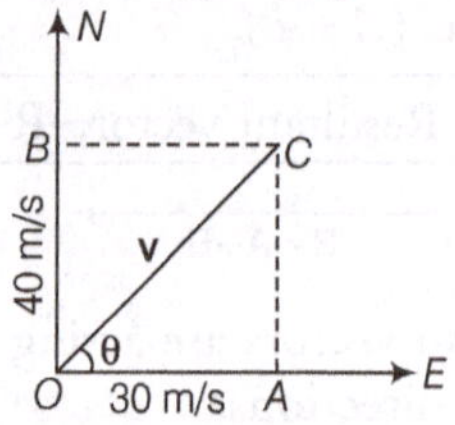

$\mathbf{v}_A = 30\,\text{m/s}$, due East; $\mathbf{v}_B = 40\,\text{m/s}$, due North

According to parallelogram law, **OC** is the resultant velocity. Its magnitude is given by

$$\mathbf{v} = \sqrt{v_A^2 + v_B^2}$$

$$= \sqrt{(30)^2 + (40)^2}$$

$$= \sqrt{900 + 1600} = 50 \text{ m/s}$$

Since, the resultant velocity **v** makes an angle θ with the East direction.

$$\text{Then, } \theta = \tan^{-1}\frac{CA}{OA} = \tan^{-1}\left(\frac{40}{30}\right) = 53^\circ 8'$$

3. Polygon Law of Vector Addition

This law states that **when the number of vectors are represented in both magnitude and direction by the sides of an open polygon taken in an order,** then their resultant is represented in both magnitude and direction by the closing side of the polygon taken in opposite order.

Consider four vectors **A**, **B**, **C** and **D** be acting in different directions that lie in a plane as shown in Fig. (a). Draw a vector **OP** parallel and equal to vector **A**. Move vectors **B**, **C** and **D** parallel to themselves, so that the tail of **B** touches the head of **A**, the tail of **C** touches the head of **B** and the tail of **D** touches the head of **C** as shown in Fig. (b).

According to the polygon law of vector addition, the closing side OT of the polygon taken in the reverse order represent the resultant **R**.

Thus, $$\mathbf{R} = \mathbf{A} + \mathbf{B} + \mathbf{C} + \mathbf{D}$$

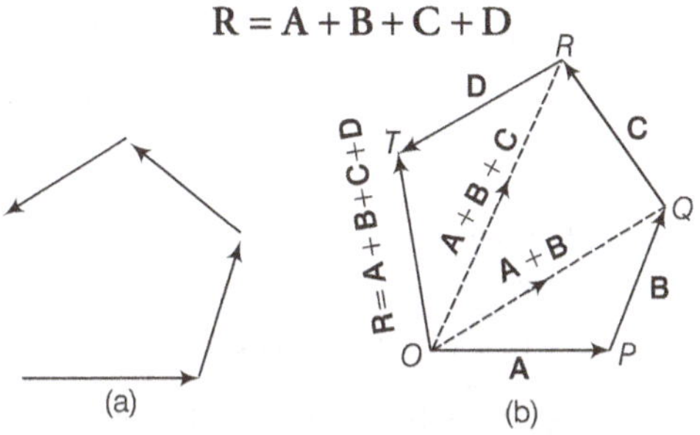

Polygon law of vector addition

Example 3 A particle has a displacement of 12 m towards East and 5 m towards the North and then 6 m vertically upwards. Find the magnitude of the sum of these displacements.

Sol. Suppose initially the particle is at origin O. Then, its displacement vectors are

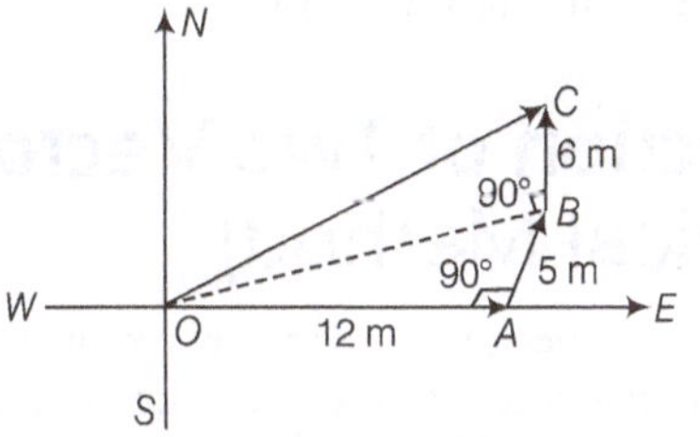

$$OA = 12\,\text{m},\ AB = 5\,\text{m},\ BC = 6\,\text{m}$$

According to polygon law of vector addition, **OC** is the resultant displacement.

$\therefore$ From $\Delta\, OAB$, have

$$\text{OB} = \sqrt{OA^2 + AB^2} = \sqrt{(12)^2 + (5)^2} = 13\,\text{m}$$

Again from $\Delta\, OBC$, we have

$$\text{OC} = \sqrt{OB^2 + BC^2} = \sqrt{(13)^2 + (6)^2} = \sqrt{205} = 14.32\,\text{m}$$

Addition of Vectors (Analytical Method)

Consider two vectors **A** and **B** inclined at an angle θ be acting on a particle at the same time. Let they be represented in magnitude and direction by two sides **OP** and **PQ** of ΔOPQ, taken in the same order.

Then, according to triangle law of vector addition, the resultant (**R**) is given by the closing side **OQ**, taken in opposite order.

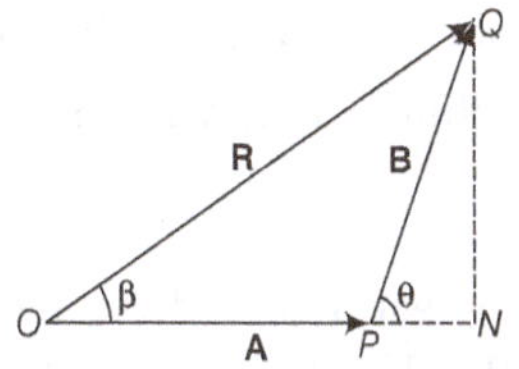

Draw QN perpendicular to OP produced.

From ΔQNP, $\dfrac{PN}{PQ} = \cos\theta$

$$\Rightarrow \quad PN = PQ\cos\theta = B\cos\theta \qquad [\because PQ = B] \ldots\text{(i)}$$

and $$\frac{QN}{PQ} = \sin\theta$$

$$\Rightarrow \quad QN = PQ\sin\theta = B\sin\theta \qquad \ldots\text{(ii)}$$

In right angled ΔONQ, we have

$$OQ^2 = QN^2 + NO^2 = QN^2 + (OP + PN)^2$$

or $$R^2 = (B\sin\theta)^2 + (A + B\cos\theta)^2$$
$$= B^2\sin^2\theta + A^2 + B^2\cos^2\theta + 2\,AB\cos\theta$$
$$= A^2 + B^2 + 2A\,B\cos\theta$$

$$\Rightarrow \quad \boxed{\text{Resultant, } R = \sqrt{A^2 + B^2 + 2AB\cos\theta}}$$

This represents the magnitude of resultant vector **R**.

If the resultant vector **R** makes an angle (β) with the direction of vector **A**, then from right angle ΔQNO,

$$\tan\beta = \frac{QN}{ON} = \frac{QN}{OP + PN} = \frac{B\sin\theta}{A + B\cos\theta}$$

or $$\boxed{\text{Direction of resultant } \mathbf{R},\ \tan\beta = \frac{B\sin\theta}{A + B\cos\theta}}$$

Regarding the Magnitude of R

(i) When $\theta = 0°$, then $R = A + B$ (maximum).

(ii) When $\theta = 90°$, then $R = \sqrt{A^2 + B^2}$.

(iii) When $\theta = 180°$, then $R = A - B$ (minimum).

This can be extended to any number of vectors if vectors **a**, **b** and **c** are given, then

$$\mathbf{a} = a_x\hat{\mathbf{i}} + a_y\hat{\mathbf{j}} + a_z\hat{\mathbf{k}}$$
$$\mathbf{b} = b_x\hat{\mathbf{i}} + b_y\hat{\mathbf{j}} + b_z\hat{\mathbf{k}}$$
$$\mathbf{c} = c_x\hat{\mathbf{i}} + c_y\hat{\mathbf{j}} + c_z\hat{\mathbf{k}}$$

where, $\mathbf{r}_x = a_x + b_x + c_x$, $\mathbf{r}_y = a_y + b_y + c_y$

and $\mathbf{r}_z = a_z + b_z + c_z$

Properties of Addition of Vectors

(i) It follows commutative law, i.e. $\mathbf{A}+\mathbf{B}=\mathbf{B}+\mathbf{A}$

(ii) It follows associative law, $(\mathbf{A}+\mathbf{B})+\mathbf{C}=\mathbf{A}+(\mathbf{B}+\mathbf{C})$

(iii) It obeys distributive law, $\lambda(\mathbf{A}+\mathbf{B})=\lambda\mathbf{A}+\lambda\mathbf{B}$

(iv) $\mathbf{A}+0=\mathbf{A}$

Example 4 Two vectors **C** and **D** having magnitude 5 units and angle $\theta = 30°$ with each other. Find the resultant vector.

Sol. We have to find the resultant of given two vectors **C** and **D**. For the magnitude of resultant vector

$$R=|\mathbf{R}|=|\mathbf{C}+\mathbf{D}|=\sqrt{C^2+D^2+2CD\cos\theta}$$
$$=\sqrt{(5)^2+(5)^2+2\times5\times5\times\cos30°}$$
$$=\sqrt{25+25+25\sqrt{3}} \quad \left(\because \cos 30°=\frac{\sqrt{3}}{2}\right)$$
$$=5\sqrt{2+\sqrt{3}} \text{ units}$$

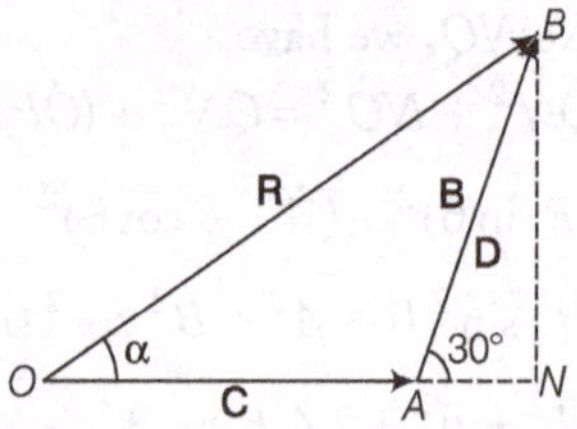

Now, for the direction of resultant vector

$$\tan\alpha=\frac{D\sin\theta}{C+D\cos\theta}=\frac{5\times\sin30°}{5+5\times\cos30°}$$
$$\tan\alpha=\frac{5\times1/2}{5+5\times\frac{\sqrt{3}}{2}}=\left(\frac{1}{2+\sqrt{3}}\right)$$
$$=2-\sqrt{3}=0.268$$
$$\Rightarrow \quad \alpha=\tan^{-1}(0.268)\simeq15°$$

Example 5 Three vectors are given by

$$\mathbf{A}=A_x\hat{\mathbf{i}}+A_y\hat{\mathbf{j}}+A_z\hat{\mathbf{k}}$$
$$\mathbf{B}=B_x\hat{\mathbf{i}}+B_y\hat{\mathbf{j}}+B_z\hat{\mathbf{k}}$$
$$\mathbf{C}=C_x\hat{\mathbf{i}}+C_y\hat{\mathbf{j}}+C_z\hat{\mathbf{k}}$$

Determine the magnitude of resultant vector.

Sol. Given, $\mathbf{A}=A_x\hat{\mathbf{i}}+A_y\hat{\mathbf{j}}+A_z\hat{\mathbf{k}}$

$$\mathbf{B}=B_x\hat{\mathbf{i}}+B_y\hat{\mathbf{j}}+B_z\hat{\mathbf{k}}$$
$$\mathbf{C}=C_x\hat{\mathbf{i}}+C_y\hat{\mathbf{j}}+C_z\hat{\mathbf{k}}$$

We can add these easily by analytical method.

The resultant of these three vectors are $\mathbf{R}=\mathbf{A}+\mathbf{B}+\mathbf{C}$

$$=A_x\hat{\mathbf{i}}+A_y\hat{\mathbf{j}}+A_z\hat{\mathbf{k}}+B_x\hat{\mathbf{i}}+B_y\hat{\mathbf{j}}+B_z\hat{\mathbf{k}}+C_x\hat{\mathbf{i}}+C_y\hat{\mathbf{j}}+C_z\hat{\mathbf{k}}$$
$$=(A_x+B_x+C_x)\hat{\mathbf{i}}+(A_y+B_y+C_y)\hat{\mathbf{j}}+(A_z+B_z+C_z)\hat{\mathbf{k}}$$

The magnitude of **R** is given by

$$R=\sqrt{(A_x+B_x+C_x)^2+(A_y+B_y+C_y)^2+(A_z+B_z+C_z)^2}$$

Example 6 A motor boat is racing towards North at 25 km/h and the water current in that region is 10 km/h in the direction of 60° East to South. Find the resultant velocity of the boat. [NCERT]

Sol. Given, velocity of motor boat, $v_b = 25$ km/h (towards North)

Velocity of water current, $v_c = 10$ km/h (towards East to South)

Direction, $\theta = 180° - 60° = 120°$

We know that,

$$v=\sqrt{v_b^2+v_c^2+2v_bv_c\cos\theta}$$
$$v=\sqrt{(25)^2+(10)^2+2\times25\times10\times\cos120°}$$
$$v=\sqrt{625+100+500\left(-\frac{1}{2}\right)}$$
$$v=21.8 \text{ km/h}$$

Suppose the resultant velocity v makes angle ϕ with the North direction. Then,

$$\tan\phi=\frac{v_c\sin120°}{v_b+v_c\cos120°}=\frac{10\times(\sqrt{3}/2)}{25+10\times(-1/2)}=0.433$$
$$\therefore \quad \phi=\tan^{-1}(0.433)=23.4°$$

Subtraction of Two Vectors (Graphical Method)

If a vector **B** is to be subtracted from vector **A**, then we have to invert the vector **B** and then add it with vector **A** according to laws of addition of two vectors.

Hence, the subtraction of vector **B** from a vector **A** is defined as the addition of vector (−**B**) (i.e. negative of vector **B**) to vector **A**.

It is expressed as $\mathbf{R}=\mathbf{A}+(-\mathbf{B})=\mathbf{A}-\mathbf{B}$

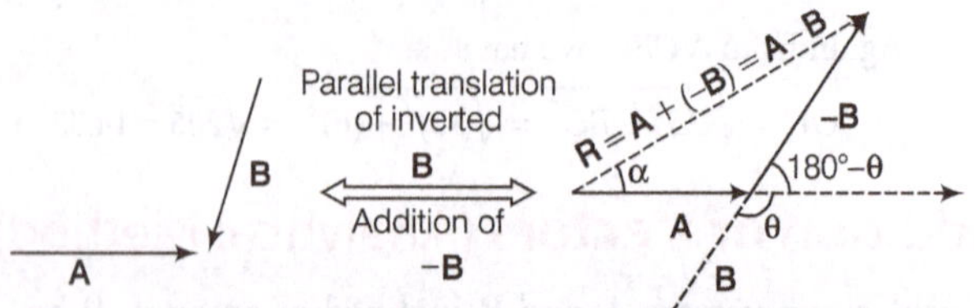

Graphical method of subtraction of two vectors

Subtraction of Vectors
(Analytical Method)

There are two vectors **A** and **B** at an angle θ. If we have to subtract **B** from **A**, then first invert the vector **B** and then add with **A** as shown in figure.

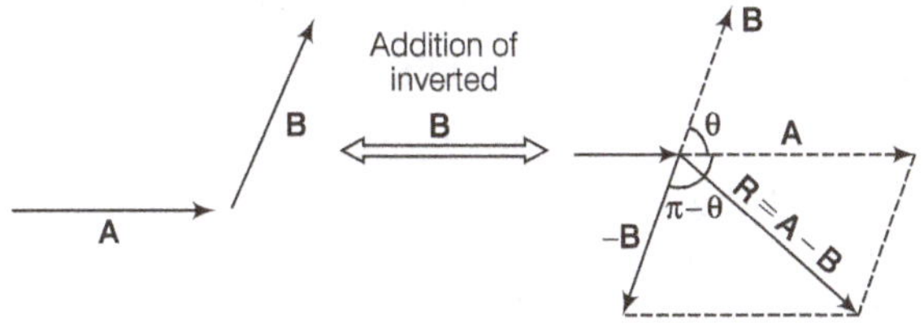

Subtraction of vectors

The resultant vector is $\mathbf{R} = \mathbf{A} + (-\mathbf{B}) = \mathbf{A} - \mathbf{B}$

The magnitude of resultant in this case is

$$R = |\mathbf{R}| = \sqrt{A^2 + B^2 + 2AB\cos(\pi - \theta)}$$

$$\boxed{\text{Resultant, } R = \sqrt{A^2 + B^2 - 2AB\cos\theta}}$$

Here, θ = angle between **A** and **B**.

Regarding the magnitude of R

(i) When $\theta = 0°$, then $R = A - B$ (minimum).

(ii) When $\theta = 90°$, then $R = \sqrt{A^2 + B^2}$.

(iii) When $\theta = 180°$, then $R = A + B$ (maximum).

Properties of Subtraction of Vectors

(i) Subtraction of vectors does not follow commutative law,

i.e. $\mathbf{A} - \mathbf{B} \neq \mathbf{B} - \mathbf{A}$

(ii) It does not follow associative law,

i.e. $\mathbf{A} - (\mathbf{B} - \mathbf{C}) \neq (\mathbf{A} - \mathbf{B}) - \mathbf{C}$

(iii) It follows distributive law, $\lambda(\mathbf{A} - \mathbf{B}) = \lambda\mathbf{A} - \lambda\mathbf{B}$

Example 7 Two forces of 5 N towards East and −7 N towards South acts on a particle. Find the resultant force.

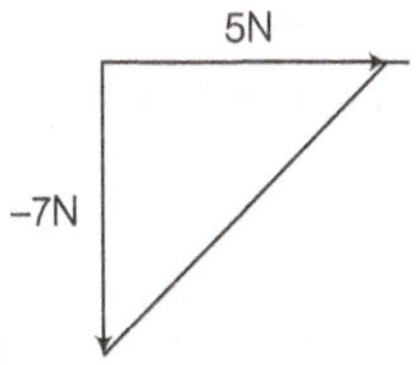

Sol. The two forces be $A = 5$ N and $B = -7$ N

Then, the magnitude of the resultant force is given by

$$F = \sqrt{A^2 + (-B)^2} = \sqrt{5^2 + (-7)^2}$$

$$F = \sqrt{25 + 49} = \sqrt{74} = 8.6 \text{ N}$$

Example 8 Two vectors of magnitude 3 units and 4 units are at angle 60° between them. Find the magnitude of their difference.

Sol. Let the vectors are **A** and **B**.

Given, $|\mathbf{A}| = 3$ unit, $|\mathbf{B}| = 4$ unit and $\theta = 60°$

The magnitude of resultant of **A** and **B**

$$R = |\mathbf{R}| = \sqrt{A^2 + B^2 - 2AB\cos\theta}$$

$$= \sqrt{3^2 + 4^2 - 2 \times 3 \times 4\cos 60°}$$

$$R = \sqrt{25 - 12} = \sqrt{13} = 3.61 \text{ units}$$

Example 9 Consider vectors *A* and *B* having equal magnitude of 5 units and are inclined to each other at 60°. Find the magnitude of sum and difference of these vectors.

Sol. Given, $\mathbf{A} = 5$ units, $\mathbf{B} = 5$ units, $\theta = 60°$

$\mathbf{A} + \mathbf{B} = ?$ and $\mathbf{A} - \mathbf{B} = ?$

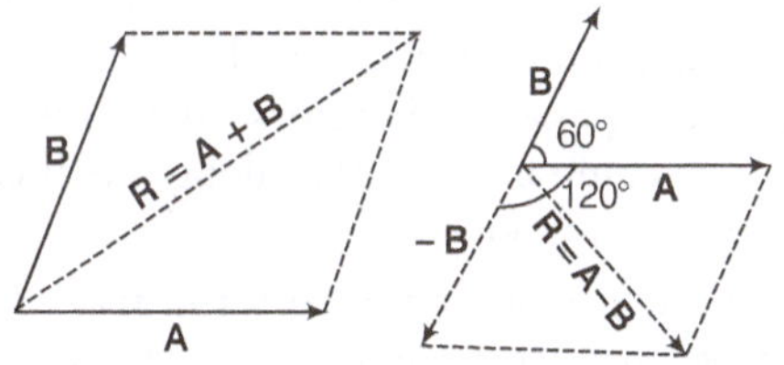

The magnitude of the resultant vectors of the sum,

$$R = \sqrt{A^2 + B^2 + 2AB\cos\theta}$$

$$= \sqrt{5^2 + 5^2 + 2 \times 5 \times 5 \times \cos 60°}$$

$$= 5\sqrt{3} \text{ unit}$$

The magnitude of the resultant vector of the difference,

$$R = \sqrt{A^2 + (-B)^2 + 2AB\cos\theta}$$

$$= \sqrt{5^2 + 5^2 + 2 \times 5 \times 5\cos 120°}$$

$$= 5 \text{ unit}$$

Multiplication of a Vector by a Scalar

When we multiply a vector **A** by a real number λ, then we get a new vector along the direction of vector **A**. Its magnitude becomes λ times the magnitude of the given vector.

Similarly, if we multiply vector **A** with a negative real number − λ, then we get a vector whose magnitude is λ times the magnitude of vector **A** but direction is opposite to that of vector **A**.

Hence, $\boxed{\lambda(\mathbf{A}) = \lambda\mathbf{A}}$ and $\boxed{-\lambda(\mathbf{A}) = -\lambda\mathbf{A}}$

e.g. (i) Consider a vector A is multiplied by a real number $\lambda = 3$ or -4, we get 3A or -4 A

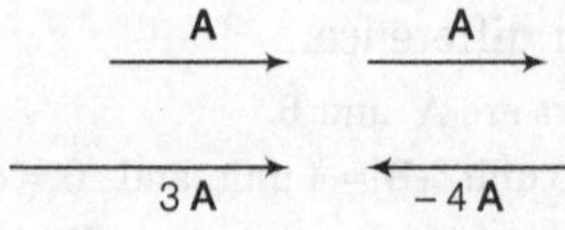

Multiplication of a vector by a real number

(ii) If we multiply a constant velocity vector by time, we will get a displacement vector in the direction of velocity vector.

Resolution of Vectors in Plane (In Two Dimensions)

The process of splitting a single vector into two or more vectors in different directions which collectively produce the same effect as produced by the single vector alone is known as **resolution of a vector.**

The various vectors into which a single vector is splitted are known as **components of vectors.** Resolution of a vector into two component vectors along the directions of two given vectors is unique.

To understand the resolution of vector in the components vectors, let us discuss the vector as a combination of unit vectors.

Any vector **r** can be expressed as a linear combination of two unit vectors $\hat{\mathbf{i}}$ and $\hat{\mathbf{j}}$ at right angle, i.e. $\mathbf{r} = x\hat{\mathbf{i}} + y\hat{\mathbf{j}}$

The vectors $x\hat{\mathbf{i}}$ and $y\hat{\mathbf{j}}$ are called the **perpendicular components** of r. The scalars x and y are called components or resolved parts of r in the directions of X-axis and Y-axis.

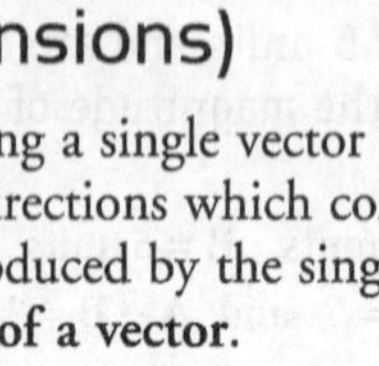

$\therefore$ Resultant vector, $\mathbf{r} = \sqrt{x^2 + y^2}$

If θ is the inclination of r with X-axis, then

Angle, $\theta = \tan^{-1}\left(\dfrac{y}{x}\right)$

Resolving a Vector into Two Component Vectors Along Given Directions

Now, draw **OQ** to represent the resultant vector **R** in magnitude and direction. From point O, draw a line **OP** parallel to the vector A and from point P, draw a line PQ parallel to vector B.

Then, these two lines intersect at point P as shown below.

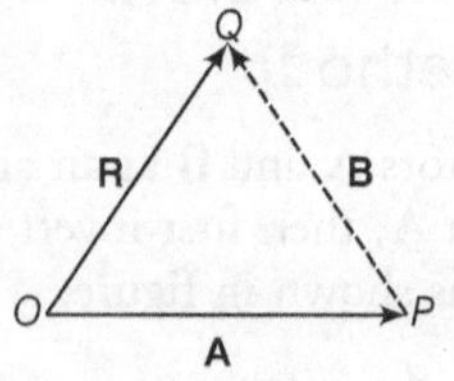

From triangle law of vector addition, we have

$$\mathbf{OQ} = \mathbf{OP} + \mathbf{PQ}$$

But OP and PQ are two component vectors of R in the direction of A and B, respectively.

Let $\mathbf{OP} = \lambda\mathbf{A}$ and $\mathbf{PQ} = \mu\mathbf{B}$, where λ and μ are two real numbers. This is also illustrated in the figure as shown below.

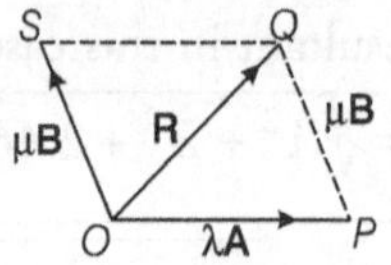

Now, the resultant vector becomes

$$\mathbf{R} = \lambda\mathbf{A} + \mu\mathbf{B}$$

Rectangular Components of a Vector in a Plane

When a vector in a plane is splitted into two component vectors at right angle to each other. Then, the component vectors are called **rectangular components** of that vector. The resultant vector is given by

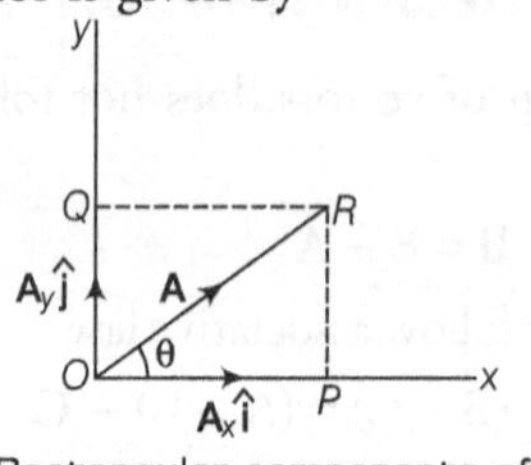

Rectangular components of **A**

$$\mathbf{A} = A_x\hat{\mathbf{i}} + A_y\hat{\mathbf{j}}$$

where, Magnitude of vector, $A = \sqrt{A_x^2 + A_y^2}$

We can also find the angle (θ) between them.

From $\tan\theta = \left(\dfrac{A_y}{A_x}\right)$

$\Rightarrow$ Angle, $\theta = \tan^{-1}\left(\dfrac{A_y}{A_x}\right)$

Where, A_y and A_x are the splitted vectors component of A in the direction of $\hat{\mathbf{j}}$ and $\hat{\mathbf{i}}$, respectively.

Example 10 The greatest and the least resultant of two forces acting at a point are 29 N and 5 N, respectively. If each force is increased by 3 N. Find the resultant of two new forces acting at right angle to each other.

Sol. Let P and Q be the two forces.

Greatest resultant, $R_1 = P + Q = 29$ N

Least resultant, $R_2 = P - Q = 5$ N

$$P + Q = 29 \quad \text{...(i)}$$

$$P - Q = 5 \quad \text{...(ii)}$$

Solving Eqs. (i) and (ii), we get

$$P = 17 \text{ N}, Q = 12 \text{ N}$$

When each force is increased by 3N, then

$$P' = P + 3 = 17 + 3 = 20 \text{ N}$$

$$\Rightarrow \quad Q' = 12 + 3 = 15 \text{ N}$$

The resultant of new forces is

$$R' = \sqrt{(20)^2 + (15)^2} = \sqrt{400 + 225} = 25 \text{ N}$$

Let the resultant R', makes an angle θ with P', then

$$\tan\theta = \frac{15}{20} = 0.75$$

$$\Rightarrow \quad \theta = \tan^{-1}(0.75) = 36°52'$$

Thus, the resultant of two new forces P' and Q' is 25 N and angle between them is 36°52′.

Example 11 A person walks in the following pattern 3.1 km North, then 2.4 km West and finally 5.2 km South.

(i) Sketch the vector diagram that represents this motion.

(ii) How far the person will be from its initial point?

(iii) In what direction would a bird fly in a straight line from the same starting point to the same final point?

Sol. (i) The vector diagram representing the motion is shown below.

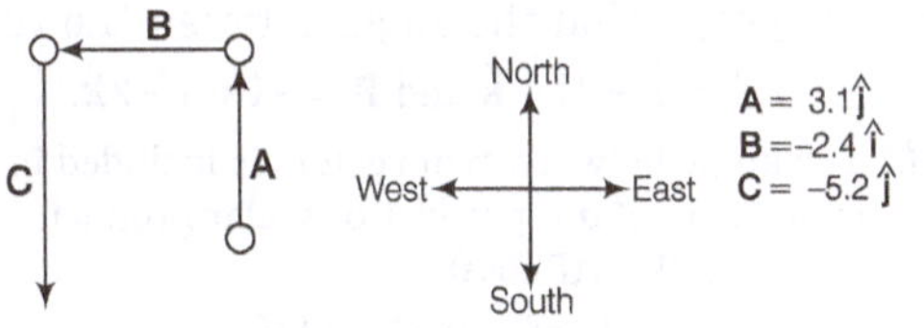

(ii) The final point is represented by

$$\mathbf{r} = \mathbf{A} + \mathbf{B} + \mathbf{C} = 3.1\hat{\mathbf{j}} - 2.4\hat{\mathbf{i}} - 5.2\hat{\mathbf{j}}$$

$$= -2.4\hat{\mathbf{i}} - 2.1\hat{\mathbf{j}}$$

whose magnitude is $|\mathbf{r}| = \sqrt{(-2.4)^2 + (-2.1)^2} \approx 3.2$ km

Hence, the person will be 3.2 km away from the initial point.

(iii) There are two possibilities for the angle.

$$\theta = \tan^{-1}\left(\frac{A_y}{A_x}\right) = \tan^{-1}\left(\frac{-3.1}{-2.4}\right) = 41° \text{ or } 221°$$

$\because$ r is in the third quadrant, hence $\theta = 221°$

Resolution of a Space Vector (In Three Dimensions)

Similarly, we can resolve a general vector **A** into three components along X, Y and Z-axes in three dimensions (i.e. space). Let α, β and γ are the angles between **A** and the X, Y and Z-axes, respectively as shown in figure. Let $\hat{\mathbf{i}}, \hat{\mathbf{j}}, \hat{\mathbf{k}}$ be the unit vectors, along X, Y and Z-axes, respectively.

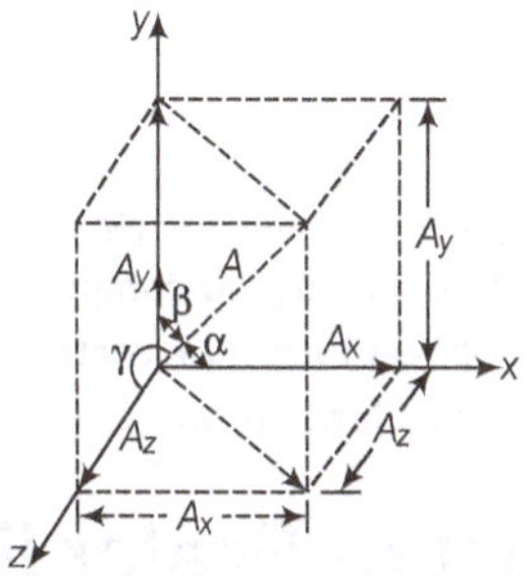

While resolving, we have,

$$A_x = A\cos\alpha, A_y = A\cos\beta, A_z = A\cos\gamma$$

$\therefore$ Resultant vector, $\mathbf{A} = A_x\hat{\mathbf{i}} + A_y\hat{\mathbf{j}} + A_z\hat{\mathbf{k}}$

Magnitude of vector **A** is $A = \sqrt{A_x^2 + A_y^2 + A_z^2}$

Example 12 Find the magnitude of the sum of the three coplanar vectors **a**, **b** and **c**, which are given as $\mathbf{a} = 2\hat{\mathbf{i}} + 3\hat{\mathbf{j}} + \hat{\mathbf{k}}$, $\mathbf{b} = -\hat{\mathbf{i}} + 2\hat{\mathbf{j}} - \hat{\mathbf{k}}$ and $\mathbf{c} = -2\hat{\mathbf{i}} - \hat{\mathbf{j}} - \hat{\mathbf{k}}$.

Sol. Given, $\mathbf{a} = 2\hat{\mathbf{i}} + 3\hat{\mathbf{j}} + \hat{\mathbf{k}}$

$$\mathbf{b} = -\hat{\mathbf{i}} + 2\hat{\mathbf{j}} - \hat{\mathbf{k}}$$

$$\mathbf{c} = -2\hat{\mathbf{i}} - \hat{\mathbf{j}} - \hat{\mathbf{k}}$$

Sum of given coplanar vectors,

$$\mathbf{a} + \mathbf{b} + \mathbf{c} = (2\hat{\mathbf{i}} + 3\hat{\mathbf{j}} + \hat{\mathbf{k}}) + (-\hat{\mathbf{i}} + 2\hat{\mathbf{j}} - \hat{\mathbf{k}}) + (-2\hat{\mathbf{i}} - \hat{\mathbf{j}} - \hat{\mathbf{k}})$$

$$= -\hat{\mathbf{i}} + 4\hat{\mathbf{j}} - \hat{\mathbf{k}}$$

$$\therefore \quad |\mathbf{a} + \mathbf{b} + \mathbf{c}| = |-\hat{\mathbf{i}} + 4\hat{\mathbf{j}} - \hat{\mathbf{k}}|$$

$$= \sqrt{(-1)^2 + 4^2 + (-1)^2}$$

$$= \sqrt{1 + 16 + 1}$$

$$= \sqrt{18} = 3\sqrt{2}$$

Example 13 Can the walk of a man be an example of resolution of forces?

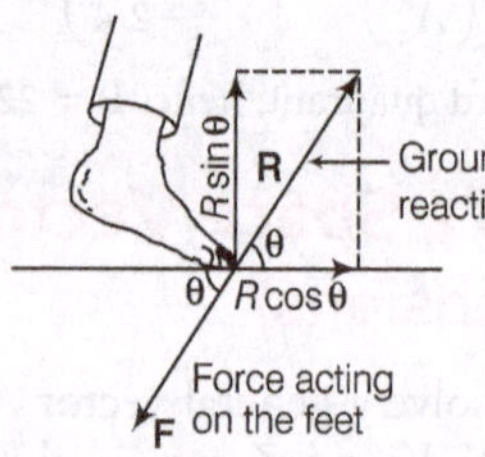

Sol. Walking of a man is an example of resolution of forces. A man while walking presses the ground with his feet backward by a force F at an angle θ with ground, in action.

The ground in reaction exerts an equal and opposite force R (= F) on the feet.

Its horizontal component $H = R\cos\theta$ enables the person to move forward while the vertical component $V = R\sin\theta$ balances his weight. This is because R is resolved into two rectangular components.

Application of resolution of vector

It is easier to pull a lawn mower than to push.

Dot Product or Scalar Product

It is defined as the product of the magnitudes of vectors **A** and **B** and the cosine of the angle θ between them. It is represented by

$$\mathbf{A}\cdot\mathbf{B} = AB\cos\theta$$

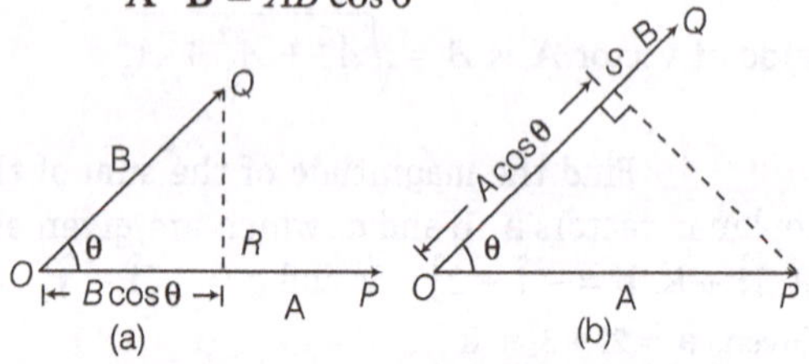

(a) $B\cos\theta$ is the projection of **B** onto **A**.
(b) $A\cos\theta$ is the projection of **A** onto **B**.

Case I When the two vectors are parallel, then $\theta = 0°$.
We have, $\mathbf{A}\cdot\mathbf{B} = AB\cos 0° = AB$

Case II When the two vectors are mutually perpendicular, then $\theta = 90°$.
We have, $\mathbf{A}\cdot\mathbf{B} = AB\cos 90° = 0$

Case III When the two vectors are anti-parallel, then $\theta = 180°$.
We have, $\mathbf{A}\cdot\mathbf{B} = AB\cos 180° = -AB$

e.g. A force **F** making an angle θ with horizontal, is applied on a body which is free to move on a horizontal surface. If s be the displacement caused by the force **F**, then the work done by the force on the body is given by

$$W = F\cos\theta\cdot s = Fs\cos\theta$$

$$W = \mathbf{F}\cdot\mathbf{s}$$

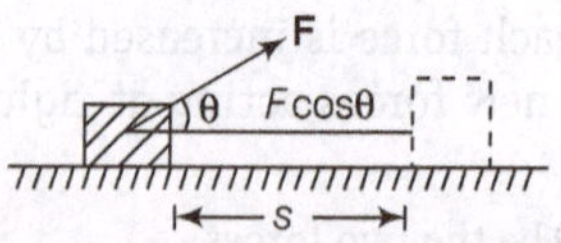

Hence, work done is an example of dot product.

Dot Product of Two Vectors in Terms of Their Components

It is defined as the product of the magnitude of one vector and the magnitude of the component of other vector in the direction of first vector.

If $\mathbf{a} = a_1\hat{\mathbf{i}} + a_2\hat{\mathbf{j}} + a_3\hat{\mathbf{k}}$ and $\mathbf{b} = b_1\hat{\mathbf{i}} + b_2\hat{\mathbf{j}} + b_3\hat{\mathbf{k}}$

then
$$\mathbf{a}\cdot\mathbf{b} = (a_1\hat{\mathbf{i}} + a_2\hat{\mathbf{j}} + a_3\hat{\mathbf{k}})\cdot(b_1\hat{\mathbf{i}} + b_2\hat{\mathbf{j}} + b_3\hat{\mathbf{k}})$$
$$= (a_1\cdot b_1)\hat{\mathbf{i}}^2 + (a_1\cdot b_2)\hat{\mathbf{i}}\cdot\hat{\mathbf{j}} + (a_1\cdot b_3)\hat{\mathbf{i}}\cdot\hat{\mathbf{k}}$$
$$+ (a_2\cdot b_1)\hat{\mathbf{j}}\cdot\hat{\mathbf{i}} + (a_2\cdot b_2)\hat{\mathbf{j}}^2 + (a_2\cdot b_3)\hat{\mathbf{j}}\cdot\hat{\mathbf{k}}$$
$$+ (a_3\cdot b_1)\hat{\mathbf{k}}\cdot\hat{\mathbf{i}} + (a_3\cdot b_2)\hat{\mathbf{k}}\cdot\hat{\mathbf{j}} + (a_3\cdot b_3)\hat{\mathbf{k}}^2.$$
$$\mathbf{a}\cdot\mathbf{b} = a_1\cdot b_1 + a_2\cdot b_2 + a_3\cdot b_3$$

where, $\hat{\mathbf{i}}\cdot\hat{\mathbf{i}} = \hat{\mathbf{j}}\cdot\hat{\mathbf{j}} = \hat{\mathbf{k}}\cdot\hat{\mathbf{k}} = 1$

and $\hat{\mathbf{i}}\cdot\hat{\mathbf{j}} = \hat{\mathbf{j}}\cdot\hat{\mathbf{k}} = \hat{\mathbf{k}}\cdot\hat{\mathbf{i}} = 0$

Properties of Dot Product

(i) $\mathbf{a}\cdot\mathbf{a} = (\mathbf{a})^2$
(ii) $\mathbf{a}\cdot\mathbf{b} = \mathbf{b}\cdot\mathbf{a}$
(iii) $\mathbf{a}\cdot(\mathbf{b}+\mathbf{c}) = \mathbf{a}\cdot\mathbf{b} + \mathbf{a}\cdot\mathbf{c}$
(iv) $(\mathbf{c}\cdot\mathbf{a})\cdot\mathbf{b} = \mathbf{c}\cdot(\mathbf{a}\cdot\mathbf{b})$
(v) $\mathbf{a}\cdot\mathbf{b} = |\mathbf{a}||\mathbf{b}|\cos\theta$

Example 14 Find the angle between the vectors $\mathbf{A} = \hat{\mathbf{i}} - 2\hat{\mathbf{j}} - \hat{\mathbf{k}}$ and $\mathbf{B} = -\hat{\mathbf{i}} + \hat{\mathbf{j}} - 2\hat{\mathbf{k}}$.

Sol. The angle between two vectors is included in the expression of dot product or scalar product.

$$\mathbf{A}\cdot\mathbf{B} = AB\cos\theta \quad \text{...(i)}$$

The magnitude of **A** is given by

$$A = \sqrt{(1)^2 + (2)^2 + (-1)^2} = \sqrt{6} \quad \text{...(ii)}$$

The magnitude of **B** is given by

$$B = \sqrt{(-1)^2 + (1)^2 + (-2)^2} = \sqrt{6} \quad \text{...(iii)}$$

We can separately evaluate the left side of Eq. (i) by writing the vectors in unit vector notation and using the distributive law.

$$\mathbf{A}\cdot\mathbf{B} = (\hat{\mathbf{i}} + 2\hat{\mathbf{j}} - \hat{\mathbf{k}})\cdot(-\hat{\mathbf{i}} + \hat{\mathbf{j}} - 2\hat{\mathbf{k}})$$
$$= 1\cdot(-1) + 2\cdot 1 + (-1)(-2) = -1 + 2 + 2 = 3$$

Substituting the values of **A** from Eq. (ii) and **B** from Eq. (iii) and $\mathbf{A}\cdot\mathbf{B}=3$ in Eq. (i), we get

$$3=(\sqrt{6})(\sqrt{6})\cos\theta$$

$$\Rightarrow \quad \cos\theta=\frac{3}{6}=\frac{1}{2}$$

$$\Rightarrow \quad \theta=\cos^{-1}\left(\frac{1}{2}\right)=60^\circ$$

Example 15 A force of $(7\hat{\mathbf{i}}+6\hat{\mathbf{k}})$ N makes a body move on a rough plane with a velocity of $(3\hat{\mathbf{i}}+4\hat{\mathbf{k}})\ \text{ms}^{-1}$. Calculate the power in watt.

Sol. Using $\hat{\mathbf{i}}\cdot\hat{\mathbf{i}}=1$, $\hat{\mathbf{i}}\cdot\hat{\mathbf{k}}=0$ and $\hat{\mathbf{k}}\cdot\hat{\mathbf{k}}=1$

$\therefore$ Power, $P=\mathbf{F}\cdot\mathbf{v}=(7\hat{\mathbf{i}}+6\hat{\mathbf{k}})\cdot(3\hat{\mathbf{i}}+4\hat{\mathbf{k}})$

$$=21+24=45\ \text{W}$$

Vector Product or Cross Product

It is defined as the product of the magnitudes of vectors **A** and **B** and the sine of the angle θ between them.

It is represented as

> Cross product of vectors **A** and **B**, $\mathbf{A}\times\mathbf{B}=AB\sin\theta\,\hat{\mathbf{n}}$

where, $\hat{\mathbf{n}}$ is a unit vector in the direction of $(\mathbf{A}\times\mathbf{B})$

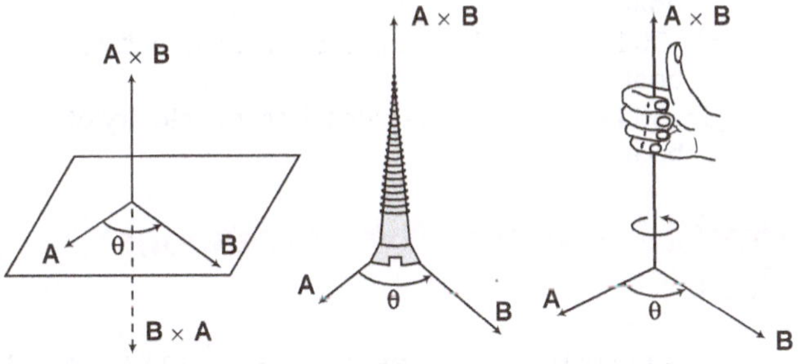

Right hand rules for direction of vector product

e.g. Torque (τ) acting on a particle about a point is equal to vector product of **r** and **F**, i.e.

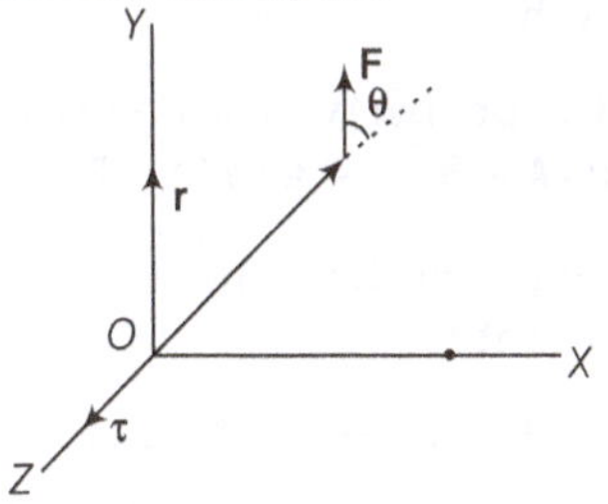

$$\tau=\mathbf{r}\times\mathbf{F}$$

$$\tau=rF\sin\theta$$

where, θ is the angle between **r** and **F**.

Therefore, torque is an example of vector product.

Cross Product of Two Vectors in Terms of Their Components

If $\mathbf{a}=a_1\hat{\mathbf{i}}+a_2\hat{\mathbf{j}}+a_3\hat{\mathbf{k}}$ and $\mathbf{b}=b_1\hat{\mathbf{i}}+b_2\hat{\mathbf{j}}+b_3\hat{\mathbf{k}}$, then

$$\mathbf{a}\times\mathbf{b}=\begin{vmatrix}\hat{\mathbf{i}} & \hat{\mathbf{j}} & \hat{\mathbf{k}}\\ a_1 & a_2 & a_3\\ b_1 & b_2 & b_3\end{vmatrix}$$

$$\boxed{\mathbf{a}\times\mathbf{b}=(a_2b_3-a_3b_2)\hat{\mathbf{i}}-(a_1b_3-a_3b_1)\hat{\mathbf{j}}+(a_1b_2-a_2b_1)\hat{\mathbf{k}}}$$

where, $\hat{\mathbf{i}}\times\hat{\mathbf{i}}=\hat{\mathbf{j}}\times\hat{\mathbf{j}}=\hat{\mathbf{k}}\times\hat{\mathbf{k}}=0$

and $\quad \hat{\mathbf{i}}\times\hat{\mathbf{j}}=\hat{\mathbf{k}},\ \hat{\mathbf{j}}\times\hat{\mathbf{k}}=\hat{\mathbf{i}},\ \hat{\mathbf{k}}\times\hat{\mathbf{i}}=\hat{\mathbf{j}},$

$\quad \hat{\mathbf{j}}\times\hat{\mathbf{i}}=-\hat{\mathbf{k}},\ \hat{\mathbf{k}}\times\hat{\mathbf{j}}=-\hat{\mathbf{i}},\ \hat{\mathbf{i}}\times\hat{\mathbf{k}}=-\hat{\mathbf{j}}$

***Case* I** Cross product of two parallel or anti-parallel vectors is zero.

***Case* II** Cross product of two mutually perpendicular vector is equal to product of the magnitude of two vectors.

If **A** and **B** are two sides of Δ, then area of $\Delta=\frac{1}{2}|\mathbf{A}\times\mathbf{B}|$

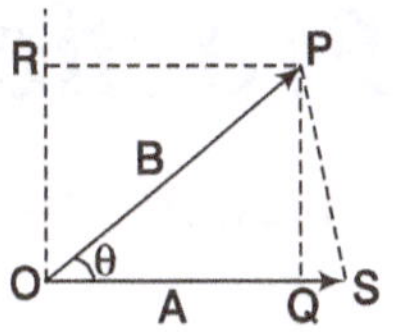

Representation of vectors **A** and **B**

As, area of $\Delta=\frac{1}{2}\times\text{base}\times\text{height}=\frac{1}{2}OS\times PQ$

$$\left(\because\ \sin\theta=\frac{PQ}{OP}\ \Rightarrow\ PQ=OP\sin\theta=B\sin\theta \text{ and } OS=A\right)$$

$$=\frac{1}{2}A\times B\sin\theta=\frac{1}{2}AB\sin\theta=\frac{1}{2}|\mathbf{A}\times\mathbf{B}|$$

Properties of Cross Product

(i) $\mathbf{a}\times\mathbf{b}=-\mathbf{b}\times\mathbf{a}$

(ii) $\mathbf{a}\times(\mathbf{b}+\mathbf{c})=\mathbf{a}\times\mathbf{b}+\mathbf{a}\times\mathbf{c}$

(iii) $(\mathbf{a}\times\mathbf{b})+(\mathbf{c}\times\mathbf{d})=(\mathbf{a}\times\mathbf{c})+(\mathbf{a}\times\mathbf{d})+(\mathbf{b}\times\mathbf{c})+(\mathbf{b}\times\mathbf{d})$

(iv) $m\mathbf{a}\times\mathbf{b}=\mathbf{a}\times m\mathbf{b}$

(v) $(\mathbf{b}+\mathbf{c})\mathbf{a}=\mathbf{b}\times\mathbf{a}+\mathbf{c}\times\mathbf{a}$

(vi) $\mathbf{a}\times\mathbf{a}=0$

(vii) $\mathbf{a}\times(\mathbf{b}-\mathbf{c})=\mathbf{a}\times\mathbf{b}-\mathbf{a}\times\mathbf{c}$

(viii) $|\mathbf{a}\times\mathbf{b}|^2=|\mathbf{a}|^2|\mathbf{b}|^2-|\mathbf{a}\cdot\mathbf{b}|^2$

(ix) $\mathbf{a}\times(\mathbf{b}\times\mathbf{c})=(\mathbf{c}\cdot\mathbf{a})\mathbf{b}-(\mathbf{b}\cdot\mathbf{a})\mathbf{c}$

Example 16 The vector **A** has a magnitude of 5 unit, **B** has a magnitude of 6 unit and the cross product **A** and **B** has the magnitude of 15 unit. Find the angle between **A** and **B**.

Sol. If the angle between **A** and **B** is θ, then cross product will have a magnitude,

$$|\mathbf{A}\times\mathbf{B}| = AB\sin\theta \Rightarrow 15 = 5\times 6\sin\theta$$

$$\sin\theta = \frac{1}{2} \Rightarrow \theta = 30°$$

Representation of Unit Vectors in a Circle

Unit vectors along three axes of cartesian coordinate system (i.e. $\hat{i}$, $\hat{j}$, $\hat{k}$) can be represented on a circle in such a way that if we rotate our eyes in anti-clockwise direction product of two consecutive vector will produce the third unit vector.

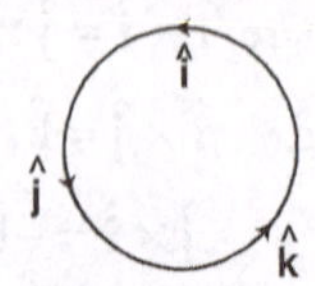

Representation of unit vectors

e.g. $\hat{i}\times\hat{j} = \hat{k}$ and $\hat{j}\times\hat{i} = -\hat{k}$

and similarly for other possibilities.

Topic Practice 1

Multiple Choice Questions

1 Mark

1. Choose the correct option/s.
   (a) To represent two-dimensional motion we need vectors
   (b) To represent one-dimensional motion we use positive and negative signs
   (c) To represent 3-dimensional motion we need vectors
   (d) All (a), (b) and (c)

2. *A* and *B* are two inclined vectors. *R* is their sum. Choose the correct figure for the given description.

(a)
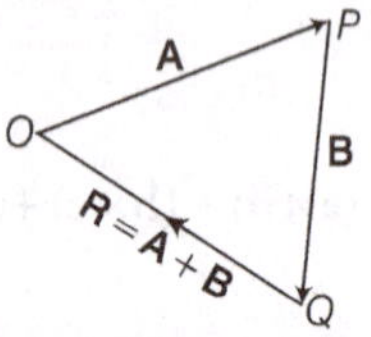

(b)
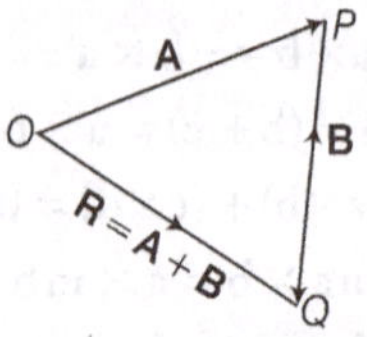

(c)
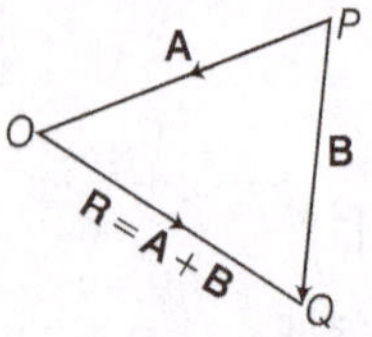

(d)
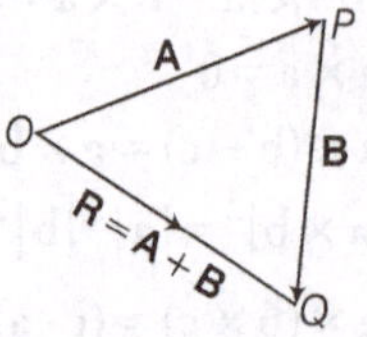

3. If **A** = **B** + **C** and the values of A, B and C are 13, 12, 5 respectively, then the angle between **A** and **C** will be
   (a) $\cos^{-1}(5/13)$
   (b) $\cos^{-1}(13/12)$
   (c) $\pi/12$
   (d) $\sin^{-1}(5/12)$

4. If magnitude of the vector **A** + **B** is equal to that of vector **A** − **B**, then angle between **A** and **B** is
   (a) 30°   (b) 45°
   (c) 60°   (d) 90°

5. The value of difference of unit vectors **A** and **B** whose angle of intersection is θ.
   (a) $2\sin\theta/2$ (b) $2\cos\theta/2$
   (c) $\sin\theta/2$ (d) $\cos\theta/2$

6. A motorboat is racing towards North at 25 kmh^{-1} and the water current in that region is 10 kmh^{-1} in the direction of 60° East of South. The resultant velocity of the boat is
   (a) 24 kmh^{-1}, with an angle 23.4° from velocity of boat
   (b) 22 kmh^{-1}, with an angle 23.4° from velocity of boat
   (c) 30 kmh^{-1}, with an angle 25° from velocity of boat
   (d) 36 kmh^{-1}, with an angle 25° from velocity of boat

Very Short Answer Type Questions

1 Mark

7. Three vectors not lying in a plane can never end up to give a null vector. Is it true? **NCERT**

8. The total path length is always equal to the magnitude of the displacement vector of a particle. Why? **NCERT**

9. What is the property of two vectors **A** and **B** such that $(\mathbf{A}+\mathbf{B})^2 = \mathbf{C}$ and $(\mathbf{A}-\mathbf{B})^2 = \mathbf{C}$?

10. Under what condition, the three vectors give zero resultant?

11. When do we say two vectors are orthogonal?

12. What are the minimum number of forces which are numerically equal whose vector sum can be zero?

13. Can the scalar product of two vectors be negative?

Short Answer Type I Questions

(2 Marks)

14. We can order events in time and there is no sense of time, distinguishing past, present and future. Is time a vector?

15. The sum and difference of two vectors are perpendicular to each other. Prove that the vectors are equal in magnitude.

16. Can we apply the commutative and associative laws of vectors subtraction also?

17. If $\mathbf{R} = (\mathbf{A} + \mathbf{B})$, show that
$R^2 = A^2 + B^2 + 2AB\cos\theta$
where, θ is the smaller angle between **A** and **B**.

18. **A**, **B** and **C** are three non-collinear, non-coplanar vectors. What can you say about direction of $\mathbf{A} \times (\mathbf{B} \times \mathbf{C})$?

Short Answer Type II Questions

(3 Marks)

19. Can you associate vectors with?
    (i) The length of a wire bent into a loop
    (ii) A plane area
    (iii) A sphere **NCERT**

20. Define scalar product of two vectors. Write its different cases.

21. Explain
    (i) Triangle law of vector addition.
    (ii) Parallelogram law of vector addition.

Long Answer Type Questions

(5 Marks)

22. State with reasons, whether the following algebric operations with scalar and vector physical quantities are meaningful.
    (i) Adding any two scalars.
    (ii) Adding a scalar to a vector of the same dimensions.
    (iii) Multiplying any vector by any scalar.
    (iv) Multiplying any two scalars.
    (v) Adding any two vectors.
    (vi) Adding a component of a vector to the same vector. **NCERT**

23. Establish the following inequalities geometrically or otherwise.
    (i) $|\mathbf{A} + \mathbf{B}| \le |\mathbf{A}| + |\mathbf{B}|$ (ii) $|\mathbf{A} + \mathbf{B}| \ge ||\mathbf{A}| - |\mathbf{B}||$
    (iii) $|\mathbf{A} - \mathbf{B}| \le |\mathbf{A}| + |\mathbf{B}|$ (iv) $|\mathbf{A} - \mathbf{B}| \ge ||\mathbf{A}| - |\mathbf{B}||$
    When does the equality sign above apply? **NCERT**

Numerical Problems

24. What is the value of m in $\hat{\mathbf{i}} + m\hat{\mathbf{j}} + \hat{\mathbf{k}}$ to be unit vector? **[1 M]**

25. Two equal forces having their resultant equal to either. At what angle are they inclined? **[1 M]**

26. What is the angle made by vector, $\mathbf{A} = 2\hat{\mathbf{i}} + 2\hat{\mathbf{j}}$ with X-axis? **[1 M]**

27. The magnitude of vectors **A**, **B** and **C** are 12, 5 and 13 units respectively and **A** + **B** = **C**, find the angle between **A** and **B**. **[1M]**

28. What is the angle between **A** and **B**, if **A** and **B** denote the adjacent sides of a parallelogram drawn from a point and the area of the parallelogram is 1/2 AB? **[1M]**

29. If $\mathbf{A} \cdot \mathbf{B} = |\mathbf{A} \times \mathbf{B}|$, find the value of angle between A and B. **[1 M]**

30. Suppose you have two forces **F** and **F**. How would you combine them in order to have resultant force of magnitudes? **[2M]**
    (i) Zero. (ii) **F**.

31. Determine that vector which when added to the resultant of $\mathbf{A} = 3\hat{\mathbf{i}} - 5\hat{\mathbf{j}} + 7\hat{\mathbf{k}}$ and $\mathbf{B} = 2\hat{\mathbf{i}} + 4\hat{\mathbf{j}} - 3\hat{\mathbf{k}}$ gives unit vector along y-direction. **[2M]**

32. The angle between vectors **A** and **B** is 60°. What is the ratio of $\mathbf{A} \cdot \mathbf{B}$ and $|\mathbf{A} \times \mathbf{B}|$? **[2M]**

33. Two forces whose magnitudes are in the ratio 3 : 5 give a resultant of 28 N. If the angle of their inclination is 60°. Find the magnitude of each force. **[2 M]**

34. Two forces 5 kg-wt. and 10 kg-wt. are acting with an inclination of 120° between them. Find the angle which the resultant makes with 10 kg-wt. **[2 M]**

35. There are two displacement vectors, one of magnitude 3 m and the other of 4 m. How would the two vectors be added so that the magnitude of the resultant vector be (i) 7 m (ii) 1 m and (iii) 5 m? **[3 M]**

36. If unit vectors $\hat{a}$ and $\hat{b}$ are inclined at angle θ, then prove that $|\hat{a}-\hat{b}| = 2\sin\frac{\theta}{2}$. NCERT [3M]

37. Show that vectors $\mathbf{A} = 2\hat{i} - 3\hat{j} - \hat{k}$ and $\mathbf{B} = -6\hat{i} + 9\hat{j} + 3\hat{k}$ are parallel. [3M]

38. On an open ground, a motorist follows a track that turns to his left by an angle of 60° after every 500 m. Starting from a given turn, specify the displacement of the motorist at the third, sixth and eighth turn. Compare the magnitude of the displacement with the total path length covered by the motorist in each case. [5 M]

39. $\hat{i}$ and $\hat{j}$ are unit vectors along X and Y-axes, respectively. What is the magnitude and direction of vectors $\hat{i}+\hat{j}$ and $\hat{i}-\hat{j}$? What are the components of a vector $A = 2\hat{i} + 3\hat{j}$ along the direction $\hat{i}+\hat{j}$ and $\hat{i}-\hat{j}$? (You may use graphical method). [5M]

Hints & Solutions

1. (d) In order to describe two-dimensional motion and three-dimensional motion, we need vectors.

2. (d) Correct figure is

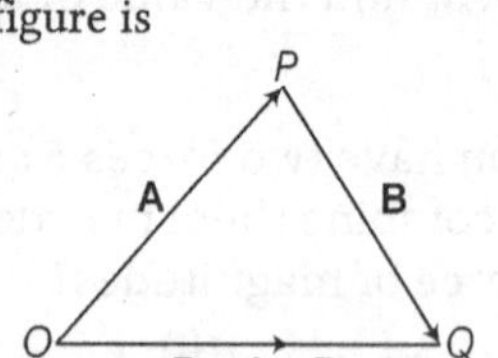

3. (a) Here, $(13)^2 = (12)^2 + (5)^2$, according to Pythagoras theorem, angle between **B** and **C** = 90°, $\cos\theta = \frac{5}{13}$

$$\Rightarrow \quad \theta = \cos^{-1}\left(\frac{5}{13}\right)$$

4. (d) Given $|\mathbf{A}+\mathbf{B}| = |\mathbf{A}-\mathbf{B}|$

$$A^2 + B^2 + 2AB\cos\theta = A^2 + B^2 - 2AB\cos\theta$$

$$\Rightarrow \quad \cos\theta = 0 \Rightarrow \theta = 90^\circ$$

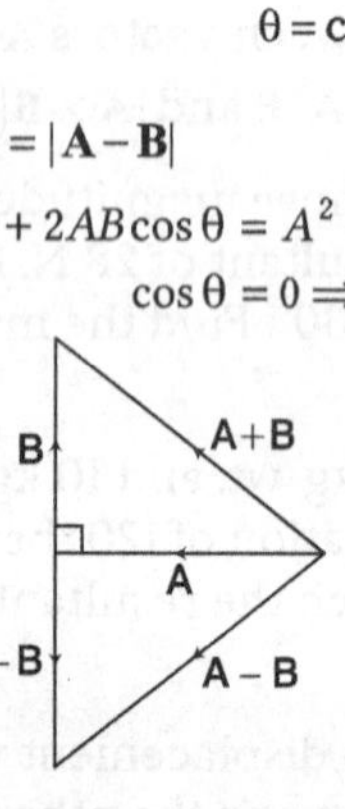

5. (a) Difference of vectors **A** and **B** can be given as

$$(\mathbf{A}-\mathbf{B})^2 = A^2 + B^2 - 2AB\cos\theta$$

$$= 1 + 1 - 2\cos\theta$$

$$= 2 - 2\cos\theta = 2(1-\cos\theta)$$

$$= 2 \times 2\sin^2\theta/2 = 4\sin^2\frac{\theta}{2}$$

$$|\mathbf{A}-\mathbf{B}| = 2\sin\theta/2$$

6. (b) The vector $\mathbf{v}_b$ representing the velocity of the motorboat and the vector $\mathbf{v}_c$ representing the water current are shown in figure in direction specified by the problem. Using the parallelogram method of addition, the resultant **R** is obtained in the direction shown in the figure.

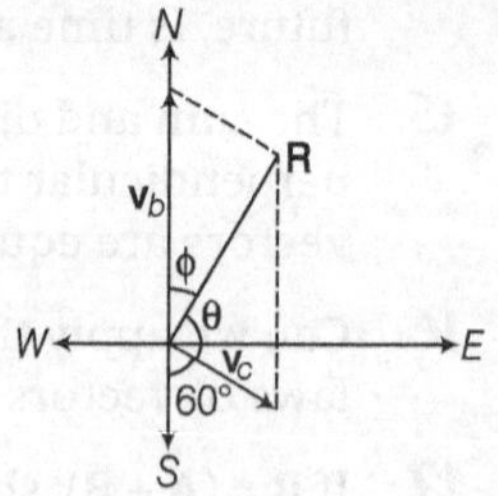

$$\theta = 180^\circ - 60^\circ = 120^\circ$$

We can obtain the magnitude of **R** using the law of cosine

$$R = \sqrt{v_b^2 + v_c^2 + 2v_b v_c \cos 120^\circ}$$

$$= \sqrt{25^2 + 10^2 + 2 \times 25 \times 10(-1/2)}$$

$$= 21.8 \text{ kmh}^{-1} \approx 22 \text{kmh}^{-1}$$

To obtain the direction, we apply the law of sine

$$\frac{R}{\sin\theta} = \frac{v_c}{\sin\phi}$$

or $\sin\phi = \frac{v_c}{R}\sin\theta = \frac{10 \times \sin 120^\circ}{21.8} = \frac{10\sqrt{3}}{2 \times 21.8} = 0.397$

$$\Rightarrow \quad \phi = 23.4^\circ$$

7. Yes, because they cannot be represented by the three sides of a triangle taken in the same order.

8. It is only true if the particle moves along a straight line in the same direction, otherwise the statement is false.

9. The two vectors are parallel and acting in the same direction, i.e. θ = 0°.

10. If three vectors acting on a point object at the same time are represented in magnitude and direction by the three sides of a triangle taken in the same order, their resultant is zero. The object is said to be in equilibrium.

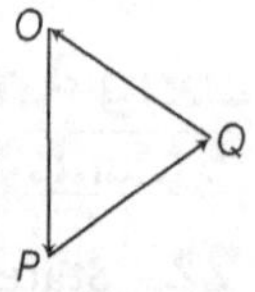

11. If the dot product of two vectors is zero, then the vectors are orthogonal.

12. Two only, provided that they are acting in opposite directions.

13. Yes, it will be negative if the angle between the two vectors lies between 90° to 270°.

14. We know that time always flows on and on i.e. from past to present and then to future.

Therefore, a direction can be assigned to time. Since, the direction of time is unique and it is unspecified or unstated. That is why, time cannot be a vector though it has a direction. [2]

15. As the vectors $\mathbf{A}+\mathbf{B}$ and $\mathbf{A}-\mathbf{B}$ are perpendicular to each other, therefore

$$(\mathbf{A}+\mathbf{B})\cdot(\mathbf{A}-\mathbf{B})=0 \quad [1]$$

$$\mathbf{A}\cdot\mathbf{A}-\mathbf{A}\cdot\mathbf{B}+\mathbf{B}\cdot\mathbf{A}-\mathbf{B}\cdot\mathbf{B}=0$$

or $$\mathbf{A}-\mathbf{B}=0 \quad [\because \mathbf{A}\cdot\mathbf{B}=\mathbf{B}\cdot\mathbf{A}]$$

$\Rightarrow$ $$\mathbf{A}=\mathbf{B} \quad [1]$$

16. Refer to text on page 77 (Properties of subtraction of vectors)

17. Given, $\mathbf{R}=\mathbf{A}+\mathbf{B}$

Taking dot product of $\mathbf{R}$ with itself, we get

$$\mathbf{R}\cdot\mathbf{R}=(\mathbf{A}+\mathbf{B})\cdot(\mathbf{A}+\mathbf{B})$$

$$R^2=\mathbf{A}\cdot\mathbf{A}+2\mathbf{A}\cdot\mathbf{B}+\mathbf{B}\cdot\mathbf{B}$$

$\Rightarrow$ $$R=A^2+2AB\cos\theta+B^2 \quad [2]$$

18. $(\mathbf{B}\times\mathbf{C})$ will act perpendicular to the plane containing $\mathbf{B}$ and $\mathbf{C}$, and directed in a direction given by right hand rule.

$\mathbf{A}\times(\mathbf{B}\times\mathbf{C})$ will lie in the plane of $\mathbf{B}$ and $\mathbf{C}$ and is perpendicular to vector $\mathbf{A}$. [2]

19. (i) We cannot associate a vector with the length of a wire bent into a loop.

(ii) We can associate a vector with a plane area.
Such a vector is called **area vector** and its direction is represented by outward drawn normal to the area.

(iii) We cannot associate a vector with volume of sphere, however, a vector can be associated with the area of sphere. [1 × 3]

20. Refer to text on page 80 (Dot product or scalar product).

21. (i) Refer to text on pages 73 and 74 (Triangle law of vector addition).

(ii) Refer to text on page 74 (Parallelogram law of vector addition).

22. (i) No, adding any two scalars is not meaningful because only the scalars of same dimensions i.e. having same unit can be added. [1/2]

(ii) No, adding a scalar to a vector of the same dimensions is not meaningful because a scalar cannot be added to a vector. [1/2]

(iii) Yes, multiplying any vector by any scalar is meaningful. When a vector is multiplied by a scalar, we get a vector, whose magnitude is equal to the product of magnitude of vector and the scalar and direction remains the same as the direction of the given vector.

e.g. A body of mass 4 kg is moving with a velocity 20 m/s towards East, then, product of velocity and mass gives the momentum of the body which is also a vector quantity.

$$\mathbf{p}=m\mathbf{v}=4\text{ kg}\times(20\text{ m/s})\text{ (East)}=80\text{ kg-m/s, East} \quad [1]$$

(iv) Yes, multiplying any two scalars is meaningful.
Density ρ and volume V both are scalar quantities. When density is multiplied by volume, then we get $\rho\times V=m$, mass of the body, which is a scalar quantity. [1]

(v) No, adding any two vectors is not meaningful because only vectors of same dimensions i.e. having same unit can be added. [1]

(vi) Yes, adding a component of a vector to the same vector is meaningful because both vectors are of same dimensions. [1]

23. Consider two vectors $\mathbf{A}$ and $\mathbf{B}$ be represented by the sides $\mathbf{OP}$ and $\mathbf{OQ}$ of a parallelogram $OPSQ$. According to parallelogram law of vector addition, $(\mathbf{A}+\mathbf{B})$ will be represented by $\mathbf{OS}$ as shown in figure. [1]

Thus, $OP=|\mathbf{A}|,\ OQ=PS=|\mathbf{B}|$

and $OS=|\mathbf{A}+\mathbf{B}|$

(i) To prove $|\mathbf{A}+\mathbf{B}|\leq|\mathbf{A}|+|\mathbf{B}|$

We know that the length of one side of a triangle is always less than the sum of the lengths of the other two sides. Hence from $\Delta\, OPS$, we have

$$OS<OP+PS$$

$\Rightarrow$ $$OS<OP+OQ$$

or $$|\mathbf{A}+\mathbf{B}|<|\mathbf{A}|+|\mathbf{B}| \quad ...(i)$$

If the two vectors $\mathbf{A}$ and $\mathbf{B}$ are acting along the same straight line and in the same direction.

or $$|\mathbf{A}+\mathbf{B}|=|\mathbf{A}|+|\mathbf{B}| \quad ...(ii)$$

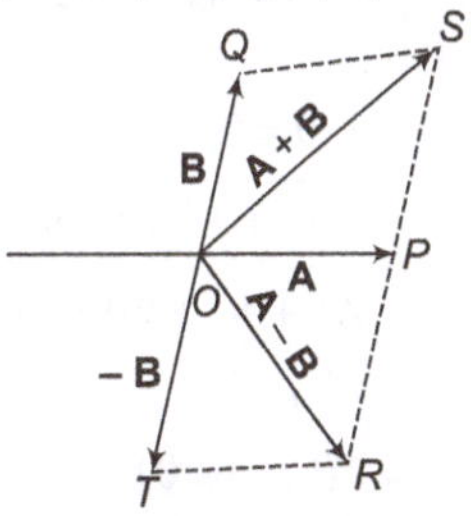

[1]

Combining the conditions mentioned in Eqs. (i) and (ii), we have $|\mathbf{A}+\mathbf{B}|\leq|\mathbf{A}|+|\mathbf{B}|$

(ii) To prove $|\mathbf{A}+\mathbf{B}|\geq||\mathbf{A}|-|\mathbf{B}||$

From $\Delta\, OPS$, we have

$$OS+PS>OP \text{ or } OS>|OP-PS|$$

or $$OS>|OP-OQ| \quad ...\text{(iii)}$$

$$[\because PS=OQ]$$

The modulus of $(OP-PS)$ has been taken because the LHS is always positive but the RHS may be negative if $OP<PS$. Thus, from Eq. (iii) we have

$$|\mathbf{A}+\mathbf{B}|>||\mathbf{A}|-|\mathbf{B}|| \quad ...\text{(iv)}$$

If the two vectors $\mathbf{A}$ and $\mathbf{B}$ are acting along a straight line in opposite directions, then

$$|\mathbf{A}+\mathbf{B}|=||\mathbf{A}|-|\mathbf{B}|| \quad ...\text{(v)}$$

Combining the conditions mentioned in Eqs. (iv) and (v) we get $|\mathbf{A}+\mathbf{B}|\geq||\mathbf{A}|-|\mathbf{B}||$ [1]

(iii) To prove $|\mathbf{A}-\mathbf{B}|\leq|\mathbf{A}|+|\mathbf{B}|$

In figure, $\mathbf{A}=(\mathbf{OP})$, $-\mathbf{B}=\mathbf{OT}=\mathbf{PR}$
and $(\mathbf{A}-\mathbf{B})=\mathbf{OR}$

From, ΔORP we note that $OR<OP+PR$.

or $$|\mathbf{A}-\mathbf{B}|<|\mathbf{A}|+|-\mathbf{B}|$$

or $$|\mathbf{A}-\mathbf{B}|<|\mathbf{A}|+|\mathbf{B}| \quad ...\text{(vi)}$$

If the two vectors are acting along a straight line. But in the opposite direction, then

$$|\mathbf{A}-\mathbf{B}| = |\mathbf{A}|+|\mathbf{B}| \quad \text{...(vii)}$$

Combining the conditions mentioned in Eqs. (vi) and (vii), we get $|\mathbf{A}-\mathbf{B}| \le |\mathbf{A}|+|\mathbf{B}|$ [1]

(iv) To prove $|\mathbf{A}-\mathbf{B}| \ge \big||\mathbf{A}|-|\mathbf{B}|\big|$

In figure from $\Delta\ OPR$, we note that

$OR + PR > OP$ or $OR > |OP - PR|$

or $OR > |OP - OT|$ $[\because OT = PR]$ ...(viii)

The modulus of $(OP - OT)$ has been taken because LHS is positive and RHS may be negative if $OP < OT$.

From Eq. (viii), we have

$$|\mathbf{A}-\mathbf{B}| > \big||\mathbf{A}|-|\mathbf{B}|\big| \quad \text{...(ix)}$$

If the two vectors **A** and **B** are acting along the same straight line in the same direction, then

$$|\mathbf{A}-\mathbf{B}| = |\mathbf{A}|-|\mathbf{B}| \quad \text{...(x)}$$

Combining the conditions mentioned in Eqs. (ix) and (x), we get $|\mathbf{A}-\mathbf{B}| \ge |\mathbf{A}|-|\mathbf{B}|$ [1]

24. For unit vector

$$|\hat{\mathbf{i}}+m\hat{\mathbf{j}}+\hat{\mathbf{k}}| = \sqrt{1+m^2+1} = 1$$

$$m^2+2 = 1$$

$$m^2 = -1 \Rightarrow m = \sqrt{-1}$$

$\therefore$ m is imaginary.

25. $A = F, B = F, R = F, \theta = ?$

$$R = \sqrt{A^2+B^2+2AB\cos\theta}$$

$$\Rightarrow R^2 = A^2+B^2+2AB\cos\theta$$

$$F^2 = F^2+F^2+2F^2\cos\theta$$

$$1 = 2(1+\cos\theta)$$

$$\Rightarrow \cos\theta = \frac{1}{2}-1 = \frac{-1}{2}$$

$$\theta = \cos^{-1}\left(-\frac{1}{2}\right) = 120°$$

26. For the vector, $A_x = 2, A_y = 2$

We know that angle is given by

$$\theta = \tan^{-1}\left(\frac{A_y}{A_x}\right) = \tan^{-1}\left(\frac{2}{2}\right)$$

$$\theta = \tan^{-1}(1) = 45°$$

27. We know that $C^2 = A^2+B^2$ or $13^2 = 12^2+5^2$

Thus, the angle between **A** and **B** is 90°.

28. Area of parallelogram $|\mathbf{A}\times\mathbf{B}| = \text{AB}\sin\theta = \frac{1}{2}\text{AB}$ [given]

$$\therefore \sin\theta = \frac{1}{2} = \sin 30° \text{ or } \theta = 30°$$

29. As $\mathbf{A}\cdot\mathbf{B} = |\mathbf{A}\times\mathbf{B}|$

$\therefore$ $\mathbf{AB}\cos\theta = \mathbf{AB}\sin\theta$ or $\tan\theta = 1$ or $\theta = \pi/4$

30. (i) If they act at opposite direction, resultant is zero. [1]

(ii) For the resultant to be **F**,

$$F^2 = F^2+F^2+2F^2\cos\theta$$

$$\Rightarrow \cos\theta = \frac{-1}{2} \Rightarrow \theta = 120°$$

[1]

31. We are given, $\mathbf{A} = 3\hat{\mathbf{i}}-5\hat{\mathbf{j}}+7\hat{\mathbf{k}}$ and $\mathbf{B} = 2\hat{\mathbf{i}}+4\hat{\mathbf{j}}-3\hat{\mathbf{k}}$

Thus, the resultant vector is given by

$$\mathbf{R} = \mathbf{A}+\mathbf{B} = (3\hat{\mathbf{i}}-5\hat{\mathbf{j}}+7\hat{\mathbf{k}})+(2\hat{\mathbf{i}}+4\hat{\mathbf{j}}-3\hat{\mathbf{k}})$$

$$= 5\hat{\mathbf{i}}-\hat{\mathbf{j}}+4\hat{\mathbf{k}}$$

[1]

But the unit vector along y-direction $= \hat{\mathbf{j}}$

$\therefore$ Required vector $= \hat{\mathbf{j}}-(5\hat{\mathbf{i}}-\hat{\mathbf{j}}+4\hat{\mathbf{k}}) = -5\hat{\mathbf{i}}+2\hat{\mathbf{j}}-4\hat{\mathbf{k}}$ [1]

32. The dot product, $\mathbf{A}\cdot\mathbf{B} = AB\cos\theta$

and cross product $|\mathbf{A}\times\mathbf{B}| = AB\sin\theta$. [1]

$$\therefore \text{Ratio is } \frac{\mathbf{A}\cdot\mathbf{B}}{|\mathbf{A}\times\mathbf{B}|} = \frac{AB\cos\theta}{AB\sin\theta} = \cot\theta = \cot 60° = \frac{1}{\sqrt{3}}$$

[1]

33. Let A and B be the two forces.

Then, $A = 3x, B = 5x, R = 28$ N and $\theta = 60°$

Thus, $\frac{A}{B} = \frac{3}{5}$

Now, $R = \sqrt{A^2+B^2+2AB\cos\theta}$ [1]

$$\Rightarrow 28 = \sqrt{9x^2+25x^2+30x^2\cos 60°} = 7x \Rightarrow x = 4$$

$\therefore$ Forces are $A = 12$ N and $B = 20$ N. [1]

34. Given, $A = 5$ kg-wt, $B = 10$ kg-wt, $\theta = 120°$ then $\beta = ?$

$$\tan\beta = \frac{B\sin\theta}{A+B\cos\theta} = \frac{10\sin 120°}{5+10\cos 120°} = \frac{5\sin 60°}{10-5\cos 60°}$$ [1]

$$= \frac{5\times\sqrt{3}/2}{10-5/2} = \frac{1}{\sqrt{3}} = \tan 30°$$

$\therefore$ $\beta = 30°$ [1]

35. The magnitude of resultant **R** of two vectors **A** and **B** is given by, $R = \sqrt{A^2+B^2+2AB\cos\theta}$

$$= \sqrt{3^2+4^2+2\times3\times4\cos\theta} = \sqrt{25+24\cos\theta}$$

[1½]

(i) R is 7 m, if $\theta = 0°$

(ii) R is 1 m, if $\theta = 180°$

(iii) R is 5 m, if $\theta = 90°$ [½ × 3]

36. For any vector $\mathbf{a} \Rightarrow |\mathbf{a}|^2 = \mathbf{a}\cdot\mathbf{a}$

$$\therefore |\hat{\mathbf{a}}-\hat{\mathbf{b}}|^2 = (\hat{\mathbf{a}}-\hat{\mathbf{b}})\cdot(\hat{\mathbf{a}}-\hat{\mathbf{b}})$$ [1]

$$= \hat{\mathbf{a}}\cdot\hat{\mathbf{a}}-\hat{\mathbf{a}}\cdot\hat{\mathbf{b}}-\hat{\mathbf{b}}\cdot\hat{\mathbf{a}}+\hat{\mathbf{b}}\cdot\hat{\mathbf{b}}$$

$$= 1-2\hat{\mathbf{a}}\cdot\hat{\mathbf{b}}+1 \quad [\because \hat{\mathbf{a}}\cdot\hat{\mathbf{a}} = 1\times1\times\cos 0° = 1]$$

$$= 2-2\times1\times1\times\cos\theta$$

$$= 2(1-\cos\theta)$$

$$= 2.2\sin^2\frac{\theta}{2} = 4\sin^2\frac{\theta}{2} \quad [\because 1-\cos 2\theta = 2\sin^2\theta]$$

[1]

Hence, $|\hat{\mathbf{a}}-\hat{\mathbf{b}}| = 2\sin\frac{\theta}{2}$.

[1]

37. The given vectors are

$\mathbf{A} = 2\hat{\mathbf{i}} - 3\hat{\mathbf{j}} - \hat{\mathbf{k}}$ and $\mathbf{B} = -6\hat{\mathbf{i}} + 9\hat{\mathbf{j}} + 3\hat{\mathbf{k}}$

Then, the vectors are parallel, if $\mathbf{A} \times \mathbf{B} = 0$ [1]

$$\therefore \quad \mathbf{A} \times \mathbf{B} = \begin{vmatrix} \hat{\mathbf{i}} & \hat{\mathbf{j}} & \hat{\mathbf{k}} \\ 2 & -3 & -1 \\ -6 & 9 & 3 \end{vmatrix}$$

$$= \hat{\mathbf{i}}(-9+9) - \hat{\mathbf{j}}(6-6) + \hat{\mathbf{k}}(18-18) = 0$$ [1]

But $|\mathbf{A} \times \mathbf{B}| = 0$ or $AB \sin \theta = 0$ $[\because \mathbf{A} \neq 0 \text{ and } \mathbf{B} \neq 0]$

$\therefore \quad \sin \theta = 0$ or $\theta = 0$

Hence, the vectors **A** and **B** are parallel. [1]

38. As motorist is taking turn to his left at an angle 60° after every 500 m, therefore, he is moving on a regular hexagon.

The distance after which motorist take a turn = 500 m

As motorist takes a turn at an angle of 60° each time, therefore motorist is moving on a regular hexagonal path. Let the motorist starts from point A and reaches at point D at the end of third turn and at initial point A at the end of sixth turn and at point C at the end of eighth turn. [1/2]

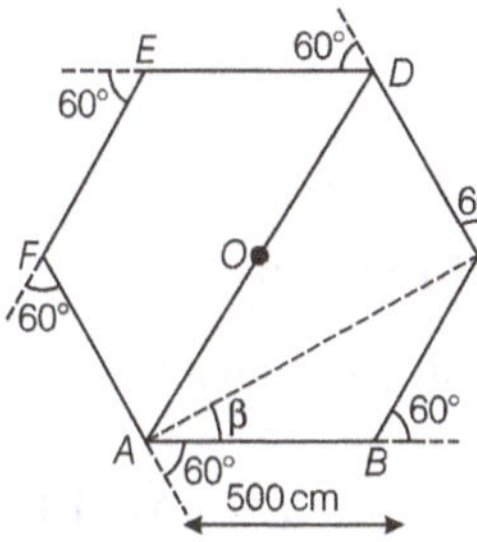

Displacement of the motorist at the third turn = AD [1/2]

$$= AO + OD = 500 + 500 = 1000 \text{ m}$$

Total path length $= AB + BC + CD$

$$= 500 + 500 + 500 = 1500 \text{ m}$$

$$\therefore \frac{\text{Magnitude of displacement}}{\text{Total path length}} = \frac{1000}{1500} = \frac{2}{3} = 0.67$$ [1/2]

At the sixth turn motorist is at the starting point A.

$\therefore$ Displacement of the motorist at the sixth turn = 0

Total path length $= AB + BC + CD + DE + EF + FA$

$$= 500 + 500 + 500 + 500 + 500 + 500 = 3000 \text{ m}$$

$$\therefore \frac{\text{Magnitude of displacement}}{\text{Total path length}} = \frac{0}{3000} = 0$$ [1]

At the eighth turn, the motorist is at point C.

$\therefore$ Displacement of the motorist = AC

Using triangle law of vector addition,

$$AC = \sqrt{AB^2 + BC^2 + 2AB \cdot BC \cos 60°}$$

$$= \sqrt{(500)^2 + (500)^2 + 2 \times 500 \times 500 \times \frac{1}{2}}$$

$$= \sqrt{3 \times (500)^2} = 500\sqrt{3} \text{ m}$$

$$AC = 500 \times 1.732 \text{ m} = 866 \text{ m}$$ [1]

If it is inclined at an angle β from the direction of **AB**,

$$\text{then } \tan\beta = \frac{500 \sin 60°}{500 + 500 \cos 60°} = \frac{500 \times \frac{\sqrt{3}}{2}}{500 + 500 \times \frac{1}{2}}$$

$$= \frac{500 \times \frac{\sqrt{3}}{2}}{500\left(1 + \frac{1}{2}\right)} = \frac{\frac{\sqrt{3}}{2}}{\frac{3}{2}} = \frac{1}{\sqrt{3}} = \tan 30°$$

or $\beta = 30°$ [1/2]

$\therefore$ Displacement of the motorist at the end of eighth turn is 866 m making an angle 30° with the initial direction of motion.

Total path length $= 8 \times 500 = 4000$ m

$$\therefore \frac{\text{Magnitude of displacement}}{\text{Total path length}} = \frac{500\sqrt{3}}{4000} = \frac{\sqrt{3}}{8} = 0.22$$ [1]

39. (i) Magnitude of $(\hat{i} + \hat{j}) = \sqrt{(1)^2 + (1)^2} = \sqrt{2}$

If vector $(\hat{\mathbf{i}} + \hat{\mathbf{j}})$ makes an angle θ, with the X-axis, then

$$\tan\theta = \frac{A_y}{A_x} = \frac{1}{1} = 1 = \tan 45° \text{ or } \theta = 45°$$

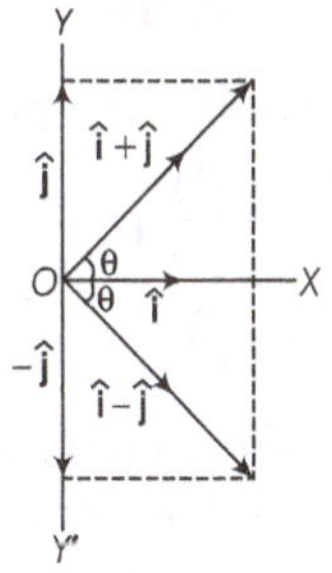

[1]

(ii) Magnitude of

$$(\hat{\mathbf{i}} - \hat{\mathbf{j}}) = \sqrt{(1)^2 + (-1)^2} = \sqrt{2}$$

If vector $(\hat{\mathbf{i}} - \hat{\mathbf{j}})$ makes an angle θ, with X-axis, then

$$\tan\theta = \frac{A_y}{A_x} = \frac{(-1)}{1} = -1$$

$$= -\tan 45°$$

$\Rightarrow \quad \theta = -45°$ with $\hat{\mathbf{i}}$

Hence, vector $(\hat{\mathbf{i}} - \hat{\mathbf{j}})$ makes an angle of 45° from X-axis in negative direction. [1]

(iii) To determine the component of $\mathbf{A} = 2\hat{\mathbf{i}} + 3\hat{\mathbf{j}}$ in the direction of $(\hat{i} + \hat{j})$.

Let $\quad \mathbf{B} = (\hat{\mathbf{i}} + \hat{\mathbf{j}})$

$$\mathbf{A} \cdot \mathbf{B} = AB \cos\theta = (A \cos\theta) \cdot B$$

or $\quad A \cos\theta = \dfrac{\mathbf{A} \cdot \mathbf{B}}{B}$

∴ Magnitude of the component of **A** in the direction of

$$\mathbf{B} = A\cos\theta = \frac{\mathbf{A}\cdot\mathbf{B}}{B} = \frac{(2\hat{\mathbf{i}}+3\hat{\mathbf{j}})\cdot(\hat{\mathbf{i}}+\hat{\mathbf{j}})}{\sqrt{(1)^2+(1)^2}}$$

$$= \frac{2\hat{\mathbf{i}}\cdot\hat{\mathbf{i}}+3\hat{\mathbf{j}}\cdot\hat{\mathbf{j}}}{\sqrt{2}} = \frac{2+3}{\sqrt{2}} = \frac{5}{\sqrt{2}}$$ [1]

Unit vector along $(\hat{\mathbf{i}}+\hat{\mathbf{j}})$, $\hat{\mathbf{n}} = \frac{(\hat{\mathbf{i}}+\hat{\mathbf{j}})}{|\hat{\mathbf{i}}+\hat{\mathbf{j}}|} = \frac{(\hat{\mathbf{i}}+\hat{\mathbf{j}})}{\sqrt{2}}$

Component of **A** along $(\hat{\mathbf{i}}+\hat{\mathbf{j}})$

= Magnitude of the component of **A** along $(\hat{\mathbf{i}}+\hat{\mathbf{j}})\cdot\hat{\mathbf{n}}$

$$= \frac{5}{\sqrt{2}}\cdot\frac{(\hat{\mathbf{i}}+\hat{\mathbf{j}})}{\sqrt{2}} = \frac{5}{2}(\hat{\mathbf{i}}+\hat{\mathbf{j}})$$ [1/2]

(iv) Magnitude of the component of **A** in the direction of

$$(\hat{\mathbf{i}}-\hat{\mathbf{j}}) = \frac{(2\hat{\mathbf{i}}+3\hat{\mathbf{j}})\cdot(\hat{\mathbf{i}}-\hat{\mathbf{j}})}{|\hat{\mathbf{i}}-\hat{\mathbf{j}}|} = \frac{2\hat{\mathbf{i}}\cdot\hat{\mathbf{i}}-3\hat{\mathbf{j}}\cdot\hat{\mathbf{j}}}{\sqrt{(1)^2+(-1)^2}}$$

$$= \frac{2-3}{\sqrt{2}} = -\frac{1}{\sqrt{2}}$$ [1/2]

Unit vector along $(\hat{\mathbf{i}}-\hat{\mathbf{j}})$

$$\hat{\mathbf{n}} = \frac{(\hat{\mathbf{i}}-\hat{\mathbf{j}})}{|\hat{\mathbf{i}}-\hat{\mathbf{j}}|} = \frac{(\hat{\mathbf{i}}-\hat{\mathbf{j}})}{\sqrt{2}}$$

∴ Component of **A** along $(\hat{\mathbf{i}}-\hat{\mathbf{j}})$

= Magnitude of the component of **A** along $(\mathbf{i}-\mathbf{j})\cdot\hat{\mathbf{n}}$

$$= -\frac{1}{\sqrt{2}}\cdot\frac{(\hat{\mathbf{i}}-\hat{\mathbf{j}})}{\sqrt{2}} = -\frac{1}{2}(\hat{\mathbf{i}}-\hat{\mathbf{j}})$$ [1]

TOPIC 02 Projectile Motion

Velocity in Two Dimensional Motion

Velocity can be expressed in the component form as

$$\mathbf{v}_{av} = \frac{\Delta x}{\Delta t}\hat{\mathbf{i}} + \frac{\Delta y}{\Delta t}\hat{\mathbf{j}}$$

$$= v_x\hat{\mathbf{i}} + v_y\hat{\mathbf{j}}$$

where, v_x and v_y are the components of velocity along x-direction and y-direction, respectively.

The magnitude of $\mathbf{v}_{av}$ is given by

$$v_{av} = \sqrt{v_x^2+v_y^2}$$

and the direction of $\mathbf{v}_{av}$ is given by angle θ

$$\tan\theta = \frac{v_y}{v_x}$$

⇒ Direction of average velocity, $\theta = \tan^{-1}\left(\frac{v_y}{v_x}\right)$

Instantaneous Velocity

The velocity at an instant of time (t) is known as **instantaneous velocity.**

Instantaneous velocity, $\mathbf{v}_i = \lim_{\Delta t\to 0}\frac{\Delta\mathbf{r}}{\Delta t} = \frac{d\mathbf{r}}{dt}$

Acceleration in Two Dimensional Motion

Average acceleration in component form can be expressed as

$$\text{Average acceleration, } \mathbf{a}_{av} = \frac{\Delta \mathrm{v}}{\Delta t} = \frac{\Delta v_x\hat{\mathbf{i}}+\Delta v_y\hat{\mathbf{j}}}{\Delta t}$$

$$= \frac{\Delta v_x}{\Delta t}\hat{\mathbf{i}} + \frac{\Delta v_y}{\Delta t}\hat{\mathbf{j}}$$

Average acceleration, $\mathbf{a}_{av} = a_x\hat{\mathbf{i}} + a_y\hat{\mathbf{j}}$

Which is expressed in component form.

In terms of x and y, a_x and a_y can be expressed as

$$a_x = \frac{d}{dt}\left(\frac{dx}{dt}\right) = \frac{d^2x}{dt^2} \text{ and } a_y = \frac{d}{dt}\left(\frac{dy}{dt}\right) = \frac{d^2y}{dt^2}$$

Instantaneous Acceleration

Instantaneous acceleration, $\mathbf{a}_i = a_x\hat{\mathbf{i}} + a_y\hat{\mathbf{j}}$

where, $a_x = \frac{dv_x}{dt}$, $a_y = \frac{dv_y}{dt}$

The magnitude of instantaneous acceleration is given by

$$a_i = \sqrt{a_x^2+a_y^2}$$

Example 1 A train is moving with a velocity of 30 km/h due West and a car is moving with a velocity of 40 km/h due North. What is the velocity of car as appear to a passenger in the train?

Sol. Given, $\mathbf{v}_T = 30$ km/h due West, $\mathbf{v}_C = 40$ km/h due North,

$\mathbf{v}_{CT} = ?, \theta = ?$

According to question,

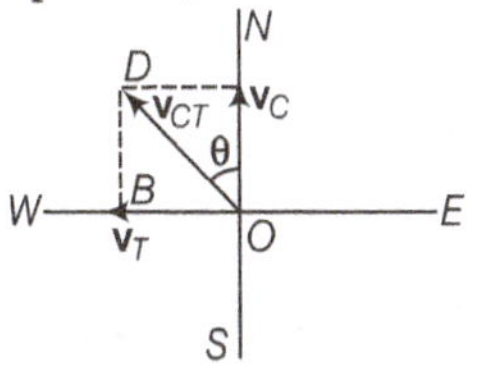

In the figure,

$$\mathbf{v}_{CT} = OD = \sqrt{OB^2 + BD^2} = \sqrt{v_T^2 + v_C^2}$$

Then, $$\mathbf{v}_{CT} = \sqrt{(30)^2 + (40)^2} = \sqrt{900 + 1600} = 50 \text{ km/h}$$

$$\tan\theta = \frac{OB}{BD} = \frac{v_T}{v_C} \Rightarrow \tan\theta = \frac{30}{40}$$

$$\theta = \tan^{-1}\left(\frac{30}{40}\right) = 36°52' \text{ West of North}$$

Example 2 A particle starts from origin at $t = 0$ with a velocity $5\hat{\mathbf{i}}$ m/s and moves in *xy*-plane under action of a force which produces a constant acceleration of $(3\hat{\mathbf{i}} + 2\hat{\mathbf{j}})$ m/s^2.

(i) What is the *y*-coordinate of the particle at the instant its *x*-coordinate is 84 m?

(ii) What is the speed of the particle at this time? **NCERT**

Sol. Given, $v_0 = 5\hat{\mathbf{i}}$ m/s, $a = 3\hat{\mathbf{i}} + 2\hat{\mathbf{j}}$ m/s^2

$y(t) = ?$, $x(t) = 84$ m (ii) Speed $v = ?$

(i) Then, $s(t) = v_0 t + \frac{1}{2}at^2$ and $v = \sqrt{v_x^2 + v_y^2}$

$$s(t) = 5\hat{\mathbf{i}}\,t + \frac{1}{2}(3\hat{\mathbf{i}} + 2\hat{\mathbf{j}})t^2 = \left(5t + \frac{3}{2}t^2\right)\hat{\mathbf{i}} + t^2\hat{\mathbf{j}}$$

On comparing, $x(t) = 5t + \frac{3}{2}t^2 = 84$

On solving it, we get

$$t = 6, \quad y(t) = 1\,t^2 = 36 \text{ m}$$

(ii) The speed of the particle can be find by differentiating the position vector w.r.t. time.

If $x(t) = 84$ m, then $t = 6$ s

$\therefore \quad y(6) = 36$ m

$$v = \frac{dy}{dt} = \frac{d(5t + \frac{3}{2}t^2)\hat{\mathbf{i}} + t^2\hat{\mathbf{j}}}{dt} = (5 + 3t)\hat{\mathbf{i}} + 2t\hat{\mathbf{j}}$$

At $\quad t = 6\text{s}, \quad v = 23\hat{\mathbf{i}} + 12\hat{\mathbf{j}}$

$\therefore \quad v = \sqrt{(23)^2 + (12)^2} = 25.94$ m/s

Example 3 A particle is moving Eastwards with a velocity of 5 m/s in 10 second, the velocity changes to 5 m/s Northwards. Find the average accelaration of the particle in this time interval.

Sol.

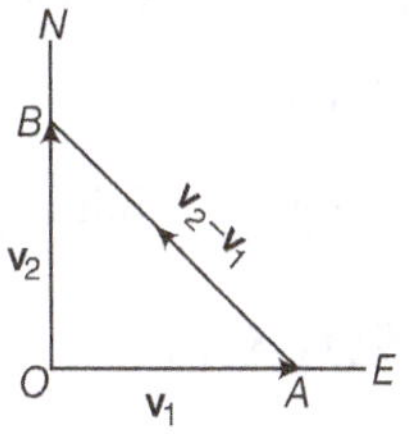

According to triangle law of vector addition,

$$\mathbf{OA} + \mathbf{AB} = \mathbf{OB}$$

$$\mathbf{AB} = \mathbf{OB} - \mathbf{OA} = \mathbf{v}_2 - \mathbf{v}_1$$

= Change in velocity

$$\therefore \quad |\mathbf{v}_2 - \mathbf{v}_1| = \mathbf{AB} = \sqrt{(\mathbf{OA})^2 + (\mathbf{OB})^2}$$

$$= \sqrt{(5)^2 + (5)^2}$$

$$= 5\sqrt{2} \text{ m/s}$$

Hence, average acceleration $= \dfrac{|\mathbf{v}_2 - \mathbf{v}_1|}{t}$

$$= \frac{5\sqrt{2}}{10} = \frac{1}{\sqrt{2}} \text{ m/s}^2$$

Along North-West direction.

Example 4 The position of a particle is given by

$$\mathbf{r} = 3.0\,t\,\hat{\mathbf{i}} - 2.0\,t^2\hat{\mathbf{j}} + 4.0\,\hat{\mathbf{k}}$$

where, t is in seconds and the coefficients have the proper units for $\mathbf{r}$ to be in metres.

(i) Find $v(t)$ and $a(t)$ of the particles.

(ii) Find the magnitude and direction of $v(t)$ at $t = 2.0$ s. **[NCERT]**

Sol. Position of particle, $\mathbf{r} = 3.0\,t\,\hat{\mathbf{i}} - 2.0t^2\hat{\mathbf{j}} + 4.0\,\hat{\mathbf{k}}$

(i) $$\mathbf{v}(t) = \frac{dr}{dt} = \frac{d}{dt}(3.0\,t\,\hat{\mathbf{i}} - 2.0t^2\,\hat{\mathbf{j}} + 4.0\,\hat{\mathbf{k}})$$

$$= 3.0\,\hat{\mathbf{i}} - 4.0t\,\hat{\mathbf{j}}$$

$$\mathbf{a}(t) = \frac{dv}{dt} = -4.0\hat{\mathbf{j}} \text{ ms}^{-2}$$

(ii) At $t = 2.0$ s

$$\mathbf{v}(t) = 3.0\,\hat{\mathbf{i}} - 8.0\,\hat{\mathbf{j}}$$

$$v = \sqrt{v_x^2 + v_y^2} = \sqrt{(3.0)^2 + (-8)^2}$$

$$= \sqrt{73} = 8.54 \text{ ms}^{-1}$$

$$\theta = \tan^{-1}\left(\frac{v_y}{v_x}\right) = \tan^{-1}\left(\frac{-8}{3}\right)$$

$$= -\tan^{-1}(2.667) = -69.5°$$

$\theta = 69.5°$ below *X*-axis

Equations of Motion for Motion in a Plane

For motion in a plane, equations of motion can be given as

(i) $v_x = v_{0x} + a_x t$ and $v_y = v_{0y} + a_y t$

(ii) $r = r_0 + v_0 t + \frac{1}{2}at^2$, $x = x_0 + v_0 t + \frac{1}{2}a_x t^2$

(iii) $y = y_0 + v_0 t + \frac{1}{2}a_y t^2$

Here, v_0 = initial velocity, r_0 = initial position.

Projectile Motion

Projectile motion is a form of motion in which an object or particle is thrown with some initial velocity near the earth's surface and it moves along a curved path under the action of gravity alone. The path followed by a projectile is called its **trajectory**. An object that is in flight after being thrown is called projectile.

(i) A tennis ball or a baseball in a flight.

(ii) A bullet fired from a rifle.

(iii) A body dropped from the window of a moving train.

(iv) A jet of water flowing from a hole near the bottom of water tank.

(v) A javelin thrown by an athlete.

Mathematical Analysis of Projectile Motion

Let OX be a horizontal line on the ground, OY be a vertical line perpendicular to ground and O be the origin for XY-axes on a plane.

Suppose an object is projected from point O with velocity (u), making an angle (θ) with the horizontal direction OX, such that $x_0 = 0$ and $y_0 = 0$ when $t = 0$.

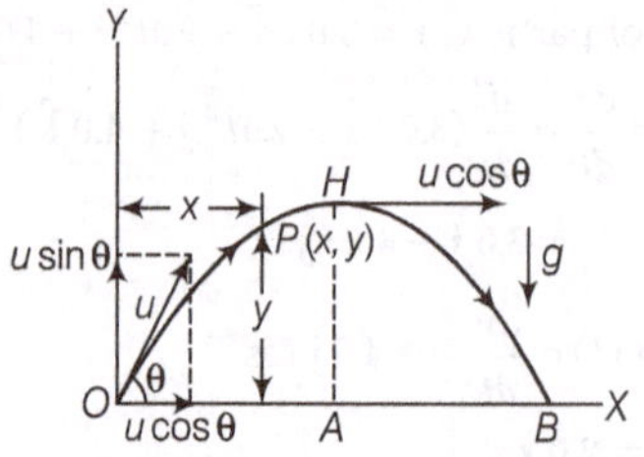

A projectile motion

While resolving velocity (u) into two components, we get (a) $u\cos\theta$ along OX and (b) $u\sin\theta$ along OY.

As the horizontal component of velocity ($u\cos\theta$) is constant throughout the motion, so there is a constant acceleration and hence force is in the horizontal direction, if air resistance is assumed to be zero. As the vertical components of velocity ($u\sin\theta$) decreases continuously with height, from O to H, due to downward force of gravity and becomes zero at H.

At point H, the object has only horizontal component velocity ($u\cos\theta$). It attains a maximum height at AH. OB is the maximum horizontal range.

Equation of Path of a Projectile

Suppose at any time t_1, the object reaches at point $P(x, y)$.

So, x = horizontal distance travelled by object in time t.

y = vertical distance travelled by object in time t.

Motion Along Horizontal Direction (OX)

The velocity of an object in horizontal direction i.e. OX is constant, so the acceleration a_x in horizontal direction is zero.

$\therefore$ Position of the object at time t along horizontal direction is given by $x = x_0 + u_x t + \frac{1}{2}a_x t^2$

But $x_0 = 0, u_x = u\cos\theta, a_x = 0$ and $t = t$

$\therefore \quad x = u\cos\theta\, t$

$$\Rightarrow \quad \boxed{\text{Time, } t = \frac{x}{u\cos\theta}} \quad \ldots\text{(i)}$$

Motion Along Vertical Direction (OY)

The vertical velocity of the object is decreasing from O to H due to gravity, so acceleration a_y is $-g$.

$\therefore$ Position of the object at any time t along the vertical direction i.e. OY is given by

$$y = y_0 + u_y t + \frac{1}{2}a_y t^2$$

But $\quad y_0 = 0, u_y = u\sin\theta, a_y = -g$

and $\quad t = t$

So, $\quad y = u\sin\theta\, t + \frac{1}{2}(-g)t^2$

$$= u\sin\theta\, t - \frac{1}{2}gt^2 \quad \ldots\text{(ii)}$$

Substituting the value of t from Eq. (i) in Eq. (ii), we get

$$y = u\sin\theta\left(\frac{x}{u\cos\theta}\right) - \frac{1}{2}g\left(\frac{x}{u\cos\theta}\right)^2$$

$$= x\tan\theta - \frac{1}{2}g\left(\frac{x}{u\cos\theta}\right)^2$$

$$\boxed{\text{Total vertical distance, } y = x\tan\theta - \left(\frac{1}{2}\frac{g}{u^2\cos^2\theta}\right)x^2}$$

This equation represents a parabola and is known as equation of trajectory of a projectile..

Note The path of a projectile projected at some angle with the horizontal (i.e. ground) is a parabolic path.

Time of Flight

It is defined as the total time for which projectile is in flight i.e. time during the motion of projectile from O to B. It is denoted by T.

Total time of flight consists of two parts such as

(a) Time taken by an object to go from point O to H. It is also known as **time of ascent** (t).

(b) Time taken by an object to go from point H to B. It is also known as **time of descent** (t).

Total time can be expressed as

$$T = t + t = 2t \Rightarrow t = \frac{T}{2}$$

The vertical component of velocity of object becomes zero at the highest point H.

Let us consider vertical upward motion of an object from O to H, we have

$$u_y = u\sin\theta,\ a_y = -g,\ t = \frac{T}{2} \text{ and } v_y = 0$$

Since, $v_y = u_y + a_y t \Rightarrow 0 = u\sin\theta - g\frac{T}{2}$

$$\text{Total time of flight, } T = \frac{2u\sin\theta}{g}$$

Note For a projectile, time of ascent equals time of descent.

Maximum Height of a Projectile

It is defined as the maximum vertical height attained by an object above the point of projection during its flight. It is denoted by H.

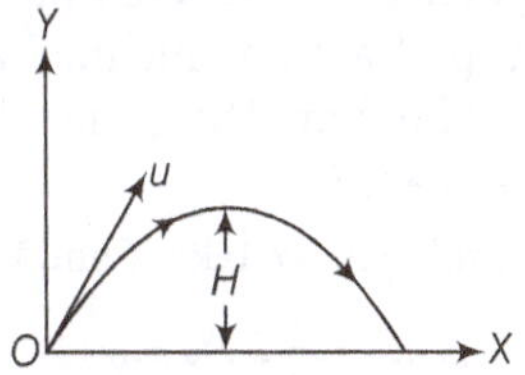

Maximum height of motion

Let us consider the vertical upward motion of the object from O to H.

We have,

$$u_y = u\sin\theta,\ a_y = -g, y_0 = 0,\ y = H,\ t = \frac{T}{2} = \frac{u\sin\theta}{g},$$

Using this relation, $y = y_0 + u_y t + \frac{1}{2}a_y t^2$

We have, $H = 0 + u\sin\theta\frac{u\sin\theta}{g} + \frac{1}{2}(-g)\left(\frac{u\sin\theta}{g}\right)^2$

$$= \frac{u^2}{g}\sin^2\theta - \frac{1}{2}\frac{u^2\sin^2\theta}{g}$$

$$\text{Maximum height, } H = \frac{u^2\sin^2\theta}{2g}$$

Horizontal Range of a Projectile

The horizontal range of the projectile is defined as the horizontal distance covered by the projectile during its time of flight. It is denoted by R.

If the object having uniform velocity $u\cos\theta$ (i.e. horizontal component) and the total time of flight T, then the horizontal range covered by the objective,

$$R = u\cos\theta \times T = u\cos\theta \times 2u\frac{\sin\theta}{g}$$

$$= \frac{u^2}{g}2\sin\theta\cos\theta$$

$$\text{Horizontal range, } R = \frac{u^2\sin 2\theta}{g}$$

$[\because \sin 2\theta = 2\sin\theta\cos\theta]$

The horizontal range will be maximum, if

$\sin 2\theta = \text{maximum} = 1$

$\sin 2\theta = \sin 90° \text{ or } \theta = 45°$

$$\therefore \quad \text{Maximum horizontal range, } R_m = \frac{u^2}{g}$$

Note Horizontal range, $R = \frac{u^2\sin 2\theta}{g}$ ...(i)

Put $90° - \theta$ in Eq. (i) in the place of θ, we get

$$R' = \frac{u^2\sin[2(90° - \theta)]}{g}$$

$$= \frac{u^2\sin(180° - 2\theta)}{g}$$

$$R' = \frac{u^2\sin 2\theta}{g} \quad [\because \sin(180° - 2\theta) = \sin 2\theta] \text{...(ii)}$$

From Eqs. (i) and (ii), it is clear that, if we through a body either at an angle of θ or $90° - \theta$, then body will cover same horizontal range.

Example 5 A soccer player kicks a ball at an angle of 30° with an initial speed of 20 m/s. Assuming that the ball travels in a vertical plane. Calculate (i) the time at which the ball reaches the highest point, (ii) the maximum height reached, (iii) the horizontal range of the ball and (iv) the time for which the ball is in the air. $g = 10\ \text{m/s}^2$.

Sol. Given, $\theta = 30°, u = 20\ \text{m/s}, g = 10\ \text{m/s}^2$

(i) $t = ?$ (ii) $H = ?$

(iii) $R = ?$ (iv) $T = ?$

(i) $t = \frac{T}{2} = \frac{u \sin\theta}{g} = \frac{20 \times \sin 30°}{10} = 2 \times \frac{1}{2} = 1\ \text{s}$

(ii) $H = \frac{u^2 \sin^2\theta}{2g} = \frac{(20)^2 \times \sin^2 30°}{2 \times 10} = 5\ \text{m}$

(iii) $R = \frac{u^2 \sin 2\theta}{g} = \frac{(20)^2 \times \sin 2 \times 30°}{10} = 34.64\ \text{m}$

(iv) $T = \frac{2u \sin\theta}{g} = \frac{2 \times 20 \times \sin 30°}{10} = 2\ \text{s}$

Example 6 A cricket ball is thrown at a speed of $28\ \text{ms}^{-1}$ in a direction 30° above the horizontal. Calculate

(i) the maximum height

(ii) the time taken by the ball to return to the same level and

(iii) the distance from the thrower to the point where the ball returns to the same level. **[NCERT]**

Sol. (i) The maximum height attained by the ball is

$$H_m = \frac{(v_0 \sin\theta_0)^2}{2g}$$

$$= \frac{(28 \sin 30°)^2}{2(9.8)} = \frac{14 \times 14}{2 \times 9.8} = 10.0\ \text{m}$$

(ii) The time taken by the ball to return the same level is

$$T = (2v_0 \sin\theta_0)/g = (2 \times 28 \times \sin 30°)/9.8$$

$$= 28/9.8 = 2.9\ \text{s}$$

(iii) The distance from the thrower to the point where the ball returns to the same level is

$$R = \frac{(v_0^2 \sin 2\theta_0)}{g} = \frac{28 \times 28 \times \sin 60°}{9.8} = 69\ \text{m}$$

Projectile Fired at an Angle with the Vertical

Let a particle be projected vertically with an angle θ with vertical and its muzzle speed (i.e. speed of projection) is u. The projectile has two components of its velocity at all the points during its motion.

The components are along X-axis (horizontal) and along Y-axis (vertical). Clearly, the angle made by the velocity of projectile at point of projection is $(90° - \theta)$ with the horizontal. In this case

(i) Time of flight $= \frac{2u \sin(90° - \theta)}{g} = \frac{2u}{g} \cos\theta$

(ii) Maximum height $= \frac{u^2 \sin^2(90° - \theta)}{2g} = \frac{u^2 \cos^2\theta}{2g}$

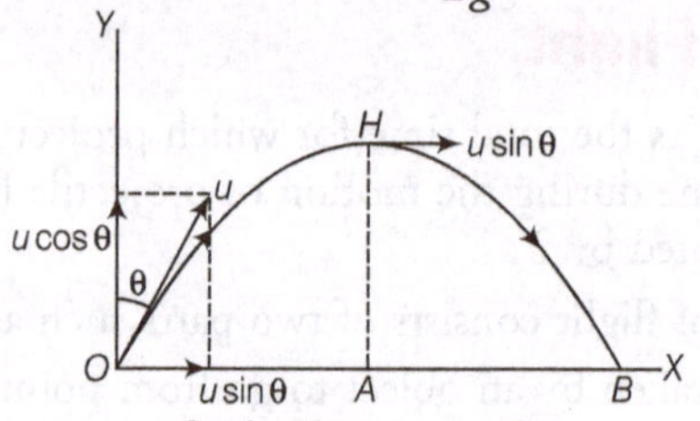

Angle after projection

(iii) Horizontal range $= \frac{u^2}{g} \sin 2(90° - \theta)$

$$= \frac{u^2}{g} \sin(180° - 2\theta) = \frac{u^2}{g} \sin 2\theta$$

(iv) Path of projectile

$$y = x \tan(90° - \theta) - \frac{1}{2} \frac{gx^2}{u^2 \cos^2(90° - \theta)}$$

$$= x \cot\theta - \frac{gx^2}{2u^2 \sin^2\theta}$$

(v) Velocity at any time, t

$$= \sqrt{[u\cos(90 - \theta)]^2 + [u\sin(90 - \theta) - gt]^2}$$

$$= \sqrt{u^2 + g^2t^2 - 2ugt \sin(90° - \theta)}$$

$$= \sqrt{u^2 + g^2t^2 - 2u\,gt \cos\theta}$$

This velocity makes an angle β with the horizontal direction, then

$$\tan\beta = \frac{u \sin(90° - \theta) - gt}{u \cos(90° - \theta)} = \frac{u \cos\theta - gt}{u \sin\theta}$$

Example 7 A particle is projected horizontally with a speed v from the top of a plane inclined at angle θ with the horizontal. How far from the point of projection will the particle hit the plane?

Sol. To solve this problem, we take X and Y-axes as shown in figure.

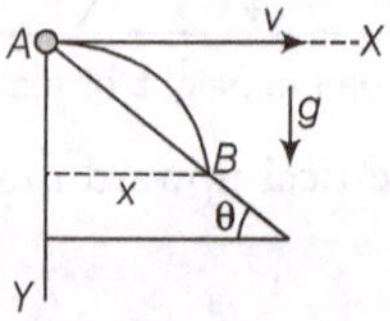

Consider the motion of particle from A to B.

Motion of particle along X-axis is given by

$$x = ut \quad \text{...(i)}$$

where, t = time to reach the particle from A to B.
Motion of particle along Y-axis is given by

$$y = \frac{1}{2}gt^2 \quad \text{...(ii)}$$

Eliminating t from Eqs. (i) and (ii), we get

$$y = \frac{1}{2}g\frac{x^2}{u^2} \text{ and } y = x\tan\theta$$

Thus, $\frac{gx^2}{2u^2} = x\tan\theta$, giving, $x = 0$ or $\frac{2u^2\tan\theta}{g}$,

$x = 0$ at point A and point B correspond to $x = \frac{2u^2\tan\theta}{g}$,

then $$y = x\tan\theta = \frac{2u^2\tan^2\theta}{g}$$

Now, $$AB = \sqrt{x^2 + y^2}$$

$$= \frac{2u^2}{g}\tan\theta\sqrt{1+\tan^2\theta} = \frac{2u^2}{g}\tan\theta\sec\theta$$

Uniform Circular Motion

When an object follows a circular path at a constant speed, the motion of the object is called **uniform circular motion**. The word uniform refers to the speed which is uniform (constant) throughout the motion. Although the speed does not vary, the particle is accelerating because the velocity changes its direction at every point on the circular track.

The figure shows a particle P which moves along a circular track of radius r with a uniform speed u.

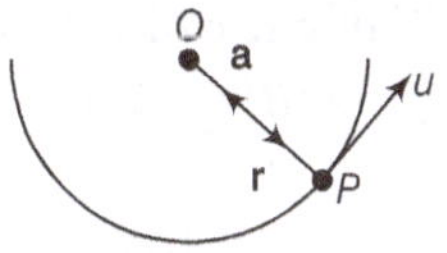

A circular motion

Examples

(i) Motion of the tip of the second hand of a clock.
(ii) Motion of a point on the rim of a wheel rotating uniformly.

Terms Related to Circular Motion

Angular Displacement

It is defined as the the angle traced out by the radius vector at the centre of the circular path in the given time. It is denoted by $\Delta\theta$ and expressed in radian. It is a dimensionless quantity. It is a vector quantity, direction is given by Right-hand rule.

Angular Velocity

It is defined as the time rate of change of its angular position, denoted by ω and is measured in radian per second. Its dimensional formula is $[M^0L^0T^{-1}]$. It is a vector quantity.

If a point object moving along a circular path, with centre (i.e. axis of rotation) at O. Let the object move from P to Q in a small time interval Δt, where $\angle POQ = \Delta\theta$.

Now, angular velocity $\omega = \frac{\text{Angle traced}}{\text{Time taken}} = \lim_{\Delta t \to 0}\frac{\Delta\theta}{\Delta t} = \frac{d\theta}{dt}$

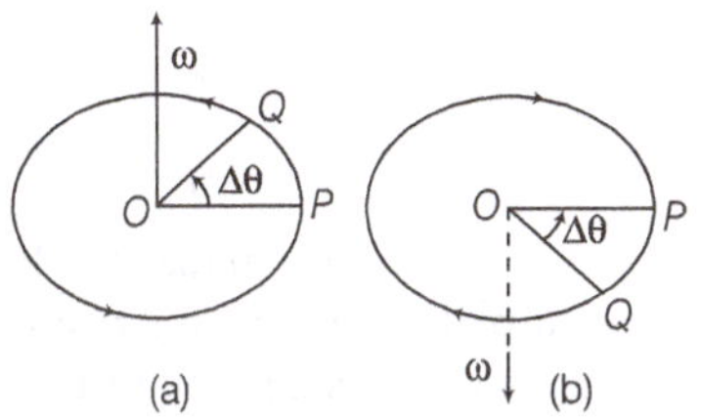

Time Period

It is defined as the time taken by a particle to complete one revolution along its circular path. It is denoted by T and is measured in second.

Frequency

It is defined as the number of revolutions completed per unit time. It is denoted by f and is measured in Hz.

Angular Acceleration

It is defined as the time rate of change of angular velocity of a particle. It is measured in radian per second square and has dimensions $[M^0L^0T^{-2}]$.

It is denoted by α, where

$$\alpha = \lim_{\Delta t \to 0}\frac{\Delta\omega}{\Delta t} = \frac{d\omega}{dt}$$

Relation between Time Period and Frequency

Let f be the frequency of an object in circular motion, then the object will complete one revolution in $\frac{1}{f}$ second which is known as time period (T).

$$\boxed{\text{Time period, } T = \frac{1}{f}}$$

Relation among Angular Velocity, Frequency and Time Period

Suppose a point object illustrating a uniform circular motion with frequency (f) and time period (T). When the object completes one revolution, the angle traced at its axis of circular motion is 2π in radian.

If time $t = T, \theta = 2\pi$ radian.

Thus, the angular velocity ω is given by

$$\text{Angular velocity, } \omega = \frac{\theta}{t} = \frac{2\pi}{T} = 2\pi f$$

Relation between Linear Velocity (v) and Angular Velocity (ω)

Suppose the particle moving on circular track of radius r is showing angular displacement $\Delta\theta$ in Δt time and in this time period, it covers a distance Δs along the circular track, then

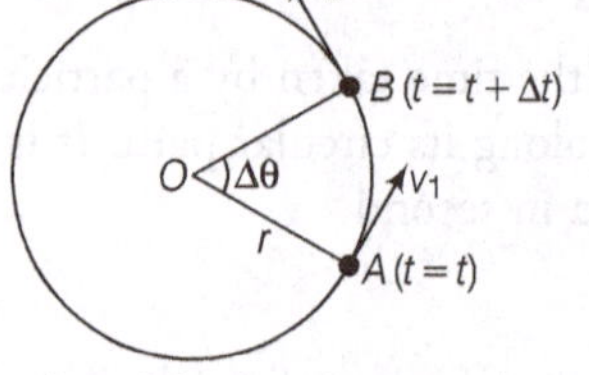

Representation of linear velocity and angular velocity

$$\omega = \frac{\Delta\theta}{\Delta t} \quad \ldots\text{(i)}$$

and $$v = \frac{\Delta s}{\Delta t} \quad \ldots\text{(ii)}$$

But $$\Delta s = r\,\Delta\theta \quad \ldots\text{(iii)}$$

(Since, angle = arc/radius)

From above three equations, we get

$$\text{Linear velocity, } v = r\frac{\Delta\theta}{\Delta t} = r\,\omega$$

Centripetal Acceleration

The acceleration associated with uniform circular motion is called a **centripetal acceleration.** Consider a particle of mass (m) moving with a constant speed (v) and uniform angular velocity (ω) on a circular path of radius (r) with centre at O. Suppose at any time t, the particle be at P, where $\mathbf{OP} = r_1$ and at time $t + \Delta t$ the particle be at Q, where $\mathbf{OQ} = r_2$ and $\angle POQ = \Delta\theta$ as shown in the figure. But $|\mathbf{r}_1| = |\mathbf{r}_2| = r$

Angular speed of the particle, $$\omega = \frac{\Delta\theta}{\Delta t} \quad \ldots\text{(i)}$$

Let $\mathbf{v}_1$ and $\mathbf{v}_2$ be the velocity vectors of the particle at locations P and Q respectively. The magnitude and direction of $\mathbf{v}_1$ and $\mathbf{v}_2$ is represented by the tangent **PA** and **QB**.

Since the particle is moving with a uniform speed (v), the length of tangents at P and Q are equal

i.e. $$|\mathbf{PA}| = |\mathbf{QB}| = |\mathbf{v}|$$

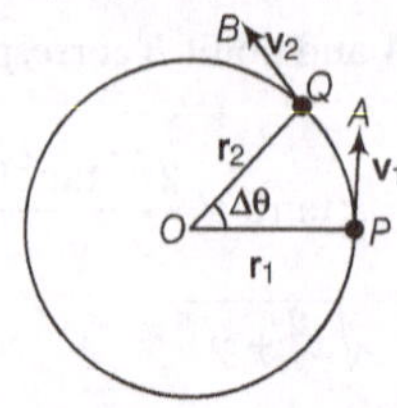

Centripetal acceleration

These two vectors have been separately shown in the following figures

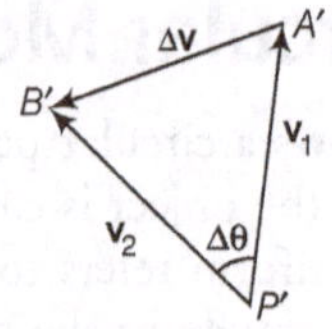

A triangle made of vectors

From triangle law of vectors, we have

$$\mathbf{P'A'} + \mathbf{A'B'} = \mathbf{P'B'}$$

$$\Rightarrow \quad \mathbf{A'B'} = \mathbf{P'B'} - \mathbf{P'A'} = \mathbf{v}_2 - \mathbf{v}_1 = \Delta\mathbf{v}$$

If $\Delta t \to 0$, then A' lies close to B'. Then, $A'B'$ can be taken as an arc $A'B'$ of circle of radius $P'A' = |\mathbf{v}|$

$$\therefore \quad \Delta\theta = \frac{A'B'}{P'A'} = \frac{|\Delta\mathbf{v}|}{|\mathbf{v}|}$$

From Eq. (i), we have $\omega\Delta t = \dfrac{|\Delta\mathbf{v}|}{|\mathbf{v}|} \Rightarrow \omega|\mathbf{v}| = \dfrac{|\Delta\mathbf{v}|}{\Delta t}$

$$\Rightarrow \quad \frac{|\Delta\mathbf{v}|}{\Delta t} = (\omega r)\,\omega = \omega^2 r \qquad [\because v = \omega r]$$

As $\Delta t \to 0$, then $\dfrac{|\Delta\mathbf{v}|}{\Delta t}$ represents the magnitude of centripetal acceleration at P which is given by

$$|\mathbf{a}| = \frac{|\Delta\mathbf{v}|}{\Delta t} = \omega^2 r = \left[\frac{v}{r}\right]^2 r = \frac{v^2}{r}$$

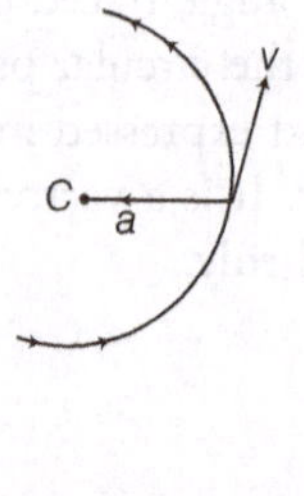

> Centripetal acceleration, $a = \dfrac{v^2}{r}$

It is towards the centre of circle.

Example 8 A body of mass 10 kg revolves in a circle of diameter 0.4 m making 1000 revolutions per minute. Calculate its linear velocity and centripetal acceleration.

Sol. $m = 10$ kg, $d = 0.4$ m, $r = 0.2$ m,

Revolutions per min, $\nu = 1000/\text{min} = \dfrac{1000}{60}$ s, linear velocity, $v = ?$, centripetal acceleration, $a = ?$

$$\omega = 2\pi\nu = 2\pi \times \frac{1000}{60} = \frac{100\,\pi}{3} \text{ rad / s}$$

$$v = r\omega = 0.2 \times \frac{100\,\pi}{3} = \frac{20\,\pi}{3} \text{ m/s}$$

$$a = r\omega^2 = 0.2 \times \left(\frac{100\,\pi}{3}\right)^2 = \frac{2000\,\pi^2}{9} \text{ m/s}^2$$

Topic Practice 2

Multiple Choice Questions

(1 Mark)

1. The direction of instantaneous velocity is shown by

(a)
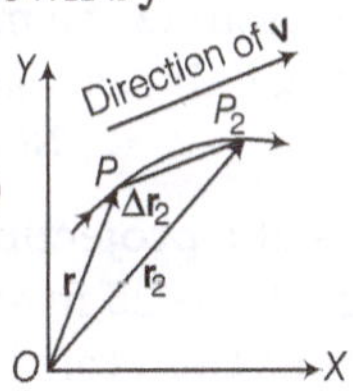

(b)
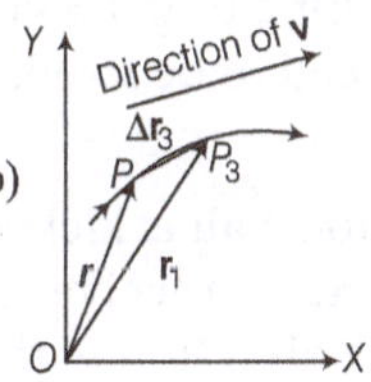

(c)
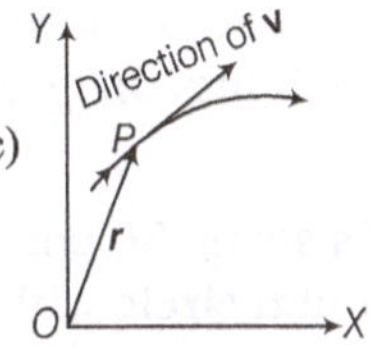

(d) None of these

2. At what point of a projectile motion, acceleration and velocity are perpendicular to each other?
   (a) At the point of projection
   (b) At the point of drop
   (c) At the top most point
   (d) Anywhere in between the point of projection and top most points

3. The displacement of a particle moving on a circular path when it makes 60° at the centre is
   (a) $2r$ (b) r
   (c) $\sqrt{2}r$ (d) None of these

4. Two cars of masses m_1 and m_2 are moving in circles of radii r_1 and r_2, respectively. Their speeds are such that they make complete circles in the same time t. The ratio of their centripetal accelerations is
   (a) $m_1r_1 : m_2r_2$ (b) $m_1 : m_2$ (c) $r_1 : r_2$ (d) 1 : 1

Very Short Answer Type Questions

(1 Mark)

5. A stone is thrown vertically upwards and then it returns to the thrower. Is it a projectile?

6. At what point in its trajectory does a projectile have its
   (i) minimum speed (ii) maximum speed?

7. A football is kicked into the air vertically upwards. What is its
   (i) acceleration and
   (ii) velocity at the highest point? **NCERT Exemplar**

8. Two bodies are projected at an angle θ and $(\pi/2 - \theta)$ to the horizontal with the same speed. Find the ratio of their time of flight.

9. Is the rocket in flight is an illustration of projectile?

10. Galileo, in his book 'Two new sciences', stated that for elevations which exceed or fall short of 45° by equal amounts, the ranges are equal. Prove this statement. **NCERT**

11. Can a body move on a curved path without having acceleration? Why?

12. The magnitude and direction of the acceleration of a body both are constant. Will the path of the body be necessarily be a straight line?

13. A stone tied at the end of string is whirled in a circle. If the string breaks, the stone flies away tangentially. Why?

Short Answer Type I Questions

(2 Marks)

14. Why is it easier for an airplane to take off into the wind?

15. How does the knowledge of projectile help, a player in the baseball game?

16. A skilled gun man always keeps his gun slightly tilted above the line of sight while shooting. Why?

Short Answer Type II Questions

(3 Marks)

17. A vector has magnitude and direction
   (i) Does it have a location in the space?
   (ii) Can it vary with time?
   (iii) Will two equal vectors **a** and **b** at different locations in space necessarily have identical physical effects? Give examples in support of your answer. **NCERT**

18. Read each statement below carefully and state with reasons, if it is true or false.
   (i) The magnitude of a vector is always a scalar.
   (ii) Each component of a vector is always a scalar.
   (iii) The average speed of a particle (defined as total path length divided by the time taken to cover the path) is either greater or equal to the magnitude of average velocity of the particle over the same interval of time. **NCERT**

19. Read each statement below carefully and state, with reasons, if it is true or false.
   (i) The net acceleration of a particle in circular motion is always along the radius of the circle towards the centre.
   (ii) The velocity vector of a particle at a point is always along the tangent to the path of the particle at that point.
   (iii) The acceleration vector of a particle in uniform circular motion averaged over one cycle is a null vector.

Long Answer Type Questions

(5 Marks)

20. (i) Show that for a projectile, the angle between the velocity and the X-axis as function of time is given by

$$\theta_{(t)} = \tan^{-1}\left(\frac{v_{oy} - gt}{v_{ox}}\right)$$

where the various symbols have their usual meanings.

(ii) Show that projection angle θ_0 for a projectile launched from the origin is given by

$$\theta_0 = \tan^{-1}\left(\frac{4h_m}{R}\right)$$

where the symbols have their usual meanings. **NCERT**

21. Derive an expression for centripetal acceleration of an object in uniform circular motion in a plane. What will be the direction of the velocity and acceleration at any instant?

22. Derive an expression for horizontal range of a projectile. Also, show that there are two angles of projection for the same horizontal range.

Numerical Problems

23. An aircraft is flying at a height of 3400 m above the ground. If the angle subtended at a ground observation point by the aircraft positions 10 s apart is 30°, what is the speed of the aircraft? **[2 M]**

24. Find the angle of projection at which horizontal range and maximum height are equal. **[2M]**

25. A cricketer can throw a ball to a maximum horizontal distance of 100 m. With the same speed, how high above the ground can the cricketer throw the same ball? **[2M]**

26. A bullet fired at an angle of 30° with the horizontal hits the ground 3 km away. By adjusting its angle of projection, can one hope to hit a target 5 km away? Assume the muzzle speed to be fixed, and neglect air resistance. **NCERT [2 M]**

27. A football is kicked 20 m/s at a projection angle of 45°. A receiver on the goal line 25 m away in the direction of the kick runs the same instant to meet the ball. What must be his speed, if he has to catch the ball before it hits the ground? **[2 M]**

28. A stone tied to the end of a string 80 cm long is whirled in a horizontal circle with a constant speed. If the stone makes 14 revolutions in 25 s, what is the magnitude and direction of acceleration of the stone? **[2 M]**

29. An aircraft executes a horizontal loop of radius 1 km with a steady speed of 900 kmh^{-1}. Compare its centripetal acceleration with the acceleration due to gravity. **[2 M]**

30. The position vector of a particle is

$$(\mathbf{r} = 2.0t\hat{\mathbf{i}} + t^2\hat{\mathbf{j}} + 3.0\hat{\mathbf{k}})$$

where t is in seconds and the coefficients have the proper units for r to be in metres. What will be the value of $\mathbf{v}(t)$ and $\mathbf{a}(t)$ for the particle and the magnitude and direction of $v(t)$ at $t = 2.0$ s? **NCERT [3 M]**

31. Figure shows a pirateship 560 m from a fort defending a harbour entrance. A defence cannon, located at sea level, fires balls at initial speed, $u_0 = 82$ m/s.

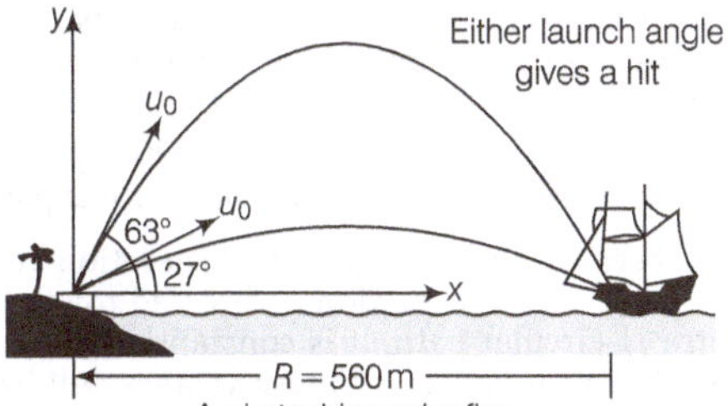

A pirateship under fire

(i) At what angle, θ_0 from the horizontal must a ball be fired to hit the ship?

(ii) What is the maximum range of the cannon balls? **[3 M]**

32. A boy stands at 78.4 m from a building and throws a ball which just enters a window 39.2 m above the ground. Calculate the velocity of projection of the ball. **[3 M]**

33. A cyclist is riding with a speed of 27 kmh^{-1}. As he approaches, a circular turn on the road of radius 80 m, he applies brakes and reduces his speed at the constant rate of 0.5 ms^{-2}. What is the magnitude and direction of the net acceleration of the cyclist on the circular turn? **NCERT [3 M]**

34. A fighter plane flying horizontally at an altitude of 1.5 km with speed 720 km h^{-1} passes directly over an anticraft gun. At what angle from the vertical should the gun be fired from the shell with muzzle speed 600 $\text{ms}^{-1}$to hit the plane?
At what minimum altitude should the pilot fly the plane to avoid being hit? (Take, $g = 10\text{ ms}^{-2}$)? **NCERT [5 M]**

Hints & Solutions

1. (c) Direction of instantaneous velocity on a radial vector curve is represented by the tangent at the point.

2. (c) At the topmost point of the projectile there is only horizontal component of velocity and acceleration due to gravity is vertically, downward, so velocity and acceleration are perpendicular to each other.

3. (b) In the figure AB is the required displacement.
In triangle OAB, $OA = OB$, and $\angle AOB = 60°$

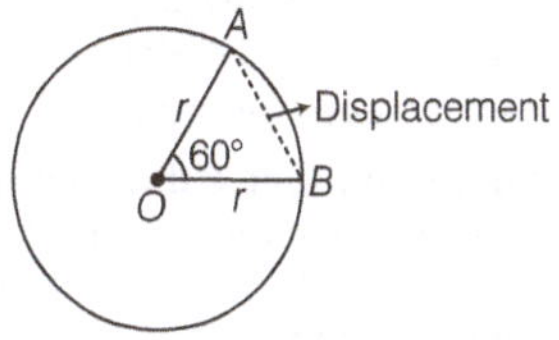

Therefore ΔAOB is a equilateral triangle.

So, $OA = OB = r = AB$.

4. (c) As, centripetal acceleration is given as, $a_c = \dfrac{v^2}{r}$

For the first body of mass m_1, $a_{c_1} = \dfrac{v_1^2}{r_1}$

For the second body of mass m_2, $a_{c_2} = \dfrac{v_2^2}{r_2}$

Also time to complete one revolution by both body is same.

Hence, $\dfrac{2\pi r_1}{v_1} = \dfrac{2\pi r_2}{v_2} \Rightarrow \dfrac{v_1}{v_2} = \dfrac{r_1}{r_2}$ ...(i)

i.e., $a_{c_1} : a_{c_2} = \dfrac{v_1^2}{r_1} \times \dfrac{r_2}{v_2^2}$ [from Eq. (i)]

$$= \frac{r_1^2}{r_2^2} \times \frac{r_2}{r_1} = \frac{r_1}{r_2} = r_1 : r_2$$

5. No, it is not a projectile, because a projectile should have two component velocities in two mutually perpendicular directions but in this case, the body has velocity only in one direction while going up or coming down.

6. (i) Projectile has minimum speed at the highest point of its trajectory.
(ii) Projectile has maximum speed at the point of projection.

7. (i) Acceleration at the highest point $= -g$

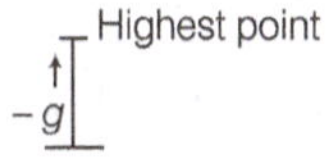

(ii) Velocity at the highest point = 0.

8. The times of flights are, $T_1 = \dfrac{2u\sin\theta}{g}$

and $T_2 = \dfrac{2u\sin\left(\dfrac{\pi}{2} - \theta\right)}{g} = \dfrac{2u\cos\theta}{g}$

$\therefore \dfrac{T_1}{T_2} = \dfrac{\sin\theta}{\cos\theta} = \tan\theta.$

9. No, because it is propelled by combustion of fuel and does not move under the effect of gravity alone.

10. For a projectile launched with velocity v_0 at an angle θ_0, the range is given by $R = \dfrac{v_0^2 \sin 2\theta_0}{g}$.

Now, for angles, $(45°+\alpha)$ and $(45°-\alpha)$, $2\theta_0$ is $(90°+2\alpha)$ and $(90°-2\alpha)$, respectively. The values of and $\sin(90°-2\alpha)$ are the same, equal to that of $\cos 2\alpha$. Therefore, ranges are equal for elevations which exceed or fall short of 45° by equal amount α.

11. No, a body cannot move on a curved path without acceleration because while moving on a curved path, the velocity of the body changes with time as the direction changes at each point.

12. No, the acceleration of a body remains constant, the magnitude and direction of the velocity of the body may change like in a circular motion.

13. When a stone is going around a circular path, the instantaneous velocity of stone is acting as tangent to the circle. When the string breaks, the centripetal force stops to act. Due to inertia, the stone continues to move along the tangent to circular path. So, the stone flies off tangentially to the circular path.

14. For an airplane to generate aerodynamic lift, there must be a high enough relative velocity between the winds and the air. If an airplane takes off by travelling into the wind, it does not have to travel as quickly with respect to ground. This in turns means that it can take off over a shorter travel distance over the runway than, if there was no wind present. [2]

15. In the baseball game, a player has to throw a ball so that it goes a certain distance in the minimum time. The time would depend on velocity of ball and angle of throw with the horizontal. Thus, while playing a baseball game, the speed and angle of projection have to be adjusted suitably so that the ball covers the desired distance in minimum time. So, a player has to see the distance and air resistance while playing with a baseball game. [2]

16. When a bullet is fired from a gun with its barrel directed towards the target, it starts falling downwards on account of acceleration due to gravity.

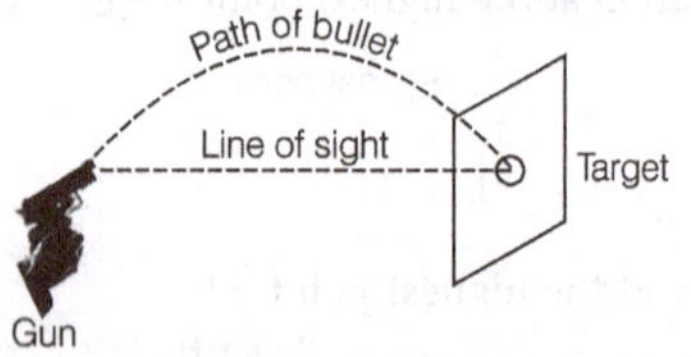

[1]

Due to which the bullet hits below the target. Just to avoid it, the barrel of the gun is lined up little above the target, so that the bullet after travelling in parabolic path hits the distant target. [1]

17. (i) A vector in general has no definite location in space because a vector remains unaffected whenever it is displaced anywhere in space provided its magnitude and direction do not change. However, a position vector has a definite location in space.

(ii) A vector can vary with time e.g. the velocity vector of an accelerated particle varies with time.

(iii) Two equal vectors at different locations in space do not necessarily have same physical effects. e.g. two equal forces acting at two different points on a body which can cause the rotation of a body about an axis will not produce equal turning effect. [1 × 3]

18. (i) **True,** because magnitude is a pure number.

(ii) **False,** each component of a vector is also a vector.

(iii) **True,** because the total path length is either greater than or equal to the magnitude of the displacement vector. [1 × 3]

19. (i) False, because the net acceleration of a particle is towards the centre only in case of a uniform circular motion.

(ii) True, because while leaving the circular path, the particle moves tangentially to the circular path.

(iii) True, because the direction of acceleration vector in a uniform circular motion is directed towards the centre of circular path. It is constantly changing with time. The resultant of all these vectors will be a zero vector. [1 × 3]

20. (i) Let v_{ox} and v_{oy} be the initial component velocities of the projectile at O along OX direction and OY direction respectively, where OX is horizontal and OY is vertical. Let the projectile go from O to P in time t and v_x, v_y be the component velocity of projectile at P along horizontal and vertical directions as shown in figure. [1]

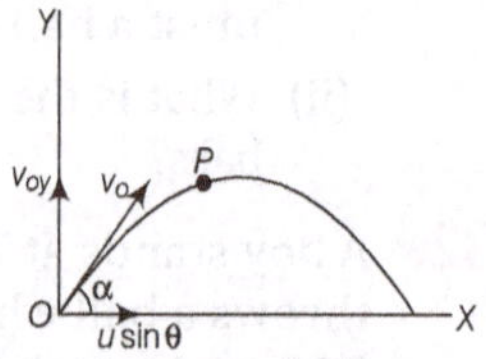

Then, $v_y = v_{oy} - gt$ and $v_x = v_{ox}$ [1]

If θ is the angle which the resultant velocity **v** makes with horizontal direction, then

$$\tan\theta = \frac{v_y}{v_x} = \frac{v_{oy} - gt}{v_{ax}} \Rightarrow \theta = \tan^{-1}\left(\frac{v_{oy} - gt}{v_{ox}}\right)$$ [1]

(ii) In angular projection,

Maximum vertical height, $h_m = \dfrac{u^2 \sin^2\theta_0}{2g}$

Horizontal range, [1/2]

$$R = \frac{u^2 \sin 2\theta_0}{g} = \frac{u^2}{g} 2\sin\theta_0 \cos\theta_0$$ [1/2]

So, $$\frac{h_m}{R} = \frac{\tan\theta_0}{4} \text{ or } \tan\theta_0 = \frac{4h_m}{R}$$

or $$\theta_0 = \tan^{-1}\left(\frac{4h_m}{R}\right)$$ [1]

21. Refer to text on page 94 (Centripetal acceleration).

22. Refer to text on page 91 (Horizontal range of a projectile and note).

23. In figure, O is the observation point at the ground, A and B are the positions of aircraft for which $\angle AOB = 30°$. Draw a perpendicular OC on AB. Here $OC = 3400$ m and $\angle AOC = \angle COB = 15°$. Time taken by aircraft from A to B is 10 s. [1/2]

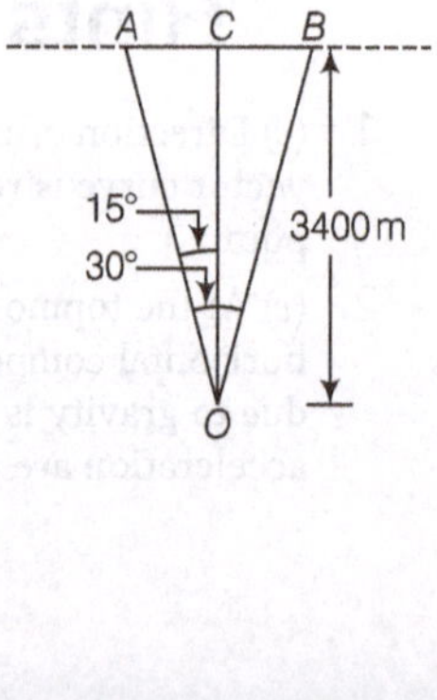

In ΔAOC, $AC = OC \tan 15°$

$= 3400 \times 0.2679 = 910.86$ m

$AB = AC + CB = AC + AC = 2AC$

$= 2 \times 910.86$ m [1/2]

Speed of the aircraft

$$v = \frac{\text{distance } AB}{\text{time}} = \frac{2\times 910.86}{10}$$

$= 182.17 \text{ ms}^{-1} = 182.2 \text{ ms}^{-1}$ [1]

24. Horizontal range = Maximum height (given)

$$\therefore \quad \frac{u^2}{g}\sin 2\theta = \frac{u^2 \sin^2\theta}{2g}$$ [1]

$$\Rightarrow \quad 2\sin\theta\cos\theta = \frac{\sin^2\theta}{2} \qquad [\because \sin 2\theta = 2\cos\theta\sin\theta]$$

$\tan\theta = 4 \Rightarrow \theta = 75°58'$ [1]

25. Let u be the velocity of projection of the ball. The ball will cover maximum horizontal distance when angle of projection with horizontal, $\theta = 45°$.

Then, $R_{max} = u^2/g$.

Here, $u^2/g = 100$ m. ...(i) [1/2]

In order to study the motion of the ball along vertical direction, consider a point on the surface of Earth as the origin and vertical upward direction as the positive direction of Y-axis. Taking motion of the ball along vertical upward direction, we have

$u_y = u, a_y = -g, v_y = 0, t = ?, y_0 = 0, y = ?$

As, $v_y = u_y + a_y t$

$\therefore \quad 0 = u + (-g)t \Rightarrow t = u/g$

Also, $y = y_0 + u_y t + \frac{1}{2}a_y t^2$

$\therefore \; y = 0 + u(u/g) + \frac{1}{2}(-g)u^2/g^2$

$$= \frac{u^2}{g} - \frac{1}{2}\frac{u^2}{g} = \frac{1}{2}\frac{u^2}{g} = \frac{100}{2} = 50 \text{ m [from Eq. (i)]}$$ [1½]

26. Horizontal range,

$$R = \frac{u^2\sin 2\theta}{g} \text{ or } 3 = \frac{u^2 \sin 60°}{g} = \frac{u^2}{g}\sqrt{3}/2 \text{ or } \frac{u^2}{g} = 2\sqrt{3}$$

Since, the muzzle velocity is fixed [1]

Therefore, maximum horizontal range,

$$R_{max} = \frac{u^2}{g} = 2\sqrt{3} = 3.464 \text{km}$$

So, the bullet cannot hit the target at 5 km away. [1]

27. Given, $u = 20$ m/s, $\theta = 45°$, $d = 25$ m

Horizontal range is given by

$$R = \frac{u^2}{g}\sin 2\theta = \frac{(20)^2}{9.8}\sin 2(45°)$$

$$= \frac{400}{9.8} \times 1 = 40.82 \text{ m}$$ [1/2]

Time of flight,

$$T = \frac{2u\sin\theta}{g} = \frac{2\times 20}{9.8}\sin 45° = 2.886 \text{ s}$$ [1/2]

The goal man is 25 m away in the direction of the ball, so to catch the ball, he is to cover a distance

$= 40.82 - 25 = 15.82$ m in time 2.886 s.

$\therefore$ Velocity of the goal man to catch the ball

$$v = \frac{15.82}{2.886} = 5.48 \text{ m/s}$$ [1]

28. Here, $r = 80$ cm $= 0.8$ m, $f = 14/25 \text{ s}^{-1}$

$$\therefore \quad \omega = 2\pi f = 2\times\frac{22}{7}\times\frac{14}{25} = \frac{88}{25} \text{ rad/s}$$

The centripetal acceleration

$$a = \omega^2 r = \left(\frac{88}{25}\right)^2 \times 0.80 = 9.90 \text{ ms}^{-2}$$ [1]

The direction of centripetal acceleration is along the string directed towards the centre of circular path. [1]

29. Here, $r = 1$ km $= 1000$ m,

$v = 900 \text{ kmh}^{-1} = 900 \times (1000 \text{ m})/(60 \times 60 \text{ s}) = 250 \text{ ms}^{-1}$

Centripetal acceleration, $a = \frac{v^2}{r} = \frac{(250)^2}{1000}$ [1]

Now, $\frac{a}{g} = \frac{(250)^2}{1000} \times \frac{1}{9.8} = 6.38$ [1]

30. The position vector, $\mathbf{r} = 2.0t\hat{\mathbf{i}} + t^2\hat{\mathbf{j}} + 3.0\hat{\mathbf{k}}$

$$\therefore \quad \mathbf{v}(t) = \frac{d\mathbf{r}}{dt} = \frac{d}{dt}(2.0t\hat{\mathbf{i}} + t^2\hat{\mathbf{j}} + 3.0\hat{\mathbf{k}})$$

$\mathbf{v}(t) = 2.0\hat{\mathbf{i}} + 2t\hat{\mathbf{j}}$ [1]

$$\mathbf{a}(t) = \frac{d\mathbf{v}(t)}{dt} = \frac{d}{dt}(2.0\hat{\mathbf{i}} + 2t\hat{\mathbf{j}}) = 2\hat{\mathbf{j}}$$ **[1/2]**

At $t = 2.0$ s, the magnitude of the $\mathbf{v}(t)$ can be given as

$\mathbf{v}(t) = 2.0\hat{\mathbf{i}} + 2\times 2\hat{\mathbf{j}} = 2.0\hat{\mathbf{i}} + 4\hat{\mathbf{j}}$ [1/2]

$v = \sqrt{4+16} = \sqrt{20}$ and direction is

$$\theta = \tan^{-1}\left(\frac{v_y}{v_x}\right) = \tan^{-1}\left(\frac{4}{2}\right) \approx 63°$$ **[1]**

31. (i) A fired cannon ball is a projectile and we want an equation that relates the launch angle θ_0 to the ball horizontal displacement i.e. range as it moves from the cannon to the ship.

$$\therefore \quad \theta_0 = \frac{1}{2}\sin^{-1}\left(\frac{gR}{u_0^2}\right) = \frac{1}{2}\sin^{-1}\left(\frac{9.8\times 560}{(82)^2}\right)$$

$$= \frac{1}{2}\sin^{-1}(0.816) = 27°$$ [1]

If one angle is 27°, then other angle $(90° - \theta_0)$ is

$= 90° - 27° = 63°$ [1/2]

(ii) Maximum range at $\theta_0 = 45°$

$$\therefore \quad R = \frac{u^2}{g}\sin 2\theta_0 = \frac{(82)^2}{9.8} \times \sin 90° = 686 \text{ m}$$ [1½]

32. Consider a boy standing at P throw a ball with a velocity u at an angle θ with the horizontal which just enters window W. [1]

As the boy is at 78.4 m from the building and the ball just enters the window 39.2 m above the ground.

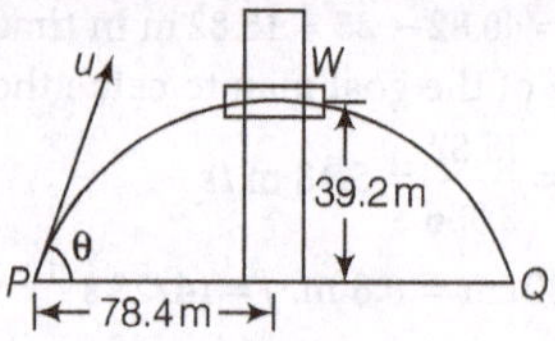

$\therefore$ Maximum height, $H = \dfrac{u^2 \sin^2 \theta}{2g}$

$\Rightarrow \quad 39.2 = \dfrac{u^2 \sin^2 \theta}{2g}$ ...(i)

and horizontal range, $R = \dfrac{u^2 \sin 2\theta}{g}$

$\Rightarrow \quad 2 \times 78.4 = \dfrac{u^2 \sin 2\theta}{g}$ ...(ii) [1]

Dividing Eq. (i) by Eq. (ii), we get

$$\frac{u^2 \sin^2 \theta}{2g} \times \frac{g}{u^2\, 2 \sin\theta \cos\theta} = \frac{39.2}{2 \times 78.4}$$

$\Rightarrow \quad \dfrac{1}{4} \tan\theta = \dfrac{1}{4} \quad \Rightarrow \quad \theta = 45°$

Substituting $\theta = 45°$ in Eq. (ii), we get

$$\frac{u^2 \sin 90°}{9.8} = 2 \times 78.4$$

$\Rightarrow \quad u = \sqrt{2 \times 78.4 \times 9.8} = 39.2$ m/s [1]

33. Here, $v = 27 \text{ kmh}^{-1} = 27 \times (1000 \text{ m}) \div (60 \times 60 \text{ s})^{-1}$

$= 7.5 \text{ ms}^{-1}$, $r = 80$ m

Centripetal acceleration,

$$a_c = \frac{v^2}{r} = \frac{(7.5)^2}{80} = 0.7 \text{ ms}^{-2}$$ [1]

Let the cyclist applies the brakes at the point P of the circular turn, then tangential acceleration a_T will act opposite to velocity.

Acceleration along the tangent, $a_T = 0.5 \text{ ms}^{-2}$

Angle between both the accelerations is 90°

Therefore, the magnitude of resultant acceleration

$$a = \sqrt{a_c^2 + a_T^2} = \sqrt{(0.7)^2 + (0.5)^2} = 0.86 \text{ ms}^{-2}$$ [1]

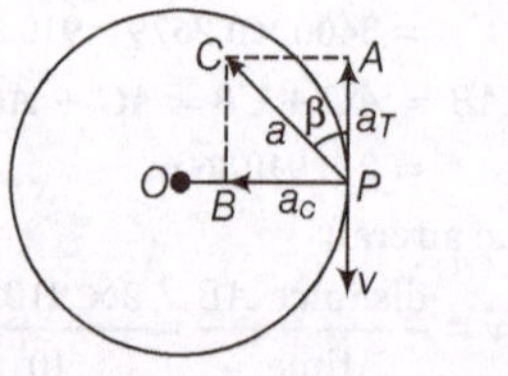

Let the resultant acceleration make an angle β with the tangent, i.e. the direction of net acceleration of the cyclist then, $\tan\beta = \dfrac{a_c}{a_T} = \dfrac{0.7}{0.5} = 1.4$ or $\beta = 54° 28'$ [1]

34. From the figure, let O be the position of gun and A be the position of plane.

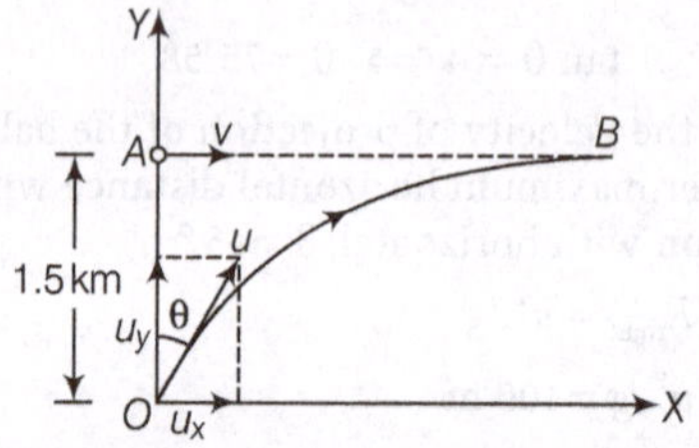

The speed of the plane,

$$v = \frac{720 \times 1000}{60 \times 60} = 200 \text{ ms}^{-1}$$ [1]

The speed of the shell, $u = 600 \text{ ms}^{-1}$

Let the shell hit the plane at B after time t if fired at an angle θ with the vertical from O. Then, the horizontal distance travelled by shell in time t is the same as the distance covered by the plane during the same period. [1]

i.e. $u_x \times t = vt$ or $u \sin\theta\, t = vt$

or $\quad \sin\theta = \dfrac{v}{u} = \dfrac{200}{600} = 0.33333 = \sin 19.5°$

or $\quad \theta = 19.5°$ with the vertical [1]

The plane will not be hit by the bullet from the gun if it is flying at a minimum height which is the maximum height (H) attained by bullet after firing from gun. [1/2]

Here, $H = \dfrac{u^2 \sin^2 (90° - \theta)}{2g} = \dfrac{u^2 \cos^2\theta}{2g}$

$= \dfrac{(600)^2 \times (\cos 19.5°)^2}{2 \times 10}$ $[\because \sin\theta = 1/3, \cos\theta = \sqrt{8}/3]$

$= \dfrac{(600)^2 \times (\sqrt{8}/3)^2}{20} = 16000 \text{ m} = 16 \text{ km}$ [1½]

Summary

- **Scalar quantities** are quantities with magnitudes only. Examples are distance, speed, mass and temperature.
- **Vector quantities** are quantities with magnitude and direction both. Examples are displacement, velocity and acceleration. They obey special rules of vector algebra.
- A **null** or **zero vector** is a vector with zero magnitude. Since the magnitude is zero, we don't have to specific its direction.
- **Negative vector** Two vectors are said to be negative of each other if their magnitudes are equal but directions are opposite.
- **Collinear vectors** The vectors which either act along the same line or along parallel lines are called collinear vectors.
- **Coplanar vectors** The vectors which act in the same plane are called coplanar vectors.
- **Position vector** A vector which gives position of an object with reference to the origin of a coordinate system is called position vector. It is given by $\mathbf{r} = x\hat{\mathbf{i}} + y\hat{\mathbf{j}}$
- **Displacement vector** It is that vector which tells how much and in which direction an object has changed its position in a given time interval.
- **Multiplication of vector by a real number** When a vector **A** is multiplied by a real number λ, we get $\lambda(A) = \lambda A$ and $-\lambda(A) = -\lambda A$.
- **Addition of vectors** Vectors can by added by using Triangle law / Parallelogram law / Polygon law
- **Properties of vector addition**
  - (i) Vectors representing physical quantities of same nature can only be added.
  - (ii) Vector addition is **commutative** $\mathbf{A} + \mathbf{B} = \mathbf{B} + \mathbf{A}$.
  - (iii) Vector addition is **associative** $(\mathbf{A} + \mathbf{B}) + \mathbf{C} = \mathbf{A} + (\mathbf{B} + \mathbf{C})$.
- **Subtraction of vectors** The subtraction of a vector **B** from vector **A** is defined as the addition of vector $-\mathbf{B}$ to **A**.

  Thus, $$\mathbf{A} - \mathbf{B} = \mathbf{A} + (-\mathbf{B})$$
- **Resolution of a vector** The process of splitting a vector into two or more vectors is known as resolution of the vector.
- A vector **A** can be expressed as $$\mathbf{A} = A_x\hat{\mathbf{i}} + A_y\hat{\mathbf{j}}$$

  where A_x, A_y are its components along X-axis and Y-axis. If vector **A** makes an angle θ with the x-axis, then $A_x = A\cos\theta$, $A_y = A\sin\theta$ and $A = |\mathbf{A}| = \sqrt{A_x^2 + A_y^2}$, $\tan\theta = \dfrac{A_y}{A_x}$.
- Any vector in three dimensions can be expressed in terms of its rectangular components as $$\mathbf{A} = A_x\hat{\mathbf{i}} + A_y\hat{\mathbf{j}} + A_z\hat{\mathbf{k}}$$

  Its magnitude, $A = \sqrt{A_x^2 + A_y^2 + A_z^2}$
- **Scalar or dot product** The scalar or dot product of two vectors **A** and **B** is defined as the product of the magnitudes of **A** and **B** and cosine of the angle θ between them. Thus $\mathbf{A}\cdot\mathbf{B} = |\mathbf{A}|\,|\mathbf{B}|\cos\theta = AB\cos\theta$

  It can be positive, negative or zero depending upon the value of θ.
- **Vector or cross product** For two vectors **A** and **B** inclined at an angle θ, the vector or cross product is defined as $$\mathbf{A}\times\mathbf{B} = AB\sin\theta\,\hat{\mathbf{n}}$$

  where $\hat{\mathbf{n}}$ is a unit vector perpendicular to the plane of **A** and **B** and its direction is that in which a right handed screw advances when rotated from **A** to **B**.
- Equations of motion in vector form. For motion with constant acceleration,

  (i) $\mathbf{v} = \mathbf{v}_0 + \mathbf{a}\,t$ (ii) $\mathbf{r} = \mathbf{r}_0 + \mathbf{v}_0\,t + \frac{1}{2}\mathbf{a}\,t^2$ (iii) $v^2 - v_0^2 = 2\mathbf{a}\cdot(\mathbf{r} - \mathbf{r}_0)$
- The motion in a plane with uniform acceleration can be treated as the superposition of two separate simultaneous one-dimensional motions along two perpendicular directions.

- **Projectile fired at an angle with the horizontal** Suppose a projectile is fired with velocity u at an angle θ with the horizontal. Let it reach the point (x, y) after time t. Then
  (i) Components of initial velocity $u_x = u\cos\theta,\ u_y = u\sin\theta$
  (ii) Components of acceleration at any instant $a_x = 0,\ a_y = -g$
  (iii) Position after time t, $x = (u\cos\theta)\,t,\ y = (u\sin\theta)\,t - \frac{1}{2}gt^2$
  (iv) Equation of trajectory: $y = x\tan\theta - \dfrac{g}{2u^2\cos^2\theta}\cdot x^2$
  (v) Maximum height, $H = \dfrac{u^2\sin^2\theta}{2g}$
  (vi) Time of flight, $T = \dfrac{2u\sin\theta}{g}$
  (vii) Horizontal range, $R = \dfrac{u^2\sin 2\theta}{g}$
  (viii) Maximum horizontal range is attained at $\theta = 45°$ and its value is $R_{max} = \dfrac{u^2}{g}$
  (ix) Velocity after time t, $v_x = u\cos\theta,\ v_y = u\sin\theta - gt$

  $$\therefore \quad v = \sqrt{v_x^2 + v_y^2} \text{ and } \tan\beta = \frac{v_y}{v_x}$$

  (x) The velocity with which the projectile reaches the horizontal plane through the point of projection same as the velocity of projection.
- **Uniform circular motion** When a body moves along a circular path with uniform speed, its motion is said to be uniform circular motion.
- **Angular displacement** It is the angle swept out by a radius vector in a given time interval.

  $$\theta\,(\text{Rad}) = \frac{\text{Arc}}{\text{Radius}} = \frac{s}{r}$$

- **Angular velocity** The angle swept out by the radius vector per second is called angular velocity.

  $$\omega = \frac{\theta}{t} \text{ or } \omega = \frac{\theta_2 - \theta_1}{t_2 - t_1}$$

- **Time period and frequency** Time taken for one complete revolution is called time period (T).
  The number of revolutions completed per second is called frequency.

  $$\omega = \frac{2\pi}{T} = 2\pi\nu$$

  Relationship between v and ω. It is given by $v = r\omega$
- Angular acceleration and its relation with linear acceleration. The rate of change of angular velocity is called angular acceleration. It is given by Linear acceleration $=$ Radius $\times$ Angular acceleration

  $$\alpha = \frac{\omega_2 - \omega_1}{t_2 - t_1}; \quad a = r\alpha$$

- **Centripetal acceleration** A body moving along a circular path is acted upon by an acceleration directed towards the centre along the radius. This acceleration is called centripetal acceleration. It is given by

  $$\alpha = \frac{v_2 - v_1}{r} = r\omega^2$$

Chapter Practice

Multiple Choice Questions

1 Mark

1 Find the correct option about vector subtraction.
(a) $\mathbf{A}-\mathbf{B}=\mathbf{A}+\mathbf{B}$ (b) $|\mathbf{A}-\mathbf{B}|=|\mathbf{B}-\mathbf{A}|$
(c) $\mathbf{A}-\mathbf{B}=\mathbf{A}+(-\mathbf{B})$ (d) None of these

2 Position vectors of three particles are given as $\mathbf{P}=3\hat{\mathbf{i}}-4\hat{\mathbf{j}}, \mathbf{Q}=6\hat{\mathbf{i}}-8\hat{\mathbf{j}}, \mathbf{R}=(3/4)\hat{\mathbf{i}}-\hat{\mathbf{j}}$, which of the following is correct?
(a) P, Q, R are equal vectors
(b) P, Q are parallel but R is not parallel
(c) P, Q, R are parallel
(d) None of the above

3 The equation of motion of a projectile are given by $x=18t$ and $2y=54t-9.8t^2$. The angle ϕ of projection is
(a) $\tan^{-1}(3)$ (b) $\tan^{-1}(1.5)$
(c) $\sin^{-1}\frac{2}{3}$ (d) $\cos^{-1}\frac{2}{3}$

4 Two cars A and B move along a concentric circular path of radius r_A and r_B with velocities v_A and v_B maintaining constant distance, then $\frac{v_A}{v_B}$ is equal to
(a) $\frac{r_B}{r_A}$ (b) $\frac{r_A}{r_B}$ (c) $\frac{r_A^2}{r_B^2}$ (d) $\frac{r_B^2}{r_A^2}$

Assertion and Reason

Directions (Q. Nos. 5-9) *In the following questions, two statements are given- one labelled Assertion (A) and the other labelled Reason (R). Select the correct answer to these questions from the codes (a), (b), (c) and (d) as given below*
(a) Both Assertion and Reason are true and Reason is the correct explanation of Assertion.
(b) Both Assertion and Reason are true but Reason is not the correct explanation of Assertion.
(c) Assertion is true but Reason is false.
(d) Assertion is false but Reason is true.

5 **Assertion (A)** Two balls of different masses are thrown vertically upward with same speed. They will pass through their point of projection in the downward direction with the same speed.
Reason (R) The maximum height and downward velocity attained at the point of projection are independent of the mass of the ball.

6 **Assertion** (A) In javelin throw, the athlete throws the projectile at an angle slightly more than 45°.
Reason (R) The maximum range does not depend upon angle of projection.

7 **Assertion** (A) Generally the path of a projectile from the earth is parabolic but it is elliptical for projectiles going to a very great height.
Reason (R) Upto ordinary height, the projectile moves under a uniform gravitational force but for great heights, projectile moves under a variable force.

8 **Assertion** (A) The projectile has, only vertical component of velocity at the highest ponit of its trajectory.
Reason (R) At the highest point, only one component of velocity is present.

9 **Assertion** (A) In a non-uniform circular motion, the acceleration of the particle is equal to sum of the tangential acceleration and the centripetal acceleration.
Reason (R) The two accelerations are perpendicular to each other.

Very Short Answer Type Questions

1 Mark

10 Is it necessary to mention the direction of vector having zero magnitude?

11 Displacement vector is fundamentally a position vector. Comment on this statement.

12 Does the nature of a vector change when it is multiplied by a scalar? Explain with example.

13 When the component of a vector **A** along the direction of **B** is zero, what can you conclude about the two vectors?

14 Can the walk of a man be an example of resolution of vectors? If yes, how?

15 For what angle between **P** and **Q**, the value of **P**+**Q** is maximum?

Short Answer Type I Questions

2 Marks

16 A rabbit runs across a parking lot on which a set of coordinates axes has been drawn. The coordinates (in metres) of the rabbit's position as functions of time t (in seconds) are given by

$x = -0.31t^2 + 7.2t + 28$ and

$y = 0.22t^2 - 9.1t + 30$

(i) At $t = 15$ s, what is the rabbit's position vector **r**?

(ii) Find the rabbit's velocity **v** at time $t = 15$ s.

(iii) Find the rabbit's acceleration a at time $t = 15$ s.

17 A biker stands on the edge of a cliff 490 m above the ground and throws a stone horizontally with an initial speed of 15 m/s. Neglecting air resistance, find the time taken by the stone to reach the ground and the speed with which it hits the ground. Consider $g = 9.8\ m/s^2$. NCERT

18 A woman rides a carnival ferris wheel of radius 15 m, completing five turns about its horizontal axis every minute. What are (i) the period of the motion, (ii) the magnitude and (iii) direction of her centripetal acceleration at the highest point and (iv) direction of her centripetal acceleration at the lowest point?

19 A boy whirls a stone in a horizontal circle of radius 1.5 m and at height 2.0 m above level ground. The string breaks, and the stone flies off horizontally and strikes the ground after travelling a horizontal distance of 10 m.

What is the magnitude of the centripetal acceleration of the stone during the circular motion?

Short Answer Type II Questions

3 Marks

20 A projectile is fired at an angle θ with the vertical with velocity u as shown in the figure.

Write the expression for

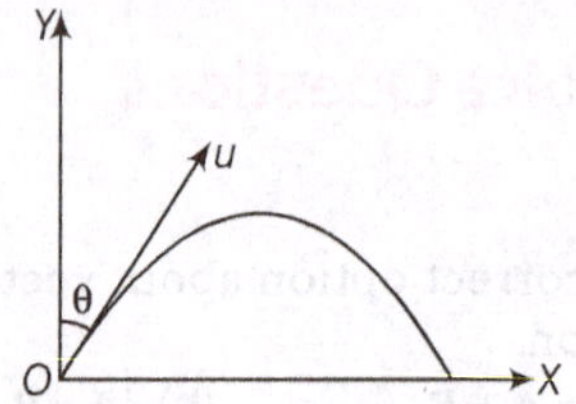

(i) maximum height (ii) total time of flight

(iii) horizontal range

21 A particle starts from the origin at $t = 0$ with a velocity of $10.0\ \hat{j}$ m/s and moves in the x-y plane with a constant acceleration of $(8.0\ \hat{i} + 2.0\ \hat{j})\ ms^{-2}$.

(i) At what time is the x-coordinate of the particle 16 m? What is the y-coordinate of the particle at that time ?

(ii) What is the speed of the particle at that time? NCERT

22 An aeroplane is flying in a horizontal direction with a velocity of 600 km/h and at a height of 1960 m. When it is vertically above the point A on the ground, a body is dropped from it. The body strikes the ground at point B. Calculate the distance AB.

23 The ceiling of a long hall is 25 m high. What is the maximum horizontal distance that a ball thrown with a speed of 40 m/s can go without hitting the ceiling of the hall? NCERT

24 Water from a sprinkler comes out with a constant velocity u in all the directions. What is the maximum area of the grassland that can be watered at any time?

Long Answer Type Questions

5 Marks

25 A projectile is fired horizontally with a velocity of 98 ms^{-1} from the hill 490 m high. Find (i) time taken to reach the ground (ii) the distance of the target from the hill and (iii) the velocity with which the body strikes the ground.

26 A hunter aims his gun and fires a bullet directly at a monkey in a tree. At the instant, the bullet leaves the barrel of the gun, the monkey drops. Will the bullet hit the monkey? Substantiate your answer with proper reasoning.

27 A marble rolls along a table at a constant speed of 1.00 m/s and then falls off the edge of the table to the floor 1.00 m below. (i) How long does the marble take to reach the floor? (ii) At what horizontal distance from the edge of the table does the marble land? (iii) What is its velocity as it strikes the floor?

Case Based Questions

Directions (Q. No. 28) *These questions are case study based questions. Read the following paragraph and answer the questions.*

28 **Projectile Motion**

Projectile motion is a form of motion in which an object or particle is thrown with some initial velocity near the earth's surface and it moves along a curved path under the action of gravity alone. The path followed by a projectile is called its trajectory, which is shown below.

While resolving velocity (u) into two components, we get (a) $u\cos\theta$ along OX and (b) $u\sin\theta$ along OY.

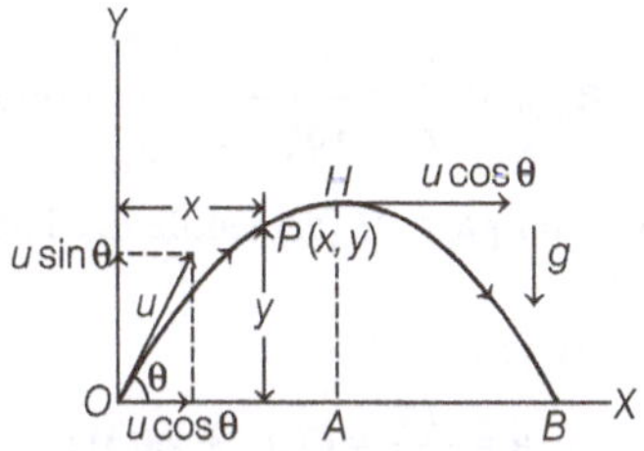

(i) What is the example of such type of motion?

(ii) What is the acceleration of the object in horizontal direction.

(iii) Find the magnetiude of vertical component of velocity at point H.

(iv) A cricket ball is thrown at a speed of 28 m/s in a direction 30° with the horizontal.

What will be the time taken by the ball to return to the same level?

(v) In above case, find the distance from the thrower to the point where the ball returns to the same level.

Answers

1 (c) To subtract **B** from **A**, we can add − **B** and **A**.

So, $\mathbf{A} + (-\mathbf{B}) = \mathbf{A} - \mathbf{B} = \mathbf{R}_2$

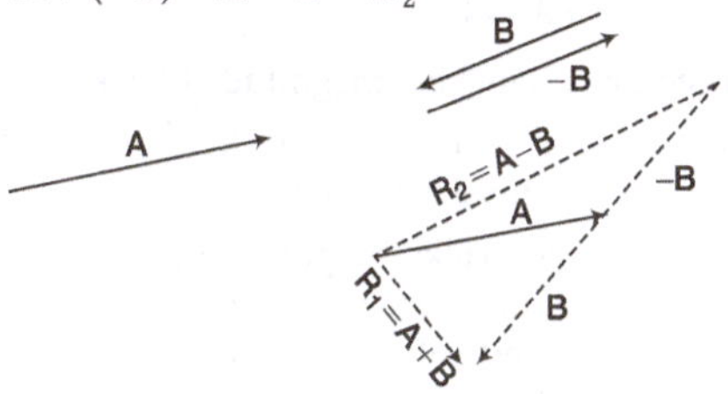

(a) (b)

$R_1 = \mathbf{A} + \mathbf{B}$ is also, shown for the comparison.

2 (c) Given, $\mathbf{P} = 3\hat{\mathbf{i}} - 4\hat{\mathbf{j}}$ and $\mathbf{Q} = 2(3\hat{\mathbf{i}} - 4\hat{\mathbf{j}}) = 2\mathbf{P}$

Also, $\mathbf{R} = \frac{1}{4}(3\hat{\mathbf{i}} - 4\hat{\mathbf{j}}) = \frac{\mathbf{P}}{4}$

So, **P**, **Q** and **R** are parallel with unequal magnitude.

3 (b) Equation of projectile is

$$x = u\cos\theta . t \Rightarrow y = u\sin\theta . t - \frac{1}{2}gt^2$$

Comparing it with given equation, we have

$$u\cos\theta = 18 \text{ and } 4\sin\theta = \frac{54}{2}$$

$$\therefore \quad \tan\theta = \frac{54}{2\times 18} = 1.5 \Rightarrow \theta = \tan^{-1}(1.5)$$

4 (b) Angular velocity ω is constant.

$$\therefore \quad v \propto r \text{ or } \frac{v_A}{v_B} = \frac{r_A}{r_B} \qquad (\because v = r\,\omega)$$

5 (a) Maximum height attained,

$$h = ut - \frac{1}{2}gt^2$$

Downward velocity attained,

$$v = \sqrt{u^2 - 2gh}$$

Both h and v are independent of mass m.

6 (d) When a body is projected from a place above the earth's surface, the angle of projection must be slightly less than 45° for the maximum horizontal angle.

7 (a) A is true and the R is its correct explanation. At greater heights, the gravitational force varies in inverse proportion to the square of the distance of the projectile from the centre of the earth. Under such a variable force, the path of the projectile is elliptical.

8 (d) A is false but the R is correct. At the highest point, the projectile has only the horizontal component of velocity.

9 (a) Both the A and R are true and the R is the correct explanation of the A.

10 A zero magnitude vector is not pointing in any particular direction, so it has an undefined direction.

11 Displacement vector is a change in position vector.

12 It does not effect nature but only effect its magnitude.
For a vector $\mathbf{A} = |\mathbf{A}| \cdot \hat{\mathbf{A}}$

$$k\mathbf{A} = k|\mathbf{A}|\,\hat{\mathbf{A}}$$

So, direction is same but magnitude is $k|\mathbf{A}|$.

13 If component of vector A is zero in direction of B, then both are perpendicular to each other.

14 Yes, when a man walks, he pushes the ground with his foot. The reaction is resolved in two components: horizontal and vertical component.

15 As, $|\mathbf{P}+\mathbf{Q}| = \sqrt{P^2 + Q^2 + 2PQ\cos\theta}$

For maximum $\mathbf{P}+\mathbf{Q}$, $\cos\theta = 1$

So, $\theta = 0°$

16 As for $t = 15$ s,

$$x = -0.31\times(15)^2 + 7.2\times 15 + 28 = 66.25$$

$$y = 0.22\times(15)^2 - 9.1\times 15 + 30 = -57$$

(i) So, position vector at $t = 15$ s is, $\mathbf{r} = 66.25\,\hat{\mathbf{i}} - 57\,\hat{\mathbf{j}}$

(ii) Velocity vector $= \left[\frac{dx}{dt}\hat{\mathbf{i}} + \frac{dy}{dt}\hat{\mathbf{j}}\right]$ at $t = 15$ s,

$$\left.\begin{aligned}\frac{dx}{dt} &= -0.62t + 7.2 = -2.1\\ \frac{dy}{dt} &= 0.44t - 91 = -2.5\end{aligned}\right| \text{ at } t = 15\text{s}$$

So, $\mathbf{v} = -2.1\,\hat{\mathbf{j}} - 2.5\hat{\mathbf{j}}$

(iii) So, $\mathbf{a} = \frac{d^2x}{dt^2}\hat{\mathbf{i}} + \frac{d^2y}{dt^2}\hat{\mathbf{j}}$

$$= -0.62\,\hat{\mathbf{i}} + 0.44\,\hat{\mathbf{j}}$$ [2]

17 Given, $h = 490$ m, $u_x = 15$ m/s,

$a_y = 9.8$ m/s, $a_x = 0, u_y = 0$

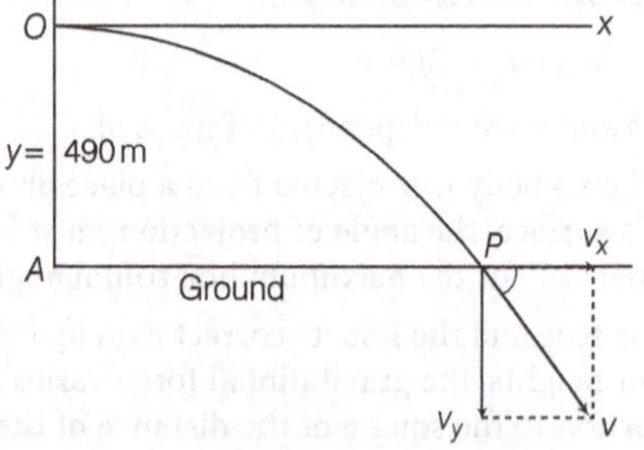

Time taken by the stone is

$$t = \sqrt{\frac{2h}{g}} = \sqrt{\frac{2\times 490}{9.8}} = 10\text{ s}$$ [1]

$$v_x = u_x + a_x t = 15 + 0\times 10 = 15 \text{ m/s}$$

$$v_y = u_y + a_y t = 0 + 9.8\times 10 = 98 \text{ m/s}$$

$$v = \sqrt{v_x^2 + v_y^2} = \sqrt{15^2 + 98^2} = 99.14 \text{ m/s}$$ [1]

18 Given, radius = 15 m, 5 rotation in one minute.

So, time period $= \frac{1 \text{ minute}}{5 \text{ cycles}} = \frac{60}{5}$s $= 12$ sec per cycle.

Centripetal acceleration $= \omega^2 r = \left(\frac{2\pi}{T}\right)^2 r$

$$= \left(\frac{2\pi}{12}\right)^2 \times 15 = 4.1 \text{ m/s}^2$$ [1]

The direction of centripetal force at highest point is downward and at lowest point is upward towards the centre of rotation. [1]

19 Given, horizontal circle of radius = 1.5 m

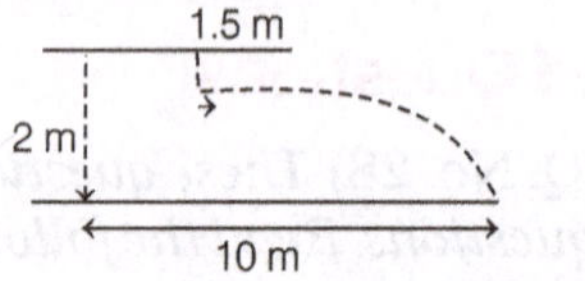

Vertical height = 2 m

and the range = 10 m

Time of fall of stone by 2 m is

$$t = \sqrt{\frac{2H}{g}} = \sqrt{\frac{2\times 2}{10}} = \frac{2}{\sqrt{10}}\text{ s}$$ [1/2]

Velocity to cover range of 10 m in $\frac{2}{\sqrt{10}}$ s is

$$v = \frac{\text{Range}}{\text{Time}} = \frac{10}{\frac{2}{\sqrt{10}}} = \frac{10\sqrt{10}}{2}$$ [1/2]

So, the centripetal acceleration,

$$\mathbf{a}_{\text{cent}} = \frac{v^2}{r} = \frac{1}{1.5}\left(\frac{10\sqrt{10}}{2}\right)^2 = 166.66 \text{ m/s}^2$$ [1]

20 Refer to text on page 92 (Projectile fired at an angle with the vertical).

21 Here, $\mathbf{u} = 10.0\,\hat{\mathbf{j}}$ ms^{-1} at $t = 0$.

$$\mathbf{a} = \frac{d\mathbf{v}}{dt} = (8.0\,\hat{\mathbf{i}} + 2.0\,\hat{\mathbf{j}}) \text{ ms}^{-2}$$

So, $\quad d\mathbf{v} = (8.0\,\hat{\mathbf{i}} + 2.0\,\hat{\mathbf{j}})\,dt$

Integrating it within the limits of motion i.e. as time changes from 0 to t, velocity changes from u to v, we have

$$\mathbf{v} - \mathbf{u} = (8.0\,\hat{\mathbf{i}} + 2.0\,\hat{\mathbf{j}})\,t$$

$\Rightarrow \quad \mathbf{v} = \mathbf{u} + 8.0t\,\hat{\mathbf{i}} + 2.0t\,\hat{\mathbf{j}}$

As, $\quad \mathbf{v} = \frac{d\mathbf{r}}{dt} \Rightarrow d\mathbf{r} = \mathbf{v}\,dt$

So, $\quad d\mathbf{r} = (\mathbf{u} + 8.0\,t\,\hat{\mathbf{i}} + 2.0t\,\hat{\mathbf{j}})\,dt$ [1]

Integrating it within the conditions of motion i.e. as time changes from 0 to t, displacement is from 0 to r, we have

$$\mathbf{r} = \mathbf{u}\,t + \frac{1}{2}\times 8.0\,t^2\,\hat{\mathbf{i}} + \frac{1}{2}\times 2.0\,t^2\,\hat{\mathbf{j}}$$

or $x\,\hat{\mathbf{i}} + y\,\hat{\mathbf{j}} = 10\,\hat{\mathbf{j}}\,t + 4.0\,t^2\,\hat{\mathbf{i}} + t^2\,\hat{\mathbf{j}}$

$$= 4.0\,t^2\,\hat{\mathbf{i}} + (10\,t + t^2)\,\hat{\mathbf{j}}$$

Here, we have, $x = 4.0\,t^2$ and $y = 10\,t + t^2$

$$\therefore \quad t = (x/4)^{\frac{1}{2}}$$

(i) At $x = 16$ m, $t = (16/4)^{\frac{1}{2}} = 2$s

$$y = 10 \times 2 + 2^2 = 24 \text{ m}$$ [1]

(ii) Velocity of the particle at time t is

$$\mathbf{v} = 10\,\hat{\mathbf{j}} + 8.0\,t\,\hat{\mathbf{i}} + 2.0t\,\hat{\mathbf{j}}$$

When $t = 2$ s, then

$$\mathbf{v} = 10\,\hat{\mathbf{j}} + 8.0 \times 2\,\hat{\mathbf{i}} + 2.0 \times 2\,\hat{\mathbf{j}} = 16\,\hat{\mathbf{i}} + 14\,\hat{\mathbf{j}}$$

$\therefore$ Speed $= |\,\mathbf{v}\,| = \sqrt{16^2 + 14^2} = 21.26 \text{ ms}^{-1}$ [1]

22 Velocity of the aeroplane in the horizontal direction is

$$u_{ax} = 600 \text{ km/h} = 600 \times \frac{5}{18} = \frac{500}{3} \text{ m/s}$$ [1]

Velocity remains constant throughout the flight of the body.

$$u_{0y} = 0 \text{ and } y = h = 1960 \text{ m}$$

Let t = time taken by the body to reach the ground

Now, $y = u_{0y}t + \frac{1}{2}gt^2$

$$\therefore \quad 1960 = \frac{1}{2} \times 9.8 \times t^2$$

$$\Rightarrow \quad t = \sqrt{\frac{1960}{4.9}} = \sqrt{400} = 20 \text{ s}$$ [1]

Distance travelled by the body in the horizontal direction,

$$AB = x = v_{ax}\,t = \frac{500}{3} \times 20$$

$$= \frac{10000}{3} = 3333 \text{ m} = 3.33 \text{ km}$$ [1]

23 Given, initial velocity $(u) = 40$ m/s

Height of the hall $(H) = 25$ m

Let the angle of projection of the ball be θ, when maximum height attained by it be 25 m.

Maximum height attained by the ball [2]

$$H = \frac{u^2 \sin^2\theta}{2g} \Rightarrow 25 = \frac{(40)^2 \sin^2\theta}{2 \times 9.8}$$

or $\sin^2\theta = \frac{25 \times 2 \times 9.8}{1600} = 0.3063$

or $\sin\theta = 0.5534 = \sin 33.6°$ [1/2]

or $\theta = 33.6°$

$\therefore$ Horizontal range $(R) = \frac{u^2 \sin 2\theta}{g}$

$$= \frac{(40)^2 \sin 2 \times 33.6°}{9.8} = \frac{1600 \times \sin 67.2°}{9.8}$$

$$= \frac{1600 \times 0.9219}{9.8} = 150.5 \text{ m}$$ [1/2]

24 Let the sprinkler has velocity u in horizontal direction and same u in verticle direction.

$$\mathbf{R}_{\max} = u_x t = u \cdot \frac{u}{g} = \frac{u^2}{g} \qquad \left[\because t = \frac{u_y}{g}\right]$$ [2]

Maximum area, $A_{\max} = \pi R_{\max}^2 = \pi \frac{u^4}{g^2}$ [1]

25 Let OX and OY be two perpendicular axes and $YO = 490$ m. A body projected horizontally from O with velocity $u\ (= 98 \text{ ms}^{-1})$ meets the ground at A following a parabolic path shown in figure. [1]

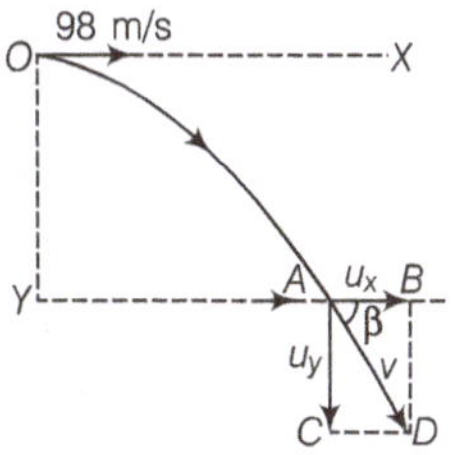

(i) Let T be the time of flight of the projectile i.e. time taken by projectile to go from O to A.

Taking vertical downward motion (i.e. motion along OY axis) of projectile from O to A, we have

$$y_0 = 0,\ y = 490 \text{ m},\ u_y = 0,\ a_y = 9.8 \text{ m/s}^2,\ t = T$$

As, $y = y_0 + u_y t + \frac{1}{2}a_y t^2$

$$\therefore \quad 490 = 0 + 0 \times T + \frac{1}{2} \times 9.8 \times T^2 = 4.9\,T^2$$

or $T = \sqrt{\frac{490}{4.9}} = 10$ s [1]

(ii) Taking horizontal motion (i.e. motion along OX-axis) of projectile from O to A, we have

$$x_0 = 0,\ x = R \text{ (say)},\ u_x = 98 \text{ m/s},\ t = T = 10 \text{ s},\ a_x = 0$$

As, $x = x_0 + u_x t + \frac{1}{2}a_x t^2$

$$\therefore \quad R = 0 + 98 \times 10 + \frac{1}{2} \times 0 \times 10^2 = 980 \text{ m}$$ [1]

(iii) Let v_x, v_y be the horizontal and vertical component velocity of the projectile at A.

Using the relation,

$$v_x = u_x + a_x t = 98 + 0 \times 10 = 98 \text{ m/s}$$

Represented by AB

Using the relation,

$$v_y = u_y + a_y t = 0 + 9.8 \times 10 = 98 \text{ m/s}$$

Represented by AC.

$\therefore$ Resultant velocity

$$v = \sqrt{v_x^2 + v_y^2} = \sqrt{98^2 + 98^2} = 98\sqrt{2} \text{ m/s}$$ [1]

If β is the angle which $\mathbf{v}$ makes with the horizontal direction, then $\tan\beta = \frac{v_y}{v_x} = \frac{98}{98} = 1$ or $\beta = 45°$ with the horizontal. [1]

26 Let the monkey stationed at A, be fired with a gun from O with a velocity u at an angle θ with the horizontal direction OX.

Draw AC, perpendicular to OX. Let the bullet cross the vertical line AC at B after time t and coordinates of B (x, y) be w.r.t. origin O as shown in figure. [1]

$\therefore\ t = \dfrac{OC}{u\cos\theta} = \dfrac{x}{u\cos\theta}$ ...(i) **[1]**

[where, $OC = x$]

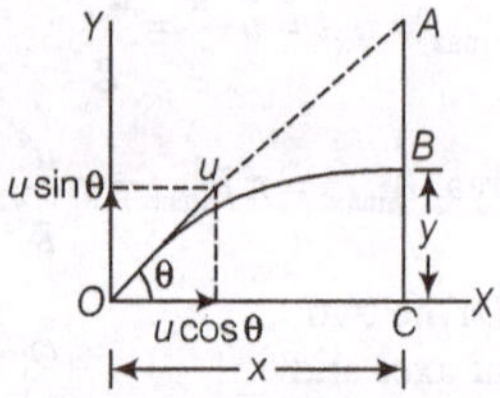

In ΔOAC, $AC = OC \tan\theta = x\tan\theta$ ...(ii)

Clearly, $CB = y$ = the vertical distance travelled by the bullet in time t.

Taking motion of the bullet from O to B along Y-axis, we have $y_0 = 0,\ y = y,\ u_y = u\sin\theta,\ a_y = -g,\ t = t$

As, $y = y_0 + u_y t + \dfrac{1}{2}a_y t^2$ [1]

$\therefore\ y = 0 + u\sin\theta\, t + \dfrac{1}{2}(-g)t^2$

$= u\sin\theta\, t - \dfrac{1}{2}gt^2$ ...(iii)

$\therefore\ AB = AC - BC = x\tan\theta - y$

$= x\tan\theta - \left(u\sin\theta t - \dfrac{1}{2}gt^2\right)$

$= x\tan\theta - \left(u\sin\theta \times \dfrac{x}{u\cos\theta} - \dfrac{1}{2}gt^2\right)$

[from Eq. (i)]

$AB = x\tan\theta - x\tan\theta + \dfrac{1}{2}gt^2 = \dfrac{1}{2}gt^2$ [1]

It means the bullet will pass through the point B on vertical line AC at a vertical distance $\dfrac{1}{2}gt^2$ below point A.

The distance through which the monkey falls vertically in time $t = \dfrac{1}{2}gt^2 = AB$. It means the bullet and monkey will pass through the point B simultaneously.

Therefore, the bullet will hit the monkey. [1]

27 Projectile motion of the marble begins as it leaves the table as shown. Since, the marble is initially moving horizontally, $v_{y_0} = 0$ and $v_{x_0} = 1.00$ m/s. We must consider the origin to be at the edge of the table, so that $x_0 = y_0 = 0$ [1]

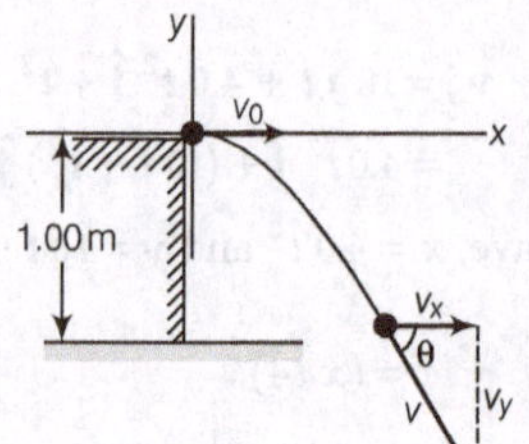

(i) $t = ?$, if $y = -1.00$ m; $y = \dfrac{-1}{2}gt^2$ $[\because v_{y_0} = 0]$

$\Rightarrow\ t = \sqrt{\dfrac{-2y}{g}} = \sqrt{\dfrac{(-2)(-1.00)}{9.8}} = 0.452$ s [1]

(ii) $x = ?$, when $t = 0.452$ s

$\therefore\ x = v_{x_0}t = 1.00 \times 0.452$ s $= 0.452$ m [1]

(iii) $v = ?,\ \theta = ?$ at $t = 0.452$ s

The x-component of velocity is constant throughout the motion, $v_x = v_{x_0} = 1.00$ m/s

The y-component of velocity

$v_y = v_{y_0} - gt = 0 - 9.8 \times .452 = -4.43$ m/s

$\therefore\ v = \sqrt{v_x^2 + v_y^2} = \sqrt{(1.00)^2 + (-4.43)^2} = 4.54$ m/s [1]

$\theta = \tan^{-1}\left|\dfrac{v_y}{v_x}\right| = \dfrac{4.43}{1.00} = 77.3^\circ$

As the marble hits the floor, its velocity is 4.54 m/s directed 77.3° below the horizontal. [1]

28 (i) Example of such type of motion is

(a) A javelin thrown by an athletic.

(b) A stone thrown away in the sky.

(ii) In the projectile motion, object is only acted upon by the vertical gravitational force. Since there is no force in the horizontal direction, acceleration in horizontal direction is zero.

(iii) The vertical component of velocity of a projectile at maximum height (H) is zero. It has only horizontal component of velocity.

(iv) Time taken to return to same level,

$T = \dfrac{2u\sin\theta}{g} = \dfrac{2 \times 28 \times \sin 30^\circ}{9.8} = \dfrac{28}{9.8} = 2.85 \approx 2.9$ s

(v) Distance from the thrower to the point where the ball returns to the same level,

$d = \dfrac{u^2 \sin 2\theta}{g} = \dfrac{28 \times 28 \times \sin 60^\circ}{9.8} = 69.2$ m

CHAPTER

04

Laws of Motion

Motion is an integral part of most of the natural phenomena. Galaxies, Stars, Planets, Satellites all are in continuous motion. Motion of these bodies is governed and regulated by certain laws. Laws hidden behind these motions in nature were discovered first by Issac Newton. Therefore, these laws are known as Newton's laws of motion.

- Newton's Laws of Motion
- Friction and Circular Motion

TOPIC 01 Newton's Laws of Motion

Force

Force may be defined as an external agency (a push or a pull) which changes or tends to change the state of rest or of uniform motion or the direction of motion of a body.

The dimension of force is $[MLT^{-2}]$ and its SI unit is **Newton.**

A force applied on an object can produce four types of effects such as

(i) Force can start or stop a motion.

(ii) Force can change speed of an object, making it to move slower or faster.

(iii) Force can change the direction of motion of an object.

(iv) Force can change the shape of an object.

Law of Inertia

Galileo first asserted that objects move with constant speed when no external forces act on them.

Inertia

The term inertia means resistance of any physical object. It is defined as the inherent property of a material body by virtue of which it remains in its state of rest or of uniform motion in a straight line. This term was first used by Galileo.

Various Types of Inertia

The various types of inertia are as below

(i) Inertia of Rest

It is defined as the tendency of a body to remain in its position of rest.

e.g. A person standing in a train falls backward when the train suddenly starts moving forward. It depicts, when train moves, the lower part of his body begins to move alongwith the train while the upper part of his body continues to remain at rest due to inertia.

(ii) Inertia of Motion

It is defined as the tendency of a body to remain in its state of uniform motion in a straight line.

e.g. When a moving bus suddenly stops or apply the brake, a person standing in it falls forward. As the bus stops, the lower part of his body comes to rest alongwith the bus while upper part of his body continues to remain in motion due to inertia and falls forward.

(iii) Inertia of Direction

It is defined as inability of a body to change by itself its direction of motion.

e.g. An umbrella protects us from rain.

The rain drops falling vertically downwards cannot change their direction of motion and wet us, without the umbrella on.

Newton's Laws of Motion

Sir Isaac Newton (1642-1727) made a systematic study of motion and extended the views of Galileo. He arrived at three laws of motion which are called **Newton's law of motion.** These laws are as follows

Newton's First Law of Motion

This law states that **every body continues in its state of rest or of uniform motion in a straight line unless it is compelled by some external force to change that state.**

The state of rest or uniform linear motion both imply zero acceleration. The first law of motion can therefore be simply expressed as:

If the net external force on a body is zero, its acceleration is zero. Acceleration can be non-zero, only if there is a net external force on the body. Newton's first law defines force qualitatively.

The Newton's first law is categorised in three parts

(i) **First part** If a body at rest continues in its state of rest. An external force has to be applied on it to make it move.

(ii) **Second part** If a body is in motion it continues moving in a straight path with a uniform speed unless an external force is applied.

(iii) **Third part** says that a body moving with a uniform speed in a straight line cannot change itself its direction of motion.

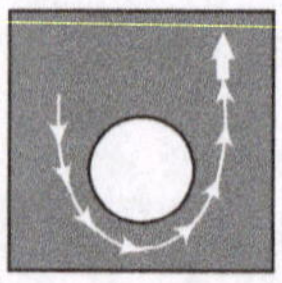

Moon changes its direction continuously

Newton's First Law Defines the Inertia

According to Newton's first law of motion, everybody continues in its state of rest or uniform motion unless an external force acts upon it. This depicts that a body by itself cannot change its state of rest or of uniform motion along a straight line.

Thus, first law defines inertia and so it is rightly inspired by the **law of inertia.**

Example 1 An astronaut accidentally gets separated out of his small spaceship accelerating in interstellar space at a constant rate of 100 m/s^2. What is the acceleration of the astronaut the instant after he is outside the spaceship? (Assume that there are no nearby stars to exert gravitational force on him). **NCERT**

Sol. Since, there are no nearby stars to exert gravitational force on him and the small spaceship exerts negligible gravitational attraction on him. The net force acting on the astronaut, once he is out of the spaceship, is zero. By the first law of motion, the acceleration of the astronaut is zero.

Momentum

Momentum of a body is the quantity of motion possessed by the body. It is defined as the product of its mass m and velocity $\mathbf{v}$ and is denoted by $\mathbf{p}$.

$$\text{Momentum, } \mathbf{p} = m\mathbf{v}$$

Unit and Dimensional Formula

SI unit of momentum = kg m/s or kg m s^{-1}

CGS unit of momentum = g cm/s or g cm s^{-1}

The dimensional formula of momentum is $[MLT^{-1}]$.
It is a vector quantity.

Newton's Second Law of Motion

This law states that **the rate of change of momentum of a body is directly proportional to the external force applied on the body and the change takes place in the direction of the applied force.**

Let F be external force applied on the body in the direction of motion of the body for time interval Δt, then the velocity of a body of mass m changes from v to $\mathbf{v} + \Delta \mathbf{v}$, i.e. change in momentum $\Delta \mathbf{p} = m\Delta \mathbf{v}$. According to Newton's second law,

$$\mathbf{F} \propto \frac{\Delta \mathbf{p}}{\Delta t} \quad \text{or} \quad \mathbf{F} = k\frac{\Delta \mathbf{p}}{\Delta t}$$

where, k is a constant of proportionality.

If limit $\Delta t \to 0$, then the term $\frac{\Delta \mathbf{p}}{\Delta t}$ becomes the derivative $\frac{d\mathbf{p}}{dt}$.

Thus, $$\boxed{\mathbf{F} = k\frac{d\mathbf{p}}{dt}}$$

For a body of fixed mass m, we have

$$\mathbf{F} = k\frac{d(m\mathbf{v})}{dt} = km\frac{d\mathbf{v}}{dt}$$

$$\mathbf{F} = km\mathbf{a} \qquad \left(\because \frac{dv}{dt} = a\right)$$

Let, $k = 1$

So, Force, $\mathbf{F} = m\mathbf{a}$

In scalar form, this equation can be written as

$$F = ma$$

$\therefore$ 1 unit force = 1 unit mass × 1 unit acceleration

A unit force may be defined as the force which produces unit acceleration in a body of unit mass.

The force is a vector quantity and its SI unit is Newton.
One newton is defined as that much force which produces an acceleration of 1 m/s^2 in a body of mass 1 kg.

$$1\text{ N} = 1\text{ kg} \times 1\text{ m/s}^2$$

$$1\text{ N} = 1\text{ kg m/s}^2$$

In CGS system, absolute unit of force is dyne. One dyne is that much force which produces an acceleration of 1 cm/s^2 in a body of mass 1 g.

$$1\text{ dyne} = 1\text{ g} \times 1\text{ cm/s}^2$$

$$1\text{ dyne} = 1\text{ g cm/s}^2$$

In SI unit, gravitational unit of force is kilogram weight (kg-wt). It is defined as that much force which produces an acceleration of 9.80 m/s^2 in a body of mass 1 kg.

$$1\text{ kg-wt} = 1\text{ kgf} = 9.8\text{ N}$$

In CGS system, gravitational unit of force is gram weight (g-wt) or gram force (gf). It is defined as that force which produces an acceleration of 980 cm/s^2 in a body of mass 1 g.

$$1\text{ g-wt} = 1\text{ gf} = 980\text{ g cm/s}^2$$

Note

- For $v \to c$, m is not constant according to the theory of relativity. Let mass of a body is m_0 at rest with respect to an observer. Now, the body moves with velocity v w.r.t. observer and its mass is m, then $m = \dfrac{m_0}{\sqrt{1 - \dfrac{v^2}{c^2}}}$.

Relation between Newton and Dyne

$$1\text{ N} = 1\text{ kg} \times 1\text{ m/s}^2 = 1000\text{ g} \times 100\text{ cm/s}^2$$

$$= 10^5\text{ g cm/s}^2 \qquad [\because 1\text{ dyne} = 1\text{ g cm/s}^2]$$

$$1\text{ N} = 10^5\text{ dyne}$$

Note

- A gravitational unit is g times the corresponding absolute unit.
- A gravitational unit of force is used to express the weight of a body. e.g. The weight of a body of mass 10 kg is 10 kg-wt or 10 kgf. For this reason, the gravitational units are also called practical units.

Example 2 If an electron is subjected to a force of 10^{-25} N in an X-ray machine, then find out the time taken by the electron to cover a distance of 0.2 m. Take mass of the electron = 10^{-30} kg.

Sol. The acceleration of the electron

$$a = \frac{F}{m} = \frac{10^{-25}}{10^{-30}} = 10^5\text{ m/s}^2$$

The time taken by the electron (t) to cover the distance (s) of 0.2 m can be given by

$$s = ut + \frac{1}{2}at^2$$

$$0.2 = 0 + \frac{1}{2} \times 10^5 \times t^2$$

$$t^2 = 0.4 \times 10^{-5} = 4 \times 10^{-6}\text{ s}^2$$

$$t = 2 \times 10^{-3}\text{ s}$$

Newton's Second Law in Component Form and its Significance

In terms of their rectangular components, the force, momentum and acceleration vectors can be expressed as

$$\mathbf{F} = F_x\hat{\mathbf{i}} + F_y\hat{\mathbf{j}} + F_z\hat{\mathbf{k}}$$

$$\mathbf{p} = p_x\hat{\mathbf{i}} + p_y\hat{\mathbf{j}} + p_z\hat{\mathbf{k}}$$

and $$\mathbf{a} = a_x\hat{\mathbf{i}} + a_y\hat{\mathbf{j}} + a_z\hat{\mathbf{k}}$$

From the formula of force in vector form, for constant m,

$$\mathbf{F} = \frac{d\mathbf{p}}{dt} = m\mathbf{a}$$

$$\therefore \quad F_x\hat{\mathbf{i}} + F_y\hat{\mathbf{j}} + F_z\hat{\mathbf{k}} = \frac{d}{dt}(p_x\hat{\mathbf{i}} + p_y\hat{\mathbf{j}} + p_z\hat{\mathbf{k}})$$

$$= m(a_x\hat{\mathbf{i}} + a_y\hat{\mathbf{j}} + a_z\hat{\mathbf{k}})$$

Equating the components along the three coordinate axes, we get

$$F_x = \frac{dp_x}{dt} = ma_x,$$

$$F_y = \frac{dp_y}{dt} = ma_y \text{ and } F_z = \frac{dp_z}{dt} = ma_z$$

The above three equations represent the component form of Newton's second law.

Example 3 A force applied on an object of mass 1 kg produces an acceleration of 8 m/s². When a force of the same magnitude is applied to a carton of ice cream of mass m_2, it produces an acceleration of 12 m/s². What is the mass of the carton of ice cream and the magnitude of the force?

Sol. Given, $a_1 = 8\,\text{m/s}^2$, $a_2 = 12\,\text{m/s}^2$, $m_1 = 1\,\text{kg}$

and Force, $F = ?$

Apply $\Sigma\mathbf{F} = m\mathbf{a}$ to each object.

$$F_1 = m_1 a_1$$

and $$F_2 = m_2 a_2$$

$$F_1 = F_2 = F$$

or $$m_1 a_1 = m_2 a_2$$

$$\Rightarrow \quad \frac{m_2}{m_1} = \frac{a_1}{a_2} = \frac{8}{12}$$

$$m_2 = \frac{8}{12} = 0.67\,\text{kg}$$

$$F = m_1 a_1 = 1 \times 8 = 8\,\text{N}$$

Example 4 A bullet of mass 0.04 kg moving with a speed of 90 m/s enters a heavy wooden block and is stopped after a distance of 60 cm. What is the average resistive force exerted by the block on the bullet? NCERT

Sol. Given, $s = 60\,\text{cm} = 0.6\,\text{m}$, $u = 90\,\text{m/s}$

The retardation a of the bullet is given by

$$a = -\frac{u^2}{2s} = \frac{-90 \times 90}{2 \times 0.6}$$

$$\Rightarrow \quad a = -6750\,\text{m/s}^2$$

The retarding force by the second law of motion is

$$F = ma$$

or $$F = 0.04 \times 6750$$

or $$F = 270\,\text{N}$$

Actual resistive force and retardation of the bullet may not be uniform. It indicates only average force.

Example 5 The motion of a particle of mass m is described by $y = ut + \frac{1}{2}gt^2$. Find the force acting on the particle. NCERT

Sol. We know, $$y = ut + \frac{1}{2}gt^2$$

Now, by differentiating the above equation w.r.t. t, we get

$$v = \frac{dy}{dt} = u + gt$$

and acceleration, $$a = \frac{dv}{dt} = g$$

Then, the force is given by

$$F = ma = mg$$

Thus, the given equation describes the motion of a particle under acceleration due to gravity and y is the position coordinate in the direction of g.

Impulse

The measure of the action of a large force acting for a short duration of time to produce a finite change in momentum is called an **impulse.** Impulse is defined as the product of the average force and the time interval for which the force acts on the body. It is denoted by **I**.

Thus, Impulse = Average force × time

Impulse is a vector quantity. The direction of impulse is same as that of the force.

Its SI unit is newton-second (N-s).

Its dimensional formula is $[\text{MLT}^{-1}]$.

Expression for an Impulse

Consider a constant force **F** which acts on a body for time dt. The impulse is given by

$$d\mathbf{I} = \mathbf{F}\,dt$$

If the force acts on the body for a time interval from t_1 to t_2, the impulse is given by

$$\mathbf{I} = \int d\mathbf{I} = \int_{t_1}^{t_2} \mathbf{F}\,dt$$

If F_{av} is the average force, then

$$I = F_{av} \int_{t_1}^{t_2} dt = F_{av} [t]_{t_1}^{t_2}$$

$$I = F_{av} [t_2 - t_1]$$

$$\text{Impulse, } I = F_{av}\, \Delta t$$

According to Newton's second law of motion,

$$F = \frac{dp}{dt} \Rightarrow F\,dt = dp$$

Integrating both sides with limits, we get

$$\int_0^t F\,dt = \int_{p_1}^{p_2} dp$$

$$\Rightarrow \quad F \times t = p_2 - p_1$$

$$\Rightarrow \quad \text{Impulse, } I = p_2 - p_1$$

Thus, **the impulse of a force is equal to the total change in momentum produced by the force.**

Example 6 A batsman hits back a ball straight in the direction of the bowler without changing its initial speed of 12 m/s. If the mass of the ball is 0.15 kg, determine the impulse imparted to the ball. (Consider a ball in linear motion).

NCERT

Sol. Given, $m = 0.15$ kg, $v = 12$ m/s, $u = -12$ m/s

Change in momentum $= p_2 - p_1 = m[v - u]$

$= 0.15\,[12 - (-12)] = 0.15 \times 24$

$p_2 - p_1 = 3.60$ kg-m/s

Impulse, $I = p_2 - p_1 \Rightarrow I = 3.6$ N-s

Newton's Third Law of Motion

When we press a coiled spring, the spring is compressed by the force of our hand. In turn, the compressed spring exerts a force on our hand, and we can feel it. Also, the earth pulls a stone downwards due to gravity. But according to Newton, the stone exerts an equal and opposite force on the earth. We do not notice it since the earth is very massive and the effect of a small force on its motion is negligible.

Thus, forces always occur in pairs as a result of mutual interaction between two bodies. Thus, **Newton's third law states that for every action, there is always an equal and opposite reaction.**

In simple terms, the third law can be stated as follows

Force in nature always occurs in pairs. Force on body *A* by body *B* is equal and opposite to the force on the body *B* by *A*.

As shown in figure if F_{BA} is the force exerted by body A on B and F_{AB} is the force exerted by B on A, then according to Newton's third law,

$$F_{AB} = -F_{BA}$$

Force on A by $B = -$ Force on B by A

The condition is shown in figure.

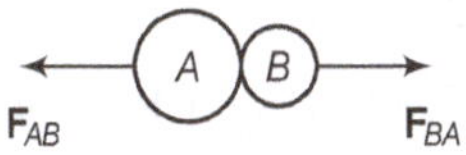

Forces acting on bodies *A* and *B* (*A* colliding with *B*)

Conservation of Momentum

This principle is a consequence of Newton's second and third law of motion.

According to this principle

'In the absence of an external force the total momentum of a system remains constant or conserved and does not change with time.'

If $\quad F_{ext} = 0$

The total momentum of an isolated system of interacting particle is conserved. Now, we will show that the total momentum of a system remains constant in the absence of external force. Internal forces acting among constituent particles of a system do not affect momentum of system as a whole.

Explanation of Conservation of Momentum

Let us consider the momenta of two particles system of masses m_1 and m_2 are p_1 and p_2 respectively, then the net momentum of the whole system

$$p = p_1 + p_2 \quad \ldots(i)$$

Suppose F_1 and F_2 are two forces acting on particles of masses m_1 and m_2. Let in a small time interval Δt the change produced by the forces F_1 and F_2 are Δp_1 and Δp_2.

Thus, net change in momentum

$$\Delta p = \Delta p_1 + \Delta p_2$$

or $$\frac{\Delta p}{\Delta t} = \frac{\Delta p_1}{\Delta t} + \frac{\Delta p_2}{\Delta t} \text{ or } \frac{dp}{dt} = \frac{dp_1}{dt} + \frac{dp_2}{dt} \quad [\text{as } \Delta t \to 0]$$

or $$\frac{dp}{dt} = F_1 + F_2 \quad \ldots(ii)$$

where, $\quad F_1 = F_{1\,ext} + F_{1\,int}$

and $\quad F_2 = F_{2\,ext} + F_{2\,int}$

or $$\frac{dp}{dt} = (F_{1\,ext} + F_{1\,int}) + (F_{2\,ext} + F_{2\,int})$$

or $$\frac{dp}{dt} = (F_{1\,ext} + F_{2\,ext}) + (F_{1\,int} + F_{2\,int}) \quad ...(iii)$$

From Newton's third law, the internal forces always occur in pair so

$$(F_{1\,int} + F_{2\,int}) = 0$$

or $$F_{1\,int} = -F_{2\,int}$$

From Eq. (iii), we get

Thus, $$\frac{dp}{dt} = (-F_{2\,int} + F_{2\,int}) + (-F_{1\,ext} + F_{2\,ext})$$

or $$\frac{dp}{dt} = 0 + F_{1\,ext} + F_{2\,ext} \quad \text{or} \quad \frac{dp}{dt} = F_{ext}$$

where, $$F = F_{1\,ext} + F_{2\,ext},\ F_{ext} = 0$$

Then, $$\frac{dp}{dt} = 0$$

or Momentum, $\mathbf{p}$ = constant

This equation shows that the law of conservation of linear momentum holds true, i.e. linear momentum of the system remains conserved.

Conservation of momentum theorem is applicable for $F_{ext} = 0$, it does not depend on internal forces. e.g.

(i) Let us consider a bullet fired from a gun. Then, force on the bullet by the gun is F and according to third law of motion, the force on the gun by bullet will be – F. The two forces act for a common interval of time Δt.

According to second law, $F\,\Delta t$ is the change in momentum of the bullet and $-F\,\Delta t$ is the change in momentum of the gun. Because bullet and gun are initially at rest and then change in momentum of the system is zero, so the sum of their final momenta must be zero.

Thus, if $\mathbf{p}_b$ is the momentum of the bullet after firing and $\mathbf{p}_g$ is the recoil momentum of the gun, then $\mathbf{p}_g = -\mathbf{p}_b$ or $\mathbf{p}_b + \mathbf{p}_g = 0$

(ii) Let a bomb be at rest, then its momentum will be zero. If the bomb explodes into two equal parts, then the parts fly off in exactly opposite directions with the same speed so that the total momentum is still zero. Here no external force is applied on the system of particles (bomb). Forces created are internal only.

Example 7 A moving neutron with speed 10^6 m/s collides with a deuteron at rest and sticks to it. Find the speed of the combination if masses of the neutron and deuteron are 1.67×10^{-27} kg and 3.34×10^{-27} kg, respectively.

Sol. Given, for neutron,

Mass, $m_1 = 1.67 \times 10^{-27}$ kg

Speed, $u_1 = 10^6$ m/s

For deuteron,

Mass, $m_2 = 3.34 \times 10^{-27}$ kg

Speed, $u_2 = 0$ [∵ the deuteron is at rest]

From principle of conservation of momentum,

$$m_1 u_1 + m_2 u_2 = (m_1 + m_2)\, v$$

$$1.67 \times 10^{-27} \times 10^6 + 3.34 \times 10^{-27} \times 0 = (3.34 + 1.67) \times 10^{-27} \times v$$

$$v = \frac{1.67 \times 10^{-27} \times 10^{+6}}{5.01 \times 10^{-27}} = 33.33 \times 10^4 \text{ m/s}$$

Some Important Implications About the Third Law of Motion

(i) **Newton's third law of motion is applicable irrespective of the nature of the forces** The forces of action and reaction may be mechanical, gravitational, electric or of any other nature.

(ii) **Action and reaction always act on two different bodies** If they acted on the same body, the resultant force would be zero and there could never be accelerated motion.

(iii) **The force of action and reaction cannot cancel each other** This is because action and reaction, though equal and opposite forces always act on different bodies and so cannot cancel each other.

(iv) **No action can occur in the absence of a reaction** In a tug of war, one team can pull the rope only if the other team is pulling the other end of the rope, no force can be exerted if the other end is free.

One team can exert the force of action because the other team provides the force of reaction.

Some Important Concepts about Newton's Third Law of Motion

(i) While walking we press the ground (action) with our feet slightly slanted in the backward direction. The ground exerts an equal and opposite force on us. The vertical component of the force of reaction balances our weight and the horizontal component enables us to move forward as shown in figure.

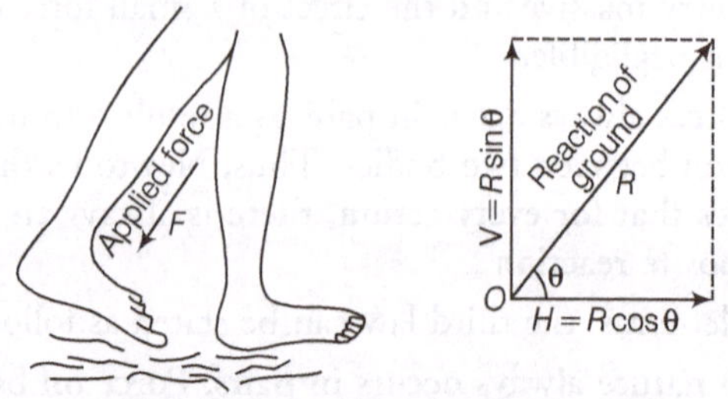

Applied force by the feet and its reaction force along with its components

(ii) **Rotatory lawn sprinkler** The action of rotatory lawn sprinkler is based on third law of motion. As water forces way out of its nozzle, it exerts an equal and opposite force in the backward direction, causing the sprinkler to rotate in the opposite direction. Thus, water is scattered in all directions as shown in figure.

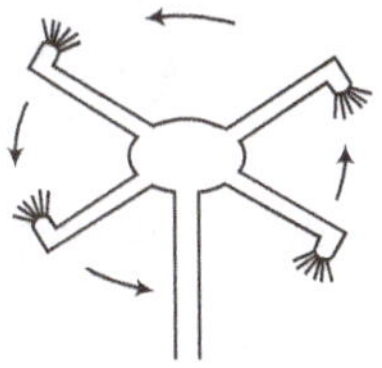

Water Rotatory lawn sprinkler

Newton's Second Law is the Real Law of Motion

Newton's first law and third law both are combined in second law and hence Newton's second law is the real law.

Newton's First Law Derived from Second Law

Let a body of mass m is subjected to an external force $\mathbf{F}$. If the acceleration produced in the body be $\mathbf{a}$, then from Newton's second law, $\mathbf{F} = m\mathbf{a}$.

Now, we assume that external force $\mathbf{F} = 0$, then from above equation, we get $\mathbf{a} = 0$.

Newton's Third Law Derived from Second Law

When two bodies A and B collide with each other, then during collision they exert forces on each other. Suppose the force exerted on the body A is $\mathbf{F}_{AB}$ and that on the body B is $\mathbf{F}_{BA}$. Suppose, due to these forces, the change in the momentum of the body A is $\Delta\mathbf{p}_1$ and that of the body B is $\Delta\mathbf{p}_2$. If the bodies remain in contact with each other for a time interval Δt, then we have

Impulse = Change in momentum

$$\mathbf{F}_{AB}\Delta t = \Delta\mathbf{p}_1 \text{ and } \mathbf{F}_{BA}\Delta t = \Delta\mathbf{p}_2$$

During collision, the bodies are the two parts of one combined body, and no external force is acting on this combined body.

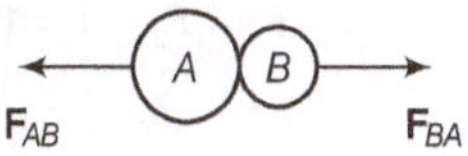

Hence, by Newton's second law, there should be no change in the momentum of the combined body, i.e.

$$\Delta\mathbf{p}_1 + \Delta\mathbf{p}_2 = 0$$
$$\mathbf{F}_{AB}\Delta t + \mathbf{F}_{BA}\Delta t = 0$$
$$\mathbf{F}_{AB} + \mathbf{F}_{BA} = 0$$
$$\mathbf{F}_{AB} = -\mathbf{F}_{BA}$$

Hence, the force exerted by the body B on the body A is equal and opposite to the force exerted by the body A on the body B. This is Newton's third law.

Equilibrium of a Particle

Forces which are acting at the same point or on a particle, are called **concurrent forces.** These forces are said to be in equilibrium when their resultant is zero.

Representation of concurrent forces

(i) If two forces $\mathbf{F}_1$ and $\mathbf{F}_2$ act on a particle, then they will be in equilibrium if $\mathbf{F}_1 = -\mathbf{F}_2$ i.e. two forces on the particle must be equal and opposite.

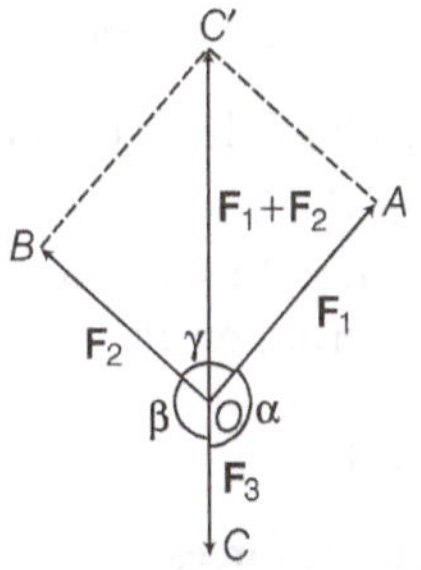

Equilibrium under concurrent forces

(ii) Three concurrent forces $\mathbf{F}_1, \mathbf{F}_2$ and $\mathbf{F}_3$ will be in equilibrium when the resultant of two forces $\mathbf{F}_1$ and $\mathbf{F}_2$ is equal and opposite to the third force $\mathbf{F}_3$.

Given, figure shows that three concurrent forces $\mathbf{F}_1, \mathbf{F}_2$ and $\mathbf{F}_3$ are acting at a point O and represented by OA, OB and OC, respectively. Let us complete the parallelogram $OAC'B$.

The diagonal OC' of the parallelogram represents $\mathbf{F}_1 + \mathbf{F}_2$, the resultant of $\mathbf{F}_1$ and $\mathbf{F}_2$ from law of parallelogram of forces.

If OC' is equal and opposite to OC, then

$$\mathbf{F}_1 + \mathbf{F}_2 = -\mathbf{F}_3 \text{ or } \mathbf{F}_1 + \mathbf{F}_2 + \mathbf{F}_3 = 0$$

i.e. three concurrent forces are in equilibrium when the resultant of any two of them is equal and opposite to the third.

A particle under the action of forces $\mathbf{F}_1, \mathbf{F}_2, \mathbf{F}_3, \ldots, \mathbf{F}_n$ will be in equilibrium if these forces can be represented by the sides of a closed n sided polygon in the same sense, i.e.

$$\mathbf{F}_1 + \mathbf{F}_2 + \mathbf{F}_3 + \ldots\ldots + \mathbf{F}_n = 0$$

This equation implies that

$$F_{1x} + F_{2x} + F_{3x} + ...+ F_{nx} = 0$$
$$F_{1y} + F_{2y} + F_{3y} + ...+ F_{ny} = 0$$
$$F_{1z} + F_{2z} + F_{3z} + ...+ F_{nz} = 0$$

where, F_{1x}, F_{1y} and F_{1z} are the rectangular components of F_1 along x, y and z-directions.

Free Body Diagram

A free body diagram (FBD) consists of a diagrammatic representation of a single body or a sub-system of bodies isolated from its surroundings showing all the forces acting on it.

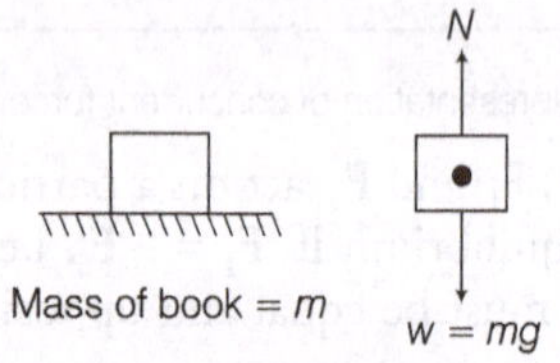

Free body diagram

Consider, for example, a book lying on a horizontal surface. A free body diagram of the book alone would consist of its weight ($w = mg$), acting through the centre of gravity and the reaction (N) exerted on the book by the surface.

Lami's Theorem

Equilibrium of concurrent forces :

According to this theorem, when three concurrent forces F_1, F_2 and F_3 acting on a body are in equilibrium, then

$$\frac{F_1}{\sin\alpha} = \frac{F_2}{\sin\beta} = \frac{F_3}{\sin\gamma}$$

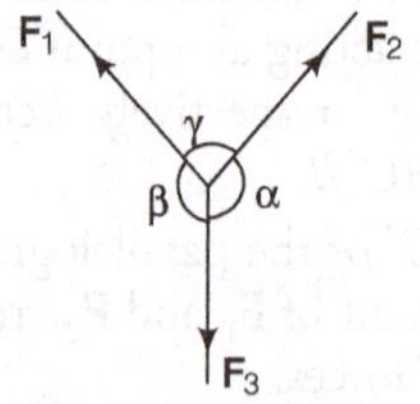

Three concurrent forces acting at some angles

where, α = angle between F_2 and F_3

β = angle between F_3 and F_1

γ = angle between F_1 and F_2

Proof As shown in given figure, the forces F_1, F_2 and F_3 can be represented by sides of ΔABC, taken in the same order.

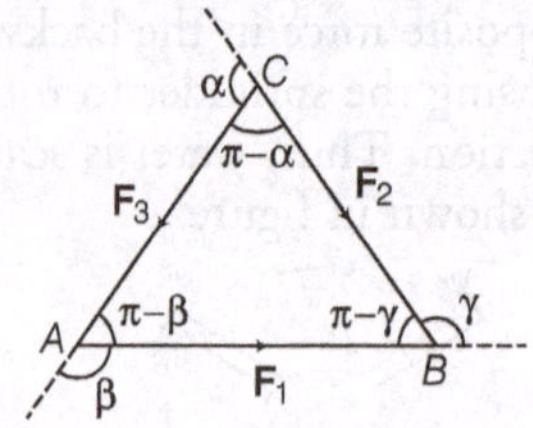

Applying law of sines to ΔABC, we get

$$\frac{F_1}{\sin(\pi-\alpha)} = \frac{F_2}{\sin(\pi-\beta)} = \frac{F_3}{\sin(\pi-\gamma)}$$

or $$\frac{F_1}{\sin\alpha} = \frac{F_2}{\sin\beta} = \frac{F_3}{\sin\gamma} \quad [\because \sin(\pi-\theta) = \sin\theta]$$

Example 8 The below figure is the part of a horizontal stretched net. Section AB is stretched with a force of 10 N, then determine the forces in the sections BC and BF.

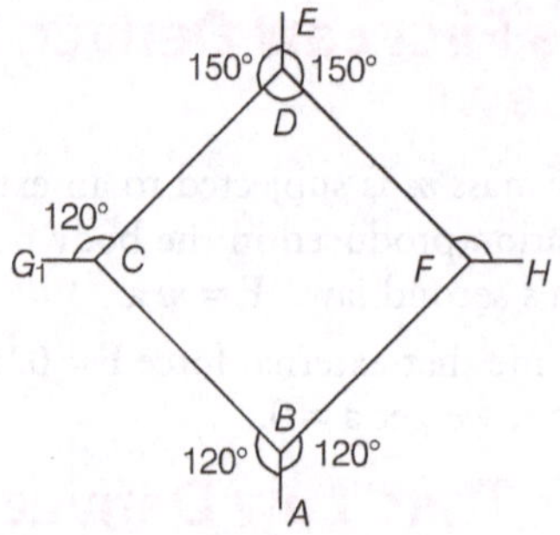

Sol. By drawing the free body diagram of point B.

Let the force in the section BC and BF are F_1 and F_2 respectively.

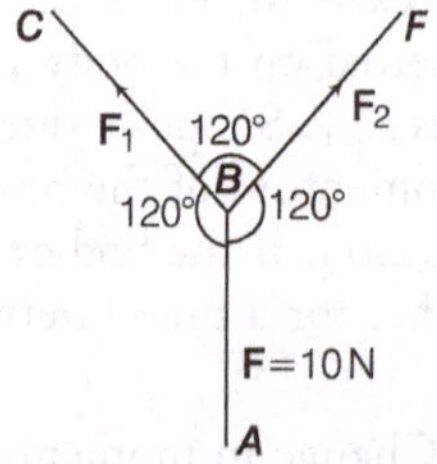

Three concurrent forces acting at some angles

From Lami's theorem, $\frac{F_1}{\sin 120°} = \frac{F_2}{\sin 120°} = \frac{F}{\sin 120°}$

$$F_1 = F_2 = F = 10\text{ N}$$

Common Forces in Mechanics

In mechanics, we encounter several kinds of forces.

(i) **Normal reaction** When bodies are in contact (e.g. a book resting on a table, a system of rigid bodies connected by ropes), there are mutual contact forces (for each pair of bodies) satisfying the third law of motion. The component of contact force normal to the surfaces in contact is called **normal reaction.** The component parallel to the surfaces in contact is called **friction.**

(ii) **Tension force** When a body of mass m is fastened with the string, then the weight of the body acts downwards while a force acts just opposite to the downwards force for balancing the downwards force, this force is called **tension.**

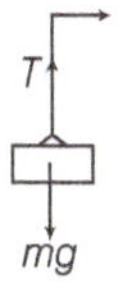

Tension force

$$T = mg$$

where, g = acceleration due to gravity,
T = tension in the string.

Note If the rope is not light, we will consider its weight as well.

Some Examples of Connected Motion

(i) Unequal masses $(m_1 > m_2)$ suspended from a pulley

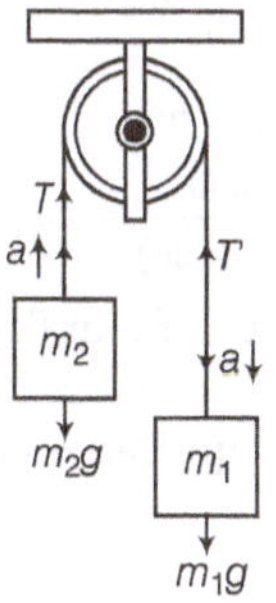

For mass m_2, applying Newton's second law,

$$T - m_2 g = m_2 a \quad \text{...(i)}$$

For mass m_1, $\quad m_1 g - T = m_1 a \quad$ ...(ii)

On adding Eqs. (i) and (ii), we get

$$(m_1 - m_2)\, g = (m_1 + m_2)\, a$$

$$\Rightarrow \quad a = \frac{(m_1 - m_2)\, g}{(m_1 + m_2)} \quad \text{...(iii)}$$

Putting the value of a from Eq. (iii) into Eq. (i), we get

$$T = m_2 a + m_2 g = \frac{(m_1 - m_2)\, m_2 g}{(m_1 + m_2)} + m_2 g$$

$$= m_2 g \left(\frac{(m_1 - m_2)}{(m_1 + m_2)} + 1 \right) = \frac{2 m_1 m_2}{(m_1 + m_2)}\, g$$

(ii) Body accelerated on a horizontal surface (m_2) by a falling body (m_1) through a pulley

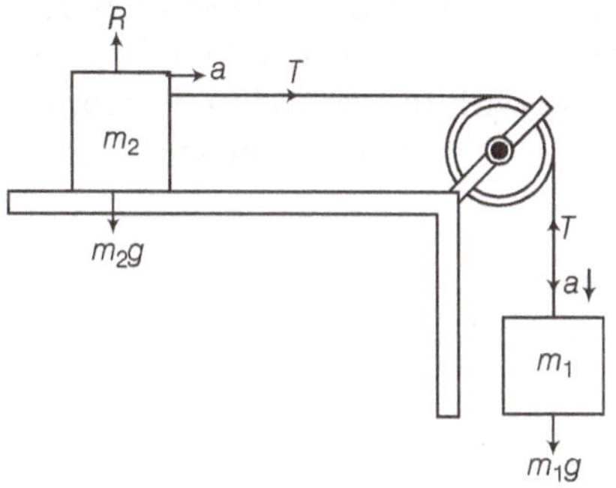

For mass m_2, $\quad T - 0 = m_2 a \quad$ ...(i)

For mass m_1, $\quad m_1 g - T = m_1 a \quad$ ...(ii)

On adding Eqs. (i) and (ii), we get

$$m_1 g = (m_1 + m_2) a$$

$$\Rightarrow \quad a = \left[\frac{m_1}{(m_1 + m_2)} \right] g \quad \text{...(iii)}$$

Putting the value of a from Eq. (iii) into Eq. (i), we get

$$T = \left(\frac{m_1 m_2}{m_1 + m_2} \right) g$$

(iii) Motion on a smooth inclined plane

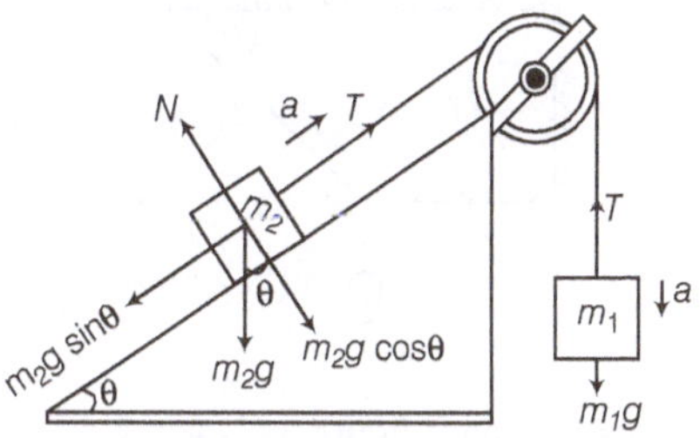

For mass m_1, $\quad m_1 g - T = m_1 a \quad$ ...(i)

For mass m_2, $\quad T - m_2 g \sin\theta = m_2 a \quad$ ...(ii)

On adding Eqs. (i) and (ii), we get

$$m_1 g - m_2 g \sin\theta = (m_1 + m_2)\, a$$

$$\Rightarrow \quad a = \left(\frac{m_1 - m_2 \sin\theta}{m_1 + m_2} \right) g \quad \text{...(iii)}$$

Putting the value of a from Eq. (iii) into Eq. (i), we get

$$T = m_1 g - m_1 a = m_1 \left[g - \left(\frac{m_1 - m_2 \sin\theta}{m_1 + m_2} \right) g \right]$$

$$= \left[\frac{m_1 m_2 (1 + \sin\theta)}{(m_1 + m_2)} \right] g$$

Example 9 See in figure a mass of 6 kg is suspended by a rope of length 2 m from the ceiling. A force of 50 N in the horizontal direction is applied at the mid-point P of the rope as shown. What is the angle, the rope makes with the vertical in equilibrium? (Take $g = 10\ ms^{-2}$). Neglect the mass of the rope. **NCERT**

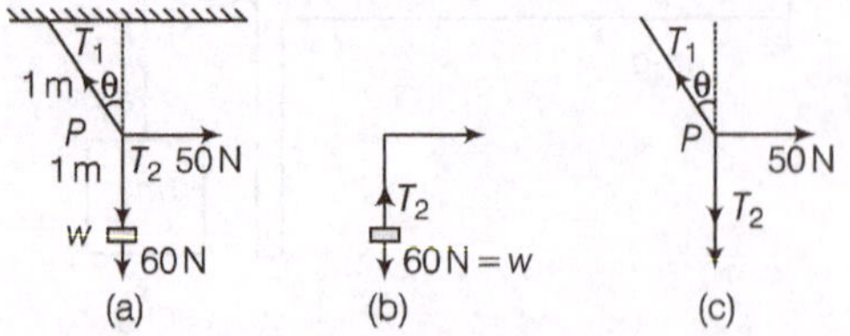

Sol. Fig. (b) is the free body diagram of w and Fig. (c) is the free body diagram of point P.

Consider the equilibrium of the weight w. Clearly,

$$T_2 = 6 \times 10 = 60\ \text{N}$$

Consider the equilibrium of the point P under the action of three forces, the tensions T_1 and T_2 and the horizontal force 50 N. The horizontal and vertical components of the resultant force must vanish separately.

$$T_1 \cos\theta = T_2 = 60\ \text{N and } T_1 \sin\theta = 50\ \text{N}$$

Which gives that $\tan\theta = \frac{5}{6}$ or $\theta = \tan^{-1}\left(\frac{5}{6}\right) = 40°$

Example 10 Determine the tensions T_1 and T_2 in the strings as shown in the figure.

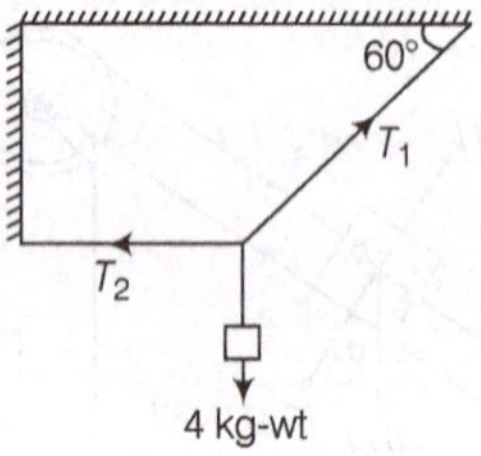

Sol. We redraw the above figure

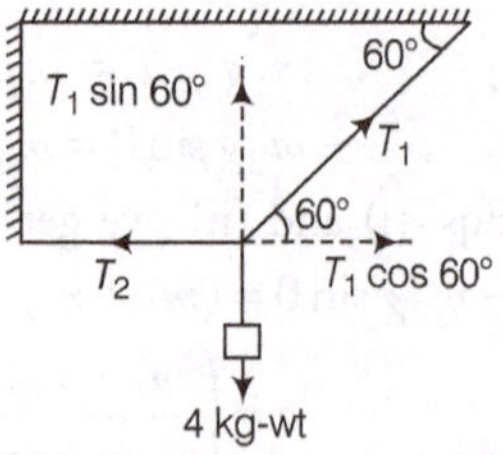

While resolving the tension T_1 along horizontal and vertical directions. As, in equilibrium,

$T_1 \sin 60° = 4\text{kg-wt} = 4 \times 9.8\text{N}$ ...(i)

$T_1 \cos 60° = T_2$ ...(ii)

Solving Eq. (i), we get

$$T_1 = \frac{4 \times 9.8}{\sin 60°} = 45.26\text{N}$$

Solving Eq. (ii), we get

$$T_2 = T_1 \cos 60°$$
$$= 45.26 \times 0.5$$
$$= 22.63\text{N}$$

Example 11 Two bodies of masses 10 kg and 20 kg respectively kept on a smooth, horizontal surface are tied to the ends of a light string. A horizontal force $F = 600$ N is applied to (i) A, (ii) B along the direction of string. What is the tension in the string in each case? **NCERT**

Sol. (*i*) **When force is applied on** A, then

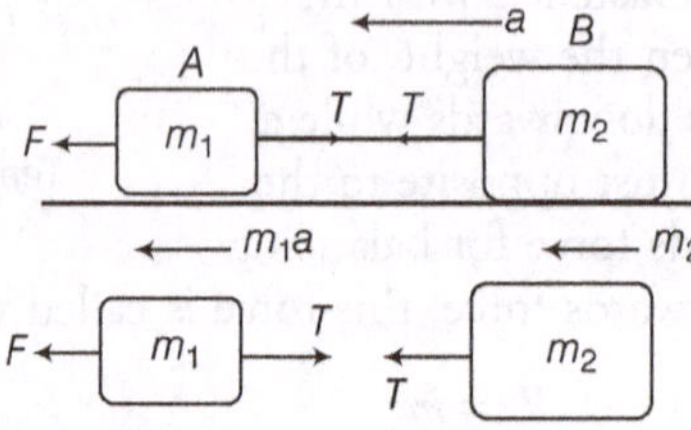

∵ Mass of body $A\ (m_1) = 10$ kg

Mass of body $B\ (m_2) = 20$ kg

Force applied $(F) = 600$ N

For body $A, F - T = m_1a$ ...(i)

For body $B, T = m_2a$ ...(ii)

Adding Eqs. (i) and (ii), we get

$$F = (m_1 + m_2)a$$

or $$a = \frac{F}{m_1 + m_2}$$

$$= \frac{600}{(10 + 20)} = 20\ \text{m/s}^2$$

Substituting value of a in Eq. (ii), we get

$$T = m_2a = 20 \times 20\ \text{N} = 400\ \text{N}$$

(*ii*) **When force is applied on** B, then

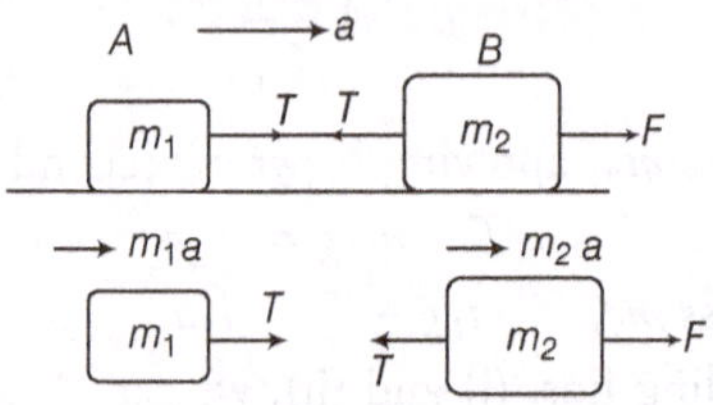

For body $A, T = m_1a$ ...(iii)

For body $B, F - T = m_2a$ ...(iv)

Adding Eqs. (iii) and (iv), we get

$$F = (m_1 + m_2)a$$

or $$a = \frac{F}{m_1 + m_2}$$

$$= \frac{600}{10 + 20} = 20\ \text{m/s}^2$$

Substituting the value of a in Eq. (iii), we get

$$T = m_1a = 10 \times 20 = 200\ \text{N}$$

Example 12 A body of mass m_1 equal to 20 kg is placed on a smooth horizontal table. This body is connected to a string which passes over a frictionless pulley. The string also carries another body of mass m_2 equal to 10 kg at the other end.

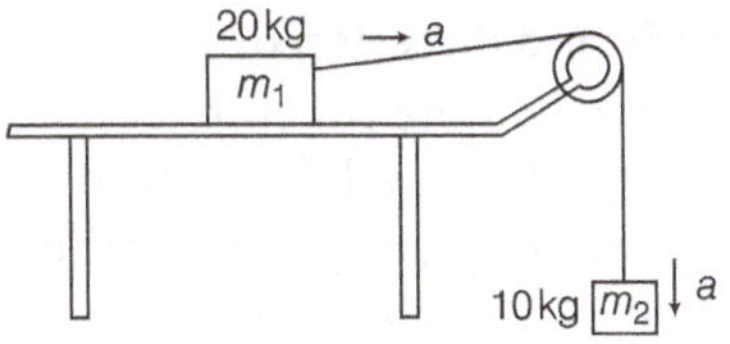

Find out the acceleration which will be produced when the nail fixed on the table is removed, also find out the tension in the string during the motion of the bodies. What is the result, when the bodies stop? Take $g = 10$ N/kg.

Sol. When the nail fixed on the table is removed, system of two bodies moves with an acceleration a in the forward direction. The acceleration can be found by using Newton's second law.

Draw the FBD for each body as shown in the figure

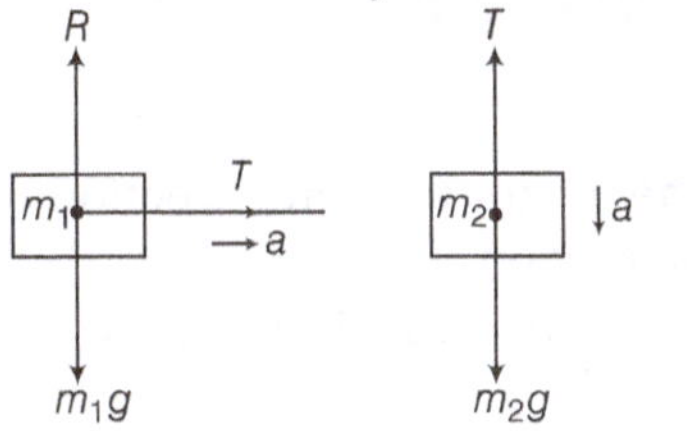

For mass m_1, $T = m_1 a$ ...(i)

For mass m_2, $m_2 g - T = m_2 a$ ...(ii)

Adding Eqs. (i) and (ii), we get

$$m_1 a + m_2 a = m_2 g$$

$$a = \frac{m_2 g}{m_1 + m_2} = \frac{10 \times 10}{20 + 10} = \frac{100}{30} = 3.33 \text{ m/s}^2$$

Tension, $T = m_1 a = 20 \times 3.33 = 66.6$ N

When the bodies stop, acceleration, a will be zero. Suppose, the tension becomes T'. As the net force on each body is zero, so for body m_2

$$T' = m_2 g = 10 \times 10 = 100 \text{ N}$$

Topic Practice 1

Multiple Choice Questions

1 Mark

1. Inertia is also called
   (a) resistance to force
   (b) resistance to change
   (c) resistance to momentum
   (d) None of the above

2. The mud guards over the wheels of a bike work on the basis of
   (a) inertia of rest
   (b) inertia of motion
   (c) inertia of direction
   (d) Newton's second law of motion

3. Newton's first law is based upon
   (a) law of gravitation
   (b) law of inertia given by Galileo
   (c) Both (a) and (b)
   (d) None of the above

4. The state of rest and state of uniform linear motion are equivalent because
   (a) no force is acting on both of them
   (b) two equal forces acting in opposite direction are acting on both of them
   (c) Both (a) and (b)
   (d) None of the above

5. When a body is dropped from rest, the motion is
   (a) uniform accelerated
   (b) uniform retarded
   (c) uniform
   (d) None of the above

6. The motion of a particle of mass m is described by $y = ut + gt^2$. Find the force acting on the particle.
   (a) Zero (b) mg (c) $2\,mg$ (d) $3\,mg$

7. A student attempts to pull himself up by tugging on his hair. He will not succeed
   (a) as the exerted force is small
   (b) the frictional force while gripping, is small
   (c) Newton's law of inertia is not applicable to living beings
   (d) as the force applied is internal to the system

8. For a given change in linear momentum, when time of impact decrease, force
   (a) decreases
   (b) increases
   (c) remains same
   (d) first decreases then increases

9. The dimensional formula of impulse is
   (a) $[ML^2T^{-2}]$ (b) $[MLT^{-2}]$
   (c) $[ML^2T^{-1}]$ (d) $[MLT^{-1}]$

10. A book is lying on the table. What is the angle between the action of the book on the table and reaction of the table on the book?
   (a) 0° (b) 30° (c) 45° (d) 180°

Very Short Answer Type Questions
(1 Mark)

11. Why fruits fall down from a tree, when its branches are shaken?

12. Why an athlete runs some steps before taking a jump?

13. A man jumping out of a moving train falls with his head forward. Why?

14. Bodies of larger mass need greater initial effort to put them in motion. Why?

15. The distance travelled by a moving body is directly proportional to time. Is any external force acting on it?

16. A body is acted upon by a number of external forces. Can it remain at rest?

Short Answer Type I Questions
(2 Marks)

17. If you jerk a piece of a paper placed under a book very quickly, the book will not move. Why?

18. A person driving a car suddenly applies the brakes on seeing a child on the road ahead. If he is not wearing seat belt, he falls forward and hits his head against the steering wheel. Why? **NCERT**

19. Why are porcelain objects wrapped in paper or straw before packing for transportation?

20. Define one newton.

21. Why does a child feel more pain when she falls down on a hard cement floor, than when she falls on the soft muddy ground in the garden? **NCERT**

22. Action and reaction forces do not cancel each other. Why?

23. Can a body in linear motion be in equilibrium?

Short Answer Type II Questions
(3 Marks)

24. State second law of motion and show that second law is the real law of motion.

25. Explain the term impulse. Show that impulse of a variable force is equal to the total change in momentum produced by the force.

26. Ten one-rupee coins are put on top of each other on a table. Each coin has mass m. Give the magnitude and direction of
   (i) the force on the 7th coin (counted from the bottom) due to all the coins on its top,
   (ii) the force on the 7th coin by the 8 coin, (counted from the bottom)
   (iii) the reaction of the 6th coin on the 7th coin. (counted from the bottom) **NCERT**

27. State and explain Newton's second law of motion. Deduce the relation $F = ma$ from it.

28. What are concurrent forces? Prove that under the action of three concurrent forces $\mathbf{F}_1$, $\mathbf{F}_2$ and $\mathbf{F}_3$; a body will be in equilibrium when $\mathbf{F}_1 + \mathbf{F}_2 + \mathbf{F}_3 = 0$.

Long Answer Type Questions
(5 Marks)

29. Give the magnitude and direction of the net force acting on
   (i) a drop of rain falling down with a constant speed.
   (ii) a cork of mass 10 g floating on water.
   (iii) a kite skillfully held stationary in the sky.
   (iv) a car moving with a constant velocity of 30 km/h on a rough road.
   (v) a high speed electron in space far from all gravitational (material) objects and free of electric and magnetic fields. **NCERT**

30. Figure shows (x, t), (y, t) diagram of a particle moving in 2-dimensions.

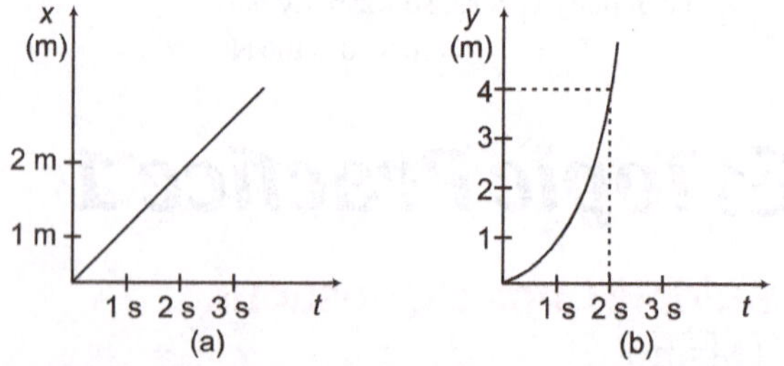

If the particle has a mass of 500 g, find the force (direction and magnitude) acting on the particle. **NCERT Exemplar**

31. Explain why?
(i) A horse cannot pull a cart and run in empty space.
(ii) Passengers are thrown forward from their seats when a speeding bus stops suddenly.
(iii) It is easier to pull a lawn mower than to push it.
(iv) A cricketer moves his hands backwards while holding a catch. **NCERT**

Numerical Problems

32. A force of 1 N acts on a body of mass 1 g. Calculate the acceleration produced in the body. **[1 M]**

33. Calculate the force acting on a body which changes the momentum of the body at the rate of 1 kg-m/s^2. **[1 M]**

34. A force of 36 dyne is inclined to the horizontal at an angle of 60°. Find the acceleration in a mass of 18 g that moves in a horizontal direction. **[1 M]**

35. A woman throws an object of mass 500 g with a speed of 25 m/s.
(i) What is the impulse imparted to the object?
(ii) If the object hits a wall and rebounds with half the original speed, what is the change in momentum of the object? **[2 M]**

36. A passenger of mass 72.2 kg is riding in an elevator while standing on a platform scale. What does the scale read when the elevator cab is (i) descending with constant velocity (ii) ascending with constant acceleration, 3.5 m/s^2? **[2 M]**

37. A person of mass 50 kg stands on a weighing scale on a lift. If the lift is descending with a downwards acceleration of 9 m/s^2, what would be the reading of the weighing scale? ($g = 10$ m/s^2) **NCERT Exemplar [2 M]**

38. A pebble of mass 0.05 kg is thrown vertically upwards. Give the direction and magnitude of the net force on the pebble
(i) during its upward motion.
(ii) during its downward motion.
(iii) at the highest point where it is momentarily at rest.
Do your answer change if the pebble was thrown at an angle of 45° with the horizontal direction? Ignore air resistance. **NCERT [3 M]**

39. A stream of water flowing horizontally with a speed of 15 m/s gushes out of a tube of cross-sectional area 10^{-2} m^2 and hits a vertical wall nearby. What is the force exerted on the wall by the impact of water, assuming it does not rebound? **[3 M]**

40. A helicopter of mass 1000 kg rises with a vertical acceleration of 15 m/s^2. The crew and the passengers weigh 300 kg. Give the magnitude and direction of the
(i) force on floor by the crew and passengers.
(ii) action of the rotor of the helicopter on the surrounding air
(iii) force on the helicopter due to the surrounding air, take $g = 10$ m/s^2. **NCERT [3 M]**

41. A girl riding a bicycle along a straight road with a speed of 5 m/s throws a stone of mass 0.5 kg which has a speed of 15 m/s with respect to the ground along her direction of motion. The mass of the girl and bicycle is 50 kg. Does the speed of the bicycle change after the stone is thrown? What is the change in speed, if so? **NCERT Exemplar [3 M]**

42. Give the magnitude and direction of the net force acting on a stone of mass 0.1 kg.
(i) Just after it is dropped from the window of a stationary train.
(ii) Just after it is dropped from the window of a train running at a constant velocity of 36 km/h.
(iii) Just after it is dropped from the window of a train accelerating with 1 m/s^2.
(iv) Lying on the floor of a train which is accelerating with 1 m/s^2, the stone being at rest relative to the train. Neglect air resistance throughout. **[5 M]**

43. Figure below shows the position-time graph of a particle of mass 4 kg. What is the (i) force on the particle for $t < 0$, $t > 4$ s, $0 < t < 4$ s? (ii) impulse at $t = 0$ and $t = 4$ s? (Consider one-dimensional motion only).

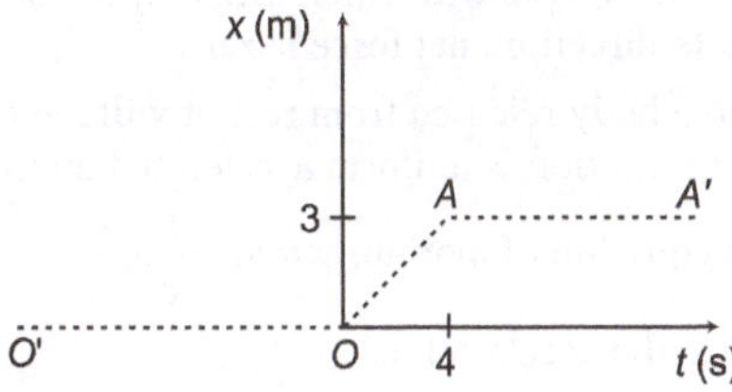

NCERT [5 M]

44. A block of mass 25 kg is raised by a 50 kg man in two different ways as shown in figure. What is the action on the floor by the man in the two cases? If the floor yields a normal force of 700 N, which mode should the man adopt to lift the block without the floor yielding? **NCERT [5 M]**

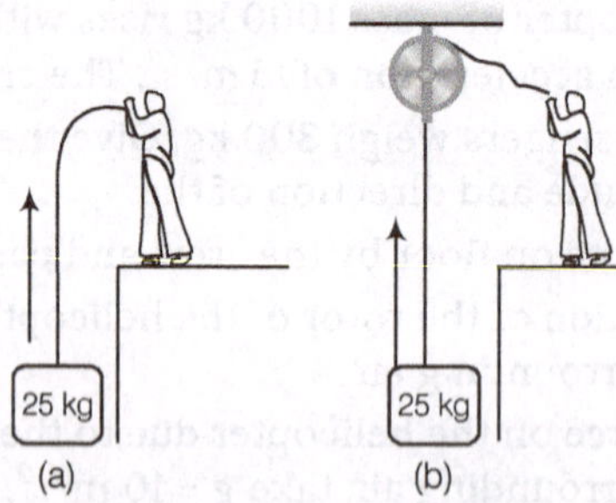

45. Figure below shows the position-time graph of a body of mass 0.04 kg. Suggest a suitable physical context for this motion. What is the time between two consecutive impulses received by the body?

What is the magnitude of each impulse? **NCERT [5 M]**

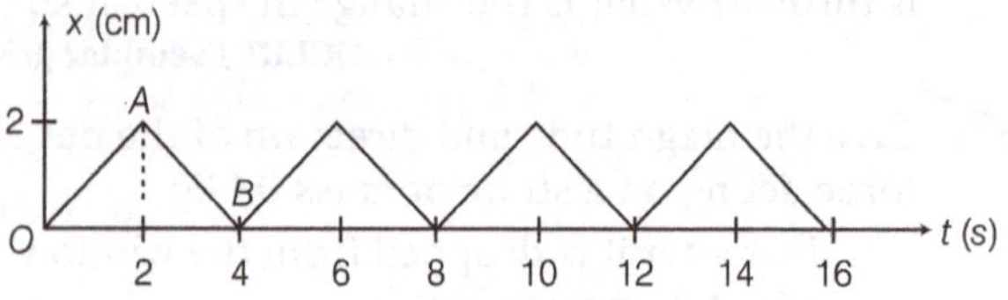

Hints & Solutions

1. (*b*) Inertia is a property which resist to change. A body does not change its state of rest or uniform motion unless an external force compels it to change that state.

2. (*c*) The rotating wheels of any vehicle throw out mud, if any, tangentially due to directional inertia. The mud guards over the wheels stop this mud and protect the clothes, etc.

3. (*b*) According to Newton's first law, a body at rest remains at rest or in uniform motion continue in motion till an external force is not applied on it. Galileo's law of inertia is the base of Newton's first law.

4. (*c*) When two forces with equal intensity act on a body in opposite direction, net force is zero.

5. (*a*) When a body released from rest, it will move under gravity, i.e. motion is uniform accelerated motion.

6. (*c*) From equation of motion, $y = ut + \frac{1}{2}at^2$ ...(i)

where, a is the acceleration

Given equation is, $y = ut + \frac{1}{2} \cdot 2gt^2$ ...(ii)

Comparing Eqs. (i) and (ii), we get

Acceleration $= 2g$

Force $= m.2g = 2mg$

7. (*d*) As by an internal force, momentum of the system cannot be changed.

8. (*b*) Since, force

$$= \frac{\text{change in momentum } (dp)}{\text{change in time } (dt)} \text{ or } F \propto \frac{1}{dt}$$

Thus, when time decreases, force increases.

9. (*d*) The dimensional formula of impulse is impulse = force × time = $[MLT^{-2}] \times [T] = [MLT^{-1}]$

10. (*d*) Since, action and reaction act in opposite directions on same line, hence angle between them is 180°.

11. Before shaking the branches, fruits are at rest. When branches are shaken, they come in motion, while the fruits tend to remain at rest due to inertia of rest. As a result, fruits get detached from the branches and fall down.

12. An athlete always runs for some distance before taking a jump, so that inertia of motion may help him in his muscular efforts to take a longer jump.

13. As the man jumps out from a moving train, his feet suddenly come to rest on touching the ground, while the upper part of his body continues to move forward. That is why he falls with his head forward.

14. According to the Newton's second law of motion, $F = ma$, for given acceleration a, if m is large, F should be more i.e. greater force will be required to put a larger mass in motion.

15. When $S \propto t$, so acceleration = 0, Therefore, no external force is acting on the body.

16. Yes, if the external forces acting on the body can be represented in magnitude and direction by the sides of a closed polygon taken in the same order.

17. As the time duration is very small, so the force applied on the piece of paper does not produce any displacement in the book. The book continues in its state of rest due to inertia. [2]

18. When a person driving a car suddenly applies the brakes, the lower part of the body slower down with the car while upper part of the body continues to move forward due to inertia of motion. If driver is not wearing seat belt, then he falls forward and his head hits against the steering wheel. [1 + 1]

19. Porcelain objects are wrapped in paper or straw before packing to reduce the chances of damage during transportation. During transportation sudden jerks or even fall can take place. Forces are created at the point of collision and the force takes longer time to reach the porcelain objects through paper or straw for same change in momentum as $F = \Delta p / \Delta t$ and therefore a lesser force acts on object. [1 + 1]

20. Refer to text on page 111 (Newton's second law of motion).

21. When a child falls on a cement floor, her body comes to rest instantly.

But $F \times \Delta t$ = change in momentum = constant.

As time of stopping Δt decreases, therefore. F increases and hence child feel more pain. When she falls on a soft muddy ground in the garden, the time of stopping increases and hence F decreases and she feels lesser pain. [2]

22. This is because forces of action and reaction always act on two different bodies. [2]

23. Yes, provided the vector sum of the forces acting upon the body is zero. [2]

24. Refer to text on pages 111 and 115 (Newton's second law of motion and Newton's second law is the real law of motion).

25. Refer to text on pages 112 and 113 (Impulse).

26. $\because$ Mass of each coin = m

Number of total coins = 10

(i) Force acting on 7th coin (counted from the bottom)

= Weight of the coins above it

= Weight of 3 coins = 3 mg N (downward) [1]

(ii) Force acting on 7th coin by the 8th coin = weight of the 8 coins + weight of two coins supported by 8 coins

= $mg + 2mg$ = 3 mg N (downward) [1]

(iii) Reaction of the 6th coin on the 7th coin

= – (force exerted on 6th coin)

= – (weight of 4 coins)

= – 4 mg N (vertically upward) [1]

27. Refer to text on page 111 (Newton's second law of motion).

28. Refer to text on page 115 (Equilibrium of a particle).

29. (i) As drop of rain is falling downward with a constant speed, therefore its acceleration is zero.

According to Newton's second law of motion, net force acting on drop $F = ma = 0$.

(ii) In floating condition, the weight of the body is balanced by the upthrust. Therefore, net force acting on a cork floating on water $F = 0$.

(iii) As kite is held stationary in the sky, therefore acceleration of the kite is zero. Therefore, net force acting on the kite $F = ma = 0$.

(iv) As car is moving with a constant velocity, therefore, its acceleration is zero i.e. $a = 0$ therefore, net force acting on the car $F = ma = 0$.

(v) As electron is in a space where there is no electric field, magnetic field and gravitational (material) objects, therefore, no electric, magnetic and gravitational force is acting on it. Hence, net force acting on electron is zero. [1 × 5]

30. Given, mass of the particle (m) = 500 g = 0.5 kg

x-t graph of the particle is a straight line.

Hence, particle is moving with a uniform velocity along X-axis, i.e. its acceleration along X-axis is zero and hence, force acting along X-axis is zero.

y-t graph of particle is a parabola. Therefore, particle is in accelerated motion along y-axis. [2½]

At $t = 0, u_y = 0$

Along Y-axis, at $t = 2$ s, $y = 4$ m

Using equation of motion,

$$y = u_y t + \frac{1}{2} a_y t^2$$

$$4 = 0 \times 2 + \frac{1}{2} \times a_y \times (2)^2 \text{ or } a_y = 2 \text{ m/s}^2$$

$\therefore$ Force acting along Y-axis $(f_y) = ma_y$

$= 0.5 \times 2 = 1.0$ N (along Y-axis) [2½]

31. (i) When a horse is trying to pull a cart, he pushes the ground backward at an angle from the horizontal. According to Newton's third law of motion, the ground also apply equal reaction force on the feet of the horse in opposite direction. The vertical component of reaction balances the weight of the horse and horizontal component is responsible for motion of the cart. In empty space, there is no reaction force, therefore, a horse cannot pull a cart. [1]

(ii) When bus is moving, the passengers sitting in it are also in motion and moving with the speed of the bus. When bus stops suddenly then lower part of the body of passengers which is in contact with the bus slow down with the bus but upper part of the bodies of the passengers continue to remain in motion in initial direction due to its inertia of motion and hence are thrown forward. [1]

(iii) In pulling a lawn mower, a force F is applied in upward direction, making an angle θ with the horizontal [Fig. (a)]. Its vertical component in upward direction decreasing the effective weight of the mower. [1]

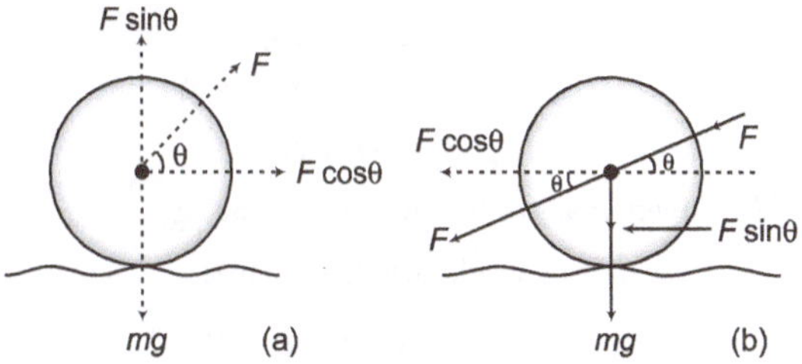

(a) (b)

In pushing a lawn mower, a force F is applied in downward direction, making an angle θ with the horizontal [Fig. (b)]. Its vertical component is in downward direction increasing the effective weight of the mower. Therefore, it is easier to pull a lawn mower than to push it. [1]

(iv) In holding a catch, the impulse imparted to the hands = $F \times \Delta t$ = change in momentum of the ball. When a cricketer lowers his hands to take a catch, he increases the time taken to stop the ball. As time t increases the force F applied on the hands of the cricketer by the ball decreases and his hands feel less hurt. [1]

32. Given, $F = 1\text{N}, m = 1\text{g} = 10^{-3}\text{kg}$

Now, $F = ma \Rightarrow a = \frac{F}{m} = \frac{1}{10^{-3}} = 10^3 \text{ m/s}^2$

33. We know that, F = rate of change of momentum

$F = 1 \text{ kg-m/s}^2 = 1\text{N}$

34. Given, $F = 36$ dyne at an angle of 60°.

$\therefore$ Component of force along x-direction

$F_x = F\cos 60° = 36 \times \frac{1}{2} = 18$ dyne

But $F_x = ma_x$,

$a_x = \frac{F_x}{m} = \frac{18}{18} = 1 \text{ cm/s}^2$

35. Given, mass of the object $(m) = 500 \text{ g} = 0.5$ kg

Speed of the object $(v) = 25$ m/s

(i) Impulse imparted to the object

= change in the momentum $= mv - mu$

$= m(v - u) = 0.5\,(25 - 0) = 12.5$ N-s [1]

(ii) Velocity of the object after rebounding $= -\frac{25}{2}$ m/s

$v' = -12.5$ m/s

$\therefore$ Change in momentum $= m(v' - v)$

$= 0.5\,(-12.5 - 25) = -18.75$ N-s [1]

36. Given, mass, $m = 72.2$ kg

Gravity acceleration, $g = 9.8 \text{ m/s}^2$

Scale reading = apparent weight = R = ?

(i) While descending with constant velocity, $a = 0$

$\therefore R = mg$

$R = 72.2 \times 9.8$

$\Rightarrow R = 707.56$ N [1]

(ii) While ascending with $a = 3.2 \text{ m/s}^2$

$R = m(g + a)$

$R = 72.2\,(9.8 + 3.2)$

$= 938.6$ N [1]

37. Given, mass of the person, $m = 50$ kg

Descending acceleration, $a = 9 \text{ m/s}^2$

Acceleration due to gravity, $g = 10 \text{ m/s}^2$ [1/2]

Apparent weight of the person,

$R = m(g - a) = 50\,(10 - 9) = 50$ N

$\therefore$ Reading of the weighing scale $= \frac{R}{g} = \frac{50}{10} = 5$ kg [1½]

38. When an object is thrown vertically upward or it falls vertically downward under gravity, then an acceleration $g = 10 \text{ m/s}^2$ acts downward due to the earth's gravitational pull.

Mass of pebble $(m) = 0.05$ kg

(i) **During upward motion**

Net force acting on pebble $(F) = mg = 0.05 \times 10$ N

$= 0.50$ N (vertically downward) [1]

(ii) **During downward motion**

Net force acting on pebble $(F) = mg = 0.05 \times 10$ N

$= 0.50$ N (vertically downward) [1/2]

(iii) **At the highest point**

Net force acting on pebble

$(F) = mg = 0.05 \times 10$ N

$= 0.50$ N (vertically downward)

If pebble was thrown at an angle of 45° with the horizontal direction, then acceleration acting on it and therefore force acting on it will remain unchanged, i.e. 0.50 N (vertically downward). In case (c), at the highest point the vertical component of velocity will be zero but horizontal component of velocity will not be zero. [1½]

39. Given, speed of the stream of water, $v = 15$ m/s

Area of cross-section of the tube, $A = 10^{-2} \text{ m}^2$

Volume of water coming out per second from the tube

$V = Av = 10^{-2} \times 15 = 15 \times 10^{-2} \text{ m}^3$ [1]

Density of water $= 10^3 \text{ kg/m}^3$

$\therefore$ Mass of the water coming out of the tube per second

$m = V\rho$ $\left[\because \text{Density} = \frac{\text{mass}}{\text{volume}}\right]$

$= 15 \times 10^{-2} \times 10^3 \text{ kg} = 150$ kg/s [1]

Force exerted on the wall by the impact of water

= change in momentum per second

$= mv = 150 \times 15 \text{ N} = 2250$ N [1]

40. $\because$ Mass of the helicopter, $m_1 = 1000$ kg

Mass of the crew and the passengers, $m_2 = 300$ kg

Acceleration of the helicopter, $a = 15 \text{ m/s}^2$

Acceleration due to gravity, $g = 10 \text{ m/s}^2$

(i) Let R_1 be the reaction applied by the floor on the crew and the passengers.

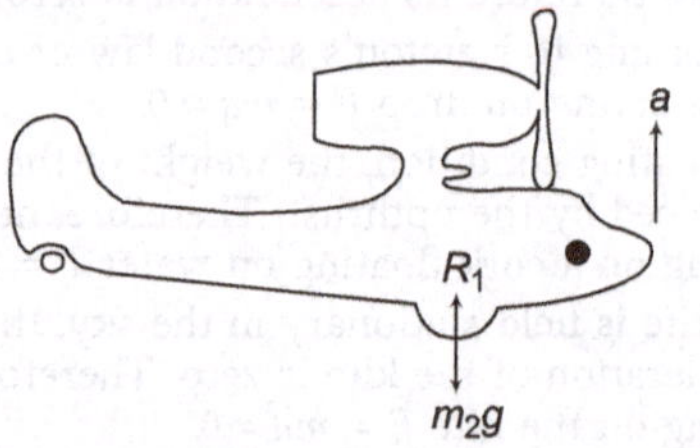

$\therefore R_1 - m_2 g = m_2 a$

or $R_1 = m_2 g + m_2 a = m_2(g + a)$

$= 300\,(10 + 15)$

$= 7500$ N (upward direction) [1]

(ii) Action of the rotor of the helicopter on the surrounding air

$= (m_1 + m_2)\,g + (m_1 + m_2)a$

$= (m_1 + m_2)(g + a)$

$= (1000 + 300) \times (10 + 15)$

$= 1300 \times 25 = 32500$ N

Force (action) of the rotor of the helicopter on the surrounding air $= 32500$ N (downward) [1]

(iii) According to Newton's third law of motion, for every action there is an equal and opposite reaction.

$\therefore$ Force on the helicopter due to the surrounding air

$= 32500$ N (upward direction) [1]

41. Total mass of girl, bicycle and stone,

$$m_1 = (50 + 0.5) \text{ kg} = 50.5 \text{ kg}$$

Velocity of bicycle, $u_1 = 5$ m/s

Mass of stone, $m_2 = 0.5$ kg

Velocity of stone, $u_2 = 15$ m/s

Mass of girl and bicycle, $m = 50$ kg

Yes, the speed of the bicycle changes after the stone is thrown.

Let, after throwing the stone the speed of bicycle be v m/s.

According to the law of conservation of linear momentum,

$$m_1u_1 = m_2u_2 + mv \quad [1]$$

$$50.5 \times 5 = 0.5 \times 15 + 50 \times v$$

$$252.5 - 7.5 = 50v \quad \text{or} \quad v = \frac{245.0}{50}$$

$$v = 4.9 \text{ m/s} \quad [1]$$

Change in speed $= 5 - 4.9 = 0.1$ m/s [1]

42. $\because$ Mass of stone $(m) = 0.1$ kg

(i) When stone is dropped from the window of a stationary train, it falls freely under gravity.

$\therefore$ Net force acting on stone (F)

$= mg = 0.1 \times 10$

$= 1.0$ N(vertical downward) [1½]

(ii) Just after the stone is dropped from the window of a train running at a constant velocity, i.e. acceleration of the train is zero. So, no force acts on the stone due to motion it falls freely under gravity. The force acts on it is due to its weight only, i.e. acceleration of the train is zero, so no force acts, on the stone due to this motion. [1½]

(iii) The train accelerates horizontally by 1 m/s^2, but as the stone is left it moves under gravity only so the net force on it will be due to gravity only. [1]

(iv) As the stone is accelerating with the train, so there must be a net horizontal force on it. Its weight also acts but is balanced by reaction force of the floor.

$$F = m \times a_{(\text{train})} = 0.1 \times 1 = 0.1 \text{ N} \quad [1]$$

43. (i)

(a) For $t < 0$, the position-time graph is OO', for which displacement of the particle is zero, therefore, particle is at rest at the origin. Hence, acceleration and force acting on particle will also be zero.

(b) For $t > 4$s, the position-time graph AA' is parallel to time axis. Therefore, for $t > 4$s particle remains at a fixed distance of 3 m from the origin. It means particle is at rest. Therefore, acceleration and force acting on particle will be zero.

(c) For $0 < t < 4$s, the position-time graph OA is a straight line inclined at an angle from time axis, which is representing uniform motion of the particle, i.e. the particle is moving with a constant velocity. Therefore, acceleration and force acting on the particle will be zero. [1 × 3]

(ii) Impulse at $t = 0$

(a) Impulse = change in momentum

$= mv - mu = m(v - u)$

Before $t = 0$, particle is at rest, hence $u = 0$

After $t = 0$, particle is moving with a constant velocity.

Velocity of the particle = slope of position-time graph

$$= \frac{3 \text{ m}}{4 \text{ s}} = 0.75 \text{ m/s}$$

$\therefore$ Impulse = change in momentum

$= 4(0.75 - 0) = 3$ kg-m/s

(b) Impulse at $t = 4$s

Before $t = 4$s, particle is moving with a constant speed, $u = 0.75$ m/s

After $t = 4$s, particle is again at rest

$\because$ $v = 0$

$\therefore$ Impulse = Change in momentum $= m(v - u)$

$= 4(0 - 0.75)$

$= -3$ kg-m/s [1 × 2]

44. $\because$ Mass of block, $m = 25$ kg

Mass of the man, $M = 50$ kg

Force required to lift the block (F) = weight of the block

$$F = mg = 25 \times 10 = 250 \text{ N}$$

Weight of the man, $w = Mg = 50 \times 10 = 500$ N

Case (a) If the block is raised by the man as shown in Fig. (a), then, force is applied by the man in the upward direction due to which apparent weight of the man increases. When man applies force on block in upward direction, block applies force on man in downward direction, according to 3rd law of motion. Therefore, action on the floor by the man $= F + w$

$= 250 + 500 = 750$ N [2½]

Case (b) If the block is raised by the man as shown in Fig. (b), then, force is applied by the man in the downward direction due to which apparent weight of the man decreases.

Therefore, action on the floor by the man

$= mg - F = 500 - 250 = 250$ N

The floor yields a normal force of 700 N. Action on the floor in case (a) exceeds 700 N, and less than 700 N in case (b). Therefore, mode (b) has to be adopted by the man to lift the block. [2½]

45. Mass of the body, $m = 0.04$ kg

The position-time graph OA from $t = 0$ to $t = 2$s is a straight line, therefore body is moving with a constant velocity.

Velocity of the body, v = Slope of x - t graph

$$= \frac{2 - 0}{2 - 0} = 1 \text{ cm/s}$$

$$= 10^{-2} \text{ m/s} \quad [\because 1 \text{ cm} = 10^{-2} \text{ m}]$$

Part AB of position-time graph is also a straight line, therefore, velocity of the body

$$v' = \frac{0-2}{0-2} = -1 \text{ cm/s}$$
$$= -10^{-2} \text{ cm/s}$$

Negative sign shows that the direction of velocity is reversed after 2 s and it is being repeated. [3]

A suitable physical context for this motion is a ball moving with a constant velocity of 10^{-2} m/s between two walls located at $x = 0$ and at $x = 2$ m and rebounded repeatedly on striking each wall.

Magnitude of the impulse imparted to the ball after every two seconds

$$= \text{change in momentum of the ball}$$
$$= mv - mv' = m(v - v')$$
$$= 0.04\,[10^{-2} - (-10^{-2})]$$
$$= 8 \times 10^{-4} \text{ kg-m/s}$$ [2]

TOPIC 02 Friction and Circular Motion

Friction

Whenever a body moves or tends to move over the surface of another body, a force comes into play which acts parallel to the surface of contact and opposes the relative motion. This opposing force is called **friction.**

Consider a wooden block placed on a horizontal surface and give it a gentle push. The block slides through a small distance and comes to rest, then according to Newton's second law, a retarding force must be acting on the block. This retarding force or opposing force is called **friction** or **friction force.** As shown in figure, the force of friction always acts tangential to the surface in contact and in a direction opposite to the direction of (relative) motion of the body.

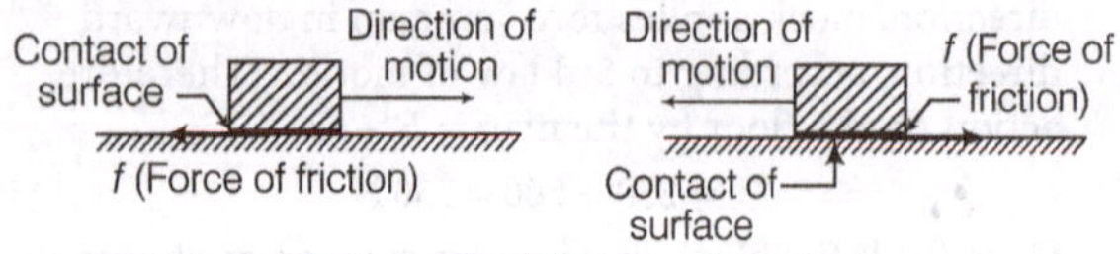

Friction in different directions

There are mainly two types of friction such as

1. Internal Friction

It arises on account of relative motion between two layers of a liquid. Internal friction is also referred as **viscosity** of liquid.

2. External Friction

It arises when two bodies in contact with each other try to move or there is an actual relative motion between the two bodies. This external friction is also called **contact friction.**

Further, external friction is of three types as given below

(i) Static Friction

Let us consider a wooden block placed over a horizontal table. Apply a small force F on it as shown in figure. The block does not move. The force of friction f_s comes into action which balances the applied force F.

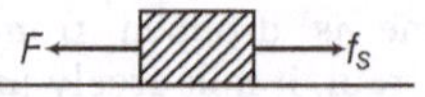

Static friction

Thus, force of friction which comes into play between two bodies before one body actually starts moving over the other is called **static friction** and it is denoted by f_s.

Therefore, static friction opposes the **impending motion** i.e. the motion that would take place under the applied force, if friction were absent. The static friction does not exist by itself. When there is no applied force, there is no static friction. It is a self adjusting force.

Laws of static friction

(i) The force of static friction is proportional to the normal force exerted by other surface normally on the former.

(ii) The static frictional force is given by $f_s \le \mu_s N$, where μ_s is the coefficient of static friction.

(iii) The 'less than or equal to' sign in the above equation represents the adjusting nature of the force of static friction.

(iv) The equality sign in the equation holds only when the static frictional force has its maximum value.

(v) It is independent of the area of contact between the two surfaces.

(ii) Limiting Friction

As we increase the applied force on the block, static friction f_s also increases to balance the applied force and the block does not move.

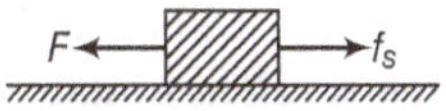

Static friction

Once the applied force is increased beyond a certain limit, the block just begins to move. At this stage, static friction is maximum.

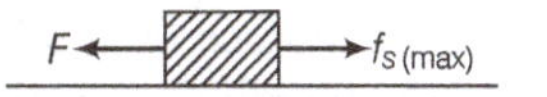

Maximum limiting friction acting on a body

Hence, maximum force of static friction which comes into play when a body just starts moving over the surface of another body is called **limiting friction**. Thus, $f_s \le f_{s\,(max)}$.

The value of limiting friction ($f_{s(max)}$) between two given surfaces is directly proportional to the normal reaction (R) between the two surfaces

i.e. $f_{s\,(max)} \propto R$ or $f_{s\,(max)} = \mu_s R$

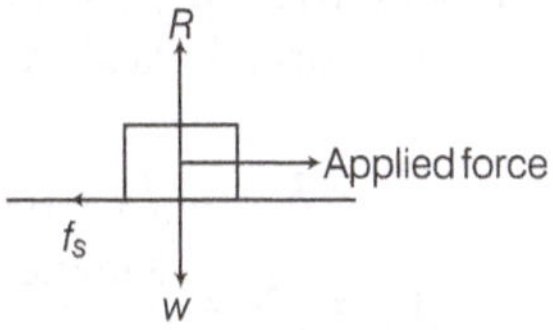

where, $R = w = mg$, m = mass of the block

or $$\mu_s = \frac{f_{s(max)}}{R} = \frac{\text{Limiting friction}}{\text{Normal reaction}}$$

The proportionality constant μ_s is called **coefficient of static friction**. It is defined as the ratio of limiting friction to the normal reaction.

Laws of limiting friction

(i) The direction of limiting friction force is always the opposite of the motion of the body.

(ii) The magnitude of the friction force is equal to the force that tends to move the body.

(iii) The magnitude of the limitng friction always have a constant ratio with the normal reaction force which acts between two surfaces.

(iv) Limiting friction force depends on the roughness of the surface.

(v) Area between the surfaces is not responsible for the magnitude of the frictional force.

Example 1 A horizontal force of 980 N is required to slide a sledge weighing 1200 kgf over a flat surface. Calculate the coefficient of friction.

Sol. Given, $f_s = 980$ N, $R = Mg = 1200\,\text{kgf} = 1200 \times 9.8$ N

Now, coefficient of static friction

i.e. $$\mu_s = \frac{f_s}{R} = \frac{980}{1200 \times 9.8} = 0.083$$

Example 2 A block of mass 2 kg is placed on the floor, the coefficient of static friction is 0.4. A force of 2.5 N is applied on the block as shown in figure. Calculate the force of friction between the block and the floor.

Sol. Here $m = 2\,\text{kg}, \mu_s = 0.4, g = 9.8\,\text{m/s}^2$

The value of limiting friction

$F_{s\,(max)} = \mu_s R = \mu_s\, mg = 0.4 \times 2 \times 9.8 = 7.84$ N

As the applied force of 2.5 N is less than the limiting friction (7.84 N), so the block does not move.

In this situation, Force of friction = Applied force = 2.5 N

Angle of Friction

The angle of friction may be defined as the angle which the resultant of the limiting friction and the normal reaction makes with the normal reaction.

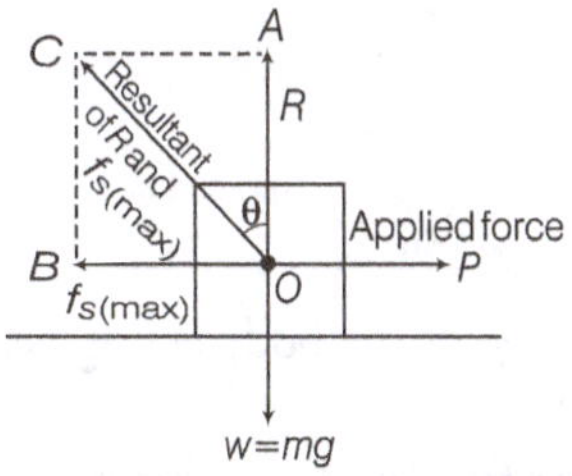

In the above figure, OA represents the normal reaction R which balances the weight of the body. OB represents the limiting friction. P is the applied force and OC is the resultant of limiting friction and normal reaction. The angle θ between the normal reaction R and the resultant OC is the angle of friction.

The value of angle of friction depends on the nature of materials of the surfaces in contact and the nature of the surfaces (smooth or rough).

Relation between angle of friction (θ) and coefficient of friction (μ_s)

In ΔAOC, $$\tan\theta = \frac{AC}{OA} = \frac{OB}{OA} = \frac{f_{s\,(max)}}{R}$$

But $$\frac{f_{s\,(max)}}{R} = \mu_s = \text{coefficient of static friction}$$

$\therefore$ $$\tan\theta = \mu_s \quad \text{or} \quad \theta = \tan^{-1}(\mu_s)$$

Hence, coefficient of static friction is equal to tangent of the angle of friction.

Example 3 A force of 49 N is just sufficient to pull a block of wood weighing 10 kg on a rough horizontal surface, so calculate the coefficient of friction and angle of friction.

Sol. Here, F = applied force= 49 N, m = 10 kg, g = 9.8 m/s^2

Coefficient of friction,

$$\mu = \frac{F}{R} = \frac{F}{mg} = \frac{49}{10 \times 9.8} = 0.5$$

As $\tan\theta = \mu = 0.5$

$\therefore$ $\theta = \tan^{-1}(0.5) = 26°34'$

Angle of Repose

Angle of repose is defined as the minimum angle of inclination of a plane with the horizontal, such that a body placed on the plane just begins to slide down the incline. It is represented by α and its value depends on material and nature of the surfaces in contact.

Consider a body of mass m placed on an inclined plane. The angle of inclination α of the inclined plane is so adjusted that a body placed on it just begins to slide down. Thus, α is the angle of repose the various forces acting on the body are

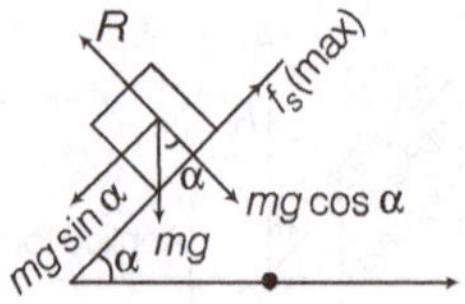

(i) The weight mg of the body acting vertically downwards.

(ii) The limiting friction $f_{s(\max)}$ acting along the inclined plane in the upward direction. It balances the component $mg\sin\alpha$ of the weight mg perpendicular to the inclined plane. Thus,

$$f_{s(\max)} = mg\sin\alpha \quad \text{...(i)}$$

(iii) The normal reaction R acting at right angle to the inclined plane in the upward direction. It balances the component $mg\cos\alpha$ of the weight mg perpendicular to the inclined plane. Thus

$$R = mg\cos\alpha \quad \text{...(ii)}$$

Dividing the Eq. (i) by Eq. (ii), we get

$$\frac{f_{s\,(\max)}}{R} = \frac{mg\sin\alpha}{mg\cos\alpha} \text{ or } \mu_s = \tan\alpha$$

Thus, the coefficient of static friction is equal to the tangent of the angle of repose.

As $\mu_s = \tan\theta = \tan\alpha$

$\therefore$ $\theta = \alpha$

Thus, the angle of friction is equal to the angle of repose.

(iii) Kinetic Friction

When we increase the applied force slightly beyond limiting friction, the actual motion starts and force of friction decreases. This means that the applied force is now greater than the force of limiting friction. The force of friction at this stage is called **kinetic friction** or **dynamic friction** which is actually a little bit less than the value of limiting friction.

Hence, kinetic friction or dynamic friction is the opposing force that comes into play when one body is actually moving over the surface of another body. Thus, kinetic friction opposes the **relative motion**.

There are four laws of kinetic friction such as

(a) The kinetic friction opposes the relative motion and has a constant value which depends on the nature of two surfaces in contact.

(b) The value of kinetic friction f_k is independent of the area of contact so long as the normal reaction remains the same.

(c) The kinetic friction does not depend on velocity.

(d) The value of kinetic friction f_k is directly proportional to the normal reaction R between the two surfaces.

i.e. $f_k \propto R$ or $f_k = \mu_k R$

$$\mu_k = \frac{f_k}{R} = \frac{\text{Kinetic friction}}{\text{Normal reaction}}$$

The proportionality constant μ_k is called **coefficient of kinetic friction** and it is defined as the ratio of kinetic friction to the normal reaction.

Variation of Frictional Force with Applied Force

The figure shows the variation of force of friction (f) with the applied force (F). As the applied force (F) increases, the static friction (f_s) increases to balance it. This shows that static friction is a self adjusting force. The kinetic friction is always less than the limiting friction $f_s^{\max}$. i.e. $f_k < f_s^{\max}$

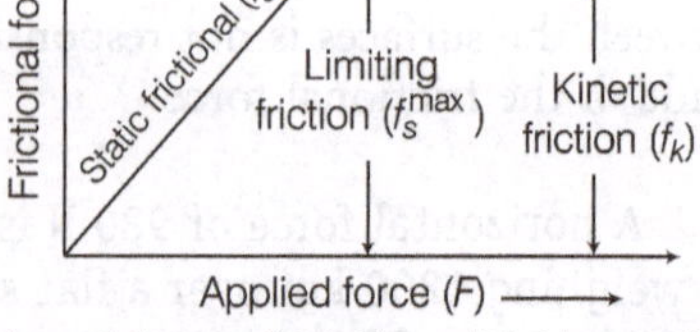

Variation of force of friction with the applied force

Note

- This can be shown as $f_k < f_{s(max)}$ or $\mu_k R < \mu_s R$
  $\therefore \quad \mu_k < \mu_s$
- Thus, the coefficient of kinetic friction is less than the coefficient of static friction.

Example 4 A hockey puck is given an initial speed of 20 m/s on a frozen pond as shown in figure. The puck remains on the ice and slides 120 m before coming to rest. Determine the coefficient of kinetic friction between the puck and the ice.

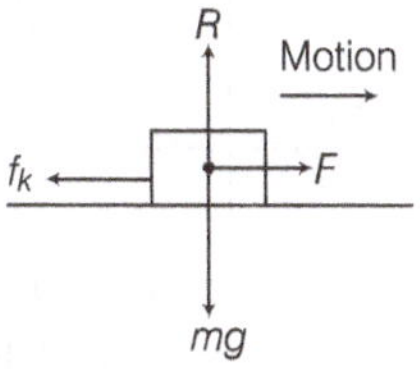

Sol. Given,

The initial speed, $u = 20$ m/s

Distance travelled, $x = 120$ m

$$v^2 = u^2 + 2ax \quad \text{[third equation of motion]}$$

$$0 = (20 \text{ m/s})^2 + 2a\,(120 \text{ m})$$

$$a = -1.67 \text{ m/s}^2$$

The negative sign shows that the acceleration is towards left, i.e. opposite the direction of the velocity.

$$\Sigma F_y = R - w = 0 \Rightarrow R = w = mg$$

Thus, $f_k = \mu_k R = \mu_k mg$

$$\Sigma F_x = -f_k = ma \Rightarrow -\mu_k mg = m(-1.67 \text{ m/s}^2)$$

$$\mu_k = \frac{1.67 \text{ m/s}^2}{9.80 \text{ m/s}^2} = 0.170$$

Example 5 A block *P* of mass 4 kg is placed on another block *Q* of mass 5 kg, and the block *Q* rests on a smooth horizontal table. For sliding block *P* on *Q*, horizontal force of 12 N is required to be applied on *P*. How much maximum force can applied on *Q* so that both *P* and *Q* move together? Also, find out acceleration produced by this force.

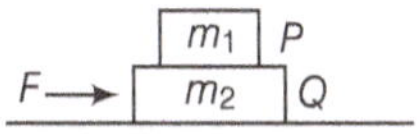

Sol. Here, $m_1 = 4$ kg, $m_2 = 5$ kg

Force applied on block $P = 12$ N

This force must be equal to the kinetic friction applied on *P* by *Q*.

$$\therefore \quad 12 = F_k = \mu_k R = \mu_k m_1 g$$

or $\quad 12 = \mu_k \times 4g \quad$ or $\quad \mu_k = \dfrac{12}{4g} = \dfrac{3}{g}$

Acceleration of $P = \dfrac{12}{4} = 3 \text{ m/s}^2$

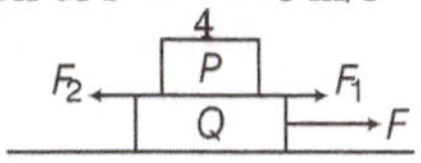

When force *F* is applied on *Q* to create common motion in *P* & *Q*, the forces created (friction) is shown in the diagram above. F_1 force will be created on *P* and F_2 force will be created on *Q*.

Considering forces on *Q*, we have

$$F - F_2 \text{ (net force)} = m_2 \times a = m_2 \times 3$$

Since, $\quad F_1 = F_2 = \mu_k m_1 g \Rightarrow F - \mu_k m_1 g = m_2 \times 3$

$$F = \mu_k m_1 g + m_2 \times 3 = \frac{3}{g} \times 4 \times g + 5 \times 3 = 12 + 15 = 27 \text{ N}$$

As this force moves both the blocks together on a smooth table, so the acceleration produced is

$$a = \frac{F}{m_1 + m_2} = \frac{27}{4+5} = 3 \text{ m/s}^2$$

Types of Kinetic Friction

(i) Sliding Friction

The force of friction that comes into play when a body slides over the surface of another body is called **sliding friction**. e.g. When a flat block is moved over the flat surface of a table, then the opposing force acting on it is known as sliding friction.

Example 6 What is the acceleration of the block and trolley system shown in a figure. If the coefficient of kinetic friction between the trolley and the surface is 0.04, what is the tension in the string? (Take, $g = 10 \text{ ms}^{-2}$). Neglect the mass of the string. **NCERT**

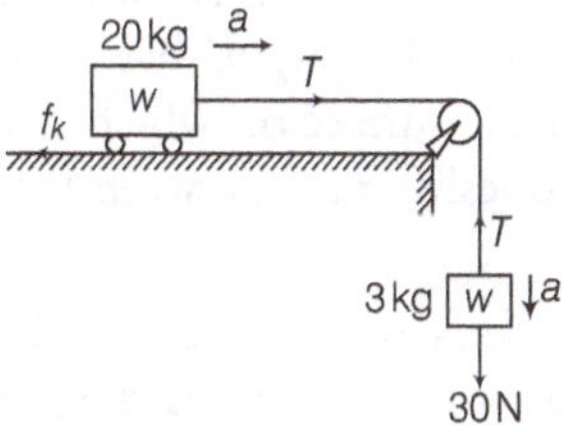

Sol. Applying the second law of motion to the block.

$$30 - T = 3a \quad \text{...(i)}$$

Apply the second law of motion to the trolley.

$$T - f_k = 20a$$

Now, $\quad f_k = \mu_k R = \mu_k mg$

Here, $\quad \mu_k = 0.04$

$$f_k = 0.04 \times 20 \times 10 = 8 \text{ N}$$

Thus, the equation for the motion of the trolley is

$$T - 8 = 20a \quad \text{...(ii)}$$

On adding Eqs.(i) and (ii), we get

$$22 = 23a$$

or $\quad a = \dfrac{22}{23} = 0.96 \text{ m/s}^2$

From Eq. (i), we get

$$30 - T = 3 \times 0.96$$

$$T = 30 - 2.88 = 27.12 \text{ N}$$

(ii) **Rolling Friction**

The force of friction that comes into play when a body rolls over the surface of another body is called **rolling friction.** e.g. When a wheel, circular disc or a ring or a sphere or a cylinder roll over a surface, the force that opposes it is the rolling friction.

When a wheel rolls without slipping over a horizontal plane, the surfaces at contact do not rub each other. The relative velocity of the point of contact of the wheel with respect to the plane is zero, if there is no slipping. There is no sliding or static friction in such an ideal situation. We need to overcome rolling friction only which is much smaller than sliding friction. For this reason, wheel has been considered as one of the greatest inventions. It conversly sliding into rolling friction thus lowers friction.

Rolling friction is directly proportional to normal reaction and inversely proportional to radius of rolling wheel.

So, $f_r \propto \frac{R}{r}$ or $f_r = \mu_r \frac{R}{r}$

where, μ_r = coefficient of rolling friction.

Cause of Rolling Friction Let us consider a wheel rolling along a road. As the wheel rolls, it exerts a large pressure due to its small area.

This causes a depression in the surface below and a mount or bump in front of it is shown in figure. In addition to this, the rolling wheel has a continuously detach itself from the surface on which it rolls. This is opposed by the adhesive force between the two surfaces in contact.

On account of these factors, a force originates which retards the rolling motion. This retarding force is known as **rolling friction.**

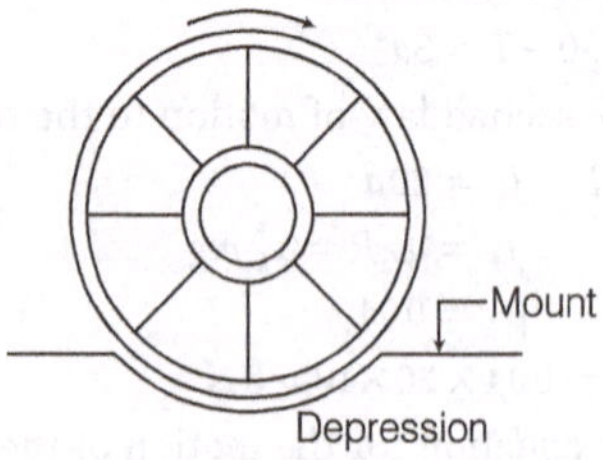

Cause of rolling friction

Pulling and Pushing of a Roller

(i) Suppose a force F is applied to pull a lawn roller of weight w as shown in figure below.

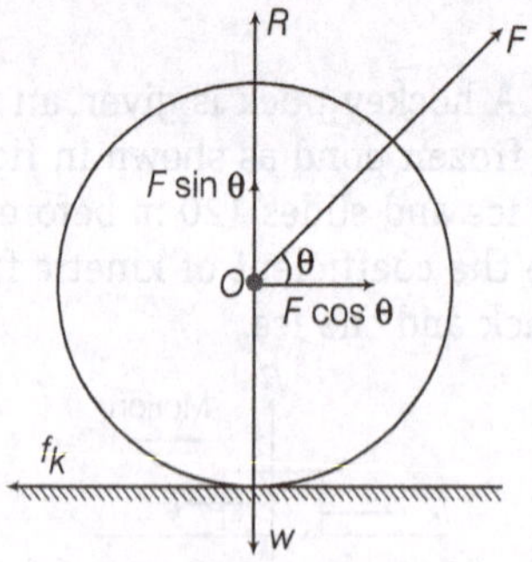

The force F has two rectangular components

(a) Horizontal component $F\cos\theta$ helps in moving the roller forward.

(b) Vertical component $F\sin\theta$ acts in upward direction. If R is the normal reaction, then

$$R + F\sin\theta = w$$

$$R = w - F\sin\theta$$

Force of kinetic friction,

$$f_k = \mu_k R = \mu_k (w - F\sin\theta) \quad \text{...(i)}$$

(ii) As shown in figure below, if force F is applied to push roller of weight w, then the normal reaction is

$$R' = w + F\sin\theta$$

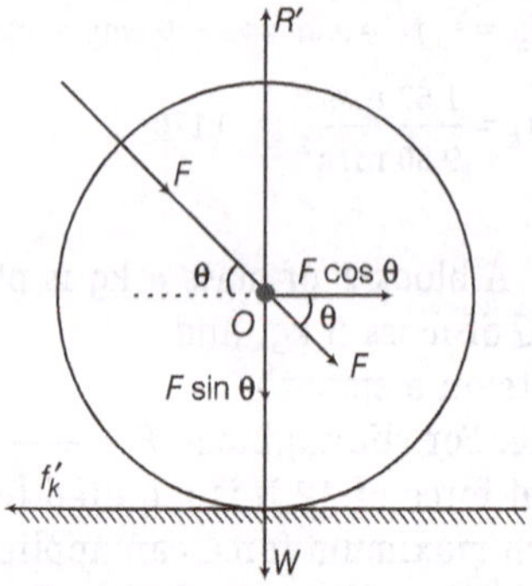

Force of kinetic friction,

$$f_k' = \mu_k R' = \mu_k (w + F\sin\theta) \quad \text{...(ii)}$$

Comparing f_k and f_k' from Eqs. (i) and (ii), we can conclude that it is easier to pull a roller than to push it $(f_k' > f_k)$.

Motion of a Body on a Rough Inclined Plane

(a) When body is moving downward with a acceleration 'a'. f is the force of friction between inclined plane and the body.

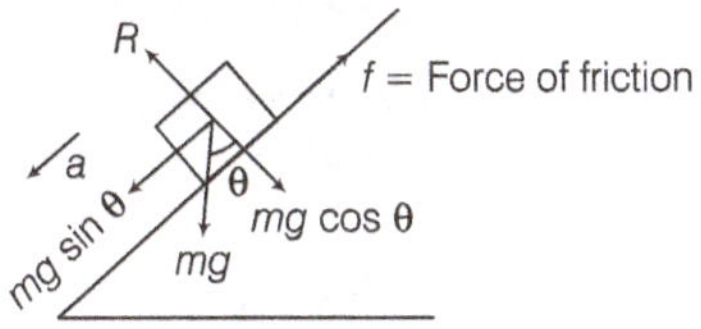

Downward motion of a body (FBD)

From FBD,

$$\boxed{R = mg\cos\theta}$$

As the body is moving downward with acceleration a, then net force in downward direction $= ma$

$$mg\sin\theta - f = ma \quad \dots\text{(i)}$$

We know that, $f = \mu R = \mu mg\cos\theta$ ...(ii)

Putting value from Eq. (ii) into Eq. (i), we get

$$\boxed{a = (\sin\theta - \mu\cos\theta)\, g}$$

(b) When body is moving upward when a force F is applied on it as shown in the figure.

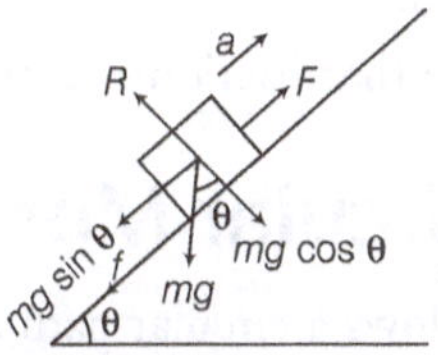

Upward motion of body (FBD)

From FBD,

$$\boxed{R = mg\cos\theta} \quad \dots\text{(i)}$$

$$F = mg\sin\theta + f \quad \dots\text{(ii)}$$

$$f = \mu R = \mu mg\cos\theta \text{ [From Eq. (i)]} \quad \dots\text{(iii)}$$

Putting the value of Eq (iii) in Eq. (ii)

$$\Rightarrow \quad F = mg(\sin\theta + \mu\cos\theta)$$

$$\Rightarrow \quad a = g(\sin\theta + \mu\cos\theta)$$

Note

- To calculate the work done over a rough inclined surface, multiply force with distance travelled by the body, i.e. $W = F \times s \Rightarrow ma \times s$ $mgs[\sin\theta + \mu\cos\theta]$ (For body moving upwards) and $W = mgs(\sin\theta - \mu\cos\theta)$ (For body moving downwards)

Example 7 A block of mass 5 kg rests on a inclined plane at an angle of 30° with the horizontal. If the block just begins to slide, then what is the coefficient of static friction between the block and the surface?

Sol. In equilibrium, the resultant of these forces must be zero.

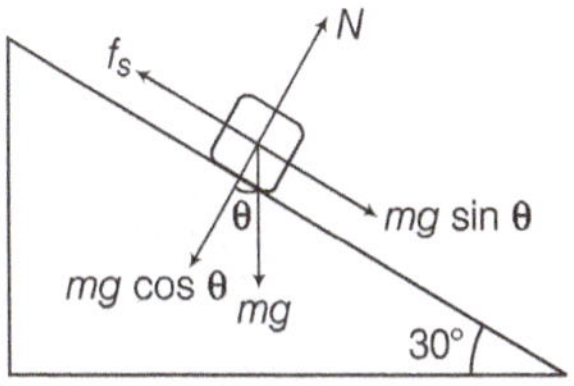

$\therefore \quad mg\sin\theta = f_s$ ...(i)

and $\quad mg\cos\theta = N$ ...(ii)

$\therefore \quad \tan\theta = \dfrac{f_s}{N}$ [Dividing Eq. (i) and (ii)]

As $\quad f_s = \mu_s N$

$\therefore \quad \tan\theta = \mu_s$

$\therefore \quad \mu_s = \tan 30°$

$\therefore \quad \mu_s = 0.577$

Example 8 A block of wood of 1 kg resting on an inclined plane of angle 30°, just starts moving down. If the coefficient of friction is 0.2, then find its velocity (in ms^{-1}) after 5 s (Take, $g = 10\ ms^{-2}$)

Sol. Acceleration of block down the plane is given by

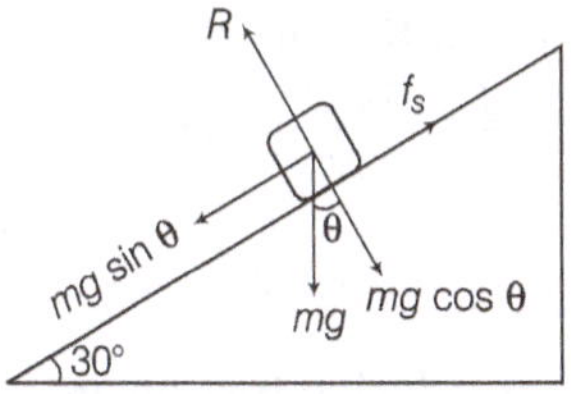

For the motion of body along the incline,

$$a = \frac{mg\sin\theta - \mu mg\cos\theta}{m}$$

(as, $R = mg\cos\theta$ and $f_s = \mu R$)

$$= 10 \times \sin 30° - 0.2 \times 10\cos 30°$$

$$= 10 \times \frac{1}{2} - 2 \times \frac{\sqrt{3}}{2}$$

$$= 3.268\ ms^{-2}$$

From equation of motion, $v = u - at$

Velocity after 5 s,

$$v = 0 + 3.268 \times 5$$

$$= 16.34\ ms^{-1}$$

Example 9 A 4 m long ladder weighing 25 kg rests with its upper end against a smooth wall and lower end on rough ground. What should be the minimum coefficient of friction between the ground and the ladder for it to be inclined at 60° with the horizontal without slipping? (Take, $g = 10\ ms^{-2}$)

Sol. In figure, AB is a ladder of weight w which acts at its centre of gravity G.

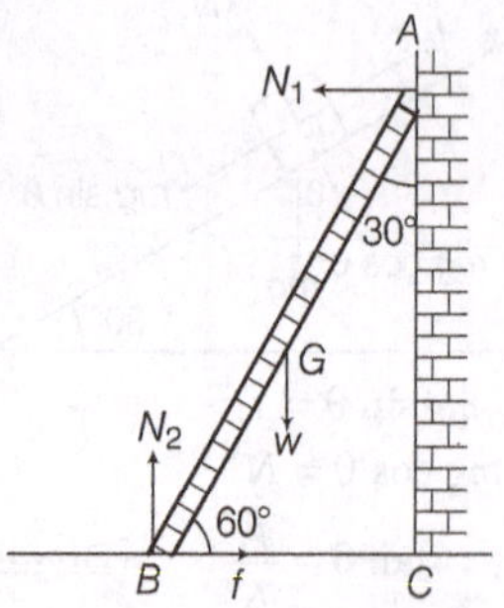

$$\angle ABC = 60^\circ \quad \therefore \quad \angle BAC = 30^\circ$$

Let N_1 be the reaction of the wall, and N_2 the reaction of the ground.

Force of friction f between the ladder and the ground acts along BC.

For horizontal equilibrium, $f = N_1$ ...(i)

For vertical equilibrium, $N_2 = w$ ...(ii)

Taking moments about B, we get for equilibrium,

$$N_1(4 \cos 30^\circ) - w(2 \cos 60^\circ) = 0 \quad \text{...(iii)}$$

Here, $w = 250\text{N}$

Solving these three equations, we get

$$f = 72.17\text{ N} \quad \text{and} \quad N_2 = 250\text{ N}$$

$$\therefore \quad \mu = \frac{f}{N_2} = \frac{72.17}{250} = 0.288$$

Ways for Reducing Friction

The various ways of reducing friction are

(i) **Lubrication** They are used to reduce kinetic friction in a machine. Lubricants like oil, grease, etc. fill the irregularities of the surface to make them smoother. Thus, friction decreases.

(ii) **Polishing** They are used to make the surface smoother.

(iii) **Ball Bearing** The ball bearing arrangement consists of two co-axial cylinders P and R between which suitable number of hard steel balls are arranged. When the wheel rotates, the ball B rotates in the direction as shown.

The wheel thus rolls on the balls instead of sliding on the axle. Thus, power dissipation is reduced.

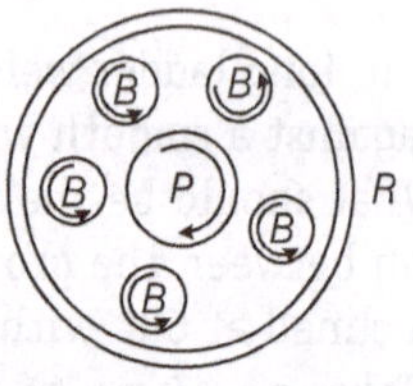

Ball bearing arrangement

(*iv*) A thin cushion of air maintained between solid surfaces in relative motion.

(*v*) **Streamlining** Friction due to air is considerably reduced by streamlining the shape of the body moving through air.

Friction is a Necessary Evil

Friction is a non-conservative force which opposes the motion of one object over another. Due to this following changes occur

(i) Wear and tear of machinery parts.

(ii) A large power is wasted to overcome friction and thus the efficiency of machines decreases.

(iii) In rotating part excessive heat is produced and cause damage to machine.

Thus it is an evil.

Also it has following advantages :

(i) We are able to walk due to friction between our feet and ground.

(ii) A vehicle stops on applying brakes due to friction.

(iii) Various parts of machine rotates due to friction between belt and pulley.

(iv) Due to friction we are able to write on a paper with a pen or pencil.

Hence, we conclude that friction is a necessary evil.

Uniform Circular Motion

When an object follows a circular path at a constant speed, the motion of the object is called **uniform circular motion**. The word uniform refers to the speed which is uniform (constant) throughout the motion. Although the speed does not vary, the particle is accelerating because the velocity changes its direction at every point on the circular track.

The figure shows a particle P which moves along a circular track of radius r with a uniform speed u.

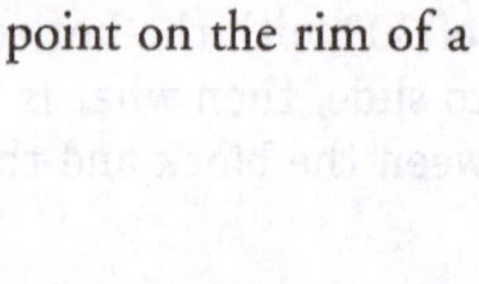

A circular motion

Examples

(i) Motion of the tip of the second hand of a clock.

(ii) Motion of a point on the rim of a wheel rotating uniformly.

Dynamics of Circular Motion

Angular Displacement

It is defined as the the angle traced out by the radius vector at the centre of the circular path in the given time. It is denoted by $\Delta\theta$ and expressed in radian. It is a dimensionless quantity. It is a vector quantity and its direction is given by Right-hand rule.

Angular Velocity

It is defined as the time rate of change of its angular position, denoted by ω and is measured in radian per second. Its dimensional formula is $[M^0L^0T^{-1}]$. It is a vector quantity.

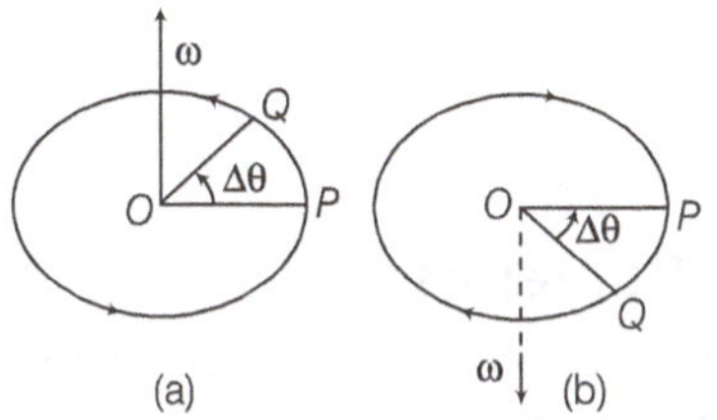

If a point object moving along a circular path, with centre (i.e. axis of rotation) at O. Let the object move from P to Q in a small time interval Δt, where $\angle POQ = \Delta\theta$.

$$\text{Now, angular velocity } \omega = \frac{\text{Angle traced}}{\text{Time taken}} = \lim_{\Delta t \to 0} \frac{\Delta\theta}{\Delta t} = \frac{d\theta}{dt}$$

Time Period

It is defined as the time taken by a particle to complete one revolution along its circular path. It is denoted by T and is measured in second.

Frequency

It is defined as the number of revolutions completed per unit time. It is denoted by f and is measured in Hz.

Angular Acceleration

It is defined as the time rate of change of angular velocity of a particle. It is measured in radian per second square and has dimensions $[M^0L^0T^{-2}]$.

It is denoted by α, where

$$\alpha = \lim_{\Delta t \to 0} \frac{\Delta\omega}{\Delta t} = \frac{d\omega}{dt}$$

Relation between Time Period and Frequency

Let f be the frequency of an object in circular motion, then the object will complete one revolution in $\frac{1}{f}$ second which is known as time period (T).

$$\text{Time period, } T = \frac{1}{f}$$

Relation among Angular Velocity, Frequency and Time Period

Suppose a point object illustrating a uniform circular motion with frequency (f) and time period (T). When the object completes one revolution, the angle traced at its axis of circular motion is 2π in radian.

If time $t = T, \theta = 2\pi$ radian.

Thus, the angular velocity ω is given by

$$\text{Angular velocity, } \omega = \frac{\theta}{t} = \frac{2\pi}{T} = 2\pi f$$

Relation between Linear Velocity (v) and Angular Velocity (ω)

Suppose the particle moving on circular track of radius r is showing angular displacement $\Delta\theta$ in Δt time and in this time period, it covers a distance Δs along the circular track, then

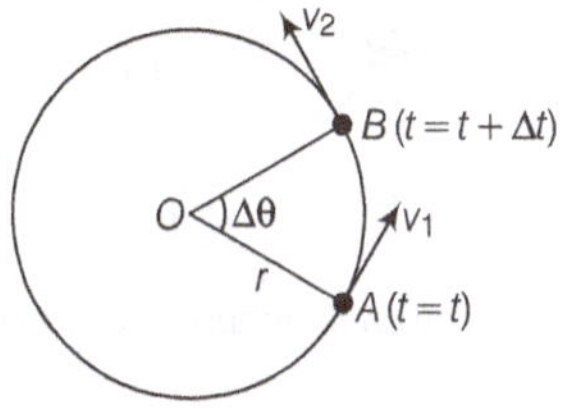

Representation of linear velocity and angular velocity

$$\omega = \frac{\Delta\theta}{\Delta t} \quad \text{...(i)}$$

and $$v = \frac{\Delta s}{\Delta t} \quad \text{...(ii)}$$

But $$\Delta s = r\Delta\theta \quad \text{...(iii)}$$

(Since, angle = arc/radius)

From above three equations, we get

$$\text{Linear velocity, } v = r\frac{\Delta\theta}{\Delta t} = r\omega$$

Centripetal Acceleration

The acceleration associated with uniform circular motion is called a **centripetal acceleration.** Consider a particle of mass (m) moving with a constant speed (v) and uniform angular velocity (ω) on a circular path of radius (r) with centre at O. Suppose at any time t, the particle be at P, where $\mathbf{OP} = r_1$ and at time $t + \Delta t$ the particle be at Q, where $\mathbf{OQ} = r_2$ and $\angle POQ = \Delta\theta$ as shown in the figure. But $|\mathbf{r}_1| = |\mathbf{r}_2| = r$

Angular speed of the particle, $\omega = \dfrac{\Delta\theta}{\Delta t}$ ...(i)

Let $\mathbf{v}_1$ and $\mathbf{v}_2$ be the velocity vectors of the particle at locations P and Q respectively. The magnitude and direction of $\mathbf{v}_1$ and $\mathbf{v}_2$ is represented by the tangent **PA** and **QB**.

Since the particle is moving with a uniform speed (v), the length of tangents at P and Q are equal

i.e. $$|\mathbf{PA}| = |\mathbf{QB}| = |\mathbf{v}|$$

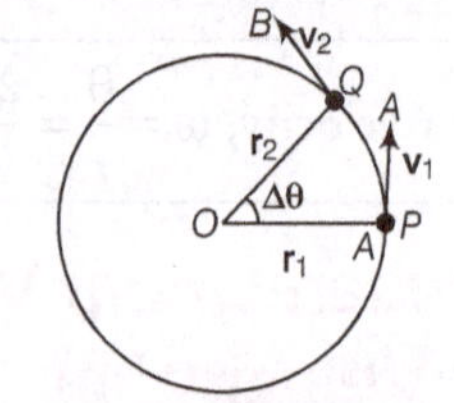

Centripetal acceleration

These two vectors have been separately shown in the following figure

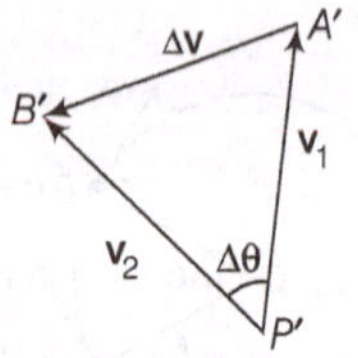

A triangle made of vectors

From triangle law of vectors, we have

$$\mathbf{P'A'} + \mathbf{A'B'} = \mathbf{P'B'}$$

$$\Rightarrow \quad \mathbf{A'B'} = \mathbf{P'B'} - \mathbf{P'A'}$$

$$= \mathbf{v}_2 - \mathbf{v}_1 = \Delta\mathbf{v}$$

If $\Delta t \to 0$, then A' lies close to B'. Then, $A'B'$ can be taken as an arc $A'B'$ of circle of radius $P'A' = |\mathbf{v}|$

$$\therefore \quad \Delta\theta = \frac{A'B'}{P'A'} = \frac{|\Delta\mathbf{v}|}{|\mathbf{v}|}$$

From Eq. (i), we have

$$\omega\Delta t = \frac{|\Delta\mathbf{v}|}{|\mathbf{v}|} \Rightarrow \omega|\mathbf{v}| = \frac{|\Delta\mathbf{v}|}{\Delta t}$$

$$\Rightarrow \quad \frac{|\Delta\mathbf{v}|}{\Delta t} = (\omega r)\,\omega = \omega^2 r \qquad [\because v = \omega r]$$

As $\Delta t \to 0$, then $\dfrac{|\Delta\mathbf{v}|}{\Delta t}$ represents the magnitude of centripetal acceleration at P which is given by

$$|\mathbf{a}| = \frac{|\Delta\mathbf{v}|}{\Delta t} = \omega^2 r = \left[\frac{v}{r}\right]^2 r = \frac{v^2}{r}$$

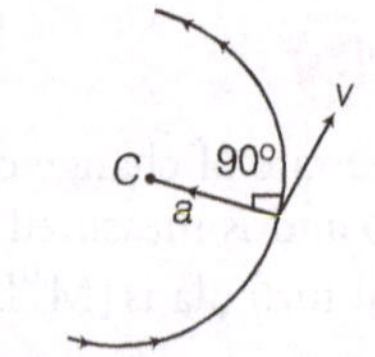

> Centripetal acceleration, $a = \dfrac{v^2}{r}$

It is towards the centre of circle.

Radius of Curvature

Any curved path can be assume to be a part of circular arc. Radius of curvature at a point is defined as the radius of that circular arc which fits at the particular point on the curve as shown in figure.

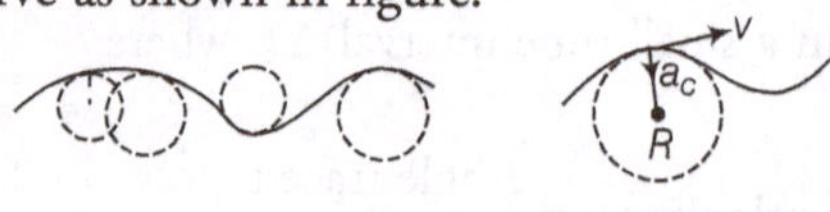

In the expression, $a_c = v^2/R$, the term R is known as radius of curvature.

Example 10 An insect trapped in a circular groove of radius 12 cm moves along the groove steadily and completes 7 revolutions in 100 s.

(i) What is the angular speed and the linear speed of the motion?

(ii) Is the acceleration vector, a constant vector? What is its magnitude? **NCERT**

Sol. The given question is based on uniform circular motion. Here, radius $R = 12$ cm.

The angular speed ω is given as

$$\omega = 2\pi / T = 2\pi \times 7/100 = 0.44 \text{ rad/s}$$

and linear speed v is $v = \omega R = 0.44 \times 12 = 5.3 \text{ cm s}^{-1}$

The direction of velocity v is along the tangent to the circle at every point. The acceleration is directed towards the centre of the circle. Since, this direction changes continuously, acceleration, is not a constant vector.

However, the magnitude of acceleration is constant.

$$a = \omega^2 R = (0.44)^2 \times 12 = 2.3 \text{ cm s}^{-2}$$

Example 11 A body of mass 10 kg revolves in a circle of diameter 0.4 m making 1000 revolutions per minute. Calculate its linear velocity and centripetal acceleration.

Sol. $m = 10\,\text{kg}, d = 0.4\text{ m}, r = 0.2\text{ m},$

Revolutions per min, $f = 1000/\text{min} = \frac{1000}{60}$ s,

Linear velocity, $v = ?$, centripetal acceleration, $a = ?$

$$\omega = 2\pi f = 2\pi \times \frac{1000}{60} = \frac{100\,\pi}{3}\text{ rad / s}$$

$$v = r\omega = 0.2 \times \frac{100\,\pi}{3} = \frac{20\,\pi}{3}\text{ m/s}$$

$$a = r\omega^2 = 0.2 \times \left(\frac{100\,\pi}{3}\right)^2 = \frac{2000\,\pi^2}{9}\text{ m/s}^2$$

Centripetal and Centrifugal Force

Earlier, we have studied that acceleration of a body moving in a circle of radius r with uniform speed v is $\frac{v^2}{r}$ directed towards the centre. From second law of motion, the force F_c is given by

Centripetal force, $F_c = \frac{mv^2}{r}$

where, m is the mass of the body. This force directed forward the centre is called **centripetal force.**

But $\frac{v^2}{r}$ is centripetal acceleration or radial acceleration.

$\therefore$ Centripetal force, $F_c = mr\omega^2$ $\quad [\because v = \omega r]$

For a stone rotated in a circle by a string, the centripetal force is provided by the tension in the string.

The centripetal force for motion of a planet around the sun is the gravitation force on the planet due to the sun.

For a car taking a circular turn on a horizontal road, the centripetal is the force of friction. Thus it is not a new type of force.

There are certain situations in which we feel that a body is acted upon by a force, but actually there is no force on the body. Such an apparent force is called **centrifugal force** (Pseudo force).

Example 12 An artificial satellite of mass 2500 kg is orbiting around the earth with a speed of 4 kms^{-1} at a distance of 10^4 km from the earth. Calculate the centripetal force acting on it.

Sol. Given, $r = 10^4\,\text{km} = 10^4 \times 1000\text{ m} = 10^7\text{ m}, m = 2500\text{ kg},$

$$v = 4\text{ kms}^{-1} = 4 \times 10^3\text{ ms}^{-1}$$

Now, centripetal force is $F = \frac{mv^2}{r}$

$$F = \frac{2500 \times (4 \times 10^3)^2}{10^7} = \frac{2500 \times 16 \times 10^6}{10^7}$$

$$F = \frac{250 \times 16 \times 10^7}{10^7} = 4000\text{ N}$$

Interesting Applications of Laws of Motion

The circular motion of a car on a flat and banked road are explained below

(i) Circular Motion of a Car on Level Road

When a vehicle goes round a curved road, it requires some centripetal force. While rounding the curve, the wheels of the vehicle have a tendency to leave the curved path and regain the straight line path. The force of friction between the road and the tyres provided the centripetal force required to keep the car in motion around the curve.

There are three forces acting on the car such as

(i) The weight of the car mg, acting vertically downwards.

(ii) Normal reaction R of the road on the car, acting vertically upwards.

(iii) Frictional force F, along the surface of the road, i.e. towards the centre of the turn.

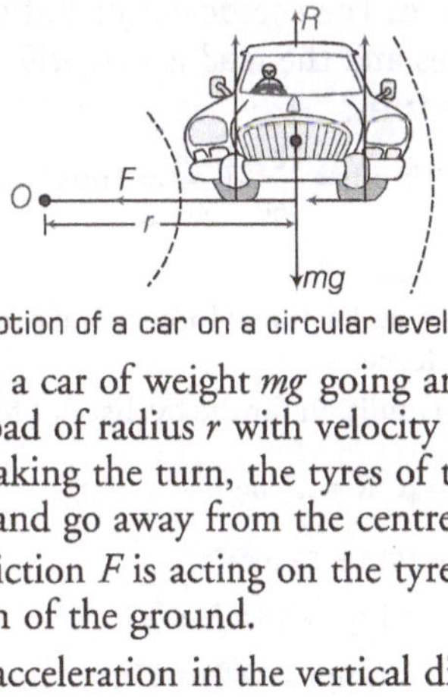

Motion of a car on a circular level road

Let us consider a car of weight mg going around a circular level road of radius r with velocity v as shown in figure. While taking the turn, the tyres of the car tend to leave the road and go away from the centre of the curve. The force of friction F is acting on the tyre and R is the normal reaction of the ground.

As there is no acceleration in the vertical direction, then

$$R - mg = 0 \Rightarrow R = mg$$

For circular motion, the centripetal force is along the surface of the road towards the centre of the turn. The static friction opposes the impending motion of the car moving away from the circle. Thus, $\frac{mv^2}{r} \le F$

where v is the velocity of car while turning and r is the radius of the circular track.

As, $F = \mu_s R = \mu_s mg$

Here, F is limiting friction to get maximum possible velocity of car, where μ_s is the coefficient of static friction between the tyres and the road.

$$\therefore \quad \frac{mv^2}{r} \le \mu_s mg \Rightarrow v \le \sqrt{\mu_s rg}$$

or **Maximum velocity of the vehicle, $v_{max} = \sqrt{\mu_s rg}$**

Hence, the maximum velocity with which a vehicle can go round a level curve without skidding is

$$v = \sqrt{\mu_s r g}.$$

Example 13 A bend in a level road has a radius of 100 m. Find the maximum speed which a car turning this bend may have without skidding, if the coefficient of friction between the tyres and road is 0.8.

Sol. The maximum speed which the car can have without skidding is given by

$$\mu = \frac{v^2}{rg} \Rightarrow v = \sqrt{\mu rg}$$

Here, $r = 100$ m, $\mu = 0.8$, $g = 9.8$ ms^{-2}

$$v = \sqrt{0.8 \times 100 \times 9.8} = \sqrt{4 \times 2 \times 2 \times 49}$$

$$v = 2 \times 2 \times 7 = 28 \text{ m/s}$$

Example 14 A cyclist speeding at 18 km/h on a level road takes a sharp circular turn of radius 3m without reducing the speed. The coefficient of static friction between the tyres and the road is 0.1. Will the cyclist slip while taking the turn? **NCERT**

Sol. Here, $v = 18 \text{ km/h} = \frac{18 \times 1000}{60 \times 60} = 5 \text{ m/s}$

$r = 3$ m, $\mu_s = 0.1$

On a level road, frictional force alone can provide the centripetal force.

Therefore, condition for the cyclist not to slip is that

$$\frac{mv^2}{r} \le F_s \ (= \mu_s R = \mu_s mg); \ v^2 \le \mu_s rg$$

$$v^2 = (5)^2 = 25 \text{ m}^2\text{s}^{-2}$$

and $\mu_s rg = 0.1 \times 3 \times 10 = 3 \text{ m}^2\text{s}^{-2}$

$\therefore$ The condition is not satisfied. Hence, the cyclist will slip.

(ii) Motion of a Car on a Banked Road

The large amount of friction between the tyres and the road produces considerable wear and tear of the tyres. To avoid this, the curved road is given an inclined sloping upwards towards the outer circumference. This reduces wearing out of the tyres because the horizontal component of normal reaction provides the necessary centripetal force. The system of raising the outer edge of a curved road above its inner edge is called **banking of the curved road.** So, the angle through which the outer edge of the curved road is raised above the inner edge is called **angle of banking.**

Let us consider a car of weight mg going along a curved path of radius r with speed v on a road banked at an angle θ, as shown in figure.

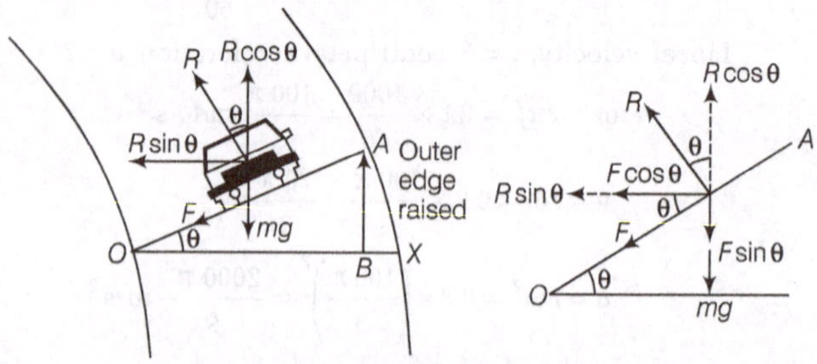

Circular motion of a car on a banked road

The forces acting on the car are

(i) Weight mg acting vertically downwards.

(ii) Normal reaction R acting upwards in a direction perpendicular to inclined plane making angle θ with the horizontal plane.

(iii) Force of friction F acting downwards along the inclined plane because car tends to slip outwards.

Reaction R can be resolved into two rectangular components

(i) $R\cos\theta$, along vertically upward direction.

(ii) $R\sin\theta$, along the horizontal towards the centre of the curved road.

Force of friction F, can also be resolved into two rectangular components.

(i) $F\cos\theta$, along the horizontal, towards the centre of curved road.

(ii) $F\sin\theta$, along vertically downward direction.

Since, there is no motion along vertical, so

$$R\cos\theta = mg + F\sin\theta \quad \text{...(i)}$$

Let v is velocity of the car. The centripetal force is now provided by the components $R\sin\theta$ and $F\cos\theta$, i.e.

$$R\sin\theta + F\cos\theta = \frac{mv^2}{r} \quad \text{...(ii)}$$

We know $F = \mu_s R$

Then, we can write Eqs. (i) and (ii) as

$$R\cos\theta = mg + \mu_s R\sin\theta \quad \text{...(iii)}$$

and $$R\sin\theta + \mu_s R\cos\theta = \frac{mv^2}{r} \quad \text{...(iv)}$$

From Eq. (iii), we get

or $R\cos\theta - \mu_s R \cdot \sin\theta = mg$

or $R(\cos\theta - \mu_s \sin\theta) = mg$

or $$R = \frac{mg}{\cos\theta - \mu_s \sin\theta} \quad \ldots(v)$$

From Eq. (iv), we get

$$R(\sin\theta + \mu_s \cos\theta) = \frac{mv^2}{r} \quad \ldots(vi)$$

From Eq. (v) and (vi), we get

$$\frac{mg(\sin\theta + \mu_s \cos\theta)}{\cos\theta - \mu_s \sin\theta} = \frac{mv^2}{r}$$

$$\therefore \quad v^2 = \frac{rg(\sin\theta + \mu_s \cos\theta)}{(\cos\theta - \mu_s \sin\theta)}$$

$$v^2 = \frac{rg\cos\theta\left(\frac{\sin\theta}{\cos\theta} + \frac{\mu_s \cos\theta}{\cos\theta}\right)}{\cos\theta\left(\frac{\cos\theta}{\cos\theta} - \mu_s \frac{\sin\theta}{\cos\theta}\right)}$$

$$v^2 = \frac{rg\cos\theta(\tan\theta + \mu_s)}{\cos\theta(1 - \mu_s \tan\theta)} = \frac{rg(\tan\theta + \mu_s)}{(1 - \mu_s \tan\theta)}$$

Maximum velocity of vehicle on banked road, $v = \sqrt{\frac{rg(\mu_s + \tan\theta)}{(1 - \mu_s \tan\theta)}}$ ...(vii)

Special case When there is no friction between the road and the tyres, then the safe limit for maximum velocity is $\mu_s = 0$,

Substituting the value of μ_s in Eq. (vii), we get

$$v = \sqrt{\frac{rg(0 + \tan\theta)}{1 - (0 \times \tan\theta)}}$$

$$v = \sqrt{rg\tan\theta} \quad \ldots(viii)$$

This is the speed at which car does not slide down even if, track is smooth. If track is smooth and speed is less than $\sqrt{rg\tan\theta}$, vehicle will move down so that r gets decreased and if speed is more than this vehicle will move up.

The angle of banking θ for minimum wear and tear of tyres is given by Eq. (viii), we get

$\tan\theta = \frac{v^2}{rg}$ or Angle of banking, $\theta = \tan^{-1}\left(\frac{v^2}{rg}\right)$

Example 15 A circular race track of radius 300 m is banked at angle of 15°. If the coefficient of friction between the wheels of a race car and the road is 0.2, what is the (i) optimum speed of the race car to avoid wear and tear on its tyres and (ii) maximum permissible speed to avoid slipping? [Take, tan 15° = 0.2679] **NCERT**

Sol. The optimum speed v_o is given by equation

$$v_o = (R\,g\tan\theta)^{1/2}$$

Here, $R = 300\text{ m}, \theta = 15°, g = 9.8\text{ ms}^{-2}, \mu_s = 0.2$,

We have $v_o = 28.1\text{ m s}^{-1}$

The maximum permissible speed v_{max} is given by equation.

$$v_{max} = \left(Rg\frac{\mu_s + \tan\theta}{1 - \mu_s \tan\theta}\right)^{1/2}$$

$$v_{max} = \left(\frac{300 \times 9.8 \times (0.2 + \tan 15°)}{1 - (0.2 \times \tan 15°)}\right)^{1/2}$$

[here, tan15° = 0.2679]

$$v_{max} = \left(\frac{2940 \times (0.4679)}{0.9464}\right)^{1/2}$$

$$= (1453.535)^{1/2} = 38.1\text{ ms}^{-1}$$

Example 16 The radius of curvature of a railway track at a place, where the train is moving at a speed of 72 kmh^{-1} is 625 m. The distance between the rails is 1.5 m. Find the angle and the elevation of the outer rail, so that there may be no side pressure on the rails. Take, $g = 9.8\text{ m/s}^2$[$\tan^{-1}(0.0653) = 3.74°$, $\sin 3.74° = 0.06522$]

Sol. Here, $r = 625\text{ m}, \ v = 72\text{ kmh}^{-1}$

$$v = 72 \times \frac{5}{18}\text{ m/s}$$

$$v = 20\text{ m/s}, \ g = 9.8\text{ m/s}^2, l = 1.5\text{ m}$$

Now, angle of elevation of outer rail, i.e. $\tan\theta = \frac{v^2}{rg}$

$$\tan\theta = \frac{20 \times 20}{625 \times 9.8} = 0.0653$$

$$\theta = \tan^{-1}(0.0653) \Rightarrow \theta = 3.74°$$

Also, elevation of outer rail $h = l\sin\theta$

$$h = 1.5\sin 3.74°$$

$$h = 0.0978\text{ m} = 9.78\text{ cm}$$

Example 17 If a car having speed 50 km/h can round the curve banked at an angle θ. Find out the value of θ, if radius of the curve is 40 m and consider the friction is negligible. [Take, $\tan^{-1}(0.5) = 26.5$]

Sol. Here, given,

$$v = 50\text{ km/h} = 50 \times \frac{5}{18}\text{ m/s} = 13.88\text{ m/s}$$

$$r = 40\text{ m}, \ \theta = ?$$

Draw the FBD of the car.

Now, apply $\Sigma F_g = ma_y$ to the car

$$R\cos\theta - mg = 0 \Rightarrow R = \frac{mg}{\cos\theta}$$

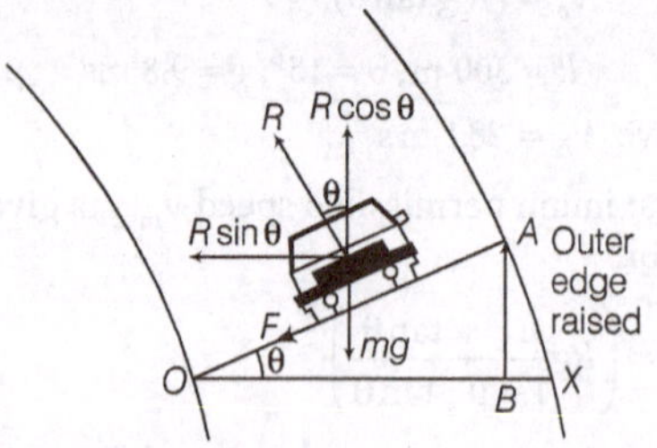

Similarly, apply $\Sigma F_x = ma_x$ to the car

$$R\sin\theta = \frac{mv^2}{r}$$

Put the value of R and then solve for θ.

$$\frac{mg}{\cos\theta}\cdot\sin\theta = \frac{mv^2}{r}$$

$$\Rightarrow \quad \tan\theta = \frac{v^2}{rg}; \theta = \tan^{-1}\left(\frac{v^2}{rg}\right)$$

Put all given values to get θ

$$\theta = \tan^{-1}\left[\frac{(13.88)^2}{40\times 9.8}\right] = \tan^{-1}(0.4916)$$

$$\theta = 2618°$$

Motion in a Vertical Circle

Suppose a particle of mass m is attached to an inextensible light string of length L. The particle is moving in a vertical circle of radius L about a fixed point O. It is imparted a velocity u in horizontal direction at lowest point A. Let v be its velocity at point B, the circle as shown in figure.

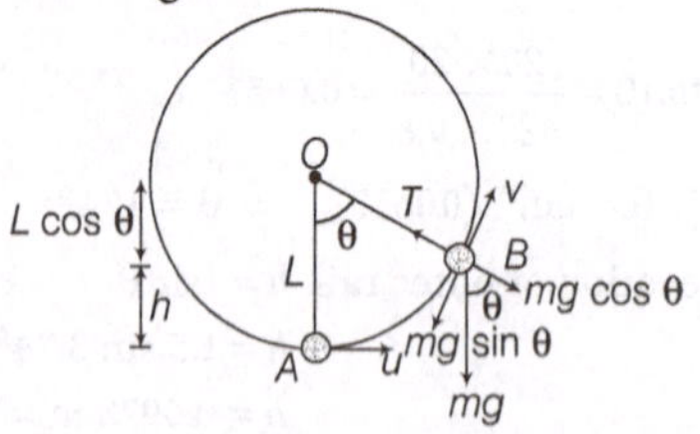

Motion of a particle in vertical circle

Here, we have

$$h = L(1-\cos\theta)$$

Now from conservation of mechanical energy, we have

$$\frac{1}{2}m(u^2 - v^2) = mgh \qquad \ldots(i)$$

The necessary centripetal force is provided by the resultant of tension T and $mg\cos\theta$.

$$\therefore \quad T - mg\cos\theta = \frac{mv^2}{L} = m\omega^2 L \quad [\because v = L\omega] \ldots(ii)$$

As speed of the particle decreases with height, tension in the string is maximum at the bottom. The particle will complete the circle if the string does not slack even at the highest point.

Now following conclusions can be made using above Eqs. (i) and (ii).

(i) **Minimum velocity at highest point** so that particle complete the circle $v_{\min} = \sqrt{gL}$, at this velocity, tension in the string is zero.

(ii) **Minimum velocity at lowest point** so that particle complete the circle, $v_{\min} = \sqrt{5gL}$, at this velocity, tension in the string is 6 mg.

(iii) **When string is horizontal**, then minimum velocity is $\sqrt{3Lg}$ and tension in this condition is $3mg$.

(iv) If velocity at lowest point is less than $\sqrt{5\,gL}$, then tension in the string becomes zero before reaching the highest point, now the particle will leave the circle and will move on parabolic path.

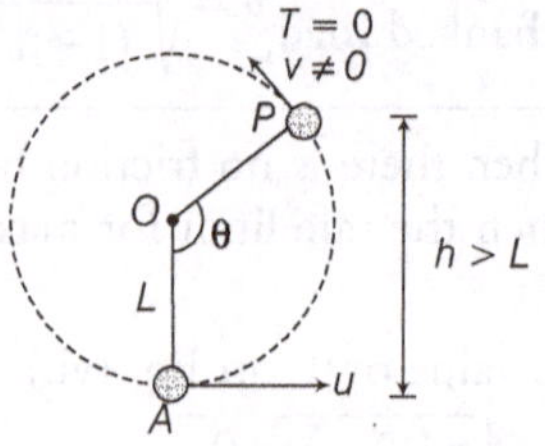

In this condition, if $\sqrt{2gL} < v < \sqrt{5\,gL}$, then tension in the string becomes zero but velocity is not zero, the particle will leave circle at $90° < \theta < 180°$ or $h > L$.

(v) If velocity at lowest point is $0 < v \le \sqrt{2\,gL}$, the particle will oscillate, in this condition velocity becomes zero but tension is not zero. The particle will oscillate in lower half of circle, i.e. $0° < \theta < 90°$

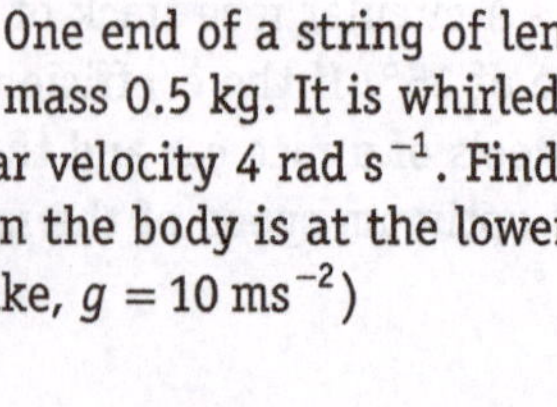

Example 18 One end of a string of length 1 m is tied to a body of mass 0.5 kg. It is whirled in a vertical circle with angular velocity 4 rad s^{-1}. Find the tension in the string when the body is at the lower most point of its motion. (Take, $g = 10$ ms^{-2})

Sol. At lower most point, the tension in the string,

$$T = m\omega^2 r + mg$$
$$= 0.5 \times (4)^2 \times 1 + 0.5 \times 10 = 13 \text{ N}$$

Example 19 A ball of mass 0.6 kg attached to a light inextensible string rotates in a vertical circle of radius 0.75 m such that it has speed of 5 ms^{-1} when the string is horizontal. Tension in string when it is horizontal on other side is (Take, $g = 10 \text{ m/s}^2$).

Sol. Tension in the string when it makes angle θ with the vertical,

$$T = \frac{mv^2}{r} + mg\cos\theta$$

When the string is horizontal, θ = 90°

$$\therefore \quad T = \frac{mv^2}{r} + mg \times 0 = \frac{mv^2}{r} = \frac{0.6 \times (5)^2}{0.75} = 20 \text{ N}$$

Topic Practice 2

Multiple Choice Questions

1 Mark

1. Which force is dissipative force?
(a) Electrostatic force (b) Magnetic force
(c) Gravitational force (d) Frictional force

2. A boy prevents fall of his book on the ground by pressing it against a vertical wall. If weight of his book is 10 kg and μ_s of the wall is 2. Find the minimum force needed by him in his attempt.
(a) 300 N (b) 400 N
(c) 500 N (d) 600 N

3. When a car is taking a circular turn on a horizontal road the centripetal force is the force of
(a) friction (b) weight of the car
(c) weight of the tyres (d) None of these

4. When a car is moving along a circle on a level road the centripetal force is provided by f, where f denotes as
(a) $f < \mu_s N = \frac{mv^2}{r}$ (b) $\frac{mv^2}{r} = f \le \mu_s N$
(c) $f = \mu_s N = \frac{mv^2}{r}$ (d) $f = \mu_k N = \frac{mv^2}{r}$

5. A body of mass m slides down on a rough inclined plane of inclination θ. If μ is the coefficient of friction, then acceleration of the body will be
(a) $g\sin\theta$ (b) $\mu\cos\theta$
(c) $g(\sin\theta - \mu\cos\theta)$ (d) $g(\cos\theta - \mu\sin\theta)$

6. A cyclist bends, while taking turn for
(a) reduce friction
(b) generate required centripetal force
(c) reduce speed
(d) reduce apparent weight

7. A car when passes through a bridge exerts a force on it which is equal to
(a) $mg + \frac{mv^2}{r}$ (b) $mg - \frac{mv^2}{r}$
(c) $\frac{mv^2}{r}$ (d) $\frac{mv^2}{r} + mgh$

8. A motor cyclist rides around the well with a round vertical wall and does not fall down, while riding because
(a) the force of gravity disappears
(b) he loses weight some how
(c) the frictional force of the wall balances his weight
(d) the force exerted by the surrounding

Very Short Answer Type Questions

1 Mark

9. Why is static friction called a self-adjusting force?

10. What is the unit of coefficient of limiting friction?

11. Write the relation between coefficient of friction and angle of friction?

12. Does the force of friction depend on the area of contact?

13. does the angle of banking depend on the mass of the vehicle?

14. Sand is spread on tracks covered with snow. Why?

15. Write the name of various methods of reducing friction.

16. A body is moving in a circular path such that its speed always remains constant. Should there be a force acting on the body?

Short Answer Type I Questions

2 Marks

17. Is large brake on a wheel more effective than a small one? Explain.

18. A block of mass m is held against a rough vertical wall by pressing it with a finger. If the coefficient of friction between the block and the wall is μ and the acceleration due to gravity is g, calculate the minimum force required to be applied by finger to hold the block against the wall? **NCERT Exemplar**

19. How does a lubricant help in reducing friction?

20. If a force is acting on a moving body in a direction perpendicular to the direction of motion, what will be its effect on the speed and direction of the body?

21. What is the cause of rolling friction?

22. Establish the relation between linear velocity (v) and angular velocity (ω).

23. If the speed of stone is increased beyond the maximum permissible value and the string breaks suddenly, which of the following correctly describes the trajectory of the stone after the string breaks

(i) the stone moves radially outwards,

(ii) the stone flies off tangentially from the instant the string breaks,

(iii) the stone flies off at an angle with the tangent whose magnitude depends on the speed of the particle? **NCERT**

Short Answer Type II Questions

3 Marks

24. A stone of mass m tied to the end of a string revolves in a vertical circle of radius R. The net forces at the lowest and highest points of the circle directed vertically downwards are (choose the correct alternative).

	Lowest point	Highest point
(i)	$mg - T_1$	$mg + T_2$
(ii)	$mg + T_1$	$mg - T_2$
(iii)	$mg + T_1 - (mv_1^2)/R$	$mg - T_2 + (mv_2^2)/R$
(iv)	$mg - T_1 - (mv_1^2)/R$	$mg + T_2 + (mv_2^2)/R$

Here (T_1, T_2) and (v_1, v_2) denote the tension in the string and the speed of the stone at the lowest and the highest point respectively. **NCERT**

25. You may have seen in a circus a motorcyclist driving in vertical loops inside a death well (a hollow spherical chamber with holes, so the spectators can watch from outside). Explain clearly, why the motorcyclist does not drop down when he is at the uppermost point, with no support from below. What is the minimum speed required at the uppermost position to perform a vertical loop if the radius of the chamber is 25 m? **NCERT**

26. Explain static friction, limiting friction and kinetic friction. Represent these frictional forces on a graph and hence explain static friction is a self adjusting force.

27. Derive an expression for acceleration of a body up a rough inclined plane.

28. Why are the curved roads banked? Obtain an expression for angle of banking of a curved road.

29. Explain the meaning of coefficient of friction and angle of friction. Establish a relation between them.

30. Friction is a necessary evil. Comment.

Long Answer Type Questions

5 Marks

31. When a body slides down from rest along a smooth inclined plane making an angle of 45° with the horizontal, it takes time T. When the same body slides down from rest along a rough inclined plane making the same angle and through the same distance, it is seen to take time pT, where p is some number greater than 1. Calculate the coefficient of friction between the body and the rough plane. **NCERT Exemplar**

32. A block of mass 15 kg is placed on a long trolley. The coefficient of static friction between the block and the trolley is 0.18. The trolley accelerates from rest with 0.5 m/s^2 for 20s and then moves with uniform velocity. Discuss the motion of the block as viewed by (i) stationary observer on the ground (ii) an observer moving with the trolley. **NCERT**

33. A monkey of mass 40 kg climbs on a rope which can stand a maximum tension of 600 N. In which of the following cases will the rope break? The monkey

(i) climbs up with an acceleration of 6 m/s^2.

(ii) climbs down with an acceleration of 4 m/s^2.

(iii) climbs up with a uniform speed of 5 m/s.

(iv) falls down the rope nearly freely under gravity. (Ignore the mass of the rope) and take $g = 10\ \text{m/s}^2$. NCERT

34. In a rotor, a hollow vertical cylinder rotates about its axis and a person rests against the inner wall. At a particular speed of the rotor, the floor below the person is removed and the person hangs resting against the wall without any floor.

If the radius of the rotor is 2 m and the coefficient of static friction between the wall and the person is 0.2.

(i) Find the minimum speed at which the floor may be removed.

(ii) What type of speciality is associated with this question? [take $g = 10\ \text{m/s}^2$]

Numerical Problems

35. What is the acceleration of a train travelling at $50\ \text{ms}^{-1}$ as it goes round a curve of 250 m radius? [1 M]

36. A heavy point mass tied to the end of string is whirled in a horizontal circle of radius 20 cm with a constant angular speed. What is angular speed if the centripetal acceleration is $980\ \text{cms}^{-2}$? [1 M]

37. A body placed on a rough inclined plane just begins to slide, when the slope of the plane equal to 1 in 4. Calculate the coefficient of friction. [2 M]

38. A body of mass 2 kg is being dragged with a uniform velocity of $2\ \text{ms}^{-1}$ on a rough horizontal plane. The coefficient of friction between the body and the surface is 0.2. Calculate the amount of heat generated per second. Take $g = 9.8\ \text{ms}^{-2}$ and $J = 4.2\ \text{Jcal}^{-1}$. [2 M]

39. A stone tied to the end of a string 80 cm long is whirled in a horizontal circle with a constant speed. If the stone makes 14 revolutions in 25 s, what is the magnitude and direction of acceleration of the stone? NCERT [2 M]

40. An aircraft executes a horizontal loop of radius 1 km with a steady speed of $900\ \text{kmh}^{-1}$. Compare its centripetal acceleration with the acceleration due to gravity. NCERT [2 M]

41. A motor cyclist moving with a velocity of $72\ \text{km h}^{-1}$ on a flat road takes a turn on the road at a point, where the radius of curvature of the road is 20 m. The acceleration due to gravity is $10\ \text{ms}^{-2}$. In order to avoid skidding, he must not bend with respect to the vertical plane by what angle? [2 M]

42. If mass, speed and radius of the circle of a particle moving uniformly in a circular path are all increased by 50%. By what percentage, the necessary force required to maintain the body moving in the circular path will have to be increased? [2 M]

43. A motorcyclist wants to drive on the vertical surface of wooden 'well' of radius 5 m, with a minimum speed of $5\sqrt{5}\ \text{ms}^{-1}$. Find the minimum value of coefficient of friction between the tyres and the wall of the well. (Take, $g = 10\ \text{ms}^{-2}$) [2 M]

44. A particle starts moving along a circle of radius $(20/\pi)$ m with constant tangential acceleration. If velocity of the particle is 50 m/s at the end of the second revolution after motion has began, then find the tangential acceleration (in ms^{-2}). [3 M]

45. Figure below shows a man standing stationary with respect to a horizontal conveyor belt that is accelerating with $1\ \text{m/s}^2$.
What is the net force on the man? If the coefficient of static friction between the man's shoes and the belt is 0.2, up to what acceleration of the belt can the man continue to be stationary relative to the belt? (Mass of the man = 65 kg). NCERT [3 M]

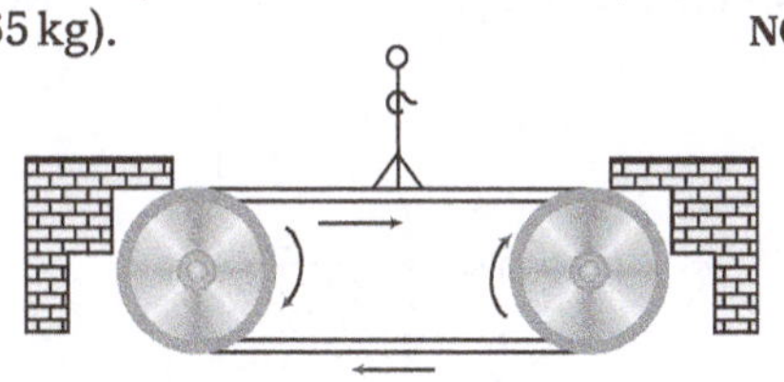

46. A stone of mass 0.25 kg tied to the end of a string is whirled round in a circle of radius 1.5 m with speed 40 rev/min in a horizontal plane. What is the tension in the string? What is the maximum speed with which the stone can be whirled around if the string can withstand a maximum tension of 200 N? NCERT [3 M]

47. An aircraft executes a horizontal loop at a speed of 720 km/h with its wings banked at 15°. What is the radius of the loop? NCERT [3 M]

48. A train rounds an unbanked circular bend of radius 30 m at a speed of 54 km/h. The mass of the train is 10^6 kg. What provides the centripetal force required for this purpose, the engine or the rails? What is the angle of banking required to prevent wearing out of the rail? **NCERT [3 M]**

49. The rear side of a truck is open and a box of 40kg mass is placed 5 m away from the open end as shown. The coefficient of friction between the box and the surface below it, is 0.15. On a straight road, the truck starts from rest and accelerates with 2 m/s^2.

At what distance from the starting point does the box fall off the truck? (ignore the size of the box). **NCERT [5 M]**

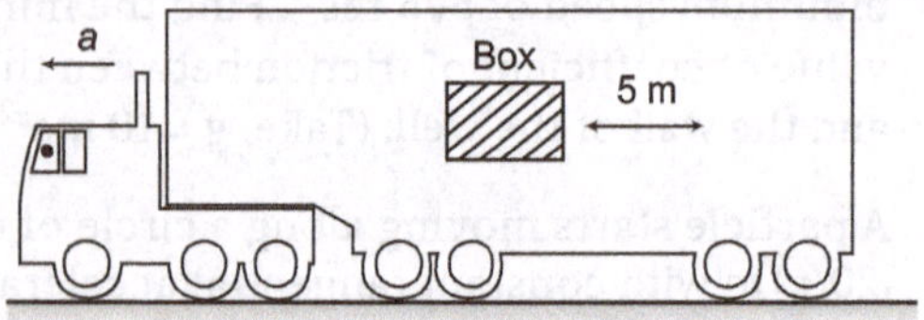

50. Two bodies A and B of masses 5 kg and 10 kg in contact with each other rest on a table is against a rigid wall as shown in figure. The coefficient of friction between the bodies and the table 0.15. A force of 200 N is applied horizontally at A.
What are (i) the reaction of the partition or wall (ii) the action- reaction forces between A and B? What happens when the partition is removed? Does the answer to (ii) change, when the bodies are in motion? Ignore difference between μ_s and μ_k. **NCERT [5 M]**

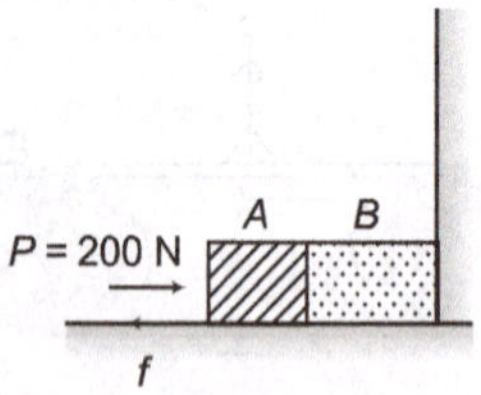

51. A disc revolves with a speed of $33\frac{1}{3}$ rev/min and has a radius of 15 cm. Two coins are placed at 4 cm and 14 cm away from the centre of the record. If the coefficient of friction between the coins and the record is 0.15, which of the coins will revolve with the record? **NCERT [5 M]**

52. A 70 kg man stands in contact against the inner wall of a hollow cylindrical drum of radius 3 m rotating about its vertical axis with 200 rev/min. The coefficient of friction between the wall and his clothing is 0.15. What is the minimum rotational speed of the cylinder to enable the man to remain stuck to the wall (without falling) when the floor is suddenly removed? **NCERT [5 M]**

Hints & Solutions

1. (*d*) Frictional force is a non-conservative force because work done by it is dissipated (wasted) as heat energy. This is not the case with other forces.

2. (*c*) The figure depends on the forces in action on the book.

$$R = N$$
$$\mu R = mg$$
$$0.2R = 10 \times 10$$
$$R = \frac{100}{0.2} = 500\text{N}$$
$$N = 500\text{N}$$

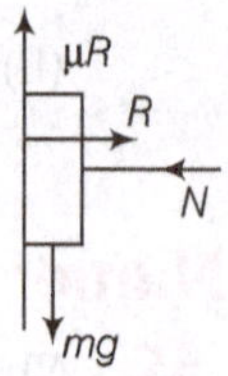

3. (*a*) Centripetal force is provided by force of friction when a car is taking a circular turn on a horizontal road.

4. (*b*) Centripetal force $f \le \mu_s N = \frac{mv^2}{r}$ used in moving a car on a circular road.

5. (c) Hence, $N = mg\cos\theta$

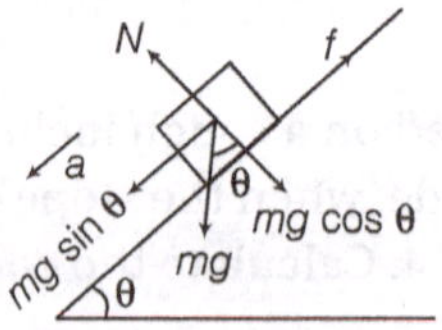

Force of friction, $f = \mu N = \mu mg\cos\theta$

$\therefore$ Net force acting on the body in downward direction,
$$F = mg\sin\theta - \mu mg\cos\theta$$
or $$F = ma = mg(\sin\theta - \mu\cos\theta)$$
or $$a = g(\sin\theta - \mu\cos\theta)$$

6. (*b*) At turning, cyclist requires centripetal force. Bending of cyclist with respect to vertical direction provides the necessary force.

7. (*b*) For a curved bridge, various forces acting on the car is

(i) weight of car acting vertically downward, i.e. mg.

(ii) Centrifugal force, $F = \frac{mv^2}{r}$ acting upward.

(iii) Normal reaction (N) acting vertically upward, i.e.
$$N + \frac{mv^2}{r} = mg$$
or $$N = mg - \frac{mv^2}{r}$$

8. (c) Various forces acting on the motor cyclist are
   (i) Weight of motor cyclist, acting downward.
   (ii) Normal reaction by wall towards the centre.
   (iii) Frictional force parallel to wall of the well.
   This frictional force balances the weight of motor cyclist.

9. As the applied force increases, the static friction also increases and becomes equal to the applied force to make the object stationary. That is why static friction is called a self-adjusting force.

10. Since, limiting friction is the ratio between force of friction and normal reaction, hence it is unitless.

11. Coefficient of friction = Tangent of the angle of friction
    or $\mu = \tan\theta$

12. No, force of friction does not depend on the area of contact.

13. No, the angle of banking does not depend on the mass of the vehicle.

14. Covering of snow laid tracks with sand increases the force of friction between the road and the wheels. Hence, chances of slipping and skidding reduce.

15. Various methods of reducing friction are
    (i) Lubrication (ii) Polishing
    (iii) Ball bearing (iv) Stream lining

16. When a body is moving along a circular path, speed always remains constant and a centripetal force is acting on the body.

17. No, the large brake on a wheel is not more effective than a small one, because the force of friction is independent of the surface area of contact. However, chances of failure of brake decreases when area of contact is larger. [2]

18. Given, mass of the block = m

    Coefficient of friction between the block and the wall = μ

    Let a force F be applied on the block to hold the block against the wall. The normal reaction of mass be N and force of friction acting upward be f.

    In equilibrium, vertical and horizontal forces should be balanced separately.

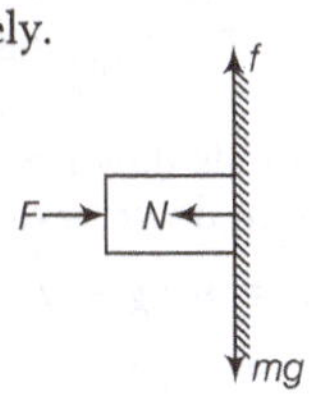

$$\therefore \quad f = mg \quad \text{...(i)}$$

$$\text{and} \quad F = N \quad \text{...(ii)}$$

But force of friction $(f) = \mu N$

$= \mu F$ [using Eq. (ii)] ...(iii) [1]

From Eqs. (i) and (iii), we get

$$\mu F = mg \quad \text{or} \quad F = \frac{mg}{\mu}$$ [1]

19. When a lubricant is added to a moving parts of a machine, it spreads between the two surfaces and fills the irregularities present on the surfaces and forms a thin layer between the surfaces in contact. As a result of it, the contact between the two hard surfaces is replaced by the contact between the hard surface and lubricating thin surface. Due to it, the force of friction is reduced considerably. [2]

20. Since, force is perpendicular to the direction of motion, there will be no change in speed of the body, but the direction of motion of the body will keep on changing continuously. [2]

21. Refer to text on page 130 (Cause of rolling friction).

22. Refer to text on page 133 (Relation between linear velocity (v) and angular velocity (ω)).

23. The second part correctly describes the trajectory of the stone after the string breaks because when a stone tied to one end of a string is whirled round in a circle then velocity of the stone at any point is along the tangent at that point. If the string breaks suddenly, then stone flies off tangentially, along the direction of its velocity. [2]

24. Let tension in the string be T_1 and T_2 at lowest and highest points of the vertical circle. [1]

    At lowest point T_1 acts towards the centre of the circle ($\because$ at the lowest point string will be stretched downward due to weight of the stone) and mg acts vertically downward (weight of an object always acts downward) [1]

    $\therefore$ Net force acting on the stone in downward direction $(F_L) = mg - T_1$

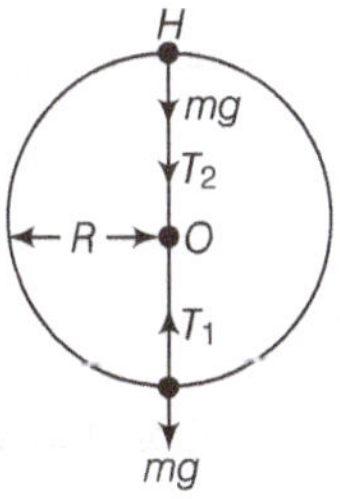

    At highest point Both T_2 and mg act vertically downward ($\because$ at the highest point string is stretched away from the centre) towards the centre of the vertical circle. Net force acting on the stone in downward direction $(F_H) = mg + T_2$

    $\therefore$ Correct option is (i). [1]

25. When the motorcyclist is at the uppermost point of the death well, then weight of the cyclist as well as the normal reaction R of the ceiling of the chamber is in downward direction. These forces are balanced by the outward centrifugal force acting on the motorcyclist.

$$\therefore \quad R + mg = \frac{mv^2}{r}$$ [1]

where, v = speed of the motorcyclist
m = mass of (motorcycle + driver)
r = radius of the death well.

As the forces acting on the motorcyclist are balanced, therefore, motorcyclist does not fall down.

The minimum speed required to perform a vertical loop is given by

$$mg = \frac{mv_{min}^2}{r}$$ [1]

[$\because$ In the case weight of the object = centripetal force]

$$\text{or} \quad v_{min} = \sqrt{rg} = \sqrt{25 \times 9.8} = 15.65 \text{ m/s}$$ [1]

26. Refer to text on pages 126, 127 and 128 (Static friction, limiting friction, kinetic friction and variation of frictional force with applied force).

27. Refer to text on page 131 (Motion of a body on a rough inclined plane).

28. Refer to text on pages 136 and 137 (Motion of a car on a banked road).

29. Refer to text on pages 127 and 128 (Angle of friction).

30. Refer to text on page 132 (Friction is a necessary evil).

31. On smooth inclined plane Acceleration of a body sliding down a smooth inclined plane, $a = g\sin\theta$

Here, $\theta = 45°$

$\therefore \quad a = g\sin 45° = \frac{g}{\sqrt{2}}$ [1]

Let the travelled distance be s.

Using the equation of motion, $s = ut + \frac{1}{2}at^2$, we get

$$s = 0.t + \frac{1}{2}\frac{g}{\sqrt{2}}T^2 \text{ or } s = \frac{gT^2}{2\sqrt{2}} \quad \text{...(i)}$$ [1]

On rough inclined plane

Acceleration of the body,

$$a = g(\sin\theta - \mu\cos\theta)$$
$$= g(\sin 45° - \mu\cos 45°)$$ [1]
$$= \frac{g(1-\mu)}{\sqrt{2}} \quad \left[\text{as } \sin 45° = \cos 45° = \frac{1}{\sqrt{2}}\right]$$

Again using equation of motion, $s = ut + \frac{1}{2}at^2$, we get

$$s = 0(pT) + \frac{1}{2}\frac{g(1-\mu)}{\sqrt{2}}(pT)^2$$

or $$s = \frac{g(1-\mu)p^2T^2}{2\sqrt{2}} \quad \text{...(ii)}$$

From Eqs. (i) and (ii), we get

$$\frac{gT^2}{2\sqrt{2}} = \frac{g(1-\mu)p^2T^2}{2\sqrt{2}}$$ [1]

or $$(1-\mu)p^2 = 1 \text{ or } 1-\mu = \frac{1}{p^2} \text{ or } \mu = \left(1 - \frac{1}{p^2}\right)$$ [1]

32. Mass of the block, $m = 15$ kg

Coefficient of friction between the block and the trolley

$$\mu = 0.18$$

Acceleration of the trolley, $a = 0.5 \text{ m/s}^2$

Time, $t = 20$ s

(i) As block is placed on the trolley, therefore, friction force is applied on the block by the trolley

$$F = ma = 15 \times 0.5 = 7.5 \text{ N}$$ [1]

Force on the block is the friction applied by trolley on the block, its direction is in the direction of motion of the trolley. [1]

For the stationary observer on the ground, the block will appear to move with acceleration initially and then with uniform velocity as given in the question. [1]

(ii) For an observer on the trolley, the block is always at rest either initially or finally. Trolley always becomes inertial frame with respect to block because both have the same acceleration initially and same velocity finally. [2]

33. Given, mass of the monkey, $m = 40$ kg

Maximum tension which can be withstood by the rope $(T)_{max} = 600$ N

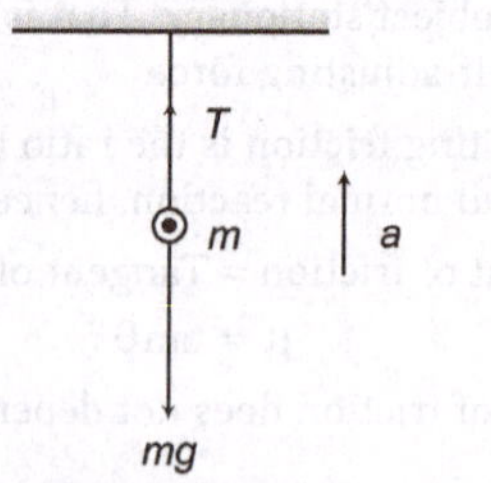

(i) When monkey climbs up with an acceleration $a = 6 \text{ m/s}^2$, then

$$T - mg = ma; \; T = mg + ma$$
$$T = m(g+a) = 40(10+6) = 640 \text{ N}$$

In this condition, $T > T_{max}$, therefore the rope will break. [1½]

(ii) When monkey climbs down with an acceleration $a = 4 \text{ m/s}^2$, then

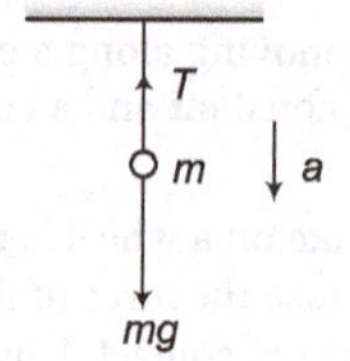

$$mg - T = ma$$
or $$T = mg - ma = m(g-a)$$
$$= 40(10-4) \text{ N} = 240 \text{ N}$$

In this condition, $T < T_{max}$,

Therefore, the rope will not break. [1]

(iii) When monkey climbs up with a uniform speed of 5 m/s, then its acceleration a is zero.

$\therefore \quad T = mg = 40 \times 10 = 400$ N

In this condition $T < T_{max}$, therefore, the rope will not break. [1]

(iv) When monkey falls down freely under gravity, then its acceleration in downward direction is g.

$$\therefore \quad T = m(g-a)$$
$$= m(g-g) \quad [\because a = g]$$
$$= 0$$

In this condition, monkey will be in a state of weightlessness and tension in the rope is zero. [1/2]

Therefore, the rope will not break.

In this problem, T actually represents friction force which is generated, when the monkey pushes the rope in downward direction with a view to climb up. [1]

34. The situation is shown in figure below

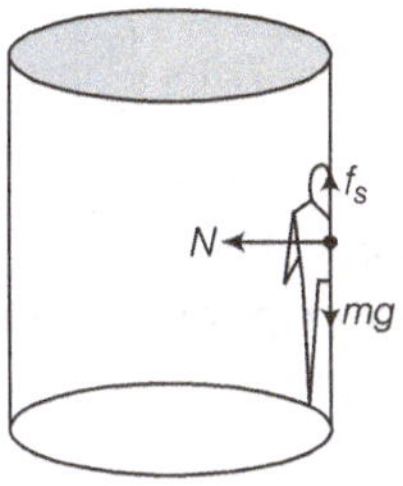

(i) When the floor is removed, the forces on the person are
(a) weight mg downward.
(b) normal force N due to the wall towards the centre.
(c) frictional force f_s parallel to the wall, upwards. [1]

The person is moving in a circle with a uniform speed, so its acceleration is v^2/r towards the centre.

Newton's law for the horizontal direction (second law) and for the vertical direction (first law) give

$$N = mv^2/r \quad \text{...(i)}$$

and $$f_s = mg \quad \text{...(ii)}$$

For the minimum speed, when the floor may be removed, the friction is limiting one and so equals $\mu_s N$. [1]

This gives $\mu_s N = mg$

or $\dfrac{\mu_s mv^2}{r} = mg$ [using Eq. (i)]

or $v = \sqrt{\dfrac{rg}{\mu_s}} = \sqrt{\dfrac{2\text{m} \times 10 \text{ m/s}^2}{0.2}} = 10 \text{ m/s}$ [1]

(ii) Speciality is that without the floor an object may be align with a vertical wall provided, it is set to be in circular motion (horizontal) with properly required speed. [2]

35. Given, velocity, $v = 50 \text{ ms}^{-1}$

Radius, $r = 250$ m

Centripetal acceleration, $a = \dfrac{v^2}{r} \Rightarrow a = \dfrac{50 \times 50}{250} = 10 \text{ ms}^{-2}$

36. Here, radius $r = 20$ cm

Centripetal acceleration, $= 980 \text{ cms}^{-2}$

We know that centripetal acceleration, $a = r\omega^2$

$$\omega = \sqrt{\frac{a}{r}} = \sqrt{\frac{980}{20}} \Rightarrow \omega = \sqrt{49} = 7 \text{ rad/s}$$

37. The slope of the plane equal to 1 in 4 implies that if $BC = 4$ and $AB = 1$. Suppose that the plane is inclined at angle θ with the horizontal AC. From the relation between the coefficient of friction and angle of repose, we have [1]

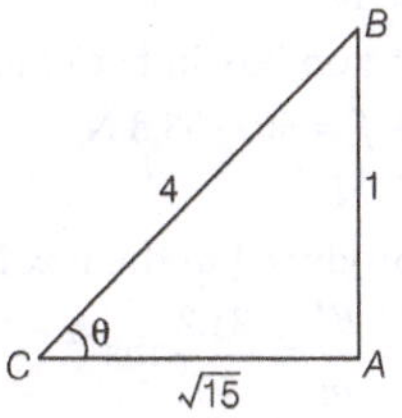

$\mu = \tan\theta$ [here, θ is angle of repose]

or $\mu = \dfrac{AB}{AC} = \dfrac{AB}{\sqrt{BC^2 - AB^2}} = \dfrac{1}{\sqrt{4^2 - 1^2}} = \dfrac{1}{\sqrt{16-1}}$

or $\mu = \dfrac{1}{\sqrt{15}}$ or $\mu = 0.258$ [1]

38. Given, $m = 2$ kg, $u = 2\text{ms}^{-1}$, $\mu = 0.2$

Force of friction, $F = \mu R$

$F = \mu mg$ [$\because R = mg$]

$F = 0.2 \times 2 \times 9.8$

$F = 3.92$ N [1/2]

Distance moved per second $s = ut$

$s = 2 \times 1 = 2$ [1/2]

Work done by friction per second, $W = Fs$

$W = 3.92 \times 2 = 7.84$ J [1/2]

Heat produced, $H = \dfrac{W}{J} \Rightarrow H = \dfrac{7.84}{4.2}$

$H = 1.87$ cal [1/2]

39. Here, $r = 80$ cm $= 0.8$ m, $f = 14/25 \text{ s}^{-1}$

$\therefore \quad \omega = 2\pi f = 2 \times \dfrac{22}{7} \times \dfrac{14}{25} = \dfrac{88}{25}$ rad/s

The centripetal acceleration

$$a = \omega^2 r = \left(\frac{88}{25}\right)^2 \times 0.80 = 9.90 \text{ ms}^{-2}$$ [1]

The direction of centripetal acceleration is along the string directed towards the centre of circular path. [1]

40. Here, $r = 1$ km $= 1000$ m,

$v = 900 \text{ kmh}^{-1} = 900 \times (1000 \text{ m})/(60 \times 60 \text{ s}) = 250 \text{ ms}^{-1}$

Centripetal acceleration,

$$a = \frac{v^2}{r} = \frac{(250)^2}{1000}$$ [1]

Now, $\dfrac{a}{g} = \dfrac{(250)^2}{1000} \times \dfrac{1}{9.8} = 6.38$ [1]

41. To avoid skidding

$$\tan\theta = \frac{v^2}{gr} = \frac{20 \times 20}{10 \times 20} = 2 \Rightarrow \theta = \tan^{-1}(2)$$ [2]

42. $F = \dfrac{mv^2}{r}$, $F' = \dfrac{(1.5m)(1.5v)^2}{(1.5r)} = 2.25\dfrac{mv^2}{r} = 2.25F$ [1]

Percentage increase $= \dfrac{2.25F - F}{F} \times 100 = 125\%$

Therefore, F has to be increased by 125%. [1]

43. $N = \dfrac{mv^2}{R}$, $mg = \mu N = \dfrac{\mu mv^2}{R}$ [1]

$\therefore$ Coefficient of friction between the tyres and wall of the well will be $\mu = \dfrac{Rg}{v^2} = \dfrac{5 \times 10}{(5\sqrt{5})^2} = 0.40$ [1]

44. As $v = \omega r$

$\Rightarrow \quad 50 = \omega\left(\frac{20}{\pi}\right)$

$\Rightarrow \quad \omega = \frac{50\pi}{20} = \frac{5\pi}{2}$

$\Rightarrow \quad \frac{2\pi}{T} = \frac{5\pi}{2} \Rightarrow T = \frac{4}{5}\text{s}$ [1½]

Given, $t = 2T = \frac{8}{5}\text{s}$

$\therefore \quad \omega = \alpha t$

$\Rightarrow \quad \frac{5\pi}{2} = \alpha \times \frac{8}{5} \Rightarrow \alpha = \frac{25\pi}{16}\text{rads}^{-2}$

$\therefore \quad a_t = r(\alpha) = \left(\frac{20}{\pi}\right)\left(\frac{25\pi}{16}\right) = 31.2 \text{ rads}^{-2}$ [1½]

45. Acceleration of the conveyor belt, $a = 1\text{ m/s}^2$

As man is standing stationary with respect to the horizontal conveyor belt therefore, acceleration of the man = acceleration of the belt

$\therefore \quad a = 1\text{ m/s}^2$

Mass of the man, $m = 65$ kg

$\therefore$ Net force acting on the man $F = ma = 65 \times 1 = 65$ N

This force is actually the force of friction (static) between man and the belt. Force of friction is actually supporting motion of man.

The direction of this force is in the direction of motion of the belt. Coefficient of friction between the man's shoes and the belt $\mu = 0.2$

Let a' be the acceleration of the belt upto which the man can continue to be stationary relative to the belt.

In this condition

$\therefore \quad ma'$ = maximum static friction

$ma' = \mu R = \mu mg \quad \left[\because \mu = \frac{\text{Limiting friction}}{\text{Normal reaction}}\right]$

or $\quad a' = \mu g = 0.2 \times 9.8 = 1.96\text{ m/s}^2$ [3]

46. Mass of stone, $m = 0.25$ kg, radius of the string, $r = 1.5$ m

Frequency, $f = 40\text{ rev/min} = \frac{40}{60}\text{ rev/s} = \frac{2}{3}\text{ rev/s}$

Centripetal force required for circular motion is obtained from the tension in the string.

$\therefore$ Tension in the string = centripetal force

$T = mr\omega^2 = mr(2\pi f)^2 \quad [\because \omega = 2\pi f]$ [1]

$= mr4\pi^2 f^2$

$T = 0.25 \times 1.5 \times 4 \times \left(\frac{22}{7}\right)^2 \times \left(\frac{2}{3}\right)^2 = 6.6\text{N}$ [1]

Maximum tension which can be withstand by the string

$T_{\max} = 200\text{ N} = \frac{mv^2_{\max}}{r}$

$v_{\max} = \sqrt{\frac{T_{\max} \times r}{m}} = \sqrt{\frac{200 \times 1.5}{0.25}}$

$= 34.6$ m/s [1]

47. Speed of the aircraft, $v = 720$ km/h

$= 720 \times \frac{5}{18}\text{ m/s} \quad \left[\because 1\text{ km/h} = \frac{5}{18}\text{ m/s}\right]$

$= 200$ m/s [1]

Angle of banking, $\theta = 15°$

Acceleration due to gravity, $g = 9.8\text{ m/s}^2$

At turn, $\tan\theta = \frac{v^2}{rg}$

or $\quad r = \frac{v^2}{g\tan\theta} = \frac{(200)^2}{9.8 \times \tan 15°} = \frac{40000}{9.8 \times 0.2679}$

$r = 15235\text{ m} = 15.24 \times 10^3\text{ m} = 15.24\text{ km}$ [2]

48. Radius of circular bend, $r = 30$ m

Speed of the train, $v = 54$ km/h

$= 54 \times \frac{5}{18}\text{ m/s} \quad \left[\because 1\text{ km/h} = \frac{5}{18}\text{ m/s}\right]$

$= 15$ m/s [1]

Mass of the train, $m = 10^6$ kg

The centripetal force is provided by the lateral thrust of the outer rail on the flanges of wheels.

Let θ be the angle of banking required to prevent wearing out the rails, then

$\tan\theta = \frac{v^2}{rg} = \frac{(15)^2}{30 \times 9.8} = \frac{225}{30 \times 9.8} = 0.7653$ [1]

$\theta = \tan^{-1}(0.7653) = 37.4°$ [1]

49. $\because$ Mass of the box, $m = 40$ kg

Coefficient of friction between the box and the surface, $\mu = 0.15$

Acceleration of the truck, $a = 2\text{ m/s}^2$

Truck is a non-inertial frame for the box, so motion of box can be studied by assuming a pseudo force acting on it in a direction opposite to the direction of acceleration of truck i.e. in backward direction.

pseudo force applied by the truck on the box due to its accelerated motion, $F = ma = 40 \times 2 = 80$ N [1]

Due to this pseudo force on the box, the box tries to move in backward direction but limiting friction force opposes its motion.

Limiting friction force between the box and the surface

$= \mu R = \mu mg$

$f = 0.15 \times 40 \times 9.8$ N

$= 58.8$ N [in forward direction]

Net force acting on box in backward direction [1]

$F' = F - f = 80 - 58.8$ N

$= 21.2$ N

Acceleration produced in the box in backward direction

$a' = \frac{F'}{m} = \frac{21.2}{40}\text{ ms}^{-2}$

$a' = 0.53\text{ ms}^{-2}$ [1]

Using equation of motion for travelling $s = 5$ m to fall off the truck, $s = ut + \frac{1}{2}at^2$

$$5 = 0 \times t + \frac{1}{2} \times 0.53 \times t^2$$

or $$t = \sqrt{\frac{5 \times 2}{0.53}} = \sqrt{\frac{1000}{53}} = 4.34 \text{ s}$$ [1]

Distance travelled by the truck in time,

$t = 4.34$ s

$$s' = ut + \frac{1}{2}at^2 = 0 \times t + \frac{1}{2} \times 2 \times (4.34)^2$$

$$= (4.34)^2 = 18.84 \text{ m}$$ [1]

50. Mass of body $A(m_1) = 5$ kg

Mass of body $B(m_2) = 10$ kg

Coefficient of friction between the bodies and the table $(\mu) = 0.15$

Force applied horizontally at A, $F = 200$ N

(i) **Reaction of partition**

Limiting friction acting to the left

$$f = \mu R = \mu (m_1 + m_2) g$$ [1]

$$= 0.15 (5 + 10) \times 9.8 = 22.05 \text{ N}$$

∴ Net force acting on the partition towards the right

$$F' = F - f$$

$$= 200 - 22.05 = 177.95 \text{ N}$$

According to the Newton's third law of motion,

Reaction of partition = Net force acting on the partition

= 177.95 N [towards the left] [1]

(ii) **Action-reaction forces between A and B**

Let f_1 be the force of limiting friction acting on body A and F_1 be the net force applied by body A on body B.

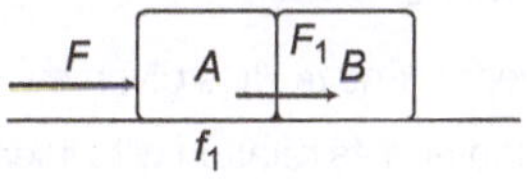

[1]

$$f_1 = \mu R_1 = \mu m_1 g \quad [\because R_1 = m_1 g]$$

$$= 0.15 \times 5 \times 9.8$$

$$= 7.35 \text{ N (towards the left)}$$ [1]

∴ Net force applied by body A on body B,

$$F_1 = F - f_1 = 200 - 7.35 = 192.65 \text{ N [towards the right]}$$

According to Newton's third law of motion, reaction force applied by body B on body, i.e.

$$A = F_1 = 192.65 \text{ N (towards left)}$$ [1]

51. Given, $(\nu) = 33\frac{1}{3} = \frac{100}{3}$ rev/min $= \frac{100}{3 \times 60}$ rev/s $= \frac{5}{9}$ rev/s

∴ Angular velocity $(\omega) = 2\pi\nu = 2 \times \frac{22}{7} \times \frac{5}{9} = \frac{220}{63}$ rad/s

Radius of the disc $(r) = 15$ cm. [1]

Distance of first coin A from the centre $(x_1) = 4$ cm

Distance of the second coin B from the centre $(x_2) = 14$ cm

Coefficient of friction between the coins and the record = 0.15.

If force of friction between the coin and the record is sufficient to provide the centripetal force, then coil will revolve with the record.

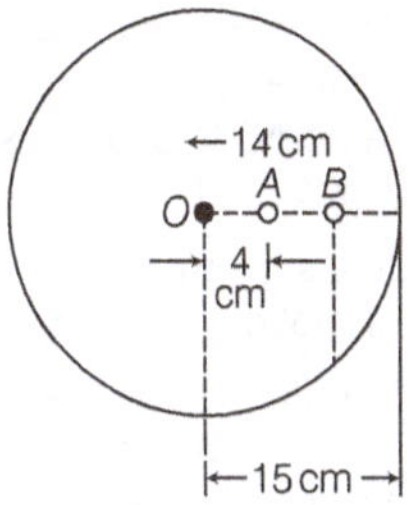

[1]

∴ To prevent slipping (or to revolve the coin alongwith record) the force of friction $f \geq$ centripetal force (f_c)

or $$\mu mg \geq mr\omega^2$$

or $$\mu g \geq r\omega^2$$ [1]

For first coin A

$$r\omega^2 = \frac{4}{100} \times \left(\frac{220}{63}\right)^2 = \frac{4 \times 220 \times 220}{100 \times 63 \times 63} = 0.488 \text{ m/s}^2$$

and $\mu g = 0.15 \times 9.8 = 1.47$ m/s^2 [1]

Here, $\mu g > r\omega^2$, therefore, this coin will revolve with the record.

For second coin B

$$r\omega^2 = \frac{14}{100} \times \left(\frac{220}{63}\right)^2 = \frac{14 \times 220 \times 220}{100 \times 63 \times 63} = 1.707 \text{ m/s}$$

and $\mu g = 1.47$ m/s

Here, $\mu g < r\omega^2$, therefore, centripetal force will not be obtained from the force of friction, hence this coin will not revolve with the record. [1]

52. Given, radius of the cylindrical drum $(r) = 3$ m

Coefficient of friction between the wall and his clothing $(\mu) = 0.15$.

Frequency $(\nu) = 200$ rev/min $= \frac{200}{60}$ rev/s $= \frac{10}{3}$ rev/s [1]

The normal reaction of the wall on the man acting horizontally provides the required centripetal force.

$$R = mr\omega^2 \quad \text{...(i)}$$

The frictional force F, acting upwards balances his weight

i.e. $$F = mg \quad \text{...(ii)}$$ [1]

The man will remain stuck to the wall without slipping, if

$$\mu R \geq F \quad \text{or} \quad F \leq \mu R$$ [1]

$$mg \leq \mu \times mr\omega^2 \quad \text{or} \quad \omega^2 \geq \frac{g}{\mu r}$$ [1]

$$\omega \geq \sqrt{\frac{g}{\mu R}}$$

For minimum angular speed of rotation,

$$\omega_{\min} = \sqrt{\frac{g}{\mu R}} = \sqrt{\frac{9.8}{0.15 \times 3}} = 4.67 \text{ rad/s}$$ [1]

SUMMARY

- Force is an external agency (a pull or a push) which changes or tends to change the state of rest or of uniform motion or the direction of motion of a body. Its SI units is Newton and dimensional formula is $[MLT^{-2}]$.
- Sir Issac Newton made a systematic study of motion and proposed three laws of motion.
- **Newton's first law of motion** states that every body continues in its state of rest or of uniform motion in a straight line unless it is compelled by some external force to change that state.
- **Newton's second law of motion** states that the rate of change of linear momentum of a body is directly proportional to the external force applied on the body and the change takes place in the direction of the applied force, $F = k\frac{dp}{dt} = ma$
- **Newton's third law of motion** states that for every action there is always an equal and opposite reaction, i.e. $F_{AB} = -F_{BA}$.
- **Linear momentum** is the quantity of motion possessed by the body. It is the product of its mass and velocity, $p = mv$ SI units is kg-m/s and dimensional formula is $[MLT^{-1}]$.
- **Impulse** is the product of the average force and the time interval for which the force acts on the body, $\mathbf{I} = \mathbf{F} \times \Delta t = \mathbf{p}_2 - \mathbf{p}_1$. Its SI unit is N-s and dimensional formula is $[MLT^{-1}]$.
- **Conservation of linear momentum**, if there are no external forces acting on a system, the total linear momentum of the system remains constant. $F_{ex} = 0$, then $\Delta \mathbf{p} = \text{constant}$
$$\mathbf{p} = \mathbf{p}_1 + \mathbf{p}_2$$
- **Equilibrium of a particle** the forces which are acting at the same point or on a particle are called concurrent forces. These forces are said to be in equilibrium when their resultant is zero.
- **Lami's theorm** According to this theorem when three concurrent forces F_1, F_2 and F_3 acting on a body are in equilibrium, then $\frac{F_1}{\sin\alpha} = \frac{F_2}{\sin\beta} = \frac{F_3}{\sin\gamma}$
- **Some common forces in mechanics are** Weight $w = mg$, Tension force, $T = mg$
- **Friction** is the opposing force which comes into play when a body moves or tries to move over the surface of another body.
- **Internal friction** are arises due to relative motion between two layers of liquid.
- **External friction** are arises when two bodies in contact with each other try to move or there is an actual relative motion between the two bodies.
- **Static Friction** The opposing force which comes into play between two bodies before one body actually starts moving over the other. It is denoted by f_s.
- **Limiting friction** The maximum opposing force which comes into play when a body just starts moving over the surface of another body. There are four laws of limiting friction.
$$\mu_s = \frac{f_s}{R} = \frac{\text{Limiting friction}}{\text{Normal reaction}}$$
- **Kinetic friction** The opposing force that comes into existence when one object is actually moving over the surface of the other object. it is also known as dynamic friction.
$$\mu_s = \frac{f_R}{R} = \frac{\text{Kinetic friction}}{\text{Normal reaction}}$$
- **Angle of friction** (θ) may be defined as the angle which the resultant of the limiting friction and the normal reaction makes with the normal reaction.
- **Angle of repose** is defined as the minimum angle of inclination of a plane with the horizontal such that a body placed on the plane just begins to slide down the incline. It is represented by α
- **Types of kinetic friction/ sliding friction** The force that comes into play when a body slides over the surface of another body.
- **Rolling Friction** The force of friction that comes into play when a body rolls over the surface of another body.
- **Angular displacement** It is the angle swept out by a radius vector in a given time interval.
$$\theta\,(\text{Rad}) = \frac{\text{Arc}}{\text{Radius}} = \frac{s}{r}$$
- **Angular velocity** The angle swept out by the radius vector per second is called angular velocity.
$$\omega = \frac{\theta}{t} \text{ or } \omega = \frac{\theta_2 - \theta_1}{t_2 - t_1}$$
- **Time period and frequency** Time taken for one complete revolution is called time period (T).
The number of revolutions completed per second is called frequency.
$$\omega = \frac{2\pi}{T} = 2\pi f$$
Relationship between v and ω. It is given by $v = r\omega$
- Angular acceleration and its relation with linear acceleration. The rate of change of angular velocity is called angular acceleration. It is given by
Linear acceleration = Radius × Angular acceleration
$$\alpha = \frac{\omega_2 - \omega_1}{t_2 - t_1}; \quad a = r\alpha$$
- **Centripetal acceleration** A body moving along a circular path is acted upon by an acceleration directed towards the centre along the radius. This acceleration is called centripetal acceleration. It is given by
$$\alpha = \frac{v_2 - v_1}{r} = r\omega^2$$
- For circular motion of car on level road Centripetal force
$$F_c = mr\omega^2 = \frac{mv^2}{r} \text{ and } v_{max} = \sqrt{\mu r g}$$
- For motion of a car on banked road, $v_{max} = \sqrt{\frac{rg(\mu_s + \tan\theta)}{1 - (\mu_s \tan\theta)}}$

Angle of banking, $\theta = \tan^{-1}\left(\frac{v^2}{rg}\right)$

Chapter Practice

Multiple Choice Type Questions

1 Mark

1 When we cut the thread tied to a ball which is in circular motion, the ball flies off tangentially to the circular path. It is due to
(a) inertia of motion
(b) inertia of direction
(c) Both (a) and (b)
(d) None of the above

2 The state of rest and state of uniform linear motion are not equivalent, when
(a) both are on frictionless surface
(b) both are on rough surface
(c) Both (a) and (b)
(d) None of the above

3 Suppose the earth suddenly stops attracting objects placed near surface. A person standing on the surface of the earth will
(a) remain standing
(b) fly up
(c) sink into earth
(d) Either (b) or (c)

4 A bullet of mass 0.04 kg moving with a speed of 90 ms^{-1} enters a heavy wooden block and stopped after 3s. What is the average resistive force exerted by the block on the bullet?
(a) 1 N
(b) 1.2 N
(c) 2 N
(d) 3 N

5 A rocket is going upwards with accelerated motion. A man sitting in it, feels his weight increased 5 times his own weight. If the mass of the rocket including that of the man is 1.0×10^4 kg, how much force is being applied by rocket engine? (Take, $g = 10 \, ms^{-2}$)
(a) 5×10^4 N
(b) 5×10^5 N
(c) 5×10^8 N
(d) 2×10^4 N

6 A particle is in equilibrium under the action of any number of forces $F_1, F_2, \ldots, F_n$, if
(a) all the forces form a closed *n* sided polygon with arrows directed in the same sense
(b) $F_1 + F_2 + F_3 + \ldots + F_n = 0$
(c) Both (a) and (b)
(d) None of the above

7 The coefficient of friction between tyres and the road is 0.1. Find the maximum speed allowed by traffic police for cars to cross a circular turn of radius 10 m to prevent accident.
(a) $\sqrt{10}$ ms^{-1}
(b) $\sqrt{20}$ ms^{-1}
(c) 5 ms^{-1}
(d) 9 ms^{-1}

Assertion and Reason

Directions (Q. Nos. 8-12) *In the following questions, two statements are given- one labelled Assertion (A) and the other labelled Reason (R). Select the correct answer to these questions from the codes (a), (b), (c) and (d) as given below*
(a) Both Assertion and Reason are true and Reason is the correct explanation of Assertion.
(b) Both Assertion and Reason are true but Reason is not the correct explanation of Assertion.
(c) Assertion is true but Reason is false.
(d) Assertion is false but Reason is true.

8 **Assertion (A)** A body is momentarily at rest still some force is acting on it at that time.
Reason (R) When a force acts on a body, it may not have some acceleration.

9 **Assertion (A)** During the action of an impulsive force, change in the momentum is very high even though force acts for a very short period.
Reason (R) The amount of force is very high.

10 **Assertion (A)** Action and reaction forces do not cancel out each other.
Reason (R) It is because both do not act on the same body.

11 **Assertion (A)** Angle of repose is equal to angle of limiting friction.
Reason (R) When a body is just at the point of motion, the force of friction in this stage is called as limiting friction.

12 **Assertion (A)** It is always necessary that external agency of force is in contact with the object while applying force on object.

Reason (R) A stone released from top of a building accelerates downward due to gravitational pull of the earth.

Very Short Answer Type Questions

1 Mark

13 $F = ma$, this expression represents Newton's second law. What is the condition behind this expression? (1)

14 Write the formula of the speed of the car on a banked circular road, when friction force acting on the tyres is zero.

15 Calculate the impulse necessary to stop 1500 kg car travelling at 90 km/h.

16 A box is lying on a rough floor. What is the maximum value of F_{max}, so that box do not slip relative to the floor?

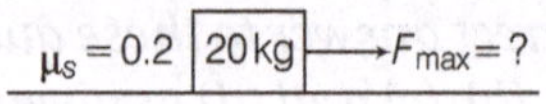

Short Answer Type I Question

2 Marks

17 A boy is trying to push a truck but not able to push it. His friend explains the situation with the help of Newton's third law. His friend says that according to Newton's third law action-reaction forces are equal and opposite, so they will cancel each other and the net force on the truck will become zero. That's why the truck will not move.
Analyse the explanation of his friend and comment that his explanation is right or wrong.

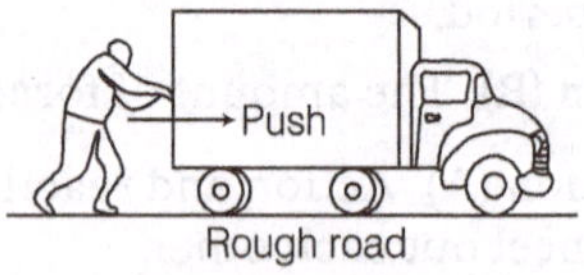

Short Answer Type II Questions

3 Marks

18 Briefly explain static friction, limiting friction and kinetic friction. How do they vary with the applied force?

19 Discuss the equilibrium of concurrent forces acting on a rigid body.

Case Based Questions

Directions (Q. No. 20) *These questions are case study based questions. Read the following paragraph and answer the questions.*

20 Newton has given three laws to describe the motion of objects. According to Newton's first law, when the net external force on a body is zero, then the body is either at rest or moving with constant velocity. The first law gives the definition of inertia. Inertia means resistance to change in state of rest or motion.
According to Newton's second law, the rate of change of momentum of a body is directly proportional to the external applied force on the body. The second law gives the measurement of force. According to Newton's third law, for every action, there is always equal and opposite reaction.

(i) Name the property by which any body tries to maintain its original state.

(ii) Why does a cricket player lower his hands while catching a ball?

(iii) An object of mass 50 kg is initially at rest. It gets the speed of 10 m/s in 5 s. Calculate the force applied by engine of the car.

(iv) A object of mass 10 kg jumps on a floor. Calculate the average force applied by the floor to the object.

Numerical Problems

21 A batsman deflects a ball by an angle of 45° without changing its initial speed, which is equal to 54 km/h. What is the impulse imparted to the ball? Mass of the ball is 0.15 kg. [2 M]

22 Forces of 16 N and 12 N are acting on a mass of 200 kg in mutually perpendicular direction. Find the magnitude of acceleration produced. [2 M]

23 The wheel of a truck has a radius of $r = 0.29$ m and is being rotated at 830 revolutions per minute (rpm) on a tyre balancing machine. Determine the speed (in m/s) at which the outer edge of the wheel is moving. [2 M]

24 What is the smallest radius of an unbanked (flat) track around which a bicyclist can move if her speed is 29 km/h and the μ_s between tyres and track is 0.32? [2 M]

25 For the given pulley block system, find the acceleration of 2 kg block.

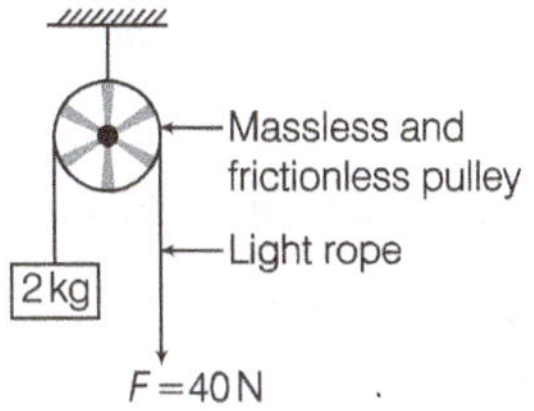

[2 M]

26 Two blocks are placed over a horizontal smooth plane as shown in the figure. Find the minimum value of μ_2, so that block could move together.

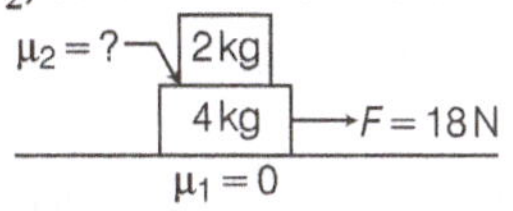

[2 M]

27 Find the maximum speed at which a car can turn around a curve of 30 m radius on a level road, given the coefficient of friction between the tyres and the road is 0.4.
$[g = 10 \text{ m/s}^2]$ **[2 M]**

28 For traffic moving at 60 km/h, if the radius of a curve is 0.1 km, then what is the correct angle of banking of the road? [take $g = 10 \text{ m/s}^2$] **[2 M]**

29 A shell of mass 0.020 kg is fired by a gun of mass 100 kg. If the muzzle speed of the shell is 80 m/s, what is the recoil speed of the gun? **[2 M]**

30 A body of mass 10 kg is placed on an inclined plane of angle 30°. If the coefficient of static friction is $1/\sqrt{3}$. find the force required to just push the body up the inclined surface. **[3 M]**

31 A disc revolves in a horizontal plane at a steady rate of 3 revolutions per second. A coin of mass 6 g just remains on the disc if kept at a mean distance of 2 cm from the axis of rotation. What is the coefficient of friction between the coin and the disc? $(g = 10 \text{ m/s}^2)$ **[3 M]**

32 For the system below, find the values of T_1, T_2 and T_3. Also, find the acceleration of every block.

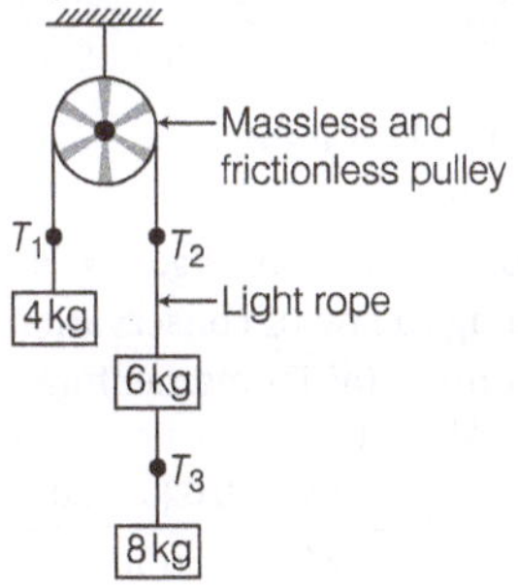

[5 M]

33 A circular motion addict of mass 80 kg slides a feris wheel around in a vertical circle of radius 10 m at a constant speed of 6.1 m/s. (i) What is the period of motion? What is the magnitude of the normal force on the addict from the seat when both go through (ii) the highest point of the circular path and (iii) lowest point? **[5 M]**

Answers

1 (*c*) Once the thread is cut, force acting on the circulating body becomes zero. So due to inertia of motion ball fly off with the same pace (inertia of motion) and of the same instantaneous direction.

2 (*b*) They are not equivalent on rough surface because a body at rest on rough surface experiences no force but a body in uniform motion on a rough surface required a uniform force to counts frictional force.

3 (*a*) If downward force on the earth stops, so upward self adjusting force also stop, in vertical direction there is no force. Due to inertia person resists any change to its state of rest. Person will remain standing.

4 (*b*) From the formula,

$$F \times t = mv_1 - mv_2$$

$$F \times 3 = 0.04 \times 90 - 0 \Rightarrow F \times 3 = 3.6$$

$$F = \frac{3.6}{3} \Rightarrow F = 1.2 \text{ N}$$

5 (*b*) As the weight of man increased by 5 times, so acceleration of the rocket,

$$a = 5,\ g = 5 \times 10 = 50 \text{ ms}^{-2}$$

Force applied by rocket engine is

$$F = ma = 1.0 \times 10^4 \times 50 = 5 \times 10^5 \text{ N}$$

6 (*c*)

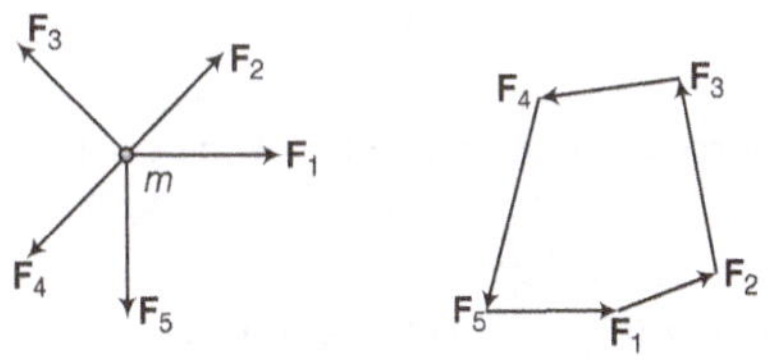

Mass m (assumed particle) is equilibrium under of forces $\mathbf{F}_1, \mathbf{F}_2, \mathbf{F}_3, \cdots, \mathbf{F}_n$.
When $\mathbf{F}_1, \mathbf{F}_2, \cdots, \mathbf{F}_n$ can be represented in magnitude and direction by sides of a closed polygon, with arrows in same sense. (Here $n = 5$; a particular case)

7 (*a*) $v_{\max} = \sqrt{\mu g r} = \sqrt{0.1 \times 10 \times 10} = \sqrt{10} \text{ ms}^{-1}$

8 (*c*)

9 (*a*)

10 (*a*)

11 (*a*)

12 (*a*)

13 The condition is that the constant of proportionality, $k = 1$.

14 $v = \sqrt{rg \tan\theta}$

15 Given, $m = 1500$ kg, $u = 90$ km/h $= 25$ m/s, $v = 0$

Impulse = Change in momentum $= m(v - u)$

$= 1500(0 - 25) = -37500 \text{ kg ms}^{-1}$

16 Here, $m = 20$ kg, $\mu_s = 0.2$, $g = 10 \text{ ms}^{-2}$

Then $F_{max} = \mu_s R = \mu_s mg$

$= 0.2 \times 20 \times 10 = 40$ N

17 The explanation is not right as the forces of action and reaction cannot cancel each other. This is because action and reaction though equal and opposite forces always act on different bodies and so cannot cancel each other. When force is applied on the massive truck, then it is not sufficient to overcome the force of friction between tyre of truck and ground. Hence the truck does not move. [2]

18 Refer to text on pages 126, 127, 128 (Static friction, limiting friction, kinetic friction and variation of frictional force with applied force).

19 Refer to text on pages 115 and 116 (Equilibrium of a particle).

20 (i) Inertia is the property of a body by virtue of which the body tries to maintain its either, the state of rest or motion. i.e. original state.

(ii) As, force $= \dfrac{\text{change in momentum}}{\text{time interval}}$

So, a cricket player lowers his hand while catching a ball in order to increase time interval to reduce zero velocity. Hence, the force on his hands is reduced and the hands of the players is protected from injury.

(iii) Given, $u = 0$, $v = 10$ m/s,

$t = 5$ s, $m = 50$ kg

$\therefore \quad a = \dfrac{v - u}{t} = \dfrac{10 - 0}{5} = 2 \text{ m/s}^2$

$\therefore$ Force applied by engine of the car is

$F = ma = 50 \times 2 = 100$ N

(iv) Given, $m = 10$ kg

$\therefore$ According to Newton's third law,

Force applied by floor to the body is the weight of the body.

$\therefore \quad w = mg = 10 \times 10$

$= 100$ N

21 Here, $m = 0.15$ kg, $u = 54$ km/h $= 15$ m/s

$\theta = \dfrac{45^\circ}{2} = 22.5^\circ$ [1]

Impulse $= mu\cos\theta - (-mu\cos\theta) = 2mu\cos\theta$

$= 2 \times 0.15 \times 15 \cos 22.5^\circ$

$= 4.5 \times 0.9239 = 4.16 \text{ kg ms}^{-1}$ [1]

22 $F_1 = 16$ N, $F_2 = 12$ N, $m = 200$ kg

Resultant force $\mathbf{F} = \sqrt{16^2 + 12^2} = 20$ N [1]

Magnitude of acceleration, $a = \dfrac{F}{m} = \dfrac{20}{200} = 0.1 \text{ ms}^{-2}$ [1]

23 Here, $r = 0.29$ m,

$T = \dfrac{1}{830} \text{ min} = 1.2 \times 10^{-3} \text{ min} = 0.072$ s [1]

Speed, $v = \dfrac{2\pi r}{T} = \dfrac{2\pi \times 0.29}{0.072} = 25$ m/s [1]

24 Here, $v = 29$ km/h $= 8.05$ m/s, $\mu_s = 0.32$

The bicycle will move on circular track when static friction becomes equal to centripetal force, i.e.

$\dfrac{mv^2}{r} = \mu_s R = \mu_s mg$ [1]

$\Rightarrow \quad r = \dfrac{v^2}{\mu_s g} = \dfrac{(8.05)^2}{0.32 \times 9.8} = 20.6 \text{ m} \simeq 21$ m [1]

25 Given, $m_1 = 2$ kg, $F = 40$ N

$\therefore$ Weight of block $= 2 \times 10 = 20$N

Hence, net effective force on the block $= 40 - 20 = 20$N

$\therefore$ Acceleration $= \dfrac{20}{2} = 10 \text{ m/s}^2$ [2]

26 Given, $m = 2$ kg, $m_2 = 4$ kg, $\mu_1 = 0$, $\mu_2 = ?$

$F = 18$ N

To move the blocks together the force applied must be atleast equal to the force of kinetic friction applied on 2 kg block by 4 kg block.

i.e. $\quad F = f_k = \mu_k R = \mu_2 m_1 g$

$18 = \mu_2 \times 2 \times 10 \Rightarrow \mu_2 = 0.9$ [2]

27 Given, $r = 30$ m, $\mu = 0.4$, $g = 10 \text{ ms}^{-2}$

To turn around a curve, the necessary centripetal force is provided by force of friction.

i.e. $\dfrac{mv^2}{r} = F = \mu R = \mu mg$

$\Rightarrow v = \sqrt{\mu rg} = \sqrt{0.4 \times 30 \times 10} = \sqrt{120} = 10.95 \simeq 11 \text{ ms}^{-1}$ [2]

28 Given, $v = 60 \text{ kmh}^{-1} = 60 \times \dfrac{5}{18} = \dfrac{50}{3} \text{ ms}^{-1}$

$r = 0.1$ km $= 100$ m, $g = 10 \text{ ms}^{-2}$

Angle of banking,

$\tan\theta = \dfrac{v^2}{rg} = \dfrac{50}{3} \times \dfrac{50}{3} \times \dfrac{1}{100 \times 10} = \dfrac{5}{18}$

$\Rightarrow \theta = \tan^{-1}\left(\dfrac{5}{18}\right) = 15^\circ 32'$ [2]

29 Here, $m = 0.020$ kg, $M = 100$ kg, $v = 80$ m/s

Then, according to law of conservation of momentum,

Final momentum = Initial momentum

$mv - Mv' = 0$

$\Rightarrow \quad v' = \dfrac{mv}{M} = \dfrac{0.020 \times 80}{100} = 0.016 \text{ ms}^{-1}$ [2]

30 Given, $m = 10$ kg, $\theta = 30°$, $\mu = \frac{1}{\sqrt{3}}$

Take, $g = 10\ ms^{-1}$

Force acting on the body down the plane

$$= mg\sin\theta = 10\times10\times\sin 30° = 100\times\frac{1}{2} = 50\ N$$ [1]

Force of friction $= f = \mu R = \mu\ mg\cos\theta$

$$= \frac{1}{\sqrt{3}}\times10\times10\times\cos 30° = \frac{100}{\sqrt{3}}\times\frac{\sqrt{3}}{2}$$

$= 50$ N [1]

Thus the greatest force required to just push the body up the inclined plane is

$$= mg\sin\theta + f = 50 + 50 = 100\ N$$ [1]

31 Given, $r = 2\ cm = \frac{2}{100}$ m, $m = 6$ g

$n = 3$ rev/sec, $g = 10\ ms^{-2}$

$$\omega = 2\pi n = 2\pi\times3 = 6\pi\ s^{-1}$$ [1/2]

The coin will stay on the disc, when force of friction is enough to provide centripetal force.

Force of friction $= \mu\ mg$ [1]

Centripetal force $= \frac{mv^2}{r}$ or $mr\omega^2$ [1/2]

$\therefore$ $\mu mg = mr\omega^2$

$\Rightarrow$ $\mu = \frac{r\omega^2}{g} = \frac{2}{100}\times\frac{(6\times3.14)^2}{10} = 0.71$ [1]

32 Let a be the acceleration as shown in figure.

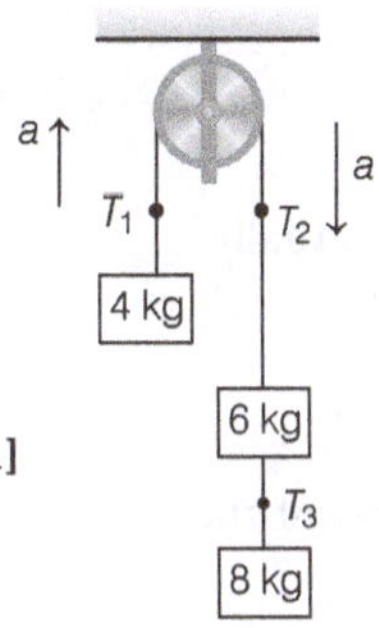

As T_1 and T_2 are on same level, thus they are equal in magnitude. Then

$4a = T_1 - 4g$ ...(i)

$14a = 14g - T_2$ ...(ii)

and $8a = 8g - T_3$ ...(iii)

On adding Eqs. (i) and (ii) and put $T_1 = T_2$ [1]

$18a = 10g$

$\Rightarrow$ $a = \frac{5}{9}g$

$\therefore$ $T_1 = T_2 = \frac{56}{9}g$ [2]

From Eq. (iii), we get

$$8\times\frac{5}{9}g = 8g - T_3$$

$\Rightarrow$ $T_3 = 8\times\frac{4}{9}g = \frac{32}{9}g$ [1]

$\therefore$ $4a_1 = \frac{56}{9}g - 4g = \frac{20g}{9} \Rightarrow a_1 = \frac{5}{9}g = 5.55\ ms^{-2}$

or $a_2 = \frac{14g - \frac{56}{9}g}{14} = 5.55\ m/s^2$

and $a_3 = \frac{8g - \frac{32}{9}g}{8} = 5.55\ m/s^2$

$\therefore$ $a_1 = a_2 = a_3 = 5.55\ m/s^2$ [2]

33 Given, $m = 80$ kg, $r = 10$ m, $v = 6.1\ ms^{-1}$,

Take $g = 10\ ms^{-1}$

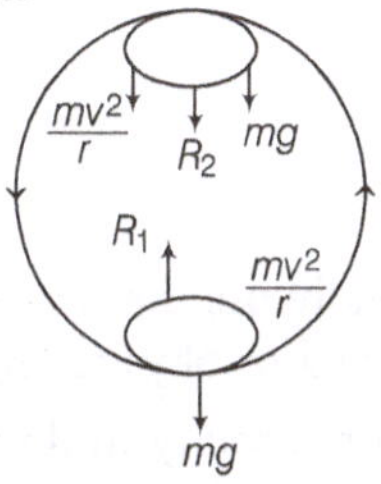

[1]

(i) $\omega = \frac{2\pi}{T} = \frac{v}{r} \Rightarrow T = \frac{2\pi r}{v} \Rightarrow T = \frac{2\times3.14\times10}{6.1} \simeq 10$ s [1]

(ii) At highest point,

$$R_2 + mg = \frac{mv^2}{r}$$

$\Rightarrow$ $R_2 = m\left(\frac{v^2}{r} - g\right) = 80\left[\frac{(6.1)^2}{10} - 10\right]$

$= -5.02\times10^{-2}$ N [1½]

(iii) At lowest point,

$$R_1 - mg = \frac{mv^2}{r}$$

$\Rightarrow$ $R_1 = m\left(\frac{v^2}{r} + g\right) = 80\left[\frac{(6.1)^2}{10} + 10\right]$

$= 1.1\times10^3$ N [1½]

CHAPTER

05

Work, Energy and Power

In daily life, we generally use the terms work, energy and power. Work is any activity involving mental or physical effort.

Whereas, energy is our **capacity** to do work. The word power is also used in everyday life with different shades of meaning. In this chapter, we will study these terms from the vision of science.

- Work
- Energy
- Power and Collision

TOPIC 01 Work

Work is said to be done by a force, when the body is displaced actually through some distance in the direction of the applied force. Thus, work is done on a body only if the following two conditions are satisfied:

(i) A force acts on the body.

(ii) The point of application of the force moves in the direction of the force.

e.g. Work is done when an engine pulls a train, a man goes up a hill, a horse pulls a cart, etc.

Work Done by a Constant Force

Work done by the force (constant force) is the product of component of force in the direction of the displacement and the magnitude of the displacement. If a constant force F is applied on a body and the body has a displacement s in the direction of the force as shown in figure.

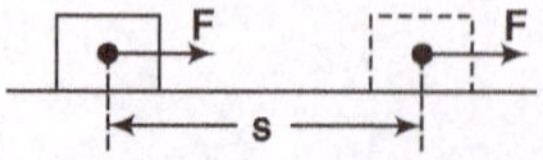

Work done, when force and displacement are in the same direction

Then, the work done on the body by the force is given by

$$\boxed{\text{Work done, } W = \mathbf{F} \cdot \mathbf{s}}$$

Thus, work done by a force is the **dot product** of force and displacement.

Work Done When Force and Displacement are Inclined to Each Other

Sometimes the displacement **s** is not in the direction of **F** as shown in figure.

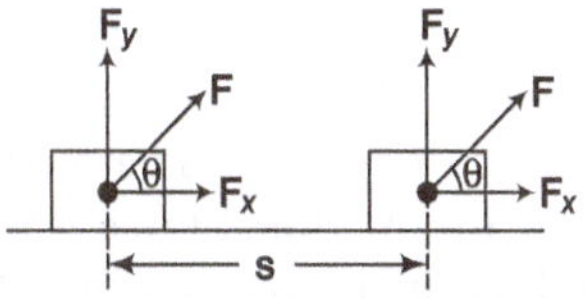

Work done when force and displacement are inclined to each other

In such a case, we find the work done by resolving **F** into two rectangular components.

(i) $\mathbf{F}_x$ along the direction of displacement **s**, such that

$$|\mathbf{F}_x| = F\cos\theta$$

(ii) $\mathbf{F}_y$ along perpendicular to displacement **s**, such that

$$|\mathbf{F}_y| = F\sin\theta$$

The component $\mathbf{F}_y$ does not work as the body does not move up or down. All the work is done by the component $\mathbf{F}_x$.

$$\text{Work done } (W) = |\mathbf{F}| \cdot |\mathbf{s}| = (F\cos\theta) \cdot s$$

$$\boxed{\text{Work done, } W = Fs\cos\theta}$$

Thus, work done is the dot product of force and displacement vector. Hence, work is a scalar quantity.

Two cases can be considered for the maximum and minimum work.

Case I When F and s are in the same direction, i.e. $\theta = 0°$, then work done is

$$W = Fs\cos 0° = Fs(1) = Fs$$

i.e. maximum work done by the force.

Case II When **F** and **s** are in opposite direction to each other, i.e. $\theta = 180°$, then

$$W = \mathbf{F} \cdot \mathbf{s} = Fs\cos 180° = -Fs$$

i.e. minimum work done by the force.

Dimensions and Units of Work

As, work = force × distance $= [MLT^{-2}] \times [L] = [ML^2T^{-2}]$

This is the dimensional formula of work.

The units of work are of types:

1. Absolute units 2. Gravitational units

(i) **Joule** It is the **absolute unit** of work in SI.

One joule of work is said to be done when a force of one newton displaces a body through a distance of one metre in its own direction.

From work done $(W) = Fs\cos\theta$,

$$1\text{ J} = 1\text{ N} \times 1\text{ m} \times \cos 0° = 1\text{ N-m}$$

(ii) **Erg** It is the **absolute unit** of work in CGS system. One erg of work is said to be done if a force of one dyne displaces a body through a distance of one centimetre in its own direction.

From work done $(W) = Fs\cos\theta$

$$1\text{ erg} = 1\text{ dyne} \times 1\text{ cm} \times \cos 0° = 1\text{ dyne-cm}$$

Relation between Joule and Erg

$$1\text{ J} = 1\text{ N} \times 1\text{ m}$$
$$= 10^5\text{ dyne} \times 10^2\text{ cm}$$
$$= 10^7\text{ dyne-cm}$$

or $\boxed{\mathbf{1\ J = 10^7\ erg}}$

(iii) **Kilogram-metre** (kg-m) It is the **gravitational unit** of work in SI system. One kilogram-metre of work is said to be done when a force of one kilogram weight displaces a body through a distance of one metre in its own direction.

We know work done $(W) = Fs\cos\theta$

$$1\text{ kg-m} = 1\text{ kg wt} \times \cos 0°$$
$$= 9.8\text{ N} \times 1\text{m} \times 1 = 9.8\text{ J}$$

(iv) **Gram-centimetre** (g-cm) It is in CGS system. One gram-centimetre of work is said to be done when a force of one gram-centimetre weight displaces a body through a distance of one centimetre in its own direction.

$$\therefore 1\text{ g-cm} = 1\text{ g-wt} \times 1\text{cm} = 980\text{ dyne} \times 1\text{ cm}$$
$$= 980\text{ erg}$$

Example 1 A lawn roller has been pushed by a gardener through a distance of 30 m. What will be the work done by him if he applies a force of 30 kg-wt in the direction inclined at 60° to the ground? Take $g = 10\text{ m/s}^2$

Sol. Given, Displacement $s = 30$ m

Force, $F = 30\text{ kg-wt} = 30 \times 10 = 300\text{N}$

Angle between force and ground, $\theta = 60°$

The work done by the gardener,

$$W = F \cdot s = Fs\cos\theta = 300 \times 30 \times \cos 60°$$
$$W = 4500\text{ J}$$

Example 2 A coolie is holding a bag by applying a force of 15 N. He moves forward and covers the horizontal distance of 8 m and then he climbs up and covers the vertical distance of 10 m. What will be the work done by him?

Sol. Given, $F = 15\text{ N}, s_1 = 8\text{ m}$ and $s_2 = 10\text{m}$

As coolie is walking horizontally, therefore, the angle between the bag and distance covered is 90°.

$\therefore$ Work done to cover the distance of 8 m.

$$W_1 = Fs_1 \cos\theta = 15 \times 8 \cos 90° = 0\text{ J}$$

When the coolie climb.

Thus, $\theta = 0°$

The work done, $W_2 = Fs_2 \cos\theta = 15 \times 10 \times \cos 0° = 150\text{ J}$

The net work done by him

$$W = W_1 + W_2 = 0 + 150 = 150\text{ J}$$

Nature of Work Done in Different Situations

Although work done is a scalar quantity, its value may be positive, negative or even zero, as discussed below:

1. Positive Work

If a force acting on a body has a component in the direction of the displacement, then the work done by the force is positive. As shown in figure, when θ is acute, then $\cos\theta$ is positive i.e. $0 \le \theta < 90°$.

$\therefore$ Work done $(W) = Fs\cos\theta$ = positive value $[0 \le \theta < 90°]$

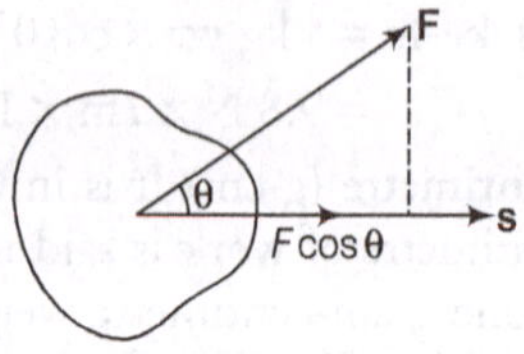

Positive work done (θ < 90°)

e.g.

(i) When a horse pulls a cart, the applied force and the displacement are in the same direction. So, work done by horse is positive.

(ii) When a load is lifted, then the lifting force and displacement act in the same direction. So, work done by the lifting force is positive.

(iii) When a spring is stretched, work done by the stretching force is positive.

2. Negative Work

If a force acting on the body has a component in the opposite direction of displacement, then work done is negative. As shown in figure, when θ is obtuse, then $\cos\theta$ is negative.

Work done $(W) = Fs\cos\theta$ = negative value $[90° < \theta < 180°]$

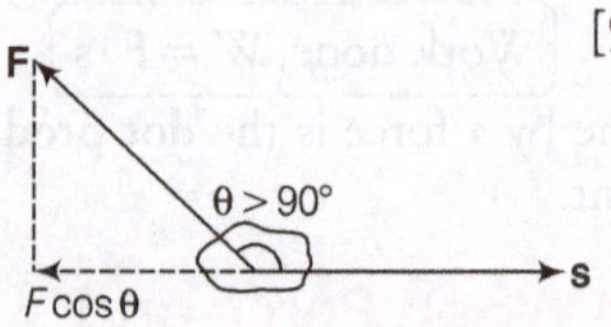

Negative work done (θ > 90°)

e.g.

(i) When brakes are applied to a moving vehicle, the work done by the braking force is negative, this is because the braking force and the displacement act in opposite directions.

(ii) When a body is dragged along a rough surface, then work done by the frictional force is negative. This is because the frictional force acts in a direction opposite to that of the displacement.

(iii) When a body is lifted, then work done by gravitational force is negative. This is because the gravitational force acts vertically downwards while the displacement is in the vertically upward direction.

3. Zero Work

Work done by force is zero, if the body gets displaced in the direction perpendicular to the direction of the applied force.

$$\text{Work done } (W) = Fs\cos 90° = Fs \cdot 0 = \text{zero}$$

e.g.

(i) Consider a body sliding over a horizontal surface. The work done by the force of gravity and the normal reaction of the surface will be zero. This is because both the forces of gravity and reaction act normally to the displacement as shown in figure.

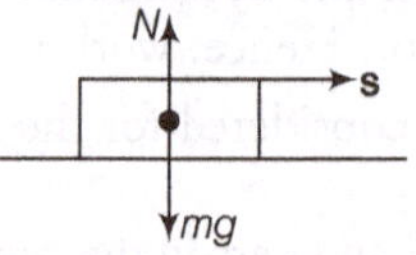

Work done by force of gravity and normal force reaction of surface

(ii) Consider a body moving in a circle with constant speed. At every point of the circular path, the centripetal force and the displacement are mutually perpendicular as shown in figure.

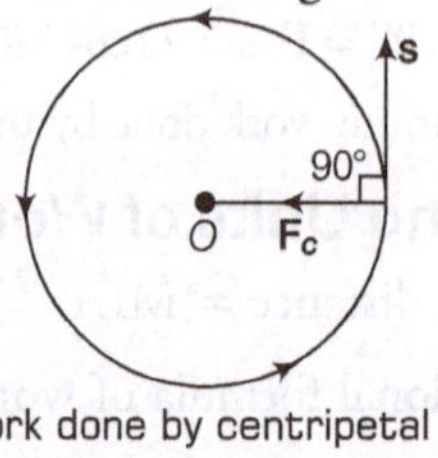

Work done by centripetal force

So, the work done by the centripetal force is zero. The same argument can be applied to a satellite moving in a circular orbit. In this case, the gravitational force is always perpendicular to displacement. So, work done by gravitational force is zero.

(iii) As shown in figure, the tension in the string of simple pendulum is always perpendicular to displacement. So, work done by the tension is zero.

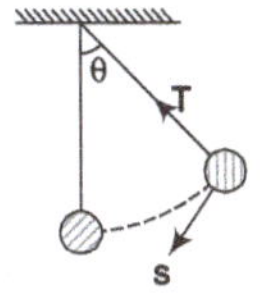

Work done by tension

Example 3 A cyclist comes to a skidding stop in 10 m. During this process, the force on the cycle due to the road is 200 N and is directly opposite to the motion. (i) How much work does the road do on the cycle? (ii) How much work does the cycle do on the road? **NCERT**

Sol. (i) The stopping force and the displacement make an angle of 180° with each other. Thus, work done by the road or the work done by the stopping force is

$$W_r = Fs\cos\theta = 200\times 10\times \cos 180° = -2000\text{ J}$$

Negative sign shows that work done by road-on cycle.

(ii) According to Newton's third law, an equal and opposite force acts on the road due to the cycle. Its magnitude is 200 N. However, the road undergoes no displacement. So, work done by the cycle on the road is zero.

Work Done by a Variable Force

Let a variable force F acts on a body along the fixed direction, say x-axis. The magnitude of the force F depends on x, as shown by force-displacement graph in figure. Let us calculate the work done when the body moves from the initial position x_i to the final position x_f under a force $F(x)$.

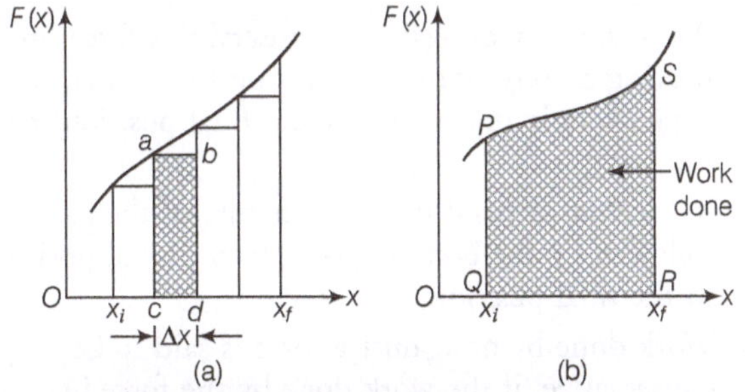

Calculation of work done by a variable force

The displacement can be divided into a large number of small equal displacements, i.e. Δx. During small displacement Δx, the force F can be assumed to be constant.

Then, the work done is

$$\Delta W = F(x)\,\Delta x = \text{Area of rectangle } abcd.$$

Adding areas of all the rectangles in figure (a), we get the total work done as $W \cong \sum_{x_i}^{x_f} F(x)\,\Delta x$

If the displacements are much small (i.e. are allowed to approach zero), then the number of terms in the sum increases without limit, but the sum approaches to definite value equal to the area under the curve. Thus, the total work done is

$$W = \lim_{\Delta x\to 0} \sum_{x_i}^{x_f} F(x)\,\Delta x = \int_{x_i}^{x_f} F(x)\,dx$$

$$W_{x_i\to x_f} = \int_{x_i}^{x_f} \mathbf{F}\cdot d\mathbf{x} = \int_{x_i}^{x_f} (F\cos\theta)\cdot dx$$

$$= \text{Area of } PQRS$$

$$W_{x_i\to x_f} = \textbf{Area under the force-displacement curve}$$

Hence, for a varying force the work done is equal to the definite integral of the force over the given displacement as shown in figure.

When the magnitude and direction of a force vary in three dimensions. So, it can be expressed in terms of rectangular components, we get

Force, $\mathbf{F} = F_x\hat{\mathbf{i}} + F_y\hat{\mathbf{j}} + F_z\hat{\mathbf{k}}$ and

Displacement, $d\mathbf{x} = dx\,\hat{\mathbf{i}} + dy\,\hat{\mathbf{j}} + dz\,\hat{\mathbf{k}}$

So, work done from x_i to x_f

$$\text{Work done, } W = \int_{x_i}^{x_f} F_x dx + \int_{y_i}^{y_f} F_y dy + \int_{z_i}^{z_f} F_z dz$$

where, F_x, F_y and F_z are the rectangular components of force in x, y and z-directions, respectively.

Example 4 Force $\mathbf{F} = [3x^2\hat{\mathbf{i}} + 4\hat{\mathbf{j}}]$ N with x in metres, acts on a particle. How much work is done on the particles as it moves from coordinates (2m, 3m) to (3m, 0m)?

Sol. Given, force $F = 3x^2\,\hat{\mathbf{i}} + 4\,\hat{\mathbf{j}}$

Coordinates $= (\underset{x_i}{2\text{m}}, \underset{y_i}{3\text{m}})$ to $(\underset{x_f}{3\text{m}}, \underset{y_f}{0\text{m}})$

Here, the force is variable force. Thus, work done is

$$W = \int_{x_i}^{x_f} F_x\cdot dx + \int_{y_i}^{y_f} F_y dy$$

$$= \int_2^3 3x^2\,dx + \int_3^0 4\,dy = 3\left[\frac{x^3}{3}\right]_2^3 + 4\,[y]_3^0$$

$$= \frac{3}{3}\times[27-8] + 4[0-3] = 19 - 12 = 7.0\text{ J}$$

Example 5 A woman pushes a trunk on railway platform which has a rough surface. She applies a force of 100 N over a distance of 10 m. Thereafter, she gets progressively tired and her applied force reduces linearly with distance to 50 N. The total distance by which the trunk has been moved is 20 m. Plot the force applied by the woman and the frictional force, which is 50 N. Calculate the work done by the two forces over 20 m. NCERT

Sol. Plots of force F applied by the woman and the opposing frictional force F are shown in figure.

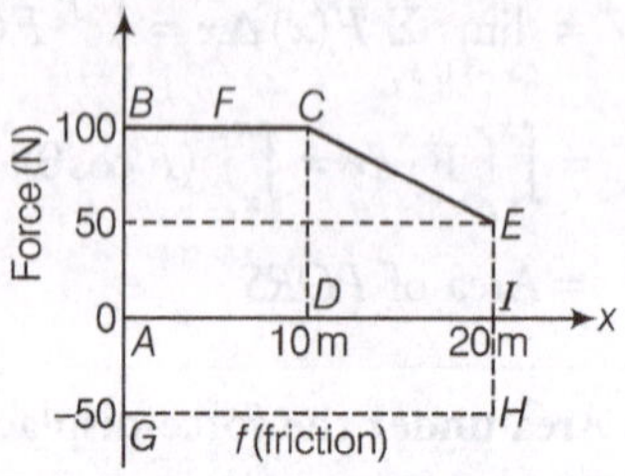

Clearly, at $x = 20$ m, $F = 50$ N

As we know the force of friction f opposes the applied force F, so it has been shown on the negative side of the force-axis.

Work done by the force F applied by the woman

W_F = Area of rectangle $ABCD$ + Area of trapezium $CEID$

$$= 100 \times 10 + \frac{1}{2}(100 + 50) \times 10 = 1000 + 750 = 1750 \text{ J}$$

Work done by the frictional force,

W_f = Area of rectangle $AGHI = (-50) \times 20 = -1000$ J

Example 6 The force applied by a man in pushing a block varies with displacement as shown in figure. If the force is expressed in Newton and displacement in metres, find the work done by him.

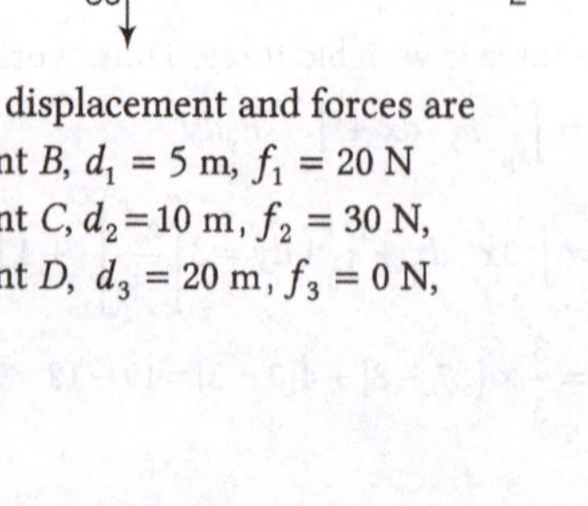

Sol. Given, displacement and forces are

At point B, $d_1 = 5$ m, $f_1 = 20$ N

At point C, $d_2 = 10$ m, $f_2 = 30$ N,

At point D, $d_3 = 20$ m, $f_3 = 0$ N,

At point E, $d_4 = 30$ m, $f_4 = -30$ N

Work done by the man = ?

Area under the rectangle $OABL$ is equal to work done W_{OABL}. $W_{OABL} = 20 \times 5 = 100$ J

[∵ Area = length × breadth]

Area under the trapezium $BCML$ is equal to work done W_{BCML}.

$$W_{BCML} = \frac{1}{2} \times [20 + 30] \times 5$$

$$\left[\because \text{ area} = \frac{1}{2} \times (\text{sum of parallel side}) \times \text{height}\right]$$

$$W_{BCML} = \frac{1}{2} \times 50 \times 5 = 125 \text{ J}$$

Area under the $\Delta\, CDM$ is equal to work done W_{CDM}.

$$W_{CDM} = \frac{1}{2} \times 10 \times 30 = 150 \text{ J}$$

$$\left[\because \text{ area} = \frac{1}{2} \times \text{base} \times \text{height}\right]$$

Area under the $\Delta\, DEN$ is equal to work done W_{DEN}.

$$W_{DEN} = \frac{1}{2} \times (10) \times (-30) = -150 \text{ J}$$

$$\left[\because \text{ area} = \frac{1}{2} \times \text{base} \times \text{height}\right]$$

Total amount of work done

$$= 100 \text{ J} + 125 \text{ J} + 150 \text{ J} - 150 \text{ J} = 225 \text{ J}$$

Conservative Force

If the work done by the force in displacing an object depends only on the initial and final positions of the object and not on the nature of the path followed between the initial and final positions, such a force is known as **conservative force.**

e.g. Gravitational force is a conservative force.

Work Done by Conservative Forces

(i) Work done by or against a conservative force, in moving a body from one position to another, depends only on the initial and final positions of the body.

(ii) It does not depend upon the nature of the path followed by the body in going from initial position to the final position.

(iii) Work done by or against a force is said to be conservative, if the work done by the force in moving a particle along a closed path (round trip), net work done is zero.

Example 7 Gravitational force is a conservative force. Explain it qualitatively.

Sol. Suppose a body of mass m is raised to a height h vertically upwards from position P to Q as shown in Fig. (a) given below. The work done on the body against gravity is

$$W_1 = mg \times PQ = mgh$$
$$W_1 = mgh \quad ...(i)$$

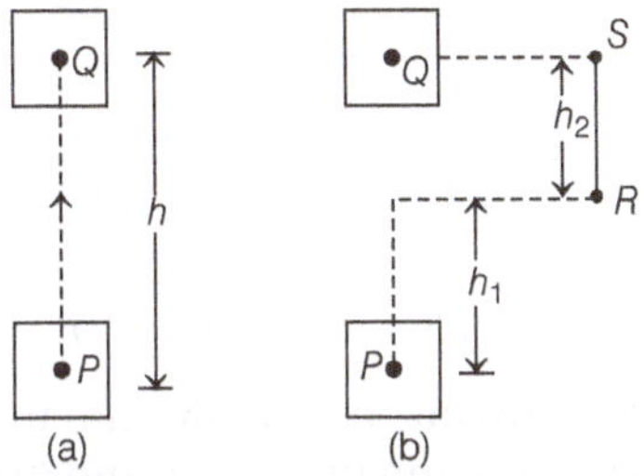

Gravitational force as conservative force

As shown in Fig. (b), now suppose the body is taken from position P to Q along the path $PTRSQ$, then during horizontal path TR and SQ, the gravity is perpendicular to the displacement, therefore work done along TR and SQ is zero. Work done is only due to vertical path PT and RS. The total work done is

$$W = W_{PT} + W_{TR} + W_{RS} + W_{SQ}$$
$$= mgh_1 + 0 + mgh_2 + 0$$
$$= mg(h_1 + h_2)$$
$$W = mgh \quad ...(ii) \quad [\because h_1 + h_2 = h]$$

Thus, the work done in moving a body against gravity does not depend on path and depends only on the initial and final positions of the body.

Example 8 A body of mass 5 kg is taken up an inclined plane to length 20 m and height 10 m and then allowed to slide down to the bottom again, then find

(i) work done by the gravitational force on moving the body from bottom to top.

(ii) work done by the gravitational force over the round trip.

Sol. Here, $m = 5$ kg

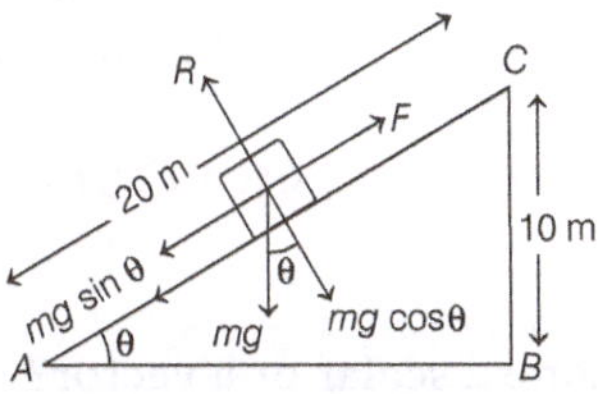

From figure,

$$\sin\theta = \frac{BC}{AC} = \frac{10}{20} = \frac{1}{2}$$

$$\sin\theta = \frac{1}{2} = \sin 30° \Rightarrow \theta = 30°$$

(i) Work done by the gravitational force in moving the body up the inclined plane,

$$W = Fs = -mg \times (20 \sin 30°)$$
$$= -5 \times 9.8 \times 20 \times \frac{1}{2} = -490 \text{ J}$$

(ii) Since, gravitational force is a conservative force, therefore work done by the gravitational force over the round trip is zero.

Non-conservative Force

If work done by a force in displacing an object from one position to another, depends upon the path between the two positions. Such a force is known as **non-conservative force.**

Let W_1, W_2 and W_3 denote the net work done in moving a body from A to B along three different path 1, 2 and 3 respectively as shown in figure. If the force is non-conservative, then $W_1 \neq W_2 \neq W_3$

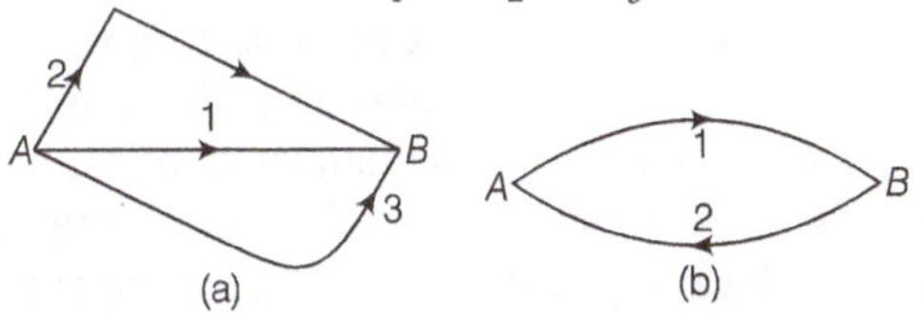

If Fig. (b), a particle is moving in a closed path $A \to 1 \to B \to 2 \to A$. If W_1 is work done in moving the particle from $A \to 1 \to B$, and W_2 is work done in moving the particle from $B \to 2 \to A$, then for a non-conservative force $|W_1| \neq |W_2|$

Hence, net work done along the closed path, $A \to B \to A$ is not zero.

The common examples of non-conservative forces are

(i) Force of friction (ii) Viscous force

(iii) Tension

Work Done by Non-conservative Forces (Friction Forces)

As we know that friction force is always opposite to the relative motion so that the work done by friction may be positive, zero and negative.

Work Done due to Friction Forces

Case I	Case II	Case III
Fig. (a) shows a situation where a block is pulled by a force F which is insufficient to overcome the friction f_{max} i.e. $F < f_{max}$	Fig. (b) shows a situation where a block is pulled by a force F which is large to overcome friction f_{max} i.e. $F > f_{max}$. Here, the work done by friction force is negative.	Fig. (c) shows that block A is placed on block B and when block A is pulled with a force F, friction force does positive work on block B and negative work on block A.
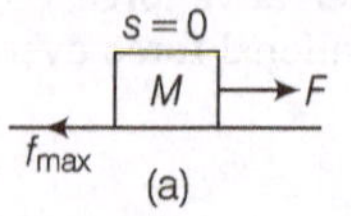 (a)	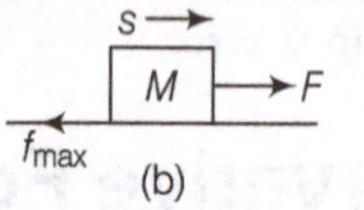 (b)	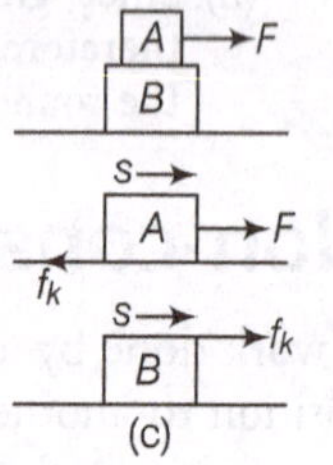 (c)
$F < f_{max}$ $F < \mu_s N$ $F < \mu_s Mg$ $\therefore$ Work done, $W = 0$	$F > f_{max}$ $f_{max} = Mg$ $W = -\mu_k Mgs$	Work done $W_{Friction}$ = – ve for A. Work done $W_{Friction}$ = + ve for B.

Example 9 A wooden block of mass 1 kg is pushed up a surface inclined to horizontal at angle of 30° by a force of 10 N parallel to the inclined surface [figure]. The coefficient of friction between block and the incline is 0.1. If the block is pushed up by 10 m along the incline. Calculate

(i) Work done against gravity.

(ii) Work done against force of friction.

(iii) Acceleration of block when it moves upward.

Sol. Given, $m = 1$ kg, $\theta = 30°$, $F = 10$ N, $\mu = 0.1$, $s = 10$ m,

$W_g = ?, W_f = ?, a = ?$

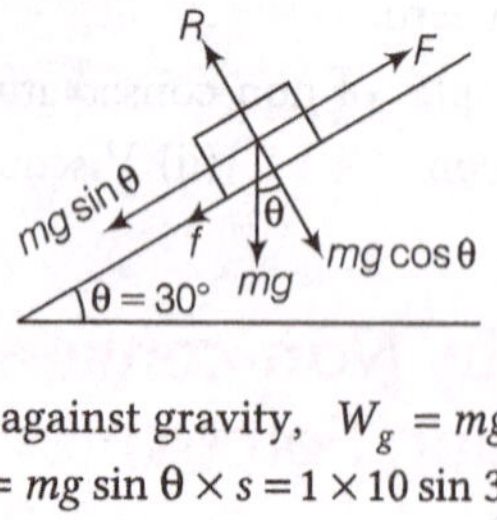

Work done against gravity, $W_g = mg \sin\theta \times s$

$$W_g = mg\sin\theta \times s = 1 \times 10 \sin 30° \times 10$$

$$= \frac{100}{2} = 50 \text{ J}$$

Work done against friction, i.e. $W_f = F \times s$

$$W_f = F \times s = \mu R \times s = \mu mg \cos\theta \times s$$

$$= 0.1 \times 1 \times 10 \cos 30° \times 10 = 10 \times 0.866 = 8.66 \text{ J}$$

Acceleration of block up the inclined plane, i.e.

$$F = ma + (mg\sin\theta + \mu\, mg\cos\theta)$$

$$\Rightarrow a = \frac{F - (mg\sin\theta + \mu\, mg\cos\theta)}{m}$$

$$a = \frac{10 - \left(1 \times 10 \times \frac{1}{2} + 0.1 \times 10 \times 0.866\right)}{1} = 4.13 \text{ m/s}^2$$

Topic Practice 1

Multiple Choice Questions

1 Mark

1. 1 kilowatt hour (kWh) = ...A... joule. Here, A refers to

(a) 4×10^2 (b) 3.6×10^6 (c) 4×10^4 (d) 3.6×10^5

2. The earth, moving around the sun in a circular orbit, is acted upon by a force and hence work done on the earth by the force is

(a) zero (b) + ve

(c) – ve (d) None of these

3. In which case, work done will be zero?

(a) a weight-lifter while holding a weight of 100 kg on his shoulders for 1 min

(b) a locomotive against gravity when it is running on a level plane with a speed of 60 kmh^{-1}

(c) a person holding a suitcase on his head and standing at a bus terminal

(d) All of the above

4. A force $\mathbf{F} = 5\hat{i} + 6\hat{j} - 4\hat{k}$ acting on a body produces a displacement $\mathbf{s} = 6\hat{i} + 5\hat{k}$. The work done by the force is

(a) 18 units (b) 15 units

(c) 12 units (d) 10 units

5. A particle is pushed by forces $2\hat{i} + 3\hat{j} - 2\hat{k}$ and $5\hat{i} - \hat{j} - 3\hat{k}$ simultaneously and it is displaced from point $\hat{i} + \hat{j} + \hat{k}$ to point $2\hat{i} - \hat{j} + 3\hat{k}$. The work done is

(a) 7 units (b) –7 units

(c) 10 units (d) –10 units

Very Short Answer Type Questions

1 Mark

6. Is work done a scalar or a vector?

7. Under what condition is the work done by a force is zero inspite of displacement being taking place?

8. Can acceleration be produced without doing any work? Give example.

9. What is the amount of work done by an electron moving with half the speed of light in empty space free of electromagnetic fields and far from all matter?

10. Does the work done in moving a body depend upon how fast the body is moved?

11. In a game of tug of war, one team is slowly giving way to the other. Which team is doing positive work and which team negative?

12. Give the conditions under which a force is called conservative force.

13. Friction is a non-conservative force. Why?

Short Answer Type I Questions

(2 Marks)

14. What are the conditions for work is to be done?

15. Under what conditions, the work done is minimum and maximum for inclination between force and displacement?

16. Define gravitational unit of work. How much it is in joules?

17. Explain with diagram, the work done by tensile force in a simple pendulum.

Short Answer Type II Questions

(3 Marks)

18. Define the term work. Show that work done is equal to the dot product of force and displacement vectors.

19. What is meant by positive work, negative work and zero work? Give one example of each.

20. Explain qualitatively that how is the gravitational force a conservative force.

21. Define conservative and non-conservative forces with example.

22. Discuss different cases of work done by friction forces.

Long Answer Type Questions

(5 Marks)

23. The sign of work done by a force on a body is important to understand. State carefully if the following quantities are positive or negative.
    (i) Work done by a man in lifting a bucket out of a well by means of a rope tied to the bucket.
    (ii) Work done by gravitational force in the above case.
    (iii) Work done by friction on a body sliding down on inclined plane.
    (iv) Work done by an applied force on a body moving on a rough horizontal plane with uniform velocity.
    (v) Work done by the resistive force of air on a vibrating pendulum in bringing it to rest. **NCERT**

24. Obtain mathematically and graphically the work done by a variable force.

25. What is a conservative force? Prove that gravitational force is conservative, while frictional force is non-conservative.

26. (i) A body is moving in a circular path of a given diameter with number of rotations per second (a) increasing (b) decreasing
    (c) constant. What happens to work done in three cases?
    (ii) Why is the work done by the centripetal force is zero?

Numerical Problems

27. A body constrained to move along the z-axes of a coordinate system is subject to a constant force **F** given by $\mathbf{F} = (-\hat{\mathbf{i}} + 2\hat{\mathbf{j}} + 3\hat{\mathbf{k}})$ N, where $\hat{\mathbf{i}}, \hat{\mathbf{j}}, \hat{\mathbf{k}}$ are unit vectors along the *x*, *y* and *z*-axes of the system, respectively. What is the work done by this force in moving the body a distance of 4 m along the *z*-axis? **NCERT [2M]**

28. Find the work done in pulling and pushing a roller through 100 m horizontally when a force of 1500 N is acting along a chain making an angle of 60° with ground. Assume the floor to be smooth. **[2M]**

29. A man moves on a straight horizontal road with a block of a mass 2 kg in his hand. If he moves a distance of 40 m with acceleration of 0.5 m/s^2. Calculate work done by the man on the block during motion. **[1M]**

30. A body of mass of 2 kg initially at rest moves under the action of an applied horizontally force of 7 N on a table with coefficient of kinetic friction = 0.1.

Compute the **NCERT [3M]**

(i) work done by the applied force in 10 s,

(ii) work done by friction in 10 s,

(iii) work done by the net force on the body in 10 s.

31. A boy has a bag of sand of mass 20 kg. First of all, he keeps the bag on his head and moves 10 m. Second time, he drags the bag through 10 m on a frictionless surface with coefficient of friction $\mu = 0.1$. In which case, he does more work? **[3M]**

32. A man weighing 50 kg supports a body of 25 kg on his head. What is the work done when he moves a distance of 20 m up an incline of 1 in 10? Take $g = 9.8\ m/s^2$. **[3M]**

33. A body of mass 3 kg is under a constant force, which causes a displacement s in metre in it, given by the relation $s = \frac{1}{3}t^2$, where t is in second. Find the work done by the force in 2s. **[3M]**

34. A particle moves along the x-axis from $x = 0$ to $x = 5$m under the influence of a force given by $f(x) = 7 - 2x + 3x^2$. Calculate the work done. **[3M]**

35. Calculate work done in raising a stone of mass 5 kg of specific gravity 3 immersed in water from a depth of 6 m to 1 m below surface of water ($g = 10\ ms^{-2}$). **[5M]**

36. A trolley of mass 300 kg carrying a sand bag of 25 kg is moving uniformly with a speed of 27 km/h on a frictionless track. After a while, sand starts leaking out of a hole on the floor of the trolley at the rate of 0.05 kgs^{-1}. What is the speed of the trolley after the entire sand bag is empty? **NCERT [2M]**

37. Calculate the work done by a car against gravity in moving along a straight horizontal road. The mass of the car is 400 kg and the distance moved is 2 m. **NCERT Exemplar [2M]**

Hints & Solutions

1. (*b*) 1 kilowatt hour (kWh) = 10^3 (W) × 3600 (s)
$$= 3.6 \times 10^6\ J$$

2. (*a*) When earth is moving around the sun in a circular orbit, the gravitational attraction on earth due to the sun is the requisite centripetal force, which is in radially inward direction, i.e. in a direction perpendicular to the direction of motion of the earth in its circular orbit around the sun.

As a result, the work done on the earth by the force will be zero because
$$W = Fs\cos 90° = 0$$

3. (*d*) Work done by weight-lifter is zero because there is no displacement. In a locomotive, work done is zero because force and displacement are mutually perpendicular to each other.

While a person holding a suitcase, work done is zero because there is no displacement.

4. (*d*) Work done, $W = \mathbf{F} \cdot \mathbf{s} = (5\hat{i} + 6\hat{j} - 4\hat{k}) \cdot (6\hat{i} + 0\hat{j} + 5\hat{k})$
$$= 30 + 0 - 20 = 10 \text{ units}$$

5. (*b*) Net force, $\mathbf{F} = 2\hat{i} + 3\hat{j} - 2\hat{k} + 5\hat{i} - \hat{j} - 3\hat{k}$
$$= 7\hat{i} + 2\hat{j} - 5\hat{k}$$
Displacement, $\mathbf{d} = 2\hat{i} - \hat{j} + 3\hat{k} - \hat{i} - \hat{j} - \hat{k} = \hat{i} - 2\hat{j} + 2\hat{k}$

Work done $= \mathbf{F} \cdot \mathbf{d} = (7\hat{i} + 2\hat{j} - 5\hat{k}) \cdot (\hat{i} - 2\hat{j} + 2\hat{k})$
$$= 7 - 4 - 10 = -7 \text{ units}$$

6. Work done by a force for a certain displacement is a scalar quantity.

7. Work done by a force is zero inspite of displacement being taking place, if displacement is in a direction perpendicular to that of force applied.

8. Yes, for uniform circular motion, no work done but a centripetal acceleration is present.

9. Zero, because electron moves on circular path with uniform speed.

10. No, time is not involved in work done.

11. The winning team (i.e. the team which is pulling the other team towards itself) is doing positive work and the losing team (i.e. the team slowly giving way to the other) is doing negative work.

12. (i) Work done by conservative force depends only on the initial and final position of the object.
(ii) Work done by the force along a closed path is zero.

13. Friction is a non-conservative force, because work done against friction along a closed path is non-zero.

14. Refer to text on page 154 (Work).

15. Refer to text on page 155 (Work done when force and displacement are inclined to each other).

16. Refer to text on page 155 (Dimensions and units of work).

17. Refer to text on page 157 (Case iii) of zero work).

18. Refer to text on pages 154 and 155 (Work and work done by a constant force).

19. Refer to text on page 156 (Positive work, negative work and zero work).

20. Refer to example 7 on page 159.

21. Refer to text on pages 158 to 159 (Conservative and Non-conservative force).

22. Refer to text on page 160 (Work done due to friction forces).

23. (i) Work done by the man against the force of gravity while lifting a bucket out of a well by means of a rope tied to the bucket is + ve, because force and displacement are in same direction. [1]

(ii) Work done by gravitational force in the above case is – ve because direction of gravitational force is opposite to the displacement. [1]

(iii) Work done is – ve because direction of friction force is opposite to sliding motion. [1]

(iv) Work done by an applied force on a body moving on a rough horizontal plane is positive because force is being applied in the direction of motion so as to overcome friction. [1]

(v) Work done is negative because the resistive force of air acts in a direction opposite to the direction of motion of the vibrating pendulum. [1]

24. Refer to text on page 157 (Work done by a variable force).

25. Refer to text on page 158 (Conservative force) and example 7 on page 159.

Hint Friction force is non-conservative force depends upon the path followed by the object.

26. (i) We know that, work done is equal to change in kinetic energy, therefore

(a) When speed of a body increases, kinetic energy also increases, therefore work is done by exerting force. [1]

(b) When the speed decreases, then kinetic energy also decreases, therefore work is done by the body on the force. [1]

(c) When speed is constant, the change in kinetic energy will be zero, hence work done is zero. [1]

(ii) Refer to text on pages 156 and 157 (Zero work). [2]

27. Here, $\mathbf{F} = (-\hat{\mathbf{i}} + 2\hat{\mathbf{j}} + 3\hat{\mathbf{k}})$ N and $\mathbf{s} = (4\,\hat{\mathbf{k}})$ m [1]

$$W = \mathbf{F} \cdot \mathbf{s} = \mathbf{F}_z \cdot \mathbf{s}_z$$
$$= 3 \times 4 = 12 \text{ N-m} = 12 \text{ J}$$ [1]

28. Here, force $F = 1500$ N

and Displacement, $s = 100$ m, $\theta = 60°$ [1/2]

$\therefore$ Work done, $W = Fs \cos\theta$

$$= 1500 \times 100 \times \cos 60°$$ [1/2]

$$= 1500 \times 100 \times \frac{1}{2}$$

$$= 75000 \text{ J} = 75 \text{ kJ}$$ [1]

29. Here, mass, $m = 2$ kg, acceleration, $a = 0.5 \text{ m/s}^2$ and displacement, $s = 40$ m

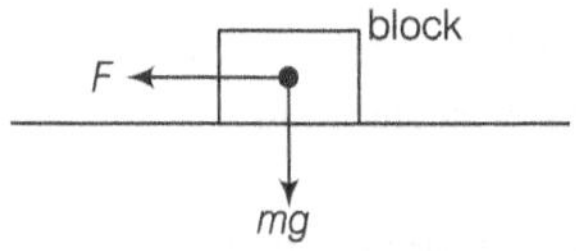

Force on the block, $F = ma = 2 \times 0.5 = 1$ N

$\therefore$ Work done, $W = F \cdot s = 1 \times 40 = 40$ J

[$\because$ Work done by mg is zero ($\theta = 90°$)]

30. Here, applied force $F = 7$ N

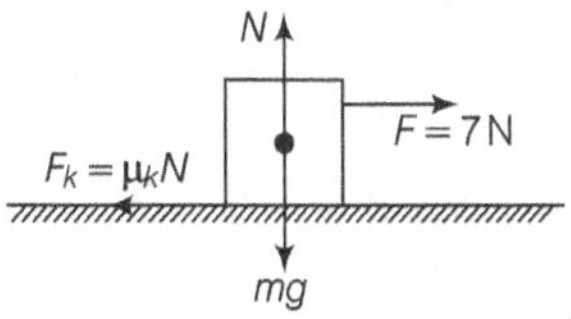

and opposing friction force, $f = \mu_k \cdot N = \mu_k \cdot mg$

$$= 0.1 \times 2 \times 9.8 = 1.96 \text{ N}$$ [1/2]

$\because$ Net accelerating force $= F - f = 7 - 1.96 = 5.04$ N

$\therefore$ Acceleration, $a = \frac{\text{force}}{\text{mass}} = \frac{5.04 \text{ N}}{2 \text{ kg}} = 2.52 \text{ ms}^{-2}$ [1/2]

(i) Distance covered in 10 s (assuming $u = 0$)

$$s = 0 + \frac{1}{2}at^2 = \frac{1}{2} \times 2.52 \times (10)^2 = 126 \text{ m}$$ [1/2]

$\therefore$ Work done by the applied force

$$W = Fs = 7 \times 126 = +882 \text{ J}$$ [1/2]

(ii) Work done by friction in 10 s

$$W' = fs \cos 180° = -1.96 \times 126 = -247 \text{ J}$$ [1/2]

(iii) Work done by net force in

$$10 \text{ s} = W - W' = 882 - 247$$
$$= +635 \text{ J}$$ [1/2]

31. We know, work done is given by $W = Fs \cos\theta$ [1]

In first case, angle (θ) between F and s is 90° because weight of the bag, i.e. force acts perpendicular to the displacement.

$\therefore$ $W = Fs \cos 90° = 0$ [1]

In second case, F and s are in the same direction, so $\theta = 0°$.

Here, $F = \mu\, mg = 0.1 \times 20 \times 9.8 = 19.6$ N

$\therefore$ $W = 19.6 \times 10 \times \cos 0° = 196$ J

So, work done in second case is more. [1]

32. Here, mass of body $= 50 + 25 = 75$ kg

$$\sin\theta = \frac{1}{10}$$

Distance, $s = 20$ m, $g = 9.8 \text{ m/s}^2$ [1]

Force needed to be applied against gravity

i.e. $F = mg \sin\theta$ [1]

Work done, $W = Fs = mg \sin\theta \times s$

$$= 75 \times 9.8 \times \frac{1}{10} \times 20 = 1470 \text{ J}$$ [1]

33. Work done by the force = force × displacement

or $W = F \times s$ ...(i)

But from Newton's 2nd law, we have

Force = mass × acceleration

i.e. $F = ma$ ...(ii)

Hence, from Eqs. (i) and (ii), we get

$$W = m\left(\frac{d^2s}{dt^2}\right)s \quad \left[\because a = \frac{d^2s}{dt^2}\right] \quad ...(iii)$$ [1]

Now, we have

$$s = \frac{1}{3}t^2$$

$$\therefore \quad \frac{d^2s}{dt^2} = \frac{d}{dt}\left[\frac{d}{dt}\left(\frac{1}{3}t^2\right)\right] = \frac{d}{dt}\times\left(\frac{2}{3}t\right) = \frac{2}{3}\frac{dt}{dt} = \frac{2}{3}$$

Hence Eq. (iii) becomes

$$W = \frac{2}{3}ms = \frac{2}{3}\times m \times \frac{1}{3}t^2 = \frac{2}{9}mt^2$$ [1]

We have, $m = 3$ kg, $t = 2s$

$$\therefore \quad W = \frac{2}{9}\times 3 \times (2)^2 = \frac{8}{3}\text{ J}$$ [1]

34. As work done, $dW = Fdx$ [1]

$$W = \int_0^5 F \cdot dx = \int_0^5 (7 - 2x + 3x^2)dx$$ [1]

$$= \left[7x - \frac{2x^2}{2} + \frac{3x^3}{3}\right]_0^5$$

$$= 7(5-0) - (5^2 - 0) + (5^3 - 0) = 135\text{ J}$$ [1]

35. As the stone weight acts downwards and upthrust acts upwards.

Thus, net weight of stone can be calculated.

$$\text{Specific gravity} = \text{Relative density} = \frac{\text{Density of stone}}{\text{Density of water}}$$

Thus, density of stone $= 3 \times 10^3$ kg /m^3 [1]

$$\text{Volume of stone} = \frac{\text{Mass of stone}}{\text{Density of stone}}$$

$$= \frac{5}{3\times 10^3} = \frac{5}{3}\times 10^{-3}\text{ m}^3$$ [1]

Upthrust on stone = Weight of liquid displaced

$$= \frac{5}{3}\times 10^{-3} \times \rho_{\text{water}} \times g = \frac{5}{3}\times 10^{-3}\times 10^3 \times 10 = \frac{50}{3}\text{ N}$$ [1]

Thus, net weight of stone,

$$mg' = mg - \text{upthrust}$$

$$mg' = \left(5\times 10 - \frac{50}{3}\right) = \frac{100}{3}\text{ N}$$ [1]

Now, force required to raise the stone,

$$F = \frac{100}{3}\text{ N}$$

Work required to raise the stone

$$W = Fd = \frac{100}{3}\times 5 = \frac{500}{3}\text{ J} = 166.6\text{ J}$$ [1]

36. In present problem, there are no net external forces. The sand is slowly leaking downwards from the hole. Consequently, normal reaction acting vertically upwards also slowly decreases. [1]

But it does not do any work because it is at right angle to trolley's motion. Thus, there is no change in speed of the trolley and it will continue among moving with a uniform speed of 27 kmh^{-1}. [1]

37. The work done by a car against gravity is zero because force of gravity is vertical and motion of car is along a straight horizontal road. [1]

As angle θ between directions of force and displacement is 90°, hence work done is zero. [1]

TOPIC 02 Energy

The energy of a body is defined as its capacity or ability for doing work.

(i) Like work, energy is a scalar quantity.

(ii) The dimensions of energy are the same as the dimensions of work i.e. $[M^1L^2T^{-2}]$.

(iii) It is measured in the same unit as work i.e. joule in SI and erg in CGS system.

Kinetic Energy

The energy possessed by a body by virtue of its motion is called **kinetic energy**. In other words, the amount of work done, i.e. a moving object can do before coming to rest is equal to its kinetic energy.

Let a body of mass m be in rest position. When a constant force is applied on the body, then it starts moving with acceleration a, then by Newton's second law of motion,

$$a = \frac{F}{m} \quad ...(i)$$

After travelling a distance s, body acquires a velocity v. Then, from relation $v^2 = u^2 + 2as$

$$v^2 = 0 + 2as$$

$$\Rightarrow \quad s = \frac{v^2}{2a} \quad ...(ii)$$

Since, capacity of doing work due to motion of the body is equal to kinetic energy.

$\therefore$ Kinetic energy, K = Work done

$$= F \cdot s$$

$$= mas \qquad [\because F = ma]$$

$$= m \cdot a \cdot \frac{v^2}{2a} \qquad \text{[from Eq. (ii)]}$$

$$\boxed{K = \frac{1}{2}mv^2}$$

where, m is a mass and v is the velocity of a body, e.g.

(i) A bullet fired from a gun can pierce a target due to its kinetic energy.

(ii) The kinetic energy of a fast stream of water is used to run water mills.

The units and dimensions of KE are Joule (in SI) and $[ML^2T^{-2}]$ respectively.

- Kinetic energy of a body is always positive. It can never be negative.
- Kinetic energy of a body depends upon the frame of reference, e.g. KE of a person of mass m sitting in a train moving with velocity v is $\frac{1}{2}mv^2$ in the frame of earth and KE of the same person = 0 , in the frame of the train.

Relation between Kinetic Energy and Linear Momentum

Kinetic energy

$$(K) = \frac{1}{2}mv^2$$

$$= \frac{(mv)^2}{2m}$$

$$\boxed{K = \frac{p^2}{2m}} \qquad [\because p = mv]$$

$$\Rightarrow \quad \boxed{p = \sqrt{2mK}}$$

Example 1 In a ballistics demonstration, a police officer fires a bullet of mass 50.0 g with speed 200 ms^{-1} on soft plywood of thickness 2.00 cm. The bullet emerges with only 10% of its initial kinetic energy. What is the emergent speed of the bullet? **NCERT**

Sol. Here, $m = 50.0 \text{ g} = 0.05 \text{ kg}, u = 200 \text{ ms}^{-1}$

$$\text{Initial KE} = \frac{1}{2}mu^2 = \frac{1}{2} \times 0.05 \times (200)^2 = 1000 \text{ J}$$

$$\text{Final KE} = 10\% \text{ of } 1000 \text{ J} = \frac{10 \times 1000}{100} = 100 \text{ J}$$

or $$\frac{1}{2}mv^2 = 100 \text{ J}$$

$$\therefore \quad v = \sqrt{\frac{2 \times 100}{m}} = \sqrt{\frac{2 \times 100}{0.05}} = 63.2 \text{ ms}^{-1}$$

Clearly, the speed reduces nearly by 68% and not by 90% by which the KE reduces.

Note We observed that KE $\propto m$ and also KE $\propto v^2$. Thus, a heavier body and a body moving faster possess greater energy. The reverse is also true.

Example 2 A toy rocket of mass 0.1 kg has a small fuel of mass 0.02 kg which it burns out in 3 s. Starting from rest on horizontal smooth track it gets a speed of 20 ms^{-1} after the fuel is burnt out. What is the approximate thrust of the rocket? What is the energy content per unit mass of the fuel? (Ignore the small mass variation of the rocket during fuel burning). **NCERT**

Sol. Here, $m = 0.1 \text{ kg}, u = 0, v = 20 \text{ ms}^{-1}, t = 3\text{s}$

$$\text{Thrust of the rocket} = ma = m\frac{v-u}{t}$$

$$= 0.1 \times \frac{20-0}{3} = \frac{2}{3} \text{ N} \qquad \left[\because v = u + at \text{ or } a = \frac{v-u}{t}\right]$$

Kinetic energy gained by the rocket

$$K = \frac{1}{2}mv^2 = \frac{1}{2} \times 0.1 \times (20)^2 = 20 \text{ J}$$

Energy content per unit mass of the fuel

$$= \frac{\text{Total energy}}{\text{Mass of the fuel}} = \frac{20 \text{ J}}{0.02 \text{ kg}} = 1000 \text{ Jkg}^{-1}$$

Example 3 Two bodies A and B having masses in the ratio of 3 : 1 possess the same kinetic energy. Obtain the ratio of linear momentum of B to A. **NCERT**

Sol. Kinetic energy of body is given by

$$E_K = \frac{1}{2}mv^2 \qquad \text{...(i)}$$

and linear momentum, $p = mv$ ...(ii)

From Eqs. (i) and (ii), we get

$$E_K = \frac{m^2v^2}{2m} = \frac{p^2}{2m}$$

When $$E_{K_1} = E_{K_2}$$

$$\Rightarrow \quad \frac{p_1^2}{2m_1} = \frac{p_2^2}{2m_2}$$

or $$\frac{p_1}{p_2} = \sqrt{\frac{m_1}{m_2}}$$

or $$\frac{p_1}{p_2} = \sqrt{\frac{3}{1}} \text{ or } \frac{p_2}{p_1} = \frac{1}{\sqrt{3}}$$

Example 4 If the momentum of a moving body is suddenly increased to 20%, find the percentage increase in its kinetic energy.

Sol. Let p_1 be the initial momentum of the body and m be the mass of the body.

$\therefore$ Final momentum, $p_2 = p_1 + 20\%$ of p_1

$$= p_1 + \frac{20}{100}p_1 = \frac{6p_1}{5}$$

Initial kinetic energy of the body, $K_1 = \frac{p_1^2}{2m}$

Final kinetic energy of the body, $K_2 = \frac{p_2^2}{2m}$

$\therefore$ Percentage increase in kinetic energy $= \frac{K_2 - K_1}{K_1} \times 100$

$$= \frac{\frac{p_2^2}{2m} - \frac{p_1^2}{2m}}{\frac{p_1^2}{2m}} \times 100 = \frac{p_2^2 - p_1^2}{p_1^2} \times 100$$

$$= \frac{\left(\frac{6p_1}{5}\right)^2 - p_1^2}{p_1^2} \times 100 = \frac{\frac{36}{25}p_1^2 - p_1^2}{p_1^2} \times 100$$

$$= \frac{11}{25} \times 100 = 44\%$$

Work Energy Theorem or Work Energy Principle

It states that work done by the net force acting on a body is equal to the change produced in the kinetic energy of the body.

Work Energy Theorem for a Constant Force

When a force F acting on a body of mass m produces acceleration a in it. After covering distance s, suppose the velocity of the body changes from u to v. We use the equation of motion $v^2 - u^2 = 2as$

Multiply both sides by $\frac{1}{2}m$, we get

$$\frac{1}{2}mv^2 - \frac{1}{2}mu^2 = mas$$

By Newton's second law, $F = ma$

$$\therefore \quad \frac{1}{2}mv^2 - \frac{1}{2}mu^2 = Fs$$

or $\boxed{K_f - K_i = W}$ $\quad [\because W = Fs]$

or $\boxed{W = \Delta K}$

where, K_f and K_i are the final and initial kinetic energies of the body.

Work energy theorem is true for any system of particles in the presence of all types of force (conservative or non-conservative).

When KE increases, then work done is positive and when KE decreases, then work done is negative.

Example 5 **A 8 kg block initially at rest is pulled to the right along a frictionless horizontal surface by a constant, horizontal force of 12 N, as shown in figure. Find the velocity of the block after it has moved a distance of 3 m. Also, find out the acceleration of the block.**

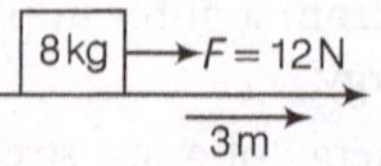

Sol. First of all draw the free body diagram of the block.

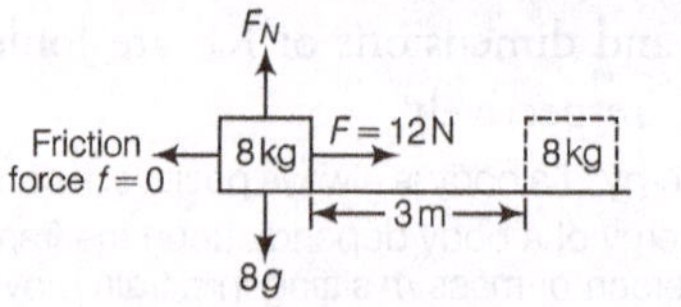

Find out the work done by the force 12 N.

$$W = Fs = Fs\cos 0° = 12 \times 3 = 36 \text{ J}$$

The work done by the normal and the weight of body will be zero.

If K_f and K_i are the final and initial kinetic energies of the block respectively, then according to work energy theorem.

$$W = K_f - K_i = \frac{1}{2}mv^2 - \frac{1}{2}mu^2 = \frac{1}{2}mv^2$$

[$\because$ initial velocity of the block $u = 0$]

Velocity of the block,

$$v = \sqrt{\frac{2W}{m}} = \sqrt{\frac{2 \times 36}{8}} \quad [\because \text{given, } m = 8 \text{ kg}]$$

$$v = 3 \text{ m/s}$$

The acceleration of the block can be calculated using the kinematic equation.

$$v^2 = u^2 + 2as$$

$$\therefore \quad a = \frac{v^2 - u^2}{2s}$$

$$= \frac{9}{2 \times 3} = 1.5 \text{ m/s}^2$$

Work-Energy Theorem for a Variable Force

Suppose a variable force **F** acts on a body of mass m and produces displacement ds in its own direction $(\theta = 0°)$. Then, the small work done is

$$dW = \mathbf{F} \cdot ds = Fds\cos 0° = Fds$$

The time rate of change of kinetic energy is

$$\frac{dK}{dt} = \frac{d}{dt}\left[\frac{1}{2}mv^2\right] = \frac{1}{2} \times 2v \times m\frac{dv}{dt}$$

$$= m\frac{dv}{dt}(v) = (ma)\,v$$

$$\left[\because \text{force, } F = ma \text{ and } v = \frac{ds}{dt}\right]$$

$$\therefore \quad \frac{dK}{dt} = F \cdot \frac{ds}{dt}$$

Thus, $dK = F\,ds$

Integrating from the initial position (x_i) to final position (x_f), we have

$$\int_{K_i}^{K_f} dK = \int_{x_i}^{x_f} F\,ds$$

where, K_i and K_f are the initial and final kinetic energies corresponding to x_i and x_f, respectively.

or $\boxed{\text{Change in kinetic energy, } K_f - K_i = \int_{x_i}^{x_f} F\,ds}$

$\therefore \quad K_f - K_i =$ work done on the body (W)

$=$ increase in KE of body.

This proves the work energy theorem for a variable force.

Note

- The work-energy theorem is not independent of Newton's second law.
- Newton's second law in two or three dimensions is in vector form, but the work energy theorem is in scalar form.

Example 6 Consider a drop of small pebble of mass 1.00 g falling from a cliff of height 1.00 km. It hits the ground with a speed of 50.0 ms^{-1}. What is the work done by the unknown resistive force? **NCERT**

Sol. We assume that the pebble is initially at rest on the cliff.

$\therefore \quad u = 0,\ m = 1.00\text{ g} = 10^{-3}\text{ kg}$

$v = 50\text{ ms}^{-1},\ h = 1.00\text{ km} = 10^3\text{ m}$

The change in KE of the pebble is

$$\Delta K = \frac{1}{2}mv^2 - \frac{1}{2}mu^2 = \frac{1}{2} \times 10^{-3} \times (50)^2 - 0 = 1.25\text{ J}$$

Assuming that $g = 10\text{ ms}^{-2}$ is constant, the work done by the gravitational force is

$$W_g = F \cdot h = mgh = 10^{-3} \times 10 \times 10^3 = 10.0\text{ J}$$

If W_r is the work done by the resistive force on the pebble, then from the work energy theorem,

$$\Delta K = W_g + W_r$$

or $W_r = \Delta K - W_g$

$= 1.25 - 10.0 = -8.75\text{ J}$

Potential Energy

The potential energy of a body is defined as the energy possessed by the body by virtue of its position or configuration in some field.

Thus, the potential energy of a system that can be associated with the configuration of a system of objects that exert forces on one another. So, configuration of the system changes, then its potential energy changes. e.g.

(i) A body lying on the roof of a building has some potential energy. When allowed to fall down it can do work.

(ii) When a spring is compressed or stretched, work done in compressing or stretching spring is stored in the spring in the form of potential energy.

Units and Dimensions of Potential Energy

The units and dimensions of potential energy are same as that of kinetic energy given as,

Dimensions $= [ML^2T^{-2}]$

Unit = Joule (J) in SI

Potential Energy Converted into Kinetic Energy

The notion of potential energy applies to only those forces where the work done against the force gets stored up as energy by virtue of position or configuration of the body when external constraints are removed.

This energy appears as kinetic energy, when the position or configuration of the body gets change under the action of external constraints.

Gravitational Potential Energy

Consider a body of mass m lying at A is moving upward at B agains gravity, then during this process, required work done is conserved in the form of gravitational potential energy.

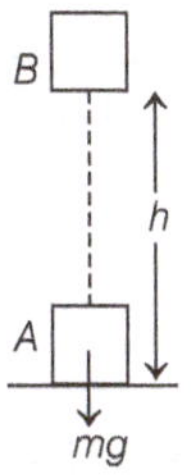

$\therefore$ Gravitational potential energy = Work done

U = Force × Displacement

$U = mgh$

Potential Energy of a Spring

There are many types of spring. Important among these are helical and spiral springs as shown in figure.

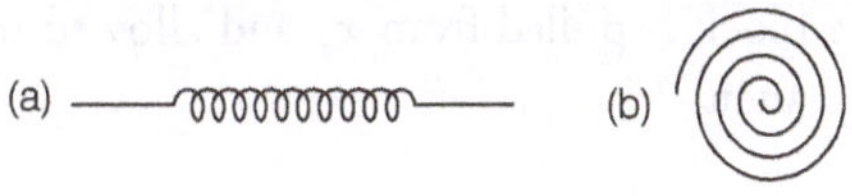

(a) Helical spring and (b) Spiral spring

Usually, we assume that the springs are massless. Therefore, work done is stored in the spring in the form of elastic potential energy of the spring. Thus, potential energy of a spring is the energy associated with the state of compression or expansion of an elastic spring.

Consider an elastic spring of negligibly small mass with its one end attached to a rigid support and its other end is attached to a block of mass m can slide over a smooth horizontal surface. At $x = 0$, the position is in the state of equilibrium as shown in Fig. (a), when the spring is stretched in Fig. (b) and compressed by pushing the block as shown in Fig. (c). So, spring force F_s begins to act in equilibrium position.

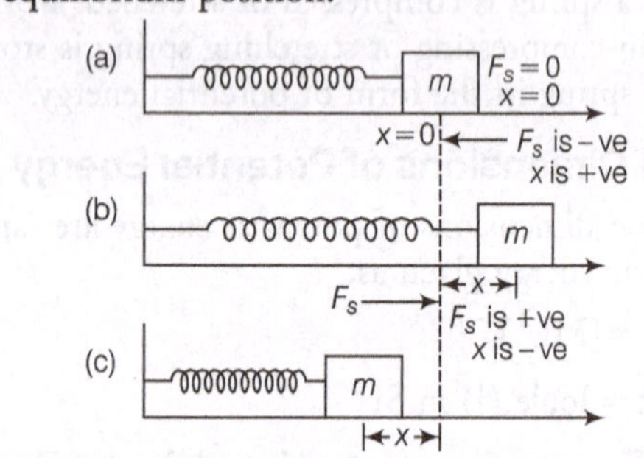

Equilibrium, stretched and compressed states of an elastic spring

For a small stretch or compression, spring obeys Hooke's law, i.e. restoring force $\propto$ stretch or compression

$$-F_s \propto x \quad \Rightarrow \quad F_s = -k\,x$$

where, k is called **spring constant**. Its SI unit is N/m. The negative sign shows F_s acts in the opposite direction of displacement x. The work done by the spring force for the small extension is

$$dW_s = F_s\,dx = -kx\,dx$$

If the block is moved from an initial displacement x_i to final displacement x_f, then work done by spring force is

$$W_s = \int dW_s = -\int_{x_i}^{x_f} kx\,dx = -k\left[\frac{x^2}{2}\right]_{x_i}^{x_f}$$

or $\boxed{\text{Net work done by the spring, } W_s = \frac{1}{2}kx_i^2 - \frac{1}{2}kx_f^2}$

(i) If $x_i = 0$ (i.e. for mean position) then, work done by the spring force is

$$W_s = -\frac{1}{2}kx_f^2$$

(ii) If the block is pulled from x_i and allowed to return to x_i, then

$$W_s = \frac{1}{2}kx_i^2 - \frac{1}{2}kx_i^2 = \text{zero}$$

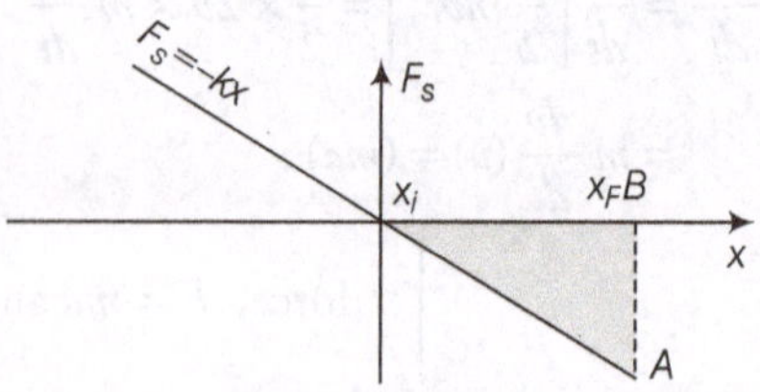

Plot of F_s *versus* x

Conclusion

(i) Spring force F_s is position dependent as it is clear in Hooke's law.
i.e. $F_s = -kx$

(ii) The work done by the spring force depends on initial and final position.

(iii) The work done by the spring force in a cyclic process is zero.

(iv) It can be expressed as the difference between the initial and final values of a potential energy function.

Hence, spring force is a **conservative force.**

Example 7 As shown in figure, a canister of mass $m = 0.40$ kg slides across a horizontal frictionless counter with speed $v = 0.50$ m/s. It then runs into and compresses a spring of spring constant $k = 750$ N/m. When the canister is momentarily stopped by the spring, by what distance d is the spring compressed ?

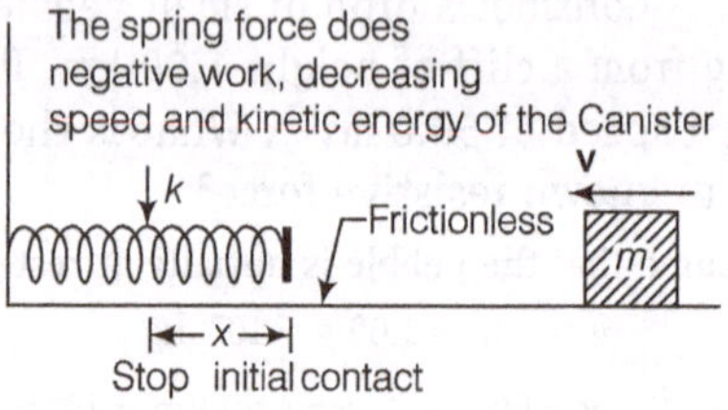

Sol. Write the work energy theorem for the canister as

$$K_f - K_i = \frac{1}{2}k\,x^2$$

Substituting according to the third key idea gives us the expression

$$0 - \frac{1}{2}mv^2 = -\frac{1}{2}kx^2$$

$$x = v\sqrt{\frac{m}{k}} = (0.50\text{ m/s})\sqrt{\frac{0.40\text{ kg}}{750\text{ N/m}}}$$

$$= 0.50 \times 0.02 = 0.0115\text{ m} = 1.15\text{ cm}$$

Conservation of Mechanical Energy

This principle states that if only the conservative forces are doing work on a body, then its mechanical energy (KE + PE) remains constant.

Suppose that a body undergoes displacement Δx under the action of a conservative force $F(x)$. Then, from work energy theorem, the change in KE, is

$$\Delta K = F(x) \cdot \Delta x$$

As the force is conservative, then change in potential energy is given by

$$\Delta U = - F(x)\, \Delta x = \text{Negative of the work done}$$

Combining the above two equations, we get

$$\Delta K = - \Delta U$$

$$\Delta K + \Delta U = 0$$

or $$\Delta (K + U) = 0$$

i.e. $$\boxed{K + U = \text{constant} = E}$$

$\therefore$ $$K_i + U_i = K_f + U_f$$

The quantity $K + U$, is called the **total mechanical energy** of the system. Although, individually the kinetic energy K and potential energy U may change from one state to another, but their sum or the total mechanical energy of the system remains constant under the conservative forces.

Mechanical Energy of a Oscillating Spring

If the block of mass m is extended to position x_m from mean position and released from rest, then its total mechanical energy at any arbitrary point x, where x lies between $-x_m$ and $+x_m$ will be given by

$$\frac{1}{2}kx_m^{\,2} = \frac{1}{2}kx^2 + \frac{1}{2}mv^2$$

Thus, speed and kinetic energy will be maximum at the equilibrium position $x = 0$, i.e.

$$\frac{1}{2}mv_m^{\,2} = \frac{1}{2}kx_m^{\,2}$$

$\Rightarrow$ $$v_m = \sqrt{\frac{k}{m}}\, x_m$$

where, v_m is the maximum speed.

Hence, the kinetic energy is converted to potential energy and *vice-versa* however, the total mechanical energy remains constant.

This is graphically shown below.

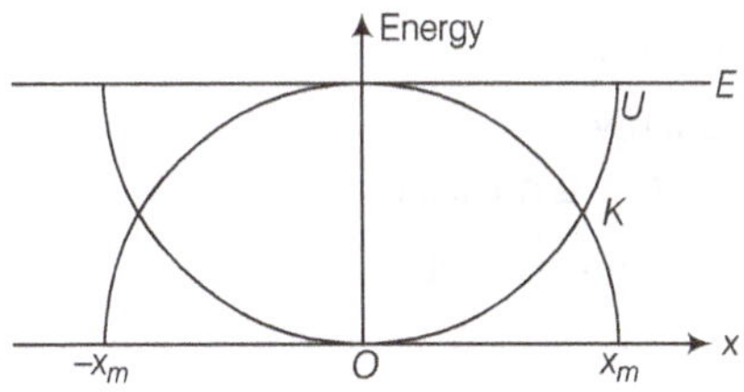

Plots of U, K and E

Example 8 To simulate car accidents, auto manufacturers study the collisions of moving cars with mounted springs of different spring constants. Consider a typical simulation with a car of mass 1000 kg moving with a speed of 18.0 kmh $^{-1}$ on a smooth road and colliding with a horizontally mounted spring of spring constant 6.25×10^3 Nm^{-1}. What is the maximum compression of the spring? **NCERT**

Sol. Here, $m = 1000$ kg, $k = 6.25 \times 10^3$ Nm^{-1},

$$v = 18 \text{ kmh}^{-1} = \frac{18 \times 5}{18} \text{ ms}^{-1} = 5 \text{ m/s}$$

At the maximum compression x_m, the kinetic energy of the car is covered entirely into the potential energy of the spring. Therefore,

Gain in PE of the spring = Loss in KE of the car

or $$\frac{1}{2}k\,x_m^2 = \frac{1}{2}mv^2$$

or $$x_m^2 = \frac{mv^2}{k} = \frac{1000 \times 5 \times 5}{6.25 \times 10^3} = 4$$

$\therefore$ $$x_m = 2.0 \text{ m}$$

Conservation of Mechanical Energy in a Freely Falling Body

Consider a body of mass m lying at position A at a height h above the ground. As the body falls, its kinetic energy increases at the expense of potential energy as shown in figure.

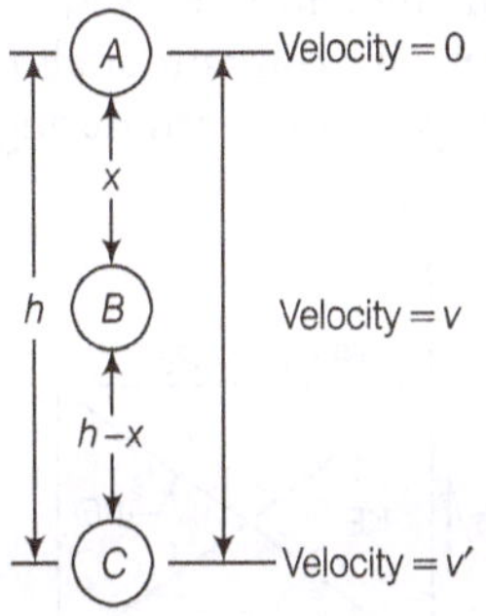

Conservation of energy in a freely falling body

At point A The body is at rest

KE of the body, $K_A = 0$

PE of the body, $U_A = mgh$

Total mechanical energy

$$E_A = K_A + U_A = 0 + mgh$$

Mechanical energy at position A, $E_A = mgh$

At point B Suppose the body falls freely through height x and reaches the point B with velocity v.

Then, $v^2 - 0^2 = 2as$ [$\because$ using $v^2 - u^2 = 2as$]

or $v^2 = 2gx$

$$\therefore \quad K_B = \frac{1}{2}mv^2$$

$$= \frac{1}{2} \times m \times 2gx = mg\,x$$

$$U_B = mg\,(h - x)$$

$$E_B = K_B + U_B$$

$$= mgx + mg\,(h - x) = mgh$$

Mechanical energy at position B, $E_B = mgh$

At point C Suppose the body finally at point C on the ground with velocity v'. Then, considering motion from A to C,

$$v'^2 - 0^2 = 2gh$$

or

$$v'^2 = 2gh$$

$$K_C = \frac{1}{2}mv^2 = \frac{1}{2} \times m \times 2gh = mgh$$

$$U_C = mg \times 0 = 0$$

$$\therefore \quad E_C = U_C + K_C = 0 + mgh = mgh$$

Mechanical energy at position C, $E_C = mgh$

Clearly, as the body falls, its PE decreases and KE increases by an equal amount. However, its total mechanical energy remains constant at all points. Thus, total mechanical energy is conserved during free fall of the body as shown in figure.

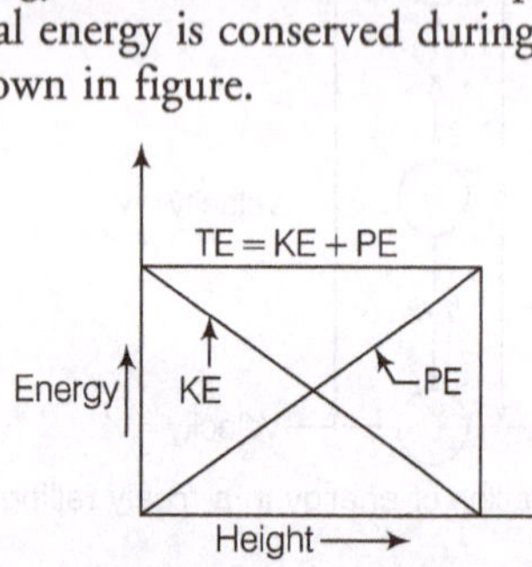

Plot of PE and KE during free fall of a body

Note

- The vibratory motion of a simple pendulum is another example of conversion of PE into KE and *vice-versa* and hence conservation of mechanical energy.
- The value of mechanical energy of a body depends upon frame of reference.
- $E - U = K$ and K is always positive, therefore for a system to exist. $E - U \geq 0$ or $E \geq U$.

Topic Practice 2

Multiple Choice Questions

(1 Mark)

1. The result of work-energy theorem for a variable force is

(a) $K_i - K_f = W$

(b) $K_f - K_i = W$

(c) $K_f - K_i > W$

(d) $K_i - K_f > W$

2. Two moving objects having same kinetic energy are stopped by application of equal retarding force. Which further will come to rest at short distance?

(a) Bigger

(b) Smaller

(c) Both at same distance

(d) Cannot say

3. The potential energy, i.e. $U(x)$ can be assumed zero when

(a) $x = 0$

(b) gravitational force is constant

(c) infinite distance from the gravitational source

(d) All of the above

4. The ratio of spring constants of two springs is 2 : 3. What is the ratio of their potential energy if they are stretched by the same force?

(a) 2 : 3 (b) 3 : 2

(c) 4 : 9 (d) 9 : 4

Very Short Answer Type Questions

(1 Mark)

5. Is it possible to exert a force which does work on a body without changing its kinetic energy. If so, give example.

6. What is the source of kinetic energy of the bullet coming out of the bullet of a rifle?

7. When an air bubble rises in water, what happens to its potential energy?

8. How the potential energy is converted into kinetic energy?

9. Is it practically possible to have situation where $(E - U) < 0$?

Short Answer Type I Questions

2 Marks

10. Can a body have energy without momentum? If yes, then explain how they are related with each other?

11. A shot fired from a gun explodes in air. What will be the changes in the momentum and the kinetic energy?

12. Derive relation between kinetic energy and linear momentum.

13. Define potential energy. How it is converted into kinetic energy?

Short Answer Type II Questions

3 Marks

14. Define kinetic energy. Prove that KE associated with a mass m moving with velocity v is $\frac{1}{2}mv^2$.

15. If a light body and heavy body are moving with same momentum, then which body is having more kinetic energy and why?

16. Explain work-energy theorem for a variable force.

17. Define gravitational potential energy and derive expression for it.

18. State and explain the principle of conservation of mechanical energy.

19. Underline the correct alternative.
    (i) When a conservative force does positive work on a body, the potential energy of the body increases, decreases/remains unaltered.
    (ii) Work done by a body against friction always results in a loss of its kinetic/potential energy.
    (iii) The rate of change of total momentum of a many particle system is proportional to the external force/ sum of the internal forces on the system. **NCERT**

Long Answer Type Questions

5 Marks

20. Given in figure are examples of some potential energy functions in one dimension. The total energy of the particle is indicated by a cross on the ordinate axis. In each case, specify the regions, if any, in which the particle cannot be found for the given energy. Also, indicate the minimum total energy the particle must have in each case. Think of simple physical contexts for which these potential energy shapes are relevant. **NCERT**

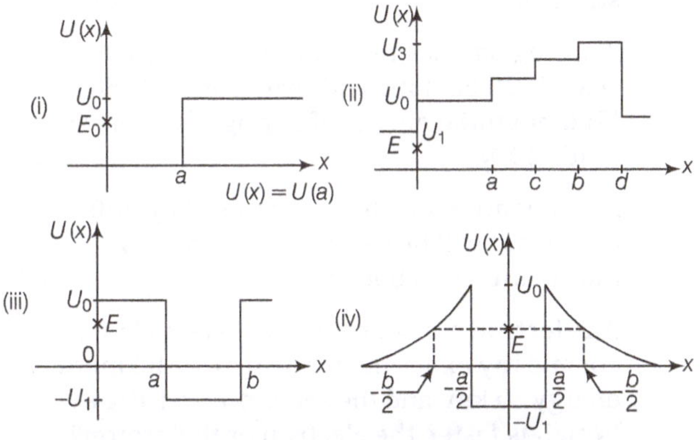

21. Find the potential energy in a spring. Draw graph showing variation of spring force with displacement.

22. How mechanical energy is conserved when a body is falling freely from a height? Show variation of energy with height.

Numerical Problems

23. The position (x) of a particle of mass 1 kg moving along X-axis at time t is given by $(x = 1/2\, t^2)$ metre. Find the work done by force acting on it in time interval from $t = 0$ to $t = 3$ s. **[2M]**

24. A bullet weighing 10 g is fired with a velocity 800 ms^{-1}. After passing through a mud wall 1 m thick, its velocity decreases to 100 ms^{-1}. Find the average resistance offered by the mud wall. **[2M]**

25. A body of mass 1.0 kg initially at rest is moved by a horizontal force of 0.5 N on a smooth frictionless table. Calculate the work done by the force in 10 s and show that this is equal to the change in kinetic energy of the body. **[2M]**

26. A body of mass 0.5 kg travels in a straight line with velocity $v = ax^{3/2}$, where $a = 5\ m^{-\frac{1}{2}} s^{-1}$. What is the work done by the net force during its displacement from $x = 0$ to $x = 2$ m? **NCERT [2M]**

27. A bolt of mass 0.3 kg falls from the ceiling of an elevator moving down with an uniform speed of $7\ ms^{-1}$. It hits the floor of the elevator (length of the elevator = 3 m) and does not rebound. What is the heat produced by the impact? Would your answer be different if the elevator were stationary? **NCERT [2M]**

28. A spring balance reads forces in Newtons. The scale is 20 cm long and read from 0 to 60 N. Find potential energy of spring when the scale reads 20 N. **[2M]**

29. If momentum of a body increased by 300%, then what will be percentage increase in momentum of a body? **[3M]**

30. An electron and a proton are detected in a cosmic ray experiment, the first with kinetic energy 10 keV and the second with 100 keV. Which is faster, the electron or the proton? Obtain the ratio of their speeds. (Electron mass $= 9.11 \times 10^{-31}$ kg, proton mass $= 1.67 \times 10^{-27}$ kg, $1 eV = 1.60 \times 10^{-19}$ J). **NCERT [3M]**

31. An object is displaced from position vector $r_1 = (2\hat{i} + 3\hat{j})$ m to $r_2 = (4\hat{i} + 6\hat{j})$ m under a force $F = (3x^2\hat{i} + 2y\hat{j})$N. Find

(i) the work done by this force.

(ii) the nature of force. **[3M]**

32. When a 300 g mass is hung from a vertical spring, it stretches from equilibrium by 10 cm. What work is required to stretch it by next 5 cm? **[3M]**

33. A block of mass 8 kg is released from the top of an inclined smooth surface as shown in figure. If spring constant of spring is $200\ Nm^{-1}$ and block comes to rest after compressing spring by 1 m then find the distance travelled by block before it comes to rest.

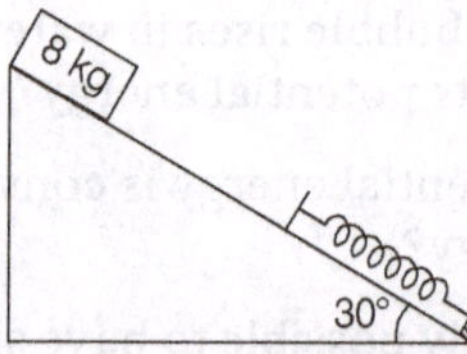

[3M]

34. In the arrangement shown in figure, string is light and inextensible and friction is absent everywhere. Find the speed of both the blocks after the block A has ascended a height of 1 m. Given that, $m_A = 1$ kg and $m_B = 2$ kg (Take, $g = 10\ ms^{-2}$). **[3M]**

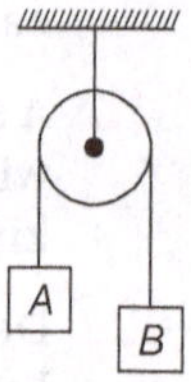

35. The bob of a pendulum is released from a horizontal position. If the length of the pendulum is 1.5 m, what is the speed with which the bob arrives at the lowermost point, given that it dissipated 5% of its initial energy against air resistance? **NCERT [3M]**

36. A rain drop of radius 2 mm falls from the height of 500 m above the ground. It falls with decreasing acceleration (due to viscous resistance of the air) until at half its original height, it attains its maximum (terminal) speed, and moves with uniform speed thereafter. What is the work done by the gravitational force on the drop in the first and second half of its journey? What is the work done by the resistive force in the entire journey if its speed on reaching the ground is $10\ ms^{-1}$? **NCERT [3M]**

37. A helicopter lifts a 72 kg astronaut 15 m vertically from the ocean by means of a cable. The acceleration of the astronaut is $\frac{g}{10}$.

How much work is done on the astronaut by

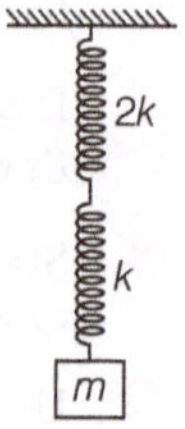

(i) the force from the helicopter and

(ii) the gravitational force on him?

(iii) what are the kinetic energy and

(iv) the speed of the astronaut just before he reaches the helicopter? (Take, $g = 10\ ms^{-2}$) **[5M]**

38. Two inclined frictionless tracks, one gradual and the other steep meet at A from where two stones are allowed to slide down from rest, one on each track figure. Will the stones reach the bottom at the same time? Will they reach there with the same speed? Explain. Given

$\theta_1 = 30°, \theta_2 = 60°$ and $h = 10$ m, what are the speeds and times taken by the two stones. NCERT [5M]

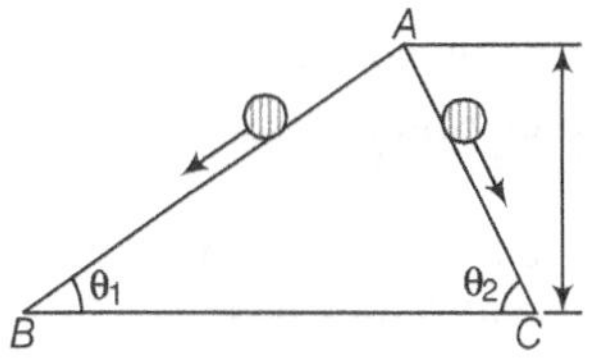

39. (i) An object of mass 5 kg falls from rest through a vertical distance of 20 m and attains a velocity of 10 ms^{-1}. How much work is done by the resistance of the air on the object? (Take, $g = 10$ ms^{-2})

(ii) A vehicle of mass 10 kg is moving in x-direction with a constant speed of 10 ms^{-1}. It is subjected to a retarding force $F = -0.1x$ Jm^{-1} during its travel from $x = 20$ m to $x = 30$ m. Evaluate its final kinetic energy. [5M]

40. A 1 kg block situated on a rough incline is connected to a spring of spring constant 100 N m^{-1} as shown in figure. The block is released from rest with the spring in the unstretched position. The block moves 10 cm down the incline before coming to rest. Find the coefficient of friction between the block and the incline. Assume that the spring has a negligible mass and the pulley is frictionless.

[Given, sin 37° = 0.6 and cos 37° = 0.8] NCERT [5M]

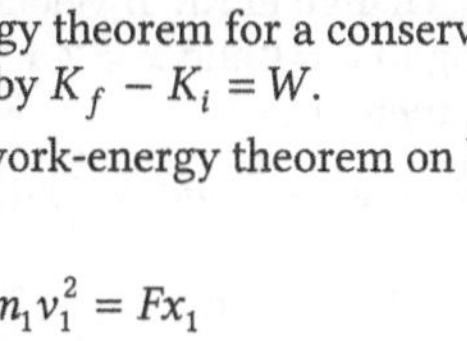

Hints & Solutions

1. (*b*) Work-energy theorem for a conservative variable force is given by $K_f - K_i = W$.

2. (*c*) Applying work-energy theorem on both moving objects.

$$\frac{1}{2} m_1 v_1^2 = Fx_1$$

and $$\frac{1}{2} m_2 v_2^2 = Fx_2$$

Since, $$\frac{1}{2} m_1 v_1^2 = \frac{1}{2} m_2 v_2^2$$

$$\Rightarrow \quad x_1 = x_2$$

3. (*d*) The zero of the potential energy is arbitrary. It is set according to convenience. For the spring force, we took $U(x) = 0$, at $x = 0$, i.e. the unstretched spring had zero potential energy.

For the constant gravitational force mg, we took $U = 0$ on the earth's surface. In a later chapter, we shall see that for the force due to the universal law of gravitation, the zero is best defined at an infinite distance from the gravitational source.

4. (*b*) $F = k_1 x_1$, $F = k_2 x_2$

$$k_1 x_1 = k_2 x_2$$

$$\Rightarrow \quad \frac{k_1}{k_2} = \frac{x_2}{x_1}$$

$$\frac{\text{PE(1)}}{\text{PE(2)}} = \frac{k_1 x_1^2}{k_2 x_2^2} = \frac{k_1}{k_2} \times \left(\frac{k_2}{k_1}\right)^2 = \frac{k_2}{k_1} = \frac{3}{2}$$

5. Yes, when spring is compressed or when a body is pulled with a constant velocity on a rough horizontal surface.

6. The source of kinetic energy of bullet is the potential energy of the compressed spring in the loaded rifle.

7. Potential energy of air bubble decreases because work is done by upthrust on the bubble.

8. Due to conservation of mechanical energy

$$K_i + U_i = K_f + U_f \quad [\because K_i \text{ is zero}]$$

$$\Rightarrow \quad U_i = K_f + U_f \quad [\because U_f < U_i]$$

$$\Rightarrow \quad K_f > 0$$

So, kinetic energy (K_f) increases.

9. No, it is practically not possible because $(E - U)$ represents KE, which cannot be negative.

10. Yes, when $p = 0$,

Then, $$K = \frac{p^2}{2m} = 0$$ [1]

But $E = K + U = U$(potential energy), which may or may not be zero. [1]

11. The linear momentum will be conserved, because explosion occurs from within, i.e. under internal forces only. However, kinetic energy will increase due to potential energy of the explosives. [2]

12. Refer to text on page 165 (Relation between kinetic energy and linear momentum).

13. Refer to text on page 167 (Potential energy and potential energy converted into kinetic energy).

14. Refer to text on pages 164 and 165 (Kinetic energy).

15. Let m_1 and m_2 be the masses of lighter and heavier body and v_1 and v_2 be their respective velocities.

Since, momentum of both bodies is same.

$$\therefore \quad m_1 v_1 = m_2 v_2 \quad \text{...(i)}$$

Kinetic energy of first body,

$$K_1 = \frac{1}{2} m_1 v_1^2$$ [1]

Kinetic energy of second body,

$$K_2 = \frac{1}{2} m_2 v_2^2$$

$$\therefore \quad \frac{K_1}{K_2} = \frac{\frac{1}{2} m_1 v_1^2}{\frac{1}{2} m_2 v_2^2} = \frac{\frac{(m_1 v_1)^2}{m_1}}{\frac{(m_2 v_2)^2}{m_2}}$$

$$\frac{K_1}{K_2} = \frac{m_2}{m_1} \quad \text{[from Eq. (i)]}$$ [1½]

Since, $m_2 > m_1$

$$\therefore \quad K_1 > K_2$$

i.e. Lighter body has more kinetic energy than heavier body. [½]

16. Refer to text on pages 166 and 167 (Work-energy theorem for a variable force).

17. Refer to text on page 167 (Gravitational potential energy).

18. Refer to text on page 169 (Conservation of mechanical energy).

19. (i) The potential energy decreases, because $\Delta U = -\int \mathbf{F} \cdot d\mathbf{x}$. If work done by conservative force is positive, then obviously ΔU is – ve. [1]

(ii) Friction always opposes motion. Hence, work done by a body against friction causes loss in its kinetic energy. [1]

(iii) The total (net) momentum can change only when some net external force acts on the system. Hence, its rate of change is proportional to the external force. [1]

20. The total energy of the particle is

$$E = K + U$$ [1]

where K is the kinetic energy.

Thus, $\quad K = E - U$ [1]

The kinetic energy $K = \left(\frac{1}{2} mv^2\right)$ can never be negative.

It means that potential energy U cannot be greater than the total energy E.

In Fig. (i), in the region $x > a$, the PE is U_0 which is greater than the total energy E. Hence, the particle cannot be found in the region $x > a$. The particle exists in the region $x = 0$ to $x = a$ in which the minimum total energy is 0. [1]

In Fig. (ii), in the entire region of the curve, i.e. x lying between $-\infty$ and $+\infty$ the total energy E is less than the potential energy $U(x)$. The particles cannot be found in these states. Minimum energy is U_1. [1]

In Fig. (iii), in the region $x < a$ and $x > b$, the PE is U_0 which is greater than E. Hence, the particle cannot be found in the region $x < a$ and $x > b$. The particle exists in the region from $x = a$ to $x = b$ in which the minimum total energy is $-U_1$.

In Fig. (iv), the particle cannot be found in the region $\frac{a}{2} < x < \frac{b}{2}$ because total energy is less than potential energy. The minimum energy is $-U_1$. [1]

21. Refer to text on pages 167 and 168 (Potential energy of a spring).

22. Refer to text on page 170 (Conservation of mechanical energy in a freely falling body).

23. $x = \frac{1}{2} t^2 \Rightarrow v = \frac{dx}{dt} = \frac{1}{2}(2t) = t$

$\therefore$ At $t = 0$, $v_i = 0 \Rightarrow$ At $t = 3$ s, $v_f = 3 \text{ ms}^{-1}$ [1]

According to work-energy theorem,

$$W = \Delta K = K_f - K_i$$

$$= \frac{1}{2} mv_f^2 - \frac{1}{2} mv_i^2 = \frac{1}{2} \times 1 \times 3^2 = 4.5 \text{ J}$$ [1]

24. According to work-energy theorem, work done by the average resistance offered by the wall = change in KE of the bullet.

$$\therefore \quad W = F \cdot s = \frac{1}{2} mv^2 - \frac{1}{2} mu^2$$ [1]

$$\Rightarrow \quad F = \frac{m(v^2 - u^2)}{2s} = \frac{0.01(100^2 - 800^2)}{2 \times 1} = -3150 \text{ N}$$

$\Rightarrow$ Resistance offered = 3150 N [1]

25. Acceleration of a body,

$$a = F/m = \frac{0.5}{1.0} = 0.5 \text{ ms}^{-2}$$ [1/2]

Distance travelled, $s = ut + \frac{1}{2} at^2$

$$s = 0 + \frac{1}{2} \times 0.5 \, (10)^2 = 25 \text{ m}$$

Work done $= F \times s = 0.5 \times 25 = 12.5$ J [1]

$$v = u + at = 0 + 0.5 \times 10 = 5 \text{ ms}^{-1}$$

Change in KE $= 1/2 \, m \, (v^2 - u^2)$

$$= 1/2 \times 1.0 \, (5^2 - 0) = 12.51$$ [1/2]

26. Given, $m = 0.5$ kg, $v = ax^{\frac{3}{2}}$, where $a = 5 \text{ m}^{-\frac{1}{2}} \text{ s}^{-1}$.

We know that work done by net force acting on a body is equal to its change in KE. If velocity of body corresponding to $x = 0$ and $x = 2$ m be u and v respectively, then

$$W = \frac{1}{2} mv^2 - \frac{1}{2} mu^2 = \frac{1}{2} m(v^2 - u^2)$$ [1]

Now, $\quad u = a \cdot (0)^{3/2} = 0$ and $v = a \cdot (2)^{3/2}$

$$\therefore \quad W = \frac{1}{2} \times 0.5 \, [\{a(2)^{3/2}\}^2 - 0]$$

$$= \frac{1}{2} \times 0.5 \times a^2 \times (2)^3$$

$$= \frac{1}{2} \times 0.5 \times (5)^2 \times 8 = 50 \text{ J}$$ [1]

27. Given, mass of bolt, $m = 0.3$ kg, height through which bolt falls $h = 3$ m.

When the bolt falls on floor of elevator and does not rebound, it suffers a loss of potential energy

$$\Delta U = mgh = 0.3 \times 9.8 \times 3 = 8.82 \text{ J} \quad [1]$$

∴ Amount of heat produced = Loss of potential energy = 8.82 J, because there is no gain in KE at all.

The answer is true when either the elevator is at rest or in state of uniform motion because potential energy of bolt has no connection with velocity of elevator. [1]

28. We can calculate the spring constant of spring, as it is extended by 20 cm under 60 N force.

$$F = kx$$

$$\Rightarrow \quad 60 = k \times 20 \times 10^{-2}$$

$$k = 300 \text{ N/m} \quad [1]$$

At a force of 20 N, the extension in spring is

$$F = kx \quad \Rightarrow 20 = 300x$$

$$x = \frac{2}{30} = \frac{1}{15} \text{ m} \quad [1]$$

29. Consider a particle of mass m moving with a velocity v so, that its KE $= \frac{1}{2}mv^2$ and momentum, $p = mv$.

Thus, $\quad \text{KE} = \frac{p^2}{2m}$

or $\quad p = \sqrt{2m\text{KE}}$ [1]

when KE is increased by 300%, then new KE

$\text{KE}' = \text{KE} + 300\% \text{ of } E = \text{KE} + 3\text{KE} = 4\text{KE}$ [1]

New momentum, $p' = \sqrt{2m\text{KE}'}$

$$= \sqrt{2m \times 4\text{KE}} = 2\sqrt{2m\text{KE}} = 2p$$

∴ Percentage increase in momentum

$$= \frac{p'-p}{p} \times 100 = \frac{2p-p}{p} \times 100 = 100\% \quad [1]$$

30. Here, $K_e = 10$ keV and $K_p = 100$ keV

$$m_e = 9.11 \times 10^{-31} \text{ kg}$$

and $m_p = 1.67 \times 10^{-27}$ kg [1]

As $\quad K = \frac{1}{2}mv^2 \quad \text{or} \quad v = \sqrt{\frac{2K}{m}}$,

Hence, $\frac{v_e}{v_p} = \sqrt{\frac{K_e}{K_p} \times \frac{m_p}{m_e}}$ [1]

$$= \sqrt{\frac{10 \text{ keV}}{100 \text{ keV}} \times \frac{1.67 \times 10^{-27} \text{ kg}}{9.11 \times 10^{-31} \text{ kg}}}$$

$\Rightarrow \quad v_e = 13.54 v_p$ [1]

Thus, electron is travelling faster.

31. (i) Work done, $W = \int_{\mathbf{r}_1}^{\mathbf{r}_2} \mathbf{F} \cdot d\mathbf{r}$

$$= \int_{\mathbf{r}_1}^{\mathbf{r}_2} (3x^2\hat{\mathbf{i}} + 2y\hat{\mathbf{j}}) \cdot (dx\hat{\mathbf{i}} + dy\hat{\mathbf{j}} + dz\hat{\mathbf{k}})$$

$$= \int_{\mathbf{r}_1}^{\mathbf{r}_2} (3x^2\,dx + 2y\,dy)$$

$$= [x^3 + y^2]_{(2,\,3)}^{(4,\,6)} = 83 \text{ J} \quad [1½]$$

(ii) While calculating the work done we did not mention the path through which the object was displaced.

Only initial and final coordinates were required.

It shows that in both the examples, the work done is path independent or work done will be equal to whichever path we follow.

Therefore, above two forces in which work done is path independent are example of **conservative forces**. [1½]

32. We can calculate spring constant of spring by first information.

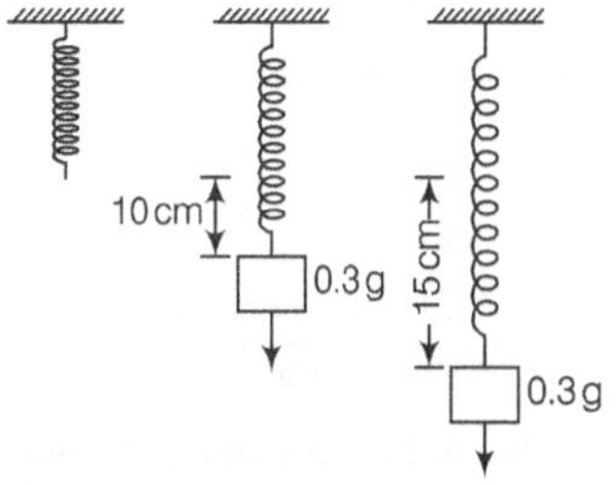

Work done by a vertical spring is

$$0.3 \text{ g} = k[10 \times 10^{-2}] \quad [1]$$

$$2 = k \times 0.1 \Rightarrow k = \frac{3}{0.1} = 30 \text{ N/m}^{-1}$$

Extra work required to stretch it by next 5 cm. [1]

$$W = \frac{1}{2}kx_2^2 - \frac{1}{2}kx_1^2$$

$$W = \frac{1}{2} \times 30\,[(15 \times 10^{-2})^2 - (10 \times 10^{-2})^2]$$

$$W = 15\,[225 - 100] \times 10^{-4} = 15 \times 125 \times 10^{-4} \text{ J}$$

$$W = 0.1875 \text{ J} \quad [1]$$

33. Consider d is the distance travelled by block along the plane and height it come in downward direction $h = d\sin 30°$.

Now, when block will comes to rest, the decrease in its potential energy will store in spring [1½]

∴ $mgh = \frac{1}{2}ky^2$ (y is compression in spring)

$$\Rightarrow mg\,d\sin 30° = \frac{1}{2}ky^2$$

$$\Rightarrow 8 \times 10 \times \frac{d}{2} = \frac{1}{2} \times 200 \times 1^2$$

$$\Rightarrow \quad 40d = 100 \Rightarrow d = 2.5 \text{ m} \quad [1½]$$

34. Friction is absent. Therefore, mechanical energy of the system will remain conserved. From constraint relations, we see that speed of both the blocks will be same. Suppose it is v. Here, gravitational potential energy of

2 kg block is decreasing while gravitational potential energy of 1 kg block is increasing.
Similarly, kinetic energy of both the blocks is also increasing. [1½]

$\therefore\ m_B gh = m_A gh + \frac{1}{2} m_A v^2 + \frac{1}{2} m_B v^2$

or $(2)(10)(1) = (1)(10)(1) + \frac{1}{2}(1)v^2 + \frac{1}{2}(2)v^2$

or $20 = 10 + 0.5\,v^2 + v^2$ or $1.5\,v^2 = 10$

$\therefore\ v^2 = 6.67\ \text{m}^2\text{s}^{-2}$ or $v = 2.58\ \text{ms}^{-1}$ [1½]

35. On releasing the bob of pendulum from horizontal position, it falls vertically downward by a distance equal to length of pendulum i.e. $h = l = 1.5$ m. [1]
As 5% of loss in PE is dissipated against air resistance, the balance 95% energy is transformed into KE. Hence,

$$\frac{1}{2}mv^2 = \frac{95}{100} \times mgh$$ [1]

$$\Rightarrow v = \sqrt{2 \times \frac{95}{100} \times gh}$$

$$= \sqrt{\frac{2 \times 95 \times 9.8 \times 1.5}{100}} = 5.3\ \text{ms}^{-1}$$ [1]

36. If r be the radius of the drop and ρ the density of water, then the mass of the drop is

$$m = \frac{4}{3}\pi r^2 \rho = \frac{4}{3} \times 3.14 \times (2 \times 10^{-3}\ \text{m})^3 \times 10^3\ \text{kg m}^{-3}$$

$$= 3.35 \times 10^{-5}\ \text{kg}$$ [1]

The weight of the drop is

$$mg = (3.35 \times 10^{-5}\ \text{kg}) \times 9.8\ \text{ms}^{-2} = 3.283 \times 10^{-4}\ \text{N}$$

The work done by the force in each half journey

$$W = mgh = (3.283 \times 10^{-4}\ \text{N}) \times 250\ \text{m} = 0.082\ \text{J}$$ [1]

The work done by the resistive force in the entire journey is equal to loss in energy of drop. If there were no resistive force, energy of drop on reaching the ground is equal to work done on the drop by gravity force

$$E_1 = mgh = 3.35 \times 10^{-5} \times 9.8 \times 500\ \text{J} = 0.164\ \text{J}$$

But the actual energy of drop is its kinetic energy

$$E_2 = \frac{1}{2}mv^2 = \frac{1}{2} \times 3.35 \times 10^{-5} \times (10)^2 = 1.675 \times 10^{-3}\ \text{J}$$

$\therefore$ Work done by resistive force

$$= E_1 - E_2 = 0.164 - 1.675 \times 10^{-3} = 0.163\text{J}$$ [1]

37. Here, mass of astronaut $m = 72$ kg, vertical distance $h = 15$ m and acceleration of astronaut $a = \frac{g}{10}$.

(i) Force from the helicopter

$$F = mg + ma = mg + \frac{mg}{10} = \frac{11\,mg}{10}$$ [1]

$\therefore$ Work done by force from the helicopter

$$W = F \times h = \frac{11mg}{10} \times h$$

$$W = \frac{11 \times 72 \times 10 \times 15}{10}$$

$$= 11880\ \text{J}$$ [1]

(ii) Work done by gravitational force

$$W' = (mg)(h)(\cos 180°)$$
$$W' = -\,mgh$$
$$= -72 \times 10 \times 15 = -10800\ \text{J}$$ [1]

(iii) KE of astronaut K = net work done on him

$$= W + W' = (11880 - 10800)\ \text{J}$$
$$= +1080\ \text{J}$$ [1]

(iv) As $\text{KE} = \frac{1}{2}mv^2$, hence

$$v = \sqrt{\frac{2K}{m}}$$

$$= \sqrt{\frac{2 \times 1080}{72}} = 5.48\ \text{ms}^{-1}$$ [1]

38. As height of both the planes is the same, both stones will reach the bottom with same speed.

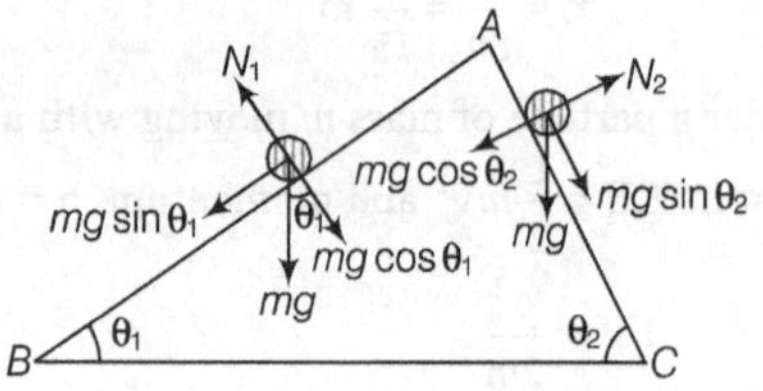

Loss in PE = Gain in KE [1]

$$m_1 gh = \frac{1}{2}m_1 v_1^2,\ m_2 gh = \frac{1}{2}m_2 v_2^2$$ [1]

$$v_1 = v_2 = \sqrt{2\,gh}$$
$$= \sqrt{2 \times 9.8 \times 10}$$
$$= 14\ \text{ms}^{-1}$$

From the figure, acceleration of the two blocks are $a_1 = g\sin\theta_1$ and $a_2 = g\sin\theta_2$ [1]

Again $v = u + at = 0 + at$

$$\Rightarrow t = \frac{v}{a} = \frac{v}{g\sin\theta}$$

$$\frac{t_1}{t_2} = \frac{\sin\theta_2}{\sin\theta_1}$$ [1]

i.e. second stone will have lesser time and reach the bottom earlier than first stone.

Value of $t_1 = \frac{v_1}{g\sin\theta_1} = \frac{14.1}{9.8 \times \sin 30°} = 2.88$ s

Value of $t_2 = \frac{v}{g\sin\theta_2} = \frac{14.1}{9.8 \times \sin 60°} = 1.66$ s [1]

39. (i) Applying work-energy theorem,
work done by all the forces = change in kinetic energy

or $W_{mg} + W_{\text{air}} = \frac{1}{2}mv^2$ [1]

$$\therefore\ W_{\text{air}} = \frac{1}{2}mv^2 - W_{mg} = \frac{1}{2}mv^2 - mgh$$

$$= \frac{1}{2} \times 5 \times (10)^2 - (5) \times (10) \times (20)$$

$$= -750 \text{ J}$$ [1]

(ii) According to work-energy theorem,
work done = change in kinetic energy of the vehicle

$$\therefore \quad W = K_f - K_i \text{ or } F \cdot dx = K_f - \frac{1}{2} mv_i^2$$ [1]

$$\text{or} \quad F \cdot dx = K_f - \frac{1}{2} \times 10 \times (10)^2$$

$$\text{or} \quad F \cdot dx = K_f - 500$$

$$\text{or} \quad \int_{x=20}^{x=30} (-0.1)x \, dx = K_f - 500$$

$$\text{or} \quad -0.1 \left[\frac{x^2}{2} \right]_{x=20}^{x=30} = K_f - 500$$ [1]

$$\text{or} \quad -0.1 \left[\frac{(30)^2}{2} - \frac{(20)^2}{2} \right] = K_f - 500$$

$$\text{or} \quad K_f - 500 = -0.1\,(450 - 200)$$

$$\text{or} \quad K_f - 500 = -25$$

$$\therefore \quad K_f = 500 - 25 = 475 \text{ J}$$ [1]

40. Here, force constant, $k = 100 \text{ Nm}^{-1}$,
Mass of block, $m = 1$ kg, $\theta = 37°$
and distance moved by block, $x = 10$ cm $= 0.1$ m
As shown in figure, the net accelerating force acting on block is $F = mg\sin\theta - f = mg\sin\theta - \mu N$

$$= mg\sin\theta - \mu\, mg\cos\theta$$ [1]

$\therefore$ Work done by the force F for motion of block,

$$W = Fx = mg(\sin\theta - \mu \cos\theta)x$$ [1/2]

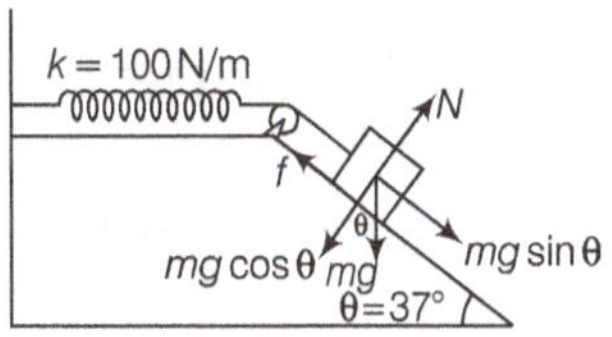

When the block stops, the work done is stored in the spring in the form of its potential energy,

$$U = \frac{1}{2} kx^2$$ [2]

$$\therefore \quad mg\,(\sin\theta - \mu \cos\theta)\,x = \frac{1}{2} kx^2$$

$$\Rightarrow \quad \mu = \frac{1}{\cos\theta} \left[\sin\theta - \frac{kx}{2\,mg} \right]$$ [1/2]

Substituting the values, we get

$$\mu = \frac{1}{\cos 37°} \left[\sin 37° - \frac{100 \times 0.1}{2 \times 1 \times 10} \right]$$ [1]

$$= \frac{1}{0.8} [0.6 - 0.5] = 0.125$$

TOPIC 03 Power and Collision

Power

Power of a person or machine is defined as the time rate at which work is done or energy is transferred by it.

If a person does work W in time t, then its average power is given by

$$\text{Average power } (P_{av}) = \text{Rate of doing work}$$

$$= \frac{\text{Work done}}{\text{Time taken}} = \frac{W}{t}$$

$$\boxed{\text{Average power, } P_{av} = \frac{W}{t}}$$

Thus, the average power of a force is defined as the ratio of the work, W to the total time t.

The **instantaneous power** of an agent is defined as the limiting value of the average power of an agent in a small time interval, when the time interval approaches to zero.

When work done by a force **F** for a small displacement $d\mathbf{r}$ is $dW = \mathbf{F} \cdot d\mathbf{r}$. Then, instantaneous power can be given as

$$P = \lim_{\Delta t \to 0} \frac{\Delta W}{\Delta t} = \frac{dW}{dt}$$

Now, $\quad dW = \mathbf{F} \cdot d\mathbf{r} \quad \therefore P = \mathbf{F} \cdot \frac{d\mathbf{r}}{dt}$

Again $\frac{d\mathbf{r}}{dt} = \mathbf{v}$, instantaneous velocity of an agent.

Therefore, $\quad P = \mathbf{F} \cdot \mathbf{v}$

Thus, the power of an agent at any instant is equal to the dot product of force and its velocity vectors at that instant.

Dimensional Formula of Power

Power is a scalar quantity, because it is the ratio of two scalar quantities work (W) and time (t). The dimensional formula of power is $[ML^2T^{-3}]$.

Units of Power

The SI unit of power is watt (W). The power of an agent is one watt if it does work at the rate of 1 joule per second.

$$1 \text{ watt} = \frac{1 \text{ joule}}{1 \text{ second}} = 1 \text{ Js}^{-1}$$

Another popular units of power are kilowatt and horsepower.

1 kilowatt = 1000 watt or 1 kW = 10^3 W

1 horsepower = 746 watt or 1 hp = 746 W

This unit is used to describe the output of automobiles, motorbikes, engines, etc.

Note

- Kilowatt hour (kWh) *or* Board of Trade (BOT) is the commercial unit of electrical energy.
- Relation between kWh and joule.

$$1 \text{ kWh} = 1 \text{ kW} \times 1 \text{ h} = 1000 \text{ W} \times 1 \text{ h} = 1000 \text{ Js}^{-1} \times 3600 \text{ s}$$

or $$1 \text{ kWh} = 3.6 \times 10^6 \text{ J}$$

Example 1 An elevator which can carry a maximum load of 1800 kg (elevator + passenger) is moving up with a constant speed of 2 ms^{-1}. The frictional force opposing the motion is 4000 N. Determine the minimum power delivered by the motor to the elevator in watts as well as in horsepower. **NCERT**

Sol. The downward force on the elevator is

$$F = mg + F_f$$

where, F_f is the frictional force

$$= 1800 \times 10 + 4000 = 22000 \text{ N}$$

The motor must supply enough power to balance this force. Hence, $P = Fv = 22000 \times 2 = 44000$ W

$$= \frac{44000}{746} \text{ hp} \simeq 59 \text{ hp}$$

Example 2 In generation of hydroelectric power 7.2×10^4 kg of water falls per hour from height 100 m and half of potential energy is converted to electric energy. How much power is generated? (Take, $g = 10 \text{ ms}^{-2}$)

Sol. $\therefore$ Potential energy = mgh

$$= 7.2 \times 10^4 \times 10 \times 100 = 7.2 \times 10^7 \text{ J}$$

$$\therefore \text{ Electric energy} = \frac{1}{2} \times 7.2 \times 10^7 = 3.2 \times 10^7 \text{J}$$

$$\therefore \text{ Power, } P = \frac{3.6 \times 10^7}{t} = \frac{3.6 \times 10^7}{3600} = 10^4 \text{ W}$$

Collision

A collision is an isolated event in which two or more colliding bodies exert strong forces on each other for a relatively short time. For a collision to take place, the actual physical contact is not necessary.

Collision between particles have been divided into two types

1. Elastic collision 2. Inelastic collision

	Elastic Collision	Inelastic Collision
(i)	A collision in which there is absolutely no loss of kinetic energy.	A collision in which there occurs some loss of kinetic energy.
(ii)	Forces involved during elastic collision must be conserved in nature.	Some or all forces involved during collision may be non-conservative in nature.
(iii)	The mechanical energy is not converted into heat, light, sound etc.	A part of the mechanical energy is converted into heat, light, sound, etc.
(iv)	e.g. Collision between subatomic particles, collision between glass balls, etc.	e.g. Collision between two vehicles, collision between a ball and floor.

Conservation of Linear Momentum in Collision

Consider two bodies 1 and 2 collide against each other. They exert mutual impulsive forces on each other during the collision time Δt. The changes produced in momenta of the two bodies will be

$$\Delta \mathbf{p}_1 = \mathbf{F}_{12} \, \Delta t$$

and $$\Delta \mathbf{p}_2 = \mathbf{F}_{21} \, \Delta t$$

where, $\mathbf{F}_{12}$ is the force exerted on body 1 by body 2 and $\mathbf{F}_{21}$ is the force exerted on body 2 by body 1.

According to Newton's third law of motion, we have

$$\mathbf{F}_{12} = -\mathbf{F}_{21}$$

$\therefore$ $$\mathbf{F}_{12} \, \Delta t = -\mathbf{F}_{21} \, \Delta t$$

or $$\mathbf{F}_{12} \, \Delta t + \mathbf{F}_{21} \, \Delta t = 0$$

$$\Delta \mathbf{p}_1 + \Delta \mathbf{p}_2 = 0$$

$$\Delta (\mathbf{p}_1 + \mathbf{p}_2) = 0$$

$$\boxed{\mathbf{p}_1 + \mathbf{p}_2 = \text{constant}}$$

Hence, **total linear momentum is conserved at each instant during collision.**

Elastic Collision in One Dimension

It involves two bodies moving initially along the same straight line, striking against each other without loss of kinetic energy and continuing to move along the same straight line after collision.

Suppose two bodies A and B of masses m_1 and m_2 moving along the same straight line with velocities u_1 and u_2, respectively. Let $u_1 > u_2$.

After collision, bodies A and B moving with velocities v_1 and v_2 in the same direction such that $v_2 > v_1$ as shown in figure.

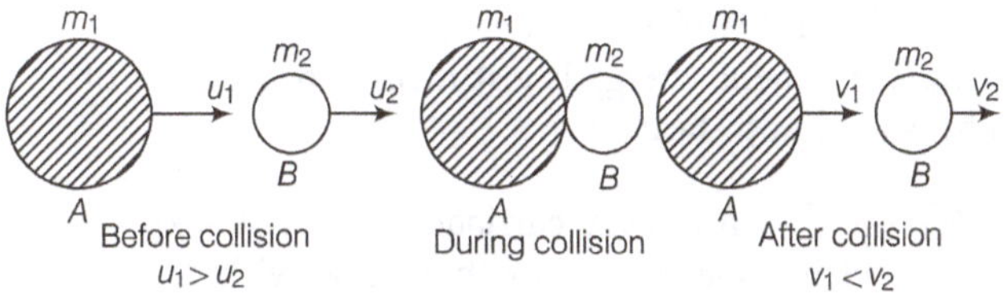

Elastic collision in one dimension

As linear momentum is conserved in any collision, we get

$$m_1u_1 + m_2u_2 = m_1v_1 + m_2v_2 \quad \ldots(i)$$

or $$m_1u_1 - m_1v_1 = m_2v_2 - m_2u_2$$

or $$m_1(u_1 - v_1) = m_2(v_2 - u_2) \quad \ldots(ii)$$

Since, **KE is also conserved in an elastic collision,** we get

$$\frac{1}{2}m_1u_1^2 + \frac{1}{2}m_2u_2^2 = \frac{1}{2}m_1v_1^2 + \frac{1}{2}m_2v_2^2$$

or $$m_1u_1^2 - m_1v_1^2 = m_2v_2^2 - m_2u_2^2$$

or $$m_1(u_1 + v_1)(u_1 - v_1) = m_2(v_2 - u_2)(v_2 + u_2) \ldots(iii)$$

Dividing Eq. (iii) by Eq. (ii), we get

$$u_1 + v_1 = v_2 + u_2$$

or $$u_1 - u_2 = v_2 - v_1 \quad \ldots(iv)$$

Hence, in one-dimensional elastic collision, relative velocity of separation after collision is equal to relative velocity of approach before collision.

Velocities of the Bodies After the Collision

From Eq. (iv), we get

$$v_2 = u_1 - u_2 + v_1 \quad \ldots(v)$$

Putting this value of v_2 in Eq. (i), we get

$$m_1u_1 + m_2u_2 = m_1v_1 + m_2(u_1 - u_2 + v_1)$$
$$= m_1v_1 + m_2u_1 - m_2u_2 + m_2v_1$$

or $$(m_1 - m_2)u_1 + 2m_2u_2 = (m_1 + m_2)v_1$$

Velocity of body A after collision,

$$v_1 = \left(\frac{m_1 - m_2}{m_1 + m_2}\right)u_1 + \left(\frac{2m_2}{m_1 + m_2}\right)u_2 \quad \ldots(vi)$$

Putting the value of v_1 in Eq. (v), we get

Velocity of body B after collision,

$$v_2 = \left(\frac{m_2 - m_1}{m_1 + m_2}\right)u_2 + \left(\frac{2m_1}{m_1 + m_2}\right)u_1 \quad \ldots(vii)$$

Eqs. (vi) and (vii) give the final velocities of the colliding bodies in terms of their initial velocities.

The two cases under the action of same and different masses can be considered as given below.

Case I When two bodies of equal masses collide.

i.e. $m_1 = m_2 = m$ say

From Eq. (vi), $v_1 = \dfrac{2mu_2}{2m} = u_2$

= velocity of body of mass m_2 before collision

From Eq. (vii), $v_2 = \dfrac{2mu_1}{2m} = u_1$

= velocity of body of mass m_1 before collision.

Hence, when two bodies of equal masses undergo perfectly elastic collision in one dimension, their velocities are just interchanged.

Case II When a light body collides against a massive stationary body.

Here, $m_1 << m_2$ and $u_2 = 0$

Neglecting m_1 in Eq. (vi), we get

$$v_1 = -\frac{m_2u_1}{m_2} = -u_1$$

From Eq. (vii), $v_2 \simeq 0$.

Hence, when a light body collides against a massive body at rest, the light body rebounds after the collision with an equal and opposite velocity while the massive body practically remains at rest.

In an elastic collision, the kinetic energy conservation holds only after the collision is over. It does not hold during the short duration of actual collision.

At the time of collision, the two colliding objects are deformed and may be momentarily at rest with respect to each other.

If the initial velocities and final velocities of both the bodies are along the same straight line, then it is called a one-dimensional collision or head-on collision.

Example 3 Two ball bearings of mass m each moving in opposite directions with equal speed collide head on with each other. Predict the outcome of the collision, assuming it to be perfectly elastic. **NCERT**

Sol. Here, $m_1 = m_2 = m$ (say)

$$u_1 = v, u_2 = -v$$

We have taken $u_1 = v$ and $u_2 = -v$ because both the ball bearings moving with same velocity but in opposite directions.

As the collision is perfectly elastic, velocities after the collision will be

$$v_1 = \frac{m_1 - m_2}{m_1 + m_2} \cdot u_1 + \frac{2m_2}{m_1 + m_2} \cdot u_2$$

$$= \frac{m - m}{m + m} \cdot v + \frac{2m}{m + m}(-v) = 0 - v = -v$$

$$v_2 = \frac{2m_1}{m_1 + m_2} \cdot u_1 + \frac{m_2 - m_1}{m_1 + m_2} \cdot u_2$$

$$= \frac{2m}{m + m} \cdot v + \frac{m - m}{m + m} \cdot (-v) = v + 0 = v$$

Thus, the two balls bounce back with equal speed after the collision.

Perfectly Inelastic Collision in One Dimension

When the two colliding bodies stick together and move as a single body with a common velocity after the collision, then the collision is **perfectly inelastic**.

As shown in figure, perfectly inelastic collision between two bodies of masses m_1 and m_2. The body of mass m_2 happens to the initially at rest ($u_2 = 0$). After the collision, the two bodies move together with common velocity v.

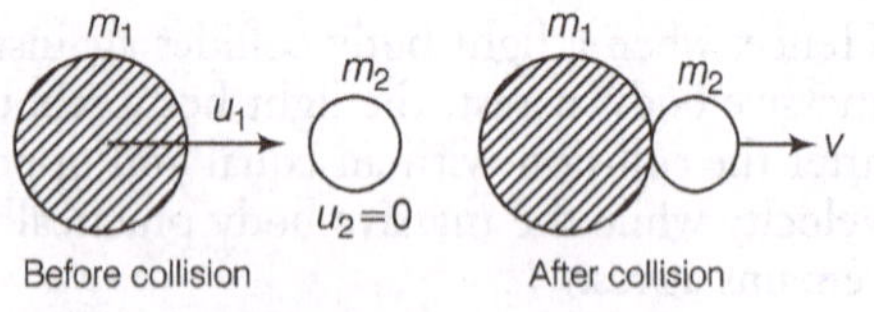

Perfectly inelastic collision

As the total linear momentum of the system remains constant, therefore $p_i = p_f$

i.e. $$m_1 u_1 + m_2 u_2 = (m_1 + m_2)\, v$$

$\therefore$ $$v = \frac{m_1 u_1}{m_1 + m_2} \qquad [\because u_2 = 0]$$

Total KE before collision, $$E_1 = \frac{1}{2} m_1 u_1^2 \qquad \text{...(i)}$$

Total KE after collision, $$E_2 = \frac{1}{2}(m_1 + m_2) v^2 \qquad \text{...(ii)}$$

On putting the value of v in Eq. (ii), we get

$$E_2 = \frac{1}{2}(m_1 + m_2)\left[\frac{m_1 u_1}{m_1 + m_2}\right]^2 = \frac{1}{2} \frac{m_1^2 u_1^2}{(m_1 + m_2)}$$

$$\text{Loss of KE} = E_1 - E_2 = \frac{1}{2} m_1 u_1^2 - \frac{m_1^2 u_1^2}{2\,(m_1 + m_2)}$$

$$\Delta\, \text{KE} = \frac{m_1^2 u_1^2 + m_1 m_2\, u_1^2 - m_1^2 u_1^2}{2\,(m_1 + m_2)} = \frac{m_1 m_2 u_1^2}{2\,(m_1 + m_2)}$$

$\therefore$ **ΔKE is a positive quantity.**

Therefore, kinetic energy is lost mainly in the form of light, sound and heat.

Example 4 A railway carriage of mass 9000kg moving with a speed of 36km/h collides with a stationary carriage of the same mass. After the collision, the carriage get coupled and move together. What is their common speed after collision? What type of collision is this?

Sol. Given, $m_1 = 9000\text{ kg}, u_1 = 36\text{ km/h} = 36 \times \frac{5}{18} = 10\text{ m/s}$

$$m_2 = 9000\text{ kg}, u_2 = 0, v_1 = v_2 = v$$

By conservation of momentum

$$m_1 u_1 + m_2 u_2 = (m_1 + m_2) v$$

$$9000 \times 10 + 9000 \times 0 = (9000 + 9000) v$$

or $$v = \frac{90000}{18000} = 5\text{ m/s}$$

$$\text{Total KE before collision} = \frac{1}{2} m_1 u_1^2 + \frac{1}{2} m_2 u_2^2$$

$$= \frac{1}{2} \times 9000 \times 10 \times 10 + 0 = 450000\text{ J}$$

$$\text{Total KE after collision} = \frac{1}{2}(m_1 + m_2) v^2$$

$$= \frac{1}{2} \times 2 \times 9000 \times (5)^2 = 225000\text{ J}$$

Thus, total KE after collision < Total KE before collision

Hence, the collision is inelastic.

Elastic Collision in Two Dimensions or Oblique Collision

Consider two objects A and B of masses m_1 and m_2 kept on the x-axis as shown in figure. Initially, the object B is at rest and A moves towards B with a speed u_1. If the collision is not head-on (the force during the collision is not along the initial velocity), the objects move along different lines.

Suppose the object A moves with a velocity $\mathbf{v}_1$ making an angle θ with the x-axis and the object B moves with a velocity $\mathbf{v}_2$ making an angle ϕ with the same axis as shown in figure.

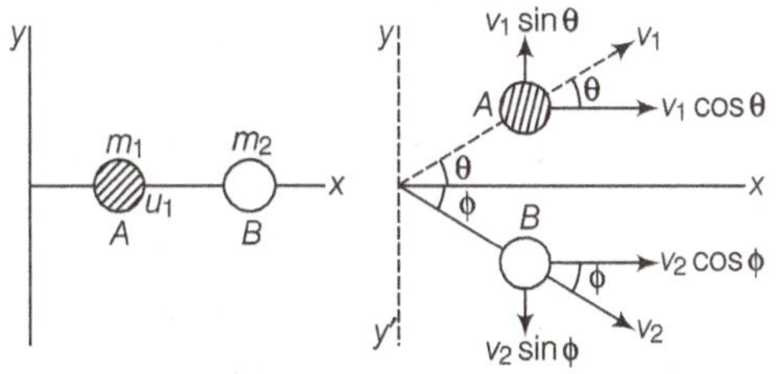

Elastic collision in two dimensions

Also, suppose $\mathbf{v}_1$ and $\mathbf{v}_2$ lie in xy-plane. Using conservation of momentum in x and y-directions, we get

$$m_1u_1 = m_1v_1\cos\theta + m_2v_2\cos\phi \quad [\because u_2 = 0] \quad \ldots\text{(i)}$$

$\because$ The initial momentum of m_1 and m_2 along y-axis is zero, then

$$0 = m_1v_1\sin\theta - m_2v_2\sin\phi \quad \ldots\text{(ii)}$$

If the collision is elastic, the final kinetic energy is equal to the initial kinetic energy.

Thus, $$\frac{1}{2}m_1u_1^2 = \frac{1}{2}m_1v_1^2 + \frac{1}{2}m_2v_2^2$$

or $$m_1u_1^2 = m_1v_1^2 + m_2v_2^2 \quad \ldots\text{(iii)}$$

The four unknown quantities v_1, v_2, θ and ϕ cannot be calculated by using the three equations (i), (ii) and (iii). But by measuring one of the four unknowns, say θ experimentally. The value of other three unknowns can be solved.

The three cases can be considered as given below.

Case I Glancing collision In a glancing collision, the incident particle does not lose any kinetic energy and is scattered almost undeflected. Thus, for such collision, when $\theta \simeq 0°$ and $\phi \simeq 90°$

From Eqs. (i) and (ii), we get

$$u_1 = v_1 \text{ and } v_2 = 0$$

$$\text{KE of the target particle} = \frac{1}{2}m_2v_2^2 = 0$$

Case II Head-on collision In this type of collision, the target particle moves in the direction of the incident particle, i.e. $\phi = 0°$. Then, Eqs. (i) and (ii), become

$$m_1u_1 = m_1v_1\cos\theta + m_2v_2$$

and $$0 = m_1v_1\sin\theta$$

Eq. (iii) for the kinetic energy remains unchanged.

Case III Elastic collision of two identical particles When two particles of same mass undergo perfectly elastic collision in two dimensions, i.e. $m_1 = m_2$.

Let us take $u_1 = u$

From Eq. (iii),

$$v_1^2 + v_2^2 = u^2 \quad \ldots\text{(iv)}$$

From Eq.(i),

$$v_1\cos\theta + v_2\cos\phi = u \quad \ldots\text{(v)}$$

From Eq. (ii),

$$v_1\sin\theta - v_2\sin\phi = 0 \quad \ldots\text{(vi)}$$

Using Eq. (v), we obtain from Eq. ... (iv)

$$v_1^2 + v_2^2 = (v_1\cos\theta + v_2\cos\phi)^2$$

$$= v_1^2\cos^2\theta + v_2^2\cos^2\phi + 2v_1v_2\cos\theta\cos\phi$$

$$\Rightarrow v_1^2(1-\cos^2\theta) + v_2^2(1-\cos^2\phi) = 2v_1v_2\cos\theta\cos\phi$$

$$v_1^2\sin^2\theta + v_2^2\sin^2\phi = 2v_1v_2\cos\theta\cos\phi \quad \ldots\text{(vii)}$$

From Eq. (vi), $v_2\sin\phi = v_1\sin\theta$

Put in Eq. (vii), $2v_1^2\sin^2\theta = 2v_1v_2\cos\theta\cos\phi$

or $$\cos\theta = \frac{2v_1^2\sin^2\theta}{2v_1v_2\cos\phi} = \left[\frac{v_1}{v_2}\right] \times \frac{\sin^2\theta}{\cos\phi} \quad \ldots\text{(viii)}$$

We know

$\cos(\theta+\phi) = \cos\theta\cos\phi - \sin\theta\sin\phi$

Using Eq. (viii) and Eq. (vi), we get

$$\cos(\theta+\phi) = \frac{v_1\sin^2\theta}{v_2\cos\phi}\cos\phi - \frac{v_1}{v_2}\sin^2\theta = 0$$

$$\therefore \quad \theta + \phi = 90°$$

Hence, we conclude that in a perfectly elastic collision, when a moving particle of mass m collides elastically in two dimensions with another particle of mass m, after collision the two particles will move at right angle to each other.

Example 5 A particle of mass m moving on a smooth surface with velocity 10 m/s strike another particle of mass $2m$ moving with 5 m/s in the same direction. If the collision is elastic and head-on, find the velocities of particle after the collision.

Sol. Given, $m_1 = m$, $m_2 = 2m$, $u_1 = 10$ m/s, $u_2 = 5$ m/s

By law of conservation of momentum,

$$m \times 10 + 2m \times 5 = mv_1 + 2mv_2$$

$$\Rightarrow \quad v_1 + 2v_2 = 20 \quad \ldots\text{(i)}$$

For head-on collision,

$$v_1 + u_1 = v_2 + u_2$$

$$\Rightarrow \quad v_1 - v_2 = 5 - 10 = -5 \quad \ldots\text{(ii)}$$

Solving Eqs. (i) and (ii), we get

$$v_1 = \frac{10}{3}\text{ m/s},$$

$$v_2 = \frac{25}{3}\text{ m/s}$$

Inelastic Collision in Two Dimensions

When two bodies travelling initially along the same straight line collide involving some loss of kinetic energy and move after collision along different directions in a plane.

Steps to be used for Solving Problems based on Two Dimensional Collision

Step I Firstly find out both x and y-coordinates. It is convenient to have either the x-axis or y-axis coincide with the direction of one of the initial velocities.

Step II Draw a diagram, labelling velocity vectors and masses.

Step III Write a separate conservation of momentum equation for each of the x and y-axes. In each case, total initial momentum in a given direction equal to the final momentum in that direction.

Step IV If the collision is in elastic, then write a general expression for the total energy before and after the collision. Equate both the equations to get unknown value.

Step V There are two equations for inelastic collisions and three for elastic collision.

Example 6 **Inelastic Collision between Two Balls**

A ball moving with a speed of 9 m/s strikes an identical ball at rest, such that after collision, the direction of each ball makes an angle of 30° with the original line of motion. Find the speed of the two balls after collision.

Sol. Given, $m_1 = m_2 = m$, $u_1 = 9$ m/s, $u_2 = 0$

$\theta_1 = \theta_2 = 30°$, $v_1 = ?$, $v_2 = ?$

According to principle of conservation of linear momentum.

$$m_1u_1 + m_2u_2 = m_1v_1 \cos\theta_1 + m_2v_2 \cos\theta_2$$

Along the direction of motion in x-axis

$$m \times 9 + 0 = mv_1 \cos 30° + mv_2 \cos 30°$$

$$9 = v_1 \frac{\sqrt{3}}{2} + v_2 \frac{\sqrt{3}}{2} = \frac{(v_1 + v_2)\sqrt{3}}{2}$$

$$v_1 + v_2 = \frac{18}{\sqrt{3}} \quad \text{...(i)}$$

Along the direction of motion in y-axis

$$0 + 0 = m_1v_1 \sin\theta_1 - m_2 v_2 \sin\theta_2$$

$$m_1v_1 \sin\theta_1 = m_2v_2 \sin\theta_2$$

$$\Rightarrow \quad mv_1 \sin 30° = mv_2 \sin 30° \Rightarrow v_1 = v_2 \quad \text{...(ii)}$$

Substituting value from Eq. (ii) in Eq. (i), then find out values of v_1 and v_2

$$2v_1 = \frac{18}{\sqrt{3}} \Rightarrow v_1 = \frac{9}{\sqrt{3}} \times \frac{\sqrt{3}}{\sqrt{3}} = \frac{9\sqrt{3}}{3} = 3\sqrt{3} \text{ m/s}$$

Hence, two balls move with same velocity = $3\sqrt{3}$ m/s after collision.

Topic Practice 3

Multiple Choice Questions

(1 Mark)

1. Which quantity of the following is force times the velocity?
(a) Work (b) Energy
(c) Power (d) Kinetic energy

2. A one kilowatt motor is used to pump water from a well 10 m deep. The quantity of water pumped out per second is nearly
(a) 1kg (b) 10 kg
(c) 100 kg (d) 1000 kg

3. A ball of mass m elastically collides with a wall with velocity v, then change in its momentum is equal to
(a) $2m$ (b) $2mv$
(c) $8mv$ (d) zero

4. A bomb of mass 30 kg at rest explodes into two pieces of masses 18 kg and 12 kg. The velocity of 18 kg mass is 6 ms^{-1}. The velocity of the other mass is
(a) 3 m/s (b) 9 m/s (c) 12 m/s (d) 6 m/s

5. A molecule in a gas container hits a horizontal wall with speed 200 ms^{-1} and at an angle 30° with the normal and rebounds with the same speed. Which statement is true?
(a) Momentum is conserved (b) Elastic collision
(c) Inelastic collision (d) Both (a) and (b)

6. From the following example, which is not a perfectly inelastic collision?
(a) A bullet fired into a block and gets embedded into it
(b) Capture of an electron by an atom
(c) A man jumping onto a moving boat
(d) A ball bearing striking another ball bearing

Very Short Answer Type Questions

(1 Mark)

7. Out of joule, calorie, kilowatt and electron volt, which one is the unit of power?

8. A bullet gets embedded in a wooden block, where does its kinetic energy go?

9. Is the total linear momentum conserved during the short time of an elastic collision of two balls ?

10. Which physical terms remain conserved in an inelastic collision?

11. Is collision between two particles possible even without any physical contact between them?

12. In what type of collision, maximum kinetic energy is transferred?

13. In which of the two types of collision i.e. elastic or inelastic, the momentum is conserved? What about KE?

14. If two bodies collide and one is initially at rest. Is it possible for any one to be at rest after collision?

Short answer Type I Questions

2 Marks

15. Show that the instantaneous power is given by the scalar product of force and velocity.

16. Throwing mud on a wall is an example of perfectly inelastic collision. Comment.

17. Two ball bearings of mass m each moving in opposite directions with equal speed v collide head-on with each other. Predict the outcome of the collision, assuming it to be perfectly elastic.

18. What is glancing collision? Find kinetic energy of target particle in it.

Short Answer Type II Questions

3 Marks

19. Explain the principle of conservation of linear momentum in collision.

20. Write differences between elastic and inelastic collision.

21. Which of the following potential energy curves in figure cannot possibly describe the elastic collision of two billiard balls? Here, r is the distance between centres of the balls. **NCERT**

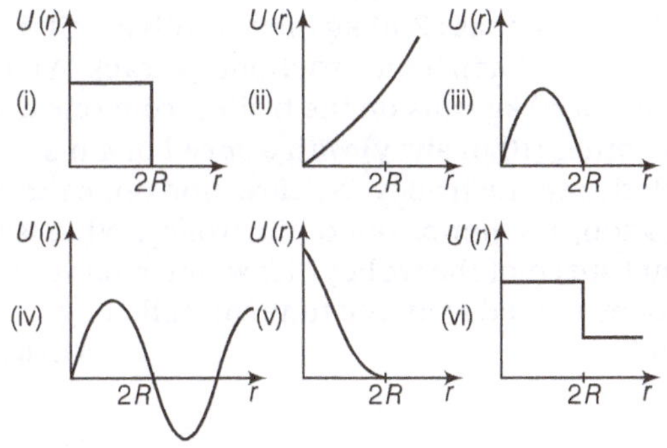

22. Two identical ball bearings in contact with each other and resting on a frictionless table are hit head-on by another ball bearing of the same mass moving initially with a speed v. If the collision is elastic, which of the following (figure) is a possible result after collision? **NCERT**

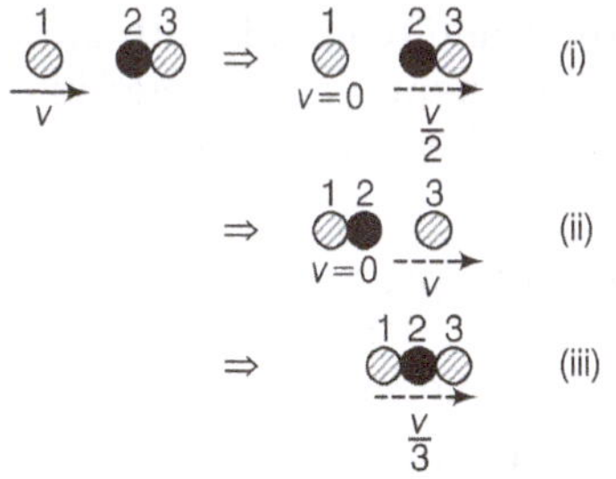

23. Explain perfectly inelastic collision in one dimension. Find the velocity after collision.

Long Answer Type Questions

5 Marks

24. State if each of the following statements is true or false. Give reasons for your answer.
   (i) In an elastic collision of two bodies, the momentum and energy of each body is conserved.
   (ii) Total energy of a system is always conserved, no matter what internal and external forces on the body are present?
   (iii) Work done in the motion of a body over a closed loop is zero for every force in nature.
   (iv) In an inelastic collision, the final kinetic energy is always less than the initial kinetic energy of the system. **NCERT**

25. Answer carefully with reasons
   (i) In an elastic collision of two billiard balls, is the total kinetic energy conserved during the short time of collision of the balls i.e. when they are in contact? **NCERT**
   (ii) Is the total linear momentum conserved during the short time of an elastic collision of two balls?
   (iii) What are the answer to (i) and (ii) for an inelastic collision?
   (iv) If the potential energy of two billiard balls depends only on the separation distance between their centres, is the collision elastic or inelastic? (Note : We are talking here of potential energy corresponding to the force during collision, not gravitational potential energy.)

Numerical Problems

26. A train has a constant speed of 40 ms^{-1} on a level road against resistive force of magnitude 3×10^4 N. Find the power of the engine. [1M]

27. A molecule in a gas container hits a horizontal wall with speed 200 ms^{-1} and angle 30° with the normal, and rebounds with the same speed. Is momentum conserved in the collision? Is the collision elastic or inelastic? NCERT [2M]

28. The bob *A* of a pendulum released from 30° to the vertical hits another bob *B* of the same mass at rest on a table as shown in figure. How high does the bob *A* rise after the collision? Neglect the size of the bobs and assume the collision to be elastic. NCERT [2M]

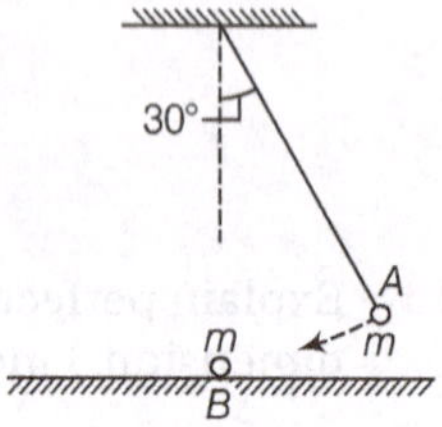

29. A ball is moving with velocity 2 ms^{-1} towards a heavy wall moving towards the ball with speed 1 ms^{-1} as shown in figure. Assuming collision to be elastic, find the velocity of ball immediately after the collision.

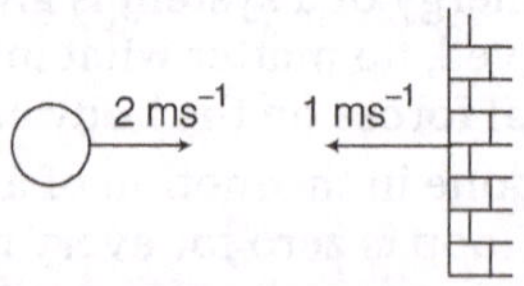

[2M]

30. Calculate the power of an electric engine which can lift 20 tonne of coal per hour from a mine 180 m deep. [1M]

31. Calculate the power of a motor which is capable of raising of water in 5 min from a well 120 m deep. [2M]

32. A spherical ball *A* of mass 4 kg, moving along a straight line strikes another spherical ball *B* of mass 1 kg at rest. After the collision, *A* and *B* move with velocity v_A and v_B respectively, making angle of 30° and 60° with respect to the original direction of motion *A*, then find the ratio $\frac{v_A}{v_B}$. [3M]

33. A pump on the ground floor of a building can pump up water to fill a tank of volume 30 m^3 in 15 min. If the tank is 40 m above the ground, and the efficiency of the pump is 30%, how much electric power is consumed by the pump? NCERT [3M]

34. A simple pendulum of length 1 m has a wooden bob of mass 1 kg. It is struck by a bullet of mass 10^{-2} kg moving with a speed of 2×10^2 ms^{-1}. The bullet gets embedded into the bob. Obtain the height to which the bob rises before swinging back. [3M]

35. A train of mass 2×10^5 kg has a constant speed of 20 ms^{-1} up a hill inclined at $\theta = \sin^{-1}\left(\frac{1}{50}\right)$ to the horizontal when the engine is working at 8×10^5 W. Find the resistance to motion of the train. (Take, $g = 9.8 ms^{-2}$). [3M]

36. A family uses 8 kW of power. (i) Direct solar energy is incident on the horizontal surface at an average rate of 200 W per square metre. If 20% of this energy can be converted to useful electrical energy, how large an area is needed to supply 8 kW? (ii) Compare this area to that of the roof of a typical house. NCERT [3M]

37. The blades of a windmill sweep out a circle of area *A*. (i) If the wind flows at a velocity *v* perpendicular to the circle, what is the mass of the air passing through it in time *t*? (ii) What is the kinetic energy of the air? (iii) Assume that the windmill converts 25% of the wind's energy into electrical energy, and that $A = 30\ m^2$, $v = 36$ km/h and the density of the air is 1.2 kg m^{-3}. What is the electrical power produced? [3M]

38. A bullet of mass 0.012 kg and horizontal speed 70 ms^{-1} strikes a block of wood of mass 0.4 kg and instantly comes to rest with respect to the block. The block is suspended from the ceilling by means of thin wires. Calculate the height to which the block rises. Also, estimate the amount of heat produced to the block. NCERT [3M]

39. A trolley of mass 200 kg moves with a uniform speed of 36 km/h on a frictionless track. A child of mass 20 kg runs on the trolley from one end to the other (10 m away) with a speed of 4 ms^{-1} relative to the trolley in a direction opposite to its motion, and jumps out of the trolley. What is the final speed of the trolley? How much has the trolley moved from the time the child begins to run? NCERT [3M]

40. (i) In unloading grain from the hold of a ship, an elevator lifts the grain through a distance of 12 m. Grain is discharged at the top of the elevator at a rate of 2 kg each second and the discharge speed of each grain particle is 3 ms^{-1}. Find the minimum horsepower of the motor that can elevate grain in this way. (Take, $g = 10 \text{ ms}^{-2}$)

(ii) An engine pumps 400 kg of water through height of 10 m in 40 s. Find the power of the engine, if its efficiency is 80%. (Take, $g = 10 \text{ ms}^{-2}$) **[5M]**

Hints & Solutions

1. (*c*) Power, $P = Fv$

2. (*b*) As, power $(P) = \dfrac{\text{Work done}}{\text{Time taken}}$

$$P = \frac{W}{t} = \frac{mgh}{t} \Rightarrow \frac{P}{gh} = \frac{m}{t}$$

$$\Rightarrow \frac{1000}{10 \times 10} = \frac{m}{t} \Rightarrow \frac{1000}{100} \times 1 = m \qquad (\because t = 1 \text{ s})$$

$$\Rightarrow m = 10 \text{ kg}$$

So, quantity of water pumped out per second is 10 kg.

3. (*b*) Let the direction in which ball is moving be taken as positive, after collision with the wall the direction of velocity is reversed.

Hence, change in momentum

= initial momentum-final momentum.

$= mv - (-mv) = 2\,mv$

4. (*b*) Applying conservation of linear momentum, we write,

$$m_1 u_1 = m_2 u_2$$

Here, $m_1 = 18 \text{ kg}, m_2 = 12 \text{ kg}$

$u_1 = 6 \text{ ms}^{-1}, u_2 = ?$

$\therefore \quad 18 \times 6 = 12 u_2$

$$\Rightarrow u_2 = \frac{18 \times 6}{12} = 9 \text{ ms}^{-1}$$

5. (*d*) Linear momentum remains conserved in elastic collision as well as in inelastic collision but kinetic energy remains conserved only in an elastic.

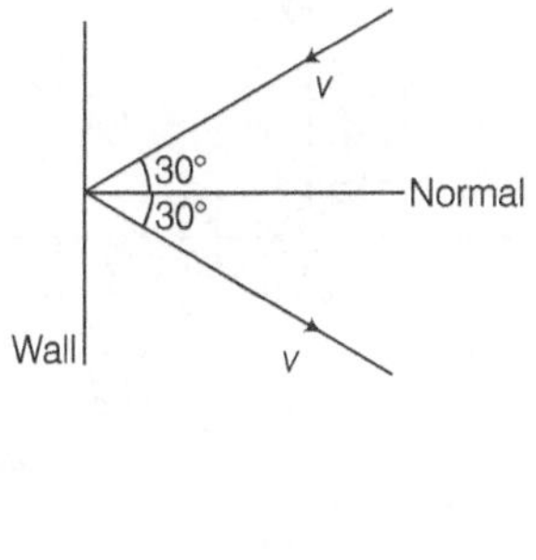

Given that the speed of the molecule of gas is same before and after the collision, therefore its kinetic energy is conserved. Hence, the collision is elastic.

6. (*d*) When a ball bearing striking against another ball bearing, whole kinetic energy is not lost. So, it is not a perfectly inelastic collision.

7. Kilowatt is the unit of power and rest are units of energy.

8. Kinetic energy of bullet gets converted into heat and sound energy.

9. During the short interval of an elastic collision, total linear momentum is conserved.

10. In an inelastic collision, total momentum as well as total energy remain conserved.

11. Yes, in atomic and subatomic particles collision without any physical contact between the colliding particles is taking place e.g. Rutherford's alpha particles scattering.

12. Maximum kinetic energy is transferred when two bodies of equal mass collide.

13. Momentum is conserved in both the types of collisions, but KE is conserved only in elastic collision.

14. Yes, when masses of two objects are equal and collision is perfectly elastic.

15. Refer to text on page 177 (Power).

16. True, when mud is trown on a wall, it sticks to it. The kinetic energy of the mud becomes zero and it cannot separates from the wall on its own. So, it is an example of perfectly inelastic collision. [2]

17. Here, $M_1 = M_2 = m, u_1 = v$ and $u_2 = -v$

Now, $v_1 = \dfrac{(M_1 - M_2)u_1 + 2M_2 u_2}{M_1 + M_2}$

$= \dfrac{(m - m)v + 2m(-v)}{m + m} = -v$ [1]

and $v_2 = \dfrac{(M_2 - M_1)u_2 + 2M_1 u_1}{M_1 + M_2}$

$= \dfrac{(m - m)(-v) + 2mv}{m + m} = v$

After collision, the two ball bearings will move with same speed but their directions of motion will be reversed. [1]

18. Refer to text on page 181 (Elastic collision in two dimensions or oblique collision-Case I).

19. Refer to text on page 178 (Conservation of linear momentum in collision).

20. Refer to text on page 178 (Collision).

21. When two billiard balls collide then distance between their centres is $2R$. Due to impact of collision there is small temporary deformation of balls. In this process, KE of ball is gradually reduced to zero and converted into elastic potential energy of balls. [1½]

When KE is zero, the balls regain their original configuration due to elasticity. The phenomenon can be successfully explained only by potential energy curve number (v), because here as $r < 2R$, the potential energy function $U(r)$ is increasing gradually on decreasing value of r. [1½]

22. We know that when two bodies of same mass collide, they interchange their velocities. When first ball collides with the combinations of balls 2 and 3, the first ball comes to rest while ball number 2 moves with velocity v again it collides with ball number 3 and hence ball number 2 comes to rest while ball number 3 moves with velocity v. [2]

Hence, the situation shown in Fig. (ii) is the correct result of collision. [1]

23. Refer to text on page 180 (Perfectly inelastic collision in one dimension).

24. (i) False, in elastic collision the linear momentum and kinetic energy of the system as a whole is conserved, but momentum and kinetic energy of each of individual body change. [1]

(ii) False, internal as well as external forces can change the kinetic energy. Again forces if conservative may change the potential energy of a system. [1]

(iii) False, for non-conservative force the work done over a closed loop is not zero. [1]

(iv) It is usually true but not always true. As an example in the explosion of a cracker final kinetic energy is greater than the initial kinetic energy.
Again final kinetic energy of gun-bullet system after firing is more than initial kinetic energy before collision. [2]

25. (i) No, the total kinetic energy, does not remain conserved during the short time when two billiard balls are in contact. At that time, balls are at rest and their KE is zero. In fact, all this KE has been transformed into elastic potential energy of balls. [1]

(ii) Yes, total linear momentum remains conserved during the short time of an elastic collision of two balls. The balls exert forces on one another due to which individual momenta of two balls change but total linear momentum remains conserved. [1]

(iii) For an inelastic, collision kinetic energy is not conserved but total linear momentum is conserved even now. [1]

(iv) As the potential energy depends only on the separation distance between the centres of balls, it means that conservative forces are in action (because PE changes due to conservative forces only). Hence, collision is surely inelastic collision. [2]

26. At constant speed, there is no acceleration, so the forces acting on the train are in equilibrium.

Therefore, $F = R$

$\therefore$ $F = 3\times10^4$ N or $P = Fv$

We have, power $= 3\times10^4 \times 40 = 1.2\times10^6$ W [1]

27. Yes, momentum remains conserved in the collision. To check whether the collision is elastic or inelastic, we consider the kinetic energy of the molecule. [1]

We find that the initial kinetic energy $\left(\frac{1}{2}mu^2\right)$ is the same as final KE. $\left(\frac{1}{2}mv^2\right)$ of the molecule as

$u = v = 200$ m / s i.e. thus the collision is elastic collision. [1]

28. When the pendulum bob A reaches the position B, its velocity is horizontal and it strikes the mass m placed at B. Since, the collision is one-dimensional and elastic, the bob exchange their velocities being of the same mass. The bob A does not rise at all and the bob B begins to move with the velocity of A. [2]

29. The speed of wall will not change after the collision. So, let v be the velocity of the ball after collision in the direction shown in figure. Since, collision is elastic ($e = 1$),

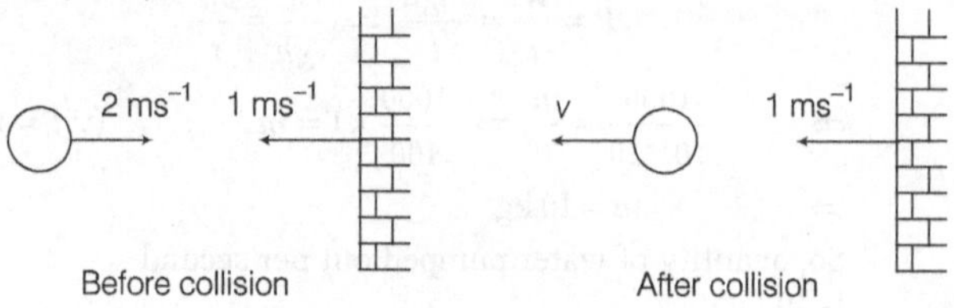

[1]

separation speed = approach speed

or $v - 1 = 2 + 1$ or $v = 4$ ms^{-1} [1]

30. Power $= \dfrac{\text{Work done}}{\text{Time taken}} = \dfrac{mgh}{t} = \dfrac{20\times1000\times9.8\times180}{60\times60}$

$= 9800$ W $= 9.8$ kW

31. Here, the volume of water raised $V = 2000$ L

Density of water, $\rho = 1$ kg/L [1]

$\therefore$ Mass of water raised, $m = V\rho = 2000\times1 = 2000$ kg

Power, $P = \dfrac{W}{t} = \dfrac{mgh}{t}$

$= \dfrac{2000\times9.8\times120}{5\times60} = 7840$ W

$= 7.840$ kW [$\because$ 1kW = 1000 W] [1]

32. According to given condition, following figure represents required situation.

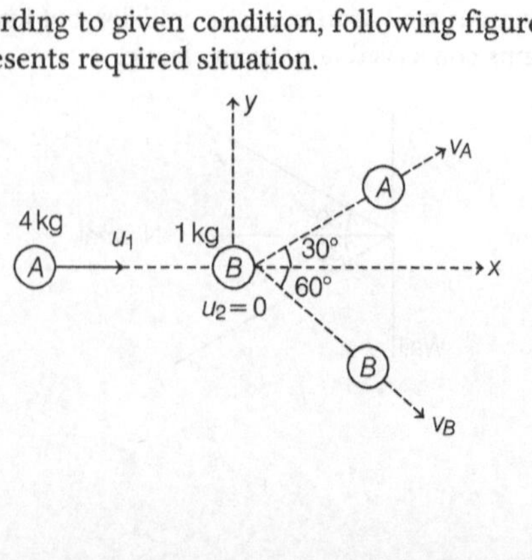

[1]

Applying the law of conservation of linear momentum along a direction perpendicular to the direction of motion (i.e. along y-axis), we get

$$0+0 = 4v_A \sin 30° - 1 \cdot v_B \sin 60° \quad [1]$$

$$4v_A \sin 30° = v_B \sin 60°$$

$$\Rightarrow \quad \frac{v_A}{v_B} = \frac{\sin 60°}{4\sin 30°} = \frac{(\sqrt{3}/2)}{(4 \times 1/2)}$$

$$\therefore \quad \frac{v_A}{v_B} = \frac{\sqrt{3}}{4} \quad [1]$$

33. Here, volume of water lifted V = volume of tank $= 30 \text{ m}^3$, time $t = 15 \text{ min} = 900 \text{ s}$,

Height of tank, $h = 40$ m and efficiency of motor, $\eta = 30\%$

$\therefore$ Output of motor = work done to raise water

$$= mgh = V\rho gh \quad [1]$$

$$\therefore \text{ Output power} = \frac{V\rho gh}{t} = \frac{30 \times 10^3 \times 9.8 \times 40}{900}$$

$$= 1.307 \times 10^4 \text{ W} \quad [1]$$

$$\therefore \quad \text{Input power} = \frac{\text{Output power}}{\eta} = + \frac{1.307 \times 10^4}{\frac{30}{100}}$$

$$= \frac{1.307 \times 10^4 \times 100}{30} = 4.357 \times 10^4 \text{ W}$$

$$= 43.57 \text{ kW} \quad [\because 1\text{kW}=1000\text{W}] \quad [1]$$

34. Applying principle of conservation of linear momentum,

$$mu = (M+m)v$$

$$\Rightarrow \quad 10^{-2} \times (2 \times 10^2) = (1 + 0.01)\, v$$

$$\Rightarrow \quad v = \frac{2}{1.01}$$

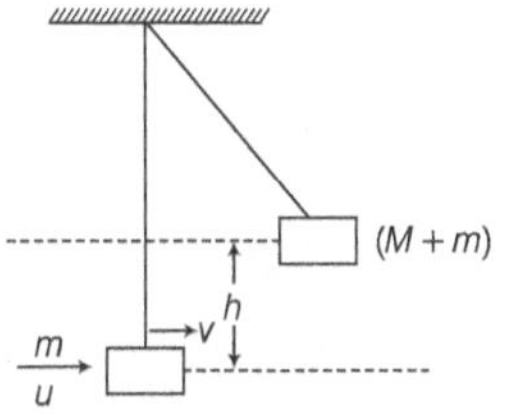

[1½]

KE_1 of the block with bullet in it, is converted into PE as it rises through a height h,

$$\frac{1}{2}(M+m)v^2 = (M+m)gh$$

$$\Rightarrow \quad h = \frac{v^2}{2g} = \left(\frac{2}{1.01}\right) \times \frac{1}{2 \times 9.8} = 0.2 \text{ m} \quad [1½]$$

35. Since, $P = Fv$

$$\Rightarrow \ F = \frac{P}{v} = \frac{8 \times 10^5}{20}$$

$$= 4 \times 10^4 \text{ N}$$

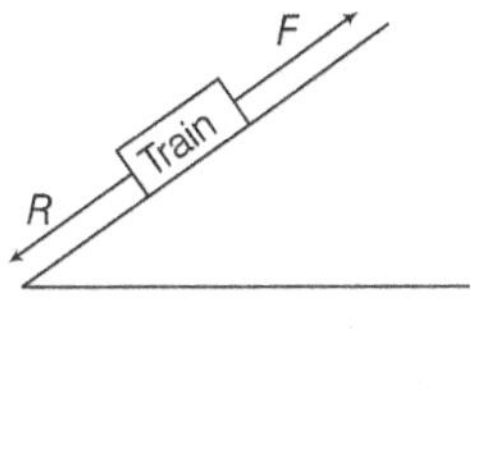

At constant speed, the forces acting on the train are in equilibrium. Resolving the forces parallel to the hill,

$$F = R + (2.0 \times 10^5) g \times \frac{1}{50}$$

$$4 \times 10^4 = R + 39200 \ \text{ or } \ R = 800 \text{ N}$$

Therefore, the resistance is 800 N.

36. (i) Power used by family, $P = 8 \text{ kW} = 8000 \text{ W}$

As only 20% of solar energy can be converted to useful electrical energy, hence power to be supplied by solar energy $\frac{8000 \text{ W}}{20\%} = 40000 \text{ W}$ [1]

As solar energy is incident at a rate of 200 Wm^{-2}, hence the area needed

$$A = \frac{40000 \text{ W}}{200 \text{ Wm}^{-2}} = 200 \text{ m}^2 \quad [1]$$

(ii) The area needed is comparable to roof area of a large sized house. [1]

37. (i) Area swept by blades of windmill = A and wind velocity = v [1]

$\therefore$ Volume of air passing per unit time = Av

$\therefore$ Mass of air passing per unit time = $Av\rho$

and mass of air passing in time t, $M = Av\rho t$

(ii) KE of said quantity of air, $K = \frac{1}{2} Mv^2 = \frac{1}{2} A\rho t v^3$ [1]

(iii) If efficiency of windmill be 25%, then

Output electrical power = 25% of input power

$$= \frac{25}{100} \times \frac{1}{2} A\rho v^3$$

As $A = 30 \text{ m}^2$, $v = 36 \text{ km/h} = 36 \times \frac{5}{18} \text{ m/s}$

$= 10$ m/s and $\rho = 1.2 \text{ kgm}^{-3}$ [1/2]

$\therefore$ Output electrical power $= \frac{25}{100} \times \frac{1}{2} \times 30 \times 1.2 \times (10)^3$

$= 4500 \text{ W} = 4.5 \text{ kW}$ [1 kW = 1000 W] [1/2]

38. Here, mass of bullet $m = 0.012$ kg, initial speed of bullet $u = 70 \text{ ms}^{-1}$, mass of wood block $M = 0.4$ kg. [1]

As on collision, the bullet comes to rest w.r.t. block, it means that after collision bullet and block are moving with a common speed v.

From conservation law of momentum $mu = (M + m)\, v$

$$\Rightarrow \quad v = \frac{mu}{(M+m)} = \frac{0.012 \times 70}{(0.4 + 0.012)} = 2.04 \text{ m s}^{-1} \quad [1]$$

If the block now rises to a maximum height of h, then using conservation law of mechanical energy, we have

$$\frac{1}{2}(M+m)\, v^2 - 0 = (M+m)\, gh$$

$$\Rightarrow \quad h = \frac{v^2}{2g} = \frac{(2.04)^2}{2 \times 9.8} = 0.212 \text{ m} = 21.2 \text{ cm} \quad [1]$$

39. Let there be an observer travelling parallel to the trolley with the same speed. He will observe the initial momentum of the trolley of mass M and child of mass m as zero. When the child jumps in opposite direction, he will observe the increase in the velocity of the trolley by

Δv. Let u be the velocity of the child. He will observe child landing at velocity $(u - \Delta v)$.

Therefore, final momentum $= M\Delta v - m(u - \Delta v)$

From the law of conservation of momentum, we have

$$M\Delta v - m(u - \Delta v) = 0 \Rightarrow \Delta v = \frac{mu}{M + m}$$

Putting various values, we have [1]

$$\Delta v = \frac{4 \times 20}{20 + 220} = 0.33 \text{ ms}^{-1}$$ [1]

$\therefore$ Final speed of trolley is 10.36 ms^{-1}

The child take 2.5 s to run on the trolley.

Therefore, the trolley moves a distance

$$= 2.5 \times 10.36 \text{ m} = 25.9 \text{ m}$$ [1]

40. (i) The work done by the motor each second, i.e.

$$\text{Power} = mgh + \frac{1}{2}mv^2, \text{ as } t = 1 \text{ s}.$$ [1]

Given, $m = 2$ kg, $v = 3 \text{ ms}^{-1}$ and $h = 12$ m.

$$\therefore \text{Power} = 2 \times (10) \times (12) + \frac{1}{2}(2)(3)^2$$

$$= 249 \text{ W} = \frac{249}{746} = 0.33 \text{ HP}$$ [1]

The motor must have an output of at least 0.33 HP.

(ii) Work done by engine against gravity,

$$W = mgh = 400 \times 10 \times 10 = 40 \text{ kJ}$$ [1]

Power used by engine (output power) $= \frac{W}{\Delta t}$

$$= \frac{40 \times 10^3}{40} W = 1 \text{ kW}$$ [1]

If power of the engine is P (input power), then

$$\eta = \frac{\text{Output power}}{\text{Input power}}$$

$$P = \frac{1 \text{ kw}}{80\%} \Rightarrow P = \frac{1000 \times 100}{80} \text{ W} = 1.25 \text{ kW}$$ [1]

Summary

- Work is said to be done whenever a force acts on a body and the body moves through some distance in the direction of the force. It is the dot product of force and displacement i.e. $W = \mathbf{F} \cdot \mathbf{s} = Fs\cos\theta$, where θ is the angle between $\mathbf{F}$ and s.
  (i) If $\theta = 90$; then $W = 0$, (ii) $\theta < 90$, then $W = +$ ve, (iii) $\theta > 90$; then $W = -$ve
- Work done is a scalar quantity measured in newton-metre. Its dimension is $[ML^2T^{-2}]$.
- The SI unit of work is joule and the CGS unit of work is erg. $1\,\text{joule} = 10^7$ erg
- Work done by variable force F is given by $W = \int F \cdot ds =$ Area under the force-displacement curve.
  (a) Forces are **conservative** if,
    (i) Work done in a closed path is zero.
    (ii) Work done is independent of path.
  (b) Forces are **non-conservation** if,
    (i) Work done in a closed path is not zero.
    (ii) Work done depends upon the path.
- The energy of a body is defined as its ability of doing work. It is a scalar quantity. Like work, SI unit of energy is joule and the CGS unit is erg.
- The energy possessed by a body by virtue of its motion is called kinetic energy. The KE of a body of mass m moving with velocity v is given by $KE = \frac{1}{2}mv^2$ or $\frac{p^2}{2m}$
- **According to work-energy theorem**, the work done by the net force acting on a body is equal to the change in kinetic energy of the body. $W =$ Change in $KE = \frac{1}{2}mv^2 - \frac{1}{2}mu^2$
- The energy possessed by a body by virtue of its position or configuration is called its **potential energy**.
- The gravitational potential energy of an object of mass m at height h from the earth's surface is given by $u = mgh$, where g is acceleration due to gravity.
- The energy associated with the state of compression or extension of an elastic (spring like) object is called elastic potential energy. If a spring is stretched through a distance x, then the elastic potential energy of the spring is given by
- $u = \frac{1}{2}kx^2$, where k is the force constant of the spring.
- **Power** is the rate of doing work. $P = \frac{\text{Energy}}{\text{Time}}$ or $\frac{\text{Work done}}{\text{Time}}$. It is a scalar quantity and it is measured in Js^{-1} or watt.
- A collision in which both the momentum and kinetic energy of the body remains conserved is called **elastic collision**.
- A collision in which only the momentum of the system is conserved but kinetic energy is not conserved is called **inelastic collision**.
- If the colliding bodies move along the same straight line path before and after the collision, then the collision is said to be one dimensional collision.
- If the two bodies do not move along the same straight line path before and after the collision, then the collision is said to be two dimensional or oblique collision.
- If two bodies of masses m_1 and m_2 moving with velocities u_1 and u_2 $(u_2 > u_1)$ in the same direction suffer head-on elastic collision such that v_1 and v_2 be their respective velocities after collision, then

$$v_1 = \left(\frac{m_1 - m_2}{m_1 + m_2}\right)u_1 + \left(\frac{2m_2}{m_1 + m_2}\right)u_2 \text{ and}$$

$$v_2 = \left(\frac{2m_1}{m_1 + m_2}\right)u_1 + \left(\frac{m_2 - m_1}{m_1 + m_2}\right)u_2$$

- If a body of mass m_1 moving with velocity u_1 collides with another body of mass m_2 and sticks to it (i.e. collision is perfectly inelastic collision), then the final common velocity is given by $v = \frac{m_1u_1}{m_1 + m_2}$
- In such a case loss in kinetic energy of the system is

$$\Delta KE = \frac{m_1m_2u_1^2}{2(m_1 + m_2)}$$

- If a particle of mass m_1 moving with velocity u_1 collides with another particle of mass m_2 at rest, then after the collision the two particles move with velocities v_1 and v_2, making angles θ_1 and θ_2 with x-axis

$$m_1v_1\sin\theta_1 = m_2v_2\sin\theta_2 \text{ (along } y\text{-axis)}$$

$$m_1u_1 = m_1v_1\cos\theta + m_1v_2\cos\theta_2 \text{ (along } x\text{-axis)}$$

Chapter Practice

Multiple Choice Questions

1 Mark

1. A thin rod of mass m elongates by l when a body of mass m is suspended from it. The work done is
(a) mgl (b) $\frac{1}{2}mgl$ (c) $2\,mgl$ (d) zero

2. A force which is inversely proportional to the speed is acting on a body. The kinetic energy of the body starting from rest is
(a) a constant
(b) inversely proportional to time
(c) directly proportional to time
(d) directly proportional to square of time

3. The negative of the work done by the conservative internal forces on a system equals to the change in
(a) total energy (b) kinetic energy
(c) potential energy (d) None of these

4. A bent bow used for shooting an arrow possesses
(a) potential energy (b) kinetic energy
(c) heat energy (d) chemical energy

5. Two springs have their force constants as k_1 and k_2 $(k_1 > k_2)$. When both the springs are stretched by same amount of length, the work done is
(a) equal in both (b) greater for k_1
(c) greater for k_2 (d) incomplete data

6. Consider the collision depicted in figure to be between two billiard balls with equal masses $m_1 = m_2$. The first ball is called the cue while the second ball is called the target. The billiard player wants to 'sink' the target ball in a corner pocket, which is at an angle $\theta_2 = 37°$.

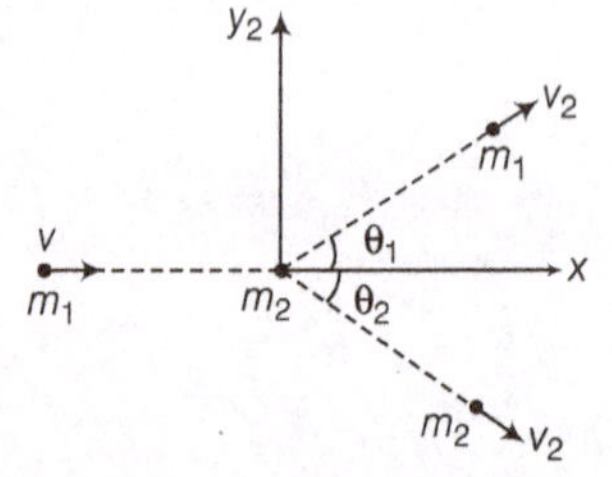

Assume that the collision is elastic and that friction and rotational motion are not important. Obtain θ_1.
(a) 58° (b) 54° (c) 53° (d) 90°

Assertion and Reason

Directions (Q. Nos. 7-11) *In the following questions, two statements are given- one labelled Assertion (A) and the other labelled Reason (R). Select the correct answer to these questions from the codes (a), (b), (c) and (d) as given below*

(a) Both Assertion and Reason are true and Reason is the correct explanation of Assertion.
(b) Both Assertion and Reason are true but Reason is not the correct explanation of Assertion.
(c) Assertion is true but Reason is false.
(d) Assertion is false but Reason is true.

7. **Assertion (A)** Two springs of force constants k_1 and k_2 are stretched by the same force. If $k_1 > k_2$, then work done in stretching the first (W_1) is less than work done in stretching the second (W_2).

Reason (R) $F = k_1x_1 = k_2x_2$

8. **Assertion (A)** If momentum of a body increases by 50%, its kinetic energy will increase by 125%.

Reason (R) Kinetic energy is proportional to square of velocity.

9. **Assertion (A)** Stopping distance
$$= \frac{\text{Kinetic energy}}{\text{Stopping force}}$$

Reason (R) Work done in stopping a body is equal to change in kinetic energy of the body.

10. **Assertion (A)** Mass and energy are not conserved separately but are conserved as a single entity called 'mass-energy'.

Reason (R) This is because one can be obtained at the cost of the other as per Einstein's equation
$$E = mc^2$$

11. **Assertion (A)** Force applied on a block moving in one dimension is producing a constant power, then the motion should be uniformly accelerated.

Reason (R) This constant power multiplied with time is equal to the change in kinetic energy.

Very Short Answer Type Questions

(1 Mark)

12. How much work is done by mass M moving once around a horizontal circle of radius r?

13. Does the work done in moving a body depend upon how fast the body is moved?

14. A person walking on a horizontal road with a load on his head does no work. Why?

15. Friction is a non-conservative force. Why?

16. Define spring constant of a spring. Give its SI unit.

17. What do you meant by conservation of linear momentum?

Short Answer Type I Questions

(2 Marks)

18. Work done in moving a body over a closed loop is zero. Is this statement true for all forces?

19. Can a body have momentum without energy? Explain.

20. If two objects collide and one is initially at rest
    (i) is it possible for both to be at rest after collision?
    (ii) is it possible for any one to be at rest after collision?

21. Is it possible to have a collision in which the whole of the kinetic energy is lost?

22. Define conservation of mechanical energy.

23. A man raises a mass m to a height h and then shifts it horizontally by a length x. What is the work done against the force of gravity?

24. Two balls of mass m, each moving in opposite direction with a speed v collide head-on with each other. How will they move after collision, assuming it to be perfectly elastic?

Short Answer Type II Questions

(3 Marks)

25. What is a conservative and non-conservative forces? Explain various properties.

26. Briefly describe the mechanism of the functioning of heavy water as moderator in nuclear reactors.

27. Explain perfectly inelastic collision in one dimension.

28. Is frictional force always negative? Comment.

29. Two protons are brought towards each other, will the potential energy of the system decrease or increase? If a proton and an electron be brought nearer, then?

30. Explain the nature of work done in different situations with example.

31. What are the characteristics of work done by conservative forces?

Long Answer Type Questions

(5 Marks)

32. A mass m is moving with a speed u collides with a similar mass m at rest, elastically and obliquely. Prove that they will move in directions making an angle $\pi/2$ with each other.

33. Explain what is meant by potential energy of a spring? Obtain an expression for it and discuss the nature of its variation.

34. (i) What are the elastic and inelastic collisions?
    (ii) Obtain relations for velocities of two spherical bodies after an elastic collision and discuss for $m_1 = m_2$, $m_1 >> m_2$ and $m_2 >> m_1$.

35. Derive an expression for work done when force and displacement are inclined to each other. Discuss different cases. Explain two absolute units of work and find relation between them.

Case Based Questions

Directions (Q. No. 36) *These questions are case study based questions. Read the following paragraph and answer the questions.*

36. There are many types of spring. Important among these are helical and spiral springs as shown in figure.

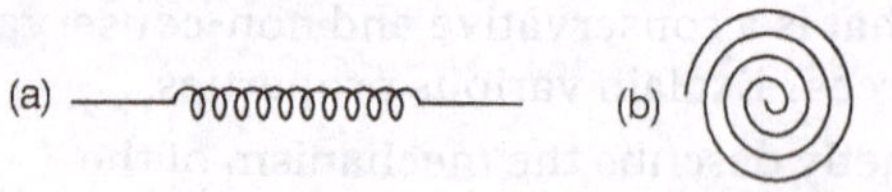

Usually, we assume that the springs are massless. Therefore, work done is stored in the spring in the form of elastic potential energy of the spring. Thus, potential energy of a spring is the energy associated with the state of compression or expansion of an elastic spring.

(i) The potential energy of a body increases in which of the following cases?
(a) If work is done by conservative force
(b) If work is done against conservative force
(c) If work is done by non-conservative force
(d) If work is done against non- conservative force

(ii) The potential energy, i.e. $U(x)$ can be assumed zero when
(a) $x = 0$
(b) gravitational force is constant
(c) infinite distance from the gravitational source
(d) All of the above

(iii) The ratio of spring constants of two springs is 2 : 3. What is the ratio of their potential energy, if they are stretched by the same force?
(a) 2 : 3 (b) 3 : 2
(c) 4 : 9 (d) 9 : 4

(iv) The potential energy of a spring increases by 15 J when stretched by 3 cm. If it is stretched by 4 cm, the increase in potential energy is
(a) 27 J (b) 30 J
(c) 33 J (d) 36 J

(v) The potential energy of a spring when stretched through a distance x is 10 J. What is the amount of work done on the same spring to stretch it through an additional distance x?
(a) 10 J (b) 20 J
(c) 30 J (d) 40 J

Numerical Proplems

37. Find the work done in moving a particle along a vector $\mathbf{s} = (2\hat{i} - 3\hat{j} + \hat{k})$ m, if applied force is $\mathbf{F} = (\hat{i} - 2\hat{j} + 3\hat{k})$N. **[1 M]**

38. Calculate the kinetic energy of a body of mass 0.1 kg, if its linear momentum is 20 kg-m/s. **[1 M]**

39. Find the average frictional force needed to stop a car weighing 800 kg running with an initial speed of 54 km/h with a distance of 25 m. **[2 M]**

40. Momentum of a body is doubled. What is the percentage increase in kinetic energy ? **[2 M]**

41. A fast moving neutron make a head-on elastic collision with a stationary deuteron. What fraction of initial kinetic energy is delivered by the neutron during collision? **[2 M]**

42. Two balls A and B of masses 0.3 kg and 0.2 kg respectively are moving along positive x-axis and negative x-axis with velocity 20 m/s. They collide and thereafter move in the direction opposite to their original direction. Find the velocity of A and B after collision. Also, calculate total KE of the balls before and after collision **[3 M]**

43. A body of mass 2 kg makes an elastic collision with another body at rest and continuous to move in the original direction but one-fourth of its original speed. (i) what is the mass of the other body ? (ii) what is the speed of the other body? **[3 M]**

Answers

1 (*b*) As we know that work done for stretching, $W = \frac{1}{2}kx^2$

$$= \frac{1}{2} \times \frac{F}{x} \times x^2 = \frac{1}{2}Fx$$

($\because$ Though rod is not a spring yet it will behave as a spring. So, $F = kx$)

$$= \frac{1}{2}Fx = \frac{1}{2}mg \times l = \frac{1}{2}mgl$$

2 (*c*) $$F = \frac{K}{v} \quad \text{(given)}$$

$$m\frac{dv}{dt} = \frac{K}{v} \Rightarrow \int mv\,dv = \int K\,dt$$

$$\Rightarrow \quad m\frac{v^2}{2} = Kt \quad \Rightarrow \quad \text{KE} \propto t$$

3 (*c*) Negative of the work by the conservative interval force causes potential energy to increase.

4 (*a*) When the bow is bent by stretching, its shape gets changed. So, it possess potential energy.

5 (*b*) The work done in a spring is

$$W_s = \frac{1}{2}k(x_i^2 - x_f^2)$$

As elongation is same in both, so

$$W_s \propto k$$

$$\Rightarrow \quad W_s(k_1) > W_s(k_2)$$

$\therefore$ Greater work is done in case of k_1.

6 (*c*) When two equal masses undergo a glancing elastic collision with one of them at rest, after the collision, they will move at right angles to each other.

$\therefore \quad \theta_1 = 90° - \theta_2 = 53°$

7 (*a*)

8 (*a*)

9 (*a*)

10 (*a*)

11 (*d*)

12 Zero work is done in a complete circle.

13 No, work done for moving body depend on the shortest path length between the initial and final position.

14 Work done by the person is zero, because there is right angle between the direction of force and displacement

15 Work done by frictional force depends upon the path followed by the object.

16 For a small stretch or compression, the restoring force is directly proportional to stretch or compression

$$-F \propto x \quad \Rightarrow \quad F = -kx$$

where, k = spring constat. Its SI unit is Nm^{-1}.

17 Refer to text on page 178 (Conservation of linear momentum in collision).

18 No, the statement is true only when motion is under conservative forces. [2]

19 Yes, when $E = K + U = 0$, either both are zero or $K = -U$. Thus, kinetic energy may or may not be zero.

As, $p = \sqrt{2mK}$

$\therefore p = 0$, only when $K = 0$ and $P \neq 0$, when $K = -U$. [2]

20 (i) No, because momentum will not be conserved in that case. [1]

(ii) Yes, when masses of two objects are equal and collision is perfectly elastic. [1]

21 Yes, for example in perfectly inelastic collision of two bodies moving towards each other with equal linear momenta. [2]

22 Refer to text on page 169 (Conservation of mechanical energy).

23 There is only potential energy, which is mgh and no effect of horizontal movement. ($\because h$ = same) [2]

24 Refer to example 3 on page 180.

25 Refer to text on pages 158 and 159 (Conservative and non-conservative force).

26 Heavy water is used in certain types of nuclear reactor, where it acts as a neutron moderator to slow down neutron. Heavy water contains normal amount of hydrogen isotope deuterium.

In collision between neutron and deutrium is elastic and 90% of the neutron's kinetic energy transferred to deuterium. [3]

27 Refer to text on page 180 (Perfectly inelastic collision in one dimension).

28 No, unlike any other force friction can be zero, positive and negative depending on situation. Work is zero, when the point of application of force does not move. It is positive when the friction force produces motion and negative when it opposes motion. [3]

29 Potential energy increases as in bringing two protons closer, work is done against force of repulsion.

However, the potential energy decreases when a proton and an electron are brought nearer, as work done is due to the force of attraction. [3]

30 Refer to text on pages 156 and 157 (Nature of work done in different situations).

31 Refer to text on page 158 (Work done by conservative forces) .

32 Refer to text on page 181 (Case III-Elastic collision of two indentical particles).

33 Refer to text on pages 167 and 168 (Potential energy of a spring).

34 (i) Refer to table in text on pages 178 (Collision).

(ii) Refer to text on page 179 (Velocities of the bodies after the collision).

35 Refer to text on page 155 (Work done when force and displacement are inclined to each other, dimensions and units of work).

36 (i) (*b*) (ii) (*c*) (iii) (*d*) (iv) (*a*) (v) (*c*)

37 As $W = \mathbf{F}\cdot\mathbf{s} = (\hat{\mathbf{i}} - 2\hat{\mathbf{j}} + 3\hat{\mathbf{k}})\cdot(2\hat{\mathbf{i}} - 3\hat{\mathbf{j}} + \hat{\mathbf{k}})$

$$= 2 + 6 + 3 = 11\,\text{J}$$

38 As, $\text{KE} = \dfrac{p^2}{2m}$

Here, p = 20kg-m/s and m = 0.1 kg

$$\therefore \quad \text{KE} = \frac{(20)^2}{2\times 0.1} = 2000\,\text{J}$$

39 As, we know work done by frictional force $= F_f x$

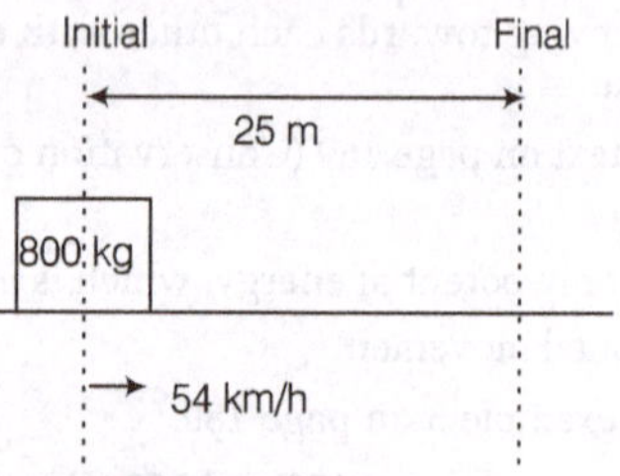

So, from energy conservation,

$$\frac{1}{2}mv^2 = F_f x \qquad [1]$$

$$\frac{800}{2}\times 15\times 15 = F_f\, 25 \quad [\because 54\text{ km h}^{-1} = 15\text{ms}^{-1}]$$

$$F_f = 3600\,\text{N} \qquad [1]$$

40 As $\text{KE} \propto p^2$

So, 2 times the momentum

$$\Rightarrow \quad \text{KE} \propto 4p^2 \qquad [1]$$

$$\text{So\% increase in KE} = \frac{4p - p^2}{p^2}\times 100 = 300\% \qquad [1]$$

41 Let the mass of neutron = m, mass of deutron = $2m$ and initial velocity of neutron = u_i

So velocity of neutron after the collision

$$v = \frac{(m_1 - m_2)}{m_1 + m_2}u_i = \frac{m - 2m}{3m} = u_i = -\frac{u_i}{3} \qquad [2]$$

42 Given, $m_A = 0.3$ kg, $m_B = 0.2$ kg and $u_A = 20$ m/s

$u_B = -20$ m/s

So $\quad v_A = \dfrac{(m_A - m_B)u_A + 2m_B u_B}{m_1 + m_2}$

$$= \frac{(0.3 - 0.2)20 + 2(0.2)(-20\text{m}/\text{s})}{0.5} = -12\text{ m/s} \qquad [1½]$$

Similarly, $v_B = 28$ m/s

So, initial kinetic energy $= \dfrac{1}{2}m_A v_A^2 + \dfrac{1}{2}m_B v_B^2$

$$= \frac{1}{2}m_A u_A^2 + \frac{1}{2}m_B u_B^2 = 100\,\text{J} \qquad [1½]$$

43 Given, $m_1 = 2$ kg, velocity $= u_1$, after collision

$$v_1 = \frac{u_1}{4}$$

So, we know $\quad v_1 = \left(\dfrac{m_1 - m_2}{m_1 + m_2}\right)u_1 \qquad [\because u_2 = 0]$

$$\Rightarrow \quad \frac{v_1}{4} = \left[\frac{2 - m_2}{2 + m_2}\right]u_1$$

$$\Rightarrow \quad 5m_2 = 6 \Rightarrow m_2 = 1.2\,\text{kg} \qquad [1½]$$

So by applying momentum conservation

$$m_1u_1 = m_1v_1 + m_2v_2$$

$$2u_1 = 2\frac{u_1}{4} + 1.2v_2$$

$$v_2 = \frac{15}{12}u \qquad [1½]$$

CHAPTER

06

System of Particles and Rotational Motion

In earlier cases, we considered every object as point mass. Even the finite size objects are considered as **point mass** to understand their motion.

An extended body (any finite size body) is a system of particles. When an extended body moves, motion of individual point masses composing the body might be different for each point mass. To understand the motion of a system (extended body), we must understand the concept of **centre of mass** of a system of particles.

- Centre of Mass and Rotational Inertia
- Moment of Inertia

TOPIC 01 Centre of Mass and Rotational Inertia

Rigid Body

A moving body is rigid when it has a perfectly definite shape and size during its entire motion. The distance between all pairs of particles of such a body do not change while applying any force on it.

e.g. A wheel in rotation can be considered as rigid body by ignoring a little change in its shape.

Centre of Mass

The centre of mass of a body or a system of bodies is the point which moves as though all of the mass were concentrated there and all external forces were applied to it.

Hence, a point at which the entire mass of the body or system of bodies is supposed to be concentrated is known as the **centre of mass.**

Centre of Mass for Two Particle System

Let the distances of the two particles be x_1 and x_2 respectively from origin O. Let m_1 and m_2 be their masses. The centre of mass of the system is that point C which is at a distance x_{CM} from O, where x_{CM} is given by

$$x_{CM} = \frac{m_1x_1 + m_2x_2}{m_1 + m_2}$$

$$\text{Centre of mass, } x_{CM} = \frac{m_1x_1 + m_2x_2}{M}$$

where, $M = m_1 + m_2 =$ total mass of system.

Example 1 Two bodies of masses 1 kg and 2 kg are located at (1, 2) and (−1, 3), respectively. Calculate the coordinates of the centre of mass.

Sol. Given, $m_1 = 1\,\text{kg}, \quad m_2 = 2\,\text{kg}$

$$x_1 = 1\,\text{m}, \; x_2 = -1\,\text{m}$$

$$y_1 = 2\,\text{m}, \; y_2 = 3\,\text{m}$$

$$\therefore \quad x_{CM} = \frac{m_1x_1 + m_2x_2}{m_1 + m_2} = \frac{1\times1 + 2\times-1}{1+2}$$

$$= \frac{1-2}{3} = \frac{-1}{3} = -0.33$$

$$\text{and } y_{CM} = \frac{m_1y_1 + m_2y_2}{m_1 + m_2} = \frac{1\times2 + 2\times3}{1+2} = \frac{2+6}{3} = \frac{8}{3} = 2.66$$

Thus, the coordinates of centre of mass are (−0.33, 2.66).

Note The centre of mass of a system of two particles lies on the straight line joining the two particles.

For a System of *n* Particles

Suppose a system of n particles having masses $m_1, m_2, m_3, \ldots, m_n$ situated at points $(x_1, y_1), (x_2, y_2), (x_3, y_3) \ldots (x_n, y_n)$.

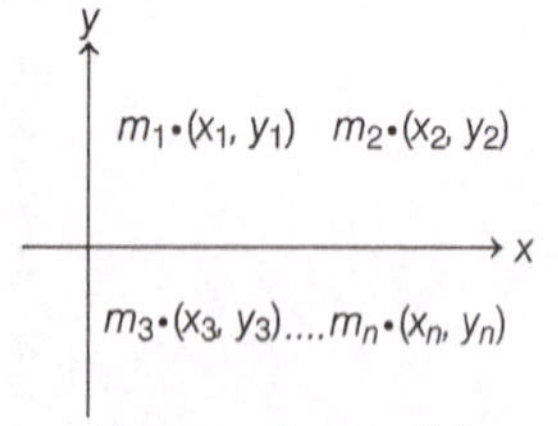

System of *n* particles

i.e. $x_{CM} =$ *x*-coordinates of centre of mass of system

$$= \frac{m_1x_1 + m_2x_2 + m_3x_3 + \cdots + m_nx_n}{m_1 + m_2 + m_3 + \cdots + m_n}$$

$$\text{Centre of mass, } x_{CM} = \frac{\sum_{i=1}^{n} m_ix_i}{\Sigma m_i}$$

and $y_{CM} =$ *y*-coordinates of centre of mass of system

$$= \frac{m_1y_1 + m_2y_2 + m_3y_3 + \cdots + m_ny_n}{m_1 + m_2 + m_3 + \cdots + m_n}$$

$$\text{Centre of mass, } y_{CM} = \frac{\sum_{i=1}^{n} m_iy_i}{\Sigma m_i}$$

Example 2 Three masses 3 kg, 4 kg and 5 kg are located at the corners of an equilateral triangle of side 1m , then what are the coordinates of centre of mass of this system.

Sol. Suppose the equilateral triangle lies in the *xy*-plane with mass 3 kg at the origin.

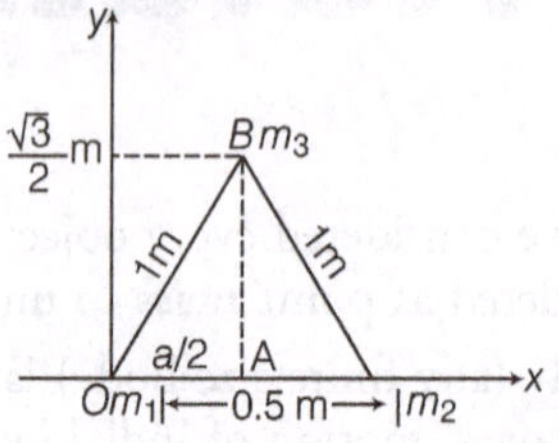

$$\text{In } \Delta OAB, AB = \sqrt{(OB)^2 - (OA)^2} = \sqrt{(1)^2 - \left(\frac{1}{2}\right)^2} = \frac{\sqrt{3}}{2}\text{m}$$

Now, $\quad x_1 = 0, \; x_2 = 1\text{m}, \; x_3 = OA = 0.5\text{m}$

$m_1 = 3\,\text{kg}, \; m_2 = 4\,\text{kg}, \; m_3 = 5\,\text{kg}$

$\therefore$ *x*-coordinate of centre of mass is

$$x = \frac{m_1x_1 + m_2x_2 + m_3x_3}{m_1 + m_2 + m_3}$$

$$= \frac{3\times0 + 4\times1 + 5\times0.5}{3+4+5} = \frac{6.5}{12} = 0.54\text{ m}$$

Again, $\quad y_1 = 0, \; y_2 = 0, \; y_3 = AB = \frac{\sqrt{3}}{2}$,

$\therefore$ *y*-coordinate of centre of mass is

$$y = \frac{m_1y_1 + m_2y_2 + m_3y_3}{m_1 + m_2 + m_3}$$

$$= \frac{3\times0 + 4\times0 + 5\times\left(\frac{\sqrt{3}}{2}\right)}{3+4+5} = \frac{5\times\sqrt{3}}{2\times12} = 0.36\text{ m}$$

Thus, the coordinates of centre of mass are (0.54 m, 0.36 m).

Example 3 Six particles are placed at different points of a square as shown in the figure. Find the location of centre of mass for the system of six particles.

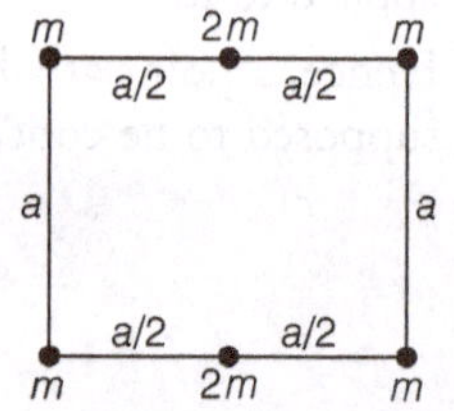

Sol. First of all consider a coordinate system for the given system of particles.

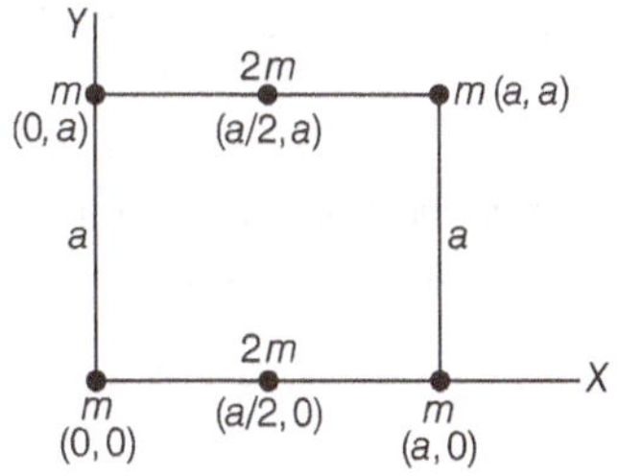

Now, apply the formula for the X-component of centre of mass.

$$X_{CM} = \frac{2m \times a/2 + 2m \times a/2 + m \times a + m \times a}{m + 2m + m + m + 2m + m} = \frac{4ma}{8m} = \frac{a}{2}$$

Now, apply the formula for the Y-component of centre of mass.

$$Y_{CM} = \frac{m \times a + 2m \times a + m \times a}{8m} = \frac{4ma}{8m} = \frac{a}{2}$$

So, the coordinates of centre of mass should be written as

$$(X_{CM}, Y_{CM}) = \left(\frac{a}{2}, \frac{a}{2}\right)$$

Hence, centre of mass of given system lies at centre of square.

Centre of Mass of Rigid Continuous Bodies

For a real body which is a continuous distribution of matter, point masses are then differential mass elements dm and centre of mass is defined as

$$x_{CM} = \frac{1}{M}\int x\, dm, \quad y_{CM} = \frac{1}{M}\int y\, dm$$

$$z_{CM} = \frac{1}{M}\int z\, dm$$

where, M is total mass of the body.

If we choose the origin of coordinates axes at centre of mass then,

$$\int x\, dm = \int y dm = \int z dm = 0$$

Centre of Mass of a Uniform Thin Rod

Let us consider a uniform thin rod AB of mass M and length L. The rod is held along x-axis with its end A at the origin, where $x = y = 0$, as shown in figure.

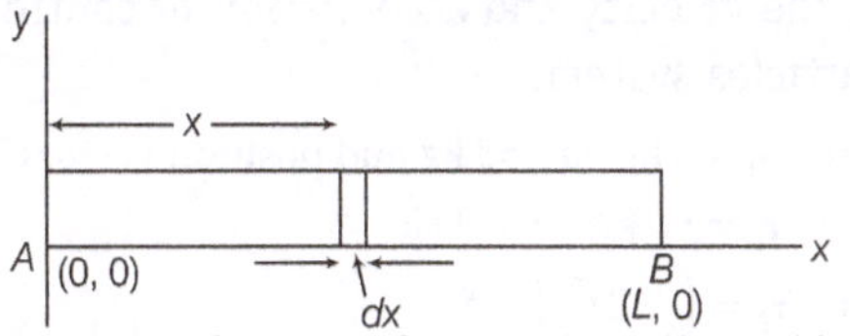

Calculation of centre of mass of a uniform thin rod

Suppose the element is placed side by side of length dx at distance i.e. x from the origin.

Then, mass of element $dm = \frac{M}{L} dx$

Let (x_{CM}, y_{CM}) be the coordinates of centre of mass of thin rod from origin. Then,

$$x_{CM} = \frac{1}{M}\int_0^L x\, dm = \frac{1}{M}\int_0^L x\left(\frac{M}{L}\right) dx = \frac{1}{L}\frac{x^2}{2}\Bigg|_0^L = \frac{L}{2}$$

Centre of mass, $x_{CM} = \frac{L}{2}$

and $\quad y_{CM} = \frac{1}{M}\int y\, dm = 0 \qquad [\because y = 0 \text{ for thin rod}]$

$$y_{CM} = 0$$

Thus, it means that the centre of mass of thin rod AB lies at point $\left(\frac{L}{2}, 0\right)$ i.e. centre between its ends A and B.

Thus, the centre of mass coincides with geometric centre.

Motion of Centre of Mass

As already defined for a system of n particles, we can relate position vector of centre of mass and that of individual masses as

$$M \cdot \mathbf{r}_{CM} = m_1\mathbf{r}_1 + m_2\mathbf{r}_2 + m_3\mathbf{r}_3 + \cdots + m_n\mathbf{r}_n$$

Differentiating with respect to time, we get

$$M \cdot \frac{d}{dt}\mathbf{r}_{CM} = m_1\frac{d}{dt}\mathbf{r}_1 + m_2\frac{d}{dt}\mathbf{r}_2 + \cdots + m_n\frac{d}{dt}\mathbf{r}_n$$

$$\Rightarrow M \cdot \mathbf{v}_{CM} = m_1\mathbf{v}_1 + m_2\mathbf{v}_2 + m_3\mathbf{v}_3 + \cdots + m_n\mathbf{v}_n$$

So, Velocity about centre of mass, $\mathbf{v}_{CM} = \dfrac{\sum_{i=1}^{n} m_i\mathbf{v}_i}{M}$

where, $\mathbf{v} = \frac{d\mathbf{r}}{dt}$, rate of change of position vector is velocity.

Again differentiating the result, we get

$$M\frac{d}{dt}\mathbf{v}_{CM} = m_1\frac{d}{dt}\mathbf{v}_1 + m_2\frac{d}{dt}\mathbf{v}_2 + m_3\frac{d}{dt}\mathbf{v}_3 + \cdots + m_n\frac{d}{dt}\mathbf{v}_n$$

As rate of change of velocity is acceleration, we write

$$a = \frac{dv}{dt}$$

$$M\mathbf{a}_{CM} = m_1\mathbf{a}_1 + m_2\mathbf{a}_2 + \cdots + m_n\mathbf{a}_n$$

So, $$\text{Acceleration about centre of mass, } \mathbf{a}_{CM} = \frac{\sum_{i=1}^{n} m_i \mathbf{a}_i}{M}$$

But, $m_i \mathbf{a}_i$ is the resultant force on the ith particle, so

$$M\mathbf{a}_{CM} = \mathbf{F}_1 + \mathbf{F}_2 + \mathbf{F}_3 + \cdots + \mathbf{F}_n$$

or $$M\mathbf{a}_{CM} = \mathbf{F}_{\text{net, ext}} \quad \ldots\text{(i)}$$

where, $\mathbf{F}_{\text{net, ext}} = \mathbf{F}_1 + \mathbf{F}_2 + \mathbf{F}_3 + \cdots + \mathbf{F}_n$ is net force of all external forces that act on the system.

From the expression (i), it is clear that the centre of mass of a system of particles moves as if whole mass of the system was concentrated at the centre of mass and all the external forces were applied at that point.

Linear Momentum of a System of Particles

For a system of n particles, total linear momentum is vector sum of linear momenta of individual particles. Where linear momentum of an individual particle is product of its mass and velocity ($\mathbf{p} = m\mathbf{v}$).

So, linear momentum of system is

$$\mathbf{p} = \mathbf{p}_1 + \mathbf{p}_2 + \mathbf{p}_3 + \ldots + \mathbf{p}_n$$

or $$\mathbf{p} = m_1\mathbf{v}_1 + m_2\mathbf{v}_2 + m_3\mathbf{v}_3 + \cdots + m_n\mathbf{v}_n \quad \ldots\text{(i)}$$

From the concept of centre of mass, we know that

$$m_1\mathbf{v}_1 + m_2\mathbf{v}_2 + m_3\mathbf{v}_3 + \cdots + m_n\mathbf{v}_n = M \cdot \mathbf{V}_{CM} \quad \ldots\text{(ii)}$$

From Eqs. (i) and (ii), we get

$$\text{Total linear momentum, } \mathbf{p} = M\mathbf{V}_{CM} \quad \ldots\text{(iii)}$$

Thus, the total momentum of a system of particles is equal to the product of the total mass and velocity of its centre of mass.

Newton's Second Law for System of Particles

Now, differentiating Eq. (iii) with respect to time, we get

$$\frac{d}{dt}\mathbf{p} = \frac{d}{dt} M\,\mathbf{V}_{CM}$$

or $$\frac{d\mathbf{p}}{dt} = M\frac{d}{dt}\mathbf{V}_{CM} \quad [\text{if } M \text{ is constant}]$$

or $$\frac{d\mathbf{p}}{dt} = M\mathbf{A}_{CM} \quad \ldots\text{(iv)}$$

From centre of mass concept, we know

$$M\mathbf{A}_{CM} = \text{net external force} \quad \ldots\text{(v)}$$

From Eqs. (iv) and (v), we get

$$\therefore \quad \text{Net external force, } \mathbf{F}_{ext} = \frac{d\mathbf{p}}{dt} = M\mathbf{A}_{CM} \quad \ldots\text{(vi)}$$

Above expression represents Newton's second law for system of particles. Here, $\mathbf{p}$ is net momentum of the system and $\mathbf{F}_{ext}$ is the net external force applied on the system.

Conservation of Linear Momentum for System of particles

If external force is not acting on the system of particles,

$$\mathbf{F}_{ext} = 0, \text{ then } \frac{d\mathbf{p}}{dt} = 0$$

or **rate of change of momentum is zero**, i.e. **momentum of system remains constant.**

So, $$\mathbf{p}_{\text{initial}} = \mathbf{p}_{\text{final}}, \text{ if } \mathbf{F}_{ext} = 0 \quad \ldots\text{(vii)}$$

Above expression represents the law of conservation of linear momentum for system of particles.

If mass of the system is constant, then

$$M\mathbf{V}_{CM} = \text{constant} \quad [\because \mathbf{F}_{ext} = 0]$$

$$\mathbf{V}_{CM} = \text{constant} \quad \ldots\text{(viii)}$$

Eq. (viii) shows that if the mass of system of particles is constant and if **net external force on the system is zero, then the velocity of centre of mass of the system will remain constant.**

Example 4 A child sits stationary at one end of a long trolley moving uniformly with a speed v on smooth horizontal floor. If child gets up and runs about on the trolley in any manner, what is the speed of CM of the (trolley + child) system? **NCERT**

Sol. When the child gets up and runs about on the trolley, he is exerting an internal force on the trolley.

Thus, no external force acts on the system. So, centre of mass is not accelerated. Hence, speed of centre of mass of trolley-child system remains same as before, i.e. v.

Example 5 If two particles of masses $m_1 = 2$ kg and $m_2 = 3$ kg have position vectors $\mathbf{r}_1 = t\hat{i} + 2t^2\hat{j} + 2t\hat{k}$ and $\mathbf{r}_2 = \hat{\mathbf{i}} + 2t^3\hat{\mathbf{j}} + 5\hat{\mathbf{k}}$ respectively, then the position vector of r_1 and r_2 is in metres and time is in seconds. Calculate the velocity and acceleration of centre of mass of two particles system.

Sol. Here, $m_1 = 2$ kg, $m_2 = 3$ kg and position vectors

$$\mathbf{r}_1 = t\hat{i} + 2t^2\hat{j} + 2t\hat{k}$$

and $$\mathbf{r}_2 = \hat{i} + 2t^3\hat{j} + 5\hat{k}$$

Now, velocity of first particle, $\mathbf{v}_1 = \dfrac{d}{dt}(\mathbf{r}_1)$

$$= \frac{d}{dt}(t\hat{\mathrm{i}} + 2t^2\hat{\mathrm{j}} + 2t\hat{\mathrm{k}})$$

$$= \hat{\mathrm{i}} + 4t\hat{\mathrm{j}} + 2\hat{\mathrm{k}}$$

Velocity of second particle, $\mathbf{v}_2 = \dfrac{d}{dt}(\mathbf{r}_2)$

$$= \frac{d}{dt}(\hat{\mathrm{i}} + 2t^3\hat{\mathrm{j}} + 5\hat{\mathrm{k}}) = 6t^2\hat{\mathrm{j}}$$

∴ Velocity of centre of mass of two particles system is

$$\mathbf{v}_{CM} = \frac{m_1\mathbf{v}_1 + m_2\mathbf{v}_2}{m_1 + m_2}$$

$$= \frac{2\times(\hat{\mathrm{i}} + 4t\hat{\mathrm{j}} + 2\hat{\mathrm{k}}) + 3\times(6t^2\hat{\mathrm{j}})}{2+3}$$

$$= \frac{2\hat{\mathrm{i}} + (8t + 18t^2)\hat{\mathrm{j}} + 4\hat{\mathrm{k}}}{5}$$

$$= \left[\frac{2}{5}\hat{\mathrm{i}} + \frac{(8t+18t^2)}{5}\hat{\mathrm{j}} + \frac{4}{5}\hat{\mathrm{k}}\right]\text{m/s}$$

Now, acceleration of first particle,

$$\mathbf{a}_1 = \frac{d}{dt}(\mathbf{v}_1) = \frac{d}{dt}(\hat{\mathrm{i}} + 4t\hat{\mathrm{j}} + 2\hat{\mathrm{k}}) = 4\hat{\mathrm{j}}$$

Acceleration of second particle

$$\mathbf{a}_2 = \frac{d}{dt}(\mathbf{v}_2) = \frac{d}{dt}(6t^2\hat{\mathrm{j}}) = 12t\,\hat{\mathrm{j}}$$

∴ Acceleration of centre of mass of given system of particles is

$$\mathbf{a}_{CM} = \frac{m_1\mathbf{a}_1 + m_2\mathbf{a}_2}{m_1 + m_2}$$

$$= \frac{2(4\hat{\mathrm{j}}) + 3(12t\hat{\mathrm{j}})}{2+3}$$

$$\mathbf{a}_{CM} = \left[\frac{(8+36t)}{5}\hat{\mathrm{j}}\right]\text{m/s}^2$$

Centre of Gravity

The centre of gravity of a rigid body is a point through which the total weight of the body act. Centre of gravity can lie within the body or not. For small objects, centre of mass always coincides with centre of gravity. But in case of large bodies whose dimensions are comparable to the size of earth, centre of mass and centre of gravity will be at different locations.

Torque and Angular Momentum

The two physical quantities torque and angular momentum are to be discussed as vector products of two vectors.

Moment of Force (Torque)

Torque is also known as **moment of a force** or a **couple.** When a force acts on a particle, the particle does not merely move in the direction of the force but it also turns about some point.

So, we can define the torque for a particle about a point as the vector product of position vector of the point where the force acts with the force itself. Let us consider a particle P and force $\mathbf{F}$ acting on it.

Let the position vector of point of application of force about O is $\mathbf{r}$.

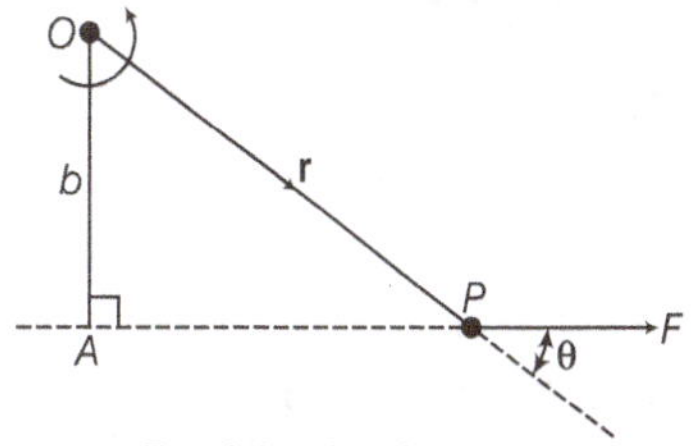

Particle showing torque, position vector and force

From figure, the torque τ acting on the particle relative to the fixed point O is a vector quantity and is defined as

$$\boxed{\text{Torque, } \boldsymbol{\tau} = \mathbf{r}\times\mathbf{F}}$$

The magnitude of torque $|\tau|$ is

$$\tau = rF\sin\theta = Fr\sin\theta$$

$$\tau = Fr_\perp = Fb \text{ (from figure)}$$

Here, $r_\perp$ is the perpendicular distance of the line of action of $\mathbf{F}$ from the point O.

Magnitude of torque can also be described as

$$\tau = rF\sin\theta$$

$$\tau = rF_\perp$$

Here, $F_\perp$ is the component of $\mathbf{F}$ in the direction perpendicular to $\mathbf{r}$.

Rectangular Components of Torque

Suppose the applied force $\mathbf{F}$ rotates the body in three dimensions, then to obtain x, y, z-components of the torque. We may apply the equation,

$$\boldsymbol{\tau} = \mathbf{r}\times\mathbf{F}$$

From this, we can write

$$\tau_x\hat{\mathrm{i}} + \tau_y\hat{\mathrm{j}} + \tau_z\hat{\mathrm{k}} = (x\hat{\mathrm{i}} + y\hat{\mathrm{j}} + z\hat{\mathrm{k}})\times(F_x\hat{\mathrm{i}} + F_y\hat{\mathrm{j}} + F_z\hat{\mathrm{k}})$$

$$= \begin{vmatrix} \hat{\mathrm{i}} & \hat{\mathrm{j}} & \hat{\mathrm{k}} \\ x & y & z \\ F_x & F_y & F_z \end{vmatrix}$$

$$= \hat{\mathbf{i}}(yF_z - zF_y) + \hat{\mathbf{j}}(zF_x - xF_z) + \hat{\mathbf{k}}(xF_y - F_z y)$$

$\therefore \quad \tau_x = yF_z - zF_y, \tau_y = (zF_x - xF_z)$

and $\quad \tau_z = xF_y - yF_x$

Note Torque could be zero ($\tau = 0$), if

$r = 0$ or $F = 0$ or $\theta = 0, 180°$

In SI system, torque is expressed in Newton-metre (N-m), it has same dimensions as that of workdone. Dimensions of torque are $[ML^2T^{-2}]$.

Example 6 Find the torque of a force $7\hat{\mathbf{i}} + 3\hat{\mathbf{j}} - 5\hat{\mathbf{k}}$ about the origin. The force acts on a particle whose position vector is $\hat{\mathbf{i}} - \hat{\mathbf{j}} + \hat{\mathbf{k}}$. NCERT

Sol. Given, position vector, $\mathbf{r} = \hat{\mathbf{i}} - \hat{\mathbf{j}} + \hat{\mathbf{k}}$

Force, $\mathbf{F} = 7\hat{\mathbf{i}} + 3\hat{\mathbf{j}} - 5\hat{\mathbf{k}}$

Torque, $\tau = ?$

$$\tau = \mathbf{r} \times \mathbf{F} = \begin{vmatrix} \hat{\mathbf{i}} & \hat{\mathbf{j}} & \hat{\mathbf{k}} \\ 1 & -1 & 1 \\ 7 & 3 & -5 \end{vmatrix}$$

$$= (5-3)\hat{\mathbf{i}} - (-5-7)\hat{\mathbf{j}} + (3+7)\hat{\mathbf{k}} = 2\hat{\mathbf{i}} + 12\hat{\mathbf{j}} + 10\hat{\mathbf{k}}$$

Angular Momentum of a Particle

Angular momentum (L) can be defined as **moment of linear momentum** about a point.

The angular momentum of a particle of mass m moving with velocity $\mathbf{v}$ (having a linear momentum $\mathbf{p} = m\mathbf{v}$) about a point O is defined by the following vector product.

$$\mathbf{L} = \mathbf{r} \times \mathbf{p}$$

or $\quad$ Angular momentum, $\mathbf{L} = m(\mathbf{r} \times \mathbf{v})$

$\mathbf{L}$ is angular momentum of particle about point O.

$\mathbf{r}$ is position vector of the particle about point O.

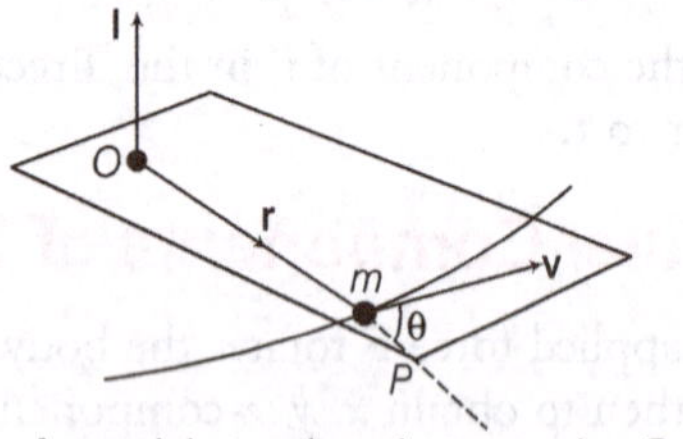

A particle moving about a point O

Magnitude of angular momentum depends on the position of point O and is given by $L = mvr\sin\theta$

where, θ = angle between $\mathbf{r}$ and $\mathbf{v}$

L can be represented as $L = rp\sin\theta = rp_\perp$

where, $p_\perp$ ($p\sin\theta$) is the component of $\mathbf{p}$ in a direction perpendicular to $\mathbf{r}$.

and $\quad L = pr\sin\theta = pr_\perp$

where, $r_\perp$ is the perpendicular distance of the linear momentum vector ($\mathbf{p}$) from origin.

Example 7 In a hydrogen atom, electron revolves in a circular orbit of radius 0.53 Å with a velocity of 2.2×10^6 m/s with an angle 30°. If the mass of electron is 9×10^{-31} kg. Find its angular momentum.

Sol. Given, $r = 0.53\text{Å} = 0.53 \times 10^{-10}$ m

$m = 9 \times 10^{-31}$ kg, $v = 2.2 \times 10^6$ m/s,

$\theta = 30°$, $L = ?$

$$L = mvr\sin\theta$$

$$= 9 \times 10^{-31} \times 2.2 \times 10^6 \times 0.53 \times 10^{-10} \times \sin 30°$$

$$= 5.247 \times 10^{-35} \text{ kg-m}^2/\text{s}$$

Relation between Torque and Angular Momentum

As angular momentum,

$$\mathbf{L} = \mathbf{r} \times \mathbf{p}$$

or $\quad \mathbf{L} = m(\mathbf{r} \times \mathbf{v})$

Differentiating with respect to time,

$$\frac{d\mathbf{L}}{dt} = \frac{d}{dt} m(\mathbf{r} \times \mathbf{v})$$

or $\quad \dfrac{d\mathbf{L}}{dt} = m\left(\dfrac{d\mathbf{r}}{dt} \times \mathbf{v} + \mathbf{r} \times \dfrac{d\mathbf{v}}{dt}\right)$

[from product rule of differentiation]

But $\quad \dfrac{d\mathbf{r}}{dt} = \mathbf{v}$ and $\mathbf{v} \times \mathbf{v} = 0$

and $\quad \dfrac{d\mathbf{v}}{dt} = a$ = acceleration

So, $\quad \dfrac{d\mathbf{L}}{dt} = m(\mathbf{r} \times \mathbf{a}) = (\mathbf{r} \times m\mathbf{a}) = \mathbf{r} \times \mathbf{F}$

$\therefore$ Rate of change of angular momentum, $\dfrac{d\mathbf{L}}{dt} = \tau$

Above equation gives Newton's second law of motion for angular motion, **rate of change of angular momentum is equal to the torque applied.**

Torque and Angular Momentum for a System of Particles

For a system of particles or a rigid body with n-particles, the total angular momentum of the system is the vector sum of the angular momenta of the individual particles.

$$\mathbf{L} = \mathbf{L}_1 + \mathbf{L}_2 + \mathbf{L}_3 + \cdots + \mathbf{L}_n = \sum_{i=1}^{n} \mathbf{L}_i$$

Differentiating the above expression with time,

$$\frac{d\mathbf{L}}{dt} = \sum_{i=1}^{n} \frac{d\mathbf{L}_i}{dt}$$

But $\sum_{i=1}^{n} \frac{d\mathbf{L}_i}{dt}$ is the net torque on the system so,

$$\frac{d\mathbf{L}}{dt} = \tau_{net}$$

Above expression shows Newton's second law for system of particles which state that the net external torque τ_{net} acting on a system of particles is equal to the time rate of change of the system's total angular momentum **L**.

> Rate of change of angular momentum, $\frac{d\mathbf{L}}{dt} = \tau_{ext}$

Thus, **the time rate of the total angular momentum of a system of particles about a point is equal to the sum of the external torques acting on the system taken about the same point.**

Conservation of Angular Momentum

As, $\frac{d\mathbf{L}}{dt} = \tau_{net}$ for the rigid body which can be treated as a system of n-particles. If $\tau_{ext} = 0$, then $\frac{d\mathbf{L}}{dt} = 0$, that means **L** = constant with time, i.e. $I\omega$ = constant

$$\boxed{I_1\omega_1 = I_2\omega_2}$$

Hence, **without any external torque, angular momentum of a system of particles remain constant.** This is known as the conservation of angular momentum.

If $\quad \tau_{ext} = 0 \Rightarrow \boxed{\mathbf{L}_{initial} = \mathbf{L}_{final}}$

Applications of Law of Conservation of Angular Momentum

- A circus acrobat performs beats involving spin by bringing her arms and legs closer to her body or *vice-versa*. On bringing the arms and legs closer to the body, her moment of inertia I decreases, hence angular velocity ω increases. The same principle is applied by ice skater or a ballet dancer.
- All helicopters are provided with two propellers. If there were only one propeller, the helicopter would rotate itself in opposite direction.
- A diver performs somersaults by jumping from a high diving board keeping his legs and arms out stretched first and then curling his body. On doing so, the moment of inertia I of his body decreases. As angular momentum remains constant, therefore, angular velocity ω of his body increases. He, then, performs somersaults. As the diver is about to touch the surface of water, he stretches out his limbs and slows down rotation.

Example 8 At a certain time, a 0.25 kg object has a position vector $\mathbf{r} = 2\hat{\mathbf{i}} - 2\hat{\mathbf{k}}$ m. At that instant, its velocity is $\mathbf{v} = -5\hat{\mathbf{i}} + 5\hat{\mathbf{k}}$ m/s and the force acting on it is $\mathbf{F} = 4\hat{\mathbf{j}}$ N.

(i) What is the angular momentum of the object about the origin?

(ii) What is torque on it?

Sol. Angular momentum, $\mathbf{L} = \mathbf{r} \times \mathbf{p} = \mathbf{r} \times m\mathbf{v} = m(\mathbf{r} \times \mathbf{v})$

Now, $\mathbf{r} \times \mathbf{v} = \begin{vmatrix} \hat{i} & \hat{j} & \hat{k} \\ 2 & 0 & -2 \\ -5 & 0 & 5 \end{vmatrix}$

$$= \hat{i}[(0 \times 5) - (0 \times -2)] - \hat{j}[(2 \times 5) - (-2 \times -5)] + \hat{k}[2 \times 0 - (0 \times -5)]$$

$$= 0$$

So, angular momentum of particle is zero.

and τ = torque = $\mathbf{r} \times \mathbf{F} = \begin{vmatrix} \hat{i} & \hat{j} & \hat{k} \\ 2 & 0 & -2 \\ 0 & 4 & 0 \end{vmatrix}$

$$= 8\hat{i} + 8\hat{k} \text{ N-m}$$

Example 9 If the radius of the earth contracts to half of its present value without change in its mass, what will be the new duration of the day? **NCERT Exemplar**

Sol. Present angular momentum of earth, $L_1 = I\omega = \frac{2}{5} MR^2\omega$

New angular momentum because of change in radius,

$$L_2 = \frac{2}{5} M\left(\frac{R}{2}\right)^2 \omega'$$

If external torque is zero, then angular momentum must be conserved $L_1 = L_2$

$$\frac{2}{5} MR^2\omega = \frac{1}{4} \times \frac{2}{5} MR^2\omega'$$

i.e. $\quad \omega' = 4\omega$

$$T' = \frac{1}{4} T = \frac{1}{4} \times 24 = 6 \text{ h}$$

Equilibrium of a Rigid Body

A rigid body is said to be in equilibrium, if both of its linear momentum and angular momentum are not changing with time.

Thus, equilibrium body does not possess linear acceleration or angular acceleration.

This means,

(i) The total force, i.e. the vector sum of all forces acting on the rigid body is zero.

$$\mathbf{F}_1 + \mathbf{F}_2 + \cdots + \mathbf{F}_n = \sum_{i=1}^{n} \mathbf{F}_i = 0$$

If the total force acting on the body is zero, then the linear momentum of body remains constant, so body must be in translatory equilibrium.

The above equations can be written in scalar form as

$$\sum_{i=1}^{n} \mathrm{F}_{ix} = 0, \sum_{i=0}^{n} \mathrm{F}_{iy} = 0 \text{ and } \sum_{i=0}^{n} \mathrm{F}_{iz} = 0$$

where, F_{ix}, F_{iy} and F_{iz} are x, y and z-components of force $\mathbf{F}_i$.

(ii) The total torque, i.e. the vector sum of all torques acting on the body must be zero.

$$\tau_1 + \tau_2 + \tau_3 + \cdots + \tau_n = \sum_{i=1}^{n} \tau_i = 0$$

The above equation can be written in scalar form as

$$\sum_{i=0}^{n} \tau_{ix} = 0, \sum_{i=0}^{n} \tau_{iy} = 0$$

and $$\sum_{i=0}^{n} \tau_{iz} = 0.$$

where, τ_{ix}, τ_{iy} and τ_{iz} are x, y and z-components of torque τ_i.

Note

Rotational equilibrium condition remains valid for any origin.

A body may remain in **partial equilibrium** as well. It means that body may remain only in **translational equilibrium** or only in **rotational equilibrium.**

(iii) The sum of the components of the torques along any axis perpendicular to the plane of the forces must be zero.

Rotational Equilibrium Only

If the net torque acting on the rigid body is zero but net force is non-zero, then rigid body is in **rotational equilibrium only.**

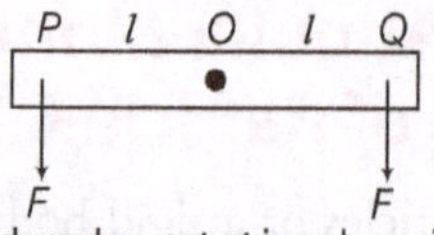

A rod under rotational equilibrium

Two equal forces are acting at the ends of a rod. In this case, the net torque produced by two forces will be zero, but net force is non-zero. It means that rigid body will have zero angular acceleration but non-zero linear acceleration.

Translational Equilibrium Only

If the net force acting on the rigid body is zero but net torque is non-zero, then rigid body is in **translational equilibrium only.**

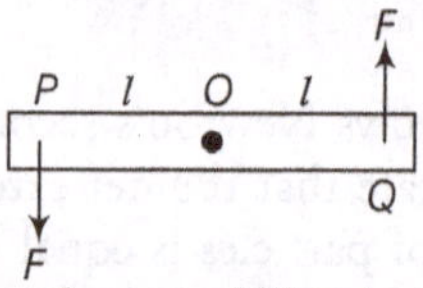

A rod under translational equilibrium

Two equal and opposite forces are acting at the ends of a rod. In this case the net force is zero, but both the forces will produce a non-zero torque. It means that rigid body will have zero linear acceleration but non-zero angular acceleration.

Couple

A pair of equal and opposite forces with parallel lines of action are known as a **couple.** A couple produces rotation without translation.

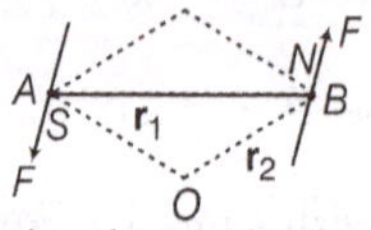

Equal and opposite forces on the poles S and N

Let a couple with forces $-\mathbf{F}$ and $\mathbf{F}$ acting at A and B points with position vectors $\mathbf{r}_1$ and $\mathbf{r}_2$ with respect to some origin O.

The moment of couple = total torque

$$= \mathbf{r}_1 \times (-\mathbf{F}) + \mathbf{r}_2 \times \mathbf{F}$$

$$= \mathbf{r}_2 \times \mathbf{F} - \mathbf{r}_1 \times \mathbf{F} = (\mathbf{r}_2 - \mathbf{r}_1) \times \mathbf{F}$$

$\because$ Moment of couple = $\mathbf{AB} \times \mathbf{F}$

By triangle law, $\mathbf{r}_1 + \mathbf{AB} = \mathbf{r}_2$

So, $\mathbf{AB} = \mathbf{r}_2 - \mathbf{r}_1$

So, moment of couple is independent of choice of origin.

Principle of Moment

When an object is in rotational equilibrium, then algebraic sum of all torques acting on it is zero. Clockwise torques are taken negative and anti-clockwise torques are taken positive.

e.g. Consider a rod of negligible mass is provided at some point like a see-saw or a lever. Pivot of lever is called **fulcrum.**

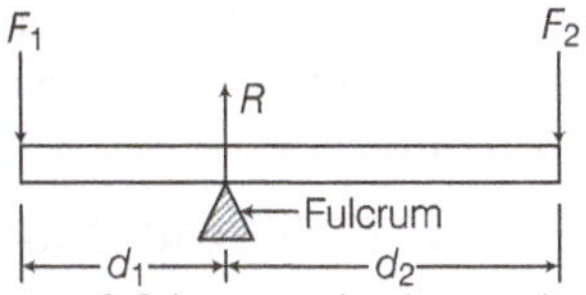

A fulcrum point in a rod

For translational equilibrium,

$$\Sigma F = 0 \text{ or } R - F_1 - F_2 = 0$$

For rotational equilibrium, $\Sigma\tau = 0$ or $F_1 d_1 - F_2 d_2 = 0$

In case of levers, F_1 is called load, d_1 is **load arm**, F_2 is called **effort**, d_2 is **effort arm.**

As, $F_1 d_1 - F_2 d_2 = 0$

or $F_1 d_1 = F_2 d_2$

or load × load arm = effort × effort arm.

This is called **principle of moment** for a lever.

Also, Mechanical advantage, $\dfrac{F_1}{F_2} = \dfrac{d_2}{d_1}$

The ratio $\dfrac{F_1}{F_2}$ is called **mechanical advantage** (MA).

Mechanical advantage greater than one is usually required as this means a small effort is required to lift a large load.

Example 10 The body in figure shown is pivoted at O and two forces act on it as shown.

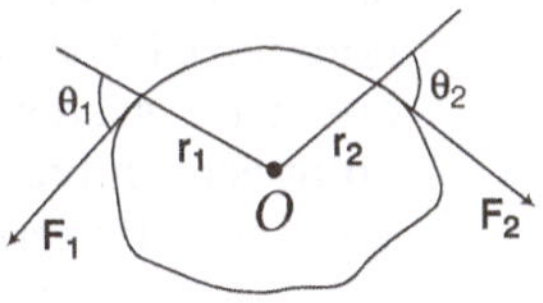

(i) Find an expression of the net torque on the body about the pivot.

(ii) If $r_1 = 1.30$ m, $r_2 = 2.15$ m, $F_1 = 4.20$ N, $F_2 = 4.90$ N, $\theta_1 = 75°$ and $\theta_2 = 60°$, what is the net torque about the pivot?

Sol. (i) Take a torque that tends to cause a counter clockwise rotation from rest to be positive and a torque that tends to cause a clockwise rotation from rest to be negative. Thus, a positive torque of magnitude $r_1 F_1 \sin\theta_1$ is associated with $\mathbf{F}_1$ and a negative torque of magnitude $r_2 F_2 \sin\theta_2$ is associated with $\mathbf{F}_2$. Both of these are about O. The net torque about O is $\tau = r_1 F_1 \sin\theta_1 - r_2 F_2 \sin\theta_2$.

(ii) Substitute the given values to obtain

$$\tau = (1.30 \text{ m})(4.20 \text{ N}) \sin 75° - (2.15 \text{ m})(4.90 \text{ N}) \sin 60°$$
$$= -3.85 \text{ N-m}$$

Example 11 A small ball of mass 1 kg is attached to one end of a 1 m long massless string and the other end of the string is hung from a point. When the resulting pendulum is 30° from the vertical, what is the magnitude of torque about the point of suspension? [Take, $g = 10 \text{ ms}^{-2}$]

Sol. Two forces are acting on the ball

(i) tension (T) (ii) weight (mg)

Torque of tension about point O is zero, as it passes through O.

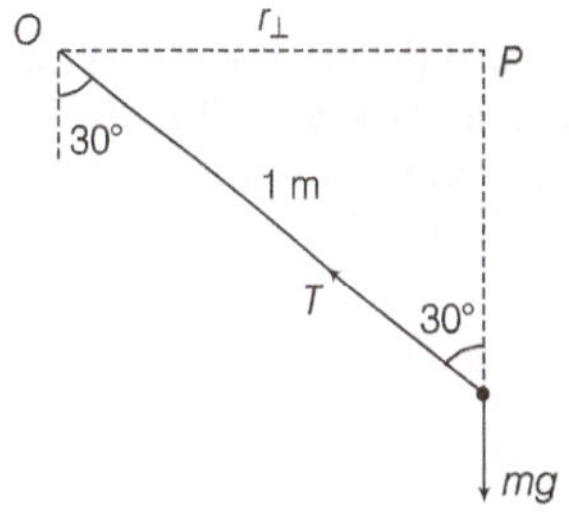

$$\tau_{mg} = F \times r_\perp$$

Here, $r_\perp = OP = 1 \sin 30° = 0.5$ m

$\therefore$ $\tau_{mg} = (mg)(0.5) = (1)(10)(0.5) = 5$ N-m

Topic Practice 1

Multiple Choice Questions

1 Mark

1. For n particles in a space, the suitable expression for the x-coordinate of the centre of mass of the system is
(a) $\dfrac{\Sigma m_i x_i}{m_i}$ (b) $\dfrac{\Sigma m_i x_i}{M}$ (c) $\dfrac{\Sigma m_i y_i}{M}$ (d) $\dfrac{\Sigma m_i z_i}{M}$
Here, M is the total mass of the system.

2. Torque vector is directed along
(a) the tangent to the circular path
(b) the inward radius
(c) the outward radius
(d) the axis of rotation

3. If $\tau_{ext} = 0$, means $\mathbf{L} \rightarrow$ constant, it is
(a) rotational analogue of conservation of linear momentum
(b) rotational analogue of force
(c) rotational analogue of linear momentum
(d) None of the above

4. In translational equilibrium,

(a) $\sum_{i=1}^{n} \mathbf{F}_{net} = 0$

(b) $\sum_{i=1}^{n} \tau_{net} = 0$

(c) Both (a) and (b) are the necessary conditions for the translational equilibrium

(d) Particle may be in equilibrium when (a) and (b) are not fulfilled.

5. For rotational equilibrium,

(a) $\sum_{i=1}^{n} \mathbf{F}_{net} = 0$

(b) $\sum_{i=1}^{n} \tau_{net} = 0$

(c) Both (a) and (b) are the necessary conditions for the rotational equilibrium

(d) Both (a) and (b) are not necessary for rotational equilibrium

Very Short Answer Type Questions

1 Mark

6. Should there necessarily be any mass at centre of mass of system?

7. Is centre of mass a reality?

8. In which case centre of mass of a body lie outside it? Give one example.

9. A cricket bat is cut through its centre of mass into two parts as shown in figure.

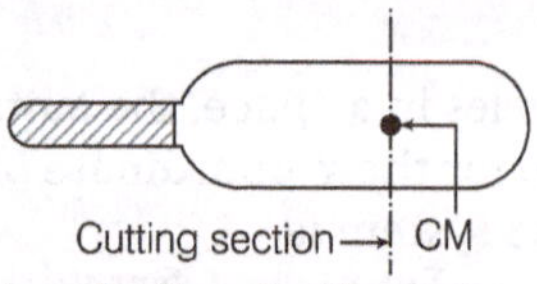

Then, state whether both parts are of same mass or not. Also, give reason.

10. $(n-1)$ equal point masses each of mass m are placed at the vertices of a regular n-polygon. The vacant vertex has a position vector a with respect to the centre of the polygon. Find the position vector of centre of mass. **NCERT Exemplar**

11. Find centre of mass of a triangular lamina. **NCERT**

12. How two particles appear to move when viewed from their centre of mass?

13. What is the value of total momentum of n particles with reference to a frame attached to its centre of mass ?

14. If only an external force can change the momentum of the centre of mass of an object how can the internal force of engine accelerates a car?

15. A bomb explodes when it reaches topmost point of its trajectory. What change in its momentum occurs?

16. An external force is applied to a rigid body and it produces only translation. What is the perpendicular distance of centre of mass from line of action of force?

17. Why a long handle is provided with car jacks?

18. If no external torque act on a body, will its angular velocity remain conserved?

19. Which component of linear momentum does not contribute to angular momentum?

20. If net torque on a rigid body is zero, does it linear momentum necessary remain conserved?

Short Answer Type I Questions

2 Marks

21. What happens to the moment of force about a point, if the line of action of the force moves towards the point?

22. A door is hinged at one end and is free to rotate about a vertical axis. Does its weight cause any torque about its axis? Give reason for your answer. **NCERT Exemplar**

23. The vector sum of a system of non-collinear forces acting on a rigid body is given to be non-zero. If the vector sum of all the torques due to the system of forces about a certain point is found to be zero, does this mean that it is necessarily zero about any arbitrary point? **NCERT**

24. When is a body lying in a gravitation field in stable equilibrium?

25. Is centre of mass and centre of gravity body always coincide?

26. Is the angular momentum always parallel to the angular velocity of a rigid body?

27. Is the change in angular momentum of a rigid body always parallel to the external torque?

Short Answer Type II Questions

3 Marks

28. Define centre of mass. If two particles of mass m_1 and m_2 are at positions with coordinates (x_1, y_1) and (x_2, y_2) respectively, then give an expression of position vector of centre of mass.

29. How can you say that orbit of moon around earth is elliptical?

30. Give the location of the centre of mass of a

(i) sphere (ii) cylinder

(iii) ring and

(iv) cube each of uniform mass density.

Does the centre of mass of a body necessarily lie inside the body? **NCERT**

31. Figure shows momentum *versus* time graph for a particle moving along x-axis. In which region, force on the particle is large. Why?

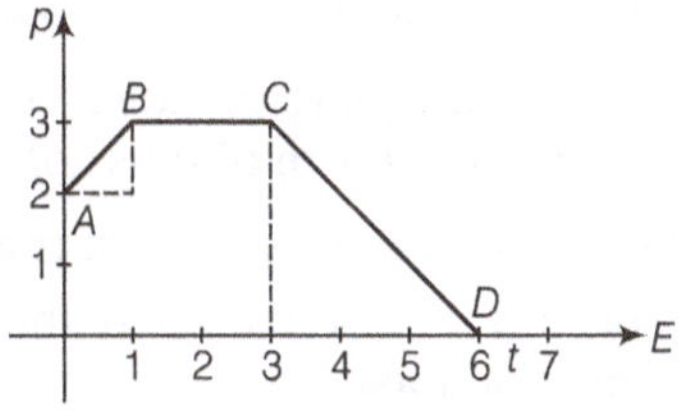

32. Find components along X, Y and Z-axes of the angular momentum $\mathbf{L}$ of a particle whose position vector is $\mathbf{r}$ and momentum is $\mathbf{p}$ with components p_x, p_y and p_z. Show if the particle moves only in xy-plane, the angular momentum has only a z-component. **NCERT**

33. Two cylindrical hollow drums of radii R and $2R$, and of a common height h, are rotating with angular velocities ω (anti-clockwise) and ω (clockwise), respectively.

Their axes, fixed are parallel and in a horizontal plane separated by $(3R + \delta)$. They are now brought in contact $(\delta \to 0)$.

(i) Show the frictional forces just after contact.

(ii) Identify forces and torques external to the system just after contact.

(iii) What would be the ratio of final angular velocities when friction ceases? **NCERT Exemplar**

34. A particle of mass m is projected from origin O with speed u at an angle θ with positive X-axis. Find the angular momentum of particle at any time t about O before the particle strikes the ground again.

35. Why equation $\mathbf{L} = \mathbf{I}\omega$ is not always correct? State the condition, if $\mathbf{L} = I\omega$ is obeyed by a system of masses.

36. State and explain law of conservation of angular momentum.

37. A system is in stable equilibrium. What can we say about its potential energy, what about the net force on the system?

38. A particle is moving with a constant speed around a circle. Locate a point (i) about which angular momentum remains constant with time (ii) about which angular momentum changes with time.

Long Answer Type Questions

5 Marks

39. A disc of radius R is removed from a disc of radius $2R$ as shown.

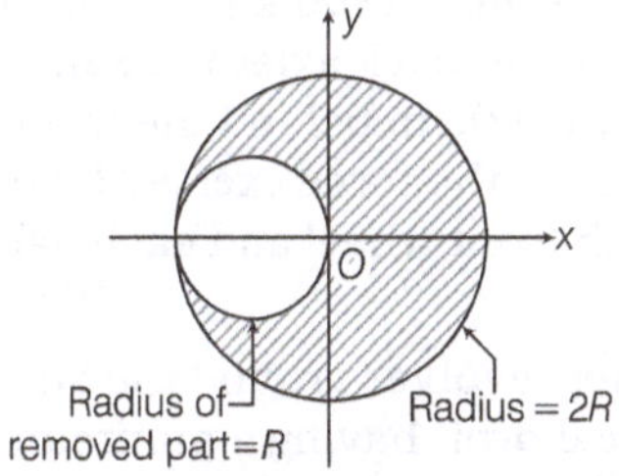

Find centre of mass of above disc with hole. **NCERT**

40. Two particles each of mass m and speed v travel in opposite direction along parallel lines, separated by a distance d. Show that vector angular momentum of the two particles system is same whatever be the point about which angular momentum is taken. **NCERT**

41. Find position of centre of mass of a semicircular disc of radius r. **NCERT Exemplar**

42. Why does the equilibrium of a rigid body require more conditions than the equilibrium of a particle?

Numerical Problems

43. A metre stick is balanced on a knife edge at its centre. When two coins, each of mass 5 g are put one on top of the other at the 12 cm mark, the stick is found to be balanced at 45.0 cm. What is the mass of the metre stick? **NCERT [2 M]**

44. A torque of 10 N-m is applied on a wheel having angular momentum of 2 kg-m^{2}s^{-1}, calculate the angular momentum of the wheel after 4 s. **[2 M]**

45. In HCl molecule, separation of nuclei of the two atoms is about 1.27Å (1Å = 10^{-10}m). Find the centre of mass of molecule given that a chlorine atom is about 35.5 times massive than a hydrogen atom. **NCERT [2 M]**

46. A 40 kg flywheel in the form of a uniform circular disc of 1m radius is making 120 rpm. Determine the angular momentum. **[2 M]**

47. A particle on a rotating disc have initial and final angular positions are
(i) – 2 rad, + 6 rad
(ii) – 4 rad, – 8 rad
(iii) 6 rad, – 2 rad,
In which case, particle undergoes a negative displacement. **[3 M]**

48. A car of weight 1800 kg. The distance between its front and back axles is 1.8 m. Its centre of gravity is 1.05 m behind the front axle. Determine the force exerted by the level ground on each front wheel and each back wheel. **NCERT Exemplar [3 M]**

49. A comet revolves around the Sun in a highly elliptical orbit having a minimum distance of 7×10^{10} m and a maximum distance of 1.4×10^{13} m. If its speed while nearest to the sun is 60 kms^{-1}, find its linear speed when situated farthest from the sun. **[3 M]**

50. The linear density of a thin rod of length 1 m varies as $\lambda = (1 + 2x)$, where x is the distance from its one end. Find the distance of its centre of mass from this end. **[3 M]**

51. If the radius of the earth contracts of the fourth of its present value without change in its mass, what will be the new duration of the day? **[3 M]**

52. A beam of uniform cross-section and uniform mass-density of mass 20 kg is supported at ends. A mass of 5 kg is placed at a distance of $L/5$ m from one of its end. If beam is L m long, what are reactions of supports? **[5 M]**

53. As shown in the figure, the two sides of a step ladder BA and CA are 1.6 m long and hinged at A. A rope DE, 0.05 m is tied half way up. A weight 40 kg is suspended from a point F, 1.2 m from B along the ladder BA. Assuming the floor to be frictionless and neglecting the weight of the ladder, find the tension in the rope and forces exerted by the floor on the ladder. (Take $g = 9.8$ m/s^2) **NCERT [5 M]**

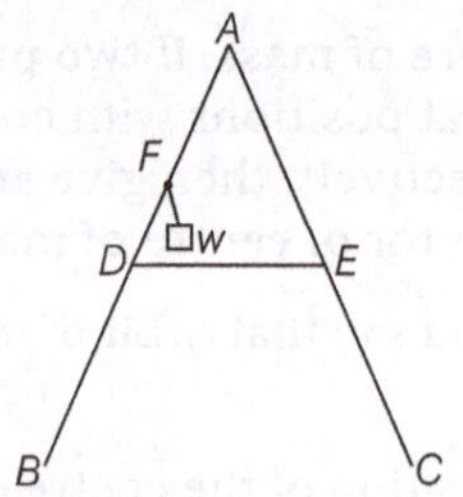

54. From a uniform disc of radius R, a circular section of radius $\frac{R}{2}$ is cut out. The centre of the hole is at $\frac{R}{2}$ from the centre of the original disc. Locate the centre of gravity of the resulting flat body. **NCERT [5 M]**

55. (i) Four particles of masses 1 kg, 2 kg, 3 kg and 4 kg are placed at the four vertices A, B, C and D of a square of side 1 m. Find the position of centre of mass of the particles.
(ii) Two identical rods each of mass m and length L are connected as shown. Locate centre of mass.

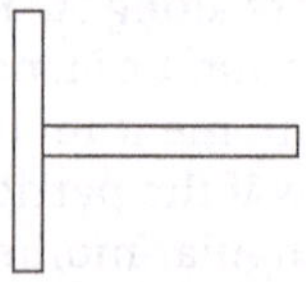

[5 M]

Hints & Solutions

1. (*b*) For system of n- particles in space, the centre of mass of such a system is at (X, Y, Z), where

$$X = \frac{\Sigma m_i x_i}{M}, \quad Y = \frac{\Sigma m_i y_i}{M} \text{ and } Z = \frac{\Sigma m_i z_i}{M}$$

Here, $M = \Sigma m_i$ is the total mass of the system. The index i runs from 1 to n.

$m_i \rightarrow$ Mass of the ith particle and position of ith particle is (x_i, y_i, z_i).

2. (*d*) The direction of the torque vector is along the axis of rotation.

3. (*a*) If $\tau_{ext} = 0$, means **L** is constant. Total angular momentum of the system is constant and remains conserved. It means that conservation of angular momentum is rotational analogue of the conservation law of the total linear momentum for a system of particles.

4. (*a*) For translational equilibrium, $\sum_{i=1}^{n} \mathbf{F}_{\text{net}} = 0$

It means $\mathbf{p}_{\text{total}} = \text{constant}$

5. (*b*) For rotational equilibrium, $\sum_{i=1}^{n} \tau_i = 0$

It means $\mathbf{L}_{\text{total}} = \text{constant}$

6. No, the centre of mass of a ring lies at its centre.

7. No, the centre of mass of a system is a hypothetical point which acts as a single mass particle of the system for an external force.

8. If geometrical centre of a body lies outside it, then centre of mass of body lies outside the body.

Centre of mass of a *L*-shaped lamina lies outside it on the line of symmetry.

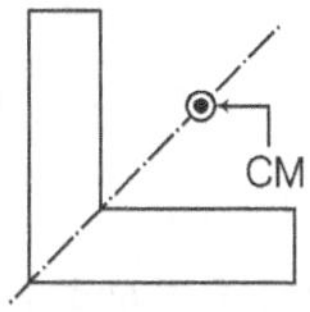

9. Centre of mass of a body lies towards region of heavier mass.
So, if bat is cut through its centre of mass, both parts are not of equal masses.

10. Suppose, **b** be the position vector of centre of mass of regular *n*-polygon.

As $(n-1)$ equal point masses each of mass m are placed at $(n-1)$ vertices of regular polygon, therefore

$$\frac{(n-1)\,mb + ma}{(n-1+1)m} = 0$$

$$\Rightarrow \quad (n-1)\,mb + ma = 0 \Rightarrow b = \frac{-a}{(n-1)}$$

11. For any planar solid, centre of mass always lies at its geometrical centre.

Geometrical centre of a triangle is intersection point of its medians. So, for any given triangular lamina

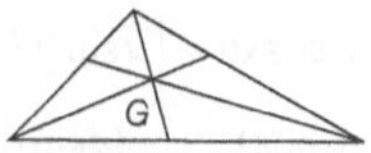

Centre of mass is at its centroid, i.e. at point of intersection of its medians. [1]

12. They appear to move in opposite directions.

13. Zero

14. This occurs due to presence of friction which is an external force.

15. Its momentum remains constant as explosion force is an internal force.

16. Zero, as torque $\tau = r_{\perp} \times F$ is zero, i.e. $r_{\perp} = 0$.

17. To produce a large torque.

18. No, angular velocity is not conserved but angular momentum is conserved.

19. The radial component of linear momentum does not contribute to angular momentum.

20. The linear momentum remain conserved if the net force on the system is zero.

21. Moment of force = force × the perpendicular distance of the line of action of force from the axis of rotation.
Hence, the moment of force about a point decreases if the line of action of the force moves towards that point. [2]

22. As torque = $\mathbf{r} \times \mathbf{F}$

That means torque produced by force is in a plane perpendicular to plane containing **r** and **F**.

So, if door is in *xy*-plane, torque produced by weight is in ± *z*-direction.

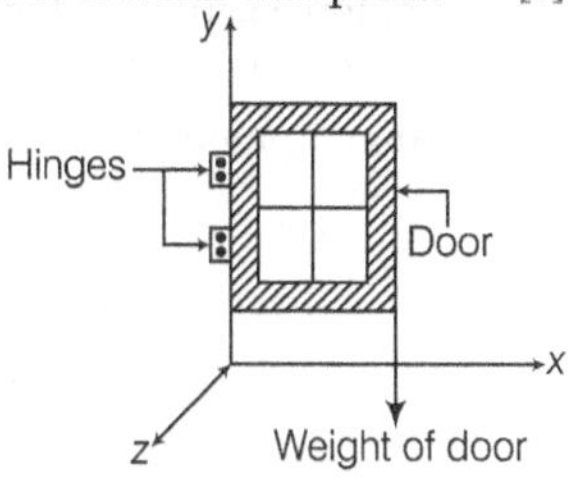

It is never about an axis passing through *y*-direction. [2]

23. No, given $\sum_i \mathbf{F}_i \neq 0$

The sum of torques about a certain point *O*

$$\sum_i \mathbf{r}_i \times \mathbf{F}_i = 0$$

The sum of torques about any other point *O′*.

$$\sum_i (\mathbf{r}_i - \mathbf{a}) \times \mathbf{F}_i = \sum_i \mathbf{r}_i \times \mathbf{F}_i - \mathbf{a} \times \sum_i \mathbf{F}_i$$

Here, the second term need not vanish. Hence, sum of torques about any other point may not be zero. [2]

24. A body in a gravitation field will be in stable equilibrium, if the vertical line through its centre of gravity passes through the base of the body. [2]

25. No, if the body is large such that *g* varies from one point to another, then centre of gravity is offset from centre of mass. But for small bodies, centre of mass and centre of gravity lies at their geometrical centres. [2]

26. No, refer to text on page 200 (Angular momentum of a particle).

27. Yes, refer to text on page 201 (Conservation of angular momentum).

28. Refer to text on pages 195 and 196 (Centre of mass and centre of mass for two particle system).

29. Both earth and moon revolves around their centre of mass. As earth is much heavier, centre of mass of system lies near surface of earth but not at its centre. Hence, moon's orbit is eccentric with respect to centre of earth. **[3]**

30. (i) Centre of mass of a sphere lies at its geometrical centre. [1/2]

(ii) Centre of mass of a cylinder lies at its geometrical centre, i.e. at the mid-point of its axis of symmetry. [1/2]

(iii) Centre of mass of a ring lies at its geometrical centre. [1/2]

(iv) Centre of mass of a cube lies at its geometrical centre, i.e. at the point of intersection of its diagonals. [1/2]

No, it is not necessary that centre of mass of a body lie inside it, because in some cases such as a ring, a hollow cylinder, a hollow sphere and a hollow cube centre of mass lies outside. [1]

31. Net force is given by $F_{\text{net}} = \dfrac{dp}{dt}$

Also, rate of change of momentum = slope of graph. [1]

As from graph, slope AB= slope CD

And slope (BC) = slope $(DE) = 0$ [1]

So, force acting on the particle is equal in regions AB and CD and in regions BC and DE (which is zero). [1]

32. Angular momentum of a particle is $\mathbf{l} = \mathbf{r} \times \mathbf{p}$

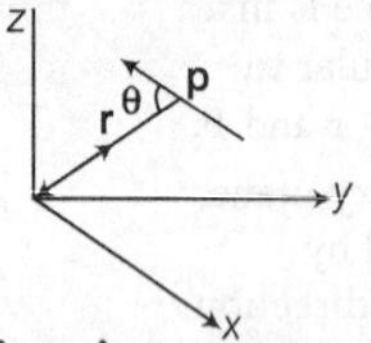

Let, $\mathbf{r} = x\hat{\mathbf{i}} + y\hat{\mathbf{j}} + z\hat{\mathbf{k}}$, where (x, y, z) is the location of particle at some instant and $\mathbf{p} = p_x\hat{\mathbf{i}} + p_y\hat{\mathbf{j}} + p_z\hat{\mathbf{k}}$, is the linear momentum of particle at that instant. [1]

Then, angular momentum of particle is given by

$$\mathbf{L} = \mathbf{r} \times \mathbf{p} = \begin{vmatrix} \hat{\mathbf{i}} & \hat{\mathbf{j}} & \hat{\mathbf{k}} \\ x & y & z \\ p_x & p_y & p_z \end{vmatrix}$$

$$= \hat{\mathbf{i}}\,(p_z \cdot y - p_y \cdot z) - \hat{\mathbf{j}}\,(p_z \cdot x - p_x \cdot z) + \hat{\mathbf{k}}\,(p_y \cdot x - p_x \cdot y) \quad \text{...(i)}$$

So, components of angular momentum along x, y and z-axes are

$$L_x = p_z y - p_y z$$
$$L_y = p_z x - p_x z$$

and $L_z = p_y x - p_x y$, respectively [1]

Now, if particle is confined to xy-plane, then

$$\mathbf{r} = x\hat{\mathbf{i}} + y\hat{\mathbf{i}} \Rightarrow z = 0$$

and $\mathbf{p} = p_x\hat{\mathbf{i}} + p_y\hat{\mathbf{j}} \Rightarrow p_z = 0$

Substituting $z = 0$ and $p_z = 0$ in Eq. (i), we get

$$\mathbf{L} = \hat{\mathbf{k}}\,(p_y x - p_x y)$$

So, angular momentum only has a z-component. As angular momentum is cross-product of **r** and **p**.

∴ It is always perpendicular to plane containing **r** and **p**. [1]

33. (i)

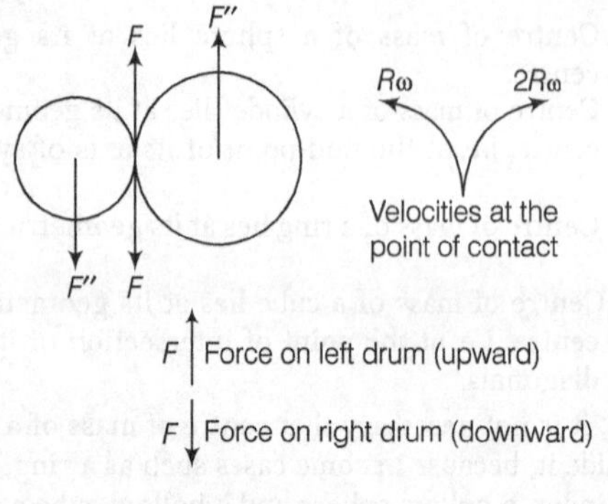

[1/2]

[1/2]

(ii) $F' = F = F''$ where F and F'' are external forces through support.

$$F_{\text{net}} = 0$$

External torque $= F \times 3R$, anti-clockwise. [1]

(iii) Let ω_1 and ω_2 be final angular velocities (anti-clockwise and clockwise respectively). Finally, there will be no friction.

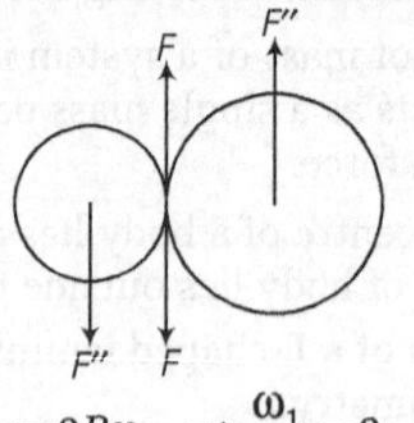

Hence, $R\omega_1 = 2R\omega_2 \Rightarrow \dfrac{\omega_1}{\omega_2} = 2$ [1]

34. Let particle is at P at any instant t and its position vector is **r**.

Then, $\mathbf{r} = x\,\hat{\mathbf{i}} + y\,\hat{\mathbf{j}}$

where, $x = u\cos\theta \cdot t$ and $y = u\sin\theta \cdot t - \dfrac{1}{2}gt^2$

and if $\mathbf{v}$ = velocity vector of particle at that instant.

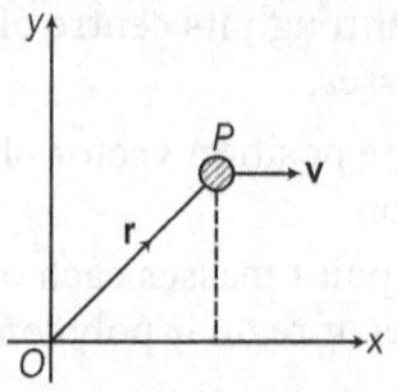

[1]

Then, $\mathbf{v} = \mathbf{v}_x\hat{\mathbf{i}} + \mathbf{v}_y\hat{\mathbf{j}}$

where, $v_x = u\cos\theta$ and $v_y = u\sin\theta - gt$

So, $\mathbf{r} = (u\cos\theta)t\,\hat{\mathbf{i}} + \left((u\sin\theta)\cdot t - \dfrac{1}{2}gt^2\right)\hat{\mathbf{j}}$

and $\mathbf{v} = u\cos\theta\,\hat{\mathbf{i}} + (u\sin\theta - gt)\,\hat{\mathbf{j}}$ [1]

Hence, $\mathbf{L}$ = angular momentum of particle $= m\,(\mathbf{r} \times \mathbf{v})$

$$= m \begin{vmatrix} \hat{\mathbf{i}} & \hat{\mathbf{j}} & \hat{\mathbf{k}} \\ u\cos\theta t & \left(u\sin\theta - \frac{1}{2}gt\right)t & 0 \\ u\cos\theta & (u\sin\theta - gt) & 0 \end{vmatrix}$$

$$= -\frac{1}{2}m\,(u\cos\theta)\,gt^2 \cdot \hat{\mathbf{k}}$$

So, angular momentum is along Z-axis. [1]

35. Refer to text on page 200 (Angular momentum of a particle).

36. Refer to text on page 201 (Conservation of angular momentum).

37. Its potential energy is minimum as the body is in stable equilibrium.

As, $|\mathbf{F}| = |\dfrac{dU}{dr}|$ and $U = U_{\min}$ [1]

So, $\dfrac{dU}{dr} = 0$ or $F_{\text{net}} = 0$ [1]

When the particle system is in stable equilibrium. [1]

38. (i) Angular momentum is constant about any point on axis of rotation.

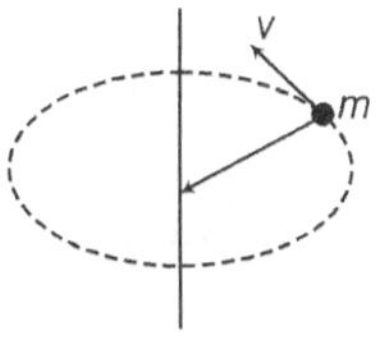

[1½]

(ii) Angular momentum about any point which is not on axis is a variable that change with time. [1½]

39. First consider the composite plate,

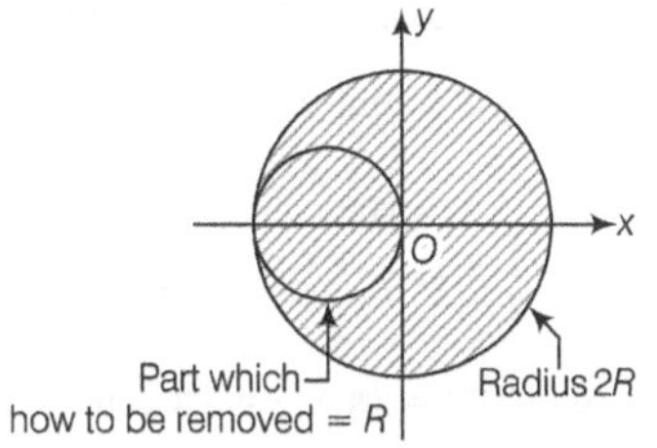

[1]

x-coordinate of centre of mass of composite plate is given by $$x_{CM} = \frac{m_1 x_1 + m_2 x_2}{m_1 + m_2}$$ [1]

where,

m_1 = mass of disc of radius $2R$

x_1 = position of centre of mass of disc with hole

m_2 = mass of part removed of radius R

x_2 = position of centre of mass of part removed.

Now, as centre of mass of composite plate is at origin,

so $$x_{CM} = 0 = \frac{m_1 x_1 + m_2 x_2}{m_1 + m_2}$$

or $$m_1 x_1 + m_2 x_2 = 0$$ [1]

Now, we are finding x_1.

So, $$x_1 = -\frac{m_2 x_2}{m_1}$$

Now, $$\frac{m_2}{m_1} = \frac{\text{density} \times \text{volume of portion 2}}{\text{density} \times \text{volume of portion 1}} = \frac{\text{thickness} \times \text{area of portion 2}}{\text{thickness} \times \text{area of portion 1}}$$

$$\Rightarrow \frac{m_2}{m_1} = \frac{A_2}{A_1} = \frac{\pi R^2}{\pi (2R)^2 - \pi R^2} = \frac{1}{3}$$ [1]

Also, $x_2 = -R$, (negative sign is w.r.t. coordinate axes)

Hence, $$x_1 = -\frac{m_2}{m_1} \cdot x_2 = -\frac{1}{3}(-R) = \frac{1}{3}R$$

So, centre of mass located at $\left(x = \frac{1}{3}R,\ y = 0\right)$ point. [1]

40. A sketch of system of particles at any instant is shown. Let, O be the origin chosen.

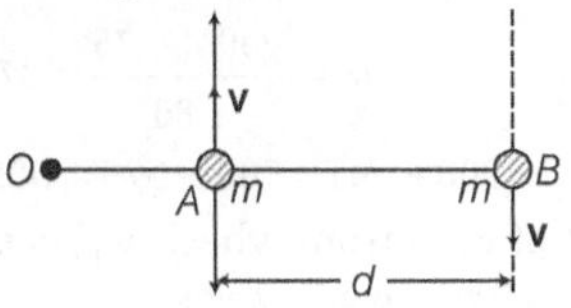

[1]

Then, angular momentum of particle at A about O is
$$\mathbf{l}_1 = \mathbf{OA} \times \mathbf{p} = \mathbf{OA} \times m\mathbf{v} = m(\mathbf{OA} \times \mathbf{v})$$ [1]

and angular momentum of particle at B about O is
$$\mathbf{l}_2 = \mathbf{OB} \times \mathbf{p} = \mathbf{OB} \times (-m\mathbf{v}) = -m(\mathbf{OB} \times \mathbf{v})$$ [1]

So, total angular momentum of the system of particles is
$$\mathbf{L} = \mathbf{l}_1 + \mathbf{l}_2 = m(\mathbf{OA} \times \mathbf{v}) - m(\mathbf{OB} \times \mathbf{v}) = m(\mathbf{OA} \times \mathbf{v} - \mathbf{OB} \times \mathbf{v}) = m(\mathbf{OA} - \mathbf{OB}) \times \mathbf{v} = m(\mathbf{BA}) \times \mathbf{v}$$ [1]

{As, **BA** = position vector of **A** − position vector of **B**}

Above expression is independent of choice of origin.

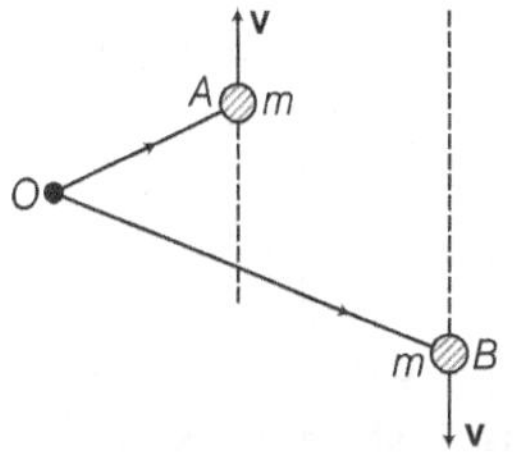

This is true even when particles are not in a straight line.

$$\mathbf{L}_i = \mathbf{l}_1 + \mathbf{l}_2 = m(\mathbf{OA} \times \mathbf{v} - \mathbf{OB} \times \mathbf{v}) = m(\mathbf{BA}) \times \mathbf{v}$$

Which is same as previous result. So, angular momentum of system is independent of choice of origin. [1]

41. As semicircular disc is symmetrical about its one of diameter, we take axes as shown. So, now we only have to calculate Y_{CM} $\cdot$(As, X_{CM} is zero by symmetry and choice of origin).

Now, $$Y_{CM} = \frac{\int y\,dm}{\int dm}$$

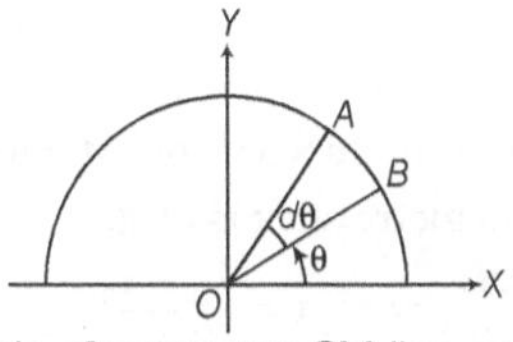

Axis of symmetry CM lies on this

Now, for a small element OAB, as element is small and it can be treated as a triangle so,

Area of sector $OAB = \frac{1}{2} \times r \times r d\theta$ [1]

Height of triangle = r

Base of triangle = $AB = r d\theta$

So, its mass $dm = \frac{1}{2} r^2 d\theta \cdot \rho$ $\quad \left[\because \rho = \frac{\text{mass}}{\text{area}}\right]$

As centre of mass of a triangle is at a distance of $\frac{2}{3}$ from its vertex (at centroid, intersection of medians).

So, $y = \frac{2}{3} r \sin\theta$ (location of CM of small sector AOB).

$$\text{So, } Y_{CM}=\frac{\int_0^{\pi} y\,dm}{\int_0^{\pi} dm}=\frac{\int_0^{\pi}\frac{2}{3}r\sin\theta\times\frac{1}{2}r^2 d\theta\cdot\rho}{\int_0^{\pi}\frac{1}{2}r^2\rho d\theta}$$ [2]

$$=\frac{\frac{1}{2}\times\frac{2}{3}r^3\cdot\rho\int_0^{\pi}\sin\theta d\theta}{\frac{1}{2}r^2\rho\cdot\int_0^{\pi}d\theta}=\frac{\frac{2r}{3}\int_0^{\pi}\sin\theta d\theta}{\int_0^{\pi}d\theta}$$

$$=\frac{\frac{2r}{3}[-\cos\theta]_0^{\pi}}{[\theta]_0^{\pi}}=\frac{\frac{-2r}{3}(\cos\pi-\cos 0^\circ)}{(\pi-0)}$$ [1]

$=4r/3\pi$

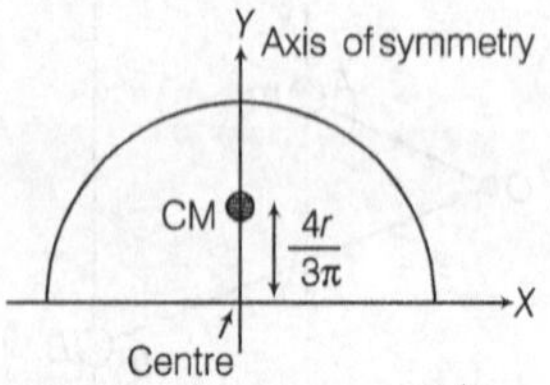

So, CM of disc is at a distance of $\frac{4r}{3\pi}$ from its centre on its axis of symmetry. [1]

42. Refer to text on page 202 (Equilibrium of a rigid body).

43. Let total mass of the metre stick be M kg.

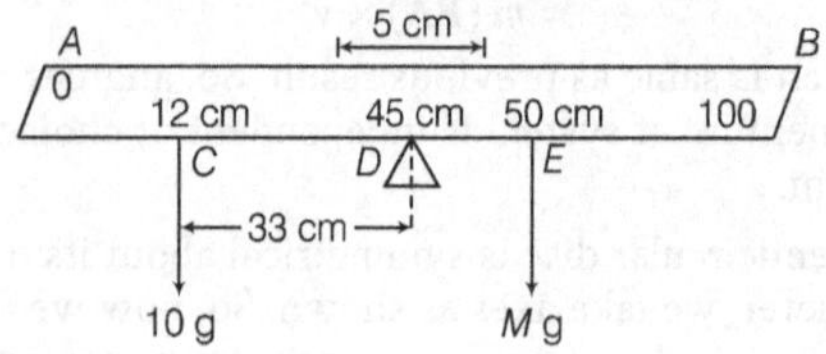

Distance between mid-point E and new centre of gravity $(DE)=50-45=5$ cm

Distance between 12 cm mark and new centre of gravity $(CD)=45-12=33$ cm [1]

From principle of moments in equilibrium,

$$M\times DE=(2\times 5)\times CD$$

$$M\times 5=10\times 33 \quad\text{or}\quad M=66\text{ g}$$

$\therefore$ Mass of the metre stick is 66 g. [1]

44. Torque, $\tau=\frac{d\mathbf{L}}{dt} \Rightarrow \tau=\frac{\mathbf{L}_2-\mathbf{L}_1}{t}$ [1]

Angular moment of the wheel,

$$\mathbf{L}_2=\tau t+\mathbf{L}_1=10\times 4+2=40+2=42\text{ kgm}^2\text{s}^{-1}$$ [1]

45. Mass of an atom is concentrated at its nucleus, they can be treated as point masses.

We take nucleus of hydrogen atom at origin and nucleus of chlorine atom on x-axis.

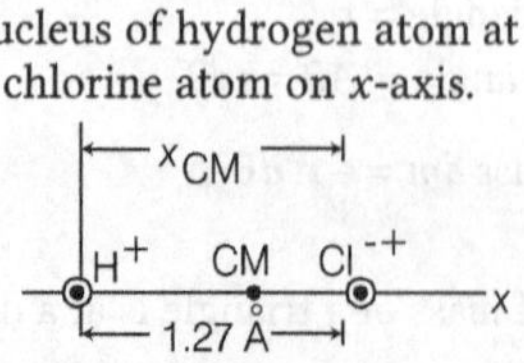

where, m_1 = mass of hydrogen = 1

m_2 = mass of chlorine = 35.5

$x_1=0,\ x_2=1.27$ Å [1]

As the system is symmetrical about x-axis, its centre of mass lies on x-axis.

Using $\quad x_{CM}=\frac{m_1x_1+m_2x_2}{m_1+m_2}$

$$=\frac{1\times 0+35.5\times 1.27}{1+35.5}$$

$=1.235$ Å

$=1.235\times 10^{-10}$ m (from origin)

So, centre of mass of HCl molecule is nearly 1.235 Å from the H-nucleus on the line joining H and Cl nuclei. [1]

46. Here, $M=40$ kg, $R=1$m, $\nu=120$ rpm $=\frac{120}{60}$ rps

$\Rightarrow$ Frequency, $\nu=2$ rps

Therefore, $I=\frac{1}{2}MR^2=\frac{1}{2}\times 40\times(1)^2=20\text{ kg - m}^2$

and $\quad\omega=2\pi\nu=2\pi\times 2=4\pi\text{ rads}^{-1}$ [1]

So, angular momentum,

$$L=I\omega=20\times 4\pi=20\times 4\times 3.14$$

$$L=251.2\text{ kg - m}^2\text{s}^{-1}$$ [1]

47. (i) Angular displacement is

$\Delta\theta=\theta_f-\theta_i=6-(-2)=8$ rad

(ii) $\Delta\theta=\theta_f-\theta_i=-8\text{ rad}-(-4\text{ rad})=-4$ rad

(iii) $\Delta\theta=-2\text{ rad}-(+6\text{ rad})=-8$ rad

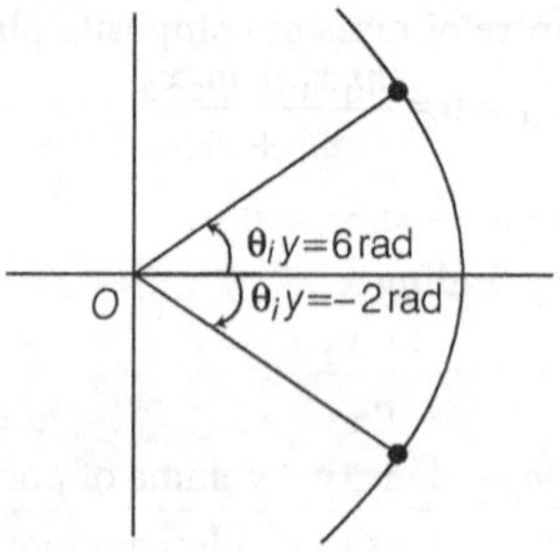

In cases (ii) and (iii), angular displacement is negative. [2 + 1]

48. Total mass of the car = 1800 kg

Let m and $(900-m)$ kg be the masses of each front wheel and each back wheel, respectively.

Distance of centre of gravity from the front axle = 1.05 m

$\therefore$ Distance of centre of gravity from the back axle $=1.80-1.05=0.75$m [1/2]

Taking torque about centre of gravity,

$$m\times 1.05=(900-m)\times 0.75$$

or $\quad 1.05\,m+0.75\,m=900\times 0.75$

or $\quad 1.80\,m=900\times 0.75$

or $\quad m=\frac{900\times 0.75}{1.80}=375$ kg

$\therefore\quad (900-m)=900-375=525$ kg [1]

$\therefore$ Weight of each front wheel $(w_1)=m_1g$

$$w_1=375\times 9.8=3675\text{ N}$$ [1/2]

Force exerted by the level ground on each front wheel.
= force exerted by each front wheel on the level ground
$(w_1) = 3675$ N

Weight of each back wheel $(w_2) = m_2 g$

$$w_2 = 525 \times 9.8 = 5145 \text{ N}$$

∴ Force exerted by the level ground on each back wheel.
= force exerted by each back wheel on level ground (w_2)
= 5145 N. [1]

49. Let mass of comet be M and its angular speed be ω when situated at a distance r from the Sun, then its angular momentum

$$L = I\omega = Mr^2\omega$$

If v be the linear speed, then $L = Mr^2\omega = Mrv$ [1]

In accordance with conservation law of angular momentum, we can write that

$$mr_1v_1 = mr_2v_2$$ [1]

$$\therefore \quad v_2 = \frac{r_1 v_1}{r_2} = \frac{7 \times 10^{10} \times 60}{1.4 \times 10^{13}} = 0.3 \text{ km/s or } 300 \text{ m/s}$$ [1]

50. Let the x-axis be along the length of the rod and origin at one of its end as shown in figure.

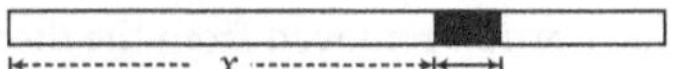

As rod is along x-axis, for all points on it y and z will be zero, so $y_{CM} = 0$ and $z_{CM} = 0$, i.e. centre of mass will be on the rod. Now, consider an element of rod of length dx at a distance x from the origin.

Mass of this element, $dm = \lambda dx = (1 + 2x)dx$ [1]

$$x_{CM} = \frac{\int x\,dm}{\int dm} = \frac{\int_0^1 x(1+2x)dx}{\int_0^1 (1+2x)dx} = \frac{\left[\frac{x^2}{2} + \frac{2x^3}{3}\right]_0^1}{[x + x^2]_0^1}$$ [1]

$$= \left[\frac{\frac{(1)^2}{2} + \frac{2(1)^3}{3} - 0 - 0}{1 + (1)^2 - 0 - 0}\right] = \frac{\frac{1}{2} + \frac{2}{3}}{2} = \frac{7}{12} \text{ m}$$ [1]

51. Refer to example 9 on page 201.

52.

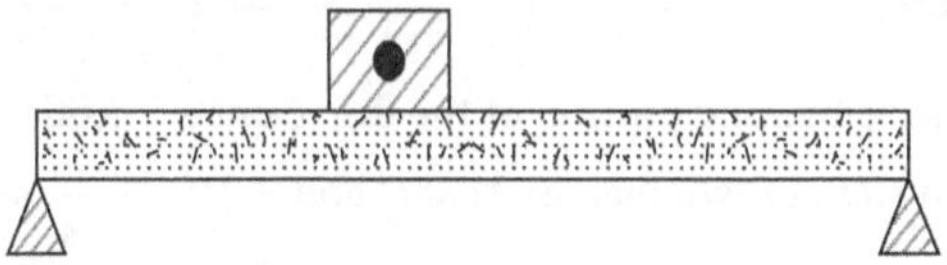

Forces involved are (i) weight of beam = $F_1 = m_1 g$.
(ii) weight of mass placed over beam = $F_2 = m_2 g$.
(ii) Reactions of supports F_3 and F_4 which we have to found. Free body diagram of our system is

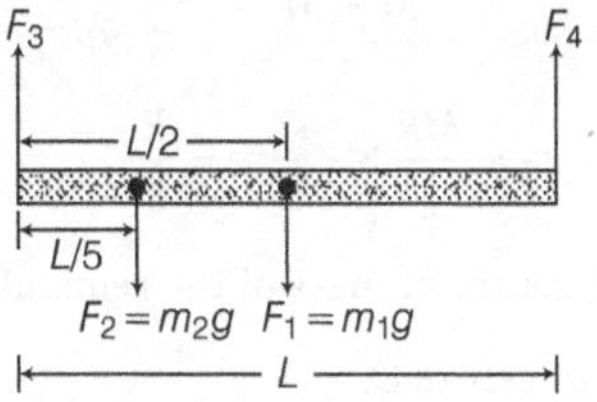

[1]

In static equilibrium problem, calculation involves the following equations

Sum of all vertical (or vertical component of) forces is zero,

$$\Sigma F_V = 0$$

Sum of all horizontal forces or horizontal components of forces is zero, $\Delta F_H = 0$

Sum of all torques is zero.

$$\Sigma\tau = 0$$ [1]

You may take signs as
All forces along + y-direction are positive.
All forces along + x-direction are positive.
All forces along − y-direction are negative.
All forces along −x-direction are negative.
All anti-clockwise torques are positive.
All clockwise torques are negative.

In given problem, as the beam is in equilibrium,

$$\Sigma F_V = 0$$ [1]

or $\quad F_3 + F_4 - F_2 - F_1 = 0$

or $\quad F_3 + F_4 - m_2 g - m_1 g = 0 \quad$ ...(i)

and $\quad \Sigma\tau = 0$

Let us choose rotation axis through right hand corner of beam.

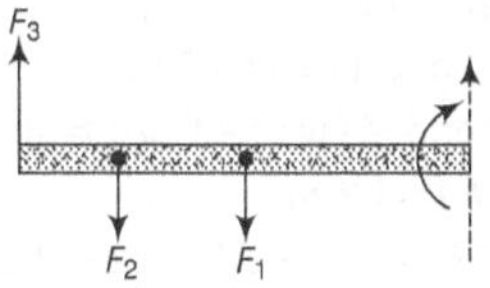

Sum of all torques is

$$F_2 \times \frac{4}{5}L + F_1 \times \frac{L}{2} - F_3 \times L = 0$$

(no torque due to force F_4) [1]

From above equation,

$$\frac{4}{5}F_2 + F_1 - F_3 = 0$$

or $\quad \frac{4}{5} m_2 g + m_1 g - F_3 = 0 \quad$ ...(ii)

When all the equations are formed, solve them like linear simultaneous equations to get desired results.

In given problem, from Eq. (ii) we get

$$F_3 = \frac{4}{5} m_2 g + m_1 g = \frac{4}{5} \times 5 \times 10 + 20 \times 10$$
$$= 20 \times 12 = 240 \text{ N}$$

Here, $m_1 = 20$ kg, $m_2 = 5$ kg, $g = 10 \text{ m/s}^2$

Substituting value of F_3, m_1 and m_2 in Eq. (i), we get

$$240 + F_4 - 5 \times 10 - 20 \times 10 = 0$$

or $\quad F_4 = 50 + 200 - 240$

$$F_4 = 10 \text{ N}$$

So, support reactions are 240 N on left support and 10 N on right support. [1]

53. Different forces acting on the system are

(i) Normal reaction of the floor at point B, N_B acting in vertically upward direction.

(ii) Normal reaction of the floor at point C, N_C acting in vertically upward direction.

(iii) Weight at point F, acting vertically downward.

(iv) Tensions in the string, as the ladder will have a tendency to slide at point B and point C (as the floor is frictionless) so, at both points D and E the string will be stretched in outward direction, therefore the tensions at both points will be along inward. [2]

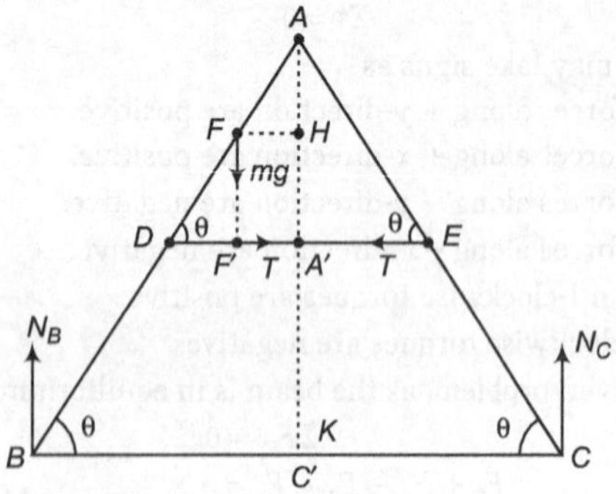

[1/2]

Given, length of each side of ladder

$$AB = AC = 1.6 \text{ m}$$

Let the sides of the ladder subtend an angle θ with the horizontal and forces exerted by the floor on the ladder at points B and C be N_B and N_C, respectively.

Length of the rope $(DE) = 0.5$ m

Weight suspended $(w) = 40$ kg-f $= 40 \times 9.8 = 392$ N

Distance $(BF) = 1.2$ m

$\therefore$ Distance $(AF) = AB - BF = 1.6 - 1.2 = 0.4$ m

$$\angle ABC = \angle ADE = \angle ACB = \angle AED = \theta$$

Let A' be the mid-point of the rope

$$\therefore \quad DA' = \frac{0.5}{2} = 0.25 \text{ m}$$

$$\therefore \quad DF' = F'A' = \frac{1}{2} DA' = \frac{1}{2} \times 0.25 = 0.125 \text{ m}$$

For translational equilibrium of the step ladder,

$$N_B + N_C = W \Rightarrow N_B + N_C = 392 \text{ N} \quad \text{...(i)}$$

Taking moment of forces about point A for side AB,

$$N_B \times BC' = W \times F'A' + T \times AA'$$

But $BC' = AB\cos\theta$ and $AA' = AD\sin\theta$

$$N_B \times AB\cos\theta = W \times 0.125 + T \times AD\sin\theta \quad \text{...(ii)}$$

But from $\Delta DFF'$,

$$\cos\theta = \frac{DF'}{DF} = \frac{0.125}{0.4} = 0.3125$$

$$\theta = 72.8^\circ$$

$$\therefore \quad \cos\theta = \cos 72.8^\circ = 0.3125 \quad [1]$$

$$\sin\theta = \sin 72.8^\circ = 0.9553$$

$$\tan\theta = \tan 72.8^\circ = 3.2350$$

Substituting values in Eq. (ii), we get

$$N_B \times 1.6 \times 0.3125 = (392 \times 0.125) + (T \times 0.8 \times 0.9553)$$

or $\quad 0.5\, N_B = 0.764T + 49 \quad$ ...(iii)

Now, taking moment of forces about point A, for side AC.

$$N_C \times CC' = T \times AA'$$

But $CC' = AC\cos\theta$ and $AA' = AE\sin\theta$

$$\therefore \quad N_C \times AC\cos\theta = T \times AE\sin\theta$$

$$N_C \times 1.6 \times 0.3125 = T \times 0.8 \times 0.9553$$

$$0.5\, N_C = 0.764\, T \quad \text{...(iv)}$$

Substituting value from Eq. (iv) in Eq. (iii), we get

$$0.5\, N_B = 0.5\, N_C + 49$$

$$0.5\,(N_B - N_C) = 49$$

$$\frac{1}{2}(N_B - N_C) = 49$$

$$N_B - N_C = 98 \quad \text{...(v)} \quad [1]$$

Adding Eqs. (i) and (v), we get

$$2N_B = 392 + 98 = 490 \text{ or } N_B = 245 \text{ N}$$

From Eq. (i),

$$N_C = 392 - 245 \text{ N} = 147 \text{ N}$$

From Eq (iv), $\quad T = \dfrac{0.5 \times 147}{0.764} = 96.2$ N [1/2]

54. Let mass per unit area of the disc be m.

$\therefore$ Mass of the disc (M) = total area of disc × mass per unit area $= \pi R^2 m$.

Mass of the portion removed from the disc (M')

$$= \pi\left(\frac{R}{2}\right)^2 m \Rightarrow \frac{\pi R^2}{4} m = \frac{M}{4} \quad [1]$$

The centre of mass of the original disc is O and the centre of mass of the removed part is O_1 and let centre of mass of the remaining part be O_2. [1/2]

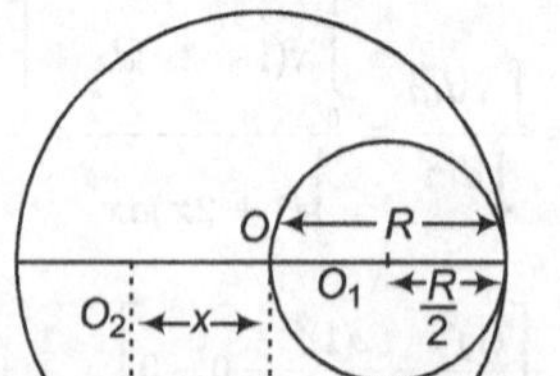

According to the question, figure can be drawn as [1]

Here, $\quad OO_1 = \dfrac{R}{2}$

The remaining portion of the disc can be considered as a system of two masses M at O and $-M' = -\dfrac{M}{4}$ at O_1. [1]

If the distance of the centre of mass of the remaining part from the centre O is at a distance x, then

$$x = \frac{M \times 0 - M' \times \frac{R}{2}}{M - M'} = \frac{-\frac{M}{4} \times \frac{R}{2}}{M - \frac{M}{4}}$$

$$= -\frac{MR}{8} \times \frac{4}{3M} = -\frac{R}{6} \quad [1]$$

Therefore, centre of mass of the remaining part is at $\dfrac{R}{6}$ to the left of centre O. [1/2]

55. (i) Assuming D as the origin, DC as x-axis and DA as Y-axis, we have

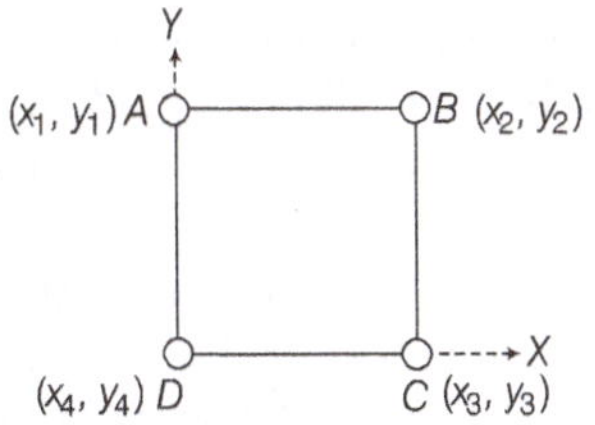

$$m_1 = 1 \text{ kg}; (x_1, y_1) = (0, 1 \text{ m})$$
$$m_2 = 2 \text{ kg}; (x_2, y_2) = (1 \text{ m}, 1 \text{ m})$$
$$m_3 = 3 \text{ kg}; (x_3, y_3) = (1 \text{ m}, 0)$$
and $m_4 = 4 \text{ kg}; (x_4, y_4) = (0, 0)$ [1]

Coordinates of their CM are

$$x_{CM} = \frac{m_1x_1 + m_2x_2 + m_3x_3 + m_4x_4}{m_1 + m_2 + m_3 + m_4}$$
$$= \frac{1(0) + 2(1) + 3(1) + 4(0)}{1 + 2 + 3 + 4} = \frac{5}{10} = \frac{1}{2} \text{ m} = 0.5 \text{ m}$$

Similarly, $y_{CM} = \frac{m_1y_1 + m_2y_2 + m_3y_3 + m_4y_4}{m_1 + m_2 + m_3 + m_4}$

$$= \frac{1(1) + 2(1) + 3(0) + 4(0)}{1 + 2 + 3 + 4} = \frac{3}{10} \text{m}$$
$$= 0.3 \text{ m}$$

$\therefore$ Centre of mass is at $(x_{CM}, y_{CM}) = (0.5 \text{ m}, 0.3 \text{ m})$ [1½]

(ii) This system is symmetrical about the x-axis. Hence, we need to find x_{CM}. Here, we will take coordinates of CM of rods.

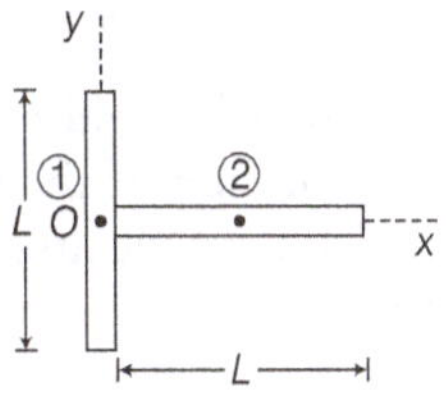

[1]

For rod 1, mass $m_1 = m$

x-coordinate $x_1 = 0$

For rod 2, mass $m_2 = m$

x-coordinate $x_2 = L/2$

$$\therefore \quad x_{CM} = \frac{m_1x_1 + m_2x_2}{m_1 + m_2}$$

$$x_{CM} = \frac{m \times 0 + m \times \frac{L}{2}}{m + m} = \frac{m\frac{L}{2}}{2m} = \frac{L}{4}$$

Similarly, $y_{CM} = 0$

$\therefore$ Centre of mass $\equiv \left(\frac{L}{4}, 0\right)$ [1½]

TOPIC 02 Moment of Inertia

The property of a body by virtue of which a rigid body opposes the torque tending to change its state of rest or of uniform rotation about an axis is called **rotational inertia** or **moment of inertia.**

To understand moment of inertia, let us consider a rigid body rotating about a fixed axis. For a rotating rigid body, kinetic energy is the sum of kinetic energies of individual particles.

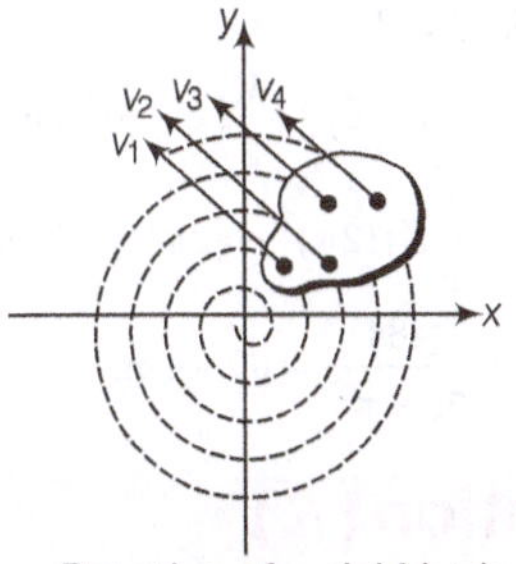

Rotation of a rigid body

So, kinetic energy of a rotating body,

$$K = \frac{1}{2}m_1v_1^2 + \frac{1}{2}m_2v_2^2 + \cdots + \frac{1}{2}m_nv_n^2$$

or $$K = \sum_{i=1}^{n} \frac{1}{2}m_iv_i^2$$

Substituting $v = r\omega$, $K = \Sigma \frac{1}{2}m_ir_i^2\omega^2$

where m_i is the mass of particle, v_i is the linear velocity. As, the angular velocity ω is same for all the particles of rigid body.

So, $$K = \frac{1}{2}\omega^2 \left(\sum_{i=1}^{n} m_ir_i^2\right) \quad \ldots\text{(i)}$$

The quantity $\Sigma (m_ir_i^2)$ depends on distribution of mass around axis of rotation. This quantity is called **moment of inertia** (I).

$$\boxed{\text{Kinetic energy, } K = \frac{1}{2}I\omega^2} \quad \ldots\text{(ii)}$$

For translational motion, the kinetic energy of a particle of mass m and speed v is

$$\text{KE} = \frac{1}{2}mv^2 \quad \ldots\text{(iii)}$$

By comparing Eqs. (ii) and (iii), we can get that moment of inertia in the rotational analogue of mass. So, for a rotating body, its moment of inertia

$$I = \sum_{i=1}^{n} m_i r_i^2$$

Hence, **moment of inertia of a rigid body about a fixed axis is defined as the sum of the products of the masses of the particles constituting the body and the squares of their respective distances from the axis of rotation.**

Some Important Points about Moment of Inertia

Moment of inertia is a measure of rotational inertia and it plays same role as played by mass in translational motion.

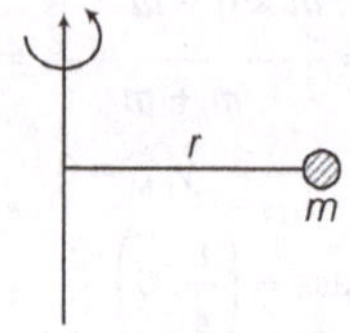

Particle revolving in a path

So, for a particle of mass m revolving in a path of radius r, moment of inertia is $I = mr^2$.

For a system of n particles, $I = \sum_{i=1}^{n} m_i r_i^2$

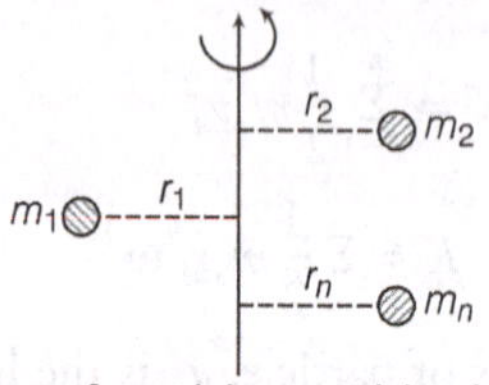

Number of particles revolving in a path

For continuous mass distributions, treating a differentially small mass as a particle moment of inertia of complete body

$$I = \int r^2 dm$$

where, integral is taken for complete body.

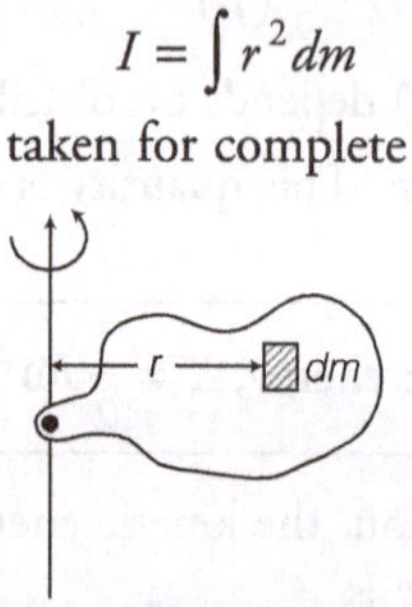

A small particle in a rigid body to find moment of inertia of the whole body

A heavy wheel called flywheel is attached to the shaft of steam engine, automobile engine etc. because of its large moment of inertia, the flywheel opposes the sudden increase or decrease of the speed of the vehicle. It allows a gradual change in the speed and prevents jerky motion and hence ensure smooth ride of passengers.

In a bicycle, bullock-cart etc., the moment of inertia is increased by concentrating most of the mass at the rim of the wheel and connecting the rim to the axle through the spokes. Even after we stop paddling, the wheels of a bicycle continue to rotate for sometime due to their large moment of inertia.

Relation between Rotational Kinetic Energy and Moment of Inertia

For system of n particles rotational kinetic energy,

$$\text{KE} = \Sigma\left(\frac{1}{2}mv^2\right) = \frac{1}{2}(\Sigma\, mr^2)\,\omega^2$$

But $\quad \Sigma\, mr^2 = I$

Therefore, rotational $\text{KE} = \frac{1}{2} I\omega^2$

When $\omega = 1$, rotational $\text{KE} = \frac{1}{2} I$

Hence, **the moment of inertia of a rigid body about an axis of rotation is numerically equal to twice the rotational kinetic energy of the body when it is rotating with unit angular velocity about that axis.**

Example 1 An energy of 484 J is spent in increasing the speed of a flywheel from 60 rpm to 360 rpm. Calculate moment of inertia of flywheel.

Sol. Energy spent, $W = 484$ J

Initial speed, $\omega_1 = 60 \text{ rpm} = \frac{60}{60} \times 2\pi = 2\pi$ rad/s

Final speed, $\omega_2 = 360 \text{ rpm} = \frac{360}{60} \times 2\pi = 12\pi$ rad/s

Moment of inertia, $I = ?$

Energy spent, $W = E_2 - E_1 = \frac{1}{2}I\omega_2^2 - \frac{1}{2}I\omega_1^2$

$$= \frac{1}{2}I[(12\pi)^2 - (2\pi)^2] = 70I\pi^2$$

$$\Rightarrow \quad I = \frac{484}{70 \times \pi^2} = 0.7 \text{ kg-m}^2.$$

Radius of Gyration (K)

The radius of gyration of a body about an axis may be defined as the distance from the axis of a point mass whose mass is equal to the mass of whole body and whose moment of inertia is equal to the moment of inertia of the body about the axis.

When square of radius of gyration is multiplied with the mass of the body, gives the moment of inertia of the body about the given axis.

$$I = MK^2$$

$$\boxed{\text{Radius of gyration, } K = \sqrt{\frac{I}{M}}}$$

where, K is radius of gyration of the body.

Note Factors on which radius of gyration of a body depend are

(a) Position and direction of the axis of rotation.

(b) Distribution of mass about the axis of rotation.

Example 2 Four masses are rotated about an axis as shown. Find radius of gyration of the system. **NCERT**

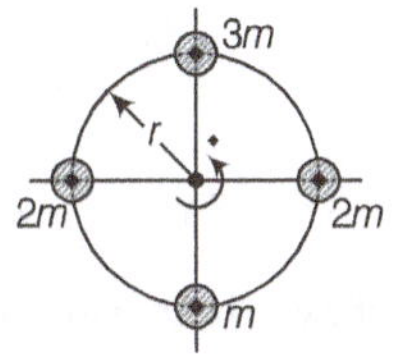

Sol. Moment of inertia of a mass about axis = mass × (distance)^2

∴ Moments of inertia of masses are

$$I_1 = 2mr^2$$

$$\Rightarrow \quad I_2 = 3m \cdot r^2$$

$$I_3 = 2m \cdot r^2$$

$$\Rightarrow \quad I_4 = m \cdot r^2$$

So, total moment of inertia of system of masses

$$= I_1 + I_2 + I_3 + I_4$$

$$= 8\,mr^2$$

Total mass of system = $8m$

If radius of gyration is K, then

$$I = MK^2$$

or $$K^2 = \frac{I}{M} = \frac{8\,mr^2}{8\,m}$$

or $$K = r$$

Moment of Inertia in Some Standard Cases

Body	Axis of rotation	Figure	Moment of inertia	K	K^2/R^2
Thin circular ring, radius R	About an axis passing through CG and perpendicular to its plane	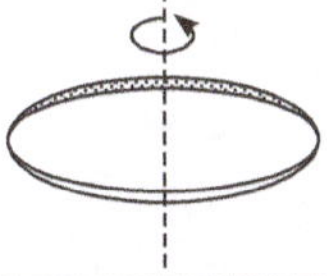	MR^2	R	1
Thin circular ring, radius R	About its diameter	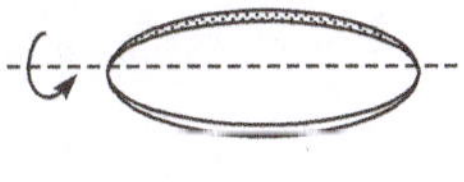	$\frac{1}{2}MR^2$	$\frac{R}{\sqrt{2}}$	$\frac{1}{2}$
Thin rod length, L	Perpendicular to rod at mid-point	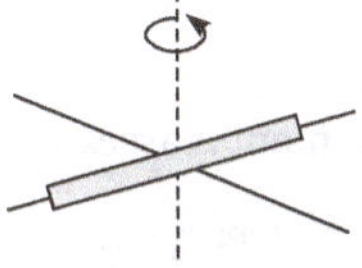	$\frac{1}{12}ML^2$	$\frac{L}{\sqrt{12}}$	
Circular disc, radius R	Perpendicular to disc at centre	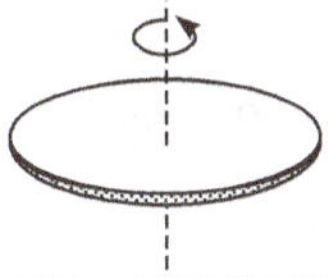	$\frac{1}{2}MR^2$	$\frac{R}{2}$	$\frac{1}{2}$
Circular disc, radius R	Diameter	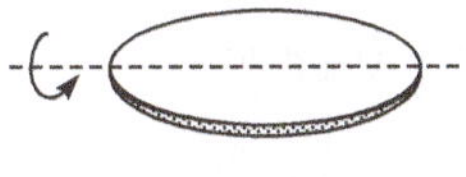	$\frac{1}{4}MR^2$	$\frac{R}{4}$	$\frac{1}{4}$
Hollow cylinder, radius R	About its own axis	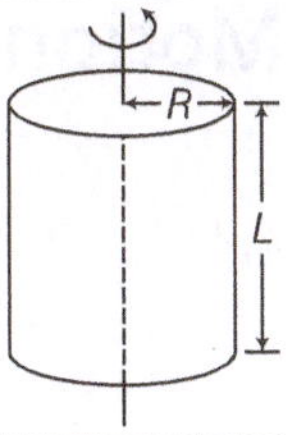	MR^2	R	1

Body	Axis of rotation	Figure	Moment of inertia	K	K^2/R^2
Solid cylindrical, radius R	About its own axis		$\frac{MR^2}{2}$	$\frac{R}{2}$	$\frac{1}{2}$
Solid sphere, radius R	About its diametric axis	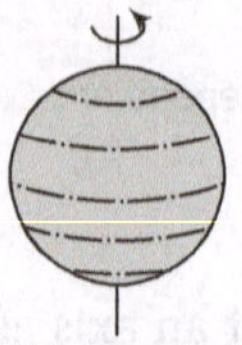	$\frac{2}{5}MR^2$	$\sqrt{\frac{2}{5}}R$	$\frac{2}{5}$
Hollow sphere, radius R	About its diametric axis	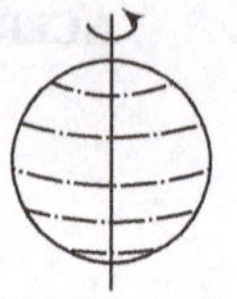	$\frac{2}{3}MR^2$	$\sqrt{\frac{2}{3}}R$	$\frac{2}{3}$

Example 3 Three masses m_1, m_2 and m_3 are located at the vertices of an equilateral triangle of length a. What is moment of inertia of the system about an axis along the altitude of the triangle passing through m_1.

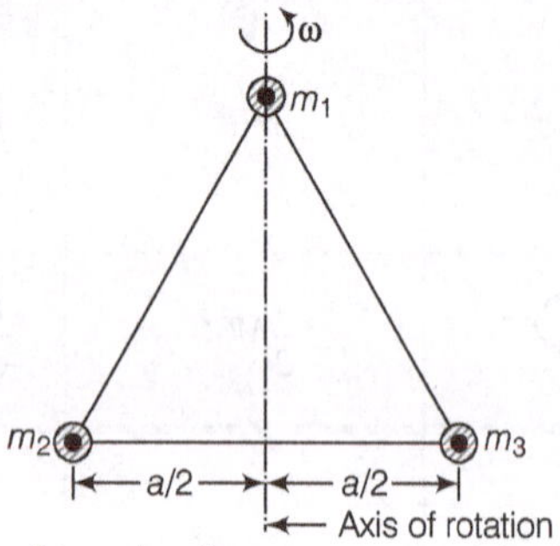

Sol. Moment of inertia of a system containing point masses is

$$I = \sum_{i=1}^{n} m_i r_i^2 \Rightarrow I = m_1 r_1^2 + m_2 r_2^2 + m_3 r_3^2 + \ldots$$

where,

m_i = mass of particle, r_i = distance from axis of rotation.

Now, $r_1 = 0, r_2 = \frac{a}{2}, r_3 = \frac{a}{2}$

$$\therefore \quad I = m_1(0)^2 + m_2\left(\frac{a}{2}\right)^2 + m_3\left(\frac{a}{2}\right)^2 = \frac{a^2}{4}(m_1 + m_2)$$

Equations of Rotational Motion

The three equations of linear motion are

(i) $v = u + at$ (ii) $s = ut + \frac{1}{2}at^2$

(iii) $v^2 - u^2 = 2as$

where, the symbols have their usual meaning.

In the similar way, we can write equations of motion for rotational motion such as

(i) $\omega = \omega_0 + \alpha t$

(ii) $\theta = \omega_0 t + \frac{1}{2}\alpha t^2$

(iii) $\omega^2 - \omega_0^2 = 2\alpha(\theta - \theta_0)$

where θ_0 and ω_0 are the initial angular displacement and initial angular velocity of the body and α is angular acceleration, respectively.

Example 4 The angular speed of a motor wheel is increased from 1200 rpm to 3120 rpm in 16s.

(i) What is its angular acceleration, assuming the acceleration to be uniform?

(ii) How many revolutions does the engine make during this time? **NCERT**

Sol. (i) Given,

Initial revolution of the wheel, $N_0 = 1200$ rpm

Final revolution of the wheel, $N = 3120$ rpm

Time, $t = 16$ s

Angular acceleration, $\alpha = ?$

Number of revolutions of the engine = ?

Initial angular speed, $\omega_0 = \frac{2\pi N_0}{60} = \frac{2\pi \times 1200}{60}$

$= 40\pi$ rad/s

Final angular speed, $\omega = \frac{2\pi N}{60} = \frac{2\pi \times 3120}{60}$

$= 104\pi$ rad/s

Angular acceleration, $\alpha = \frac{\omega - \omega_0}{t}$,

$$\alpha = \frac{104\pi - 40\pi}{16} = 4\pi \text{ rad/s}^2$$

(ii) Now, evaluate the angular displacement of the motor wheel because the number of revolutions of the wheel of the engine is

$$N_E = \frac{\theta}{2\pi}$$

The angular displacement in time t is

$$\theta = \omega_0 t + \frac{1}{2}\alpha t^2$$

$$\theta = 40\pi \times 16 + \frac{1}{2} \times 4\pi \times (16)^2 = 1152\pi \text{ rad}$$

Determine the number of revolutions done by the wheel of the engine in time, $t = 16$ s.

$$N_E = \frac{\theta}{2\pi} = \frac{1152\pi}{2\pi}$$

$$N_E = 576$$

Example 5 A wheel has a constant angular acceleration of 4.2 rad/s^2. During a certain 8.05 s interval, it turns through angle of 140 rad. Assuming that wheel started from rest, how long it had been in motion before the start of the 8.0 s?

Sol. Let ω_0 = initial angular speed at $t = 0$

Then, angle turned at end of 8.0 s is 140°.

Using $$\theta = \omega_0 t + \frac{1}{2}\alpha t^2$$

We have $$\omega_0 = \frac{\theta - \frac{1}{2}\alpha t^2}{t}$$

$$\omega_0 = \frac{140 - \frac{1}{2}(4.2)(8.0)^2}{8.0}$$

$$\omega_0 = 0.7 \text{ rad/s}$$

Now, using $\omega = \omega_0 + \alpha t$ and taking $\omega = 0$.

We have, $$t = \frac{\omega - \omega_0}{\alpha} = \frac{0 - \omega_0}{4.2} = -\frac{0.7}{4.2} = -0.16 \text{ s}$$

So, wheel starts from rest 0.16 s before.

Dynamics of Rotational Motion about a Fixed Axis

From the given table, we compare linear motion and rotational motion about a fixed axis.

Comparison of Translational and Rotational Motion

Pure translation	Pure rotational
Position, x	Angular position, θ
Velocity, $v = \frac{dx}{dt}$	Angular velocity, $\omega = \frac{d\theta}{dt}$
Acceleration, $a = \frac{dv}{dt}$	Angular acceleration, $\alpha = \frac{d\omega}{dt}$
Mass, m	Rotational inertia, I
Newton's second law, $F = ma$	Newton's second law, $\tau = I\alpha$
Work done, $W = \int F\,dx$	Work done, $W = \int \tau\,d\theta$
Kinetic energy, $K = \frac{1}{2}mv^2$	Kinetic energy, $K = \frac{1}{2}I\omega^2$
Power, $P = Fv$	Power, $P = \tau\omega$
Linear momentum, $p = mv$	Angular momentum, $L = I\omega$

Relation between Torque and Moment of Inertia

The rotational kinetic energy of a rigid body is represented by

$$\text{KE} = \frac{1}{2}I\omega^2$$

If the body has an angular acceleration α, its rotational kinetic energy will be change.

We know, power, $P = \frac{d}{dt}(\text{KE})$

[rate of change of KE is power]

$$= \frac{d}{dt}\left(\frac{1}{2}I\omega^2\right)$$

$$= \frac{1}{2}I\frac{d}{dt}(\omega^2) \quad \text{[if } I \text{ is constant]}$$

$$= \frac{1}{2}I(2\omega)\frac{d\omega}{dt}$$

$$P = I\omega\alpha \quad \left[\because \alpha = \frac{d\omega}{dt}\right]$$

$$\tau\omega = I\omega\alpha \quad [\because P = \tau\omega]$$

$$\boxed{\text{Torque, } \tau = I\alpha} \quad [I \text{ is constant}]$$

It is similar to the expression of Newton's second law for translational motion with constant mass.

Relation between Angular Momentum and Moment of Inertia

For a rigid body (about an fixed axis),

L = sum of angular momenta of all particles

$$= m_1v_1r_1 + m_2v_2r_2 + \ldots\ldots$$

$$= m_1 r_1^2 \omega + m_2 r_2^2 \omega + \ldots\ldots \quad [\because v = \omega r]$$

$$= (m_1 r_1^2 + m_2 r_2^2 + m_3 r_3^2 + \ldots\ldots)\omega$$

i.e. $L = I\omega$

Example 6 A cord of negligible mass is wound round the rim of a flywheel of mass 20 kg and radius 20 cm. A steady pull of 25 N is applied on the cord as shown in the figure. The flywheel is mounted on a horizontal axle with frictionless bearings.

(i) Compute angular acceleration of the flywheel.

(ii) Find the work done by the pull, when 2 m of the cord is unwound.

(iii) Find also the KE of the flywheel at this point. Assume that the flywheel starts from rest.

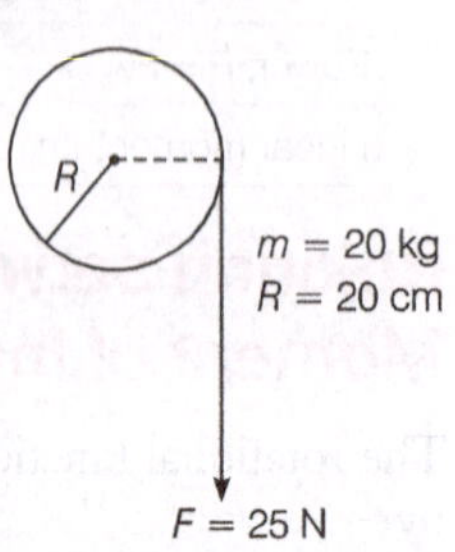

(iv) Compare the answers of parts (ii) and (iii).

Sol. (i) Torque, $\tau = FR = 25 \times 0.20 = 5$ N-m $[\because R = 20 \text{ cm} = 0.2 \text{ m}]$

Moment of inertia,

$$I = \frac{MR^2}{2} = \frac{20 \times (0.2)^2}{2} = 0.4 \text{ kg-m}^2$$

$$\text{Angular acceleration, } \alpha = \frac{\tau}{I} = \frac{5}{0.4} = 12.5 \text{ rad/s}^2$$

(ii) Work done by the pull, $W = F \times s = 25 \times 2 = 50$ J

(iii) $\text{KE} = \frac{1}{2} I\omega^2$

$$\omega^2 = \omega_0^2 + 2\alpha\theta = 0 + 2 \times 12.5 \times 10$$

$$\left[\because \omega_0 = 0, \theta = \frac{2}{0.2} = 10 \text{ rad}\right]$$

$$\therefore \quad \text{KE} = \frac{1}{2} \times 0.4 \times 250 = 50 \text{ J}$$

(iv) From parts (*ii*) and (*iii*), KE = W

$\therefore$ No loss of energy due to friction.

Work Done by Torque

Consider a rigid body acted upon by a force F at a perpendicular distance r from the axis of rotation. Let under the action of this force, the body rotates through an angle $\Delta\theta$.

Work done = Torque × Displacement = $\tau d\theta$

The power associated with the work done by a torque acting on a rotating body is given by

$$\text{Power} = \frac{dW}{dt} = \tau \frac{d\theta}{dt} = \tau\omega$$

where, $\tau\omega$ is also known as instantaneous rotational power.

Example 7 To maintain a rotor at a uniform angular speed of 100 rads^{-1} an engine needs to transmit a torque of 200 N-m. What is the power required by engine? Assume 100% efficiency of engine.

Sol. Work done by torque in turning rotor by an angle $d\theta$ is $= \tau d\theta$

So, power delivered by engine,

$$P = \frac{\text{Work done}}{\text{Time taken}} = \tau \frac{d\theta}{dt},$$

(dt = time taken for turning by angle $d\theta$)

or $P = \tau\omega$

So, power required $= 100 \times 200 = 20000$ W

$= 20$ kW $[\because 1 \text{ kW} = 1000]$

Example 8 To maintain a rotor at a uniform angular speed of 200 rads^{-1}, an engine needs to transmit a torque of 180 N-m. What is the power required by engine? Assume 100% efficiency of engine.

Sol. Work done by torque in turning rotor by angle $d\theta$ is $= \tau d\theta$

So, power delivered by engine

$$P = \frac{\text{Work done}}{\text{Time taken}} = \tau \frac{d\theta}{dt}$$

[dt = time for turning by angle $d\theta$.]

or $P = \tau\omega$

So, power required $= 180 \times 200 = 36000$ W

$= 36$ kW $[\because 1 \text{ kW} = 1000 \text{ W}]$

Example 9 A child stands at centre of a turntable with his arms out stretched. The turntable is set rotating with an angular speed of 40 rev/min.

(i) How much is the speed of child if he folds his hands and thereby reduces his MI to 2/5 times of initial value? Assume turntable is frictionless.

(ii) Show that child's new kinetic energy of rotation is more than the initial kinetic energy. How do you account for this increase in kinetic energy? **NCERT Exemplar**

Sol. (i) As no external torque is involved with child + turntable system, so angular momentum of system remains constant.

or $I_i\omega_i = I_f\omega_f$ ...(i)

$I_i\omega_i$ = initial angular momentum, $I_f\omega_f$ = final angular momentum

Here, $\omega_i = 40 \text{ rpm} \Rightarrow I_f = \frac{2}{5} I_i$

Substituting in Eq. (i), we get

$$I_i \times 40 = \frac{2}{5} I_i \times \omega_f$$

or $$\omega_f = \frac{5 \times 40}{2} = 100 \text{ rpm}$$

(ii) Initial $\text{KE} = \frac{1}{2} I_i \omega_i^2 = \frac{1}{2} \times I_i \times (40)^2$

$= \frac{1}{2} \times I_i \times 1600 = 800\, I_i$

Final $\text{KE} = \frac{1}{2} I_f \omega_f^2 = \frac{1}{2} \times \frac{2}{5} I_i \times (100)^2$

$= \frac{1}{2} \times \frac{2}{5} \times I_i \times 100 \times 100 = 2000\, I_i$

Clearly, final KE > initial KE. This energy is obtained from conversion of muscular work in KE. Muscular work has to be done in folding of arms.

Topic Practice 2

Multiple Choice Questions

(1 Mark)

1. The angular velocity of second's hand of a watch will be
   (a) $\frac{\pi}{60}$ rads^{-1} (b) $\frac{\pi}{30}$ rads^{-1}
   (c) $60\,\pi$ rads^{-1} (d) $30\,\pi$ rads^{-1}
2. If frictional force is neglected and girl drops her hand, then (initially girl is rotating with her arms outstretched on chair)

   (a) I_{girl} will reduce (b) I_{girl} will increase
   (c) ω_{girl} will reduce (d) None of these
3. The torque of a force $\mathbf{F} = 2\hat{i} - 3\hat{j} + 5\hat{k}$ acting at a point whose position vector $\mathbf{r} = 3\hat{i} - 3\hat{j} + 5\hat{k}$ about the origin is
   (a) $-5\hat{j} - 3\hat{k}$ (b) $3\hat{i} + 5\hat{j} - 3\hat{k}$
   (c) $5\hat{i} - 3\hat{k}$ (d) $5\hat{j} + 3\hat{k}$

Very Short Answer Type Questions

(1 Mark)

4. Why is moment of inertia also called rotational inertia?
5. Does the moment of inertia of a rigid body change with the speed of rotation?
6. Two solid spheres of the same mass are made of metals of different densities. Which of them has a larger moment of inertia about the diameter? Why?
7. In a flywheel, most of the mass is concentrated at the rim. Explain why?
8. Does the radius of gyration depend upon the speed of rotation of the body?
9. About which axis would a uniform cube have a minimum rotational inertia?
10. A ballet dancer stretches her hand out for slowing down. Name the conservation obeyed.
11. Two wheels A and B ($I_A > I_B$) are initially rotating with same angular speed. If they are deaccelerated by applying same torque, then which of them stops earlier?
12. About which axis rotating an object is eariest?
13. Is angular displacement is a vector or a scalar?
14. How we find direction of angular velocity ?
15. Give dimensions of angular displacement, angular velocity and angular acceleration.
16. Are torque and angular acceleration are parallel vectors?

Short Answer Type I Questions

(2 Marks)

17. Show that kinetic energy of an object rotating about a fixed axis with angular momentum $L = I\omega$, can be expressed as $K = \frac{L^2}{2I}$.
18. A person is standing on a rotating table with metal spheres in his hands. If he withdraw his hands to his chest, what will be the effect on his angular velocity?
19. Two boys of the same weight sit at the opposite ends of a diameter of a rotating circular table. What happens to the speed of rotation if they move nearer to the axis of rotation?
20. If ice on poles melts, then what is the change in duration of day?
21. The speed of a whirl wind in a tornado is alarmingly high. Why?

Short Answer Type II Questions

3 Marks

22. A uniform square plate S (side c) and a uniform rectangular plate R (sides b, a) have identical areas and masses (figure).

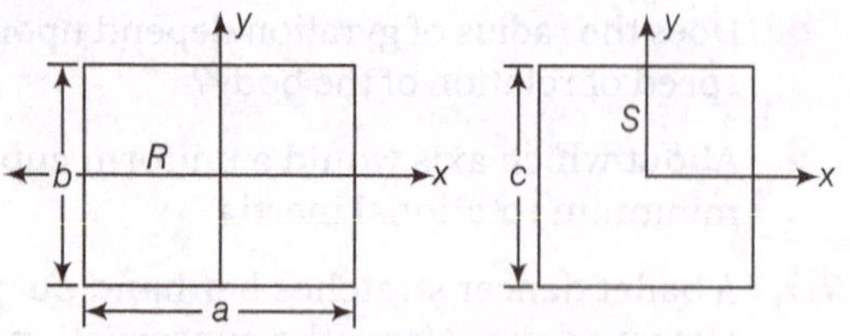

Show that (i) $I_{xR}/I_{xS} < 1$ (ii) $I_{yR}/I_{yS} > 1$ and (iii) $I_{zR}/I_{zS} > 1$ **NCERT Exemplar**

23. A uniform disc of radius R is resting on a table on its rim. The coefficient of friction between disc and table is μ (figure). Now, the disc is pulled with a force **F** as shown in the figure. What is the maximum value of **F** for which the disc rolls without slipping? **NCERT Exemplar**

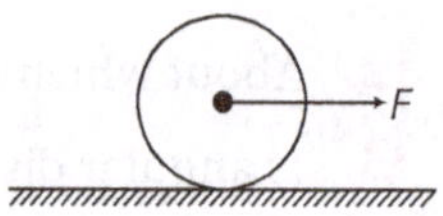

24. Explain why friction is necessary to make the disc in figure rolling in the direction indicated.

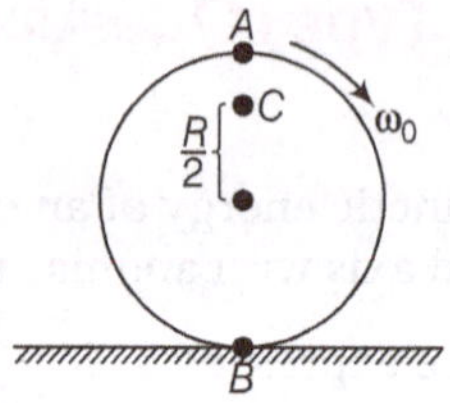

(i) Give the direction of frictional force at B and the sense of frictional torque before perfect rolling begins.
(ii) What is the force of friction after perfect rolling begins? **NCERT**

Long Answer Type Questions

5 Marks

25. Two discs of moment of inertia I_1 and I_2 (about their axes normal to plane of disc and passing through centre) are rotating with angular speeds ω_1 and ω_2 are brought into contact face to face with their axes coinciding.
(i) What is angular speed of two discs system?
(ii) Show that the kinetic energy of combined system is less than the sum of initial kinetic energies of the two discs.
(iii) How do you account for loss of energy? **NCERT**

26. A disc of radius R is rotating with an angular speed ω, about a horizontal axis. It is placed on a horizontal table. The coefficient of kinetic friction is μ_k.
(i) What was the velocity of its centre of mass before being brought in contact with the table?
(ii) What happens to the linear velocity of a point on its rim when placed in contact with the table?
(iii) What happens to the linear speed of the centre of mass when disc is placed in contact with the table?
(iv) Which force is responsible for the effects in (ii) and (iii)?
(v) What condition should be satisfied for rolling to begin?
(vi) Calculate the time taken for the rolling to begin. **NCERT Exemplar**

Numerical Problems

27. What is the moment of inertia of a sphere of mass 20 kg and radius $\frac{1}{4}$ m about its diameter? **[1 M]**

28. A constant torque of 120 N-m rotates its point of action by an angle of 30°. What is the work done by the torque? **[1 M]**

29. A wheel of moment of inertia 50 kg-m^2 about its own axis is revolving at a rate of 5 revolutions per second. What is its angular momentum? **[1 M]**

30. A solid cylinder of mass 20 kg rotates about its axis with angular speed of 100 rad/s. The radius of cylinder is 0.25 m. What is KE of rotation of cylinder? **NCERT Exemplar [2 M]**

31. The power output of an automobile engine is advertised to be 200 HP at 6000 rpm. What is the corresponding torque? **[2 M]**

32. A flywheel of moment of inertia 10 kg-m^2 is rotating at 50 rad/s. It must be brought to stop in 10 s.
(i) How much work must be done to stop it?
(ii) What is the required average power? **[3 M]**

33. A rope of negligible mass is wound round a hollow cylinder of mass 3 kg and radius 40 cm. What is angular acceleration of the cylinder, if the rope is pulled with a force of 30 N? What is linear acceleration of the rope? Assume no slipping. **[3 M]**

34. A solid cylinder of mass 20 kg rotates about its axis with angular speed (100 rad/s). The radius of cylinder is 0.25 m. What is the kinetic energy associated with the rotation of the cylinder? What is the magnitude of angular momentum of the cylinder about its axis? **NCERT [3 M]**

35. The oxygen molecule has a mass of 5.30×10^{-26}kg and a moment of inertia of 1.94×10^{-46}kg-m^2 about an axis through its centre perpendicular to the lines joining the atoms. Suppose the mean speed of such a molecule in gas is 500 m/s and its KE of rotation is 2/3 of its KE of translation. Find average angular velocity of the molecule. **NCERT Exemplar [3 M]**

36. A hoop of radius 2 m weighs 100 kg. It rolls along a horizontal floor so that its centre of mass has a speed of 20 cm/s. How much work has to be done to stop it? **[3 M]**

37. A bullet of mass 10 g and speed 500 m/s is fired into a door and gets embedded exactly at the centre of the door. The door is 1.0 m wide and weight 12 kg. It is hinged at one end and rotates about a vertical axis practically without friction. Find the angular speed of the door just after the bullet embeds into it. **NCERT [3 M]**

38. A cylinder of mass 10 kg and radius 15 cm is rolling perfectly on a plane of inclination 30°. The coefficient of static friction, $\mu_s = 0.25$.

(i) How much is the force of friction acting on the cylinder?

(ii) What is the work done against friction during rolling?

(iii) If the inclination θ of the plane is increased, at what value of θ does the cylinder begin to skid and not roll perfectly? **[3 M]**

39. A solid disc and a ring, both of radius 10 cm are placed on a horizontal table simultaneously, with initial angular speed equal to 10π rads^{-1}. Which of the two will start to roll earlier? The coefficient of kinetic friction is $\mu_k = 0.2$? **[5 M]**

40. A man stands on a rotating platform with his arms stretched horizontally holding a 5 kg weight in each hand. The angular speed of the platform is 30 rpm. The man then brings his arms close to his body with the distance of each weight from the axis changing from 90 cm to 20 cm. The moment of inertia of the man together with the platform may be taken to be constant and equal to 7.6 kg-m^2.

(i) What is his new angular speed? (Neglect friction)

(ii) Is kinetic energy conserved in the process? If not, from where does the change come about? **NCERT [5 M]**

41. A solid cylinder rolls up an inclined plane of angle of inclination 30°. At the bottom of inclined plane, the CM of cylinder has a speed of 5 m/s.

(i) How far will the cylinder go up the plane?

(ii) How long it will take to return to the bottom? **NCERT [5 M]**

Hints & Solutions

1. (b) Second's hand covers 2π radians in 60 seconds.

$$\therefore \quad \omega = \frac{\theta}{t} = \frac{2\pi}{60} = \frac{\pi}{30} \text{ rads}^{-1}$$

2. (a) As there is no external torque, if the girl bends her hands, her MI about the rotational axis will decrease. By conservation of angular momentum,

if $L = I\omega =$ constant, then ω will increase.

3. (a) Given, force, $\mathbf{F} = 2\hat{i} - 3\hat{j} + 5\hat{k}$

Position vector of point, $\mathbf{r} = 3\hat{i} - 3\hat{j} + 5\hat{k}$

$$\therefore \text{ Torque, } \tau = \mathbf{r} \times \mathbf{F} = \begin{vmatrix} \hat{i} & \hat{j} & \hat{k} \\ 3 & -3 & 5 \\ 2 & -3 & 5 \end{vmatrix}$$

$$= \hat{i}(-15+15) - \hat{j}(15-10) + \hat{k}(-9+6)$$

$$= 0 - 5\hat{j} - 3\hat{k} = -5\hat{j} - 3\hat{k}$$

4. The moment of inertia gives a measure of inertia in rotational motion.

So, it is also called rotational inertia.

5. No, because the moment of inertia depends upon the axis of rotation and distribution of mass.

6. The sphere with smaller density will have larger radius and hence larger moment of inertia.

7. Concentration of mass at the rim increases the moment of inertia and thereby brings uniform motion.

8. No, it depends only on the distribution of mass of the body.

9. In a uniform cube, the mass is more concentrated about a diagonal.

10. This is based on the conservation of angular momentum.

11. B stops earlier.

12. About an axis through its centre of mass.

13. Angular momentum is a vector, if it is differentiably small. Large values of angular displacement are scalars.

14. By right hand thumb rule.

15. Refer to Example 7 on page 218 (Equations of rotational motion).

16. Yes, $\tau = I\alpha$

17. Refer to text on page 213 (Moment of inertia).

18. When the person withdraws his hands to his chest, his moment of inertia decreases. No external torque is acting on the system. So, to conserve angular momentum, the angular velocity increases. [2]

19. The moment of inertia of the system (circular table + two boys) decreases. To conserve angular momentum ($L = I\omega$ = constant), the speed of rotation of the circular table increases. [2]

20. Molten ice from poles goes into ocean and so mass is going away from axis of rotation. So, moment of inertia of earth increases and to conserve angular momentum, angular velocity (ω) decreases. So, time period of rotation increases ($T = 2\pi/\omega$). So, net effect of global warming is increasing in the duration of day. [2]

21. In a whirl wind, the air from nearby region gets concentrated in a small space thereby decreasing the value of moment of inertia considerably. Since, $I\omega$ = constant, due to decrease in moment of inertia, the angular speed becomes quite high. [2]

22. By given question

Area of square = Area of rectangular plate

$$\Rightarrow \quad c^2 = a \times b \Rightarrow c^2 = ab$$

Now, by definition,

(i) $$\frac{I_{xR}}{I_{xS}} = \frac{b^2}{c^2} \qquad [\because I \propto (\text{area})^2]$$

From the diagram $b < c$,

$$\Rightarrow \quad \frac{I_{xR}}{I_{xS}} = \left(\frac{b}{c}\right)^2 < 1 \Rightarrow I_{xR} < I_{xS}$$ [1]

(ii) $$\frac{I_{yR}}{I_{yS}} = \frac{a^2}{c^2}$$

as $a > c$

$$\frac{I_{yR}}{I_{yS}} = \left(\frac{a}{c}\right)^2 > 1$$ [1]

(iii) $$I_{zR} - I_{zS} \propto (a^2 + b^2 - 2c^2)$$
$$= a^2 + b^2 - 2ab = (a-b)^2 \quad [\because c^2 = ab]$$

$$\Rightarrow (I_{zR} - I_{zS}) > 0 \Rightarrow \frac{I_{zR}}{I_{zS}} > 1$$ [1]

23. Let the acceleration of the centre of mass of disc be a, then

$$Ma = F - f \qquad \text{...(i)}$$ [1]

The angular acceleration of the disc is $\alpha = a/R$ (if there is no sliding).

Then, $$\left(\frac{1}{2}MR^2\right)\alpha = Rf \Rightarrow Ma = 2f$$ [1]

Thus, From Eq. (i), $2f = F - f$, $f = F/3$.

Since, there is no sliding.

$$\Rightarrow \quad f \le \mu mg \Rightarrow F \le 3\mu Mg$$ [1]

24. To roll a disc, one require a linear velocity which can be provided only by a tangential force. As frictional force is the only tangential force in this case, so it is necessary for the rolling of the disc. Initially, friction will be kinetic. [1]

(i) As frictional force at B opposes the angular velocity of B. So, frictional force is in the forward direction, the sense of frictional torque is such as to oppose the angular motion and produce some linear motion, so that the condition of pure rolling ($v_{CM} = R\omega$) should be fulfilled. [1]

(ii) After pure rolling starts there will be no need of friction, so friction force will become zero. [1]

25. Let ω be the final angular velocity of two discs system.

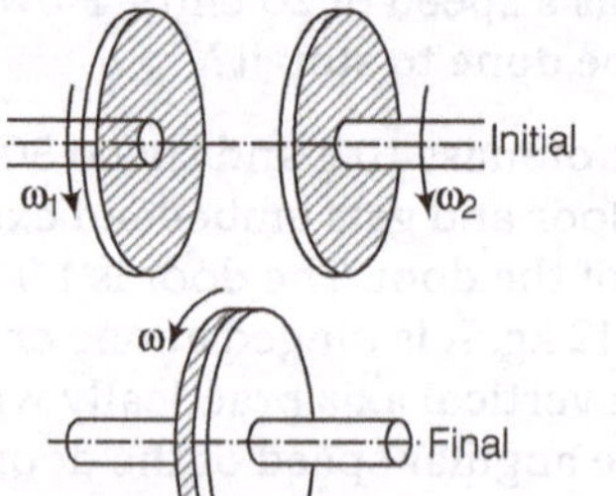

(i) According to conservation of angular momentum, we get

Total initial angular momentum = Final angular momentum

$$\Rightarrow \quad I_1\omega_1 + I_2\omega_2 = (I_1 + I_2)\omega$$

$$\Rightarrow \quad \omega = \left(\frac{I_1\omega_1 + I_2\omega_2}{I_1 + I_2}\right)$$ [1]

(ii) Initial KE of disc $= K_1 + K_2 = \frac{1}{2}I_1\omega_1^2 + \frac{1}{2}I_2\omega_2^2$

Final KE of disc system $= \frac{1}{2}(I_1 + I_2)\omega^2$

$$= \frac{1}{2}(I_1 + I_2)\cdot\left(\frac{I_1\omega_1 + I_2\omega_2}{I_1 + I_2}\right)^2$$ [1]

Loss of KE = Initial KE − Final KE

$$= \left(\frac{1}{2}I_1\omega_1^2 + \frac{1}{2}I_2\omega_2^2\right) - \frac{1}{2}(I_1 + I_2)\cdot\left(\frac{I_1\omega_1 + I_2\omega_2}{I_1 + I_2}\right)^2$$

$$= \frac{1}{2(I_1 + I_2)}(I_1^2\omega_1^2 + I_1I_2\omega_2^2 + I_1I_2\omega_1^2$$ [1]

$$+ I_2^2\omega_2^2 - I_1^2\omega_1^2 - I_2^2\omega_2^2 - 2I_1I_2\omega_1\omega_2)$$

$$= \frac{1}{2(I_1 + I_2)}(I_1I_2\omega_2^2 + I_1I_2\omega_1^2 - 2I_1I_2\omega_1\omega_2)$$

$$= \frac{1}{2(I_1 + I_2)} \cdot I_1I_2 \cdot (\omega_2^2 + \omega_1^2 - 2\omega_1\omega_2)$$

$$= \frac{I_1I_2}{2(I_1 + I_2)} \cdot (\omega_1 - \omega_2)^2$$ [1]

As above quantity is positive, so a loss of energy occurs.

(iii) When 2 discs come in contact, they rub against each other till both reach same angular speed. So, part of energy is converted into heat due to friction. [1]

26. (i) Before the disc is brought in contact with table, it is only rotating about its horizontal axis. So, its centre of mass is at rest, i.e. $v_{CM} = 0$. [1/2]

(ii) When rim is placed in contact with the table, then its linear velocity at any point on the rim of disc will reduce due to kinetic friction. [1/2]

(iii) If rotating disc is placed in contact with the table, its centre of mass acquires some velocity (which was zero before contact) due to kinetic friction. So, linear velocity of CM will increase. [1/2]

(iv) Kinetic friction. [1/2]

(v) Rolling will begin when $v_{CM} = R\omega$. [1/2]

(vi) Acceleration produced in centre of mass due to friction $a_{CM} = \frac{F}{m} = \frac{\mu_k mg}{m} = \mu_k g$ [1/2]

Angular acceleration produced by the torque due to friction. $\alpha = \frac{\tau}{I} = \frac{\mu_k mgR}{I}$

$\therefore \quad v_{CM} = u_{CM} + a_{CM}t \Rightarrow v_{CM} = \mu_k gt$

and $\quad \omega = \omega_0 + \alpha t$

$\Rightarrow \quad \omega = \omega_0 - \frac{\mu_k mgR}{I}t$ [1]

For rolling without slipping,

$$\frac{v_{CM}}{R} = \omega_0 - \frac{\mu_k mgR}{I}t$$

$$\Rightarrow \frac{\mu_k gt}{R} = \omega_0 - \frac{\mu_k mgR_t}{I}$$

$$t = \frac{R\omega_0}{\mu_k g\left(1 + \frac{mR^2}{I}\right)}$$ [1]

27. Moment of inertia of a sphere about its diameter,

$$I = \frac{2}{5}mR^2 = \frac{2}{5} \times 20 \times \left(\frac{1}{4}\right)^2 = 0.5 \text{ kg-m}^2$$

28. Work done by the torque, $W = \tau\theta$

$$= 120 \times \left(\frac{30 \times \pi}{180}\right) = 20\pi \text{ J}$$

29. Here, $I = 50\text{kg-m}^2$, $\omega = 5$ rps $= 5 \times 2\pi$ rad/s

$\therefore$ Angular momentum $L = I\omega = 50 \times 10\pi = 500\pi$J-s

30. $M = 20$ kg, $\omega = 100$ rad/s, $R = 0.25$ m

Moment of inertia of cylinder about its own axis

$$= \frac{1}{2}MR^2 = \frac{1}{2} \times 20 \times (0.25)^2 = 0.625 \text{ kg-m}^2$$ [1]

Rotational KE $= \frac{1}{2}I\omega^2 = \frac{1}{2} \times 0.625 \times (100)^2 = 3125$ J [1]

31. Given, $P = 200$ HP $= 200$ HP $\times \frac{746}{1 \text{ HP}} = 1.49 \times 10^5$ W [1]

and $\omega_z = 6000$ rev/min $= 6000 \times \frac{2\pi}{60} = 628$ rad / s

$$\tau = \frac{P}{\omega} = \frac{1.49 \times 10^5}{628} = 237.5 \text{ N-m}$$ [1]

32. Given, $\omega_0 = 50$ rad/s, $t = 10$ s,

From the equation, $\omega = \omega_0 - \alpha t$

$$0 = 50 - \alpha \times 10$$

$$\alpha = 5 \text{ rad/s}^2$$

Again, $\theta = \omega_0 t - \frac{1}{2}\alpha t^2$

$$= 50 \times 10 - \frac{1}{2} \times 5 \times (10)^2$$

$$= 500 - 250 = 250 \text{ rad}$$ [1½]

Retarding torque, $\tau = I\alpha = 10 \times 5 = 50$ cm

Work done by retarding torque,

$$W = \tau\theta = 50 \times 250 = 12500 \text{ J}$$

Required average power,

$$P = \frac{W}{t} = \frac{12500}{10} = 1250 \text{ W}$$ [1½]

33. Torque on cylinder, τ = force $\times$ radius

$$= 30 \times 0.4 = 12 \text{ N-m}$$

Moment of inertia of hollow cylinder about its axis

$$I = MR^2 = 3 \times (0.4)^2 = 0.48 \text{ kg-m}^2$$ [1]

Also, $\quad \tau = I\alpha \Rightarrow \alpha = \frac{\tau}{I}$

$\therefore \quad \alpha = \frac{12}{0.48} = 25 \text{ s}^{-2}$ [1]

Linear acceleration of rope

$$a = \frac{F}{m} = \frac{30}{3} = 10 \text{ m/s}^2$$ [1]

34. Moment of inertia of cylinder about its axis $= \frac{1}{2}MR^2$

M = mass, R = radius

$$= \frac{1}{2} \times 20 \times (0.25)^2 \text{kg-m}^2$$

$$= 0.625 \text{ kg-m}^2$$ [1]

Kinetic energy of rotating cylinder

$$= \frac{1}{2} I\omega^2 = \frac{1}{2}(0.625)(100)^2 \text{ J} = 3125\text{J}$$ [1]

Angular momentum of cylinder about its own axis

$$= I\omega = 0.625 \times 100 = 62.5 \text{ kg-m}^2/\text{s}$$ [1]

35. Taking atoms as point masses, moment of inertia of molecule is

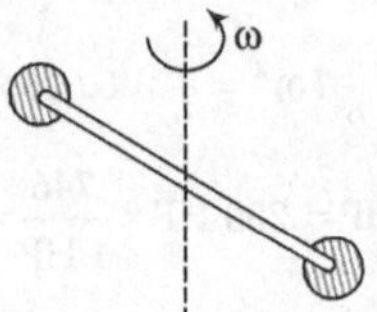

$$I = \frac{m}{2}r^2 + \frac{m}{2}r^2 = mr^2 \Rightarrow I = mr^2$$

or $$r = \sqrt{\frac{I}{m}}$$ [1]

Now, given that

$$KE_{(rot)} = \frac{2}{3} KE_{(trans.)}$$

$$\frac{1}{2} I\omega^2 = \frac{2}{3} \times \frac{1}{2} mv^2$$

$$I\omega^2 = \frac{2}{3} mv^2$$

$$\Rightarrow \quad mr^2\omega^2 = \frac{2}{3} mv^2$$

or $$\omega = \sqrt{\frac{2}{3}}\left(\frac{v}{r}\right) = \sqrt{\frac{2}{3}} \times v \times \sqrt{\frac{M}{I}}$$ [1]

Here, $v = 500$ m/s

$$I = 1.94 \times 10^{-46} \text{ kg-m}^2$$

$$\Rightarrow \quad m = 5.36 \times 10^{-26} \text{ kg}$$

So, average angular velocity of the molecule is

$$= \sqrt{\frac{2}{3}} \times 500 \times \sqrt{\frac{5.36 \times 10^{-26}}{1.94 \times 10^{-46}}}$$

$$= 6.7 \times 10^{12} \text{ rad/s}$$ [1]

36. Moment of inertia of hoop about its centre

$$I = MR^2$$ [1/2]

and energy of loop = translational kinetic energy of CM and rotational kinetic energy about axis through CM. [1]

$$= \frac{1}{2} mv_{CM}^2 + \frac{1}{2} I\omega^2 \qquad \left[I = mR^2 \text{ and } \omega = \frac{v}{R}\right]$$

$$= \frac{1}{2} mv_{CM}^2 + \frac{1}{2} mR^2 \times \frac{v_{CM}^2}{R^2} = mv_{CM}^2$$ [1/2]

Work done is stopping the hoop

= total KE of loop

$$= mv_{CM}^2 = 100 \times (0.2)^2 = 4 \text{ J}$$ [1]

37. Given, mass of bullet $(m) = 10$ g $= 0.01$ kg

Speed of bullet $(v) = 500$ m/s

Width of the door $(l) = 1.0$ m

Mass of the door $(M) = 12$ kg [1/2]

As bullet gets embedded exactly at the centre of the door, therefore its distance from the hinged end of the door,

$$r = \frac{l}{2} = \frac{1}{2} \text{m}$$ [1/2]

Angular momentum transferred by the bullet to the door,

$$L = mv \times r = 0.01 \times 500 \times \frac{1}{2} = 2.5 \text{ Js}$$ [1]

Moment of inertia of the door about the vertical axis at one of its end, $I = \frac{Ml^2}{3} = \frac{12 \times (1)^2}{3} = 4 \text{ kg-m}^2$

But angular momentum, $L = I\omega$

$$2.5 = 4 \times \omega$$

$$\omega = \frac{2.5}{4} = 0.625 \text{ rad/s}$$ [1]

38. Given, mass of the cylinder $m = 10$ kg

Radius, $r = 15$ cm $= 0.15$ m

Inclination of plane, $\theta = 30°$

Coefficient of static friction, $\mu_s = 0.25$

(i) Force of friction acting on the cylinder on the inclined plane, $F = \frac{1}{3} mg \sin\theta$

$$= \frac{1}{3} \times 10 \times 9.8 \times \sin 30°$$

$$= \frac{1}{3} \times 10 \times 9.8 \times \frac{1}{2}$$

$$= 16.3 \text{ N}$$ [1]

(ii) Force of friction acts perpendicular to the direction of displacement.

∴ Work done against friction during rolling

$$W = Fs \cos 90° = 0$$

(iii) For rolling without slipping, [1]

$$\mu = \frac{1}{3} \tan\theta$$

or $\tan\theta = 3\mu = 3 \times 0.25 = 0.75$

$= \tan 36°54'$

or $\theta = 36°54' = 37°$

So, for skidding, $\theta > 37°$. [1]

39. Thus, the force of friction $\mu_k mg$ produces an acceleration a in the centre of mass. So, the equation of motion for centre of mass is

$$\mu_k mg = ma \quad \text{...(i)}$$

The torque due to force of friction is $\mu_k mg \times R$. It produces angular retardation given by

$$\mu_k mgR = -I\alpha \quad \text{...(ii)}$$ [1]

Rolling begins when

$$v = R\omega$$

But $$v = 0 + at = \mu_k gt \quad \text{...(iii)}$$

[from Eq. (i), $a = \mu_k g$]

and $\omega = \omega_0 + \alpha t = \omega_0 - \frac{\mu_k mgR}{I} t$ [using Eq. (ii)] [1]

or $\frac{v}{R} = \omega_0 - \frac{\mu_k mgR}{I} t$

$\Rightarrow \frac{\mu_k gt}{R} = \omega_0 - \frac{\mu_0 mgRt}{I}$

or $\frac{\mu_k gt}{R}\left[1 + \frac{mR^2}{I}\right] = \omega_0$ or $t = \frac{R\omega_0}{\mu_k g\left(1 + \frac{mR^2}{I}\right)}$ [1]

For a disc, $I = mR^2/2$

$\therefore \quad t = \frac{R\omega_0}{3\mu_k g} = \frac{0.10 \times 10\pi}{3 \times 0.2 \times 9.8} = 0.53$ s [1]

For a ring, $I = mR^2$

$\therefore \quad t = \frac{R\omega_0}{2\mu_k g} = \frac{0.10 \times 10\pi}{2 \times 0.2 \times 9.8} = 0.80$ s

Thus, the disc begins to roll earlier than the ring. [1]

40. (i) Moment of inertia of man and platform system

$I_i = 7.6$ kg-m^2

Change in moment of inertia of man and platform system when he stretches his hands to a distance of 90 cm $= 2 \times mr^2 = 2 \times 5 \times (0.9)^2$ [1]

$= 8.1$ kg-m^2

$I_i = I + 8.1 = 7.6 + 8.1 = 15.7$ kg-m^2

Initial angular velocity, $\omega_i = 30$ rpm

Initial angular momentum of system,

$L_i = I_i\omega_i = 15.7$ kg-m$^2 \times 30$ rpm [1]

When man folds his hands to a distance of 20 cm,

Moment of inertia of man $= 2 \times mr^2 = 2 \times 5 \times (0.2)^2$

$= 0.4$ kg-m^2

So, final moment of inertia of man and platform system

$= 7.6 + 0.4 = 8$ kg-m^2 [1]

Final angular momentum of system

$L_f = I_f\omega_f = 8 \times \omega_f$

Equating initial and final values

$L_i = L_f$

$\Rightarrow \quad \omega_f = \frac{15.7 \times 30}{8}$ [1]

$= 58.88$ rpm

(ii) KE is not conserved in process.

$K_{\text{final}} > K_{\text{initial}}$

Muscular work done by the man in folding his arms is converted into KE. [1]

41. (i) Energy at point $A = \frac{1}{2} mv^2 + \frac{1}{2} I\omega^2$ [1]

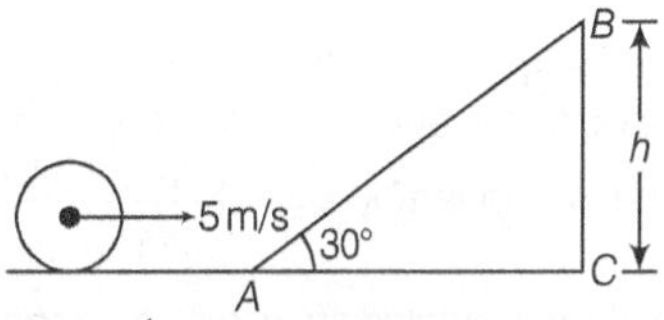

where, $I = \frac{1}{2} mr^2$ and $\omega = \frac{v}{r}$

So, energy at point $A = \frac{1}{2} mv^2 + \frac{1}{2} \times \frac{1}{2} mr^2 \times \frac{v^2}{r^2}$

$= \frac{1}{2} mv^2 + \frac{1}{4} mv^2 = \frac{3}{4} mv^2$ [1 + 1]

and energy at point $B = mgh$

Equating we get, $\frac{3}{4} mv^2 = mgh$

or $h = \frac{3}{4}\frac{v^2}{g} = \frac{3}{4} \times \frac{5^2}{9.8} = 1.91$ m [1]

(ii) In ΔABC, $AB = \frac{h}{\sin 30°}$

or $AB = \frac{1.91}{0.5} = 3.82$ m

So, cylinder rolls a direction of 3.82 m up the incline. [1]

SUMMARY

- A body is said to be a rigid body when it has a perfectly definite shape and size. The distance between all pairs of particles of such a body do not change while applying any force on it.
- The centre of mass of a body or a system of bodies is the point which moves as through all of the mass were concentrated there and all external forces were applied to it.
- For a system of n-particles, the centre of mass is given by

$$x_{CM} = \frac{m_1x_1 + m_2x_2 + \ldots + m_nx_n}{m_1 + m_2 + \ldots + mn} = \frac{\sum_{i=1}^{n} m_ix_i}{\Sigma m_i}$$

- If in a two particles system, particles of masses m_1 and m_2 are moving with velocities v_1 and v_2, respectively, then velocity of the centre of mass is given by $v_{CM} = \frac{m_1v_1 + m_2v_2}{m_1 + m_2}$
- If acceleration of the particles are a_1 and a_2 respectively, then acceleration of the centre of mass is given by

$$a_{CM} = \frac{m_1a_1 + m_2a_2}{m_1 + m_2}$$

- The centre of mass of an object need not to lie within the object.
- The turning effect of a force about the axis of rotation is called moment of force or torque due to the force.
  Torque = Force × its perpendicular distance from the axis of rotation.
- The moment of linear momentum is called **angular momentum**. It is denoted by τ.
  Angular momentum (τ) = linear momentum (p) × its perpendicular distance from the axis of rotation (r).
- The rate of change of angular momentum of a system of particles about a fixed point is equal to the total external torque acting on the system about that point. $\tau_{total} = \frac{d\mathbf{L}}{dt}$
- **For translational equilibrium of a rigid body**, the vector sum of all the forces acting on a rigid body must be zero.

  i.e. $$F_1 + F_2 + \ldots + F_n = \sum_{i=1}^{n} F_i = 0$$

- **For rotational equilibrium**, the vector sum of torques of all the forces acting on the rigid body about the reference point must be zero.

  i.e. $$\tau_1 + \tau_2 + \ldots + \tau_n = \sum_{i=1}^{n} \tau_i = 0$$

- The moment of couple is equal to the product of either of the forces and the perpendicular distance, called the arm of the couple, between their lines of action.
  Moment of couple = Force × arm of the couple
  or $\tau = Fd$
- In rotational equilibrium, Clockwise moment = Anti-clockwise moment
  or $F_1 \times d_1 = F_2 \times d_2$
  or load × load arm = effort × effort arm
- The moment of inertia of a body about a given axis is equal to the sum of the products of the masses of its constituent particles and the square of their respective distances from the axis of rotation.
  Moment of inertia of a body is given by

$$I = m_1r_1^2 + m_2r_2^2 + m_3r_3^2 + \ldots = \sum_{i=1}^{n} m_ir_i^2$$

  Its unit is kg - m^2 and its dimensional formula is $[ML^2]$.
- Radius of gyration, $K = \sqrt{\frac{I}{M}}$

Chapter Practice

Multiple Choice Questions

1 Mark

1 Distance of the centre of mass of a solid uniform cone from its vertex is z_0. If the radius of its base is R and its height is h, then z_0 is equal to

(a) $\frac{h^2}{4R}$ (b) $\frac{3h}{4}$ (c) $\frac{5h}{8}$ (d) $\frac{3h^2}{8R}$

2 The centre of mass of a system of two particles divides the distance between them.

(a) In inverse ratio of square of masses of particles
(b) In direct ratio of square of masses of particles
(c) In inverse ratio of masses of particles
(d) In direct ratio of masses of particles

3 A nucleus explodes into two lighter nuclei as shown in the figure. The ratio of v_1 and v_2 is

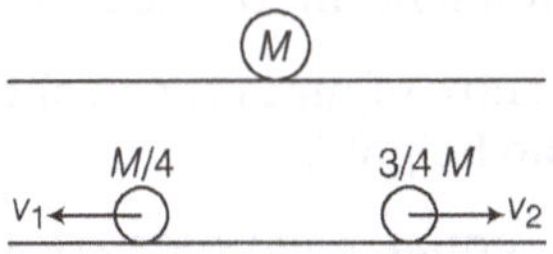

(a) $v_1 = v_2/2$ (b) $v_1 = 3v_2$
(c) $v_1 = 2v_2$ (d) $v_1 = v_2$

4 A body is rotating with angular velocity $\omega = (3\hat{i} - 4\hat{j} - \hat{k})$. The linear velocity of a point having position vector $\mathbf{r} = (5\hat{i} - 6\hat{j} + 6\hat{k})$ is

(a) $6\hat{i} + 2\hat{j} - 3\hat{k}$ (b) $-18\hat{i} - 23\hat{j} + 2\hat{k}$
(c) $-30\hat{i} - 23\hat{j} + 2\hat{k}$ (d) $6\hat{i} - 2\hat{j} + 8\hat{k}$

5 Newton's second law for rotational motion of a system of particles can be represented as ($\mathbf{L}$ for a particle, $\mathbf{L}$ for a system of particles)

(a) $\frac{d\mathbf{p}}{dt} = \tau_{ext}$ (b) $\frac{d\mathbf{L}}{dt} = \tau_{ext}$
(c) $\frac{d\mathbf{L}}{dt} = \tau_{ext}$ (d) $\frac{d\mathbf{L}}{dt} = \tau_{int} + \tau_{ext}$

6 Two masses are joined with a light rod and the system is rotating about the fixed axis as shown in the figure. The MI of the system about the axis is

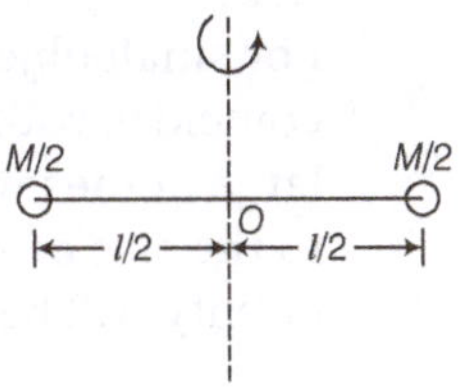

(a) $Ml^2/2$ (b) $Ml^2/4$
(c) Ml^2 (d) $Ml^2/6$

7 A rod is rotating about an axis passing through its centre and perpendicular to its length. The radius of gyration for the rod is

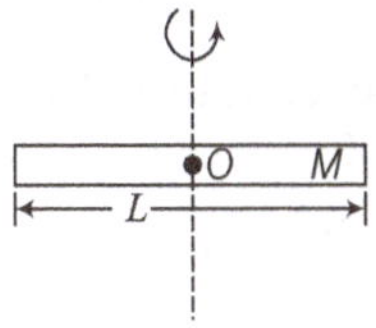

(a) $\frac{L}{12}$ (b) $\frac{L}{\sqrt{12}}$
(c) $\frac{L}{6}$ (d) $\frac{L}{\sqrt{6}}$

8 A disc of mass M and radius R is rotating about one of its diameter. The value of radius of gyration for the disc is

(a) $R/4$ (b) $R/2$
(c) $R/6$ (d) None of these

9 The angular velocity of a wheel increases from 100 rps to 300 rps in 10 s. The number of revolutions made during that time is

(a) 600 (b) 1500
(c) 1000 (d) 2000

10 To maintain a rotor at a uniform angular speed of 100 rads^{-1}, an engine needs to transmit torque of 100 Nm. The power of the engine is

(a) 10 kW (b) 100 kW
(c) 10 MW (d) 100 MW

Assertion and Reason

Direction (Q. No. 11-15) *In the following questions , two statements are given- one labelled Assertion* (A) *and the other labelled Reason* (R). *Select the correct answer to these questions from the codes* (a), (b), (c) *and* (d) *as given below*

(a) Both Assertion and Reason are true and Reason is the correct explanation of Assertion.
(b) Both Assertion and Reason are true but Reason is not the correct explanation of Assertion.
(c) Assertion is true but Reason is false.
(d) Assertion is false but Reason is true.

11. **Assertion (A)** The CM of a body must lie on the body.
Reason (R) The CM of a body lie at the geometric centre of body.

12. **Assertion (A)** The motion of the CM describes the translational part of the motion.
Reason (R) Translational motion always means straight line motion.

13. **Assertion (A)** At the centre of earth, a body has centre of mass, but no centre of gravity.
Reason (R) Acceleration due to gravity is zero at the centre of earth.

14. **Assertion (A)** Inertia and moment of inertia are same quantities.
Reason (R) Inertia represents the capacity of a body to oppose its state of motion of rest.

15. **Assertion (A)** Moment of inertia of a particle is same, whatever be the axis of rotation.
Reason (R) Moment of inertia depends on mass and distance of the particle from the axis of rotation.

Very Short Answer Type Questions

(1 Mark)

16 What is the basic difference between pure translation motion and pure rotational motion?

17 What is the significance of centre of mass?

18 State conservation of angular momentum theorem for a rigid body.

19 On which factors, moment of inertia of a rigid body depends?

20 If the value of acceleration due to gravity (g) varies, will the centre of mass and centre of gravity coincide?

21 Write one example of conservation of angular momentum theorem.

Short Answer Type I Questions

(2 Marks)

22 If two point masses are placed at ($+2\,m$), and ($-2\,m$), is it necessary that the centre of mass of system must lie at origin?

23 Write two differences between centre of mass and centre of gravity.

Short Answer Type II Questions

(3 Marks)

24 Three identical spheres each of radius r and mass m are placed touching each other on a horizontal floor. Locate the position of centre of mass of the system.

25 Moment of inertia of a thin rod of length l about an axis passing through its one end and perpendicular to its length is $MR^2/3$. Find radius of gyration of rod about given axis.

26 Derive the relation between angular momentum and moment of inertia for a rigid body rotating about a fixed axis.

27 Write three practical applications of conservation of angular momentum for a rigid body.

Long Answer Type Questions

(5 Marks)

28 Derive expressions for (i) Linear momentum, (ii) Newton's second law and (iii) Conservation of linear momentum for the system of particles.

29 Find the centre of mass for a solid cone of base radius r and height h.

30 Torques of equal magnitude are applied to a hollow cylinder and a solid sphere, both having same masses and radii. The cylinder is free to rotate about its standard axis of symmetry and sphere is free to rotate about an axis passing through its centre. Which of the two will acquire a greater angular speed after a given time?

Case Based Questions

Directions (Q. No. 31) *These questions are case study based questions. Read the following paragraph and answer the questions.*

31. The centre of gravity of a rigid body is a point through which the total weight of the body acts. Centre of gravity can lie within the body or not. For small objects, centre of mass always coincides with centre of gravity. But in case of large bodies whose dimensions are comparable to the size of earth, centre of mass and centre of gravity will be at different locations.

In the given figure, balancing of a cardboard on the tip of a pencil is done. The point of support, G is the centre of gravity.

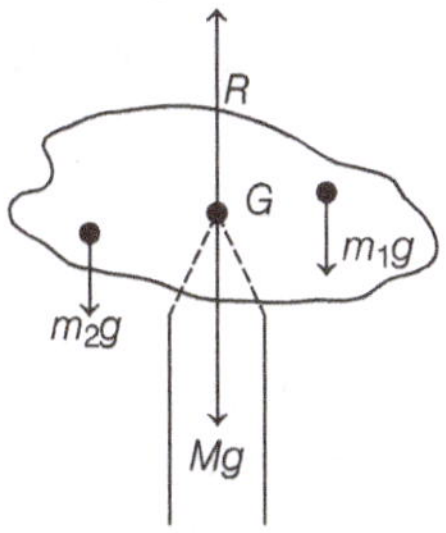

(i) If the $\mathbf{F}_{\text{net, ext}}$ is zero on the cardboard, it means

(a) $R = Mg$ (b) $m_1 g = Mg$
(c) $m_2 g = Mg$ (d) $R = m_1 / g$

(ii) Choose the correct option.

(a) τ_{Mg} about CG = 0
(b) τ_R about CG = 0
(c) Net τ due to $m_1 g, m_2 g \cdots m_n g$ about CG = 0
(d) All of the above

(iii) The centre of gravity and the centre of mass of a body coincide when

(a) g is negligible
(b) g is variable
(c) g is constant
(d) g is zero

(iv) If value of g varies, the centre of gravity and the centre of mass will

(a) coincide
(b) not coincide
(c) become same physical quantities
(d) None of the above

(v) Where will be the centre of gravity of the following rigid body?

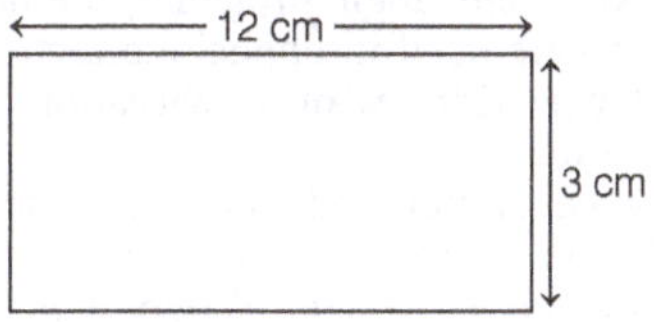

(a) (6,3) (b) (6,6)
(c) (6,1.5) (d) (1.5,3)

Numerical Problems

32 Three point masses of 1 kg, 2 kg and 3 kg lie at (1, 2), (0, – 1) and (2, – 3), respectively. Calculate the coordinates of the centre of mass of the system. **[2 M]**

33 Find the value of torque, if $\mathbf{F} = (4\hat{\mathbf{i}} - 10\hat{\mathbf{j}})$ N and $\mathbf{r} = (-5\hat{\mathbf{i}} - 3\hat{\mathbf{j}})$ m **[1 M]**

34 An automobile engine develops 100 kW when rotating at a speed of 1800 rpm. Find the torque produced. **[2 M]**

35 A fan of moment of inertia is 0.6 kg-m^2 is to be run upto a working speed of 0.5 rps. What is the angular momentum of the fan? **[2 M]**

Hints & Solutions

1 (*b*) We know that centre of mass of a uniform solid cone of height h is at height $\frac{h}{4}$ from base, therefore,

As, $h - z_0 = \frac{h}{4}$ or $z_0 = h - \frac{h}{4} = \frac{3h}{4}$

2 (*c*) We have $m_1 r_1 = m_2 r_2 \Rightarrow \frac{r_1}{r_2} = \frac{m_2}{m_1}$

$\therefore \quad r \propto 1/m$

3 (*b*) From conservation of linear momentum,
Initial linear momentum = Final linear momentum

$$0 = \frac{M}{4} v_1 - \frac{3}{4} M v_2$$

$$\frac{v_1}{4} = \frac{3}{4} v_2$$

$$\Rightarrow \quad v_1 = 3 v_2$$

4 (*c*) Here, $\omega = 3\hat{\mathbf{i}} - 4\hat{\mathbf{j}} - \hat{\mathbf{k}}$, $\mathbf{r} = 5\hat{\mathbf{i}} - 6\hat{\mathbf{j}} + 6\hat{\mathbf{k}}$

As, $\mathbf{v} = \omega \times \mathbf{r} = \begin{vmatrix} \hat{\mathbf{i}} & \hat{\mathbf{j}} & \hat{\mathbf{k}} \\ 3 & -4 & -1 \\ 5 & -6 & 6 \end{vmatrix}$

$$= \hat{\mathbf{i}}(-24 - 6) - \hat{\mathbf{j}}(18 + 5) + \hat{\mathbf{k}}(-18 + 20)$$

$$= -30\hat{\mathbf{i}} - 23\hat{\mathbf{j}} + 2\hat{\mathbf{k}}$$

5 (*c*) Newton's second law for rotational motion is

$$\tau_{\text{ext}} = \frac{d\mathbf{L}}{dt}$$

6 (*b*) Total moment of inertia is

$$I = \frac{M}{2}\left(\frac{l}{2}\right)^2 + \frac{M}{2}\left(\frac{l}{2}\right)^2 = \frac{Ml^2}{8} + \frac{Ml^2}{8} = \frac{Ml^2}{4}$$

7 (*b*) As, $I_{\text{rod}} = \frac{ML^2}{12}$ ...(i)

Using $I = MK^2$ ...(ii)

Comparing Eqs. (i) and (ii), we get

$$K = L/\sqrt{12}$$

8 (*b*) I_{disc} about the axis along its diameter $= \frac{MR^2}{4}$ ...(i)

Using radius of gyration, $I = MK^2$ ...(ii)

Comparing Eqs. (i) and (ii), we get $K = \frac{R}{2}$

9 (*d*) Angular displacement θ during time *t*, assuming constant acceleration be.

$$\theta = \frac{\omega_0 + \omega_t}{2} = \frac{100+300}{2} \times 10 = 2000 \text{ revolutions}$$

10 (*a*) Here, $\omega = 100 \text{ rad s}^{-1}, \tau = 100 \text{ Nm}$

Power of the engine, $P = \tau\omega$

$\therefore\ P = (100 \text{ N-m})(100 \text{ rad s}^{-1}) = 10 \times 10^3 \text{ W} = 10 \text{kW}$

11 (*d*) **12** (*a*)

13 (*a*) **14** (*d*)

15 (*d*)

16 In pure translational motion, every particle of a body moves through the same linear distance in a straight line. While in pure rotational motion, every particle moves in circles of different radii about a fixed line or axis of rotation.

17 Analysis of motion of a large object is a complex process but its motion can be viewed as motion of a point mass with the help of centre of mass analysis. So, analysing motion as motion of centre of mass is a simple process.

18 Refer to text on page 201 (Conservation of angular momentum).

19 Moment of inertia of a rigid body depends on
(i) mass of the body. (ii) size of body.
(iii) axis of rotation of the body.
(iv) distribution of mass of the body about the axis of rotation.

20 No, if the body is so large that the value of acceleration due to gravity (g) varies, then centre of mass and centre of gravity will be offset from each other.

21 The angular velocity of revolution of a planet around the sun in an elliptical orbit increases, when the planet comes closer to the sun and *vice-versa* but its angular momentum remains constant.

22 No, the position of the centre of mass of a system is independent of the choice of coordinate system. The position of centre of mass depends on the shape and size of the body and distribution of its mass. [2]

23 (i) Centre of mass is the point at which the distribution of mass is equal in all direction, whereas the centre of gravity is the point at which the distribution of weight is equal in all direction. [1]

(ii) The centre of mass does not depend on gravitational field, while centre of gravity does depend on gravitational field. [1]

24 This situation can be shown in figure. The centre of spheres are joined to form an equilateral triangle *ABC* with side 2*r*.

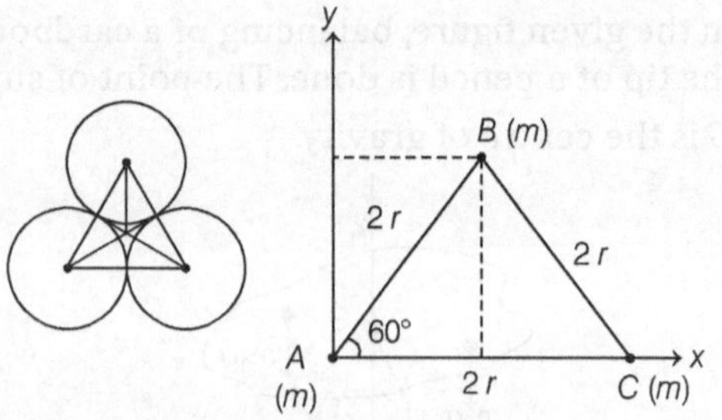

Then, coordinates of $A(0, 0)$ and $C(2r, 0)$ and of $B = (2r\cos 60°, 2r\sin 60°) = (r, \sqrt{3}r)$

$$\therefore x_{CM} = \frac{m \times 0 + m \times r + m \times 2r}{3m} = r$$

$$y_{CM} = \frac{m \times 0 + m \times \sqrt{3}r + m \times 0}{3m} = \frac{\sqrt{3}r}{3} = \frac{r}{\sqrt{3}}$$

Coordinates of centre of mass $= \left(r, \frac{r}{\sqrt{3}}\right)$. [3]

25 The radius of gyration of a body about an axis may be defined as the distance from the axis of a mass point whose mass is equal to the mass of whole body and whose moment of inertia is equal to the moment of inertia of the body about its axis. When square of radius of gyration is multiplied with the mass of the body, give the moment of inertia of the body about the given axis.

$$I = MK^2 \Rightarrow K = \sqrt{\frac{I}{M}}$$

Given, $I = \frac{MR^2}{3}$

$$\Rightarrow K = \sqrt{\frac{MR^2}{3 \times M}} = \frac{R}{\sqrt{3}}$$ [3]

26 Refer to text on pages 217 and 218 (Relation between angular momentum and moment of inertia).

27 (i) A circus acrobat performs feats involving spin by bringing her arms and legs closer to her body or *vice-versa.* [1]

(ii) All helicopters are provided with two propellers. If there were one single propeller, the helicopter would rotate itself in opposite direction in accordance with law of conservation of angular momentum. [1]

(iii) A flywheel is mounted rigidly on a space craft for orientation control. The space craft and fly wheel form an isolated system. When neither the space craft nor the flywheel is turning, the total angular momentum *L* of the system is zero. [1]

28 (i) Refer to text on page 198 (Linear momentum of a system of particles).

(ii) Refer to text on page 198 (Newton's second law for system of particles).

(iii) Refer to text on page 198 (Conservation of linear momentum for system of particles).

29 The cone is supposed to be made up of large number of circular discs of different radii and masses.

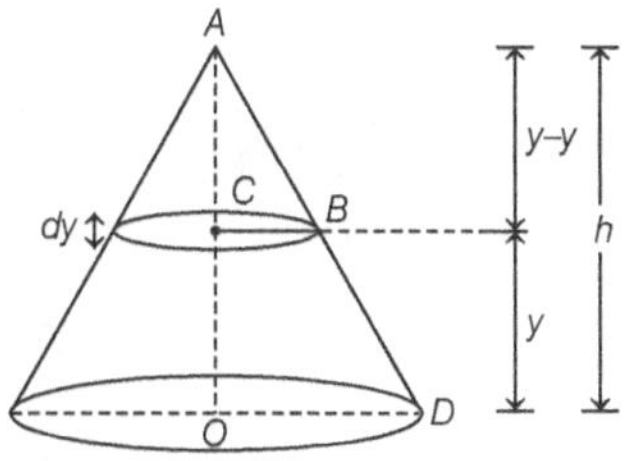

Consider a disc of radius $BC = x$ and mass dm at a height y from the base. [1]

ΔABC and ΔADO are similar,

$$\therefore \quad \frac{AO}{AC} = \frac{DO}{BC}$$

or $$\frac{h}{h-y} = \frac{r}{x} \text{ or } x = \frac{r(h-y)}{h} \quad \text{... (i)}$$ [1]

Mass of elementary disc, dm = Volume × Density

$$dm = \pi x^2 \times dy \times \rho = \pi \rho \frac{r^2(h-y)^2}{h^2} dy$$ [1/2]

∴ Coordinates of centre of mass of cone are

$$y_{CM} = \frac{1}{M}\int y\,dm = \frac{1}{M}\int y \cdot \frac{\pi \rho r^2}{h^2}(h-y)^2 dy$$

$$= \frac{\pi \rho r^2}{Mh^2}\int_0^h (h^2 y + y^3 - 2hy^2)\,dy$$

$$y_{CM} = \frac{\pi \rho r^2}{\frac{1}{3}\pi R^2 h \rho \times h^2} \times \frac{h^4}{12} = \frac{h}{4} \quad \left[\because M = \frac{1}{3}\pi r^2 h\rho\right]$$

Similarl y, $x_{CM} = 0, z_{CM} = 0$ [1½]

Hence, centre of mass lies at $\frac{h}{4}$ from the point O at the centre of the base of the cone. [1]

30 If M is mass and R is the radius of hollow cylinder and the solid sphere, then moment of inertia of hollow cylinder about its axis of symmetry, $I_1 = MR^2$.

Moment of inertia of solid sphere about an axis passing through its centre, $I_2 = \frac{2}{5}MR^2$ [2]

Torque applied, $\tau = I_1\alpha_1 = I_2\alpha_2$

$$\therefore \quad \frac{\alpha_2}{\alpha_1} = \frac{I_1}{I_2} = \frac{MR^2}{\frac{2}{5}MR^2} = \frac{5}{2} \Rightarrow \alpha_2 > \alpha_1$$ [1]

From equation of rotational motion, $\omega = \omega_0 + \alpha t$

For a given value of ω_0 and t, $\omega_2 > \omega_1$

i.e. Angular speed of solid sphere will be greater than the angular speed of hollow cylinder. [2]

31 (i) (*a*) (ii) (*d*) (iii) (*c*) (iv) (*b*) (v) (*c*)

32 Given, $m_1 = 1$ kg, $m_2 = 2$ kg, $m_3 = 3$ kg,

Then, $$X_{CM} = \frac{m_1x_1 + m_2x_2 + m_3x_3}{m_1 + m_2 + m_3} = \frac{1+0+6}{1+2+3} = \frac{7}{6}$$ [1]

$$Y_{CM} = \frac{m_1y_1 + m_2y_2 + m_3y_3}{m_1 + m_2 + m_3} = \frac{2-2-9}{1+2+3} = \frac{-9}{6} = \frac{-3}{2}$$ [1]

Thus, coordinates of centre of mass is $\left(\frac{7}{6}, \frac{-3}{2}\right)$. [1]

33 Given, $\mathbf{F} = 4\hat{\mathbf{i}} - 10\hat{\mathbf{j}}$, $\mathbf{r} = -5\hat{\mathbf{i}} - 3\hat{\mathbf{j}}$

∴ Torque, $\tau = \mathbf{r} \times \mathbf{F} = (-5\hat{\mathbf{i}} - 3\hat{\mathbf{j}}) \times (4\hat{\mathbf{i}} - 10\hat{\mathbf{k}})$

$$= \hat{\mathbf{k}}(50+12) = 62\,\hat{\mathbf{k}}$$ [1]

34 Given, $P = 100$ kW, $n = 1800$ rpm $= 30$ rps

$$\omega = 2\pi n = 60\pi \text{ rad s}^{-1}$$ [1]

∴ Power, $P = \tau\omega$

$$\Rightarrow \quad \tau = \frac{P}{\omega} = \frac{100 \times 1000 \times 7}{60 \times 22} = 530.3 \text{ N-m}$$ [1]

35 Given, $I = 0.6$ kg-m^2, $n = 0.5$ rps

$$\omega = 2\pi n = \pi \text{ rad s}^{-1}$$ [1]

∴ Angular momentum,

$$L = I\omega = 0.6 \times 3.14 = 1.9 \text{ kg-m}^2\text{s}^{-1}$$ [1]

CHAPTER

07

Gravitation

Every object in the universe attracts every other object with a force which is called force of gravitation.

Galileo was the first to recognise the fact that all bodies, irrespective of their masses fall towards the earth with a constant acceleration. Kepler believed all heavenly bodies obey a mathematical order unlike anything on the earth.

- Theory of Planetary Motion
- Acceleration due to Gravity and Gravitational Potential Energy
- Escape Velocity, Geostationary and Solar Satellites

TOPIC 01 Theory of Planetary Motion

In early days, people were observing the heavenly bodies like sun, moon, stars, planets etc., and their movement. The heavenly bodies which move around the sun are called planets. Earth, mercury, venus, etc., are planets. Generally, all the planets move around the sun in elliptical path.

The earliest recorded model for planetary motions proposed by **Ptolemy** about 2000 years ago was a **geocentric model**. It states that the description of the cosmos where the earth is at the orbital centre of all celestial bodies.

However, a more elegant model in which the sun was at the centre around which the planet revolved is called **heliocentric model**. This theory was later on supported by Galileo from his experimental study on the moon and other planets. Tycho Brahe (1546-1601) spent his entire lifetime recording observations of the planets with the naked eyes. His assistant Johannes Kepler compiled his data and analysed. He extracted three elegant laws that are now known as Kepler's law.

Kepler's Laws of Planetary Motion

Kepler's laws of planetary motion are three scientific laws describing motion of planets around the sun.

Kepler's First Law of Orbits

According to this law, all planets move in elliptical orbits with the sun situated at one of the foci of the ellipse.

This law identifies that the distance between the sun and the earth is constantly changing as the earth goes around its orbit as shown in figure.

It shows an ellipse traced out by a planet around the sun, S. The closest point is P and the farthest point is A. P is called the **perihelion** and A is the **aphelion**.

The length of the major axis is equal to the sum of the planet-sun distance at perihelion plus the planet-sun distance at aphelion. The length of the major axis is $2a$. Half the distance AP is length a of the semi-major axis.

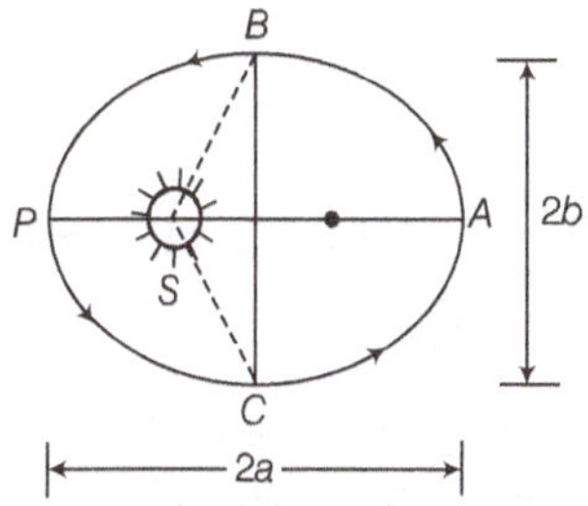

An ellipse traced out by a planet around the sun

Kepler's Second Law of Areas

According to this law, the speed of planet varies in such a way that the radius vector drawn from the sun to a planet sweeps out equal areas in equal interval of time. i.e. The areal velocity of the planet around the sun is constant.

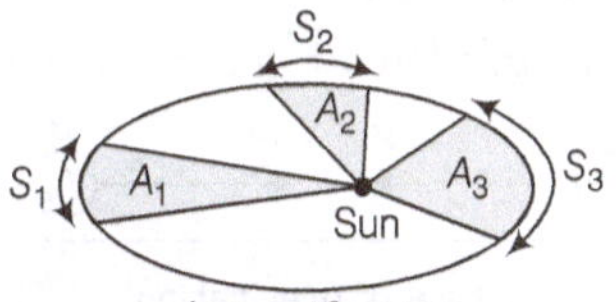

Laws of areas

The elliptical orbit of a planet around the sun is shown in figure. The areas A_1, A_2 and A_3 are swept out by the radius vector in equal intervals of time Δt. According to Kepler's second law, $A_1 = A_2 = A_3$

Note Areal velocity may be defined as the area swept by the radius vector in unit time.

This law is identical with the law of conservation of angular momentum.

Proof Consider a small area ΔA described in a small time interval Δt and let the position of the planet be denoted by r.

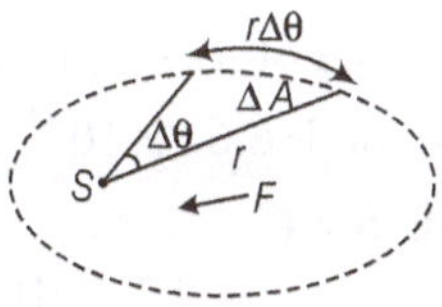

Now, $$\Delta A = \frac{1}{2} r (r \Delta \theta)$$

$\therefore$ $$\frac{\Delta A}{\Delta t} = \frac{1}{2} r^2 \frac{\Delta \theta}{\Delta t}$$

Proceeding to limit as $\Delta t \to 0$, we get

$$\lim_{\Delta t \to 0} \frac{\Delta A}{\Delta t} = \frac{1}{2} r^2 \lim_{\Delta t \to 0} \frac{\Delta \theta}{\Delta t}$$

or $$\frac{dA}{dt} = \frac{1}{2} r^2 \omega \qquad \left[\because \omega = \frac{\Delta \theta}{\Delta t}\right] \quad \ldots \text{(i)}$$

Instantaneous angular momentum,

$$L = mr^2 \omega \quad \ldots \text{(ii)}$$

From Eqs. (i) and (ii), we get

$$\frac{dA}{dt} = \frac{L}{2m} \text{ or } L = 2m \times \frac{dA}{dt} \quad \ldots \text{(iii)}$$

The line of action of the gravitational force passes through the axis. Therefore, angle between **r** and **F** is 180°.

Now, $$\tau_{\text{ext}} = \mathbf{r} \times \mathbf{F} = rF \sin 180° \, \hat{\mathbf{n}} = 0$$

$\therefore$ $$\tau_{\text{ext}} = 0$$

$$L = \text{constant} \qquad \left[\therefore \frac{dL}{dt} = \tau_{\text{ext}}\right] \quad \ldots \text{(iv)}$$

From Eqs. (iii) and (iv), we get

$\therefore$ Areal velocity, $$\frac{dA}{dt} = \text{constant}$$

i.e. **The areal velocity of the planet around the sun is constant.** This proved the Kepler's second law of planetary motion.

Kepler's Third Law of Period

According to this law, the square of the time period of revolution of a planet around the sun is proportional to the cube of the semi-major axis of its elliptical orbit.

T = time period of revolution of a planet

i.e. $$\boxed{T^2 \propto a^3}$$

Proof of Third Law

Kepler's third law can be readily proved by assuming that the orbit of the planet is a circle of radius r with sun at the centre. The sun's gravitational attraction provides the necessary centripetal force for the planet to orbit around the sun.

Thus, $$\frac{GM_s m}{r^2} = \frac{mv^2}{r} \text{ or } \frac{GM_s}{r^2} = \frac{v^2}{r} \quad \ldots \text{(i)}$$

where, M_s is the mass of the sun and v is the orbital speed of the planet. The planet completes one revolution of the orbit in a time period (T) given by

$$v = 2\pi r / T \quad \ldots \text{(ii)}$$

Substituting the value of v in Eq. (i), we get

$$\frac{GM_s}{r^2} = \frac{4\pi^2 r^2}{T^2 r}$$

or $$T^2 = \frac{4\pi^2}{GM_s} r^3 \text{ or } T^2 = kr^3 \text{ or } T^2 \propto r^3$$

This is the third law of Kepler. The constant k is same for all planets and has a value $2.97 \times 10^{-19} \text{ s}^2\text{m}^{-3}$. If the orbit is an ellipse, then r may be replaced by semi-major axis a of the ellipse.

Example 1 A satellite revolves round a planet in an elliptical orbit. Its maximum and minimum distances from the planet are 1.5×10^7 m and 0.5×10^7 m, respectively. If the speed of the satellite at the farthest point be 5×10^3 m/s, calculate the speed at the nearest point.

Sol. We know that, $L = \mathbf{r} \times m\mathbf{v}$

As the two above mentioned points **r** and **v** are mutually perpendicular.

Therefore, $|\mathbf{r} \times m\mathbf{v}| = rmv \sin 90° = rmv$

$$L = mv_1 r_1 = mv_2 r_2$$

$$\Rightarrow \quad \frac{v_1}{v_2} = \frac{r_2}{r_1}$$

$$\Rightarrow \quad \frac{5 \times 10^3}{v_2} = \frac{0.5 \times 10^7}{1.5 \times 10^7}$$

$$\Rightarrow \quad v_2 = 1.5 \times 10^4 \text{ m/s}$$

Example 2 Calculate the period of revolution of the neptune around the sun, given that diameter of its orbit is 30 times the diameter of the earth's orbit around the sun. Assume both the orbits to be circular.

Sol. According to Kepler's third law,

$$\frac{T_n^2}{T_e^2} = \frac{R_n^3}{R_e^3}$$

where subscripts n and e refer to the neptune and the earth respectively.

$$\therefore \quad T_n^2 = T_e^2 \times \left(\frac{R_n}{R_e}\right)^3 = 1 \times (30)^3$$

[∵ time period of the earth's revolution = 1 year and ratio of radii (hence, diameters) of the neptune and the earth is 30]

$$\therefore \quad T_n = 1 \times \sqrt{(30)^3}$$

$$T_n = 30\sqrt{30} = 164.3 \text{ yr}$$

Example 3 Suppose there existed a planet that went around the sun twice as fast as the earth. What would be its orbital size as compared to that of the earth? **[NCERT]**

Sol. Let T_P and T_E denote the time periods of the planet and the earth, respectively. If R_P and R_E denote the corresponding orbital size as, then

$$\frac{T_P^2}{T_E^2} = \frac{R_P^3}{R_E^3}$$

or $$\left(\frac{R_P}{R_E}\right)^3 = \left(\frac{T_P}{T_E}\right)^2 \Rightarrow \frac{R_P}{R_E} = \left(\frac{T_P}{T_E}\right)^{2/3}$$

Since, $$T_P = \frac{1}{2} T_E, \frac{T_P}{T_E} = \frac{1}{2}$$

Thus, $$\frac{R_P}{R_E} = \left(\frac{1}{2}\right)^{2/3} = 0.63 \Rightarrow R_P = 0.63 R_E$$

Newton's Universal Law of Gravitation

It states that, Every body in this universe attracts each other body with a force whose magnitude is directly proportional to the product of their masses and inversely proportional to the square of the distance between their centres. This force acts along the line joining the centres of two bodies.

Consider two bodies of masses m_1 and m_2 with their centres mutually separated by a distance r as shown in figure. Let F be the force (in magnitude) of gravitational attraction between two bodies.

According to Newton's law of gravitation, we get

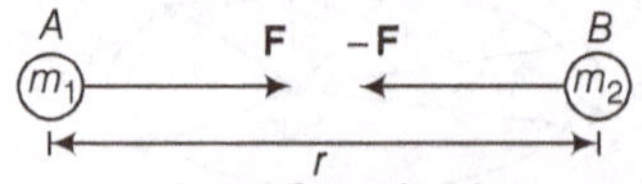

Law of gravitation

So, $$F \propto m_1 m_2 \quad \text{...(i)}$$

and $$F \propto \frac{1}{r^2} \quad \text{...(ii)}$$

From Eqs. (i) and (ii), we get

or $$F \propto \frac{m_1 m_2}{r^2}$$

or $$\boxed{\text{Gravitational force, } F = G\frac{m_1 m_2}{r^2}} \quad \text{...(iii)}$$

where G is a constant of proportionality known as **gravitational constant**. It is also known as **universal gravitational constant.**

In CGS system, the value of G is 6.67×10^{-8} dyne cm^2 g^{-2} and its SI value is 6.67×10^{-11} Nm^{2}kg^{-2}.

Dimensional formula for G

$$G = \frac{F r^2}{m_1 m_2} = \frac{[\text{MLT}^{-2}][\text{L}^2]}{[\text{M}^2]}$$

$$= [\text{MLT}^{-2}][\text{L}^2][\text{M}^{-2}]$$

$$= [\text{M}^{-1}\text{L}^3\text{T}^{-2}]$$

Suppose $m_1 = m_2 = 1$ unit and $r = 1$ unit, then from Eq. (iii), we get

$$F = \frac{G \times 1 \times 1}{(1)^2} \Rightarrow F = G$$

Thus, universal gravitational constant (G) is numerically equal to the force of attraction acting between two bodies, each of unit mass separated by unit distance apart.

Important Points about Gravitational Force

- It is always attractive in nature while electric and magnetic force can be attractive or repulsive.
- It is independent of the intervening medium between the particles while electric and magnetic force depend on the nature of the medium between the particles.
- The gravitational force is a conservative force.
- The value of G does not depend on the nature and size of the masses.
- The force of attraction between a hollow spherical shell of uniform density and a point mass situated outside is just as if the entire mass of the shell is concentrated at the centre of the shell. Gravitational force possesses spherical symmetry.
- The force of attraction due to a hollow spherical shell of uniform density on a point mass situated inside it, is zero.

Example 4 A sphere of mass 40 kg is attracted by a second sphere of mass 60 kg with a force equal to 4 mgf. If G is 6×10^{-11} Nm^2/kg^2, then calculate the distance between them. Consider acceleration due to gravity is 10 m/s^2.

Sol. Given, $M = 40 kg$, $m = 60 kg$,

$$F = 4 \text{ mgf} = 4 \times 10^{-6} \times 10 = 4 \times 10^{-5} \text{N},$$

$$G = 6 \times 10^{-11} \text{ Nm}^2/\text{kg}^2, g = 10 \text{m/s}^2.$$

According to universal law, $F = \frac{GMm}{r^2}$

$$\Rightarrow \quad r = \sqrt{\frac{GMm}{F}} = \sqrt{\frac{6 \times 10^{-11} \times 40 \times 60}{4 \times 10^{-5}}}$$

$$= 0.06 \text{ m} = 6 \text{ cm}$$

Vector Form of Newton's Law of Gravitation

Consider two particles A and B of masses m_1 and m_2, respectively.

Let $\mathbf{r}_{12}$ = displacement vector from A to B,

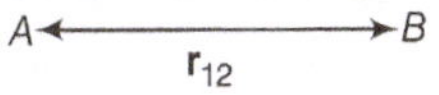

$\mathbf{r}_{21}$ = displacement vector from B to A,

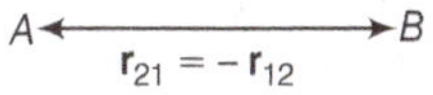

$\mathbf{F}_{21}$ = gravitational force exerted on B by A

$\mathbf{F}_{12}$ = gravitational force exerted on A by B

On vector notation, Newton's law of gravitation is written as follows

$$\mathbf{F}_{12} = -G\frac{m_1 m_2}{r_{21}^2}\hat{\mathbf{r}}_{21} \quad \text{...(i)}$$

where $\hat{\mathbf{r}}_{21}$ is a unit vector pointing towards A. The negative sign indicates that the direction of $\mathbf{F}_{12}$ is opposite to that of $\hat{\mathbf{r}}_{21}$.

The negative sign also shows that the gravitational force is attractive in nature.

Similarly, $\quad \mathbf{F}_{21} = -G\frac{m_1 m_2}{r_{12}^2}\hat{\mathbf{r}}_{12}$

where, $\hat{\mathbf{r}}_{12}$ is a unit vector pointing towards B.

But, $\quad \hat{\mathbf{r}}_{21} = -\hat{\mathbf{r}}_{12}$

Also, $\quad r_{21}^2 = r_{12}^2$

$$\therefore \quad \mathbf{F}_{21} = G\frac{m_1 m_2}{r_{21}^2}\hat{\mathbf{r}}_{21} \quad \text{...(ii)}$$

Equating Eqs. (i) and (ii), we have

$$\mathbf{F}_{12} = -\mathbf{F}_{21}$$

As $\mathbf{F}_{12}$ and $\mathbf{F}_{21}$ are directed towards the centres of the two particles, so, **gravitational force is a central force.**

Topic Practice 1

Multiple Choice Questions

1 Mark

1. In planetary motion, the areal velocity of position vector of a planet depends on angular velocity (ω) and the distance of the planet from sun (r). If so the correct relation for areal velocity is

(a) $\frac{dA}{dt} \propto \omega r$ (b) $\frac{dA}{dt} \propto \omega^2 r$

(c) $\frac{dA}{dt} \propto \omega r^2$ (d) $\frac{dA}{dt} \propto \sqrt{\omega r}$

2. The orbital angular momentum of a satellite revolving at a distance r from the centre is L. If the distance is increased to $16r$, then the new angular momentum will be

(a) $16\,L$ (b) $64\,L$

(c) $\frac{L}{4}$ (d) $4\,L$

3. According to Kepler's law of planetary motion, if T represents time-period and r is orbital radius, then for two planets these are related as

(a) $\left(\frac{T_1}{T_2}\right)^3 = \left(\frac{r_1}{r_2}\right)^2$ (b) $\left(\frac{T_1}{T_2}\right)^{3/2} = \frac{r_1}{r_2}$

(c) $\left(\frac{T_1}{T_2}\right)^2 = \left(\frac{r_1}{r_2}\right)^3$ (d) $\left(\frac{T_1}{T_2}\right) = \left(\frac{r_1}{r_2}\right)^{2/3}$

4. Two equal point masses are separated by a distance d_1. The force of gravitation acting between them is F_1. If the separation is decreased to d_2, then the new force of gravitation F_2 is given by

(a) $F_2 = F_1$ (b) $F_2 = F_1\left(\frac{d_1}{d_2}\right)^2$

(c) $F_2 = F_1\left(\frac{d_2}{d_1}\right)^2$ (d) $F_2 = F_1\left(\frac{d_1}{d_2}\right)$

5. Two sphere of masses m and M are situated in air and the gravitational force between them is F. The space around the masses is now filled with a liquid of specific gravity 3. The gravitational force will now be

(a) F (b) $\frac{F}{3}$

(c) $\frac{F}{9}$ (d) $3\,F$

Very Short Answer Type Questions

1 Mark

6. By which law is the Kepler's law of areas identical?

7. Draw areal velocity versus time graph for mars. **NCERT Exemplar**

8. What is the direction of areal velocity of the earth around the sun?

9. Out of aphelion and perihelion, where is the speed of the earth more and why ?

10. From Kepler's second law and observations of the sun's motion as seen from the earth, we can conclude that the earth is closer to the sun during winter in the Northern hemisphere than during summer. Explain.

11. Is the Kepler's law kinematic ?

12. Assume that the law of gravitation changes from inverse square to inverse cube. Does the angular momentum of a planet about the sun will remain constant ?

13. How earth retains most of the atmosphere?

14. Do the force of friction and other contact forces arise due to gravitational attraction? If not, then what is the origin of these forces ?

15. Why does tides arise in the oceans ?

16. If you compare the gravitational force on the earth due to the sun to that due to the moon, you would find that sun's pull is greater than the moon's pull. However, the tidal effect of the moon's pull is greater than the tidal effect of the sun. Why ? **NCERT**

17. How is the gravitational force between two point masses affected when they are dipped in water keeping the separation between them the same ?

Short Answer Type I Questions

2 Marks

18. Write down the statement of Kepler's first law of orbits.

19. A planet moving along an elliptical orbit is closest to the Sun at a distance r_1 and farthest away at a distance of r_2. If v_1 and v_2 are the linear velocities at these points respectively, then find the ratio $\frac{v_1}{v_2}$.

20. Write down the Newton's universal law of gravitation with its formula.

21. Write down the formula of gravitation constant and derive its dimensional formula.

22. Imagine what would happen if the value of G becomes

(i) 100 times of its present value.

(ii) $\frac{1}{100}$ times of its present value.

Short Answer Type II Questions

3 Marks

23. Two identical heavy spheres are separated by a distance 10 times their radius. Will an object placed at the mid-point of the line joining their centres be in stable equilibrium or unstable equilibrium? Give reasons for your answer. **NCERT Exemplar**

24. Two stationary particles of masses M_1 and M_2 are a distance d apart. A third particle lying on the line joining the particles, experiences no resultant gravitational force. What is the distance of this particle from M_1?

25. Give the proof to Kepler's third law.

26. What is gravitational constant? Find out its dimension.

27. Compare the gravitational force and electric force.

Long Answer Type Questions

5 Marks

28. Write the Kepler's law and prove the second law of Kepler.

29. What is the Newton's universal law of gravitation? Derive its expression.

30. Four particles each of mass M and equidistant from each other, move along a circle of radius R. Under the action of their mutual gravitational attraction. What is the speed of each particle?

Numerical Problems

31. The hydrogen atom consists of a proton of mass 1.67×10^{-27} kg and orbiting electron of mass 9.11×10^{-31} kg. In one of its orbits, the electron is 5.3×10^{-11}m from the proton and in another orbit, it is 10.6×10^{-11}m from the proton. What are the mutual attractive forces when the electron is in these orbits, respectively? **[2 M]**

32. If earth be at one half its present distance from the sun, then how many days will there be in a year? **[1 M]**

33. In Kepler's law of periods, $T^2 = kr^3$, the constant, $k = 10^{-13}$ s^{2}m^{-3}. Express the constant k in days and kilometres. The moon is at a distance of 3.84×10^5 km from the earth. Obtain its time period of revolution in days. **NCERT [2 M]**

34. The time period of a satellite of earth is 5 h. If the separation between the earth and the satellite is increased to four times the previous value, then what will be the new time period? **[2 M]**

35. A geostationary satellite is orbiting the earth at a height of $5R$ above the surface of the earth, R being the radius of the earth. Find the time period of another satellite (in hours) at a height of $2R$ from the surface of the earth. **[3 M]**

36. A saturn year is 29.5 times the earth year. How far is the saturn from the sun of the earth is 1.50×10^8 km away from the sun? **NCERT [3 M]**

37. A rocket is fired from the earth towards the sun. At what distance from the earth's centre is the gravitational force on the rocket zero? Mass of the sun $= 2 \times 10^{30}$ kg, mass of the earth $= 6 \times 10^{24}$ kg. Neglect the effect of other planets etc. (Orbital radius $= 1.5 \times 10^{11}$ m). **NCERT [5 M]**

Hints & Solutions

1. (c) $\frac{dA}{dt} = \frac{L}{2m} \Rightarrow \frac{dA}{dt} \propto vr \propto \omega r^2$

2. (d) $L = mvr = m\sqrt{\frac{GM}{r}}\, r = m\sqrt{GMr}$

$\therefore \quad L \propto \sqrt{r}$

$\therefore \quad L' \propto \sqrt{16r} \Rightarrow L' = 4L$

3. (c) From Kepler's third law of planetary motion,

$$T^2 \propto r^3 \Rightarrow \frac{T^2}{r^3} = \text{constant}$$

$$\Rightarrow \frac{T_1^2}{r_1^3} = \frac{T_2^2}{r_2^3} = \text{constant or } \left(\frac{T_1}{T_2}\right)^2 = \left(\frac{r_1}{r_2}\right)^3$$

4. (b) From Newton's law of gravitation,

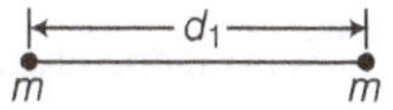

$$F_1 = \frac{Gm \cdot m}{d_1^2} = \frac{Gm^2}{d_1^2} \quad \text{...(i)}$$

Similarly,

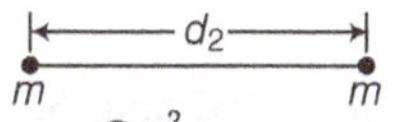

$$F_2 = \frac{Gm^2}{d_2^2} \quad \text{...(ii)}$$

From Eqs. (i) and (ii), we get

$$\frac{F_1}{F_2} = \left(\frac{d_2}{d_1}\right)^2$$

$$\therefore \quad F_2 = F_1\left(\frac{d_1}{d_2}\right)^2$$

5. (a) Gravitational force does not depend on the medium between the masses.
So, it will remain same, i.e. F.

6. The law of conservation of angular momentum.

7. Areal velocity of planet revolving around the sun is constant with time (kepler's second law).

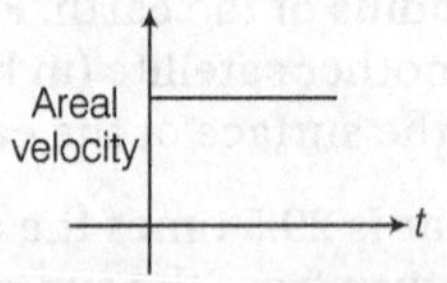

8. It is normal to the plane containing the earth and the sun as areal velocity.

$$\frac{\Delta A}{\Delta t} = \frac{1}{2} r \times v\Delta t$$

and directed according to right hand rule.

9. At perihelion, because the earth has to cover greater linear distance to keep the areal velocity constant.

10. The earth is closer to the sun during winter. But heating effect is less because the sun's rays fall obliquely.

11. Yes, because kepler's third law is the relation between distance and time.

12. The torque on a planet is zero so long as the force is a central force. The angular momentum of planet remains constant so long as torque remains zero.

13. Earth retains most of the atmosphere due to force of gravity.

14. Contact forces have electrical region.

15. Tides arise in the oceans due to the force of attraction between the moon and sea water.

16. Even though the sun is much farther away from the earth than moon, it exerts a stronger gravitational pull because it is so huge. However, the sun exerts a smaller tidal influence on the earth than the moon because earth is more closer to the moon.

17. Gravitational force acting between two point masses m_1 and m_2, $F = \frac{Gm_1 m_2}{r^2}$, is independent of the nature of medium between them.
Therefore, gravitational force acting between two point masses will remain unaffected when they are dipped in water.

18. Refer to text on pages 232 and 233 (Kepler's first law of orbits)

19. From the law of conservation of angular momentum

$$mr_1v_1 = mr_2v_2 \Rightarrow r_1v_1 = r_2v_2 \text{ or } \frac{v_1}{v_2} = \frac{r_2}{r_1}$$ [2]

20. Refer to text on pages 234 and 235 (Newton's universal law of gravitation).

21. Refer to text on pages 234 and 235 (Newton's universal law of gravitation)

22. (i) Earth's attraction would be so large that you would be crushed to the earth. [1]
(ii) Earth's attraction would be so less that we can easily jump from the top of a multi-storey building. [1]

23. If F_L and F_R are the forces exerted on mass m lying at O (after displacing it from O to O'), by masses M lying on left and right, respectively. Then, from figure,

$$F_L = G\frac{Mm}{(x+\Delta x)^2} \text{ and } F_R = G\frac{Mm}{(x-\Delta x)^2}$$ [1]

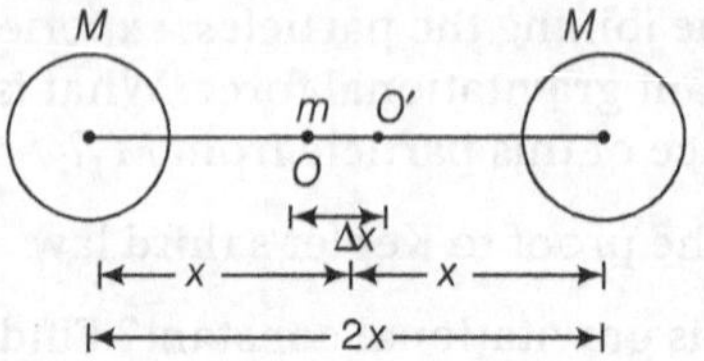

[1]

Since $F_R > F_L$, the net force on m is towards right.
Hence, the equilibrium is unstable. [1]

24. The force on m towards M_1 is $F = G\frac{M_1 m}{r^2}$

The force on m towards M_2 is $F = G\frac{M_2 m}{(d-r)^2}$ [1]

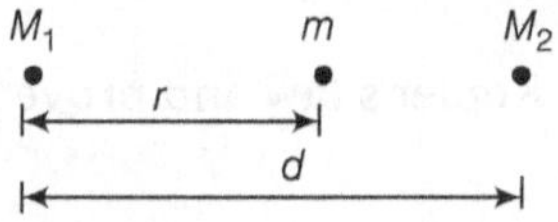

[1/2]

Equating two forces, we have

$$G\frac{M_1 m}{r^2} = G\frac{M_2 m}{(d-r)^2}$$ [1/2]

$$\left(\frac{d-r}{r}\right)^2 = \frac{M_2}{M_1} \text{ or } \frac{d}{r} - 1 = \frac{\sqrt{M_2}}{\sqrt{M_1}}$$

$$\Rightarrow \qquad \frac{d}{r} = \frac{\sqrt{M_2} + \sqrt{M_1}}{\sqrt{M_1}}$$

So, distance of an particle from m is

$$r = d\left(\frac{\sqrt{M_1}}{\sqrt{M_1} + \sqrt{M_2}}\right)$$ [1]

25. Refer to text on pages 233 and 234 (Proof of third law).

26. Refer to text on pages 234 and 235 (Newton's universal law of gravitation).

27. Refer to text on page 235 (Important points about gravitational force).

28. Refer to text on pages 232 and 233 (Kepler's laws of planetary motion and Kepler's second law of areas).

29. Refer to text on pages 234 and 235 (Newton's universal law of gravitation).

30. Gravitational force = Centripetal force

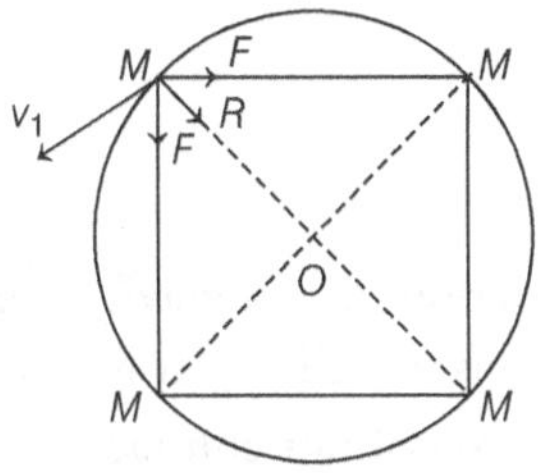

[1]

$$\sqrt{2}F + \frac{GMM}{(2R)^2} = \frac{Mv^2}{R}$$ [1]

$$\sqrt{2}\cdot\frac{GMM}{(R\sqrt{2})^2} + \frac{GMM}{4R^2} = \frac{Mv^2}{R} \Rightarrow \frac{GM}{R}\left(\frac{2\sqrt{2}+1}{4}\right) = v^2$$ [2]

Speed of the particle, $v = \frac{1}{2}\sqrt{\frac{GM}{R}(1+2\sqrt{2})}$ [1]

31. Given, $m_1 = 1.67\times10^{-27}$ kg, $m_2 = 9.11\times10^{-31}$ kg,

$r_1 = 5.3\times10^{-11}$ m, $r_2 = 10.6\times10^{-11}$ m

$\therefore$ Newton's law of gravitation,

$$F_1 = \frac{Gm_1m_2}{r_1^2} = \frac{(6.67\times10^{-11})\times(1.67\times10^{-27})\times(9.11\times10^{-31})}{(5.3\times10^{-11})^2}$$

Since, $r_2 = 2r_1$ [1]

$$F \propto \frac{1}{r^2}$$

$$\because \quad \frac{F_1}{F_2} = \frac{r_1^2}{r_2^2} = \frac{1}{2^2} = \frac{1}{4}$$

$$\therefore \quad F_2 = \frac{F_1}{4} = \frac{1}{4}(3.6\times10^{-47}) = 9.0\times10^{-48}\text{N}$$ [1]

32. According to Kepler's third law

$$T^2 \propto R^3$$

Hence, $\frac{T_1^2}{T_2^2} = \frac{R_1^3}{R_2^3} \Rightarrow T_2^2 = \left[\frac{R_2}{R_1}\right]^3 T_1^2$ [1/2]

$$\Rightarrow T_2 = T_1\left[\frac{R_2}{R_1}\right]^{3/2} = 365\left(\frac{R/2}{R}\right)^{3/2} = 365\times\frac{1}{2\sqrt{2}} = 129 \text{ days}$$ [1/2]

33. Given, $k = 10^{-13}\text{s}^2/\text{m}^3$

As, $1\text{ s} = \frac{1}{24\times60\times60}$ day and $1\text{m} = \frac{1}{1000}$ km [1/2]

$$\therefore \quad k = 10^{-13}\times\frac{1}{(24\times60\times60)^2}(\text{day})^2\frac{1}{(1/1000)^3}\text{km}^{-3}$$

$$= 1.33\times10^{-14}\ (\text{day})^2\text{km}^{-3}$$ [1/2]

For the moon, $r = 3.84\times10^5$ km

$$\therefore \quad T^2 = kr^3 = 1.33\times10^{-14}\times(3.84\times10^5)^3$$

$$= 753.087$$

$$T = 27.3 \text{ days}$$ [1]

34. $T_2 = T_1\left[\frac{R_2}{R_1}\right]^{3/2} = T_1[4]^{3/2} = 8T_1 = 40\text{h}$ [2]

35. From Kepler's third law,

$$T^2 \propto r^3$$

Hence, $T_1^2 \propto r_1^3$ and $T_2^2 \propto r_2^3$ [1]

So, $\frac{T_2^2}{T_1^2} = \frac{r_2^3}{r_1^3} = \frac{(3R)^3}{(6R)^3} \Rightarrow \frac{T_2}{T_1} = \frac{1}{2\sqrt{2}}$ $[\because T_1 = 24\text{ h}]$

$$\therefore \quad T_2 = \frac{24}{2\sqrt{2}} = \frac{12}{\sqrt{2}}$$ [2]

36. According to Kepler's third law of planetary motion, $T^2 \propto r^3$ [1/2]

Thus, $\frac{T_S^2}{T_E^2} = \frac{r_S^3}{r_E^3}$ or $\left(\frac{T_S}{T_E}\right)^2 = \left(\frac{r_S}{r_E}\right)^3$

or $\left(\frac{r_S}{r_E}\right) = \left(\frac{T_S}{T_E}\right)^{2/3}$ [1]

or $r_S = \left(\frac{T_S}{T_E}\right)^{2/3}\times r_E$ [1/2]

As, $\frac{T_S}{T_E} = 29.5$ and $r_E = 1.5\times10^8$ km,

$$r_S = (29.5)^{2/3}(1.5\times10^8 \text{ km})$$

$$= 14.3\times10^8 \text{ km}$$ [1]

37. We are given that

Mass of the sun, $M_s = 2\times10^{30}$ kg

Mass of the earth, $M_e = 6\times10^{24}$ kg [1]

Distance between the centres of the sun and the earth,

$$r = 1.5\times10^{11} \text{ m}$$

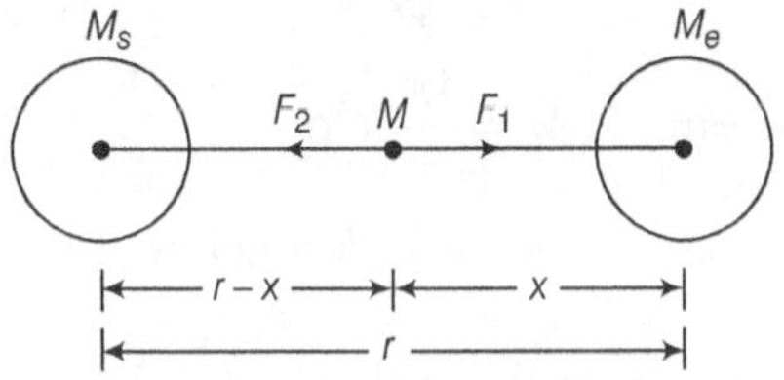

[1]

Let x be the distance of the required point from the centre of the earth. Clearly, at this point the gravitational force (F_1) on the rocket of mass m due to the earth = gravitational force (F_2) on the rocket due to the sun, i.e. $F_1 = F_2$. [1]

or $\frac{GmM_e}{x^2} = \frac{GmM_s}{(r-x)^2}$

or $\frac{(r-x)^2}{x^2} = \frac{M_s}{M_e} = \frac{2\times10^{30}\text{ kg}}{6\times10^{24}\text{ kg}} = \frac{10^6}{3}$

or $\frac{r-x}{x} = \frac{10^3}{\sqrt{3}}$ or $\frac{r}{x} - 1 = \frac{10^3}{\sqrt{3}}$ [1]

or $\frac{r}{x} = \frac{10^3}{\sqrt{3}} + 1 \approx \frac{10^3}{\sqrt{3}}$

or $x = \frac{\sqrt{3}r}{10^3} = \frac{1.732(1.5\times10^{11})\text{ m}}{10^3} = 2.6\times10^8$ m [1]

TOPIC 02 Acceleration Due to Gravity and Gravitational Potential Energy

Acceleration due to Gravity of Earth

The force of gravity acting on a body having unit mass placed on or near the surface of the earth is known as **acceleration due to gravity.** It is represented by symbol g and its value is 9.8 m/s^2 on the surface of the earth.

Consider the earth to be made up of concentric shells and a point mass m situated at a distance r from the centre.

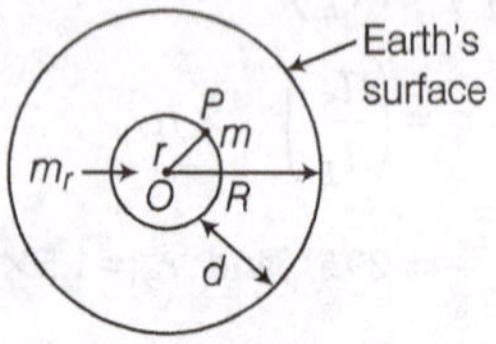

Determination of acceleration due to gravity of earth

The point P lies outside, if the shell's radius is less than r and the point P lies inside if the shell's radius is greater than r. The smaller sphere exerts a force on a mass m at P as if its mass m_r is concentrated at the centre. The force on the mass m at P has a magnitude

$$F = \frac{Gm(m_r)}{r^2} \quad \ldots(i)$$

Mass on the earth is $M = \frac{4\pi}{3}R^3\rho$

where, M = mass of the earth, R = radius of the earth and

ρ = density of the earth.

Mass on sphere is $m_r = \frac{4\pi}{3}\rho r^3$

Substituting the value of m_r in Eq. (i), we have

$$F = \frac{Gm}{r^2}\frac{4\pi}{3}\rho r^3 = Gm\frac{M}{R^3}r$$

$$\Rightarrow \quad F = G\frac{Mm}{R^2} \quad [\because r = R]$$

From Newton's second law, we know, $F = mg$

$$\therefore \quad g = \frac{F}{m} = \frac{GM}{R^2}$$

Acceleration due to gravity, $g = \frac{GM}{R^2}$

The unit of acceleration due to gravity is ms^{-2} or Nkg^{-1} and g has the dimension $[\text{LT}^{-2}]$. It is a vector quantity and it is neither universal nor constant.

Computation of Mass and Density of Earth

We may compute the mass and density of earth from Newton's law of gravitation from the relation, we get,

$$g = \frac{GM_e}{R_e^2}$$

The mass of the earth M_e is given by

$$M_e = \frac{gR_e^2}{G} \quad \ldots(i)$$

Substitute the values; $g = 9.8 \text{ ms}^{-2}$, $R_e = 6.37 \times 10^6 \text{m}$ and $G = 6.67 \times 10^{-11} \text{ m}^3 \text{ kg}^{-1}\text{s}^{-2}$ in Eq (i), we get

$$M_e = \frac{9.8 \times (6.37 \times 10^6)^2}{6.67 \times 10^{-11}}$$

$$= 6.0 \times 10^{24} \text{ kg (approx.)}$$

If ρ is the average density, then mass,

$$M_e = \text{volume} \times \text{density} = \frac{4}{3}\pi R_e^3 \times \rho \quad \ldots(ii)$$

From Eqs. (i) and (ii), we get

$$\frac{gR_e^2}{G} = \frac{4}{3}\pi R_e^3 \times \rho$$

$$\Rightarrow \quad \rho = \frac{3g}{4\pi R_e G}$$

Substitute the value of g, R_e, G, we get

$$\rho = \frac{3 \times 9.8}{4 \times 3.14 \times 6.37 \times 10^6 \times 6.67 \times 10^{-11}}$$

$$= 5.5 \times 10^3 \text{ kgm}^{-3} \text{ (approx.)}$$

Note

- The value of g on the surface of the moon is equal to 1/6 times the value of g on the surface of the earth.
- The value of g is independent of mass, shape, size etc., of the body and depends upon the mass and radius of the earth.
- Weight of a body, $w = mg$.

Example 1 The acceleration due to gravity at the moon's surface is 1.67 ms^{-2}. If the radius of the moon is 1.74×10^6 m, then calculate the mass of the moon.

Sol. As we know, gravitational aceeleration,

$$g = \frac{GM}{R^2} \quad \text{or} \quad M = \frac{gR^2}{G}$$

This relation is true not only to the earth but for any heavenly body which is assumed to be spherical.

Now, $g = 1.67 \text{ ms}^{-2}, R = 1.74 \times 10^6 \text{ m}$

$G = 6.67 \times 10^{-11} \text{ Nm}^{-2} \text{ kg}^{-2}$

$\therefore$ Mass of the moon, $M = \frac{1.67 \times (1.74 \times 10^6)^2}{6.67 \times 10^{-11}}$ kg

$= 7.58 \times 10^{22}$ kg

Example 2 A star 2.5 times the mass of the sun and collapsed to a size of 12 km and rotates with a speed of 1.2 revolutions per second. (Extremely compact stars of this kind are known as neutron stars. Certain stellar objects, called pulsars, belong to this category.) Will an object placed on its equator remain stuck to its surface due to gravity ?
(mass of the sun = 2×10^{30} kg) **[NCERT]**

Sol. We are given mass of neutron star,

i.e. $M = 2.5 \times 2 \times 10^{30}$ kg

$= 5 \times 10^{30}$ kg

Radius of star, $R = 12 \text{ km} = 1.2 \times 10^4$ m

Frequency of rotation, $\nu = 1.5$

If g is the acceleration due to gravity on the surface of the star,

$$g = \frac{GM}{R^2} = \frac{6.67 \times 10^{-11} \times 5 \times 10^{20}}{(1.2 \times 10^4)^2} \text{ m/s}^2$$

$= 2.3 \times 10^{12} \text{ m/s}^2$

Centrifugal acceleration (a_c) produced in the object at the equator,

i.e. $a_c = R\omega^2 = R \times (2\pi\nu)^2 = 4\pi^2\nu^2 R$

or $a_c = 4 \times 9.87 \times (1.5)^2 \times 1.2 \times 10^4 \text{ m/s}^2$

$a_c = 1.1 \times 10^6 \text{ m/s}^2$

Since $g > a_c$, the object will remain stuck to its surface due to gravity.

Example 3 A spherical mass of 20 kg lying on the earth's surface is attracted by another spherical mass of 150 kg with a force equal to the weight of 0.25 mg. The centre of the two masses are 0.30 m apart. Calculate the mass of the earth.

Sol.

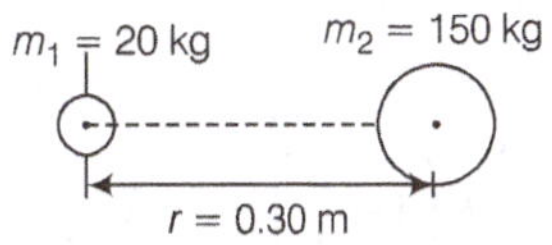

Given, $m_1 = 20 \text{ kg}, m_2 = 150 \text{ kg}$

$F = 0.25$ mg-wt

$g = 9.80 \text{ ms}^{-2}$

$R = 6 \times 10^6$ m

Now, kg-wt multiply by 9.8 to get in Newton.

$F = 0.25 \text{ mg-wt} = 0.25 \times 10^{-3}$ g-wt

$= 0.25 \times 10^{-3} \times 10^{-3} \text{ kg-wt} = 0.25 \times 10^{-6}$ kg-wt

$= 0.25 \times 10^{-6} \times 9.8$ N $\quad [\because 1 \text{ kg-wt} = 9.8 \text{ N}]$

From universal law, $F = G\frac{m_1 m_2}{r^2}$

or $G = \frac{Fr^2}{m_1 m_2}$

$$G = \frac{0.25 \times 10^{-6} \times 9.8 \times (0.3)^2}{20 \times 150}$$

$G = 75 \times 9.80 \times 10^{-13} \text{ Nm}^2 \text{ kg}^{-2}$

$\therefore \quad g = \frac{GM}{R^2}$

$$\therefore \quad M = \frac{g \times R^2}{G} = \frac{9.80 \times (6 \times 10^6)^2}{75 \times 9.80 \times 10^{-13}} = 4.8 \times 10^{24} \text{ kg}$$

Acceleration due to Gravity above the Surface of Earth

Consider a body of mass m lying on the surface of the earth of mass M and radius R. Acceleration due to gravity at the surface of the earth.

i.e. $$g = \frac{GM}{R^2} \quad \text{...(i)}$$

Suppose the body is taken to a height h above the surface of the earth where the value of acceleration due to gravity is g_h as shown in figure.

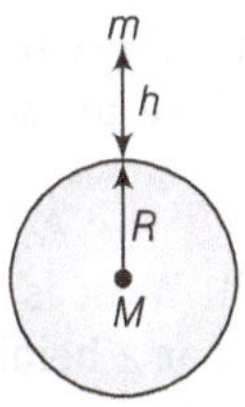

Variation of g with altitude

Then, $$g_h = \frac{GM}{(R+h)^2} \quad \text{...(ii)}$$

where, $(R+h)$ is the distance between the centres of body and the earth.

Dividing Eq. (ii) by Eq. (i), we get

$$\frac{g_h}{g} = \frac{GM}{(R+h)^2} \times \frac{R^2}{GM}$$

or $$\frac{g_h}{g} = \frac{R^2}{(R+h)^2} \quad \text{...(iii)}$$

As $h << R$, we can derive an expression for g_h

$$\frac{g_h}{g} = \frac{R^2}{\left[R\left(1+\frac{h}{R}\right)\right]^2} = \frac{R^2}{R^2\left(1+\frac{h}{R}\right)^2}$$

or

$$\frac{g_h}{g} = \frac{1}{\left(1+\frac{h}{R}\right)^2} = \left(1+\frac{h}{R}\right)^{-2}$$

Acceleration due to gravity at height h, $g_h = \dfrac{g}{\left(1+\frac{h}{R}\right)^2}$

If $h << R$, therefore h/R is very small, then expanding the right hand side of the above equation by Binomial theorem and neglecting squares and higher power of h/R, we get

$$\frac{g_h}{g} = 1 - \frac{2h}{R}$$

Acceleration due to gravity at height h, $g_h = g\left(1-\dfrac{2h}{R}\right)$ ...(iv)

or $gh = g - \dfrac{2h}{R} g$ or $g - g_h = \dfrac{2h}{R} g$ ...(v)

From Eq. (v), we know that the value of acceleration due to gravity decreases with height.

Since, the value of g at a given place on the earth is constant and R is also constant,

$\therefore$ $g - g_h \propto h$

From the above equation, we note that if h increases, g_h must decrease because g is constant. **Thus, the value of acceleration due to gravity decreases with increase in height above the surface of the earth.**

Example 4 A body weighs 63 N on the surface of the earth. What is the gravitational force on it due to the earth at a height equal to half the radius of the earth? **[NCERT]**

Sol. Let g_h be the acceleration due to gravity at a height equal to half the radius of the earth $\left(h = \frac{R}{2}\right)$ and g is its value on the earth's surface. Let the body have mass m.

We know that

$$\frac{g_h}{g} = \left(\frac{R}{R+h}\right)^2 \text{ or } \frac{g_h}{g} = \left(\frac{R}{R+\frac{R}{2}}\right)^2 = \left(\frac{2}{3}\right)^2 = \frac{4}{9}$$

Let w be the weight of body on the surface of the earth and w_h be the weight of the body at height h.

Then, $\dfrac{w_h}{w} = \dfrac{mg_h}{mg} = \dfrac{g_h}{g} = \dfrac{4}{9}$ or $w_h = \dfrac{4}{9} w = \dfrac{4}{9} \times 63$ N

$= 28$ N

Example 5 If an object at the altitude of the space shuttle's orbit, about 400 km about the earth's surface, then find out the free fall acceleration of that object.

Sol. The acceleration, $g = \dfrac{F}{m} = \dfrac{GMm/R^2}{m} = \dfrac{GM}{R^2}$

If the object is at height h above the earth's surface, then

$$g_h = \frac{GM}{(R+h)^2}$$

$$\Rightarrow \quad g_h = \frac{6.67 \times 10^{-11} \times 5.98 \times 10^{24}}{(6.4 \times 10^6 + 0.4 \times 10^6)^2} = 8.70 \text{ m/s}^2$$

Acceleration due to Gravity below the Surface of Earth

Assume the earth to be a homogeneous sphere (i.e. a sphere of uniform density). Let ρ be the mean density of the earth and a body be lying on the surface of the earth where the value of acceleration due to gravity is g.

Then, $g = \dfrac{GM}{R^2}$ or $g = \dfrac{G \times \frac{4}{3}\pi R^3 \rho}{R^2}$

$\left[\because \text{ mass of the earth, } M = \frac{4}{3}\pi R^3 \rho\right]$

$$g = \frac{4}{3}\pi G R \rho \quad \text{...(i)}$$

Now, the body be taken to a depth d below the free surface of the earth, where the acceleration due to gravity is g_d. Here, the force of gravity acting on the body is only due to the inner solid sphere of radius $(R - d)$.

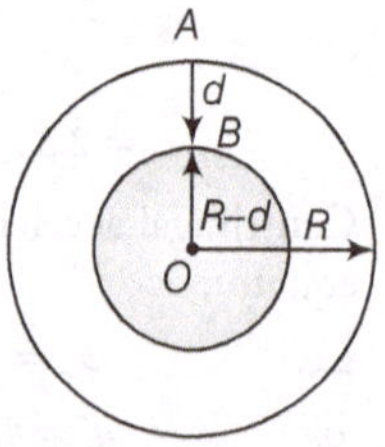

Variation of g with depth

$$\therefore \quad g_d = \frac{GM'}{(R-d)^2}$$

where M' is the mass of inner solid sphere of radius $(R - d)$.

or $g_d = \dfrac{G}{(R-d)^2} \times \dfrac{4}{3}\pi (R-d)^3 \times \rho$

or $g_d = \dfrac{4}{3}\pi G (R-d) \rho$ ...(ii)

Dividing Eq. (ii) by Eq. (i), we get

$$\frac{g_d}{g} = \frac{\frac{4}{3}\pi G(R-d)\rho}{\frac{4}{3}\pi GR\rho} = \frac{R-d}{R}$$

or $$\frac{g_d}{g} = 1 - \frac{d}{R}$$

Acceleration due to gravity at depth d, $g_d = g\left(1-\frac{d}{R}\right)$

or $$g_d - g = -\frac{d}{R_t}g \quad \text{or} \quad g - g_d = \frac{d}{R}g$$

Here, $(g - g_d)$ gives the decrease in the value of g.

Since, g is constant at a given place of the earth and R is also a constant.

$\therefore$ $$(g - g_d) \propto d$$

From the above equation, it is clear that if d increases, g_d must decrease because g is constant. **Hence, the acceleration due to gravity decreases as we move down into the surface of the earth.** i.e. g decreases with the increase in depth d.

At the centre O of the earth, $d = R$

Thus, we get $$g_d = g\left(1-\frac{R}{R}\right) = \text{zero}$$

Hence, acceleration due to gravity at the centre of the earth is zero.

Hence, the weight of a body at the centre of the earth is zero though its mass is constant.

Variation in the Value of *g* Due to Gravity (Graphical Representation)

Given below figure the variation of g as function of r, where r is the distance from the centre of earth.

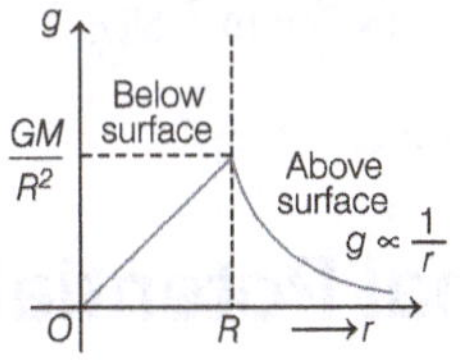

Variation of g above and below the surface of the earth

Example 6 What will be the value of g at the bottom of sea 7 km deep? Diameter of the earth is 12800 km and g on the surface of the earth is 9.8 ms^{-2}.

Sol. Depth of sea, $d = 7$ km, $g = 9.8\ ms^{-2}$

Radius of the earth, $R = \frac{D}{2} = \frac{12800}{2}$ km $= 6400$ km

Value of g at bottom of sea

$$g_d = g\left(1-\frac{d}{R}\right) = 9.8\left(1-\frac{7}{6400}\right) ms^{-2}$$

$$g_d = \frac{9.8 \times 6393}{6400} ms^{-2} = 9.789\ ms^{-2}$$

Variation in the Value of *g* Due to Rotation of the Earth (Effect of Latitude)

Acceleration due to gravity also vary due to the rotation of earth, if a body of mass m lying at a point whose latitude is λ, then rotation of earth (angular speed ω), the apparent acceleration due to gravity on body is given by $g' = g - \omega^2 R\cos^2\lambda$

Following conclusions can be drawn from the above discussion

(i) The effect of centrifugal force due to rotation of the earth is to reduce the effective value of g.

(ii) The effective value of g is not truely in vertical direction.

(iii) At the equators, $\lambda = 0°$

Therefore, $g' = g - R\omega^2$ (minimum value)

(iv) At the poles, $\lambda = 90°$

Therefore, $g' = g$ (maximum value)

Gravitational Field

The space surrounding a material body in which its gravitational force of attraction can be experienced is called its gravitational field.

Intensity of Gravitational Field at a Point

Intensity of gravitational field at a point can be defined as the force experienced by a unit mass placed at that point.

Let, M be the mass of a body around which a gravitational field exists. In order to get the gravitational field intensity at a point P in the gravitational field, a test mass m is placed at the point P.

The test mass is supposed to be so small that it does not alter the gravitational field in any manner. If a test mass m at a point P in a gravitational field experience a force F, then

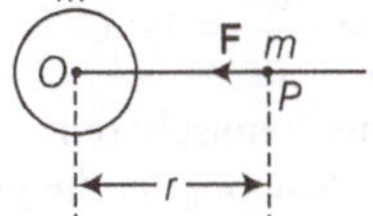

Gravitational field intensity

Intensity of gravitational field, $I = \frac{F}{m} = \frac{GMm/r^2}{m}$

$$\text{Intensity of gravitational field, } I = \frac{GM}{r^2}$$

where, r is the distance of P from the centre of the body producing the gravitation field.
If $r = \infty$, $I = 0$. It means the intensity of gravitational field is zero only at infinite distance from the body.
If a unit mass (m) is placed on the surface of earth, then the gravitational force acting on the test mass m will be equal to the weight w of the test mass.

Now, $I = \frac{w}{m} = \frac{mg}{m} = g$ or $I = g$

Example 7 The mass of 5 kg is placed at the surface of the earth. Calculate the magnitude of the gravitational field intensity acting on the mass.

Sol. Given, $m = 5$ kg, $R = 6400$ km $= 6.4 \times 10^6$ m

$\therefore$ Intensity, $I = \frac{GM}{R^2}$

$$I = \frac{6.67 \times 10^{-11} \times 6.0 \times 10^{24}}{(6.4 \times 10^6)^2}$$

$$= 0.977 \times 10 = 9.77 \approx 9.8 \text{ N/kg}$$

Example 8 The gravitational intensity at the centre of a hemispherical shell of uniform mass density, (in figure) has the direction indicated by arrow (i) a, (ii) b, (iii) c, (iv) zero. Choose the correct answer. **[NCERT]**

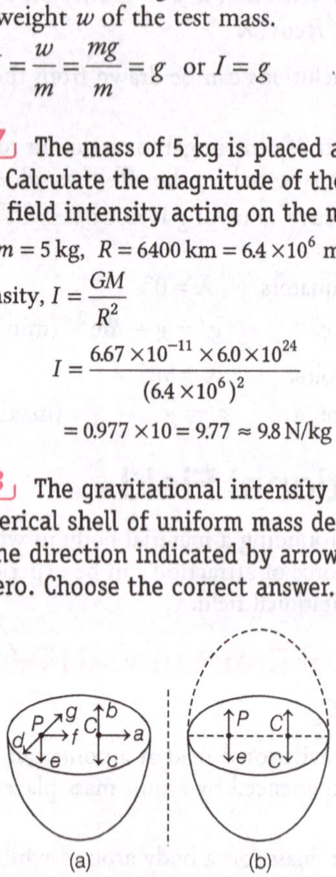

Hemispherical shell

Sol. Complete the hemisphere, Fig. (b). The gravitational intensity (gravitational force per unit mass) is zero at all points in a spherical shell.
This implies that at any point inside the spherical shell, the gravitational forces are symmetrically placed. As gravitational potential v is constant, hence intensity,

$$E = -\frac{dv}{dr} = 0 \text{ at } C.$$

Thus, if the upper hemisphere is removed, the net gravitational force acting on the particle at C will be downward as shown by arrow c.

Hence, option (iii) is correct. It is to be remembered that the net gravitational force acting on particle C due to upper hemisphere (shown by dotted arrow), is equal and opposite to that acting due to lower hemisphere in order that the total gravitational force due to entire spherical shell is zero.

Example 9 Two masses 800 kg and 600 kg, are at a distance 0.25 m apart. Calculate the magnitude of the gravitational field intensity at a point distance 0.20 m from the 800 kg mass and 0.15 m from the 600 kg mass. Given, $G = 6.6 \times 10^{-11}$ Nm^{2}kg^{-2}.

Sol. Let I_A be the gravitational field intensity at P due to 800 kg mass at A.

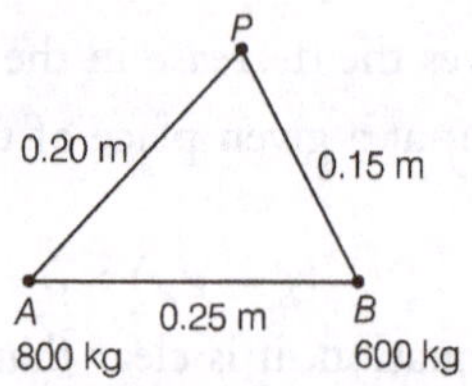

Then, $I_A = G\frac{800}{(0.2)^2} = 2 \times 10^4 G$ along PA

Let I_B be the gravitational field intensity at P due to 600 kg mass at B

Then, $I_B = G\frac{600}{(0.15)^2}$ along $PB = \frac{80000\,G}{3}$ along PB

The angle between I_A and I_B is 90°.
If I be the magnitude of the resultant intensity, then

$$I = \sqrt{I_A^2 + I_B^2} = \sqrt{(2 \times 10^4\, G)^2 + \left(\frac{80000\,G}{3}\right)^2}$$

$$= G\sqrt{4 \times 10^8 + \frac{64}{9} \times 10^8}$$

$$= 6.6 \times 10^{-11} \times 2 \times 10^4 \sqrt{1 + \frac{16}{9}}$$

$$= 6.6 \times 2 \times \frac{5}{3} \times 10^{-7} \text{ Nkg}^{-1}$$

$$I = 2.22 \times 10^{-6} \text{ Nkg}^{-1}$$

Gravitational Potential

Gravitational potential at a point in the gravitational field is defined as the amount of work done in bringing a body of unit mass from infinity to that point without acceleration

i.e. Gravitational potential, $V = -\frac{W}{m}$

where, W is the amount of work done in bringing a body of mass m from infinity to that point and I is the intensity of field.

$$V = -\int \frac{\mathbf{F} \cdot d\mathbf{r}}{m} = -\int \mathbf{I} \cdot d\mathbf{r} \qquad \left[\text{as, } \frac{F}{m} = I\right]$$

$\therefore$ $$I = -\frac{dV}{dr}$$

i.e. negative gradient of potential gives intensity of field or potential which is a scalar function of position whose space derivative gives intensity.

Negative sign indicates that the direction of intensity is in the direction where the potential decreases.

Gravitational potential is a scalar quantity and SI is joule/kg and in CGS system is erg/g.

Dimensional formula for gravitational potential.

i.e. $$V = \frac{W}{m} = \frac{[ML^2T^{-2}]}{[M]} = [M^0L^2T^{-2}]$$

Expression for Gravitational Potential of Earth

Suppose the earth be perfect sphere of radius R and mass M, can be supposed to be concentrated at its centre O. Then, the gravitational potential at point Q can be calculated, where $OQ = r$ and $r > R$.

Take two points A and B, so $OA = x$ and $AB = dx$ as shown in figure.

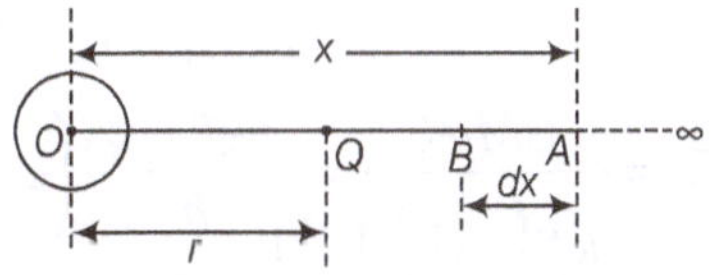

Calculation for gravitational potential

At point A, gravitational force of attraction on a body of unit mass will be $F = \dfrac{GM \times 1}{x^2} = \dfrac{GM}{x^2}$

Small amount of work done in bringing the unit mass body without acceleration through a small distance ($AB = dx$) is

$$dW = Fdx = \frac{GM}{x^2}dx$$

Total amount of work done in bringing a body from infinity to point Q, we get

$$\text{Work done } (W) = \int_{\infty}^{r} \frac{GM}{x^2} dx = -\left[\frac{GM}{x}\right]_{\infty}^{r}$$

$$= -GM\left[\frac{1}{r} - \frac{1}{\infty}\right] = \frac{-GM}{r}$$

$\because$ $V = W$

$$\boxed{\text{Gravitational potential, } V = \frac{-GM}{r}} \qquad \ldots\text{(i)}$$

where, V is total gravitational potential at point Q.

Special Cases

(i) When $r = \infty$ from Eq. (i), then $V_Q = 0$, hence gravitational potential is maximum (zero) at infinity.

(ii) At surface of the earth, $r = R$, then $V_Q = \dfrac{-GM}{R}$.

Gravitational potential difference between two points in gravitational field can be defined as the work done in moving a unit mass from one point to other.

Suppose a unit mass is displaced from point A to point B in earth's gravitational field, then gravitational potential difference $= V_B - V_A$

$$= \left(\frac{-GM}{r_A}\right) - \left(\frac{-GM}{r_B}\right) = GM\left(\frac{1}{r_B} - \frac{1}{r_A}\right)$$

Note

Potential due to a large number of particles is given by scalar addition of all the potentials as shown in figure.

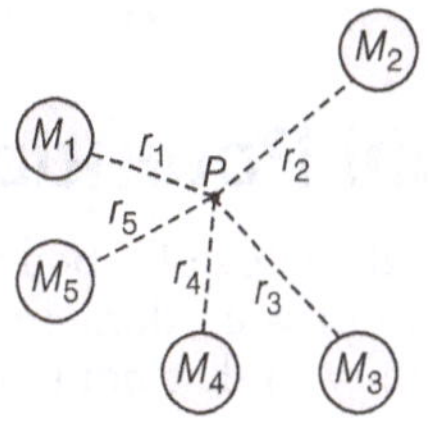

Superposition of different potentials

$$V = V_1 + V_2 + V_3 + \ldots$$

$$= \frac{-GM_1}{r_1} - \frac{GM_2}{r_2} - \frac{GM_3}{r_3} \ldots = -G\sum_{i=1}^{i=n} \frac{M_i}{r_i}$$

Example 10 As you will learn in the text, a geostationary satellite orbits the earth at a height of nearly 36000 km from the surface of the earth. What is the potential due to the earth's gravity at the site of this satellite? (take the potential energy at infinity to be zero). Mass of the earth $= 6.0 \times 10^{24}$ kg, radius = 6400 km. **[NCERT]**

Sol. We are given that

Mass of the earth, $M = 6.0 \times 10^{24}$ kg

Radius of the earth, $R = 6400$ km

Height of the satellite from the earth's surface,

$h = 36000$ km

Distance of the satellite from the centre of the earth,

$r = R + h = 6400 \text{ km} + 36000 \text{ km}$

$r = 42400 \text{ km} = 4.24 \times 10^7$ m

If V is the potential at the site of the satellite,

$$V = -\frac{GM}{r} = -\frac{(6.67 \times 10^{-11}) \times (6.0 \times 10^{24})}{(4.24 \times 10^7)}$$

$$V = -9.4 \times 10^6 \text{ J/kg}$$

Example 11 At a point above the surface of the earth, the gravitational potential is -5.12×10^7 J/kg and the acceleration due to gravity is 6.4 m/s^2. Assuming the mean radius of the earth to be 6400 km, calculate the height of the point above the earth's surface.

Sol. If r is the distance of the given point from the centre of the earth, then gravitational potential at the point,

$$V=-\frac{GM}{r}=-5.12\times10^7\ \text{J/kg}$$

Acceleration due to gravity at this point,

$$g=\frac{GM}{r^2}=6.4\ \text{m/s}^2$$

Clearly, $\frac{|V|}{g}=\frac{GM/r}{GM/r^2}=r$

Thus, $r=\frac{5.12\times10^7\ \text{J/kg}}{6.4\ \text{m/s}^2}=8\times10^6\ \text{m}=8000\ \text{km}$

Obviously, height of the point from the earth's surface

$=(r-R)=8000\ \text{km}-6400\ \text{km}=1600\ \text{km}$

Gravitational Potential Energy

Gravitational potential energy of a body at a point is defined as the amount of work done in bringing the given body from infinity to that point against the gravitational force.

Let a body of mass m is placed at P in the gravitational field of a body of mass M.

Let r be the distance of P from the centre O of the body of mass M as shown in figure. Then, the total work done (W) by the gravitational field when a body of mass m is moved from infinity to a distance r from O is given by

$$W=mV=-\frac{GmM}{r}$$

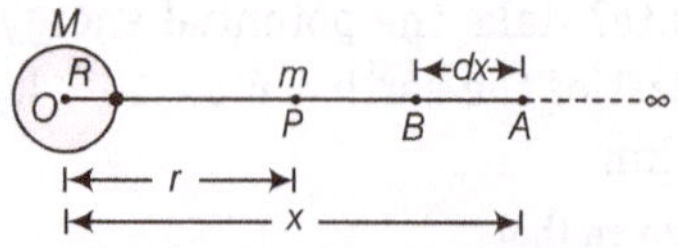

Gravitational potential energy

This work done is equal to the gravitational potential energy U of mass m.

$\therefore$ Gravitational potential energy, $U=-\frac{GMm}{r}$

$\Rightarrow$ Gravitational potential energy, $U=\left(-\frac{GM}{r}\right)\times m$

$\therefore$ **Gravitational potential energy = Gravitational potential × mass of the body.**

Some Cases

(i) According to the superposition principle, if there are three particles of masses m_1, m_2 and m_3 in an isolated system, then total gravitational potential energy of the system is

$$U=-\left(\frac{Gm_1m_2}{r_{12}}+\frac{Gm_2m_3}{r_{23}}+\frac{Gm_1m_3}{r_{13}}\right)$$

(ii) Gravitational potential energy at earth's surface,

$$U_e=\frac{-GM_em}{R_e}$$

where, M_e and R_e are mass and radius of earth, respectively.

(iii) If the body of mass m is moved from the surface of the earth to a point distance h above the surface of the earth.

Then, change in potential energy or work done against gravity will be

$$W=\Delta U=GMm\left(\frac{1}{r_1}-\frac{1}{r_2}\right)$$

Change in gravitational potential energy at height h

$$\Delta U=GMm\left(\frac{1}{R}-\frac{1}{R+h}\right)$$

[as, $r_1=R$ and $r_2=R+h$]

$$\Rightarrow\quad \Delta U=\frac{GMmh}{R^2\left(1+\frac{h}{R}\right)}=\frac{mgh}{1+\frac{h}{R}}\quad\left(\text{as, }\frac{GM}{R^2}=g\right)$$

$$\Delta U=mgh\left(1+\frac{h}{R}\right)^{-1}=mgh\left(1-\frac{h}{R}\right)$$

$\because\ h<<R$

$\therefore\ \Delta U=mgh$

(iv) When $h=R$, then work done $=\frac{mgR}{1+R/R}=\frac{1}{2}mgR$

Example 12 Assuming gravitational potential to be zero at infinity. Compute the potential energy of a body of mass 0.1 kg at the surface of the earth. (Take, mass of the earth, $m=5.98\times10^{24}$ kg, and $R_e=6.37\times10^6$ m

Sol. The gravitational potential energy of a body of mass m (= 0.1 kg) at the surface of earth is

$$U=-\frac{GM_em}{R_e}=\frac{6.67\times10^{-11}\times0.1\times5.98\times10^{24}}{6.37\times10^6}\ \text{kg}$$

$$=-6.26\times10^6\ \text{J}$$

Example 13 A particle of mass 1 kg is placed at a distance of 4 m from the centre and on the axis of a uniform ring of mass 5 kg and radius 3 m. Calculate the work required to be done to increase the distance of the particle from 4 m to $3\sqrt{3}$ m.

Sol. $U_1 = -\dfrac{G \times 5 \times 1}{5}$ J or $U_1 = -G$ J

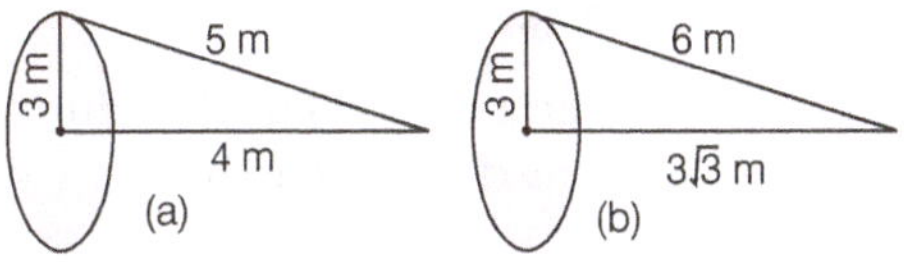

$$U_2 = \frac{-G \times 5 \times 1}{6} \text{ J} = -\frac{5G}{6} \text{ J}$$

$$\text{Work done} = \left(-\frac{5G}{6}\right) - (-G) = G - \frac{5G}{6} = \frac{G}{6}$$

Topic Practice 2

Multiple Choice Questions

1 Mark

1. If g is the acceleration due to gravity at the surface of the earth. The force acting on the particle of mass m placed at the surface is
   (a) mg (b) $\dfrac{GmM_E}{R_E^2}$
   (c) Data insufficient (d) Both (a) and (b)
2. The height at which the weight of a body becomes 1/16th, its weight on the surface of the earth (radius R), is
   (a) $5R$ (b) $15\,R$ (c) $3\,R$ (d) $4\,R$
3. Assuming the earth to have a constant density, point out which of the following curves show the variation of acceleration due to gravity from the centre of earth to the points far away from the surface of earth.

(a)
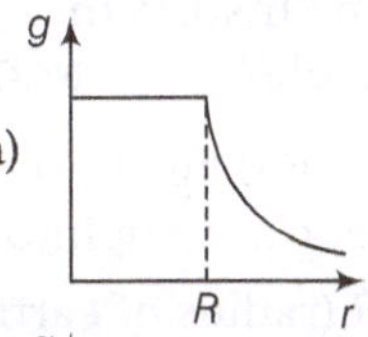

(b)
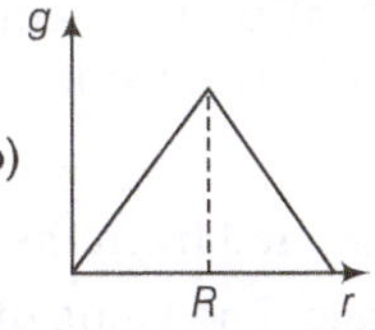

(c)
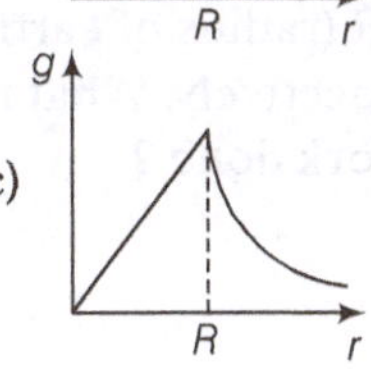

(d) None of these

4. The gravitational potential at a distance r from the centre of the earth ($r > R$) is given by (consider, mass of the earth = M_e, radius of the earth = R)
   (a) $\dfrac{-GM_e}{R}$ (b) $\dfrac{GM_e}{R}$
   (c) $\dfrac{-GM_e}{r}$ (d) $\dfrac{+GM_e}{r}$
5. Two point masses m_1 and m_2 are separated by a distance r. The gravitational potential energy of the system is G_1. When the separation between the particles is doubled, the gravitational potential energy is G_2. Then, the ratio of $\dfrac{G_1}{G_2}$ is
   (a) 1 (b) 2 (c) 3 (d) 4

Very Short Answer Type Questions

1 Mark

6. Where does a body weigh more; at the surface of the earth or in a mine?
7. If the earth is regarded as a hollow sphere, then what is the weight of an object below surface of the earth?
8. If the force of gravity acts on all bodies in proportion to their masses, then why doesn't a heavy body fall faster than a light body?
9. What would happen if the force of gravity were to disappear suddenly?
10. When a pendulum clock is taken to a mountain, it becomes slow. But a wrist watch controlled by a spring remains unaffected. Explain.
11. Would we have more sugar to the kilogram at the pole or at the equator?
12. Why a body weighs more at poles and less at equator?
13. How the value of g is change with change in shape of earth?
14. What is the amount of work done in bringing a mass from the surface of the earth on one side to a point diametrically opposite on the other side?

Short Answer Type I Questions

2 Marks

15. Why a tennis ball bounces higher on hills than on plains?

16. The acceleration due to gravity on a planet is 1.96 ms^{-2}. If it is safe to jump from a height of 2 m on the earth, then what will be the corresponding safe height on the planet?

17. Does the concentration of the earth's mass near its centre change the variation of g with height compared with a homogeneous sphere, how?

18. What is the gravitational potential energy of a body at height h from the earth surface?

19. A spherical planet has mass M_P and diameter D_P. A particle of mass m falling freely near the surface of this planet will experience an acceleration due to gravity, equal to whom?

Short Answer Type II Questions

3 Marks

20. What do you mean by acceleration due to gravity? Derive its formula.

21. What is the gravitational field? Derive an expression of intensity of gravitational field at a point.

22. An object of mass m is raised from the surface of the earth to a height equal to the radius of the earth, that is, taken from a distance R to $2R$ from the centre of the earth. What is the gain in its potential energy? **NCERT Exemplar**

23. Derive an expression for work done against gravity.

24. Two bodies of m and $4m$ are placed at a distance r. The gravitational field is zero at a point on the line joining the two masses. What will be the gravitational potential at this point?

Long Answer Type Questions

5 Marks

25. Choose the correct alternatives.
    (i) Acceleration due to gravity increases/decreases with increasing altitude.
    (ii) Acceleration due to gravity increases/decreases with increasing depth (assume the earth to be a sphere of uniform density).
    (iii) Acceleration due to gravity is independent of the mass of the earth/mass of the body.
    (iv) The formula, $-GMm\left(\frac{1}{r_2}-\frac{1}{r_1}\right)$ is more/less accurate than the formula $mg\,(r_2 - r_1)$ for the difference of potential energy between two points r_2 and r_1 distance away from the centre of the earth. **NCERT**

26. Derive an expression of acceleration due to gravity above the surface of earth.

27. What is the gravitational potential? Derive an expression for gravitational potential of earth.

Numerical Problems

28. What is the apparent weight of a man of 60 kg who is standing in a lift which is moving up with a uniform speed ? **[1 M]**

29. Assuming the earth to be a sphere of uniform mass density, how much would body weight half way down to the centre of the earth if it weighted 250 N on the surface? **NCERT [3 M]**

30. Determine the speed with which the earth would have to rotate on its axis so that a person on the equator would weight $\frac{3}{5}$th as much as at present. Take the equatorial radius as 6400 km. **[2 M]**

31. What will be the potential energy of a body of mass 67 kg at a distance of 6.6×10^{10} m from the centre of the earth? Find gravitational potential at this distance. **[3 M]**

32. Two heavy spheres, each of mass 100 kg and radius 0.10 m are placed 1.0 m apart on a horizontal table. What is the gravitational force and potential at the mid-point of the line joining the centres of the spheres? Is an object placed at that point in equilibrium? If so, is the equilibrium stable or unstable? **NCERT [3 M]**

33. The mass of a spaceship is 1000 kg. It is to be launched from the earth's surface out into free space. The value of g and R (radius of earth) are 10 m/s^2 and 6400 km, respectively. What is the required energy for this work done ? **[3 M]**

Hints & Solutions

1. (*d*) Force on particle at surface is $F = mg$

   where, g = acceleration due to gravity at the earth's surface

   Also, $g = \frac{GM_e}{R_e^2} \Rightarrow F = mg = \frac{GmM_e}{R_e^2}$

2. (*c*) According to the question,

   $$\frac{GMm}{(R+h)^2} = \frac{1}{16}\frac{GMm}{R^2}$$

   where, m = mass of the body

   and $\frac{GM}{R^2}$ = gravitational acceleration

   $$\frac{1}{(R+h)^2} = \frac{1}{16R^2}$$

   or $\frac{R}{R+h} = \frac{1}{4}$ or $\frac{R+h}{R} = 4$

   $$h = 3R$$

3. (*c*) $g \propto r$ inside and $g \propto \frac{1}{r^2}$ outside

4. (*c*) The gravitational potential at a distance r from the centre of the earth.

   $$V(r) = -\frac{GM_e}{r}$$

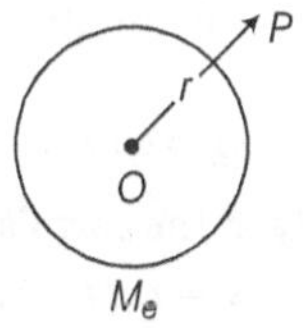

5. (*b*) As we know, $G_1 = \frac{-Gm_1m_2}{r}$ ...(i)

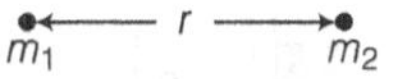

   $$G_2 = -\frac{Gm_1m_2}{2r} \quad ...(ii)$$

   $\Rightarrow \frac{G_1}{G_2} = 2$ [dividing Eq. (i) by Eq. (ii)]

6. The value of g in mine is less than that on the surface of the earth.

7. The weight of an object below surface of the earth is zero.

8. Acceleration due to gravity is independent of the mass of the body.

9. The universe would collapse. We would be thrown away because of the centrifugal force. Eating, drinking and infact all activities would become impossible.

10. At the mountain, g decreases and time period of the pendulum clock increases at $T = 2\pi\sqrt{l/g}$. On the other hand, a spring in the wrist watch remains unaffected by the variation of g.

11. $mg_p = m'g_e$ since, $g_p > g_e$,

    $\therefore m' > m$. So, we shall have greater mass of sugar at the equator.

12. The value of g is more at poles than at the equator. Therefore, a body weighs more at poles than at equator.

13. At the surface of the earth, g is maximum at the poles and minimum at the equator i.e. the value of g decreases from poles to equator.

14. Since, gravitational potential difference is zero, therefore the work done is zero.

15. As the acceleration due to gravity on hills is less than that on the surface of the earth (effect of height), therefore, a tennis ball bounces higher on hills than on plains. [2]

16. Acceleration due to gravity on planet $(g_p) = 1.96 \text{ m/s}^2$

    Acceleration due to gravity on earth $(g_e) = 9.8 \text{ m/s}^2$

    Safe height on the surface of earth $(h_e) = 2$ m

    If h_p be the safe height on the planet and u be the velocity of jumping, then from

    $$v^2 = u^2 - 2gh$$

    On the surface of earth, at maximum height, $v = 0$

    $\therefore \quad 0 = u^2 - 2g_eh_e \Rightarrow h_e = \frac{u^2}{2g_e}$ ...(i)

    On the surface of earth, at maximum height, $v = 0$

    $\therefore \quad 0 = u^2 - 2g_ph_p \Rightarrow h_p = \frac{u^2}{2g_p}$ ...(ii) [1]

    Dividing Eq. (ii) by Eq. (i), we get

    $$\frac{h_p}{h_e} = \frac{g_e}{g_p}$$

    $$\Rightarrow \quad h_p = h_e \times \frac{g_e}{g_p} = 2 \times \frac{9.8}{1.96}$$

    $\therefore \quad h_p = 10$ m [1]

17. Any change in the distribution of the earth's mass will not affect the variation of acceleration due to gravity with height. This is because for a point outside the earth, the whole mass of the earth is effective and the earth behaves as a homogeneous sphere. [2]

18. Gravitational potential energy, i.e.

    $$U_h = -\frac{GMm}{R+h} = -\frac{gR^2m}{R+h} \quad \left[\text{where, } g = \frac{GM}{R^2}\right]$$ [1]

    $$= -\frac{gR^2m}{R\left(1+\frac{h}{R}\right)} = -\frac{mgR}{1+\frac{h}{R}}$$ [1]

19. Force is given by

    $$F = \frac{GM_em}{R^2} = \frac{GM_pm}{(D_p/2)^2} = \frac{4GM_pm}{D_p^2}$$ [1]

    $$\frac{F}{m} = \frac{4GM_p}{D_p^2}$$

Since, acceleration due to gravity,

$$g_p = \frac{F}{m} = \frac{4GM_p}{D_p^2}$$ [1]

20. Refer to text on page 240 (Acceleration due to gravity of earth)

21. Refer to text on pages 243 and 244 (Gravitational field and intensity of gravitational field at a point).

22. Gain in PE, $\Delta U = U_f - U_i$

$$= -\frac{GMm}{2R} - \left(-\frac{GMm}{R}\right)$$ [1]

$$= \frac{GMm}{R}\left(-\frac{1}{2}+1\right) = \frac{GMm}{2R}$$ [1]

$$= \frac{(gR^2)\,m}{2R} = \frac{1}{2}mgR \quad \left[\text{as } g = \frac{GM}{R^2}\right]$$ [1]

23. Potential energy of the body on the surface of the earth

$$= \frac{-GMm}{R}$$ [1/2]

Potential energy of the body at a height h from the surface of the earth $= -\frac{GMm}{(R+h)}$

$$\text{Work done} = \left(-\frac{GMm}{R+h}\right) - \left(-\frac{GMm}{R}\right)$$ [1]

$$= \frac{GMm}{R} - \frac{GMm}{R+h}$$

$$= GMm\left(\frac{1}{R} - \frac{1}{R+h}\right)$$ [1/2]

$$= \frac{GMmh}{R(R+h)} = \frac{MgR^2h}{R(R+h)} \quad \left[\because g = \frac{GM}{R^2}\right]$$

$$= \frac{(Mgh)R}{(R+h)} = \frac{Mgh}{1+\frac{h}{R}}$$ [1]

24.

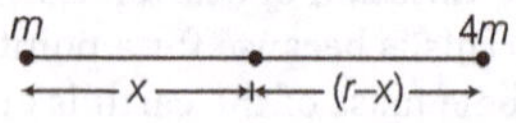

$$\frac{Gm}{x^2} = \frac{G(4m)}{(r-x)^2}$$ [1]

$$\frac{1}{x} = \frac{2}{r-x} \Rightarrow r - x = 2x$$

$$\Rightarrow \quad 3x = r \Rightarrow x = \frac{r}{3}$$ [1]

$$\therefore \text{ The gravitational potential} = \frac{-Gm}{r/3} + \frac{-G(4m)}{2r/3}$$

$$= \frac{-3Gm}{r} - \frac{6Gm}{r}$$

$$= \frac{-9Gm}{r}$$ [1]

25. (i) Acceleration due to gravity at altitude h from the earth's surface is given by

$$g' = \frac{g}{\left(1+\frac{h}{R_e}\right)^2}$$ [1]

where, R_e is the radius of the earth.

Therefore, acceleration due to gravity decreases with increasing altitude. [1/2]

(ii) Acceleration due to gravity at depth d from the earth's surface is given by

$$g' = g\left(1 - \frac{d}{R_e}\right)$$

Therefore, acceleration due to gravity decreases with increasing depth. [1]

(iii) Acceleration due to gravity is independent of the mass of the body. [1]

(iv) The formula, $-GMm\left(\frac{1}{r_2} - \frac{1}{r_1}\right)$

is more accurate than the formula $mg(r_2 - r_1)$ for the difference of potential energy between two points r_2 and r_1, distance away from the centre of the earth. [1½]

26. Refer to text on pages 241 and 242 (Acceleration due to gravity above the surface of earth).

27. Refer to text on pages 244 and 245 (Gravitational potential and expression for gravitational potential of earth).

28. Apparent weight $= mg = 60 \times 9.8 = 588$ N

29. Weight of the body at the earth's surface

$$w = mg = 250\text{ N} \quad \text{...(i)}$$

Acceleration due to gravity at depth d from the earth's surface

$$g' = g\left(1 - \frac{d}{R}\right)$$ [1]

Here, $d = \frac{R}{2}$

$$\therefore \quad g' = g\left(1 - \frac{R/2}{R}\right) = g\left(1 - \frac{1}{2}\right)$$ [1]

$$\Rightarrow \quad g' = \frac{g}{2}$$

$\therefore$ Weight of the body at depth d

$$\Rightarrow \quad w' = mg = \frac{mg}{2}$$ [1/2]

Using Eq. (i), we get

$$w' = \frac{250}{2} = 125\text{ N}$$

$\therefore$ Weight of the body will be 125 N. [1/2]

30. Acceleration due to gravity at the equator is

$$g_e = g - R\omega^2$$ [1/2]

$$mg_e = mg - mR\omega^2$$ [1/2]

or $\frac{3}{5} mg = mg - mR\omega^2$ $\left[\because mg_e = \frac{3}{5} mg\right]$ [1/2]

$\therefore \omega = \sqrt{\frac{2g}{5R}} = \sqrt{\frac{2\times 9.8}{5\times 6400\times 10^3}}$

$= 7.8\times 10^{-4}$ rad/s [1/2]

31. Mass of the earth, $M = 6.0\times 10^{24}$ kg, $m = 67$ kg

$G = 6.67\times 10^{-11}$ Nm^2 kg^{-2} [1]

Gravitational potential, $V = -\frac{GM}{R}$

$= -\frac{6.67\times 10^{-11}\times 6\times 10^{24}}{6.6\times 10^{10}}$

$V = -6.1\times 10^3$ Jkg^{-1} [2]

32. Let A and B be the two given spheres and O be the mid-point on the line joining their centres.

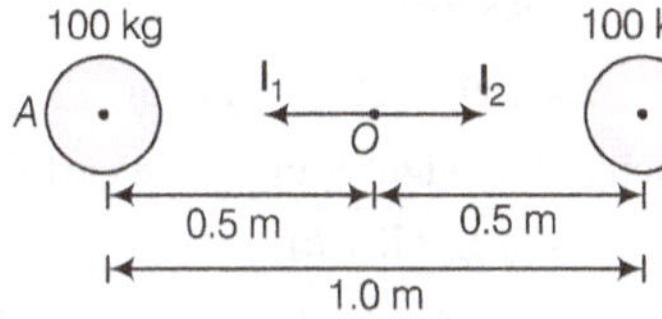

[1]

If I_1 and I_2 are the gravitational fields at O due to A and B respectively,

$I_1 = \frac{G\times 100}{(0.5)^2}$, $I_2 = \frac{G\times 100}{(0.5)^2}$

Since, I_1 and I_2 are equal and opposite, then resultant gravitational field at O is zero. [1]

If V is the gravitational potential at O due to A and B

$V = -\frac{G\times 100}{0.5} - \frac{G\times 100}{0.5} = -\frac{2G\times 100}{0.5}$

or $V = \frac{-2\times 6.67\times 10^{-11}\times 100}{0.5}$

$= -2.7\times 10^{-8}$ J/kg

The object placed at O is in equilibrium as there is no net force acting on the object. But it will be in an unstable equilibrium as once displaced from O, it will not come back to O. [1]

33. $W = 0 - \left[\frac{-GMm}{R}\right] = \frac{GMm}{R} = gR^2 \times \frac{m}{R} = mgR$ [1]

$= 1000\times 10\times 6400\times 10^3$

$= 64\times 10^9$ J $= 6.4\times 10^{10}$ J [2]

TOPIC 03 Escape Velocity, Geostationary and Solar Satellites

Escape Velocity

The minimum velocity with which a particle or body should be launched from the earth's gravitational field such that it never comes back to the earth, is known as escape velocity.

Escape Velocity from Principle of Conservation of Energy

Let the object of mass m reach at infinity and its velocity be v_f. The energy of an object is the sum of potential energy and kinetic energy. Then, the total energy of the projectile at infinity is given by

$$E(\infty) = W_1 + \frac{mv_f^2}{2} \quad \ldots(i)$$

where, W_1 is gravitational potential energy of the object at infinity. If the object was thrown initially with a velocity v_i from a point at a distance $(h+R)$ from the centre of the earth, then its initial energy is given by

$$E(h+R) = \frac{1}{2} m v_i^2 - \frac{GmM}{h+R} + W_1 \quad \ldots(ii)$$

According to principle of energy conservation Eqs.(i) and (ii) are equal. So, $\frac{mv_i^2}{2} - \frac{GmM}{(h+R)} = \frac{mv_f^2}{2}$

If $\frac{mv_f^2}{2}$ is zero, then $\frac{mv_i^2}{2} - \frac{GmM}{h+R} = 0$

Thus, the minimum velocity required for an object to reach infinity i.e. escape from the earth corresponds to

$$\frac{1}{2} m(v_i^2)_{\min} = \frac{GmM}{h+R}$$

If the object is thrown from the surface of the earth, h is zero, so we get

$$(v_i)_{\min} = \sqrt{\frac{2GM}{R}} \quad \ldots(iii)$$

Thus, the escape speed of a body depends upon the mass and radius of the planet from which the body is projected.

Using the relation, $g = GM/R^2$, we get

Escape velocity, $v_e = (v_i)_{\min} = \sqrt{2gR}$

If $g = 9.8$ m/s^2 and $R = 6.4 \times 10^6$m, then

$$(v_i)_{min} = 11.2 \text{ km/s}$$

From above equation, $v_e = \sqrt{\frac{2G}{R} \times \frac{4}{3}\pi R^3 \times \rho}$

$$\left[\text{where, } M = \frac{4}{3}\pi R^3 \cdot \rho\right]$$

where, ρ is the mean density of the earth.

$$\boxed{\text{Escape velocity, } v_e = R\sqrt{\frac{8}{3}\pi G\rho}} \quad \ldots\text{(iv)}$$

Important points

(i) Orbital velocity (v_0) of a satellite is the velocity required to put the satellite into its orbit around the earth, $v_0 = \sqrt{gR}$, i.e. $v_e = \sqrt{2}\, v_0$

(ii) Since, mass of moon is less than mass of earth. Hence, escape velocity (v_e) for moon is less than escape velocity for earth.
For moon, $v_e = 2.354$ km/s

Example 1 Calculate the escape speed of a body from the solar system from following data

(i) Mass of the sun $= 2 \times 10^{30}$ kg.

(ii) Separation of the earth from the sun $= 1.5 \times 10^{11}$ m.

Sol. If M be the mass of the sun and R be the distance of the earth from the sun, then escape velocity,

$$v_e = \sqrt{\frac{2GM}{R}} = \sqrt{\frac{2 \times 6.67 \times 10^{-11} \times 2 \times 10^{30}}{1.5 \times 10^{11}}} \text{ m s}^{-1}$$

$$= \sqrt{\frac{4 \times 6.67}{1.5}} \times 10^4 \text{ ms}^{-1} = 4.217 \times 10^4 \text{ ms}^{-1}$$

$$v_e = 42.17 \text{ kms}^{-1} \quad [\because 1 \text{ km} = 1000 \text{ m}]$$

$\therefore$ The escape speed for solar system is 42.17 kms^{-1}.

Example 2 Estimate the size of a rockey sphere with a density of 3.0 g/cm^3 from the surface of which you could barely throw a golf ball and have it never back. (assume your best throw is 40 m/s).

Sol. Let us consider that the rockey sphere has mass M and radius R. The escape speed for such a sphere is given by

$$v_e = \sqrt{\frac{2GM}{R}} = \sqrt{\frac{2G\left(\frac{4\pi}{3}\right)R^3\rho}{R}} = \sqrt{\frac{8\pi G\rho}{3}}R \text{ or } R = v_e\sqrt{\frac{3}{8\pi G\rho}}$$

Here, $\rho = 3.0 \text{ g/cm}^3 = 3.0 \times 10^3 \text{ kg/m}^3$, $v_e = 40$ m/s

Thus, $R = 40\sqrt{\frac{3}{8 \times 3.14 \times 6.67 \times 10^{-11} \times 3 \times 10^3}}$ m

or $R = 40 \times 772.6 \text{ m} = 30904 \text{ m} = 30.904 \text{ km}$

Example 3 Calculate the escape velocity for an atmospheric particle 1000 km above the earth's surface, given that the radius of the earth $= 6.4 \times 10^6$ m and acceleration due to gravity on the surface of the earth $= 9.8$ ms^{-2}.

Sol.

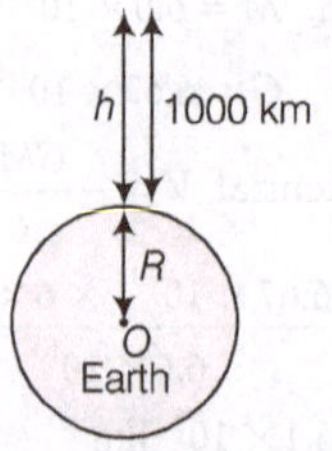

Here, Height, $h = 1000$ km,

$R = 6.4 \times 10^6$ m,

$g = 9.8$ ms^{-2}

$h = 1000 \times 1000 = 10^6$ m

Escape velocity at a height h above the earth's surface

$$v_e = \sqrt{2g_h(R+h)}$$

Substitute the value of g_h in the above formula, we get

$$g_h = \frac{gR^2}{(R+h)^2}$$

$$\Rightarrow \quad v_e = \sqrt{\frac{2 \times gR^2}{(R+h)^2}(R+h)} = \sqrt{\frac{2gR^2}{R+h}}$$

$$v_e = \sqrt{\frac{2 \times 9.8 \times (6.4 \times 10^6)^2}{(6.4 + 1)\, 10^6}} \text{ ms}^{-1}$$

$$= 10.42 \text{ kms}^{-1}$$

Earth Satellites

A **satellite** is a body which is constantly revolving in an orbit around a comparatively much larger body.

e.g. The moon is a natural satellite while INSAT-1B is an artificial satellite of the earth.

Orbital Velocity and Time Period of Satellite

Consider a satellite of mass m is revolving in circular orbit around earth at height h from its surface.

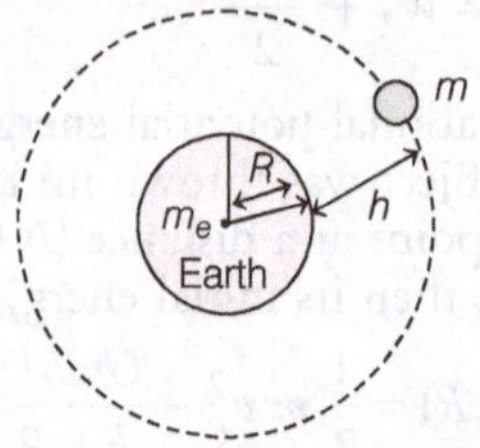

As we have already discussed that the centripetal force required for circular orbit is given by

$$F_e = \frac{mv^2}{r}$$

Here, v = orbital velocity of satellite

and r = radius of circular path = $F_e + h$

$$\therefore \quad F_e = \frac{mv^2}{R+h} \quad \ldots\text{(i)}$$

and is directeds toward the centre. This centripetal force is provided by the gravitational force which is expressed as

$$F_g = \frac{GmM}{r^2} = \frac{GmM}{(R+h)^2} \quad \ldots\text{(ii)}$$

Equating both these Eqs. (i) and (ii), we get

$$v^2 = \frac{GM}{R+h} \Rightarrow v = \sqrt{\frac{GM}{R+h}}$$

$$\Rightarrow \quad v = R\sqrt{\frac{g}{R+h}} \quad \left[\because g = \frac{GM}{R^2}\right]$$

Thus, v decreases as h increases.

When, $h = 0$

$$\therefore \quad v = \sqrt{\frac{GM}{R}} = \sqrt{gR}$$

In every orbit, the satellite traverses a distance $2\pi(R+h)$ with velocity v.

Then, its time period is given by

$$T = \frac{2\pi r}{v} = \frac{2\pi(R+h)}{v}$$

$$= \frac{2\pi(R+h)^{3/2}}{\sqrt{GM}} \quad \ldots\text{(iii)} \left[\because v^2 = \frac{GM}{R+h}\right]$$

On squaring both sides in Eq. (iii), we get

$$\boxed{T^2 = k(R+h)^3} \quad \left[\because k = \frac{4\pi^2}{GM}\right]$$

Thus, it is Kepler's law of periods. For a satellite, very close to surface of earth, h can be neglected in comparison to R. If $h = 0$ and T is T_0, then

$$T_0 = 2\pi\sqrt{R/g}$$

For earth, $R = 6400$ km

and $g = 9.8 \text{ m/s}^2$

$$T_0 = 2\pi\sqrt{\frac{6.4 \times 10^6}{9.8}} \cong 85 \text{ min}$$

Calculation of Mass of Earth

We can calculate the mass of earth by knowing the period of revolution T of an earth's satellite.

From Eq. (iii), we have

$$T = \frac{2\pi(R_e + h)^{3/2}}{\sqrt{GM}}$$

On squaring both sides, we get

$$T^2 = \frac{4\pi^2(R_e + h)^3}{GM} \quad \text{or} \quad M = \frac{4\pi^2(R_e + h)^3}{T^2 G}$$

Thus, if the radius $(R_e + h)$ of the orbit of a satellite and its period of revolution T is known , then mass of earth can be calculated.

Calculation of height of a satellite above the earth's surface

Squaring both sides of Eq. (iii), we get

$$T^2 = \frac{4\pi^2(R_e + h)^3}{gR_e^2}$$

$$(R_e + h)^3 = \frac{T^2 gR_e^2}{4\pi^2}$$

$$(R_e + h) = \left[\frac{T^2 gR_e^2}{4\pi^2}\right]^{1/3}$$

$$h = \left[\frac{T^2 gR_e^2}{4\pi^2}\right]^{1/3} - R_e$$

Thus, knowing T, g and R_e the height h of the satellite above the surface of the earth be calculated.

Energy of an Orbiting Satellite

When a satellite revolves around a planet in its orbit, it possesses both potential energy (due to its position against gravitational pull of the earth) and kinetic energy (due to orbital motion).

If m is the mass of the satellite and v is its orbital velocity.

Then, KE of the satellite

$$K = \frac{1}{2}mv^2 = \frac{1}{2}m\frac{GM}{r}$$

$$\boxed{\text{Kinetic energy of satellite, } K = \frac{GMm}{2(R+h)}} \quad \ldots\text{(i)}$$

$$[\because r = R+h]$$

PE of the satellite, $U = mV$

$$\text{Potential energy of satellite, } U = -\frac{GMm}{R+h} \quad \ldots\text{(ii)}$$

Total mechanical energy of satellite, $E = K + U$

or
$$E = \frac{GMm}{2(R+h)} - \frac{GMm}{(R+h)}$$

$$E = -\frac{GMm}{2(R+h)} \quad \ldots\text{(iii)}$$

$$\therefore \text{Total energy of satellite, } E = -\frac{GMm}{2(R+h)}$$

Satellites are always at finite distance from the earth and hence, their energy cannot be positive or zero.

Example 4 A 400 kg satellite is in a circular orbit of radius $2R$ about the earth. How much energy is required to transfer it to a circular orbit of radius $4R$? What are the changes in the kinetic and potential energies? **NCERT**

Sol. Given

Mass of satellite, $m = 400$ kg

The initial energy is given by, $E_i = \frac{-GMm}{4R}$

Final energy is given by, $E_f = \frac{-GMm}{8R}$

$\therefore$ Change in the total energy is given by

$$\Delta E = E_f - E_i = \frac{-GMm}{8R} - \left(\frac{-GMm}{4R}\right)$$

$$\Delta E = \frac{GMm}{8R} = \left(\frac{GM}{R^2}\right)\frac{mR}{8}$$

$$= \frac{gmR}{8} = \frac{9.81 \times 400 \times 6.37 \times 10^6}{8}$$

$$\Delta E = 3.13 \times 10^9 \text{ J}$$

The kinetic energy is reduced,

$\therefore \quad \Delta K = K_f - K_i = -3.13 \times 10^3$ J

Change in potential energy,

$$\Delta U = -2 \times \Delta E = -2 \times 3.13 \times 10^9 = -6.25 \times 10^9 \text{ J}$$

Example 5 The planet mars has two moons, phobos and delmos.

(i) Phobos has a period 7h, 39 min and an orbital radius of 9.4×10^3 km. Calculate the mass of mars.

(ii) Assume that earth and mars move in circular orbits around the sun with the martian orbit being 1.52 times the orbital radius of the earth. What is the length of the martian year in days?

Sol. (i) Given, $T =$ 7 h 39 min $= 459 \times 60$ s

$R = 9.4 \times 10^3$ km $= 9.4 \times 10^6$ m, $M_m = ?$

$$\therefore \text{Mass of mars, } M_m = \frac{4\pi^2}{G} \cdot \frac{R^3}{T^2}$$

$$= \frac{4 \times (3.14)^2 \times (9.4 \times 10^6)^3}{6.67 \times 10^{-11} \times (459 \times 60)^2}$$

$$= 6.48 \times 10^{23} \text{ kg}$$

(ii) From Kepler's third law, $\frac{T_m^2}{T^2} = \frac{R_{MS}^3}{R_{ES}^3}$

where, R_{MS} is the mass-sun distance and R_{ES} is the earth-sun distance

$\therefore \quad T_m = (1.52)^{3/2} \times 365$

$= 684$ days

Example 6 Express the constant k in equation $T^2 = k(R+h)^3$ in days and kilometres. Given, $k = 10^{-13}$ s^2/m^3. The moon is at a distance of 3.84×10^5 km from the orbit. Obtain its time period of revolution in days. **NCERT**

Sol. $\quad k = 10^{-13} s^2/m^3$

$$= 10^{-13}\left[\frac{1}{(24 \times 60 \times 60)^2} d^2\right]\left[\frac{1}{(1/1000)^3 \text{ km}^3}\right]$$

$$= 1.33 \times 10^{-14} d^2 / \text{km}^3$$

$$T^2 = k(R+h)^3 = 1.33 \times 10^{-14} \times (3.84 \times 10^5)^3 = 27.3 \text{ days}$$

Topic Practice 3

Multiple Choice Questions

1 Mark

1. An object is thrown from the surface of the moon. The escape speed for the object is

(a) $\sqrt{2g'R_m}$, where g' = acceleration due to gravity on the moon and R_m = radius of the moon

(b) $\sqrt{2g'R_e}$, where g' = acceleration due to gravity on the moon and R_e = radius of the earth

(c) $\sqrt{2gR_m}$, where g = acceleration due to gravity on the earth and R_m = radius of the moon

(d) None of the above

2. The orbital velocity of a satellite orbiting near the surface of the earth is given by

(a) $v = \sqrt{gR_e}$, where $g = \frac{GM_e}{R_e^2}$

(b) $v = \sqrt{gR_e}$, where $g = \frac{GM_e}{R_e}$

(c) $v = \sqrt{\frac{gh}{R_e}}$, where $g = \frac{GM_e}{R_e^2}$

(d) $v = \sqrt{gh}$, where $g = \frac{GM_e}{R_e}$

3. If the gravitational potential energy at infinity is assumed to be zero, the potential energy at distance $(R_e + h)$ from the centre of the earth is

(a) $PE = \frac{GmM_e}{(R_e + h)}$ (b) $PE = \frac{-GmM_e}{(R_e + h)}$

(c) $PE = mgh$ (d) $PE = \frac{-GmM_e}{2(R_e + h)}$

Very Short Answer Type Questions

1 Mark

4. What velocity will you give to a donkey and what velocity to a monkey so that both escape the gravitational field of the earth?

5. Can we determine the mass of a satellite by measuring its time period?

6. Why is the atmosphere much rarer on the moon than on the earth?

7. Does the speed of a satellite remain constant in a particular orbit (circular) ?

Short Answer Type I Questions

2 Marks

8. On what factor does the escape speed from a surface depend?

9. A satellite of mass *m* is revolving around the earth at height *h* with orbital velocity *v*. Find the expression for the potential energy of satellite.

10. If the kinetic energy of a satellite revolving around the earth in any orbit is doubled, then what will happen to it?

11. If suddenly the gravitational force of attraction between the earth and a satellite revolving around it becomes zero, then what will happen to the satellite?

12. The earth is acted upon by the gravitational attraction of the sun. Why don't the earth fall into the sun?

Short Answer Type II Questions

3 Marks

13. Does the escape speed of a body from the earth depend on
 (i) mass of the body
 (ii) the location from where it is projected
 (iii) the direction of projection
 (iv) the height of the location from where the body is launched? **NCERT**

14. Which of the following symptoms is likely to affect an astronaut in space (i) swollen feet (ii) swollen face, (iii) headache, (iv) orientational problem. **NCERT**

15. Define period of revolution. Derive an expression of period of revolution or time period of satellite.

16. Choose the correct alternatives.
 (i) If the zero of potential energy is at infinity, the total energy of an orbiting satellite is negative of the kinetic/potential energy.
 (ii) The energy required to rocket an orbiting satellite out of the earth's gravitational influence is more/less than the energy required in project a stationary object at the same height (as the satellite) of the earth's influence. **NCERT**

Long Answer Type Questions

5 Marks

17. What do you mean by escape velocity? Derive its expression in terms of density.

18. A comet orbits the sun in highly elliptical orbit. Does the comet has a constant
 (i) linear speed,
 (ii) angular speed,
 (iii) angular momentum,
 (iv) kinetic energy,
 (v) potential energy and
 (vi) total energy throughout its orbit? Neglect any mass loss of the comet when it comes very close to the sun. **NCERT**

Numerical Problems

19. The orbiting velocity of an earth-satellite is 8 kms^{-1}. What will be the escape velocity? [2 M]

20. The escape speed of a projectile on the earth's surface is 11.2 km/s. A body is projected out with thrice this speed. What is the speed of the body far away from the earth? Ignore the presence of the sun and other planets. [3 M]

21. Two uniform solid spheres of equal radii R, but mass M and $4M$ have a centre of separation $6R$, as shown in figure. The two spheres are held fixed. A projectile of mass m is projected from the surface of the sphere of mass M directly towards the centre of the second sphere. Obtain an expression for the minimum speed v of the projectile so that it reaches the surface of the second sphere. NCERT [5 M]

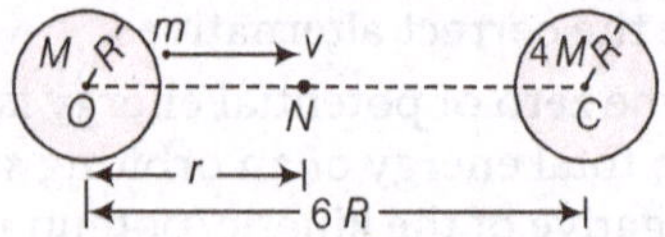

22. If one satellite of Jupiter has an orbital period of 1.769 days and the radius of the orbit is 4.22×10^8m. Show that the mass of jupiter is about one-thousandth that of the sun. NCERT [5 M]

23. How will you weigh the sun i.e. estimate its mass? The mean orbital radius of the earth around the sun is 1.5×10^8km. [3 M]

24. Let us assume that our galaxy consists of 2.5×10^{11} stars each of one solar mass. How long will a star at a distance of 50000 ly from the galactic centre take to complete one revolution? [3 M]

25. A rocket is fired vertically with a speed of 5 km/s from the earth surface. How far from the earth does the rocket go before returning to the earth? Mass of the earth $= 6.0 \times 10^{24}$ kg. Mean radius of the earth $= 6.4 \times 10^6$ m; $G = 6.67 \times 10^{-11} \text{ Nm}^2/\text{kg}^2$. NCERT [5 M]

26. A satellite is in an elliptic orbit around the earth with aphelion of $6R$ and perihelion of $2R$, where $R = 6400$ km is the radius of the earth. Find eccentricity of the orbit. Find the velocity of the satellite at apogee and perigee. What should be done if this satellite has to be transferred to a circular orbit of radius $6R$? NCERT Exemplar [5 M]

27. The escape speed on the earth is 11.2 km/s. What is its value for a planet having double the radius and eight times the mass of the earth? [2 M]

28. The asteroid pallas has an orbital period of 4.62 yr. Find the semi-major axis of its orbit. Given, $G = 6.67 \times 10^{-11} \text{ Nm}^2\text{kg}^{-2}$, mass of the sun $= 1.99 \times 10^{30}$kg and $1 \text{ yr} = 3.156 \times 10^7$ s [2 M]

29. A satellite orbits the earth at a height of 400 km above the surface. How much energy must be expanded to rocket, the satellite out of the earth's gravitational influence?
Mass of the satellite = 200 kg, mass of the earth, $M = 6.0 \times 10^{24}$ kg, radius of the earth $= 6.4 \times 10^6$m, $G = 6.67 \times 10^{-11} \text{ Nm}^2/\text{kg}^2$. [3 M]

30. Calculate the change in the energy of a 500 kg satellite when it falls from an altitude of 200 km to 199 km. If this change takes place during one orbit. Calculate the retarding force on the satellite. Given, mass of the earth $= 6 \times 10^{24}$ kg and radius of the earth = 6400 km [3 M]

31. A rocket is fired vertically from the surface of the mars with the speed of 2 km/s. If 20% of its initial energy is lost due to Martian atmospheric resistance, how far will the rocket go from the surface of the mars before returning to it. Mass of the mars $= 6.4 \times 10^{23}$ kg; radius of the mars = 3395 km; $G = 6.67 \times 10^{-11} \text{ Nm}^2/\text{kg}^2$ NCERT [5 M]

32. A spaceship is stationed on the mars. How much energy must be expanded on the spaceship to launch it out of the solar system. The mass of the spaceship = 1000 kg; mass of the sun $= 2 \times 10^{30}$ kg; mass of the mars $= 6.4 \times 10^{23}$ kg; radius of the mars = 3395 km; radius of the orbit of mars $= 2.28 \times 10^8$ km, $G = 6.67 \times 10^{-11} \text{ Nm}^2/\text{kg}^2$. [5 M]

Hints & Solutions

1. (a) Escape speed from the moon

$$= \sqrt{2g'R_m}$$

where, g' = acceleration due to gravity on the surface of moon

and R_m = radius of the moon.

2. (*a*) Orbital velocity of satellite,

$$v = \sqrt{\frac{GM_e}{(R_e + h)}}$$

If the satellite is close to the surface of the earth, $h = 0$

$$\Rightarrow \quad v = \sqrt{\frac{GM_e}{R_e}}$$

$$\Rightarrow \quad v = \sqrt{\left(\frac{GM_e}{R_e^2}\right) R_e} = \sqrt{gR_e}, \quad \text{where } g = \frac{GM_e}{R_e^2}$$

3. (*b*) Gravitational Potential Energy (GPE) $= -\dfrac{GmM_e}{r}$

where, r = distance from centre of the earth.

$$\because \quad r = R_e + h$$

$$\Rightarrow \quad \text{GPE} = -\frac{GmM_e}{(R_e + h)}$$

4. The escape velocity does not depend upon the mass of the body.

$$v_e = \sqrt{2gR}$$

5. No, we cannot determine the mass of a satellite by measuring its time period.

6. The value of escape velocity on the moon is small as compared to the value of the earth only 2.5 kms^{-1}. So, the molecules of air escape easily from the surface of moon, hence there is no atmosphere.

7. Yes, as $v = \sqrt{\dfrac{GM}{r}}$, v depends only upon r. For a particular orbit, r is constant and so is v.

8. Value of escape speed at the surface of a planet is given by the relation

$$v_{es} = \sqrt{\frac{2GM}{R}} = \sqrt{2gR}$$

Thus, the value of escape speed from the surface of a planet depends upon (*i*) value of acceleration due to gravity g at the surface and (*ii*) the size (i.e. radius) R of the planet only. It is independent of all other factors. e.g. The mass and size of the body to be projected, angle of projection, etc. [2]

9. Refer to text on pages 253 and 254 (Energy of an orbiting satellite).

10. The total energy of a satellite in any orbit, $E = -K$, where K is its KE in that orbit. [1]

If its kinetic energy is doubled, i.e. an additional kinetic energy (K) is given to it, $E = -K + K = 0$ and the satellite will leave its orbit and go to infinity. [1]

11. If suddenly the gravitational force of attraction between the earth and a satellite revolving around it becomes zero, satellite will not be able to revolve around the earth. Instead, the satellite will start moving along a straight line tangentially at that point on its orbit, where it is at the time of gravitational force becoming zero. **[2]**

12. The earth is orbiting round the sun in a stable orbit (nearly circular) such that the gravitational attraction of the sun just provides the required centripetal force to the earth for its orbital motion. So, net force on the earth is zero and consequently, the earth does not fall into the sun. **[2]**

13. (i) No, escape velocity is independent of the mass of the body. [1/2]

(ii) Yes, escape velocity depends (through slightly) on the location from where the body is projected because with location g changes and so should $v_e (= \sqrt{2gR})$ change. [1]

(iii) No, escape velocity is independent of the direction of projection. [1/2]

(iv) Yes, escape velocity depends (through slightly) on the height of location from where the body is projected as g depends on height. [1]

14. (i) We know that the legs carry the weight of the body in the normal position due to gravity pull. The astronaut in space is in weightlessness state. Hence, swollen feet may not affect his working. [1/2]

(ii) In the conditions of weightlessness, the face of the astronaut is expected to get more affect. Due to it, the astronaut may develop swollen face. As eyes, ears, nose, mouth etc., are all embedded in the face, hence swollen face may affect to great extent the seeing/hearing/ smelling/eating capabilities of the astronaut in space. [1]

(iii) Headache is due to mental strain. It will persist whether a person is an astronaut in space or he is on earth. It means headache will have the same effect on the astronaut in space as on a person on earth. [1]

(iv) Space also has orientation. We also have the frames of reference in space. Hence, orientational problem will affect the astronaut in space. [1/2]

15. Period of revolution of a satellite is the time taken by the satellite to complete one revolution round the earth. It is denoted by T.

$$\therefore \quad T = \frac{\text{Circumference of circular orbit}}{\text{Orbital velocity}}$$ [1]

$$\text{or} \quad T = \frac{2\pi r}{v_o}$$

$$\text{or} \quad T = \frac{2\pi(R+h)}{v_o} \quad [\because r = R + h]$$

$$\text{or} \quad T = 2\pi(R+h)\sqrt{\frac{R+h}{GM}} \quad \left[\because v_o = \sqrt{\frac{GM}{R+h}}\right]$$

$$\text{or} \quad T = 2\pi\sqrt{\frac{(R+h)^3}{GM}}$$ [1]

$$\text{Also,} \quad T = 2\pi\sqrt{\frac{(R+h)^2(R+h)}{GM}}$$

or $T = 2\pi\sqrt{\dfrac{(R+h)^3}{gR^2}}$

$\because$ $gR^2 = GM$

$\therefore$ $T = 2\pi\sqrt{\dfrac{(R+h)^3}{gR^2}}$ [1]

16. (i) Potential energy of satellite, $U = -\dfrac{GMm}{r}$ [1/2]

Kinetic energy of satellite, $K = \dfrac{GMm}{2r}$ [1/2]

Total energy, $E = U + K$ [1/2]

$$= \frac{GMm}{r} + \frac{GMm}{2r} = \frac{-GMm}{2r} = -K$$

i.e. negative of kinetic energy. [1/2]

(ii) The energy required to rocket an orbiting satellite out of gravitational influence is less than the energy required to project a stationary object, because in case of orbiting satellite, the gravitational pull of the earth acting on it is balanced by centripetal force, so work is required only in rocketing it (no work is required against the gravitational pull). [1]

17. Refer to text on pages 251 and 252 (Escape velocity and escape velocity from principle of conservation of energy).

18. (i) According to law of conservation of angular momentum, $L = mvr =$ constant, therefore the comet moves faster when it is close to the sun and moves slower when it is farther away from the sun. Therefore, the speed of the comet does not remain constant. [1]

(ii) As the linear speed varies, the angular speed also varies. Therefore, angular speed of the comet does not remain constant. [1/2]

(iii) As no external torque is acting on the comet, therefore, according to law of conservation of angular momentum, the angular momentum of the comet remain constant. [1]

(iv) Kinetic energy of the comet $= \dfrac{1}{2}mv^2$

As the linear speed of the comet changes, its kinetic energy also changes. Therefore, its KE does not remain constant. [1]

(v) Potential energy of the comet changes as its kinetic energy changes. [1/2]

(vi) Only angular momentum and total energy of a comet remain constant throughout its orbit. [1]

19. Escape velocity, $v_e = \sqrt{2}\, v_o$ [1]

$\therefore$ $v_e = \sqrt{2} \times 8 = 11.31 \text{ kms}^{-1}$ [1]

20. Let v_e be the escape velocity and v be the velocity of the body outside the gravitational field of the earth.

According to law of conservation of energy,

Initial KE of the body = energy spent by the body in crossing the earth's gravitational field + kinetic energy left with the body once outside the earth's gravitational field, i.e. [1]

$$\frac{1}{2}m(3v_e)^2 = \frac{1}{2}mv_e^2 + \frac{1}{2}mv^2$$

or $\dfrac{9}{2}mv_e^2 = \dfrac{1}{2}mv_e^2 + \dfrac{1}{2}mv^2$

or $v^2 = 8v_e^2$

or $v = \sqrt{8v_e^2} = 2\sqrt{2}\,v_e$ [1]

As $v_e = 11.2$ km/s

$\Rightarrow$ $v = 2\sqrt{2} \times 11.2$ km/s

or $v = 31.7$ km/s [1]

21. The two spheres exert gravitational forces on the projectile in mutually opposite directions. At the neutral point N, these two forces cancel each other. If $ON = r$, then

$$\frac{GMm}{r^2} = \frac{G(4M)\,m}{(6R-r)^2}$$

or $(6R - r)^2 = 4r^2$

$\Rightarrow$ $6R - r = \pm\, 2r$

or $r = 2R$ or $-6R$ [1]

The neutral point, $r = -6R$ is inadmissible.

$\therefore$ $ON = r = 2R$

It will be sufficient to project the particle m with a minimum speed v which enables it to reach the point N. Therefore, the particle m gets attracted by the gravitational pull of $4\,M$. [1]

The total mechanical energy of m at surface of left sphere is

E_i = KE of m + PE due to left sphere + PE due to right sphere

$$= \frac{1}{2}mv^2 - \frac{GMm}{R} - \frac{4\,GMm}{5R}$$ [1]

At the neutral point, speed of the particle becomes zero. The energy is purely potential.

$\therefore$ E_N = PE due to left sphere + PE due to right sphere

$$= -\frac{GMm}{2R} - \frac{4GMm}{4R}$$ [1]

By conservation of mechanical energy,

$$E_i = E_N$$

or $\dfrac{1}{2}mv^2 - \dfrac{GMm}{R} - \dfrac{4\,GMm}{5R} = -\dfrac{GMm}{2R} - \dfrac{4GMm}{4R}$

or $v^2 = \dfrac{2GM}{R}\left(\dfrac{4}{5} - \dfrac{1}{2}\right) = \dfrac{3GM}{5R}$

$\therefore$ $v = \sqrt{\dfrac{3GM}{5R}}$ [1]

22. Here, orbital period of the satellite of jupiter, $T_s = 1.769$ days $= 1.769 \times 24 \times 60 \times 60$ s

Orbital period of the earth, $T_e = 1\text{y} = 365.25$ d

Radius of the orbit of the satellite, $r_s = 4.22 \times 10^8$ m [1]

Radius of the orbit of the earth,

$r_e = 1$ AU $= 1.496 \times 10^{11}$ m

According to Kepler's third law, $T^2 = \left(\frac{4\pi^2}{Gm}\right)r^3$

Let M_s and M_j represent the masses of the sun and the jupiter.

For the Sun-Earth system, $T_e^2 = \left(\frac{4\pi^2}{GM_s}\right)r_e^3$ [1]

For Jupiter-Satellite system,

$$T_s^2 = \left(\frac{4\pi^2}{GM_j}\right)r_s^3$$ [1]

Thus, $$\frac{T_e^2}{T_s^2} = \left(\frac{M_j}{M_s}\right)\left(\frac{r_e}{r_s}\right)^3 \text{ or } \frac{M_j}{M_s} = \left(\frac{T_e}{T_s}\right)^2\left(\frac{r_s}{r_e}\right)^3$$

or $$\frac{M_j}{M_s} = \left(\frac{365.25\text{d}}{1.769\text{ d}}\right)^2\left(\frac{4.22 \times 10^8\text{ m}}{1.496 \times 10^{11}\text{ m}}\right)^3$$ [1]

$$= (4.26 \times 10^4)(22.4 \times 10^{-9}) \times 10^{-3}$$

or $$M_j \approx 10^{-3} M_s$$

Thus, M_j (mass of the jupiter) $= \frac{1}{1000} M_s$ (mass of the sun) [1]

23. We can weight the sun i.e. find its mass (M) using Kepler's third law of planetary motion according to which

$$T^2 = \left(\frac{4\pi^2}{GM}\right)r^3 \text{ or } M = \frac{4\pi^2 r^3}{GT^2}$$ [1]

Here, r (radius of the earth's orbit around the sun)

$= 1.5 \times 10^8$ km $= 1.5 \times 10^{11}$ m [1/2]

T (time period of earth's revolution around the sun)

$= 1\text{y} = 3.156 \times 10^7$ s

Thus, $$M = \frac{39.5\,(1.5 \times 10^{11}\text{ m})^3}{(6.67 \times 10^{-11}\text{ Nm}^2/\text{kg}^2)(3.156 \times 10^7\text{ s})^2}$$ [1]

[as $5\pi^2 = 39.5$]

$$M = 2.0 \times 10^{30}\text{ kg}$$ [1/2]

24. Mass of the galaxy, $m = (2.5 \times 10^{11})$ solar mass

$= (2.5 \times 10^{11})(2 \times 10^{30}\text{ kg})$

$= 5 \times 10^{41}$ kg [1]

Radius of the path of the star, $r = 50000$ ly

$= 50000(9.46 \times 10^{15}\text{ m}) = 4.73 \times 10^{20}$ m

If T is the time taken by the star to complete one revolution, then $T = \left(\frac{4\pi^2 r^3}{Gm}\right)^{1/2}$ [1]

$$T = \left[\frac{39.5\,(4.73 \times 10^{20}\text{ m})^3}{(6.67 \times 10^{-11}\text{ Nm}^2/\text{kg}^2)(5 \times 10^{41}\text{ kg})}\right]^{1/2}$$

$$T = 11.194 \times 10^{15}\text{ s}$$

or $$T = \frac{11.194 \times 10^{15}}{3.156 \times 10^7}\text{ y}$$

$$= 3.55 \times 10^8\text{ y}$$

[as $1\text{y} = (365.24 \times 24 \times 60 \times 60)\text{ s} = 3.156 \times 10^7$ s] [1]

25. Here, speed of the rocket, $v = 5$ km/s $= 5 \times 10^3$ m/s

Mass of the earth, $M = 6.0 \times 10^{24}$ kg

Radius of the earth, $x = 6.4 \times 10^6$ m

Gravitational constant, $G = 6.67 \times 10^{-11}$ Nm^2/kg^2

Let m be the mass of the rocket and h be the maximum height gained by the rocket.

Change in potential energy of the rocket

= PE at a height h – PE at the surface of the earth [1]

$$= -\frac{GMm}{(R+h)} - \left(-\frac{GMm}{R}\right)$$

$$= GMm\left(\frac{1}{R} - \frac{1}{R+h}\right)$$

$$= GMm\left[\frac{h}{R(R+h)}\right] \quad \text{...(i)}$$ [1]

Initial KE of rocket $= \frac{1}{2}mv^2$

Final KE of the rocket when at the height, $h = 0$

Thus, change in KE of the rocket $= \frac{1}{2}mv^2$ ...(ii)

According to law of conservation of energy, from Eqs. (i) and (ii), we get

$$GMm\left[\frac{h}{R(R+h)}\right] = \frac{1}{2}mv^2$$ [1]

or $$\frac{v^2}{2GM} = \frac{h}{R^2 + Rh}$$

or $$v^2R^2 + v^2Rh = 2GMh$$

or $$h(2GM - v^2R) = v^2R^2$$

or $$h = \frac{v^2R^2}{2GM - v^2R}$$ [1]

or $$h = \frac{(5 \times 10^3\text{ m/s})^2(6.4 \times 10^6\text{ m})^2}{[\{2 \times (6.67 \times 10^{-11}\text{ Nm}^2/\text{kg}^2)(6.0 \times 10^{24}\text{ kg})\} - \{(5 \times 10^3\text{ m/s})^2(6.4 \times 10^6\text{ m})\}]}$$

$= 1.6\times 10^6$ m

Distance of the rocket from the centre of the earth

$= 6.4\times 10^6 \text{ m} + 1.6\times 10^6 \text{ m} = 8\times 10^6$ m [1]

26. If r_a and r_p denote the distances of aphelion and perihelion of the elliptical orbit (of eccentricity) of the satellite, then from the geometry of the ellipse.

$$r_a = a(1+e) \text{ and } r_p = a(1-e)$$

[where, a is the semi-major axis of the ellipse]

As $r_a = 6R$ and $r_p = 2R$,

$$\frac{a(1+e)}{a(1-e)} = \frac{6R}{2R} = 3, \text{ where } e = \frac{1}{2}$$ [1]

If v_a and v_p are the velocities of the satellite (of mass m) at aphelion and perihelion respectively, then from the law of conservation of angular momentum,

$$mv_ar_a = mv_pr_p \text{ or } \frac{v_a}{v_p} = \frac{r_p}{r_a} = \frac{2R}{6R} = \frac{1}{3}$$ [1]

From the law of conservation of energy,

(KE + PE) at aphelion = (KE + PE) at perihelion

or $\frac{1}{2}mv_a^2 - \frac{GMm}{r_a} = \frac{1}{2}mv_p^2 - \frac{GMm}{r_p}$

or $v_p^2 - v_a^2 = -2GM\left(\frac{1}{r_a} - \frac{1}{r_p}\right)$ [1]

$= 2GM\left(\frac{1}{r_p} - \frac{1}{r_a}\right)$

or $v_p^2\left(1 - \frac{v_a^2}{v_p^2}\right) = 2GM\left(\frac{r_a - r_p}{r_pr_a}\right)$

$= 2GM\left(\frac{6R - 2R}{6R\times 2R}\right) = \frac{2}{3}\frac{GM}{R}$

or $v_p^2\left(1 - \frac{1}{9}\right) = \frac{2}{3}\frac{GM}{R}$ or $v_p = \sqrt{\frac{3}{4}\frac{GM}{R}}$ [1/2]

$= \frac{\sqrt{3}}{2}\sqrt{\frac{GM}{R}} = 0.8666\ (7.9 \text{ km/s}) = 6.84$ km/s

Also, $v_a = \frac{v_p}{3} = \frac{6.84 \text{ km/s}}{3} = 2.28$ km/s

Velocity of the satellite in a circular orbit.

$v_c = \sqrt{\frac{GM}{r}} = \sqrt{\frac{GM}{6R}}$ [as $r = 6R$]

or $v_c = \frac{1}{\sqrt{6}}\sqrt{\frac{GM}{R}} = 0.408\ (7.9 \text{ km/s}) = 3.22$ km/s [1]

The amount by which velocity is to be increased in transferring the satellite into a circular orbit at apogee.

$= v_c - v_a = 3.22 \text{ km/s} - 2.28 \text{ km/s} = 0.94$ km/s

This is accomplished by suitably firing rockets from the satellites. [1/2]

27. v_P (escape speed on a planet) $= \sqrt{\frac{GM_P}{R_P}}$ [1/2]

v_e (escape speed on the earth) $= \sqrt{\frac{GM_e}{R_e}}$ [1/2]

Clearly, $\frac{v_P}{v_e} = \sqrt{\frac{M_P}{M_e}\times\frac{R_e}{R_P}} = \sqrt{8\times\frac{1}{2}} = 2$ [1/2]

or $v_P = 2v_e = 22.4$ km/s [1/2]

28. $T^2 = \frac{4\pi^2a^3}{GM_s}$ or $a = \left[\frac{GM_sT^2}{4\pi^2}\right]^{1/3}$

Substituting values, we get $a = 4.15\times 10^{11}$ m. [2]

29. Mass of the earth, $M = 6.0\times 10^{24}$ kg

Mass of the satellite, $m = 200$ kg

Radius of the earth, $R = 6.4\times 10^6$ m

Height of the satellite above the earth's surface,

$h = 400 \text{ km} = 0.4\times 10^6$ m

Radius of the orbit of the satellite, $r = R + h$

$= 6.4\times 10^6 + 0.4\times 10^6$

$= 6.8\times 10^6$ m [1]

Total energy of the satellite,

$E = -\frac{GMm}{2r}$

$= -\frac{6.67\times 10^{-11}\times 6.0\times 10^{24}\times 200}{2\times 6.8\times 10^6}$

$= -5.9\times 10^9$ J [1½]

Negative total energy denoted that the satellite is round to the earth. Therefore, to pull the satellite out of the earth's gravitational influence, energy required $= 5.9\times 10^6$ J. [1/2]

30. Given, $M_e = 6\times 10^{24}$ kg, $r_e = 6400$ km

$r_1 = 6400 + 200 = 6600 \text{ km} = 6.6\times 10^6$ m

$r_2 = 6400 + 199 = 6599 \text{ km} = 6.599\times 10^6$ m

Change in energy $= GMm\left(\frac{1}{r_1} - \frac{1}{r_2}\right)$

$= 6.67\times 10^{-11}\times 6\times 10^{24}\times 500$ [1]

$\left(\frac{1}{6.6\times 10^6} - \frac{1}{6.599\times 10^6}\right)$

$= 2\times 10^{17}\ (1.5152\times 10^{-7} - 1.5154\times 10^7)$ J

$= -4\times 10^6$ J [1]

If this occurs during one orbit, then the energy lost = force × distance. If we take the distance as being the circumference of one orbit.

Then, Retarding force

$= \frac{4\times 10^6}{2\pi\times 6.6\times 10^6}$

$= \frac{4\times 10^6}{2\times 6.6\times 3.14\times 10^6} = 0.1$ N [1]

31. We are given that

Mass of the mars, $M = 6.4 \times 10^{23}$ kg

Radius of the mars, $R = 3395$ km $= 3.395 \times 10^6$ m

Velocity of the rocket, $v = 2$ km/s $= 2 \times 10^3$ m/s [1]

Let h be the maximum height attained by the rocket.

Change in potential energy of rocket.

PE = final potential energy – initial potential energy

$$= -G\frac{Mm}{(R+h)} - \left(-G\frac{Mm}{R}\right) \quad [1]$$

$$= -G\frac{Mm}{(R+h)} + G\frac{Mm}{R}$$

$$= GMm\left(\frac{1}{R} - \frac{1}{R+h}\right)$$

$$= GMm\frac{h}{R(R+h)} \quad [1]$$

Here, 20% of the kinetic energy of the rocket is lost due to Martian atmosphere.

KE of the rocket which is converted into its potential energy $= \frac{80}{100} \times \frac{1}{2}mv^2 = 0.4\ mv^2$ [1]

Applying law of conservation of energy,

$$\Rightarrow \quad GMm\frac{h}{R(R+h)} = 0.4\ mv^2$$

$$\Rightarrow \quad GM\frac{h}{R^2 + Rh} = 0.4\ v^2$$

or
$$h = \frac{R^2}{\left(\frac{GM}{0.4\ v^2}\right) - R}$$

$$\Rightarrow \quad h = \frac{11.526 \times 10^{12}}{26.68 \times 10^6 - 3.395 \times 10^6}\ \text{m}$$

$$\Rightarrow \quad h = 495 \times 10^3\ \text{m} = 495\ \text{km} \quad [1]$$

32. Given, mass of the sun, $M = 2 \times 10^{30}$ kg

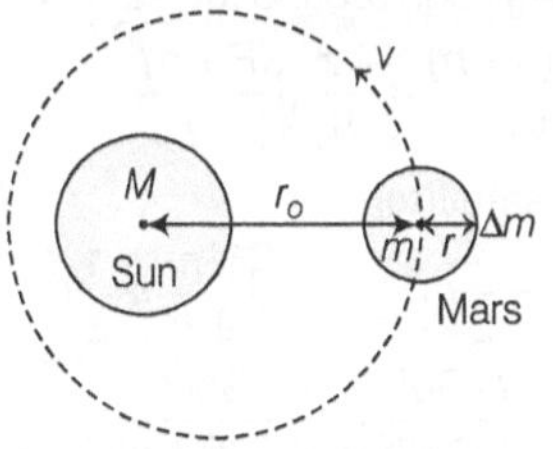

[1]

Mass of the mars, $m = 6.4 \times 10^{23}$ kg

Mass of spaceship, $\Delta m = 1000$ kg

Radius of orbit of the mars, $r_o = 2.28 \times 10^{11}$ m

Radius of the mars, $r = 3.395 \times 10^6$ m

If v is the orbital velocity of mars.

$$\frac{mv^2}{r_o} = G\frac{Mm}{r_o^2}$$

or
$$v^2 = \frac{GM}{r_o} \quad [1]$$

Since, the velocity of the spaceship is the same as that of the mars.

Kinetic energy of the spaceship,

$$K = \frac{1}{2}(\Delta m)v^2$$

$$= \frac{1}{2}(\Delta m)\frac{GM}{r_o} = \frac{GM(\Delta m)}{2r_o}$$

or
$$K = \frac{(6.67 \times 10^{-11})(2 \times 10^{30}) \times 1000}{2 \times (2.28 \times 10^{11})}\ \text{J}$$

$$= 2.925 \times 10^{11}\ \text{J} \quad [1]$$

Total potential energy of the spaceship.

U = potential energy of the spaceship due to its being in the gravitational field of the mars + potential energy of the spaceship due to its being in the gravitational field of the sun.

$$= -G\frac{m \times \Delta m}{r} - G\frac{M \times \Delta m}{r_o}$$

$$= -G\Delta m\left(\frac{m}{r} + \frac{M}{r_o}\right)$$

or
$$U = -6.67 \times 10^{-11} \times 10^3 \times \left(\frac{6.4 \times 10^{23}}{3.395 \times 10^6} + \frac{2 \times 10^{30}}{2.28 \times 10^{11}}\right)\text{J}$$

$$= -6.67 \times 10^{-8}\ (1.885 \times 10^{17} + 87.719 \times 10^{17})\ \text{J}$$

$$= -6.67\ (89.604 \times 10^9)\ \text{J} = -5.977 \times 10^{11}\ \text{J} \quad [1]$$

Total energy of the spaceship,

$$E = K + U = 2.925 \times 10^{11}\ \text{J} - 5.997 \times 10^{11}\ \text{J}$$

$$= -3.072 \times 10^{11}\ \text{J}$$

$$= -3.1 \times 10^{11}\ \text{J} \quad [1/2]$$

Negative energy denotes that the spaceship is bound to the solar system.

Thus, the energy needed by the spaceship to escape from the solar system $= 3.1 \times 10^{11}$ J. [1/2]

SUMMARY

- **Kepler's laws of planetary motion.**
  (i) **Kepler's first law** (law of orbit) Every planet revolves around the sun in an elliptical orbit. The sun is situated at one focus of the ellipse.
  (ii) **Kepler's second law** (law of area) The radius vector drawn from the sun to a planet sweeps out equal areas in equal intervals of time, i.e. the areal velocity of the planet around the sun is constant.
  (iii) **Kepler's third law** (law of period) The square of the time period of revolution of a planet around the sun is directly proportional to the cube of semi-major axis of the elliptical orbit, i.e. $T^2 \propto r^3$, where r is the semi-major axis of the elliptical orbit of the planet around the sun.
  The period T and radius R of the circular orbit of a planet about the sun are related by
  $$T^2 = \left(\frac{4\pi^2}{G M_s}\right) R^3$$
  where, M_s is the mass of the sun. Most planets have nearly circular orbits about the sun. For elliptical orbits, the above equation is valid if R is replaced by the semi-major axis a.
- **Universal law of gravitation** Every body in the universe attracts every other body with a force which is directly proportional to the product of their masses and inversely proportional to the square of the distance between them.
- **Newton's Universal law of gravitation**
  Gravitational force, $F = G\dfrac{m_1 m_2}{r^2}$
  where, G = constant of proportionality,
  = universal gravitational constant
  $= 6.67 \times 10^{-11}\ \text{N-m}^2\text{kg}^{-2}$ (in SI unit)
  Dimensional formula of $G = \text{M}^{-1}\text{L}^3\text{T}^{-2}$
- **Principle of superposition** Resultant force,
  $$F = -Gm_1\left[\frac{m_2}{r_{12}^2}\mathbf{r}_{21} + \frac{m_3}{r_{13}^2}\mathbf{r}_{31} + \ldots + \frac{m_n}{r_{1n}^2}\mathbf{r}_{n1}\right]$$
- The acceleration due to gravity (g) is related with gravitational constant (G) by the relation, $g = \dfrac{GM}{R^2}$ where, M and R are the mass and radius of the earth, respectively.
- **Variation of acceleration due to gravity**
  (i) **Effect of altitude,** $g' = \dfrac{g R^2}{(R+h)^2}$
  and $g' = g\left(1 - \dfrac{2h}{R}\right)$
  (ii) **Effect of depth,** $g' = g\left(1 - \dfrac{d}{R}\right)$
- Acceleration due to gravity also vary due to the rotation of earth,
  $$g' = g - \omega^2 R\cos^2\lambda$$
- Intensity of Gravitational field at a point is, $I = \dfrac{F}{m} = \dfrac{GM}{r^2}$
- **Gravitational potential,** $V = -\dfrac{W}{m} = -\int I \cdot dr \left[\text{as } \dfrac{F}{m} = I\right]$
- **Gravitational potential energy,** U = gravitational potential × mass of body $= -\dfrac{GM}{r} \times m$.
- **Escape velocity** The minimum velocity with which a particle or body should be launched from the earth's gravitation field is known as escape velocity.
  $$v_e = \sqrt{\frac{2GM}{R}} = \sqrt{2gR}.$$
- For Earth, the value of escape speed is $11.2\ \text{kms}^{-1}$.
  For a point close to the Earth's surface, the escape speed and orbital speed are related as $v_e = \sqrt{2}\, v_o$, where v_o = the velocity required to put the satellite into its orbit.
- **Orbital speed of a satellite** It is the speed required to put the satellite into given orbit around Earth. Orbital speed of satellite, when it is revolving around earth at height h is given by
  $$v_0 = R\sqrt{\frac{g}{R+h}}$$
  Time period of satellite (T) It is the time taken by satellite to complete one revolution around the earth.
  $$T = \frac{2\pi(R+h)}{v_0} = \frac{2\pi}{R}\sqrt{\frac{(R+h)^3}{g}}$$
  Total energy of satellite,
  $$E = -\frac{GMm}{(R+h)} + \frac{1}{2}mv_0^2 = -\frac{GMm}{(R+h)} + \frac{1}{2}m\left(\frac{GM}{R+h}\right) = -\frac{GMm}{2(R+h)}$$
  Binding energy of satellite $= -E = \dfrac{GMm}{(R+h)}$.

Chapter Practice

Multiple Choice Questions

1 Mark

1. The period of a planet around the sun is 27 times that of the earth. The ratio of radius of planet's orbit to the radius of the earth's orbit is
(a) 4 (b) 9
(c) 64 (d) 27

2. A point mass m is placed outside a hollow spherical shell of mass M and uniform density at a distance d from centre of the big sphere. Gravitational force on point mass m at P is

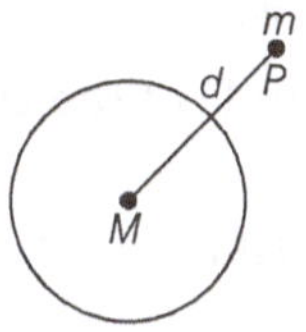

(a) $\frac{GmM}{d^2}$ (b) zero
(c) $\frac{2\,GmM}{d^2}$ (d) Data insufficient

3. The value of acceleration due to gravity at a height h above the surface of the earth of radius R is g', then
(a) $g' < g$ (b) $g' > g$
(c) $g' = g$ (d) $g' = g\left(1 - \frac{2h}{R}\right)$

4. Three particles each of mass m are kept at vertices of an equilateral triangle of side L. The gravitational potential at the centre due to these particles is
(a) $-\frac{3Gm}{L}$ (b) $\frac{-9\,Gm}{\sqrt{3}\,L}$
(c) $-\frac{3\sqrt{3}\,Gm}{L}$ (d) Both (b) and (c)

5. A particle is kept at rest at a distance R_e (earth's radius) above the earth's surface. The minimum speed with which it should be projected so that it does not return is (mass of earth = M_e)
(a) $\sqrt{\frac{6M_e}{4R_e}}$ (b) $\sqrt{\frac{GM_e}{2R_e}}$
(c) $\sqrt{\frac{GM_e}{R_e}}$ (d) $\sqrt{\frac{2\,GM_e}{R_e}}$

Assertion and Reason

Directions (Q. Nos. 6-10) *In the following questions, two statements are given- one labelled Assertion (A) and the other labelled Reason (R). Select the correct answer to these questions from the codes (a), (b), (c) and (d) as given below*

(a) Both Assertion and Reason are true and Reason is the correct explanation of Assertion.
(b) Both Assertion and Reason are true but Reason is not the correct explanation of Assertion.
(c) Assertion is true but Reason is false.
(d) Assertion is false but Reason is true.

6. **Assertion (A)** The force of attraction due to a hollow spherical shell of uniform density, on a point mass situated inside it is zero.

Reason (R) Various region of the spherical shell attract the point mass inside it in various directions. These forces cancel each other completely.

7. **Assertion (A)** There is a popular statement regarding Cavendish: 'Cavendish weighed the earth'.
Reason (R) The measurement of G by Cavendish's experiment, combined with the knowledge of g and R_e enables one to estimates M_e from equation.

$$g = \frac{GM_e}{R_e^2}$$

8. **Assertion (A)** The velocity of the satellite decreases as its height above earth's surface increases and is maximum near the surface of the earth.

Reason (R) The velocity of the satellite is inversely proportional to its height above earth's surface.

9. **Assertion (A)** The total energy of the satellite is always negative irrespective of the nature of its orbit i.e., elliptical or circular and it cannot be positive or zero.

Reason (R) If the total energy is positive or zero, the satellite would leave its orbit.

10. **Assertion (A)** As we go up the surface of the earth, we feel light weighed than on the surface of the earth.

Reason (R) The acceleration due to gravity decreases on going up above the surface of the earth.

Very Short Answer Type Questions

1 Mark

11. What is Kepler's second law of planetary motion?
12. Acceleration due to gravity is also called gravitational field intensity. Why?
13. Why moon has no atmosphere?
14. What is relation between orbital and escape velocities?

Short Answer Type I Questions

2 Marks

15. State Newton's law of gravitation. Distinguish between g and G.
16. How are gravity and gravitation different?
17. Give an expressions for variation of g in different cases.

Long Answer Type Questions

5 Marks

18. Derive an expression for variation of g above and below the surface of earth.
19. (i) Define the escape velocity.

(ii) Derive an expression for the escape velocity of earth using energy consideration.

Case Based Questions

Directions (Q. No. 20) *These questions are case study based questions. Read the following paragraph and answer the questions.*

20. Let the speed of the planet at the perihelion P in following figure be v_P and the sun planet distance SP be r_P. The corresponding quantity at the aphelion A is (r_A, v_A). The mass of the planet is m_P.

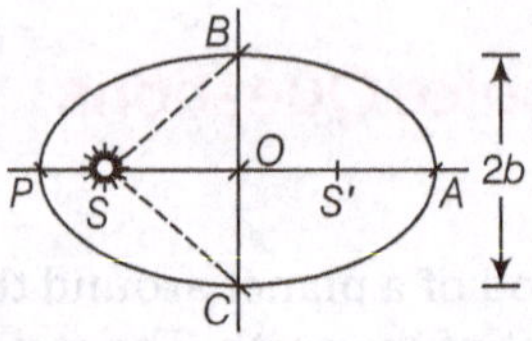

(i) The magnitude of the angular momentum at P is

(a) $L_P = \dfrac{m_P r_P}{v_P}$

(b) $L_P = \dfrac{m_P v_P}{r_P}$

(c) $L_P = m_P r_P v_P$

(d) $L_P = m_P v_P$

(ii) The magnitude of the angular momentum at A is

(a) $L_A = m_P r_A v_A$ (b) $L_A = \dfrac{m_P r_A}{v_A}$

(c) $L_A = m_P v_A$ (d) $L_A = \dfrac{m_P v_A}{r_A}$

(iii) The vectors $\mathbf{r}_p$ and $\mathbf{v}_p$ are

(a) parallel

(b) mutually perpendicular

(c) anti-parallel

(d) coincident

(iv) The relation for conservation of angular momentum at P and A is

(a) $m_P r_P v_P = m_P r_A v_A$ (b) $\dfrac{m_P r_P}{v_P} = \dfrac{m_P r_A}{v_A}$

(c) $m_P v_P = m_P v_A$ (d) $\dfrac{m_P v_P}{r_P} = \dfrac{m_P v_A}{r_A}$

(v) The magnitude of the angular momentum as the planet goes round the sun

(a) is constant

(b) is variable

(c) depends on magnitude of velocity

(d) increases as planet goes near to sun

Numerical Problems

21. How much below the surface does the acceleration due to gravity become 70% of its value on the surface of earth? [2 M]

22. If the earth stops rotating about its axis, what will be the change in the value of g at a place on the equator?

(Take, radius of earth, $R = 6.4 \times 10^6$ m) **[2 M]**

23. A remote sensing of the earth revolves in a circular orbit at a height of 250 km above the earth's surface. What is the (i) orbital velocity and (ii) period of revolution of satellite? (Take, radius of the earth $= 6.38 \times 10^6$ m and acceleration due to gravity at the surface of earth $= 9.8\ \text{ms}^{-2}$) **[2M]**

Answers

1. (*b*) Given, $T_p = 27\ T_e \Rightarrow T_p / T_e = 27$ ...(i)

where, T_p = Time-period of the planet,

T_e = Time-period of the earth

Let r_p and r_e be the radius of planet and the earth's orbit, respectively. From Kepler's third law of planetary motion,

$$T^2 \propto r^3$$

$$\Rightarrow \quad \frac{T_p^2}{r_p^3} = \frac{T_e^2}{r_e^3}$$

$$\Rightarrow \quad \left(\frac{T_p}{T_e}\right)^2 = \left(\frac{r_p}{r_e}\right)^3$$

$$\text{or} \quad \left(\frac{T_p}{T_e}\right)^{2/3} = \frac{r_p}{r_e} \quad \text{...(ii)}$$

$$\text{or} \quad \frac{r_p}{r_e} = \left(\frac{T_p}{T_e}\right)^{2/3} = (27)^{2/3} \quad \text{[From Eq. (i)]}$$

$$\Rightarrow \quad \frac{r_p}{r_e} = (3)^2 = 9$$

2. (*a*) For a point outside the spherical shell,

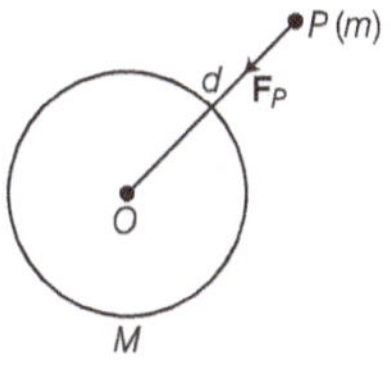

$$|\mathbf{F}_p| = \frac{GmM}{d^2}$$

3. (a) $g' = \dfrac{GM_e}{(R_e + h)^2}$ ...(i)

where, g' = Acceleration due to gravity at height 'h' above the earth's surface.

At the earth's surface; $g = \dfrac{GM_E}{R^2}$ ...(ii)

From Eqs. (i) and (ii), it is evident that $g' < g$

4. (*c*) Gravitational potential at centre, *i.e.*, centroid of triangle G,

$$V_T = V_A + V_B + V_C$$

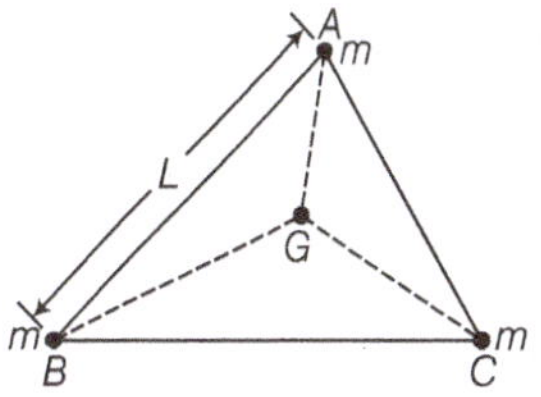

$$\Rightarrow \quad V_T = -\frac{Gm}{AG} - \frac{Gm}{BG} - \frac{Gm}{CG}$$

Also, $AG = BG = CG = \dfrac{2}{3} \times \left(\dfrac{\sqrt{3}\,L}{2}\right) = \dfrac{\sqrt{3}\,L}{3}$

$$\Rightarrow \quad V_T = -Gm\left(\frac{1}{AG} + \frac{1}{BG} + \frac{1}{CG}\right)$$

$$= -Gm\left(\frac{3 \times 3}{\sqrt{3}\,L}\right) = -\frac{9\,Gm}{\sqrt{3}\,L} \quad \text{or} \quad \frac{-3\sqrt{3}\,Gm}{L}$$

5. (*c*) Escape speed $= v_{\min} = \sqrt{\dfrac{2GM_e}{(h + R_e)}}$

where, h = height above the earth's surface.

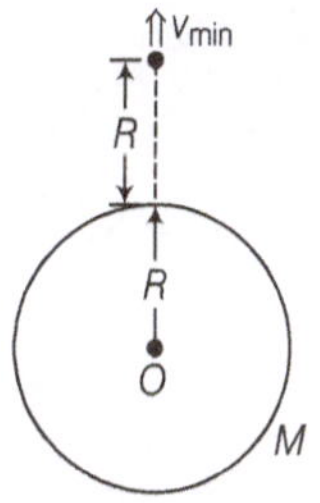

In this case, $h = R$

$$\Rightarrow \quad v_{\min} = \sqrt{\frac{2\,GM_e}{2R_e}} = \sqrt{\frac{GM_e}{R_e}}$$

6. (*a*) **7.** (*a*)

8. (*a*) **9.** (*a*)

10. (*a*)

11. Refer to text on page 233 (Kepler's second law of areas).

12. By definition, gravitational field intensity measures force of gravity per unit mass (*F*/*m*). Numerically, this quantity equals acceleration due to gravity.

13. Escape velocity from the surface of the moon is very small. (It is only 2.354 km/s). For the temperature on the surface of the moon, the calculated rms. velocity of all gas molecules is more than this escape velocity. Hence, all of them escaped from moon's surface.

14. For near to earth orbits, $v_o = \sqrt{gR}$ and escape velocity, $v_e = \sqrt{2gR}$, hence $v_e = \sqrt{2}v_o$.

15. Refer to text on pages 234 and 235 (Newton's universal law of gravitation).

16. Attraction between general bodies is called gravitation. The force remains balanced and bodies do not move towards each other. Attraction between a planet (or sub-planet) and a body is called gravity. The force of gravity is not balanced and body falls towards the planet (or sub-planet). [2]

17. Refer to text on page 243 [Variation in the value of g due to gravity (graphical representation) and variation in the value of g due to rotation of the earth (effect of latitude)].

18. Refer to text on pages 241 and 242 (Acceleration due to gravity above and below the surface of earth).

19. (i) Refer to text on page 251 (Escape velocity).
(ii) Refer to text on pages 251 and 252 (Escape velocity from principle of conservation of energy).

20. (i) (*c*) (ii) (*a*) (iii) (*b*) (iv) (*a*) (v) (*a*)

21. Here, $g'/g = 70/100 = 7/10$

$\therefore \quad g' = g(1 - d/R)$

$\Rightarrow \quad \frac{g'}{g} = 1 - d/R$ or $\frac{7}{10} = 1 - \frac{d}{R}$ [1]

$\Rightarrow \quad \frac{d}{R} = 1 - \frac{7}{10} = \frac{3}{10}$

$\Rightarrow \quad d = \frac{3R}{10} = \frac{3 \times 6.4 \times 10^6}{10}$

$= 1.92 \times 10^6$ m [1]

22. $g_\lambda = g - \omega^2 R_E \cos \lambda$

where, λ is a latitude.

At equator $\lambda = 0$, so at equator,

$g_{eq} = g - \omega^2 R_E$ [1]

$\therefore \Delta g = g - g_{eq} = \omega^2 R_E = \left(\frac{2\pi}{24 \times 3600}\right)^2 \times 6.4 \times 10^6$

$= 0.034$ m/s^2. [1]

23. (i) $v_0 = R\sqrt{\frac{g}{R+h}}$

$= 6.38 \times 10^6 \sqrt{\frac{9.8}{6.38 \times 10^6 + 0.250 \times 10^6}}$

$= 7756.6$ m/s [1]

(ii) $T = \frac{2\pi(R+h)}{v_0} = 2 \times \frac{22}{7} \frac{(6.38 \times 10^6 + 0.250 \times 10^6)}{7756.6}$

$= 5373.16$ s [1]

CHAPTER

08

Mechanical Properties of Solids

In construction of structures for buildings, bridges, pillars, beams, etc., knowledge of strength of materials is of great importance. For efficient design of building structures and machine parts, we must have knowledge about behaviour of materials when they are subjected to external forces.

- Elastic and Plastic Behaviour of Solids
- Modulus of Elasticity or Elastic Modulus

TOPIC 01 Elastic and Plastic Behaviour of Solids

Elastic Body and Elasticity

A body that returns to its original shape and size after the removal of the deforming force (when deformed within elastic limit) is called an **elastic body**. Quartz fibre, ivory ball and phospher bronze are the elastic bodies.

The property of matter by virtue of which it regains its original shape and size, when the deforming forces have been removed is called **elasticity**. e.g. If we stretch a spring, and release, then it will regain its original size.

Plastic Body and Plasticity

A body that does not regain its original shape and size after the removal of deforming force, is called a **plastic body**. Putty, paraffin wax, mud and quartz are nearly perfectly plastic bodies.

The property of a body by virtue of which it does not regain its original shape and size even after the removal of deforming force, is known as **plasticity**. e.g. If we stretch a piece of chewing gum and release, it will not regain its original shape and size.

Elastic Limit

Elastic limit is the upper limit of deforming force up to which, if deforming force is removed, the body regains its original form completely. Beyond elastic limit, if deforming force is increased, the body loses its property of elasticity and gets permanently deformed. Elastic limit is the property of a body whereas elasticity is the property of material of a body.

Deforming Force

A force acting on a body, instead of producing a change in its state of rest or of uniform motion, produces a change in the shape of the body, such a force is called **deforming force.**

Stress

When a deforming force is applied on a body, it changes the configuration of the body by changing the normal positions of the molecules or atoms of the body. As a result, an internal restoring force comes into play which tends to bring the body back to its initial configuration.

The internal restoring force acting per unit area of a deformed body is called **stress.**

i.e. $$\text{Stress} = \frac{\text{Restoring force } (F)}{\text{Area of cross-section } (A)}$$

If there is no permanent change in the configuration of the body i.e. in the absence of plastic behaviour of the body, the restoring force is equal and opposite to the external deforming force applied. Thus, quantitatively, stress can be given as

$$\text{Stress, } S = \frac{\text{External deforming force}}{\text{Area of cross-section}}$$

Units and Dimensional Formula of Stress

SI unit of stress is N/m^2 or pascal (Pa) and in CGS system unit is dyne/cm^2. The dimensional formula of stress is $[ML^{-1}T^{-2}]$

Note

- Stress is not a vector quantity. Since, unlike a force, the stress cannot be assigned a specific direction.
- Breaking stress is constant for a material.

On the basis of applied forces on the body, the stress can be classified as

1. Normal Stress or Longitudinal Stress

It is defined as the restoring force per unit area acting perpendicular to the cross-section of the body. It is of two types

(i) Tensile Stress

When two equal and opposite forces are applied at the ends of a circular rod to increase its length, then a restoring force equal to the applied force F normal to the cross-sectional area A of the rod comes into existence. This restoring force per unit area of cross-section is known as **tensile stress.**

$$\text{Tensile stress} = \frac{F}{A}$$

(ii) Compressive Stress

When two equal and opposite forces are applied at the ends of a rod to decrease its length or compress it, then again restoring force equal to the applied force comes into existence. This restoring force per unit area of cross-section of the rod is known as **compressive stress.**

$$\text{Compressive stress} = \frac{F}{A}$$

Note

- Tensile stress or compressive stress is also termed as **longitudinal stress.**
- Tensile stress and compressive stress are equal for small loads.

2. Tangential or Shearing Stress

When a deforming force acts tangentially to the surface of a body, it produces a change in the shape of the body without any change in volume. This tangential force applied per unit area of cross-section is known as **tangential stress.**

$$\text{Tangential stress} = \frac{F}{A}$$

3. Hydraulic or Bulk Stress

If a body is subjected to a uniform force from all sides, then the corresponding stress is called **hydraulic stress** or bulk stress. There is a change in volume of the body but not change in geometrical shape.

$$\text{Bulk stress} = \frac{F}{A}$$

Note

- The hydraulic stress is also known as volumetric stress.
- The effect of stress is to produce distortion or change in size, volume and shape (i.e. configuration of the body).

Example 1 Calculate the value of stress in a wire of steel having radius of 2 mm, if 10 kN of force is applied on it.

Sol. Given, force, $F = 10 \text{ kN} = 1 \times 10^4 \text{ N}$

Radius, $r = 2 \text{ mm} = 2 \times 10^{-3} \text{ m}$

Area, $A = \pi r^2 = \pi \times (2 \times 10^{-3})^2$

$= 12.56 \times 10^{-6} \text{ m}^2$

$\therefore$ Stress $= \dfrac{\text{Force}}{\text{Area}} = \dfrac{1 \times 10^4 \text{ N}}{12.56 \times 10^{-6} \text{ m}^2}$

$= 0.0796 \times 10^{10} = 7.96 \times 10^8 \text{ N/m}^2$

Breaking Stress

Breaking force per unit area of cross-section of a wire is called breaking stress.

$$\text{Breaking stress} = \frac{\text{Breaking force}(F)}{\text{Area of cross - section}(A)}$$

$$= \frac{FL}{AL} = \frac{MgL}{V} \qquad [\because F = mg \text{ and } V = AL]$$

$$\boxed{\text{Breaking stress} = \rho g L} \qquad \left[\because \rho = \frac{M}{V}\right]$$

where, L = length of wire and ρ = density of wire.

Note Breaking stress is fixed for a material but breaking force will vary, depending on area of cross-section of the wire.

Strain

When a deforming force acts on a body, the body undergoes a change in its shape and size. The ratio of the change in configuration of the body to the original configuration is called **strain.**

$$\boxed{\text{Strain} = \frac{\text{Change in configuration}}{\text{Original configuration}}}$$

If there is a change in any of the configuration of the body due to the applied deforming force on it, then the body is said to be strained or deformed.

Strain is the ratio of two like quantities, so it has no unit and dimension.

According to type of change in configuration i.e. change in length, volume or shape of the body, the strain can be classified as

1. Longitudinal Strain

It is defined as the change in length per unit original length, when the body is deformed by external longitudinal force.

$$\boxed{\text{Longitudinal strain} = \frac{\text{Change in length}}{\text{Original length}} = \frac{\Delta L}{L}}$$

Example 2 Consider a steel rod having radius of 8 mm and the length of 2m. If a force of 150 kN stretches it along its length, then calculate the stress, percentage strain in the rod if the elongation in length is 7.46 mm.

Sol. If the rod stretches along its length, then the stress produced is the tensile stress whereas the strain produced is longitudinal strain.

Radius, $r = 8 \text{ mm} = 8 \times 10^{-3} \text{ m}$, Length, $L = 2 \text{ m}$

Force, $F = 150 \text{ kN} = 15 \times 10^4 \text{ N}$

Area, $A = \pi r^2 = \pi \times (8 \times 10^{-3})^2 = 201 \times 10^{-6} \text{ m}^2$

$\Delta L = 7.46 \text{ mm} = 7.46 \times 10^{-3} \text{ m}$, percentage strain = ?

Stress $= \dfrac{F}{A} = \dfrac{15 \times 10^4}{201 \times 10^{-6}} = 0.0746 \times 10^{10} \text{ N/m}^2$

$= 7.46 \times 10^8 \text{ N/m}^2$

Longitudinal strain $= \dfrac{\Delta L}{L} = \dfrac{7.46 \times 10^{-3}}{2} = 3.73 \times 10^{-3}$

Percentage strain $= 3.73 \times 10^{-3} \times 100 = 0.37$ %

Example 3 The greatest length of aluminium wire that can hang vertically without breaking is 2.83×10^3 m. If density of aluminium wire is $2.7 \times 10^3 \text{ kg/m}^3$, then find the breaking stress of aluminium. (Take, $g = 9.8 \text{ m/s}^2$)

Sol. Given, length $(L) = 2.83 \times 10^3$ m

Density $(\rho) = 2.7 \times 10^3 \text{ kg/m}^3$

$g = 9.8 \text{ m/s}^2$

$\therefore$ Breaking stress $= L\rho g = 2.83 \times 10^3 \times 2.7 \times 10^3 \times 9.8$

$= 7.49 \times 10^7 \text{ N/m}^2$

2. Volumetric Strain

It is defined as the change in volume per unit original volume, when the body is deformed by external forces.

$$\boxed{\text{Volumetric strain} = \frac{\text{Change in volume}}{\text{Original volume}} = \frac{\Delta V}{V}}$$

Example 4 Consider a solid cube which is subjected to a pressure of 6×10^5 N/m^2. Due to this pressure, each side of the cube is shortened by 2%. Find out the volumetric strain of the cube.

Sol. Let L be the initial length of the each side of the cube.

Volume, $V = L \times L \times L = L^3$

$= \text{Initial volume } (V_i \text{ say})$

If the each side of the cube is shortened by 2%, then final length of the cube $= L - 2\%$ of L

$$= \left(L - \frac{2L}{100}\right) = L\left(1 - \frac{2}{100}\right)$$

$$\therefore \quad \text{Final volume, } V_f = L^3\left(1 - \frac{2}{100}\right)^3 = V\left(1 - \frac{2}{100}\right)^3$$

$$\text{Change in volume, } \Delta V = V_f - V_i = V\left(1 - \frac{2}{100}\right)^3 - V$$

$$= V\left[\left(1 - \frac{2}{100}\right)^3 - 1\right]$$

$$\frac{\Delta V}{V} = \left(1 - \frac{2}{100}\right)^3 - 1 \simeq \left[1 - \frac{2 \times 3}{100}\right] - 1$$

$$[\because (1-x)^n \simeq 1 - nx \text{ for } x << 1]$$

$$\therefore \quad \text{Volumetric strain} = \frac{\Delta V}{V} = 1 - 0.06 - 1 = -0.06$$

Here, negative sign shows decrease in volume.

3. Shear Strain

If the deforming forces produce a change in the shape of the body, then the strain is called **shear strain.**

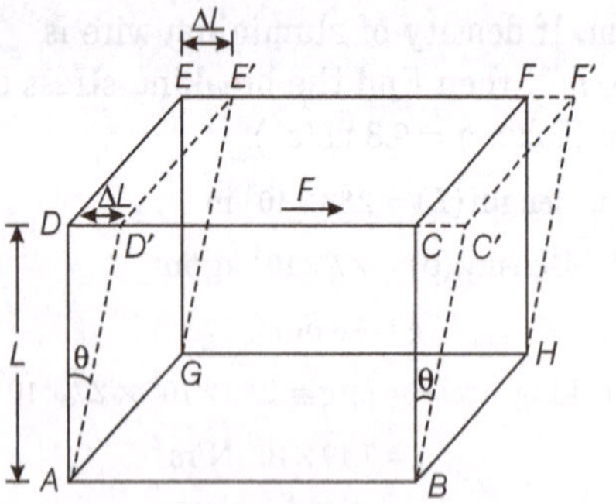

Shear strain

The angle of deformation θ is called **angle of shear.**

$$\text{Shear strain } (\theta) = \tan\theta = \frac{\Delta L}{L}$$

Note

- The strain produced in a spring is longitudinal as well as shear if the spring is stretched by suspending a load at its free end.
- The strain persists even when the stress is removed and thus lags behind the stress.

Example 5 If the angle of shear is 30° for a cubical body and the change in length is 250 cm, then what must be the volume of this cubical body?

Sol. Given, angle of shear = 30°

and change in length $\Delta L = 250$ cm $= 2.5$ m

$$\therefore \quad \text{Shear strain, } \tan\theta = \frac{\Delta L}{L} \Rightarrow \tan 30° = \frac{2.5}{L}$$

$$L = \frac{2.5}{\tan 30°} = \frac{2.5}{0.577} = 4.332 \text{ m}$$

$$\text{Volume, } V = L^3 = 81.309 \text{ m}^3$$

Hooke's Law

Within elastic limit, the stress developed is directly proportional to the strain produced in a body.

i.e. Stress ∝ Strain ⇒ Stress = E × Strain

or $$E = \frac{\text{Stress}}{\text{Strain}}$$

where E is a constant and is known as **modulus of elasticity** of the material of the body.

Example 6 After a fall, a 95 kg rock climber finds himself dangling from the end of a rope that had been 15 m long and 9.6 mm in diameter but has stretched by 2.8 cm. For the rope, calculate

(i) the strain,

(ii) the stress and

(iii) the modulus of elasticity.

Sol. Here, $L = 1500$ cm is the unstretched length of the rope, $\Delta L = 2.8$ cm is the amount of length stretches.

$$\text{The strain} = \frac{\Delta L}{L} = \frac{2.8 \text{ cm}}{1500 \text{ cm}} = 1.9 \times 10^{-3}$$

Stress = Force/Area

Force, F = force of gravity on the rock climber

$= mg = 95 \times 9.8$ N

$$\text{Area, } A = \pi r^2 = \pi \times \left(\frac{D}{2}\right)^2 = \pi \times \left(\frac{9.6}{2} \times 10^{-3} \text{ m}\right)^2$$

$$\text{Stress} = \frac{95 \times 9.8}{\pi \times (4.8)^2 \times 10^{-6}} \simeq 1.29 \times 10^7 \text{ N/m}^2$$

$$\text{Hence, } E = \frac{\text{Stress}}{\text{Strain}} = \frac{1.3 \times 10^7}{1.9 \times 10^{-3}} = 6.84 \times 10^9 \text{ N/m}^2$$

Stress-Strain Curve

When a wire is stretched by a load as in Fig. (a), it is seen that for small value of load, the extension produced in the wire is proportional to the load.

Hence, stress ∝ strain

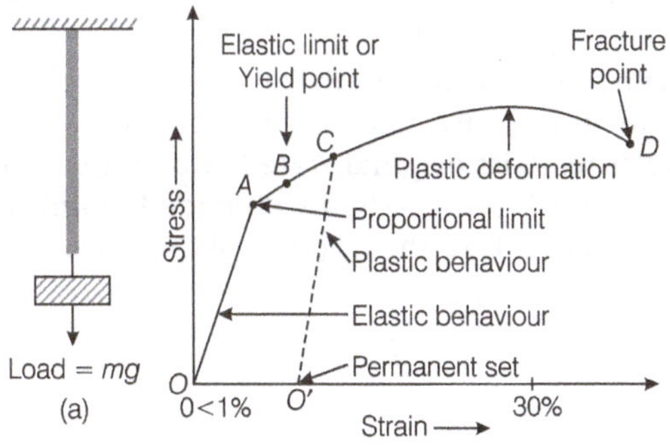

A typical stress-strain curve

(i) In drawing, a stress *vs* strain graph, the stress is found to be proportional to strain (% elongation) up to point *A*. Thus, Hooke's law is fully obeyed in this region, the point *A* is known as point of **proportional limit.**

(ii) When stress is increased beyond *A*, then for small stress, there is a large strain in the wire upto point *B*.

(iii) When the load is gradually removed between points *O* to *B*, the wire return to its original length. The wire regains its original dimension only when load applied is less than or equal to certain limit. This limit is called **elastic limit**. The point *B* on stress-strain curve is known as **elastic limit** or **yield point.** The material of the wire in the region *OB* shows the elastic behaviour, hence known as **elastic region.**

(iv) If the stress or load increases beyond point *B*, the strain further increases. This increase in strain represented by *BC* part of the curve. Now, if the load is removed, the wire does not regain its original length. But the increase in the length of the wire is permanent.

In other words, there is permanent strain equal to OO' in the wire even when the stress is zero. This permanent strain in the wire is known as permanent set.

(v) Now, as the stress beyond *C* is increased, there is large strain in the wire. This large increase in the strain for small stress is represented by *CD* part of the curve. The wire breaks at point *D* which is known as **fracture point.**

The material of the wire from point *C* to point *D* shows the **plastic behaviour** or **plastic deformation.** The stress needed to cause the actual fracture of the material is known as **breaking stress** or **ultimate tensile strength.**

On the basis of elastic and plastic properties, materials can be classified as

(i) **Ductile Materials** The materials which have large plastic range of extension.

(ii) **Brittle Materials** The materials which have small range of plastic extension.

(iii) **Elastomers** Materials like rubber for which stress and strain are not directly proportional.

Note

- Hooke's law is valid only in the linear portion of the stress-strain curve. The law is not valid for large values of strain.
- Elastic limit and limit of proportionality are very close to each other, so that Hooke's law is nearly applicable upto elastic limit.

Topic Practice 1

Multiple Choice Questions

1 Mark

1. The property of a body by virtue of which it tends to regain its original size and shape of a body when applied force is removed, is known as
   (a) fluidity (b) elasticity
   (c) plasticity (d) rigidity

2. *A* and *B* are two wires. The radius of *A* is twice that of *B*. They are stretched by the same load. Then, the stress on *B* is
   (a) equal to that on *A* (b) four times that on *A*
   (c) two times that on *A* (d) half that on *A*

3. On suspending a weight *Mg*, the length *l* of elastic wire having area of cross-section *A*, becomes double the initial length. The instantaneous stress action on the wire is
   (a) Mg/A (b) $Mg/2A$
   (c) $2Mg/A$ (d) $4Mg/A$

4. In plotting stress *versus* strain curves for two materials *P* and *Q*, a student by mistake puts strain on the *Y*-axis and stress on the *X*-axis as shown in the figure.

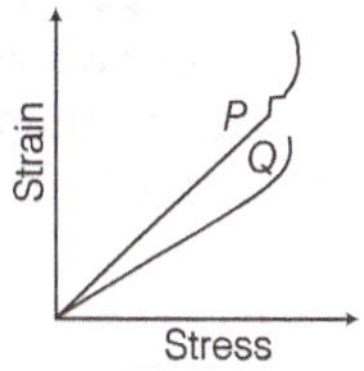

Then, the correct statement is/are
   (a) *P* has more tensile strength than *Q*
   (b) *P* is more ductile than *Q*
   (c) *P* is more brittle than *Q*
   (d) The Young's modulus of *P* is more than that of *Q*

5. Upto which point on stress-strain graph of a metal wire, the material remain elastic?
(a) Proportional limit (b) Yield point
(c) Ultimate point (d) Breaking point

Very Short Answer Type Questions

1 Mark

6. Two identical solid balls, one of ivory and the other of wet-clay, are dropped from the same height on the floor. Which will rise to a greater height after striking the floor and why?

7. Is stress a vector quantity? **NCERT Exemplar**

8. Stress and pressure are both forces per unit area. Then, in what respect does stress differ from pressure?

9. Which type of strain is there, when a spiral spring is stretched by a force?

10. What does the slope of stress *versus* strain graph indicate?

11. A thick wire is suspended from a rigid support, but no load is attached to its free end. Is this wire under stress?

12. Is it possible to double the length of a metallic wire by applying a force over it?

Short Answer Type I Questions

2 Marks

13. Define stress. Give its types and state which type of force produces that type of stress.

14. Define strain. Give its dimensions and units, also classify different types of strain.

15. A wire elongates by l mm when a load W is hanged from it. If the wire goes over a pulley and two weights W each are hung at the two ends, then what will be the elongation of the wire in mm?

Long Answer Type Questions

5 Marks

16. Represent graphically the variation of extension with load in an elastic body. On the graph, mark
(i) Hooke's law region
(ii) elastic limit
(iii) yield point
(iv) breaking point

17. The stress-strain graph for a metal wire is shown in figure. Upto the point E, the wire returns to its original state O along the curve EPO when it is gradually unloaded. Point B corresponds to the fracture of the wire.

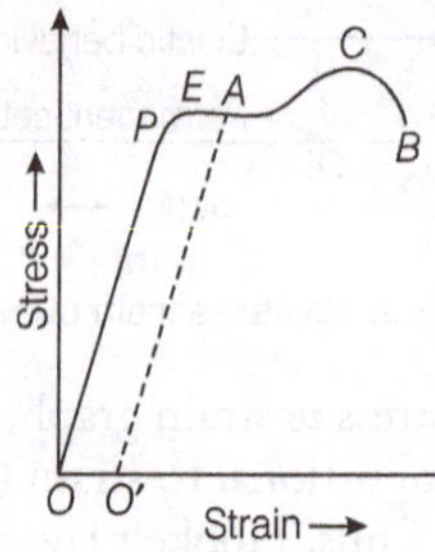

(i) Up to which point on the curve is Hooke's law obeyed? This point is sometimes called proportionality limit.
(ii) Which point on the curve corresponds to elastic limit and yield point of the wire?
(iii) Indicate the elastic and plastic regions of the stress-strain graph.
(iv) Describe what happens when the wire is loaded up to a stress corresponding to the point A on the graph and then unloaded gradually. In particular, explain the dotted curve.
(v) What is peculiar about the portion of the stress-strain graph from C to B? Upto what stress can the wire be subjected without causing fracture?

18. Differentiate between elastic materials, brittle materials and elastomers and also give their stress-strain curves.

Numerical Problems

19. A steel cable with a radius of 1.5 cm supports a chair lift at a ski area. If the maximum stress is not to exceed 10^8 N/m^2, then what is the maximum load the cable can support? **NCERT [2 M]**

20. A wire of length 2.5 m has a percentage strain of 0.012% under a tensile force. Determine the extension in the wire. **[2 M]**

21. Two wires made of same material are subjected to forces in the ratio 1 : 4. Their lengths are in the ratio 2 : 1 and diameters in the ratio 1 : 3. What is the ratio of their extensions? **[2 M]**

22. When a metallic cube of side 20 cm is subjected to a shearing force of 200 kg-f. The top face is displaced through 0.2 mm with respect to the bottom. Find the shearing strain. **[2 M]**

23. A normal face is applied on a cube such that its side decreased by 1%. Determine the value of bulk strain. **[2 M]**

24. The breaking stress of a metallic wire is $7.2\times10^8\,N/m^2$ and its density is $7.8\times10^3\,kg/m^3$. The wire is held vertically to the rigid support. Find the maximum length, so that the wire does not break. (Take, $g = 10\,m/s^2$) **[3 M]**

25. A steel wire of length $2l$ and cross-sectional area A is stretched within elastic limit as shown in figure. Calculate the strain and stress in the wire.

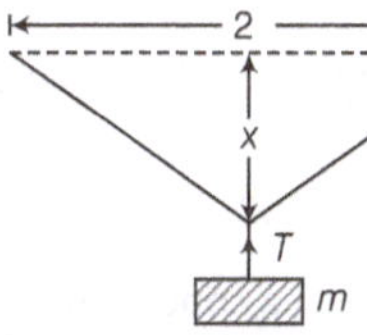

[5 M]

Hints & Solutions

1. (*b*) The property of a body, by virtue of which it tends to regain its original size and shape when the applied force is removed, is known as elasticity and the deformation caused is known as elastic deformation.

2. (*b*) $\text{Stress} = \frac{\text{Force}}{\text{Area}} = \frac{F}{\pi r^2}$

$\therefore$ $\text{Stress} \propto \frac{1}{r^2}$

$\Rightarrow \frac{(\text{Stress})_B}{(\text{Stress})_A} = \left(\frac{r_A}{r_B}\right)^2 = (2)^2$

$\Rightarrow (\text{Stress})_B = 4\times(\text{Stess})_A$ (as, F = constant)

3. (*c*) When the length of wire becomes double, its area of cross-section will become half because volume of wire is constant ($V = AL$).

So, the instantaneous stress $= \frac{\text{Force}}{\text{Area}} = \frac{Mg}{A/2} = \frac{2Mg}{A}$

4. (*b*) Form graph, P has more strain so P is more ductile with respect to Q.

5. (*b*) Upto yield point, the material shows elastic behaviour, however Hooke's law is obeyed upto proportional limit.

6. The ball of ivory will rise to a greater height because, ivory is more elastic than wet-clay.

7. No, stress is a scalar quantity, not a vector quantity.

$$\text{Stress} = \frac{\text{Magnitude of internal reaction force}}{\text{Area of cross - section}}$$

8. Pressure is an external force per unit area, while stress is the internal restoring force per unit area which comes into play in a deformed body, when stress is acting transversely per unit area of a body.

9. Shear strain.

10. The slope of stress (on Y-axis) and strain (on X-axis) gives modulus of elasticity.

The slope of stress (on X-axis) and strain (on Y-axis) gives the reciprocal of modulus of elasticity.

11. Yes, the wire is under stress due to its own weight.

12. Yes, it is possible, if diameter of wire is comparatively large and having high ductility.

13. Refer to text on pages 268 and 269 (Stress and its types).

14. Refer to text on pages 269 and 270 (Strain and its types).

15. According to Hooke's law,

Modulus of elasticity, $E = \frac{W}{A}\times\frac{L}{l}$

where, L = original length of the wire

A = cross-sectional area of the wire

$\therefore$ Elongation, $l = \frac{WL}{AE}$ ...(i)

In given arrangement, either side of the wire, tension is W and length is $\frac{L}{2}$. [1]

So, elongation in each part is

$$\Delta l = \frac{W\,L/2}{AE} = \frac{WL}{2AE} = \frac{l}{2} \quad \text{[from Eq. (i)]}$$

$\therefore$ Total elongation in the wire $= \frac{l}{2}+\frac{l}{2} = l$ [1]

16. Refer to text on pages 170 and 271 (Stress-strain curve).

17. Refer to text on pages 170 and 271 (Stress-strain curve).

18. Refer to text on pages 170 and 271 (Stress-strain curve and properties).

19. Given, radius of steel cable $(r) = 1.5\text{ cm} = 1.5\times10^{-2}$ m

$$\text{Maximum stress} = 10^8\ \text{N/m}^2$$

Area of cross-section of steel cable $(A) = \pi r^2$

$$= 3.14\times(1.5\times10^{-2})^2\ \text{m}^2$$

$$= 3.14\times2.25\times10^{-4}\ \text{m}^2 \quad [1/2]$$

$$\text{Maximum stress} = \frac{\text{Maximum force}}{\text{Area of cross-section}} \quad [1/2]$$

or Maximum force = Maximum stress × Area of cross-section

$$= 10^8\times(3.14\times2.25\times10^{-4})\ \text{N}$$

$$= 7.065\times10^4\ \text{N} = 7.1\times10^4\ \text{N} \quad [1]$$

20. Here, original length, L = 2.5 m

$$\text{Strain} = \frac{\Delta L}{L} = 0.012\% = \frac{0.012}{100}$$

$$\Delta L = \text{Strain}\times L \quad [1]$$

or $\Delta L = \text{extension} = \frac{0.012}{100} \times L$

$= \frac{0.012 \times 2.5}{100} = 3 \times 10^{-4}$ m = 0.3 mm [1]

21. According to Hooke's law,

Modulus of elasticity, $E = \frac{F}{\pi r^2} \times \frac{l}{\Delta l}$ or $\Delta l = \frac{Fl}{\pi r^2 E}$

or $\Delta l \propto \frac{Fl}{r^2}$ [$\because E$ is same for two wires] [1]

$\therefore \quad \frac{\Delta l_1}{\Delta l_2} = \frac{F_1}{F_2} \times \frac{l_1}{l_2} \times \frac{r_2^2}{r_1^2} = \frac{1}{4} \times \frac{2}{1} \times \left(\frac{3}{1}\right)^2 = \frac{9}{2}$

So, $\Delta l_1 : \Delta l_2 = 9:2.$ [1]

22. Given, side of metallic cube (l) = 20 cm

Displacement in top face of cube, Δl = 0.2 mm = 0.02 cm [1]

$\therefore$ Shearing strain $= \frac{\Delta l}{l} = \frac{0.02}{20} = 0.001$ [1]

23. Given that, when a normal force is applied on a cube of side l, then its side is decreased by 1%, i.e. $\frac{\Delta l}{l} = 0.01$

Volume of cube, $V = l^3$ [1]

Bulk strain $= \frac{\Delta V}{V} = 3\frac{\Delta l}{l} = 3 \times 0.01 = 0.03$ [1]

24. Given, density of wire (ρ) $= 7.8 \times 10^3$ kg/m^3, $g = 10$ m/s^2

Breaking stress $= 7.2 \times 10^8$ N/m^2

$\therefore$ Breaking stress $= \frac{F}{A}$ [1]

$7.2 \times 10^8 = \frac{Mg}{A}$

$= \frac{LMg}{AL} = L\left(\frac{M}{V}\right)g$ [$\because V = AL$]

$\Rightarrow \quad 7.2 \times 10^8 = L\rho g$ $\left[\because \rho = \frac{M}{V}\right]$ [1]

$\Rightarrow \quad L = \frac{7.2 \times 10^8}{\rho g}$

$= \frac{7.2 \times 10^8}{7.8 \times 10^3 \times 10}$

$= 9.23 \times 10^3$ m [1]

25. Total length $L = 2l$. Increase in length of the wire, when it is stretched from its mid-point.

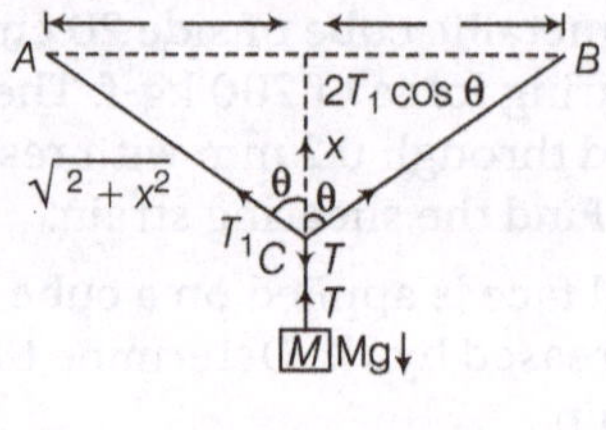

[1]

From Pythagoras theorem, $BC^2 = l^2 + x^2$

$BC = \sqrt{l^2 + x^2}$ [1]

Similarly, $AC = \sqrt{l^2 + x^2}$

Change in length, of the wire

$\Delta L = (AC + CB) - AB = (\sqrt{l^2 + x^2} + \sqrt{l^2 + x^2}) - 2l$

$= 2(l^2 + x^2)^{1/2} - 2l = 2l\left(1 + \frac{x^2}{l^2}\right)^{1/2} - 2l$ ...(i)

Since $x << l$, so using Binomial expansion, we have

$\left(1 + \frac{x^2}{l^2}\right)^{1/2} = \left(1 + \frac{x^2}{2l^2}\right)$

[neglecting terms containing higher powers of x]

$\therefore \quad \Delta L = 2l\left(1 + \frac{x^2}{2l^2}\right) - 2l = \frac{x^2}{l}$ [1]

Hence, strain $= \frac{\Delta L}{L} = \frac{x^2}{l \times 2l} = \frac{x^2}{2l^2}$ [1]

$\because \quad T = 2T_1 \cos\theta$

$\therefore \quad T_1 = \frac{Mg}{2\cos\theta}$ [$\because T = Mg$]

Putting $\cos\theta = \frac{x}{\sqrt{l^2 + x^2}}$

$T_1 = \frac{Mg}{2x}(\sqrt{l^2 + x^2}) = \frac{Mgl}{2x}\left(1 + \frac{x^2}{l^2}\right)^{1/2}$

$= \frac{Mgl}{2x}\left(1 + \frac{x^2}{2l^2}\right)$ [using $(1 + x)^x = 1 + xx$]

$\because \quad x << l \quad \therefore \quad \frac{x^2}{2l^2} \to 0$

Thus, $1 + \frac{x^2}{2l^2} = 1$

$\therefore \quad T_1 = \frac{Mgl}{2x}$

Stress in the wire $= \frac{T_1}{A} = \frac{Mgl}{2xA}$ [1]

TOPIC 02 Modulus of Elasticity or Elastic Modulus

Elastic Modulus

The modulus of elasticity or coefficient of elasticity of a body is defined as the ratio of stress to the corresponding strain within the elastic limit.

$$\text{Modulus of elasticity} = \frac{\text{Stress}}{\text{Strain}}$$

Its SI unit is Nm^{-2} or Pascal (Pa) and its dimensional formula is $[ML^{-1}T^{-2}]$.

- Modulus of elasticity depends on the nature of the material of the body.
- Modulus of elasticity of a body is independent of its dimensions (i.e. length, area, volume etc.)
- Dimensional formula of modulus of elasticity is same as that of the stress or pressure.

There are three types of modulus of elasticity

1. Young's Modulus of Elasticity

Within the elastic limit, the ratio of longitudinal stress to the longitudinal strain is called Young's modulus of the material of the wire.

i.e. $$\text{Young's modulus } (Y) = \frac{\text{Longitudinal stress}}{\text{Longitudinal strain}}$$

$$\text{Young's modulus, } Y = \frac{\text{Tensile (or compressive) stress } (\sigma)}{\text{Longitudinal strain } (\varepsilon)}$$

Consider a wire of radius r and length L. Let a force F be applied on the wire along its length i.e. normal to the surface of the wire as shown in figure.

If ΔL be the change in length of the wire,

Longitudinal stress = F/A, where A is the area of cross-section of the wire.

Longitudinal strain = $\Delta L / L$

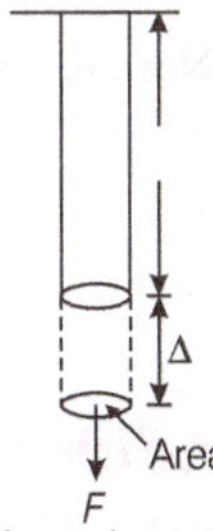

Young's modulus of elasticity

∴ Young's modulus,

$$Y = \frac{F/A}{\Delta L / L} = \frac{FL}{A\Delta L} \quad \text{...(i)}$$

If extension is produced by hanging a mass m, then $F = mg$

Also, $A = \pi r^2$

Substituting these values in Eq.(i), we get

$$Y = \frac{mgL}{\pi r^2 \Delta L}$$

or $$\text{Young's modulus, } Y = \frac{FL}{\pi r^2 \Delta L}$$

If $L = 1\text{m}$, $A = 1\text{m}^2$ and $\Delta L = 1\text{m}$, then $Y = F$

Thus, **Young's modulus of elasticity is equal to the force required to extend a wire of unit length and unit area of cross-section by unit amount.**

Extension is proportional to the deforming force and length of rod. Greater the force, larger the deformation and longer the rod larger, the extension.

Example 1 If a wire of length 4 m and cross-sectional area of 2m^2 is stretched by a force of 3 kN, then determine the change in length due to this force. Given Young's modulus of material of wire is 110×10^9 N / m^2.

Sol. Given, area of cross-section, $A = 2$ m^2

Force, $F = 3 \text{ kN} = 3 \times 10^3$ N

Length, $L = 4$ m

Young's modulus, $Y = 110 \times 10^9$ N / m^2

Change in length, $\Delta L = ?$

Apply, $Y = \frac{FL}{A\Delta L}$

$$\Rightarrow \Delta L = \frac{FL}{AY} = \frac{3 \times 10^3 \times 4}{2 \times 110 \times 10^9}$$

$$= 0.0545 \times 10^{-6} \text{ m}$$

$$\Delta L = 54.5 \times 10^{-3} \text{ mm}$$

Example 2 In a physics department, a Foucault pendulum consists of a 130 kg steel ball which swings at the end of a 8.0 m long steel cable having the diameter of 3.0 mm. If the ball was first hung from the cable, then determine how much did the cable stretch?

The amount by which the cable stretches depends on the elasticity of the steel cable. Young's Modulus for steel is given as $Y = 20 \times 10^8$ N/m^2

Sol. Given, diameter, $D = 3.0 \text{ mm} = 3.0 \times 10^{-3}$ m

Length, $L = 8.0$ m, mass, $m = 130$ kg

Radius, $r = \frac{D}{2} = \frac{3.0 \times 10^{-3}}{2} = 1.5 \times 10^{-3}$ m

The area of cross-section of the cable

$$A = \pi r^2 = \pi \times (1.5\times10^{-3})^2 = 7.065\times10^{-6}\ \text{m}^2$$

Thus,

$$F = mg = 130\times9.8$$
$$F = 1274\ \text{N}$$

The change in length

$$Y = \frac{\text{Stress}}{\text{Strain}} = \frac{F/A}{\Delta L/L} \Rightarrow \Delta L = \frac{LF}{AY}$$

$$\Rightarrow \quad \Delta L = \frac{8.0\times1274}{7.065\times10^{-6}\times20\times10^{8}} = 0.72\ \text{m} = 720\ \text{mm}$$

Example 3 **The ball of 200 g is attached to the end of a string of an elastic material (say rubber) and having length and cross-sectional area of 51 cm and 22 mm², respectively. Find the Young's modulus of this material if string is whirled round, horizontally at a uniform speed of 50 rpm in a circle of diameter 104 cm.**

Sol. Mass of the ball, $M = 200\ \text{g} = 0.2\ \text{kg}$

Area of cross-section, $A = 22\ \text{mm}^2 = 22\times10^{-6}\ \text{m}^2$

Radius of the circle, $r = \frac{D}{2} = \frac{104}{2} = 52\ \text{cm} = 0.52\ \text{m}$

Length of the string, $l = 51\ \text{cm} = 0.51\ \text{m}$

Revolution per second, $= 50\times60\ \text{rps} = 3000\ \text{rps}$

Centripital force, $F = mr\omega^2 = 0.2\times0.52\times(2\pi\times N)^2$

$$F = 36.95\times10^{6}\ \text{N}$$

The change in length Δl

= radius of the circle − length of the string $= 0.52 - 0.51$

$\Delta l = 0.01\ \text{m}$

Young's modulus of the material

$$Y = \frac{F}{A}\frac{l}{\Delta l} = \frac{36.95\times10^{6}}{22\times10^{-6}}\times\frac{0.51}{0.01} = 85.67\times10^{12}\ \text{Nm}^{-2}$$

2. Bulk Modulus of Elasticity

Within the elastic limit, the ratio of normal stress to the volumetric strain is called bulk modulus of elasticity.

Consider a body of volume V and surface area A. Suppose a force F acts uniformly over the whole surface of the body and it decreases the volume by ΔV as shown in figure.

The Bulk modulus of elasticity is given by

$$B = \frac{\text{Normal stress}}{\text{Volumetric strain}} = \frac{F/A}{\Delta V/V}$$

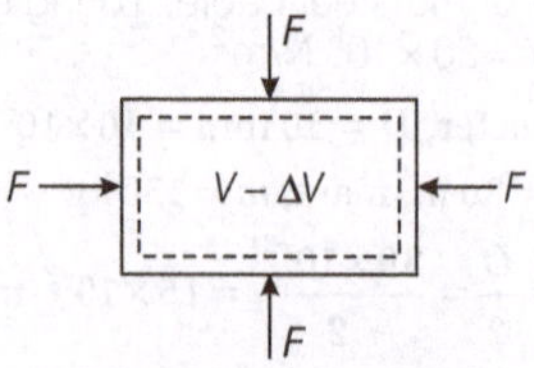

Bulk modulus of elasticity

$\therefore$ Bulk modulus, $B = \frac{-F}{A}\frac{V}{\Delta V}$

$$\Rightarrow \quad \boxed{\text{Bulk modulus, } B = -\frac{pV}{\Delta V}}$$

where, $p = \frac{F}{A}$ is the normal pressure.

Note

- Negative sign shows that the volume decreases with the increase in stress.
- Bulk modulus for a perfect rigid body and ideal liquid is infinite.

Compressibility

The reciprocal of the Bulk modulus of a material is called its compressibility.

Compressibility, $k = \frac{1}{B} = \frac{-\Delta V}{pV}$

SI unit of compressibility $= \text{N}^{-1}\text{m}^2$

CGS unit of compressibility $= \text{dyne}^{-1}\text{cm}^2$

The dimensional formula of compressibility is $[\text{M}^{-1}\text{LT}^2]$

Example 4 **What will be the decrease in volume of 100 cm³ of water under pressure of 100 atm if the compressibility of water is 4×10^{-5} per unit atmospheric pressure?**

Sol. Bulk modulus $(B) = \frac{1}{\text{Compressibility}} = \frac{1}{k}$

$$= \frac{1}{4\times10^{-5}} = 0.25\times10^{5}\ \text{atm}$$
$$= 0.25\times10^{5}\times1.013\times10^{5}\ \text{N/m}^2$$
$$= 2.533\times10^{9}\ \text{N/m}^2$$

Volume, $V = 100\ \text{cm}^3 = 10^{-4}\ \text{m}^3$

Pressure, $p = 100\ \text{atm} = 100\times1.013\times10^{5}\ \text{N/m}^2$

$= 1.013\times10^{7}\ \text{N/m}^2$

Now, apply $\frac{1}{B} = k = \frac{\Delta V}{pV}$

$$\therefore \quad \Delta V = \frac{pV}{B} = \frac{1.013\times10^{7}\times10^{-4}}{2.533\times10^{9}}$$

$$\Delta V = 0.4\times10^{-6}\ \text{m}^3 = 0.4\ \text{cm}^3$$

3. Modulus of Rigidity or Shear Modulus

Within the elastic limit, the ratio of tangential stress (shear stress) to shear strain is called modulus of rigidity. It is denoted as G or η. Let us consider a cube whose lower face is fixed and a tangent force F acts on the upper face whose area is A, as shown in figure.

$\therefore$ $$\boxed{\text{Tangential stress (shear stress)} = \frac{F}{A}}$$

Let the vertical sides of the cube shifts through an angle θ, called shear strain.

$\therefore$ Modulus of rigidity is given by

$$\eta \text{ or } G = \frac{\text{Tangential stress (shear stress)}}{\text{Shear strain}}$$

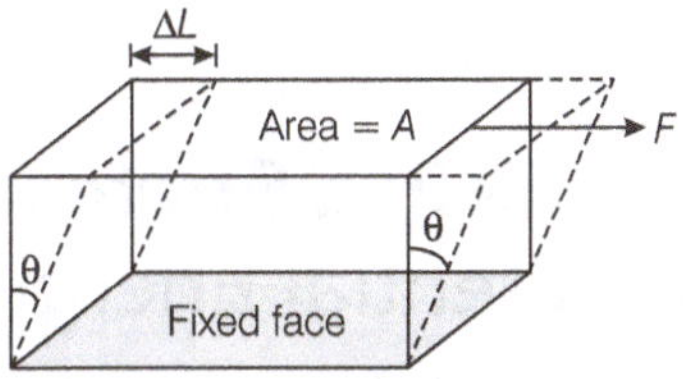

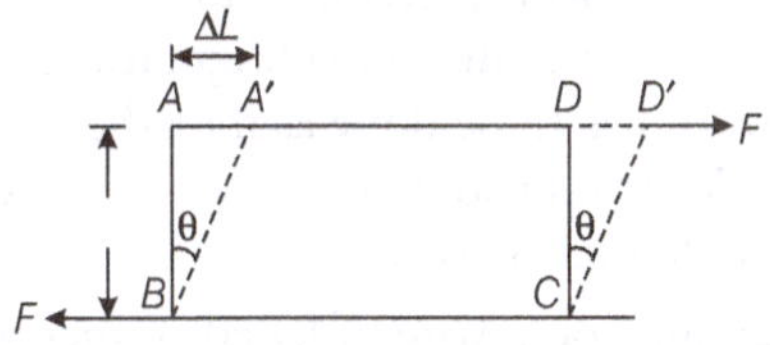

According to diagram, by displacing its upper face through distance $AA' = \Delta L$

Let $AB = DC = L$ and $\angle ABA' = \theta$,

$$\eta = \frac{F/A}{\theta} = \frac{F}{A\theta}$$

Shear strain, $\theta \approx \tan\theta = \frac{AA'}{AB} = \frac{\Delta L}{L}$

$$\boxed{\text{Shear modulus, } \eta = \frac{F}{A} \cdot \frac{L}{\Delta L}}$$

Example 5 Consider an Indian rubber cube having modulus of rigidity of 2×10^7 dyne/cm^2 and of side 8 cm. If one side of the rubber is fixed, while a tangential force equal to the weight of 300 kg is applied to the opposite face, then find out the shearing strain produced and distance through which the strain side moves.

Sol. Given, modulus of rigidity, $\eta = 2 \times 10^7$ dyne/cm^2

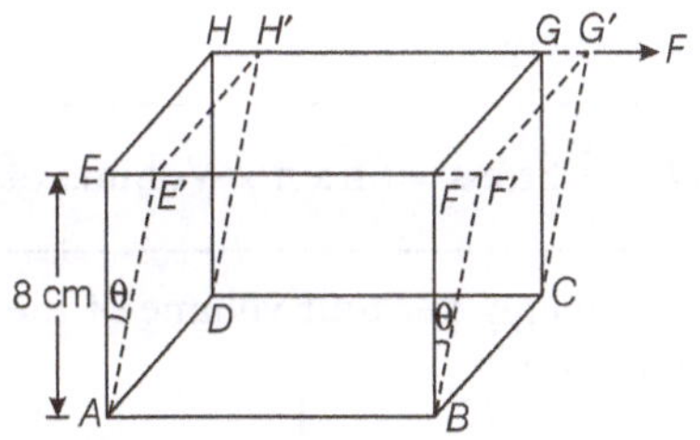

Side of the cube, $l = 8$ cm

Area, $A = l^2 = 64$ cm^2

Force or load, $F = 300$ kgf $= 300 \times 1000 \times 981$ dyne

As, $\eta = \frac{F}{A\theta} \Rightarrow \theta = \frac{F}{A\eta}$

$$\theta = \frac{300 \times 1000 \times 981}{64 \times 2 \times 10^7} \simeq 0.23 \text{ rad}$$

As, $\eta = \frac{F}{A}\frac{l}{\Delta l} \Rightarrow \frac{\Delta l}{l} = \theta$

$\Rightarrow$ $\Delta l = l\theta = 8 \times 0.23 \Rightarrow \Delta l = 1.84$ cm

Poisson's Ratio

When a wire is loaded, its length increases but its diameter decreases. The strain produced in the direction of applied force is called **longitudinal strain** and strain produced in the perpendicular direction is called **lateral strain.**

Within the elastic limit, the ratio of lateral strain to the longitudinal strain is called **Poisson's ratio.**

Let the length of the loaded wire increases from L to $L + \Delta L$ and its diameter decreases from D to $D - \Delta D$.

Longitudinal strain $= \frac{\Delta L}{L}$

Lateral strain $= \frac{-\Delta D}{D}$

Poisson's ratio $\sigma = \frac{\text{Lateral strain}}{\text{Longitudinal strain}}$

$$= \frac{-\Delta D / D}{\Delta L / L}$$

$$\boxed{\text{Poisson's ratio, } \sigma = \frac{-L}{D} \cdot \frac{\Delta D}{\Delta L}}$$

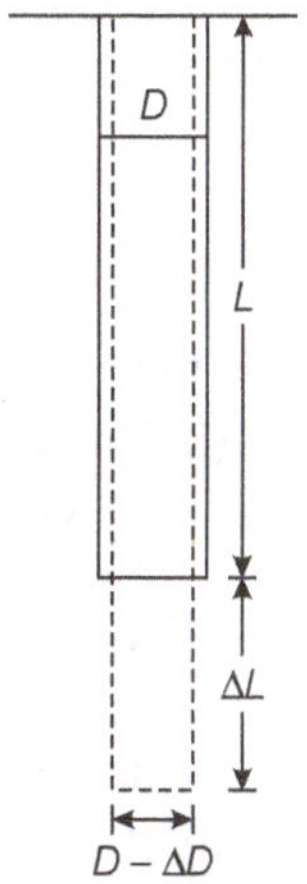

Poisson's ratio

The negative sign indicates that longitudinal and lateral strain are in opposite sense, it has no unit and dimensions.

Theoretically value of poisson's ratio lies between -1 to 0.5 but practical values of poisson's ratio is from 0 to 0.5.

Poisson's ratio is a constant provided a material remains elastic, homogeneous and isotropic in nature.

Example 6 A material having Poisson's ratio 0.2. A load is applied on it, due to which it suffers the longitudinal strain 3.0×10^{-3}, then find out the percentage change in its volume.

Sol. Given, Poisson's ratio, $\sigma = 0.2$

Longitudinal strain $= \frac{\Delta L}{L} = 3.0 \times 10^{-3}$

As, $\sigma = -\dfrac{\Delta D/D}{\Delta L/L}$ or $\sigma = \dfrac{-\Delta R/R}{\Delta L/L}$

$\Rightarrow$ $\dfrac{\Delta R}{R} = -\sigma \times \dfrac{\Delta L}{L} = -0.6 \times 10^{-3}$

Volume, $V = \pi R^2 L$

Then, percentage change in volume,

$$\left(\frac{\Delta V}{V} \times 100\right) = \left(\frac{2\Delta R}{R} + \frac{\Delta L}{L}\right) \times 100$$

$$= [2 \times (-0.6 \times 10^{-3}) + 3.0 \times 10^{-3}] \times 100 = 0.18\ \%$$

Relation between Y, B, η and σ

The different elastic constants exhibit the following relationship.

(i) $Y = 3B(1 - 2\sigma)$

(ii) $Y = 2\eta(1 + \sigma)$

(iii) $\sigma = \dfrac{3B - 2\eta}{2\eta + 6B}$

(iv) $\dfrac{9}{Y} = \dfrac{1}{B} + \dfrac{3}{\eta}$

Above relations are approximate and valid for metals only.

Factors Affecting Elasticity of Material

The following factors affect the elasticity of a material

(i) **Hammering and rolling** In both of these processes, the crystal grains are broken into small units and the elasticity of the material increases.

(ii) **Annealing** This process result in the formation of larger crystal grains and elasticity of the material decreases.

(iii) **Presence of impurities** Depending on the nature of impurity, the elasticity of material can be increased or decreased.

(iv) **Temperature** Elasticity of most of the materials decreases with increase in the temperature but elasticity of invor steel (alloy) does not change with change of temperature.

Elastic After Effect

When the deforming force is removed from the elastic bodies, the bodies tend to return to their respective original state. It has been found that bodies which kept loaded for a long time take appreciably long time in regaining their original shape. The delay in regaining the original shape is known as elastic after effect.

Elastic Fatigue

The elastic fatigue is defined as the loss in the strength of a material caused due to repeated alternating strains to which the material is subjected.

e.g. A hard wire can be broken by bending it repeatedly in opposite directions, as it loses strength due to elastic fatigue. For the same reason, the railway bridges are declared unsafe after a reasonably long period to avoid the risk of a mishappening.

Work Done in a Stretched Wire : Elastic Potential Energy

When a wire is stretched, interatomic forces come into play which oppose the change in configuration of the wire. Hence, work has to be done against these restoring forces. The work done in stretching the wire is stored in it as its elastic potential energy.

Let a force F applied on a wire of length L increases its length by ΔL. Initially, the internal restoring force in the wire is zero. When the length is increased by ΔL, the internal force increases from 0 to F. Within elastic limit this internal force is equals to externally applied force.

$\therefore$ Average internal force for an increase in length

$$\Delta L \text{ of wire} = \frac{0 + F}{2} = \frac{F}{2}$$

Work done on the wire,

$$W = \text{Average force} \times \text{Increase in length}$$

$$= \frac{F}{2} \times \Delta L$$

This work done is stored as elastic potential energy U in the wire,

$$U = \frac{1}{2} F \times \Delta L = \frac{1}{2} \text{Stretching force} \times \text{Increase in length}$$

If area of cross-section of wire is A, then

$$U = \frac{1}{2} \frac{F}{A} \times \frac{\Delta L}{L} \times AL$$

Elastic potential energy,

$$\boxed{U = \frac{1}{2} \text{Stress} \times \text{Strain} \times \text{Volume of wire}}$$

Elastic potential energy per unit volume of the wire or elastic energy density is

$$u = \frac{U}{\text{Volume}} = \frac{1}{2} \text{Stress} \times \text{Strain}$$

But $\quad$ Stress = Young's modulus × Strain

Elastic energy density,

$$u = \frac{1}{2} \text{Young's modulus} \times (\text{Strain})^2$$

Example 7 When the load of a wire is increased from 3 kg wt to 5 kg wt, the length of that wire changes from 0.61 mm to 1.02 mm. Calculate the change in the elastic potential energy of the wire.

Sol. Here, $F_1 = 3 \text{ kgf} = 3 \times 9.8 \text{N} = 29.4 \text{N}$

$l_1 = 0.61 \text{ mm} = 6.1 \times 10^{-4} \text{m}$

$F_2 = 5 \text{ kgf} = 5 \times 9.8 = 49 \text{N}$

$l_2 = 1.02 \text{ mm} = 1.02 \times 10^{-3} \text{m}$

∴ Change in elastic potential energy of the wire,

$$\Delta U = W_2 - W_1 = \frac{1}{2} F_2 l_2 - \frac{1}{2} F_1 l_1$$

$$= \frac{1}{2} \times 5 \times 9.8 \times 1.02 \times 10^{-3} - \frac{1}{2} \times 3 \times 9.8 \times 0.61 \times 10^{-3}$$

$$= 24.99 \times 10^{-3} - 8.967 \times 10^{-3}$$

$$= 16.03 \times 10^{-3} \text{ J}$$

Applications of Elastic Behaviour of Solids

(i) Any metallic part of a machinery is never subjected to a stress beyond the elastic limit of the material.

In case, the metallic part of the machinery is subjected to a stress beyond the elastic limit, it will get permanently deformed and hamper its working.

(ii) The thickness of metallic ropes used in cranes to lift and move heavy weights is decided on the basis of the elastic limit of the rope and the factor of safety.

(iii) **Force constant of a wire** For a wire, force that produces a unit elongation is called force constant of wire.

Force constant, $k = \frac{F}{\Delta l}$

$\Rightarrow \quad k = \frac{YA}{L}$

where, L = length of unstretched wire

and $\quad A$ = area of cross-section.

(iv) **Maximum height of a mountain on earth** At base of a mountain of height h, rocks and material of mountain are subjected to a pressure p.

$$p = h\rho g$$

where, ρ = density of material.

Now, when this pressure exceeds elastic limit of earth's supporting material and rocks, then they tend to flow away from base of mountain.

So, elastic limit > p > $h\rho g$

or $\quad h_{max} = \frac{k}{\rho g}$

(v) **Depression of a beam** Depression δ of a beam of length l, width b and thickness d under a load w is given by empirical formula,

$$\delta = \frac{wl^3}{4Ybd^3}$$

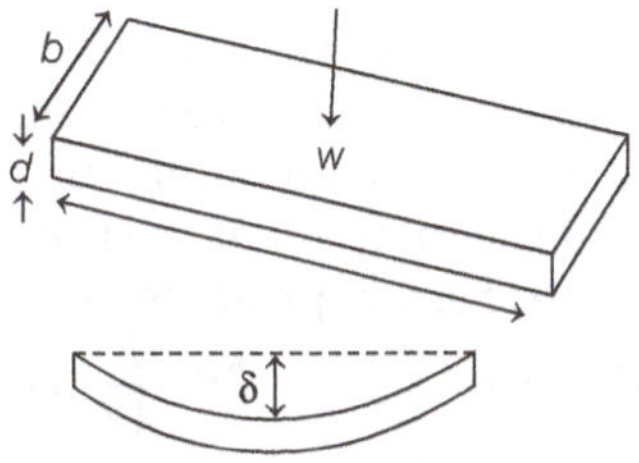

So, depression is minimised by increasing dimension d instead of dimension b.

(vi) **Thermal stress** When a rigidly fixed rod is heated due to expansion or compression a compressive or tensile stress is developed into it.

Thermal strain = $\frac{\Delta L}{L} = \alpha \Delta \theta$

where, α = coefficient of linear expansion

and $\quad \Delta\theta$ = rise in temperature.

So, thermally generated stress = $Y\alpha\Delta\theta$

Topic Practice 2

Multiple Choice Questions

1 Mark

1. A uniform rod of length L and density ρ is being pulled along a smooth floor with a horizontal acceleration α. The magnitude of the stress at the transverse cross-section through the mid-point of the rod is

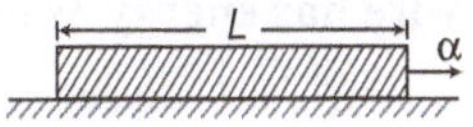

(a) $L\rho\alpha$ (b) $\frac{L\rho\alpha}{2}$ (c) $\frac{2}{3} L\rho\alpha$ (d) None of these

2. A metal wire of length L_1 and area of cross-section A is attached to a rigid support. Another metal wire of length L_2 and of the same cross-sectional area is attached to the free end of the first wire. A body of mass M is then suspended from the free end of the second wire.

If Y_1 and Y_2 are the Young's moduli of the wires respectively, the effective force constant of the system of two wires is

(a) $\frac{[(Y_1Y_2)A]}{[2(Y_1L_2+Y_2L_1)]}$ (b) $\frac{[(Y_1Y_2)A]}{(L_1L_2)^{1/2}}$

(c) $\frac{[(Y_1Y_2)A]}{(Y_1L_2+Y_2L_1)}$ (d) $\frac{[(Y_1Y_2)^{1/2}A]}{(L_1L_2)^{1/2}}$

3. A uniform rod of length (L) and area of cross-section (A) is subjected to tensile load (F). If σ be the Poisson's ratio and Y be the Young's modulus of the material of the rod, then find the volumetric strain produced in the rod.

(a) $\frac{F}{AY}(1+2\sigma)$ (b) $\frac{F}{AY}(1-2\sigma)$

(c) zero (d) None of these

4. If the volume of a wire remains constant when subjected to tensile stress, the value of Poisson's ratio of the material of the wire is

(a) 0.1 (b) 0.2 (c) 0.4 (d) 0.5

5. A material has Poisson's ratio 0.5. If a uniform rod of it suffers a longitudinal strain of 2×10^{-3}, then the percentage change in volume is

(a) 0.6 (b) 0.4 (d) 0.2 (d) zero

Very Short Answer Type Questions

1 Mark

6. What is the Young's modulus for a perfect rigid body?

7. A metal bar of length L, area of cross-section A, Young's modulus Y and coefficient of linear expansion α, is clamped between two stout pillars. What is the force exerted by the bar when it is heated through t°C?

8. What is Bulk modulus for a perfectly rigid body?

9. A stretched wire has energy. Is it potential or kinetic?

10. The shear modulus of a material is always considerably smaller than the Young's modulus for it. What does it signify?

Short Answer Type I Questions

2 Marks

11. State modulus of elasticity, give its unit and dimensions and also state its types.

12. The Young's modulus for steel is much more than that for rubber. For the same longitudinal strain, which one will have greater tensile stress? **NCERT Exemplar**

13. A solid sphere of radius R made of a material of bulk modulus B is surrounded by a liquid in a cylindrical container. A massless piston of area A floats on the surface of the liquid. When a mass M is placed on the piston to compress the liquid, find fractional change in the radius of the sphere?

Short Answer Type II Questions

3 Marks

14. Identical springs of steel and copper are equally stretched. On which, more work will have to be done? **NCERT Exemplar**

15. A uniform heavy rod of weight W, cross-sectional area A and length l is hanging from a fixed support. Young's modulus of the material of the rod is Y. Neglecting the lateral contraction, find the elongation produced in the rod.

16. What is meant by Young's modulus of elasticity? Determine the Young's modulus of the material of a wire?

Numerical Problems

17. A wire increases by 10^{-3} of its length when a stress of 10^8 Nm^{-2} is applied to it. What is the Young's modulus of the material of the wire? **[1 M]**

18. Figure shows the strain-stress curve for a given material. What are (i) Young's modulus and (ii) approximate yield strength for this material?

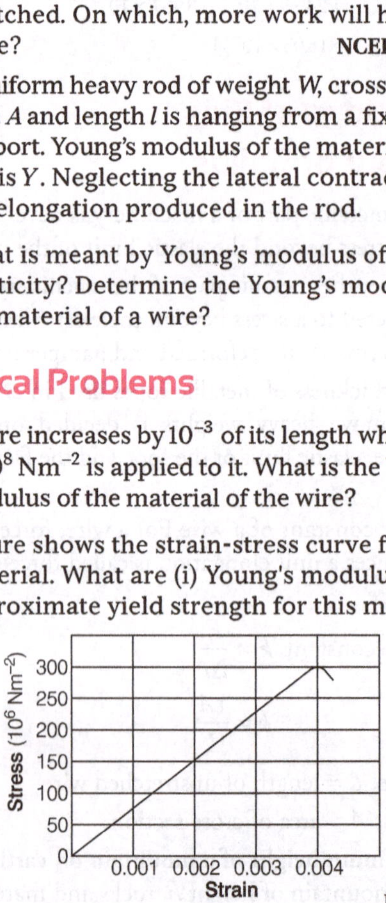

NCERT [2 M]

19. Calculate the percentage increase in length of a wire of diameter 2.5 mm stretched by a force of 100 kg weight. Young's modulus of elasticity of wire is 12.5×10^{11} dyne/sq cm. **[2 M]**

20. A steel wire of length 4.7 m and cross-sectional area 3.0×10^{-5} m^2 stretches by the same amount as a copper wire of length 3.5 m and cross-sectional area 4.0×10^{-5} m^2 under a given load.

What is the ratio of the Young's modulus of steel to that of copper? **NCERT [3 M]**

21. A rod of length 1.05 m having negligible mass is supported at its ends by two wires of steel (wire *A*) and aluminium (wire *B*) of equal lengths as shown in Fig. The cross-sectional areas of wires *A* and *B* are 1 mm^2 and 2 mm^2, respectively. Young's modulus of elasticity for steel and aluminium are 2×10^{11} and $7 \times 10^{11} N/m^2$, respectively. At what point along the rod should a mass *m* be suspended in order to produce (i) equal stresses and (ii) equal strains in both steel and aluminium wires.

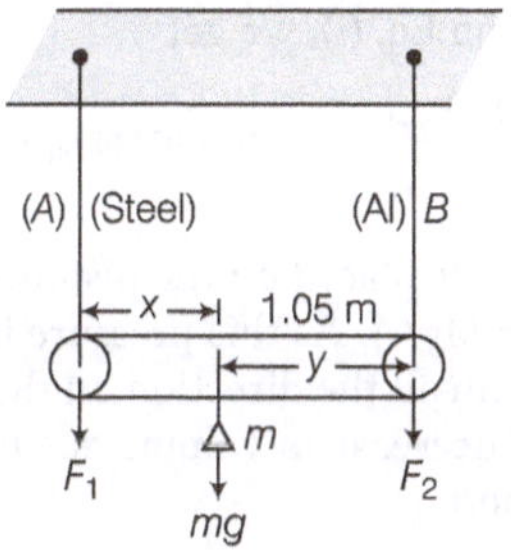

NCERT [5 M]

22. A rubber string 10 m long is suspended from a rigid support at its one end. Calculate the extension in the string due to its own weight. The density of rubber is 1.5×10^3 kg/m^3 and Young's modulus for the rubber is 5×10^6 N/m^2. The breaking stress for a metal is $7.8 \times 10^9 N/m^2$. Calculate the maximum length of the wire made of this metal which may be suspended without breaking. The density of metal $= 7.8 \times 10^3 kg/m^3$. **[5 M]**

23. The Marina trench is located in the Pacific ocean and at one place, it is nearly 11 km beneath the surface of water. The water pressure at the bottom of the trench is about 1.1×10^8 Pa. A steel ball of initial volume 0.32 m^3 is dropped into the ocean and falls to the bottom of trench. What is the change in the volume of the ball when it reaches to the bottom if the Bulk modulus of steel is $1.6 \times 10^{11} N/m^2$? **NCERT [2 M]**

24. To what depth must a rubber ball be taken in deep sea so that its volume is decreased by 0.1%? (The Bulk modulus of rubber is 9.8×10^8 N/m^2; and the density of seawater is 10^3 kg/m^3.) **[2 M]**

25. The edge of an aluminium cube is 10 cm long. One face of the cube is firmly fixed to a vertical wall. A mass of 100 kg is then attached to the opposite face of the cube.
The shear modulus of aluminium is 25 GPa. What is the vertical deflection of this face? **[5M]**

26. One end of a nylon rope, of length 4.5 cm and diameter 6 mm, is fixed to a free limb. A monkey, weighing 100 N, jumps to catch the free end and stays there. Find the elongation of the rope and the corresponding change in the diameter. Given Young's modulus of nylon $= 4.8 \times 10^{11}$ N/m^2 and Poisson's ratio of nylon $= 0.2$. **[3 M]**

27. Determine the volume contraction of a solid copper cube, 10 cm on an edge, when subjected to a hydraulic pressure of 7×10^6 Pa. Bulk modulus for copper $= 140 \times 10^9$ Pa. **[3 M]**

28. A mild steel wire of length 1 m and cross-sectional area 0.5×10^{-2} cm^2 is stretched, well within its elastic limit, horizontally between two pillars. A mass of 100 g is suspended from the mid-point of the wire. Calculate the depression at the mid-point. Given Young's modulus for steel $(Y_S) = 2 \times 10^{11}$ Pa. **NCERT [3 M]**

Hints & Solutions

1. (*b*) The force at the cross-section through the mid-point of the rod is

$$F = \frac{L}{2} A\rho\alpha$$

$$\therefore \quad \text{Stress} = \frac{F}{A} = \frac{1}{2} L\rho\alpha$$

2. (*c*) Using the usual expression for the Young's modulus, the force constant for the wire can be written as

$$k = \frac{F}{\Delta L} = \frac{YA}{L}$$

where, the symbols have their usual meanings.
When the two wires are connected together in series, the effective force constant is given by

$$k_{eq} = \frac{k_1 k_2}{k_1 + k_2}$$

Substituting the corresponding lengths, area of cross-section and the Young's moduli, we get

$$k_{eq} = \frac{\left(\frac{Y_1 A}{L_1}\right)\left(\frac{Y_2 A}{L_2}\right)}{\frac{Y_1 A}{L_1} + \frac{Y_2 A}{L_2}} = \frac{(Y_1 Y_2) A}{Y_1 L_2 + Y_2 L_1}$$

3. (*b*) Young's modulus, i.e. $Y = \frac{\text{Stress}}{\text{Strain}} = \frac{F/A}{\Delta L/L}$

$$\Rightarrow \quad Y \times \frac{\Delta L}{L} = \frac{F}{A} \quad \text{...(i)}$$

Now, by definition of Poisson's ratio

$$\sigma = \frac{\text{Lateral strain}}{\text{Longitudinal strain}} = -\frac{\Delta r/r}{\Delta L/L}$$

$$\Rightarrow \quad \frac{\Delta r}{r} = -\frac{\sigma \cdot \Delta L}{L} = -\frac{\sigma F}{AY} \quad \text{[by using Eq. (i)]}$$

$$\Rightarrow \quad \frac{\Delta r}{r} = -\frac{\sigma F}{AY} \quad \text{...(ii)}$$

Now, $V = \pi r^2 L \Rightarrow \frac{\Delta V}{V} = \frac{2\Delta r}{r} + \frac{\Delta L}{L}$

By using Eqs. (i) and (ii), we get

$$\Rightarrow \quad \frac{\Delta V}{V} = 2\left(-\frac{\sigma F}{AY}\right) + \frac{F}{AY}$$

$$\Rightarrow \quad \frac{\Delta V}{V} = \frac{F}{AY}(1 - 2\sigma)$$

4. (*d*) Let L be the length, r be the radius of the wire.

Volume of the wire, $V = \pi r^2 L$

Differentiating on both sides, we get

$$\Delta V = \pi(2r\Delta r)L + \pi r^2 \Delta L$$

As the volume of the wire remains unchanged when it gets stretched, so $\Delta V = 0$. Hence,

$$0 = 2\pi r L \Delta r + \pi r^2 \Delta L$$

$$\therefore \quad \frac{\Delta r/r}{\Delta L/L} = -\frac{1}{2}$$

$$\text{Poisson's ratio} = \frac{\text{Lateral strain}}{\text{Longitudinal strain}} = \frac{\Delta r/r}{\Delta L/L} = \frac{1}{2} = 0.5$$

5. (*d*) As, the Poisson's ratio of material is 0.5, so there is no change in volume.

6. Young's modulus $(Y) = \frac{F}{A} \times \frac{l}{\Delta l}$

For a perfectly rigid body, change in length $\Delta l = 0$

$$\therefore \quad Y = \frac{F}{A} \times \frac{l}{0} = \infty$$

Therefore, Young's modulus for a perfectly rigid body is ∞.

7. $Y = \frac{FL}{Al}$, where $l = L\alpha\Delta t$ and l = change in length.

$$Y = \frac{FL}{AL\alpha\Delta t} = \frac{F}{A\alpha\Delta t} = \frac{F}{A\alpha\Delta t}$$

$$\therefore \quad F = YA\alpha \cdot \Delta t$$

8. Bulk modulus $(B) = \frac{p}{\Delta V/V} = \frac{pV}{\Delta V}$

For perfectly rigid body, change in volume $\Delta V = 0$

$$\therefore \quad B = \frac{pV}{0} = \infty$$

Therefore, Bulk modulus for a perfectly rigid body is ∞.

9. Refer to text on page 278 (Work done in a stretched wire : Elastic potential energy).

10. **η of a material is smaller than its Y.** As, we know that it is easier to slide layers of atoms of solids over one another than to pull them apart or to squeeze them to close together.

11. Refer to text on pages 275, 276 and 277 (Elastic modulus and its types).

12. Young's modulus $(Y) = \frac{\text{Stress}}{\text{Longitudinal strain}}$

For same longitudinal strain, $Y \propto$ stress [1]

$$\therefore \quad \frac{Y_{\text{steel}}}{Y_{\text{rubber}}} = \frac{(\text{stress})_{\text{steel}}}{(\text{stress})_{\text{rubber}}} \quad \text{...(i)}$$

But $Y_{\text{steel}} > Y_{\text{rubber}}$

$$\therefore \quad \frac{Y_{\text{steel}}}{Y_{\text{rubber}}} > 1$$

Therefore, from Eq. (i), we get

$$\frac{(\text{stress})_{\text{steel}}}{(\text{stress})_{\text{rubber}}} > 1 \text{ or } (\text{stress})_{\text{steel}} > (\text{stress})_{\text{rubber}}$$ [1]

13. When mass M is placed on the piston, the excess pressure, $p = Mg/A$. As this pressure is equally applicable from all the direction on the sphere, hence there will be decrease in volume due to decrease in radius of sphere.

Volume of the sphere, $V = \frac{4}{3}\pi R^3$. [1/2]

Differentiating it, we get,

$$\Delta V = \frac{4}{3}\pi(3R^2)\Delta R = 4\pi R^2 \Delta R$$

$$\therefore \quad \frac{\Delta V}{V} = \frac{4\pi R^2 \Delta R}{\frac{4}{3}\pi R^3} = \frac{3\Delta R}{R}$$ [1/2]

We know that,

$$B = \frac{P}{dV/V} = \frac{Mg}{A} \Big/ \frac{3\Delta R}{R} \quad \text{or} \quad \frac{\Delta R}{R} = \frac{Mg}{3BA}$$ [1]

14. Work done in stretching a wire is given by

$$W = \frac{1}{2}F \times \Delta l$$ [1]

As springs of steel and copper are equally stretched. Therefore, for same force (F),

$$W \propto \Delta l \quad \text{...(i)}$$

Young's modulus $(Y) = \frac{F}{A} \times \frac{l}{\Delta l}$ [1/2]

or $\Delta l = \frac{F}{A} \times \frac{l}{Y}$

As both springs are identical,

$$\therefore \quad \Delta l \propto \frac{1}{Y} \quad \text{...(ii)}$$

From Eqs. (i) and (ii), we get $W \propto \frac{1}{Y}$ [1/2]

$$\therefore \quad \frac{W_{steel}}{W_{copper}} = \frac{Y_{copper}}{Y_{steel}} < 1 \quad [\text{as } Y_{steel} > Y_{copper}]$$

or $W_{steel} < W_{copper}$ [1/2]

Therefore, more work will be done for stretching copper spring. [1/2]

15. As shown in figure, consider a small element of thickness dx at distance x from the fixed support. Force acting on the element dx is

$$F = \text{Weight of length } (l - x) \text{ of the rod} = \frac{W}{l}(l - x)$$ [1]

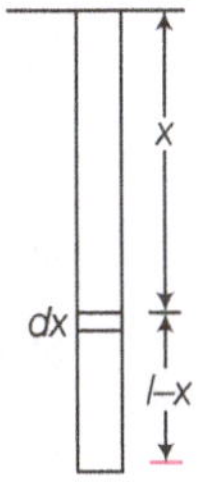

Elongation of the element

$$= \text{Original length} \times \frac{\text{Stress}}{Y}$$

$$= dx \times \frac{F/A}{Y} = \frac{W}{l\,Ay}(l - x)dx$$ [1]

Total elongation produced in the rod

$$= \frac{W}{l\,AY}\int_0^l (l - x)dx = \frac{W}{l\,Ay}\left[lx - \frac{x^2}{2}\right]_0^l$$

$$= \frac{W}{l\,Ay}\left[l^2 - \frac{l^2}{2}\right] = \frac{Wl}{2Ay}$$ [1]

16. Refer to text on page 275 (Young's modulus of elasticity).

17. Given, $\Delta L = 10^{-3} L$, with L as the original length

$$\text{Strain} = \frac{\Delta L}{L} = 10^{-3} \text{ and Stress} = \frac{F}{A} = 10^8 \text{ N/m}^2$$

$$\because \quad Y = \frac{\text{Stress}}{\text{Strain}} = \frac{F/A}{\Delta L / L}$$ [1/2]

$$Y = \frac{1 \times 10^8}{10^{-3}} = 10^{11} \text{ N/m}^2$$ [1/2]

18. (i) Young's modulus of the given material (Y)

= Slope of strain-stress curve [1/2]

$$Y = \frac{150 \times 10^6}{0.002} = 75 \times 10^9 \text{ N/m}^2$$ [1/2]

$$= 7.5 \times 10^{10} \text{ N/m}^2$$

(ii) Yield strength of the given material

= Maximum stress, the material can sustain [1/2]

$= 300 \times 10^6 \text{ N/m}^2 = 3 \times 10^8 \text{ N/m}^2$ [1/2]

19. Here, $2r = 2.5\text{mm} = 0.25\text{cm}$ or $r = 0.125$ cm

$$\therefore \quad a = \pi r^2 = \frac{22}{7} \times (0.125)^2 \text{ sq. cm}$$

$$F = 100 \text{ kg} = 100 \times 1000 \text{ g}$$

$$F = 10 \times 1000 \times 980 \text{ dyne}$$

$$Y = 12.5 \times 10^{11} \text{ dyne/sq. cm}$$ [1/2]

As $\quad Y = \dfrac{F \times l}{a \times \Delta l}$

$$\therefore \quad \frac{\Delta l}{l} = \frac{F}{aY}$$ [1/2]

Hence, % increase in length $= \dfrac{\Delta l}{l} \times 100 = \dfrac{F}{aY} \times 100$

$$= \frac{(100 \times 1000 \times 980) \times 7 \times 100}{22 \times (0.125)^2 \times 12.5 \times 10^{11}}$$

$$= 0.1812\%$$ [1]

20. Given, **for steel wire** Length $(l_1) = 4.7$ m [1/2]

Area of cross-section $(A_1) = 3.0 \times 10^{-5}$ m^2

For copper wire Length $(l_2) = 3.5$ m

Area of cross-section $(A_2) = 4.0 \times 10^{-5}$ m^2 [1/2]

Let F be the given load under which steel and copper wires be stretched by the same amount Δl.

$$\text{Young's modulus } (Y) = \frac{F/A}{\Delta l / l} = \frac{F \times l}{A \times \Delta l}$$ [1]

For steel, $\quad Y_s = \dfrac{F \times l_1}{A_1 \times \Delta l}$ ...(i)

For copper, $\quad Y_c = \dfrac{F \times l_2}{A_2 \times \Delta l}$ ...(ii)

Dividing Eq. (i) by Eq. (ii), we get

$$\frac{Y_s}{Y_c} = \frac{F \times l_1}{A_1 \times \Delta l} \times \frac{A_2 \times \Delta l}{F \times l_2}$$ [1/2]

$$= \frac{l_1}{l_2} \times \frac{A_2}{A_1} = \frac{4.7}{3.5} \times \frac{4.0 \times 10^{-5}}{3.0 \times 10^{-5}}$$

$$\frac{Y_s}{Y_c} = \frac{18.8}{10.5} = 1.79 = 1.8$$ [1/2]

21. Let the length of wires A and B is equal to L and their area of cross-section be A_1 and A_2, respectively.

Given, $\quad A_1 = 1 \text{ mm}^2 = 1 \times 10^{-6} \text{ m}^2$

$$A_2 = 2 \text{ mm}^2 = 2 \times 10^{-6} \text{ m}^2$$ [1]

$$Y_{steel} = 2 \times 10^{11} \text{ N/m}^2$$

$$Y_{Al} = 7.0 \times 10^{10} \text{ N/m}^2$$

Let F_1 and F_2 be the tensions in the two wires, respectively.

(i) When equal stresses are produced, then

$$\frac{F_1}{A_1} = \frac{F_2}{A_2}$$ [1/2]

or $\quad \dfrac{F_1}{F_2} = \dfrac{A_1}{A_2} = \dfrac{1 \times 10^{-6}}{2 \times 10^{-6}}$

or $\quad \dfrac{F_1}{F_2} = \dfrac{1}{2}$ ...(i) [1/2]

Let mass m be suspended at distance x from steel wire A.

Taking moment of forces about the point of suspension of mass from the rod, we get

$$F_1 \times x = F_2 \times (1.05 - x) \quad [1/2]$$

or $$\frac{F_1}{F_2} = \frac{(1.05 - x)}{x} \quad ...(ii)$$

From Eqs. (i) and (ii), we get

$$\frac{1}{2} = \frac{(1.05 - x)}{x}$$

$$x = 2.10 - 2x$$

or $3x = 2.10$ or $x = 0.70$ m

∴ The mass m must be suspended at a distance 0.70 m from steel wire A. [1/2]

(ii) Young's modulus $(Y) = \dfrac{\text{Stress}}{\text{Strain}}$

∴ $$\text{Strain} = \frac{\text{Stress}}{Y} = \frac{F/A}{Y}$$

For steel wire A, $(\text{Strain})_{\text{steel}} = \dfrac{F_1}{A_1 Y_1}$ [1/2]

For aluminium wire B,

$$(\text{Strain})_{\text{Al}} = \frac{F_2}{A_2 Y_2}$$

When equal strains are produced in both wires, then

$$\frac{F_1}{A_1 Y_1} = \frac{F_2}{A_2 Y_2} \quad [1/2]$$

or $$\frac{F_1}{F_2} = \frac{A_1 Y_1}{A_2 Y_2} \quad ...(iii)$$

∴ From Eqs. (ii) and (iii), we get

$$\frac{(1.05 - x)}{x} = \frac{A_1 Y_2}{A_2 Y_2} \quad [1/2]$$

$$= \frac{1 \times 10^{-6}}{2 \times 10^{-6}} \times \frac{2 \times 10^{11}}{7 \times 10^{10}}$$

$$\frac{(1.05 - x)}{x} = \frac{10}{7}$$

$$10x = 7.35 - 7x \Rightarrow 17x = 7.35$$

or $$x = \frac{7.35}{17}$$

$$x = 0.43 \text{ m}$$

∴ The mass m must be suspended at a distance 0.43 m from the steel with A. [1/2]

22. $l = 10$ m, $\rho = 1.5 \times 10^3$ kg/m^3

$Y = 5 \times 10^6$ N/m^2

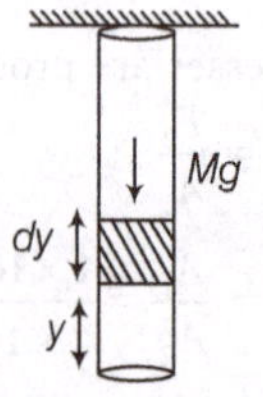

[1]

We know, $Y = \dfrac{Fl}{A \Delta l}$

Efficient force = Mg

Consider a small length dy at a distance y from free end. The length above this, $(l - y)$ will experience a force of

$$F_{dy} = \frac{M}{l}(dy).gdy \quad [1]$$

∴ Extension $dl = \dfrac{Fl}{AY}$

$$\Rightarrow \quad dl = \frac{(l-y)}{AY} \cdot \frac{M}{l} gdy = \frac{Mg}{lAY}(l-y)dy \quad [1]$$

Net extension due to its own weight $= \int dl$

$$= \frac{Mg}{AYl}\int_0^l (l-y)dy = \frac{Mg}{lAY}\left[ly - \frac{y^2}{2}\right]_0^l = \frac{Mgl}{2AY}$$

$$\text{Net extension} = \frac{Mgl}{2AY} = \frac{Mgl^2}{2YV} = \frac{\rho g l^2}{2Y}$$

$$\text{Extension of rubber string} = \frac{1.5 \times 10^3 \times 10 \times 10^2}{2 \times 5 \times 10^6} = 0.15 \text{ m} \quad [1]$$

Breaking stress for a metal $= 7.8 \times 10^9$ N/m^2

Density $= 7.8 \times 10^3$ kg/m^3.

$$\text{Stress} = \frac{\text{Force}}{\text{Area}} = \frac{Mg}{A} = \frac{Mgl}{Al} = \frac{Mgl}{\text{Volume}} = \rho g l$$

If $\rho gl >$ Breaking stress, the wire will break.

or $$l \le \frac{\text{Breaking stress}}{\rho g}$$

∴ $$l \le \frac{7.8 \times 10^9}{\rho g}, \; l \le \frac{7.8 \times 10^9}{7.8 \times 10^3 \times 10}$$

i.e. $$l \le 10^5 \text{ m}$$

Maximum length of wire $= 10^5$ m [1]

23. Depth $(h) = 11$ km $= 11 \times 10^3$ m

Pressure at the bottom of the trench $(p) = 1.1 \times 10^8$ Pa

Initial volume of the ball $(V) = 0.32$ m^3

Bulk modulus of steel $(B) = 1.6 \times 10^{11}$ N/m^2

$$\text{Bulk modulus of steel } (B) = \frac{p}{(\Delta V/V)} = \frac{pV}{\Delta V} \quad [1/2]$$

$$\Delta V = \frac{pV}{B} = \frac{1.1 \times 10^8 \times 0.32}{1.6 \times 10^{11}} \quad [1]$$

$$\Delta V = 2.2 \times 10^{-4} \text{ m}^3 \quad [1/2]$$

24. Bulk modulus of rubber $(B) = 9.8 \times 10^8$ N/m^2

Density of seawater $(\rho) = 10^3$ kg/m^3

Percentage decrease in volume,

$$\left(\frac{\Delta V}{V} \times 100\right) = 0.1 \text{ or } \frac{\Delta V}{V} = \frac{0.1}{100} \quad [1/2]$$

or $$\frac{\Delta V}{V} = \frac{1}{1000}$$

Let the rubber ball be taken up to depth h.

∵ Change in pressure $(p) = h\rho g$

$\therefore$ Bulk modulus $(B) = \dfrac{p}{(\Delta V/V)} = \dfrac{h\rho g}{(\Delta V/V)}$ [1/2]

or $h = \dfrac{B \times (\Delta V/V)}{\rho g} = \dfrac{9.8 \times 10^8 \times \dfrac{1}{1000}}{10^3 \times 9.8} = 100\text{ m}$ [1]

25.

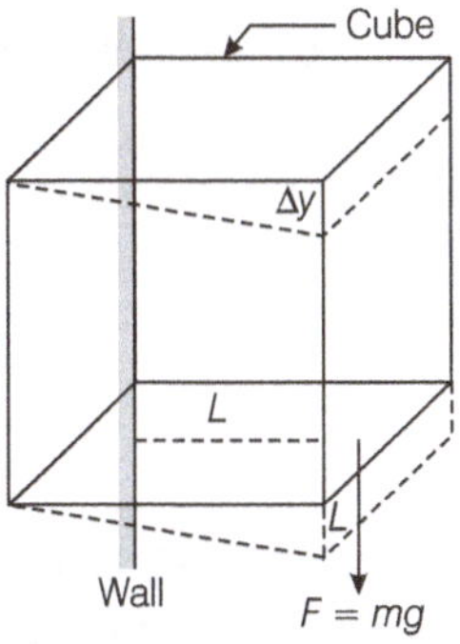

Given, side of a cube $(l) = 10\text{ cm} = 0.1\text{ m}$

Area of its each face $(A) = l^2 = (0.1)^2 = 0.01\text{ m}^2$ [1/2]

Load $(m) = 100\text{ kg}$

Tangential force acting on one face of the cube,

$F = mg = 100 \times 9.8 = 980\text{ N}$ [1/2]

Shear stress acting on this face $= \dfrac{F}{A} = \dfrac{980}{0.01}\text{ N/m}^2$

$= 9.8 \times 10^4\text{ N/m}^2$ [1]

Shear modulus of aluminium $(\eta) = 25\text{ GPa}$

$= 25 \times 10^9\text{ N/m}^2$

Shear modulus $(\eta) = \dfrac{\text{Shearing stress}}{\text{Shearing strain}}$ [1/2]

or shearing strain $\left(\dfrac{\Delta L}{L}\right) = \dfrac{\text{Shearing stress}}{\text{Shear modulus}}$

or $\Delta L = \dfrac{\text{Shearing stress}}{\text{Shear modulus}} \times L = \dfrac{9.8 \times 10^4}{25 \times 10^9} \times 0.1$ [1½]

$= 0.0392 \times 10^{-5}\text{ m} = 3.92 \times 10^{-7}\text{ m}$ [1]

26. Here, $l = 4.5\text{ m}$; $D = 6\text{ mm} = 6 \times 10^{-3}\text{ m}$, $F = Mg = 100\text{ N}$,

$Y = 4.8 \times 10^{11}\text{ N/m}^2$; $\Delta l = ?$; $\Delta D = ?$

$Y = \dfrac{F}{(\pi D^2/4)} \times \dfrac{l}{\Delta l}$ [1]

or $\Delta l = \dfrac{4Fl}{\pi D^2 Y} = \dfrac{4 \times 100 \times 4.5}{3.14 \times (6 \times 10^{-3})^2 \times (4.8 \times 10^{11})}$

$= 3.315 \times 10^{-5}\text{ m}$

Given, poisson's ratio is 0.2, so

$\sigma = \dfrac{\Delta D/D}{\Delta l/l}$ (in magnitude) [1]

or $\Delta D = \sigma \dfrac{\Delta l}{l} \times D = 0.2 \times \dfrac{(3.315 \times 10^{-5})}{4.5} \times (6 \times 10^{-3})$

$= 8.84 \times 10^{-9}\text{ m}$ [1]

27. Given, each side of cube $(l) = 10\text{ cm} = 0.1\text{ m}$

Hydraulic pressure $(p) = 7 \times 10^6\text{ Pa}$ [1/2]

Bulk modulus for copper $(B) = 140 \times 10^9\text{ Pa}$

Volume contraction $(\Delta V) = ?$ [1/2]

Volume of the cube $(V) = l^3 = (0.1)^3 = 1 \times 10^{-3}\text{ m}^3$ [1/2]

Bulk modulus for copper $(B) = \dfrac{p}{\Delta V/V} = \dfrac{pV}{\Delta V}$ [1/2]

or $\Delta V = \dfrac{pV}{B}$ [1/2]

$\Delta V = \dfrac{7 \times 10^6 \times 1 \times 10^{-3}}{140 \times 10^9}$

$= \dfrac{1}{20} \times 10^{-6}\text{ m}^3$

$= 0.05 \times 10^{-6}\text{ m}^3 = 5 \times 10^{-8}\text{ m}^3$ [1/2]

28. When a load w is suspended from a stretched wire of length l, then depression at the mid-point is given by

$$\delta = \frac{wl^3}{12\pi r^4 Y}$$

where, r = radius of the wire,
Y = Young's modulus of the material of the wire.

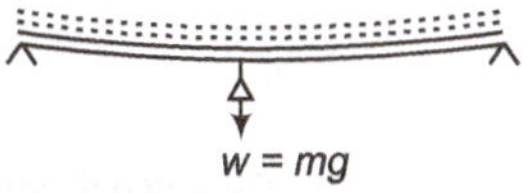

Given, length $(l) = 1\text{ m}$

Area of cross-section $(A) = 0.5 \times 10^{-2}\text{ cm}^2$ [1/2]

$= 0.5 \times 10^{-6}\text{ m}^2$

Mass $(m) = 100\text{ g} = 0.1\text{ kg}$

$\therefore$ Load $(w) = mg = 0.1 \times 9.8\text{ N} = 0.98\text{ N}$ [1/2]

Young's modulus for steel $(Y) = 2 \times 10^{11}\text{ Pa}$

Area $(A) = \pi r^2$ or $r^2 = \dfrac{A}{\pi} = \dfrac{0.5 \times 10^{-6}}{\pi}$ [1/2]

Depression in a wire when a load is suspended at its centre

$\delta = \dfrac{wl^3}{12\pi r^4 Y} = \dfrac{0.98 \times (1)^3}{12\pi \times \left(\dfrac{0.5 \times 10^{-6}}{\pi}\right)^2 \times 2 \times 10^{11}}$ [1]

$\delta = \dfrac{0.98 \times \pi}{12 \times 0.25 \times 2 \times 10^{-1}}$

$= 5.12\text{ m}$ [1/2]

Summary

- Materials having a definite shape and volume are known as **solids** or rigid bodies.
- A body that returns to its original shape and size on the removal of deforming force is called elastic body and this property is called **elasticity**.
- If a body does not show any tendency to regain its original shape and size even after the removal of deforming force are called plastic body and this property is called **plasticity**.
- The internal restoring force acting per unit area of a deformed force is called **stress**.

  i.e $$\text{Stress} = \frac{F}{A}$$

  SI unit of stress is N/m^2 or pascal
- The restoring forces per unit area act perpendicular to the surface of the body are called **normal forces**.
- When there is an increase in the length or the extension of the body in the direction of the force applied then it is called **tensile stress**.
- When there is a decrease in the length or the compression of the body due to the deforming force applied normally on the body then it is called **compressive stress.**
- If a body is subjected to a uniform force from all sides, then the corresponding stress is called **bulk stress** or **hydraulic stress** or volumetric stress.
- **Strain** is defined as the ratio of change in configuration to the original configuration.
- The materials which can be elastically stretched to large values of strain are called **elastomers**.
- **Longitudinal strain** (ε) is the change in length per unit original length, when the body is deformed by external forces,

  i.e. $$\varepsilon = \frac{\Delta L}{L}$$
- **Volumetric strain** is the change in volume per unit original volume, when the body is deformed by external forces. i.e. $\varepsilon = \frac{\Delta V}{V}$.
- **Shearing strain** is the deforming forces produce a change in the shape of the body, i.e. $\theta = \tan\theta = \frac{\Delta L}{L}$.
- The material which have large plastic range of extension are called **ductile material.**
- The materials which have very small range of plastic extension are called **brittle material.**
- Within elastic limit, the stress developed is directly proportional to the strain produced in a body. This is **Hooke's law.**
- From **Hooke's law**, stress ∝ strain.

  ⇒ $$\text{Stress} = E \times \text{Strain}, \text{ here } E \text{ is modulus of elasticity.}$$
- The ratio of longitudinal stress (σ) to the longitudinal strain (ε) within the elastic limit is called **Young's modulus** (Y).

  i.e. $$Y = \frac{\sigma}{\varepsilon}$$
- Ratio of normal stress to the volumetric strain within the elastic limit is called **Bulk modulus** (B),

  i.e. $B = \frac{F}{A} \Big/ \frac{\Delta V}{V} = \frac{1}{k}$, where k = compressibility
- The ratio of tangential stress to the shear strain within elastic limit is called shear modulus or **modulus of rigidity** (η).

  i.e. $$\eta = \frac{F}{A} \cdot \frac{L}{\Delta L}$$
- The ratio of lateral strain to the longitudinal strain within the elastic limit it is called **Poisson's ratio.**
- Potential energy stored in a stretched wire $= \frac{1}{2}$ stress × strain × volume.

Chapter Practice

Multiple Choice Questions

1 Mark

1 The maximum load a wire can withstand without breaking, when its length is reduced to half of its original length, will
(a) be double (b) be half
(c) be four times (d) remains same

2 A spring is stretched by applying a load to its free end. The strain produced in the spring is
(a) volumetric (b) shear
(c) longitudinal and shear (d) longitudinal

3 A rigid bar of mass M is supported symmetrically by three wires each of length l. Those at each end are of copper and the middle one is of iron. The ratio of their diameters, if each is to have the same tension, is equal to

(a) $Y_{\text{copper}} / Y_{\text{iron}}$ (b) $\sqrt{\dfrac{Y_{\text{iron}}}{Y_{\text{copper}}}}$

(c) $\dfrac{Y^2_{\text{iron}}}{Y^2_{\text{copper}}}$ (d) $\dfrac{Y_{\text{iron}}}{Y_{\text{copper}}}$

4. For an ideal liquid,
(a) the bulk modulus is infinite
(b) the bulk modulus is zero
(c) the shear modulus is infinite
(d) the shear modulus is zero

5. A copper and a steel wire of the same diameter are connected end to end. A deforming force F is applied to this composite wire which causes a total elongation of 1 cm. The two wires will have
(a) the same stress (b) different stress
(c) the same strain (d) different strain

Assertion and Reason

Directions (Q. Nos. 6-10) *In the following questions, two statements are given- one labelled Assertion (A) and the other labelled Reason (R). Select the correct answer to these questions from the codes (a), (b), (c) and (d) as given below*

(a) Both Assertion and Reason are true and Reason is the correct explanation of Assertion.
(b) Both Assertion and Reason are true but Reason is not the correct explanation of Assertion.
(c) Assertion is true but Reason is false.
(d) Assertion is false but Reason is true.

6. **Assertion (A)** Stress is the internal force per unit area of a body.

Reason (R) Rubber is less elastic than steel.

7. **Assertion (A)** When a solid is deformed, the atoms or molecules are displaced from their equilibrium position.
Reason (R) Due to change in interatomic spacing, intermolecular/interatomic forces arise.

8. **Assertion (A)** The restoring force F, on a stretched string for extension x is related to potential energy U as

$$F = \frac{-dU}{dx}$$

Reason (R) $F = -kx$ and $U = (1/2)kx^2$, where k is a spring constant for the given stretched string.

9. **Assertion (A)** The strain produced by a hydraulic pressure is volumetric in nature.
Reason (R) It is a ratio of change in volume (ΔV) to the original volume (V).

10. **Assertion (A)** Young's modulus for a perfectly plastic body is zero.

Reason (R) For a perfectly plastic body, restoring force is zero.

Very Short Answer Type Questions

1 Mark

11 What is rigidity modulus?

12 Which of the three types of elasticity (Y, K and η) is possessed by all the three states of matter (solid, liquid and gas)?

13 What do you understand by elastic after effect?

14 Why do springs become slack after a prolonged use?

15 What is the work done in streching a wire?

Short Answer Type I Questions

(2 Marks)

16 Why is a solid ductile or brittle? Explain on the basis of stress *versus* strain graph.

17 Two wire of same length and material but of different radii are suspended from a rigid support. Both carry the same load. With the stress, strain and extension in them be same or different?

Short Answer Type II Question

(3 Marks)

18 The length of a metallic wire is L_1, when the tension in the wire is T_1; and is L_2, when the tension is T_2. Find the original length of the wire.

Case Based Questions

Directions (Q. No. 19) *These questions are case study based questions. Read the following paragraph and answer the questions.*

19 When a bar of cross-section A is subjected to equal and opposite tensile forces at its ends, then a restoring force equal to the applied force normal to its cross-section comes into existence. This restoring force per unit area of cross-section is known as tensile stress. While when the deforming force acts tangentially to the surface, then this tangential force applied per unit area of cross-section is known as tangential stress. Consider a plane section of the bar whose normal makes an angle θ with the axis of the bar.

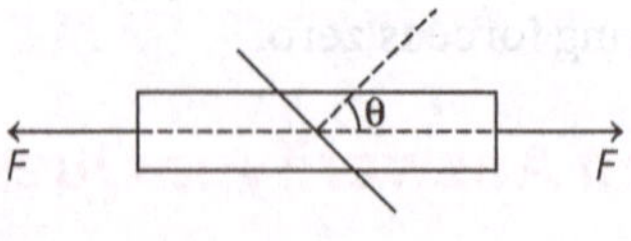

(i) Which of the following property of the bar does not change due to this force?
(a) Area (b) Volume
(c) Shape (d) Size

(ii) What is the tensile stress on this plane?
(a) $(F/A)\cos^2\theta$ (b) F/A
(c) $(F/A)\tan\theta$ (d) $(F/A)\sec^2\theta$

(iii) What is the shearing stress on this plane?
(a) $\frac{F}{2A}\sin 2\theta$ (b) $\frac{F}{A}\cos 2\theta$
(c) $\frac{F}{2A}\cos^2\theta$ (d) $\frac{F}{4A^2}$

(iv) For what value of θ is the tensile stress maximum?
(a) 0° (b) 90°
(c) 45° (d) 30°

(v) For what value of θ is the shearing stress maximum?
(a) 45° (b) 30°
(c) 90° (d) 60°

Numerical Problems

20 A wire of length 50 cm and cross-sectional area 1 mm^2 is made of a material of Young's modulus 2×10^{10} N/m^2. How much work is done in stretching the wire through 1 mm? [1 M]

21 A 5 cm cube has its upper face displaced by 0.2 cm by a tangential force of 8 N. Calculate the shearing strain, shearing stress and modulus of rigidity of the material of cube. [2 M]

Answers

1 (*d*) We know that,

$$\text{Breaking stress} = \frac{\text{Breaking force}}{\text{Area of cross - section}}$$

When length of the wire changes, area of cross-section remains same.

Hence, breaking force will be same when length changes.

2 (*c*) Consider the diagram where a spring is stretched by applying a load to its free end. Clearly the length and shape of the spring changes.

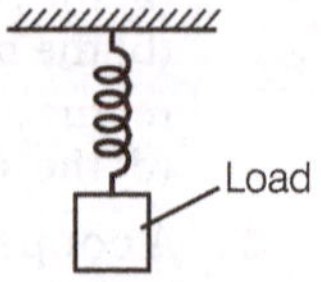

The change in length corresponds to longitudinal strain and change in shape corresponds to shearing strain.

3 (*b*) We know that Young's modulus

$$Y = \frac{\text{Stress}}{\text{Strain}} = \frac{F/A}{\Delta L/L} = F/A \times \frac{L}{\Delta L}$$

$$= \frac{F}{\pi(D/2)^2} \times \frac{L}{\Delta L} = \frac{4FL}{\pi D^2 \Delta L}$$

$$\Rightarrow D^2 = \frac{4FL}{\pi \Delta L Y} \Rightarrow D = \sqrt{\frac{4FL}{\pi \Delta L Y}}$$

As F and $\frac{L}{\Delta L}$ are constants.

Hence, $D \propto \sqrt{\frac{1}{Y}}$

Now, we can find ratio as $\frac{D_{copper}}{D_{iron}} = \sqrt{\frac{Y_{iron}}{Y_{copper}}}$

4 (*a, d*) As an ideal liquid is not compressible.
Hence, change in volume, $\Delta V = 0$

$$\text{Bulk modulus } B = \frac{\text{Stress}}{\text{Volume strain}} = \frac{F/A}{\Delta V/V} = \frac{F}{A} \times \frac{V}{\Delta V}$$
$$= \infty$$

$$\text{Compressibility, } K = \frac{1}{B} = \frac{1}{\infty} = 0$$

As there is no tangential (viscous) force exists in case of an ideal fluid, hence, shear modulus = 0.

5 (*a, d*) Consider the diagram where a deforming force F is applied to the combination.

$$\text{For steel wire, } Y_{\text{steel}} = \frac{\text{Stress}}{\text{Strain}} = \frac{F/A}{\text{Strain}}$$

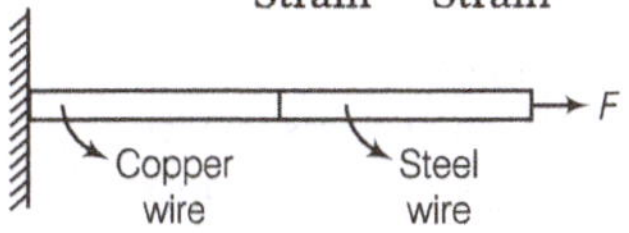

where F is tension in each wire and A is cross-section area of each wires.

As F and A are same for both the wire, hence, stress will be same for both the wire.

$$(\text{Strain})_{\text{steel}} = \frac{\text{Stress}}{Y_{\text{steel}}}, (\text{Strain})_{\text{copper}} = \frac{\text{Stress}}{Y_{\text{copper}}}$$

As, $Y_{\text{steel}} \neq Y_{\text{copper}}$

Hence, the two wires will have differents strain.

6 (*b*) Stress is defined as internal force per unit area of a body. Also, rubber is less elastic than steel because restoring force is less for rubber than steel.

7 (*a*) When a solid is deformed, the atoms or molecules are displaced from their equilibrium positions causing a change in the inter atomic (or inter molecular distances).

8 (*a*) When a string is stretched for an extension x, then stored potential energy U is given by

$$F = -\frac{dU}{dx} \text{ and } U = \frac{1}{2}kx^2$$

where, k is a spring constant.

9 (*b*) The strain produced by a hydraulic pressure is called volume strain as pressure creates a normal force on every point and is defined as the ratio of change in volume (ΔV) to the original volume (V).

i.e., volume strain $= \dfrac{\Delta V}{V}$

10 (*a*) Young's modulus of a material, $Y = \dfrac{\text{Stress}}{\text{Strain}}$

$$\therefore \quad \text{Stress} = \frac{\text{Restoring force}}{\text{Area}}$$

As, restoring force is zero.

$$\therefore \quad Y = 0$$

11 Refer to text on page 276 (Modulus of rigidity or Shear modulus).

12 The volume elasticity (K) is possessed by all the three states of the matter.

13 Refer to text on page 278 (Elastic after effect).

14 The elasticity of the material decreases due to repeated deformation in the long run. The elastic limit also decreases and springs become deformed permanently.

15 Work done in stretching a wire is

$$= \frac{1}{2} \times \text{stress} \times \text{strain} \times \text{volume}$$

or $$= \frac{1}{2} \times Y \times (\text{strain})^2 \times \text{volume}$$

16 In the stress *versus* strain graph for a wire, the portion of graph between elastic limit and breaking point is called plastic region. A solid is said to be more ductile, if the plastic region of the graph is longer and brittle, if the plastic region is shorter. [2]

17 Stress $= \dfrac{F}{A} = \dfrac{F}{\pi r^2}$

Since, the two wires carry the same load (F) but are of different radii, the stress in the two wires will be different.

Now, extension, $l = \dfrac{F \times L}{A \times Y} = \dfrac{F \times L}{\pi r^2 \times Y}$ [1]

Since, for the two wires, F, L and Y are same but r is different, the extension in the two wires will be different.

Also, strain, $\dfrac{l}{L} = \dfrac{F}{A \times Y} = \dfrac{F}{\pi r^2 \times Y}$

Obviously, strain will also be different in two wires. [1]

18 Let L and a be the original length and the area of cross-section of the wire. If on applying a force F, extension produced is l, then

$$Y = \frac{F/a}{l/L} = \frac{FL}{al}$$

In the first case, $F = T_1$ and $l = L_1 - L$

$$\therefore \quad Y = \frac{T_1 L}{a(L_1 - L)} \quad \text{...(i)}$$

In the second case, $F = T_2$ and $l = L_2 - L$

$$\therefore \quad Y = \frac{T_2 L}{a(L_2 - L)} \quad \text{...(ii)}$$ [1½]

From Eqs. (i) and (ii), we get

$$\frac{T_1 L}{a(L_1 - L)} = \frac{T_2 L}{a(L_2 - L)}$$

or $$T_1(L_2 - L) = T_2(L_1 - L)$$

or $$L(T_2 - T_1) = T_2 L_1 - T_1 L_2 \text{ or } L = \frac{T_2 L_1 - T_1 L_2}{T_2 - T_1}$$ [1½]

19 (i) (*b*) This force produces a change in shape of the body without change in volume.

(ii) (*a*) The resolved part of F along the normal is the tensile force on this plane and the resolved part parallel to the plane is the shearing force on the plane.

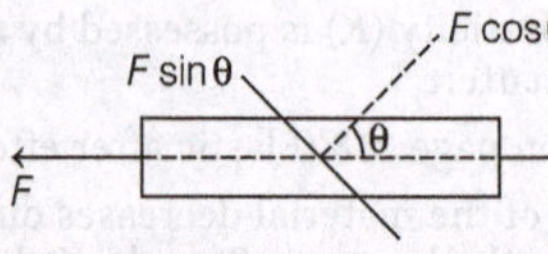

$\because$ Area of plane section = $A \sec\theta$

Tensile stress

$$= \frac{\text{Force}}{\text{Area}} = \frac{F\cos\theta}{A\sec\theta} = \frac{F}{A}\cos^2\theta \qquad \left(\because \sec\theta = \frac{1}{\cos\theta}\right)$$

(iii) (a) Shearing stress $= \frac{\text{Force}}{\text{Area}} = \frac{F\sin\theta}{A\sec\theta}$

$$= \frac{F}{A}\sin\theta\cos\theta = \frac{F}{2A}\sin 2\theta$$

(iv) (a) Tensile stress will be maximum when $\cos^2\theta$ is maximum, i.e. $\cos\theta = 1$ or $\theta = 0°$.

(v) (a) Shearing stress will be maximum when $\sin 2\theta$ is maximum, i.e. $\sin 2\theta = 1$ or $2\theta = 90°$ or $\theta = 45°$.

20 $\therefore F = \frac{YA\Delta l}{l} = \frac{2\times10^{10}\times10^{-6}\times10^{-3}}{0.5}$

Work done $= \left(\frac{1}{2}F\right)\Delta l = \left(\frac{1}{2}\times40\right)\times10^{-3}$

$= 2\times10^{-2}$ [1/2]

Force is taken as $F/2$, because when extension is zero, force is zero and when it is l, force is F.

Hence, average force $= \frac{F}{2}$. [1/2]

21 Given, $l = 5\text{ cm} = 5\times10^{-2}\text{ m}$, $\Delta l = 0.2\text{ cm} = 0.2\times10^{-2}\text{ m}$, $F = 8\text{ N}$

Shearing strain $= \frac{\Delta l}{l} = \frac{0.2}{5} = 0.04$ [1/2]

Shearing stress $= \frac{F}{l\times l} = \frac{8}{(5\times10^{-2})^2} = 3200\text{ N/m}^2$ [1/2]

Modulus of rigidity,

$$\eta = \frac{\text{Shearing stress}}{\text{Shearing strain}} = \frac{3200}{0.04} = 8\times10^4\text{ N/m}^2$$ [1]

CHAPTER

09

Mechanical Properties of Fluids

Liquids and gases are collectively known as **fluids.** Fluid flows under the action of an applied force as fluids do not withstand shearing stress.

In this chapter, we shall study hydrostatics and hydrodynamics. The study of fluids at rest is known as **hydrostatics** or **fluid statics.** The study of fluids in motion is named as **hydrodynamics** or **fluid dynamics.**

- Hydrostatics
- Hydrodynamics
- Surface Tension and Surface Energy

TOPIC 01 Hydrostatics

The key property of fluids is that they offer very little resistance to shear stress; their shape changes by application of very small shear stress.

Fluid Thrust

The molecules of a fluid kept in a container are in random motion due to their thermal velocities. So, they constantly collide with the walls of the container and rebounding from them, suffering a change in momentum normal to the colliding walls due to which some normal change in momentum is transferred to the walls, thus a force is exerted on the walls of the container.

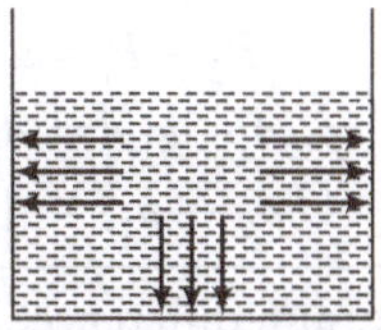

Liquid in a container is exerting thrust

The total normal force exerted by a fluid at rest on a given surface in contact with it, is called thrust of the fluid on that surface.

Fluid Pressure

The pressure of liquid at a point is the thrust (or normal force) exerted by the liquid at rest per unit area around that point.

If the total force F acts normally over a flat area A, then, the pressure is

$$p = \frac{\text{thrust}}{\text{area}} \quad \text{or} \quad \boxed{\text{Pressure, } p = \frac{F}{A}}$$

The unit of pressure is **dyne/cm^2** in CGS system and **N/m^2** in SI system and dimensional formula of pressure is $[ML^{-1}T^{-2}]$.

Pressure of 1 N/m^2 is called **1 pascal** in the honour of the French scientist **Blaise Pascal** (1623-1662) who carried out the pioneering studies on fluid pressure.

$$1\,\text{Pa (or } 1\,\text{N/m}^2) = 10\,\text{dyne/cm}^2 = 10^{-5}\,\text{bar}$$

The another common unit of pressure is atmosphere (atm). 1 atm is defined as the pressure exerted by the atmosphere at sea level.

$$1\,\text{atm} = 1.013 \times 10^5\,\text{Pa} = 760\,\text{torr} = 1.013\,\text{bar}$$

Pressure is a scalar quantity, because liquid pressure at a particular point in liquid has same magnitude in all directions. This shows that a definite direction is not associated with liquid pressure.

Example 1 The two thigh bones (femurs), each of cross-sectional area 10 cm^2 support the upper part of a human body of mass 40 kg. Estimate the average pressure sustained by the femurs. **NCERT**

Sol. Given, $A = 20 \times 10^{-4}\,\text{m}^2$

Weight of body acting vertically downwards = Force of bones

Force on bones, $F = 40\,\text{kg-wt} = 400\,\text{N}$ $[\because g = 10\,\text{m/s}^2]$

$$p_{av} = \frac{F}{A} = \frac{400}{20 \times 10^{-4}} = 2 \times 10^5\,\text{N/m}^2$$

Example 2 Consider a spring having spring constant of 81.75 N/m of pressure measuring device. A force acting on the piston compresses the spring downward and the area of the piston is 3m^2. Find out the compression in the spring, if the upthrust force exerted by the fluid on the piston is 12 N.

Sol. As the force acting on the piston compresses the spring. This force will be balanced by the force acting upward by the fluid known as **upthrust force**.

$$\therefore \quad p = \frac{F}{A} = \frac{kx}{A}$$

Given, $F = 12\,\text{N}$, $A = 3\text{m}^2$ and $k = 81.75\,\text{N/m}$

From $F = kx$

$$\Rightarrow \quad x = \frac{F}{k} = \frac{12}{81.75}$$

$$x = 0.146\,\text{m}$$

Hence, compression in the spring is $x = 14.6\,\text{cm}$

Pressure Exerted by a Liquid Column

Consider a fluid at rest having density ρ contained in a cylindrical vessel as shown in figure. Let the two points A and B separated by a vertical distance h.

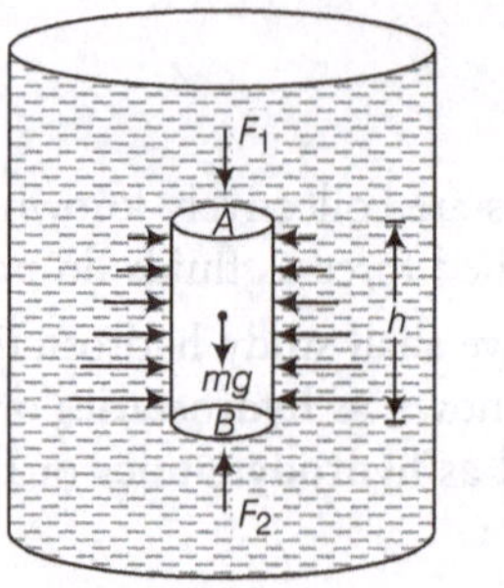

Fluid under gravity

Now, we consider an imaginary cylinder of fluid of cross-sectional area a, such that points A and B lie on its upper and lower circular faces, respectively. Then, weight of fluid cylinder acting downwards,

$$w = m \times g = \text{volume} \times \text{density} \times g = Ah\rho g$$

where, $V = A \times h$

As the fluid is at rest, the resultant horizontal forces should be zero and the resultant vertical forces should balance the weight of the element.

$\therefore$ Net downward force = net upward force

$$F_1 + w = F_2$$

where, F_1 is the force acting downwards at the top and F_2 is the force acting upward at the bottom.

$$F_2 - F_1 = w$$

$$p_2 A - p_1 A = Ah\rho g$$

$$A(p_2 - p_1) = A(h\rho g)$$

$$\boxed{\text{Pressure difference, } p_2 - p_1 = h\rho g}$$

Hence, the pressure difference depends on the vertical height of liquid column, (i.e. distance between point A and point B), density of the fluid and the acceleration due to gravity.

If point A is shifted to the fluid surface, which is open to the atmosphere, then replace p_1 by atmospheric pressure p_a and p_2 by p, we get

$$\text{Pressure, } p = p_a + h\rho g$$

Thus, the pressure p at depth below the surface of a liquid open to the atmosphere is greater than atmospheric pressure by an amount ρgh. This excess of pressure at depth h in liquid $p - p_a = h\rho g$, i.e. called **gauge pressure** at point B, while point A is at the liquid surface.

Thus, gauge pressure at a point in a fluid is the difference of total pressure at that point and atmospheric pressure.

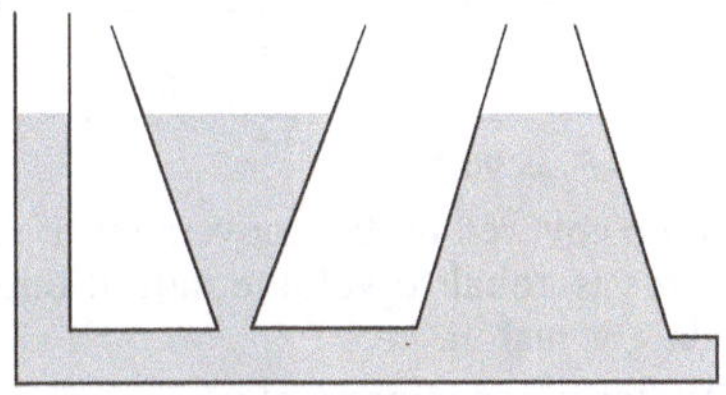

Three vessels A, B and C containing different amounts of liquids but pressure is same at bottom of each of them

Hence, the pressure exerted by a liquid depends only on the height of fluid column and is independent of the shape of the containing vessel, which is quite unexpected, hence it is known as hydrostatic paradox.

Note Fluid pressure is zero in gravity free regions.

Example 3 What is the pressure on a swimmer 10 m below the surface of a lake? **NCERT**

Sol. Here, $h = 10\,\text{m}$ and $\rho = 1000\,\text{kg/m}^3$

$$g = 10\,\text{m/s}^2$$

$$p = p_a + \rho gh$$

$$= 1.01\times10^5\ \text{Pa} + 1000\ \text{kg/m}^3 \times 10\ \text{m/s}^2 \times 10\ \text{m}$$

$$= 2.01\times10^5\,\text{Pa}$$

$$\simeq 2\text{atm}$$

Example 4 At a depth 1000 m in an ocean

(i) What is the absolute pressure?

(ii) What is the gauge pressure?

(iii) Find the force acting on the window of area 20 cm × 20 cm of a submarine at this depth, the interior of which is maintained at sea-level atmospheric pressure. (The density of sea water is $1.03\times10^3\,\text{kgm}^{-3}$, $g = 10\ \text{ms}^{-2}$) **NCERT**

Sol. Given, $h = 1000$ m and $\rho = 1.03\times10^3\ \text{kg/m}^3$

We know, $p = p_a + \rho gh$

$$p = 1.01\times10^5 + 1.03\times10^3 \times 10\times1000$$

$$p = 104.01\times10^5\ \text{Pa} \approx 104\ \text{atm}$$

Now, $p_g = p - p_a$

$$p_g = 104\ \text{atm} - 1\text{atm}$$

$$p_a = 1\ \text{atm}$$

$\because$ $p_g = 103\ \text{atm}$

The pressure outside the submarine while pressure inside, it is p_a.

Given, $A = 400\ \text{cm}^2 = 0.04\ \text{m}^2$.

The net pressure acting on the window is gauge pressure, then $p_g = \dfrac{F}{A} \Rightarrow F = p_g A$

or $F = 103\times10^5 \times 0.04 = 4.12\times10^5$ N

Pascal's Law

The French scientist **Blaise Pascal** observed that *pressure in* a fluid at rest is the same at all points if they are at same height. This is known as **Pascal's law.**

Proof of Pascal's Law

It can be proved by using two principles as given below:

(i) The force on any layer of a fluid at rest is normal to the layer.

(ii) Newton's first law of motion

In given figure, consider an element in the interior of a fluid at rest. This element ABC-DEF is in the form of a right angled prism. This prismatic element is very small so that every part of it can be considered at the same depth from the liquid surface and therefore, the effect of the gravity is the same at all these points.

Let we extend this element for our clarification. The forces on this element are those exerted by the rest of the fluid and they must be normal to the surfaces of the element as discussed earlier. Suppose, the fluid exert pressures p_a, p_b and p_c on the faces $BEFC$, $ADFC$ and $ADEB$, respectively, of this element and the corresponding normal forces on these faces are F_a, F_b and F_c.

Let A_a, A_b and A_c be the respective areas of the three faces.

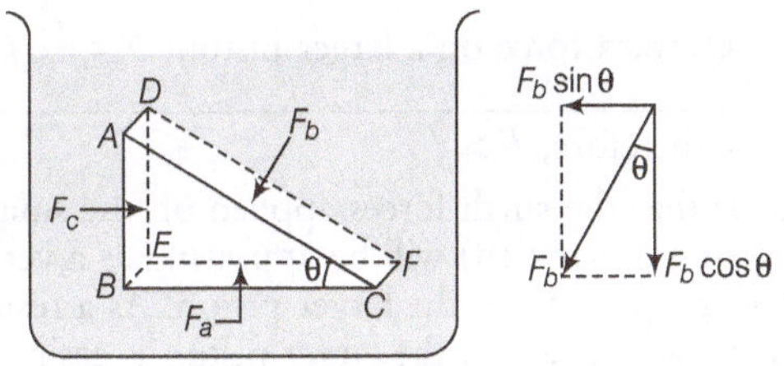

Proof of Pascal's law

In right triangle ABC, $\angle ACB = \theta$

Along horizontal direction, $F_b \sin\theta = F_c$

Along vertical direction, $F_b \cos\theta = F_a$ ...(i)

From the geometry, we have

$A_b \sin\theta = A_c$ and $A_b \cos\theta = A_a$ ...(ii)

From the above equations, we have

$$\frac{F_b \sin\theta}{A_b \sin\theta} = \frac{F_c}{A_c} \text{ and } \frac{F_b \cos\theta}{A_b \cos\theta} = \frac{F_a}{A_a}$$

$$\therefore \quad \frac{F_a}{A_a} = \frac{F_b}{A_b} = \frac{F_c}{A_c}$$

$$\Rightarrow \quad \boxed{p_a = p_b = p_c}$$

Hence, the pressure exerted by the fluid at rest on a body in the fluid is same in all directions. Thus, pressure is not a vector quantity because no direction can be assigned to it.

Applications of Pascal's Law

(i) Hydraulic Lift

Hydraulic lift is an application of Pascal's law. It is used to lift heavy loads. It is a force multiplier.

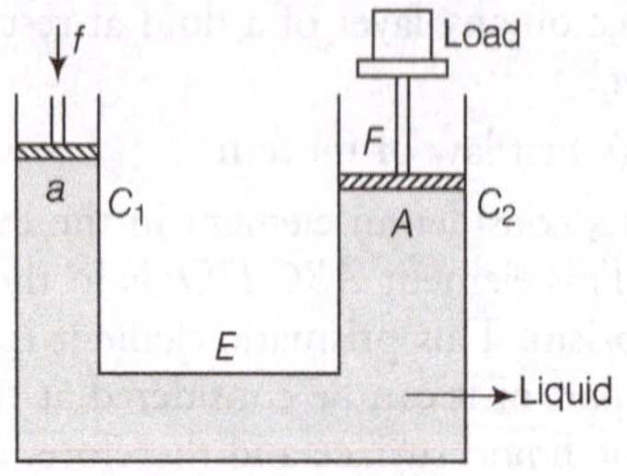

Hydraulic lift

It consists of two cylinders C_1 and C_2 connected to each other by a pipe E. These cylinders are fitted with water-tight frictionless pistons of different cross-sectional areas. These cylinders and the pipe contain a liquid.

According to Pascal's law, this pressure p is transmitted to the larger piston of cross-sectional area A, then upward force on larger piston C_2 is

$$F = p \times A = \frac{f}{a} \times A = \frac{A}{a} \times f \quad \left[\because p = \frac{f}{a}\right]$$

$$\boxed{\text{Upward force on a larger piston, } F = \frac{A}{a} f}$$

As, $A > a$, therefore, $F > f$.

This shows that the small forces applied on the smaller piston (acting downward) will be appearing as a very large force (acting upward) on the larger piston. As a result of it, a heavy load placed on the larger piston is easily lifted upwards.

Example 5 Two syringes of different cross-sections (without needles) filled with water are connected with a tightly fitted rubber tube. Diameters of the smaller and larger piston are 1.0 cm and 3.0 cm, respectively.

(i) Find the force exerted on the larger piston when a force of 10 N is applied to the smaller piston.

(ii) If the smaller piston is pushed in through 6.0 cm, how much does the larger piston move out? **NCERT**

Sol. (i) Here, $A_1 = \pi\left(\frac{D_1}{2}\right)^2, A_2 = \pi\left(\frac{D_2}{2}\right)^2$

$$A_1 = \pi\left(\frac{3}{2}\times 10^{-2}\right)^2 \text{ m}^2,\ A_2 = \pi\left(\frac{1}{2}\times 10^{-2}\right)^2 \text{ m}^2$$

$\because$ Pressure is transmitted undiminished through water, so,

$$\therefore \quad F_2 = \frac{A_2}{A_1} F_1 = \frac{\pi\left(\frac{3}{2}\times 10^{-2}\right)^2}{\pi\left(\frac{1}{2}\times 10^{-2}\right)^2} \times 10$$

$$\Rightarrow \quad F_2 = 90 \text{ N}$$

(ii) Volume covered by the movement of smaller piston inwards is equal to volume moved outwards due to the larger piston.

$\because$ Water is incompressible

$$\therefore \quad L_1 A_1 = L_2 A_2$$

$$L_2 = \frac{A_1}{A_2} L_1 = \frac{\pi\left(\frac{1}{2}\times 10^{-2}\right)^2}{\pi\left(\frac{3}{2}\times 10^{-2}\right)^2} \times 6 \times 10^{-2}$$

$$L_2 = 0.67 \times 10^{-2} \text{ m} = 0.67 \text{ cm}$$

Atmospheric pressure is common to both pistons and has been ignored.

Example 6 In a car lift compressed air exerts a force F_1 on a small piston having a radius of 5.0 cm. This pressure is transmitted to a second piston of radius 15 cm. If the mass of the car to be lifted to 1350 kg, calculate F_1. What is the pressure necessary to accomplish this task? ($g = 9.8 \text{ ms}^{-2}$). **NCERT**

Sol. Since, the pressure is transmitted undiminished through the fluid, calculate the force F_2 exerting by the car.

Given, $r_1 = 5 \text{ cm} = 0.05 \text{ m}$, $r_2 = 15 \text{cm} = 0.15 \text{ m}$, $m = 1350 \text{ kg}$

$$F_2 = mg = 1350 \times 9.81 \text{ N}$$

As the pressure through air is transmitted equally in all directions, so that the pressure p_1 and p_2 will be same.

$$p_1 = p_2 \quad \Rightarrow \frac{F_1}{A_1} = \frac{F_2}{A_2} \quad \Rightarrow \frac{F_1}{\pi r_1^2} = \frac{F_2}{\pi r_2^2}$$

$$\therefore\ F_1 = F_2 \times \left(\frac{r_1}{r_2}\right)^2 = 1350 \times 9.81 \times \left(\frac{5}{15}\right)^2 \simeq 1.5 \times 10^3 \text{ N}$$

Now, the required air pressure necessary to lift the car can be calculated.

The air pressure p which will produce the force of

$$1.5 \times 10^3 \text{ N is } p = \frac{F_1}{A_1} = \frac{1.5 \times 10^3}{\pi (0.05)^2}$$

$$\Rightarrow \qquad p = 1.9 \times 10^5 \text{ Pa}$$

(ii) Hydraulic Brakes

The working of the hydraulic brakes is also based on the Pascal's law. It consists of a tube T containing brake oil. One end of the tube is connected to the wheel cylinder having two pistons P_1 and P_2. The pistons P_1 and P_2 are connected to the brake shoes S_1 and S_2, respectively and the other end of tube is connected to master cylinder fitted with the piston P.

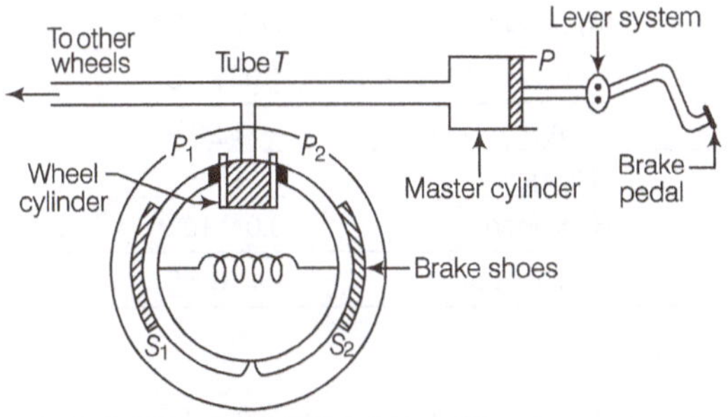

Constructional details of hydraulic brakes

The piston P is connected to the brake pedal through the lever system. The area of cross-section of the wheel cylinder is greater than that of master cylinder. The arrangement is shown in above figure.

Working of Hydraulic Brakes

(i) When the brake pedal is pressed, the lever system operates. The piston P is pushed. The pressure is transmitted to pistons P_1 and P_2 in accordance with Pascal's law.

(ii) The pistons (P_1 and P_2) push the brake shoes away from each other. The brake shoes press against the inner rim of the wheel and retard the motion of the wheel.

(iii) Since, the area of the pistons of the wheel cylinder is greater than the area of piston P, therefore, a small force applied to the brake pedal produces a large thrust on the wheels and hence, the brake becomes operative.

(iv) When the pressure on the brake pedal is released, the brake shoes return to their normal pistons by the action of spring (i.e., it pulls the brake shoes away from the rim) which in turn forces back the oil from wheel cylinder into the master cylinder.

(v) In order to apply equal pressure to all the wheels, the master cylinder is connected to all the wheels of the vehicle through tubes.

(vi) Hence, small force applied to the pedal exerts a much larger force on the wheel drums, which enables the driver to keep the vehicle under control.

Note The total or actual pressure p at a point is called absolute pressure. Gauge pressure is the difference between the actual pressure (or absolute pressure) at a point and the atmospheric pressure, i.e. $p_g = p - p_a = h\rho g$. The gauge pressure is proportional to h.

Example 7 What is the absolute and gauge pressure of the gas above the liquid surface in the tank shown in figure? Density of oil = 820 kg-m^{-3}, density of mercury $= 13.6 \times 10^3 \text{ kgm}^{-3}$.

Given, 1 atm pressure = 1.01×10^5 Pa. **NCERT**

Sol. As the points A and B are at the same level in the mercury column, so $p_A = p_B$

Now, $p_A = p + (1.50 + 1.00) \times 820 \times 9.8$

where, p is the pressure of the gas in the tank.

And $p_B = p' + (1.50 + 0.75) \times 13.6 \times 10^3 \times 9.8$

where, p' is the atmospheric pressure.

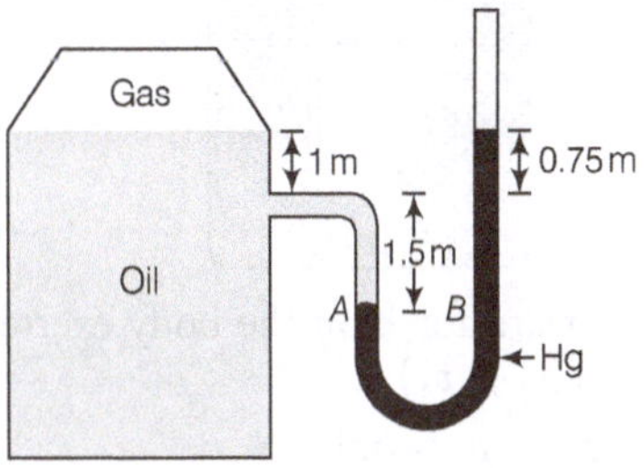

As, $p_A = p_B$

$$p - p' = 2.25 \times 13.6 \times 10^3 \times 9.8 - 2.50 \times 820 \times 9.8$$
$$= 3 \times 10^5 - 0.2 \times 10^5$$
$$= 2.8 \times 10^5 \text{ Pa}$$

$\therefore$ Gauge pressure

= absolute pressure − atmospheric pressure.

$p_g = p - p' = 2.8 \times 10^5$ Pa $\qquad [\because p' = p_a]$

Absolute pressure

= gauge pressure + atmospheric pressure

$p = 2.8 \times 10^5 + 1.01 \times 10^5 = 3.81 \times 10^5$ Pa

Buoyancy

When a body is partially or wholly immersed in a fluid at rest, it displaces the fluid. The displaced fluid exerts a thrust or an upward force on the body.

The upward force acting on the body immersed in a fluid is called **upward thrust** or **buoyant force** and the phenomenon is called **buoyancy**.

We know the weight of the body acts at its centre of gravity. But the buoyant force acts at the **centre of buoyancy** which is the centre of gravity of the liquid displaced by the body, when immersed in the liquid.

Archimedes' Principle

The Archimedes' principle gives the magnitude of buoyant force on a body. It states that, when a body is immersed wholly or partially in a liquid at rest, it experiences an upthrust. The upthrust is equal to the weight of the liquid displaced by the immersed part of the body and this upthrust acts through the centre of gravity of the displaced fluid.

Explanation of Archimedes' Principle

Consider a cylindrical body of height h immersed in a fluid. The upward force (F_2) on the bottom of the body is more than the downward force (F_1) on its top. If p_1 and p_2 are the pressures at upper face and lower face of the body, respectively.

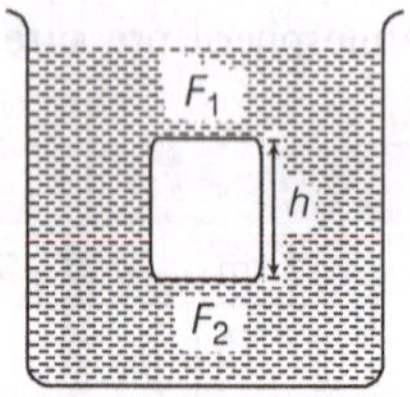

The resultant upward force on the body exerted by the fluid is equal to $(p_2 - p_1)A$.

As we know, $p_2 - p_1 = \rho g h$

So, $(p_2 - p_1) A = h\rho g A = mg$ $\quad [\because m = Ah\rho]$

where, ρ = density of fluid and

A = cross-sectional area of the body

Thus, the upward force exerted by the fluid on the body is equal to the weight of the displaced fluid.

The following three cases are possible when the body is immersed in the fluid.

(i) If the weight of the body is greater than the upward force or upthrust by the fluid acting upwards, then the body sinks.

(ii) If the weight of the body is equal to the upthrust or the weight of the body is just balanced by upthrust, then the body floats fully immersed.

(iii) If the weight of the body is less than the upward force, then the body floats partly immersed.

If the total volume of the body is V_S and a part V_P of it is submerged in the fluid, then at equilibrium,

Weight of the body = Weight of fluid displaced

$$V_S \rho_S g = V_P \rho_l g$$

where, ρ_S and ρ_l are the densities of the body and fluid, respectively.

$$\boxed{\frac{\rho_S}{\rho_l} = \frac{V_P}{V_S}}$$

Densities of Some Common Fluids at STP

Fluid	Density ρ (gm^{-3})
Water	1.00×10^3
Sea water	1.03×10^3
Mercury	13.6×10^3
Ethyl alcohol	0.806×10^3
Whole blood	1.06×10^3
Air	1.29
Oxygen	1.43
Hydrogen	9.0×10^{-2}
Interstellar space	$\approx 10^{-22}$

Example 8 A tank contains water and mercury as shown in figure. An iron cube of edge 6 cm is in equilibrium as shown in figure.

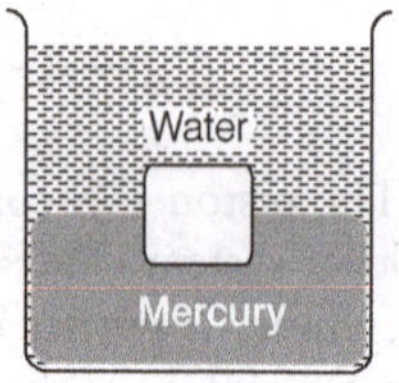

What is the fraction of cube inside the mercury?

Given, density of iron = 7.7×10^3 kgm^{-3}

and density of mercury = 13.6×10^3 kgm^{-3}.

Sol. Let y be the depth of cube in mercury. The depth of cube in water will be $(0.06 - y)$ m. The buoyant force on cube due to mercury can be find out by using Archimedes' principle.

$$B_1 = (0.06)^2 \times y \times (13.6 \times 10^3) \times 9.8 \text{ N}$$

Similarly, due to water the buoyant force on cube is

$$B_2 = (0.06)^2 \times (0.06 - y) \times 10^3 \times 9.8 \text{ N}$$

When cube is in equilibrium, the sum of both the buoyant forces will be equal to the total weight of iron cube.

$B_1 + B_2$ = weight of iron cube

or $(0.06)^2 \times 10^3 \times 9.8\,[13.6\,y + (0.06 - y)]$

$$= (0.06)^3 \times 7.7 \times 10^3 \times 9.8 \Rightarrow y = \frac{0.396}{12.6} = 0.032 \text{ m}$$

$$\text{Fraction of cube inside mercury} = \frac{0.032}{0.06} = 0.533 = 53\,\%$$

Example 9 What is the principle behind the up and down motion of a fish in water?

Sol. An object can float on water if its density is less than water. A fish can adjust its density by expanding or contracting itself. The fish can move upward by decreasing its density and downward by increasing its density.

Note

- When ice (density ρ_w) floats in a liquid (density ρ_l) and completely melts, then there could be following cases
  - (i) If $\rho_l > \rho_w$, the level of liquid will rise.
  - (ii) If $\rho_l < \rho_w$, the level of liquid decreases.
  - (iii) If $\rho_l = \rho_w$, the level of liquid will remain the same.
- Archimedes' principle is not applicable for a falling beaker containing fluid or in gravity free space.

Topic Practice 1

Multiple Choice Questions

1 Mark

1. Average pressure p_{av} is defined as
   (a) $p_{av} = \frac{F}{A}$ (b) $p_{av} = \frac{V}{F}$
   (c) $p_{av} = \frac{A}{F}$ (d) $p_{av} = \frac{F}{V}$

2. Dimensions of pressure are
   (a) $[ML^{-1}T^{-2}]$ (b) $[ML^2T^{-2}]$
   (c) $[ML^3T^{-1}]$ (d) $[M^2L^{-1}T^{-2}]$

3. The density of water at 4°C is
   (a) $1.0 \times 10^3 \text{ kgm}^{-3}$ (b) $4 \times 10^2 \text{ kgm}^{-3}$
   (c) $6 \times 10^3 \text{ kgm}^{-3}$ (d) $3.2 \times 10^3 \text{ kgm}^{-3}$

4. Pascal's law states that pressure in a fluid at rest is the same at all points, if
   (a) they are at the same height
   (b) they are along same plane
   (c) they are along same line
   (d) Both (a) and (b)

5. A square tank each having size l is filled with a liquid of height h. The thrust experienced by the vertical surface and bottom surface of the tank are
   (a) glh^2 and $h\rho gl$ (b) $\frac{1}{2}h\rho gl$ and $h\rho g^2 l$
   (c) $\frac{1}{2}glh^2$ and $h\rho gl^2$ (d) $2glh^2$ and $h\rho gl^2$

6. An aluminium block of mass 1 kg and volume $3.6 \times 10^{-4} \text{ m}^3$ is suspended from a string and then completely immersed in a container of water. The decrease in tension in the string after immersion is (Take, $g = 10 \text{ ms}^{-2}$)
   (a) 9.8 N (b) 6.2 N
   (c) 3.6 N (d) 1.0 N

7. The height h of oil in the U-tube as shown in following figure will be

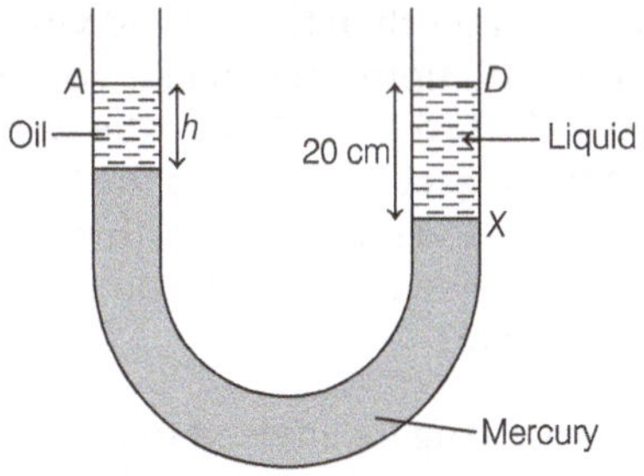

   (Take, density of oil = 0.9 g/cc, density of liquid = 1.6 g/cc, density of mercury = 13.6 g/cc)
   (a) 19.8 cm (b) 19.9 cm
   (c) 18.9 cm (d) 10.9 cm

Very Short Answer Type Questions

1 Mark

8. Why pressure is a scalar quantity?

9. Express one atmospheric pressure in terms of pascals.

10. The thrust due to atmospheric pressure on us is around 15 tonne. How do we withstand such a thrust?

11. What is gauge pressure?

12. Three vessels have same base area and different neck area. Equal volume of liquid is poured into them, which will possess more pressure at the base?

13. A vessel filled with water is kept on a weighing pan and the scale adjusted to zero. A block of mass M and density ρ is suspended by a massless spring of spring constant k. This block is submerged inside into the water in the vessel. What is the reading of the scale? **NCERT**

14. Will a ship ride higher in water of an inland lake or in the ocean. Why?

15. Density of lead is more than that of iron. What will be the ratio of loss of weight of a lead sphere to that of an iron sphere when placed in water? Radius of both spheres is 10 cm.

Short Answer Type I Questions

(2 Marks)

16. A balloon with hydrogen in it rises up but a balloon with air comes down, Why?

17. Two vessels have the same base area but different shapes. The first vessel takes twice the volume of water than the second vessel required to fill upto a particular common height. Is the force exerted by the water on the base of the vessel the same in the two cases? If so, why do the vessels filled with water to that same height give different readings on a weighing scale? **NCERT**

18. Why are passengers advised to remove the ink from their pens while going up in an aeroplane?

19. A block of wood floats in a bucket of water in a lift. Will the block sink more or less, if the lift starts accelerating up?

20. What is the fractional volume submerged for an iceberg floating on a freshwater lake of a planet whose gravity is five times that of earth? Ice floats in water with about nine-tenths of its volume submerged.

Short Answer Type II Questions

(3 Marks)

21. Explain why?
    (i) The blood pressure in humans is greater at the feet than the brain.
    (ii) Atmospheric pressure at a height of about 6 km decreases to nearly half its value at the sea level though the height of the atmosphere is more than 100 km.
    (iii) Hydrostatic pressure is a scalar quantity even though pressure is force divided by area. **NCERT**

22. State Pascal's law for fluids with the help of a neat labelled diagram. Explain principle of hydraulic brakes.

23. State and prove Archimedes' principle.

24. Why does mercury is preferred as a barometric substance over water?

25. An U-tube having A area of cross-section and g the acceleration due to gravity contains a liquid which stands at the same level when at rest. What will be the difference in height h of the liquid in two limbs of U-tube, when the system is given an acceleration a towards right?

26. A piece of ice with a stone in it floats on water when taken in a vessel. When ice melts completely, the level of water in vessel will increase, decrease or remain unchanged? Justify your answer.

Numerical Problems

27. A container of area 0.02 m^2 is filled with water. Find the pressure at the bottom of the container if a weight is placed on the piston. (as shown in the figure). **[2 M]**

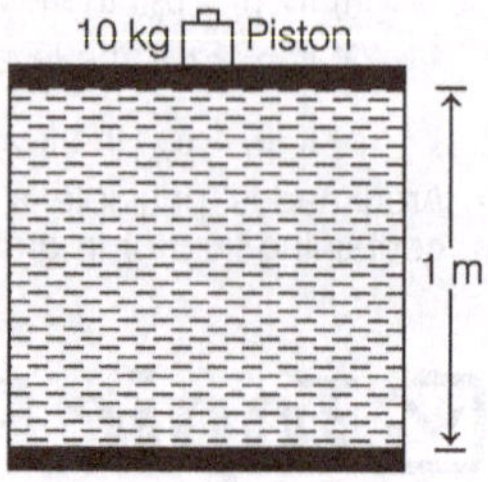

28. A 50 kg girl wearing high heels shoes balances on a single heel. The heel is circular with a diameter 1.0 cm. What is the pressure exerted on the horizontal floor? **NCERT [2 M]**

29. A body of mass 6 kg is floating in a liquid with 2/3 of its volume inside the liquid. Find ratio between the density of the body and density of liquid. Take $g = 10 \text{m/s}^2$. **[2 M]**

30. If the required pressure in the tyre of a car is 199 kPa, then
    (i) what is the gauge pressure?
    (ii) what is the absolute pressure? **[2 M]**

31. A hydraulic automobile lift is designed to lift cars with a maximum mass of 3000 kg. The area of cross-section of the piston carrying the load is 425 cm^2. What maximum pressure would the smaller piston have to bear? **NCERT [2 M]**

32. Torricelli's barometer used mercury. Pascal duplicated it using French wine of density 948 kg/m^3. Determine the height of the wine column for normal atmospheric pressure. The pressure exerted by a liquid column where, $p = h\rho g$, h = height of liquid column
    ρ = density of liquid
    g = acceleration due to gravity. **[2 M]**

33. A vertical off-shore structure is built to withstand a maximum stress of 10^9 Pa. Is the structure suitable for putting up on top of an oil well in the ocean? Take the depth of the ocean to be roughly 3 km and ignore ocean currents. **NCERT [2 M]**

34. An U-tube contains water and methylated spirit separated by mercury. The mercury columns in the two arms are in level with 10.0 cm of water in one arm and 12.5 cm of spirit in the other. What is the specific gravity of spirit? **NCERT [3 M]**

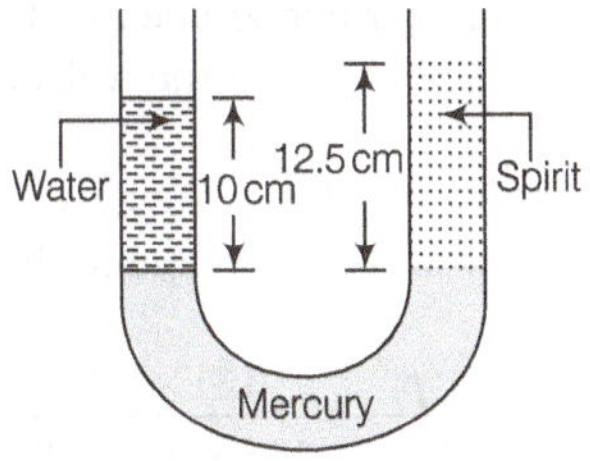

35. In the previous question, if 15.0 cm of water and spirit each are further poured into the respective arms of the tube, what is the difference in the levels of mercury in the two arms? (specific gravity of mercury = 13.6) **NCERT [3 M]**

36. During blood transfusion, the needle is inserted in a vein where the gauge pressure is 2000 Pa. At what height must the blood container be placed so that blood may just enter the vein? (Use the density of whole blood from table). **NCERT [3 M]**

37. A tank with a square base of area 1.0 m^2 is divided by a vertical partition in the middle. The bottom of the partition has a small hinged door of area 20 cm^2. The tank is filled with water in one compartment and an acid (of relative density 1.7) in the other, both to a height of 4.0. Compute the force necessary to keep the door close. **NCERT [3 M]**

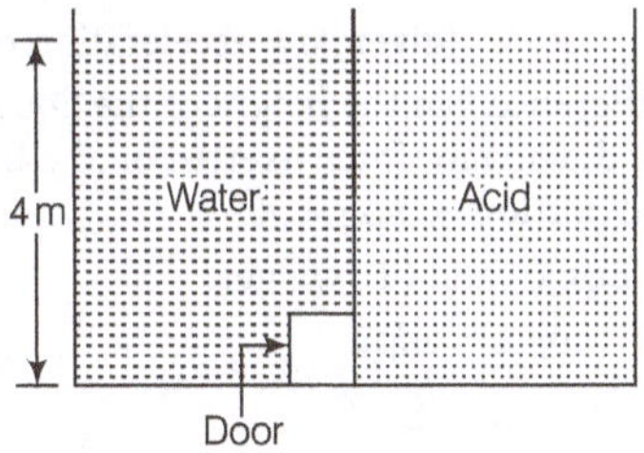

Hints & Solutions

1. (*a*) If F is the magnitude of the normal force acting over an area A, then the average pressure p is defined as the normal force acting per unit area.

$$p_{av} = \frac{F}{A}$$

2. (*a*) Dimensions of pressure are $[ML^{-1}T^{-2}]$. The SI unit of pressure is Nm^{-2}.

3. (*a*) The density of water at 4° C (277 K) is 1.0×10^3 kgm^{-3}.

4. (*a*) Pascal's law states that pressure in a fluid at rest is the same at all points if they are at the same height.

5. (*c*) As we know, pressure increases with depth, average pressure on the vertical surface of tank in contact with liquid, $p_{av} = \frac{0 + h\rho g}{2} = \frac{1}{2}h\rho g$

$\therefore$ Thrust on the vertical surface of tank = $p_{av} \times$ area

$$= \left(\frac{h\rho g}{2}\right) \times hl = \frac{1}{2}glh^2$$

Over the bottom surface, the pressure due to liquid is uniform at all points, hence $p = h\rho g$

$\therefore$ Thrust on the bottom $= p \times l^2 = h\rho g l^2$

Hence, option (c) is correct answer.

6. (*c*) As the aluminium block is immersed in container filled with water, it will experience buoyant force and loss in weight.

The decrease in weight or tension in string

$$= V \times d \times g = 3.6 \times 10^{-4} \times 10^3 \times 1 = 3.6 \text{ N}$$

7. (*c*) Taking pressure at level X in both arms of U-tube, we have

Pressure due to h cm of oil + Pressure due to $(20 - h)$ cm of mercury = Pressure of 20 cm of liquid

$$h \times 0.9 \times g + (20 - h) \times 13.6 \times g = 20 \times 1.6 \times g$$

$$\Rightarrow \quad 0.9h + (20 - h)13.6 = 20 \times 1.6$$

$$\Rightarrow \quad 0.9h + 272 - 13.6h = 32$$

$$\Rightarrow \quad 12.7h = 240$$

$$\Rightarrow \quad h = \frac{240}{12.7} = 18.9 \text{ cm}$$

8. Refer to text on page 292 (Fluid pressure).

9. Refer to text on page 292 (Fluid pressure).

10. Because, there is equal and opposite pressure exerted by our body, which gets counter balanced by the atmospheric pressure.

11. The difference between absolute pressure and atmospheric pressure is known as gauge pressure.

As, $p_{absolute} = p_a + \rho g h$

where, $p_{absolute}$ = the total or actual pressure at a point

and p_a = atmospheric pressure.

So, $p_{absolute} - p_a = \rho g h$ i.e. $p_{gauge} = \rho g h$

Here, ρ is the density of a fluid of depth h.

12. If the volumes are same, then height of the liquid will be highest in which the cross-sectional area is least at the top. So, the vessel having least cross-sectional area at the top possess more pressure at the base ($\because p = \rho g h$).

13. The scale is adjusted to zero, therefore, when block suspended to a spring is immersed in water, then the reading of the scale will be equal to the thrust on the block due to water.

Thrust $= V\rho_w g = \frac{m}{\rho}\rho_w g$ $\quad\left[\because V = \frac{m}{\rho}\right]$

14. Salt water of ocean is denser than lake water, so upthrust is more in ocean. Thus, ship rides higher in ocean.

15. Loss of weight

= Volume displaced × Density of water × g

So, ratio is one.

16. The density of hydrogen is less than air. So, the buoyant force on the balloon will be more than its weight in case of the hydrogen. So, in this case the balloon rises up. In case of air, the weight of balloon is more than the buoyant force acting on it, so balloon will come down. [2]

17. The pressure exerted by a liquid column depends upon its height. The height of water in both vessels are same, therefore, the pressure on the base of each vessel will be same. [1]

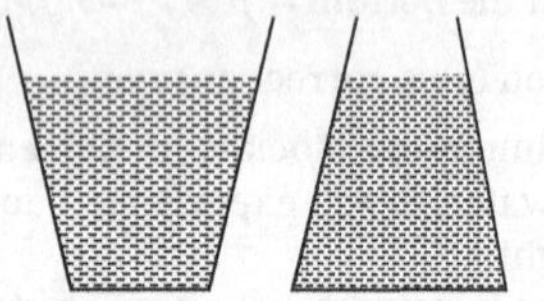

The area of the base of each vessel is also same and hence, force exerted by the water on the base of the vessels is same. As vessels hold different mass of fluid so they give different reading (mg) on a weighing scale. [1]

18. As atmospheric pressure decreases with height, hence ink inside the pen tends to come out to balance or equalise the atmospheric pressure outside, because ink inside the pen is filled at the atmospheric pressure existing on the earth's surface. If the ink comes out it may spoil the clothes, thus to avoid this, passengers are advised to remove the ink. [2]

19. The block will float at the same level in a bucket of water in a lift, because floating body is unaffected by the variation in acceleration due to gravity g. [2]

20. The fractional volume of ice submerged in water is independent of the value of acceleration due to gravity g. So, ice will float in water with about nine-tenths of its volume on the new planet also. [2]

21. (i) The pressure of liquid column is given by $p = h\rho g$, where h is depth, ρ is density and g is acceleration due to gravity.

Therefore, pressure of liquid column increases with depth. The height of blood column in human body is more at feet than at the brain. Therefore, the blood pressure in humans is greater at the feet than the brain. [1]

(ii) The density of air is maximum near the surface of the earth and decreases rapidly with height. At a height of 6 km, the density of air decreases to nearly half of its value at the sea level. Beyond 6 km height, the density of air decreases very slowly with height. Hence, the atmospheric pressure at a height of about 6 km decreases to nearly half of its value at the sea level. [1]

(iii) When force is applied on a liquid, the pressure is transmitted equally in all directions inside the liquid. Therefore, hydrostatic pressure has no fixed direction and hence, it is a scalar quantity. [1]

22. Refer to text on pages 293, 294 and 295 (Pascal's law and hydraulic brakes).

23. Refer to text on page 296 (Archimedes' principle).

24. Mercury is used in barometer due to following reasons

(i) Mercury does not stick to the walls of the barometer tube. [1]

(ii) Its density is too high, roughly 13.6×10^3 kg/m^3. Hence, height of mercury column in barometer tube will be

$$h_{Hg} = \frac{p}{\rho_{Hg} g} = \frac{1.01 \times 10^5}{13.6 \times 10^3 \times 9.8} = 0.76 \text{ m}$$

($\because p = 1.01 \times 10^5$ Pa = atmospheric pressure)

Whereas for water,

$$h_{water} = \frac{1.01 \times 10^5}{10^3 \times 9.8} = 10.3 \text{ m}$$

Hence, tube length for water barometer is too high compared to mercury barometer, will cause inconvenience. [1]

(iii) Its vapour pressure is quite small. [1]

25. From the diagram, if l is the horizontal portion of the tube,

Mass of liquid in this portion

= Volume × density (where, ρ = density of liquid)

$= Al \times \rho$

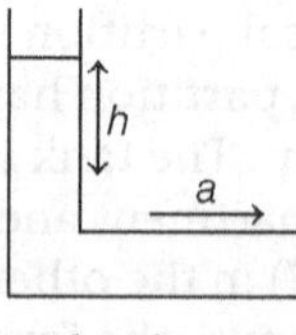

Force exerted on the above mass towards left

$= ma = Al\rho \times a$ ...(i)

(given, a = acceleration of U-tube) [1½]

Due to difference h in the height of the liquid in the two limbs, the downward force exerted on the liquid in horizontal portion $= h\rho g \times A$ ...(ii)

Equating Eqs. (i) and (ii), we get

$$h\rho g A = Al\rho a$$

$$\therefore \quad h = \frac{la}{g}$$

[1½]

26. The level of water in the vessel will come down which can be explained as follows

If m and M are the mass of stone and ice-piece respectively, then mass of water displaced by ice-piece with stone will be $m + M$.

If ρ_w is the density of water, then volume of water displaced is

$$V = \frac{M + m}{\rho_w} \quad \text{...(i)}$$

[1]

When ice melts completely, there will be extra water of mass M and volume $\dfrac{M}{\rho_w}$ in vessel.

Now, the stone will sink and will displace water equal to volume $\dfrac{m}{\rho_s}$, where ρ_s = density of stone. [1]

Thus, the total volume of extra water obtained by melting of ice and displaced by sinking stone is

$$V' = \frac{M}{\rho_w} + \frac{m}{\rho_s} \quad \text{...(ii)}$$

As $\rho_s > \rho_w$, $\dfrac{1}{\rho_s} < \dfrac{1}{\rho_w}$ and $\dfrac{m}{\rho_s} < \dfrac{m}{\rho_w}$

From Eqs. (i) and (ii), we note that $V' < V$, the level of water in vessel will come down. [1]

27. The net force acting on the base

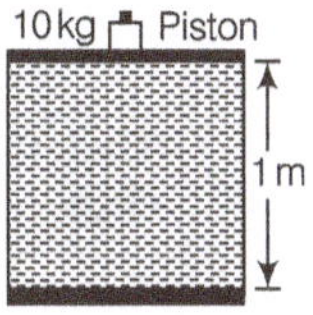

$$= (\rho g h)A + mg$$

$$F = 1000 \times 9.8 \times 1 \times 0.02 + 10 \times 9.8$$

$$= 294 \text{ N}$$

$$\therefore \quad \text{Pressure} = \frac{\text{thrust}}{\text{area}} = \frac{294 \text{ N}}{0.02}$$

$$= 14700 \text{N}$$ [2]

28. Given, mass of girl $(m) = 50$ kg

Diameter of circular heel $(2r) = 1.0$ cm

$\therefore$ Radius $(r) = 0.5$ cm $= 5 \times 10^{-3}$ m [1]

Area of circular heel $(A) = \pi r^2 = 3.14 \times (5 \times 10^{-3})^2 \text{m}^2$

$$= 78.50 \times 10^{-6} \text{m}^2$$

$\therefore$ Pressure exerted on the horizontal floor

$$p = \frac{F}{A} = \frac{mg}{A} = \frac{50 \times 9.8}{78.50 \times 10^{-6}} = 6.24 \times 10^6 \text{ Pa}$$ [1]

29. As we know that, for a floating body

Buoyant force = Weight of liquid displaced

Let V be the volume of the body $\dfrac{2}{3} V \rho_l g = V \rho_b g$ [1]

where, ρ_b = density of floating body

and ρ_l = density of liquid

$$\therefore \quad \frac{\rho_b}{\rho_l} = \frac{2}{3}$$ [1]

30. (i) Gauge pressure

$$\therefore \quad p_g = 199 \text{ kPa}$$ [1]

(ii) Absolute pressure

$$p = p_a + p_g \quad \text{[from Eq. (i)]}$$

$$= 101 \text{ kPa} + 199 \text{ kPa} = 300 \text{ kPa}$$ [1]

31. Given, maximum mass that can be lifted $(m) = 3000$ kg

Area of cross-section $(A) = 425 \text{ cm}^2 = 4.25 \times 10^{-2} \text{m}^2$

$\therefore$ Maximum pressure on the bigger piston

$$p = \frac{F}{A} = \frac{mg}{A} = \frac{3000 \times 9.8}{4.25 \times 10^{-2}} = 6.92 \times 10^5 \text{ Pa}$$ [1]

According to Pascal's law, the pressure applied on an enclosed liquid is transmitted equally in all directions.

$\therefore$ Maximum pressure on smaller piston

= maximum pressure on bigger piston

$$p' = p = 6.92 \times 10^5 \text{ Pa}$$ [1]

32. Atmospheric pressure $(p) = 1.013 \times 10^5$ Pa

Density of French wine $(\rho) = 984 \text{ kg/m}^3$

Let h be the height of wine column,

$$p = h\rho g, \quad h = \frac{p}{\rho g} = \frac{1.013 \times 10^5}{984 \times 9.8} = 10.5 \text{ m}$$ [2]

33. Given, depth of ocean $(h) = 3$ km $= 3000$ m

Density of water $(\rho) = 10^3 \text{ kg/m}^3$

Pressure exerted by water column

$$p = h\rho g = 3000 \times 10^3 \times 9.8$$ [1]

$$= 29.4 \times 10^6 \text{ Pa} = 2.94 \times 10^7 \text{ Pa}$$

Maximum stress which can be withstand by the vertical off-shore structure $= 10^9$ Pa

As, $\quad 10^9 \text{ Pa} > 2.9 \times 10^7 \text{ Pa}$

Therefore, the vertical structure is suitable for putting up on top of an oil well in the ocean. [1]

34. Height of water column, $h_1 = 10.0$ cm

Density of water, $\rho_1 = 1 \text{ g/cm}^3$

Height of spirit column, $h_2 = 12.5$ cm

Density of spirit, $\rho_2 = ?$

The mercury column in both arms of the U-tube are at same level, therefore, pressure in both arms will be same. [1]

$\therefore$ Pressure exerted by water column = pressure exerted by spirit column

$$\therefore \quad p_1 = p_2$$

$$h_1 \rho_1 g = h_2 \rho_2 g$$

$$\text{or} \quad \rho_2 = \frac{h_1 \rho_1}{h_2} = \frac{10 \times 1}{12.5} = 0.80 \text{ g/cm}^3$$ [1]

$$\text{Specific gravity of spirit} = \frac{\text{Density of spirit}}{\text{Density of water}}$$

$$= \frac{0.80}{1} = 0.80$$ [1]

35. When 15.0 cm of water is poured in each arm, then

Height of water column $(h_1) = 10 + 15 = 25$ cm

Height of spirit column $(h_2) = 12.5 + 15 = 27.5$ cm

Density of water $(\rho_w) = 1 \text{ g/cm}^3$

Density of spirit $(\rho_s) = 0.80 \text{ g/cm}^3$

Density of mercury $(\rho_m) = 13.6 \text{ g/cm}^3$ [1]

Let in equilibrium, the difference in the level of mercury in both arms be h cm.

$$\therefore \quad h\rho_m g = h_1 \rho_w g - h_2 \rho_s g$$ [1]

or $h = \dfrac{h_1\rho_w - h_2\rho_s}{\rho_m} = \dfrac{25\times 1 - 27.5\times 0.80}{13.6}$

$= 0.221$ cm

Therefore, mercury will rise in the arm containing spirit by 0.221 cm. [1]

36. Given, gauge pressure $(p) = 2000$ Pa

Density of whole blood $(\rho) = 1.06\times 10^3 \text{ kg/m}^3$

$g = 9.8 \text{ m/s}^2$ [1]

Let the container be placed at height h metre.

Pressure exerted by the blood $(p) = h\rho g$ [1]

or $h = \dfrac{p}{\rho g}$

$= \dfrac{2000}{1.06\times 10^3 \times 9.8}$

$= 0.193 \text{ m} \simeq 0.20$ m [1]

37. Given, height of water and acid $(h) = 4.0$ m

Density of water $(\rho_w) = 1\times 10^3 \text{ kg/m}^3$

Density of acid $(\rho_a) = 1.7\times 10^3 \text{ kg/m}^3$

Pressure exerted by water at the door

$p_1 = h\rho_w g = 4\times 1\times 10^3 \times 9.8$

$= 39.2\times 10^3$ Pa [1]

Pressure exerted by acid at the door

$p_2 = h\rho_a g = 4\times 1.7\times 10^3 \times 9.8$

$= 66.64\times 10^3$ Pa

$\therefore$ Difference in pressure $(\Delta p) = p_2 - p_1$

$= 66.64\times 10^3 - 39.2\times 10^3$

$= 27.44\times 10^3$ Pa [1]

Area of the door $(A) = 20 \text{ cm}^2$

$= 20\times 10^{-4} \text{ m}^2$

Force acting on the door $= \Delta p \times A \left[\because \text{pressure} = \dfrac{\text{force}}{\text{area}}\right]$

$= 27.44\times 10^3 \times 20\times 10^{-4}$

$= 54.88 \text{ N} \approx 55$ N

Therefore, 55 N force is necessary to keep the door close. [1]

TOPIC 02 Hydrodynamics

Branch of Physics which deals with the study of fluids in motion called **fluid dynamics** or **hydrodynamics**.

Ideal liquid

A liquid is said to be ideal, if

(i) It is incompressible (density remains constant irrespective of pressure)

(ii) It is non-viscous and

(iii) Its flow is steady, cannot withstand any shearing stress.

Streamline Flow

Streamline flow or laminar flow of a liquid is that flow in which each particle of the liquid passing through a point travels along the same path and with the same velocity as the preceding particle passing through the same point. A streamline is defined as a curve whose tangent at any point is in the direction of the fluid velocity at that point.

Trajectory of a fluid particle

Properties of Streamlines

(i) In streamline flow, no two streamlines can cross each other. If they do so, the particles of the liquid at the point of intersection will have two different directions for their flow, which will destroy the steady nature of the liquid flow.

(ii) The greater is the crowding of streamline at a place greater is the velocity of the liquid particles at that place and *vice-versa*.

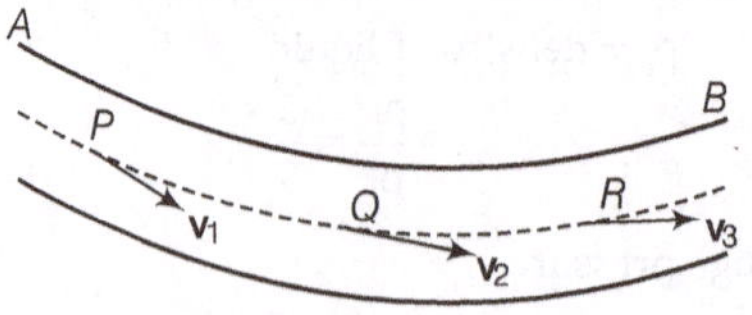

A region of streamline flow

Turbulent Flow

Turbulent flow of liquid is that flow in which each particle of the liquid passing through a point change their path and velocity continuously and haphazardly with time.

For example, in rivers and canals, where speed of water is quite high or the boundary surfaces cause abrupt changes in velocity of the flow, then the flow becomes irregular.

Such flow of liquid is known as **turbulent flow.**

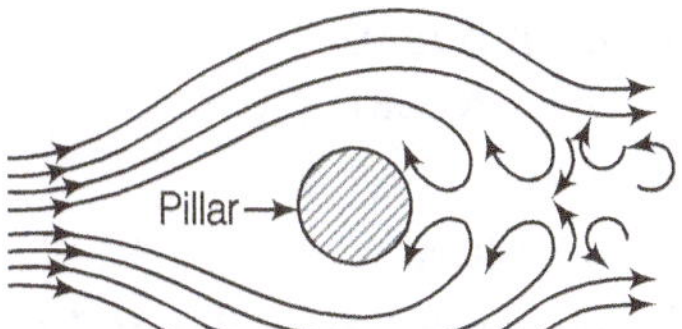

turbulent flow of liquid

Viscosity

When a solid body slides over another solid body, the force of friction opposes the relative motion of the solid bodies. In the same way, when a layer of fluid slides over another layer of the same fluid, a force of friction comes into play which is called **viscous force.** This force opposes the relative motion of the different layers of a fluid.

So, the tendency of fluids to oppose the relative motion of its layers is called **viscosity of fluid.** The backward dragging force called **viscous drag** or **viscous force.**

Cause of Viscosity

The velocities of the layers of the liquid increases uniformly from bottom to the top layer. For any layer of liquid, its lower layer pulls it backward while its upper layer pulls it forward direction. This type of flow is known as **laminar flow.**

Similar cases arise when the liquid, flowing in a pipe or a tube, then the velocity of the liquid is maximum along the axis of the tube and decreases gradually, as it moves towards the walls where it becomes zero.

Velocity Gradient

When a liquid volume flows over a solid surface, different layers of fluid have different speed.

Layer in contact with the solid is at rest and as we move up towards upward free layer, velocity of successive layers increases. If layers at distances x and $x + dx$ have speeds
v and $v + dv$, then we define a quantity called velocity gradient. Velocity gradient $= \dfrac{dv}{dx}$

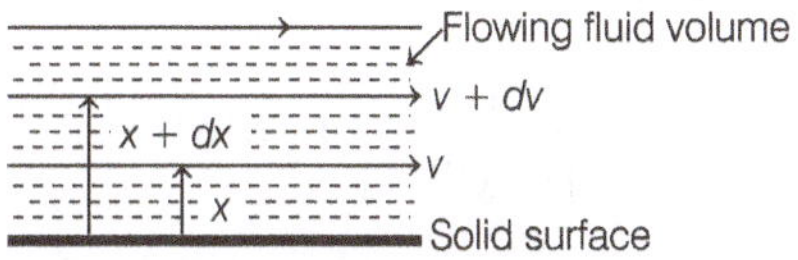

Velocity gradient occurs due to different amount of resistance on different fluid layers.

Velocity gradient can be defined as rate of change of velocity with respect to depth. It is also called shear strain rate of flowing fluid. Unit of velocity gradient is second^{-1} and its dimension is $[T^{-1}]$.

Viscous Force and Coefficient of Viscosity

Tangential force acting parallel to any layer of a flowing fluid is proportional to

(i) area A of layer.

(ii) velocity gradient $\dfrac{dv}{dx}$ of layer.

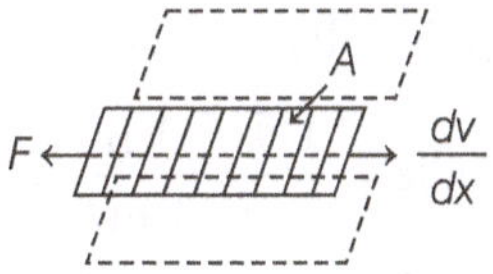

So, $F \propto A$ and $F \propto \dfrac{dv}{dx} \Rightarrow F \propto -A\dfrac{dv}{dx}$

Negative sign appears as F and $\dfrac{dv}{dx}$ have different directions. As tangential force opposing the flow also depends on fluid properties, so

$$\boxed{\text{Viscous force, } F = -\eta A \frac{dv}{dx}}$$

where, η is a constant that depends on fluid properties and is called coefficient of viscosity.

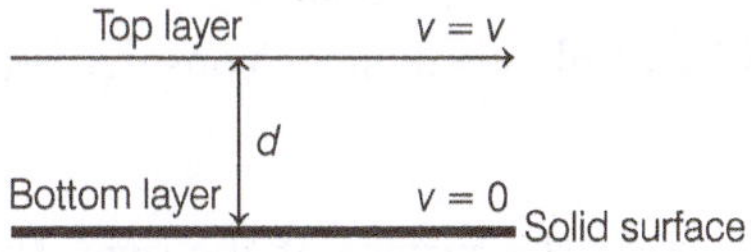

Hence, the coefficient of viscosity is defined as the ratio of shearing stress to the strain rate

$$\eta = \frac{F/A}{v/d} = \frac{Fd}{vA}$$

$$\boxed{\text{Coefficient of viscosity, } \eta = \frac{Fd}{vA}}$$

or it can be written as, $\eta = \dfrac{F/A}{\dfrac{dv}{dx}}$

Dimension of η

$$\eta = \frac{F}{A}\cdot\frac{l}{v} = \frac{[MLT^{-2}]}{[L^2 LT^{-1}]}[L] = [ML^{-1}T^{-1}]$$

Units of η

(i) In CGS system, the unit of η is **dyne-s/cm^2** and it is called **poise.**

$$1 \text{ poise} = \frac{1 \text{ dyne}}{1 \text{ cm}^2} \times \frac{1 \text{ cm}}{1 \text{ cm/s}}$$

$$1 \text{ poise} = 1 \text{ dyne-s/cm}^2$$

The coefficient of viscosity of a liquid is said to be 1 poise, if a tangential force of 1 dyne cm^{-2} of the surface is required to maintain a relative velocity of 1 cm s^{-1} between two layers of the liquid 1 cm apart.

(ii) The SI unit of η is **Ns/m^2** or **kg/ms** and it is called **decapoise** or **poiseuille.**

$$1 \text{ poiseuille} = \frac{1 \text{ N}}{1 \text{ m}^2}\cdot\frac{1 \text{ m}}{1 \text{ m/s}} = 1 \text{ Ns/m}^2$$

The coefficient of viscosity of a liquid is said to be 1 poiseuille or decapoise if a tangential force of 1 Nm^{-2} of the surface is required to maintain a relative velocity of 1 ms^{-1} between two layers of the liquid 1 m apart.

(iii) Relation between poiseuille and poise

1 poiseuille or 1 decapoise = 10 poise

The coefficient of viscosity is a scalar quantity.

Relative Viscosity

$$\text{Relative viscosity of liquid} = \frac{\eta_{liquid}}{\eta_{water}}$$

Relative viscosity of bloods remains constant between 0°C and 37°C.

Example 1 Near the surface of the river, the velocity of water is 160 kmh^{-1}. Find the shearing stress between horizontal layers of water, if the river is 6 m deep and the coefficient of viscosity of water is 10^{-2} poise.

Sol. Given, $v = 160 \text{ km/h} = 160 \times \frac{5}{18} \text{ m/s} = 44.44 \text{ m/s}$

$d = 6$ m and $\eta = 10^{-2}$ poise $= 10^{-3}$ Pa-s

$$\text{Shearing stress} = \frac{F}{A} = \eta\frac{v}{d} = 10^{-3} \times \frac{44.44}{6}$$

$$\text{Shearing stress} = 7.407 \times 10^{-3} \text{ Nm}^{-2}$$

Example 2 A metal block of area 0.10 m^2 is connected to a 0.01 kg mass via a string that passes over an ideal pulley (considered massless and frictionless), as in figure. **NCERT**

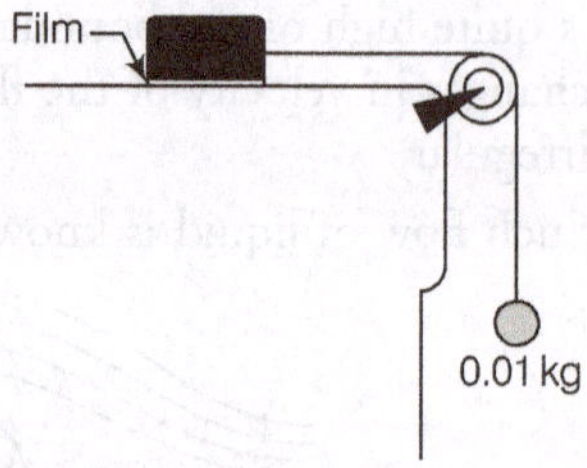

Sol. Given, $m = 0.010$ kg,

$g = 9.8 \text{ m/s}^2$, $A = 0.10 \text{ m}^2$

$$F = T = mg = 0.010 \times 9.8 = 9.8 \times 10^{-2} \text{ N}$$

$$\text{Shear stress on the fluid} = \frac{F}{A} = \frac{9.8 \times 10^{-2}}{0.10} = 0.98 \text{ N/m}^2$$

$$\text{The strain rate, } \eta = \frac{\text{Stress}}{\text{Strain rate}}$$

$$\text{Strain rate} = \frac{v}{d} = \frac{0.085}{0.30 \times 10^{-3}}$$

Now, the coefficient of viscosity of the liquid.

$$\eta = \frac{Fd}{Av} = \frac{9.8 \times 10^{-2} \times 0.30 \times 10^{-3}}{0.10 \times 0.085}$$

$$\eta = 3.45 \times 10^{-3} \text{ Pa-s}$$

Effect of Temperature on the Viscosity

The viscosity of liquids decreases with increase in temperature and increases with decrease in temperature. This is due to increase of kinetic energy of fluid particles,

i.e. $$\eta \propto \frac{1}{\sqrt{T}}$$

On the other hand, the viscosity of gases increases with the increase in temperature and *vice-versa*. This is due to increase of diffusion of molecules of one layer into another, i.e.

$$\eta \propto \sqrt{T}$$

Critical Velocity The velocity of liquid flow, below which its flow is streamlined and above which its becomes turbulent.

$$\text{Critical velocity, } v_C = \frac{K\eta}{r\rho}$$

where, K = Reynold's number,

η = coefficient of viscosity of liquid,

r = radius of capillary tube

and ρ = density of liquid.

Stokes' Law

When a small spherical body falls through a viscous fluid at rest, the layers of fluid in contact with the body are dragged alongwith it. But the layers of the fluid away from the body are at rest. This produces a relative motion between different layers of the fluid.

As a result, a **backward dragging** force (i.e. viscous force) comes into play, which opposes the motion of the body. This backward dragging force increases with the increase in velocity of the moving body. Falling of a raindrop, swinging of a pendulum bob are the examples of such type of motion.

Sir George G Stokes' (1819–1903), an English scientist found that the backward dragging force F acting on a small spherical body of radius r, moving through a fluid of coefficient of viscosity η, with velocity v is given by

$$\boxed{\text{Dragging force, } F = 6\pi\eta rv}$$

This is called **Stokes' law** of viscosity.

Dimentional formula

Coefficient of viscocity of the medium, $\eta = \dfrac{F}{6\pi rv}$

Dimension of η can also obtained by using above formula.

$$\therefore \text{ Dimention of } \eta = \frac{[\text{MLT}^{-2}]}{[\text{L}][\text{LT}^{-1}]} = [\text{ML}^{-1}\text{T}^{-1}]$$

Stokes observed that the viscous drag (F) depends on coefficient of viscosity (η), velocity of body (v) and radius of body (r), hence

let $\qquad F = K\eta^a v^b r^c$

$$[F] = [\eta]^a\,[v]^b\,[r]^c$$

Dimensionally, $[\text{MLT}^{-2}] = [\text{ML}^{-1}\text{T}^{-1}]^a\,[\text{LT}^{-1}]^b\,[\text{L}]^c$

$$[\text{MLT}^{-2}] = [\text{M}^a\text{L}^{-a-b+c}\text{T}^{-a-b}]$$

Comparing powers on both sides, we get

$$a = 1 \qquad \ldots\text{(i)}$$

$$-a + b + c = 1 \qquad \ldots\text{(ii)}$$

$$-a - b = -2 \qquad \ldots\text{(iii)}$$

Comparing Eqs. (ii) and (iii), we get

$$c = 1, \quad b = 1$$

Substituting $F = 6\pi\eta rv$,

where, $K = 6\pi$ found experimentally.

Applications of Stokes' Law

(i) **To determine the electronic charge by Millikan's experiment** Stokes' formula is used. In this method, the formula is applied for finding out the radii of small oil-drops by measuring their terminals velocities in air.

(ii) **Parachute** When a man coming down with the help of a parachute, he descends very slowly in air. Suppose the total mass of the parachute and the man is m_1 and the mass of air linked with the parachute is m_2. Then, the effective acceleration of the man is

$$g' = \frac{\text{Weight of the mass } m_1 \text{ in air} + \text{Weight of the mass } m_2 \text{ in air}}{\text{Total mass}} = \frac{m_1 g + O}{m_1 + m_2}$$

[$\because$ The weight of air of mass m_2 in air will be zero]

$$= \frac{m_1}{m_1 + mg} \times g$$

(iii) **Velocity of rain drops** When rain drops fall under gravity, their motion is opposed by the viscous drag in air. So, the drop attain a constant velocity known as terminal velocity.

Note

- This law is used in the determination of electronic charge with the help of Millikan's experiment.
- This law accounts the formation of clouds.

Example 3 Consider a drop of rain having radius 0.4 mm and velocity 2 m/s. Find the viscous force on the rain drop, if viscosity of air is 18×10^{-5} dyne cm^{-2}s.

Sol. The Stoke's law is an interesting example of retarding force which is proportional to velocity.

Given, radius, $r = 0.4 \text{ mm} = 0.4\times 10^{-3}$ m

Terminal velocity, $v = 2 \text{ ms}^{-1}$

and viscosity of air, $\eta = 18\times 10^{-5}$ dyne cm^{-2}s

$$= 18\times 10^{-6} \text{ Pa-s}$$

According to Stoke's law, the viscous force $F = 6\pi\eta rv$

$$= 6\times 3.142\times 18\times 10^{-6}\times 0.4\times 10^{-3}\times 2$$

$$F = 2.71\times 10^{-7} \text{ N}$$

Terminal Velocity

The maximum constant velocity acquired by a body while falling through a viscous fluid is called its **terminal velocity**.

Consider an example of raindrop in air. It accelerates initially due to gravity. The force of viscosity increases as the velocity of the body increases. A stage is reached, when the true weight of the body becomes just equal to the sum of the upthrust and the viscous force. Then, the body begins to fall with a constant velocity called **terminal velocity**.

Suppose a sphere of density ρ falls through a liquid of density σ.

Upward thrust = The weight of the fluid displaced

$$= \frac{4}{3}\pi r^3 \sigma g$$

Force of viscosity $= 6\pi\eta r v$, and weight of the spherical body

$$= \frac{4}{3}\pi r^3 \rho g \qquad [\because mV\rho]$$

When upthrust and viscous drag are just equals to weight, then

$$\frac{4}{3}\pi r^3 \sigma g + 6\pi\eta r v = \frac{4}{3}\pi r^3 \rho g$$

or $$6\pi\eta r v = \frac{4}{3}\pi r^3 (\rho - \sigma) g$$

or $$\boxed{\text{Terminal velocity, } v = \frac{2}{9} \cdot \frac{r^2(\rho - \sigma) g}{\eta}}$$

where, r = radius of the spherical body,

v = terminal velocity

and η = coefficient of viscosity of fluid

As net force on reaching terminal velocity is zero, body continues to fall with constant speed.

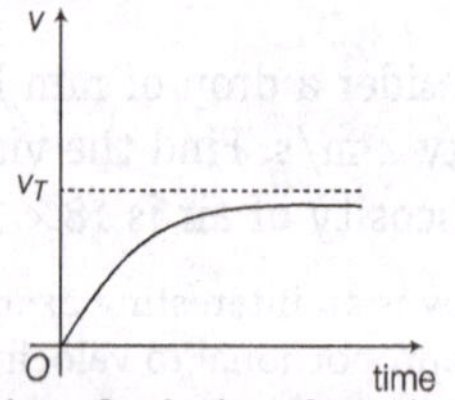

Variation of velocity of a sphere falling through a liquid, with time

Note From the above expression we can see that terminal velocity of a spherical body is directly proportional to the difference in the densities of the body and the fluid $(\rho - \sigma)$. If the density of fluid is greater than that of body (*i.e.*, $\sigma > \rho$), the terminal velocity is negative. This means that the body instead of falling, moves upward. This is why air bubbles rise up in water.

Example 4 If 27 drops of rain were to be combine to form one new large spherical drop, then what should be the velocity of this large spherical drop? Consider the terminal velocity of 27 drops of equal size falling through the air is 0.20 ms^{-1}.

Sol. Let, the radius of the small drop is r and that of big drop is R. The volume of the big drop = 27 × volume of each small drop

$$\frac{4}{3}\pi R^3 = 27 \times \frac{4}{3}\pi r^3 \Rightarrow R = 3r$$

Let, the terminal velocities of small and big drops are v_1 and v_2, respectively. Then,

$$v = \frac{2r^2(\rho - \sigma) g}{9\eta}$$

$$\Rightarrow \quad v \propto r^2$$

Hence, $$\frac{v_2}{v_1} = \frac{R^2}{r^2} \Rightarrow v_2 = v_1 \times \frac{R^2}{r^2} = 0.2\left(\frac{3r}{r}\right)^2 = 0.2 \times 9$$

$$\therefore \quad v_2 = 1.8 \text{ m/s}$$

Flow of Liquid Through Pipes: Poiseuille's Formula

The volume of a liquid flowing out per second through a horizontal capillary tube of length l, radius r, under a pressure difference p applied across its ends is given by

$$V = \frac{Q}{t} = \frac{\pi p r^4}{8\eta l}$$

This formula is called **Poiseuille's formula.**

The term $\frac{8\eta l}{\pi r^4}$ is equivalent to R. This term is known as viscous resistance, thus $R_{\text{Viscous}} = \frac{8\eta l}{\pi r^4}$

So, the above equation shows that the viscous resistance increase with increase in length of the pipe and decrease with its radius. It also depends on coefficient of viscosity, it increases with increase in viscosity of the liquid, e.g. glycerine offers more resistance than water, when flows through a pipe.

Equation of Continuity

It states that, **during the streamline flow of the non-viscous and incompressible fluid through a pipe of varying cross-section, the product of area of cross-section and the normal fluid velocity (av) remains constant throughout the flow.**

Consider a non-viscous and incompressible liquid flowing through a tube AB of varying cross-section.

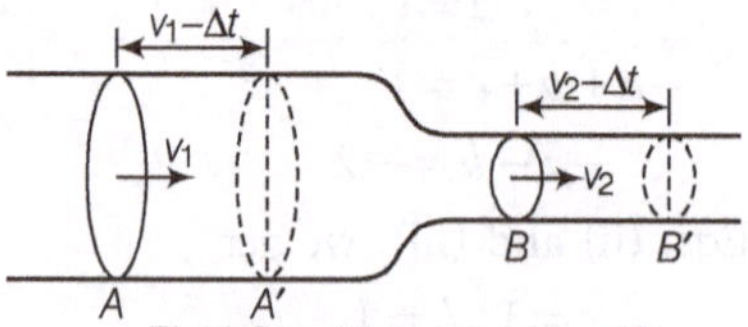

Fluid flow through pipe AB

Let a_1 be the area of cross-section, v_1 at section A and the values of corresponding quantities at section B be a_2 and v_2, respectively. The density of flowing fluid is ρ.

As the fluid is incompressible, is constant

As, mass = volume × density

= Area of cross-section × length × density

$\therefore$ Mass of fluid that entering through section A in time Δt,

$$m_1 = a_1 v_1 \Delta t \rho_1$$

Mass of fluid that leaving through section B in time Δt,

$$m_2 = a_2 v_2 \Delta t \rho_2$$

According to conservation of mass, we get

$$m_1 = m_2$$

or $\quad a_1 v_1 \Delta t \rho = a_2 v_2 \Delta t \rho$

ρ, is constant

Hence, $\quad a_1 v_1 = a_2 v_2$

or $\quad av = \text{constant}$

This is known as **equation of continuity.**

Different Energy of a Flowing Liquid

There are three types of energies in a flowing liquid.

Pressure Energy

If p is the pressure on the area A of a fluid, and the liquid moves through a distance l due to this pressure, then

Pressure energy of liquid = work done

$$= \text{force} \times \text{displacement}$$

$$= pAl$$

The volume of the liquid is Al.

Hence, pressure energy per unit volume of liquid

$$= \frac{pAl}{Al} = p$$

Kinetic Energy

If a liquid of mass m and volume V is flowing with velocity v, then the kinetic energy is $\frac{1}{2}mv^2$.

$\therefore$ Kinetic energy per unit volume of liquid $= \frac{1}{2}\left(\frac{m}{V}\right)v^2$

$$= \frac{1}{2}\rho v^2$$

Here, ρ is the density of liquid.

Potential Energy

If a liquid of mass m is at a height h from the reference line ($h = 0$), then its potential energy is mgh.

$\therefore$ Potential energy per unit volume of the liquid

$$= \left(\frac{m}{V}\right)gh = \rho gh$$

Bernoulli's Theorem

Bernoulli's principle is based on the law of conservation of energy and applied to ideal fluids. It states that **the sum of pressure energy per unit volume, kinetic energy per unit volume and potential energy per unit volume of an incompressible, non-viscous fluid in a streamlined irrotational flow remains constant at every cross-section throughout the liquid flow.**

Mathematically, it can be expressed as

$$\boxed{p + \frac{1}{2}\rho v^2 + \rho gh = \text{constant}}$$

where, p represents for pressure energy per unit volume $\frac{1}{2}\rho v^2$ for kinetic energy per unit volume and ρgh for potential energy per unit volume and ρ is density of flowing fluid (ideal).

The Swiss physicist **Daniel Bernoulli** developed this relationship in 1738.

Proof Consider an ideal fluid having streamline flow through a pipe of varying area of cross-section as shown in figure.

Let p_1, a_1, h_1, v_1 and p_2, a_2, h_2, v_2 be the pressure, area of cross-section, height and velocity of flow at points A and B, respectively. Force acting on fluid at point $A = p_1 a_1$

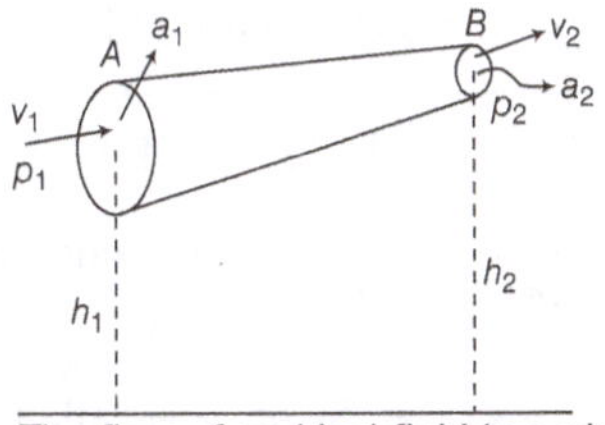

The flow of an ideal fluid in a pipe varying cross-section

Distance travelled by fluid in one second at point A

$$= v_1 \times 1 = v_1$$

Work done per second on the fluid at point A

$$= \text{Force} \times \text{distance travelled by fluid in one second.}$$

$$W_1 = p_1 a_1 \times v_1$$

Similarly, work done per second by the fluid at point B,

$$W_2 = p_2 a_2 v_2$$

$\therefore$ Net work done on the fluid by pressure energy,

$$W = p_1 a_1 v_1 - p_2 a_2 v_2$$

But, $\quad a_1 v_1 = a_2 v_2 = \frac{m}{\rho}$ (i.e. equation of continuity)

$\therefore$ Net work done on the fluid by the pressure energy,

$$W = \left(\frac{p_1 m}{\rho} - \frac{p_2 m}{\rho}\right)$$

Total work done by the pressure energy on the fluid increases the kinetic energy and potential energy of the fluid, when it flows from A to B.

$\therefore$ Increase in kinetic energy of fluid

$$= \text{KE at } B - \text{KE at } A$$

$$= \frac{1}{2}mv_2^2 - \frac{1}{2}mv_1^2 \quad [\because a_1 > a_2 \therefore v_2 > v_1]$$

Similarly, total increase in potential energy $= mgh_2 - mgh_1$

According to work energy theorem, work done on the fluid is equal to change in the energy of fluid.

i.e. work done by the pressure energy = total increase in energy

$$\therefore \quad \frac{p_1 m}{\rho} - \frac{p_2 m}{\rho} = (mgh_2 - mgh_1) + \left(\frac{1}{2}mv_2^2 - \frac{1}{2}mv_1^2\right)$$

$$\left(\frac{p_1 - p_2}{\rho}\right) = (gh_2 - gh_1) + \frac{1}{2}v_2^2 - \frac{1}{2}v_1^2$$

or $$\frac{p_1}{\rho} + \frac{1}{2}v_1^2 + gh_1 = \frac{p_2}{\rho} + \frac{1}{2}v_2^2 + gh_2$$

Hence, $$\frac{p}{\rho} + gh + \frac{1}{2}v^2 = \text{constant}$$

$$\boxed{p + \frac{1}{2}\rho v^2 + \rho gh = \text{constant}} \quad \ldots\text{(i)}$$

Dividing both sides of Eq. (i) by ρg, we get

$$\frac{p}{\rho g} + h + \frac{v^2}{2g} = \frac{\text{constant}}{\rho g} = \text{new constant} \quad \ldots\text{(ii)}$$

Here, $\frac{p}{\rho g}$ is called **pressure head**, h is called **gravitational head** and $\frac{v^2}{2g}$ is called **velocity head**.

Equation (ii) enable us to state Bernoulli's theorem in the streamline flow of an ideal liquid as the sum of pressure head, gravitational head and velocity head is always constant.

If the fluid is flowing through a horizontal tube, two ends of the tube are at the same level. Therefore, there is no gravitational head (level difference), i.e. $h = 0$.

$$p + \frac{1}{2}\rho v^2 = \text{constant}$$

This shows, if **p increases, v decreases and *vice-versa*.** Thus, Bernoulli's theorem also states that in the streamline flow of an ideal liquid through a horizontal tube, the velocity increases where pressure decreases and *vice-versa*. This is also called **Bernoulli's principle.**

Limitations of Bernoulli's Theorem

(i) Bernoulli's equation ideally applies to fluids with zero viscosity or non-viscous fluids.

(ii) The fluids must be incompressible, as the elastic energy of the fluid is also not taken into consideration.

(iii) Bernoulli's equation is applicable only to streamline flow of a fluid. It is not valid for non-steady or turbulent flow.

Example 5 Consider the two horizontal pipes of different diameters which are connected together and the water is flowing through these two pipes. In the first pipe, the pressure is $3.0 \times 10^4\ \text{N/m}^2$ and the speed of the water flowing is 5 m/s. If the diameters of the pipes are 4 cm and 6 cm, respectively, then what will be the speed and the pressure of the water in the second pipe? Density of the water is $10^3\ \text{kg/m}^3$.

Sol. According to the equation of continuity, we get

$$a_1 v_1 = a_2 v_2 \Rightarrow \pi r_1^2 v_1 = \pi r_2^2 v_2$$

$$\therefore \quad v_2 = \left(\frac{r_1}{r_2}\right)^2 v_1$$

Given, $$r_1 = \frac{4}{2} = 2\text{ cm} = 2 \times 10^{-2}\text{ m}$$

$$r_2 = \frac{6}{2} = 3\text{ cm} = 3 \times 10^{-2}\text{ m}$$

$$v_1 = 5\text{ m/s}$$

$$v_2 = \left(\frac{2}{3}\right)^2 \times 5 = 2.22\text{ m/s}$$

Now, applying the Bernoulli's theorem,

$$p_1 + \frac{1}{2}\rho v_1^2 = p_2 + \frac{1}{2}\rho v_2^2$$

$$p_2 = p_1 + \frac{1}{2}\rho(v_1^2 - v_2^2)$$

$$= 3.0 \times 10^4 + \frac{1}{2} \times 10^3(5^2 - 2.22^2)$$

$$= 3 \times 10^4 + 500 \times 20.08$$

$$p_2 \approx 4 \times 10^4\text{ N/m}^2$$

Simple Applications of Bernoulli's Theorem

(i) Speed of Efflux (Torricelli's Law)

According to Torricelli's, velocity of efflux i.e. the velocity with which the liquid flows out of an orifice (i.e. a narrow hole) is equal to that which a freely falling body would acquire in falling through a vertical distance equal to the depth of orifice below the free surface of liquid.

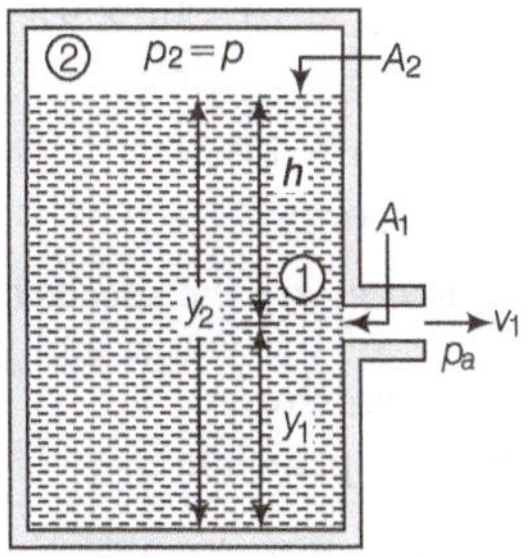

Fluid flow from an orifice

The word efflux means the outflow of a fluid as shown in figure. Consider a tank containing a liquid of density ρ with a small hole on its side at height y_1 from the bottom and y_2 be the height of the liquid surface from the bottom and p be the air pressure above the liquid surface.

If A_1, A_2 are the cross-sectional areas and v_1, v_2 are the velocities of liquid at point 1 and 2, respectively, then from the equation of continuity, we get

$$A_1 v_1 = A_2 v_2 \quad \text{or} \quad v_2 = \frac{A_1}{A_2} v_1$$

If $A_2 >> A_1$ so the liquid may be taken at rest at the top, i.e. $v_2 \approx 0$.

Applying the Bernoulli's theorem at points 1 and 2. The pressure $p_1 = p_a$ (the atmospheric pressure)

We get, $p_a + \frac{1}{2}\rho v_1^2 + \rho g y_1 = p + \rho g y_2 \qquad [\because v_2 \approx 0]$

or $$\frac{1}{2}\rho v_1^2 = \rho g (y_2 - y_1) + (p - p_a)$$

$$y_2 - y_1 = h$$

Hence, $$\frac{1}{2}\rho v_1^2 = \rho g h + (p - p_a)$$

Velocity of the liquid falls from orifice,

$$v_1 = \sqrt{2gh + \frac{2(p - p_a)}{\rho}}$$

When the tank is open to the atmosphere,

$$p = p_a \text{ and } v_1 = \sqrt{2gh}$$

Thus, the **velocity of efflux** of a liquid is equal to the velocity which a body acquires in falling freely from the free liquid surface to the orifice. This result is called **Torricelli's law.**

Example 6 If the water emerges from an orifice in a tank in which the gauge pressure is 4×10^5 N/m^2 before the flow starts then, what will be the velocity of the water emerging out? Take density of water is 1000 kgm^{-3}.

Sol. Here, $p = 4 \times 10^5$ N/m^2 and $\rho = 1000$ kgm^{-3}, $g = 10$ m/s^2

Apply $p = h\rho g$,

$$\Rightarrow \quad h = \frac{p}{\rho g} = \frac{4 \times 10^5}{1000 \times 10}$$

$$\therefore \text{Velocity of efflux, } v = \sqrt{2gh} = \sqrt{\frac{2 \times 10 \times 4 \times 10^5}{1000 \times 10}}$$

$$= \sqrt{800}$$

$$= 28.28 \text{ m/s}$$

(ii) Atomizer or Sprayer

It is based on the Bernoulli's principle. The essential parts of an atomizer are shown in figure. The forward stroke of the piston produces a stream of air past the end of the tube.

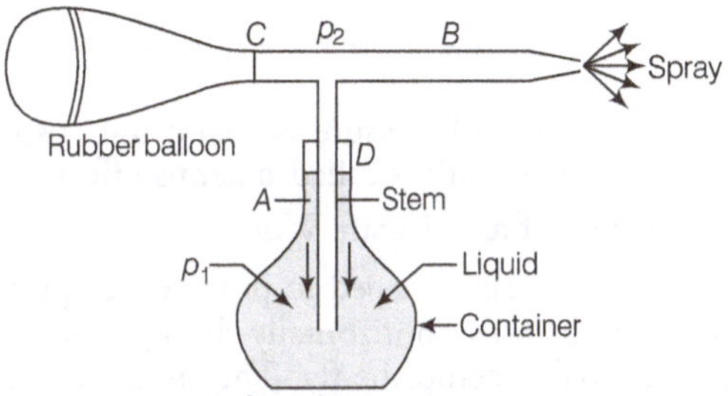

Atomizer or sprayer

The air flowing past the open end of the tube reduces the pressure on the liquid. So, the atmospheric pressure acting on the surface of liquid forces, the liquid into the tube *D*. As a result the liquid rises up in the vertical tube *A*. When it collides with the high speed air in tube *B*, it breaks up into fine spray.

(iii) Dynamic Lift

Dynamic lift is the force that acts on a body by virtue of its motion through a fluid. It is responsible for the curved path of a spinning ball and the lift of an aircraft wing.

(a) **Ball Moving without Spin**

When the velocity of the air on left the ball is same as that on right of the ball at the diametrically opposite points resulting in zero pressure difference.

The air therefore, exerts no sideways force on the ball as shown in Fig. (a)

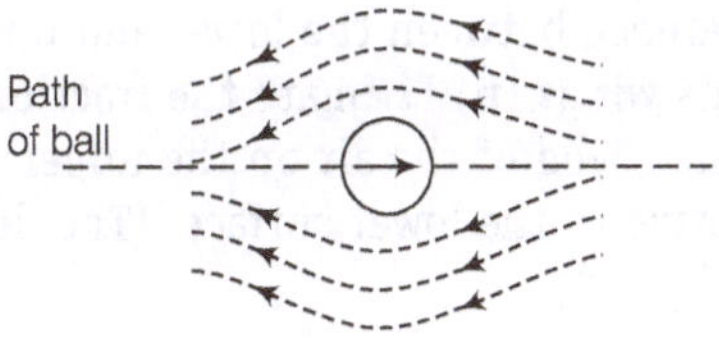

(a) Top view ball moving without spin

(b) **Ball Moving with Spin**

As the ball spins, velocity of air with respect to ball is not same on both sides. Since, the ball is spinning, it drags some air with it because of the roughness of its surface. The speed of air on right of the ball with respect to it is greater than that on left of the ball. Hence, the pressure on right of the ball is greater than that on left of the ball. The force acts on the ball which makes it follow a curved path, as shown in Fig. (b).

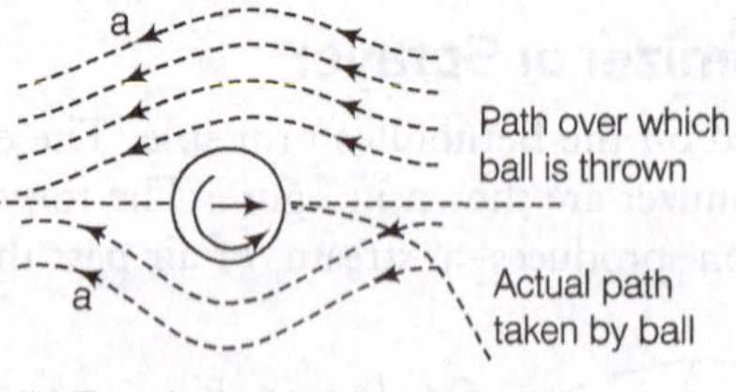

(b) Top view of ball moving with spin

The difference in lateral pressure, which causes a spinning ball to take a curved path is called **magnus effect**.

(c) **Aerofoil, Lift of an Aircraft Wing**

Aerofoil is a solid object shaped to provide an **upward dynamic lift** as it moves horizontally through air. This upward force makes aeroplane fly. The cross-section of the wing of an aeroplane looks like an aerofoil.

When the aeroplane moves through air, the air in the region above the wing moves faster than the air below as seen from the streamlines above the wing.

The difference in speed in the two regions makes the pressure in the region above lower than the pressure below the wing producing thereby a dynamic lift.

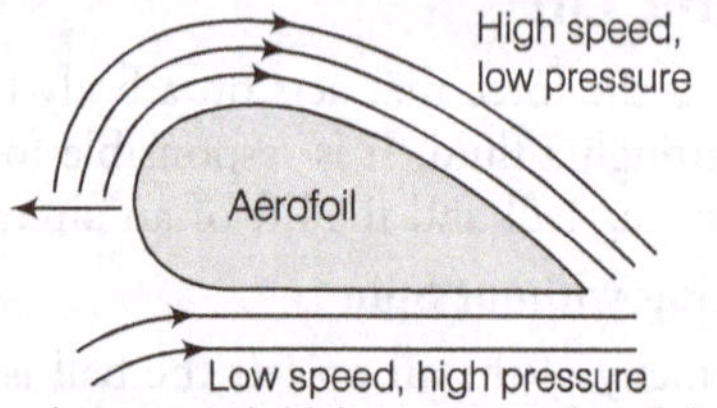

Low speed, high pressure Aerofoil

Example 8 A fully loaded Boeing aircraft has a mass of 3.3×10^5 kg. Its total wing area is 500 m^2. It is in level flight with a speed of 960 km/h. (i) Estimate the pressure difference between the lower and upper surfaces of the wings (ii) Estimate the fractional increase in the speed of the air on the upper surface of the wing relative to the lower surface. [The density of air is $\rho = 1.2$ kgm^{-3}] **NCERT**

Sol. (i) The weight of the boeing aircraft is balanced by the upward force due to the pressure difference

$$\Delta p \times A = mg = 3.3 \times 10^5 \times 9.8$$

So, $$\Delta p = \frac{mg}{A} = \frac{3.3 \times 10^5 \times 9.8}{500}$$
$$= 6.46 \times 10^3 \text{ N/m}^2$$

$\therefore$ $$\Delta p \approx 6.5 \times 10^3 \text{ N/m}^2$$

(ii) Consider v_1 and v_2 are the speeds of air on lower and upper surfaces of the wings and p_1 and p_2 are the corresponding pressures.

From Bernoulli's principle

$$p_1 + \frac{1}{2}\rho v_1^2 = p_2 + \frac{1}{2}\rho v_2^2$$

$\therefore$ $$p_1 - p_2 = \Delta p = \frac{\rho}{2}(v_2^2 - v_1^2)$$

$$(v_2 - v_1) = \frac{2\Delta p}{\rho(v_2 + v_1)}$$

Average speed, $$v_{av} = \frac{v_2 + v_1}{2} = 960 \text{ km/h} = 267 \text{ m/s}$$

So, $$\frac{v_2 - v_1}{v_{av}} = \frac{\Delta p}{\rho v_{av}^2} = \frac{6.5 \times 10^3}{1.2 \times (267)^2} \approx 0.08 = 8\%$$

Then, the speed above the wing needs to be only 8% higher than that below.

(d) **Roof can Blown off Without Damaging the House**

During wind storm, the roofs of some huts are blown off without damaging the other parts of the house. The high wind blowing over the roof creates a low pressure p_2 in accordance with Bernoulli's principle.

The pressure p_1 below the roof is equal to the atmospheric pressure which is larger than p_2. This difference of pressure provides a vertical lift to the roof of hut. When lift is sufficient the roof of the hut is blown off.

(e) **Deep Water Flows Calm**

When the water will deep, the hydrostatic pressure will be large. By Bernoulli's theorem, the velocity of water at that place will be less, i.e. the water will be run calm there.

Topic Practice 2

Multiple Choice Questions

1 Mark

1. In a streamline flow,
   (a) the speed of a particle always remains same
   (b) the velocity of a particle always remains same
   (c) the kinetic energies of all the particles arriving at a given point are the same
   (d) the potential energies of all the particles arriving at a given point are the same

2. In a turbulent flow, the velocity of the liquid molecules in contact with the walls of the tube is
(a) zero
(b) maximum
(c) equal to critical velocity
(d) may have any value

3. Two water pipes of diameters 2 cm and 4 cm are connected with the main supply line. The velocity of flow of water in the pipe of 2 cm diameter is
(a) 4 times that in the other pipe
(b) $\frac{1}{4}$ times that in the other pipe
(c) 2 times that in the other pipe
(d) $\frac{1}{2}$ times that in the other pipe

4. A small drop of water falls from rest through a large height h in air, the final velocity is proportional to
(a) $\sqrt{h}$ (b) h
(c) (1/h) (d) h°

Very Short Answer Type Questions

1 Mark

5. Give one major difference between laminar and turbulent flow.

6. Can two streamlines cross each other, why?

7. While its raining, why all raindrops falls with same speed?

8. Why does the velocity increase when liquid flowing in a wider tube enters a narrow tube? NCERT

9. Can Bernoulli's equation be used to describe the flow of water through a rapid in a river? Explain.

10. Does it matter if one uses gauge instead of absolute pressures in applying Bernoulli's equation? Explain.

11. Give an expressions of pressure head, gravitational head and velocity head of a flowing fluid.

12. A hot liquid moves faster than a cold liquid. Why?

13. On what factors does the critical speed of fluid flow depend?

Short Answer Type I Questions

2 Marks

14. Give definitions and units of
(i) coefficient of viscosity (ii) velocity gradient.

15. Fill in the blanks using the word(s) from the list appended with each statement.
(i) Viscosity of gases......with temperature, whereas, viscosity of liquids......with temperature. (increases/decreases)
(ii) For solids with elastic modulus of rigidity, the shearing force is proportional to......while for fluids, it is proportional to......(shear strain/rate of shear strain)
(iii) For a fluid in a steady flow, the increase in flow speed at a constriction follows from......while the decrease of pressure there follows from......(conservation of mass/Bernoulli's principle).
(iv) For the model of a plane in a wind tunnel, turbulence occurs at a......speed that the critical speed for turbulence for an actual plane (greater/smaller) NCERT

16. In deriving Bernoulli's equation, we equated the work done on the fluid in the tube to its change in the potential and kinetic energy.
(i) How does the pressure change as the fluid moves along the tube, if dissipative forces are present?
(ii) Do the dissipative forces become more important as the fluid velocity increases? Discuss qualitatively.

17. Figs. (a) and (b) refer to the steady flow of a non-viscous liquid. Which of two figures is incorrect Why?

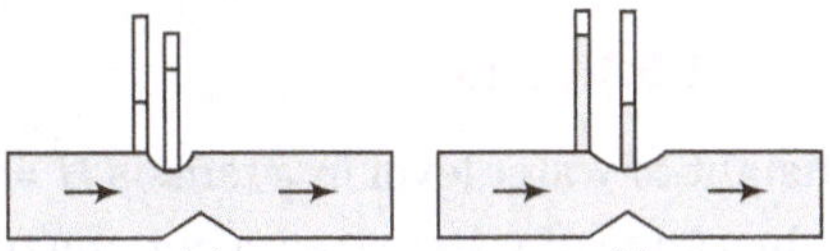
(a) (b)

Short Answer Type II Questions

3 Marks

18. State and prove Bernoulli's theorem.

19. (i) What is viscous force?
(ii) In what factor does it depend?
(iii) Define the coefficient of viscocity.

20. Define terminal velocity. Discuss the factors on which it depends.

21. (i) Why does water flow faster than honey?
(ii) The viscous force F acting on a body of radius r moving with a velocity v in a medium of coefficient of viscosity η is given by $F = 6\pi\eta rv$. Check the correctness of the formula.

22. Write three points of difference between solid friction and viscosity.

Long Answer Type Questions

5 Marks

23. Explain why?
(i) To keep a piece of paper horizontal, you should blow over, not under it.
(ii) When we try to close a water tap with our fingers, fast jets of water gush through the opening between our fingers.
(iii) The size of the needle of a syringe controls flow rate better than the thumb pressure exerted by a doctor while administering an injection.
(iv) A fluid flowing out of a small hole in a vessel results in a backward thrust on the vessel.
(v) A spinning cricket ball in air does not follow a parabolic trajectory. **NCERT**

24. If a sphere of radius r falls under gravity through a liquid of viscosity η, its average acceleration is half that of in starting of the motion. Then, show that the time taken by it to attain the terminal velocity is independent of the liquid density.

Numerical Problems

25. The height of water level in a tank is $H = 96$ cm. Find the range of water stream coming out of a hole at depth $H/4$ from upper surface of water. **[1 M]**

26. At what speed will the velocity head of stream of water be 40 cm? **[2 M]**

27. What should be the average velocity of water in a tube of radius 0.005 m so that the flow is just turbulent? The viscosity of water is 0.001 Pa-s. **[2 M]**

28. In a test experiment on a model aeroplane in a wind tunnel, the flow of speeds on the upper and lower surfaces of the wings are 70 m/s and 63 m/s respectively. What is the lift on the wings, if its area is 2.5 m^2? Take the density of air to be 1.3 kg / m^3. **NCERT [3 M]**

29. The cylindrical tube of a spray pump has a cross-section of 8.0 cm^2 one end of which has 40 fine holes each of diameter 1.00 mm. If the liquid flow inside the tube is 1.5 m/min, what is the speed of ejection of the liquid through the holes? **NCERT [3 M]**

30. A non-viscous liquid of constant density 1000 kgm^{-3} flows in a streamline motion along a tube of variable cross-section. The tube is a kept inclined in the vertical plane as shown in figure. The area of cross-section of the tube at two points P and Q at heights of 2 m and 5 m are respectively, $4\times10^{-3} m^2$ and $8\times10^{-3} m^2$. The velocity of the liquid at point P is 1 ms^{-1}. Find the work done per unit volume by the pressure and the gravity forces as the fluid flows from point P to Q. **[5 M]**

Hints & Solutions

1. (*b*) Both speed and direction of flow remain same.
2. (*d*) In turbulent flow, the velocity may have any value.
3. (*a*) From equation of continuity, av = constant

$$d_A = 2\text{ cm} \text{ and } d_B = 4\text{ cm}$$
$$\therefore \quad r_A = 1\text{ cm} \text{ and } r_B = 2\text{ cm}$$
$$\therefore \quad \frac{v_A}{v_B} = \frac{a_B}{a_A} = \frac{\pi(r_B)^2}{\pi(r_A)^2} = \left(\frac{2}{1}\right)^2 \Rightarrow v_A = 4v_B$$

4. (*d*) Final velocity is terminal velocity, it does not depend on the height of fall.
5. Refer to text on pages 302 and 303 (Streamline and turbulent flow).
6. Two streamlines can never cross each other because if they cross them at the point of intersection, there will be two possible direction of flow of fluid which is impossible for streamlines.
7. Refer to text on page 305 [Applications of Stokes' law (iii)].
8. This is due to equation of continuity, $a_1 v_1 = a_2 v_2$

$$\because \quad a_1 > a_2$$
$$\therefore \quad v_2 > v_1$$

9. No, Bernoulli's equation cannot be used to describe the flow of water through a rapid in a river because Bernoulli's equation can be utilised only for streamline flow.

10. No, it does not matter if one uses gauge instead of absolute pressures in applying Bernoulli's equation unless the atmospheric pressure at the two points where, Bernoulli's equation is applied are significantly different.

11. Refer to text on pages 307 and 308 (Proof of Bernoulli's theorem).

12. The viscosity of liquid decreases with the increase in temperature. Therefore, viscosity of hot liquid is less than that of cold liquid. Due to this, hot liquid moves faster than the cold liquid.

13. The critical speed of a fluid depends on (a) diameter of tube, (b) density of fluid, (c) coefficient of viscosity of the fluid.

14. Refer to text on pages 303 and 304 (Velocity gradient and viscous force and coefficient of viscosity).

15. (i) increases, decreases [1/2]
(ii) shear strain, rate of shear strain [1/2]
(iii) conservation of mass, Bernoulli's principle [1/2]
(iv) greater [1/2]

16. (i) If dissipative forces are present, then a part of pressure energy is utilised in overcoming these forces. Due to which, the pressure decreases as the fluid moves along the tube. [1]

(ii) Yes, the dissipative forces become more important as the fluid velocity increases.

The viscous drag is given by

$$F = -\eta A \frac{dv}{dx}$$

As the velocity of fluid increases, the velocity gradient increases and hence, viscous drag increases i.e. dissipative force also increases. [1]

17. Fig. (a) is incorrect. According to equation of continuity, the speed of liquid is larger at smaller area.

From Bernoulli's theorem due to larger speed, the pressure will be lower at smaller area and therefore, height of liquid column will also be at lesser height, while in Fig. (a) height of liquid column at narrow area is higher. [2]

18. Refer to text on pages 307 and 308 (Bernoulli's theorem and proof).

19. (i) Refer to text on page 303 (Viscous force and coefficient of viscosity).

(ii) Refer to text on page 303 (Viscous force and coefficient of viscosity).

(iii) Refer to text on page 303 (Viscous force and coefficient of viscosity).

20. Refer to text on pages 305 and 306 (Terminal velocity).

21. (i) As we know from poiseuille's formula $V = \frac{\pi p r^4}{8\eta l}$

where, V volume of liquid flowing per second through a horizontal narrow tube of radius r and length l under a pressure difference p across the two ends of the tube and η is the coefficient of viscosity of liquid. As η of honey is more than η of water, hence according to $V \propto \frac{1}{\eta}$, water flows faster than honey. [1½]

(ii) Refer to text on pages 304 and 305 (Stokes' law). [1½]

22. As viscosity and friction both opposes relative motion but they differ from each other as discussed below

Solid friction	Viscosity
Independent of the area of solid surfaces in contact.	Directly proportional to the area of liquid layers.
Independent of the relative velocity of two bodies on surfaces of contact.	Directly proportional to the relative velocity between the layers of liquid.
But depends on normal reaction between the surfaces in contact directly.	It is independent of the normal reaction between the two layers of liquid.

[3]

23. (i) When we blow over a piece of paper, the velocity of air above the paper increases. So, in accordance with Bernoulli's theorem $\left(p + \frac{1}{2}\rho v^2 = \text{constant}\right)$, the pressure of air decreases above the paper. Due to the pressure difference of air, below and above the paper a lifting force acts on paper and hence, it remains horizontal. [1]

(ii) According to equation of continuity,

$$A_1 v_1 = A_2 v_2 \text{ or } A \propto \frac{1}{V}$$

When we try to close a water tap with our fingers, the area of cross-section of the outlet of water jet is reduced due to the restriction provided by the fingers and therefore, the velocity of water increases and fast jets of water gush through the openings between our fingers. [1]

(iii) According to Bernoulli's theorem,

$$p + \frac{1}{2}\rho v^2 = \text{constant}$$

In this relation, pressure (p) occurs with exponential power of one while velocity (v) occurs with exponential powers of two. Therefore, the influence of velocity is higher than pressure. The size of the needle controls the velocity of flow and the thumb pressure controls pressure.

Therefore, size of the needle of a syringe controls flow rate better than thumb pressure. [1]

(iv) A fluid flowing out of a small hole in a vessel has a large velocity and therefore, a large momentum. As no external force is acting, therefore, according to law of conservation of momentum equal momentum in opposite direction and hence, a backward velocity is attained by the vessel. Therefore, a backward thrust $\left(F = \frac{dp}{dt}\right)$ acts on the vessel. [1]

(v) A spinning cricket ball in air does not follow a parabolic trajectory due to Magnus effect.

Let a spinning cricket ball is moving forward with a velocity v and spinning clockwise with velocity u.

As ball moves forward, it leaves, a lower pressure region behind it.

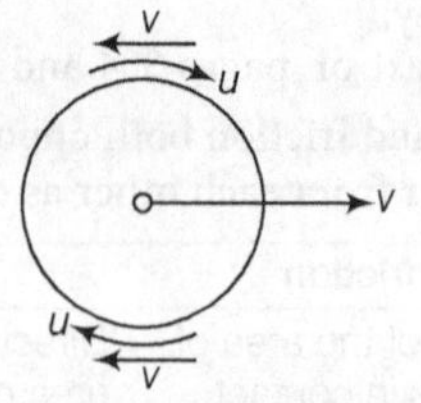

To fill this region, air moves backward with velocity v. The layers of air in contact with the ball spin with ball with velocity u. Therefore, the resultant velocity of air above the ball is $(v - u)$ and below the ball is $(v + u)$.

According to Bernoulli's theorem,

$$p + \frac{1}{2}\rho v^2 = \text{constant}$$

Therefore, pressure below the ball becomes lower than above the ball. Due to this pressure difference, a force acts on ball in downward direction. Therefore, the ball follows a curved path which is not parabolic. [1]

24. Let the density of sphere's material is ρ and that of liquid is σ.

When the sphere just enters in the liquid,

Downward force on the sphere, F = weight of the sphere − weight of the fluid displaced by it.

$$F = \frac{4}{3}\pi r^3 \cdot \rho g - \frac{4}{3}\pi r^3 \cdot \sigma g = \frac{4}{3}\pi r^3 (\rho - \sigma) g$$

$\because$ Mass = Volume × Density

Hence, $m = \frac{4}{3}\pi r^3 \rho$

$\therefore$ Acceleration of the sphere at this instant,

$$a = \frac{F}{m}$$

$$a = \frac{\frac{4}{3}\pi r^3(\rho - \sigma)g}{\frac{4}{3}\pi r^3 \rho} = \left(1 - \frac{\sigma}{\rho}\right)g$$ [2]

When the sphere approches to terminal velocity, its acceleration becomes zero.

$\therefore$ Average acceleration of the sphere $= \frac{a + 0}{2}$

$$= \frac{\left(1 - \frac{\sigma}{\rho}\right)g}{2} = \left(1 - \frac{\sigma}{\rho}\right)\frac{g}{2}$$ [1]

If time t taken by the sphere to attain the terminal velocity

As we know that,

$$\text{Terminal velocity, } v = \frac{2}{9}\frac{r^2}{\eta}(\rho - \sigma)g$$

$\because$ The sphere falls from rest,

$\therefore \quad u = 0$

Using $\quad v = u + at$

Putting values $\frac{2}{9}\frac{r^2}{\eta}(\rho - \sigma)g = 0 + \left(1 - \frac{\sigma}{\rho}\right)\frac{g}{2} \cdot t$ [1]

$$\therefore \quad t = \frac{4}{9}\frac{r^2 \rho}{\eta}$$

Thus, t is independent of the liquid density. [1]

25. The depth of hole below the upper surface of water is

$$h = \frac{H}{4} = \frac{96}{4} = 24 \text{ cm}$$

The height of hole from ground is,

$$h' = 96 - 24 = 72 \text{ cm}$$

Horizontal range $= 2\sqrt{hh'} = 2\sqrt{24 \times 72} = 48\sqrt{3}$ cm

26. Given, $h = 40$ cm, $g = 980 \text{ cm/s}^2$ [1/2]

We know that velocity head, $h = \frac{v^2}{2g}$ [1/2]

$\therefore \quad v = \sqrt{2gh} = \sqrt{2 \times 980 \times 40} = 280 \text{ cms}^{-1}$ [1]

27. Here, $r = 0.005$ m, diameter $D = 2r = 0.010$ m

$$\eta = 0.001 \text{ Pa-s}, \rho = 1000 \text{ kgm}^{-3}$$ [1]

For flow to be just turbulent, $R_e = 3000$

$$\therefore \quad v = \frac{R_e \eta}{\rho D} = \frac{3000 \times 0.001}{1000 \times 0.010} = 0.3 \text{ ms}^{-1}$$ [1]

28. Let the lower and upper surface of the wings of the aeroplane be at the same height h and speeds of air on the upper and lower surfaces of the wings be v_1 and v_2.

Speed of air on the upper surface of the wings

$$v_1 = 70 \text{ m/s}$$

Speed of air on the lower surface of the wings

$$v_2 = 63 \text{ m/s}$$

Density of the air, $\rho = 1.3 \text{ kg/m}^3$ [1]

Area, $A = 2.5 \text{ m}^2$

According to Bernoulli's theorem,

$$p_1 + \frac{1}{2}\rho v_1^2 + \rho gh = p_2 + \frac{1}{2}\rho v_2^2 + \rho gh$$ [1]

or $\quad p_2 - p_1 = \frac{1}{2}\rho(v_1^2 - v_2^2)$

$\therefore$ Lifting force acting on the wings,

$$F = (p_2 - p_1) \times A$$ [1/2]

$$= \frac{1}{2}\rho(v_1^2 - v_2^2) \times A \quad [\because \text{force} = \text{pressure} \times \text{area}]$$

$$= \frac{1}{2} \times 1.3 \times [(70)^2 - (63)^2] \times 2.5$$

$$= \frac{1}{2} \times 1.3 \, [4900 - 3969] \times 2.5$$

$$= \frac{1}{2} \times 1.3 \times 931 \times 2.5 = 1.51 \times 10^3 \text{ N}$$ [1/2]

29. Area of cross-section of tube $(A) = 8 \text{ cm}^2 = 8 \times 10^{-4} \text{ m}^2$

Number of holes, $N = 40$

Diameter of each hole, $2r = 1.0$ mm [1]

$\therefore$ Radius of each hole, $r = 0.5 \text{ mm} = 5\times 10^{-4}\text{ m}$

Velocity of liquid flow in tube, $= 1.5 \text{ m/min} = \frac{1.5}{60} \text{ m/s}$

$= 2.5\times 10^{-2}\text{ m/s}$ [1/2]

Total area of holes $= N \times \pi r^2$

$= 40\times 3.14\times (5\times 10^{-4})^2 = 3.14\times 10^{-5}\text{ m}^2$ [1/2]

From equation of continuity,

$$A_1 v_1 = A_2 v_2$$ [1/2]

or $v_2 = \frac{A_1 v_1}{A_2} = \frac{8\times 10^{-4}\times 2.5\times 10^{-2}}{3.14\times 10^{-5}} = \frac{20}{3.14}\times 10^{-1}$

$= 0.64 \text{ m/s}$ [1/2]

30. Given, $\rho = 1000\text{ kg/m}^3$, $v_1 = 1\text{ m/s}$, $a_1 = 4\times 10^{-3}\text{ m}^2$,

$a_2 = 8\times 10^{-3}\text{ m}^2$, $h_1 = 2\text{ m}$, $h_2 = 5\text{ m}$

Apply Bernoulli's theorem,

$$p_1 + \frac{1}{2}\rho v_1^2 + g\rho h_1 = p_2 + \frac{1}{2}\rho v_2^2 + g\rho h_2$$ [1]

$$(p_1 - p_2) = \frac{1}{2}\rho (v_2^2 - v_1^2) + \rho g (h_2 - h_1)$$

where,

$(p_1 - p_2)$ = Work done by pressure per unit volume

i.e. $$\left(\frac{W}{\text{Volume}}\right)_p = \frac{1}{2}\rho (v_2^2 - v_1^2) + \rho g (h_2 - h_1) \quad \text{...(i)}$$ [1]

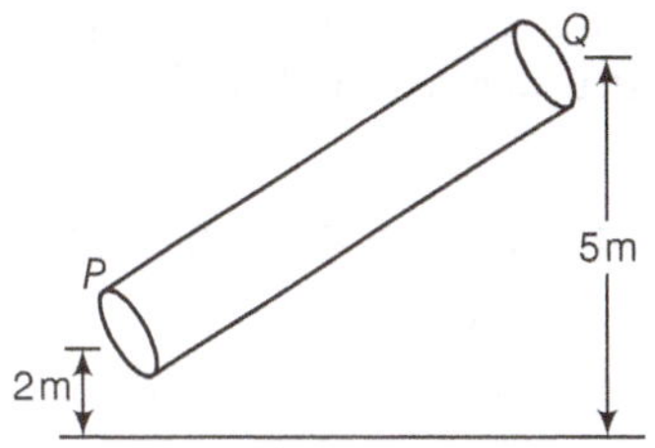

From equation of continuity,

$$a_1 v_1 = a_2 v_2$$ [1]

$$v_2 = \frac{a_1 v_1}{a_2} = \frac{4\times 10^{-3}\times 1}{8\times 10^{-3}} = 0.5 \text{ m/s}$$

$$\left(\frac{W}{\text{Volume}}\right)_p = \frac{1}{2}\times 1000\,[0.25 - 1] + 1000\times 10\,(5-2)$$

$= -375 + 30{,}000 = 29625 \text{ J/m}^3$ [1]

Work done per unit volume by the gravitational force

$= \rho g (h_1 - h_2)$

$= 1000\times 10\,(2-5) = -3\times 10^4 \text{ J/m}^3$ [1]

TOPIC 03 Surface Tension and Surface Energy

Surface Tension

Surface tension arises due to the fact that the free surface of a liquid at rest has some additional potential energy. Due to it, a liquid surface tends to occupy a minimum surface area and behaves like stretched membrane.

e.g. A steel needle may be made to float on water, though the steel is more dense than water. This is because the water surface acts as a stretched elastic membrane and supports the needle. This property of a liquid is called **surface tension.**

Consider a line AB on the free surface of a liquid. The small elements of the surface on this line are in equilibrium because they are acted upon by equal and opposite forces, acting perpendicular to the line from either side as shown in figure.

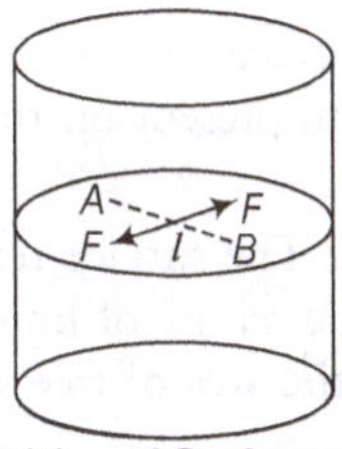

Definition of Surface tension

The force acting on this line is proportional to the length of this line. If l is the length of imaginary line and F the total force on either side of the line, then

$$F \propto l \Rightarrow F = Sl$$

$$S = \frac{F}{l}$$

or $$\boxed{\text{Surface tension, } S = \frac{\text{Force}}{\text{Length}}}$$

From this expression, **surface tension can be defined as the force acting per unit length of an imaginary line drawn on the liquid surface, the direction of force being perpendicular to this line and tangential to the liquid surface.** It is denoted by S and it is a **scalar quantity.**

Units and Dimension of Surface Tension

SI units of surface tension = N/m

CGS unit of surface tension = dyne/cm

Dimension of surface tension

$$= \frac{\text{Force}}{\text{Length}} = \frac{[\text{MLT}^{-2}]}{[\text{L}]} = [\text{ML}^0\text{T}^{-2}]$$

Factors Affecting Surface Tension

1. **Temperature** The surface tension of liquid decreases with rise in temperature and *vice-versa.*

   The surface tension of a liquid becomes zero at a particular temperature, called 'Critical temperature' of that liquid. Due to this,
   (i) Hot soup taste better than cold soup as hot soup spread over a large area of tongue.
   (ii) Machinery parts get jammed in winter as surface tension of lubricating oil increases with decrease in temperature.
2. **Addition of Impurities** The surface tension of liquids changes appreciably with addition of impurities.(a) A highly soluble substance like sodium chloride increases the surface tension of water. (b)A sparingly soluble substance like phenol or soap reduces the surface tension of water.
3. **Medium** The surface tension of liquid depends upon the medium present on the other side of liquid.
4. **Nature of liquid** The surface tension of liquid depends upon the nature of liquid and is independent of the area of free surface.

Example Showing Surface Tension

(i) Rain drops and drops of mercury placed on glass plate are spherical.
(ii) Hair of shaving brush/painting brush, when dipped in water spread out, but as soon as, it is taken out, its hairs stick together.
(iii) A greased needle placed gently on the free surface of water in a beaker does not sink.
(iv) Oil drop spreads on cold water but does not change shape on hot water.

Intermolecular Forces : Cohesive and Adhesive Forces

Between any two molecules, there exists a force of attraction. This force is called the intermolecular force.

These intermolecular forces of attraction are of two types

(i) **Cohesive force** The force of attraction between the two molecules of the same substance is called as a cohesive force and the attraction itself is called **cohesion**, e.g. attraction between water and water molecules.
(ii) **Adhesive force** The force of attraction between the two molecules of the different substance is called an adhesive force and the attraction itself is called **adhesion.**

Water wets glass but mercury does not wet glass In case of water, cohesive force between water molecules is very less compared to the adhesive force between glass and water molecules. Thus, there is a strong attraction between water and glass molecules. Hence, water wets glass.

In case of mercury, the cohesive force between its molecules is very strong compared to negligible adhesive force between glass and mercury molecules. Thus, there is a strong attraction between mercury molecules and almost no attractive force between glass and mercury molecules. Hence, mercury does not wet.

Explanation of Surface Tension on the Basis of Intermolecular Cohesive Force

Laplace explained the phenomenon of surface tension on the basis of intermolecular forces. We know that if the distance between two molecules is less than the molecular range c ($\approx 10^{-9}$ m), then they attract each other, but if the distance is more than this range, then the attraction becomes negligible.

In order to understand the tension acting in the free surface of a liquid. Consider three molecules A, B and C in a liquid, such that molecule A is well inside the liquid, molecule B is close to the free surface and the molecule C is on the free surface.

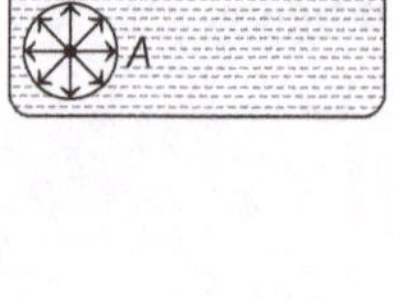

From the figure, we concluded that

(i) The sphere of influence of the molecule A is completely inside the liquid, and hence it will be acted upon by equal forces in all directions and these forces will balance one another and the net force acting on it is zero.

(ii) For the molecule B, a part of upper half of the sphere of influence is in the air, which contains air molecules. Air molecules exert very negligible adhesive forces on molecule B. Therefore, the cohesive forces due to molecules in the liquid remains unbalanced and thus a net force in downward direction acts on the molecule.

(iii) For the molecule C, the upper half of the sphere of influence is completely in the air. Due to this, the force of attraction due to the molecules inside the lower half of the sphere will remain unbalanced. This molecule experiences the maximum possible unbalanced force in the downward direction.

(iv) Thus, the molecules on the surface and in a surface film of thickness equal to the range of molecular attraction of the liquid molecule experience a net force in the downward direction. The magnitude of force depends upon the distance of the molecule from the free surface. The behaviour of this film is different from that of the rest of the liquid. It is called the surface film. This film behaves like a film which is under tension. This phenomenon is known as surface tension.

(v) If any molecule is brought to the surface from the liquid, the work is to be done against this net downward force. This work increases the potential energy of the surface. But the liquid surface will have the tendency to have minimum potential energy. So a minimum number of molecules remains on the surface of the liquid.

(vi) Thus, the free surface of a liquid behaves like a stretched elastic membrane and has a tendency to contract so as to minimise its surface area.

Shape of Menicus

If a liquid wets the sides of the vessel containing liquid, the shape of liquid meniscus is **concave upwards.** In this case, force of cohesion between liquid molecules is less than force of adhesion between liquid and vessel molecules.

If a liquid does not wet the sides of the vessel containing liquid, the shape of liquid meniscus is **convex upwards.** In this case, force of cohesion between liquid molecules is greater than the force of adhesion between liquid and vessel molecules.

The shape of liquid meniscus depends upon the molecular forces and is independent of the gravity pull.

Surface Energy

The free surface of a liquid always has a tendency to contract and possess minimum surface area. If it is required to increase the surface area of the liquid at a constant temperature, work has to be done. This **work done** is stored in the surface film of the liquid as its **potential energy**.

This potential energy per unit area of the surface film is called the **surface energy.** Hence, **the surface energy may be defined as the amount of work done in increasing the area of the liquid surface by unity**. Thus,

$$\text{Surface energy} = \frac{\text{Work done in increasing the surface area}}{\text{Increase in surface area}}$$

The SI unit of surface energy is J/m^2.

Relation between Surface Energy and Surface Tension

Consider a rectangular frame $PQRS$. Here, wire QR is movable. A soap film is formed on the frame. The film pulls the movable wire QR inward due to surface tension.

As, $$\text{Surface tension} = \frac{\text{force}}{\text{length}} = \frac{F'}{2l}$$

$$F' = S \times 2l$$

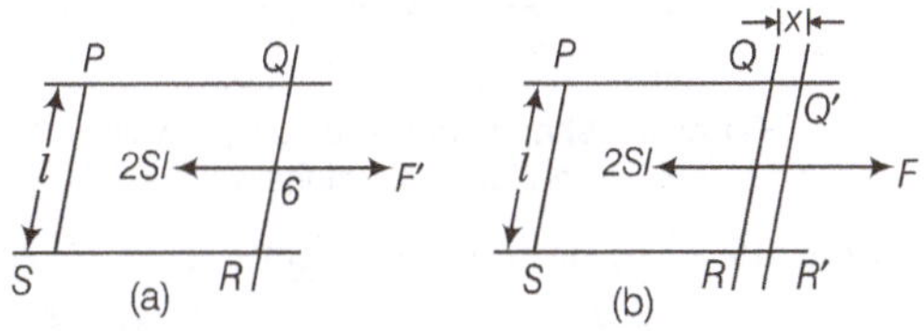

Equilibrium position of the film　　Stretched position of the film

If QR is moved through a distance x by an external force F very slowly, then some work has to be done against this force.

$\therefore$ External work done = Force × distance

$$= S \times 2l \times x \qquad [\because F' = F]$$

Increase in surface area of film $= 2l \times x$

[As soap film has two sides]

$$\text{Surface energy} = \frac{\text{Work done}}{\text{Surface area}} = \frac{S2lx}{2lx} = S$$

So, **value of surface energy of liquid is numerically equal to the value of surface tension.**

Angle of Contact

The surface of liquid near the plane of contact with another medium is in curved shape.

The angle between tangent to the liquid surface at the point of contact and the solid surface inside the liquid is called as angle of contact.

The value of angle of contact depends on the following factors

(i) Nature of the solid and liquid in contact.

(ii) Cleanliness of the surface in contact.

(iii) Medium above the free surface of the liquid.

(iv) Temperature of the liquid

e.g. Water forms droplets on lotus leaf shown in Fig. (a) while spreads over a clean plastic plate in Fig. (b).

Consider the three interfacial tensions at all the three interfaces such as

S_{sa} = surface tension between solid and air
S_{la} = surface tension between liquid and air
S_{sl} = surface tension between solid and liquid

At the line of contact, the surface forces between the three media must be in equilibrium. Resolving S_{la} into two rectangular components, we have $S_{la}\cos\theta$ acts along the solid surface and $S_{la}\sin\theta$ acts along the perpendicular to the solid surface.

As the liquid on the surface of soild is at rest, so the molecules of these interfaces are in equilibrium. Thus, the net force on them is zero.

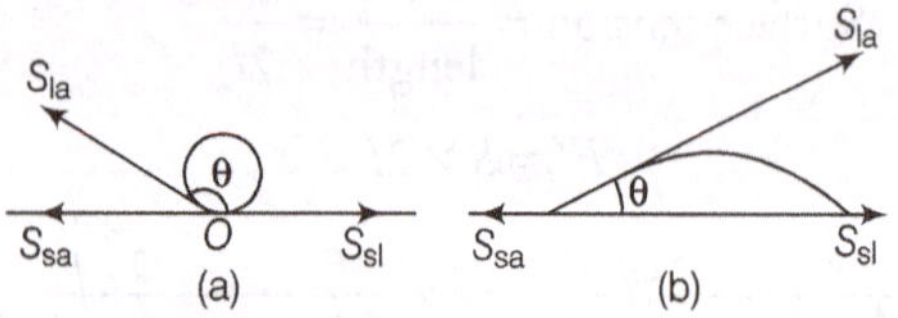

Different shapes of water drops with interfacial tensions

For the molecule O to be in equilibrium.

$$S_{sl} + S_{la}\cos\theta = S_{sa}$$

$$\cos\theta = \frac{S_{sa} - S_{sl}}{S_{la}}$$

The following cases arise

(i) If the surface tension at the solid-liquid S_{sl}, interface is greater than the surface tension at the liquid-air S_{la} interface, i.e. $S_{sl} > S_{la}$, then $\cos\theta$ is negative and $\theta > 90°$ (the angle of contact is **obtuse angle**). The molecules of a liquid are attracted strongly to themselves and weakly to those of solid. It costs a lot of energy to create a liquid-solid surface. The liquid then does not wet the solid. e.g. Water-leaf or glass-mercury interface.

(ii) If the surface tension at the solid-liquid S_{sl} interface is less than the surface tension at the liquid-air S_{la} interface, i.e. $S_{sl} < S_{la}$, then $\cos\theta$ is positive and $\theta < 90°$ (the angle of contact is **acute angle**). The molecules of the liquid are strongly attracted to those of solid and weakly attracted to themselves. It costless energy to create a liquid-solid surface and liquid wets the solid.
e.g. When soap or detergent is added to water, the angle of contact becomes small.

Capillarity

The term capilla means hair which is Latin word. A tube of very fine (hair-like) bore is called a **capillary tube.**

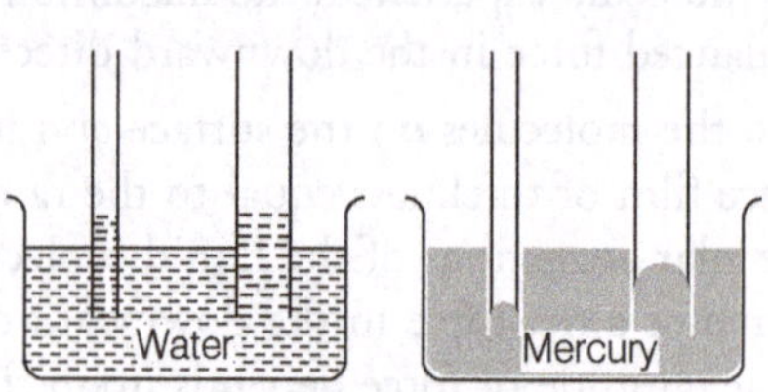

Capillarity

If a capillary tube of glass is dipped in liquid like water, the liquid rises in the tube, but when the capillary tube is dipped in a liquid like mercury, the level of liquid falls in the tube. **This phenomenon of rise or fall of a liquid in the capillary is called capillarity.**

Some examples are

1. We use towels for drying our skin.
2. In trees sap rises due to vessels. It is similar to capillary action.

Capillary Rise

One application of the pressure difference across a curved surface is the water rises up in a narrow tube (capillary) in spite of gravity. Consider a capillary of radius R is inserted into a vessel containing water.

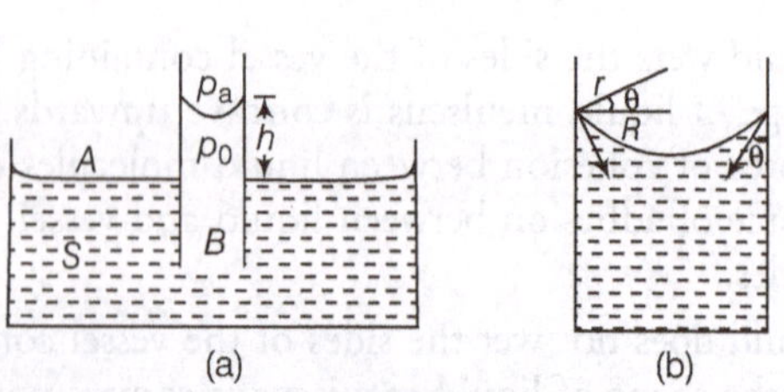

Capillary rise

The surface of water in the capillary becomes concave. It means that there must be a pressure difference between the two sides of the meniscus.

So, $(p_a - p_0) = (2S/r)$

$= 2S/(R\sec\theta)$

$= (2S/R)\cos\theta$ ...(i)

where, r = radius of curvature of the concave meniscus.

Now, consider two points A and B. According to Pascal's law, they must be at the same pressure,

$$p_0 + h\rho g = p_A = p_B = p_a$$

So, $p_a = p_0 + h\rho g$

$p_a - p_0 = \rho g h$ ...(ii)

(p_a = atmospheric pressure)

From Eqs. (i) and (ii), we get

$$\rho g h = \frac{2S}{R}\cos\theta$$

Height of rise of liquid in capillary, $h = \dfrac{2S\cos\theta}{\rho R g}$

This is the formula for the rise of liquid in a capillary. The liquids which met the glass surfaces, e.g. water, rises in the capillary and the liquids which do not wet the glass surface falls in the capillary.

Some common examples of capillarity are

(i) Blotting paper absorbs ink due to capillarity.
(ii) A towel soaks water on account of capillarity motion.
(iii) Oil rises through the wicks due to capillarity.

Example 1 A capillary of radius 0.05 cm is immersed in water. Find the value of rise of water in capillary if value for the surface tension is 0.073 N/m and angle of contact is 0°.

Sol. Given, $S = 0.073$ N/m,

$R = 0.05\,\text{cm} = 5\times10^{-4}$ m

$\theta = 0°, h = ?$

From the formula, $h = \dfrac{2S\cos\theta}{\rho g R} = \dfrac{2\times0.073\times\cos0°}{10^3\times9.8\times5\times10^{-4}}$

$= 0.02979$ m

Example 2 In a glass capillary tube, water rises upto a height of 10.0 cm while mercury fall down by 5.0 cm in the same capillary. If the angles of contact for mercury glass is 60° and water glass is 0°, then find the ratio of surface tension of mercury and water.

Sol. For water, $h_1 = 10.0\,\text{cm} = 0.1$ m

$\rho_1 = 10^3\,\text{kg/m}^3, \theta = 0°$

For mercury, $h_2 = 5.0\,\text{cm} = 0.05$ m

$\rho_2 = 13.6\times10^3\,\text{kg/m}^3, \theta = 60°$

Suppose S_1 and S_2 are the surface tensions for water and mercury, respectively, then

$$S_1 = \frac{h_1 R\rho_1 g}{2\cos\theta_1} \text{ and } S_2 = \frac{h_2 R\rho_2 g}{2\cos\theta_2}$$

The ratio of surface tension of mercury and water,

$$\frac{S_2}{S_1} = \frac{h_2 R\rho_2 g}{2\cos\theta_2}\times\frac{2\cos\theta_1}{h_1 R\rho_1 g}$$

$$\frac{S_2}{S_1} = \frac{h_2\rho_2\cos\theta_1}{h_1\rho_1\cos\theta_2}$$

$$= \frac{0.05\times13.6\times10^3\times\cos0°}{0.1\times1000\times\cos60°} = 13.6:1$$

Measuring the Surface Tension of Liquid

The arrangement for measuring h is shown in figure. It consists of a glass capillary of uniform cross-section clamped in a stand in vertical position. A beaker filled with water is placed on the horizontal base of the stand exactly below the capillary. A travelling microscope (capable of travelling in both vertical and horizontal direction) is placed in front of the capillary for height measurement.

When the capillary rise is complete, readings of water level in the beaker and that of lowest point of meniscus in the capillary are taken by travelling microscope. The difference of these readings gives h.

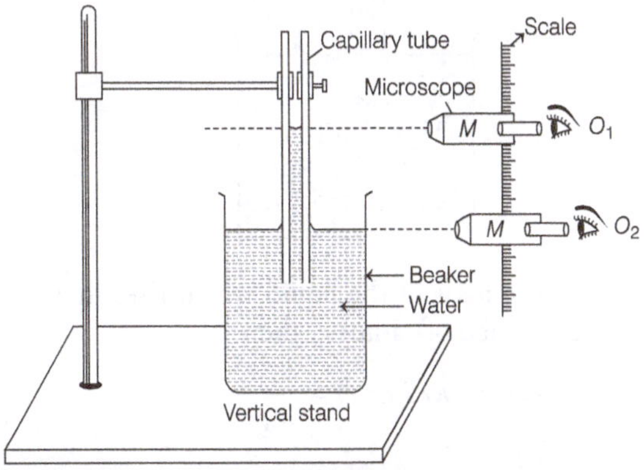

By the help of vernier caliper, the diameter can be calculated $\left(r = \dfrac{\text{diameter}}{2}\right)$.

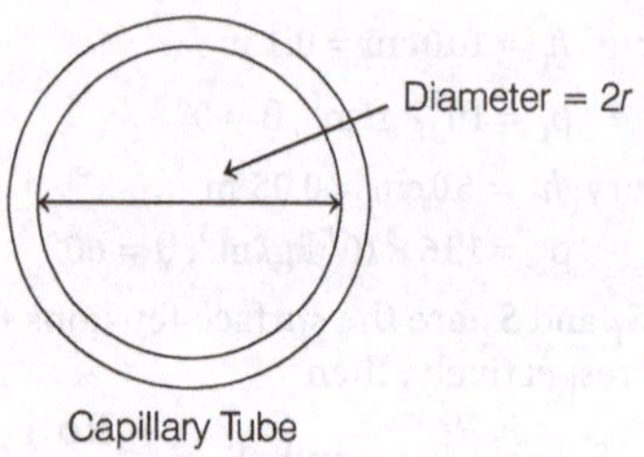

Capillary Tube

Putting the observed value of h and r in the equation given below.

$$S = \frac{rh\rho g}{2}$$

By this process value of surface tension can be calculated.

Some Special Cases of Capillary Rise

(i) If a capillary tube is of insufficient length as compared to height to which liquid can rise in the capillary tube, then the liquid rises upto the full length of capillary tube but there is no overflowing of the liquid in the form of fountain. It is so because the liquid meniscus adjusts its radius of curvature so, that $hR = a$ constant, i.e. $hR = h'R'$.

(ii) When a capillary tube dipped vertically in a liquid is tilted, length of the liquid (l) in capillary tube increases but vertical height of liquid (h) in the tube above the surface of liquid in trough remains the same.

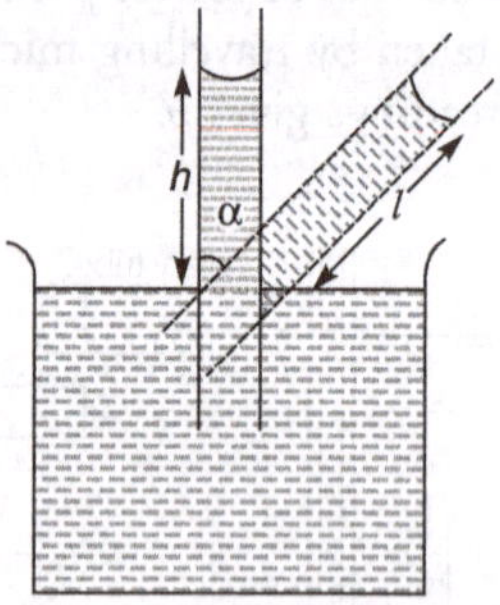

(iii) If m is the mass of the liquid which rises in a capillary tube of radius r, then

$$mg = 2\pi rS \text{ or } m = \frac{2\pi rS}{g}$$

Excess Pressure

Due to surface tension, a drop or bubble tends to contract and so compresses the matter enclosed. This in turn increases the internal pressure which prevents further contraction and equilibrium is achieved.

So, inequilibrium the pressure inside a bubble or drop is greater than outside and the difference of pressure between two sides of the liquid surface is called excess pressure.

Excess Pressure Inside a Liquid Drop

Suppose a spherical liquid drop of radius R and S be the surface tension of liquid. Due to its spherical shape, there is an excess pressure p inside the drop over that on outside. This excess pressure acts normally outwards. Due to this pressure, radius increases from R to $R + dR$, then extra surface energy can be determined.

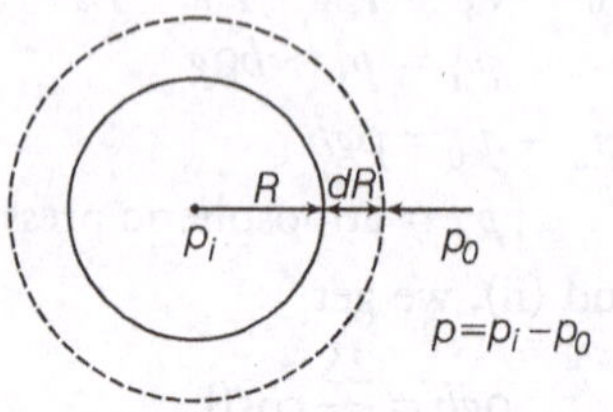

Excess pressure inside a liquid drop

Excess pressure inside the drop, $p = p_i - p_0$

where, p_i = total pressure inside the liquid drop

p_0 = atmospheric pressure

Initial surface area of the liquid $= 4\pi R^2$

Final surface area of the liquid drop

$$= 4\pi (R + dR)^2 = 4\pi (R^2 + 2R\,dR + dR^2)$$

$$= 4\pi R^2 + 8\pi R dR$$

[dR^2 is very small and hence neglected]

Increase in the surface area of liquid drop

$$= 4\pi R^2 + 8\pi R\,dR - 4\pi R^2 = 8\pi R dR$$

External work done in increasing the surface area of the drop

= Increase in surface energy

= Increase in surface area × Surface tension

$$= (8\pi R dR) \times S \quad \text{...(i)}$$

But work done

= Excess pressure × Area × Change in radius

$$= p \times 4\pi R^2 \times dR \quad \text{...(ii)}$$

From Eqs. (i) and (ii), we get

So, $$p \times 4\pi R^2 \times dR = 8\pi RdRS$$

Excess pressure, $p = \frac{2S}{R}$

So, **pressure difference in a drop bubble,**

$$p_i - p_0 = \frac{2S}{R}$$

Excess Pressure Inside a Soap Bubble

In case of a soap bubble, there are two surfaces which expands, so

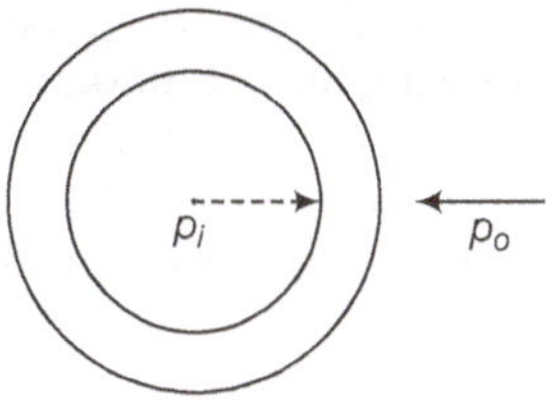

Excess pressure inside a soap bubble

Increase in surface area of a soap bubble

$$= 2 \times 8\pi R\, dR = 16\pi R\, dR \quad ...(i)$$

External work done in increasing the surface area of the soap bubble = Increase in surface energy

$$= \text{Increase in surface area} \times \text{surface tension}$$
$$= 16\pi R\, dRS$$

But, work done = Force × change in radius

where, Force = Excess pressure × area

$$= (p \times 4\pi r^2)$$

So, work done $= p \times 4\pi R^2 \times dR$ ...(ii)

From Eqs. (i) and (ii), we get

$$p \times 4\pi R^2 \times dR = 16\pi R dRS$$

$$\boxed{p = \frac{4S}{R}}$$

Pressure difference inside a soap bubble, $p_i - p_0 = \dfrac{4S}{R}$

Excess pressure inside an air bubble in a liquid is similar to a liquid drop in air, it has only one free spherical surface. Hence, excess pressure is given by

$$p = \frac{2S}{R}$$

Note

- When an air bubble of radius R lies at a depth h below the free surface of a liquid of density ρ and surface tension S, the excess pressure inside the bubble will be
$$p = \frac{2S}{R} + h\rho g$$
- When an ice-skater slides over the surface of smooth ice, some ice melts due to the pressure exerted by the sharp metal edges of the skates. The tiny water droplets act as rigid ball bearings and help the skaters to run along smoothly.

Some Important Points Regarding Excess Pressure

(i) If we have an air bubble inside a liquid, a single surface is formed. There is air on the concave side and liquid on the convex side. The pressure in the concave side (that is in the air) is greater than the pressure in the convex side (that is in the liquid) by an amount $2T/R$.

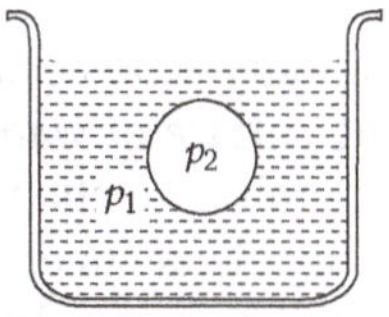

Excess pressure in an air bubble inside a liquid

$$\therefore \quad p_2 - p_1 = \frac{2T}{R}$$

(ii) From the above discussion, we can make a general statement. The pressure on the concave side of a spherical liquid surface is greater than the convex side by $2T/R$ as shown below.

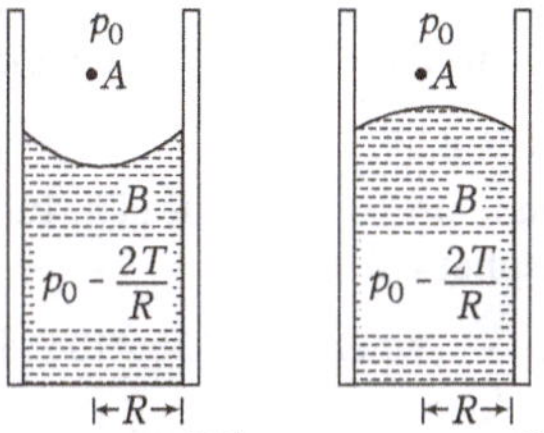

$p_A - p_B = \dfrac{2T}{R}$ $\qquad$ $p_B - p_A = \dfrac{2T}{R}$

(iii) Excess pressure inside a soap bubble can also be understood in terms of excess pressure inside a curved surface as shown below

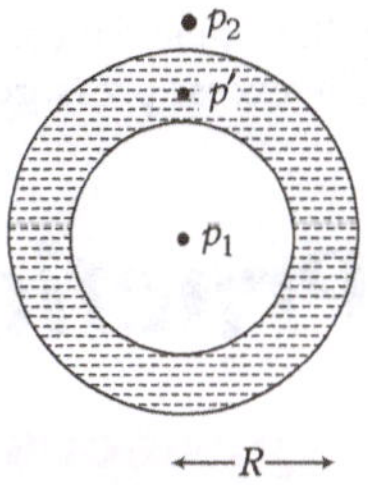

$$p_1 - p' = \frac{2T}{R} \Rightarrow p' - p_2 = \frac{2T}{R}$$

Excess pressure $\Delta p = p_1 - p_2 = \dfrac{4T}{R}$

(iv) If two bubbles of different sizes are connected with each other through a thin tube (as shown in figure) then the air will rush from smaller to larger bubble (pressure inside smaller bubble will be greater than pressure inside larger bubble), so that the smaller will shrink while the larger will expand till the smaller bubble reduces to a droplet.

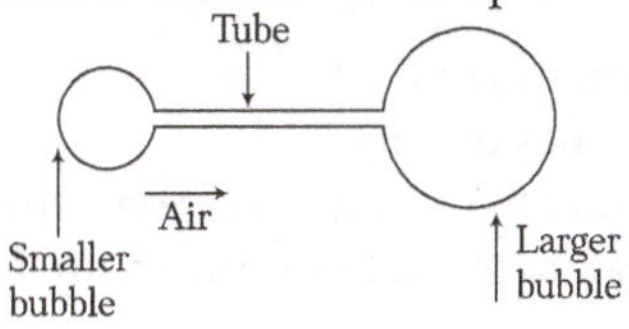

Example 3 **Excess Pressure in Hemispherical Bubble**

The lower end of a capillary tube of diameter 2 mm is dipped 8 cm below the surface of water in a beaker. What is the pressure required in the tube in order to blow a hemispherical bubble at its end in water? The surface tension of water at temperature of the experiments is $7.30 \times 10^{-2} \text{Nm}^{-1}$, 1 atm $= 1.01 \times 10^5 \text{Pa}$, density of water = 1000 kg/m^3, $g = 9.80 \text{ ms}^{-2}$. Also, calculate the excess pressure.

NCERT

Sol. Given, $h = 0.08$ m, $d = 1000 \text{ kg/m}^3$, $g = 9.80 \text{ m/s}^2$ and we know that $p_0 = p_a + hdg$

p_0 is outside pressure

$$p_0 = 1.01 \times 10^5 \text{ Pa} + 0.08 \text{ m} \times 1000 \text{ kg/m}^3 \times 9.80 \text{ m/s}^2$$

$$p_0 = 1.01784 \times 10^5 \text{ Pa}$$

Calculate inside pressure required in tube in order to blow a hemispherical bubble

$$p_i = p_0 + \frac{2S}{r}, \text{ where } S = 7.30 \times 10^{-2} \text{ Pa-m}$$

$$p_i = 1.01784 \times 10^5 + \frac{2 \times 7.3 \times 10^{-2}}{10^{-3}}$$

$$= (1.01784 + 0.00146) \times 10^5 \text{ Pa} \Rightarrow$$

$$p_i = 1.02 \times 10^5 \text{ Pa}$$

where, the radius of the bubble is taken to be equal to the radius of capillary tube. Since, the bubble is hemispherical. The excess pressure in the bubble is 146 Pa.

Topic Practice 3

Multiple Choice Questions

(1 Mark)

1. Surface tension is due to
(a) frictional forces between molecules
(b) cohesive forces between molecules
(c) adhesive forces between molecules
(d) Both (b) and (c)

2. The value of surface tension of water is minimum at
(a) 4°C (b) 25°C (c) 50°C (d) 75°C

3. The surface tension of a liquid at its boiling point
(a) becomes zero
(b) becomes infinity
(c) is equal to the value at room temperature
(d) is half to the value at the room temperature

4. Water rises to a height h in capillary tube. If the length of capillary tube above the surface of water is made less than h, then
(a) water rises upto the tip of capillary tube and then starts overflowing like a fountain
(b) water rises upto the top of capillary tube and stays there without overflowing
(c) water rises upto a point a little below the top and stays there
(d) water does not rise at all

5. A capillary tube A is dipped in water. Another identical tube B is dipped in soap-water solution. Which of the following shows the relative nature of the liquid columns in the two tubes?

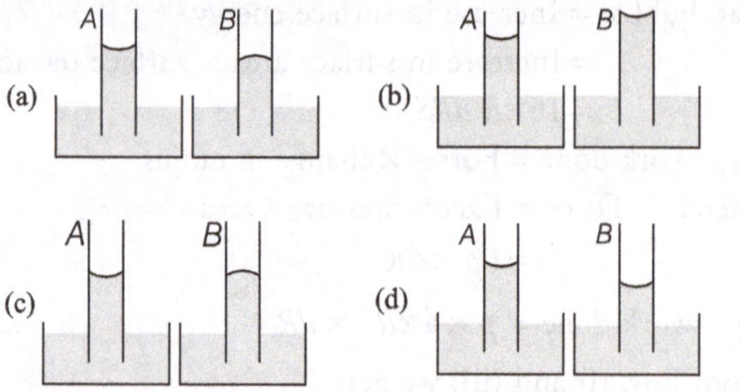

Very Short Answer Type Questions

(1 Mark)

6. If a wet piece of wood burns, then water droplets appear on the other end, why?

7. Why, surface tension of all lubricating oils and paint is kept low?

8. It becomes easier to spray the water in which some soap is dissolved, explain it.

9. Why soap bubble bursts after some time?

10. How a raincoat become waterproof?

Short Answer Type I Questions

(2 Marks)

11. What is surface tension? Give its unit and dimensions. Is it a scalar quantity or a vector?

12. What do you mean by surface energy?

Short Answer Type II Questions

(3 Marks)

13. Define 'angle of contact'. Draw labelled diagrams to show angles of contact between

(i) mercury and glass

(ii) water and glass.

14. (i) A capillary tube is immersed first in cold water and then in hot water. In which case, height of capillary is more and why?

(ii) Water gets depressed in a glass tube whose inner surface is coated with wax, why?

15. (i) The excess pressure inside a soap bubble is thrice the excess pressure inside a second soap bubble. What is the ratio between the volume of the first and second bubble?

(ii) The soap bubbles of unequal sizes are blown at the ends of a capillary tube. Which one will grow at the expense of other and why?

Long Answer Type Questions

5 Marks

16. Derive an expression for excess of pressure inside

(i) a liquid drop. (ii) a soap bubble.

17. How angle of contact decides shape of a drop of liquid over a solid surface. Explain.

18. Derive an expression for rise of a liquid in a capillary tube. Under what condition level of liquid in capillary falls below free surface of liquid?

19. If a number of little droplets of water, each of radius r, coalesce to form a single drop of radius R, and the energy released is converted into kinetic energy then find out the velocity acquired by the bigger drop.

20. Explain why?

(i) The angle of contact of mercury with glass is obtuse, while that of water with glass is acute.

(ii) Water on a clean glass surface tends to spread out while mercury on the same surface tends to form drops. (Put differently, water wets the glass while mercury does not.)

(iii) Surface tension of a liquid is independent of the area of the surface.

(iv) Water with detergents dissolved in it should have small angles of contact.

(v) A drop of liquid under no external forces is always spherical in shape. NCERT

Numerical Problems

21. Fig.(a) shows a thin liquid film supporting a small weight $= 4.5 \times 10^{-2}$N. What is the weight supported by a film of the same liquid at the same temperature in Figs. (b) and (c)? Explain your answer physically. NCERT [2 M]

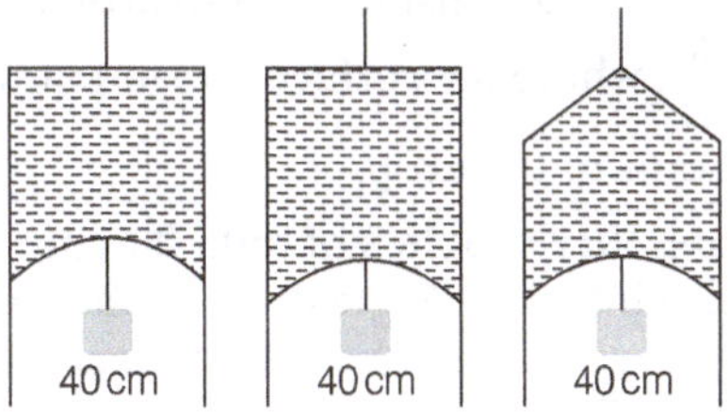

22. A liquid drop breaks into 27 small drops. If surface tension of the liquid is S, then find the energy released. [2 M]

23. Find the work done in increasing the radius of a soap bubble from 4 cm to 6 cm. The value of surface tension for the soap solution is 30 dyne cm^{-1}. [1 M]

24. Find the work done required to make a soap bubble of radius 0.02 m. Given surface tension of soap 0.03 N/m. [1 M]

25. The surface tension and vapour pressure of water at 20°C is 7.28×10^{-2}N/m and 2.33×10^{3}Pa, respectively. What is the radius of the smallest spherical water droplet which can form without evaporating at 20°C? NCERT [2 M]

26. Two soap bubbles of radii 6 cm and 8 cm coalesce to form a single bubble. Find the radius of the new bubble. [2 M]

27. A liquid drop of radius 4 mm breaks into 1000 identical drops. Find the change in surface energy. $S = 0.07$ Nm^{-1}. [2 M]

28. The sap in trees, which consists mainly of water in summer, rises in a system of capillaries of radius $r = 2.5 \times 10^{-5}$ m. The surface tension of sap is $S = 7.28 \times 10^{-2}$ N/m and angle of contact is 0°. Does surface tension alone account for the supply of water to the top of all trees? NCERT [2 M]

29. A U-shaped wire is dipped in a soap solution and removed. The thin soap film formed between the wire and a light slider supports a weight of 1.5×10^{-2}N (which includes the small weight of the slider). The length of the slider is 30 cm. What is the surface tension of the film? NCERT [3 M]

30. What is the pressure inside the drop of mercury of radius 3.00 mm at room temperature? Surface tension of mercury at that temperature (20°C) is 4.65×10^{-1} N/m. The atmospheric pressure is 1.01×10^{5} Pa. Also, give the excess pressure inside the drop.
Excess pressure inside a liquid drop is given by $\Delta p = \frac{2S}{R}$, where S = surface tension of the liquid, R = radius of the drop. **NCERT [3 M]**

31. Two mercury droplets of radii 0.1 cm and 0.2 cm collapse into one single drop. What amount of energy is released? The surface tension of mercury $S = 435.5 \times 10^{-3}$ N/m.
When two or more droplets collapse to form a bigger drop, then its surface area decreases and energy is released equal to $S\Delta A$. **NCERT [3 M]**

32. What is the excess pressure inside a bubble of soap solution of radius 5.00 mm, given that the surface tension of soap solution at the temperature (20°C) is 2.50×10^{-2} N/m? If an air bubble of the same dimension were formed at a depth of 40.0 cm inside a container containing the soap solution (of relative density 1.20), what would be the pressure inside the bubble? (1 atm pressure is 1.01×10^{5} Pa.) **NCERT [5 M]**

Hints & Solutions

1. (*d*) Both cohesive and adhesive forces result in surface tension.

2. (*a*) Value of surface tension decreases with increase in temperature.

3. (*a*) Surface tension is zero at boiling point.

4. (*b*) It is given that water rises to a height h in capillary tube. So, the length of capillary tube above the surface water is made less than h, then height of water column > length of capillary tube.
So, liquid will be stay there.

5. (*d*) Soap solution has lower surface tension, T as compared to pure water and capillary rise in tube,
i.e. $h = \frac{2T \cos\theta}{\rho r g}$, so h is less for soap solution.

The radius of curvature of concave meniscus increases till the pressure on its concave side becomes equal to the pressure exerted by the liquid column of smaller length.

6. When a piece of the wood burns, then steam formed and water appear in the form of drops due to surface tension on the other end.

7. So, they can spread over large area easily.

8. When some soap is dissolved in water, the surface tension of water decreases. Thus, the less energy required to spray water.

9. Soap bubble bursts after some time because the pressure inside it become more than the outside pressure.

10. If the angle of contact between water and the material of the raincoat is obtuse, then rain water does not wet the raincoat. Thus, the raincoat becomes waterproof. [2]

11. Refer to text on pages 315 and 316 (Surface tension and units and dimension of surface tension).

12. Refer to text on page 317 (Surface energy).

13. Refer to text on page 318 (Angle of contact). [1]
Diagrams to show angles of contact between
(i) Mercury and glass is as follows

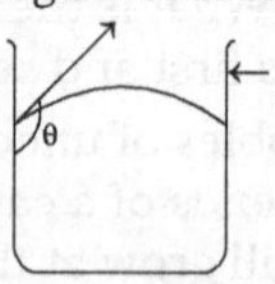

[1]

(ii) Water and glass is as follows

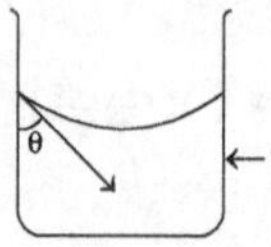

The angle of contact between mercury and glass is 138° and angle of contact between water and glass is about 8°. [1]

14. (i) The formula of capillary rise in a capillary tube is

$$h = \frac{2\sigma \cos\theta}{r\rho g}$$

where, σ = surface tension of water.
As σ of hot water is less than σ of cold water, hence water will rise more in cold water.
Also, capillary tube expands in hot water, so its radius (r) also increases because r is inversely proportional to h. [1½]

(ii) The angle of contact between water and wax is obtuse, so capillary rise $h = \frac{2\sigma \cos\theta}{r\rho g}$ will be negative because $\cos\theta$ is negative. That's why water gets depressed. [1½]

15. (i) Given, p_1, p_2 pressure inside first and second soap bubbles are related $p_1 = 3p_2$
($\because$ excess pressure inside soap bubble, $p = \frac{4S}{R}$, S = surface tension)

Now, $\frac{4S}{r_1} = \frac{3 \times 4S}{r_2} \Rightarrow r_2 = 3r_1$

$$\therefore \quad \frac{V_1}{V_2} = \frac{\frac{4}{3}\pi r_1^3}{\frac{4}{3}\pi r_2^3} = \left(\frac{r_1}{r_2}\right)^3 = \left(\frac{1}{3}\right)^3 = \frac{1}{27}$$

[1½]

(ii) The bubble with bigger size will grow compared to smaller sized bubble, because excess pressure $p = \frac{4S}{R}$, i.e. inversely proportional to radius and also air flows from higher pressure to lower pressure. [1½]

16. Refer to text on pages 320 and 321 (Excess pressure inside a liquid drop and a soap bubble).

17. Refer to text on page 318 (Angle of contact).

18. Refer to text on pages 318 and 319 (Capillary rise).

19. Let n be the number of little droplets which coalesce to form single drop. Then,

Volume of n little droplets = Volume of single drop

or $$n \times \frac{4}{3}\pi r^3 = \frac{4}{3}\pi R^3 \text{ or } nr^3 = R^3$$

Decrease in surface area $= n \times 4\pi r^2 - 4\pi R^2$

$$= 4\pi\,[nr^2 - R^2] = 4\pi\left[\frac{nr^3}{r} - R^2\right]$$

$$= 4\pi\left[\frac{R^3}{r} - R^2\right] = 4\pi R^3\left[\frac{1}{r} - \frac{1}{R}\right] \quad [\because nr^3 = R^3]$$

[2½]

The energy released,

E = Surface tension × decrease in surface area

$$= 4\pi S R^3\left[\frac{1}{r} - \frac{1}{R}\right]$$

The mass of bigger drop,

$$M = \frac{4}{3}\pi R^3 \times 1 = \frac{4}{3}\pi R^3$$

$$\therefore \quad E = \frac{4}{3}\pi S R^3 . 3\left[\frac{1}{r} - \frac{1}{R}\right] = 3SM\left[\frac{1}{r} - \frac{1}{R}\right] \quad \left[\because M = \frac{4}{3}\pi R^3\right]$$

$\because$ KE of bigger drop = Energy released

$$\frac{1}{2}MV^2 = 3SM\left[\frac{1}{r} - \frac{1}{R}\right]$$

$$\therefore \quad V = \sqrt{6S\left(\frac{R-r}{Rr}\right)}$$

[2½]

20. (i) When a small quantity of a liquid is poured on a solid, three types of interfaces namely liquid-air, solid-air and solid-liquid are occured. The surface tension corresponding to these three interfaces are S_{LA}, S_{SA} and S_{SL}, respectively.

If θ is the angle of contact between solid and liquid then,

$$S_{SL} + S_{LA}\cos\theta = S_{SA}$$

$$\Rightarrow \quad S_{LA}\cos\theta = S_{SA} - S_{SL}$$

$$\cos\theta = \frac{S_{SA} - S_{SL}}{S_{LA}} \quad \text{...(i)}$$

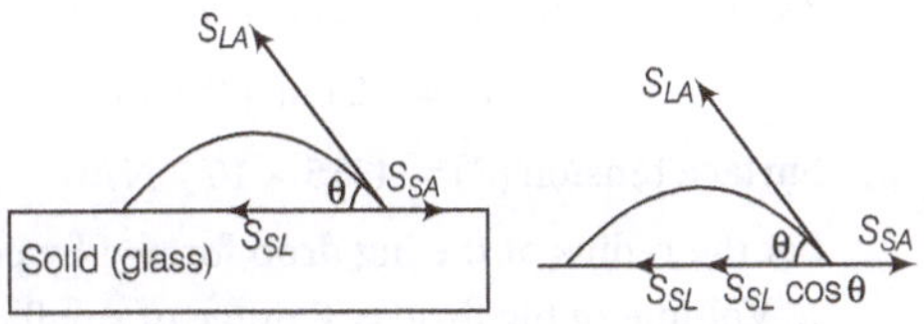

For mercury and glass $S_{SA} < S_{SL}$, therefore, from Eq. (i) $\cos\theta$ is negative and therefore, $\theta > 90°$, i.e. obtuse.

For water and glass $S_{SA} > S_{SL}$, therefore, from Eq. (i) $\cos\theta$ is positive and therefore, $\theta < 90°$, i.e. acute. [1]

(ii) For equilibrium of a liquid drop on a solid surface

$$S_{SL} + S_{LA}\cos\theta = S_{SA}$$

In case of mercury and glass, $S_{SL} > S_{SA}$, therefore, for equilibrium $\cos\theta$ should be negative, i.e. θ should be obtuse. In order to achieve this obtuse value of angle of contact, the mercury tends to form a drop. In case of water and glass, $S_{SA} > S_{SL}$, therefore, for equilibrium $\cos\theta$ should be positive, i.e. θ should be acute.

In order to achieve this value of angle of contact, the water tends to spread. [1]

(iii) Surface tension of a liquid is defined as the force acting per unit length on an imaginary line drawn tangentially to the liquid surface at rest. Therefore, surface tension is independent of the area of the liquid surface. [1]

(iv) The rise of liquid in a capillary tube is given by

$$h = \frac{2S\cos\theta}{r\rho g}, \quad \text{i.e. } h \propto \cos\theta$$

The cloth has narrow spaces in the form of fine capillaries. If angle of contact θ is small, then the value of $\cos\theta$ will be large and hence, detergent will rise more in fine capillaries in the cloth. Now, the detergent solution will penetrate more in cloth and remove stains and dust from the cloth. [1]

(v) In the absence of external forces, the size of a liquid drop is decided only by the force due to surface tension. Due to surface tension, a liquid drop tends to acquire minimum surface area. As surface area is minimum for a sphere for a given volume of liquid. Therefore, under no external force a liquid is always spherical in shape. [1]

21. As liquid is same, temperature is same and the length of the film supporting the weight is also same, therefore, in Figs. (b) and (c), the film will support same weight, i.e. 4.5×10^{-2} N. [2]

22. Let the radius of larger drop = R

and radius of each small drop = r

Volume of 27 small drops = Volume of the large drop

$$= 27 \times \frac{4}{3} \times \pi r^3 = \frac{4}{3}\pi R^3$$

So, $$r = R/3$$

Surface area of large drop $= 4\pi R^2$ [1]

Surface area of 27 small drops $= 27 \times 4\pi r^2$

$$= 27 \times 4\pi\left(\frac{R}{3}\right)^2 = 12\pi R^2$$

$\therefore$ Increase in surface area $= 12\pi R^2 - 4\pi R^2 = 8\pi R^2$

Increase in energy = Increase in surface area × Surface tension

$$= 8\pi R^2 \times S$$ [1]

23. Given, $r_1 = 4$ cm, $r_2 = 6$ cm, $S = 30$ dyne cm^{-1}

So, change in surface area $= 2 \times 4\pi\,(6^2 - 4^2)$

[Soap solution has two surfaces]

$= 8\pi \, 20 = 160 \, \pi \, cm^2$

Work done $= S \times$ change in surface area

$= 30 \times 160 \times 3.142 = 15081.6$ erg

24. Given, $S = 0.03$ N/m

Work done = surface area × surface tension

$= 2 \times 4\pi r^2 \times S$

$= 2 \times 4 \times 3.14 \times (0.02)^2 \times 0.03 = 3 \times 10^{-4}$ J

25. Given, surface tension of water, $S = 7.28 \times 10^{-2}$ N/m

Vapour pressure, $p = 2.33 \times 10^3$ Pa

The drop will evaporate, if the water pressure is greater than the vapour pressure.

Let a water droplet of radius R can be formed without evaporating. [1]

∴ Vapour pressure = Excess pressure in drop

∴ $$p = \frac{2S}{R}$$

or $$R = \frac{2S}{p} = \frac{2 \times 7.28 \times 10^{-2}}{2.33 \times 10^3} \approx 6.25 \times 10^{-5} \text{ m}$$ [1]

26. Surface energy of first soap bubble

= Surface tension × surface area

$= 2 \times 4\pi R_1^2 S = 8\pi R_1^2 S$ [1]

Surface energy of second soap bubble $= 8\pi R_2^2 S$

Let the radius of the new soap bubble is R. So, the surface energy of new bubble $= 8\pi R^2 S$

By the law of conservation of energy,

$$8\pi R^2 S = 8\pi R_1^2 S + 8\pi R_2^2 S$$

$$R^2 = R_1^2 + R_2^2 = 36 + 64$$

∴ $R^2 = 100 \text{ cm}^2 \Rightarrow R = 10$ cm [1]

27. Volume of 1000 small drops = Volume of a large drop

$$1000 \times \frac{4}{3}\pi r^3 = \frac{4}{3}\pi R^3 \Rightarrow r = \frac{R}{10}$$

Surface area of large drop $= 4\pi R^2$ [1]

Surface area of 1000 drop $= 4\pi \times 1000 \, r^2 = 40\pi R^2$

∴ Increase in surface area $= (40 - 4)\pi R^2 = 36 \, \pi R^2$

The increase in surface energy

= Surface tension × increase in surface area

$= 36\pi R^2 \times 0.07 = 36 \times 3.14 \times (4 \times 10^{-3})^2 \times 0.07$

$= 1.26 \times 10^{-4}$ J [1]

28. Given, radius $(r) = 2.5 \times 10^{-5}$ m

Surface tension $(S) = 7.28 \times 10^{-2}$ N/m

Angle of contact $(\theta) = 0°$,

density of water $(\rho) = 10^3$ kg/m³

The maximum height which sap can rise in trees through capillarity action is given by [1]

$$h = \frac{2S \cos \theta}{r \rho g}$$

$$= \frac{2 \times 7.28 \times 10^{-2} \times \cos 0°}{2.5 \times 10^{-5} \times 1 \times 10^3 \times 9.8} = 0.59 \text{ m}$$

But, the height of many trees are more than 0.59 m, therefore, the rise of sap in all trees is not possible through capillarity action alone. [1]

29. Length of the slider $(l) = 30$ cm

As a soap film has two free surfaces, therefore, total length of the film to be supported

$l' = 2l = 2 \times 30 = 60$ cm $= 0.60$ m [1]

Let S be the surface tension of the soap solution.

Total force on the slider due to surface tension,

$$F = S \times 2l$$

$$F = S \times 0.60 \text{ N} \quad \text{...(i)}$$

Weight (w) supported by the slider $= 1.5 \times 10^{-2}$ N [1]

In equilibrium,

Force on the slider due to surface tension = weight supported by the slider

∴ $$F = w$$

$$S \times 0.60 = 1.5 \times 10^{-2}$$

or $$S = \frac{1.5 \times 10^{-2}}{0.60}$$

$= 2.5 \times 10^{-2}$ N/m [1]

30. Given, radius of drop $(R) = 3.00$ mm

$= 3 \times 10^{-3}$ m

Surface tension of mercury $(S) = 4.65 \times 10^{-1}$ N/m

Atmospheric pressure $(p_0) = 1.01 \times 10^5$ Pa [1]

Pressure inside the drop = Atmospheric pressure + Excess pressure inside the liquid drop $= p_0 + \frac{2S}{R}$

$$= 1.01 \times 10^5 + \frac{2 \times 4.65 \times 10^{-1}}{3 \times 10^{-3}}$$

$= 1.01 \times 10^5 + 3.10 \times 10^2$

$= 1.01 \times 10^5 + 0.00310 \times 10^5$

$= 1.01310 \times 10^5$ Pa [1]

Excess pressure inside the drop

$$(\Delta p) = \frac{2S}{R} = \frac{2 \times 4.65 \times 10^{-1}}{3 \times 10^{-3}}$$

$= 3.10 \times 10^2 = 310$ Pa [1]

31. Radii of mercury droplets, $r_1 = 0.1 \text{ cm} = 1 \times 10^{-3}$ m

$r_2 = 0.2 \text{ cm} = 2 \times 10^{-3}$ m

Surface tension $(S) = 435.5 \times 10^{-3}$ N/m

Let the radius of the big drop formed by collapsing be R.

∴ Volume of big drop = Volume of small droplets [1]

$$\frac{4}{3}\pi R^3 = \frac{4}{3}\pi r_1^3 + \frac{4}{3}\pi r_2^3$$

or $$R^3 = r_1^3 + r_2^3$$

$= (0.1)^3 + (0.2)^3$

$= 0.001 + 0.008 = 0.009$

or $R = 0.21 \text{ cm} = 2.1 \times 10^{-3} \text{m}$

$\therefore$ Change in surface area

$\Delta A = 4\pi R^2 - (4\pi r_1^2 + 4\pi r_2^2)$

$= 4\pi [R^2 - (r_1^2 + r_2^2)]$ [1]

$\therefore$ Energy released $= S \cdot \Delta A$

$= S \times 4\pi [R^2 - (r_1^2 + r_2^2)]$

$= 435.5 \times 10^{-3} \times 4 \times 3.14 [(2.1 \times 10^{-3})^2 - (1 \times 10^{-6} + 4 \times 10^{-6})]$

$= 435.5 \times 4 \times 3.14 [4.41 - 5] \times 10^{-6} \times 10^{-3}$

$= -32.27 \times 10^{-7} = -3.22 \times 10^{-6} \text{J}$

(Negative sign shows absorption)

Therefore, 3.22×10^{-6} J energy will be absorbed. [1]

32. Given, surface tension of soap solution (S)

$= 2.5 \times 10^{-2} \text{N/m}$

Density of soap solution $(\rho) = 1.2 \times 10^3 \text{kg/m}^3$

Radius of soap bubble $(r) = 5.00 \text{ mm} = 5.0 \times 10^{-3} \text{m}$ [1]

Radius of air bubble $(R) = 5 \times 10^{-3}$ m

Atmospheric pressure $(p_0) = 1.01 \times 10^5$ Pa

Excess pressure inside the soap bubble

$= \frac{4S}{r}$

$= \frac{4 \times 2.5 \times 10^{-2}}{5.0 \times 10^{-3}} = 20 \text{ Pa}$ [1]

Excess pressure inside the air bubble

$= \frac{2S}{R} = \frac{2 \times 2.5 \times 10^{-2}}{5.0 \times 10^{-3}}$

$= 10$ Pa [1]

$\therefore$ Pressure inside the air bubble = Atmospheric pressure + Pressure due to 40 cm of soap solution column + Excess pressure inside the bubble

$= (1.01 \times 10^5) + (0.40 \times 1.2 \times 10^3 \times 9.8) + 10$

$= (1.01 \times 10^5) + 4.704 \times 10^3 + 10$

$= 1.01 \times 10^5 + 0.04704 \times 10^5 + 0.00010 \times 10^5$

$= 1.05714 \times 10^5 \text{ Pa} = 1.06 \times 10^5 \text{ Pa}$ [2]

Summary

- **Thrust** The total force exerted by the liquid at rest, on any surface in contact with it is called the thrust of the liquid on that surface.
- **Pressure,** $p = \frac{\text{Thrust}}{\text{Area}} = \frac{F}{A}$. Its SI unit is N/m^2 or Pascal (Pa).
  Pressure exerted by a liquid column, $p = \rho g h$
  where, h = height of liquid column, g = acceleration due to gravity, ρ = density of liquid.
- **Pascal's law** It states that if an external pressure is applied to an enclosed liquid, it is transmitted undiminished equally to all other points of the liquid and to the walls of container.
- **Atmospheric pressure** The pressure exerted by the atmosphere is called atmospheric pressure. At sea-level, we have atmospheric pressure = 1.013×10^5 Nm^{-2}
- **Absolute Pressure and gauge pressure** The total or actual pressure p at a point is called absolute pressure. Gauge pressure is the difference between the actual pressure (absolute pressure) at a point and the atmospheric pressure. Thus, $p_g = p - p_a$ or $p = p_a + p_g$
  Absolute pressure = Atmospheric pressure + Gauge pressure.
- **Buoyancy** It states that when a body is partially or fully dipped into a fluid, the fluid exerts an upward force on the body called as buoyant force and this phenomenon is called buoyancy.
- **Archimedes' principle** It states that when a body is partially or fully dipped in a fluid at rest, the fluid exerts an upward force of buoyancy equal to the weight of the displaced fluid.
  Weight of the body = Weight of fluid displaced
  $$V_b \rho_b g = V_f \rho_f g$$
  ∴ Denisity of body to fluid, $\frac{\rho_b}{\rho_f} = \frac{V_f}{V_b}$
- **Velocity of efflux** (Torricelli's theorem) The speed of liquid coming out through a hole at a depth (h) below the free surface is called velocity of efflux, $v = \sqrt{2hg}$
- **Viscosity** It is the property of a fluid due to which an opposing force comes into play whenever there is relative motion between its different layers.
- **Newton's formula for viscous force** The viscous drag between two parallel layers each of area A and having velocity gradient $\frac{dv}{dx}$ is given by $F = -\eta A \frac{dv}{dx}$
  where, η is the coefficient of viscosity of the liquid.
- **Stoke's law** It states that the backward dragging force of viscosity acting on a spherical body of radius r moving with velocity v through a fluid of viscosity η is
  $$F = 6\pi\eta r v$$
- **Terminal velocity** It is the maximum constant velocity attained by a spherical body while falling through a viscous medium. The terminal velocity of a spherical body of density ρ and radius r moving through a fluid of density ρ' and viscosity η is given by
  $$v = \frac{2}{9}\frac{r^2}{\eta}(\rho - \rho')g$$
- **Poiseuille's formula** The volume of a liquid flowing per second through a horizontal capillary tube of length l, radius r under a pressure difference p across its two ends is given by $V = \frac{\pi}{8} \cdot \frac{pr^4}{\eta l}$
  , where, η is coefficient of viscosity of the liquid.
- **Surface tension** (S) Surface tension is the property of a liquid due to which its free surface behaves like a stretched elastic membrane and tends to have least possible surface area.
  SI unit of surface tension is Nm^{-1} or Jm^{-2}.
- **Capillarity** The phenomenon of rise or fall of a liquid in the capillary tube is called capillarity.
  Height of rise of liquid in capillary is given by $h = \frac{2S\cos\theta}{\rho R g}$
  where, R = radius of capillary base.
- **Streamline and Turbulent Flow** Flow of a fluid is said to be streamlined if each element of the fluid passing through a particular point travels along the same path, with exactly the same velocity as that of the preceding element.
  A special case of streamline flow is laminar flow, in which a fluid has a steady flow in the form of parallel layer and these do not mix with one another.
- **A turbulent flow** is the one in which the motion of the fluid particles are disordered or irregular. In such a flow, most of the energy used up in maintaining the flow, is spent in causing eddies in the fluid and only a small part of the energy is used for the actual forward flow.
- **Equation of continuity** It states that when an incompressible and non-viscous fluid flows steadily through a tube of non-uniform cross-section, then the product of area of cross-section and the velocity of flow is same at every point in the tube. Av = constant
- **Bernoulli's theorem** It states that the sum of pressure energy, kinetic energy and potential energy per unit volume of an incompressible and non-viscous fluid in a streamlined irrotational flow remains constant at every cross-sectional throughout the liquid flow.
  $$p + \frac{1}{2}\rho v^2 + \rho g h = \text{constant}$$
  where, p = pressure, $\frac{1}{2}\rho v^2$ = kinetic energy per unit volume, $\rho g h$ = potential energy per unit volume.

Chapter Practice

Multiple Choice Questions

1 Mark

1 Pressure is applied to an enclosed fluid. It is
(a) increased and applied to every part of the fluid
(b) diminished and transmitted to the walls of the container
(c) increased in proportion to the mass of the fluid and then transmitted
(d) transmitted unchanged to every portion of the fluid and the walls of container

2 A liquid film is formed over a frame *ABCD* as shown in figure. Wire *CD* can slide without friction. Maximum value of mass that can be hanged from *CD* without breaking the liquid film is

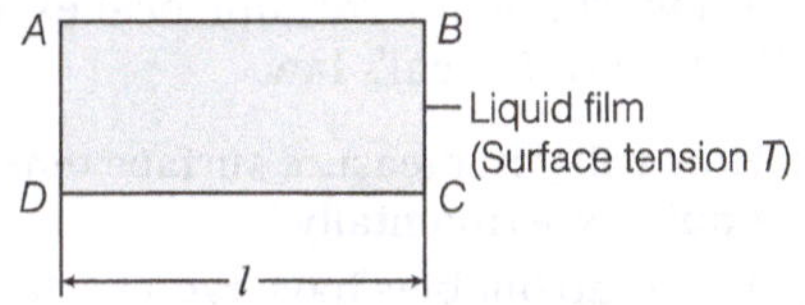

(a) $\frac{Tl}{g}$ (b) $\frac{2Tl}{g}$
(c) $\frac{g}{2Tl}$ (d) $T \times l$

3 An incompressible liquid flows through a horizontal tube as shown (areas of tubes is marked) then the velocity *v* of the fluid is

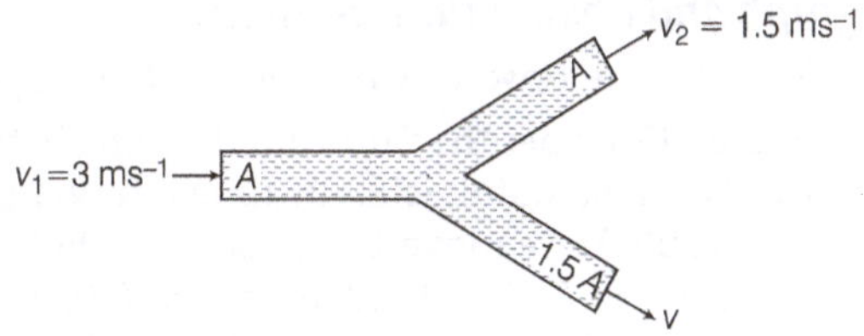

(a) $3.0\ ms^{-1}$ (b) $1.5\ ms^{-1}$
(c) $1.0\ ms^{-1}$ (d) $2.25\ ms^{-1}$

4 According to Bernoulli's equation,

$$\frac{p}{\rho g} + h + \frac{1}{2}\frac{v^2}{g} = \text{constant}$$

The terms, $\frac{p}{\rho g}$, h and $\frac{1}{2}\frac{v^2}{g}$ are generally called respectively :
(a) Gravitational head, pressure head and velocity head
(b) Gravity, gravitational head and velocity head
(c) Pressure head, gravitational head and velocity head
(d) Gravity, pressure and velocity head

5 A ball is moving in a straight line through a fluid which is spinning around its own centre of mass as shown.

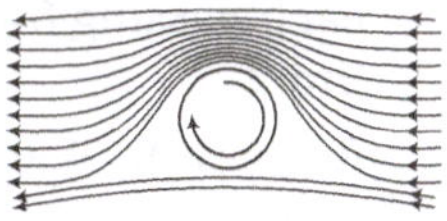

Then, the ball experiences
(a) an upward force (b) a downward force
(c) a leftward force (d) no force at all

6 For a rain drop of radius *a*, terminal velocity v_t is given by
(a) $\frac{2a^2}{9\eta}(\rho - \sigma)g$ (b) $\frac{4\pi}{3} \times a^3 (\rho + \sigma)g$
(c) $\frac{4\pi}{6} \times a^3 (\rho + \sigma)^2 g$ (d) $\frac{5\pi}{3} \times a^3 (\rho - \sigma)^2 g$

Assertion and Reason

Directions (Q. Nos. 7-11) *In the following questions, two statements are given- one labelled Assertion (A) and the other labelled Reason (R). Select the correct answer to these questions from the codes (a), (b), (c) and (d) as given below*
(a) Both Assertion and Reason are true and Reason is the correct explanation of Assertion.
(b) Both Assertion and Reason are true but Reason is not the correct explanation of Assertion.
(c) Assertion is true but Reason is false.
(d) Assertion is false but Reason is true.

7 **Assertion (A)** A fluid will stick to a solid surface.

Reason (R) Surface energy between fluid and solid is smaller than the sum of surface energies.

8 **Assertion (A)** Smaller drop of liquid resists deforming forces better than the larger drops.

Reason (R) Excess pressure inside a drop is directly proportional to its surface area.

9 **Assertion (A)** The surface of water in the capillary tube is concave.

Reason (R) The pressure difference between two sides of the tube is $\frac{2S}{a}\cos\theta$.

10 **Assertion (A)** Ploughing a field reduces evaporation of water from the ground beneath.

Reason (R) Results in lowering of surface area open to sunlight.

11 **Assertion (A)** In steady flow, the velocity of each passing fluid particle remains constant in time.

Reason (R) Each particle follows a smooth path and the paths of the particle do not cross each other.

Very Short Answer Type Questions

1 Mark

12 How is the surface tension of a liquid explained on the basis of intermolecular forces?

13 From where the energy comes when a liquid rises against gravity in a capillary tube?

14 What is the net weight of a body when it falls with terminal velocity through a viscous fluid?

15 When water flows through a pipe, which layer moves faster?

16 Why the viscosity of the liquid decreases with increase in temperature?

Short Answer Type I Question

2 Marks

17 Prove that there is always excess of pressure on the concave side of the meniscus of a liquid. Obtain expression for the excess of pressure inside a liquid drop.

Short Answer Type II Questions

3 Marks

18 State and prove Pascal's law of fluid pressure. Illustrate it by two examples.

19 If a drop of liquid breaks into smaller droplets, it results in lowering of temperature of the droplets. Let a drop of radius R, break into N small droplets each of radius r. Estimate the lowering in temperature. **NCERT**

20 (i) A liquid of density d and surface tension S rises to a height h in a capillary tube of diameter D. What is the weight of the liquid in the capillary tube? Angle of contact given is 0°.

(ii) The soap bubble formed at the end of the tube is blown very slowly. Draw the graph between excess of pressure inside the bubble with time.

21 (i) Two drops of the same radius are falling through air with a steady velocity of 5 cms^{-1}. If the two drops coalesce, what would be the terminal velocity?

(ii) Define terminal velocity and show the nature of graph showing its variation with time, during a falling of a sphere through a liquid.

Long Answer Type Questions

5 Marks

22 Explain working of hydraulic brakes as application of Pascal's law.

23 (i) How will you measure surface tension of a liquid experimentally?

(ii) Two soap bubbles have radii in the ratio 2 : 3. Compare the excess pressure inside these bubbles. Also, compare the work done in blowing these bubbles.

Case Based Questions

Directions (Q. No. 24) *These questions are case study based questions. Read the following paragraph and answer the questions.*

24 Consider the flow at two regions 1 (i.e. BC) and 2 (i.e. DE). Consider the fluid initially lying between B and D. In an infinitesimally time interval Δt, this fluid would have moved. Suppose v_1 is the speed at B and v_2 at D, then fluid initially at B has moved a distance $v_1\Delta t$ to C ($v_1\Delta t$ is small enough to assume constant cross-section along BC).

In the same interval Δt, the fluid initially at D moves to E, a distance equal to $v_2\Delta t$. Pressures p_1 and p_2 act as shown on the plane faces of areas A_1 and A_2 binding the two regions as shown in figure

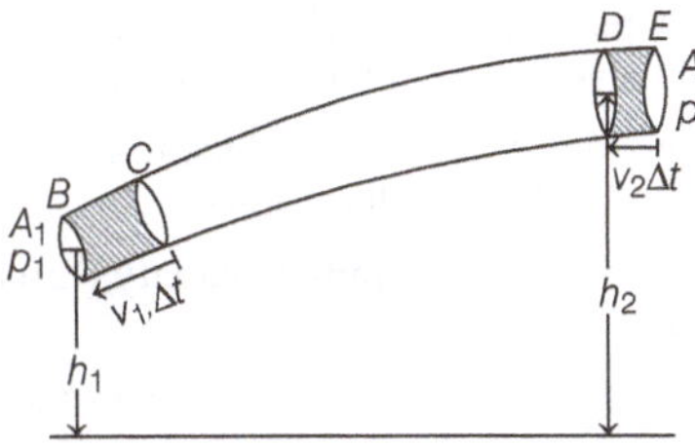

(i) Find the work done on the fluid at *BC*.
(ii) Find work done on the fluid of *DE*.
(iii) What is the total work done on the fluid?
(iv) What will the change in its kinetic energy?
(v) Find the expression of Bernoulli's equation.

Numerical Problems

25 A thin wire is bent in the form of a ring of diameter 3.0 cm. The ring is placed horizontally on the surface of soap solution and then raised up slowly. How much upward force is necessary to break the vertical film formed between the ring and the solution? $T = 3.0 \times 10^{-2} \text{Nm}^{-1}$ **[1 M]**

26 In Millikan's oil drop experiment, what is the terminal speed of an uncharged drop of radius 2.0×10^{-5} m and density 1.2×10^3 kg/m^3? Take the viscosity of air at the temperature of the experiment to be 1.8×10^{-5} Pa-s. How much is the viscous force on the drop at that speed? Neglect buoyancy of the drop due to air. **NCERT [2 M]**

27 The terminal velocity of a copper ball of radius 2.0 mm falling through a tank of oil at 20°C is 6.5 cms^{-1}. Compute the viscosity of the oil at 20°C. Density of oil is 1.5×10^3 kg m^{-3}, density of copper is 8.9×10^3 kg m^{-3}. **[2 M]**

28 The velocity of water in a river is 18 kmh^{-1} near the surface. If the river is 5 m deep, find the shearing stress between horizontal layers of water. The coefficient of viscosity of water 10^{-2} poise. **[2 M]**

29 Show that if *n* equal rain droplets falling through air with equal steady velocity of 10 cms^{-1} coalesce, the resultant drop attains a new terminal velocity of $10\, n^{2/3}$cms^{-1}. **[3 M]**

30 The flow rate of water from a tap of diameter 1.25 cm is 0.48 L/min. The coefficient of viscosity of water is 10^{-3} Pa-s. After some time the flow rate is increased to 3 L/min. Characterise the flow for both the flow rates. **NCERT [3 M]**

31 A cylindrical vessel filled with water upto a height of 2 m stands on a horizontal plane. The side wall of the vessel has a plugged circular hole touching the bottom. Find the minimum diameter of the hole so that the vessel begin to move on the floor, if the plug is removed. The coefficient of friction between the bottom of the vessel and the plane is 0.4 and total mass of water plus vessel is 100 kg. **[3 M]**

32 Mercury has an angle of contact equal to 140° with sodalime glass. A narrow tube of radius 1.00 mm made of this glass is dipped in a trough containing mercury. By what amount does the mercury dip down in the tube relative to the liquid surface outside? Surface tension of mercury at the temperature of the experiment is 0.465 N/m. Density of mercury $= 13.6 \times 10^3$ kg/m^3. **[5 M]**

33 Two narrow bores of diameter 3.0 mm and 6.0 mm are joined together to form a U-tube open at both ends. If the U-tube contains water, what is the difference in its levels in the two limbs of the tube? Surface tension of water at the temperature of the experiment is 7.3×10^{-2} N/m. Take the angle of contact to be zero and density of water to be 1.0×10^3 kg/m^3. ($g = 9.8$ m/s^2) **NCERT [5 M]**

34 Glycerine flows steadily through a horizontal tube of length 1.5 m and radius 1.0 cm. If the amount of glycerine flowing per second at one end is 4.0×10^{-3} kg/s. What is the pressure difference between the two ends of the tube? (Density of glycerine $= 1.3 \times 10^3$ kg/m^3 and viscosity of glycerine = 0.83 Pa-s). (You may also like to check, if the assumption of laminar flow in the tube is correct). **[5 M]**

Answers

1 (*d*) Hint : Pascal's law.

2 (*b*) Weight of the body hang from wire (mg)

= upward force due to surface tension ($2Tl$)

$$\Rightarrow \quad m = \frac{2Tl}{g}$$

3 (c) If the liquid is incompressible, then mass of liquid entering through left end, should be equal to mass of liquid coming out from the right end.

$\therefore \quad M = m_1 + m_2 \Rightarrow Av_1 = Av_2 + 1.5Av$

$\Rightarrow \quad A \times 3 = A \times 1.5 + 1.5Av \Rightarrow v = 1\ \text{ms}^{-1}$

4 (c) Here, pressure head $= \dfrac{p}{\rho g}$

$h =$ gravitational head, $\dfrac{1}{2}v^2/g =$ velocity head

5 (a) An upward force acts on ball : magnus effect

6 (a) In equilibrium, this terminal velocity v_t is given by

$$6\pi\eta a v_t = (4\pi/3)\, a^3 (\rho - \sigma)\, g$$

where, ρ and σ are mass densities of sphere and the fluid, respectively. We obtain

$$v_t = 2a^2 (\rho - \sigma)\, g/(9\eta)$$

7 (a) A fluid will stick to a solid surface if the surface energy between fluid and the solid is smaller than the sum of surface energies between solid-air and fluid-air, interface.

8 (c) The excess pressure inside a liquid drop, we get

$$p = \frac{2\sigma}{R}$$

i.e., $\quad p \propto \dfrac{1}{R}$

Hence, the excess pressure is large in a small drop due to which it can resist the deforming forces.

9 (a) Since, the surface of water in the capillary is concave. This means that there is a pressure difference between the two sides of the top surface. This is given by

$(p_i - p_o) = (2S/r) = 2S\,(a \sec\theta) = (2S/a)\cos\theta \qquad \text{...(i)}$

Thus, the pressure of the water inside the tube, just at the meniscus (air-water interface) is less than the atmospheric pressure. Consider the two points A and B. They must be at the same pressure, namely

$$p_o + h\rho g = p_i = p_A \qquad \text{...(ii)}$$

where, ρ is the density of water and h is called the capillary rise. Using Eqs. (i) and (ii), we have

$$h\rho g = (p_i - p_o) = (2S\cos\theta)/a$$

10 (c) Assertion is true, Reason is false. Ploughing breaks capillaries through which water vapour of earth reaches surface.

11 (a) The flow of the fluid is said to be steady if at any given point, the velocity of each passing fluid particle remains constant in time. This does not mean that the velocity at different points in space is same. The velocity of a particular particle may change as it moves from one point to another. Every other particle which passes the second point behaves exactly as the previous particle that has just passed that point.

12 It is the property of virtue of which the free surface of the liquid behaves as stretched membrane.

13 The energy comes from the surface tension and contact angle of fluid in the capillary tube.

14 Net weight is zero, at terminal velocity through a viscous fluid.

15 The layer in the centre flows faster then the layer near the wall.

16 Due to increase in temperature, the inter-molecular forces are weakened and therefore the liquid viscosity decreases.

17 (i) Pressure on the concave side is greater than the pressure on the convex side

$\because \ (p - p_0) = \dfrac{2s}{R}\cos\theta$

$p - p_0 \propto \cos\theta$ [1]

(ii) Excess pressure inside a liquid drop $(p - p_0) = \dfrac{2s}{R}$ [1]

18 **Hint** Refer to text on pages 293 and 294 (Pascal's law and proof of Pascal's law). [3]

19 When a big drop of radius R, break into N droplets each of radius r, the volume remains constant.

$\therefore$ Volume of big drop $= N \times$ Volume of small drop

$$\frac{4}{3}\pi R^3 = N \times \frac{4}{3}\pi r^3$$

or $\quad R^3 = Nr^3$ or $N = \dfrac{R^3}{r^3}$ [1]

Now, change in surface area $= 4\pi R^2 - N4\pi r^2$

$= 4\pi\,(R^2 - Nr^2)$

Energy released $= S \times \Delta A = S \times 4\pi(R^2 - Nr^2)$ [1]

Due to release of this energy, the temperature is lowered.

If ρ is the density and s is specific heat of liquid and its temperature is lowered by $\Delta\theta$, then

Energy released $= ms\Delta\theta$

$$S \times 4\pi\,(R^2 - Nr^2) = \left(\frac{4}{3}\pi \times R^3 \times \rho\right) s\Delta\theta$$

$$\Delta\theta = \frac{S \times 4\pi\,(R^2 - Nr^2)}{\frac{4}{3}\pi R^3 \rho \times s} = \frac{3S}{\rho s}\left[\frac{R^2}{R^3} - \frac{Nr^2}{R^3}\right]$$

$$= \frac{3S}{\rho s}\left[\frac{1}{R} - \frac{(R^3/r^3) \times r^2}{R^3}\right] \qquad \left[\because N = \frac{R^3}{r^3}\right]$$

$$\Delta\theta = \frac{3S}{\rho s}\left[\frac{1}{R} - \frac{1}{r}\right]$$ [1]

20 (i) Weight of the liquid in capillary tube $= mg = \pi r^2 hdg$

But capillary rise, $h = \dfrac{2S\cos\theta}{rdg} = \dfrac{2S}{rdg} \qquad (\because \cos 0° = 1)$

$\therefore$ Weight of liquid $= \pi r^2 dg \times \dfrac{2S}{rdg} = \pi r 2S = \pi DS$ [2]

(ii) As excess pressure inside the soap bubble of radius r is

$$p = \frac{4S}{r}$$

Thus, $p \propto \frac{1}{r}$

So,the graph will be as follows

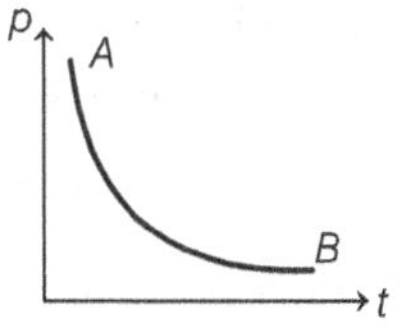

A parabolic curve showing variation of p with time because r increases ρ decreases. [1]

21 (i) As terminal velocity is expressed as $v = \frac{2}{9} r^2 \frac{(\rho - \sigma) g}{\eta}$

$$v = 5 \text{ cm/s}$$

Hence, by taking the ratio,

$$v = 5(4)^{1/3} \text{ cm/s}$$ [2]

(ii) As net force on reaching terminal velocity is zero, a body falls with constant speed.

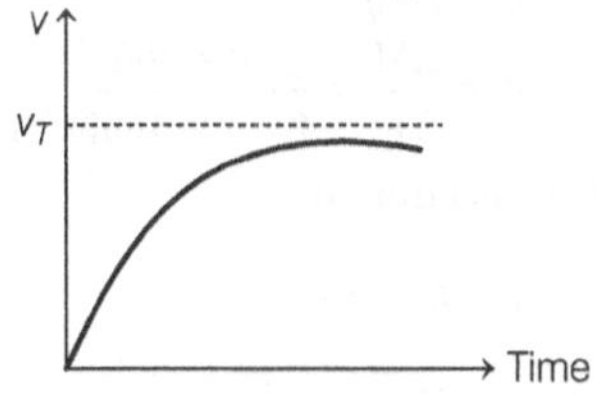

[1]

22 Refer to text on page 295 (Working of hydraulic brakes).

23 (i) Refer to text on pages 319 and 320 (Measuring the surface tension of liquid). [3]

(ii) If r_1 and r_2 are the bubble's radii, as per question,

$$\frac{r_1}{r_2} = \frac{2}{3}$$

If σ = surface tension of the soap bubble.

Excess pressure inside bubbles of radii r_1 and r_2 will be

$$p_1 = \frac{4\sigma}{r_1} \quad \text{...(i)}$$

and

$$p_2 = \frac{4\sigma}{r_2} \quad \text{...(ii)}$$

On dividing Eq. (i) by Eq. (ii), we get

$$\frac{p_1}{p_2} = \frac{4\sigma}{r_1} \times \frac{r_2}{4\sigma} = \frac{r_2}{r_1} = \frac{3}{2}$$

and work done in blowing up the two soap bubbles,

$$W_1 = 2 \times 4\pi r_1^2 \times \sigma$$

$$W_2 = 2 \times 4\pi r_2^2 \times \sigma$$

$$\therefore \quad \frac{W_1}{W_2} = \frac{r_1^2}{r_2^2} = \left(\frac{2}{3}\right)^2 = \frac{4}{9}$$ [2]

24 (i) The work done on the fluid at left end BC is

$$W_1 = p_1 A_1 (v_1 \Delta t) = p_1 \Delta V \quad (\because V = A \times x)$$

(ii) The work done on the fluid at DE is

$$W_2 = -p_2 A_2 (v_2 \Delta t) = -p_2 \Delta V$$

(as same volume passes through it)

(iii) The total work done on the fluid is

$$W = W_1 - W_2 = (p_1 - p_2) \Delta V$$

(iv) Some part of work goes into changing the kinetic energy of the fluid and other goes into changing the gravitational potential energy. If the density of the fluid is ρ and $\Delta m = \rho A_1 v_1 \Delta t = \rho \Delta V$ is the mass passing through the pipe in time Δt, the change in its kinetic energy is

$$\Delta K = \frac{1}{2} \rho \Delta V (v_2^2 - v_1^2)$$

(v) We can employ the work-energy theorem to this volume of the fluid and this yields

$$(p_1 - p_2) \Delta V = \left(\frac{1}{2}\right) \rho \Delta V (v_2^2 - v_1^2) + \rho g \Delta V (h_2 - h_1)$$

We now divide each term by ΔV to obtain

$$(p_1 - p_2) = \left(\frac{1}{2}\right) \rho (v_2^2 - v_1^2) + \rho g (h_2 - h_1)$$

We can rearrange the above terms to obtain

$$p_1 + \left(\frac{1}{2}\right) \rho v_1^2 + \rho g h_1 = p_2 + \left(\frac{1}{2}\right) \rho v_2^2 + \rho g h_2$$

This is Bernoulli's equation. Since, 1 and 2 refer to any two locations along the pipeline, we may write the expression in general as

$$p + \frac{1}{2} \rho v^2 + \rho g h = \text{constant}$$

25 As we know, $s = \frac{F}{l}$

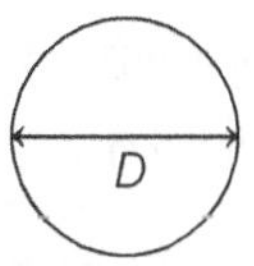

Here, $l = 2$ (perimetre of ring)

So, $F = ls = 2 \times \pi D \times 3 \times 10^{-2} = 5.65 \times 10^{-3}$ N

26 Given, radius of drop $(r) = 2.0 \times 10^{-5}$ m

Density of oil $(\rho) = 1.2 \times 10^3 \text{ kg/m}^3$

Viscosity of air $(\eta) = 1.8 \times 10^{-5}$ Pa-s

Terminal velocity, $v = \frac{2}{9} \frac{r^2 (\rho - \rho_0) g}{\eta}$

$$= \frac{2}{9} \times \frac{(2 \times 10^{-5})^2 \times (1.2 \times 10^3 - 0) \times 9.8}{1.8 \times 10^{-5}}$$

$$= 5.8 \times 10^{-2} \text{ m/s}$$ [1]

∴ Viscous force on the drop, (According to Stoke's law)

$$F = 6\pi\eta r v$$

$$= 6 \times 3.14 \times 1.8 \times 10^{-5} \times 2 \times 10^{-5} \times 5.8 \times 10^{-2}$$

$$= 3.93 \times 10^{-10} \text{ N}$$ [1]

27 Given, $v_t = 6.5 \times 10^{-2}$ m/s

$$r = 2 \times 10^{-3} \text{ m}, g = 9.8 \text{ m/s}^2$$

$$\rho = 8.9 \times 10^3 \text{ kg/m}^3, \sigma = 1.5 \times 10^3$$ [1]

$$\rho-\sigma = 8.9\times10^3 - 1.5\times10^3 = 7.4\times10^3 \text{ kg/m}^3$$

As, we know terminal velocity

i.e. $v_t = \frac{2r^2(\rho-\sigma)}{9\eta}g$

$$\eta = \frac{2}{9}\times\frac{(2\times10^{-3})^2\times9.8}{(6.5\times10^{-2})}\times7.4\times10^3$$

$\eta = 9.9\times10^{-1}$ kg/ms [1]

28 As the velocity of water at the bottom of the river is zero,

$$dv = 18 \text{ kmh}^{-1} = 18\times\frac{5}{18} = 5 \text{ ms}^{-1}$$

Also, $dx = 5$ m, $\eta = 10^{-2}$ poise $= 10^{-3}$ Pa-s [1/2]

Force of viscosity, $F = \eta A \frac{dv}{dx}$ [1/2]

We know that, shearing stress $= \frac{F}{A}$

$$\Rightarrow \frac{F}{A} = \eta\frac{dv}{dx} = \frac{10^{-3}\times5}{5} = 10^{-3} \text{ Nm}^{-2}$$

29 Volume of a bigger drop

$= n\times$ Volume of a smaller droplet [1/2]

or $\frac{4}{3}\pi R^3 = n\times\frac{4}{3}\pi r^3$ or $R^3 = nr^3$ or $R = n^{1/3}r$

Terminal velocity of a small droplet is given by

$$v_s = \frac{2}{9}\frac{r^2}{\eta}(\rho-\rho')g \quad \text{...(i)}$$ [1/2]

Terminal velocity of a bigger drop is given by

$$v_b = \frac{2}{9}\frac{R^2}{\eta}(\rho-\rho')g \quad \text{...(ii)}$$ [1/2]

Dividing Eq. (ii) by Eq. (i), we get

$$\frac{v_b}{v_s} = \frac{R^2}{r^2}$$ [1]

But $R = n^{1/3}r$

and $v_s = 10$ cm/s

$$v_b = v_s\times\left(\frac{R^2}{r^2}\right) = 10\times\frac{n^{2/3}r^2}{r^2}$$

$v_b = 10\,n^{2/3}$ cm/s [1/2]

30 Let the speed of the flow be v.

Given, diameter of tap $= d = 1.25$ cm

Volume of water flowing out per second.

$$Q = v\times\frac{\pi d^2}{4} \Rightarrow v = \frac{4Q}{d^2\pi}$$ [1]

Estimate Reynold's number, $R_e = \frac{4\rho Q}{\pi d\eta}$

$$Q = 0.48 \text{ L/min} = 8\times10^{-3} \text{ L/s} = 8\times10^{-6} \text{ m}^3\text{/s}$$

$$R_e = \frac{4\times10^3\times8\times10^{-6}}{3.14\times1.25\times10^{-2}\times10^{-3}}$$ [1]

$R_e = 815$ [i.e. below 1000, the flow is steady]

After some time, when

$$Q = 3 \text{ L/min} = 5\times10^{-5} \text{ m}^3\text{/s},$$

$$R_e = \frac{4\times10^3\times5\times10^{-5}}{3.14\times1.25\times10^{-2}\times10^{-3}} = 5095$$ [1]

$\therefore$ The flow will be turbulent.

31 Velocity of efflux through the hole, $v = \sqrt{2gh}$

$\because$ Distance moved by water in one second $v = \sqrt{2gh}$ [1]

$\therefore$ Rate of change of momentum $= (\rho A\sqrt{2gh})(\sqrt{2gh})$

$= 2\,ghA\rho$

According to Newton's second law of motion,

Force due to the velocity of efflux $= 2\,gh\,A\rho$.

Now, according to Newton's third law of motion, [1/2]

Force on the vessel = Rate of the momentum

Force on the vessel $= 2\,gh\,A\rho$

The vessel will move, if force on the vessel = force of friction

or $2gh\,A\rho = \mu Mg$

or $A = \frac{\mu M}{2h\rho} = \frac{0.4\times100}{2\times2\times1000} = \frac{1}{100}$ [1/2]

Since, the hole is circular.

$$A = \pi r^2 = \frac{\pi D^2}{4}$$

$$\therefore \quad D = \sqrt{\frac{4A}{\pi}} = \sqrt{\frac{4\times1}{100\times3.14}} = 0.113 \text{ m}$$

So, diameter of a hole $D = 0.113$ m [1]

32 Given, angle of contact $(\theta) = 140°$

Radius of tube $(r) = 1$ mm $= 10^{-3}$ m

Surface tension $(S) = 0.465$ N/m

Density of mercury $(\rho) = 13.6\times10^3$ kg/m^3 [2]

Height of liquid rise or fall due to surface tension (h)

$$= \frac{2S\cos\theta}{r\rho g}$$

$$= \frac{2\times0.465\times\cos140°}{1\times10^{-3}\times13.6\times10^3\times9.8}$$

$$= \frac{2\times0.465\times(-0.7660)}{10^{-3}\times13.6\times10^3\times9.8} = -5.34\times10^{-3} \text{ m}$$

$= -5.34$ mm [3]

Hence, the mercury level will depressed by 5.34 mm.

33 Given, surface tension of water $(S) = 7.3\times10^{-2}$ N/m

Density of water $(\rho) = 1.0\times10^3$ kg/m^3

Acceleration due to gravity $(g) = 9.8$ m/s^2

Angle of contact $(\theta) = 0°$ [1]

Diameter of one side, $2r_1 = 3.0$ mm

$\therefore \quad r_1 = 1.5$ mm $= 1.5\times10^{-3}$ m

Diameter of other side, $2r_2 = 6.0$ mm

$$r_2 = 3.0 \text{ mm} = 3.0 \times 10^{-3} \text{ m}$$ [1]

Height of water column rises in first and second tubes

$$h_1 = \frac{2S \cos\theta}{r_1 \rho g} \Rightarrow h_2 = \frac{2S \cos\theta}{r_2 \rho g}$$ [1]

∴ Difference in levels of water rises in both tubes

$$\Delta h = h_1 - h_2 = \frac{2S \cos\theta}{\rho g}\left(\frac{1}{r_1} - \frac{1}{r_2}\right)$$ [1]

$$= \frac{2 \times 7.3 \times 10^{-2} \times \cos 0°}{1.0 \times 10^3 \times 9.8} \left[\frac{1}{1.5 \times 10^{-3}} - \frac{1}{3.0 \times 10^{-3}}\right]$$

$$= \frac{14.6}{9.8} \times 10^{-2}\left[\frac{2-1}{3}\right] = \frac{14.6}{9.8 \times 3} \times 10^{-2}$$

$$= 0.497 \times 10^{-2} \text{ m}$$

$$= 4.97 \times 10^{-3} \text{ m} = 4.9 \text{ mm}$$ [1]

34 Given, length of the tube $(l) = 1.5$ m

Radius of the tube $(r) = 1.0 \text{ cm} = 1 \times 10^{-2} \text{ cm}$

Mass of glycerine flowing per second $= 4 \times 10^{-3}$ kg/s

Density of glycerine, $\rho = 1.3 \times 10^3 \text{ kg/m}^3$

Viscosity of glycerine, $\eta = 0.83$ Pa - s

Volume of glycerine flowing per second, $V = \frac{m}{\rho}$

$$\left[\because \text{density} = \frac{\text{Mass}}{\text{Volume}}\right]$$

$$= \frac{4 \times 10^{-3}}{1.3 \times 10^3} \text{ m}^3/\text{s} = \frac{4}{1.3} \times 10^{-6} \text{ m}^3/\text{s}$$ [1]

According to Poiseuille's formula, the rate of flow of liquid through a tube

$$V = \frac{\pi}{8} \frac{pr^4}{\eta l}$$

where, p is the pressure difference between the two ends of the tube.

or $$p = \frac{8\eta l V}{\pi r^4} = \frac{8 \times 0.83 \times 1.5 \times 4 \times 10^{-6}}{3.14 \times (1 \times 10^{-2})^4 \times 1.3}$$ [1]

$$= 976 \text{ Pa}$$

To check the laminar flow in the tube, the value of Reynold's number should be less than 2000.

Reynold's number, $R_e = \frac{\rho D v_c}{\eta}$ [1]

where, v_c is the critical velocity and D is the diameter of the tube.

Critical velocity, $v_c = \frac{\text{Volume flowing out per second}}{\text{Area of cross-section}}$

$$= \frac{m/\rho}{A} = \frac{m}{\rho \pi r^2} \quad [\because A = \pi r^2]$$

∴ Reynold's number, $R_e = \frac{\rho D}{\eta} \times \frac{m}{\rho \pi r^2}$ [1]

$$= \frac{2r \times m}{\eta \pi r^2} \quad [\because D = 2r]$$

$$= \frac{2m}{\pi r \eta} = \frac{2 \times 4 \times 10^{-3}}{3.14 \times 10^{-2} \times 0.83} = 0.31$$

As $R_e < 2000$, therefore, flow of glycerine is laminar. [1]

CHAPTER

10

Thermal Properties of Matter

We are known to common sense notions of heat and temperature. When heat is supplied to a body, the physical state of the body may be changed. These changes may follow certain laws. Thus, we can say that all the changes in characteristics (properties) of matter that appear due to heat are known as its **thermal properties.** In this chapter, we will deal with heat and its measurement and the process of heat transfer.

- Temperature and Its Measurement
- Calorimetry
- Heat Transfer

TOPIC 01 Temperature and Its Measurement

Temperature

Temperature is the measure of degree of hotness or coldness of a body. The measurement of temperature of a body is a relative measure.

Consider, there are two bodies with temperatures T_1 and T_2 where $T_1 > T_2$, then the body with T_1 is called hotter one with respect to another one which is known as **colder body.**

Heat

Heat is the form of energy which flows from hotter body to colder body by virtue of temperature difference. The amount of heat is measured in **joule** (SI unit). Another widely used unit for the heat is **calorie** (in CGS).

One calorie is equal to the amount of heat energy required to raise the temperature of one gram of water through 1°C (from 14.5°C to 15.5°C).

1 joule = 4.2 calorie

Measurement of Temperature

As temperature is a fundamental physical quantity, its measured by some specified scales.

These scales are commonly called **thermometers**. The thermometers are calibrated so that a numerical value may be assigned to a given temperature.

Temperature is measured in different units known as **kelvin** (K), **degree centigrade** (°C), **degree fahrenheit** (°F) etc., among which kelvin (K) is taken as the SI unit of temperature. Many physical properties of materials change sufficiently with temperature to be used as the basis for constructing thermometers.

To define a scale for temperature measurement, two physical phenomena which always occur at same temperature in nature are taken as reference temperatures. These are called fixed points, where **lower fixed point** (LFP) is temperature of melting point of ice at 1 atm pressure and **upper fixed point** (UFP) is the temperature of boiling point of water at 1 atm pressure.

For any temperature scale the quantity given by,

$$\frac{\text{Temperature of a body} - \text{LFP}}{\text{UFP} - \text{LFP}} \text{ is always a constant.}$$

In order to convert temperature from one scale to another, we use

$$\left(\frac{\text{T} - \text{LFP}}{\text{UFP} - \text{LFP}}\right)_{\text{on one scale}} = \left(\frac{\text{T} - \text{LFP}}{\text{UFP} - \text{LFP}}\right)_{\text{on other scale}}$$

Different Scales to Measure the Temperature

S. No.	Scale	Unit	Freezing or ice point (Lower fixed point)	Boiling or steam point (Upper fixed point)
1.	Celsius scale	Degree centigrade (°C)	0°C	100°C
2.	Fahrenheit scale	Degree Fahrenheit (°F)	32°F	212°F
3.	Reaumur scale	Degree Reaumur (°R)	0° R	80°R
4.	Kelvin scale	Kelvin (K)	273.15 K	373.15 K

Relation among the Temperatures Measured by Different Scales

The temperature measured by different scales is related as

$$\frac{C-0}{100} = \frac{F-32}{180} = \frac{K-273.15}{100}$$

Different Types of Thermometer

Mercury Thermometer

In mercury thermometer, length of mercury column is taken as thermometric property.

(i) **In Celsius or Centigrade scale** In Celsius scale, the reference temperatures are taken as 0°C and 100°C (number of degrees between 0°C and 100°C is 100).

Then, $$t = \frac{l_t - l_0}{l_{100} - l_0} \times 100$$

Here, l is length of mercury column at t°C, 0°C and 100°C.

(ii) **In Fahrenheit scale** In Fahrenheit scale, reference temperatures are 32°F and 212°F (number of degrees or interval between 32°F and 212°F is 180).

Then, $$t = \frac{l_t - l_{32}}{l_{212} - l_{32}} \times 180$$

Here, l is length of mercury column at t°F, 32°F and 212°F.

Gas Thermometer

In gas thermometer, the pressure of given mass of an ideal gas (at constant volume) or volume of a given mass of an ideal gas (at constant pressure) is taken as thermodynamic property. The reference points are taken as 0°C (ice point) and 100°C (steam point).

Unknown temperature is calculated as

$$t\,(°\text{C}) = \frac{p_t - p_0}{p_{100} - p_0} \times 100$$

Here, p is pressure of given mass of an ideal gas at 0°C, 100°C and t°C.

$$t\,(°\text{C}) = \frac{V_t - V_0}{V_{100} - V_0} \times 100$$

Here, V is volume of given mass of an ideal gas at 0°C, 100°C and t°C.

Platinum Resistance Thermometer

In this thermometer, the resistance of platinum wire is taken as thermodynamic property. Reference points are taken as 0°C (ice point) and 100°C (steam point).

Unknown temperature is calculated as

$$t\,(°\text{C}) = \frac{R_t - R_0}{R_{100} - R_0} \times 100$$

Here, R is resistance of platinum wire at 0°C, 100°C and t°C.

Ideal Gas Equation and Absolute Temperature

Three characteristics of a gas which describe its behaviour are pressure (p), volume (V) and temperature (T).

The relation among the characteristics of a gas is given by

(i) **Boyle's Law** It is given by English chemist Robert Boyle (1627–1691). According to this law,

$$p \propto \frac{1}{V} \quad \text{(at constant temperature)}$$

i.e. $pV = \text{constant}$

(ii) **Charles' Law** It is given by French scientist Jacques Charles (1747–1823). According to this law,

$$V \propto T \quad \text{(at constant pressure)}$$

i.e. $\frac{V}{T} = \text{constant}$

Ideal Gas Equation

On combining these two laws (above mentioned), we get

$$\frac{pV}{T} = \text{constant (for a given quantity of gas)}$$

This relation is known as **ideal gas law.** It can be written in more general forms for a given amount of gas as

$$\boxed{pV = \mu RT}$$

where, μ is number of moles of a gas and R is known as universal gas constant valued $8.31\ \text{J mol}^{-1}\ \text{K}^{-1}$. This equation is known as **ideal gas equation.**

From the ideal gas equation, $pV \propto T$

This is the cause for a gas to be used to measure temperature by a volume gas thermometer (for which $p \propto T$ as volume of the gas is constant).

Absolute Zero Temperature

Theoretically, there is no limit for maximum temperature but there is a sharp point for minimum temperature that no body can have the temperature lower than this, is known as **absolute zero temperature.** Its value is 0K or −273.16°C.

Thermal Expansion

When heat is supplied to material, its dimensions (length, area and volume) changes due to change in its temperature.

The phenomenon of change in dimensions of an object due to absorption of heat is known as **thermal expansion.**

Linear Expansion

The expansion in length of a body due to increase in its temperature is called the **linear expansion.**

If a rod having initial length l_1 at temperature T_1 and final increased length l_2 at increased temperature T_2, then fractional change in its length is given by

$$\frac{\Delta l}{l_1} = \frac{(l_2 - l_1)}{l_1} = \alpha_l (T_2 - T_1) = \alpha_l \Delta T$$

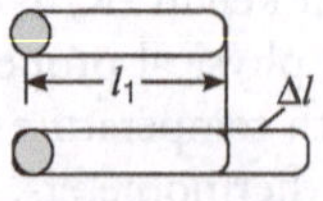

Linear expansion

Here, $\Delta l \propto l_1$ and $\Delta l \propto \Delta T$;

$\therefore \quad \Delta l \propto l_1 \Delta T$

$\Rightarrow \quad \boxed{\text{Expansion in length, } \Delta l = \alpha_l l_1 \Delta T}$

The quantity, α_l is known as **coefficient of linear expansion.** It is a characteristic of the material of the rod.

$$\alpha_l = \frac{\Delta l}{l \Delta T} = \frac{\text{Increase in length}}{\text{Original length} \times \text{Rise in temperature}}$$

Hence, the coefficient of linear expansion of a material of a solid rod is defined as increase in length per unit original length per degree rise in temperature. Its unit is $^\circ\text{C}^{-1}$ or $^\circ\text{K}^{-1}$.

Example 1 A blacksmith fixes iron ring on the rim of the wooden wheel of a bullock cart. The diameter of the rim and the iron ring are 5.243 m and 5.231 m, respectively at 27°C. To what temperature should the ring be heated so as to fit the rim of the wheel? ($\alpha = 1.20 \times 10^{-5} \text{K}^{-1}$) **NCERT**

Sol. Given, initial temperature $T_1 = 27°\text{C}$

Initial length, $l_1 = 5.231$ m

Final length, $l_2 = 5.243$ m

Now, $\quad \alpha_l = \frac{\Delta l}{l_1 \Delta T} = \frac{l_2 - l_1}{l_1 \Delta T}$

$\Rightarrow \quad l_2 = l_1 [1 + \alpha_l (T_2 - T_1)]$

i.e. $5.243 \text{ m} = 5.231\text{m} [1 + 1.20 \times 10^{-5} \text{ K}^{-1} (T_2 - 27°\text{C})]$

This gives $T_2 = 218°\text{C}$

Example 2 A large steel wheel is to be fitted on to a shaft of the same material. At 27°C, the outer diameter of the shaft is 8.70 cm and the diameter of the central hole in the wheel is 8.69 cm. The shaft is cooled using 'dry ice' (solid carbon dioxide).

At what temperature of the shaft does the wheel slip on the shaft? Assume coefficient of linear expansion of the steel to be constant over the required temperature range. $\alpha_{steel} = 1.20 \times 10^{-5}\ K^{-1}$. **NCERT**

Sol. Given, $l_1 = 8.70$ cm, $l_2 = 8.69$ cm,

$T_1 = 27 + 273 = 300$ K, $T_2 = ?$

As, $l_2 - l_1 = \alpha l_1 (T_2 - T_1)$

$\therefore \quad T_2 - T_1 = \dfrac{l_2 - l_1}{\alpha l_1}$

or $\quad T_2 - 300 = \dfrac{8.69 - 8.70}{1.20 \times 10^{-5} \times 8.70} = -95.8$

or $\quad T_2 = 300 - 95.8$

$= 204.2$ K

$= -68.95°$ C

Areal or Superficial Expansion

The expansion in the area of a surface due to increase in its temperature is called **area expansion.**

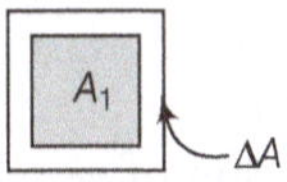

Area expansion

If a plate having initial area A_1 at temperature T_1 and final area A_2 at temperature T_2 then fractional change in its area is given by

$$\frac{\Delta A}{A_1} = \frac{(A_2 - A_1)}{A_1} = \alpha_A (T_2 - T_1) = \alpha_A \Delta T$$

Here, $\quad \Delta A \propto A_1$ and $\Delta A \propto \Delta T$

$\therefore \quad \Delta A \propto A_1 \Delta T$

$\Rightarrow$ Expansion in area, $\Delta A = \alpha_A A_1 \Delta T$

where, α_A is known as **coefficient of area expansion.** It depends on nature of the material of the plate.

$$\alpha_A = \frac{\Delta A}{A_1 \Delta T}$$

$$\alpha_A = \frac{\text{Increase in surface area}}{\text{Original surface area} \times \text{Rise in temperature}}$$

Hence, coefficient of areal expansion of metal sheet is defined as the increase in its surface area per unit original surface area per degree rise in its temperature. Its unit is $°C^{-1}$ or $°K^{-1}$.

Example 3 A metal ball having a diameter of 0.4 m is heated from 273 to 360 K. If the coefficient of area expansion of the material of the ball is 0.000034 K^{-1}, then determine the increase in surface area of the ball.

Sol. Given, Diameter = 0.4 m

Radius, $r = \dfrac{0.4}{2} = 0.2$ m

$\Delta T = T_2 - T_1$

$= 360\ K - 273\ K = 87$ K

$\alpha_A = 0.000034\ K^{-1}$

$\Delta A = ?$

Apply, $\quad \Delta A = \alpha_A A_1 \Delta T$

where, $\quad A_1 = 4\pi r^2 = 4 \times \pi \times (0.2)^2 = 0.5024\ m^2$

$\Delta A = 0.000034 \times 0.5024 \times 87$

$\Delta A = 0.001486 = 1.486 \times 10^{-3}\ m^2$

Volumetric Expansion

The expansion in the volume of an object due to increase in its temperature is known as **volumetric expansion.**

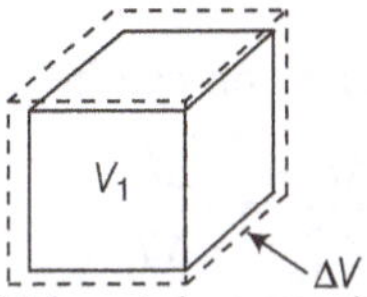

Volumetric expansion

The fractional change in volume of an object is given by

$$\frac{\Delta V}{V_1} = \frac{(V_2 - V_1)}{V_1} = \alpha_V (T_2 - T_1) = \alpha_V \Delta T$$

Here, $\quad \Delta V \propto V_1$ and $\Delta V \propto \Delta T$

$\therefore \quad \Delta V \propto V_1 \Delta T$

$\Rightarrow$ Expansion in volume, $\Delta V = \alpha_V V_1 \Delta T$

where, α_V is known as coefficient of volumetric expansion.

$$\alpha_V = \frac{\Delta V}{V_1 \Delta T}$$

Hence, the coefficient of volumetric (cubical) expansion of a substance is defined as the increase in volume per unit original volume per degree rise in its temperature. Its unit is $°C^{-1}$ or K^{-1}.

Coefficient of Thermal Expansion at High Temperature

The coefficients α_l, α_A and α_V for a given solid are constants only at a given temperature. The value of these coefficients, however changes with change in the temperature range and become constant only at a high temperature.

The coefficient of expansion α depends generally on temperature of metals, its value first increases with temperature and then becomes constant at a high temperature (above 500K).

The dependency is shown below.

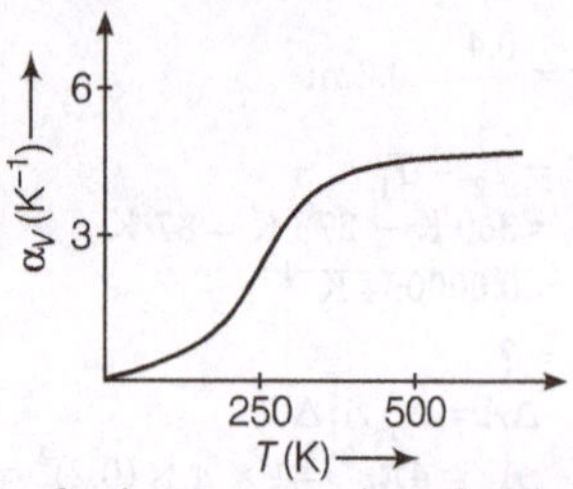

Coefficient of volume expansion of with temperature

Note The dimensions of all types of coefficients of expansion is [K^{-1}] and SI unit is per Kelvin, i.e. K^{-1}.

Relation among the Coefficients of Expansion

The coefficients of expansion can be given as

$$\alpha_l = \frac{\Delta l}{l_1 \Delta T} = \frac{\Delta l}{l \Delta T} \qquad \text{(When } l_1 = l\text{)}$$

$$\alpha_A = \frac{\Delta A}{A_1 \Delta T} = \frac{\Delta A}{A \Delta T} \qquad \text{(When } A_1 = A\text{)}$$

and
$$\alpha_V = \frac{\Delta V}{V_1 \Delta T} = \frac{\Delta V}{V \Delta T} \qquad \text{(When } V_1 = V\text{)}$$

Its ratio is given by

$$\boxed{\alpha_l : \alpha_A : \alpha_V = 1 : 2 : 3}$$

i.e. $\alpha_A = 2\alpha_l$ and $\alpha_V = 3\alpha_l$

Example 4 **The volume of a glass block initially was 15000 cm^3 but when the temperature of that glass block increases from 20°C to 45°C, then its volume increases by 5cm^3. Determine the coefficient of linear expansion.**

Sol. Given, $V_1 = 15000 \text{ cm}^3$,

$$\Delta T = T_2 - T_1 = 45°\text{C} - 20°\text{C} = 25°\text{C}$$

Change in volume, $\Delta V = 5 \text{ cm}^3$

Coefficient of volume expansion,

$$\alpha_V = \frac{\Delta V}{V_1 \Delta T} = \frac{5}{15000 \times 25}$$

$$\alpha_V = 0.0133 \times 10^{-3} \text{ °C}^{-1}$$

Coefficient of linear expansion

$$\alpha_l = \frac{\alpha_V}{3} = \frac{0.0133 \times 10^{-3}}{3}$$

$$\alpha_l = 4.4 \times 10^{-6} \text{ °C}^{-1}$$

Thermal Expansion of Liquids

Thermal expansion in liquids is identical to that of volume expansion in solids and is governed by the relationship which is $V = V_0 (1 + \gamma \Delta\theta)$, γ is coefficient of thermal expansion of liquids. γ for liquids is generally higher than that of solids.

Since, liquids are always heated in a vessel, so initially on heating the system (liquid + vessel), the level of liquid in vessel falls (as vessel expands more since it absorbs heat and liquid expands less) but later on, it starts rising due to faster expansion of the liquid. Thus, liquids have two coefficients of volume expansion.

(i) **Coefficient of real volumetric expansion γ_r**, which is due to the actual increase in volume of liquid due to heating.

(ii) **Coefficient of apparent volumetric expansion γ_a**, which is apparent increase in the volume of liquid if expansion of vessel containing the liquid is not taken into account.

$\therefore \quad \gamma_r = \gamma_a + \gamma_V$

Here, γ_V = expansion of vessel

Anomalous Expansion of Water

Water shows an anomalous behaviour, it contracts on heating between the temperature 0°C to 4°C. When water is cooled below the room temperature (i.e. normal temperature) the volume of given amount of water decreases.

Until its temperature reaches to 4°C and below 4°C, the volume increases (and hence density decreases). Water has maximum density (and hence minimum volume) at 4°C.

The curve shows the variation of density of water with respect to temperature from 0°C to 10°C as shown in figure.

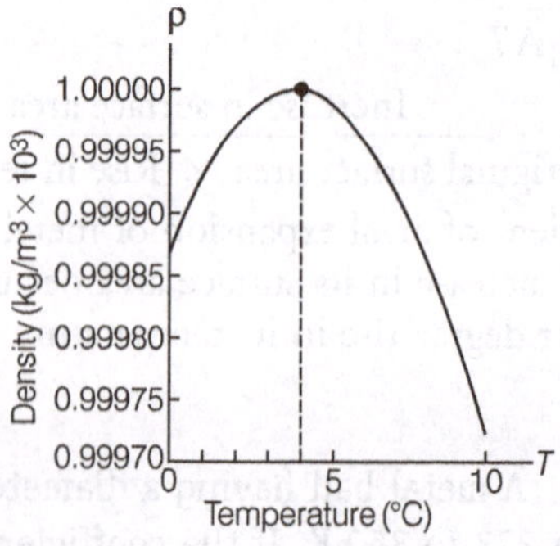

Variation of density of water w.r.t. temperature

The figure shows the variation of volume of 1 kg of water with temperature (°C).

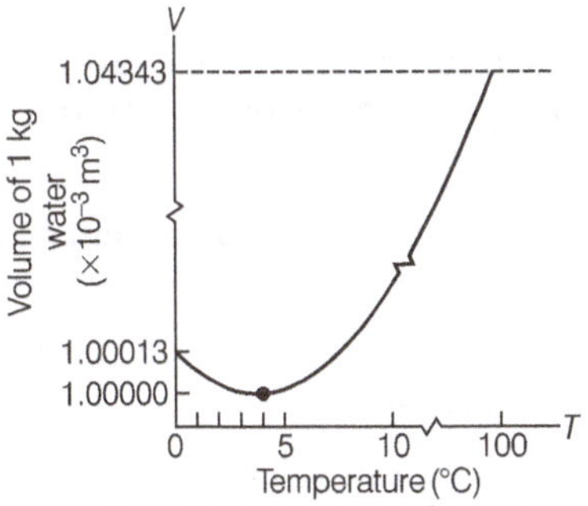

Abnormal behaviour of water

In winters, when an open water body like a lake is cooled water near the surface loses energy to the atmosphere becomes denser and sinks, the warmer, less dense water near the bottom rises.

However, once colder water on top reaches temperature below 4°C, it becomes less dense and remains at the surface, where it freezes. Ice layer formed on top is an insulator and it resists further conduction of heat. This phenomenon allows the marine animals to remain alive and move freely near the bottom.

Thermal Expansion of Gases

On heating gases expand more than solids or liquids and equal volumes of different gases expand equally, when heated by the same amount.

All gases have coefficient of volume expansion α_V with volume variation given by

$$V = V_0(1 + \alpha_V \Delta T)$$

and pressure variation given by

$$p = p_0(1 + \alpha_p \Delta T)$$

where, α_p = Coefficient of pressure expansion at constant volume

For ideal gas, $\alpha_p = \alpha_V = \dfrac{1}{273}$

Variation of Density with Temperature of Liquid

When a given mass of a liquid is heated, its volume increases; accordingly, the density of the liquid decreases. This variation in density occurs in solids also, but is insignificant.

Let V and V' be the volume of a liquid at temperatures T and $T + \Delta T$ respectively, and γ of the coefficient of volume expansion.

Then, we have

$$\Delta V = V' - V = \gamma V \Delta T$$

or $$V' = V(1 + \gamma \Delta T) \quad \ldots\text{(i)}$$

If ρ and ρ' be the densities of the liquid at temperatures T and $T + \Delta T$ respectively, then we have

$$V\rho = V'\rho' \text{ (each is mass)}$$

or $$\rho / \rho' = V' / V$$

Marking this substitutions in Eq. (i), we get

$$\rho = \rho'(1 + \gamma \Delta T) \text{ or } \rho' = \rho(1 + \gamma \Delta T)^{-1}$$

Expanding by Bionomial theorem and neglecting smaller terms, we have

$$\rho' = \rho(1 - \gamma \Delta T)$$

Thus, the density of liquids, which expand on heating, decreases with rise in temperature. However, the density of water increases with rise in temperature in the range 0-4°C.

Comparison of Expansions in Solids, Liquids and Gases

The expansion in solids and liquids is rather small as compared to the gases at ordinary temperature. The coefficient of volume expansion for the liquids is relatively independent of the temperature.

For an ideal gas, the volume expansion at constant pressure can be obtained from the equation,

$$pV = \mu RT$$

$$\Rightarrow \quad p\Delta V = \mu R \Delta T$$

$$\Rightarrow \quad \frac{\Delta V}{V} = \frac{\Delta T}{T}$$

i.e. $$\alpha_V = \frac{1}{T} \text{ for an ideal gas.}$$

At 0°C, $\alpha_V = (1/273)\text{K}^{-1} = 3.7 \times 10^{-3} \text{ K}^{-1}$

which is much larger than the solids and liquids. For a gas, room temperature and constant pressure α_V is about $3300 \times 10^{-6} \text{ K}^{-1}$.

Topic Practice 1

Multiple Choice Questions

1 Mark

1. Which of the following is a measure of hotness of a body?
   (a) Temperature (b) Heat
   (c) Specific heat (d) Latent heat

2. A glass of ice-cold water left on a table on a hot summer day eventually warms up whereas a cup of hot tea on the same table cools down because
(a) its surrounding media are different
(b) the direction of heat flow depends on the surrounding temperature with respect to the object
(c) heating or cooling does not depend on surrounding temperature
(d) Both (a) and (b)

3. The common physical property which is to be used as the basis for constructing thermometer is
(a) the variation of the volume of a liquid with temperature
(b) the variation of the pressure of a gas with temperature
(c) the variation of the resistance of a wire with temperature
(d) All of the above

4. A fully inflated balloon shrinks when it is put into cold water, because
(a) water causes lesser pressure from outside on the balloon
(b) water causes a pull on balloon which presses it
(c) air inside the balloon contracts due to cooling
(d) rubber of balloon expands on cooling and compresses air inside

5. Coefficient of volumetric expansion α_V is not a constant. It depends on temperature. Variation of α_V with temperature for metals is

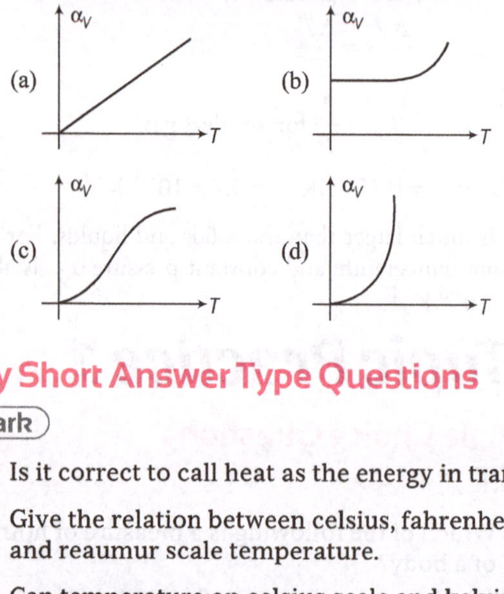

Very Short Answer Type Questions

1 Mark

6. Is it correct to call heat as the energy in transit?

7. Give the relation between celsius, fahrenheit and reaumur scale temperature.

8. Can temperature on celsius scale and kelvin scale related?

9. Two absolute scales A and B have triple points of water defined to be 200 A and 350 B. What is relation between T_A and T_B? **NCERT**

10. Why the temperature above 1200°C cannot be measured accurately by a platinum resistance thermometer?

11. Give relation between coefficient of linear, superficial and volumetric expansion.

12. Give units and dimensions of coefficient of cubical expansion.

13. At what temperature density of pure water is maximum?

14. Draw a graph to show variation of volume of a sample of pure water, when its temperature is varied.

Short Answer Type I Questions

2 Marks

15. In what ways are the gas thermometers superior to mercury thermometers?

16. Gas thermometers are more sensitive than mercury thermometers. Why?

17. There is a slight temperature difference between the water fall at the top and the bottom. Why?

18. The difference between length of a certain brass rod and that of a steel rod is claimed to be constant at all temperatures. Is this possible?

19. There are two spheres of same radius and material at same temperature but one being solid while the other hollow. Which sphere will expand more if (i) they are heated to the same temperature (ii) same amount of heat is given to each of them?

Short Answer Type II Questions

3 Marks

20. Derive a relation between coefficient of linear expansion, coefficient of superficial expansion and coefficient of volumetric expansion.

21. Show that for a gas, coefficient of cubical expansion at constant pressure is equal to reciprocal of its absolute temperature.

22. Explain expansion on the basis of potential energy curve for two molecules.

23. What is thermal stress? When a rod of length l and area A is kept between two rigid supports and its temperature is raised by ΔT, then find the value of force exerted by rod on the support. (Take, α = coefficient of linear expansion and Y = Young's modulus of rod's material).

Long Answer Type Questions

5 Marks

24. (i) Explain thermal expansion of liquid.
(ii) What is apparent volumetric expansion? What is the relation between the coefficient of real volumetric expansion and apparent volumetric expansion?

25. (i) Explain, how density of liquid varies with increases of temperature.
(ii) Compare the expansions in solids, liquids and gases with temperature.

26. (i) Explain, anamalous expansion of water with suitable graph.
(ii) Explain, thermal expansion of gases.

Numerical Problems

27. Find out the temperature which has same numerical value on celsius and fahrenheit scale. **[2 M]**

28. A celsius and fahrenheit thermometer are put in an hot bath. The reading of fahrenheit thermometer is 3/2 times the reading of celsius thermometer. What is the temperature of bath on celsius, fahrenheit and kelvin's scales. **[3 M]**

29. The triple points of neon and carbon dioxide are 24.57 K and 216.55 K, respectively. Express these temperatures on the celsius and fahrenheit scales. **NCERT [3 M]**

30. Two ideal gas thermometers A and B use oxygen and hydrogen, respectively. The following observations are made **NCERT [3 M]**

Temperature	Pressure thermometer A	Pressure thermometer B
Triple point of water	1.250×10^5 Pa	0.200×10^5 Pa
Normal melting point of sulphur	1.797×10^5 Pa	0.287×10^5 Pa

(i) What is the absolute temperature of normal melting point of sulphur as read by thermometers A and B?
(ii) What do you think is the reason for slightly different answers from A and B? **NCERT**

31. A metallic ball has a radius of 9.0 cm at 0°C. Calculate the change in its volume when it is heated to 90°C. Given that coefficient of linear expansion of metal of ball is $1.2 \times 10^{-5}\ K^{-1}$. **[3 M]**

32. A steel tape 1 m long is correctly calibrated for a temperature of 27.0°C. The length of a steel rod measured by this tape is found to be 63.0 cm on a hot day when the temperature is 45.0°C. What is the actual length of the steel rod on that day? What is the length of the same steel rod on a day when the temperature is 27.0°C? Coefficient of linear expansion of steel $= 1.20 \times 10^{-5}\ {}^\circ C^{-1}$? **NCERT [2 M]**

33. The coefficient of volume expansion of glycerine is $49 \times 10^{-5}\ {}^\circ C^{-1}$. What is the fractional change in its density for a 30°C rise in temperature? **[2 M]**

34. A brass rod of length 50 cm and diameter 3.0 mm is joined to a steel rod of the same length and diameter. What is the change in length of the combined rod at 250°C, if the original length are at 40.0°C? Is there a 'thermal stress' developed at the junction? The ends of the rod are free to expand. Coefficient of linear expansion of brass $= 2.0 \times 10^{-5}\ {}^\circ C^{-1}$ and that of steel $= 1.2 \times 10^{-5}\ {}^\circ C^{-1}$. **[5 M]**

35. A hole is drilled in a copper sheet. The diameter of the hole is 4.24 cm at 27°C. What is the change in the diameter of the hole when the sheet is heated to 227°C? Coefficient of linear expansion of copper is $1.70 \times 10^{-5}/{}^\circ C$. **NCERT [5 M]**

Hints & Solutions

1. (*a*) Temperature is a measure of hotness of a body. A body at a higher temperature when touched gives a feeling of more hotness than that at a lower temperature. But, temperature does not give the measure of content of heat in a body.

2. (*b*) When the temperature of body, ice cold water or hot tea in this case, and its surrounding medium are different, then heat transfer takes place between the system and the surrounding medium, until the body and the surrounding medium are at the same temperature.

3. (*d*) Any physical property which varies linearly with temperature can be used constructing thermometers.

4. (*c*) Air inside the balloon contracts and therefore balloon walls shrink. A change in temperature of a body causes a change in dimensions.

5. (*c*) α_V is a characteristic of the substance but is not strictly a constant. It depends in general on temperature as shown in figure. It is seen that α_V becomes constant only at a higher temperature.

6. Yes, it is perfect correct to call heat as the energy in transit because it appears only when it flows from body at higher temperature to body at lower temperature.

7. $\dfrac{C-0}{100-0} = \dfrac{F-32}{212-32} = \dfrac{R-0}{80-0}$

8. $t = T - 27315$ or $T = t + 27315$
where, t = temperature on Celsius scale
and T = temperature on Kelvin scale.

9. $\dfrac{T_A}{T_B} = \dfrac{200}{350} = \dfrac{4}{7}$ or $T_A = \dfrac{4}{7} T_B$

10. This is because platinum begins to evaporate above 1200°C.

11. Refer to text on page 340 (Relation among the coefficients of expansion).

12. Refer to text on page 339 (Volumetric expansion).

13. Refer to text on page 340 (Anomalous expansion of water).

14. Refer to text on pages 340 and 341 (Anomalous expansion of water).

15. A gas thermometer is more superior to a mercury thermometer, as its working is independent of the nature of gas (working substance) used. As the variation of pressure (or volume) with temperature is uniform, the range, in which temperature can be measured with a gas thermometer is quite large. Further, a gas thermometer is more sensitive than mercury thermometer. [2]

16. The coefficient of increase of pressure (or volume) of a gas is $\dfrac{1}{273.15}$ °C^{-1}. It is very large as compared to coefficient of expansion of mercury. Therefore, for a certain increase in temperature, increase in volume of the gas will be large compared to that of mercury and hence a gas thermometer is more sensitive. [2]

17. The potential energy of water at the top of the fall gets converted into heat kinetic energy at the bottom of the fall. When water hits the ground, a part of its kinetic energy gets converted into heat which increases its temperature slightly. [1+1]

18. Yes, it is possible to describe the difference of length to remain constant. So, the change in length of each rod must be equal at all temperature. Let L_b and L_s be the length of the brass and the steel rod and α_b and α_s be the coefficients of linear expansion of the two metals. Let there is change in temperature be ΔT.

Then, $\alpha_b L_b \Delta T = \alpha_s L_s \Delta T$ [1]

or $\alpha_b L_b = \alpha_s L_s \Rightarrow L_b / L_s = \alpha_s / \alpha_b$

Hence, the lengths of the rods must be in the inverse ratio of the coefficient of linear expansion of their materials. [1]

19. (i) As thermal expansion of isotropic solids is similar to true photographic enlargement, the expansion of a cavity is same as if it were a solid body of the same material i.e. $\Delta V = \gamma V \Delta T$. As here V, γ and ΔT are same for both solid and hollow spheres, so the expansions of both will be equal. [1]

(ii) If same amount of heat is given to the two spheres, then due to lesser mass, rise in temperature of hollow sphere will be more (as $\Delta T = Q/Mc$) and hence the expansion will be more as $\Delta V = \gamma V \Delta T$. [1]

20. Refer to text on pages 338 and 339 (Linear expansion, areal or superficial expansion and volumetric expansion).

21. For a gas, $pV = nRT$ [1]

At constant pressure,

$$p\Delta V = nR\Delta T$$ [1]

$\therefore \dfrac{\Delta V}{V} = \dfrac{\Delta T}{T}$ or $\dfrac{\Delta V}{V\Delta T} = \dfrac{1}{T}$ or $r = \dfrac{1}{T}$ [1]

22. As temperature rises potential energy of two molecule system rises and so, mean separation or the amplitude of vibration of molecules increases. This results in expansion.

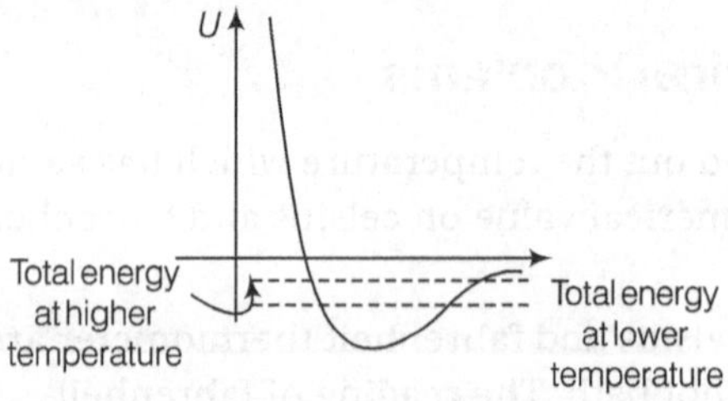

[3]

23. When expansion of a rod is restricted, the rod acquires a compressive strain due to the force exerted by expanding rod at supports. This causes a thermal stress in the rod. [1]

If l = length and A = area of rod, then

Thermal strain is

$$\frac{\Delta l}{l} = \alpha \Delta T$$

or Young's modulus of rod,

$$Y = \frac{\sigma}{\Delta l / l}$$

or thermal stress, $\sigma = Y\alpha\Delta T$

Hence, force on support is

$$F = \sigma A = Y\alpha\Delta T \cdot A$$ [2]

24. (i) Refer to text on page 340 (Thermal expansion of liquids).

(ii) Refer to text on page 341 (Comparison of expansions in solids, liquid and gases).

25. (i) Refer to text on page 341 (Variation of density with temperature of liquid).
(ii) Refer to text on page 341 (Comparison of expansions in solids, liquids and gases).

26. (i) Refer to text on pages 340 and 341 (Anamalous expansion of water).
(ii) Refer to text on page 341 (Thermal expansion of gases).

27. Let θ be the same numerical value of temperature on the both scales.

$$\therefore \quad \frac{T_C}{5} = \frac{T_F - 32}{9}$$

$$\Rightarrow \quad \frac{\theta}{5} = \frac{\theta - 32}{9} \quad [\because \theta°C = \theta°F = \theta, \text{ given}]$$

$$\theta = -40°C = -40°F$$ [2]

28. Let if reading on celsius scale is θ.

Reading on $\quad T_F = \frac{3}{2}\theta$

As $\quad \frac{\theta}{100} = \frac{T_F - 32}{180}$ [1]

$$\frac{\theta}{5} = \frac{\frac{3}{2}\theta - 32}{9}$$

On solving, we get

$$\theta = -106.67\,°C$$ [1]

Temperature on kelvin's scale,

$$T_K = -106.67 + 273.15 = 166.48 \text{ K}$$ [1]

29. For neon Triple point $T = 24.57$ K

$\therefore \; T_C = T(\text{K}) - 273.15$ [1]

$= 24.57 - 273.15 = -248.58°\text{C}$

$$T_F = \frac{9}{5}T_C + 32 = \frac{9}{5} \times (-248.58) + 32 = -415.44°\text{F}$$ [1/2]

For carbon dioxide Triple point, $T = 216.55$ K

$\therefore \; T_C = T(K) - 273.15 = 216.55 - 273.15 = -56.6°\text{C}$ [1/2]

$$T_F = \frac{9}{5}T_C + 32 = \frac{9}{5} \times (-56.6) + 32 = -69.88°\text{C}$$ [1]

30. (i) (a) For pressure thermometer A,

$T_{tr} = 273$ K, $p_{tr} = 1.250 \times 10^5$ Pa,

$p = 1.797 \times 10^5$ Pa [1]

Normal freezing point of sulphur,

$$T = \frac{p}{p_{tr}} \times T_{tr} = \frac{1.795 \times 10^5 \times 273}{1.250 \times 10^5} = 392.028 \text{ K}$$ [1]

(b) For pressure thermometer B,

$T_{tr} = 273$ K, $p_{tr} = 0.200 \times 10^5$ Pa, $p = 0.287 \times 10^5$ Pa

$$\therefore \; T = \frac{0.287 \times 10^5 \times 273}{0.200 \times 10^5} = 391.75 \text{ K}$$

(ii) The slight difference is due to the fact that oxygen and hydrogen do not behave strictly as ideal gases. [1]

31. As radius of ball, $r_0 = 9.0$ cm $= 0.090$ m at 0°C, hence its

volume, $\quad V_0 = \frac{4}{3}\pi r_0^3 = \frac{4}{3} \times 3.14 \times (0.090)^3$

$$= 3.05 \times 10^{-3}\,\text{m}^3$$ [1]

Again as, $\alpha = 1.2 \times 10^{-5}\ \text{K}^{-1}$,

$\therefore \quad \gamma = 3\alpha$

$= 3 \times 1.2 \times 10^{-5} = 3.6 \times 10^{-5}\ \text{K}^{-1}$

Moreover rise in temperature

$\Delta T = 90°\text{C} - 0°\text{C} = 90°\text{C} = 90$ K [1]

$\therefore$ Increase in volume, $\Delta V = V\gamma\Delta T$

$= 3.05 \times 10^{-3} \times 3.6 \times 10^{-5} \times 90$

$= 9.88 \times 10^{-6}\ \text{m}^3$

$= 9.88\ \text{cm}^3$ [1]

32. Here, $t_1 = 27°\text{C}$, $l_1 = 63$ cm,

$t_2 = 45°\text{C}$, $\alpha = 1.20 \times 10^{-5}\,°\text{C}^{-1}$ [1/2]

Length of the rod on the hot day is

$l_2 = l_1[1 + \alpha(t_2 - t_1)]$ [1/2]

$= 63[1 + 1.20 \times 10^{-5}(45 - 27)]$

$= 63.0136$ cm [1/2]

As the steel tape has been calibrated for a temperature of 27°C, so length of the steel rod at 27°C = 63 cm. [1/2]

33. Let M be the mass of glycerine, ρ_0 its density at 0°C, ρ_t its density at t°C.

Then, $\quad \gamma = \frac{V_t - V_0}{V_0\,\Delta T} = \frac{\frac{M}{\rho_t} - \frac{M}{\rho_0}}{(M/\rho_0)\Delta T}$

$$\gamma = \frac{\frac{1}{\rho_t} - \frac{1}{\rho_0}}{(1/\rho_0)\,\Delta T} = \frac{\rho_0 - \rho_t}{\rho_t \Delta T}$$ [1]

$\therefore$ Fractional change in density,

$$\frac{\rho_0 - \rho_t}{\rho_0} = \gamma\Delta T$$

$$= 49 \times 10^{-5} \times 30 = 0.0147$$ [1]

34. For brass rod,

$l = 50$ cm, $t_1 = 40°\text{C}$, $t_2 = 250°\text{C}$

$\alpha = 2.0 \times 10^{-5}\,°\text{C}^{-1}$ [1]

Change in length of brass rod is

$\Delta l = \alpha l(t_2 - t_1)$

$= 2.0 \times 10^{-5} \times 50 \times (250 - 40) = 0.21$ cm [1]

For steel rod, $l = 50$ cm, $t_1 = 40°\text{C}$, $t_2 = 250°\text{C}$,

$\alpha = 1.2 \times 10^{-5}\,°\text{C}^{-1}$ [1]

Change in length of steel rod is

$\Delta l' = \alpha l(t_2 - t_1)$

$= 1.2 \times 10^{-5} \times 50 \times (250 - 40)$

$= 0.13$ cm [1]

Change in length of the combined rod at 250°C

$= \Delta l + \Delta l'$

$= 0.21 + 0.13$

$= 0.34$ cm

As the rods expand freely, so no thermal stress is developed at the junction. [1]

35. Given, diameter of the hole $(d_1) = 4.24$ cm

Initial temperature $T_1 = 27 + 273 = 300$ K

Final temperature $T_2 = 227 + 273 = 500$ K [1]

Coefficient of linear expansion $(\alpha) = 1.70 \times 10^{-5}$ /°C

Coefficient of superficial expansion

$(\beta) = 2\alpha = 3.40 \times 10^{-5}$ /°C [1/2]

Initial area of hole at 27°C $(A_1) = \pi r^2 = \dfrac{\pi d_1^2}{4}$

$= \dfrac{\pi}{4}(4.24)^2$

$= 4.494\pi$ cm^2

Area of hole at 227°C $(A_2) = A_1(1 + \beta\Delta t)$ [1]

$= 4.494\pi[1 + 3.40 \times 10^{-5} \times (227 - 27)]$

$= 4.494\pi(1 + 3.40 \times 10^{-5} \times 200)$

$= 4.495\pi \times 1.0068$

$= 4.525\pi$ cm^2 [1/2]

If diameter of hole becomes d_2 at 227°C, then

$$A_2 = \frac{\pi d_2^2}{4}$$ [1]

or $4.525\pi = \dfrac{\pi d_2^2}{4}$

$\Rightarrow \quad d_2^2 = 4.525 \times 4$

$\Rightarrow \quad d_2 = 4.2544$ cm

$\therefore$ Change in diameter $(\Delta d) = d_2 - d_1 = 4.2544 - 4.24$

$= 0.0144$ cm

$= 1.44 \times 10^{-2}$ cm [1]

TOPIC 02 Calorimetry

Heat Capacity

The quantity of heat is given to any substance depends on its mass m, the change in temperature ΔT and the nature of substance which is being heated.

To change the temperature of substance, a given quantity of heat is absorbed or rejected by it, which is characterised by a quantity is known as **heat capacity**.

Thermal Capacity

The thermal capacity of a body is defined as a amount of heat required to rise the temperature of the body through 1K. If in the formula $Q = mC\Delta T$, we put $\Delta T = 1$K.

Then, $\quad Q = mC$

Thus, thermal capacity is equal to the product of mass of the body and specific heat of the substance of that body, the unit of thermal capacity is cal/°C.

Its SI unit is J/K (or J/°C).

Specific Heat Capacity

The amount of heat needed to raise the temperature of unit mass of a substance by unity is known as the **specific heat capacity** or **specific heat.** It is denoted by s and its SI unit is Jkg^{-1}K^{-1}.

$$s = \frac{S}{m} = \frac{\Delta Q}{m\Delta T}$$

$\Rightarrow$ Specific heat capacity, $s = \dfrac{1}{m}\dfrac{\Delta Q}{\Delta T}$

where, m = mass of given substance.

The SI unit of specific heat capacity is Jkg^{-1}K^{-1}.

Note Water has the highest specific heat capacity (4.18×10^3 J kg^{-1} °C^{-1}) compared to other substances. For this reason water is used as a coolant in automobile radiators as well as a heater in hot water bags.

Example 1 **A 10 kW drilling machine is used to drill a bore in a small aluminium block of mass 8.0 kg. How much is the rise in temperature of the block in 2.5 min, assuming 50% of power is used up in heating the machine itself or lost to the surroundings. Specific heat of aluminium = 0.91 Jg^{-1}°C^{-1}.** **NCERT**

Sol. Given, power, $P = 10$ kW $= 10 \times 10^3$ W

Time, $\quad t = 2.5$ min $= 2.5 \times 60$ s

Total energy used $= Pt = 10 \times 10^3 \times 2.5 \times 60$

$= 1.5 \times 10^6$ J

Energy absorbed by aluminium block,

$Q = 50\%$ of the total energy

$= \dfrac{1.5 \times 10^6}{2} = 0.75 \times 10^6$ J

Also, $m = 8.0$ kg $= 8.0 \times 10^3$g, $s = 0.91$ Jg^{-1}°C^{-1}

As, $\quad Q = ms\,\Delta T$

$\therefore \quad \Delta T = \dfrac{Q}{ms}$

$= \dfrac{0.75 \times 10^6}{8.0 \times 10^3 \times 0.91}$

$= 103.02$° C

Calorimetry

It is the branch of science that deals with the measurement of heat. When a body at higher temperature is brought in contact with another body at lower temperature, then the heat flows from the body kept at higher temperature to the body kept at lower temperature till both the bodies acquire the same temperature.

The principle of calorimetry states that total heat given by a hotter body equals to the total heat received by colder body.

i.e. Heat lost by hotter body = Heat gained by colder body

If there are two bodies of masses m_1 and m_2 and having values of specific heats s_1 and s_2 respectively, then for temperature difference ΔT.

$$\Rightarrow \quad \boxed{m_1 s_1 \, \Delta T = m_2 s_2 \, \Delta T}$$

Calorimeter

It is a device used for measuring the quantities of heat. It consists of a cylindrical vessel of copper provided with a stirrer. The vessel is kept inside a wooden jacket. The space between the calorimeter and the jacket is packed with a heat insulating material like glass, wool etc.

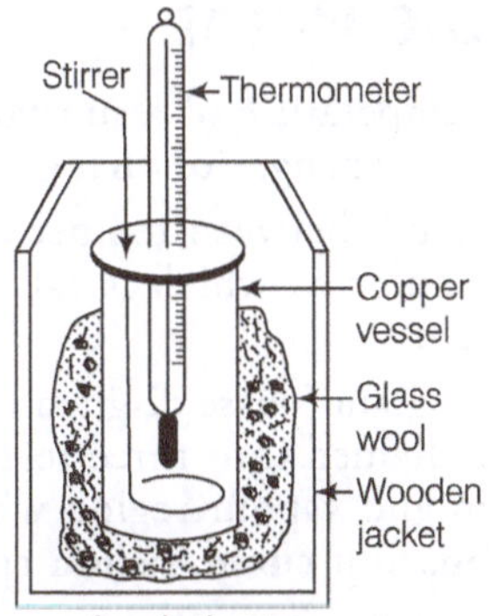

A calorimeter arrangement

Thus, the calorimeter gets thermally isolated from the surroundings.

The loss of heat due to radiation is further reduced by polishing the outer surface of the calorimeter and the inner surface of the jacket.

The lid is provided with holes for inserting a thermometer and a stirrer into the calorimeter.

When bodies at different temperatures are mixed together in the calorimeter, heat is exchanged between the bodies as well as with the calorimeter.

If there is no loss of heat to the surroundings, then according to the principle of calorimetry,

Heat gained by cold bodies = Heat lost by hot bodies

Water Equivalent of Calorimeter

The water equivalent of the calorimeter is equal to the mass of water which would increase in temperature by same amount as the calorimeter if given the same amount of heat.

water equivalent, $w = mC$

where, m = mass of calorimeter and

C = specific heat of material of calorimeter.

So, heat absorbed by calorimeter when its temperature changes by $\Delta T = mC\Delta T = w\Delta T$.

Advantages of High Specific Heat of Water in Daily Life

(i) **Fomentation** Hot water bottles are used for fomentation, as the water remains hot in the bottle for a long time in spite of giving off large quantities of heat.

(ii) **Land and sea breezes** The specific heat capacity of water is about five times more than that of sand. It therefore, takes a much longer time to heat and to cool with respect to sand.

During the day, the land cools faster than the sea. The hot air from the sea rises while the cool air from the sea moves to take its place, giving rise to a sea breeze.

During the night, the water cools faster than the land. The hot air from the land moves to take its place, giving rise to a land breeze.

(iii) **Car radiators** Water is used as coolant in car radiators. Due to its high specific heat capacity, it can absorb a large amount of heat energy from the engine of the car, but its temperature does not rise too high.

(iv) **Bottled Wines** In cold countries, wine bottles are kept under water. Due to the high specific heat capacity of water, it takes a long time for the temperature to fall to 0°C.

Example 2 In an experiment on the specific heat of a metal, a 0.20 kg block of the metal at 150°C is dropped in a copper calorimeter (of water equivalent 0.025 kg) containing 150 cm^3 of water at 27°C. The final temperature is 40°C. Compute the specific heat of the metal.

Sol. Given, mass of metal block, $m = 0.20 \text{ kg} = 200 \text{ g}$

Fall in temperature of metal block,

$$\Delta T = 150° - 40° = 110°\text{C}$$

Let specific heat of metal block = s cal g^{-1}°C^{-1}

$\therefore$ Heat lost by metal block $= mc\,\Delta T = 200 \times s \times 110$ cal

Volume of water in calorimeter = 150 cm^3

Mass of water, $m' = 150$ g

Water equivalent of calorimeter,

$$w = 0.025 \text{ kg} = 25 \text{ g}$$

Specific heat of water,

$$s' = 1 \text{ cal g}^{-1}\text{°C}^{-1}$$

$\therefore$ Heat gained by water and calorimeter

$$= (m' + w)\, s' \Delta T'$$
$$= (150 + 25) \times 1 \times (40 - 27) \text{ cal}$$
$$= 175 \times 13 \text{ cal}$$

According to principle of calorimetry, we get

Heat lost = Heat gained

$\therefore \quad 200 \times s \times 110 = 175 \times 13$

or $\quad s = \dfrac{175 \times 13}{200 \times 110} = 0.1 \text{ cal g}^{-1}\,{}^\circ\text{C}^{-1}$

Change of State

The process of converting one state of a substance into another state is known as **change of state** of a substance or matter.

Matter generally exists in three states

(i) Solid (ii) Liquid (iii) Gas

These states can be changed into one another by absorbing heat or rejecting heat. The process is called the **change of state.**

The common changes of states are

(i) Solid to liquid (and *vice-versa*)

(ii) Liquid to gas (and *vice-versa*)

The changes can occur when the exchange of heat takes place between substance and its surroundings.

Note

- Besides these three states i.e. solid, liquid and gas, the fourth state of matter also exist which is known as **plasma.**
- When a substance is heated to a very high temperature, many electrons around the nucleus of the atom of the substance are free. The collection of these free electrons and the positive ions forms a plasma.

Terms Related to Change of State

There are some important terms related to change of state as given below

Melting and Melting Point

The process of change of state from solid to liquid is called **melting.** The temperature at which solid starts to liquify is known as the **melting point** of that solid.

Note The melting point of a substance at standard atmospheric pressure is called **normal melting point.**

Fusion and Freezing Point

The process of change of state from liquid to solid is called **fusion.** The temperature at which liquid starts to freeze is known as the **freezing point** of the liquid.

Vaporisation and Boiling Point

The process of change of state from liquid to vapour (or gas) is called **vaporisation.** During the change of state (completely), the temperature remains constant which implies both liquid and vapour states of the substance co-exist in thermal equilibrium. The temperature at which the liquid and the vapour states of the substance co-exist is called the **boiling point** of the liquid.

Sublimation

The process of change of state directly from solid to vapour (or gas) without changing into liquid state is known as **sublimation.** Few common substances that shows sublimation are camphor, nepthalene balls, etc.

Effect of pressure on the boiling point of a liquid The boiling point of a liquid increases with the increase in pressure. The boiling point of water is 100°C at 1 atm pressure and it is 128°C at 2 atm pressure.

Triple Point

The temperature of a substance remains constant during its phase change (or change of state).

The graph between temperature and pressure of substance can be plotted which is called **phase diagram** or *p-T* diagram.

The diagram (phase diagram of water and CO_2) shows *p-T* plane divided into three regions i.e. solid region, liquid region and vapour region which are separated by **sublimation curve, fusion curve and vaporisation curve.**

These three curves represent the states in which solid and vapour phases, solid and liquid phases and liquid and vapour phases co-exist.

The temperature and pressure at which all three phases of a substance co-exist simultaneously is known as the **triple point** of the substance, e.g. The triple point for water is represented by temperature 273.16 K and pressure 6.11×10^{-3} Pa.

Two figures below show the phase diagram with triple point for (a) water (b) CO_2.

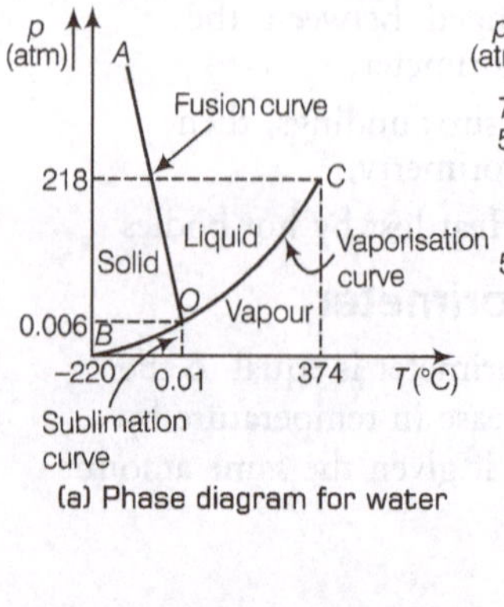

(a) Phase diagram for water

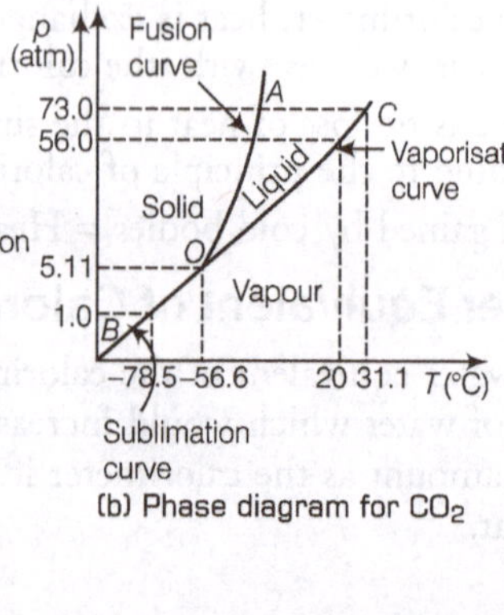

(b) Phase diagram for CO_2

The sublimation curve BO represents states in which the solid and vapour phases co-exist. The point on vaporisation curve co-represent the states in which the liquid and vapour phases co-exist. The fusion curve AO represents the states in which solid and vapour phases co-exist. Vapourisation curve OC shows all states in which liquid and vapour phases are in equilibrium.

Note A gas can be liquified by applying pressure on it only when temperature of gas is below critical temperature. The pressure required is called critical pressure. The volume occupied by unit mass of the gas at critical temperature and critical pressure is called critical volume.

Latent Heat

The amount of heat transferred per unit mass during the change of phase of a substance without any change in its temperature is called latent heat of the substance for particular change.

Latent heat is denoted by L and having SI unit J kg^{-1}.

Thus, if a mass m of a substance undergoes a change from one state to the other, then the quantity of heat required is given by

$$\boxed{Q = mL} \text{ i.e. } \boxed{\text{Latent heat, } L = Q/m}$$

Hence, during the phase change, the heat required by the substance depends on the mass m of the substance.

Types of Latent Heat

There are two types of latent heat of materials

(i) **Latent Heat of Fusion or Melting**
It is the amount of heat given (or taken out) to convert unit mass (1 kg) of substance from solid state to liquid state (or from liquid state to solid state) at its melting point (without change in temperature).

$$\boxed{\text{Latent heat of fusion, } L_f = \frac{Q}{m}}$$

Its SI unit is Jkg^{-1}.

(ii) **Latent Heat of Vaporisation**
It is the amount of heat given (or taken out) to convert unit mass (1 kg) of substance from liquid state to vapour state (or from vapour state to liquid state) at boiling point (without change in temperature).

It is denoted by L_V. It is given by

$$\boxed{\text{Latent heat of vaporisation, } L_V = \frac{Q}{m}}$$

and its SI unit is Jkg^{-1}. The latent heats of state change of some substances are given below in the table.

Variation of Temperature During Change of State

It is observed from the above graph as heat is added or removed during a change of state, the temperature remains constant, hence the slopes of the phase lines are not all the same, which indicates the specific heats of the various states are not equal.

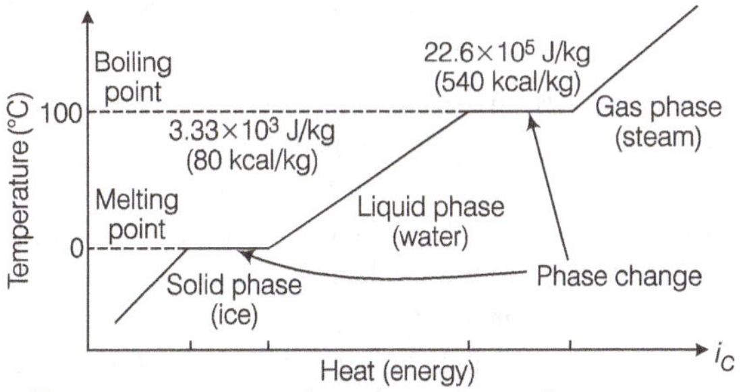

Temperature *versus* heat for water at 1 atm pressure

e.g. Water having $L_f = 3.33 \times 10^5$ Jkg^{-1} and $L_V = 22.6 \times 10^5$ Jkg^{-1}, it means 3.33×10^5 J of heat is needed to melt 1 kg of ice at 0°C and 22.6×10^5 J of heat is needed to convert 1 kg of water to steam at 100°C.

Effect of Latent Heat of Fusion of Ice in Daily Life

(i) Teeth feel ice-cream much more colder than ice-cooled water at 0°C. This is because, when ice-cream melts, it takes sufficient heat from the teeth.

(ii) Snow melts slowly on mountains because latent heat of ice were small, then in summer all the snow would have melted very quickly and the rivers would have been flooded. It is due to high latent heat, that a small piece of ice cools sufficient amount of water.

(iii) The temperature of atmosphere falls appreciably after rain of hail-stones. When hail-stones falls during rains, they take sufficient heat from the atmosphere for melting. That is why the weather is much more colder after the snowfall, than that during the snowfall.

(iv) Water in lakes and ponds in cold countries freezes slowly during a heavy cold, only the surface layer of ponds and river are frozen to ice. Since ice is a bad conductor of heat, the thickness of ice layer formed seldom exceeds many inches. Thus, the aquatic animals (like fish) gets time to more to bottom, where water remains at 4°C. Thus, they remains alive.

Example 3 The ice of 0.15 kg mass at 0°C is mixed with 0.30 kg of water at 50°C in a container. The resulting temperature of the container (after mixing) is 6.7°C. Determine the heat of fusion of ice if specific heat (s_w) for the water is 4186 $\text{Jkg}^{-1}\text{K}^{-1}$. **NCERT**

Sol. Heat lost by water $= ms_w(\theta_f - \theta_i)_w$

$$= (0.30 \text{ kg})(4186 \text{ Jkg}^{-1}\text{K}^{-1})(50.0 - 6.7)°\text{C}$$

$$= 54376.14 \text{ J}$$

Heat required to melt ice = mass of ice $\times L_f$

$$= m_I L_f$$

$$= (0.15 \text{ kg}) L_f$$

Heat required to raise temperature of ice water to final temperature (from the calorimetry)

$$= m_I s_w (\theta_f - \theta_i)_I$$

$$= (0.15 \text{ kg})(4186 \text{ Jkg}^{-1}\text{K}^{-1})(6.7°\text{C} - 0°\text{C})$$

$$= 4206.93 \text{ J}$$

Principle of calorimetry i.e. heat lost = heat gained

$$\Rightarrow \quad 54376.14 \text{ J} = (0.15 \text{ kg})L_f + 4206.93 \text{ J}$$

$$\Rightarrow \quad L_f = 3.34 \times 10^5 \text{ Jkg}^{-1}$$

This is required value of heat of fusion of ice.

Example 4 A lead bullet penetrates into a solid object and melts. If half of its kinetic energy was used to heat it, calculate the initial velocity of the bullet. The initial temperature of the bullet is 27°C and the melting point of the material of bullet is 327°C. Given that latent heat of fusion of lead is 2.5×10^4 J kg^{-1} and specific heat capacity of lead is 125 J $\text{kg}^{-1}\text{K}^{-1}$.

Sol. Let mass of bullet is m and given

$$s = 125 \text{ Jkg}^{-1}\text{ K}^{-1}$$

$$\Delta\theta = 327° - 27° = 300°\text{C}$$

Heat required by bullet to reach its melting point

$$\Rightarrow \quad \Delta Q_1 = m \times 125 \times 300$$

$$= m \times 3.75 \times 10^4 \text{ Jkg}^{-1}$$

Heat required to melt the bullet $\Delta Q_2 = mL_b$.

Latent heat of bullet, $L_b = 2.5 \times 10^4 \text{ J kg}^{-1}$

$$\Rightarrow \quad \Delta Q_2 = m \times 2.5 \times 10^4 \text{ J kg}^{-1}$$

The kinetic energy of bullet $= \frac{1}{2}mv^2$, where v is velocity.

Half of kinetic energy $= \frac{1}{2}\left(\frac{1}{2}mv^2\right) = \frac{1}{4}mv^2$

Loss in kinetic energy $= \Delta Q_1 + \Delta Q_2$

$$\therefore 1/4\, mv^2 = m(3.75 + 2.5) \times 10^4 \text{ Jkg}^{-1}$$

$$\Rightarrow \quad v = 500 \text{ ms}^{-1}$$

Topic Practice 2

Multiple Choice Questions

1 Mark

1. The latent heat of vaporisation of a substance is always
(a) greater than its latent heat of fusion
(b) greater than its latent heat of sublimation
(c) equals to its latent heat of sublimation
(d) less than its latent heat of fusion

2. If m mass of a substance undergoes a phase change, then amount of heat required will be
(a) $\Delta Q = mL$ (b) $\Delta Q = mC_p\Delta T$
(c) $\Delta = ms\Delta T$ (d) $\Delta Q = mC_V\Delta T$

3. Water is heated from –20°C to 120°C. Correct graph is

(a)
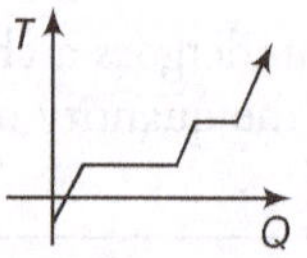

(b)
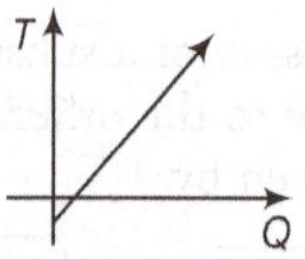

(c)
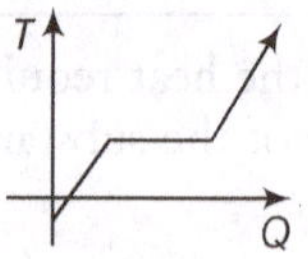

(d)
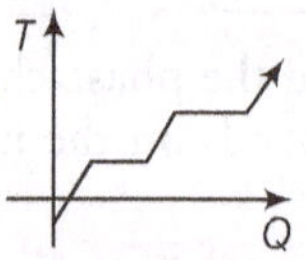

4. In a cooling tower, water enters at 6°C and leaves at 14°C. Rate of heat removal is 2.01×10^6 J per minute. Rate of flow of water is nearly, (specific heat of water = 4200 $\text{Jkg}^{-1}\text{K}^{-1}$).
(a) 1 kg s^{-1} (b) 2 kg s^{-1} (c) 3 kg s^{-1} (d) 4 kg s^{-1}

Very Short Answer Type Questions

1 Mark

5. What is difference between heat capacity and specific heat capacity?

6. Why, water is used as an coolant in the radiator of cars?

7. On which basic principle, calorimetry is based?

8. Are melting point and boiling point is a constant?

9. How melting and boiling points change, when pressure is varied?

10. Define latent heat. Give its unit.

Short Answer Type I Questions

(2 Marks)

11. Explain terms of sublimation.

12. With the help of a suitable graph, explain terms latent heat of fusion, specific heat and latent heat of vaporisation.

13. Describe a simple experiment to demonstrate boiling of water at a temperature much lower than 100°C.

14. The coolant used in a nuclear reactor should have high specific heat. Why?

15. Two bodies of specific heats C_1 and C_2 having same heat capacities are combined to form a single composite body. What is the specific heat of the composite body?

16. What are the basic requirements of a cooking utensil in respect of specific heat, thermal conductivity and coefficient of expansion?

Long Answer Type Questions

(5 Marks)

17. Answer the following questions based on the p-T phase diagram of CO_2.

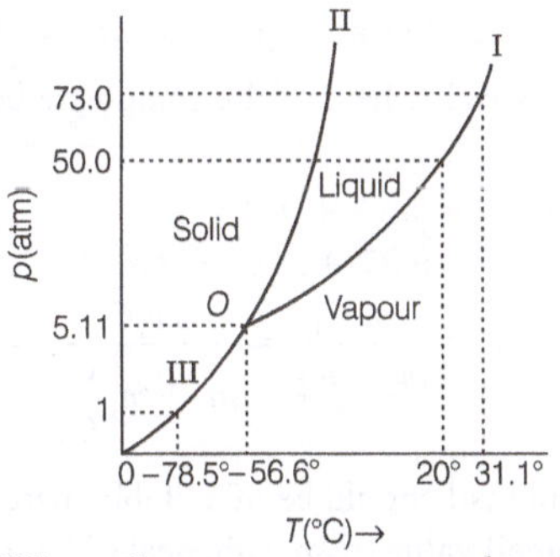

(i) CO_2 at 1 atm pressure and temperature – 60°C is compressed isothermally. Does it go through the liquid phase?

(ii) What happens when CO_2 at 4 atm pressure is cooled from room temperature at constant pressure?

(iii) Describe qualitatively the changes in a given mass of solid CO_2 at 10 atm pressure and temperature – 65°C as it heated upto room temperature at constant pressure.

(iv) CO_2 is heated to a temperature 70°C and compressed isothermally. What changes in its properties, do you expect to observe? **NCERT**

18. Answer the following questions based on the p-T phase diagram of carbon dioxide as shown in the figure.

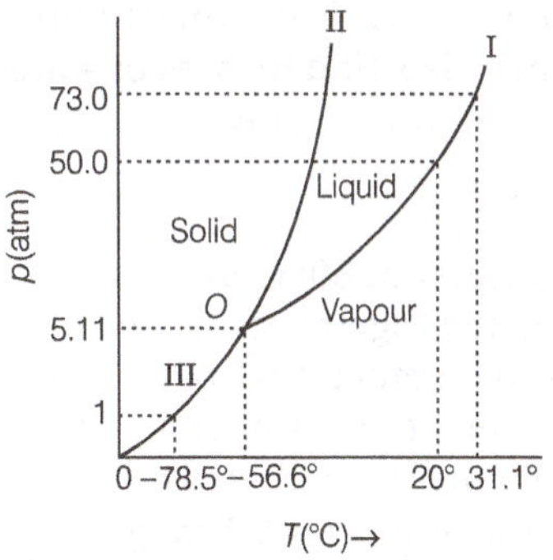

(i) At what temperature and pressure can the solid, liquid and vapour phases of CO_2 co-exist in equilibrium?

(ii) What is the effect of decrease of pressure on the fusion and boiling point of CO_2?

(iii) What are the critical temperature and pressure for CO_2? What is their significance?

(iv) Is CO_2 solid, liquid or gas at (a) – 70°C under 1 atm (b) – 60°C under 10 atm (c) 15°C under 56 atm? **NCERT**

Numerical Problems

19. A copper block of mass 2.5 kg is heated in a furnace to a temperature of 500°C and then placed on a large ice block. What is the maximum amount of ice that can melt? (specific heat of copper $= 0.39\ \text{Jg}^{-1}{}^\circ\text{C}^{-1}$, and heat of fusion of water $= 335\ \text{Jg}^{-1}$). **NCERT [3 M]**

20. A fat man is used to consuming about 3000 kcal worth of food everyday. His food contains 50 g of butter plus a plate of sweets everyday, besides items which provide him with other nutrients (proteins, vitamins, minerals, etc.) in addition to fats and carbohydrates. The calorific value of 10 g of butter is 60 kcal and that of a plate of sweets is of average 700 kcal. What dietary strategy should he adopt to cut down his calories to about 2100 kcal per day? Assume the man cannot resist eating the full plate of sweets once it is offered to him. **[3 M]**

21. A lead bullet penetrates into a solid object and melts. Assuming that 25% of its kinetic energy was used to heat it, calculate the initial speed of the bullet. The initial temperature of the bullet is 27°C and its melting point is 327°C. Latent heat of fusion of lead $= 2.5 \times 10^4\ \text{J kg}^{-1}$ and specific heat capacity of lead $= 125\ \text{J kg}^{1}\text{K}^{1}$. **[3 M]**

22. In a container of negligible mass 30 g of steam at 100°C is added to 200 g of water that has a temperature of 40°C. If no heat is lost to the surroundings, what is the final temperature of the system? Also, find masses of water and steam in equilibrium. (Take, $L_V = 539$ cal g^{-1} and $c_{water} = 1$ cal $g^{-1}\,°C^{-1}$) **[3 M]**

23. (i) 5 g of water at 30°C and 5 g of ice at −20°C are mixed together in a calorimeter. Find the final temperature of mixture. Water equivalent of calorimeter is negligible, specific heat of ice = 0.5 cal $g^{-1}\,°C^{-1}$ and latent heat of ice = 80 cal g^{-1}.

(ii) How much heat is required to convert 8.0 g of ice at − 15° C to steam at 100°C? (Given, $c_{ice} = 0.53$ cal $g^{-1}\,°C^{-1}$, $L_f = 80$ cal g^{-1} and $L_V = 539$ cal g^{-1} and $c_{water} = 1$ cal $g^{-1}\,°C^{-1}$)

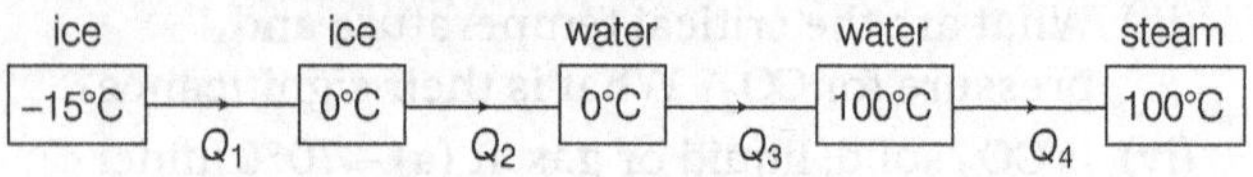

[5 M]

24. A child running a temperature of 101°F is given an antipyretic (i.e. a medicine that lowers fever) which causes an increase in the rate of evaporation of sweat from his body. If the fever is brought down to 98°F in 20 min. What is the average rate of extra evaporation caused by the drug? Assume the evaporation mechanism to be the only way by which heat is lost. The mass of the child is 30 kg. The specific heat of human body is approximately the same as that of water and latent heat of evaporation of water at that temperature is about 580 cal g^{-1}. **NCERT [5 M]**

Hints & Solutions

1. (a) As more energy is required for enormous expansion. When a substance is changed from liquid to gaseous state, latent heat of vaporisation is always greater than latent heat of fusion.

2. (a) If mass m of a substance undergoes a change from one state to the other, then the quantity of heat required is given by

$$\Delta Q = mL$$

where, L is known as latent heat and is a characteristic of the substance.

3. (d) Correct graph is (d).

4. (a) $\dfrac{\Delta Q}{\Delta t} = \dfrac{\Delta m}{\Delta t} \cdot s \cdot \Delta Q$

∴ Rate of water flow is

$$\frac{\Delta m}{\Delta t} = \frac{\Delta Q/\Delta t}{s\Delta Q} = \frac{2.01\times10^6}{60\times4200\times(14-6)} = 1\ \text{kg s}^{-1}$$

5. Refer to the text on page 346 (Heat capacity and specific heat capacity).

6. Because, specific heat of water is very high due to this it absorbs a large amount of heat. This helps in maintaining the temperature of the engine low.

7. Law of conservation of energy.

8. No, they change when pressure is changed.

9. Refer to the text on page 348 (Melting and melting point, effect of pressure on the boiling point of liquid).

10. Refer to the text on page 349 (Latent heat).

11. Refer to the text on page 348 (Sublimation).

12. Refer to the text on pages 348 and 349 (Triple point).

13. A half filled round bottom flask from which air is removed is cooled by powering cold water over the flask. Boiling can be observed in the flask. **[2]**

14. The purpose of a coolant is to absorb maximum heat with least rise in its own temperature. This is possible only if specific heat is high because $Q = mc\,\Delta T$. For a given value of m and Q, the rise in temperature ΔT will be small if c is large. This will prevent different parts of the nuclear reactor from getting too hot. **[2]**

15. As the heat capacities are equal, so $m_1C_1 = m_2C_2$. **[1]**

Let C be the specific heat of the composite body.

Then,

$$(m_1 + m_2)\,C = m_1C_1 + m_2C_2$$

$$= m_1C_1 + m_1C_1 = 2\,m_1C_1$$

or

$$C = \frac{2m_1C_1}{m_1 + m_2} = \frac{2m_1C_1}{m_1 + m_1\dfrac{C_1}{C_2}} = \frac{2C_1C_2}{C_1 + C_2}$$

[1]

16. A cooking utensil should be of suitable material, which possesses small value of specific heat (C), large value of thermal conductivity (K) and low coefficient of expansion (α). **[2]**

17. (i) No, when CO_2 at 1 atm pressure and at − 60°C is compressed isothermally, it changes directly from vapour phase to solid phase without going through the liquid phase.

This can be checked by drawing a vertical line at − 60° C which intersects the sublimation curve III. **[1]**

(ii) CO_2 at 4 atm pressure and at temperature (say 25°C) is vapour. If it is cooled at constant temperature, it condenses directly into solid without going through liquid phase.

This can be checked by drawing a horizontal line at $p = 4$ atm which intersects the sublimation curve III. **[1]**

(iii) CO_2 at 10 atm pressure and at $-65°C$ is solid. As CO_2 is heated at constant pressure, it will go to liquid phase and then to the vapour phase. It is because, the horizontal line through the initial point intersects both the fusion and the vaporisation curves. The fusion and boiling points can be known from the points, where the horizontal line at 10 atm (initial point) intersects the respective curves. [2]

(iv) When the carbon dioxide is heated to 70°C (which is greater than its critical temperature), it will not exhibit any clear phase transition to the liquid phase. At this state, it will deviate more and more from ideal gas behaviour, as its pressure increases. [1]

18. (i) The solid, liquid and vapour phases of CO_2 co-exist in equilibrium at its triple point O for which

$$p_{tr} = 5.11 \text{ atm and } T_{tr} = -56.6°C \quad [1]$$

(ii) The vaporisation curve I and fusion curve II show that both the boiling point and fusion point of CO_2 decrease with decrease of pressure. [1]

(iii) For CO_2, $p_c = 73.0$ atm and $T_c = 31.1°C$. [1]
Above its critical temperature, CO_2 gas cannot be liquefied, however large pressure may be applied.

(iv) (a) $-70°C$ under 1 atm. This point lies in vapour region. [1/2]
Therefore, at $-70°C$ under 1 atm, CO_2 is vapour.
(b) $-60°C$ under 10 atm. This point lies in solid region. Therefore, CO_2 is solid at $-60°C$ under 10 atm. [1/2]
(c) 15°C under 56 atm. This point lies in liquid region. Therefore, CO_2 is liquid at 15°C under 56 atm. [1]

19. Mass of copper block, $M = 2.5 \text{ kg} = 2.5 \times 10^3 \text{g}$

Specific heat of copper, $c = 0.39 \text{ J g}^{-1} {}^\circ\text{C}^{-1}$

Fall in temperature, $\Delta T = 500 - 0 = 500°C$ [1]

Heat lost by copper block $= mc\,\Delta T$

$$= 2.5 \times 10^3 \times 0.39 \times 500 \text{ J} \quad [1/2]$$

Let mass of ice melted = M gram

Heat of fusion of ice, $L = 335 \text{ Jg}^{-1}$

Heat gained by ice $= ML = M \times 335$ J

$\because$ Heat gained = Heat lost [1/2]

$\therefore$ $M \times 335 = 2.5 \times 10^3 \times 0.39 \times 500$

or $$M = \frac{2.5 \times 10^3 \times 0.39 \times 500}{335}$$

$$= 1455.2 \text{ g} = 1.455 \text{ kg} \quad [1]$$

20. The man intends to cut down $= 3000 - 2100$

$$= 900 \text{kcal}. \quad [1]$$

But avoiding sweets completely, he will cut down 700 kcal. To cut down another 200 kcal, he should cut down butter by $\frac{10}{60} \times 200 \simeq 33$ g per day. [1]

He should not cut down consumption of food, that provides him with vitamins and other vital nutrients. [1]

21. Let the mass of the bullet $= m$.

Heat required to take the bullet from 27°C to 327°C

$$Q = ms(T_2 - T_1) = m \times 125 \times (327 - 27)$$
$$= m \times (125)(300) = m \times (3.75 \times 10^4 \text{ Jkg}^{-1}) \quad [1]$$

Heat required to melt the bullet

$$= mL = m \times (2.5 \times 10^4 \text{ J kg}^{-1})$$

If the initial speed be v, the kinetic energy is $\frac{1}{2}mv^2$ and hence the heat developed is $\frac{1}{4}\left(\frac{1}{2}mv^2\right) = \frac{1}{8}mv^2$. [1]

Thus, $\frac{1}{8}mv^2 = Q = m(3.75 + 2.5) \times 10^4 \text{ J kg}^{-1}$

or $v = 707.11 \text{ ms}^{-1}$ [1]

22. Given, mass, $m = 200$ g, $m_1 = 30$ g

Temperature, $T_1 = 100°C$, $T_2 = 40°C$

Latent heat, $L_V = 539 \text{ cal g}^{-1}$

Specific heat, $c_w = 1 \text{ cal g}^{-1} {}^\circ\text{C}^{-1}$

Let Q be the heat required to convert 200 g of water at 40°C into 100°C, then

$$Q = mc\Delta T = (200)(1.0)(100 - 40) = 12000 \text{ cal} \quad [1]$$

Now, suppose m_0 mass of steam converts into water to liberate this much amount of heat, then

$$m_0 = \frac{Q}{L} = \frac{12000}{539} = 22.26 \text{ g} \quad [1]$$

Since, it is less than 30 g, the temperature of the mixture is 100°C.

Mass of steam in the mixture

$$= m_1 - m_0 = 30 - 22.26 = 7.74 \text{ g}$$

and mass of water in the mixture $= m + m_0$

$$= 200 + 22.26 = 222.26 \text{ g} \quad [1]$$

23. (i) In this case, heat is given by water and taken by ice. Heat available with water to cool from 30°C to 0°C

$$= mc\Delta T = 5 \times 1 \times 30 = 150 \text{ cal}$$

Heat required by 5 g ice to increase its temperature up to 0°C,

$$mc\Delta T = 5 \times 0.5 \times 20 = 50 \text{ cal} \quad [1]$$

Out of 150 cal heat available, 50 cal is used for increasing temperature of ice from $-20°C$ to $0°C$. The remaining heat 100 cal is used for melting the ice. [1]

If mass of ice melted is mg, then

$$m \times 80 = 100 \Rightarrow m = 1.25 \text{ g}$$

Thus, 1.25 g ice out of 5 g melts and mixture of ice and water is at 0°C. [1]

(ii) $Q_1 = mc_{ice}(T_f - T_i)$
$= (8.0)(0.53)[0 - (-15)] = 63.6$ cal

$Q_2 = mL_f = (8)(80) = 640$ cal [1]

$Q_3 = mc_{water}(T_f - T_i)$
$= (8.0)(1.0)[100 - 0] = 800$ cal

$Q_4 = mL_V = (8.0)(539) = 4312$ cal

$\therefore$ Net heat required,

$$Q = Q_1 + Q_2 + Q_3 + Q_4 = 5815.6 \text{ cal} \quad [1]$$

24. Mass of child, $M = 30\text{ kg} = 30 \times 10^3\text{g}$

Fall in temperature,

$$\Delta T = 101 - 98 = 3°\text{F} = 3 \times \frac{5}{9} = \frac{5}{3}°\text{C}$$ [1]

Specific heat of human body,

$$c = \text{specific heat of water} = 1\text{ cal g}^{-1}°\text{C}^{-1}$$

Heat lost by child in the form of evaporation of sweat,

$$Q = Mc\,\Delta T = 30 \times 10^3 \times 1 \times \frac{5}{3} = 50000\text{ cal}$$ [1]

If M' gram of sweat evaporates from the body of the child, then heat gained by sweat

$$Q = M'L = M' \times 580\text{ cal} \quad [\because L = 580\text{ calg}^{-1}]$$ [1]

$\because$ Heat gained = Heat lost

$$M' \times 580 = 50000 \Rightarrow M' = \frac{50000}{580} = 86.2\text{ g}$$ [1]

Time taken by sweat to evaporate = 20 min

$$\therefore \text{ Rate of evaporation of sweat} = \frac{86.2}{20} = 4.31\text{ g min}^{-1}$$ [1]

TOPIC 03 Heat Transfer

Heat is the form of energy which can flow from one body to another due to their temperature difference in the form of radiations, molecular vibrations, molecular displacement, etc. These processes of heat flow are collectively known as **heat transfer.**

The processes of heat transfer are shown in figure.

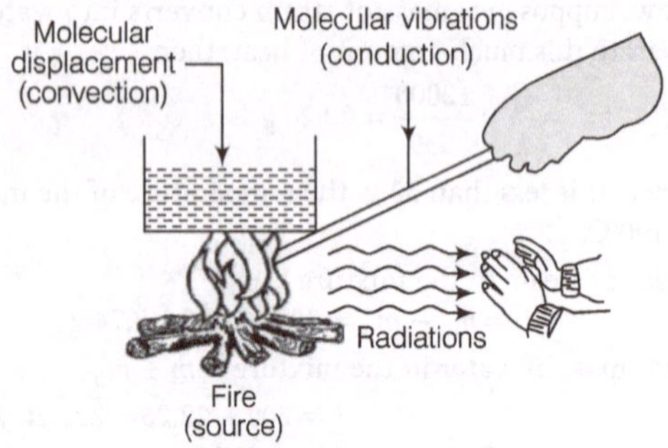

Modes of heat transfer

There are three modes of heat transfer namely (i) Conduction (ii) Convection (iii) Radiation

Conduction

The transfer of heat taking place due to molecular vibrations (i.e. molecular collisions) is known as **heat conduction.** In this process, there is no change in average position of the molecule and hence there is no mass movement of matter. Generally in solids, heat is transferred by the process of conduction.

Thermal Conductivity

The ability of material to conduct the heat through it is known as **thermal conductivity.** Heat conduction is defined as the time rate of heat flow in a material for a given temperature difference.

Consider a metal rod of length l and area of cross-section A. Let the ends of the rod are at the temperatures T_1 and T_2. Then, the rate of flow of heat H conducted through any section (in steady state) of the rod is directly proportional to the temperature difference ΔT, time t for which the heat flows and the area of cross-section A and is inversely proportional to the length L of the rod.

Thus, the rate of heat transfer is given by

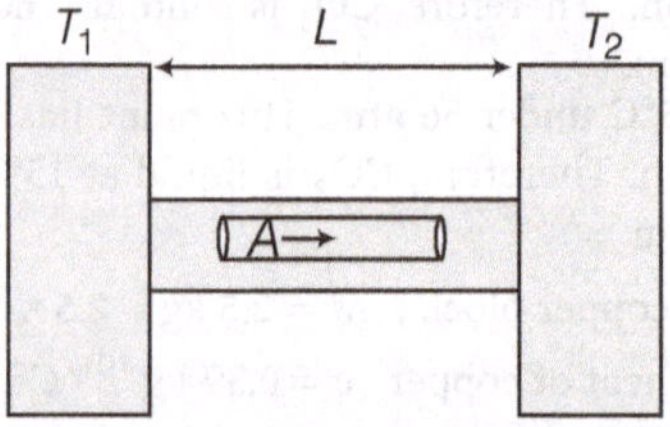

Calculation of thermal conductivity of a metal rod

$$H \propto \frac{A(T_1 - T_2)}{L}$$

$$\text{Rate of heat transfer} = \frac{\Delta Q}{\Delta t} = \frac{KA(T_1 - T_2)}{L}$$

$$H = KA\frac{\Delta T}{L}$$

$$\therefore \quad \boxed{\text{Heat transferred, } Q = KA\frac{\Delta T}{L} \cdot t}$$

Here, K is known as **coefficient of thermal conductivity** of material of rod. The greater value of K implies that material will conduct the heat more rapidly. The SI unit of K is $\text{Js}^{-1}\text{m}^{-1}\text{K}^{-1}$ or $\text{Wm}^{-1}\text{K}^{-1}$ and dimensions of K is $[\text{MLT}^{-3}\text{K}^{-1}]$. The value of thermal conductivity vary slightly with temperature, but it can be considered to be constant over normal temperature range.

The term $\frac{\Delta T}{L}$ is known as **temperature gradient.**

If $A = 1, T_1 - T_2 = \Delta T = 1, L = 1$ and $t = 1$, then $Q = K$

Hence, **the coefficient of thermal conductivity of a material may be defined as the quantity of heat that flows per unit time through a unit cube of the material when its opposite faces are kept at a temperature difference of one degree.**

Note

- Steady state means that the temperature of each part of the body remains constant during the conduction of heat through it.
- The metals are much better conductors than the non-metals. This is because the metals have large number of free electrons which can carry heat from hotter part to colder part.

Thermal Current and Thermal Resistance

The rate of flow of heat is known as **heat current.** It is denoted by H.

SI unit of thermal current is J/s or watt (W) and its dimensions $[ML^2T^{-3}]$

Thus, $H = \frac{\Delta Q}{\Delta t} = KA\frac{(T_1 - T_2)}{L} = \frac{T_1 - T_2}{\left(\frac{L}{KA}\right)}$

Thermal resistance, $R = \frac{\Delta T}{H} = \frac{T_1 - T_2}{H} = \frac{L}{KA}$

$\therefore$ $\boxed{\text{Thermal resistance, } R = \frac{L}{KA}}$

It is analogous to electric current, $i = \frac{V_1 - V_2}{R}$

where, $V_1 - V_2$ = voltage difference

and R = resistance.

So, the terms $\frac{T_1 - T_2}{(L/KA)}$ and $\frac{L}{KA}$ can be treated as thermal current (heat flow) and thermal resistance, respectively.

SI unit of thermal resistance (R) is K-s/J or K/W and its dimension is $[M^{-1}L^{-2}T^3K]$.

Example 1 Calculate the rate of loss of heat through a glass window of area 1000 cm^2 and thickness 0.4 cm. When temperature inside is 37°C and outside is −5°C. Coefficient of thermal conductivity of glass is 2.2×10^{-3} cal s^{-1} cm^{-1} K^{-1}.

Sol. Given, $A = 1000 \text{ cm}^2, L = 0.4 \text{ cm}$

$$\Delta T = T_1 - T_2 = 37 - (-5) = 42°\text{C}$$

$$K = 2.2 \times 10^{-3} \text{ cal s}^{-1}\text{cm}^{-1}\text{K}^{-1}$$

Rate of loss of heat,

$$H = \frac{Q}{T} = \frac{KA(T_1 - T_2)}{L}$$

$$= \frac{2.2 \times 10^{-3} \times 1000 \times 42}{0.4}$$

$$H = 231 \text{ cal s}^{-1}$$

Example 2 Two rods A and B are of equal length. Each rod has its ends at temperatures T_1 and T_2. What are the conditions that will ensure equal rates of flow of heat through the rods A and B?

Sol. Heat transferred rate by rod A is $\frac{\Delta Q_1}{\Delta t}$.

Length of rod A is L and temperature difference,

$$\Delta T = T_1 - T_2$$

Area of cross-section of rod, $A = A_1$,

thermal conductivity $= K_1 \Rightarrow \frac{\Delta Q_1}{\Delta t} = K_1 A_1 \frac{\Delta T}{L}$

Heat transferred rate by rod B is $\frac{\Delta Q_2}{\Delta t}$.

Length of rod B is L, temperature difference $= T_1 - T_2$, area of cross-section of rod $B = A_2$,

Thermal conductivity $= K_2$

$$\Rightarrow \quad \frac{\Delta Q_2}{\Delta t} = K_2 A_2 \frac{\Delta T}{L}$$

For equal rate of heat transfer,

$$\frac{\Delta Q_1}{\Delta t} = \frac{\Delta Q_2}{\Delta t} \Rightarrow \frac{K_1 A_1 \Delta T}{L} = \frac{K_2 A_2 \Delta T}{L}$$

$$\Rightarrow K_1 A_1 = K_2 A_2 \Rightarrow \frac{K_2}{K_1} = \frac{A_1}{A_2}$$

This is the required condition for equal rate of heat transferred from both the rods.

Combination of Rods with Different Thermal Conductivities

If two or more rods or conductors are connected with one another, then the combination has an equivalent thermal conductivity as a whole.

(a) **Series combination of two thermal conductors**

We know that the series combination of resistances gives the equivalent resistance as $R_{eq} = R_1 + R_2$

This gives $\frac{L_1 + L_2}{K_{eq}A} = \frac{L_1}{K_1 A} + \frac{L_2}{K_2 A} \quad \left[\because R = \frac{L}{KA}\right]$

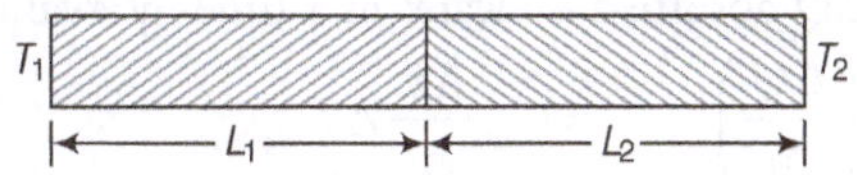

If $L_1 = L_2 = L$, then $\frac{2L}{K_{eq}A} = \frac{L}{K_1 A} + \frac{L}{K_2 A}$

$$\Rightarrow \boxed{\text{Equivalent thermal conductivity, } K_{eq} = \frac{2K_1K_2}{K_1+K_2}}$$

Here, K_{eq} is the equivalent thermal conductivity of series connection of rods (as thermal conductor).

(b) **Parallel combination of two thermal conductors**

We know that the parallel combination of resistances gives the equivalent resistances as

$$\frac{1}{R_{eq}} = \frac{1}{R_1} + \frac{1}{R_2}$$

This gives, $$\frac{1}{\frac{L}{K_{eq}2A}} = \frac{1}{\left(\frac{L}{K_1A}\right)} + \frac{1}{\left(\frac{L}{K_2A}\right)}$$

(For equal area of cross-sections and length)

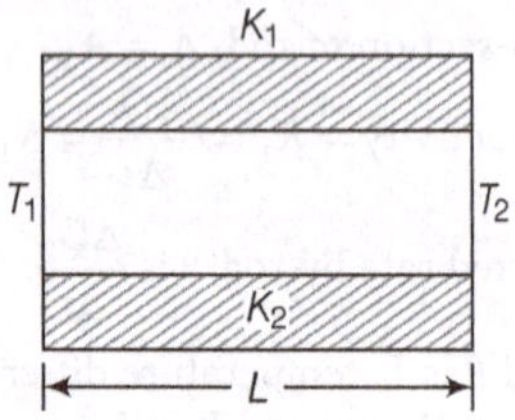

$$\Rightarrow \frac{2AK_{eq}}{L} = \frac{K_1A}{L} + \frac{K_2A}{L}$$

$$\Rightarrow \boxed{\text{Equivalent thermal conductivity, } K_{eq} = \frac{K_1+K_2}{2}}$$

Searle's Experiment

Searle's experiment is an procedure to measure thermal conductivity of material. A bar of material is being heated by steam on one side and the other side cooled down by water while the length of bar is thermally insulated.

Then the heat ΔQ propagating through the bar in a time interval Δt is given by

$$\left(\frac{\Delta Q}{\Delta t}\right)_{bar} = -KA\frac{\Delta T_{bar}}{L}$$

where, ΔQ = the heat supplied to the bar in time Δt.

K = coefficient of thermal conductivity of the bar.

A = cross-sectional area of the bar.

ΔT_{bar} = temperature difference between each end of the bar

L = length of the bar

The heat ΔQ absorbed by water in a time interval of Δt is,

$$\left(\frac{\Delta Q}{\Delta t}\right)_{water} = C_w \frac{\Delta m}{\Delta t}\Delta T_{water}$$

where, C_w = specific heat of water

Δm = mass of water collected during time Δt.

ΔT_{water} = difference in the temperature of water before and after it has gone through the bar.

Assuming perfect insulation and no energy loss,

$$\left(\frac{\Delta Q}{\Delta t}\right)_{bar} = \left(\frac{\Delta Q}{\Delta t}\right)_{water}$$

or $$K = -C_w \frac{L}{A} \cdot \frac{\Delta m}{\Delta t} \cdot \frac{\Delta T_{water}}{\Delta T_{bar}}$$

Use of Good and Poor Conductors of Heat

(i) Cooking utensils are made from good conductors of heat. Such utensils get heated up quickly. Food can be cooked efficiently in shorter time. The utensils are generally made of copper, brass, steel, aluminium etc.

(ii) The handles of kettles and utensils are made of bad conductors of heat such as wood, plastic, ebonite, etc. They help in holding them comfortably.

(iii) Woolen clothes are bad conductors. Woolen clothes are not actually warm. They do not allow heat to conduct away or to escape out and thus keep our body warm.

(iv) Building materials like bricks, asbestos, mud, grass, etc, are bad conductors of heat. They do not permit heat and cold to pass through the walls of bricks they keep the houses warm in winter and cool in summer. Roof sheds are made of asbestors for the same reason.

(v) Hair and the fur of animals are bad conductors of heat. They protect them from cold.

(vi) Vehicles carrying inflammable materials such as petrol are covered with materials of bad conductors of heat. Otherwise, the petrol can get heated up and catch fire.

Example 3 An iron bar having length L_1 =0.1 m, area of cross-section $0.02\,m^2$, thermal conductivity K_i =79 $Wm^{-1}K^{-1}$ and brass bar having length L_2 =0.1 m area of cross-section, A_2 = 0.02 m^2 and thermal conductivity K_2=109$Wm^{-1}K^{-1}$ are soldered end to end as shown in figure.

The terminal ends of two rods are maintained at 373 K and 273 K, respectively. Find the expression and compute

(i) the temperature of the junction of two bars.

(ii) equivalent thermal conductivity of composite bar and

(iii) the heat current through the composite bar **NCERT**

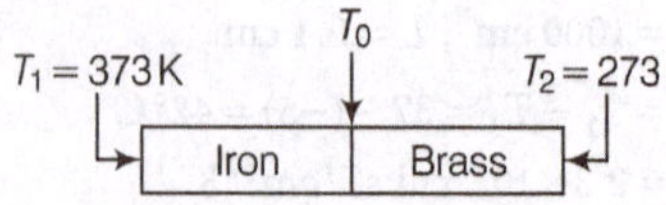

Sol. Given, $L_1 = L_2 = L = 0.1$ m

$A_1 = A_2 = A = 0.02\text{ m}^2$

$K_1 = 79\text{ Wm}^{-1}\text{K}^{-1}$, $K_2 = 109\text{ Wm}^{-1}\text{K}^{-1}$

$T_1 = 373$ K and $T_2 = 273$ K

At steady state, heat transferred from each section of thermal conductor is same i.e. $H_1 = H_2 = H$

$$\Rightarrow \quad \frac{K_1A_1(T_1 - T_0)}{L_1} = \frac{K_2A_2(T_0 - T_2)}{L_2} \quad \text{...(i)}$$

For $A_1 = A_2 = A$ and $L_1 = L_2 = L$, Eq. (i) becomes

$$K_1(T_1 - T_0) = K_2(T_0 - T_2)$$

$$\Rightarrow \quad T_0 = \frac{K_1T_1 + K_2T_2}{K_1 + K_2}$$

Therefore, heat current through each bar

$$H = \frac{K_1A(T_1 - T_0)}{L} = \frac{K_2A(T_0 - T_2)}{L}$$

$$= \frac{A(T_1 - T_2)}{L\left(\frac{1}{K_1} + \frac{1}{K_2}\right)} = \frac{K_1K_2A(T_1 - T_2)}{L(K_1 + K_2)} \quad \text{...(ii)}$$

Now, heat current through composite bar of length $L_1 + L_2 = 2L$ and equivalent thermal conductivity K', can be given by

$$H' = \frac{K'A(T_1 - T_2)}{2L} = H \quad \text{...(iii)}$$

From Eq. (ii) and Eq. (iii), we get

$$\Rightarrow \quad K' = \frac{2K_1K_2}{K_1 + K_2}$$

(i) So, the temperature of the junction of two bars is

$$T_0 = \frac{K_1T_1 + K_2T_2}{K_1 + K_2}$$

$$= \frac{79\text{Wm}^{-1}\text{K}^{-1} \times 373\text{K} + 109\text{Wm}^{-1}\text{K}^{-1} \times 273\text{K}}{79\text{Wm}^{-1}\text{K}^{-1} + 109\text{Wm}^{-1}\text{K}^{-1}}$$

$$= 315\text{ K}$$

(ii) Equivalent thermal conductivity

$$K' = \frac{2K_1K_2}{K_1 + K_2} = \frac{2 \times 79\text{ Wm}^{-1}\text{K}^{-1} \times 109\text{ Wm}^{-1}\text{K}^{-1}}{79\text{ Wm}^{-1}\text{K}^{-1} + 109\text{ Wm}^{-1}\text{K}^{-1}}$$

$$= 91.6\text{ Wm}^{-1}\text{K}^{-1}$$

(iii) Heat current through the composite bar

$$H' = H = \frac{K'A(T_1 - T_2)}{2L}$$

$$= \frac{91.6\text{ Wm}^{-1}\text{K}^{-1} \times 0.02\text{ m}^2 \times (373 - 273)\text{ K}}{2 \times 0.1\text{ m}}$$

$$= 916.1\text{ W}$$

Convection

Convection is the process in which heat is transferred from one point to another by the actual motion of matter from a region of high temperature to a region of lower temperature. This process of heat transfer takes place only in fluids. There are two types of convections

(i) **Forced Convection** Forced convection is the process in which heat is transferred from one place to other by actual transfer of heated material (or molecules). If heated material is forced to move say by a blower or a pump, the process of heat transfer is called **forced convection.** The heat transfer in human body is an example of forced convection.

(ii) **Natural or Free Convection** In the process of convection, if the heated material moves due to difference in density. This process of heat transfer is **called natural** or **free convection** such as heat transfer in water. Free convection in a fluid volume in gravitational field. Convection occurs due to density variation with temperature.

Land and Sea Breezes

During the day, the **land heats up faster than the sea.** This occurs because the water has greater specific heat and mixing currents disperse the absorbed heat throughout the great volume of water.

The hot air above the land expands and becoming less dense and hence the warmer air rises and colder air from the sea takes it place. The warmer air from the land moves towards the sea to complete the cycle. This create a breeze from the sea to the land which is called a **sea breeze.**

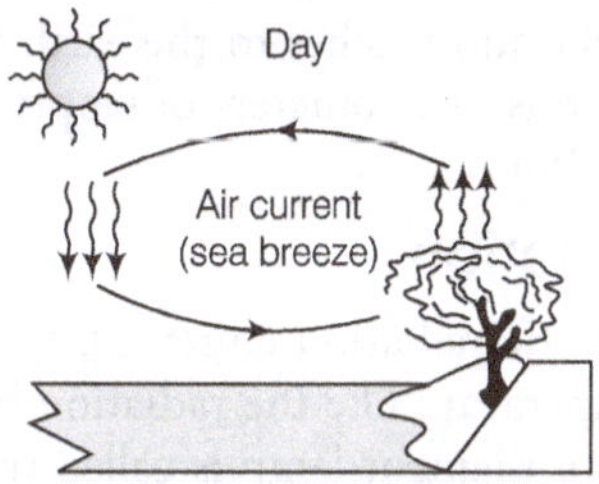

Land warmer than water

During the night, the opposite happens. The **land cools faster than sea.** The warm air above the sea rises. This warm air is replaced by colder air from the land creating a **land breeze.**

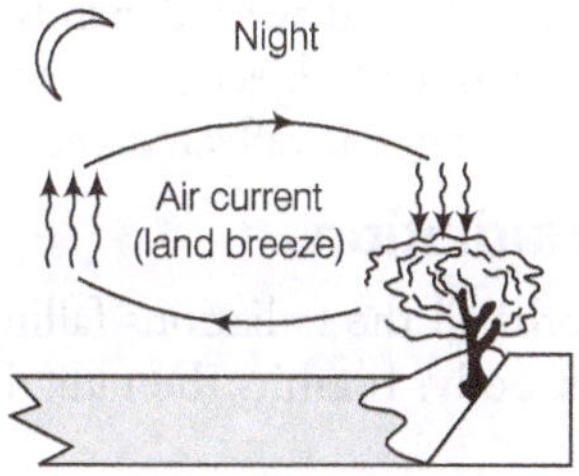

Water warmer than land

Formation of Trade Winds

As equatorial and polar regions of the earth receive unequal solar heat. At the equator, air near the earth's surface is hot while the air in upper atmosphere of the poles is cool.
So, there is a convection current in between two positions, air at the equatorial surface rises and move out towards the poles, descending and streaming in towards the equator. The rotation of the earth, however, modifies this convection current because of this, air has the Eastward speed of 1600 km/h.
While the speed of air closer to the poles is zero. So, air descends not at the poles but at 30° North latitude and returns to the equator. This is called **trade wind.** Hence, the steady wind blowing from North-East to equator, near the surface of Earth is called **trade wind.** It is an example of natural convection.

Radiation

It is a mode of heat transfer from one place to another without heating the intervening medium. The heat is transferred by the mean of thermal radiations, radiant energy or simply radiation. Here, the term radiation is used in two meanings. The first is the process by which the energy is emitted by a body, is transmitted in space and falls on another body. The second one is the energy itself is being transmitted in space.

The heat from the sun reaches to the earth by radiation. They travel millions of kilometers of empty space without any material medium.

Thermal Radiation

The electromagnetic radiation emitted by a body, by virtue of its temperature like the radiation by a red hot iron or light form filament lamp is called **thermal radiation.**

Colour of a Body

When thermal radiation falls on some other body, it may partly reflected and partly absorbed. The amount of heat that a body absorbed by radiation depends on the colour of the body. The colour of object shows that radiation of that particular wavelength is reflected back by the body.

Black Body Radiation

A body that absorbs all the radiations falling on it is known as a **black body.** It emits the radiations at the fastest rate.

The radiations emitted by a black body is known as **black body radiation** or **cavity radiation.** The black body is also called the **ideal radiator** or **cavity radiator.**

A perfect body absorbs 100% of radiations falling on it, is only an ideal concept because within the universe there is no existence of black body. However, lamp black is close to a black body because, it reflects only 1% of radiation falling on it.

Absorptive and Emissive Powers, Emissivity, Transmittance and Reflectivity

The ratio of the amount of thermal radiation absorbed by a body in a given time to the total amount of thermal radiations incident on the body in the same time is known as **absorptance** (*a*) or **absorptive power** of the body.

$$\Rightarrow \quad \frac{\text{Energy absorbed}}{\text{Energy incident}}$$

The **emissive power** of a body at a given temperature and for a given wavelength λ is defined as the amount of radiant energy per unit time per unit surface area of the body within a unit wavelength range around the wavelength λ.
The ratio of emissive power (e) of a body to the emissive power (E) of a perfect black body at the same temperature is called **emissivity.** It is denoted by ε.

Thus, $$\text{Emissivity, } \varepsilon = \frac{e}{E}$$

Spectral emissive power e_λ It is emissive power for a particular wavelength λ and is defined as the total amount of thermal energy emitted per unit time, per unit area of the body for a particular wavelengths.

Thus, $$e = \int_0^\infty e_\lambda \, d\lambda$$

Its SI unit is $\frac{\text{joule}}{\text{m}^2\text{s}}$ or $\frac{\text{watt}}{\text{m}^2}$ and dimensional formula is $[\text{MT}^{-3}]$.

Transmittance (Transmittivity) The ratio of heat energy transmitted by a body in a given time to the total radiation energy incident on it in the same interval of time is called transmittance or transmissivity. It is denoted by t.

$$\therefore \quad \text{Transmittance, } t = \frac{Q_{\text{transmitted}}}{Q_{\text{incident}}} = \frac{Q_t}{Q_i}$$

It is a dimensionless quantity.
Reflectivity The ratio of heat energy reflected by a body in a given time to the total radiation energy incident on it in the same interval of time is called reflectivity.

It is denoted by r.

$\therefore$ $$\text{Reflectivity, } r = \frac{Q_{\text{reflected}}}{Q_{\text{incident}}} = \frac{Q_r}{Q_i}$$

It is dimensionless quantity.

Relation between Absorptive Power (*a*) Transmittance (*t*) and Reflectivity (*r*)

$\because$ $$Q_a + Q_t + Q_r = Q$$

Dividing both sides by Q, we get

$$\frac{Q_a}{Q} + \frac{Q_t}{Q} + \frac{Q_r}{Q} = 1$$

$\Rightarrow$ $$a + t + r = 1$$

For a perfect reflector, $a = t = 0, r = 1$

For a perfect transmitter, $a = r = 0, t = 1$

Kirchhoff's Radiation Law

According to this law, 'the ratio of emissive power (e) to absorptive power (a) is same for all surfaces at the same temperature and is equal to emissive power (E) of a black body at that temperature.'

Then, $$\left(\frac{e}{a}\right)_{\text{for any surface}} = \text{constant} = E$$

Similarly, for a particular wavelength λ,

$$\left(\frac{e_\lambda}{a_\lambda}\right)_{\text{for any body}} = E_\lambda$$

Here, E_λ = emissive power of black body.

Stefan-Boltzmann Law

Stefan-Boltzmann law states that the total energy emitted per second by a unit area of a perfect black body is proportional to the fourth power of its absolute temperature.

i.e. $$E \propto T^4$$

i.e. $$\text{Total energy, } E = \sigma T^4$$

where σ is a universal constant called Stefan-Boltzmann constant.

$$\sigma = 5.67 \times 10^{-8} \text{ Wm}^{-2} \text{ K}^{-4}$$

It's dimensional formula is $[M^1L^0T^{-3}\theta^{-4}]$.

If the body is not a perfect black body and has emissivity ε, then above relations get modified as

$$E = \varepsilon\sigma T^4$$

where, ε = emissivity of that body

For a black body, $\varepsilon = 1$

Example 4 Calculate the temperature (in K) at which a perfect black body radiates energy at the rate of 5.67 W/cm^2.
Given, $\sigma = 5.67 \times 10^{-8} \text{ Wm}^{-2} \text{ K}^{-4}$

Sol. Given, $E = 5.67 \text{ W/cm}^2 = 5.67 \times 10^4 \text{ W/m}^2$

$$\sigma = 5.67 \times 10^{-8} \text{ Wm}^{-2} \text{ K}^{-4}$$

Apply Stefan's law, $E = \sigma T^4$

$$T^4 = \frac{E}{\sigma} \Rightarrow T = \left(\frac{E}{\sigma}\right)^{1/4} = \left(\frac{5.67 \times 10^4}{5.67 \times 10^{-8}}\right)^{1/4}$$

$$T = (10^{12})^{1/4} = 10^3$$

$$T = 1000 \text{ K}$$

Example 5 A thin brass rectangular sheet of sides 15.0 cm and 12.0 cm is heated in a furnace to 600°C, and taken out. How much electric power is needed to maintain the sheet at this temperature, given that its emissivity is 0.250? Neglect heat loss due to convection. (Stefan-Boltzmann constant, $\sigma = 5.67 \times 10^{-8} \text{ Wm}^{-2}\text{K}^{-4}$). **NCERT**

Sol. Given, $A = 2 \times 15.0 \times 12.0 \times 10^{-4} \text{ m}^2 = 3.60 \times 10^{-2} \text{ m}^2$

$$T = 600 + 273 = 873 \text{ K}$$

$$\varepsilon = 0.250,$$

$$\sigma = 5.67 \times 10^{-8} \text{ Wm}^{-2} \text{ K}^{-4}$$

The rate of heat loss by the sheet,

$$H = \frac{Q}{t} = \varepsilon\sigma A T^4$$

$$= 0.250 \times 5.67 \times 10^{-8} \times 3.60 \times 10^{-2} \times (873)^4$$

$$= 296 \text{ Js}^{-1} = 296 \text{ W}$$

Wien's Displacement Law

The radiation emitted by a body is a mixture of waves of different wavelengths. Out of these, some have major contribution to total radiant energy while others don't contribute much. Typical graph of emitter at different temperatures is shown in figure alongside.

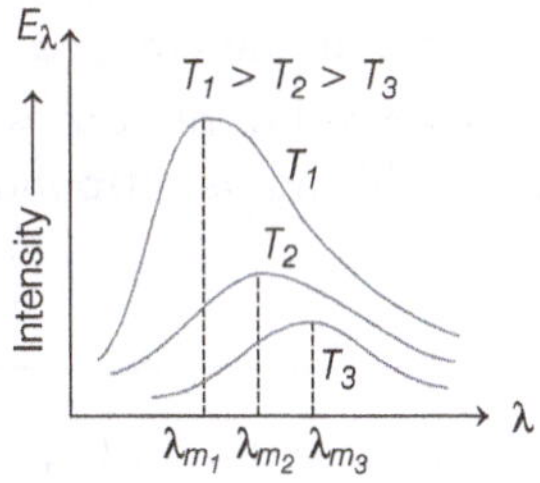

So, if the temperature is increased, then the wavelength (λ_m) corresponding to highest intensity decreases. Wien's displacement law states that 'the product of wavelength (λ_m) corresponding to highest intensity and the absolute temperature is constant'. i.e. $\lambda_m \cdot T = b$ = constant

Here, b is constant called as Wien's constant and its value is 2.88×10^{-3} mK.

Example 6 A hot body having the surface temperature 1327°C. Determine the wavelength at which it radiates maximum energy. Given Wien's constant $= 2.9\times 10^{-3}$ mK.

Sol. Given, $T = 1327 + 273 = 1600$ K

Wien's constant, $b = 2.9\times 10^{-3}$ m K

$$\lambda_m = \frac{b}{T} = \frac{2.9\times 10^{-3}}{1600} = 1.81\times 10^{-6} \text{ m}$$

Example 7 Consider a filament which is indirectly heated. The radiating maximum energy having wavelength 3.4×10^{-5} cm. Determine the amount of heat energy lost per second per unit area if the temperature of surrounding air is 17°C.

Given, $\sigma = 5.67\times 10^{-8}\ \text{Wm}^{-2}\ \text{K}^{-4}$, $b = 2.9\times 10^{-3}$ mK

Sol. Given, wavelength, $\lambda_m = 3.4\times 10^{-5}\ \text{cm} = 3.4\times 10^{-7}$ m

Temperature of surrounding,

$$T_0 = 17°\text{C} + 273 = 290 \text{ K}$$

$$\sigma = 5.67\times 10^{-8}\ \text{Wm}^{-2}\ \text{K}^{-4}$$

$$b = 2.9\times 10^{-3}\ \text{mK}$$

According to Wien's law

$$T = \frac{b}{\lambda_m} = \frac{2.9\times 10^{-3}\ \text{mK}}{3.4\times 10^{-7}} = 8529.4 \text{ K}$$

According to Stefan-Boltzmann law, $E = \sigma(T^4 - T_0^4)$

$$= 5.67\times 10^{-8}\,[(8529.4)^4 - (290)^4]$$

$$E = 30016.98\times 10^4\ \text{W/m}^2$$

Newton's Law of Cooling

Newton's law of cooling states that the rate of cooling of a body is directly proportional to the temperature difference between the body and its surroundings, provided the temperature difference is small

i.e. Rate of loss of heat $\propto$ Temperature difference between the body and its surroundings.

$$-\frac{dQ}{dt} \propto (T - T_0)$$

$$\text{Rate of loss of heat, } -\frac{dQ}{dt} = k(T - T_0)$$

Example 8 A body cools in 7 min from 60°C to 40°C. What will be its temperature after the next 7 min? The temperature of the surroundings is 10°C.

Sol. According to the Newton's law of cooling, we have

$$\frac{dQ}{dt} = k\left(\frac{T_1 + T_2}{2} - T_0\right)$$

$$\frac{ms\,(T_1 - T_2)}{t} = k\left(\frac{T_1 + T_2}{2} - T_0\right)$$

$$\frac{ms\,(60 - 40)}{7\times 60} = k\left(\frac{60 + 40}{2} - 10\right)$$

$$\frac{ms\times 20}{420} = k\times 40$$

Suppose, after the next 7 min = 420 seconds, the temperature is T. Then,

$$\frac{ms\,(40 - T)}{420} = k\left(\frac{40 + T}{2} - 10\right) \quad \text{...(ii)}$$

On dividing Eq. (i) by Eq. (ii), we get

$$\frac{20}{40 - T} = \frac{40}{\left(\frac{40 + T}{2} - 10\right)}$$

On solving, we get $T = 28°$ C

Topic Practice 3

Multiple Choice Questions

1 Mark

1. The bottoms of utensils for cooking food are blackened to
   (a) absorb minimum heat from fire
   (b) absorb maximum heat from fire
   (c) emit radiations
   (d) reflect heat to surroundings

2. The rate of loss of heat depends on
   (a) the sum of temperature of the body and its surroundings
   (b) the difference in temperature of the body and its surroundings
   (c) the product of temperature of the body and its surroundings
   (d) the ratio of temperature of the body and its surroundings

3. In equation $-\frac{d\theta}{dt} = k\,(T_2 - T_1)$, where k is a positive constant which depends upon
   (a) the area of exposed surface
   (b) the nature of the surface of the body
   (c) Both (a) and (b)
   (d) Neither (a) nor (b)

4. Three rods are joined as shown, (their ends are maintained at indicated temperatures).

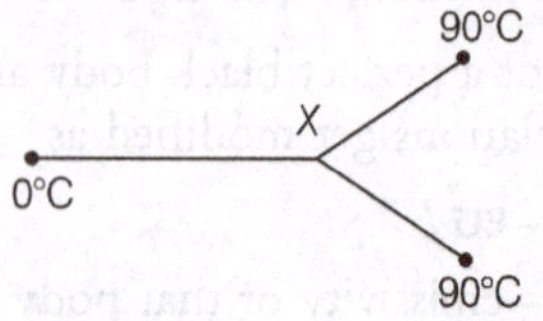

Assuming no heat loss through length of rods, temperature of junction X will be

(a) 45°C (b) 60°C
(c) 30°C (d) 20°C

5. Let temperature of sun increases from T to $2T$ and radius of earth is increased from R to $2R$ then, energy received on earth increases by

(a) 32 times (b) 16 times
(c) 4 times (d) 64 times

Very Short Answer Type Questions

1 Mark

6. If all the objects radiate electromagnetic energy, why do not the objects around us in everyday life become colder and colder?
7. White clothes are more comfortable in summer while colourful clothes are more comfortable in winter. Why?
8. Can we boil water inside in the earth's satellite?
9. Stainless steel cooking pans are preferred with extra copper bottom. Why?
10. Why an ice box is constructed with a double wall?
11. Why birds are often seen to swell their feathers in winter?
12. Two bodies at different temperatures T_1 and T_2, if brought in thermal contact do not necessarily settle at the mean temperature $\frac{T_1 + T_2}{2}$. Why?
13. Usually a good conductor of heat is a good conductor of electricity also. Give reason.
14. Place a safety pin on a sheet of paper. Hold the sheet over a burning candle, until the paper becomes yellow and charr. On removing the pin, its white trace is observed on the paper. Why?
15. Black body radiation is white. Comment.

Short Answer Type I Questions

2 Marks

16. Two thermos flasks are of the same height and same capacity. One has a circular cross-section while the other has a square cross-section. Which of the two is better?
17. On a hot day, a car is left in sunlight with all the windows closed. After some time, it is found that the inside of the car is considerably warmer than the air outside. Explain, why?
18. A piece of paper wrapped tightly on a wooden rod is observed to get charred quickly when held over a flame as compared to a similar piece of paper when wrapped on a brass rod. Explain why?
19. In a coal fire, the pockets formed by coals appear brighter than the coals themselves. Is the temperature of such a pocket higher than the surface temperature of a glowing coal?
20. Woollen clothes are warm in winter. Why?
21. Why rooms are provided with the ventilators near the roof?
22. The earth constantly receives heat radiation from the sun and gets warmed up. Why does the earth not get as hot as the sun?
23. If a drop of water falls on a very hot iron, it does not evaporate for a long time. Give reason.

Short Answer Type II Questions

3 Marks

24. Explain the following
    (i) Hot tea cools rapidly when poured into the saucer from the cup.
    (ii) Temperature of a hot liquid falls rapidly in the beginning but slowly afterwards.
    (iii) A hot liquid cools faster if outer surface of the container is blackened.
25. Two rods of the same area of cross-section, but of lengths l_1 and l_2 and conductivities K_1 and K_2 are joined in series. Show that the combination is equivalent of a material of conductivity

$$K = \frac{l_1 + l_2}{\left(\frac{l_1}{K_1}\right) + \left(\frac{l_2}{K_2}\right)}$$

Long Answer Type Questions

5 Marks

26. Explain why
    (i) a body with large reflectivity is a poor emitter.
    (ii) a brass tumbler feels much colder than a wooden tray on a chilly day.

(iii) an optical pyrometer (for measuring high temperature) calibrated for an ideal black body radiation gives too low a value for the temperature of a red hot iron piece in the open, but gives a correct value for the temperature when the same piece is in the furnace.

(iv) the earth without its atmosphere would be inhospitably cold.

(v) heating systems based on circulation of steam are more efficient in warming a building than those based on circulation of hot water. **NCERT**

27. Distinguish between conduction, convection and radiation.

Numerical Problems

28. Two vessels of different materials are identical in size and wall thickness. They are filled with equal quantities of ice at 0°C.
If the ice melts completely in 10 and 25 min respectively, compare the coefficients of thermal conductivity of the materials of the vessels. **[2 M]**

29. If wavelength of maximum intensity of radiation emitted by sun and moon are 0.5×10^{-6} m and 10^{-4} m respectively, then find the ratio of their temperatures. **[2 M]**

30. The intensity of radiation emitted by the sun has its maximum value at a wavelength of 510 nm and that emitted by the North star has the maximum value at 350 nm. If these stars behave like black bodies, then what is the ratio of the surface temperature of the sun and North star? **[2 M]**

31. In the figure, the distribution of energy density of the radiation emitted by a black body at a given temperature is shown. What is the possible temperature of the black body?

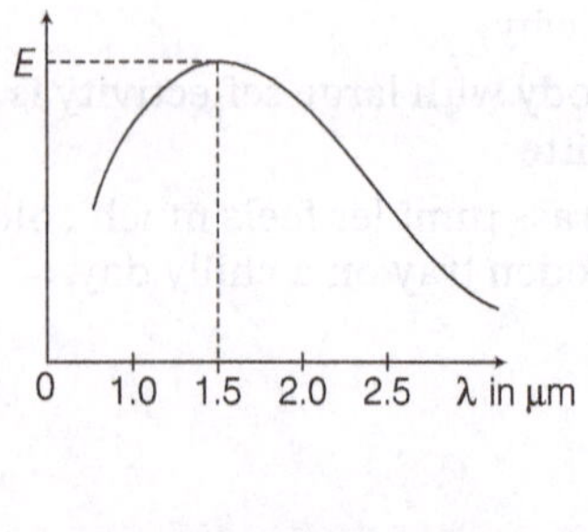

[2 M]

32. Two vessels A and B of different materials but having identical shape, size and wall thickness are filled with ice and kept at the same place. Ice melts at the rate of 100 g min^{-1} and 150g min^{-1} in A and B, respectively. Assuming that heat enters the vessels through the walls only, calculate the ratio of thermal conductivities of their materials **[3 M]**

33. A brass boiler has a base area of 0.15 m^2 and thickness 1.0 cm. It boils water at the rate of 6.0 kg min^{-1}, when placed on a gas stove.
Estimate the temperature of the part of the flame in contact with the boiler. Thermal conductivity of brass = 109 $Js^{-1}m^{-1}°C^{-1}$ and heat of vaporisation of water = 2256Jg^{-1}.
NCERT [3 M]

34. A body cools from 80°C to 50°C in 5 min. Calculate the time it takes to cool from 60°C to 30°C, the temperature of the surrounding is 20°C. **NCERT [5 M]**

35. A thermocol cubical ice box of side 30 cm has a thickness of 5.0 cm. If 4.0 kg of ice are put in the box, estimate the amount of ice remaining after 6 h. The outside temperature is 45°C and coefficient of thermal conductivity of thermocol = 0.01 $Js^{-1}m^{-1}°C^{-1}$. Given, heat of fusion of water = 335×10^3 J kg^{-1} **NCERT [3 M]**

Hints & Solutions

1. (b) Black bodies absorb and emit radiant energy better than bodies of lighter colours. The bottoms of the utensils for cooking food are blackened so that they absorb maximum heat from the fire and give it to the vegetables to be cooked.

2. (b) The rate of loss of heat depends on the difference in temperature between the body and its surroundings.

3. (c) k depends upon the area of exposed surface and the nature of the surface of the body.

4. (b) As, $Q \propto (T_1 - T_2)$
And $Q = Q_1 + Q_2$
$\Rightarrow X - 0° = 90° - X + 90° - X \Rightarrow X + X + X = 90° + 90°$
$\Rightarrow 3X = 180° \Rightarrow X = \frac{180°}{3} \Rightarrow X = 60°C$

5. (d) As $P \propto AT^4$ and $A \propto R^2$
So, $P \propto R^2T^4$
$\therefore \frac{P'}{P} = \frac{4 \times 16}{1} = 64$

6. According to the Principle of heat exchange, all the objects (above 0 K) not only radiate electromagnetic energy but also absorb at the same rate from their surroundings. Thus, they do not become colder.

7. White clothes absorb very little heat radiation and hence they are comfortable in summer. Coloured clothes absorb almost whole of the incident radiation and keep the body warm in winter.

8. No, the process of transfer of heat by convection is based on the fact that a liquid becomes lighter on becoming hot and rise up. In condition of weightlessness, this is not possible. So, transfer of heat by convection is not possible in the earth's satellite.

9. The thermal conductivity of copper is much larger than that of steel. The copper bottom allows more heat to flow into the pan and hence helps in cooking the food faster.

10. An ice box is made of double wall and the space in between the walls is filled with some non-conducting material to provide heat insulation, so that the loss of heat can be minimised.

11. When the birds swell their feathers, they are able to enclose air in the feathers. Air, being a poor conductor of heat, so it prevents the loss of heat from the bodies of the birds to the surroundings and as such they do not feel cold in winter.

12. The two bodies may have different masses and different materials i.e. they may have different thermal capacities.

In case the two bodies have equal thermal capacities, they would settle at the mean temperature $\frac{T_1 + T_2}{2}$.

13. Electrons contribute largely both towards the flow of electricity and the flow of heat. A good conductor contains a large number of free electrons. So, it is both a good conductor of heat and electricity.

14. The safety pin is made of steel which is good conductor of heat. So, the safety pin takes heat from the paper under it and transfer it away to the surroundings. The portion of the paper under the safety pin remains comparatively colder than the remaining part.

15. The statement is true. A black body absorbs radiations of all wavelengths. When heated to a suitable temperature, it emits radiations of all wavelengths. Hence, a black body radiation is white.

16. As both flasks have same height and capacity, the area of the cylindrical wall will be less than that of the square wall. Hence, the thermos flask of circular cross-section will transmit less heat as compared to the thermos flask of square cross-section and it will be better. [2]

17. Glass transmits about 50% of heat radiation coming from a hot source like the sun but does not allow the radiation from moderately hot bodies to pass through it. Due to this, when a car is left in the sun, heat radiation from the sun gets into the car but as the temperature inside the car is moderate, they do not pass back through its windows. Hence, inside of the car becomes considerably warmer. [2]

18. Brass is a good conductor of heat. It quickly conducts away the heat. So, the paper does not alter its ignition point easily. On the other hand, wood is a bad conductor of heat and is unable to conduct away the heat. So, the paper quickly reaches its ignition point and is charred. [2]

19. The temperature of pockets formed by coals are not appreciably different from the surface temperature of glowing coals.

However, the pockets formed by coals act as cavities. The radiations from these cavities are black body radiations and so have maximum intensity. Hence, the pockets appear brighter than the glowing coals. [2]

20. Woollen fibres enclose a large amount of air in them. Both wool and air are bad conductors of heat. The small coefficient of thermal conductivity prevents the loss of heat from our body due to conduction. So, we feel warm in woollen clothes. [2]

21. It is done so to remove the harmful impure air and to replace it by the cool fresh air. The air we breath out is warm and so it is lighter. It rises upwards and can go out through the ventilator provided near the roof.

The cold fresh air from outside enters the room through the doors and windows. Thus, the convection current is set up in the air. [2]

22. Because the earth is located at a very large distance from the sun, hence it receives only a small fraction of the heat radiation emitted by the sun. Further, due to loss of heat from the surface of the earth due to convection and radiation also, the earth does not become as hot as the sun. [2]

23. When a drop of water falls on a very hot iron, it gets insulated from the iron by a layer of poor conducting water vapour. As the heat is conducted very slowly through this layer, it takes quite long for the drop to evaporate. But if the drop of water falls on iron which is not very hot, then it comes in direct contact with iron and evaporates immediately. [2]

24. (i) As surface area increases on pouring hot tea in saucer from the cup and the rate of loss of heat is directly proportional to surface area of the radiating surface, so the tea will cool faster in the saucer. [1]

(ii) Temperature of a hot liquid falls exponentially in accordance with Newton's law of cooling. In other words, rate of cooling is directly proportional to the temperature difference between hot liquid and the surroundings. It is due to this reason that a hot liquid cools rapidly in the beginning but slowly afterwards. [1]

(iii) When outer surface of container is blackened, the surface becomes good emitter of heat and so the hot liquid in it cools faster. [1]

25. It is given that conductivities K_1 and K_2 are in series, so rate of flow of heat energy is same. But the sum of the difference in temperature is the difference across their free ends.

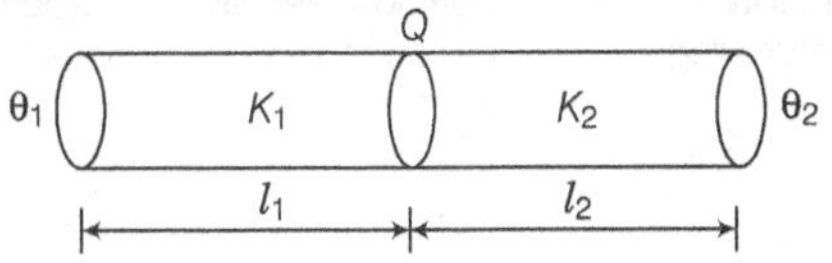

[1]

$\therefore \quad (\theta_1 - \theta) + (\theta - \theta_2) = (\theta_1 - \theta_2)$

i.e. $\dfrac{\theta}{t} \cdot \dfrac{l_1}{K_1 A} + \dfrac{\theta}{t} \dfrac{l_2}{K_2 A} = \dfrac{\theta}{t} \cdot \dfrac{(l_1 + l_2)}{K_{eq} A}$ [1]

$\Rightarrow \quad \dfrac{l_1}{K_1} + \dfrac{l_2}{K_2} = \dfrac{l_1 + l_2}{K_{eq}}$

$\therefore \quad K_{eq} = \dfrac{l_1 + l_2}{\left(\dfrac{l_1}{K_1} + \dfrac{l_2}{K_2}\right)}$ [1]

26. (i) A body with large reflectivity is a poor absorber of heat. According to Kirchhoff's law, a poor absorber of heat is a poor emitter. Hence, a body with large reflectivity is a poor emitter. [1]

(ii) Brass is a good conductor of heat. When a brass tumbler is touched, heat quickly flows from human body to tumbler. Consequently, the tumbler appears colder. Wood is a bad conductor. So, heat does not flow from the human body to the tray in this case. Thus, it appears comparatively hotter. [1]

(iii) Let T be the temperature of the hot iron in the furnace.

Heat radiated per second per unit area, $E = \sigma T^4$

When the body is placed in the open at temperature T_0, the heat radiated/second/unit area,

$$E' = \sigma (T^4 - T_0^4).$$

Clearly, $E' < E$. So, the optical pyrometer gives too low a value for the temperature in the open. [1]

(iv) Heat radiated out by the earth is reflected back by the atmosphere. In the absence of atmosphere, at night all heat would escape from the earth's surface and thereby the earth's surface would be inhospitably cold. Also, atmosphere helps in maintaining the temperature through convection current. [1]

(v) Though steam and boiling water are at the same temperature but each unit mass of steam contains a larger amount of additional heat called the latent heat. e.g. each gram of steam has 540 cal of more heat than each gram of boiling water. Hence, steam loses more heat than boiling water. [1]

27.

	Conduction	Convection	Radiation
1.	It is the transfer of heat by direct physical contact.	It is the transfer of heat by the motion of a fluid.	It is the transfer of heat by electromagnetic waves.
2.	It is due to temperature difference. Heat flows from high temperature region to low temperature region.	It is due to difference in density. Heat flows from low density region to high density region.	It occurs from all bodies at temperatures above 0 K.
3.	It occurs in solids through molecular collisions, without actual flow of matter.	It occurs in fluids by actual flow of matter.	It can take place at large distances and does not heat the intervening medium.
4.	It is a slow process.	It is also a slow process.	It propagates at the speed of light.
5.	It does not obey the laws of reflection and refraction.	It does not obey the laws of reflection and refraction.	It obeys the laws of reflection and refraction.

[1 + 1 + 1 + 1 + 1]

28. Let K_1 and K_2 be the coefficients of thermal conductivity of the materials and t_1 and t_2 be the times in which ice melts in the two vessels.

As the same quantity of ice melts in the two vessels, the quantity of heat flowed into the vessels must be same.

$\because \quad Q = \dfrac{K_1 A (T_1 - T_2) t_1}{x} = \dfrac{K_2 A (T_1 - T_2) t_2}{x}$ [1]

$\Rightarrow \quad K_1 t_1 = K_2 t_2$

$\therefore \quad \dfrac{K_1}{K_2} = \dfrac{t_2}{t_1} = \dfrac{25 \text{ min}}{10 \text{ min}} = 5 : 2$ [1]

29. According to Wien's law, $\lambda_m T =$ constant

$\therefore (\lambda_m T)_s = (\lambda_m T)_m$ or $\dfrac{T_s}{T_m} = \dfrac{(\lambda_m)_m}{(\lambda_m)_s} = \dfrac{10^{-4}}{0.5 \times 10^{-6}} = 200$ [2]

30. From Wien's law,

$$\frac{T_S}{T_N} = \frac{(\lambda_N)_{max}}{(\lambda_S)_{max}} = \frac{350}{510} = 0.69$$ [2]

31. $\lambda_m T = b$, where $b = 2.89 \times 10^{-3}$ mK

$\Rightarrow T = \dfrac{b}{\lambda_m} = \dfrac{2.89 \times 10^{-3}}{1.5 \times 10^{-6}} = 2000$ K [2]

32. Let m_1 and m_2 be the masses of ice melted in same time ($t = 1$ min) in vessels A and B, respectively.

Then, the amounts of heat flowed into the two vessels will be [1/2]

$$Q_1 = \frac{K_1 A (T_1 - T_2) t}{x} = m_1 L \quad \text{...(i)}$$ [1]

$$Q_2 = \frac{K_2 A (T_1 - T_2) t}{x} = m_2 L \quad \text{...(ii)}$$ [1/2]

where, L is latent heat of ice.

Dividing Eq. (i) by Eq. (ii), we get,

$$\frac{K_1}{K_2} = \frac{m_1}{m_2} = \frac{100 \text{ g}}{150 \text{ g}} = \frac{2}{3} = 2 : 3$$ [1]

33. Here, $A = 0.15 \text{ m}^2$, $x = 1.0 \text{ cm} = 0.01$ m,

$K = 109 \text{ Js}^{-1}\text{m}^{-1}{}^\circ\text{C}^{-1}$, $L = 2256 \text{ Jg}^{-1}$

$T_2 = 100°\text{C}$, $t = 1 \text{ min} = 60$ s [1]

Let T_1 be the temperature of the part of the flame in contact with boiler. Then, amount of heat that flows into water in 1 min.

$$Q = \frac{KA(T_1 - T_2)t}{x} = \frac{109 \times 0.15 \times (T_1 - 100) \times 60}{0.01} \text{J}$$ [1]

Mass of water boiled per min = 6 kg = 6000 g

Heat used to boil water,

$$Q = mL = 6000 \text{ g} \times 2256 \text{ Jg}^{-1} = 6000 \times 2256 \text{ J}$$

$$\therefore \quad \frac{109 \times 0.15 \times (T_1 - 100) \times 60}{0.01} = 6000 \times 2256$$

or $$T_1 - 100 = \frac{6000 \times 2256 \times 0.01}{109 \times 0.15 \times 60} = 138° \text{C}$$

or $$T_1 = 138 + 100 = 238° \text{C}$$ [1]

34. According to Newton's law of cooling, when the temperature difference is not large, rate of loss of heat is proportional to the temperature difference between the body and the surroundings.

$$mc \frac{T_1 - T_2}{t} = K(T - T_0)$$ [1]

where, $T = \frac{T_1 + T_2}{2}$ = average of the initial and final temperatures of the body and T_0 is the temperature of the surroundings. [1]

Here, $T_1 = 80°\text{C}$, $T_2 = 50°$, $T_0 = 20°\text{C}$,

$t = 5 \text{ min} = 300 \text{ s}$

$$T = \frac{T_1 + T_2}{2} = \frac{80 + 50}{2} = 65°\text{C}$$ [1]

$$\therefore \quad mc \frac{80 - 50}{300} = K(65 - 20) \quad \text{...(i)}$$

If the liquid takes t seconds to cool from 60°C to 30°C, then

$$T = \frac{60 + 30}{2} = 45°\text{C}$$

$$\therefore \quad mc \frac{60 - 30}{t} = K(45 - 20) \quad \text{...(ii)}$$ [1]

Dividing Eq. (i) by Eq. (ii), we get

$$\frac{30}{300} \times \frac{t}{30} = \frac{45}{25} \quad \text{or} \quad t = \frac{45}{25} \times 300 = 540\text{s} = 9 \text{ min}$$ [1]

35. Here, $A = 6 \times \text{side}^2 = 6 \times 30 \times 30$

$= 5400 \text{ cm}^2 = 0.54 \text{ m}^2$ [1/2]

$x = 5 \text{ cm} = 0.05 \text{ m}$

$t = 6 \text{ h} = 6 \times 3600 \text{s}$

$T_1 - T_2 = 45 - 0 = 45° \text{C}$, [1/2]

$K = 0.01 \text{ Js}^{-1}\text{m}^{-1}{}^\circ\text{C}^{-1}$

$L = 335 \times 10^3 \text{ J kg}^{-1}$

Total heat entering the box through all the six faces,

$$Q = \frac{KA(T_1 - T_2)t}{x} = \frac{0.01 \times 0.54 \times 45 \times 6 \times 3600}{0.05}$$

$= 104976 \text{ J}$ [1]

Let m kg of ice melt due to this heat. Then,

$Q = mL$ [1/2]

or $$m = \frac{Q}{L} = \frac{104976 \text{ J}}{335 \times 10^3 \text{ J kg}^{-1}} = 0.313 \text{ kg}$$

Mass of ice left after six hours = 4−0.313 = 3.687 kg [1/2]

Summary

- **Temperature** is the property of a state of matter by virtue of which we predict its hotness or coldness, relative to some body.
- **Heat** is form of energy which determines the change in thermal state of a body. It flows from the body which is at a high temperature to the other at low temperature.
- The devices which are used to measure the temperature are termed as **thermometers.**
- **Relation between C, F and K Scales** $\frac{C}{5} = \frac{F-32}{9} = \frac{K-273.15}{5}$
- **Boyle's Law** $p \propto \frac{1}{V}$ (at constant temperature) $\therefore\ pV = \text{constant}$
- **Charles'Law** $V \propto T$ (at constant pressure) $\frac{V}{T} = \text{constant}$
- **Ideal Gas Equation** $pV = \mu RT$
  where, p = pressure of gas, V = volume of gas, T = temperature of gas
  μ = number of moles, R = universal gas constant = $8.31\,\text{Jmol}^{-1}\text{K}^{-1}$.
- **Thermal Expansion** Heating a body is accompanied by an increase in size of the body is called thermal expansion. There are three types of thermal expansion:
  1. Expansion of solids 2. Expansion of liquids 3. Expansion of gases
- If a rod is having length l_0 at temperature T, then expansion in length of rod due to rise in temperature by ΔT, is given by
  $$\Delta l = l_0 \alpha \Delta T$$
  where, α is the coefficient of linear expansion, whose value depends on the nature of the material.
  Final length, $l_f = l_0 + l_0\alpha\Delta T = l_0(1+\alpha\Delta T)$
- Area expansion is valid only for solids. This is given by $A_f = A_0(1+\beta\times\Delta T)$
  where, A_f is the area of body when temperature has been changed by ΔT, A_0 is the area of body at temperature T and β is the coefficient of superficial expansion.
- Volume after expansion, $V = V_0(1+\gamma\Delta T)$, where, γ is the coefficient of cubical expansion.
- **Heat Capacity** The heat capacity of a body is the quantity of heat required by the body to raise its temperature by 1°C. It is also known as thermal capacity.
  $$\text{Heat capacity} = ms \text{ (mass} \times \text{specific heat)}$$
- **Water Equivalent** It is the quantity of water whose thermal capacity is same as the heat capacity of the body. It is denoted by W.
  $$W = ms = \text{Heat capacity of the body}$$
- **Specific Heat** The specific heat (s) of a substance is the quantity of heat in calorie required to raise the temperature of 1g of that substance by 1°C. Its unit is $\text{cal g}^{-1}\text{C}^{-1}$.
- **Calorimetry** Heat lost by hotter body = Heat gained by colder body
  $$m_1 s_1 \Delta T = m_2 s_2 \Delta T$$
- **Latent Heat** The heat required to change the state of a system is proportional to mass of the system, i.e.
  $$Q \propto m \Rightarrow Q = mL$$
  where, L = latent heat of the material.
- **Transmission of Heat** There are three different ways in which heat can be transferred-conduction, convection and radiation.

- **Conduction** It is a process by which the heat is transferred in solid. In conduction, molecules vibrate about a fixed location and transfer the heat by collision.
- **Convection** It is a process by which the heat is transferred in fluids (liquids and gases). In convection, transfer of heat takes place by transport of matter (in form of motion of particles).
- **Radiation** This mode of heat transfer does not require any medium, and it is the fastest mode of heat transfer. Instance of this mode of heat transfer is the radiation received by earth coming from sun.
- The amount of heat transmitted through a conductor is given by

$$Q = \frac{KA\Delta Tt}{l}$$

Thermal resistance of heat is given by

$$|H| = \left|\frac{\Delta Q}{\Delta t}\right| = \frac{KA}{l}\Delta T = \frac{\Delta T}{l/KA}$$

The term $\frac{l}{KA}$ is generally called the **thermal resistance.**

- **Stefan's Law** The energy emitted per second per unit area of a black body (emissive power = 1) is proportional to the fourth power of the absolute temperature.

i.e. $$E = \sigma T^4$$

Here, σ = Stefan's constant $= 5.67 \times 10^{-8}\,\text{Jm}^{-2}\text{s}^{-1}\text{K}^{-4}$

For any other body $E = \varepsilon\sigma T^{-4}$

Here, ε = emissivity of body ($\varepsilon = 1$ for a black body)

If Q is the total energy radiated by the ordinary body, then

$$E = \frac{Q}{A \times t} = \varepsilon\sigma T^{-4} \Rightarrow Q = A\varepsilon\sigma T^{-4}t$$

- **Wien's Displacement Law** It states that, "as temperature of black body T increases, the wavelength λ_m corresponding to maximum emission decreases, such that

$$\lambda_m \propto \frac{l}{T} \text{ or } \lambda_m T = b$$

where, b is known as Wien's constant and its value is 2.89×10^{-3} mK.

- According to **Newton's law of cooling**, 'rate of cooling of a body is directly proportional to the temperature difference between the body and the surroundings provided that the temperature difference is small.'

Mathematically, $-\frac{dT}{dt} \propto (T - T_0)$, $-\frac{dT}{dt} = k(T - T_0)$

where, k is a universal constant.

Chapter Practice

Multiple Choice Questions

1 Mark

1 Two temperature scales A and B are related by $\frac{A-42}{110}=\frac{B-72}{220}$. At which temperature two scales have the same reading?

(a) $-42°C$ (b) $-72°C$
(c) $12°C$ (d) $40°C$

2 Measurements on real gases deviate from the values predicted by the ideal gas law at

(a) high temperature (b) low temperature
(c) room temperature (d) All of these

3 Two absolute scales A and B have triple points of water defined to be 400 A and 300 B. The relation between T_A and T_B is (Triple point of water is 273.16 K temperature and 6.11×10^{-3} atm pressure, water coexists in gas, liquid and solid states)

(a) $T_A=\frac{4}{3}T_B$ (b) $T_B=\frac{4}{7}T_A$
(c) $T_A=\frac{4}{7}T_B$ (d) $T_B=T_A$

4 The amount of heat that a body can absorb by radiation

(a) depends on colour and temperature both of body
(b) depends on colour of body only
(c) depends on temperature of body only
(d) depends on density of body

5 The rate of cooling due to conduction, convection, and radiation combined, is proportional to the difference in temperature, for

(a) large temperature differences
(b) small temperature differences
(c) any temperature difference
(d) None of the above

Assertion and Reason

Directions (Q. Nos. 6-10) *In the following questions, two statements are given- one labelled Assertion (A) and the other labelled Reason (R). Select the correct answer to these questions from the codes (a), (b), (c) and (d) as given below*

(a) Both Assertion and Reason are true and Reason is the correct explanation of Assertion.
(b) Both Assertion and Reason are true but Reason is not the correct explanation of Assertion.
(c) Assertion is true but Reason is false.
(d) Assertion is false but Reason is true.

6 **Assertion (A)** At room temperature, water does not sublimate from ice to steam.

Reason (R) The critical point of water is much above the room temperature.

7 **Assertion (A)** A flannel keeps the ice cold but keeps people warm.

Reason (R) Bad conductors do not permit heat to flow through them.

8 **Assertion (A)** A body at 0°C is radiating heat.

Reason (R) According to Provost's. theory of heat, all bodies radiate heat when their temperature is above the temperature of surroundings.

9 **Assertion (A)** A hotter body has more heat content than a colder body.

Reason (R) Temperature is the measure of degree of hotness of a body.

10 **Assertion (A)** When heat transfer takes place between a system and surroundings, the total heat content of system or surroundings separately remains same.

Reason (R) Heat is a form of energy which follows the principle of conservation of energy.

Very Short Answer Type Questions

1 Mark

11 What is absolute zero of temperature?

12 What is the SI unit of specific heat capacity?

13 State the Newton's law of cooling.

Short Answer Type I Questions

2 Marks

14 What is difference between heat and temperature?

15 Define the specific heat of a solid or liquid.

Short Answer Type II Questions

(3 Marks)

16 Discuss the different types of thermometer.

17 Define and explain latent heat of a substance. Give its SI unit.

Long Answer Type Questions

(5 Marks)

18 Define coefficient of thermal conductivity and describe Searle's method to determine coefficient of thermal conductivity of a good conductor.

19 Describe the uses of good and poor conductors of heat?

Case Based Questions

Directions (Q. No. 20) *These questions are case study based questions. Read the following paragraph and answer the questions.*

20 Almost all substances (solids, liquids and gases) expand on heating and contract on cooling. Few exception are : water from 0°C to 4°C and silver iodide from 80°C to 141°C, contract on heating and expand on cooling. When we change the temperature of the substance, then their dimensions (length, area, volume) changes. The phenomenon is called thermal expansion. The change in length (Δl), area (ΔA) and volume (ΔV) due to temperature change is given by $\Delta l = l\alpha\Delta T$, $\Delta A = A\beta\Delta T$ and $\Delta V = V\gamma\Delta T$, where; α, β and γ are the coefficients of linear, superficial and volume expansion of the solid.

(i) When the water is heated above 4°C, then how its volume changes?

(ii) What is the relation between α, β and γ?

(iii) Draw the graph of γ *versus* temperature (T) of a solid.

(iv) If the temperature of a rod is increased by x, then what is the expression for thermal strain in the rod?

Numerical Problems

21 A steel ring of 3.000 inch inside diameter at 20°C is to be heated and slipped over a brass shaft measuring 3.002 inch in diameter at 20°C. To what temperature should the ring be heated? ($\alpha_{steel} = 1.1 \times 10^{-5}\ {}^\circ C^{-1}$) **[2 M]**

22 How much heat is required to convert 8.0 g of ice at – 15°C to steam at 100°C? (Given $c_{ice} = 0.53$ cal/g-°C, $L_f = 80\ cal/g$ and $L_v = 539$ cal/g, and $c_{water} = 1$ cal/g-°C)

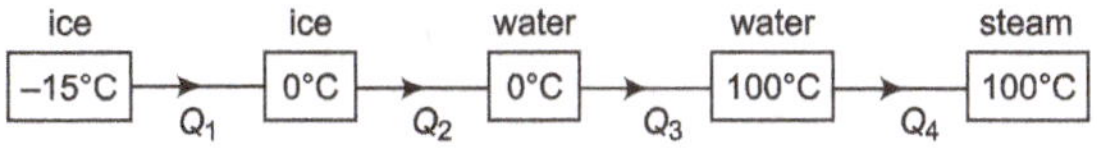

[2 M]

23 10 g of water at 70°C is mixed with 5 g of water at 30°C. Find the temperature of the mixture in equilibrium. **[2 M]**

24 A body cools from 80°C to 50°C in 5 minutes. Calculate the time it takes to cool from 60°C to 30°C. The temperature of the surrounding is 20°C. **[3 M]**

25 A black body has temperature of 1527°C and surface area 0.2 m^2. Find the energy radiated per second by the black body. (Stefan's constant, $\sigma = 5.67 \times 10^{-8}$ Js^{-1}m^{-2}K^{-4}) **[3 M]**

Answers

1 (*c*) Given, $\dfrac{A-42}{110} = \dfrac{B-72}{220}$ ...(i)

For same reading, $A = B = x$

From Eq. (i), we get

$$\frac{x-42}{110} = \frac{x-72}{220} \Rightarrow x - 42 = \frac{x-72}{2}$$

$\Rightarrow 2x - 84 = x - 72$

$\therefore \quad x = 12^\circ C$

2 (*b*) Measurements on real gases deviation from the values predicted by the ideal gas law at low temperature. But, the relationship is linear over a large temperature range, and it looks as though the pressure might reach zero with decreasing temperature, if the gas continued to be a gas.

3 (*a*) As per question triple point of water 273.16 K has a value 400 A on scale A and 300 B on scale B.

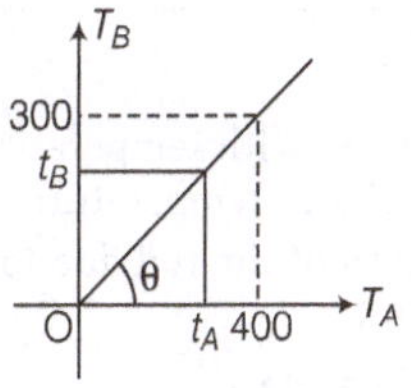

$$\tan\theta = \frac{t_B}{t_A} = \frac{300}{400} \Rightarrow t_A = \frac{4}{3}t_B \Rightarrow T_A = \frac{4}{3}T_B \quad \text{...(i)}$$

4 (*a*) The thermal radiation that falls on a body partly reflected and partly absorbed. The amount of heat that a body can absorb, by radiation depends on the colour of the body and temperature of body.

5 (*b*) For small temperature differences, the rate of cooling due to conduction, convection and radiation combined is proportional to the difference in temperature of body and surroundings.

6 (*a*) 7 (*a*)

8 (*c*) 9 (*a*)

10 (*a*)

11 Refer to text on page 338 (Absolute zero temperature).

12 Refer to text on page 346 (Specific heat capacity).

13 Refer to text on page 397 (Newton's law of cooling).

14 Refer to text on page 336 (Temperature and heat).

15 Refer to text on page 346 (Note).

16 Refer to text on page 337 (Mercury, gas and platinum resistance thermometer).

17 Refer to text on page 349 (Latent heat).

18 Refer to text on pages 354 and 356 (Thermal conductivity and Searle's experiment).

19 Refer to text on page 356 (Use of good and poor conductors of heat).

20 (i) When the water is heated above 4°C, then it gets expansion. So, the volume of the water increases.

(ii) The ratio of α, β and γ is given by $\alpha : \beta : \gamma = 1 : 2 : 3$

$\therefore \quad \alpha = k$ (say)

$$\beta = 2k \Rightarrow k = \frac{\beta}{2}$$

$$\gamma = 3k \Rightarrow k = \frac{\gamma}{3}$$

$$\therefore \quad \alpha = \frac{\beta}{2} = \frac{\gamma}{3}$$

or $\quad 6\alpha = 3\beta = 2\gamma$

(iii) The variation of coefficient of volume expansion (γ) *versus* temperature (T) is given by

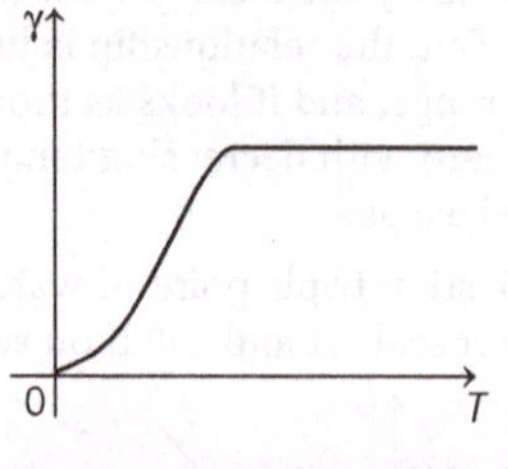

It first increases with temperature and then becomes constant at higher temperature.

(iv) The elongation of the rod due to temperature change by x is given by

$$\Delta l = l\alpha x$$

$$\therefore \quad \text{Strain} = \frac{\Delta l}{l} = \alpha x$$

21 Let θ be the temperature to which the ring must be heated.

Final diameter of ring should be 3.002 inch.

$$\Rightarrow \quad 3.002 = 3\,[1 + \alpha(\theta - 20)]$$

$$\Rightarrow \quad \theta = \frac{3.002 - 3}{3\alpha} + 20 \Rightarrow \theta = 75.6°\,\text{C}$$ [2]

22 $Q_1 = mc_{ice}(T_f - T_i) = (8.0)\,(0.53)\,[0 - (-15)] = 63.6$ cal

$Q_2 = mL_f = (8)\,(80) = 640$ cal

$Q_3 = mc_{water}(T_f - T_i) = (8.0)\,(1.0)\,[100 - 0] = 800$ cal

$Q_4 = mL_v = (8.0)\,(539) = 4312$ cal

$\therefore$ Net heat required

$$Q = Q_1 + Q_2 + Q_3 + Q_4 = 5815.6 \text{ cal}$$ [2]

23 Let t°C be the temperature of the mixture. From energy conservation,

Heat given by 10 g of water = Heat taken by 5 g of water

or $\quad m_1 c_{water}\,|\Delta t_1| = m_2 c_{water}\,|\Delta t_2|$

$\therefore \quad (10)\,(70 - t) = 5\,(t - 30)$

$\therefore \quad t = 36.67°$C [2]

24 According to Newton's law of cooling.

$$\frac{-dT}{dt} = k(T - T_0)$$

or $$\frac{T_1 - T_2}{t_2 - t_1} = k\left[\frac{T_1 + T_2}{2} - T_0\right]$$

In first case

$T_1 = 80°$C, $T_2 = 50°$C, $T_0 = 20°$C and $t_1 - t_2 = 5$ min

$$\therefore \quad \frac{80 - 50}{5\,\text{min}} = k\left[\left(\frac{80 + 50}{2} - 20\right)\right] \Rightarrow \frac{30}{5\,\text{min}} = k \times 45 \quad ...(i)$$ [1½]

In second case

$T_1 = 60°$C, $T_2 = 30°$C

$$\therefore \quad \frac{60 - 30}{t} = k\left(\frac{60 + 30}{2} - 20\right) \text{ or } \frac{30}{t} = k \times 25$$

Dividing Eq. (i) by Eq. (ii), we get

$$\frac{t}{5\,\text{min}} = \frac{45}{25} \text{ or } t = \frac{9}{5} \times 5 \text{ min} = 9 \text{ min}$$ [1½]

25 According to Stefan's law, the radiant energy (heat) emitted per second per unit surface area of a black body is given by $\quad Q = \sigma T^4$ [1]

where T is the absolute temperature of the black body and σ is Stefan's constant. If the area of the black body be A, then the energy emitted by the black body per second is

$$\sigma T^4 \times A$$ [1]

Here, $T = 1527°\text{C} = 1527 + 273 = 1800$ K and $A = 0.2\,\text{m}^2$

Therefore, the energy radiated by the body per second is,

$(5.67 \times 10^{-8}) \cdot (1800)^4 \cdot (0.2) = 1.19 \times 10^5$ J [1]

CHAPTER

11

Thermodynamics

Thermodynamics is the field of Physics relating heat, work tansfer and the associated changes in the properties (such as pressure, volume, temperature, etc) of a working substance. Thermodynamics is a macroscopic science. It involves few macroscopic variables of the system. Thermodynamics avoids the molecular description all together. The state of a gas in thermodynamics is specified by macroscopic variables such as pressure, volume, temperature, mass and composition of gas.

- Heat and First Law of Thermodynamics
- Second Law of Thermodynamics

TOPIC 01 Heat and First Law of Thermodynamics

Thermal Equilibrium

Two systems are said to be in thermal equilibrium with each other if they are at the same temperature.

Again, consider the adiabatic wall separating the two gases A and B is replaced by **diathermic wall** (i.e. a wall that allows energy flow or heat from one to another). On account of flow of heat energy, the macroscopic variables of the two gases change spontaneously, either pressure or volume or both the pressure and volume of two gases may change.

Let the pressure and volume of two gases after change are (p'_A, V'_A) and (p'_B, V'_B) such that the new states of A and B are in equilibrium with each other. There is no more energy flow from one to another. This condition is shown in figure below.

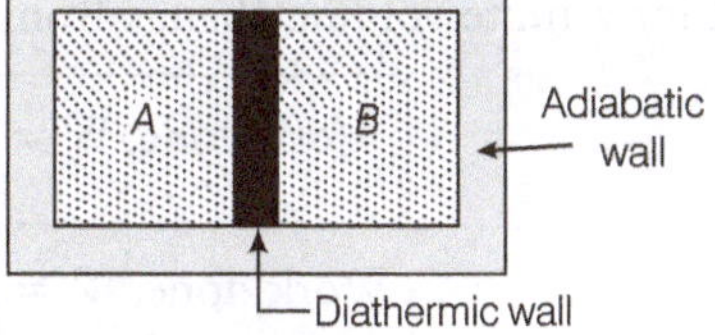

Two systems A and B in thermal equilibrium

Hence, the temperature of two gases become equal and the gases are said to be in thermal equilibrium with each other.

- If there is no unbalanced force and torque acting on the system, then the system is said to be in mechanical equilibrium.
- If the system does not undergo any spontaneous change in its internal structure due to chemical reaction, diffusion etc., then the system is said to be in chemical equilibrium.
- **Two systems are said to be in thermal equilibrium, if there is no net flow of heat between them when they are brought into thermal contact.**

Zeroth Law of Thermodynamics

This law was formulated by **RH Fowler** in 1931. The zeroth law of thermodynamics states that

'If two systems say (*A* and *B*) are separately in thermal equilibrium with a third system say (*C*), then *A* and *B* are in thermal equilibrium with each other'.

Let us consider two systems *A* and *B* separated by a fixed adiabatic wall. The two systems *A* and *B* are in contact with a third system *C* through diathermic wall. The macroscopic variables of *A* and *B* will vary until both *A* and *B* come in thermal equilibrium with the third system *C*.

This shows that two systems *A* and *B* are separately in thermal equilibrium with a third system *C*. This condition is shown in Fig. (a)

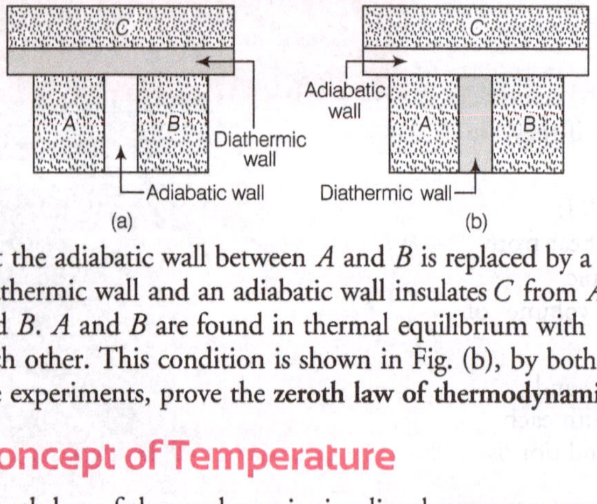

(a) (b)

Let the adiabatic wall between *A* and *B* is replaced by a diathermic wall and an adiabatic wall insulates *C* from *A* and *B*. *A* and *B* are found in thermal equilibrium with each other. This condition is shown in Fig. (b), by both the experiments, prove the **zeroth law of thermodynamics.**

Concept of Temperature

Zeroth law of thermodynamics implies that temperature is a physical quantity which has the same value for all systems which are in thermal equilibrium with each other.

Hence, zeroth law says that if systems *A* and *B* are separately in thermal equilibrium with *C*, then

$$T_A = T_C \quad \text{and} \quad T_B = T_C \quad \Rightarrow \quad T_A = T_B$$

So, systems *A* and *B* will also be in thermal equilibrium with each other.

Hence, temperature is that property of a body/system that describes whether the body/system is in thermal equilibrium with other system/body or not.

Heat, Work and Internal Energy

Heat

It is the energy that is exchanged between a system and its environment because of the temperature difference between them. SI unit of heat is joule.

The amount of heat Q given to a body to raise its temperature from T_i to T_f depends on mass, nature of substance and change in its temperature.

i.e. $\Delta Q \propto m\Delta T$ or $\Delta Q \propto m(T_f - T_i)$

or Change in heat, $\Delta Q = ms(T_f - T_i)$

where, m = mass of body, T_i = initial temperature
T_f = final temperature, s = specific heat of material

Work

By work, we mean work done by the system or on the system. Suppose, a gas is confined in a cylinder with a movable piston, if p is pressure on the piston and A is area of piston, then force exerted by the gas on the piston of cylinder, $F = pA$

When the piston is pushed outward by an infinitesimal distance dx, then the work done by the gas

$$dW = Fdx = pA\,dx = p\,dV \quad [\because Adx = dV]$$

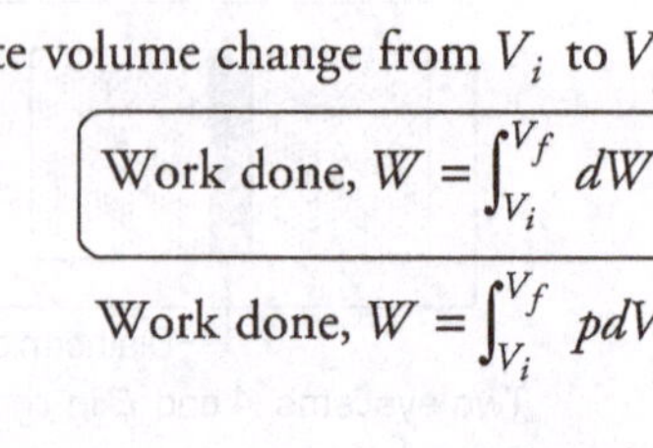

Work in a movable piston

and for a finite volume change from V_i to V_f,

$$\text{Work done, } W = \int_{V_i}^{V_f} dW$$

$$\text{Work done, } W = \int_{V_i}^{V_f} p\,dV$$

Here, p could be variable.

There are many ways to change the state of a gas. One way is represented by a plot between pressure of the gas and its volume and it is called an **indicator diagram.**

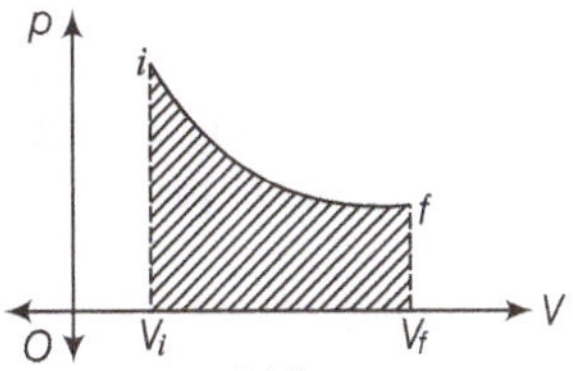

p-V diagram

The indicator diagram represents the variation of pressure (p) of the gas with the volume (V).

On indicator diagram, the area bounded by p-V graph represents the work done

$$\text{Work} = \int_{V_i}^{V_f} p dV = \text{area under } p\text{-}V \text{ graph}$$

From, $\Delta W = \int_{V_i}^{V_f} p dV$

If system expands,

$V_f > V_i$, i.e. W = **positive**

If system contracts,

$V_f < V_i$, i.e. W = **negative**

Like heat, work done is also path dependent and so it is not a state function. In case of a cyclic process, work done is equal to the area enclosed under p-V diagram and it is positive, if cycle is clockwise and negative, if the cycle is anti-clockwise.

Equivalence of Work and Heat

The mechanical equivalent of heat states that motion and heat are mutually interchangeable, i.e. a given amount of work would generate the same amount of heat. Thus, work is a form of heat energy.

Whenever heat is converted into mechanical work or mechanical work is converted into heat, then the ratio of work done to heat produced always remains constant,

i.e. $W \propto Q$

$$\frac{W}{Q} = J \Rightarrow \boxed{W = JQ}$$

J is called mechanical equivalent of heat.

Its value is 4.2 J/cal

or 4.2×10^7 erg/cal

or 4.2×10^3 J/kcal

Thus, joule conclude that 4.18×10^3 J of work is equivalent to 1 kilocalorie of heat.

$$1 \text{ kilocalorie} = 4.18 \times 10^3 \text{ J}$$

Internal Energy

Internal energy of a system is defined as the total energy possessed by the system due to molecular motion and molecular configuration. It is represented by U. The energy due to molecular motion is called **internal kinetic energy** U_K. The motion includes translational, rotational and vibrational motion of the molecules. The energy due to molecular configuration is called **internal potential energy** U_P. Then,

$$\boxed{\text{Internal energy, } U = U_K + U_P}$$

Thus, the internal energy of a system is the sum of molecular kinetic and potential energies in the frame of reference relative to which the centre of mass of the system is at rest.

Ways to Change Internal Energy of a System

There are four ways to change the internal energy of a system.

(i) By doing work on the system (ΔW = – ve).

(ii) If system is doing some work (ΔW = + ve).

(iii) If some heat energy is given to the system (ΔQ = +ve).

(iv) If some heat energy is taken out from the system. (ΔQ = – ve).

We will use these sign conventions for ΔQ and ΔW in the topics coming ahead.

First Law of Thermodynamics as Energy Balance

First law of thermodynamics is a statement of conservation of energy applied to any system in which energy transfer from or to the surroundings is taken into account.

It states that heat given to a system is either used in doing external work or it increases the internal energy of the system or both.

i.e. $\boxed{\text{Heat supplied, } \Delta Q = \Delta U + \Delta W}$

where,

ΔQ = Heat supplied to the system by the surroundings.

ΔW = Work done by the system on the surroundings

ΔU = Change in internal energy of the system.

ΔU depends only on the initial and final states.

Consider a gas in a cylinder with a massless and frictionless piston. Let the gas expands by a very small volume dV.

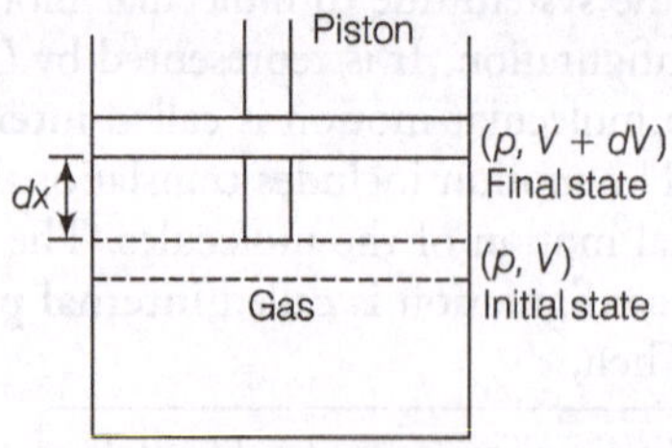

Experimental arrangement to prove first law of thermodynamics

Let p is pressure and V is volume of the gas. A is area of cross-section of the piston, dx is the distance moved by the piston. Let the volume expansion is dV.

So, the work done by the gas

$$dW = \text{force} \times dx$$

or $$dW = pA \times dx = p(A\,dx) = pdV \quad [\because A dx = dV]$$

$\therefore$ $$dW = pdV$$

[For small displacement dx, the pressure is assumed to be constant.]

Thus, from first law $\Delta Q = \Delta U + pdV$

where,

ΔQ = heat transition between system and surroundings

ΔU = change in internal energy of the system.

Example 1 The quantities in the following table represent four different paths for same initial and final states. Find the values of a, b, c, d, e, f and g.

S. No.	Q (J)	W (J)	ΔU (J)
Path I	– 80	–120	d
Path II	90	c	e
Path III	a	40	f
Path IV	b	– 40	g

Sol. For path I, $\Delta Q = \Delta W + \Delta U$

$\Rightarrow$ $\Delta U = \Delta Q - \Delta W$

$= -80 - (-120)$

$= 40$ J

As, ΔU = a state function,

So, $d = e = f = g = 40$ J

Now for path II, $\Delta Q = \Delta W + \Delta U$

$90 = c + 40$

$\Rightarrow$ $c = 50$ J

Similarly, $a = 80$ J, $b = 0$

Thermodynamic Processes

When state of a system changes or the state variables changes with time, then this process is known as **thermodynamic process.**

Some Important Processes

(i) A thermodynamic process occurring at constant temperature, is known as **isothermal process.**
e.g. Freezing of water at 0°C to form ice at 0°C.

(ii) A thermodynamic process occurring at constant pressure, is known as **isobaric process.**
e.g. Boiling of water in a open container.

(iii) A thermodynamic process occurring at constant volume, is known as **isochoric process.** In isochoric process, the work done by the system will be zero.
e.g. Heat given to a system with fixed walls.

(iv) A thermodynamic process which takes place in such a way that there is no transfer of heat into or out of the system.
e.g. Rapid compression, like filling of a cycle tube by a hand pump.

(v) **Cyclic and non-cyclic process** In cyclic process, initial and final states are same while in non-cyclic processes, they are different.

Note **Isolated system** A system which can neither do work nor can take or give heat from or to the outside is called isolated system. The internal energy of an isolated system remain constant. **Quasi-static process** is a hypothetical concept. Practically, processes that are sufficiently slow are considered as quasi-static. The system changes its variables (p, T, V) so slowly that it remains in thermal and mechanical equilibrium with its surroundings throughout.

Example 2 Give an example of each of given below

(i) Isobaric process (ii) Isochoric process

(iii) Isothermal process (iv) Adiabatic process

Sol. (i) **Isobaric process** Cooking in an open lid container.

(ii) **Isochoric process** Cooking in a pressure cooker.

(iii) **Isothermal process** Boiling of water at atmospheric pressure.

(iv) **Adiabatic process** Expulsion of air from a bursted tyre (tube).

Example 3 How an adiabatic can be carried practically?

Sol. For an adiabatic process, $\Delta Q = 0$. So, if a process is carried very fast so that heat cannot be transferred from system to surroundings and *vice-versa*, it is an adiabatic process.

Equation of State, Work Done and p-V Graph for an Isothermal Process

For an isothermal process, temperature remains constant.

For an ideal gas, the equation of state is given by

$$pV = \text{constant}$$

So, gas follows Boyle's law

$$p_iV_i = p_fV_f, \text{ for isothermal process}$$

p-V Diagram

On a p-V diagram, an isotherm is a curve that connects points of same temperature.

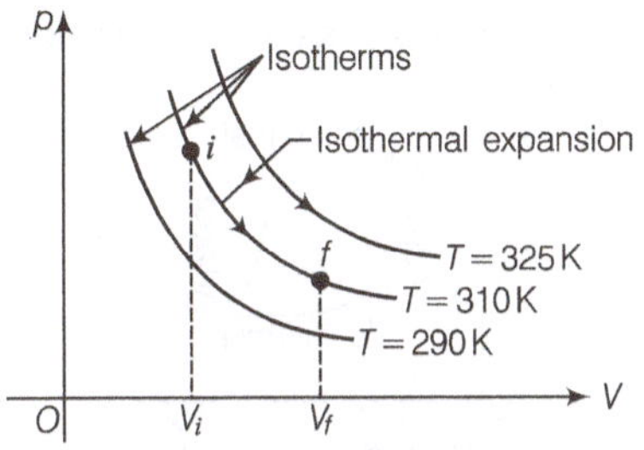

An isothermal expansion process

Work Done

Work done in an isothermal process = area under p-V graph

$$= \int_{V_i}^{V_f} p\,dV = \mu RT \int_{V_i}^{V_f} \frac{dV}{V}$$

$$\left[\because pV = \mu RT \Rightarrow p = \frac{\mu RT}{V}\right]$$

$$= \mu RT \ln(V)_{V_i}^{V_f}$$

$$= \mu RT \ln(V_f - V_i)$$

$$W_{\text{iso}} = \mu RT \ln\left(\frac{V_f}{V_i}\right)$$

Work done, $\boxed{W_{\text{iso}} = 2.303\,\mu RT \log\left(\frac{V_f}{V_i}\right)}$

As temperature of ideal gas remains constant.

$\therefore \quad \Delta U = 0$

So, by first law of thermodynamics

$$\Delta Q = \Delta W + \Delta U$$

$$\Rightarrow \quad \Delta Q = \Delta W = \mu RT \ln\left(\frac{V_f}{V_i}\right)$$

where, μ = number of moles,

R = gas constant and T = temperature

V_f and V_i are the final and initial volumes of the gas, respectively.

i.e. Heat supplied in an isothermal change is used to do work against surroundings or if the work is done on the system, then the equal amount of heat energy will be liberated by the system.

Let us consider two cases for finding the nature of the work done.

Case I If $V_f > V_i$, then $W > 0$

Thus, it is an **isothermal expansion** which means the gas absorbs heat.

Case II If $V_f < V_i$, then $W < 0$

Thus, it is an **isothermal compression**, work is done on the gas by the environment and heat is released.

Example 4 Three moles of an ideal gas kept at constant temperature of 300 K is compressed from a volume of 4 L to 1 L. Calculate the work done in the process. Take R as 8.31 J/mol-K.

Sol. Given, $\mu = 3$, $T = 300$ K, $V_i = 4$ L, $V_f = 1$ L,

$R = 8.31$ J/mol-K, $W = ?$

Work done in isothermal process is given by

$$W = 2.303\,\mu RT \log\frac{V_f}{V_i} = 2.303 \times 3 \times 8.31 \times 300 \log\frac{1}{4}$$

$$= -1.037 \times 10^4 \text{ J}$$

Equation of State, Work Done and p-V Graph for an Adiabatic Process

In an adiabatic process, there is no exchange of heat between system and the surroundings.

By first law, $\quad \Delta Q = \Delta U + \Delta W \quad$ ...(i)

For adiabatic process, $\quad \Delta Q = 0$

$\therefore \quad \Delta U = -\Delta W$

For adiabatic process,

$$\boxed{pV^\gamma = \text{constant}}$$

where, $\quad \gamma = \dfrac{C_p}{C_V}$

Thus, if we consider an ideal gas with the adiabatic range from (p_i, V_i) to (p_f, V_f), then

$$p_iV_i^\gamma = p_fV_f^\gamma = \text{constant}$$

In the propagation of sound in air, the compression and rarefaction of air molecules comes under adiabatic process. The air molecules oscillates so fast that neither the heat comes in nor comes out from the oscillating particles region. That is why oscillation of particles during sound wave propagation comes under adiabatic process.

Note

Relation between p and T; V and T in an adiabatic process

$$p^{1-\gamma} \cdot T^{\gamma} = \text{constant}$$

and $\quad V^{\gamma-1} \cdot T = \text{constant}$

p-V Diagram

On a p-V diagram, the process is represented by an adiabatic curve as shown.

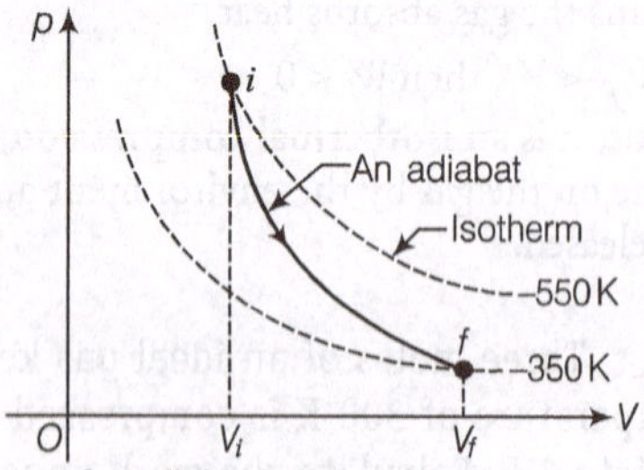

An adiabatic expansion process

A curve representing an adiabatic process is called an adiabat. If we differentiate $pV^{\gamma} =$ constant, we get

$$dp\, V^{\gamma} + p\gamma V^{\gamma-1}\, dV = 0$$

$$\Rightarrow \qquad \frac{dp}{dV} = -\gamma\left(\frac{p}{V}\right)$$

So, slope of adiabatic curve $= -\gamma\left(\frac{p}{V}\right)$, which is γ times more than slope of an isotherm.

By definition of specific heat,

$$C = \frac{\Delta Q}{m\,\Delta T} = \frac{Q}{m\,\Delta T}, \Delta Q = 0 \text{ in adiabatic process.}$$

So, $\quad C = 0$ (adiabatic process)

So, specific heat of a gas in adiabatic compression or expansion is zero.

Work Done

Also, work done in an adiabatic process

$$W = \int_{V_i}^{V_f} p\,dV = \int_{V_i}^{V_f} \frac{K}{V^{\gamma}}\,dV \quad [\because pV^{\gamma} = K \text{ (constant)}]$$

$$= K\left|\frac{V^{-\gamma+1}}{-\gamma+1}\right|_{V_i}^{V_f} = \frac{K}{1-\gamma}\left[\frac{1}{V_f^{\gamma-1}} - \frac{1}{V_i^{\gamma-1}}\right]$$

$$\text{Thus, } W = \frac{1}{1-\gamma}\left[\frac{p_f V_f^{\gamma}}{V_f^{\gamma-1}} - \frac{p_i V_i^{\gamma}}{V_i^{\gamma-1}}\right] = \frac{p_i V_i - p_f V_f}{\gamma - 1}$$

$$pV = \mu RT,\ p_i V_i = \mu R T_i \text{ and } p_f V_f = \mu R T_f$$

$$\boxed{\text{Work done, } W = \frac{\mu R(T_i - T_f)}{\gamma - 1}}$$

As, $\quad \Delta Q = 0$

$\Rightarrow \quad \Delta U = -\Delta W$

So, if work is done by the system, the internal energy and so the temperature of system falls i.e. $W > 0, T_f < T_i$. Conversely, if work is done on the system, the internal energy and so the temperature of system increases.

i.e. $\quad W < 0, T_f > T_i$

All nearly practical adiabatic processes occur so rapidly that no transfer of energy as heat occurs between the system and surroundings. e.g. Sudden bursting of bicycle tube and propagation of sound waves in air.

The p-V curves of an ideal gas for two adiabatic processes connecting two isotherms is shown in the figure

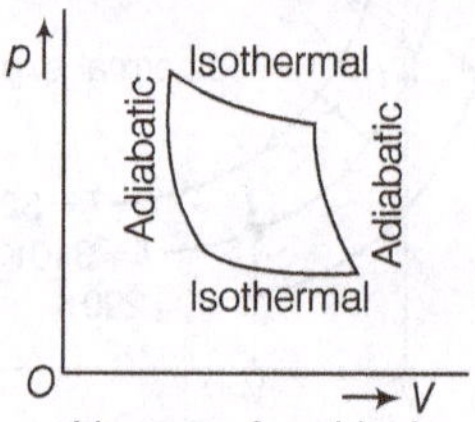

p-V curve of an ideal gas

Comparison of Work Done in Isothermal and Adiabatic Process

(Using Area Under the Curve)

Let a fixed mass of an ideal gas is expanded from volume V_1 to volume V_2, first under the isothermal conditions and then under adiabatic conditions. The curves obtained are as shown in Fig. (a). The area under the isothermal curve is more than the area under the adiabatic curve.

Since, the area bounded by the curve with volume axis represents the work done in the process, hence it is clear that for same expansion, the work done in the isothermal process will be more than the work done in the adiabatic process.

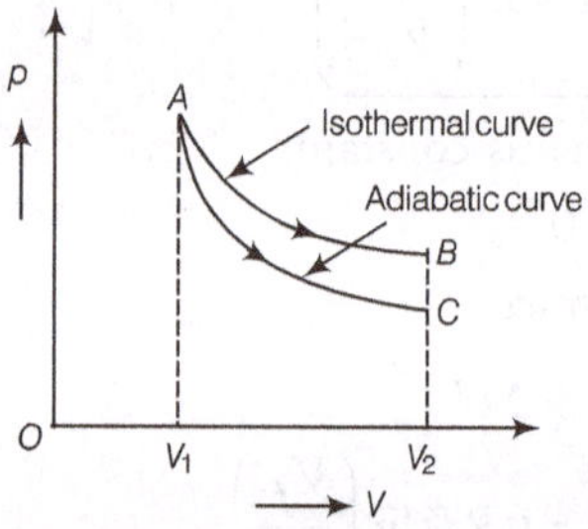

Fig. (a)

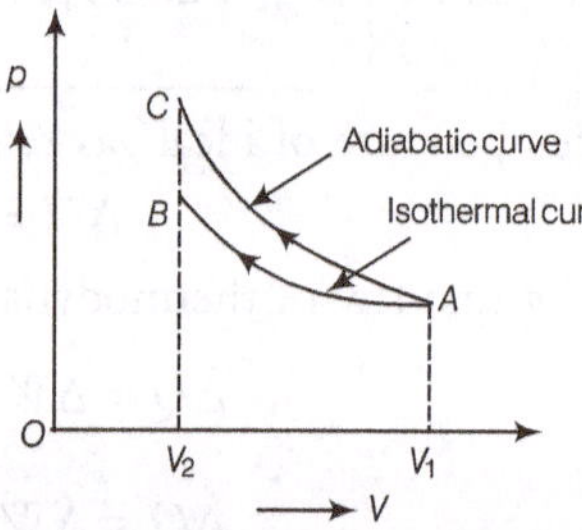

Fig. (b)

In case of compression Fig. (b) from volume V_1 to volume V_2, the adiabatic curve lies above the isothermal curve. Thus, in same compression, the work done in adiabatic process is more than that in the isothermal process.

Example 5 A cylinder containing one gram molecule of the gas was compressed adiabatically until its temperature rise from 27°C to 97°C. Calculate the work done and heat produced in the gas. Take γ as 1.5

Sol. Given, $T_i = 27°\text{C} = 27 + 273 = 300\text{ K}$

$$T_f = 97°\text{C} = 97 + 273 = 370\text{ K}, \gamma = 1.5$$

Work done in adiabatic compression is given by

$$W = \frac{R}{1-\gamma}(T_i - T_f) = \frac{8.31}{1-1.5}(300-370) = 1163.4\text{ J}$$

$$\text{Heat produced, } H = \frac{W}{J} = \frac{1163.4}{4.2} = 277\text{ cal}$$

Work Done in an Isochoric Process

In case of an isochoric process, volume of the system remains constant. So, if heat is added to system, its pressure increases and if heat is extracted from the system, pressure will be reduced.

Equation of State

In this process, p and T changes but V = constant, Gay-Lussac's law is obeyed.

$$\Rightarrow \quad p \propto T \Rightarrow \frac{p_1}{T_1} = \frac{p_2}{T_2}$$

where, V = constant

So, $\boxed{\text{Work done, } \Delta W = 0}$

$$\Rightarrow \quad \Delta W = p\,\Delta V = 0 \quad [\because \Delta V = 0]$$

From first law of thermodynamics, $\Delta Q = \Delta U$

Hence, in an isochoric process, the entire heat given to or taken from the system goes to change its internal energy and temperature of the system.

The change in temperature can be determined by the equation.

$$\boxed{\Delta U = \mu C_V\,\Delta T}$$

Work Done in an Isobaric Process

When a thermodynamic system undergoes a physical change at constant pressure, then this thermodynamic process is known as **isobaric process**.

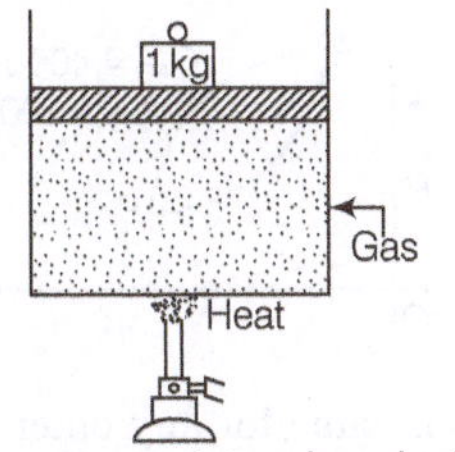

A simple arrangement to show isobaric process

e.g. A gas is heated in a piston cylinder arrangement with constant weight over the cylinder.

Suppose the pressure p of a gas remains constant and its volume changes from V_i to V_f, then the work done by the gas is

$$W = \int_{V_i}^{V_f} p\,dV = p\int_{V_i}^{V_f} dV = p(V_f - V_i)$$

$$\boxed{\text{Work done, } W = \mu R(T_f - T_i)} \quad [\because pV = \mu RT]$$

As the temperature of the gas changes, so its internal energy also changes. Hence, in an isobaric process, the absorbed heat goes partly to increase internal energy and partly to do work.

Example 6 If 70 cal of heat is required to raise the temperature of 2 mol of an ideal gas at constant pressure from 30°C to 35°C, calculate

(i) work done by the gas

(ii) increase in internal energy of gas.

Take, $R = 2$ cal/mol-K.

Sol. (i) In isobaric process, p = constant

and $\Delta W = \text{work done} = p\Delta V$

$$= nR(\Delta T) = 2 \times 2 \times (35 + 273) - (30 + 273)$$

$$= 20\text{ cal}$$

(ii) $\Delta U = \Delta Q - \Delta W$ [from first law]

$$= 70 - 20 = 50\text{ cal}$$

Example 7 Find the ratio of $\frac{\Delta Q}{\Delta U}$ and $\frac{\Delta Q}{\Delta W}$ in an isobaric process. The ratio of molar specific heats, $\frac{C_p}{C_V} = \gamma$.

Sol. In an isobaric process, p = constant

$$\therefore \quad C = C_p$$

and $$\frac{\Delta Q}{\Delta U} = \frac{nC_p\Delta T}{nC_V\Delta T} = \frac{C_p}{C_V} = \gamma$$

also $$\frac{\Delta Q}{\Delta W} = \frac{\Delta Q}{\Delta Q - \Delta U}$$

$$= \frac{nC_p\Delta T}{nC_p\Delta T - nC_V\Delta T}$$

$$= \frac{C_p}{C_p - C_V} = \frac{\gamma}{\gamma - 1}$$

Work Done in a Cyclic Process

A single process or a series of processes in which, after certain interchanges of heat and work, the system is restored to its initial state is known as a **cyclic process**.

As both initial and final states are same in a cyclic process, $\Delta U = U_f - U_i = 0$.

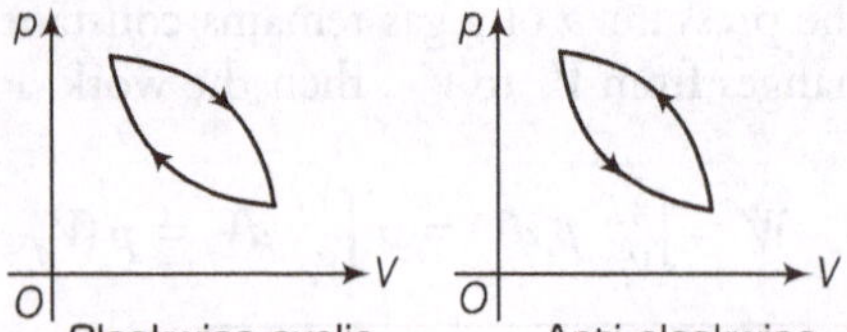

Clockwise cyclic process   Anti-clockwise cyclic process

For a cyclic process, *p*-*V* graph is a closed curve and area enclosed by the curve is equal to the work done.

From first law of thermodynamics,

$$\Delta Q = \Delta U + \Delta W$$

For cyclic process, $\Delta U = 0$ or $\boxed{\Delta Q = \Delta W}$

So, **heat supplied to the system is converted into work done and *vice-versa*.**

Let (V_1, p_1) shows the initial state of a gas and (V_2, p_2) shows the final state. The gas reached between *A* and *B* by both paths *AB* and *BA*.

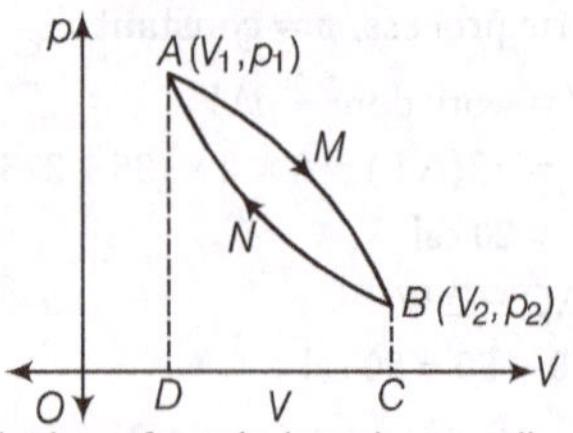

Calculation of work done in a cyclic process

So, work done by the gas for expansion from *A* to *B*, is

$$W_1 = \text{area } AMBCDA$$

Let the system return back to the initial state $A(V_1, p_1)$ by the path *BA*. The complete process is cyclic.

Work done on the gas for compression from *B* to *A* is

$$W = -\text{ area } BNADCB$$

Net work done by the gas in the cyclic process

$$W_{A \to B \to A} = W_1 + W_2 = \text{area } AMBCDA - \text{area } BNADCB$$
$$= \text{area } AMBNA$$

Hence, the work done in a cyclic process is equal to the area enclosed by the loop.

- If the cycle is clockwise, work done is positive and if the cycle is anti-clockwise, the work done is negative.
- Cyclic processes are of great importance as mechanical machines like engines and refrigerators operates in cycles; in which the system do work by using influx of heat and is restored to its initial state.
- A process in which the system do not return to its initial state after undergoing a series of change is known as non-cyclic process.

Summary of thermodynamic processes

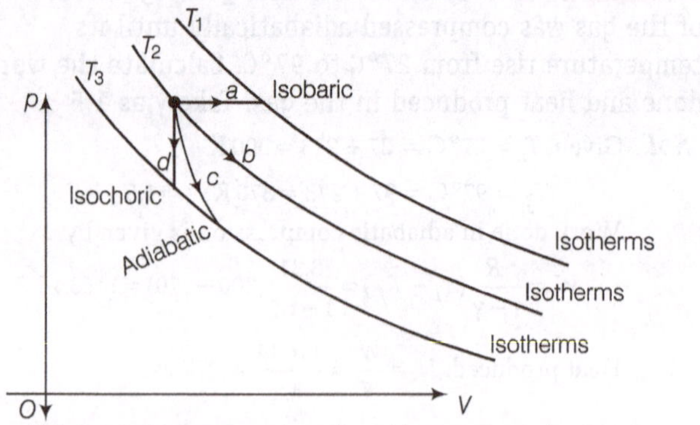

p-*V* diagram to represent various thermodynamic processes

Thermodynamic Processes

Process	Constant Quantity	Path	Heat/Work/Internal energy
Isobaric	p	a	$\Delta Q = nC_p\Delta T$, $\Delta W = p\Delta V$, $\Delta U = nC_V\Delta T$
Isochoric	V	d	$\Delta Q = \Delta U = nC_V\Delta T$, $\Delta W = 0$
Isothermal	T	b	$\Delta Q = \Delta W = nRT\ln V_f / V_i$, $\Delta U = 0$
Adiabatic	pV^γ	c	$\Delta Q = 0$; $\Delta W = -\Delta U$

Example 8 When a system goes from state *A* to state *B*, it is supplied with 400 J of heat and it does 100 J of work.

(i) For process $A \to B$, what is the change in internal energy?

(ii) If the system moves from *B* to *A*, what will be change in system, internal energy?

(iii) If in moving from *A* to *B* along a different path where, work done on the system is 400 J, how much heat does it absorb for this path?

Sol. (i) From first law of thermodynamics,

$$\Delta U_{AB} = \Delta Q_{AB} - \Delta W_{AB} = (400 - 100)\text{ J} = 300\text{ J}$$

(ii) As ΔU for a closed path is zero,

$$\Delta U_{AB} + \Delta U_{BA} = 0$$
$$\Delta U_{BA} = -\Delta U_{AB} = -300\text{ J}$$

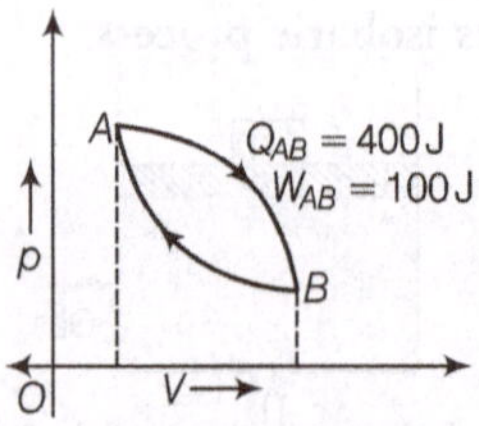

(iii) As ΔU_{AB} is same for any other path, so

$$\Delta U_{AB} = \Delta Q - \Delta W$$
$$300\text{ J} = \Delta Q - (-400\text{ J}) \Rightarrow \Delta Q = -100\text{ J}$$

Heat Capacity

If an amount of heat ΔQ is needed to change its temperature by ΔT, then **heat capacity** can be defined as

$$\text{Heat capacity, } S = \frac{\Delta Q}{\Delta T}$$

Heat capacity is numerically equal to the heat energy required to change the temperature of a body by unity. Its unit is J/K.

Specific Heat Capacity

The amount of heat required to change the temperature of unit mass of a substance by unity is known as **specific heat capacity** of heat substance.

$$s = \frac{S}{m} = \frac{1}{m}\frac{\Delta Q}{\Delta T}$$

$$\text{Specific heat capacity, } s = \frac{1}{m}\frac{\Delta Q}{\Delta T}$$

where, s = specific heat capacity of the substance.
It depends on the nature of substance and its temperature. Its unit J/kg-K. Heat capacity per kg is known as **specific heat capacity.**

Molar Specific Heat Capacity

Heat capacity per mole is known as **molar specific heat capacity.**

$$C = \frac{S}{\mu} = \frac{1}{\mu}\left(\frac{\Delta Q}{\Delta T}\right)$$

$$\text{Molar specific heat capacity, } C = \frac{1}{\mu}\frac{\Delta Q}{\Delta T}$$

where, μ = number of moles.
The amount of heat required to raise the temperature of one gram mole of a substance through a unit is called **molar specific heat** capacity of the substance.
C depends on the nature of the substance, its temperature and the conditions under which heat is supplied. Its unit is J/mol-K.
Specific and molar heat capacities of some solids at room temperature and atmospheric pressure

Substance	Specific heat ($\text{Jkg}^{-1}\text{K}^{-1}$)	Molar specific Heat ($\text{J mol}^{-1}\text{K}^{-1}$)
Aluminium	900.0	24.4
Carbon	506.5	6.1
Copper	386.4	24.5
Lead	127.7	26.5
Silver	236.1	25.5
Tungsten	134.4	24.9

Mechanical Equivalent of Heat

Mechanical equivalent of heat is defined as the amount of work needed to produce 1 calorie of heat.
It is just a conversion factor.

$$1 \text{ calorie (heat energy)} = 4.186\text{ J} \simeq 4.2\text{ J}$$

Specific Heat Capacities of Gases

For gases, their specific heat capacities depends on the process or under which condition heat exchange between the gases and the sourrounding is taking place.

There are two main specific heat capacities for a gas and defined as,

(i) **Molar heat capacity at constant volume,** (C_V) –
The amount of heat required to increase the temperature of one mole of the gas by 1°C (or 1K) at constant volume is known as molar heat capacity at constant volume. It is denoted by C_V.

(ii) **Molar heat capacity at constant pressure,** (C_p) –
The amount of heat required to increase the temperature of one mole of the gas by 1°C (or 1 K) at constant pressure is known as molar heat capacity at constant pressure. It is denoted by C_p.

Note For a gas, $C_p > C_V$ always, because at constant pressure, more heat is required to increase the temperature of one mole of the gas by 1°C (or 1K) as compare to that of at constant volume.

Relation between C_p and C_V (Mayer's Formula)

We can establish the relation between specific heat capacity at constant volume (C_V) and specific heat capacity at constant pressure (C_p) of a gas.

For an ideal gas, the relation between C_p and C_V is

$$C_p - C_V = R \quad \text{...(i)}$$

This relation is known as Mayer's Formula.

To establish the relation, we begin with first law of thermodynamics for 1 mole of the gas

$$\Delta Q = \Delta U + p\Delta V$$

If heat ΔQ is absorbed at constant volume,

$\therefore$ $p\Delta V = 0$ and $\Delta Q = C_V \Delta T$ for one mole of a gas
$\Delta V = 0$

Then,
$$C_V = \left(\frac{\Delta Q}{\Delta T}\right)_V = \left(\frac{\Delta U}{\Delta T}\right)_V = \left(\frac{\Delta U}{\Delta T}\right) \quad \text{...(ii)}$$

where the subscript V is dropped in the last step, since U of an ideal gas depends only on temperature, not on volume.

Now, heat ΔQ is absorbed at constant pressure, then

$$\Delta Q = C_p \Delta T$$

$$C_p = \left(\frac{\Delta Q}{\Delta T}\right)_p = \left(\frac{\Delta U}{\Delta T}\right)_p + p\left(\frac{\Delta V}{\Delta T}\right)_p$$

The subscript p can be dropped from the first term since U of an ideal gas depends only on T, not on pressure.

Now, by using Eq. (ii), we have

or $$C_p = C_V + p\left(\frac{\Delta V}{\Delta p}\right)_p \quad \text{...(iii)}$$

For one mole of an ideal gas, we can write $pV = RT$

If the pressure is kept constant

$$p\left(\frac{\Delta V}{\Delta T}\right)_p = R \quad \text{...(iv)}$$

From Eqs. (iii) and (iv), we get

$$\boxed{C_p - C_V = R}$$

Here, C_p and C_V are molar specific heat capacities of an ideal gas at constant pressure and volume, respectively and R is the universal gas constant.

The ratio of C_p and C_V is notified by γ.

$$\gamma = C_p / C_V$$

It is also known as heat capacity ratio, then

$$C_V = \frac{R}{\gamma - 1} \text{ and } C_p = \frac{\gamma R}{\gamma - 1}$$

Example 9 A gaseous mixture enclosed in a vessel consists of 1g mole of a gas $A\left(\gamma = \frac{5}{3}\right)$ and some amount of gas $B\left(\gamma = \frac{7}{5}\right)$ at a temperature T. The gases A and B do not react with each other and are assumed to be ideal.

Find number of gram moles of the gas B, if γ for the gaseous mixture is $\left(\frac{19}{13}\right)$.

Sol. For an ideal gas,

$$\frac{C_p}{C_V} = \gamma \text{ and } C_p - C_V = R$$

So, combining above equations we get

$$C_V = \frac{R}{\gamma - 1}$$

$$(C_V)_A = \frac{R}{\frac{5}{3} - 1} = \frac{3}{2}R$$

and $$(C_V)_B = \frac{5}{2}R$$

and $$(C_V)_{mix} = \frac{R}{\frac{19}{13} - 1} = \frac{13}{6}R$$

Now, from conservation of energy

$$U_{mix} = U_A + U_B$$

or $$\Delta U_{mix} = \Delta U_A + \Delta U_B$$

$$\Rightarrow (\mu_A + \mu_B)(C_V)_{mix}\,\Delta T = \mu_A (C_V)_A\,\Delta T + \mu_B (C_V)_B\,\Delta T$$

$$\Rightarrow (C_V)_{mix} = \frac{\mu_A (C_V)_A + \mu_B (C_V)_B}{\mu_A + \mu_B}$$

$$\Rightarrow \frac{13}{6}R = \frac{1 \times \frac{3}{2}R + \mu_B \times \frac{5}{2}R}{1 + \mu_B}$$

$$\Rightarrow 13 + 13\mu_B = 9 + 15\mu_B$$

$$\Rightarrow \mu_B = 2\text{ g-mol}$$

Example 10 Find molar specific heat for the process $p = \frac{a}{T}$ for a monoatomic gas. $\left(a = \text{constant}, C_V = \frac{3}{2}R\right)$

Sol. From first law of thermodynamics,

$$\Delta Q = \Delta W + \Delta U$$

$$\Rightarrow C = \frac{\Delta Q}{\Delta T} = \frac{\Delta W}{\Delta T} + \frac{\Delta U}{\Delta T}$$

or $$C = \frac{\Delta W}{\Delta T} + C_V \quad [\because \Delta U = C_V \Delta T]$$

$$C = \frac{p\Delta V}{\Delta T} + C_V \quad [\because \Delta W = p\Delta V] \text{ ...(i)}$$

For the process,

$$pV = RT \quad [\because \text{for monoatomic gas}, \mu = 1]$$

$$\Rightarrow V = \frac{RT}{p} = \frac{RT^2}{a}$$

$$\Rightarrow \frac{\Delta V}{\Delta T} = \frac{dV}{dT} = \frac{2RT}{a} \quad \text{...(ii)}$$

Substituting value of Eq. (ii) in Eq. (i), we get

$$C = p\left(\frac{2RT}{a}\right) + C_V = \frac{a}{T}\left(\frac{2RT}{a}\right) + C_V \quad \left[\because p = \frac{a}{T}\right]$$

$$\Rightarrow C = 2R + C_V$$

$$= 2R + \frac{3}{2}R = \frac{7}{2}R$$

Topic Practice 1

Multiple Choice Questions

1 Mark

1. According to Zeroth law, which physical quantity must have same value for the two systems to be in thermal equilibrium?
   (a) Pressure (b) Temperature
   (c) Volume (d) Composition
2. For an ideal gas, internal energy depends on
   (a) only molecular kinetic energy
   (b) only potential energy of the molecules
   (c) Both kinetic and potential energies of the molecules
   (d) None of the above
3. According to first law of thermodynamics
   (a) any process that involves energy conservation is possible in nature
   (b) $\Delta Q = \Delta U + \Delta W$
   (c) Both (a) and (b)
   (d) Neither (a) nor (b)
4. For isothermal expansion of an ideal gas,
   (a) $\Delta U = +$ ve (b) $\Delta Q = +$ ve
   (c) $\Delta W = +$ ve (d) Both (b) and (c)
5. A gas is expanded isothermally from volume V_1 to V_2 at a constant temperature T, the work done by the gas in this expansion is
   (a) $\mu RT \log \frac{V_1}{V_2}$ (b) $\mu RT \times \frac{V_1}{V_2}$
   (c) $\mu RT \log \frac{V_2}{V_1}$ (d) $\mu RT \times \frac{V_2}{V_1}$
6. In adiabatic process,
   (a) $\Delta T = 0$ (b) $\Delta U = -\Delta W, \Delta Q = 0$
   (c) $\Delta V = 0$ (d) None of these
7. Molar specific heat capacity C
   (a) can be represented by $\frac{\Delta Q}{M \Delta T}$
   (b) depends on the amount of substance
   (c) depends on the nature and temperature of the substance
   (d) Both (a) and (b)

Very Short Answer Type Questions

1 Mark

8. Can a system be heated and its temperature remain constant? **NCERT Exemplar**
9. Air pressure in a car tyre increases during driving. Explain. **NCERT Exemplar**
10. If a gas is suddenly compressed, its temperature increases, why?
11. Write conditions for an isothermal process.
12. Why a gas is cooled when it expand?
13. Apply first law of thermodynamics for isothermal expansion of an ideal gas.
14. Two isothermal curves do not intersect each other, why?
15. What is meant by free expansion?

Short Answer Type Questions

2 Marks

16. Two bodies at different temperatures T_1 and T_2 are brought in contact. Under what condition, they settle to mean temperature? (after they attain equilibrium) **NCERT Exemplar**
17. The initial state of a certain gas is (p_i, V_i, T_i). It undergoes expansion till its volume becomes V_f. Consider the following two cases
    (i) The expansion takes place at constant temperature.
    (ii) The expansion takes place at constant pressure.

    Plot the p-V diagram for each case. In which of the two cases, is the work done by the gas more? **NCERT Exemplar**
18. When ice melts, then change in internal energy is greater than the heat supplied, why?
19. Generally, a gas has two specific heat capacities, why? and which one is greater, explain it.

Short Answer Type II Questions

3 Marks

20. Explain, why?
    (i) 500 J of work is done on a gas to reduce its volume by compression adiabatically. What is the change in internal energy of the gas?
    (ii) The coolant in a chemical or a nuclear plant , i.e. the liquid used to prevent the different parts of a plant from getting too hot should have high specific heat.

(iii) Air pressure in a car tyres increases during driving.

(iv) The climate of a harbour town is more temperate than that of a town in a desert at the same latitude. **NCERT**

21. A cycle followed by an engine (made of one mole of an ideal gas in a cylinder with a piston) is shown in figure. Find heat exchanged by the engine with the surroundings for each section of the cycle. $[C_V = (3/2)R]$

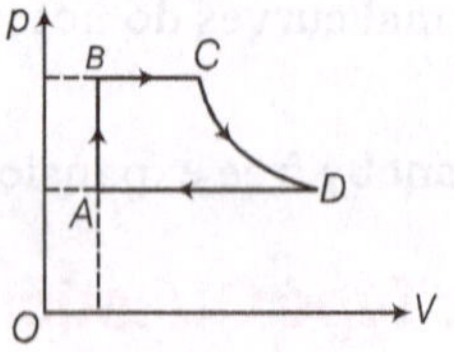

(i) AB : constant volume

(ii) BC : constant pressure

(iii) CD : adiabatic

(iv) DA : constant pressure **NCERT Exemplar**

22. Calculate the work done for adiabatic expansion of a gas.

23. Consider one mole of perfect gas in a cylinder of unit cross-section with a piston attached (figure). A spring (spring constant k) is attached (unstretched length L) to the piston and to the bottom of the cylinder. Initially, the spring is unstretched and the gas is in equilibrium. A certain amount of heat Q is supplied to the gas causing an increase of volume from V_0 to V_1.

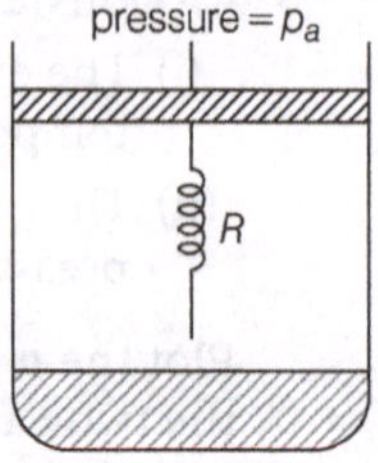

(i) What is the initial pressure of the system?

(ii) What is the final pressure of the system?

(iii) Using the first law of thermodynamics, write down a relation between Q, p_a, V, V_0 and k.

24. Consider a p-V diagram in which the path followed by one mole of perfect gas in a cylindrical container is shown.

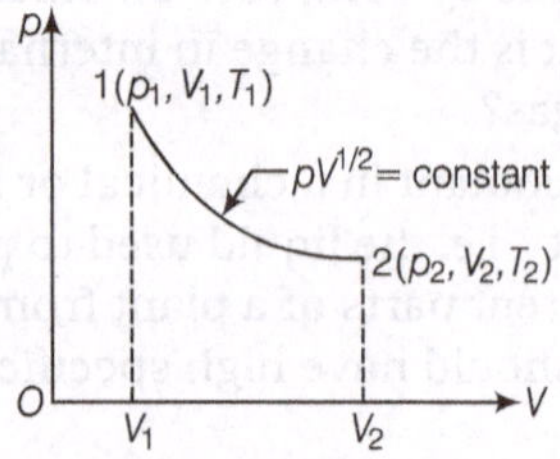

(i) Find the work done when the gas is taken from state 1 to state 2.

(ii) What is the ratio of temperatures T_1/T_2, if $V_2 = 2V_1$?

(iii) Given the internal energy for one mole of gas at temperature T is $(3/2)RT$, find the heat supplied to the gas when it is taken from states 1 to 2, with $V_2 = 2V_1$. **NCERT Exemplar**

25. Derive Mayer's formula.

Long Answer Type Questions

5 Marks

26. (i) State and explain first law of thermodynamics.

(ii) Define specific heat capacity and molar specific heat capacity.

(iii) What is mechanical equivalence of heat?

27. In the given p-V diagrams, **NCERT Exemplar**

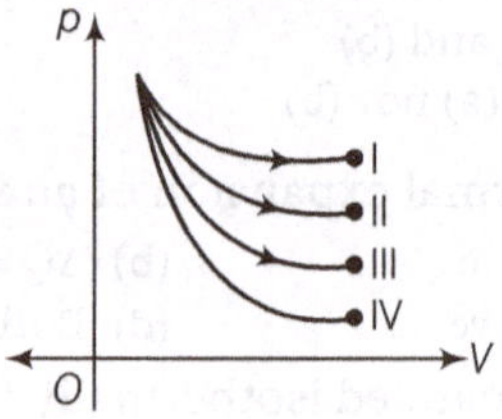

Find which curve represents

(i) isothermal process,

(ii) adiabatic process for

(a) monoatomic (b) diatomic

(c) triatomic gas.

28. Consider that an ideal gas (n moles) is expanding in a process given by $p = f(V)$, which passes through a point (V_0, p_0). Show that the gas is absorbing heat at (p_0, V_0), if the slope of the curve $p = f(V)$ is larger than the slope of the adiabat passing through (p_0, V_0).

29. A cycle followed by a machine (made of one mole of perfect gas in a cylinder with a piston) is shown in figure

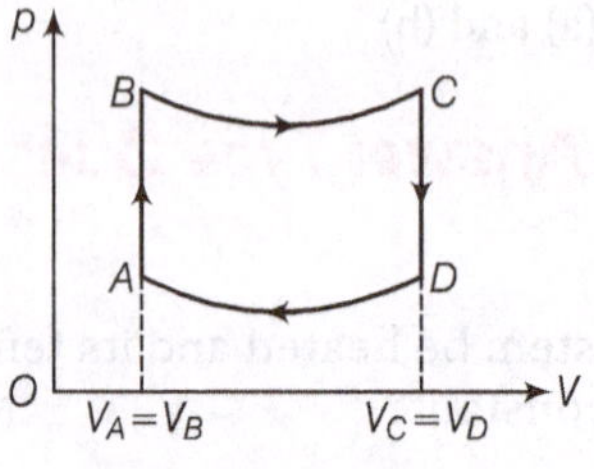

A to B : volume constant B to C : adiabatic
C to D : volume constant D to A : adiabatic

$$V_C = V_D = 2V_A = 2V_B$$

(i) In which part of the cycle, heat is supplied to the machine from outside?
(ii) In which part of the cycle, heat is being given to the surrounding by the machine?
(iii) What is the work done by the machine in one cycle? Write your answer in term of p_A, p_B, V_A.
(iv) What is the efficiency of the machine?

Take $\gamma = \frac{5}{3}$ for the gas and

$C_V = \frac{3}{2}R$ for one mole

NCERT Exemplar

Numerical Problems

30. An electric heater supplies heat to a system at a rate of 100 W. If the system performs work at a rate of 75 J/s. At what rate, is the internal energy increasing? **NCERT [1 M]**

31. Find the values of two molar specific heats of nitrogen. Given, $\gamma = 1.41$ and $R = 8.31\ \text{J mol}^{-1}\text{K}^{-1}$. **[1 M]**

32. A system goes from P to Q by two different paths in the p-V diagram as shown in figure. Heat given to the system in path 1 is 1000 J. The work done by the system along path 1 is more than path 2 by 100 J. What is the heat exchanged by the system in path 2? **NCERT Exemplar [2 M]**

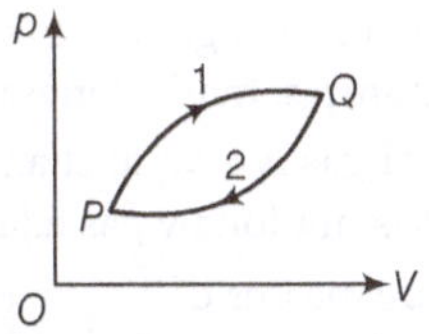

33. What amount of heat must be supplied to 2.0×10^{-2} kg of nitrogen (at room temperature) to raise its temperature by 45°C at constant pressure? (Molecular mass of $N_2 = 28$, $R = 8.3\ \text{J mol}^{-1}\text{K}^{-1}$) **[2 M]**

34. A geyser heats water flowing at the rate of 3.0 L/min from 27°C to 77°C. If the geyser operates on a gas burner, what is the rate of consumption of the fuel if its heat of combustion is 4.0×10^4 J/g?. **NCERT [2 M]**

35. A cylinder with a movable piston contains 3 moles of hydrogen at standard temperature and pressure. The walls of the cylinder are made of a heat insulator and the piston is insulated by having a pile of sand on it. By what factor, does the pressure of the gas increase if the gas is compressed to half its original volume? **NCERT [2 M]**

36. A thermodynamic system is taken from an original state D to an intermediate state E by the linear process shown in figure.

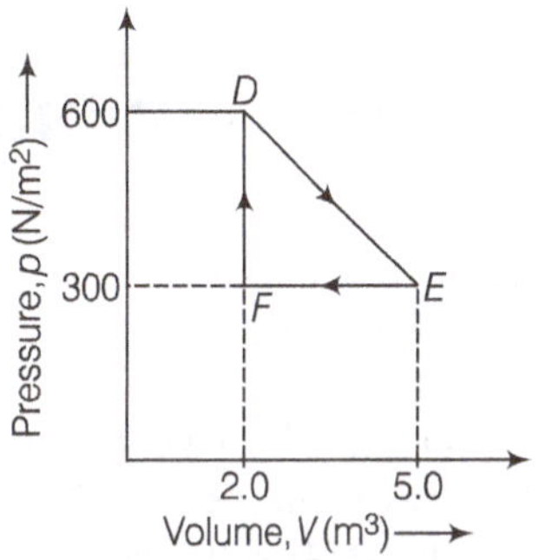

Its volume is then reduced to the original value from E to F by an isobaric process. Calculate the total work done by the gas from D to E to F. **NCERT [3 M]**

37. In changing the state of a gas adiabatically from an equilibrium state A to another equilibrium state B, an amount of work equal to 22.3 J is done on the system. If the gas is taken from state A to B *via* a process in which the net heat absorbed by the system is 9.35 cal, how much is the net work done by the system in the latter case? (Take 1 cal = 4.19 J). **[3 M]**

38. A gas is initially at a pressure of 50 kPa. Its pressure is kept constant and the volume is changed from 2 m³ to 2.5 m³. Its volume is now kept constant and the pressure is increased from 50 kPa to 150 kPa. The gas is brought back to its initial state *via* a process in which, the pressure varies linearly with its volume. Whether the heat is supplied to or extracted from the gas in the complete cycle? **[3 M]**

39. What is a cyclic process? What is change in internal energy of the system in a cyclic process? In changing the state of a gas adiabatically from an equilibrium states A to B, an amount of 40.5 J of work is done on the system. If the gas is taken from states A to B *via* a process in which net heat absorbed by the system is 12.6 cal. How much is the net work done by the system in the later case? (1 cal = 4.19 J) **[5 M]**

40. An ideal gas has a specific heat or molar heat capacity at constant pressure $C_p = 5R/2$. The gas is kept in a closed vessel of volume $0.0083\ m^3$ at a temperature of 300 K and a pressure of $1.6 \times 10^6\ Nm^{-2}$. An amount of 2.49×10^4 J of heat energy is supplied to the gas. Calculate the final temperature and pressure of the gas. **[2 M]**

Hints & Solutions

1. (*b*) According to Zeroth law, temperature should be the physical quantity that will be same for two systems to be in thermal equilibrium.
According to this law,
if $T_A = T_C$ and $T_B = T_C$, then $T_A = T_B$

2. (*a*) For an ideal gas, internal energy depends only on the molecular kinetic energy of the molecules of an ideal gas.

3. (*c*) According to first law, any process that involves energy conservation is possible in nature but in reality there are many process that are allowed by first law but never happen in nature.
According to first law, $\Delta Q = \Delta U + \Delta W$
For example, a book lying on table does no work itself. It does not rise itself by lowering its internal energy U.

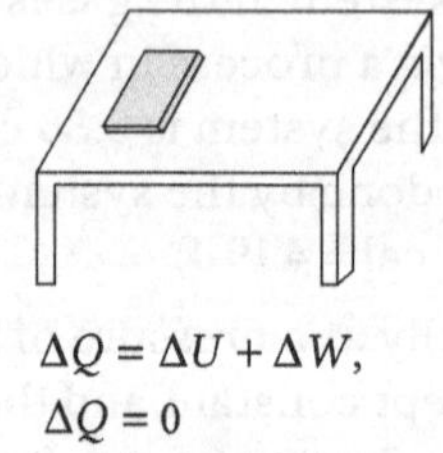

In $\Delta Q = \Delta U + \Delta W,$
for $\Delta Q = 0$

$$0 = \Delta U + \Delta W \Rightarrow \Delta W = -\Delta U$$

If ΔU is negative, then ΔW is positive. Theoretically possible, but not observed practically.

4. (*d*) For isothermal expansion,

$$\Delta U = 0 \Rightarrow \Delta Q = \Delta W$$

Here, $\Delta W \rightarrow +\text{ ve} \Rightarrow \Delta Q \rightarrow +\text{ ve}$

5. (*c*) Work done for the small expansion, $dW = p\ dV$
Net work done, $W = \int_{V_1}^{V_2} p\ dV \qquad (\because pV = \mu RT)$

$$W = \mu RT \int_{V_1}^{V_2} \frac{dV}{V} = \mu RT \log \frac{V_2}{V_1}$$

6. (*b*) In adiabatic process, there is no exchange of heat between system and surroundings.
$\Rightarrow \quad \Delta Q = 0$
By first law of thermodynamics
$\Delta Q = \Delta U + \Delta W = 0 \Rightarrow \Delta U = -\Delta W$

7. (*c*) $C = \dfrac{\Delta Q}{\mu \Delta T}$, where $\mu = \dfrac{\text{mass}}{\text{molar mass}} = \dfrac{m}{M}$
C depends on nature and temperature of substance and also varies with pressure and volume of gases.

8. If the system does work against the surroundings so that it compensates for the heat supplied, the temperature can remains constant.

9. During driving, temperature of the gas increases while its volume remains constant. So, according to Charles' law, at constant V, $p \propto T$. Therefore, pressure of gas increases.

10. Because sudden compression of a gas is an adiabatic process.
According to the first law of thermodynamics,

$$\Delta Q = \Delta U + \Delta W$$

$\because \quad \Delta Q = 0$
$\therefore \quad \Delta U = -\Delta W$
$\because \Delta W$ = negative because work done on the gas.
Thus, ΔU increases and gas temperature rises.

11. The conditions for an isothermal process are
(i) The walls should be diathermic.
(ii) The process should be quasi-static.

12. When a gas expands, it does work on the surroundings. This work is done on the expense of internal energy and that is why its internal energy and so its temperature decreases.

13. First law of thermodynamics gives

$$\Delta Q = \Delta U + \Delta W$$

For an isothermal expansion, $\Delta U = 0$.
So, $\quad \Delta Q = \Delta W$
For an isothermal expansion of the ideal gas, work done by the gas is equal to the heat given to the ideal gas.

14. If two isothermal curves intersect, this implies that the pressure and volume of a gas are the same at two different temperatures, that's impossible.

15. Free expansion of gas is a rapid change which cannot be controlled. It does not follow gas equation.

16. Let m_1 and m_2 are masses of bodies with specific heats s_1 and s_2, then if their temperature after they are in thermal equilibrium is T.

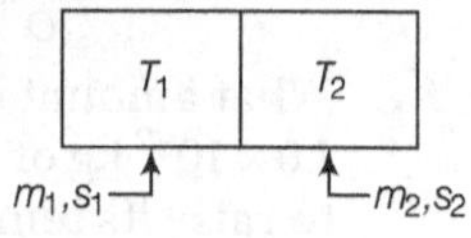

Then, if $T_1 > T > T_2$ and assuming no heat loss.
Heat lost by hot body = heat gained by cold body

$$m_1 s_1 (T_1 - T) = m_2 s_2 (T - T_2) \quad [1]$$

$$\Rightarrow \quad \frac{m_1 s_1 T_1 + m_2 s_2 T_2}{m_1 s_1 + m_2 s_2} = T \text{ [equilibrium temperature]}$$

So for, bodies to settle down to mean temperature,

$$m_1 = m_2 \text{ and } s_1 = s_2$$

means bodies have same specific heat and have equal masses.

Then, $\quad T = \dfrac{T_1 + T_2}{2}$ [mean temperature] [1]

17.

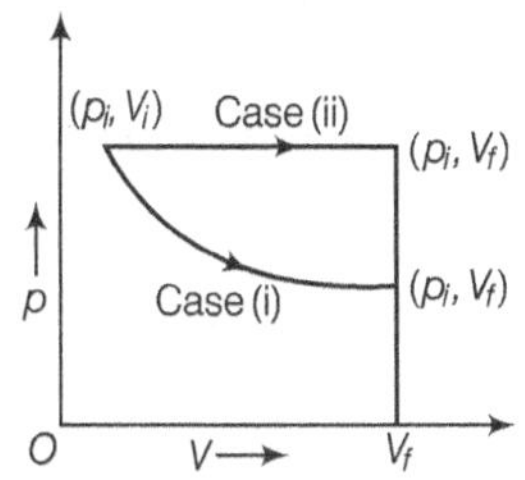

[1]

The p-V diagram for each case is shown in the figure.

In case (i) $p_iV_i = p_fV_f$, therefore process is isothermal.

In case (ii), pressure is constant, work done = area under the p-V curve, so work done is more when the gas expands at constant pressure. [1]

18. When ice melts, volume of water formed is less than that of ice. So, surroundings (environment) does work on the system (ice). And by first law,

$$\Delta Q = \Delta W + \Delta U \Rightarrow \Delta U = \Delta Q - \Delta W \quad [1]$$

(ΔW = negative as work is done on the system)

$$\Rightarrow \quad \Delta U > \Delta Q \quad [1]$$

19. Refer to text on page 379 (Specific heat capacities of gases).

20. (i) $\because$ process is adiabatic

$\therefore \quad \Delta Q = 0$

Work done on the gas, $\Delta W = -500\text{J}$

According to the first law of thermodynamics.

$$\Delta Q = \Delta U + \Delta W \Rightarrow \Delta U = -\Delta W = 500\text{J} \quad [1]$$

(ii) This is because heat absorbed by a substance (coolant) is directly proportional to the specific heat of the substance. [1/2]

(iii) Refer to Sol. 9 on page 384. [1]

(iv) This is because in a harbour town, the relative humidity is more than in a desert town. Hence, the climate of a harbour town is without extremes of hot and cold. [1/2]

21. (i) In figure, portion AB of the cycle involved increases in pressure/temperature of gas at constant volume. Therefore, the system gains heat from the surroundings.

$$Q_{AB} = U_{AB} \quad [\because W = 0]$$

$$= \frac{3}{2}R(T_B - T_A) = \frac{3}{2}(p_BV_B - p_AV_A) \quad [\because \Delta U = nC_V\Delta T]$$

$$= \frac{3}{2}(p_B - p_A)V_A \quad [\because V_B = V_A] \quad [1]$$

(ii) In the portion BC, the gas increases in volume at constant pressure. Heat required for this is gained from surroundings.

$$Q_{BC} = U_{BC} + W_{BC} = \frac{3}{2}(p_CV_C - p_BV_B) + p_B(V_C - V_B)$$

$$= \frac{5}{2}p_B(V_C - V_B) \quad [\because p_C = p_B]$$

$$Q_{BC} = \frac{5}{2}p_B(V_C - V_A) \quad [1]$$

(iii) As CD represents an adiabatic change, therefore, $Q_{CD} = 0$. [1/2]

(iv) DA involves compression of gas from V_D to V_A at constant pressure p_A. Work is done on the gas (negative).

$$\Delta Q_{DA} = \Delta U_{DA} + \Delta W_{DA}$$

$$= \frac{3}{2}R(T_A - T_D) + p_A(V_A - V_D)$$

$$= \frac{3}{2}p_A(V_A - V_D) + p_A(p_A - V_D)$$

$$= \frac{5}{2}p_A(V_A - V_D) \quad [1/2]$$

22. Consider (say μ mole) an ideal gas, which is undergoing an adiabatic expansion. Let the gas expands by an infinitesimally small volume dV, at pressure p, then the infinitesimally small work done given by

$$dW = pdV$$

The net work done from an initial volume V_1 to final volume V_2 is given by

$$W = \int_{V_1}^{V_2} pdV \quad [1]$$

For an adiabatic process, pV^γ = constant = K

$$p = \frac{K}{V^\gamma} = KV^{-\gamma}$$

$$\therefore \quad W = \int_{V_1}^{V_2}(KV^{-\gamma})\,dV = K\left[\frac{V^{-\gamma+1}}{-\gamma+1}\right]_{V_1}^{V_2}$$

$$= \frac{KV_2^{-\gamma+1} - KV_1^{-\gamma+1}}{(1-\gamma)} \quad [1]$$

For an adiabatic process,

$$K = p_1V_1^\gamma = p_2V_2^\gamma$$

$$\Rightarrow \quad W = \frac{p_2V_2^\gamma \cdot V_2^{-\gamma+1} - p_1V_1^\gamma \cdot V_2^{-\gamma+1}}{(1-\gamma)}$$

$$= \frac{1}{(1-\gamma)}(p_2V_2 - p_1V_1)$$

For an ideal gas, $p_1V_1 = \mu RT_1$ and $p_2V_2 = \mu RT_2$. So, we have

$$W = \frac{1}{(1-\gamma)}[\mu RT_2 - \mu RT_1] = \frac{\mu R}{(\gamma - 1)}[T_1 - T_2] \quad [1]$$

23. (i) $p_i = p_a$ [1/2]

(ii) $p_f = p_a + \frac{k}{A}(V - V_0)$ [1/2]

(iii) According to first law of thermodynamics,

$$\Delta Q = \Delta U + \Delta W, \text{ where}$$

$$\Delta U = C_V(T - T_0),\ \Delta W = p_a(V - V_0) + \frac{1}{2}k(V - V_0)^2$$

$$(\because A = 1 \text{ unity}^2)$$

$$\Delta Q = p_a(V - V_0) + \frac{1}{2}k(V - V_0)^2 + C_V(T - T_0)$$

where, $T_0 = p_aV_0/R$,

$$\Rightarrow \quad T = [p_a + (K/A) \times (V - V_0)]\,V/R \quad [2]$$

24. (i) Work done by the gas (let $pV^{1/2} = A$)

$$\Delta W = \int_{V_1}^{V_2} p\,dV = A\int_{V_1}^{V_2} \frac{dV}{\sqrt{V}} = A\left[\frac{\sqrt{V}}{1/2}\right]_{V_1}^{V_2}$$

$$= 2A(\sqrt{V_2} - \sqrt{V_1}) = 2p_1V_1^{1/2}[V_2^{1/2} - V_1^{1/2}] \quad [1]$$

(ii) Since, $T = pV/nR = \frac{A}{nR}\cdot\sqrt{V}$

Thus, $\frac{T_2}{T_1} = \sqrt{\frac{V_2}{V_1}} = \sqrt{2}$ [1]

(iii) Then, the change in internal energy

$$\Delta U = U_2 - U_1 = \frac{3}{2}R(T_2 - T_1) = \frac{3}{2}RT_1(\sqrt{2}-1)$$

$$\Delta W = 2A\sqrt{V_1}(\sqrt{2}-1) = 2RT_1(\sqrt{2}-1)$$

According to first law of thermodynamics,

$$\Delta Q = \Delta U + \Delta W \Rightarrow \Delta Q = (7/2)RT_1(\sqrt{2}-1) \quad [1]$$

25. Refer to text on pages 379 and 380 (Relation between C_p and C_V).

26. (i) Refer to text on pages 373 and 374 (First law of thermodynamics as energy balance).

(ii) Refer to text on page 379 (Specific heat capacity, molar specific heat capacity).

(iii) Refer to text on page 379 (Mechanical equivalence of heat).

27. For isothermal process, pV = constant

For adiabatic process, pV^{γ} = constant

$\gamma = \frac{5}{3}$ for monoatomic gas = 1.66

$\gamma = \frac{7}{5} = 1.4$ for diatomic gas

$\gamma = \frac{8}{6} = 1.33$ for triatomic gas [2]

and slope increases with γ, so

For Ist, $\gamma = 1$, an isotherm

For IInd, $\gamma = 1.33$

For IIIrd, $\gamma = 1.4$

For IVth, $\gamma = 1.66$ [2]

So, graph I is isothermal,

Graph II is triatomic adiabatic,

Graph III is diatomic adiabatic,

Graph IV is monoatomic adiabatic. [1]

28. Slope of $p = f(V)$, curve at $(V_0, p_0) = f(V_0)$

Slope of adiabat at (V_0, p_0)

$$= K(-\gamma)V_0^{-1-\gamma} = -\gamma p_0/V_0 \quad [1]$$

Now, heat absorbed in the process $p = f(V)$

$$dQ = dU + dW$$

$$= nC_V dT + p\,dV \quad [1]$$

Since, $T = (1/nR)\,pV = (1/nR)\,V\,f(V)$

$$\therefore \quad dT = (1/nR)[f(V) + V f'(V)]\,dV \quad [1]$$

Thus, $$\left.\frac{dQ}{dV}\right|_{V=V_0} = \frac{C_V}{R}[f(V_0) + V_0 f'(V_0)] + f(V_0)$$

$$= \left[\frac{1}{\gamma - 1} + 1\right] f(V_0) + \frac{V_0 f'(V_0)}{\gamma - 1}$$

$$= \frac{\gamma}{\gamma - 1}p_0 + \frac{V_0}{\gamma - 1}f'(V_0) \quad [1]$$

Heat is absorbed when $dQ/dV > 0$ when gas expands, that is when $\gamma p_0 + V_0 f'(V_0) > 0$

$$f'(V_0) > -\gamma p_0/V_0 \quad [1]$$

29. (i) A to B because $T_B > T_A$, as $p \propto T$ [$\because V$ constant] [1/2]

(ii) C to D because $T_C > T_D$, as $p \propto T$ [$\because V$ constant] [1/2]

(iii) $W_{AB} = \int_A^B p\,dV = 0$ and $W_{CD} = 0$ [$\because V$ constant]

Similarly, $$W_{BC} = \int_B^C p\,dV = K\int_B^C \frac{dV}{V^{\gamma}} = K\left[\frac{V^{-\gamma+1}}{-\gamma+1}\right]_{V_B}^{V_C}$$

[$\because pV^{\gamma} = K$]

$$= \frac{1}{1-\gamma}(p_CV_C - p_BV_B)$$

Similarly, $$W_{DA} = \frac{1}{1-\gamma}(p_AV_A - p_DV_D) \quad [1]$$

Now, $$p_C = p_B\left(\frac{V_B}{V_C}\right)^{\gamma} = 2^{-\gamma}p_B \quad [\because V_C = 2V_B]$$

Similarly, $p_D = p_A 2^{-\gamma}$

Total work done $= W_{BC} + W_{DA}$

$$= \frac{1}{1-\gamma}[p_BV_B(2^{-\gamma+1} - 1) - p_AV_A(2^{-\gamma+1} - 1)]$$

$$= \frac{1}{1-\gamma}(2^{1-\gamma} - 1)(p_B - p_A)V_A \quad [\because V_A = V_B]$$

$$= \frac{3}{2}\left[1 - \left(\frac{1}{2}\right)^{2/3}\right](p_B - p_A)V_A \quad [1]$$

(iv) Heat supplied during process A to B

$$dQ_{AB} = dU_{AB}$$

$$Q_{AB} = \frac{3}{2}nR(T_B - T_A) = \frac{3}{2}(p_B - p_A)V_A \quad [1]$$

$$\text{Efficiency} = \frac{\text{Net work done}}{\text{Heat supplied}} = \left[1 - \left(\frac{1}{2}\right)^{2/3}\right] \quad [1]$$

30. Heat energy supplied per second by the heater

$$\Delta Q = 100 \text{ W} = 100 \text{ J/s}$$

Work done by the system $(\Delta W) = +75$ J/s

Rate of change in internal energy $(\Delta U) = ?$

According to first law of thermodynamics,

$$\Delta U = \Delta Q - \Delta W = 100 - 75 = 25 \text{ J/s} = 25 \text{ W}$$

31. Given, $R = 8.31 \text{J mol}^{-1}\text{K}^{-1}$ and $\gamma = 1.41$

We know, $C_V = \dfrac{R}{(\gamma - 1)} = \dfrac{8.31}{(1.41 - 1)} = 20.3 \text{ Jmol}^{-1}\text{K}^{-1}$

$\because \quad \dfrac{C_p}{C_V} = \gamma \Rightarrow C_p = C_V \cdot \gamma$

$= 20.3 \times 1.41 = 28.623 \text{J/mol-K}$

32. For path 1, Heat given $Q_1 = +1000 \text{J}$

Work done $= W_1$ [Let]

For path 2, Work done $W_2 = (W_1 - 100) \text{J}$

Heat given $Q_2 = ?$

As change in internal energy between two states for different path is same.

$$\Delta U = Q_1 - W_1 = Q_2 - W_2$$

$$1000 - W_1 = Q_2 - (W_1 - 100)$$

$$Q_2 = 1000 - 100 = 900 \text{ J}$$ [2]

33. Here, mass of gas, $m = 2 \times 10^{-2}$ kg = 20 g

Rise in temperature, $\Delta T = 45°\text{C}$

Heat required, $\Delta Q = ?$

Molecular mass, $M = 28$

Number of moles, $n = \dfrac{m}{M} = \dfrac{20}{28} = 0.714$

As nitrogen is a diatomic gas, molar specific heat at constant pressure is

$$C_p = \frac{7}{2} R = \frac{7}{2} \times 8.3 \text{J mol}^{-1}\text{K}^{-1}$$ [1]

As $\quad \Delta Q = nC_p \Delta T$

$\therefore \quad \Delta Q = 0.714 \times \dfrac{7}{2} \times 8.3 \times 45 \text{ J} = 933.4 \text{ J}$ [1]

34. Here, volume of water heated = 3.0 L/min

Mass of water heated, $m = 3000$ g/min

Rise in temperature, $\Delta T = 77 - 27 = 50° \text{C}$

Specific heat of water, $C = 4.2 \text{ J g}^{-1} \text{°C}^{-1}$

Amount of heat used, $\Delta Q = mC \Delta T = 3000 \times 4.2 \times 50$

$= 63 \times 10^4 \text{ J/min}$

Heat of combustion $= 4 \times 10^4$ J/g [1]

Rate of combustion of fuel $= \dfrac{63 \times 10^4}{4 \times 10^4} = 15.75$ g / min [1]

35. As no heat is allowed to be exchanged, the process is adiabatic.

$\therefore \quad p_2 V_2^\gamma = p_1 V_1^\gamma$ or $\dfrac{p_2}{p_1} = \left(\dfrac{V_1}{V_2}\right)^\gamma$ [1]

As $\quad V_2 = \dfrac{1}{2} V_1$

or $\quad \dfrac{p_2}{p_1} = \left(\dfrac{V_1}{1/2 V_1}\right)^{1.4} = 2^{1.4} = 2.64$ [1]

36. From figure, change in pressure,

$$dp = DF = 600 - 300 = 300 \text{ Nm}^{-2}$$ [1]

Change in volume, $dV = EF = 5 - 2 = 3 \text{ m}^3$ [1]

Work done by the gas from D to E to F = area of ΔDEF

$$W = \frac{1}{2} \times EF \times DF = \frac{1}{2} \times 300 \times 3 = 450 \text{J}$$ [1]

37. Given, work done $(W) = -22.3$ J

Work done is taken negative as work is done on the system.

In an adiabatic change, $\Delta Q = 0$

Using first law of thermodynamics,

$$\Delta U = \Delta Q - W = 0 - (-22.3) = 22.3 \text{ J}$$ [1]

For another process between states A and B,

Heat absorbed $(\Delta Q) = +9.35$ cal

$= +(9.35 \times 4.19) \text{ J} = +39.18 \text{ J}$ [1]

Change in internal energy between two states *via* different paths are equal.

$\therefore \quad \Delta U = 22.3 \text{ J}$

$\therefore$ From first law of thermodynamics,

$\Delta U = \Delta Q - W$

or $\quad W = \Delta Q - \Delta U = 39.18 - 22.3 = 16.88 \text{ J} \approx 16.9 \text{ J}$ [1]

38. First draw p-V diagram as shown below.

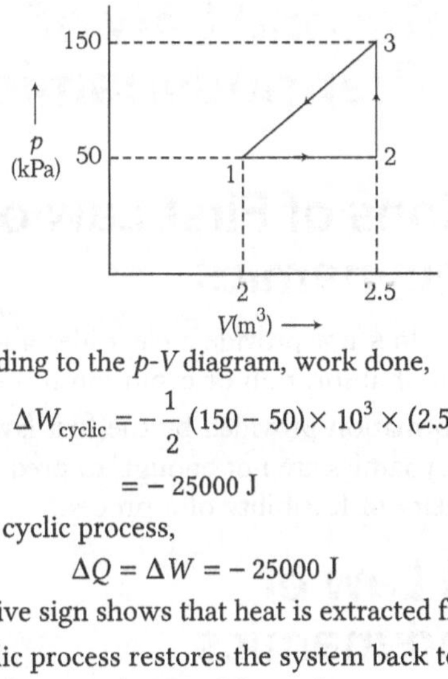

[1]

According to the p-V diagram, work done,

$$\Delta W_{\text{cyclic}} = -\frac{1}{2}(150 - 50) \times 10^3 \times (2.5 - 2.0)$$

$= -25000$ J [1]

In the cyclic process,

$$\Delta Q = \Delta W = -25000 \text{ J}$$ [1]

Negative sign shows that heat is extracted from the gas.

39. A cyclic process restores the system back to its initial state after completion of the cycle. [1]

As internal energy is a state function, so its value at initial point is same as that at final point (initial state is same as that of final state). [1]

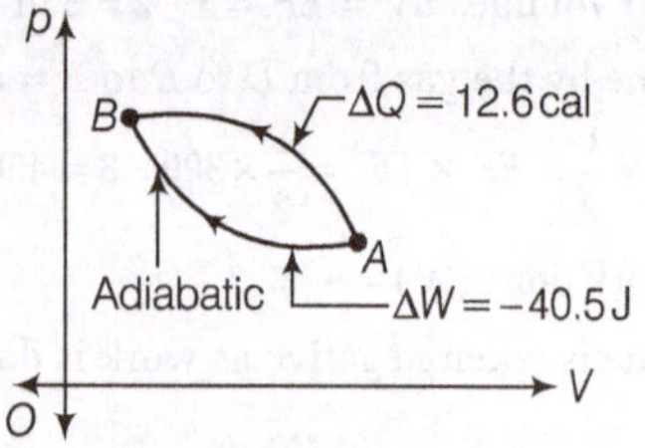

For adiabatic process $A \to B$,

$\Delta Q = 0$, so by first law of thermodynamics,

$$\Delta Q = \Delta W + \Delta U$$

or $\Delta U = -\Delta W = -(-40.5) = 40.5\text{ J}$ [1]

For another process $A \to B$,

$$\Delta Q = +12.6\text{ cal} = 12.6 \times 4.19\text{ J} = 52.8\text{ J}$$ [1/2]

and by first law of thermodynamics,

$$\Delta Q = \Delta W + \Delta U \Rightarrow \Delta W = \Delta Q - \Delta U$$

$\Rightarrow$ $\Delta W = 52.8 - 40.5 = 12.3\text{ J}$

[as ΔU is a state function, ΔU_{AB} is same for this process also] [1½]

40. According to the Mayor's formula,

$$C_V = C_p - R = \frac{5R}{2} - R = \frac{3R}{2}, \Delta V = 0, T_1 = 300\text{ K},$$

$$V = 0.0083\text{ m}^3, \; p_1 = 1.6 \times 10^6\text{ Nm}^{-2}$$ [1]

From first law of thermodynamics,

$$Q = \Delta U + p\Delta V$$

$\Rightarrow$ $\Delta U = Q = 2.49 \times 10^4\text{ J}$ [1]

From gas equation, $n = \frac{pV}{RT} = \frac{1.6 \times 10^6 \times 0.0083}{8.3 \times 300} = \frac{16}{3}$

$\therefore$ $\Delta U = nC_V\Delta T$

$\Rightarrow$ $\Delta T = \frac{\Delta U}{nC_V} = \frac{2.49 \times 10^4 \times 6}{3 \times 8.3 \times 16} = 375\text{ K}$ [1]

Final temperature $= 300 + 375 = 675\text{ K}$

As volume remains constant, $p \propto T \Rightarrow \frac{p_2}{p_1} = \frac{T_2}{T_1}$ [1]

$\Rightarrow$ $p_2 = \frac{T_2}{T_1} \times p_1 = \frac{1.6 \times 10^6 \times 675}{300}$

$= 3.6 \times 10^6\text{ Nm}^{-2}$ [1]

TOPIC 02 Second Law of Thermodynamics

Limitations of First Law of Thermodynamics

(i) First law does not provide a clear idea about the direction of absorption or evolution of heat.

(ii) The information provided by the first law of thermodynamics are not enough to predict the spontaneity of feasibility of a process.

Second Law of Thermodynamics

There are many processes which are based on energy conservation but it is not possible in nature.

e.g. A ball lying on a floor could jump upto some height by itself gaining some heat energy from the ground. This process is possible according to first law (energy conservation) but not actually possible in nature.

It means that some additional basic principle of nature forbids the above process, even though it satisfy the energy conservation. The principle that put a restriction on the first law of thermodynamics is known as the **second law of thermodynamics.**

The second law of thermodynamics gives a fundamental limitation to the efficiency of a heat engine and the coefficient of performance of a refrigerator. Two statements of Kelvin-Planck and Clausius put restrictions on the possibility of perfect heat engine and perfect refrigerator, respectively.

Kelvin-Planck's Statement

No process is possible whose sole result is the absorption of heat from a reservoir and the complete conversion of the heat into work.

Clausius' Statement

No process is possible whose sole result is the transfer of heat from a colder object to a hotter object.

PMM1 and PMM2

Any device that violates the first law of thermodynamics (by creating energy) is called a **perpetual motion machine** of the first kind (PMM1) and the device that violates the second law is called a perpetual motion machine of the second kind (PMM2).

Example 1 Is it possible to convert all the heat extracted from a hot body into work?

Sol. No, heat cannot be converted into work completely because a part of heat is rejected and remaining part is converted into work.

Reversible and Irreversible Process

Reversible Process

A process which could be reserved in such a way that the system and its surrounding returns exactly to their initial states with no other changes in the universe is known as **reversible process.**

e.g. If heat is absorbed in the direct process, then same amount of heat should be given out in the reverse process. If work is done on the working substance in the direct process, then the same amount of work should be done by the working substance in the reverse process.

The conditions for reversibility are

(i) There must be complete absence of dissipative forces such as friction, viscosity, electric resistance etc.

(ii) The direct and reverse processes must take place infinitely slowly.

(iii) The temperature of the system must not differ appreciably from its surroundings.

Ideal Engine is Practically not Possible

Irreversibility is the rule of nature. It means that a change happened in the universe cannot be exactly reversed. That is why, any engine cannot have 100% efficiency. If we could eliminate all the resistive forces, the efficiency of an engine could be maximised. For future, some trains are proposed that will move in a vacuum tunnel to eliminate the air friction and hence to increase the efficiency of the engine.

Irreversible Process

Any process which is not reversible exactly is an **irreversible process.** All natural processes such as conduction, radiation, radioactive decay etc., are irreversible processes. All practical processes such as free expansion, Joule-Thomson expansion, electrical heating of a wire are also irreversible.

Irreversibility arises mainly from two causes

(i) Many processes (like diffusion of gases, decay of organic matter) take the system to non-equilibrium states.

(ii) Many processes involve the dissipative forces like friction, viscosity, inelasticity, etc.

Carnot Engine

Carnot engine is an ideal heat engine proposed by **Sadi Carnot** in 1824. The reversible engine which operates between two temperatures of source (T_1) and sink (T_2) is known as **Carnot heat engine.**

The designed engine is a theoretical engine which is free from all the defects of a practical engine. This engine cannot be realised in actual practice, however, this can be taken as a standard against which the performance of an actual engine can be judged.

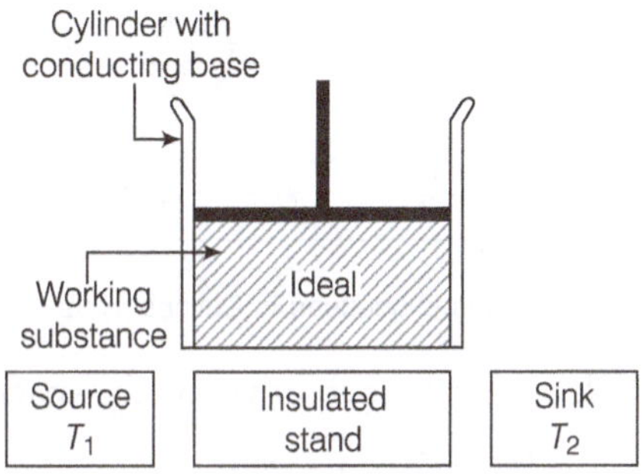

A Carnot engine

Parts of Carnot Engine

Cylinder

The cylinder has conducting base and insulating walls. It consists an ideal gas as a working substance insulating and frictionless piston is attached with it as shown in the figure.

Source

It is a hot reservoir at a temperature T_1 with conducting walls. It has infinite thermal capacity. Any amount of heat can be taken from it without changing the temperature.

Sink

It is a cold reservoir at temperature T_2. It has infinite thermal capacity so any amount of heat can be rejected to it without changing the temperature.

Working Substance

We use an ideal gas as a working substance in the cylinder.

Insulating Stand

The base of the cylinder could be placed on the insulating stand, to isolate it completely from the surroundings.

Carnot Cycle

As the engine works, the working substance of the engine undergoes a cycle known as **Carnot cycle.**

The Carnot cycle consists of the following four strokes

First Stroke (Isothermal Expansion) (Curve *AB*)

The cylinder containing one mole of an ideal gas as working substance allowed to expand slowly at the constant temperature T_1 by putting it on the source.

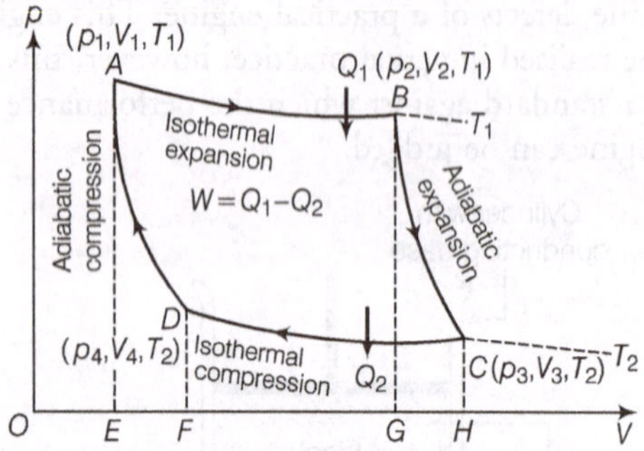

Various processes in Carnot cycle

Work done = heat absorbed by the system

$$W_1 = Q_1 = \int_{V_1}^{V_2} pdV$$

$$= RT_1 \log_e\left(\frac{V_2}{V_1}\right) = \text{area of } ABGEA$$

Second Stroke (Adiabatic Expansion) (Curve *BC*)

The cylinder is then placed on the non-conducting stand and the gas is allowed to expand adiabatically till the temperature falls from T_1 to T_2.

$$W_2 = \int_{V_2}^{V_3} pdV = \frac{R}{(\gamma - 1)}(T_1 - T_2) = \text{area } BCHGB$$

Third Stroke (Isothermal Compression) (Curve *CD*)

The cylinder is placed on the sink and the gas is compressed at constant temperature T_2.

Work done = heat released by the system

$$W_3 = Q_2 = -\int_{V_3}^{V_4} pdV = -RT_2 \log_e \frac{V_4}{V_3}$$

$$= RT_2 \log_e \frac{V_3}{V_4} = \text{area } CDFHC$$

Fourth Stroke (Adiabatic Compression) (Curve *DA*)

Finally, the cylinder is again placed on non-conducting stand and the compression is continued so that gas returns to its initial stage.

$$W_4 = -\int_{V_4}^{V_1} pdV = -\frac{R}{\gamma - 1}(T_2 - T_1)$$

$$= \frac{R}{\gamma - 1}(T_1 - T_2) = \text{area of } ADFEA$$

Efficiency of Carnot Cycle (Engine)

The efficiency of engine is defined as the ratio of work done to the heat supplied, i.e.

$$\eta = \frac{\text{Work done}}{\text{Heat input}} = \frac{W_{net}}{Q_1}$$

Net work done during the complete cycle

$$W = W_1 + W_2 + (-W_3) + (-W_4)$$

$$= W_1 - W_3 = \text{area } ABCDA \quad [\text{as } W_2 = W_4]$$

$$\therefore \quad \eta = \frac{W}{Q_1} = \frac{W_1 - W_3}{W_1} = \frac{Q_1 - Q_2}{Q_1} = 1 - \frac{Q_2}{Q_1}$$

or $$\eta = 1 - \frac{RT_2 \log_e (V_3/V_4)}{RT_1 \log_e (V_2/V_1)}$$

Since, points *B* and *C* lie on same adiabatic curve

$$\therefore \quad T_1V_2^{\gamma-1} = T_2V_3^{\gamma-1} \quad \text{or} \quad \frac{T_1}{T_2} = \left(\frac{V_3}{V_2}\right)^{\gamma-1} \quad \ldots\text{(i)}$$

Also, points *D* and *A* lie on the same adiabatic curve

$$\therefore \quad T_1V_1^{\gamma-1} = T_2V_4^{\gamma-1}$$

or $$\frac{T_1}{T_2} = \left(\frac{V_4}{V_1}\right)^{\gamma-1} \quad \ldots\text{(ii)}$$

From Eqs. (i) and (ii), we get

$$\frac{V_3}{V_2} = \frac{V_4}{V_1}$$

or $$\frac{V_3}{V_4} = \frac{V_2}{V_1}$$

$$\Rightarrow \quad \log_e\left(\frac{V_3}{V_4}\right) = \log_e\left(\frac{V_2}{V_1}\right)$$

So, $$\boxed{\text{Efficiency of Carnot engine, } \eta = 1 - \frac{T_2}{T_1}}$$

- The efficiency of the Carnot engine depends only on the temperatures of source and sink.
- The efficiency of Carnot engine does not depend on the nature of the working substance.
- The efficiency of Carnot engine will be 100%, if the temperature of the sink is 0 K. As practically, we cannot attain a sink at 0 K, so it is not possible to have 100% efficiency.

Carnot Theorems

According to Carnot theorem,

(i) A heat engine working between the two given temperatures T_1 of hot reservoir (source) and T_2 of cold reservoir (sink) cannot have efficiency more than that of the Carnot engine.

(ii) The efficiency of the Carnot engine is independent of the nature of working susbtance..

We can prove the part (ii) of Carnot theorem as below.

Suppose a reversible Carnot engine R and an irreversible heat engine I, working between the same source T_1 and same sink T_2 as shown in figure.

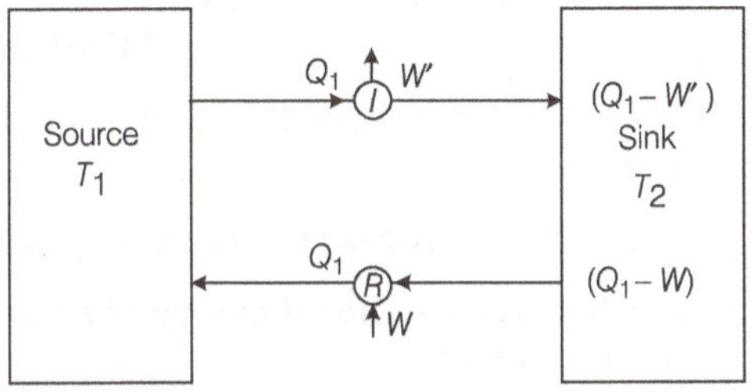

Reversible and irreversible heat engine act together

Suppose the two engines are coupled in such a way that irreversible engine I acts like a heat engine and reversible Carnot engine R acts like a refrigerator. In one complete cycle, the engine I absorbs heat Q_1 from the source, deliver work W' and release the balance $(Q_1 - W')$ to the sink. The engine R returns the same heat Q_1 to the source when work W is done on it in one full cycle. Therefore, it would take heat $(Q_1 - W)$ from the sink as shown in figure.

Let us assume that the efficiency of reversible engine R is less than that of I, i.e. $\eta_R < \eta_I$.

For Q_1, $\quad W < W'$ and $(Q_1 - W) > (Q_1 - W')$

Thus, the coupled I-R system on whole extracts heat $(Q_1 - W) - (Q_1 - W') = (W' - W)$ from the sink and delivers the same amount of work $(W' - W)$ in one cycle without any change in the source. So, it is against the second law of thermodynamics.

Hence, the assertion $\eta_I > \eta_R$ is wrong. No engine can have efficiency greater than that of the Carnot engine. Thus, this proves the first part of Carnot theorem.

Coefficient of Performance of Carnot Engine

For Carnot refrigerator, $\dfrac{Q_1}{Q_2} = \dfrac{T_1}{T_2}$

$$\Rightarrow \quad \frac{Q_1 - Q_2}{Q_2} = \frac{T_1 - T_2}{T_2} \quad \text{or} \quad \frac{Q_2}{Q_1 - Q_2} = \frac{T_2}{T_1 - T_2}$$

So, $$\boxed{\text{Coefficient of performance, } \beta = \frac{T_2}{T_1 - T_2}}$$

where, T_1 = temperature of surrounding,

T_2 = temperature of cold body.

It is clear that $\beta = 0$ when $T_2 = 0$, i.e. the coefficient of performance will be zero, if the cold body is at the temperature equal to absolute zero.

Example 2 Consider a Carnot cycle operating between $T_1 = 500$ K and $T_2 = 300$ K producing 1 kJ of mechanical work per cycle. Find the heat transferred to/by the engine by/to the reservoir. **NCERT Exemplar**

Sol. Here, $T_1 = 500\,\text{K}$, $T_2 = 300\,\text{K}$, $W = 1\,\text{kJ} = 1000\,\text{J}$

As, efficiency, $\eta = \dfrac{W}{Q} = \dfrac{T_1 - T_2}{T_1}$

So, heat transferred to engine by the hot reservoir in cycle

$$Q_1 = \frac{WT_1}{T_1 - T_2} = \frac{1000 \times 500}{500 - 300} = 2500\text{ J or } 2.5\text{ kJ}$$

and heat transferred by the engine to the cold reservoir in one cycle

$$Q_2 = Q_1 - W = 2.5\text{ kJ} - 1\text{ kJ} = 1.5\text{ kJ}$$

Example 3 A refrigerator has to transfer an average of 263 J of heat per second from temperature −10° C to 25° C. Calculate the average power consumed, assuming no energy losses in the process.

Sol. Given, $Q_2 = 263\,\text{J/s}$, $T_2 = -10°\text{C} = -10 + 273 = 263\,\text{K}$

and $T_1 = 25°\text{C} = 25 + 273 = 298\,\text{K}$,

$$\beta = \frac{Q_2}{W} = \frac{T_2}{T_1 - T_2}$$

$$\Rightarrow \text{Average power, } W = \frac{Q_2(T_1 - T_2)}{T_2} = \frac{263\,(298 - 263)}{263}$$

$$= 35\text{ J/s} = 35\text{ W}$$

Example 4 A Carnot engine takes 10^6 cal of heat from a source at 827°C and exhaust it to a sink 27°C. How much work does it gives as output? What is engine efficiency? Also, find out the coefficient of performance of the engine, if it is used in reverse direction.

Sol. Given, $T_1 = 827 + 273 = 1100\,\text{K}$

$$T_2 = 27 + 273 = 300\,\text{K}, \; Q_1 = 10^6\text{ cal}$$

$$Q_2 = \frac{T_2}{T_1} \times Q_1 = \frac{300}{1100} \times 10^6 = 2.72 \times 10^5\text{ cal}$$

$$\text{Efficiency } (\eta) = \left(1 - \frac{T_2}{T_1}\right) \times 100\% = \left(1 - \frac{300}{1100}\right) \times 100 = 72.72\%$$

As, $\beta = \dfrac{T_2}{T_1 - T_2}$ = coefficient of performance

$$= \frac{300}{1100 - 300} = \frac{300}{800} = 0.375$$

Example 5 A Carnot engine with ideal gas is used for freezing water which is at 0°C. The engine is operated by a 500 W electric motor having an efficiency of 50%. Find time to freeze 25 kg of water. Take 25°C and 0°C as the source and sink. Latent heat of ice = 333×10^3 J kg^{-1}.

Sol. Write the given

Here, $T_1 = 273$ K, $T_2 = 25 + 273 = 298$ K

$$L = 333 \times 10^3 \text{ J kg}^{-1}$$

Efficiency of electric motor = 50%

Find out the used power of the engine.

= 50% of 500 W = 250 W

Write the formula of coefficient of performance.

$$\beta = \frac{Q_2}{W} = \frac{T_2}{T_1 - T_2}$$

Heat extracted from water in unit time.

$$Q_2 = \frac{T_2}{T_1 - T_2} \times W = \frac{273}{298 - 273} \times 250 = 2730.0 \text{ Js}^{-1}$$

Total heat extracted from 25 kg water to freeze it into ice

$$Q = mL = 25 \times 333 \times 10^3 \text{ J}$$

Total time taken in freezing water into ice.

$$= \frac{Q}{Q_2} = \frac{25 \times 333 \times 10^3}{2730} = 3049.45 \text{ s}$$

Topic Practice 2

Multiple Choice Questions

(1 Mark)

1. Choose the correct option.
(a) First law of thermodynamics is the only law of thermodynamics
(b) Second law puts some limitations on first law
(c) Reversibility is the rule of nature
(d) None of the above

2. According to Carnot, which type of engine working between two temperatures T_1 and T_2 have maximum efficiency?
(a) Reversible engine (b) Irreversible engine
(c) Any heat engine (d) None of these

3. For Carnot engine, which process should be chosen to take the working substance from T_1 to T_2 or *vice-versa*?
(a) Isochoric (b) Isothermal
(c) Adiabatic (d) Isobaric

Very Short Answer Type Questions

(1 Mark)

4. Which thermodynamic law put restrictions on the complete conversion of heat into work?

5. What is the significance of second law of thermodynamics?

6. Is reversible process possible in nature?

7. What are the forces which make any process irreversible?

8. If a refrigerator's door is kept open, will the room become cool or hot? Explain. **NCERT Exemplar**

9. Can we design a reversible Carnot engine in practice?

10. What type of process is a Carnot cycle?

11. On what factors, the efficiency of a Carnot engine depends?

12. If the temperature of the sink is increased, what will happen to the efficiency of Carnot engine?

13. How is the efficiency of a Carnot engine affected by the nature of the working substance?

Short Answer Type I Questions

(2 Marks)

14. Explain the limitations of the first law of thermodynamics.

15. Draw p-V diagram of a Carnot cycle.

16. Under what condition, an ideal Carnot engine has 100% efficiency?

Short Answer Type II Questions

(3 Marks)

17. Find out whether these phenomena are reversible or not.
(i) Waterfall and (ii) Rusting of iron.

18. An ideal engine works between temperatures T_1 and T_2. It derives an ideal refrigerator that works between temperatures T_3 and T_4. Find the ratio Q_3/Q_1 in terms of T_1, T_2, T_3 and T_4.

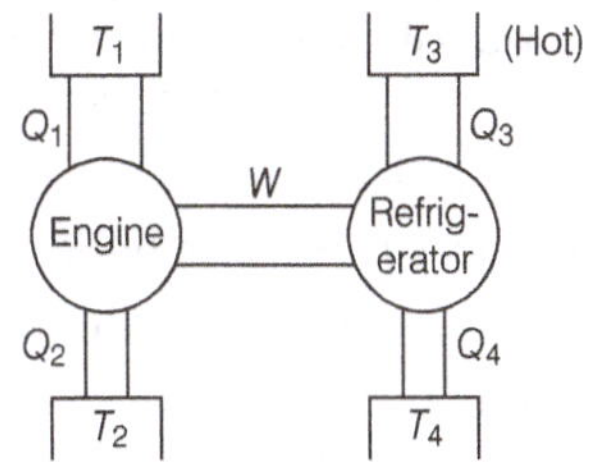

19. Temperatures of the hot and cold reservoirs of a Carnot engine is raised by equal amounts. How the efficiency of the Carnot engine affected?

Long Answer Type Questions

5 Marks

20. Two cylinders A and B of equal capacity are connected to each other *via* a stopcock. A contains a gas at standard temperature and pressure. B is completely evacuated. The entire system in thermally insulated. The stopcock is suddenly opened.

Answer the following

(i) What is final pressure of the gas in A and B?

(ii) What is the change in internal energy of the gas?

(iii) What is the change in temperature of the gas?

(iv) Do the intermediate states of the system (before settling to the final equilibrirum state) lie on its p-V-T surface? **NCERT**

21. Explain with the suitable example that a reversible process must be carried slowly and a fast process is necessarily irreversible.

22. State and prove Carnot theorems in details.

Numerical Problems

23. Find the efficiency of the Carnot engine working between boiling point and freezing point of water. **[1 M]**

24. Consider a Carnot cycle operating between $T_1 = 500$ K and $T_2 = 300$ K producing 1 kJ of mechanical work per cycle. Find the heat transferred to the engine by the reservoirs. **NCERT Exemplar [2 M]**

25. A Carnot engine is operating between 600 K and 200 K. Consider that the actual energy produced is 2 kJ per kilocalorie of heat absorbed. Compare the real efficiency with the efficiency of Carnot engine. **[2 M]**

26. A steam engine delivers 5.4×10^8 J of work per min and absorbs 3.6×10^9 J of heat per min from its boiler.

(i) What is the efficiency of the engine?

(ii) How much heat is wasted per minute? **NCERT [2 M]**

27. Two Carnot engines A and B are operated in series. The first one A receives heat at 900 K and rejects it to a reservoir at temperature T. The second engine B operates on this reservoir and rejects heat to a reservoir at 400 K. Calculate temperature T when

(i) efficiencies of both A and B are equal.

(ii) the work outputs of both A and B are equal. **[3 M]**

28. The efficiency of a Carnot engine is 1/2. If the sink temperature is reduced by 100°C, then engine efficiency becomes 2/3. Find **[5 M]**

(i) sink temperature

(ii) source temperature

(iii) Explain, why a Carnot engine cannot have 100% efficiency?

29. Two Carnot engines A and B are operated in series. The first one A receives heat at 800 K and rejects to a reservoir at temperature T K. The second engine B receives the heat rejected by the first engine and in turn rejects to a heat reservoir at 300 K. Calculate the temperature T K for the following cases.

(i) When the outputs of the two engines are equal.

(ii) When the efficiencies of the two engines are equal. **[5 M]**

Hints & Solutions

1. (*b*) Second law puts some limitation on the first law of thermodynamics. In $\Delta Q = \Delta U + \Delta W$, practically $\Delta Q > 0$ imply $\Delta U > 0$, it is not possible to keep $\Delta U = 0$ and $\Delta Q = \Delta W$.

2. (*a*) According to Carnot, for reversible engine, efficiency is maximum.

3. (*c*) For Carnot engine during temperature change, no heat should be absorbed or released from reservoirs. So, it is an adiabatic process.

4. According to second law of thermodynamics, heat energy cannot converted into work completely.

5. It gives a fundamental limitation to the efficiency of a heat engine and the coefficient of performance of a refrigerator.
6. A reversible process is never possible in nature because of dissipative forces and condition for a quasi-static process is not practically possible.
7. All sorts of dissipative forces, e.g. force of friction, viscous drag, electrical resistance, non-elasticity, thermal radiation, convection etc., make a real process irreversible.
8. Here, heat removed is less than the heat supplied and hence the room become hotter.
9. No, we cannot design an ideal Carnot engine in practice.
10. Carnot cycle is a reversible cyclic process through which heat is converted into mechanical work.
11. The efficiency of a carnot engine depends, on the temperature of source of heat and the sink.
12. Efficiency, $\eta = 1 - \frac{T_2}{T_1}$

By increasing (T_2), the efficiency of the Carnot engine will decrease.
13. The efficiency of Carnot engine is independent of the nature of working substance.
14. Refer to text on page 388 (Limitations of first law of thermodynamics).
15. p-V diagram for Carnot cycle

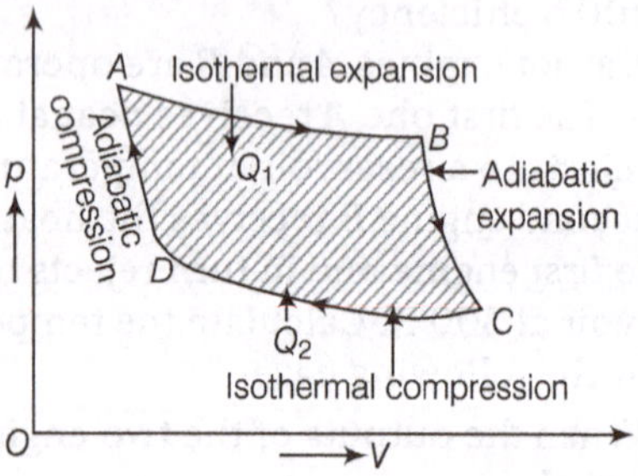

[2]

16. Efficiency of a Carnot engine is given by $\eta = \left(1 - \frac{T_2}{T_1}\right)$

where, T_2 = temperature of sink

and T_1 = temperature of sink source. [1]

So for $\eta = 1$ or 100%, $T_2 = 0$ K or heat is rejected into a sink at 0 K temperature. [1]

17. (i) **Waterfall** The falling of water cannot be reversible process. During the water fall, its potential energy convert into kinetic energy of the water.

On striking the ground, some part of potential energy converts into heat and sound which are not reversible. In nature, it automatically convert the kinetic energy and potential energy so that the water will rise back so waterfall is not a reversible process. [1 ½]

(ii) **Rusting of iron** In rusting of iron, the iron become oxidised with the oxygen of the air as it is a chemical reaction, it cannot be reversed. [1 ½]

18. W = work done by engine = $Q_1 - Q_2$

and W = work done supplied to refrigerator = $Q_3 - Q_4$

$$\Rightarrow \quad Q_1 - Q_2 = Q_3 - Q_4$$ [1]

Dividing by Q_1, $1 - \frac{Q_2}{Q_1} = \frac{Q_3}{Q_1} - \frac{Q_4}{Q_1}$

$$\Rightarrow \quad \frac{Q_3}{Q_1} = 1 - \frac{Q_2}{Q_1} + \frac{Q_4}{Q_1}$$

$$= 1 - \frac{T_2}{T_1} + \frac{T_4}{T_1}$$

$$= \frac{T_1 - T_2 + T_4}{T_1}$$ [1 + 1]

19. Let the initial temperatures of hot and cold reservoirs were T_1 and T_2. The initial efficiency of the Carnot engine is given by

$$\eta = \frac{T_1 - T_2}{T_1} \quad \text{...(i)}$$ [1]

As given, the temperature of both the reservoirs is raised by equal amount t, so $T_1' = T_1 + t$ and $T_2' = T_2 + t$. The final efficiency of the Carnot engine will be

$$\eta' = \frac{T_1' - T_2'}{T_1'} = \frac{(T_1 + t) - (T_2 + t)}{(T_1 + t)}$$

$$= \frac{T_1 - T_2}{(T_1 + t)} \quad \text{...(ii)}$$ [1]

Dividing Eq. (ii) by Eq. (i), we have

$$\frac{\eta'}{\eta} = \frac{\left(\frac{T_1 - T_2}{T_1 + t}\right)}{\left(\frac{T_1 - T_2}{T_1}\right)} = \frac{T_1}{T_1 + t}$$

As $\eta' < \eta$, i.e. the efficiency of Carnot engine decreases. [1]

20. (i) Let capacity of each cylinder be V and atmospheric pressure be p.

$$p_1 = p$$

Initial volume of gas = Volume of the cylinder A

$$\therefore \quad V_1 = V$$

When stopcock is opened, then volume available for gas becomes $2V$

$$\therefore \quad V_2 = 2V$$

Final pressure (p_2) = ?

As system is thermally insulated, therefore there is no change in temperature during the process and hence it is an isothermal process.

For an isothermal process (according to Boyle's law),

$$p_1V_1 = p_2V_2$$

or $$p_2 = p_1\frac{V_1}{V_2} = p \times \frac{V}{2V}$$

$$= \frac{p}{2} = \frac{1}{2} \text{ atm} = 0.5 \text{ atm}$$ [2]

(ii) Change in internal energy, $\Delta U = 0$, as no work is done on or by the gas. [1]

(iii) Change in temperature of the gas is zero as gas does no work in expansion. [1]

(iv) No, because free expansion of gas is rapid and cannot be controlled. The intermediate states are non-equilibrium states and do not satisfy the gas equation. Therefore, the intermediate state of the gas does not be on the p-V-T surface. [1]

21. A reversible process must pass through equilibrium states which are very close to each other so that when process is reversed, it passes back through these equilibrium states. [1]

Then, it is again decompressed or it passes through same equilibrium states, system can be restored to its initial state without any change in surroundings. [2]

e.g. If a gas is compressed as shown

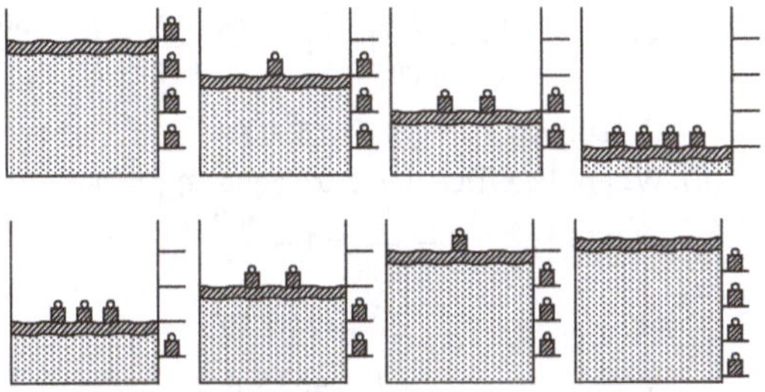

But an irreversible process can proceeds without reaching equilibrium in intermediate states. [1]

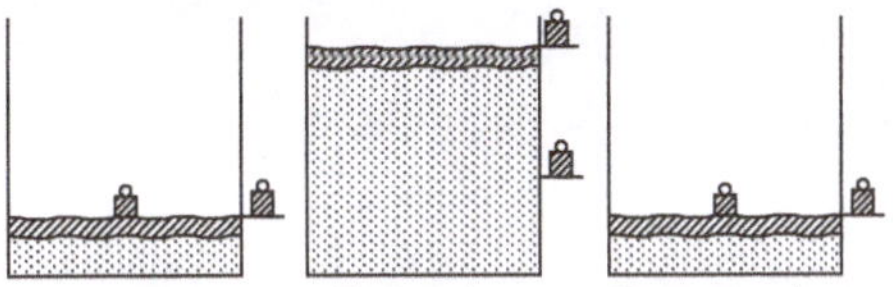

[1]

22. Refer to text on page 391 (Carnot theorems).

23. Efficiency of Carnot engine, $\eta = 1 - \frac{T_2}{T_1}$

$$= 1 - \frac{273 \text{ K}}{373 \text{ K}} = \frac{100}{373} = 0.268 = 26.8\%$$

24. As we know, $\frac{Q_2}{Q_1} = \frac{T_2}{T_1} = \frac{3}{5}$

$\because \quad 1 - \frac{Q_2}{Q_1} = 1 - \frac{T_2}{T_1}$

$\Rightarrow \quad \frac{Q_1 - Q_2}{Q_1} = \frac{500 - 300}{500} \quad [\because Q_1 - Q_2 = W]$ [1]

$\Rightarrow \quad \frac{W}{Q_1} = \frac{2}{5}$

$\therefore \quad Q_1 = 10^3 \times \frac{5}{2} = 2500 \text{J}$ [1]

25. Given, $T_1 = 600 \text{ K}$, $T_2 = 200 \text{ K}$

Efficiency of Carnot engine, $\eta = \frac{T_1 - T_2}{T_1} = \frac{600 - 200}{600}$

$$= \frac{400}{600} = \frac{2}{3} = 66\%$$ [1]

Real efficiency $= \frac{\text{Energy output}}{\text{Energy input}} = \frac{2}{1 \times 4.2} = 0.47 = 47\%$

$\therefore \quad \frac{\text{Real efficiency}}{\text{Carnot engine efficiency}} = \frac{47}{66} = 0.71$ [1]

26. (i) Work done by the engine per min

$$\Delta W = 5.4 \times 10^8 \text{ J} = 0.54 \times 10^9 \text{ J/min}$$

Heat absorbed by engine per min

$$\Delta Q_1 = 3.6 \times 10^9 \text{ J/min}$$

So, engine efficiency, $\eta = \frac{\text{Work done}}{\text{Heat delivered}}$

$$= \frac{0.54 \times 10^9}{3.6 \times 10^9} = 0.15 = 15\%$$ [1]

(ii) Heat wasted per min $=$ heat absorbed $-$ work done

$$= 3.6 \times 10^9 - 0.54 \times 10^9$$

$$= 3.06 \times 10^9 \text{ J / min}$$ [1]

27. (i) Efficiency of A = efficiency of B

$$\eta_A = \eta_B$$

$\Rightarrow \quad 1 - \frac{T}{900} = 1 - \frac{400}{T}$

$\Rightarrow \quad T^2 = 900 \times 400$

$\Rightarrow \quad T = 600 \text{ K}$ [1]

(ii) Let the first engine take Q_1 heat as input at temperature, $T_1 = 800 \ K$

and gives out heat Q_2 at temperature T_0. The second engine receive Q_2 as input and give is out heat Q_3 at temperature $T_3 = 300\text{K}$ to the sink.

Work done by first (A) engine = work done by second (B) engine.

Thus, $\quad Q_1 - Q_2 = Q_2 - Q_3$

Dividing both sides by Q_1

$$1 - \frac{Q_2}{Q_1} = \frac{Q_2}{Q_1} - \frac{Q_3}{Q_1}$$

$\Rightarrow \quad 1 - T/T_1 = \frac{Q_2}{Q_1}\left(1 - \frac{Q_3}{Q_2}\right)$ [1]

$\Rightarrow \quad 1 - T/T_1 = \frac{T}{T_1}(1 - T_3/T)$

$\Rightarrow \quad T_1/T - 1 = 1 - \frac{T_3}{T} \Rightarrow \frac{T_1}{T} + \frac{T_3}{T} = 2$

$\Rightarrow \quad \frac{1}{T}(T_1 + T_3) = 2 \Rightarrow T = \frac{T_1 + T_3}{2}$

$\Rightarrow \quad T = \frac{900 + 400}{2} = 650\text{K}$ [1]

28. (i) Efficiency, $\eta = 1 - \frac{T_2}{T_1}$

where, T_2 = sink temperature

T_1 = source temperature. [1]

$$1 - \frac{T_2}{T_1} = \frac{1}{2} \quad \text{...(i)}$$ [1]

$$1 - \left(\frac{T_2 - 100}{T_1}\right) = \frac{2}{3} \quad \text{...(ii)}$$

From Eq. (i), $\frac{T_2}{T_1} = \frac{1}{2}$

and Eq. (ii) $\frac{T_2 - 100}{T_1} = \frac{1}{3}$ [1]

On dividing, we get

$$\frac{T_2}{T_2 - 100} = \frac{3}{2} \Rightarrow T_2 = 300\text{K}$$

(ii) Substituting in Eq. (i), $T_1 = 600$ K [1]

(iii) As efficiency, $\eta_2 \Rightarrow 1 - \frac{T_2}{T_1}$

$\therefore$ It equals to 1 only when $\frac{T_2}{T_1} = 0$ or $T_2 = 0$K

But absolute zero is not possible. [1]

29. For engine *A*, $T_1 = 800$ K, $T_2 = T$ K

Efficiency, $\eta_A = 1 - \frac{T_2}{T_1} = 1 - \frac{T}{800}$

Also, $\frac{Q_2}{Q_1} = \frac{T_2}{T_1} = \frac{T}{800}$ [1]

Work output, $W_A = Q_1 - Q_2 = \eta_A \times Q_1 \quad \left[\because \eta_A = 1 - \frac{Q_2}{Q_1}\right]$

or $W_A = \left(1 - \frac{T}{800}\right) Q_1$

For engine *B*, $T_1' = T$ K, $T_2' = 300$ K

Efficiency, $\eta_B = 1 - \frac{T_2'}{T_1'} = 1 - \frac{300}{T}$ [1]

Work output, $W_B = Q_1' - Q_2' = \eta_B \times Q_1' = \left(1 - \frac{300}{T}\right) Q_1'$

Since, the engine *B* absorbs the heat rejected by the engine *A*, so

$$Q_1' = Q_2 \quad \therefore \quad W_B = \left(1 - \frac{300}{T}\right) Q_2$$

(i) When outputs of the two engines are equal,

$W_A = W_B$

or $\left(1 - \frac{T}{800}\right) Q_1 = \left(1 - \frac{300}{T}\right) Q_2$ [1½]

or $\left(1 - \frac{T}{800}\right) = \left(1 - \frac{300}{T}\right) \frac{Q_2}{Q_1} = \left(1 - \frac{300}{T}\right) \frac{T}{800}$

On solving, we get $T = 550$ K

(ii) When the efficiencies are equal, $\eta_A = \eta_B$

or $1 - \frac{T}{800} = 1 - \frac{300}{T}$

or $T^2 = 24 \times 10^4$

$\therefore \quad T = 489.9$ K [1½]

Summary

- **Thermodynamics** It is the branch of physics which deals with the study of transformation of heat energy into other forms of energy.
- Two systems are said to be in thermal equilibrium with each other if they are at the same temperature.
- **Zeroth law of thermodynamics** If two systems A and B are separately in thermal equilibrium with a third system C, then A and B are in thermal equilibrium with each other.
- **Heat** It is the energy that is transferred between a system and its environment.

$$\Delta Q = ms\,(T_f - T_i)$$

- **Internal energy** The total energy possessed by the system due to molecular motion and molecular configuration, i.e.

$$U = U_k + U_p$$

- Work done by or on the system is given by

$$W = \int_{V_i}^{V_f} p\,dV$$

where, V_i = initial volume of gas, V_f = final volume of gas, p = pressure

- **Heat capacity** An amount of heat ΔQ is needed to change its temperature ΔT. Its unit is J/K.

$$S = \frac{\Delta Q}{\Delta T}$$

- **Specific heat capacity** The amount of heat required to change the temperature of unit mass of a substance by unity. Its unit is J/kg-K.

$$S = \frac{1}{m}\frac{\Delta Q}{\Delta T}$$

- **Molar specific heat capacity** The amount of heat required to raise the temperature of one mole of a substance through a unit degree. Its unit is J/mol-K; $C = \frac{1}{\mu}\frac{\Delta Q}{\Delta T}$
- The relation between C_p and C_V is given by, $C_p - C_V = R$
- **First law of thermodynamics** The heat given to system is either used in doing work (ΔW) or it increases the internal energy (ΔU) the system, i.e. $\Delta Q = \Delta U + \Delta W$
- When state of a system changes or the state variables changes with time, then this process is known as thermodynamic system.
- An **isothermal process** occurs at constant temperature and work done in an isothermal process is given by the following equation.

$$W = 2.303\mu RT \log\left(\frac{V_f}{V_i}\right)$$

- An isobaric process occurs at constant pressure and work done is an isobaric process is given by the following equation, $W = \mu R\,(T_f - T_i)$
- An **isochoric process** is one in which volume is kept constant, meaning that the work done by the system will be zero.
- An adiabatic process does not allow transfer of heat by or to the system and work done in this process is given by the following equation

$$W = \frac{\mu R\,(T_i - T_f)}{\gamma - 1}$$

- In cyclic process, initial and final states are same while in non-cyclic processes, they are different.
- **Kelvin Planck statement** No process is possible whose sole result in the absorption of heat from a reservoir and the complete conversion of heat into work.
- **Clausius statement** No process is possible whose sole result is the transfer of heat from a colder object to hotter object.
- **Carnot engine** The reversible engine which operates between two temperatures of source and sink.
- Carnot cycle consists four strokes and each stroke having own work which is given by the following equations.

$$W_1 = RT_1 \log_e \frac{V_2}{V_1}, \qquad W_2 = (T_1 - T_2)\frac{R}{\gamma - 1}(T_1 - T_2)$$

$$W_3 = RT_2 \log_e \frac{V_3}{V_4}, \qquad W_4 = \frac{R}{\gamma - 1}(T_1 - T_2)$$

- **Carnot's theorem**

(i) A heat engine working between the two given temperature T_1 of hot reservoir, i.e. source and T_2 of cold reservoir, i.e. sink cannot have efficiency of more than that of carnot engine.

(ii) The efficiency of the carnot engine is independent of the nature of working substance.

- Coefficient of performance of carnot engine is given by the following equation, $\beta = \frac{T_2}{T_1 - T_2}$

where, T_1 = temperature of surroundings and T_2 = temperature of cold body

Chapter Practice

Multiple Choice Questions

1 Mark

1 If two systems are in thermal equilibrium with each other, it means their
(a) masses are equal, temperatures may be unequal
(b) temperatures are equal
(c) masses and temperatures are equal
(d) None of the above

2 Choose the correct option.
(a) $C_p = C_V = 2R$
(b) $C_V - C_p = R$
(c) $C_p - C_V = \frac{R}{2}$
(d) $C_p - C_V = R$

3 Choose the correct option for the *p*-*V* curve shown below.

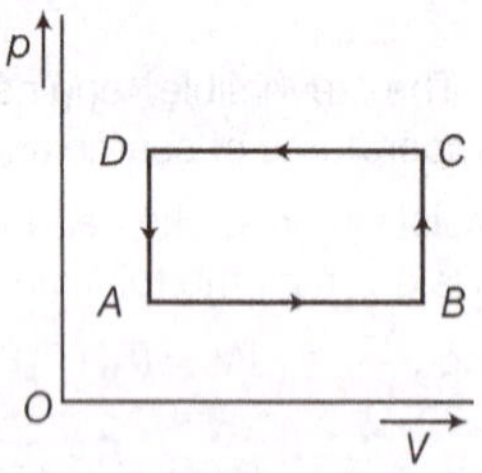

(a) For the process *ABCD*, $\Delta U = 0$
(b) For the process *ABCDA*, *W* is negative
(c) Both (a) and (b)
(d) None of the above

Assertion and Reason

Directions (Q. Nos. 4-8) *In the following questions, two statements are given- one labelled Assertion (A) and the other labelled Reason (R). Select the correct answer to these questions from the codes (a), (b), (c) and (d) as given below*
(a) Both Assertion and Reason are true and Reason is the correct explanation of Assertion.
(b) Both Assertion and Reason are true but Reason is not the correct explanation of Assertion.
(c) Assertion is true but Reason is false.
(d) Assertion is false but Reason is true.

4 **Assertion (A)** Zeroth law of thermodynamics explains the concept of energy.

Reason (R) Energy is dependent on volume.

5 **Assertion (A)** The ratio of specific heat of a gas at constant pressure and specific heat at constant volume for a diatomic gas is more than that for a monoatomic gas.

Reason (R) The molecules of a monoatomic gas have more degree of freedom than those of a diatomic gas.

6 **Assertion (A)** In an adiabatic compression, the internal energy and temperature of the system gets decreased.

Reason (R) An adiabatic compression is a quick process.

7 **Assertion (A)** When a bottle of cold carbonated drink is opened, a fog forms around opening.

Reason (R) Adiabatic expansion of gas causes lowering of temperature and condensation of water vapours.

8 **Assertion (A)** Thermodynamics deals with the concepts of heat and temperature.
Reason (R) The temperature of an ideal gas depends on its molecular kinetic energy.

Very Short Answer Type Questions

1 Mark

9 When the work done is positive?

10 Is it possible to increase the temperature of a gas without heating it?

11 What is a thermodynamic system?

12 What do you mean by an adiabatic wall and a diathermic wall?

13 Can a system be heated and its temperature remains constant?

14 Can a practical engine be as much efficient as a Carnot engine?

15 Find value of specific heat of a gas in isothermal process.

Short Answer Type I Questions

2 Marks

16 Which one a solid, a liquid or a gas of same mass and at the same temperature has greatest internal energy? Give reason.

17 Why water at the base of a waterfall is slightly warmer than the top?

18 Two blocks of same metal having masses 5 g and 10 g collide against a target with same velocity. If total energy is used in heating the balls, which will attain higher temperature?

19 Why is conversion of heat into work not possible without a sink at lower temperature?

20 Does the working of an electric refrigerator define second law of thermodynamics?

21 Explain 'coolant fluid used in a chemical plant or in a car radiator should have high specific heat'. Is water a suitable coolant?

22 Milk is poured into a cup of tea and is mixed with a spoon. Is this an example of a reversible process? Give reason.

Short Answer Type II Questions

3 Marks

23 Find work done during the cyclic process showing indicator diagram.

24 Draw indicator diagram for an adiabatic process. Find the slope of an adiabatic at any point.

25 Two identical samples of a gas are at a pressure p_1 and volume V_1. The two samples are allowed to expand so as to acquire a volume V_2. But one sample expands isothermally while the other expands adiabatically. In which case, more work is done and why?

26 State second law of thermodynamics. Write a difference between heat engine and refrigerator.

27 Define reversible process. Write two characteristics of reversible process.

Long Answer Type Questions

5 Marks

28 What do you understand by reversible and irreversible processes? Give example. What are the necessary conditions for a process to be reversible.

29 What is Carnot engine? On what factors does it depend? Also, define the efficiency of a Carnot engine.

30 Explain four strokes in Carnot cycle with p-V diagram. Find coefficient of performance of Carnot engine.

Case Based Questions

Directions (Q. No. 31) *These questions are case study based questions. Read the following paragraph and answer the questions.*

31 Two cylinders A and B of equal capacity are connected to each other *via* a stopcock. A contains a gas at standard temperature and pressure and B is completely evacuated. The entire system in thermally insulated. The stopcock is suddenly opened.

(i) What is final pressure of the gas in A and B?

(ii) What is the change in internal energy of the gas?

(iii) What is the change in temperature of the gas?

(iv) Do the intermediate states of the system (before settling to the final equilibrium state) lie on its p-V-T surface?

Numerical Problems

32 A Carnot engine is operated between $T_1 = 600$ K and $T_2 = 400$ K.

(i) What is the efficiency of carnot engine.

(ii) What is the coefficient of performance? **[2 M]**

33 If a Carnot engine whose heat sink is at 27°C has an efficiency of 40%. By how many degrees should the temperature of the source be changed to increase the efficiency by 10% of the original efficiency. **[3 M]**

Answers

1 (*b*) If two systems are in thermal equilibrium with each other, it means their temperatures must be same. Masses may be equal or unequal.

2 (*d*) We know that, $C_p = C_V + \dfrac{p\Delta V}{\mu \Delta T}$

$\Rightarrow C_p = C_V + R \Rightarrow C_p - C_V = R$

3 (*b*) For the process *ABCDA* work done,

$W = -$ (Area under the rectangular loop *ABCDA*)

For $A \rightarrow B \rightarrow C \rightarrow D$ process pressure has increased, volume is same. So, temperature also increases.

$\Rightarrow$ internal energy increases $\Rightarrow \Delta U =$ positive

4 (*d*) Zeroth law explains the concept of temperature.

5 (*d*) For a monoatomic gas, number of degree of freedom, $n = 3$ and for a diatomic gas, $n = 5$

As, $$\frac{C_p}{C_V} = x = 1 + \frac{2}{n}$$

So, for monoatonic gas,

$$\frac{C_p}{C_V} = \frac{5}{3} = 1.66$$

and for diatomic gas,

$$\frac{C_p}{C_V} = \frac{7}{5} = 1.4$$

$$\therefore \left(\frac{C_p}{C_V}\right)_{mono} > \left(\frac{C_p}{C_V}\right)_{di}$$

6 (*d*) During adiabatic compression, work is done on the system. Both the internal energy and temperature of the system increases.

An adiabatic compression is a quick process.

7 (*a*) Change is fast and also adiabatic expansion causes cooling.

8 (*b*) Thermodynamics deals with the concept of heat and temperature; kinetic energy of the molecules of an ideal gas describes its temperature.

9 When the system expands, i.e. final volume is greater than initial volume, then work done is positive.

10 Yes, during adiabatic compression, the temperature of the gas increases, while no heat is given to it.

11 A thermodynamic system is an assembly of large number of atoms or molecules, which has a certain pressure, volume and temperature.

12 The boundary walls which prevent thermal interaction between system and surrounding are adiabatic walls. While the diathermic walls are the boundaries through which exchange of heat takes place.

13 Refer to Sol. 8 on page 384.

14 No according to Carnot theorem, no heat engine can have efficiency more than that of the Carnot engine.

15 In an isothermal process, temperature remains constant, so specific heat is infinite.

16 The internal energy is the sum of molecular kinetic energy and potential energy. In solid, liquid and gas, the goseous molecules are free to move and intermolecular interactions are least. So, they have more kinetic energy and potential energy than solid and liquid. Hence, internal energy is greatest in gas. [2]

17 When water falls from a height, its potential energy is converted into kinetic energy of water molecules and at the bottom, this energy is converted to heat energy when it comes to rest. That's why water become warmer than at the top. [2]

18 The heat generated is given by

$$\Delta Q = ms\Delta T \Rightarrow \Delta Q \propto m\Delta T$$

As whole of the kinetic energy is converted into heat energy which is dependent on mass. Thus, 10 g ball will have more heat, but the temperature change is same in both. [2]

19 The transfer of heat takes place from a body to another when there is a temperature difference between them. Thus, heat is converted to work when the heat energy from a source at higher temperature moves to a sink at lower temperature to equalise it. [2]

20 No, according to second law of thermodynamics, heat can only be transferred from a hot reservoir to a cold reservoir without doing work. But in a refrigerator, the reverse process takes place by doing work (by electrical means). [2]

21 The specific heat capacity defines the capacity of a material to absorb more amount of heat for a minimum change in temperature.

The coolant in a chemical plant and in a car is used for this purpose, so they should have high specific heat.

As water is readily available and has high specific heat, so it can be used as coolant. [2]

22 No, if is an irreversible process. Because in this, some part of the energy is converted into heat, which is lost in the surrounding and cannot be recovered back. [2]

23 Refer to text on pages 377 and 378 (Work done in a cyclic process).

24 Refer to text on page 376 (*p*-*V* diagram).

25 The processes can be shown by

$$(p_1, V_1, T) \xrightarrow{\text{Adiabatic}} (p'_A, V_2, T')$$

$$(p_1, V_1, T) \xrightarrow{\text{Isothermal}} (p'_I, V_2, T)$$

In isothermal process, temperature remains same, but in adiabatic, temperature falls (i.e. $T' < T$). Using *p*-*V* diagram, [1]

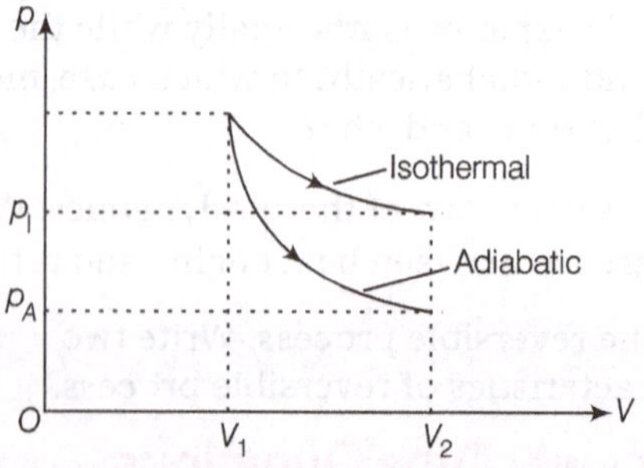

[1]

From graph, $p_I > p_A$

$\therefore$ Area under isothermal curve is greater than that of adiabatic curve. So, work done is more in isothermal process than the work done in adiabatic process. [1]

26 Refer to text on page 388 (Second law of thermodynamics). [2]

Heat engine works on the second law of thermodynamics, while refrigerator works in reverse way of this law. [1]

27 Refer to text on page 389 (Reversible process).

28 Refer to text on page 389 (Reversible and irreversible process).

29 Refer to text on pages 389 and 390 [Carnot engine and efficiency of Carnot cycle (engine)].

30 Refer to text on pages 390 and 391 (Carnot cycle and coefficient of performance of Carnot engine).

31 (i) Let capacity of each cylinder be V and atmospheric pressure be p.

$$p_1 = p$$

Initial volume of gas = Volume of the cylinder A

$$\therefore \quad V_1 = V$$

When stopcock is opened, then volume available for gas becomes $2V$

$$\therefore \quad V_2 = 2V$$

Final pressure $(p_2) = ?$

As system is thermally insulated, therefore there is no change in temperature during the process and hence, it is an isothermal process.

For an isothermal process (according to Boyle's law),

$$p_1V_1 = p_2V_2$$

or
$$p_2 = p_1\frac{V_1}{V_2} = p \times \frac{V}{2V}$$

$$= \frac{p}{2} = \frac{1}{2} \text{ atm} = 0.5 \text{ atm}$$

(ii) Change in internal energy, $\Delta U = 0$, as no work is done on or by the gas.

(iii) Change in temperature of the gas is zero as gas does no work in expansion.

(iv) No, because free expansion of gas is rapid and cannot be controlled. The intermediate states are non-equilibrium states and do not satisfy the gas equation. Therefore, the intermediate state of the gas does not be on the p-V-T surface.

32 Given, $T_1 = 600\text{K}, T_2 = 400\text{ K}$

(i) Efficiency, $\eta = \frac{1 - T_2}{T_1} = 1 - \frac{400}{600} = \frac{1}{3}$ or $33\frac{1}{3}\%$ [1]

(ii) Coefficient of performance, $\beta' = \frac{T_2}{T_1 - T_2} = \frac{400}{600 - 400}$

$$= 2$$ [1]

33 Given, $T_2 = 27 + 273 = 300\text{K}, \ \eta = 40\%$

$$\Rightarrow \quad \frac{40}{100} = 1 - \frac{T_2}{T_1} \Rightarrow \frac{T_2}{T_1} = 1 - \frac{40}{100} = \frac{3}{5}$$

$$\Rightarrow \quad T_1 = \frac{5}{3}T_2 = \frac{5}{3} \times 300 = 500\text{K}$$ [1]

$\therefore$ New efficiency, $\eta' = 40 + 10\% \text{ of } 40 = 44\%$

$$\Rightarrow \quad \eta' = 1 - \frac{T_2}{T_1'}$$

$$\Rightarrow \quad \frac{44}{100} = 1 - \frac{300}{T_1'}$$ [1]

$$\Rightarrow \quad T_1' = \frac{100 \times 300}{56} = 535.7\text{ K}$$

Increase in temperature = 535.7 − 500 = 35.7 K [1]

CHAPTER

12

Kinetic Theory of Gases

Kinetic theory of gas explains the behaviour of gases based on the idea that the gas consists of rapidly moving atoms or molecules. Interatomic forces, which are short range forces, can be neglected in gases and this explains the rapid movement of gases.

- Kinetic Interpretation of Behaviour of Gases
- Motion of Gas Molecules

TOPIC 01 Kinetic Interpretation of Behaviour of Gases

In gases, intermolecular forces are weak and its molecules move in all directions colliding with each other.

To keep our analysis simple we thought of an ideal gas with perfectly rigid spherical molecules which does not exerts any attraction or repulsion force on each other. All real gases do not behave like an ideal gas, but at low pressure and high temperatures, monoatomic gases are nearly ideal gases.

Equation of State for an Ideal Gas

An ideal gas or perfect gas strictly obeys the gas laws such as Boyle's law, Charles' law and Gay Lussac's law, etc.

For ideal gases value of $\frac{pV}{T}$ remains constant (here, p is pressure of gas, V is volume and T is absolute temperature).

$$\frac{pV}{T} = r \text{ (constant)}$$

$$pV = rT \quad \ldots\text{(i)}$$

r is a constant that varies with volume or with number of atoms or molecules N of gas in the given sample. It is called specific gas constant.

r can also be written as $\quad r = Nk \quad \ldots\text{(ii)}$

The observation tells that k is same for all gases and is denoted by k_B.

So, Eq. (ii) becomes $r = Nk_B$ ...(iii)

where, k_B = Boltzmann constant and its value in SI unit is 1.38×10^{-23} J / K.

From Eqs. (i) and (iii), we have

$$pV = Nk_BT \text{ or } \frac{pV}{NT} = k_B = \text{constant}$$

So, for different gases, we may write

$$\frac{p_1V_1}{N_1T_1} = \frac{p_2V_2}{N_2T_2} = \frac{p_3V_3}{N_3T_3} \dots = k_B = \text{constant}$$

The perfect gas equation can be written as

$$\boxed{pV = \mu RT}$$

where, μ = number of moles and $R = N_A k_B$ is universal gas constant.

$$\mu = \frac{m}{M_0} = \frac{N}{N_A}$$

where, m = mass of the gases.

In terms of density, perfect gas equation is

$$p = \frac{\rho RT}{M_0}$$

where, ρ = mass density of the gas,

M_0 = molar mass of the gas, (mass of one mole of the gas)

and $R = 8.314 \text{ J mol}^{-1}\text{K}^{-1} \approx 2 \text{ cal mol}^{-1}\text{K}^{-1}$.

Example 1 A gas at 27°C is kept in a cylinder with a movable piston.

On heating the gas simultaneously and loading its piston, it is found that pressure is doubled and its volume is three times.

Find the final temperature of the gas. Assume ideal behaviour.

Sol. Given, initial temperature of gas = 27° C = 300 K

From gas equation,

$$\frac{pV}{T} = \text{a constant}$$

$$\Rightarrow \frac{p_1V_1}{T_1} = \frac{p_2V_2}{T_2}$$

$$\text{or } \frac{T_2}{T_1} = \frac{p_2}{p_1} \times \frac{V_2}{V_1} = \frac{2p_1}{p_1} \times \frac{3V_1}{V_1}$$

$$\Rightarrow T_2 = 6T_1 = 6 \times 300 \text{ K} = 1800 \text{ K} = 1527° \text{ C}$$

Example 2 A vessel contains two non-reacting gases, i.e. neon (monoatomic) and oxygen (diatomic). The ratio of their partial pressures is 3 : 2. Estimate the ratio of (i) number of molecules and (ii) mass density of neon and oxygen in the vessel. Atomic number of Ne = 20.2, molecular mass of O_2 = 32.0. **NCERT**

Sol. (i) As V and T are same for the two gases, we can write

$$p_{Ne}V = \mu_{Ne}RT \text{ and } p_{O_2}V = \mu_{O_2}RT$$

$$\text{or } \frac{p_{Ne}}{p_{O_2}} = \frac{\mu_{Ne}}{\mu_{O_2}}$$

$$\because \frac{p_{Ne}}{p_{O_2}} = \frac{3}{2} \Rightarrow \frac{\mu_{Ne}}{\mu_{O_2}} = \frac{3}{2}$$

If N_{Ne} and N_{O_2} are the number of molecules of the two gases and N_A is Avogadro's number, then

$$\frac{\mu_{Ne}}{\mu_{O_2}} = \frac{N_{Ne}/N_A}{N_{O_2}/N_A} = \frac{3}{2}$$

$$\Rightarrow \frac{N_{Ne}}{N_{O_2}} = 1.5$$

(ii) Now, $\mu_{O_2} = \frac{m_{O_2}}{M_{O_2}}$ and $\mu_{Ne} = \frac{m_{Ne}}{M_{Ne}}$

$$\therefore \frac{\rho_{Ne}}{\rho_{O_2}} = \frac{m_{Ne}/V}{m_{O_2}/V} = \frac{m_{Ne}}{m_{O_2}} = \frac{\mu_{Ne}M_{Ne}}{\mu_{O_2}M_{O_2}} = \frac{3}{2} \times \frac{20.2}{32} = 0.947$$

Example 3 Two non-reactive gases are kept in a container. The ratio of their partial pressures is given 5 : 3. Find the ratio of number of molecules.

Sol. As two non-reactive gases are mixed in a container, so the value of V and T will be same for both with partial pressures, p_1 and p_2.

For gas I, $p_1V = \mu_1RT$ ...(i)

For gas II, $p_2V = \mu_2RT$ ...(ii)

Dividing Eq. (i) by Eq. (ii), we get

$$\frac{p_1}{p_2} = \frac{\mu_1}{\mu_2} \quad \text{...(iii)}$$

$$\mu_1 = N_1/N_A \quad \text{...(iv)}$$

$$\mu_2 = N_2/N_A \quad \text{...(v)}$$

Dividing Eq. (iv) by Eq. (v),

$$\frac{\mu_1}{\mu_2} = \frac{N_1}{N_2} \quad \text{...(vi)}$$

From Eqs. (iii) and (vi), we get

$$\frac{N_1}{N_2} = \frac{\mu_1}{\mu_2} = \frac{p_1}{p_2} \Rightarrow \frac{N_1}{N_2} = \frac{p_1}{p_2} \text{ or } \frac{N_1}{N_2} = \frac{5}{3}.$$

Behaviour of Real Gas and Ideal (Perfect) Gas

An ideal gas is a theoretical model of a gas and no real gas is truly ideal. However, a real gas behaves as an ideal gas most closely at low pressure and high temperature. This is because at low pressure and high temperature, the molecules of gas are far apart due to which molecular force of attraction is negligible.

We have, $pV = \mu RT$ (ideal gas equation)

$$\therefore \quad \frac{pV}{\mu T} = R = \text{constant}$$

The experimental graph drawn between $\frac{pV}{\mu T}$ and p is shown in the figure below.

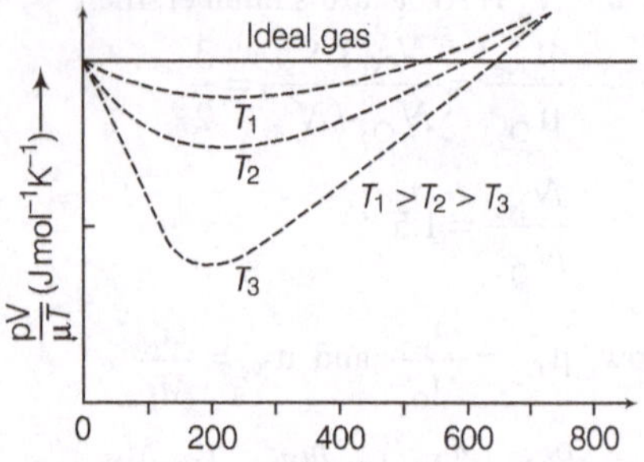

Behaviour of real gases approach ideal gas at low pressure and high temperature

If we plot same graph for real gases at three different temperatures T_1, T_2, T_3 ($T_1 > T_2 > T_3$), then we find the curve as shown in figure by dotted lines.

Solid line is showing ideal gas approach and dotted line is showing real gas approach. Here, we observe that curves of real gases meets curve of ideal gas as p approaches zero or at high temperature. From the observation of this graph, we will find that all curves for real gas approach ideal gas behaviour at low pressure and high temperature.

Gas Laws

Boyle's Law

It states that for a given mass of a gas at constant temperature, the volume of that mass of gas is inversely proportional to its pressure, i.e. $V \propto \frac{1}{p}$

According to ideal gas equation, we get $pV = \mu RT$

So, at constant temperature, pV = constant

$\Rightarrow$ Boyle's law, $p_1V_1 = p_2V_2 = p_3V_3 \cdots = \text{constant}$

The figure below shows the comparison between experimental p-V curves (bold) and the theoretical curves (dotted) predicted by Boyle's law.

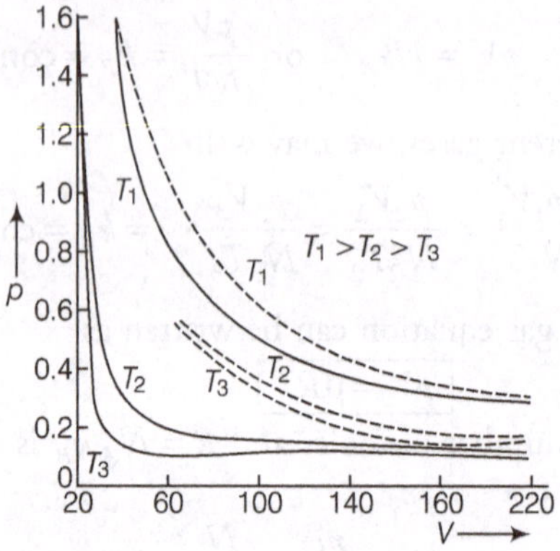

Example 4 A gas at 27°C in a cylinder has a volume of 4 L and pressure 100 N/m². If the gas is compressed at constant temperature so that the pressure is 150 N/m². Estimate the change in volume.

Sol. Given, $V_1 = 4$ L, $V_2 = ?$, $p_1 = 100$ N/m²,

$p_2 = 150$ N/m², $\Delta V = ?$

Using Boyle's law for constant temperature, we have

$$p_1V_1 = p_2V_2$$

$$\Rightarrow \quad V_2 = \frac{p_1V_1}{p_2} = \frac{100 \times 4}{150} = 2.667 \text{ L}$$

$\therefore$ Change in volume, $\Delta V = V_1 - V_2$

$= 4 - 2.667 = 1.33$ L

Charles' Law

It states that for a given mass of an ideal gas at constant pressure, volume V of a gas is directly proportional to its absolute temperature T,

i.e. $V \propto T$

From ideal gas equation, $\frac{V}{T} = \frac{\mu R}{p}$

So, at constant pressure, $\frac{V}{T}$ = constant

$\Rightarrow$ Charles' law, $\frac{V_1}{T_1} = \frac{V_2}{T_2} = \frac{V_3}{T_3} = \cdots = \text{constant}$

The figure below shows the comparison between experimental T-V curves (bold) and the theoretical curves (dotted) predicted by Charles' law.

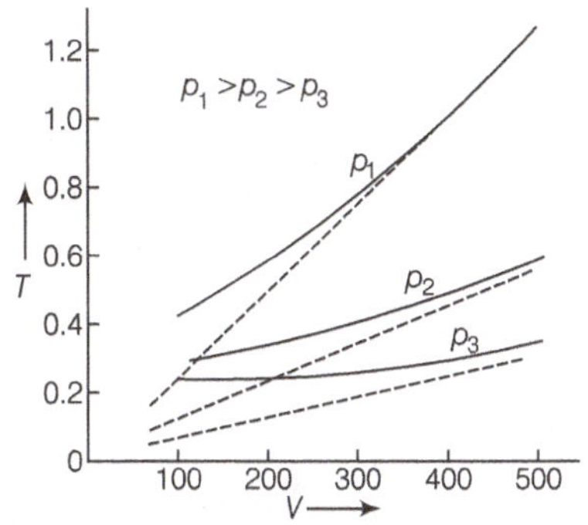

Example 5 A gas is filled in a cylinder at 300K. Calculate the temperature upto which it should be heated so that its volume becomes $\frac{4}{3}$ of its initial volume.

Sol. Given, $T_1 = 300$ K, $T_2 = ?$

$$V_1 = V,\ V_2 = \frac{4}{3}V$$

According to Charles' law, we get

$$\frac{V_2}{V_1} = \frac{T_2}{T_1} \Rightarrow T_2 = T_1 \frac{V_2}{V_1} = 300 \times \frac{4}{3} = 400 \text{ K}$$

Kinetic Theory of an Ideal Gas

Kinetic theory of gases is based on the molecular picture of matter. It correlates the macroscopic properties (e.g. pressure and temperature) of gases to microscopic properties (e.g. speed and kinetic energy) of gas molecules.

Assumptions of Kinetic Theory of Gases

(i) A given amount of gas consists of a very large number of molecules (of the order of Avogadro's number 10^{23}) and all molecules are identical in all respect.

(ii) The molecules of a gas are in a state of incessant random motion in all directions with different speeds, move freely in straight lines.

(iii) The size of a molecule is much smaller than the average separation between the molecules. At ordinary pressure and temperature, the average distance between molecules is about 20 Å, whereas size of a molecule is 2 Å.

(iv) There is no intermolecular forces between molecules of gas except during collision.

(v) The collision between molecules among themselves or between molecules and walls are perfectly elastic (i.e. total momentum and total kinetic energy of molecules are conserved, however only their velocities will change).

(vi) The duration of collision between two molecules is negligible as compared to time interval of two successive collisions, i.e. collisions are instantaneous.

(vii) The density and the distribution of molecules is uniform throughout the gas.

Concept of Pressure of an Ideal Gas

Consider an ideal gas consisting of N molecules in a container of volume V. The container is a cube with edges of length l. Consider a molecule of mass m moving with velocity (v_x, v_y, v_z).

As molecule collides with the wall parallel to yz-plane elastically, its x-component of velocity is reversed, while its y and z-components of velocity remain unaltered i.e. velocity after collision is $(-v_x, v_y, v_z)$.

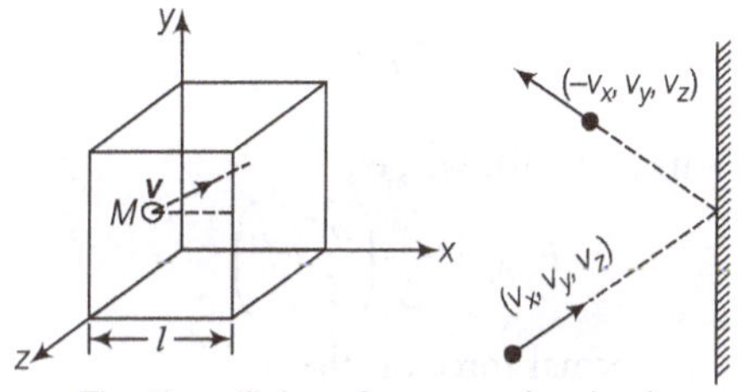

Elastic collision of a gas molecule along x-component of velocity

So, the change in momentum of the molecule is

$$\Delta p_x = (p_x)_{\text{final}} - (p_x)_{\text{initial}}$$
$$\Delta p_x = -mv_x - (mv_x)$$
$$\Delta p_x = -2mv_x$$

$\because$ Impulse = Change in momentum of molecule

$$\Rightarrow \quad F\,\Delta t = \Delta p_x = -2mv_x \quad \ldots\text{(i)}$$

where, F is the average force on the molecule by the wall. For molecule to collide with same wall, twice it must travel a distance $2l$ in x-direction (as the molecule has to travel from $+x$ to $-x$-directions between two walls).

So, time interval between two collisions with same wall is

$$\Delta t = \frac{2l}{v_x}$$

The average force exerted on a molecule by the wall for each collision is

$$F = \frac{-2mv_x}{\Delta t} = \frac{(-2mv_x)}{(2l/v_x)} = \frac{-mv_x^2}{l}$$

By Newton's Third Law,

The average force exerted by a molecule on the wall is $\frac{mv_x^2}{l}$. If there are N molecules, so total force on the wall will be $F_{wall} = \frac{m}{l}(v_{x_1}^2 + v_{x_2}^2 + \dots + v_{x_N}^2)$

It can be rewritten as

$$F_{wall} = \frac{Nm}{l}\bar{v}_x^2 \qquad \dots\text{(ii)}$$

where, $\bar{v}_x^2 = \frac{v_{x_1}^2 + v_{x_2}^2 + \dots + v_{x_N}^2}{N}$

Now, $\bar{v}^2 = \bar{v}_x^2 + \bar{v}_y^2 + \bar{v}_z^2$

[as velocity has 3 components v_x, v_y, v_z]

Since, motion is completely random, so average values $\bar{v}_x^2, \bar{v}_y^2$ and $\bar{v}_z^2$ are equal to each other [i.e. $\bar{v}_x^2 = \bar{v}_y^2 = \bar{v}_z^2$]

$\therefore$ $\bar{v}^2 = 3\bar{v}_x^2$

or $\bar{v}_x^2 = \frac{1}{3}\bar{v}^2 \qquad \dots\text{(iii)}$

From Eqs. (ii) and (iii), we get,

$$F_{wall} = \frac{N}{3}\left(\frac{m}{l}\bar{v}^2\right) \qquad \dots\text{(iv)}$$

Here, F_{wall} is normal force on the wall.

Pressure on the wall, $p = \frac{F_{wall}}{\text{Area}} = \frac{F_{wall}}{l^2}$

$\Rightarrow$ $p = \frac{1}{l^2}\left(\frac{N}{3}\frac{m\bar{v}^2}{l}\right)$ or $p = \frac{1}{l^3}\left(\frac{Nm\bar{v}^2}{3}\right)$

or $p = \frac{1}{V}\left(\frac{Nm\bar{v}^2}{3}\right)$ [$\because$ volume, $V = l^3$]

or $\boxed{p = \frac{1}{3}\left(\frac{N}{V}\right)m\bar{v}^2}$

$\Rightarrow$ Pressure exerted by an ideal gas, $\boxed{p = \frac{1}{3}nm\bar{v}^2}$ ...(v)

where, p = pressure exerted on wall,

n = number density (i.e. number of molecules per unit volume) of gas,

m = mass of one molecule,

$\bar{v}^2$ = mean square speed

and $p = \frac{1}{3}nm\bar{v}^2$ is known as expression for pressure exerted by an ideal gas and also called **kinetic gas equation.**

Let M be the mass of all molecules of a given ideal gas enclosed in a vessel of volume V having density ρ, then

$n \times m$ = Number of molecules per unit volume × Mass of one molecule

= Total mass of all molecules per unit volume

$= \frac{M}{V}$

$\Rightarrow$ $n \times m = \rho$ $\left[\because \text{Density}, \rho = \frac{\text{Mass}}{\text{Volume}}\right]$ ...(vi)

From Eqs. (v) and (vi), we get

$$\boxed{p = \frac{1}{3}\rho\bar{v}^2}$$

Example 6 **A container is filled with a gas at a pressure of 76 cm of mercury at a certain temperature. The mass of a gas is increased by 50% by introducing more gas in the container at same temperature. Calculate the final pressure of the gas.**

Sol. According to kinetic theory of gases,

$$pV = \frac{1}{3}Mv_{rms}^2$$

At constant temperature, v_{rms}^2 is constant. As V is also constant.

$\therefore$ $p \propto M$

When the mass of the gas is increased by 50%, pressure also increased by 50%.

$\therefore$ Resultant pressure $= 76 + \frac{50}{100} \times 76 = 114$ cm of Hg

Root Mean Square Speed of Gas Molecule

Root mean square is defined as the square root of the mean of square of the speed of different molecule, i.e.

$$v_{rms} = v = \sqrt{(v_1^2 + v_2^2 + \dots + v_n^2)/N}$$

According to kinetic theory of gases, it is observed that

$$v_{rms} = \sqrt{\frac{3p}{\rho}}$$

At normal pressure ($p = 1.01 \times 10^5$ Nm^{-2}), the densities of air and hydrogen are 1.29 kg m^{-3} and 0.09 kg m^{-3}, respectively.

Therefore, the rms speed of air and hydrogen molecules are

$$(v_{\text{rms}})_{\text{air}} = \sqrt{\frac{3\times(1.01\times10^5\ \text{Nm}^{-2})}{1.29\ \text{kg m}^{-3}}} = 485\ \text{ms}^{-1}$$

$$= 1746\ \text{kmh}^{-1}$$

and $$(v_{\text{rms}})_{\text{hydrogen}} = \sqrt{\frac{3\times(1.01\times10^5\ \text{Nm}^{-2})}{0.09\ \text{kg m}^{-3}}} = 1835\ \text{ms}^{-1}$$

$$= 6600\ \text{kmh}^{-1}$$

So, we can say that rms speed of gas molecules is of the order of supersonic aeroplanes and jet planes.

Example 7 The molecules of a given mass of a gas have root mean square speeds of 100 ms^{-1} at 27°C and 1.00 atm pressure. What will be the root mean square speeds of the molecules of the gas at 127°C and 2.0 atm pressure? **NCERT Exemplar**

Sol. According to ideal gas equation, we get

$$\frac{p_1V_1}{T_1} = \frac{p_2V_2}{T_2} \text{ or } \frac{V_1}{V_2} = \frac{p_2T_1}{p_1T_2} = \frac{2\times300}{1\times400} = \frac{3}{2}$$

$$p_1 = \frac{1}{3}\frac{M}{V_1}(v_{\text{rms}})_1^2,$$

$$p_2 = \frac{1}{3}\frac{M}{V_2}(v_{\text{rms}})_2^2$$

$$\therefore \quad (v_{\text{rms}})_2^2 = (v_{\text{rms}})_1^2 \times \frac{V_2}{V_1}\times\frac{p_2}{p_1} = (100)^2\times\frac{2}{3}\times2$$

or $$(v_{\text{rms}})_2 = \frac{200}{\sqrt{3}}\ \text{ms}^{-1}$$

Kinetic Interpretation of Temperature

The average KE of a molecule depends on the absolute temperature of the gas. It is the kinetic interpretation of temperature. Let us consider a sample of an ideal gas having N number of molecules. Let the volume of the gas is V, pressure is p and temperature is T.

From the pressure expression of an ideal gas

$$p = \frac{1}{3}nm\bar{v}^2 \quad \ldots\text{(i)}$$

Multiplying both sides with V, we get

$$\Rightarrow \quad pV = \frac{1}{3}(nV)m\bar{v}^2$$

or, $$pV = \frac{2}{3}(nV)\frac{1}{2}m\bar{v}^2$$

$$\Rightarrow \quad pV = \frac{2}{3}N\left(\frac{1}{2}m\bar{v}^2\right) \quad \ldots\text{(ii)}$$

Here, number of molecules in the sample, $N = nV$

Here, $\frac{1}{2}m\bar{v}^2$ is the average kinetic energy of the molecules of the gas.

So, total internal energy of the gas

$$E = N\left(\frac{1}{2}m\bar{v}^2\right) \quad \ldots\text{(iii)}$$

From Eqs. (ii) and (iii), we get

$$pV = \frac{2}{3}E \quad \ldots\text{(iv)}$$

According to equation of state for 1 mole ideal gas,

$$pV = RT$$

Hence, from equation (iv),

$$RT = \frac{2}{3}E$$

For N number of molecules,

or, $$pV = k_BNT \quad \ldots\text{(v)}$$

Combining Eqs. (iv) and (v), we get

$$\frac{2}{3}E = k_BNT \Rightarrow \frac{E}{N} = \frac{3}{2}k_BT \quad \ldots\text{(vi)}$$

or $$\frac{1}{2}mv^2 = \frac{3}{2}k_BT \quad \ldots\text{(vii)}$$

$\Rightarrow$ Average kinetic energy, $\frac{1}{2}mv^2 \propto T$

It is clear that **average kinetic energy of a molecule is directly proportional to the absolute temperature of the gas.** This is a fundamental result that relates temperature of the gas to average kinetic energy of a molecule.

If $T = 0$, then $\frac{1}{2}m\bar{v}^2 = 0$ but $m \neq 0$ so $\bar{v}^2 = 0$

Thus, **absolute zero of temperature may be defined as that temperature at which the mean square speed of an ideal gas molecules reduces to zero, which is not possible in nature.**

Example 8 A balloon has 5.0 g mole of helium at 7°C. Calculate

(i) the number of atoms of helium in the balloon.

(ii) the total internal energy of the system. **[NCERT Exemplar]**

Sol. (i) Here, $\mu = 5.0$, $T = 7°\text{C} = 273 + 7 = 280$ K

Number of atoms $= \mu N_A = 5.0\times6.02\times10^{23} \approx 30\times10^{23}$

(ii) Average kinetic energy per molecule $= \frac{3}{2}k_BT$

$\therefore$ Total internal energy $= \frac{3}{2}k_BT\times N$

$$= \frac{3}{2}\times30\times10^{23}\times1.38\times10^{-23}\times280 = 1.74\times10^4\ \text{J}$$

Example 9 In a container, two gases neon and argon are filled. Find the ratio of the root mean square speed of the molecules of the two gases. $M_{Ne} = 20.2$ and $M_{Ar} = 39.9$. The temperature of the system is 30°C.

Sol. Given, $M_{Ne} = 20.2, M_{Ar} = 39.9$

Temperature $(T) = 30°$ C

We know that, $\frac{1}{2}mv_{rms}^2 = \frac{3}{2}k_BT$

Temperature is same for both the gases. Now, we can find the ratio of v_{rms} for the two gases.

$$\frac{(v_{rms}^2)_{Ne}}{(v_{rms}^2)_{Ar}} = \frac{(M)_{Ar}}{(M)_{Ne}}$$

Now, we can easily find the numerical value of ratio of two v_{rms}.

$$\frac{(v_{rms})_{Ne}}{(v_{rms})_{Ar}} = \sqrt{\frac{39.9}{20.2}} \simeq 1.40$$

Topic Practice 1

Multiple Choice Questions

1 Mark

1. Kinetic theory of gases
   (a) correctly explains specific heat capacities of many gases
   (b) relates properties of gases such as viscosity, conduction etc., with molecular parameters
   (c) Both (a) and (b) are correct
   (d) None of the above

2. Choose the correct option.
   (a) Maxwell and Boltzmann were among the scientists who developed kinetic theory
   (b Kinetic theory gives molecular interpretation of pressure and temperature of a gas
   (c) Kinetic theory is consistent with gas laws and Avogadro's hypothesis
   (d) All of the above

3. The collisions of the molecules of an ideal gas are
   (a) elastic (b) inelastic
   (c) completely inelastic (d) partially elastic

4. If 1 mole of a diatomic gas is at a pressure of 8×10^4 Nm^{-2}. The density of the gas is 4 kgm^{-3}. What is the energy of 1 molecule gas due to its thermal motion? (Take, mass of gas = 1 kg)
   (a) 3×10^4 J (b) 5×10^4 J
   (c) 6×10^4 J (d) 7×10^4 J

5. The average translational kinetic energy of 1 molecule of a gas is
   (a) $\frac{3}{2}k_BT$ (b) k_BT
   (c) $\frac{1}{2}k_BT$ (d) $\frac{2}{3}k_BT$

Very Short Answer Type Questions

1 Mark

6. Give one difference between real and ideal gas on the basis of intermolecular space.
7. Under what conditions, real gases behave as an ideal gas?
8. If a vehicle runs on the road for a long time, then the air pressure in the tyres increases. Explain.
9. What would be the effect on rms velocity of gas molecules, if the temperature of the gas is increased by a factor 4?
10. If a gas is heated, its temperature increases. On the basis of kinetic theory of gases, explain.
11. What is the value of kinetic energy of 1 mole of a gas in terms of its temperature?
12. According to kinetic theory of gases, explain absolute zero.

Short Answer Type I Questions

2 Marks

13. When do the real gases obey more correctly the gas equation $(pV = nRT)$?
14. Three vessels of equal capacity have gases at the same temperature and pressure. The first vessel contains neon (monoatomic), the second contains chlorine (diatomic) and the third contains uranium hexafluoride (polyatomic). Do the vessels contain equal number of respective molecules? Is the root mean square speed of molecules, the same in the three cases? If not, in which case is v_{rms}, the largest? **NCERT**
15. A gas mixture consists of molecules of types A, B and C with masses, $m_A > m_B > m_C$. Rank the three types of molecules in decreasing order of (i) average KE (ii) rms speed. **NCERT Exemplar**
16. Why temperature less than absolute zero is not possible?

Short Answer Type II Questions

3 Marks

17. Write the difference between ideal gas and real gas.

18. Explain the concept of an ideal gas and give its equation of state. Show that internal energy of an ideal gas is a function of its temperature only and is independent of its volume.

19. Explain, why
   (i) there is no atmosphere on moon?
   (ii) there is fall in temperature with altitude?

NCERT Exemplar

20. Show that the average kinetic energy of gas molecule is directly proportional to the absolute temperature of the gas. Hence, give the kinetic interpretation of temperature.

Long Answer Type Questions

5 Marks

21. Deduce Boyle's law, Charles' law, Avogadro's law and Dalton's law of partial pressure starting from expression of pressure derived in kinetic theory of gases.

22. Figure shows plot of pV/T *versus* p for 1.00×10^{-3} kg of oxygen gas at two different temperatures.

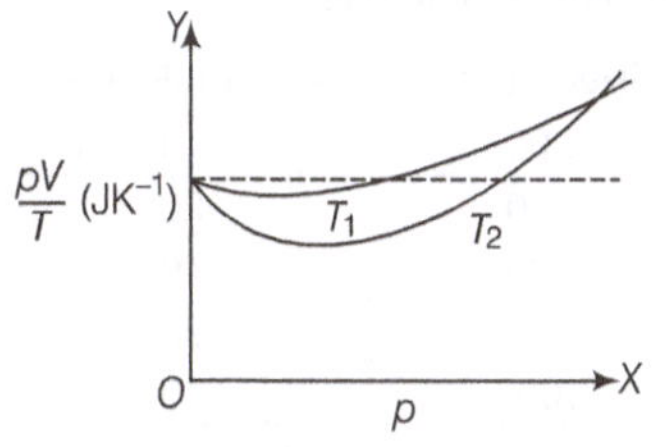

NCERT

   (i) What does the dotted plot signify?
   (ii) Which is true, $T_1 > T_2$ or $T_1 < T_2$?
   (iii) What is the value of pV/T, where the curves meet on the Y-axis?
   (iv) If we obtain similar plots for 1.00×10^{-3} kg of hydrogen, would we get the same value of pV/T at the point where the curves meet on the Y-axis? If not, what mass of hydrogen yields the same value of pV/T (for low pressure, high temperature region of the plot)? (Molecular mass of $H_2 = 2.02$ u, $O_2 = 32.0$ u, $R = 8.31$ Jmol^{-1}K^{-1}).

23. Explain the assumptions of kinetic theory of gases.

24. Prove that the pressure exerted by the gas is $p = \frac{1}{3}\rho \bar{v}^2$, where ρ is the density and $\bar{v}$ is the root mean square velocity.

25. Derive an expression for pressure exerted by an ideal gas using kinetic theory of gases. Hence, define root mean square velocity.

Numerical Problems

5 Marks

26. Calculate the number of atoms in 39.4 g gold. Molar mass of gold is 197g mol^{-1}.
NCERT Exemplar [1 M]

27. The volume of a given mass of a gas at 27°C, 1 atm is 100 cc. What will be its volume at 327°C? **[1 M]**

28. Two molecules of a gas have speeds of 9×10^6 ms^{-1} and 1×10^6 ms^{-1}, respectively. What is the root mean square speed of these molecules? **[1 M]**

29. Molar volume is the volume occupied by 1 mol of any (ideal) gas at standard temperature and pressure (STP : 1 atm pressure, 0°C). Show that, it is 22.4 L. **NCERT [2 M]**

30. Estimate the total number of air molecules (inclusive of oxygen, nitrogen, water vapour and other constituents) in a room of capacity 25.0 m^3 at a temperature of 27°C and 1 atm pressure. ($k_B = 1.38 \times 10^{-23}$ JK^{-1}) **[2 M]**

31. Estimate the fraction of molecular volume to the actual volume occupied by oxygen gas at STP. Take the diameter of an oxygen molecule to be 3 Å. **NCERT [2 M]**

32. A flask contains argon and chlorine in the ratio of 2 : 1 by mass. The temperature of the mixture is 27°C. Obtain the ratio of
   (i) average kinetic energy per molecule and
   (ii) root mean square speed (v_{rms}) of the molecules of the two gases. Atomic mass of argon = 39.9 u; Molecular mass of chlorine = 70.9 u. **[2 M]**

33. We have 0.5 g of hydrogen gas in a cubic chamber of size 3 cm kept at NTP. The gas in the chamber is compressed keeping the temperature constant till a final pressure of 100 atm. Is one justified in assuming the ideal gas law, in the final state? (Hydrogen molecules can be considered as spheres of radius 1 Å). **NCERT Exemplar [2 M]**

34. A tank used for filling helium balloons has a volume of 0.6 m^3 and contains 2.0 mol of helium gas at 20.0°C. Assuming that the helium behaves like an ideal gas.
   (i) What is the total translational kinetic energy of the molecules of the gas?
   (ii) What is the average kinetic energy per molecule? **[2 M]**

35. At what temperature, is the root mean square speed of an atom in an argon gas cylinder equal to the rms speed of a helium gas atom at −20°C? (Atomic mass of Ar = 39.9 u, He = 4.0 u). **NCERT [2 M]**

36. Determine the rms velocity of oxygen molecules at STP. The molecular weight of oxygen is 32. **[3 M]**

37. Estimate the average thermal energy of a helium atom at (i) room temperature (27°C) (ii) the temperature on the surface of the sun (6000 K), (iii) the temperature of 10 million kelvin (the typical core temperature in the case of a star). **[3 M]**

38. (i) Write ideal gas equation in terms of density.
   (ii) If molar volume is the volume occupied by 1 mole of any (ideal) gas at STP, show that it is 22.4 L (Take, $R = 8.313\ \text{mol}^{-1}\text{K}^{-1}$). **[3 M]**

39. A meter long narrow bore held horizontally (and closed at one end) contains a 76 cm long mercury thread which traps a 15 cm column of air. What happens, if the tube is held vertically with the open end at the bottom? **[3 M]**

40. The container shown in figure has two chambers, separated by a partition of volumes $V_1 = 2.0$ L and $V_2 = 3.0$ L. The chambers contain $\mu_1 = 4.0$ and $\mu_2 = 5.0$ moles of a gas at pressures $p_1 = 1.00$ atm and $p_2 = 2.00$ atm. Calculate the pressure after the partition is removed and the mixture attains equilibrium. **NCERT Exemplar [3 M]**

V_1	V_2
μ_1	μ_2
p_1	p_2

41. An oxygen cylinder of volume 30 L, has an initial gauge pressure of 15 atm and a temperature of 27 °C. After some oxygen is withdrawn from the cylinder, the gauge pressure drops to 11 atm and its temperature drops to 17 °C. Estimate the mass of oxygen taken out of the cylinder. (Take, $R = 8.31\ \text{mol}^{-1}\text{K}^{-1}$, molecular mass of $O_2 = 32$ u). **NCERT [3 M]**

42. Given below are densities of some solids and liquids. Give rough estimate of the size of their atoms.

Substance	Atomic Mass (u)	Density (10^{-3} kg m^{-3})
(i) Carbon (diamond)	12.01	2.22
(ii) Gold	197.00	19.32
(iii) Nitrogen (liquid)	14.01	1.00
(iv) Lithium	6.94	0.53
(v) Fluorine (liquid)	19.00	1.14

[5 M]

43. You are given, the following data about a group of particles, where n_i represents the number of molecules with speed v_i

n_i	2	4	8	6	3
v_i (ms^{-1})	1.0	2.0	3.0	4.0	5.0

Calculate (i) average speed. (ii) rms speed. (iii) most probable speed. **[5 M]**

44. Consider an ideal gas with following distribution of speeds.

Speed (m/s)	% of molecules
200	10
400	20
600	40
800	20
1000	10

   (i) Calculate v_{rms} and hence T (Take, $m = 3.0 \times 10^{-26}$ kg).
   (ii) If all the molecules with speed 1000 m/s escape from the system, calculate new v_{rms} and hence T. **NCERT Exemplar [5 M]**

45. Oxygen is filled in a closed metal jar of volume 10^{-3} m^3 at a pressure of 1.5×10^5 Pa and temperature 400 K. The jar has a small leak in it. The atmospheric pressure is 10^5 Pa and the atmospheric temperature is 300 K. Find the mass of the gas that leaks out by the time, the pressure and the temperature inside the jar equalise with the surrounding. **[5 M]**

Hints & Solutions

1. (c) Kinetic theory of gases correctly explains specific heat capacities of many gases and it relates properties of gases viscosity, conduction, etc. with molecular parameter.

2. (d) The kinetic theory was developed in the nineteenth century by Maxwell, Boltzmann and others. It has been remarkably successful. It gives a molecular interpretation of pressure and temperature of a gas and is consistent with gas laws and Avogadro's hypothesis.

3. (a) According to kinetic theory of gases the collision among molecules and the collision of molecule with the walls of container are elastic.

4. (a) Thermal energy corresponds to internal energy

Mass = 1 kg, density = 4 kgm^{-3}

$$\because \quad \text{Volume} = \frac{\text{Mass}}{\text{Density}} = \frac{1}{4}\ \text{m}^3$$

Pressure = $8 \times 10^4\ \text{Nm}^{-2}$

$$\therefore \text{ Internal energy of 1 molecule} = \frac{3}{2} p \times V$$

$$= \frac{3}{2} \times 8 \times 10^4 \times \frac{1}{4} = 3 \times 10^4\ \text{J}$$

5. (a) We know that, pressure of gas and internal energy are related as

$$pV = \frac{2}{3} E \qquad \text{...(i)}$$

$$\left(\begin{array}{l}\text{here, } E = \text{total internal energy of the gas} \\ \quad = N\, 1/2\, m\, \bar{v}^2\end{array}\right)$$

and from ideal gas equation, we have

$$pV = k_B N T \qquad \text{...(ii)}$$

From Eqs. (i) and (ii), we get

$$\frac{2}{3} E = k_B NT \Rightarrow \frac{E}{N} = \frac{3}{2} k_B T \Rightarrow \frac{1}{2} m\bar{v}^2 = \frac{3}{2} k_B T$$

6. Refer to text on page 402 (Kinetic interpretation of behaviour of gases).

7. At low pressure and high temperature, real gases behave as an ideal gas.

8. Due to the presence of friction between the road and tyres, the tyres get heated as a result of which temperature of air inside the tyre increases and hence pressure in tyre also increases.

9. As, $v_{rms} \propto \sqrt{T}$

If temperature of the gas is increased 4 times, then v_{rms} will be doubled.

10. If a gas is heated, then the root mean square velocity of its molecules is increased.

$$\because \quad v_{rms} \propto \sqrt{T}$$

$\therefore$ The temperature of the gas increases.

11. Refer to text on page 407 (Kinetic interpretation of temperature).

12. Absolute zero is the temperature at which the molecules of a gas becomes motionless, i.e. $\bar{v}_{rms} = 0$.

13. Refer to text on page 402 (Kinetic interpretation of behaviour of gases).

14. As three vessels are identical, i.e. they have same volume. Now at constant pressure, temperature and volume, the three vessels will contain equal number of molecules (by Avogadro's law) and is equal to Avogadro's number, $N_A = 6.023 \times 10^{23}$. [1]

$$\because \quad v_{rms} = \sqrt{\frac{3k_B T}{m}}$$

$$\Rightarrow \quad v_{rms} \propto \frac{1}{\sqrt{m}}$$

where, m is mass of single gas molecule as neon has the smallest mass, so rms speed will be greatest in case of neon. [1]

15. The average KE will be same as conditions of temperature and pressure are same.

$$v_{rms} \propto \frac{1}{\sqrt{m}}$$ [1]

$$\because \quad m_A > m_B > m_C$$

$$\Rightarrow \quad v_C > v_B > v_A$$ [1]

16. Refer to text on page 407 (Kinetic interpretation of temperature).

17.

	Ideal Gas	Real Gas
(i)	It obeys ideal gas equation, $pV = \mu RT$ at all temperatures and pressures.	It does not obey, $pV = \mu RT$ at all values of temperature and pressure.
(ii)	The volume of the molecules of an ideal gas is zero.	The volume of the molecules of a real gas is non-zero.
(iii)	There is no intermolecular force between the molecules.	There is intermolecular force of attraction or repulsion depending on whether intermolecular separation is larger or small.
(iv)	There is no intermolecular potential energy U because intermolecular force F is zero.	Potential energy U does not equal to zero as intermolecular force F is not zero.
(v)	It has only kinetic energy.	It has both kinetic and potential energy.
(vi)	At absolute zero, the volume, pressure and internal energy become zero.	All real gases get liquified before reaching absolute zero. The internal energy of the liquified gas is not zero.

[6 × ½ = 3]

18. Refer to text on pages 402 and 403 (Equation of state for an ideal gas) and page 407 (Kinetic interpretation of temperature).

19. (i) The moon has small gravitational force and hence the escape velocity is small.
As the rms speed of the air molecules is larger than escape velocity on the moon, a significant number of molecules have speed greater than escape velocity and they escape.
Now, rest of the molecules arrange the speed distribution for the equilibrium temperature. Again, a significant number of molecules escape as their speeds exceed escape speed. Hence, over a long time the moon has lost most of its atmosphere. [2]
(ii) As the molecules move higher, their potential energy increases and hence kinetic energy decreases and hence temperature reduces.
As a result, at greater height, more volume is available and gas expands and hence some cooling further takes place. [1]

20. Refer to text on page 407 (Kinetic interpretation of temperature).

21. We can deduce gas laws from kinetic theory as follows
(i) Boyle's law
$$p = \frac{1}{3}\frac{nm}{V}v_{\text{rms}}^2$$
or $$pV = \frac{1}{3}nmv_{\text{rms}}^2$$
Now, as v_{rms} is a function of temperature above, so if temperature is constant, v_{rms} is constant.
Hence, at constant temperature, the term on right hand side of equation is a constant.
$\therefore$ $pV =$ constant
when $T =$ constant [1]
(ii) Charles' law
$$p = \frac{1}{3}\frac{mn}{V}v_{\text{rms}}^2$$
or $$V = \frac{2}{3}\frac{n}{p}\left(\frac{1}{2}mv_{\text{rms}}^2\right)$$
$$= \frac{2}{3}\frac{n}{p}\cdot\frac{3}{2}k_BT$$
So, when $p =$ a constant, then
$V \propto T$ or $\frac{V}{T} =$ a constant. [1]
(iii) Avogadro's law
Let there are two gases under same condition of pressure, volume and temperature, then
For gas 1,
$$pV = \frac{1}{3}m_1n_1v_{1\text{ rms}}^2$$
and for gas 2,
$$pV = \frac{1}{3}m_2n_2v_{2\text{ rms}}^2$$
As the temperature is same, $\frac{1}{2}m_1v_{1\text{rms}} = \frac{1}{2}m_2v_{2\text{rms}}$
$\therefore$ $n_1 = n_2$
or equal volume of all gases at same pressure and temperature contains equal number of molecules. [1½]
(iv) Dalton's law of partial pressure
Let a gas mixture occupies a volume V, then partial pressure of individual gases are
$$p_1V = \frac{1}{3}m_1n_1\bar{v}_1^2,\ p_2V = \frac{1}{3}m_2n_2\bar{v}_2^2,\ \ldots,\ p_nV = \frac{1}{3}m_nn_n\bar{v}_n^2$$
On adding above equations, we get
$$(p_1 + p_2 + \ldots + p_n)V = \frac{1}{3}(m_1n_1\bar{v}_1^2 + m_2n_2\bar{v}_2^2 + \ldots)$$
As gases occupy same volume their temperatures are equal and so
$$\frac{1}{2}m_1\bar{v}_1^2 = \frac{1}{2}m_2\bar{v}_2^2 \quad \ldots,\text{ etc.}$$
or $$(p_1 + p_2 + \ldots + p_n)V = \frac{1}{3}m\bar{v}_1^2(n_1 + n_2 + \ldots) = pV$$
or $$p = p_1 + p_2 + \ldots p_n$$
So, total pressure of gas is sum of partial pressures of constituents. [1½]

22. (i) Dotted plot shows that $\frac{pV}{T}$ is a constant quantity $\left(\frac{pV}{T} = mR\right)$ which is independent of pressure. It signifies the ideal gas behaviour. [1]
(ii) As curve at temperature T_1 is closer to the dotted plot than the curve at temperature T_2. Since, the behaviour of a real gas approaches the behaviour of perfect gas when temperature is increased, so $T_1 > T_2$. [1]
(iii) The value of $\frac{pV}{T}$, where the curves meet on Y-axis is equal to μR.
Now, given mass of oxygen gas $= 1.00 \times 10^{-3}$ kg $= 1$ g
$$\therefore \quad \frac{pV}{T} = \mu R = \left(\frac{1}{32}\right) \times 8.31\ \text{JK}^{-1}$$
$$= 0.26\ \text{JK}^{-1}$$ [1]
(iv) If we use 1.00×10^{-3} kg of hydrogen, then we will not get same value of $\frac{pV}{T}$ at the point where the curves meet on Y-axis because molecular mass of hydrogen is different from oxygen.
Now, to get same value of $\frac{pV}{T}$, mass of hydrogen required is obtained from
$$\frac{pV}{T} = \mu R = \frac{m}{2.02} \times 8.31 = 0.26$$
$$\Rightarrow \quad m = \frac{2.02 \times 0.26}{8.31} = 6.32 \times 10^{-2}\ \text{g}$$ [2]

23. Refer to text on page 405 (Assumptions of kinetic theory of gases).

24. Refer to text on pages 405 and 406 (Concept of pressure of an ideal gas).

25. Refer to text on pages 405, 406 and 407 (Concept of pressure of an ideal gas and root mean square speed of gas molecule).

26. Molar mass of gold is 197g mol^{-1}, the number of atoms $= 6.0\times 10^{23}$ [1/2]

$\therefore$ Number of atoms in 39.4 g $= \dfrac{6.0\times 10^{23}\times 39.4}{197}$

$= 1.2\times 10^{23}$ [1/2]

27. Keeping p constant, we have

$$V_2 = \frac{V_1T_2}{T_1} = \frac{100\times 600}{300} = 200 \text{ cc}$$

28. $v_{\text{rms}} = \sqrt{\dfrac{v_1^2+v_2^2}{2}} = \sqrt{\dfrac{(9\times 10^6)^2+(1\times 10^6)^2}{2}}$ [1/2]

$= \sqrt{\dfrac{(81+1)\times 10^{12}}{2}} = \sqrt{41}\times 10^6 \text{ ms}^{-1}$ [1/2]

29. As, for one mole of ideal gas, $pV = \mu RT$ $[\because \mu = 1]$

$$pV = RT \Rightarrow V = \frac{RT}{p}$$ [1]

Putting, $R = 8.31 \text{ J mol}^{-1}\text{ K}^{-1}$, $T = 273\text{K}$

$p = 1 \text{ atm} = 1.013\times 10^5 \text{ N m}^{-2}$

$$V = \frac{8.31\times 273}{1.013\times 10^5} = 0.0224 \text{ m}^3$$ [1/2]

$= 22.4 \text{ L}$ $[\because 1\text{m}^3 = 10^3\text{L}]$ [1/2]

30. Given, $V = 25.0 \text{ m}^3$, $T = 273 + 27 = 300$ K [1/2]

$k_B = 1.38\times 10^{-23} \text{ JK}^{-1}$

Now, $pV = \mu RT \Rightarrow pV = \mu(N_Ak_B)T$ [1/2]

$\Rightarrow pV = N'k_BT$ [N' is total number of molecules]

$$\therefore N' = \frac{pV}{k_BT} = \frac{(1.01\times 10^5)\times 25}{(1.38\times 10^{-23})\times 300} = 6.10\times 10^{26}$$ [1]

31. Given, $d = 3\text{Å}$

$$r = \frac{d}{2} = 1.5\times 10^{-10}\text{ m} = 1.5\times 10^{-8}\text{ cm}$$

Molecular volume, $V = \dfrac{4}{3}\pi r^3 N$

$= \dfrac{4}{3}\times 3.14\times(1.5\times 10^{-8})^3\times 6.023\times 10^{23} = 8.52$ cc [1]

Actual volume occupied by 1 mole of oxygen at STP,

$V' = 22400$ cc

$$\therefore \frac{V}{V'} = \frac{8.52}{22400} = 3.8\times 10^{-4}$$ [1]

32. (i) The average kinetic energy per molecule of any gas is $\dfrac{3}{2}k_BT$. It depends only on temperature and not on the nature of the gas. As both argon and chlorine have the same temperature in the flask, the ratio of average KE per molecule of the two gases is 1 : 1. [1]

(ii) If m is mass of single molecule and M is the molecular mass, then

$$\frac{1}{2}mv_{\text{rms}}^2 = \frac{3}{2}k_BT$$

= constant at a given temperature [1/2]

$$\therefore \frac{(v_{\text{rms}}^2)_{\text{Ar}}}{(v_{\text{rms}}^2)_{\text{Cl}_2}} = \frac{(m)_{\text{Cl}_2}}{(m)_{\text{Ar}}} = \frac{M_{\text{Cl}_2}}{M_{\text{Ar}}} = \frac{70.9}{39.9} = 1.777$$

or $\dfrac{(v_{\text{rms}})_{\text{Ar}}}{(v_{\text{rms}})_{\text{Cl}_2}} = \sqrt{1.777} = 1.333$ [1/2]

33. We have, $0.25\times 6\times 10^{23}$ molecules, each of volume 10^{-30}m^3.

Molecular volume $= 2.5\times 10^{-7} \text{ m}^3$

Supposing, ideal gas law is valid.

Final volume $= \dfrac{V_{\text{in}}}{100} = \dfrac{(3)^3\times 10^{-6}}{100} \approx 2.7\times 10^{-7} \text{ m}^3$ [1]

Which is about the molecular volume. Hence, intermolecular forces cannot be neglected. Therefore, the ideal gas situation does not hold. [1]

34. (i) We know that, $(\text{KE})_{\text{trans}} = \dfrac{3}{2}nRT$

Given, $n = 2$ mol, $T = 273 + 20 = 293$ K

$\Rightarrow (\text{KE})_{\text{trans}} = \dfrac{3}{2}(2)(8.31)(293) = 7.3\times 10^3$ J [1]

(ii) Average KE per molecule

$= \dfrac{1}{2}m\bar{v}_{\text{rms}}^2 = \dfrac{3}{2}kT = \dfrac{3}{2}(1.38\times 10^{-23})(293)$

$= 6.07\times 10^{-21}$ J [1]

35. Let C and C' be the rms velocity of argon and a helium gas atoms at temperatures TK and T'K, respectively.

Here, $M = 39.9$, $M' = 4.0$, $T = ?$,

$T' = -20 + 273 = 253$ K

Now, $v = \sqrt{\dfrac{3RT}{M}} = \sqrt{\dfrac{3RT}{39.9}}$ [1]

and $v' = \sqrt{\dfrac{3RT'}{M'}} = \sqrt{\dfrac{3R\times 253}{4}}$

Since, $v = v'$, therefore

$\sqrt{\dfrac{3RT}{39.9}} = \sqrt{\dfrac{3R\times 253}{4}}$ or $T = \dfrac{39.9\times 253}{4} = 2523.7\text{K}$ [1]

36. At STP, pressure, $p = 1 \text{ atm} = 1.013\times 10^5 \text{ Nm}^{-2}$

Mass, $M = 32\text{g} = 32\times 10^{-3}$ kg

Molar volume, $V = 22.4 \text{ L} = 22.4\times 10^{+3} \text{ m}^3$ [1]

Root mean square velocity of oxygen molecules at STP,

$$v_{\text{rms}} = \sqrt{\frac{3p}{d}} = \sqrt{\frac{3pV}{M}} = \sqrt{\frac{3\times 1.013\times 10^{-5}\times 22.4\times 10^3}{32\times 10^{-3}}}$$ [1]

$v_{\text{rms}} = 461.23 \text{ ms}^{-1}$ [1]

37. (i) Given, $T = 27°\text{C} = (273.15 + 27) = 300.15$ K

Average thermal energy, $E = \dfrac{3}{2}k_BT$

(where, k_B = Boltzmann constant $= 1.38\times 10^{-23} \text{ J K}^{-1}$)

$$E = \frac{3}{2}\times 1.38\times 10^{-23}\times 300.15 = 6.21\times 10^{-21} \text{ J}$$ [1]

(ii) At the temperature, $T = 6000\text{ K}$ (surface of the sun)

Average thermal energy,

$$E = \frac{3}{2}k_B T = \frac{3}{2} \times 1.38 \times 10^{-23} \times 6000$$
$$= 1.241 \times 10^{-19}\text{ J}$$ [1]

(iii) At temperature, $T = 10^7\text{K}$

Average thermal energy,

$$E = \frac{3}{2}k_B T = \frac{3}{2} \times 1.38 \times 10^{-23} \times 10^7 = 2.07 \times 10^{-16}\text{ J}$$ [1]

38. (i) Refer to text on pages 402 and 403 (Equation of state for an ideal gas). [1]

(ii) $p = 1\text{ atm} = 0.76\text{ m of Hg}$

$$= 0.76 \times (13.6 \times 10^3) \times 9.8\text{ Pa}$$

$\Rightarrow$ $T = 273\text{ K}, R = 8.31\text{ J mol}^{-1}\text{K}^{-1}, \mu = 1\text{ mole}$

As, $pV = \mu RT$

or $$V = \frac{\mu RT}{p} = \frac{1 \times 8.31 \times 273}{0.76 \times (13.6 \times 10^3) \times 9.8}$$ [1]

$$= 22.4 \times 10^{-3}\text{ m}^3 = 22.4\text{ L}$$ [1]

39. If the tube is held horizontally, the mercury thread of length 76 cm traps a length of air = 15 cm. A length of 9 cm of the tube will be at the open end, Fig. (a). The pressure of air enclosed in tube will be atmospheric pressure. Let area of cross-section of the tube be 1 sq. cm.

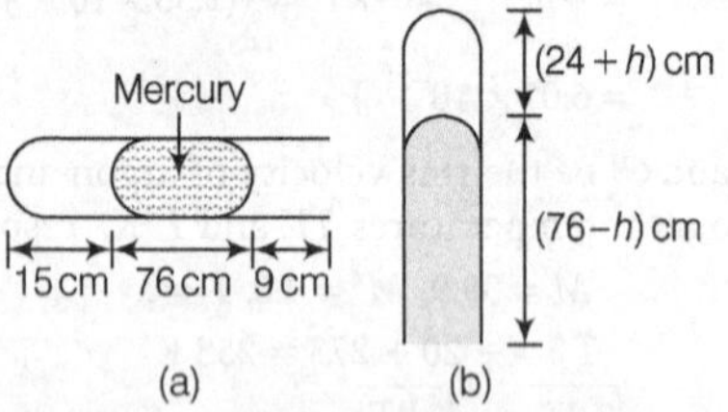

$\therefore$ $p_1 = 76\text{ cm and } V_1 = 15\text{ cm}^3$ [1]

If the tube is held vertically, 15 cm air gets another 9 cm of air (filled in the right handside in the horizontal position) and let h cm of mercury flow out to balance the atmospheric pressure, Fig. (b). Then, the heights of air column and mercury column are $(24 + h)$ cm and $(76 - h)$ cm, respectively.

The pressure of air $= 76 - (76 - h) = h$ cm of mercury

$\therefore$ $V_2 = (24 + h)\text{ cm}^3 \text{ and } p_2 = h\text{ cm}$ [1]

If we assume that temperature remains constant, then

$$p_1V_1 = p_2V_2 \text{ or } 76 \times 15 = h \times (24 + h)$$

or $$h^2 + 24h - 1140 = 0$$

or $$h = \frac{-24 \pm \sqrt{(24)^2 + 4 \times 1140}}{2}$$

$$= 23.8\text{ cm or } -47.8\text{ cm}$$

Since, h cannot be negative (because more mercury cannot flow into the tube), therefore $h = 23.8$ cm. Thus, in the vertical position of the tube, 23.8 cm of mercury flows out. [1]

40. Given, $V_1 = 2.0\text{ L}, V_2 = 3.0\text{ L}, \mu_1 = 4.0\text{ moles}, \mu_2 = 5.0\text{ moles}$

$p_1 = 1.00\text{ atm}, \; p_2 = 2.00\text{ atm}$

$$p_1V_1 = \mu_1 RT_1, \; p_2V_2 = \mu_2 RT_2$$
$$\mu = \mu_1 + \mu_2, \; V = V_1 + V_2$$

For 1 mole, $pV = \frac{2}{3}E$ [1]

For μ_1 mole, $p_1V_1 = \frac{2}{3}\mu_1 E_1$

For μ_2 mole, $p_2V_2 = \frac{2}{3}\mu_2 E_2$

Total energy, $(\mu_1 E_1 + \mu_2 E_2) = \frac{3}{2}(p_1V_1 + p_2V_2)$

$$pV = \frac{2}{3}E_{\text{total}} = \frac{2}{3}\mu E_{\text{per mole}}$$ [1]

$$p(V_1 + V_2) = \frac{2}{3} \times \frac{3}{2}(p_1V_1 + p_2V_2)$$

$$p = \frac{p_1V_1 + p_2V_2}{V_1 + V_2} \quad \text{...(i)}$$

$$= \left(\frac{1.00 \times 2.0 + 2.00 \times 3.0}{2.0 + 3.0}\right) = \frac{8.0}{5.0} = 1.60\text{ atm}$$ [1]

41. Given, absolute pressure, $p_1 = (15 + 1)$ atm [1/2]

[$\because$ absolute pressure = gauge pressure + 1 atm]

$$= 16 \times 1.013 \times 10^5\text{ Pa}$$
$$V_1 = 30\text{ L} = 30 \times 10^{-3}\text{ m}^3$$
$$T_1 = 273.15 + 27 = 300.15\text{ K}$$ [1/2]

Using ideal gas equation, $pV = nRT$

or $$n = \frac{pV}{RT} = \frac{p_1V_1}{RT_1} = \frac{16 \times 1.013 \times 10^5 \times 30 \times 10^{-3}}{8.314 \times 300.15}$$

$$= 19.48$$ [1]

Final pressure,

$$p_2 = (11 + 1) = 12\text{ atm} = 12 \times 1.013 \times 10^5\text{ Pa}$$
$$V_2 = 30\text{ L} = 30 \times 10^{-3}\text{ m}^3$$
$$T_2 = 273.15 + 17 = 290.15\text{ K}$$ [1/2]

Number of moles

$$= \frac{p_2V_2}{RT_2} = \frac{12 \times 1.013 \times 10^5 \times 30 \times 10^{-3}}{8.314 \times 290.15}$$
$$= 15.12$$

Hence, moles removed $= 19.48 - 15.12 = 4.36$

Mass removed $= 4.36 \times 32$ g

$$= 139.52\text{g} = 0.1395\text{ kg}$$ [1/2]

42. We know that, density of an element,

$$\rho = \frac{\text{Mass}}{\text{Volume}} = \frac{\text{Mass of 1 mole}}{\text{Total volume of molecules in 1 mole when closely packed}}$$ [1]

$$\rho = \frac{M(\text{in gram})}{\left(\frac{4}{3}\pi r^3\right)N_A} = \frac{3M \times 10^{-3}\text{ kg}}{4\pi r^3 \cdot N_A} \Rightarrow r = \left[\frac{3M \times 10^{-3}}{4\pi N_A \cdot \rho}\right]^{1/3}$$ [1½]

where, N_A = Avogadro's number $\simeq 6 \times 10^{23}$

(i) For carbon (diamond),

$$M = 12.01, \rho = 2.22 \times 10^3\text{ kg/m}^3$$

$\therefore$ Radius of carbon atom,

$$r = \left[\frac{3\times 12.01\times 10^{-3}}{4\times 3.14\times 6\times 10^{23}\times 2.22\times 10^{3}}\right]^{1/3}$$ [1/2]

$= 1.29\times 10^{-10}\text{m} = 1.29$ Å

(ii) For gold, $M = 197.00, \rho = 19.32\times 10^{3}$ kg/m^3

$\therefore$ Radius of gold atom,

$$r = \left[\frac{3\times 197\times 10^{-3}}{4\times 3.14\times 6\times 10^{23}\times 19.32\times 10^{3}}\right]^{\frac{1}{3}}$$ [1/2]

$= 1.59\times 10^{-10}\text{m} = 1.59$ Å

(iii) For nitrogen (liquid),

$M = 14.01, \rho = 1.00\times 10^{3}$ kg / m^3

$\therefore$ Radius of nitrogen atom,

$$r = \left[\frac{3\times 14.01\times 10^{-3}}{4\times 3.14\times 6\times 10^{23}\times 1.0\times 10^{3}}\right]^{\frac{1}{3}}$$ [1/2]

$= 1.77\times 10^{-7}$ m $= 1.77$ Å

(iv) For lithium, $M = 6.94, \rho = 0.53\times 10^{3}$ kg/m^3

$\therefore$ Radius of lithium atom,

$$r = \left[\frac{3\times 6.94\times 10^{-3}}{4\times 3.14\times 6\times 10^{23}\times 0.53\times 10^{3}}\right]^{\frac{1}{3}}$$ [1/2]

$= 1.73\times 10^{-10}$ m

$= 1.73$ Å

(v) For flourine (liquid),

$M = 19.00$ and $\rho = 1.14\times 10^{3}$ kg /m^3

$\therefore$ Radius of fluorine atom,

$$r = \left[\frac{3\times 19.0\times 10^{-3}}{4\times 3.14\times 6\times 10^{23}\times 1.14\times 10^{3}}\right]^{\frac{1}{3}}$$

$= 1.88\times 10^{-10}$ m

$= 1.88$ Å [1/2]

43. (i) Average speed

$$= \frac{n_1v_1 + n_2v_2 + n_3v_3 + n_4v_4 + n_5v_5}{n_1 + n_2 + n_3 + n_4 + n_5}$$

$$= \frac{2\times 1 + 4\times 2 + 8\times 3 + 6\times 4 + 3\times 5}{2+4+8+6+3}$$

$= 3.17$ m / s [1½]

(ii) Root mean square speed

$$= \sqrt{\frac{n_1v_1^2 + n_2v_2^2 + n_3v_3^2 + n_4v_4^2 + n_5v_5^2}{n_1 + n_2 + n_3 + n_4 + n_5}}$$

$$= \sqrt{\frac{2\times 1^2 + 4\times 2^2 + 8\times 3^2 + 6\times 4^2 + 3\times 5^2}{2+4+8+6+3}}$$

$= 3.36$ m / s [1½]

(iii) The most probable speed is that speed which is possessed by maximum number of molecules.

Most probable speed, $v_{mp} = \sqrt{\frac{2k_BT}{m}} = \sqrt{\frac{3k_BT}{m}\times\frac{2}{3}}$ [1]

$$v_{mp} = \sqrt{\frac{2}{3}}\times\sqrt{\frac{3k_BT}{m}} = \sqrt{\frac{2}{3}}v_{rms}$$

$= \sqrt{\frac{2}{3}}\times 3.36$ m/s $= 0.816\times 3.36$ m/s $= 2.74$ m/s [1]

44. This problem is designed to give an idea about cooling by evaporation

(i) $v^2_{rms} = \frac{\sum_i n_iv_i^2}{\sum n_i}$ [1]

$$= \frac{10\times(200)^2 + 20\times(400)^2 + 40\times(600)^2 + 20\times(800)^2 + 10\times(1000)^2}{100}$$

$$= \frac{10\times 100^2\times(1\times 4 + 2\times 16 + 4\times 36 + 2\times 64 + 1\times 100)}{100}$$

$= 1000\times(4 + 32 + 144 + 128 + 100)$ [1]

$= 408\times 1000$ m^2/s^2

$\therefore$ $v_{rms} = 639$ m /s ,

$\frac{1}{2}mv^2_{rms} = \frac{3}{2}kT$

$\therefore$ $T = \frac{1}{3}\frac{mv^2_{rms}}{k} = \frac{1}{3}\times\frac{3.0\times 10^{-26}\times 4.08\times 10^5}{1.38\times 10^{-23}}$

$= 2.96\times 10^2 = 296$ K [1]

(ii) $$v^2_{rms} = \frac{10\times(200)^2 + 20\times(400)^2 + 40\times(600)^2 + 20\times(800)^2}{90}$$

$$= \frac{10\times 100^2\times(1\times 4 + 2\times 16 + 4\times 36 + 2\times 64)}{90}$$

$v^2_{rms} = 10000\times\frac{308}{9}$

$v^2_{rms} = 342\times 1000$ m^2/s^2 [1]

$v_{rms} = 584$ m/s

$T = \frac{1}{3}\frac{mv^2_{rms}}{k} = 248$ K

So, temperature reduces as fast moving molecules leaves the volume considered. [1]

45. Given, volume, $V = 10^{-3}$ m^3

Pressure, $p_1 = 1.5\times 10^5$ Pa, $p_2 = 10^5$ Pa

Temperature, $T_1 = 400$ K, $T_2 = 300$ K [1]

From ideal gas equation, $p_1V = n_1RT_1 \Rightarrow n_1 = \frac{p_1V}{RT_1}$ [1]

Similarly, $p_2V = n_2RT_2 \Rightarrow n_2 = \frac{p_2V}{RT_2}$ [1/2]

$\therefore$ Number of mole leaked,

$$\Delta n = n_1 - n_2 = \left(\frac{p_1}{T_1} - \frac{p_2}{T_2}\right)\frac{V}{R} = \left(\frac{1.5}{400} - \frac{1}{300}\right)\times\frac{10^5\times 10^{-3}}{8.3}$$

$= 5.02\times 10^{-3}$ [1½]

$\therefore$ Mass of gas leaked $= \Delta n M_0 = 5.02\times 10^{-3}\times 32 = 0.16$ g [1]

TOPIC 02 Motion of Gas Molecules

Degree of Freedom

The total number of coordinates or independent quantities required to describe completely the position and configuration of a dynamical system is known as number of **degrees of freedom** of the system. It is represented by f.

Degree of freedom can also be expressed in terms of system parameters, $f = 3N - K$

where, N is the number of particles in a system and K is number of independent relations or bonds between the particles.

(i) A monoatomic gas molecule (or atom) is a rigid sphere. It can translate along X, Y and Z-axis. Thus, its velocity can have three components or molecules can undergo three independent motions. Hence, a monoatomic gas molecule has three degrees of freedom.

Here, $N = 1$ and $K = 0$, so by using above relation, $f = 3 \times 1 - 0 = 3$.

Note A monoatomic gas molecule can rotate also, but it has a very small moment of inertia and so its rotational kinetic energy is very insignificant in comparison to its translational kinetic energy.

(ii) A diatomic gas molecule is in shape of a dumbell. It can translate along X, Y and Z-axis. So, it has three degrees of freedom for translation.

A diatomic dumbell can rotate about any of three axes, but its moment of inertia along the axis joining two atoms is negligible.

So, a diatomic gas molecule can have three translational and two rotational motions.

Therefore, it has five degrees of freedom.

Here, $N = 2$ and $K = 1$

So, $\quad f = 2 \times 3 - 1 = 5$

(iii) A polyatomic gas molecule can independently translate about any of the axis and it can also rotate about any of the three axes.

So, a polyatomic gas molecule has six degrees of freedom.

Here, $N = 3$ and $K = 3$

So, $\quad f = 3 \times 3 - 3 = 6$

Note At high temperature atoms of molecule of a diatomic or a polyatomic gas molecule can vibrate also. For each vibrational mode, a molecule has two additional degrees of freedom.

Law of Equipartition of Energy

It states that, for a dynamic system in thermal equilibrium, the total energy is distributed equally amongst all the degree of freedom and the energy associated with each molecule per degree of freedom is $\frac{1}{2} k_B T$.

where, $k_B = 1.38 \times 10^{-23}\ \text{JK}^{-1}$ is Boltzmann constant and T is absolute temperature of system on the Kelvin scale.

Total Internal Energy of an Ideal Gas Sample

As pressure exerted by an ideal gas is

$$p = \frac{1}{3}\left(\frac{N}{V}\right) m v_{\text{rms}}^2$$

and for an ideal gas, $pV = \mu RT = \left(\frac{N}{N_A}\right) RT$

From above two equations, we get

$$\frac{1}{2} m v_{\text{rms}}^2 = \frac{3}{2}\left(\frac{R}{N_A}\right) T$$

where, R / N_A = Boltzmann's constant (k_B).

So, we can say that mean kinetic energy of 1 gas molecule is

$$E_1 = \frac{3}{2} k_B T$$

This expression gives law of equipartition of energy. As an ideal gas molecule has three degrees of freedom, so energy associated with each degree of freedom is $\frac{1}{2} k_B T$.

From above, we can deduce following

- Energy of 1 mole of a gas at temperature T,

$$E_{N_A} = N_A \times E_1 = \frac{3}{2} N_A k_B T = \frac{3}{2} RT$$

- Energy of μ moles of a gas,

$$E_\mu = \mu \times E_{N_A} = \frac{3}{2} \mu RT = \frac{3}{2} pV$$

- Energy of m gram of a gas,

$$E_m = \frac{3}{2}\left(\frac{m}{M_0}\right)RT$$

where, M_0 = molar mass of a gas.

Specific Heat Capacity (C)

In this topic, we will relate different specific heat capacities of gases with degrees of freedom. It can be calculated by applying the law of equipartition of energy of gases.

If a polyatomic gas molecule has f degrees of freedom, then internal energy of one mole of the gas is

$$U = f \times \left(\frac{1}{2}k_BT\right) \times N_A = \frac{f}{2}RT$$

Now, $$C_V = \frac{dU}{dT} = \frac{d}{dT}\left(\frac{f}{2}RT\right) = \frac{f}{2}R$$

$$C_V = \frac{f}{2}R$$

$\therefore$ $$C_p = C_V + R = \frac{f}{2}R + R = \left(\frac{f}{2}+1\right)R$$

$$C_p = \left(\frac{f}{2}+1\right)R$$

So, specific heat ratio is

$$\gamma = \frac{C_p}{C_V} = \frac{\left(\frac{f}{2}+1\right)R}{\frac{f}{2}R} \Rightarrow \boxed{\gamma = \left(1+\frac{2}{f}\right)}$$

which is required relation between γ and f.

Monoatomic Gases

In monoatomic gases, a molecule has three translational degrees of freedom.

So, total internal energy of one mole of monoatomic gas

$$U = \frac{3}{2}k_BT \times N_A = \frac{3}{2}RT \quad (\text{as } R = N_Ak_B)$$

$$\therefore \quad U = \frac{3}{2}RT \quad \ldots\text{(i)} \quad [\text{for monoatomic gas}]$$

If dU is a small amount of heat energy required to raise the temperature of 1g mole of the gas at constant volume through at temperature dT. Then,

$$C_V = \frac{dU}{dT} \quad [\because \mu = 1] \ldots\text{(ii)}$$

where, C_V = specific heat of gas at constant volume.

Putting, $U = \frac{3}{2}RT$ in Eq. (ii), we have

$$C_V = \frac{d}{dT}\left(\frac{3}{2}RT\right) = \frac{3}{2}R$$

$$\therefore \quad C_V = \frac{3}{2}R$$

If C_p is molar specific heat at constant pressure, then from Mayer's relation, we have

$$C_p - C_V = R \Rightarrow C_p - \frac{3}{2}R = R$$

$$\therefore \quad C_p = \frac{5}{2}R$$

Now, ratio of specific heat, $\gamma = \frac{C_p}{C_V} = \frac{\left(\frac{5}{2}\right)R}{\left(\frac{3}{2}\right)R} = \frac{5}{3} = 1.67$

Ratio of specific heat capacities for monoatomic gases

$$\gamma = 1.67$$

Example 1 Calculate the molecular kinetic energy of 1 g of helium (molecular weight 4) at 127°C. (Given, $R = 8.31\ \text{Jmol}^{-1}\text{K}^{-1}$)

Sol. Given, $T = 273 + 127 = 400\ \text{K}$

Helium is monoatomic gas.

$\therefore$ Average kinetic energy per mole of helium $= \frac{3}{2}RT$

Average kinetic energy of 1 g of helium $= \frac{3}{2}\frac{RT}{M}$

$$= \frac{3 \times 8.31 \times 400}{2 \times 4} = 1246.5\ \text{J}$$

Diatomic Gases

In case of diatomic gases, if the vibrational mode is not considered, then it has five degrees of freedom (three translational and two rotational) at room temperature. According to law of equipartition of energy, total internal energy of one mole of such type of gas is

$$U = 5 \times \left(\frac{1}{2}k_BT\right) \times N_A$$

Thus, $$U = \frac{5}{2}RT \quad [\because R = k_BN_A]$$

The molar specific heat C_V is given by,

So, $$C_V = \frac{dU}{dT} = \frac{d}{dT}\left(\frac{5}{2}RT\right)$$

$$\therefore \quad C_V = \frac{5}{2}R$$

Now, $C_p = C_V + R \Rightarrow C_p = \frac{5}{2}R + R = \frac{7}{2}R$

So, $C_p = \frac{7}{2}R$

So, $\gamma = \frac{C_p}{C_V} = \frac{\left(\frac{7}{2}\right)R}{\left(\frac{5}{2}\right)R} \Rightarrow \gamma = \frac{7}{5} = 1.40$

Ratio of specific heat capacities for diatomic gases

$$\gamma = 1.40$$

Example 2 **Calculate the total number of degrees of freedom possessed by the molecules in 1 cm^3 of H_2 gas at temperature 273 K and 1 atm pressure?** **NCERT Exemplar**

Sol. At 273 K temperature and 1 atm pressure mean STP condition.

$\therefore$ Number of H_2 molecules on 22400 cm^3 at STP $= 6.02 \times 10^{23}$

$\therefore$ Number of H_2 molecules in 1 cm^3 at STP

$$= \frac{6.02 \times 10^{23}}{22400} = 2.6875 \times 10^{19}$$

Number of degrees of freedom associated with each H_2 (diatomic) molecule = 5

$\therefore$ Total number of degrees of freedom associated with 1 cm^3 of gas $= 2.6875 \times 10^{19} \times 5 = 1.34375 \times 10^{20}$

Example 3 **Find the value of internal energy of one mole of a diatomic gas, which do not show vibrational mode. Also, find the value of C_V for the sample of above gas.**

Sol. Molecule of diatomic gas will have three translational and two rotational degrees of freedom. So,

Degrees of freedom $(f) = 3 + 2 = 5$

Total energy $(E) = 5\left(\frac{1}{2}k_BT\right) = \frac{5}{2}k_BT$

As the gas is one mole, so the total number of molecules is N_A. So, total energy of one mole of gas could be found.

$$U = \frac{5}{2}k_BT \times N_A = \frac{5}{2}k_BN_AT = \frac{5}{2}RT$$

We can find the value of C_V by applying, $C_V = \frac{dU}{dT}$

$$C_V = \frac{d}{dT}\left(\frac{5}{2}RT\right) \Rightarrow C_V = \frac{5}{2}R$$

Triatomic Gases

In case of a **linear triatomic gases** molecule has seven degrees of freedom. Using law of equipartition of energy, total internal energy of one mole of such gases is

$$U = 7 \times \left(\frac{1}{2}k_BT\right) \times N_A = \frac{7}{2}RT \; [\because k = k_AN_B]$$

Now, $C_V = \frac{dU}{dT} = \frac{d}{dT}\left(\frac{7}{2}RT\right) = \frac{7}{2}R \Rightarrow C_V = \frac{7}{2}R$

Now, $C_p = C_V + R = \frac{7}{2}R + R \Rightarrow C_p = \frac{9}{2}R$

$\therefore$ $\gamma = \frac{C_p}{C_V} = \frac{\left(\frac{9}{2}\right)R}{\left(\frac{7}{2}\right)R} = \frac{9}{7} \Rightarrow \gamma = \frac{9}{7} = 1.28$

Ratio of specific heat capacities for triatomic gases,

$$\gamma = 1.28$$

Note A **non-linear triatomic gases** molecule has only six degrees of freedom (three translational and three rotational).

So, $C_V = \frac{f}{2}R = 3R$ and $C_p = \left(\frac{f}{2} + 1\right)R = 4R$

$\therefore$ $\gamma = \frac{C_p}{C_V} = \frac{4}{3} = 1.33$

Polyatomic Gases

A polyatomic gases molecule in general has three translational, three rotational degrees of freedom and with certain number (let f) of vibrational modes

Using law of equipartition of energy, total internal energy of one mole of such gases is

$$U = \left[\frac{3}{2}k_BT + \frac{3}{2}k_BT + fk_BT\right] \times N_A \Rightarrow U = (3 + f)\,RT$$

Now, $C_V = \frac{dU}{dT} = \frac{d(3 + f)RT}{dT} = (3 + f)R$

$\Rightarrow$ $C_V = (3 + f)R$

$\therefore$ $C_p = C_V + R = (3 + f)R + R \Rightarrow C_p = (4 + f)R$

So, $\boxed{\gamma = \frac{C_p}{C_V} = \frac{(4 + f)}{(3 + f)}}$ (taking, $f = 6$)

Ratio of specific heat capacities for polyatomic gas, $\gamma = 1.11$

Example 4 **Discuss variation of molar specific heat at constant volume (C_V) for a diatomic gas with temperature.**

Sol. (i) At low temperatures (about 60 K), a diatomic gas molecule has only translatory motion. So, a diatomic gas molecule has three degrees of freedom.

So, total internal energy of 1 mole of gas,

$$U = \frac{3}{2}N_A k_B T = \frac{3}{2}RT$$

Hence, $C_V = \frac{dU}{dT} = \frac{3}{2}R$

(ii) Above 60 K, the molecules begin to rotate and around 280 K rotational energy reaches its maxima. Now, molecule has five degrees of freedom.

Hence, $U = \frac{5}{2}RT$ and $C_V = \frac{5}{2}R$

(iii) Above 750 K, vibration in molecules begins to occur and reaches maximum at about 4000 K. With vibration, number of degrees of freedom become 7 (2 degrees of freedom for vibration along molecular axis as both kinetic and potential energies of molecule changes).

So, $U = \frac{7}{2}RT$ and $C_V = \frac{7}{2}R$

Different gases show such changes at different temperatures.

Example 5 An isolated container containing monoatomic gas of molar mass m is moving with a velocity v_0. If the container is suddenly stopped, find the change in temperature. **NCERT Exemplar**

Sol. Loss in kinetic energy of gas $= \Delta E = \frac{1}{2}(mn)\,v_0^2$

where, n is number of moles and m is molar mass.

If its temperature changes by ΔT, then

$$n\frac{3}{2}R\Delta T = \frac{1}{2}mn\,v_0^2$$

$\therefore$ Change in temperature, $\Delta T = \frac{mv_0^2}{3R}$

Mean Free Path (λ)

Every gas consists of a large number of molecules undergoing frequent collision, therefore they cannot move straight or unhindered, these molecules are in a state of continuous and random motion. Also, they undergo perfectly elastic collision against each other. The average distance travelled by a molecule between two successive collisions is known as the **mean free path** of the molecule.

Expression for Mean Free Path

Let d be the diameter of each molecule of the gas, then a particular molecule will suffer collision with any molecule that comes within a distance d between centres of two molecules.

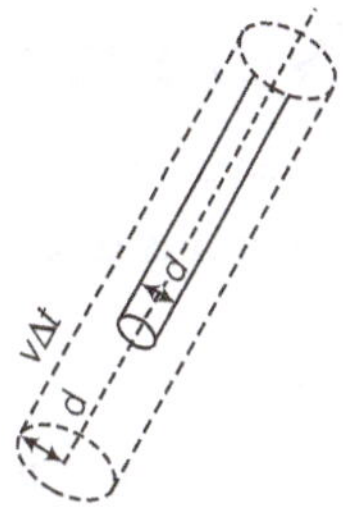

Volume swept by a molecule in time Δt

If $\bar{v}$ is average speed of molecule, then from figure, the volume swept by the molecule in small time Δt in which any molecule will collide with it $= \pi d^2 \langle v \rangle \Delta t$

If n is number of molecules per unit volume of the gas, then number of collision suffered by the molecule in time $\Delta t = \pi d^2 \langle v \rangle \Delta t \times n$.

So, number of collisions per second $= \frac{\pi d^2 \langle v \rangle \Delta t \times n}{\Delta t}$

$= n\pi d^2 \langle v \rangle$

$\therefore$ Average time between two successive collisions

i.e. $\tau = \frac{1}{n\pi d^2 \langle v \rangle}$

$\therefore$ Mean free path = average distance between two successive collision

$\Rightarrow \lambda = \tau \times$ mean velocity $= \frac{1}{n\pi d^2 \langle v \rangle} \times \bar{v} = \frac{1}{n\pi d^2}$

Mean free path, $\lambda = \frac{1}{n\pi d^2}$

where, d = diameter of each molecule

and n = number of molecules per unit volume.

In the above derivation of λ, we imagined the other molecules to be at rest. But actually all molecules are moving, which will result into the following more accurate value.

$$\lambda = \frac{1}{\sqrt{2}n\pi d^2} \quad \text{...(i)}$$

where, T = temperature of gas (in kelvin),

d = molecules diameter

and λ = mean free path.

Note

- Mean free path, $\lambda = \frac{K_B T}{\sqrt{2}\pi d^2 p}$ (in terms of temperature and pressure)
- The mean free path of a given gas is (i) directly proportional to its absolute temperature, and (ii) inversely proportional to its pressure.
- Using kinetic theory of gases, the Bulk measurable properties like viscosity, heat conductivity and rate of diffusion can be easily related to the microscopic parameters like molecular size.

Avogadro's Number

The mole is one of the seven SI base units. It is defined as '**1 mole is the number of atoms in a 12 g sample of carbon-12 (^{12}C) isotope**'.

Number of atoms or molecules in 1 mole (which is experimentally determined and proven theoretically by kinetic theory) is

$$N_A = 6.022 \times 10^{23}\ \text{mol}^{-1}$$

This number is called **Avogadro's number.**

The number of moles n contained in a sample of any substance is equal to the ratio of the number of molecules N in sample to the number of molecules N_A in one mole.

$$\Rightarrow \quad n = \frac{N}{N_A}$$

As, mass of a sample, $M = m \times N$

where, m = mass of 1 atom or molecule.

So, we can say

$$n = \frac{N}{N_A} = \frac{mN}{mN_A} = \frac{M}{M_0}$$

where, M_0 = molar mass of material of sample.

By applying gas equation, it can be shown that 1 mole of an ideal gas occupy 22.4 L of volume at STP.

Example 6 Ten small planes are flying at a speed of 150 km/h in total darkness in an air space that is $20 \times 20 \times 1.5\ \text{km}^3$ in volume. You are in one of the planes, flying at random within this space with no way of knowing where the other planes are. On the average about how long a time will elapse between near collision with your plane. Assume for this rough computation that a safety region around the plane can be approximated by a sphere of radius 10 m. **NCERT Exemplar**

Sol. Given, $v = 150$ km/h, $V = 20 \times 20 \times 1.5$,

$N = 10,\ d = 2 \times 10 = 20$ m

Time taken by plane, $t = \lambda / v$ and mean free path

i.e. $$\lambda = \frac{1}{\sqrt{2}\pi d^2 n}$$

where, d = diameter and n = number of density

So, $$n = \frac{N}{V} = \frac{10}{20 \times 20 \times 1.5} = 0.0167\ \text{km}^{-3}$$

and time elapse between collision,

$$t = \frac{1}{\sqrt{2}\pi d^2 (N/V) \times v}$$

$$= \frac{1}{1.414 \times 3.14 \times (20)^2 \times 0.0167 \times 10^{-3} \times 150} = 0.225\ \text{h}$$

Example 7 The average speed of air molecules is 485 m/s. At STP the number density is 2.7×10^{25} / m^3 and diameter of the air molecule is 2×10^{-10} m. Find the value of mean free path (λ) for the air molecule and average time (τ) between successive collisions.

Sol. To find the mean free path, we need the values of d and n. Just put these values in the formula of mean free path.

$$\lambda = \frac{1}{\sqrt{2}n\pi d^2} = \frac{1}{\sqrt{2}\pi \times 2.7 \times 10^{25} (2 \times 10^{-10})^2}$$

$$= 2.1 \times 10^{-7}\ \text{m}$$

The value of $\tau = \frac{l}{v}$

Now, put the values and get the value of τ.

$$\tau = \frac{2.9 \times 10^{-7}}{485} = 4.3 \times 10^{-10}\ \text{s}$$

Topic Practice 2

Multiple Choice Questions

1 Mark

1. The internal energy of 2 moles of a monoatomic gas is

(a) $\frac{3}{2}RT$ (b) $3RT$ (c) $2RT$ (d) $5RT$

2. The value of C_p for a monoatomic gas is

(a) $\frac{5}{2}R$ (b) $\frac{3}{2}R$ (c) $\frac{R}{2}$ (d) $5R$

3. The value of C_V for a monoatomic gas is

(a) $\frac{5}{2}R$ (b) $\frac{3}{2}R$ (c) $\frac{R}{2}$ (d) $3R$

4. Expression of mean free path, if we consider the motion of all the molecules is

(a) $\frac{1}{n\pi d^2}$ (b) $\frac{1}{\sqrt{2}n\pi d^2}$

(c) $n\pi d^2$ (d) $\sqrt{2}n\pi d^2$

5. The mean free path for air molecule with average speed 18.5 ms^{-1} at STP is ($d = 2 \times 10^{-10}$ m and $n = 2.7 \times 10^{25}\ \text{m}^{-3}$)

(a) 3.5×10^{-7} m (b) 4×10^{-7} m

(c) 2.9×10^{-7} m (d) 5×10^{-7} m

Very Short Answer Type Questions

1 Mark

6. What is the number of degree of freedom of a bee flying in a room ?

7. How degree of freedom of a gas molecule is related with the temperature ?
8. Is molar specific heat of a solid, a constant quantity ?
9. If a molecule having N atoms has k number of constraints, how many degrees of freedom does the gas possess?
10. If there are f degrees of freedom with n moles of a gas, then find the internal energy possessed at a temperature T.
11. What is mean free path of a gas ?
12. How is mean free path depends on number density of the gas ?
13. What is Avogadro's number N_A ?

Short Answer Type I Questions

(2 Marks)

14. State and explain law of equipartition of energy.
15. What is basic law followed by equipartition of energy ?
16. Is specific heat capacity of a gas is a constant quantity? If not, then why does it varry with temperature?
17. Equal masses of monoatomic and diatomic gases are supplied heat at the same temperature, pressure and volume. If same amount of heat is supplied to both the gases, which of them will undergo greater temperature rise?
18. At room temperature, diatomic gas molecule has five degrees of freedom, at high temperature. It has seven degrees of freedom, explain.
19. Prove that for a diatomic gas, the ratio of the two specific heats at room temperature is 7/5.
20. Using the law of equipartition of energy, show that for a polyatomic gas degree of freedom f is 6.
21. Give a formula for mean free path of the molecules of a gas. Briefly explain, how its value is affected by (i) change in temperature. (ii) change in pressure.

Short Answer Type II Questions

(3 Marks)

22. What do you mean by degrees of freedom? Show that the number of degrees of freedom of a system consisting of N-particles and having K independent relation between them is $(3N - K)$.
23. State the law of equipartition of energy. Determine the values of γ for diatomic gas N_2 at moderate temperature.
24. Estimate the value of γ for
    (i) monoatomic gas. (ii) diatomic gas.
    (iii) polyatomic gas.
25. Derive the relation between the ratio of two specific heats of gas and degree of freedom.
26. Draw a graph to show variation of molar specific heat at constant volume of hydrogen gas with temperature.

Long Answer Type Questions

(5 Marks)

27. State the law of equipartition energy of a dynamic system and use it to find the values of internal energy and the ratio of the specific heats of (i) monoatomic (ii) diatomic and (iii) triatomic gases.
28. What is meant by mean free path of a gas molecule? Derive an expression for it. On which factors does it depend?
29. (i) Define mean free path.
    (ii) Derive an expression for mean free path of a gas molecule.

Numerical Problems

30. Calculate the ratio of the mean free paths of the molecules of two gases having molecular diameters 1 Å and 2 Å. The gases may be considered under identical conditions of temperature, pressure and volume. **NCERT Exemplar [1 M]**
31. Calculate the number of degrees of freedom in 15 cm^3 of nitrogen at NTP. **[2 M]**
32. A diatomic gas is heated in a vessel to a temperature of 10000 K. If each molecule possess an average energy E_1. After sometime, a few molecule escape into the atmosphere at 300 K. Due to which, their energy changes to E_2. Calculate the ratio of $\frac{E_1}{E_2}$. **[2 M]**

33. What will be the internal energy of 8 g of oxygen at STP? **[2 M]**

34. Calculate the mean free path of a molecule of a gas at a room temperature and one atmospheric pressure. The radius of the gas molecules (avg) is 2×10^{-10}m. **[2 M]**

35. Calculate the temperature of atoms at which rms speed of argon gas is equal to the rms speed of helium gas atoms at $-10\,°C$? (Atomic mass of Ar= 39.9 u, that of He = 4u) **[3 M]**

36. If one mole of a monoatomic gas is mixed with three moles of a diatomic gas. What is the molar specific heat of mixture at constant value? [Take, $R = 8.31\ J\ mol^{-1}K^{-1}$] **[3 M]**

37. A cylinder of fixed capacity contains 44.8 L of helium gas at STP. Calculate the amount of heat required to raise the temperature of container by 15°C. [Given, $R = 8.31\ J\ mol^{-1}K^{-1}$] **[3 M]**

38. A gaseous mixture contain 16g of helium and 16 g of oxygen, then calculate the ratio of C_p/C_V of the mixture. **[3 M]**

39. A box of 1.00 m³ is filled with nitrogen at 1.50 atm at 300 K. The box has a hole of an area is 0.010 m m². How much time is required for the pressure to reduce by 0.10 atm, if the pressure outside is 1 atm? **NCERT Exemplar [5 M]**

40. Estimate the mean free path and collision frequency of a nitrogen molecule in a cylinder containing nitrogen at 2.0 atm and temperature 17°C. Take the radius of a nitrogen molecule to be roughly 1.0 Å. Compare the collision time with the time, the molecule moves freely between two successive collisions. (Molecular mass of nitrogen = 28.0 u) **NCERT [5 M]**

Hints & Solutions

1. (b) $U = \left(\frac{3}{2}k_BT\right)2N_A = 3(k_B \times N_A)\,T = 3RT.$

2. (a) $C_V = \frac{dU}{dT} = \frac{d}{dT}\left(\frac{3}{2}RT\right) = \frac{3}{2}R$

$C_p - C_V = R \Rightarrow C_p = \frac{5}{2}R$

3. (b) Since, monoatomic gas has only translational mode, so the value of degree of freedom $f = 3$.

We know that, $U = \frac{f}{2}RT$

$\therefore U$ (for monoatomic gas) $= \frac{3}{2}RT$

$$C_V = \frac{dU}{dT} = \frac{d}{dT}\left(\frac{3}{2}RT\right) = \frac{3}{2}R$$

4. (b) If we consider the motion of all the molecules of a gas to find mean free path, then $\lambda = \frac{1}{\sqrt{2}n\pi d^2}$.

5. (c) For air at STP, $n = 2.7\times10^{25}\ m^{-3}$

$d = 2\times10^{-10}$ m

$\Rightarrow \quad \lambda = \frac{1}{\sqrt{2}n\pi d^2}$

On putting values, $\lambda = 2.9\times10^{-7}$ m

6. Three, because bee is free to move along x-direction or y-direction or z-direction.

7. Degree of freedom will increase when temperature is very high because at high temperature, vibrational motion of the gas will contribute to the kinetic energy. Hence, there is an additional kinetic energy associated with the gas, as a result of increased degree of freedom.

8. Yes, theoretically, the molar specific heat of a solid is a constant quantity as its value is $3R$ J/mol-K.

9. Degree of freedom, $f = 3N - K$.

10. For 1 mole with f degrees of freedom,

Internal energy, $U = 1\times C_V\times T = \frac{f}{2}RT$ **[1/2]**

For n moles, $U = nC_V\,T = \frac{nf}{2}RT$ **[1/2]**

11. The average distance travelled by a molecule between two successive collisions is known as mean free path of the molecule.

12. The mean free path is inversely proportional to the number density of the gas.

13. Avogadro's number $(N_A) = 6.022\times10^{23}\ mol^{-1}$.

14. Refer to text on page 416 (Law of equipartition of energy).

15. The law of equipartition of energy for any dynamical system in thermal equilibrium, the total energy is distributed equally amongst all the degrees of freedom. **[1]**
The energy associated with each molecule per degree of freedom is $\frac{1}{2}k_BT$, where k_B is Boltzmann's constant and T is temperature of the system. **[1]**

16. Refer to text on page 417 [Specific heat capacity (C)].

17. For monoatomic gas, temperature rise will be greater because monoatomic gas possesses only translational degree of freedom whereas diatomic gas translation, rotation and vibrational (at higher temperature), so temperature rise for diatomic gases is lower. [2]

18. At low temperature, diatomic gas has three translational and two rotational degrees of freedom, so total number of degrees of freedom is 5. [1]

But at high temperature, gas molecule starts to vibrate which give two additional degrees of freedom i.e. 7. [1]

19. Refer to text on pages 417 and 418 (Diatomic gases).

20. Refer to text on page 418 (Polyatomic gas).

21. As, we know that the value of mean free path of the molecules of a given gas is given by

Mean free path, $$\lambda = \frac{1}{\sqrt{2}\pi n d^2}$$

Here, n = number of gas molecules present in unit volume of given gas and d = molecular diameter.

(i) **Effect of temperature** As temperature of a gas is increased at constant pressure, volume of gas increases and hence n, the number of molecules per unit volume decrease. In fact

$$n \propto \frac{1}{V} \text{ and } V \propto T$$

Thus, $$n \propto \frac{1}{T}$$

Due to decrease in molecular number density, the value of mean free path of the gas increase i.e. $\lambda \propto \frac{1}{n} \propto T$. Thus, pressure remaining constant, the mean free path of a gas is directly proportional to its absolute temperature. [1]

(ii) **Effect of pressure** At constant temperature, on increasing pressure, the volume V decrease, the molecular number density n increases and consequently, the mean free path decreases.

i.e. $$p \propto \frac{1}{V} \propto n$$

$\therefore$ $$\lambda \propto \frac{1}{n} \text{ or } \lambda \propto \frac{1}{p}$$

Thus, at a constant temperature, the mean free path of a gas is inversely proportional to its pressure. [1]

22. Refer to text on page 416 (Degree of freedom).

23. Refer to text on page 416 (Law of equipartition of energy). [1½]

Degree of freedom of diatomic gas (N_2) at moderate temperature is 5.

As we know, $\gamma = \left(1 + \frac{2}{f}\right) = 1 + \frac{2}{5} = \frac{7}{5} = 1.40$ [1½]

24. Refer to text on pages 417 and 418 (Monoatomic gases, diatomic gases and polyatomic gases).

25. Refer to text on page 417 (Specific heat capacity).

26. Hydrogen is a diatomic, so its molar specific heat at constant volume (C_V) changes from $\frac{3R}{2}$ (low temperatures) to its theoretical value $\frac{5R}{2}$ (mid temperatures) and becomes $\frac{7R}{2}$ (high temperatures) as shown in the graph.

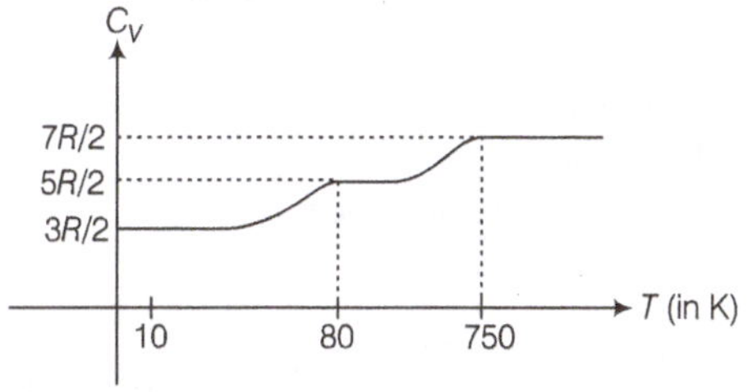

[3]

27. Refer to text on pages 416, 417 and 418 (Law of equipartition of energy, total internal energy of an ideal gas sample, monoatomic gases, diatomic gases and triatomic gases).

28. Refer to text on pages 419 (Mean free path and expression for mean free path).

29. (i) The mean free path of a gas molecule is defined as the average distance travelled by a molecule between two successive collisions.

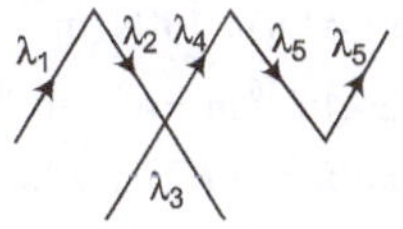

According to figure, if a molecule covers free path $\lambda_1, \lambda_2, \lambda_3 \cdots$ after successive collisions, then its mean free path is given by

$$\lambda = \frac{\lambda_1 + \lambda_2 + \lambda_3 \cdots}{\text{(Total number of collisions)}}$$ [2]

(ii) Refer to text on page 419 (Expression for mean free path). [3]

30. As, we know, mean free path, $\lambda \propto \frac{1}{d^2}$ [1/2]

Given, $d_1 = 1\text{Å}$ and $d_2 = 2\text{Å}$

$\Rightarrow$ $\lambda_1 : \lambda_2 = 4 : 1$ [1/2]

31. Number of nitrogen molecules in 22400 cm^3 of gas at NTP $= 6.023 \times 10^{23}$

$\therefore$ Number of nitrogen molecules in 15 cm^3 of gas at NTP

$$= \frac{6.023 \times 10^{23} \times 15}{22400} = 4.03 \times 10^{20}$$ [1]

Number of degrees of freedom of nitrogen (diatomic) molecule at 273 K = 5

$\therefore$ Total degrees of freedom of 15 cm^3 of gas

$$= 4.03\times 10^{20} \times 5 = 2.015\times 10^{21}$$ [1]

32. Number of degrees of freedom of diatomic gas at 10000 K = 7

Number of degrees of freedom of diatomic gas at 300 K = 5 [1]

$$\therefore \quad \frac{E_1}{E_2} = \frac{\left(\frac{7}{2}\right) k_B T_1}{\left(\frac{5}{2}\right) k_B T_2} = \frac{7}{5}\times\frac{T_1}{T_2} = \frac{7}{5}\times\frac{10000}{300} = \frac{140}{3}$$ [1]

33. Oxygen is a diatomic gas.

Number of moles of oxygen gas

$$= \frac{\text{Atomic weight}}{\text{Molecular weight}} = \frac{8}{32}$$ [1/2]

$$= \frac{1}{4} = 0.25$$

$\therefore$ Energy associated with 1 mole of oxygen, [1/2]

$$U = \frac{5}{2}RT$$

$\therefore$ Internal energy of 8 g of oxygen $= 0.25\times\frac{5}{2}RT$ [1/2]

$$= 0.25\times\frac{5}{2}\times 8.31\times 273 = 1417.9\text{ J}$$ [1/2]

34. Given, $T = 27°\text{C} = 273 + 27 = 300\text{ K}$,

$$p = 1\text{ atm} = 1.01\times10^5\text{ N/m}^2$$

and $\quad d = 2\times 2\times10^{-10}\text{ m} = 4\times10^{-10}\text{ m}$

$\because$ Mean free path, $\lambda = K_B T/\sqrt{2}\pi d^2 p$ [1]

$$= \frac{1.38\times10^{-23}\times300}{1.414\times3.14(4\times10^{-10})^2 1.013\times10^5} = 5.75\times10^{-8}\text{m}$$ [1]

35. As we know that, $v_{rms} = \sqrt{\frac{3RT}{M}}$

Thus, $\quad v_{rms}/\text{Ar} = v_{rms}/\text{He}$

$$\Rightarrow \quad \sqrt{\frac{T_{Ar}}{M_{Ar}}} = \sqrt{\frac{T_{He}}{M_{He}}}$$ [1]

Given, $T_{He} = 273 - 10 = 263\text{ K}$

$M_{Ar} = 39.9\text{u}$ and $M_{He} = 4\text{u}$ [1]

Thus, $\quad \frac{T_{Ar}}{39.9} = \frac{263}{4}$

$$T_{Ar} = \frac{263\times39.9}{4} = 2623.43\text{ K}$$ [1]

36. Given, for monoatomic gas, $\mu_1 = 1$, $C_{V_1} = \frac{3}{2}R$ and for a diatomic gas, $\mu_2 = 3$ and $C_{V_2} = \frac{5}{2}R$

$\therefore$ Total heat energy required to raise the temperature of mixture by ΔT.

$$\Delta U = \mu_1 C_{V_1}\Delta T + \mu_2 C_{V_2}\Delta T$$ [1]

$$\Delta U = 1\times\frac{3}{2}R\Delta T + 3\times\frac{5}{2}R\Delta T = 9R\Delta T \quad \text{...(i)}$$

Let C_{V_m} be the molar specific heat of the mixture at constant volume and as total number of moles of mixture.

$$\mu_m = 1 + 3 = 4$$ [1]

$\therefore$ Heat energy required

$$\Delta U = \mu_m C_{V_m}\Delta T$$

$$\Rightarrow \quad \Delta U = 4\,C_{V_m}\,\Delta T \quad \text{...(ii)}$$

From Eqs. (i) and (ii), we have

$$9R\Delta T = 4\,C_{V_m}\Delta T \Rightarrow \Delta C_{V_m} = \frac{9}{4}R = 2.25\,R$$ [1]

37. At STP, 1 mole of gas occupy 22.4 L of volume.

$\therefore$ Moles of helium in container,

$$\mu = \frac{44.8}{22.4} = 2\text{ moles}$$ [1/2]

Now, helium is monoatomic, so, $C_V = \frac{3}{2}R$ [1/2]

Change in temperature,

$$\Delta T = T_2 - T_1 = 15°\text{C} = 15\text{ K}$$ [1/2]

$\therefore$ Volume of gas remain constant

$$\therefore \quad \Delta W = p\Delta V = 0 \Rightarrow \Delta Q = \Delta U + \Delta W$$ [1/2]

Amount of heat required, $\Delta Q = \Delta U = \mu C_V \Delta T$

$$= 2\times\frac{3}{2}R\times15 = 45\,R$$

$$= 45\times8.31 = 374\text{ J}$$ [1]

38. Moles of helium, $\mu_{He} = \frac{16}{4} = 4$

Moles of oxygen, $\mu_{O_2} = \frac{16}{32} = \frac{1}{2}$

As helium is monoatomic, so degrees of freedom of helium, $f = 3$, so $C_{V_{He}} = \frac{f}{2}R = \frac{3}{2}R$ [1/2]

As oxygen is diatomic, so degrees of freedom of oxygen, $f = 5$, so

$$C_{V_{O_2}} = \frac{f}{2}R = \frac{5}{2}R$$ [1/2]

$$\therefore \quad C_{V\,\text{mixture}} = \frac{\mu_{He}C_{V_{He}} + \mu_{O_2}C_{V_{O_2}}}{\mu_{He} + \mu_{O_2}}$$

$$= \frac{4\times\frac{3}{2}R + \frac{1}{2}\times\frac{5}{2}R}{4 + \frac{1}{2}} = \frac{29}{18}R$$ [1]

$$\gamma = \frac{C_p}{C_V} \quad \text{[of mixture]}$$

$$\gamma_{\text{mixture}} = 1 + \frac{R}{C_{V\,\text{mixture}}} = 1 + \frac{R}{\frac{29}{18}R} = 1.62$$

[as $C_p - C_V = R$] [1]

39. Given, volume of the box, $V = 1.00\ \text{m}^3$

Area, $a = 0.010\text{mm}^2 = 10^{-8}\text{m}^2$

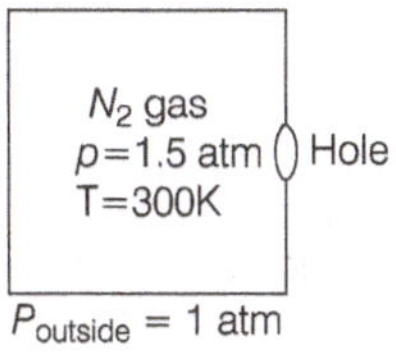

Temperature outside = Temperature inside

Initial pressure inside the box = 1.50 atm

Final pressure inside the box = 0.10 atm [1]

Assuming,

v_{ix} = Speed of nitrogen molecule inside the box along x-direction.

n_1 = Number of molecules per unit volume in a time interval of Δt, all the particles at a distance $(v_{ix}\Delta t)$ will collide the hole and the wall, the particle colliding along the hole will escape out reducing the pressure in the box. [1]

Let area of the wall is A, number of particles colliding in time, $\Delta t = \frac{1}{2} n_1 (v_{ix}\Delta t) A$

$\frac{1}{2}$ is the factor because all the particles along x- direction are behaving randomly. Hence, half of these are colliding against the walls on either side.

Inside the box, $v_{ix}^2 + v_{iy}^2 + v_{iz}^2 = v_{rms}^2$

$$\Rightarrow \quad v_{ix}^2 = \frac{v_{rms}^2}{3} \quad [\because v_{ix} = v_{iy} = v_{iz}]$$ [1]

If particles collide along hole, they move out. Similarly, outer particles colliding along hole will move in.

If a = area of hole

Then, net particle flow in time,

$$\Delta t = \frac{1}{2}(n_1 - n_2)\frac{k_B T}{m}\Delta t a \quad \left[\because v_{rms} = \sqrt{\frac{3k_B T}{m}}\right]$$

[Temperature inside and outside the box are equal]

Let n = number of density of nitrogen

$$n = \frac{\mu N_A}{V} = \frac{pN_A}{RT} \quad \left[\because \frac{\mu}{V} = \frac{p}{RT}\right]$$

where, N_A = Avogadro's number.

If after time Δt, pressure inside changes from p to p_1'

$$\therefore \quad n_1' = \frac{p_1' N_A}{RT}$$

Now, number of molecules gone out $= n_1 V - n_1' V$

$$= \frac{1}{2}(n_1 - n_2)\sqrt{\frac{k_B T}{m}}\Delta t a$$ [1]

$$\therefore \quad \frac{p_1 N_A}{RT}V - \frac{p_1' N_A}{RT}V = \frac{1}{2}(p_1 - p_2)\frac{N_A}{RT}\sqrt{\frac{k_B T}{m}}\Delta t a$$

$$\Rightarrow \quad \Delta t = 2\left(\frac{p_1 - p_1'}{p_1 - p_2}\right)\frac{V}{a}\sqrt{\frac{m}{k_B T}}$$

Putting the values from the data given,

$$\Delta t = 2\left(\frac{1.5 - 1.4}{1.5 - 1.0}\right)\frac{1 \times 1.00}{0.01 \times 10^{-6}}\sqrt{\frac{46.7 \times 10^{-27}}{1.38 \times 10^{-23} \times 300}}$$

$$= \frac{2}{5} \times 3.358 \times 10^5 = \frac{6.717}{5} \times 10^5 = 1.343 \times 10^5 \text{s}$$ [1]

40. Let n be the number of molecules per unit volume of the gas. Now, $pV = NkT$, where N = number of molecules in volume V of the gas

$$\therefore \quad n = \frac{N}{V} = \frac{p}{kT}$$ [1]

Here, $p = 2 \times 1.01 \times 10^5\ \text{N/m}^2$, $k = 1.38 \times 10^{-23}\ \text{J/K}$

and $T = 273 + 17 = 290$ K.

$$\therefore \quad n = \frac{2 \times 1.01 \times 10^5}{(1.38 \times 10^{-23}) \times (290)} = 5.05 \times 10^{25}\ \text{molecules/m}^3$$ [1]

Mean free path,

$$\lambda = \frac{1}{4\pi\sqrt{2}\, r^2 n}$$

Here, $r = 1.0$ Å $= 1.0 \times 10^{-10}$ m and

$n = 5.05 \times 10^{25}$ molecules/m^3.

$$\therefore \quad \lambda = \frac{1}{4\pi\sqrt{2} \times (1.0 \times 10^{-10})^2 \times 5.05 \times 10^{25}}$$

$$\lambda = 1.11 \times 10^{-7}\ \text{m}$$ [1]

Now, $v_{rms} = \sqrt{\frac{3RT}{M}}$

$$= \sqrt{\frac{3 \times 8.31 \times 290}{28 \times 10^{-3}}} = 508.14\ \text{m/s}$$ [1]

$\therefore$ Collision frequency,

$$f = \frac{v_{rms}}{\lambda} = \frac{508.14}{1.11 \times 10^{-7}} = 4.58 \times 10^9\ \text{collisions/s}$$ [1]

SUMMARY

- **Behaviour of gases** Ideal gas equation is

$$pV = nRT \text{ or } pV = Nk_BT \text{ or } \frac{pV}{NT} = k_B = \text{constant}$$

For different gases,

$$\frac{p_1V_1}{N_1T_1} = \frac{p_2V_2}{N_2T_2} = \frac{p_3V_3}{N_3T_3} \ldots = k_B = \text{constant}$$

where, k_B = Boltzmann's constant and its value in SI unit is 1.38×10^{-23} J/K.

- **Kinetic theory of ideal gas** Kinetic theory of gases is based on the molecular theory of matter. It correlates the macroscopic properties like pressure and temperature of gases to microscopic properties like speed and kinetic energy of gas molecules.

- **Root mean square speed** The square root of average of square velocities of gas molecules is known as root mean square speed. It is abbreviated as v_{rms}.
Root mean square speed,

$$v_{rms} = \sqrt{\frac{3k_BT}{m}}$$

where, m = mass of one molecule,
k_B = Boltzmann's constant
and T = absolute temperature of the gas.

- At normal pressure ($p = 1.01 \times 10^5 \text{Nm}^{-2}$), the rms speed of air and hydrogen molecules are

$$(v_{rms})_{air} = 485 \text{ms}^{-1},$$
$$(v_{rms})_{hydrogen} = 1835 \text{ms}^{-1}$$

- **Degree of freedom** The total number of coordinates axes of independent quantities required to describe completely the position and configuration of dynamical system (gaseous) is known as number of degrees of freedom of the system. It is represented by f and expressed as

$$f = 3N - K$$

where, f = degree of freedom, N = number of particles and K = number of coordinates of the particles.

- **Law of equipartition of energy** For a dynamic system in thermal equilibrium, the total energy is distributed equally amongst all the degree of freedom and the energy associated with each molecule per degree of freedom is

$$\frac{1}{2}k_BT.$$

where, $k_B = 1.38 \times 10^{-23}$ JK^{-1} is Boltzmann constant and T is absolute temperature of system on the kelvin scale.

- **Molar specific heat of gases** The molar specific heat of gases is the heat given per mole of the gas per unit rise in the temperature.. Molar specific heat can be

(i) Molar specific heat at constant volume,

$$C_V = \left(\frac{\Delta Q}{\Delta T}\right)_V \text{ or } C_V = \frac{f}{2}R$$

(ii) Molar specific heat at constant pressure
Relation between C_p and C_V is given by

$$C_p = C_V + R \text{ or } C_p = \left(\frac{f}{2} + 1\right)R = \frac{1}{n}\left(\frac{\Delta Q}{\Delta T}\right)_p$$

- **Mean free path** It is the average distance between two successive collisions of a gas molecules and is given by

$$\lambda = \frac{1}{\sqrt{2}\pi d^2 n}$$

where, d = diameter of a molecule and n = number of molecules per unit volume.
It is also called the number density of the molecules.

Chapter Practice

Multiple Choice Questions

1 Mark

1 The two gases with the ratio 3 : 2 of their masses in a container are at a temperature T. The ratio of the kinetic energies of the molecule of two gases is

(a) 3 : 2 (b) 9 : 4 (c) 1 : 1 (d) 4 : 9

2 The relation between the v_{rms} value of a molecule of a gas and the molecular mass of the gas is

(a) $v_{rms} \propto \frac{1}{\sqrt{M}}$ (b) $v_{rms} \propto \frac{1}{M}$

(c) $v_{rms} \propto \sqrt{M}$ (d) $v_{rms} \propto M$

3 If one mole of a monoatomic gas $\left(\gamma = \frac{5}{3}\right)$ is mixed with one mole of a diatomic gas $\left(\gamma = \frac{7}{5}\right)$, the value of γ for the mixture is

(a) 1.40 (b) 1.50 (c) 1.53 (d) 3.07

4 If γ is the ratio of specific heats and R is the universal gas constant, then the molar specific heat at constant volume C_V is given by

(a) γR (b) $\frac{(\gamma - 1)R}{\gamma}$ (c) $\frac{R}{\gamma - 1}$ (d) $\frac{\gamma R}{\gamma - 1}$

5 We took two separate gases with the same number densities for both. If the ratio of the diameters of their molecules is 4 : 1, then ratio of their mean free paths is

(a) 1 : 4 (b) 4 : 1 (c) 2 : 1 (d) 1 : 16

Assertion and Reason

Directions (Q. Nos. 6-10) *In the following questions, two statements are given- one labelled Assertion (A) and the other labelled Reason (R). Select the correct answer to these questions from the codes (a), (b), (c) and (d) as given below*

(a) Both Assertion and Reason are true and Reason is the correct explanation of Assertion.

(b) Both Assertion and Reason are true but Reason is not the correct explanation of Assertion.

(c) Assertion is true but Reason is false.

(d) Assertion is false but Reason is true.

6 **Assertion (A)** A bubble comes from the bottom of a lake to the top.

Reason (R) Its radius increases.

7 **Assertion (A)** Molecules attract when they are little distance apart and repels when they come very close to each other.

Reason (R) $F = -\frac{dU}{dr}$

8 **Assertion (A)** Total KE of any gas at temperature T would be $\frac{1}{2}mv_{rms}^2$.

Reason (R) Translational KE of any type of gas at temperature T would be $\frac{3RT}{2}$ for one mole.

9 **Assertion (A)** In gases, the molecules move faster and move long distances without colliding.

Reason (R) In gases, the interatomic forces are negligible.

10 **Assertion (A)** The total translational kinetic energy of all the molecules of a given mass of an ideal gas is 1.5 times the product of its pressure and its volume.

Reason (R) The molecules of a gas collide with each other and the velocities of the molecules change due to the collision

Very Short Answer Type Questions

1 Mark

11 Write the rms speed of molecules of a gas in terms of its pressure.

12 Name the factors on which degree of freedom of a gas depends.

13 What is the value of γ for monoatomic gas?

Short Answer Type I Questions

(2 Marks)

14 Why does specific heat of gases increases with their atomicity?

15 Find the degree of freedom for following gas.
(i) Monoatomic gas (ii) Diatomic gas

16 What do you understand by degree of freedom?

Short Answer Type II Questions

(3 Marks)

17 Establish ideal gas equation.

18 Write the assumptions of kinetic theory of gases.

19 Calculate the rms speed for air and hydrogen.

20 Kinetic energy of 1 mole of an ideal gas is $\frac{3}{2}RT$.
Prove this statement.

Long Answer Type Questions

(5 Marks)

21 What are the postulates of kinetic theory of gases? What will be expression for the pressure exerted by an ideal gas?

22 Using the law of equipartition of energy, show that for an ideal gas having f degrees of freedom is given by, $\gamma = 1 + 2/f$.

23 Find the ratio of specific heat capacities for triatomic gases.

Case Based Questions

Directions (Q. No. 24) *These questions are case study based questions. Read the following paragraph and answer the questions.*

24 Every gas consists of a large number of molecules undergoing frequent collision, therefore they cannot move straight or unhindered, there molecules are in a state of continuous and random motion. Also, they undergo perfectly elastic collision against each other.
The average distance travelled by a molecules between two successive collision is known as the mean free path of the molecule.
(i) Write the formula of mean free path.
(ii) Write the two basic assumptions on mean free path.
(iii) Write the formula of mean free path in terms of temperature and pressure.

Numerical Problems

25 What is the rms speed of hydrogen gas molecules at STP?
(Given, density is 0.09 kg m^{-3}) **[2 M]**

26 Calculate the temperature at which the rms speed of CO_2 gas molecule will be 1 kms^{-1}.
(Given, molecular mass of CO_4 = 44 u) **[3 M]**

27 What is the kinetic energy of translation of one molecule of a gas at 300 K ? Gas is having three degree of freedom.
(Given, $k_B = 1.38 \times 10^{-23}$ JK^{-1}) **[3 M]**

28 One mole of a monoatomic gas is mixed with three moles of a diatomic gas. What is the molar specific heat of the mixture at constant volume. (Take, $R = 8.31$ J mol^{-1} K^{-1}) **[3 M]**

29 Calculate the mean free path of nitrogen gas at STP. (Given, diameter of nitrogen molecule is 4 Å) **[5 M]**

Answers

1 (c) Average KE of a molecule does not depend on the molecular mass and total mass of the gas. It depends only on the temperature of the gas.

So, $\frac{(\text{KE})_1}{(\text{KE})_2} = 1$

2 (a) $v_{rms} = \sqrt{\frac{3k_BT}{m}}$

where, m is mass of the molecule.

$v_{rms} = \sqrt{\frac{3k_BTN_A}{m\,N_A}}$

where, N_A is Avogadro number.

$v_{rms} = \sqrt{\frac{3k_BT\,N_A}{M}} \Rightarrow v_{rms} \propto \frac{1}{\sqrt{M}}$

3 (*b*) $$\gamma_{mix} = \frac{\frac{\mu_1\gamma_1}{\gamma_1 - 1} + \frac{\mu_2\gamma_2}{\gamma_2 - 1}}{\frac{\mu_1}{\gamma_1 - 1} + \frac{\mu_2}{\gamma_2 - 1}} = \frac{\frac{1 \times \frac{5}{3}}{\left(\frac{5}{3} - 1\right)} + \frac{1 \times \frac{7}{5}}{\left(\frac{7}{5} - 1\right)}}{\left(\frac{1}{\frac{5}{3} - 1}\right) + \left(\frac{1}{\frac{7}{5} - 1}\right)} = \frac{3}{2} = 1.5$$

4 (*c*) From the Mayer's formula,

$$C_p - C_V = R \qquad \text{...(i)}$$

and $$\gamma = \frac{C_p}{C_V} \Rightarrow \gamma C_V = C_p \qquad \text{...(ii)}$$

On substituting Eq. (ii) in Eq. (i), we get

$$\gamma C_V - C_V = R \Rightarrow C_V(\gamma - 1) = R$$

$\therefore$ $$C_V = \frac{R}{\gamma - 1}$$

5 (*d*) $$l = \frac{1}{\sqrt{2}n\pi d^2}$$

$$\frac{l_1}{l_2} = \frac{d_2^2}{d_1^2} = \left(\frac{1}{4}\right)^2 = \frac{1}{16} \qquad [\because n_1 = n_2]$$

6 (*b*) Pressure decreases as bubble comes to top, hence volume increases.

7 (*a*) Molecules attract when they are little distance apart and repel when they come very close because $F = -dU/dr$.

8 (*b*) Only translational PE is mv_{rms}^2 and translational KE or (degree of freedom is 3) one mole is $\frac{3RT}{2}$.

9 (*a*) The interatomic forces are negligible in gases. Therefore in gases, the molecules are free and move large distance before colliding.

10 (*b*) Total translational KE $= \frac{3}{2}nRT = 1.5pV$

11 $v_{rms} = \sqrt{\frac{3p}{\rho}}$

12 Number of particle in a system and number of independent bonds between the particles.

13 $$\gamma = \frac{C_P}{C_V} = \frac{\left(\frac{5}{2}\right)R}{\left(\frac{3}{2}\right)R} = \frac{5}{3} = 1.67$$

14 Refer to text on page 417 [Specific heat capacity (*C*)].

15 Refer to text on page 416 (Degree of freedom).

16 Refer to text on page 416 (Degree of freedom).

17 Refer to text on pages 402 and 403 (Equation of state for an ideal gas).

18 Refer to text on page 405 (Assumptions of kinetic theory of gases).

19 Refer to text on pages 406 and 407 (Root mean square speed of gas molecule).

20 Refer to text on page 407 (Kinetic interpretation of temperature).

21 Refer to text on pages 405 and 406 (Kinetic theory of an ideal gas and concept of pressure of an ideal gas).

22 Refer to text on page 417 (Specific heat capacity).

23 Refer to text on page 418 (Triatomic gases).

24 (i) $\lambda = \frac{1}{\sqrt{2}n\pi d^2}$

(ii) (a) The molecules of gas are considered as hard spheres each of diameter *d*.

(b) The collision between gas molecules are perfectly elastic.

(iii) $\lambda = \frac{k_B T}{\sqrt{2}\pi d^2 p}$

25 $1.8 \times 10^3 \text{ ms}^{-1}$

26 $1.8 \times 10^3 \text{ K}$

27 $6.21 \times 10^{-21} \text{ J}$

28 $2.25\ R$

29 $5 \times 10^{-8} \text{ m}$

CHAPTER

13

Oscillations

In previous chapters, we have studied that the motion is the change in position of an object with respect to time and its reference point. On the basis of path traced and various other properties, motion can be classified into several categories, like non-repetitive, periodic and oscillatory motion.

- Simple Harmonic Motion
- Force and Energy in SHM and Systems Executing SHM

TOPIC 01 Simple Harmonic Motion

We can notice a number of phenomena in our daily life, illustrating oscillatory motion, e.g. motion of vibrating strings of sitar or guitar, vibration of air molecules helping in propagation of sound, vibration of atoms about their equilibrium positions in a solid, oscillatory motion of AC voltage (going positive and negative about the mean value).

Periodic and Oscillatory Motion

Periodic Motion

A motion that repeats itself after regular intervals of time is called **periodic motion.** e.g. Revolution of planets around the sun, rotation of the earth about its polar axis, etc.

Oscillatory Motion

A motion in which a body moves to and fro or back and forth repeatedly about a fixed point in a regular interval of time is called **oscillatory motion.** This fixed point is known as mean/equilibrium position or centre of oscillation. e.g. Motion of a simple pendulum as it moves to and fro about its mean position.

It is to be noted here that, oscillatory motion is periodic but periodic motion is not oscillatory.

If the body is given a small displacement from its mean position, a force called restoring one comes into play which tries to bring the body back to the equilibrium point. This process repeats itself again and again causing oscillation.

e.g. A ball placed in a bowl will be in equilibrium at the bottom. If it is displaced a little from the mean position, it will start oscillations in the bowl.

Period and Frequency

Period

The smallest interval of time after which a periodic motion is repeated, is called its **period**. Its SI unit is second and it is denoted by the symbol T. e.g.

(i) Period of vibration of a quartz crystal is expressed in units of microsecond (10^{-6} s) i.e. μs.

(ii) Period of revolution of the planet mercury is 88 earth days.

(iii) Period of revolution of Halleys Comet is 76 years, so it appears after every 76 years.

Frequency

The number of oscillations/vibrations preformed by a oscillating body about its mean position in a unit time is known as its frequency. The SI unit of frequency of oscillation is hertz (Hz).

Frequency can also be defined as reciprocal of time period, it is denoted by ν.

Thus, $$\boxed{\text{Frequency, } \nu = \frac{1}{T}}$$

and $1 \text{ hertz} = 1 \text{ Hz} = 1 \text{ oscillation per sec} = 1 \text{ s}^{-1}$

When frequency of an oscillatory motion is very high, then motion is called **vibrational motion.**

Example 1 On an average, a human heart is found to beat 75 times in a minute. Calculate its beat frequency and period. **NCERT**

Sol. The beat frequency of heart

$$= \frac{\text{Number of beats}}{\text{Time taken}} = \frac{75}{60} = 1.25 \text{ s}^{-1} = 1.25 \text{ Hz}$$

$$\text{Beat period, } T = \frac{1}{\text{frequency}} = \frac{1}{1.25 \text{ s}^{-1}} = 0.8 \text{ s}$$

Displacement

In oscillation, we use term displacement as the change in position with respect to mean position (or equilibrium position) or reference position.

Periodic Function

The displacement can be represented by a mathematical function of time. The function which repeats its value in regular interval of time or period is called **periodic function.** One of the simplest periodic function is given by
$$f(t) = A \sin \omega t \quad \text{...(i)}$$
The time period for this function will be, $T = 2\pi/\omega$ because when we add 2π with the argument ωt of the function, then its value remains same.

Thus, $$f(t) = f(t+T)$$

Similarly, if we consider a sine function then
$$f(t) = A \sin \omega t$$
Also, $$f_1(t) = A \sin \omega t + B \cos \omega t \quad \text{...(ii)}$$
is a periodic function with time period T.

Now taking, $A = D \cos \phi$ and $B = D \sin \phi$

Thus, Eq. (ii) can be written as
$$f_1(t) = D \sin(\omega t + \phi)$$
where, $D = \sqrt{A^2 + B^2}$ and $\phi = \tan^{-1}\left(\frac{B}{A}\right)$

An important result given by the French mathematician, Jean Baptiste Joseph Fourier (1768-1830) is that **any periodic function can be expressed as a superposition of sine and cosine function of different time periods with suitable coefficients.**

Example 2 Which of the following functions of time represent (a) periodic and (b) non-periodic motion? Give the period for each case of periodic motion. [ω is any positive constant]. **NCERT**

(i) $\sin \omega t + \cos \omega t$ (ii) $\sin \omega t + \cos 2\omega t + \sin 4\omega t$

(iii) $e^{-\omega t}$ (iv) $\log(\omega t)$

Sol. (i) Given, $x(t) = \sin \omega t + \cos \omega t$

$$= \sqrt{2}\left[\sin \omega t \cos \frac{\pi}{4} + \cos \omega t \sin \frac{\pi}{4}\right]$$

$$x(t) = \sqrt{2} \sin\left(\omega t + \frac{\pi}{4}\right)$$

$$\text{Moreover, } x\left(t + \frac{2\pi}{\omega}\right) = \sqrt{2} \sin\left[\omega\left(t + \frac{2\pi}{\omega}\right) + \frac{\pi}{4}\right]$$

$$= \sqrt{2} \sin\left(\omega t + 2\pi + \frac{\pi}{4}\right)$$

$$= \sqrt{2} \sin\left(\omega t + \frac{\pi}{4}\right) = x(t)$$

$[\because \sin(2\pi + \theta) = \sin \theta]$

Hence, $\sin \omega t + \cos \omega t$ is a periodic function with time period equal to $\frac{2\pi}{\omega}$.

(ii) Given, $x(t) = \sin \omega t + \cos 2\omega t + \sin 4\omega t$

$\sin \omega t$ is a periodic function with period

$$= \frac{2\pi}{\omega} = T$$

$\cos 2\omega t$ is a periodic function with period

$$= \frac{2\pi}{2\omega} = \frac{\pi}{\omega} = \frac{T}{2}$$

$\sin 4\omega t$ is a periodic function with period

$$= \frac{2\pi}{4\omega} = \frac{\pi}{2\omega} = \frac{T}{4}$$

Clearly, the function $x(t)$ repeats after a minimum time, $T = \frac{2\pi}{\omega}$. Hence, the given function is periodic.

(iii) The function $e^{-\omega t}$ decreases monotonically to zero as $t \to \infty$. It is an exponential function with a negative exponent of e, where $e \approx 2.71828$. It never repeat its value. So, it is non-periodic.

(iv) The function $\log(\omega t)$ increases monotonically with time. As $t \to \infty$, $\log(\omega t) \to \infty$. It never repeat its value. So, it is non-periodic.

Example 3 The equation of a wave is given by $y = 6\sin 10\pi t + 8\cos 10\pi t$, where y is in centimetre and t in second. Determine the constants involved in the standard equation of the wave.

Sol. Given, $y = 6\sin 10\pi t + 8\cos 10\pi t$ ...(i)

The general equation of wave is

$$y = A\sin(\omega t + \phi)$$
$$= A\sin \omega t \cos \phi + A\cos \omega t \sin \phi$$
$$= (A\cos \phi)\sin \omega t + (A\sin \phi)\cos \omega t \quad \text{...(ii)}$$

Comparing Eqs. (i) and (ii), we get

$$A\cos \phi = 6 \quad \text{...(iii)}$$
$$A\sin \phi = 8 \quad \text{...(iv)}$$

and $\omega t = 10\pi t$ or $\omega = 10\pi$

$\therefore$ Time period, $T = \frac{2\pi}{\omega} = \frac{2\pi}{10\pi} = 0.2\text{s}$

Squaring and adding Eqs. (iii) and (iv), we get

$$A^2(\cos^2\phi + \sin^2\phi) = 6^2 + 8^2 = 36 + 64 = 100$$

or $A^2 = 100$

$\therefore$ $A = 10\text{ cm}$

Dividing Eq. (iv) by Eq. (iii), we get

$$\tan \phi = \frac{8}{6} = 1.3333$$

$\therefore$ $\phi = \tan^{-1}(1.3333) = 53°8'$

Simple Harmonic Motion

A special type of periodic motion in which a particle moves to and fro repeatedly about a mean position under the influence of a restoring force is known as **Simple Harmonic Motion** (SHM).

Characteristic of SHM

(i) The motion of a particle is in a straight line to and fro about a fixed point, called equilibrium position.
(ii) The restoring force acting on particle is always proportional to the displacement of the particle from the equilibrium position.
(iii) The force always directed towards the equilibrium position.

Simple Harmonic Motion as a projection of Uniform Circular Motion

(Geometrical Interpretation of SHM)

Consider a particle P starting from X is moving with a uniform speed along the circumference of a circle of radius A, with centre at O. This circle is known as **circle of reference**, while the particle P is known as **reference particle**.

Let P' be the foot of perpendicular drawn from the point P to the diameter XOX'. P' is known as **projection** of the particle P at diameter XOX'.

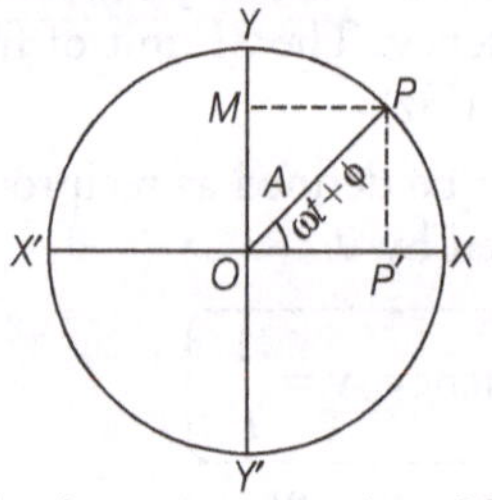

Circular representation of SHM

As P moves along the circle from X to Y, Y to X', X' to Y' and Y' to X, the projection of the particle P i.e. P' moves from X to O, O to X', X' to O and O to X, respectively.

Thus, P revolves along the circumference of the circle while its projection P' moves to and fro about the point O along the diameter XOX'. Hence, the motion of P' about point O is said to be **simple harmonic.**

Therefore, the projection of uniform circular motion upon a diameter of the circle executes simple harmonic motion.

The motion of projection of reference particle along any other diameter of the circle of reference will also be simple harmonic motion.

Hence, **SHM can be geometrically defined as the projection of a uniform circular motion on any diameter of the circle of reference.**

Example 4 Figure below shows a circular motion of a particle. All the parameters are labelled in the figure. Obtain the corresponding equation for simple harmonic motion of the revolving particle P.

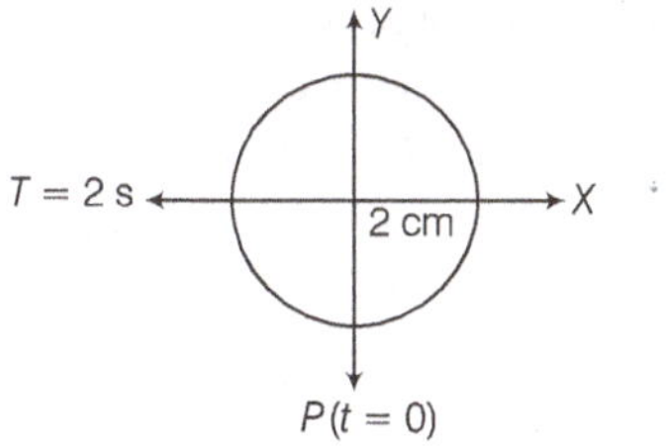

Sol. Suppose the particle moves from P to P' in time t.

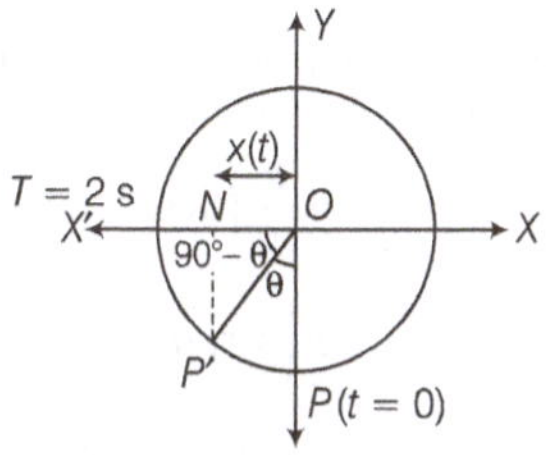

The angle swept by the radius vector

$$\theta = \omega t = \frac{2\pi}{T} t = \frac{2\pi}{2} \cdot t = \pi t \text{ rad}$$

$$\text{Displacement } ON = OP' \cos\left(\frac{\pi}{2} - \theta\right) = 2 \cos\left(\frac{\pi}{2} - \theta\right)$$

$$-x(t) = 2 \sin \theta$$

[negative sign shows displacement being to left from O]

$$\Rightarrow \quad x(t) = 2 \sin \pi t$$

Characteristics of Simple Harmonic Motion

Some of the important parameters which define the characteristics of a simple harmonic motion are given below.

(i) Displacement

The displacement of a particle executing SHM at an instant is given by the distance of the particle from the mean position at that instant.

The values of displacement as a continuous function of time can be represented as a graph given below.

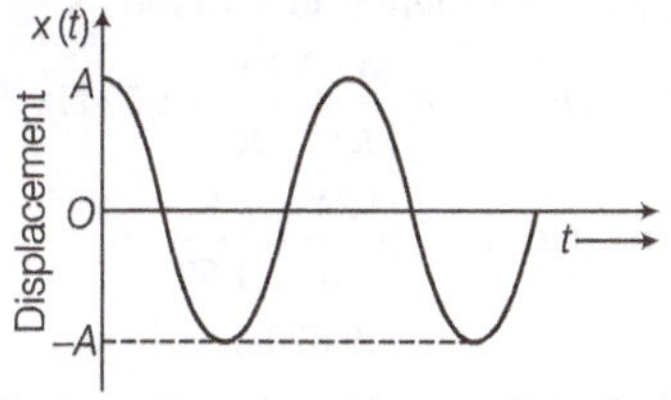

Displacement as a continuous function of time

Here, displacement, $y = A \sin \omega t$

The function containing sine or cosine term is known as sinusoidal function.

(ii) Amplitude

The magnitude of maximum displacement of a particle executing SHM is called **amplitude** of the oscillation of that particle. Amplitude is measured on either side of mean position. The displacement varies between the extremes $+A$ and $-A$ because the sinusoidal function of time varies from $+1$ to -1.

Two SHM may have same ω (angular frequency) and ϕ (phase constant) but different amplitudes A and B.

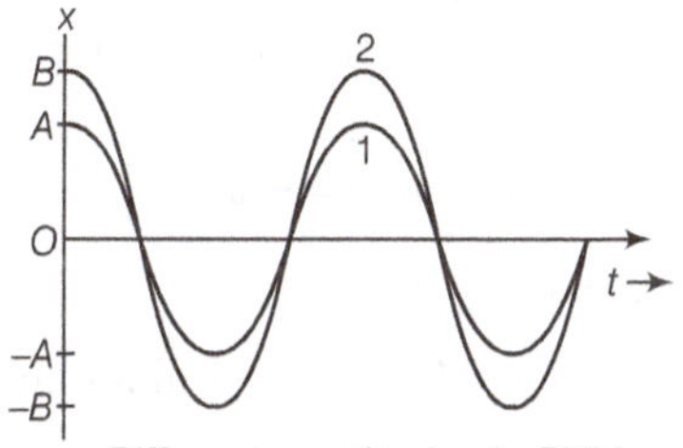

Different amplitudes in SHM

(iii) Phase

If amplitude A is fixed for a given SHM, then the state of motion i.e. position and velocity of the particle at any time t is determined by the argument $(\omega t + \phi_0)$ in the sinusoidal function. This quantity $(\omega t + \phi_0)$ is called phase of the motion.

For $t = 0$, phase $\omega t + \phi_0 = \phi$. Thus, ϕ_0 is called **phase constant** or **phase angle**. Two SHM may have the same A (amplitude) and ω (angular frequency) but different phase angle ϕ. This can be shown in the graph below

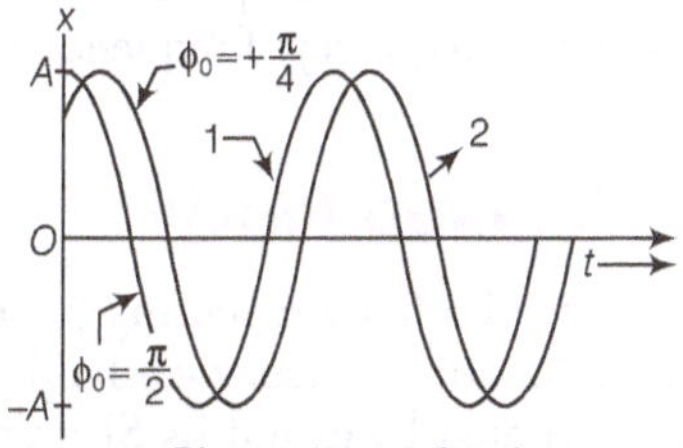

Phase determination

As in above graph, the curve 1 has phase constant of $\pi/2$ (i.e. $\phi_0 = \pi/2$) and amplitude of A, the curve 2 has phase constant of $\frac{\pi}{4}\left(\text{i.e.}\, \phi_0 = +\frac{\pi}{4}\right)$ and amplitude of A.

(iv) Velocity

The velocity of a particle executing SHM at any instant, is defined as the time rate of change of its displacement at that instant.

$$\text{Velocity, } v = \omega\sqrt{A^2 - y^2}$$

At mean position, $x = 0$

$\therefore \quad v = \omega A \quad$ [maximum velocity]

At extreme position $\quad x = A$

$\therefore \quad v = 0 \quad$ [minimum velocity]

(v) Acceleration

The acceleration of the particle executing SHM at any instant is defined as the time rate of change of its velocity at that instant.

$$\text{Acceleration, } a = -\omega^2 x$$

At mean position, $x = 0$

$\therefore \quad a = 0 \quad$ [minimum acceleration]

At extreme position $x = A$,

$\therefore \quad a = -\omega^2 A \quad$ [maximum acceleration]

(vi) Time Period

The time taken by a particle executing SHM to complete one vibration is called time period (T) of the motion. This means that the value of x at any time t is equal to the value of x at time $t + T$.

Then we can show that time period of motion is

$$T = \frac{2\pi}{\omega}.$$

The number of oscillations completed by the particle in one second is called frequency. Frequency is reciprocal of time period.

(vii) Angular Frequency

Angular frequency of a body executing periodic motion is equal to the product of frequency of the particle with factor 2π. It is denoted by ω and its SI unit is radian per second.

We know that, $\quad T = \dfrac{2\pi}{\omega}$

$$\Rightarrow \quad \omega = \frac{2\pi}{T} = 2\pi\nu$$

where, ν = frequency of the particle.

Example 5 Consider an SHM as

$$x(t) = 2\cos(4\pi t + \pi/6)$$

where x is in metres and t in seconds. Determine the time period and initial velocity of the oscillating body.

Sol. Given equation of SHM

$$x(t) = 2\cos(4\pi t + \pi/6) \quad \text{...(i)}$$

We know that, $\quad x(t) = A\cos(\omega t + \phi) \quad$ ...(ii)

Comparing Eq. (i) with Eq. (ii), we get

$\therefore$ Amplitude, $A = 2$

$$\omega = 4\pi \quad \text{or} \quad \frac{2\pi}{T} = 4\pi$$

$$\Rightarrow \quad T = \frac{1}{2} = 0.5\ \text{s}$$

The velocity of the particle can be found by differentiating displacement w.r.t time

$$\therefore \text{ Velocity, } v = \frac{dx}{dt} = \frac{d}{dt}[2\cos(4\pi t + \pi/6)]$$

$$= -2\sin\left(4\pi t + \frac{\pi}{6}\right) \times 4\pi$$

$$\text{or velocity, } v = -8\pi\sin\left(4\pi t + \frac{\pi}{6}\right)$$

The initial velocity is the velocity of the oscillating body at time $t = 0$

$$\therefore \text{ Initial velocity} = \left.\frac{dx}{dt}\right|_{t=0} = -8\pi\sin\left(4\pi \times 0 + \frac{\pi}{6}\right)$$

$$= -8\pi\sin\left(\frac{\pi}{6}\right)$$

$$\text{Initial velocity} = -4\pi \text{ m/s} \quad \left[\because \sin\frac{\pi}{6} = \frac{1}{2}\right]$$

Example 6 A simple harmonic motion is represented by

$$x = 12\sin(10t + 0.6)$$

Find out the amplitude, angular frequency, frequency, time period and initial phase if displacement is measured in metre and time in seconds.

Sol. Given equation, $x = 12\sin(10t + 0.6)$

On comparing with $x(t) = A\sin(\omega t + \phi)$

We have,

(i) Amplitude, $A = 12$ m

(ii) Angular frequency, $\omega = 10$ rad / s

(iii) Frequency, $\nu = \dfrac{\omega}{2\pi} = \dfrac{10}{2\pi} = 1.59$ Hz

(iv) Time period, $T = \dfrac{2\pi}{\omega} = \dfrac{1}{1.59}$

$= 0.628$ s

(v) Initial phase, $\omega t + \phi|_{t=0} = 10t + 0.6|_{t=0}$

$= 0.6$ rad

Example 7 A particle executes SHM with a time period of 2 s and amplitude 5 cm. Find

(i) displacement

(ii) velocity and

(iii) acceleration after 1/3 s starting from the mean position.

Sol. Here, $T = 2$ s, $A = 5$ cm, $t = \frac{1}{3}$ s

(i) For the particle starting from mean position, (i.e. $\phi = 0$) displacement,

$$x = A \sin \omega t = A \sin \frac{2\pi}{T} t$$

$$= 5 \sin \frac{2\pi}{2} \times \frac{1}{3} = 5 \sin \frac{\pi}{3} = 5 \times \frac{\sqrt{3}}{2} = 4.33 \text{ cm}$$

(ii) Velocity, $v = \frac{dx}{dt} = \frac{d(A \sin \omega t)}{dt} = A\omega \cos \omega t$

$$= \frac{2\pi A}{T} \cos \frac{2\pi}{T} t = \frac{2\pi \times 5}{2} \cos \frac{\pi}{3}$$

$$= 5 \times 3.14 \times 0.5 \qquad \left[\because \cos \frac{\pi}{3} = 0.5\right]$$

$$= 7.85 \text{ cm s}^{-1}$$

(iii) Acceleration, $a = \frac{dv}{dt} = \frac{d(A\omega \cos \omega t)}{dt} = -A\omega^2 \sin \omega t$

$$= -\frac{4\pi^2 A}{T^2} \sin \frac{2\pi}{T} t = -\frac{4 \times 9.87 \times 5}{4} \sin \frac{\pi}{3}$$

$$= -9.87 \times 5 \times \frac{\sqrt{3}}{2} = -42.73 \text{ cm s}^{-2}$$

$$\therefore \quad |a| = 42.73 \text{ cm s}^{-2}$$

Example 8 A body oscillates with SHM according to the equation,

$$x = (5.0 \text{ m}) \cos [(2\pi \text{ rad s}^{-1}) t + \pi/4].$$

At $t = 1.5$ s, calculate displacement, speed and acceleration of the body. **[NCERT]**

Sol. Equation of SHM,

$$x(t) = (5.0 \text{ m}) \cos [(2\pi \text{ rad s}^{-1}) t + \pi/4]$$

time, $t = 1.5$ s

$$x(t) = 5.0 \times \cos [2\pi \times 1.5 + \pi/4]$$

$$= 5.0 \times \cos \left(3\pi + \frac{\pi}{4}\right) = -5.0 \cos \frac{\pi}{4} = -5.0 \times 0.707$$

$$x(t) = -3.535 \text{ m}$$

$$v = \frac{dx}{dt} = \frac{d}{dt}\left[5.0 \cos \left(2\pi t + \frac{\pi}{4}\right)\right]$$

$$= -5.0 \times \sin \left(2\pi t + \frac{\pi}{4}\right) \times 2\pi$$

$$= -10\pi \sin \left(2\pi t + \frac{\pi}{4}\right)$$

$$\therefore \quad \left.\frac{dx}{dt}\right|_{t=1.5} = -10\pi \sin \left(3\pi + \frac{\pi}{4}\right) = 10\pi \times 0.707$$

$$= 22.22 \text{ m/s} \qquad [\because \sin (3\pi + \theta) = -\sin \theta]$$

$$a = \frac{dv}{dt} = \frac{d}{dt}\left[-10\pi \sin \left[2\pi t + \frac{\pi}{4}\right]\right]$$

$$= -10\pi \times 2\pi \cos \left(2\pi t + \frac{\pi}{4}\right)$$

$$\left.\frac{dv}{dt}\right|_{t=1.5} = -20\pi^2 \cos \left(3\pi + \frac{\pi}{4}\right) = 139.56 \text{ m/s}^2$$

Differential Equation of SHM

In SHM, the restoring force acting on the particle is proportional to its displacement.

Thus, $$F = -kx \qquad \text{...(i)}$$

The negative sign shows that F and x are appositively directed. Here, k is spring factor or force constant.

According to Newton second law,

$$F = m \frac{d^2x}{dt^2} \qquad \text{...(ii)}$$

From Eqs. (i) and (ii), we get

$$\frac{md^2x}{dt^2} = -kx \Rightarrow \frac{d^2x}{dt^2} = \frac{-k}{m} x$$

$$\Rightarrow \quad \frac{d^2x}{dt^2} = -\omega^2 x \qquad \left[\because \omega^2 = \frac{k}{m}\right]$$

$$\Rightarrow \quad \boxed{\frac{d^2x}{dt^2} + \omega^2 x = 0} \qquad \text{...(iii)}$$

This is the differential equation of SHM. Here, ω is the angular frequency. Clearly, x should be such a function whose second derivative is equal to the function itself multiplied with a negative constant. So, a possible solution of Eq. (iii) may be of the form

$$x = A \cos(\omega t + \phi_0) \Rightarrow \frac{dx}{dt} = -\omega A \sin(\omega t + \phi_0)$$

$$\Rightarrow \quad \frac{d^2x}{dt^2} = -\omega^2 A \cos(\omega t + \phi_0) = -\omega^2 x$$

$$\Rightarrow \quad \frac{d^2x}{dt^2} + \omega^2 x = 0$$

which is same as Eq. (iii).

Hence, the solution of the Eq. (iii) is

$$x = A \cos(\omega t + \phi_0) \qquad \text{...(iv)}$$

It gives displacement of the harmonic oscillator at any instant t.

Here, A is the amplitude of the oscillating particle,

$\phi = \omega t + \phi_0$ is the phase of the oscillating particle,

ϕ_0 is the initial phase (at $t = 0$) or epoch.

Graphical Representation of Displacement, Velocity and Acceleration

Displacement $x(t) = A\cos\omega t$	Velocity $v(t) = -\omega A\sin\omega t$	Acceleration $a(t) = -\omega^2 A\cos\omega t$
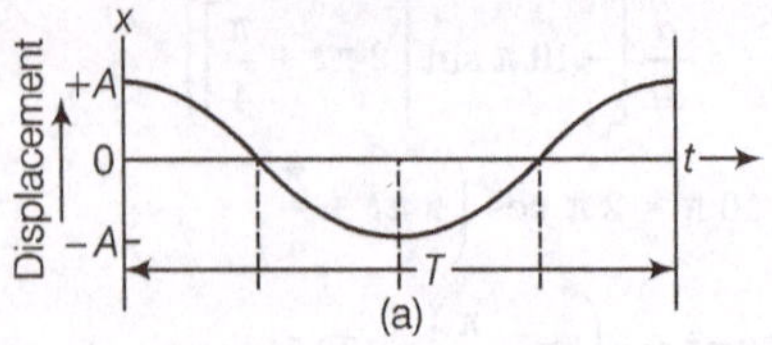 (a)	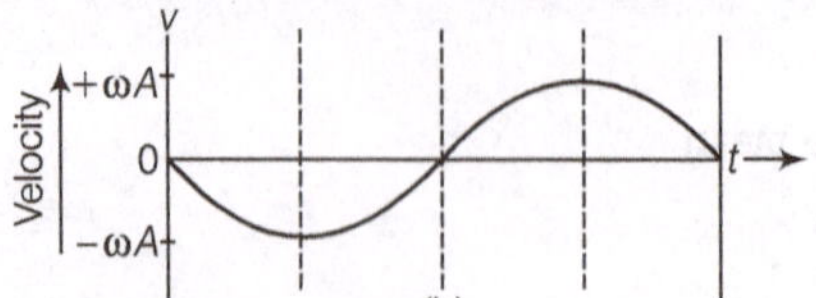 (b)	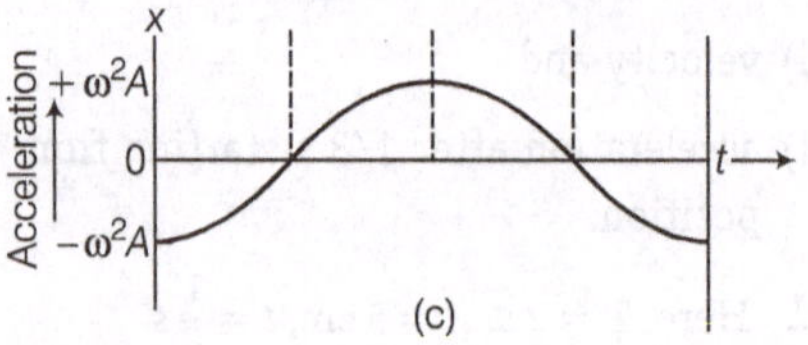 (c)
Sinusoidal in nature, x varies from $-A$ to A. It has zero phase difference.	Sinusoidal in nature. $v(t)$ varies from $-\omega A$ to ωA. It has a phase difference of $\frac{\pi}{2}$ w.r.t. $x(t)$	Sinusoidal in nature. $a(t)$ varies from $-\omega^2 A$ to $\omega^2 A$. It has a phase difference of π w.r.t. $x(t)$.

Topic Practice 1

Multiple Choice Questions

1 Mark

1. Choose the correct option.
   (a) Every periodic motion is oscillatory
   (b) Every oscillatory motion is periodic
   (c) Both (a) and (b)
   (d) Neither (a) nor (b)

2. When frequency of oscillations is high then motion is called
   (a) periodic (b) non-periodic
   (c) vibratory (d) rotatory

3. The expression that represents the motion as shown by x-t graph below, is x =

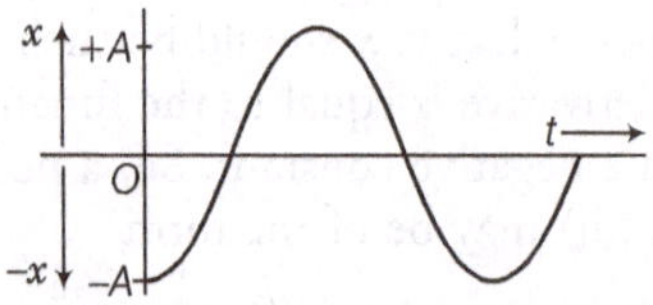

   (a) $-A\sin(\omega t)$ (b) $A\cos(\omega t)$
   (c) $-A\cos(\omega t)$ (d) $A\sin(\omega t)$

4. Choose the correct option regarding given x-t graphs.

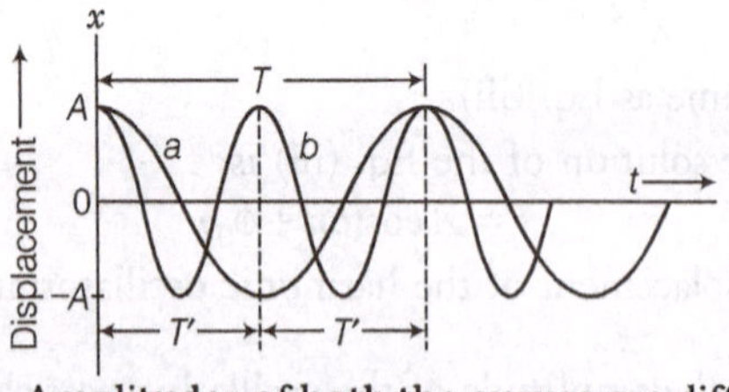

   (a) Amplitudes of both the curves are different
   (b) $T' = T/2$
   (c) Both curves have same frequeny
   (d) Both curves have same wavelengths.

5. When two displacement represented by $y_1 = a\sin(\omega t)$ and $y_2 = b\cos(\omega t)$ are superimposed, the motion is
   (a) not a simple harmonic
   (b) simple harmonic with amplitude $\frac{a}{b}$
   (c) simple harmonic with amplitude $\sqrt{a^2 + b^2}$
   (d) simple harmonic with amplitude $\frac{(a+b)}{2}$

Very Short Answer Type Questions

1 Mark

6. What are the basic properties required by a system to oscillate?
7. All oscillatory motions are periodic and *vice-versa*. Is it true?
8. State the conditions when motion of a particle can be an SHM.
9. Give the name of three important characteristics of a SHM.
10. SHM is related with uniform circular motion how?
11. What is the geometrical meaning of SHM?
12. When are two SHM said to be in anti phase?
13. When are two SHM said to be in phase?
14. Define phase of a vibrating particle.

Short Answer Type I Questions

2 Marks

15. What do you understand by simple harmonic motion? Write the general equation for SHM.

16. Write the short note on period and frequency.

17. What is the SHM and write its characteristics?

18. Which of the following examples represent periodic motion?
    (i) A swimmer completing one (return) trip from one bank of a river to the other and back.
    (ii) A freely suspended bar magnet displaced from its *N-S* direction and released.
    (iii) A hydrogen molecule rotating about its centre of mass.
    (iv) An arrow released from a bow. **NCERT**

19. Figures depict four x-t plots for linear motion of a particle. Which of the plots represent periodic motion? What is the period of motion (in case of periodic motion)? **NCERT**

(i)
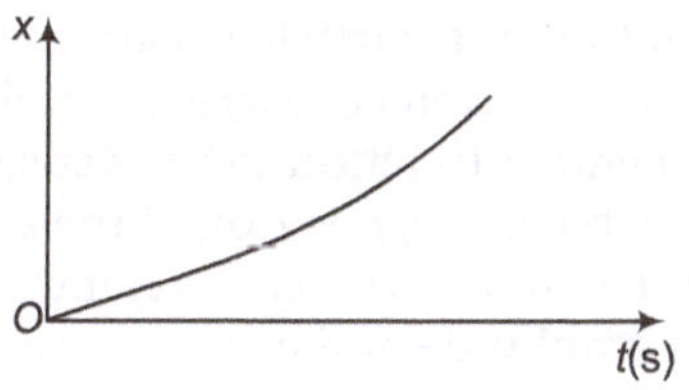

(ii)
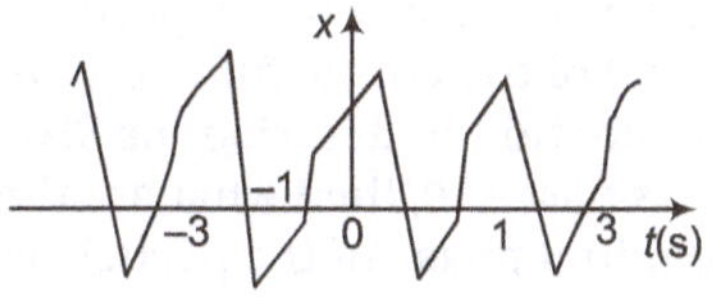

(iii)
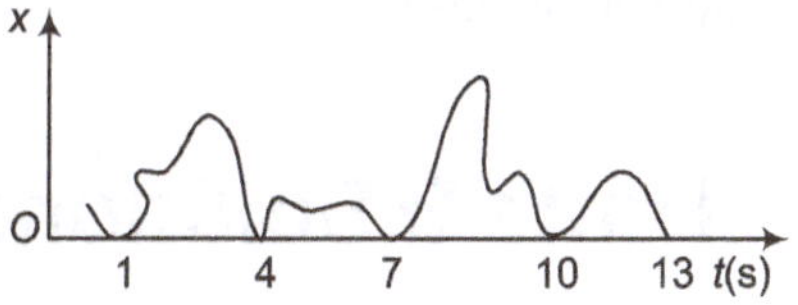

(iv)
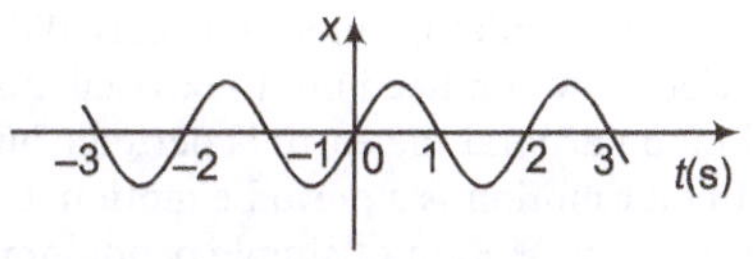

20. Which of the following examples represent (nearly) simple harmonic motion and which represent periodic but not simple harmonic motion?
    (i) The rotation of earth about its axis.
    (ii) Motion of an oscillating mercury column in a U-tube.
    (iii) Motion of a ball bearing inside a smooth curved bowl, when released from a point slightly above the lower most point.
    (iv) General vibrations of a polyatomic molecule about its equilibrium position. **NCERT**

21. Every SHM is periodic motion, but every periodic motion need not to be a simple harmonic motion. Do you agree? Give an example to justify your statement.

22. Which of the following relationships between the acceleration a and the displacement x of a particle involve simple harmonic motion?
    (i) $a = 0.7x$
    (ii) $a = -200x^2$
    (iii) $a = -10x$
    (iv) $a = 100x^3$ **NCERT**

Short Answer Type II Questions

3 Marks

23. What are oscillatory motion and periodic motion?

24. Write down the differential equation for SHM Give its solution.

25. A particle is in linear simple harmonic motion between two points A and B, 10 cm apart. Take the direction from A to B as the positive direction and give the signs of velocity, acceleration and force on the particle when it is
    (i) at the end A.
    (ii) at the end B.
    (iii) at the mid-point of AB going towards A.
    (iv) at 2 cm away from B going towards A.
    (v) at 3 cm away from A going towards B.
    (vi) at 4 cm away from B going towards A. **NCERT**

26. A particle performs SHM on a rectilinear path. Starting from rest, it travels x_1 distance in first second and in the next second, it travels x_2 distance. Find out the amplitude of this SHM.

27. Give the graphical representation of displacement, velocity and acceleration in SHM.

Long Answer Type Questions

5 Marks

28. Show that simple harmonic motion may be regarded as the projection of uniform circular motion along a diameter of the circle. Hence, derive an expression for the displacement of a particle in SHM.

29. Define the terms; harmonic motion, displacement, velocity, acceleration, amplitude, time period, frequency, angular frequency and phase with reference to oscillatory motion.

30. Which of the following functions of time represent (i) simple harmonic (ii) periodic but not simple harmonic and (iii) non-periodic motion? Give period for each case of periodic motion (ω is any positive constant).

(a) $\sin\omega t - \cos\omega t$ (b) $\sin^3 \omega t$

(c) $3\cos\left(\frac{\pi}{4} - 2\omega t\right)$ (d) $\cos\omega t + \cos 3\omega t + \cos 5\omega t$

(e) $\exp(-\omega^2 t^2)$ (f) $1 + \omega t + \omega^2 t^2$ **NCERT**

31. Plot the corresponding reference circle for each of the following simple harmonic motions. Indicate the initial ($t = 0$) position of the particle, the radius of the circle and the angular speed of the rotating particle. For simplicity, the sense of rotation may be fixed to be anti-clockwise in every case (x is in cm and t is in second).

(i) $x = -2\sin\left(3t + \frac{\pi}{3}\right)$ (ii) $x = \cos\left(\frac{\pi}{6} - t\right)$

(iii) $x = 3\sin\left(2\pi t + \frac{\pi}{4}\right)$ (iv) $x = 2\cos\pi t$ **NCERT**

Numerical Problems

32. The piston in the cylinder head of a locomotive has a stroke (twice the amplitude) of 1.0 m. If the piston executes simple harmonic motion with an angular frequency of 200 rad/min, then what is its maximum speed? **NCERT [1 M]**

33. A body describes simple harmonic motion with an amplitude of 5 cm and a period of 0.2 s. Find the acceleration and velocity of the body when the displacement is (i) 5 cm, (ii) 3 cm and (iii) 0 cm. **[3 M]**

34. Figures correspond to two circular motions. The radius of the circle, the period of revolution, the initial position and the sense of revolution (i.e. clockwise or anti-clockwise) are indicated on each figure.

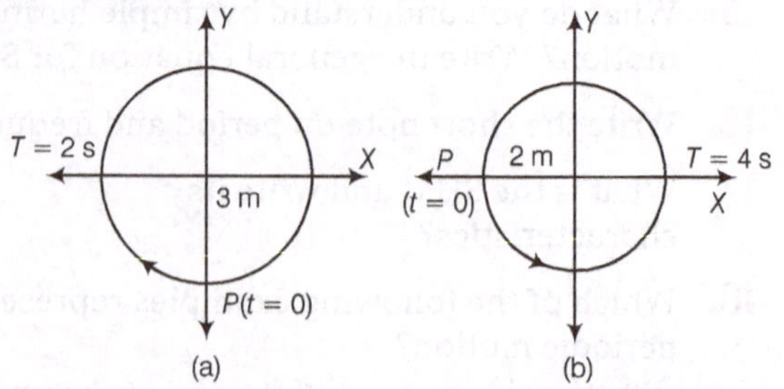

Obtain the corresponding simple harmonic motions of the X-projection of the radius vector of the revolving particle P, in each case. **[3 M]**

35. A man stands on a weighing machine placed on a horizontal platform. The machine reads 50 kg. By means of a suitable mechanism, the platform is made to execute harmonic vibrations up and down with a frequency of two vibrations per second. What will be the effect on the reading of the weighing machine? The amplitude of vibrations of platform is 5 cm. Take $g = 10\ \text{ms}^{-2}$. **[3 M]**

36. The motion of a particle executing simple harmonic motion is described by the displacement function, $x(t) = A\cos(\omega t + \phi)$
If the initial ($t = 0$) position of the particle is 1 cm and its initial velocity is ω cm/s, then what are its amplitude and initial phase angle? The angular frequency of the particle is $\pi\ \text{s}^{-1}$. If instead of the cosine function, we choose the sine function to describe the SHM, $x = B\sin(\omega t + \alpha)$, then what are the amplitude and initial phase of the particle with the above initial conditions? **NCERT [5 M]**

Hints & Solutions

1. (*b*) Every oscillatory motion is periodic but every periodic motion need not to be oscillatory. The motion of moon around the earth is periodic but not oscillatory. Circular motion is a periodic motion, but it is not oscillatory. Motion of simple pendulum is oscillatory and periodic both.

2. (*c*) When frequency of oscillations is high then the motion is called vibratory motion.

3. (*c*) The x-t graph could be represented by

$$x(t) = -A\cos(\omega t) \quad \text{...(i)}$$

On comparing graph and Eq. (i), we get

at $t = 0,\ x(0) = -A\cos 0^\circ = -A$

$$t = \frac{T}{4},\ x(T/4) = -A\cos\left(\frac{2\pi}{T}\times\frac{T}{4}\right) = 0$$

$$t = \frac{T}{2},\quad x = +A$$

Hence, Eq. (i) represents the given graph.

4. (*b*) From graphs, amplitudes of both the curves are same.

In the graph, curve *b* has half the period and twice the frequency of the curve *a*.

i.e. $$T' = \frac{T}{2}$$

5. (*c*) Given, $y_1 = a\sin\omega t$

$$y_2 = b\cos\omega t = b\sin\left(\omega t + \frac{\pi}{2}\right)$$

The resultant displacement is given by

$$y = y_1 + y_2 = \sqrt{a^2 + b^2}\sin(\omega t + \phi)$$

Hence, the motion of superimposed wave is simple harmonic with amplitude $\sqrt{a^2 + b^2}$.

6. Inertia and elasticity are the properties which are required by a system to oscillate.

7. No, there are other types of periodic motions also. Circular motion and rotatory motion are periodic but non-oscillatory.

8. For SHM, the restoring force on the particle must be proportional to its displacement and directed towards mean position.

9. Three important characteristics of an SHM are amplitude, time period (or frequency) and phase.

10. A SHM is the projection of a uniform circular motion of a particle on one of the diameter of the circle.

11. Geometrically, a uniform circular motion projected along the diameter represents a SHM.

12. If there is a phase difference on an odd integral multiple of π between them, the two SHM are said to be in anti phase.

13. If there is a phase difference of an integral multiple of 2π between them, the two SHM are said to be in phase.

14. The phase of a vibrating particle at any instant of time is the state of particle as regards to its position and state of motion.

15. In case of SHM, acceleration is always proportional to displacement in a direction opposite to that of the displacement. [1]

Equation of SHM

Acceleration $= -\omega^2 x$

$$\Rightarrow \quad \frac{d^2x}{dt^2} + \omega^2 x = 0,\ \omega = 2\pi f$$

where, ω is the angular frequency (radian/sec) and f is linear frequency (s^{-1} or hertz). [1]

16. Refer to text on page 431 (Period and Frequency).

17. Refer to text on page 432 (Simple harmonic motion).

18. (i) There is no repetition of the motion as the swimmer just completes one trip, hence not periodic. [1/2]

(ii) The motion is repeated after a certain interval of time, hence periodic. In fact, the bar magnet oscillates about its mean position with a definite period of time. [1/2]

(iii) Rotatary motion is periodic as repeating after fixed time-interval. [1/2]

(iv) There is no repetition, hence not periodic. [1/2]

19. As the graphs are plot between displacements *versus* time, we shall check for repetition to ascertain, whether periodic or not. Also, the minimum time span after which the plot repeats itself will be time period of the motion.

(i) No repetition of motion. It is a unidirectional, linear but non-uniform motion of the particle. [1/2]

(ii) Motion repeats after every 2 s. Hence, periodic with time period 2 s. [1/2]

(iii) Repetition of one position or a few positions (but not all) is not enough for motion to be periodic, the entire motion during one period must be repeated successively. Hence, the given *x-t* plot is not periodic, though there is repetition of a single position ($x = 0$ at every 3 s) but other positions are not repeated. [1/2]

(iv) Clearly, the motion repeats itself after every 2s. Hence, periodic motion having a time-period of 2s. [1/2]

20. (i) There is no to and fro motion which is a must for a periodic motion to be SHM. Hence, rotation of earth about its axis is not SHM. [1/2]

(ii) This is a periodic motion and as it follows $F = -kx$ (about mean position, to and fro motion) hence SHM. [1/2]

(iii) A periodic motion, oscillatory in nature about lower most point as mean position following SHM force law, hence, it is SHM. [1/2]

(iv) A polyatomic molecule has a number of natural frequencies. So, in general, its vibration is a superposition of SHMs of a number of different frequencies. Thus, superposition is periodic but not necessarily SHM. [1/2]

21. Yes, every periodic motion need not to be SHM, e.g. the motion of the earth round the sun is a periodic motion, but not simple harmonic motion as the back and forth motion is not taking place. [2]

22. All SHM follows the condition acceleration $\propto -$ displacement or acceleration $= -$ constant $\times$ displacement.

(i) No negative sign on RHS, hence, not SHM. [1/2]

(ii) Displacement on RHS is squared, hence not SHM. [1/2]

(iii) $a = -10x$ follows the condition of SHM, acceleration $\propto -$ displacement hence, SHM. [1/2]

(iv) No negative sign on RHS and displacement appears as cubed, hence, not SHM. [1/2]

23. Refer to text on pages 430 and 431 (Periodic and oscillatory motion).

24. Refer to text on page 435 (Differential equation of SHM).

25. At either extreme positions in SHM, the velocity is 0 but not the acceleration and force. Acceleration is always direct towards the mean position (point about which SHM is taking place). Further, acceleration decides the direction of force.

Visualise the situation using the diagram below

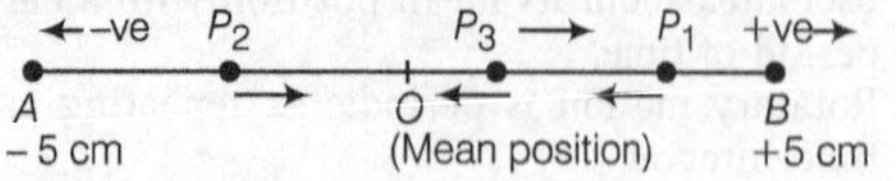

Now,

		Velocity	Acceleration	Force	
(i)	A	0	+	+	[1/2]
(ii)	B	0	−	−	[1/2]
(iii)	O	−	0	0	[1/2]
(iv)	P_1	−	−	−	[1/2]
(v)	P_2	+	+	+	[1/2]
(vi)	P_3	−	−	−	[1/2]

26. Because the particle starts from rest, so its starting point will be extreme position.

Thus, the displacement of the particle from the mean position after one second

$$A - x_1 = A\cos\omega t = A\cos\omega \quad \text{...(i) [putting } t = 1\text{ s]}$$

where, A is amplitude of the SHM and for next second

$$A-(x_1+x_2) = A\cos\omega t = A\cos 2\omega \quad \text{[putting } t = 2\text{ s]}$$

$$= A[2\cos^2\omega - 1] \quad \text{...(ii)}$$

$$[\because \cos 2\omega = 2\cos^2\omega - 1]$$

From Eq. (i) and Eq. (ii), we have [1]

$$A-(x_1+x_2) = A\left[2\cdot\left(\frac{A-x_1}{A}\right)^2 - 1\right]$$

$$= \frac{1}{A}[2A^2 + 2x_1^2 - 4Ax_1 - A^2]$$

$$\Rightarrow A^2 - A(x_1+x_2) = A^2 + 2x_1^2 - 4Ax_1$$

$$\Rightarrow \quad A[3x_1 - x_2] = 2x_1^2$$

$$\therefore \quad A = \frac{2x_1^2}{3x_1 - x_2}$$ [2]

27. Refer to text on page 436 (Graphical representation of displacement, velocity and acceleration).

28. Refer to text on pages 432 and 433 (Simple harmonic motion as a projection of uniform circular motion and displacement).

29. Refer to text on pages 433 and 434 (Characteristics of simple harmonic motion).

30. (a) Assuming $x(t) = \sin\omega t - \cos\omega t$

$$= \sqrt{2}\left[\frac{1}{\sqrt{2}}\sin\omega t - \frac{1}{\sqrt{2}}\cos\omega t\right]$$

$$= \sqrt{2}\left[\cos\frac{\pi}{4}\sin\omega t - \sin\frac{\pi}{4}\cos\omega t\right] = \sqrt{2}\sin\left(\omega t - \frac{\pi}{4}\right)$$

Clearly, the above equation is of the form

$$x = A\sin(\omega t \pm \phi)$$ [1/2]

represents SHM.

Again, if $t = \frac{2\pi}{\omega}$ is the period of SHM, then

$$x\left(t + \frac{2\pi}{\omega}\right) = \sqrt{2}\sin\left[\omega\left(t + \frac{2\pi}{\omega}\right) - \frac{\pi}{4}\right]$$

$$= \sqrt{2}\sin\left(\omega t + 2\pi - \frac{\pi}{4}\right)$$

$$= \sqrt{2}\sin\left(\omega t - \frac{\pi}{4}\right) = x(t)$$

Hence, the period $T = \frac{2\pi}{\omega}$

and phase angle $= -\frac{\pi}{4}$ or $\left(2\pi - \frac{\pi}{4}\right)$ [1/2]

(b) Let $x(t) = \sin^3 t \Rightarrow x(t) = \frac{1}{4}(3\sin\omega t - \sin 3\omega t)$

Using, $\sin 3\theta = 3\sin\theta - 4\sin^3\theta$

The above equations represent two SHMs in combination. The combination is periodic but not SHM.

Period of $\frac{3}{4}\sin\omega t = \frac{2\pi}{\omega} = T$

Period of $\frac{1}{4}\sin 3\omega t = \frac{2\pi}{3\omega} = T' = \frac{T}{3}$

Thus, period of the combination = Minimum time after which the combined function repeats

$$= \text{LCM of } T \text{ and } \frac{T}{3} = T$$ [1]

(c) $x(t) = 3\cos\left(\frac{\pi}{4} - 2\omega t\right) = 3\cos\left(2\omega t - \frac{\pi}{4}\right)$

As $\cos(-\theta) = \cos\theta$

The above equation is of the form

$$x(t) = A\cos(\omega t \pm \phi)$$

Hence, SHM with period $T = \frac{2\pi}{2\omega} = \frac{\pi}{\omega}$ [1]

(d) $x(t) = \cos\omega t + \cos 3\omega t + \cos 5\omega t$

$\cos\omega t$ represents SHM with period $= \frac{2\pi}{\omega} = T$ (say)

$\cos 3\omega t$ represents SHM with period $= \frac{2\pi}{3\omega} = \frac{T}{3}$

$\cos 5\omega t$ represents SHM with period $= \frac{2\pi}{5\omega} = \frac{T}{5}$

The minimum time after which the combined function repeats its value is T. Hence, the given function represents periodic function but not SHM, with period T. [1]

(e) $x(t) = \exp(-\omega^2 t^2)$

The given function is an exponential function. It decreases monotonically $x(t) \to 0$ as $t \to \infty$

There is no repetition of the values. Hence, it represents a non-periodic function. [1/2]

(f) $x(t) = 1 + \omega t + \omega^2 t^2$

Here, as $t \to \infty$, $x(t) \to \infty$

No repetition of values. Hence, it represents non-periodic function. [1/2]

31. (i) Given, $x = -2\sin\left(3t + \frac{\pi}{3}\right)$

$$= 2\cos\left(3t + \frac{\pi}{3} + \frac{\pi}{2}\right)$$

$$= 2\cos\left(3t + \frac{5\pi}{6}\right)$$

On comparing with standard equation for SHM,

$x = A\cos\left[\frac{2\pi}{T}t + \phi\right]$, we get amplitude $A = 2$ cm

Phase angle, $\phi = \frac{5\pi}{6} = 150°$

Angular velocity, $\omega = \frac{2\pi}{T} = 3$ rad/s

This corresponding reference circle is plotted as below

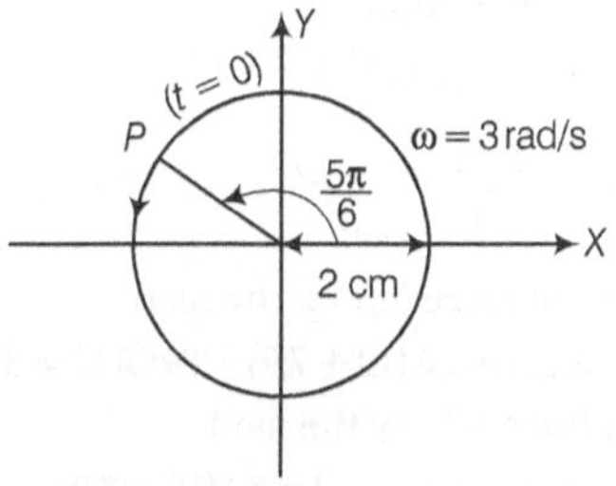

[1 ½]

(ii) $x = A\cos\left(\frac{2\pi}{T}t + \phi\right)$ is the standard SHM equation.

The given equation, $x = \cos\left(\frac{\pi}{6} - t\right)$

$$= \cos\left(t - \frac{\pi}{6}\right) \quad [\text{as } \cos(-\theta) = \cos\theta]$$

On comparison, amplitude $A = 1$ cm

Phase angle, $\phi = -\frac{\pi}{6} = -30°$

Angular velocity, $\omega = \frac{2\pi}{T} = 1$ rad/s

The reference circle is plotted below.

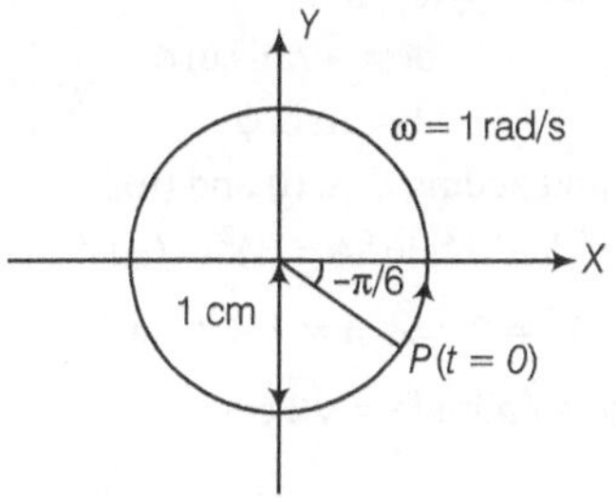

[1 ½]

(iii) Given equation,

$$x = 3\sin\left(2\pi t + \frac{\pi}{4}\right)$$

$$= -3\cos\left[\left(2\pi t + \frac{\pi}{4}\right) + \frac{\pi}{2}\right]$$

$$\left[\because \cos\left(\frac{\pi}{2} + \theta\right) = -\sin\theta\right]$$

or $x = 3\cos\left(2\pi t + \frac{3\pi}{4}\right)$

On comparing with standard SHM equation

$$x = A\cos\left(\frac{2\pi}{T}t + \phi\right)$$

We get, $A = 3$ cm

Phase angle, $\phi = \frac{3\pi}{4} = 135°$ and $\omega = \frac{2\pi}{T} = 2\pi$ rad/s

The reference circle of the motion of the particle is plotted below.

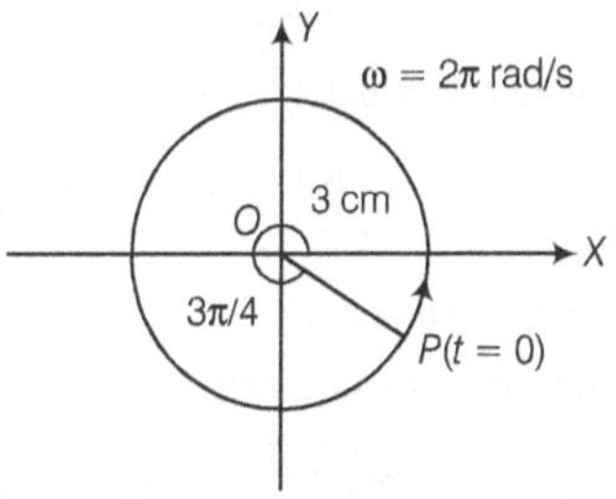

[1]

(iv) Given, $x = 2\cos\pi t$

Standard SHM equation, $x = A\cos\left(\frac{2\pi}{T}t + \phi\right)$

Then, we get amplitude, $A = 2$ cm

Phase angle, $\phi = 0$

Angular velocity, $\omega = \pi$ rad/s

The reference circle of the motion is plotted below.

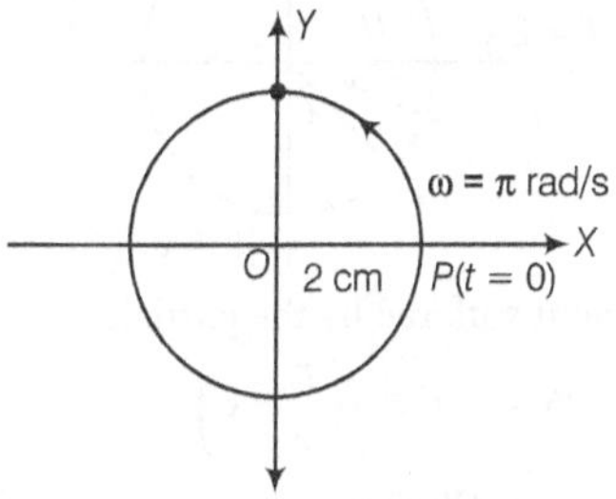

[1]

32. Given, angular frequency of the piston, $\omega = 200$ rad/min

Stroke length = 1 m

$\therefore$ Amplitude of SHM,

$$A = \frac{\text{Stroke length}}{2} = \frac{1}{2} = 0.5 \text{ m}$$ [1/2]

Now, $v_{max} = \omega A = 200 \times 0.5 = 100$ m/min [1/2]

33. Given, amplitude, $A = 5 \text{ cm} = 0.05 \text{ m}$

Time period, $T = 0.2 \text{ s}$

(i) When displacement is $x = 5 \text{ cm} = 0.05 \text{ m}$

Acceleration, $a = -\omega^2(x) = -\left(\frac{2\pi}{T}\right)^2 (x)$

$= -\left(\frac{2\pi}{0.2}\right)^2 (0.05)$

$= -5\pi^2 \text{ m/s}^2$

Velocity, $v = \omega\sqrt{A^2 - x^2}$

$= \left(\frac{2\pi}{T}\right)\sqrt{(0.05)^2 - (0.05)^2}$

$= \left(\frac{2\pi}{T}\right) \times 0 = 0$ [1]

(ii) When displacement is $x = 3 \text{ cm} = 0.03 \text{ m}$

Acceleration, $a = -\left(\frac{2\pi}{0.2}\right)^2 (0.03) = -3\pi^2 \text{ m/s}^2$

and velocity, $v = \omega\sqrt{A^2 - x^2}$

$= \left(\frac{2\pi}{0.2}\right)\sqrt{(0.05)^2 - (0.03)^2} = 0.4\pi \text{ m/s}$ [1]

(iii) When displacement is $x = 0$

Acceleration, $a = -\omega^2 x = 0$

Velocity, $v = \omega\sqrt{A^2 - x^2} = \left(\frac{2\pi}{0.2}\right)\sqrt{(0.05)^2 - (0)^2}$

$= 0.5\pi \text{ m/s}$ [1]

34. If the particle moves from P to P' in time-interval t, then angle moved by position vector (or radius vector)

$$\theta = \omega t = \frac{2\pi}{T}t = \frac{2\pi}{2}t = \pi t \text{ rad}$$

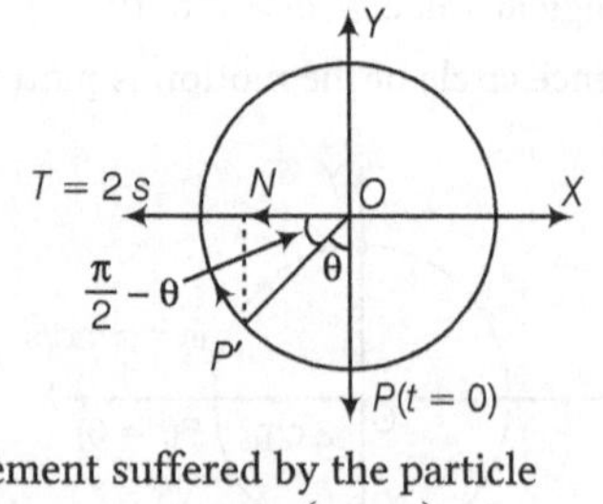

[1]

Displacement suffered by the particle

$ON = OP' \cos\left(\frac{\pi}{2} - \theta\right)$

$= OP' \sin\theta$

But $ON = -x(t)$

As it is left to mean position O, hence, negative sign.

$\Rightarrow \quad -x(t) = 3\sin\theta \quad [\because OP = 3 \text{ cm}]$

or $\quad x(t) = -3\sin\theta$

or $\quad x(t) = -3\sin \pi t$ as $\theta = \pi t$

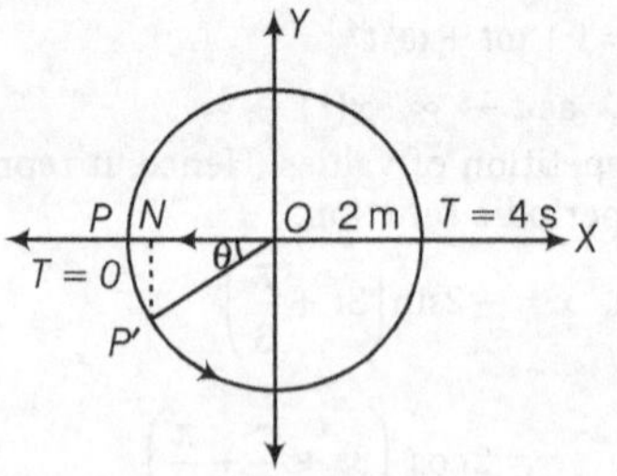

[1]

If the particle moves from P to P' in the time-interval t.

Angle swept by radius vector

$$\theta = \omega t = \frac{2\pi}{T}t = \frac{2\pi}{4}t = \frac{\pi t}{2} \text{ rad}$$

Displacement, $\quad ON = OP' \cos\theta$

or $\quad -x(t) = 2\cos\frac{\pi t}{2} \quad [\because OP = 1\text{cm}]$

Negative sign to indicate left to mean position.

$\Rightarrow \quad x(t) = -2\cos\left(\frac{\pi t}{2}\right)$ [1]

35. Here, $m = 50 \text{ kg}$, $\nu = 2 \text{ s}^{-1}$, $A = 5 \text{ cm} = 0.05 \text{ m}$

Maximum acceleration

$a_{\max} = \omega^2 A = (2\pi\nu)^2 A = 4\pi^2\nu^2 A$

$= 4 \times \left(\frac{22}{7}\right)^2 \times (2)^2 \times 0.05 = 7.9 \text{ ms}^{-2}$ [1]

$\therefore$ Maximum force felt by the man

$m(g + a_{\max}) = 50(10 + 7.9) = 895.0 \text{ N} = 89.5 \text{ kgf}$ [1]

Minimum force felt by the man

$= m(g - a_{\max}) = 50(10 - 7.9)$

$= 105.0 \text{ N} = 10.5 \text{ kgf}$

Hence, the reading of the weighing machine varies between 10.5 kgf and 89.5 kgf. [1]

36. Given, $\quad x(t) = A\cos(\omega t + \phi) \quad$ ...(i)

At $t = 0$; $x(0) = 1$ cm, velocity $v = \omega$ cm/s

Angular frequency $\omega = \pi \text{s}^{-1}$ [1]

$\Rightarrow \quad 1 = A\cos(\omega t + \phi)$

For $t = 0$, $\quad 1 = A\cos\phi \quad$ ...(i)

Now, $\quad v(t) = \frac{dx(t)}{dt} = \frac{d}{dt}A\cos(\omega t + \phi)$

$= -A\omega\sin(\omega t + \phi)$

Again at $t = 0$, $v = \omega$ cm/s

$\Rightarrow \quad \omega = -A\omega\sin\phi$

$\Rightarrow \quad -1 = A\sin\phi \quad$ ...(ii)

Squaring and adding Eqs. (i) and (ii),

$A^2\cos^2\phi + A^2\sin^2\phi = (1)^2 + (-1)^2$

$A^2 = 2 \Rightarrow A = \pm\sqrt{2} \text{ cm}$ [1½]

Hence, the amplitude $= \sqrt{2}$ cm

Dividing Eq. (ii) by Eq. (i), we have

$$\frac{A\sin\phi}{A\cos\phi} = \frac{-1}{1} \text{ or } \tan\phi = -1$$

$$\Rightarrow \quad \phi = -\frac{\pi}{4} \text{ or } \frac{7\pi}{4} \quad \text{[1/2]}$$

Now, if instead of cosine, we choose the sine function, then $x(t) = B\sin(\omega t + \alpha)$

At $t = 0$, $x = 1$ cm $\Rightarrow$ $1 = B\sin(0+\alpha)$

or $\quad B\sin\alpha = 1 \quad$ ...(iii)

$$\text{Velocity } v(t) = \frac{dx(t)}{dt} = \frac{d}{dt}[B\sin(\omega t + \alpha)]$$

$$= +B\omega\cos(\omega t + \alpha)$$

Again at $t = 0$, $v(t) = \omega$ cm/s

$$\omega = +B\omega\cos(0 + \alpha)$$

$$B\cos\alpha = +1 \quad \text{...(iv)}$$

Squaring and adding Eqs. (iii) and (iv),

$$B^2\sin^2\alpha + B^2\cos^2\alpha = (1)^2 + (+1)^2$$

$$\Rightarrow \quad B^2(\sin^2\alpha + \cos^2\alpha) = 2$$

$$B^2 1 = 2 \Rightarrow B = \pm\sqrt{2} \text{ cm} \quad \text{[1]}$$

Hence, amplitude of motion $= \sqrt{2}$ cm

Dividing Eq. (iii) by Eq. (iv), we get

$$\frac{B\sin\alpha}{B\cos\alpha} = \frac{1}{1} \text{ or } \tan\alpha = 1$$

$$\therefore \quad \alpha = \frac{\pi}{4} \quad \text{[1]}$$

TOPIC 02 Force and Energy in SHM and Systems Executing SHM

Total Energy of a particle in Simple Harmonic Motion

A particle executing SHM posseses both kinetic energy and potential energy. When a body is displaced from its equilibrium position by doing work upon it, it acquires potential energy. When the body is released, it begins to move back with a velocity, thus acquiring kinetic energy.

Both kinetic and potential energies of a particle in SHM vary between zero and their maximum values.

Kinetic Energy

The magnitude of velocity at any instant of time in SHM

$$v = \omega\sqrt{A^2 - y^2}$$

$$\therefore \text{ Kinetic energy, } K = \frac{1}{2}mv^2$$

$$= \frac{1}{2}m(\omega\sqrt{A^2 - y^2})^2$$

$$= \frac{1}{2}m\omega^2(A^2 - y^2)$$

$$\boxed{\text{Kinetic energy, KE} = \frac{1}{2}k(A^2 - y^2)}$$

Hence, kinetic energy is also a periodic function of time, being **zero when the displacement is maximum.**

Kinetic energy is maximum when the particle is at the mean position.

Period of kinetic energy is $T/2$.

Potential Energy

When the displacement of a particle from its equilibrium position is x, then restoring force acting on it given as

$$F = -ky$$

If we displace the particle further through a small distance dx, then work done against the restoring force is given by

$$dW = -Fdy = -ky\,dy$$

The total work done in moving the particle from mean position ($x = 0$) to displacement x is given by

$$W = \int dW = -\int_0^y ky\,dy = -k\left[\frac{y^2}{2}\right]_0^y = -\frac{1}{2}ky^2$$

This work done against the restoring force is stored as the potential energy of the particle. Hence, potential energy of a particle at displacement x is given by

$$U = -W = \frac{1}{2}ky^2 = \frac{1}{2}m\omega^2y^2$$

$$\boxed{\text{Potential energy, } U = \frac{1}{2}ky^2}$$

$$= \frac{1}{2}m\omega^2A^2\cos^2(\omega t + \phi)$$

$$U = \frac{1}{2}kA^2\cos^2(\omega t + \phi)$$

Thus, potential energy of a particle executing simple harmonic motion is also periodic with period $T/2$.

Potential energy is **zero at the mean position and maximum at the extreme position.**

Total Energy

At any displacement x, the total energy of a harmonic oscillation is given by

$$E = K + U = \frac{1}{2}k(A^2 - x^2) + \frac{1}{2}kx^2$$

$$\boxed{\text{Total energy, } E = \frac{1}{2}kA^2}$$

$$E = \frac{1}{2}m\omega^2 A^2 = 2\pi^2 m\nu^2 A^2 \qquad [\because \omega = 2\pi\nu]$$

Thus, **the total mechanical energy of a harmonic oscillation is independent of time or displacement, while it depends on the maximum displacement i.e. amplitude.** Hence, in the absence of any frictional force, the total energy of a harmonic oscillation is **conserved.**

Hence, the total energy of particle in SHM is directly proportional to the mass m of the particle, the square of its frequency ν, and the square of its vibrational amplitude A.

Graphical Representation of Energy in SHM

At mean position, $x = 0$

(i) Kinetic energy, $K = \frac{1}{2}k(A^2 - 0^2) = \frac{1}{2}kA^2$

(ii) Potential energy, $U = \frac{1}{2}k(0^2) = 0$

Hence, at **mean position, the entire mechanical energy is in the form of kinetic energy.**

At extreme positions, $x = \pm A$

(i) Kinetic energy, $K = \frac{1}{2}k(A^2 - A^2) = 0$

(ii) Potential energy, $U = \frac{1}{2}kA^2$

Hence, at **the two extreme positions, the energy is totally potential, i.e. kinetic energy is zero.**

From above results, the graph for kinetic energy K, potential energy U and total energy E with displacement x is given below.

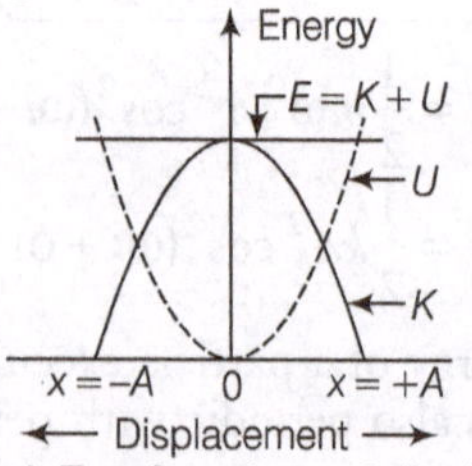

K, U and *E* as functions of displacement *x* for a harmonic oscillation

Plot for variation of energies K, U and E of a harmonic oscillator with time t is given below.

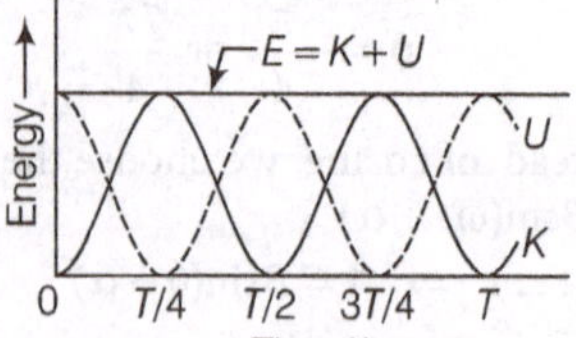

K, U and *E* as functions of time *t* for a harmonic oscillation

From the graph, we note that PE or KE completes two vibrations in a time during which SHM completes one vibration, (i.e. PE and KE both repeat after a period $T/2$) **Thus, the frequency of PE or KE is double than that of SHM. But, the total energy remains constant at all t or x.**

Example 1 **A particle is executing SHM of amplitude A. At what displacement from the mean position is the energy half kinetic and half potential?**

Sol. As, $E_k = E_p$

$$\therefore \quad \frac{1}{2}m\omega^2(A^2 - x^2) = \frac{1}{2}m\omega^2 x^2$$

$$\Rightarrow \quad A^2 - x^2 = x^2 \text{ or } 2x^2 = A^2$$

$$\Rightarrow \quad x^2 = \frac{A^2}{2}$$

$$\text{or} \quad x = \pm\frac{A}{\sqrt{2}}$$

Thus, the energy will be half kinetic and half potential at displacement $\frac{A}{\sqrt{2}}$ on either side of the mean position.

Example 2 **A body of mass 0.2 kg and velocity after 1s, when it passes through mean position is 6 m/s. Find out the total energy and potential energy of the body if time period of the body is 8s during the SHM?**

Sol. Given, $m = 0.2$ kg, $T = 8$ s

$$\omega = \frac{2\pi}{T} = \frac{2\pi}{8} = \frac{\pi}{4} \text{ rad/s}$$

When $t = 1$ s, $v = 6$ m/s

$$v(t) = \omega A \cos \omega t$$

$$6 = \frac{\pi}{4} \times A \cos\left(\frac{\pi}{4} \times 1\right)$$

$$6 = \frac{\pi}{4} \times A \times \frac{1}{\sqrt{2}}$$

$$A = \frac{4\sqrt{2} \times 6}{\pi}$$

$$= \frac{24\sqrt{2}}{\pi} \text{ m}$$

The total energy of the body

$$E = \frac{1}{2}m\omega^2A^2 = \frac{1}{2}\times 0.2\times\left(\frac{\pi}{4}\right)^2\times\left(\frac{24\sqrt{2}}{\pi}\right)^2$$

$$= \frac{230.4}{32} = 7.2\text{ J}$$

Potential energy, $PE = E - KE = 7.2 - \frac{1}{2}mv^2$

$$= 7.2 - \frac{1}{2}\times 0.2\times(6)^2 = 7.2 - 3.6$$

Potential energy = 3.6 J

Example 3 A block whose mass is 1 kg is fastened to a spring. The spring has a spring constant of 50 Nm^{-1}. The block is pulled to a distance $x = 10$ cm from its equilibrium position at $x = 0$ on a frictionless surface from rest at $t = 0$. Calculate the kinetic, potential and total energies of the block when it is 5 cm away from the mean position. **NCERT**

Sol. Given, $m = 1$ kg, $k = 50\text{Nm}^{-1}$, $A = 10\text{ cm} = 0.1\text{m}$, $x = 5\text{ cm} = 0.05\text{ m}$

Kinetic energy, $K = \frac{1}{2}k(A^2 - x^2)$

$$K = \frac{1}{2}\times 50\times[(0.1)^2 - (0.05)^2] = 0.1875\text{ J}$$

Potential energy of a block,

$$U = \frac{1}{2}kx^2 = \frac{1}{2}\times 50\times(0.05)^2 = 0.0625\text{ J}$$

Total energy, $E = K + U = 0.1875 + 0.0625$

$E = 0.25$ J

We also know that at maximum displacement, KE is zero and hence the total energy of the system is equal to PE.

Therefore, the total energy of the system

$$= \frac{1}{2}(k\times A^2) = \frac{1}{2}\times 50\text{ Nm}^{-1}\times 0.1\times 0.1$$

$$= 0.25\text{ J} \qquad [\because \text{here, } x = A = 0.1\text{m}]$$

Which is same as the sum of two energies at a displacement of 5 cm. This is in confirmity with the principle of conservation of energy.

Restoring Force

Whenever a body is displaced a little from its equilibrium position (i.e. mean position), a **restoring force** acts on the body in a direction opposite to its displacement in order to bring the body back to its equilibrium position.

This restoring force is proportional to the displacement, provided the displacement is small. If the body is left there, it returns back to its mean position, under the restoring force.

In this way, the restoring force helps in oscillating the body back and forth about the mean position with a definite period.

Now, from Newton's second law of motion

We know that, $F = ma$

For a body executing SHM, we have studied earlier that $a(t) = -\omega^2 x(t)$

Thus, $F(t) = -m\omega^2 x(t)$

$$\Rightarrow \boxed{\text{Restoring force, } F(t) = -kx(t)} \qquad \ldots\text{(i)}$$

where, $k = m\omega^2$ or $\omega = \sqrt{\frac{k}{m}}$

The force law is expressed by Eq. (i) and can be taken as an alternative definition of simple harmonic motion. **It states that simple harmonic motion is the motion executed by a particle subjected to a force, which is proportional to the displacement of the particle and is always directed towards the mean position.**

Example 4 Give expression for restoring force for a spring attached to a mass.

Sol. For a spring attached with mass, the restoring force is $-kx$ and acts on the mass.

$\therefore \quad ma = -kx$

$\Rightarrow \quad -\frac{x}{a} = \frac{m}{k}$

$\Rightarrow \quad ma = -m\omega^2 x = -\frac{m4\pi^2}{T^2}x$

$\Rightarrow \quad T = 2\pi\sqrt{\frac{x}{a}} = 2\pi\sqrt{\frac{m}{k}}$

Example 5 Two identical springs of spring constant k are attached to a block of mass m and to fixed supports as shown in figure. Show that when the mass is displaced from its equilibrium position on either side. It executes a simple harmonic motion. Find the period of oscillations.

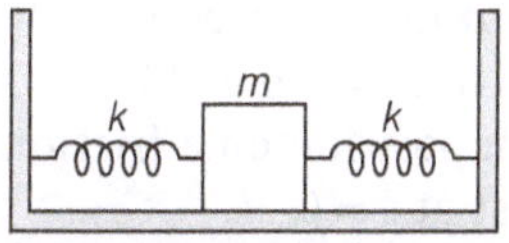

NCERT

Sol. Let the mass m is displaced by the small length x to the right side of the mean position. Then, the left spring gets elongated by distance x and right spring gets compressed by distance x.

Force exerted by left spring, trying to pull the mass towards the mean position.

$$F_1 = -kx$$

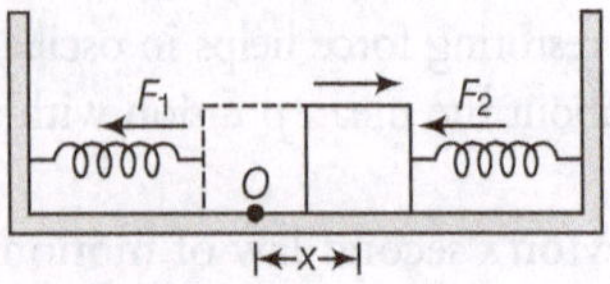

Similarly, force exerted by the right spring, trying to push the mass towards the mean position,

$$F_2 = -kx$$

The net force acting on the mass due to both the springs is

$$F = F_1 + F_2 = -2kx$$

Thus, the force acting on the mass is proportional to its displacement x and is directed towards its mean position. Hence, the motion of the mass m is simple harmonic. Comparing the equation, $F = -2kx$ with $F = -k'x$.

We have, force constant $k' = 2k$.

$\therefore$ The time period of oscillation is $T = 2\pi\sqrt{\frac{m}{k'}}$

$$= 2\pi\sqrt{\frac{m}{2k}}$$

Example 6 The vertical motion of a huge piston in a machine is simple harmonic with a frequency of $0.50\ s^{-1}$. A block of 10 kg is placed on the piston. What is the maximum amplitude of the piston's SHM for the block and the piston to remain together?

Sol. As, $\nu = \frac{1}{2\pi}\sqrt{\frac{k}{m}}$

$$\therefore \quad k = 4\pi^2 m\nu^2$$

For maximum displacement, $y_{max} = A$

Maximum restoring force,

$$F = -kA = -mg$$

or
$$A = \frac{mg}{k} = \frac{mg}{4\pi^2 m\nu^2} = \frac{g}{4\pi^2\nu^2}$$

$$= \frac{9.8}{4\times(3.14)^2\times(0.50)^2} = 0.99\ \text{m}$$

Example 7 Consider a block of mass 700 g is fastened to a spring having spring constant of 70 N/m. Find out the following parameters, if block is pulled a distance of 14 cm from its mean position on a frictionless surface and released from rest at $t = 0$.

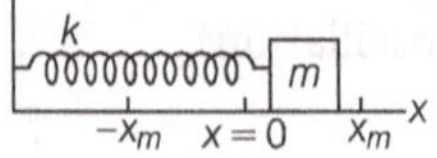

(i) The angular frequency, the frequency and the period of the resulting motion.

(ii) The amplitude of the oscillation.

(iii) The maximum speed of the oscillating block.

(iv) The maximum acceleration of the block.

(v) The phase constant and hence the displacement function $x(t)$.

Sol. The spring block system forms a linear simple harmonic oscillation with block undergoing SHM. Linear means the restoring force ($F = -kx$) is proportional to x rather than power of x. For a spring, the spring constant being, $k = m\omega^2$.

(i) The angular frequency is given by

$$\omega = \sqrt{\frac{k}{m}} = \sqrt{\frac{70\ \text{N/m}}{0.700\ \text{kg}}} = 10\ \text{rad/s}$$

$$\text{Frequency, } f = \frac{\omega}{2\pi} = \frac{10}{2\pi} \simeq 1.59\ \text{Hz}$$

$$\text{The period, } T = \frac{1}{f} = \frac{1}{1.59} = 0.63 = 630\ \text{ms}$$

Since, there is no friction involved, the mechanical energy of the spring block system is conserved. The block is released from rest 14 cm from its equilibrium or mean position. The block will have zero kinetic energy whenever it is again 14 cm from its equilibrium position, which means it will never farther than 14 cm.

(ii) The maximum amplitude of the oscillation

= maximum displacement

$$\therefore \quad x_m = 14\ \text{cm} = 0.14\ \text{m}$$

(iii) The maximum speed v_m is given by

$$v_m = \omega\, x_m = 10\times 0.14 = 1.4\ \text{m/s}$$

(iv) The maximum acceleration of the block is given by

$$a_m = \omega^2 x_m = 100\times 0.14 = 14\ \text{m/s}^2$$

At time $t = 0$, the block is located at position, $x = x_m$

(v) Then, from $x(t) = x_m \cos(\omega t + \phi)$

$$x_m = x_m \cos(0\times\omega + \phi)$$

$$\cos\phi = 1 \Rightarrow \phi = 0$$

The displacement

$$x(t) = x_m \cos(\omega t + \phi) = 0.14\times\cos(10t + 0)$$

$$x(t) = 0.14\cos 10t$$

Simple Pendulum

An ideal simple pendulum consists of a point mass suspended by an inextensible and weightless string which is fixed at the other end as shown in figure. But this type of pendulum is not possible to make practically.

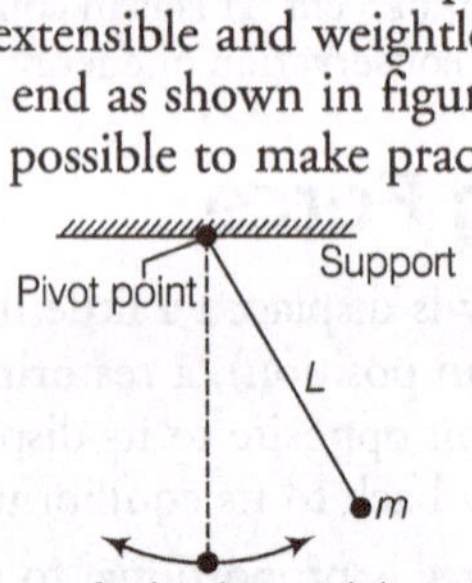

A simple pendulum

So, practically, a simple pendulum is obtained by suspending a small metal bob by a long and fine cotton thread from a support as given in the figure along side.

Expression for Time Period of a Simple Pendulum

Consider a simple pendulum, a small bob of mass m tied to an inextensible massless string of length L.

In the equilibrium position, the bob of a simple pendulum lies vertically below the point of suspension. If the bob is slightly displaced on either side and then released, it begins oscillation about the mean position.

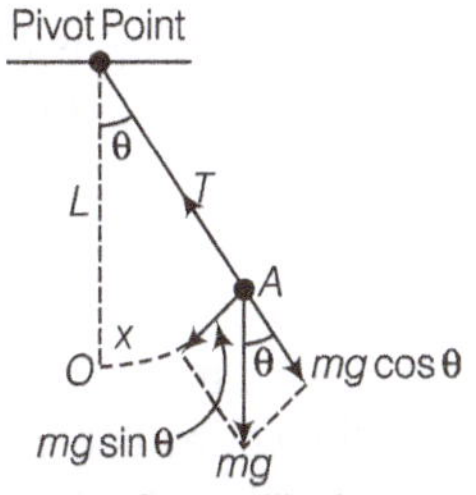

An oscillating pendulum

Let us consider that at any instant during oscillation, the bob lies at position A when its displacement is $OA = x$ and the thread makes an angle θ with the vertical.

The forces acting on the bob are

(i) Weight mg of the bob acting vertically downwards.

(ii) Tension T along the string.

The force mg has two rectangular components

(i) The component $mg \cos\theta$ acting along the thread is balanced by the tension T in the thread and

(ii) The tangential force $mg \sin\theta$ will provide the restoring torque, which tends to bring the bob back to its mean position. Thus, the restoring torque of the force $mg \sin\theta$ about the pivot point is given by

$$\tau = -(mg\sin\theta)L = -mgL\sin\theta \qquad \ldots\text{(i)}$$

where, the negative sign shows that the torque acts to reduce θ. L is the length of the simple pendulum. For rotation, the torque can be given as

$$\tau = I\alpha \qquad \ldots\text{(ii)}$$

where, I = pendulum's moment of inertia about the pivot point.

α = angular acceleration about the pivot point.

From Eqs. (i) and (ii), we get

$$-mgL\sin\theta = I\alpha$$

$$\Rightarrow \qquad \alpha = \frac{-mgL\sin\theta}{I}$$

If θ is in radian, $\sin\theta$ can be expressed as

$$\sin\theta = \theta - \frac{\theta^3}{3!} + \frac{\theta^5}{5!} - \ldots$$

Now, if θ is small, $\sin\theta$ can be approximated by θ

$$\therefore \qquad \alpha \approx \frac{-mgL\theta}{I}$$

Therefore, the acceleration of the pendulum is proportional to the angular displacement θ but in opposite sign. Thus, as the pendulum moves to the right, it's pull to the left increases until it stops and begins to return to the left.

Similarly, when it moves towards left, its acceleration to the right tends to return it to the right and so on as it swings to and fro as SHM. Hence, the motion of a simple pendulum swinging through small angles is approximately SHM.

Equation $\alpha = \frac{-mgL}{I}\theta$ is the angular analogue of equation $a = -\omega^2 x$.

On comparing these equations, we have

$$\omega = \sqrt{\frac{mgL}{I}}$$

$$\Rightarrow \qquad \frac{2\pi}{T} = \sqrt{\frac{mgL}{I}} \Rightarrow T = 2\pi\sqrt{\frac{I}{mgL}} \qquad \ldots\text{(iii)}$$

where, T = time period of pendulum.

All the masses of a simple pendulum is centered in the mass m of the bob (taken as a point) which is at a distance of L from the pivot point. Therefore, $I = mL^2$.

On putting this value in Eq. (iii)

$$T = \frac{1}{2\pi}\sqrt{\frac{mL^2}{mgL}} = \frac{1}{2\pi}\sqrt{\frac{L}{g}}$$

$$\Rightarrow \qquad \boxed{\text{Time period of pendulum, } T = 2\pi\sqrt{\frac{L}{g}}}$$

Obviously, the time period of a simple pendulum depends on its length L and acceleration due to gravity g and is independent of the mass m of the bob.

$T = 2\pi\sqrt{\frac{L}{g}}$ is valid only for small length.

If length is large, then $T = 2\pi\sqrt{\frac{R}{\left(1+\frac{R}{L}\right)g}}$

as $L \to \infty$, $T = 2\pi\sqrt{\frac{R}{g}}$

as $L = R$, $T = 2\pi\sqrt{\frac{R}{2g}}$

where, R = distance between the pivot point and the centre of mass of the pendulum.

Example 8 What is the length of a simple pendulum, which ticks seconds ?

Sol. The time period of simple pendulum which ticks seconds is 2s and called as **second pendulum**.

Given, $T = 2\text{s}$ and $g = 9.8\ \text{m/s}^2$

$$T = 2\pi\sqrt{\frac{L}{g}} = 2\pi\sqrt{\frac{L}{9.8}}$$

$$2^2 = 4\pi^2 \times \frac{L}{9.8} \Rightarrow L = \frac{9.8}{\pi^2} = 0.992\ \text{m} \simeq 1.0\ \text{m}$$

Oscillation Due to a Spring

To study oscillation due to a spring, let us consider a massless spring lying on a frictionless horizontal table. Its one end is attached to a rigid support and the other end to a block of mass m.

If the block is pulled towards right through a small distance x and released, it starts oscillating back and forth about its equilibrium position under the action of the restoring force.

$$F = -kx$$

where, k is the force constant (restoring force per unit deformation of the spring). The negative sign indicates that the force is directed opposite to x.

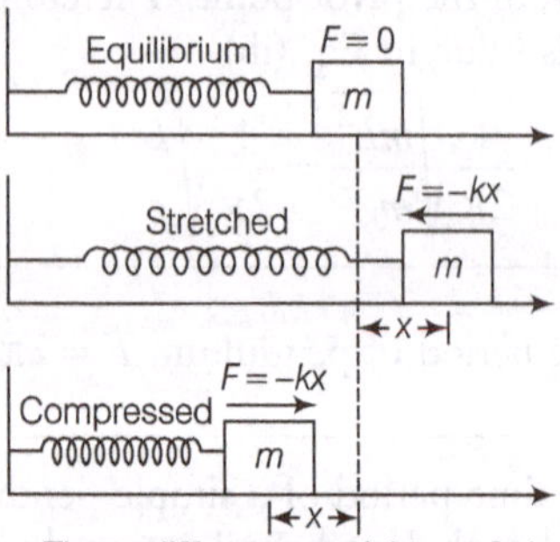

Three different positions of the oscillation due to a spring

If $\frac{d^2x}{dt^2}$ is the acceleration of the body, then

$$m\frac{d^2x}{dt^2} = -kx \qquad \left[\because F = ma = m\frac{d^2x}{dt^2}\right]$$

or

$$\frac{d^2x}{dt^2} = \frac{-k}{m}x = -\omega^2 x \Rightarrow \frac{d^2x}{dt^2} + \omega^2 x = 0$$

Thus, acceleration is proportional to displacement x and acts opposite to it.

Hence, the block executes simple harmonic motion.

Its time period is given by

$$T = \frac{2\pi}{\omega} = \frac{2\pi}{\sqrt{k/m}} \quad \text{or} \quad \boxed{\text{Time period, } T = 2\pi\sqrt{\frac{m}{k}}}$$

Frequency of oscillation can also be calculated as

$$\boxed{\text{Frequency, } \nu = \frac{1}{T} = \frac{1}{2\pi}\sqrt{\frac{k}{m}}}$$

Clearly, the time period T will be small or frequency ν large if the spring is highly stiff (high k) and attached body is light (small m)

Example 9 A 5 kg collar is attached to a spring of spring constant 500 Nm^{-1}. It slides without friction over a horizontal rod. The collar is displaced from its equilibrium position by 10.0 cm and released. Calculate

(i) the period of oscillation,

(ii) the maximum speed and

(iii) maximum acceleration of the collar. **NCERT**

Sol. Draw the figure containing collar of 5 kg attached to a spring of spring constant 500 N /m.

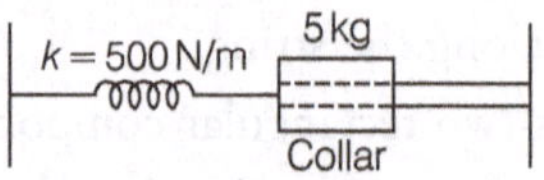

(i) Given, $m = 5\text{kg}$, $k = 500\ \text{N/m}$, $A = 10\text{cm} = 0.1\text{m}$

The period of oscillation is given by

$$T = 2\pi\sqrt{\frac{m}{k}} = 2\pi \times \sqrt{\frac{5}{500}} = 0.628\ \text{s}$$

(ii) Maximum speed of the collar, $v_{max} = \omega A$

$$v_{max} = \sqrt{\frac{k}{m}} \cdot A = \sqrt{\frac{500}{5}} \times 0.1 = 1\ \text{m/s}$$

(iii) Maximum acceleration of the collar,

$$a_{max} = \omega^2 A = \frac{k}{m} \cdot A = \frac{500}{5} \times 0.1 = 10\ \text{m/s}^2$$

Topic Practice 2

Multiple Choice Questions

1 Mark

1. A spring-mass system is oscillating on a frictionless horizontal plane. The position of the mass when its potential energy and its kinetic energy both are equal, is (let A is the amplitude of oscillation.)

   (a) A (b) $A/\sqrt{2}$ (c) $A/2$ (d) $A/\sqrt{3}$

2. The expression for displacement of an object in SHM is $x = A\cos(\omega t)$. The potential energy at $t = T/4$ is

(a) $\frac{1}{2}kA^2$ (b) $\frac{1}{8}kA^2$

(c) $\frac{1}{4}kA^2$ (d) zero

3. A body executes simple harmonic motion. The potential energy (PE), the kinetic energy (KE) and total energy (TE) are measured as function of displacement x. Which of the following statement is true?
(a) KE is maximum, when $x = 0$
(b) TE is zero, when $x = 0$
(c) KE is maximum, when x is maximum
(d) PE is maximum, when $x = 0$

4. In the figure shown below, the block is moved side ways by a distance A. The magnitude of net force on the block is

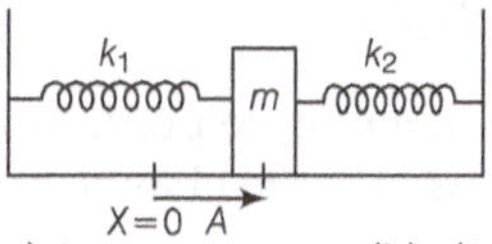

(a) $(k_1 - k_2)A$ (b) $(k_2 - k_1)A$

(c) $(k_1 + k_2)A$ (d) $\left(\frac{k_1 + k_2}{2}\right)A$

Very Short Answer Type Questions

(1 Mark)

5. What is the force equation of a SHM?

6. Under what condition is the motion of a simple pendulum be simple harmonic? **NCERT Exemplar**

7. Name the trigonometric functions which are suitable for analytical treatment of periodic and/or oscillatory motions.

8. What is the ratio between the distance travelled by the oscillator in one time period and amplitude? **NCERT Exemplar**

9. A simple pendulum is transferred from earth to the surface of moon. How will its time period be affected?

10. On which factors does the time period of a simple pendulum depend?

Short Answer Type Questions

(2 Marks)

11. How do the kinetic and the potential energies vary during one oscillating in a SHM?

12. In case of an oscillating simple pendulum what will be the direction of acceleration of the bob at (a) the mean position, (b) the end points?

13. Justify the following statements
(i) The motion of an artificial satellite around the earth cannot be taken as SHM.
(ii) The time period of a simple pendulum will get doubled if its length is increased four times.

14. Define the restoring force and it characterstic in case of an oscillating body.

Short Answer Type II Questions

(3 Marks)

15. A mass attached to a spring is free to oscillate, with angular velocity ω in a horizontal plane without friction or damping. It is pulled to a distance x_0 and pushed towards the centre with a velocity v_0 at time $t = 0$. Determine the amplitude of the resulting oscillations in terms of the parameters ω, x_0 and v_0. [**Hint** Start with the equation $x = A\cos(\omega t + \theta)$ and note that the initial velocity is negative.] **NCERT**

16. Determine the time period of oscillation of a simple pendulum.

17. Answer the following questions.
(i) Time period of a particle in SHM depends on the force constant k and mass m of thc particle $T = 2\pi\sqrt{\frac{m}{k}}$. A simple pendulum executes SHM approximately. Then, why is the time period of a pendulum independent of the mass of the pendulum?
(ii) The motion of a simple pendulum is approximately simple harmonic for small angle oscillations. For larger angles of oscillation, a more involved analysis shows that T is greater than $2\pi\sqrt{\frac{l}{g}}$. Think of a qualitative argument to appreciate this result.
(iii) A man with a wristwatch on his hand falls from the top of a tower. Does the watch give correct time during the free fall?
(iv) What is the frequency of oscillation of a simple pendulum mounted in a cabin that is freely falling under gravity? **NCERT**

18. A simple pendulum of length l and having a bob of mass M is suspended in a car. The car is moving on a circular track of radius R with a uniform speed v. If the pendulum makes small oscillations in a radial direction about its equilibrium position, then what will be its time period? **NCERT**

19. An air chamber of volume V has a neck area of cross-section a into which a ball of mass m just fits and can move up and down without any friction (see figure). Show that when the ball is pressed down a little and released, it executes SHM. Obtain an expression for the time period of oscillations assuming pressure-volume variations of air to be isothermal. **NCERT**

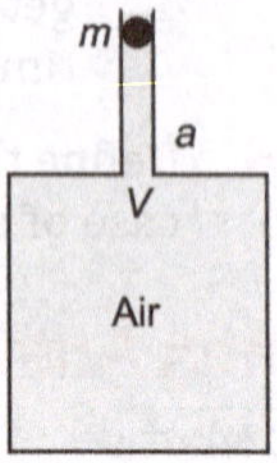

20. One end of a U-tube containing mercury is connected to a suction pump and the other end to atmosphere. A small pressure difference is maintained between the two columns. Show that when the suction pump is removed, the column of mercury in the U-tube executes simple harmonic motion.

21. Show that for a particle in linear SHM, the average kinetic energy over a period of oscillation equals the average potential energy over the same period.

Long Answer Type Questions

5 Marks

22. Prove that the sum of kinetic energy, potential energy and total energy of a particle doing SHM is constant.

23. A cylindrical piece of cork of base area A, density ρ and height L floats in a liquid of density ρ_L. The cork is depressed slightly and then released. Show that the cork oscillates up and down simple harmonically and find its time period of oscillations. **NCERT**

24. Fig. (a) shows a spring of force constant k clamped rigidly at one end and a mass m attached to its free end. A force F applied at the free end stretches the spring. Fig. (b) shows the same spring with both ends free and attached to a mass m at either end. Each end of the spring in Fig. (b) is stretched by the same force F.

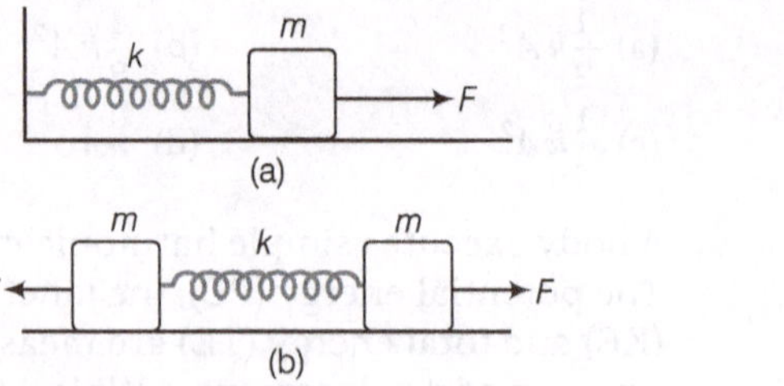

(i) What is the maximum extension of the spring in both the cases?
(ii) If the mass in Fig. (a) and the two masses in Fig. (b) are released, then what is the period of oscillation in each case? **NCERT**

25. Explain the restoring force and simple pendulum with the help of diagram.

Numerical Problems

26. If the length of a simple pendulum is increased by 25%, then what is the change in its time period? **[1 M]**

27. How much is KE for displacement equal to half the amplitude? **[1 M]**

28. A body of mass 12 kg is suspended by coil spring of natural length 50 cm and force constant 2.0×10^3 Nm^{-1}. What is the stretched length of the spring? If the body is pulled down further stretching the spring to a length of 5.9 cm and then released, then what is the frequency of oscillation of the suspended mass? (Neglect the mass of the spring) **[2 M]**

29. A spring compressed by 0.1 m develops a restoring force 10 N. A body of mass 4 kg placed on it. Deduce
(i) the force constant of the spring.
(ii) the depression of the spring under the weight of the body (take $g = 10$ N/kg)
(iii) the period of oscillation, the body is distributed and
(iv) frequency of oscillation **[2 M]**

30. A circular disc of mass 10 kg is suspended by a wire attached to its centre. The wire is twisted by rotating the disc and released. The period of torsional oscillations is found to be 1.5 s. The radius of the disc is 15 cm. Determine the torsional spring constant of the wire. (Torsional spring constant α is defined by the relation, $J = -\alpha\theta$, where J is the restoring couple and θ the angle of twist.) **NCERT [2 M]**

31. A spring balance has a scale that reads from 0 to 50 kg. The length of the scale is 20 cm. A body suspended from this spring, when displaced and released, oscillates with a period of 0.60 s. What is the weight of the body? **NCERT [3 M]**

32. A spring of force constant 1200 Nm^{-1} is mounted on a horizontal table. A mass of 3.0 kg is attached to the free end of the spring, pulled sideways to a distance of 2.0 cm and then released.

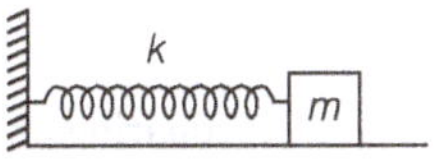

(i) What is the frequency of oscillation of the mass?
(ii) What is the maximum acceleration of the mass?
(iii) What is the maximum speed of the mass? **NCERT [3 M]**

33. In the previous question, let us take the position of mass when the spring is unstreched as $x = 0$ and the direction from left to right as the positive direction of x-axis. Given x as a function of time t for the oscillating mass, if at the moment we start the stopwatch ($t = 0$), the mass is
(i) at the mean position,
(ii) at the maximum stretched position and
(iii) at the maximum compressed position.
In what way do these functions for SHM differ from each other, in frequency, in amplitude or the initial phase? **NCERT [3 M]**

34. The acceleration due to gravity on the surface of moon is 1.7 m/s^2. What is the time period of a simple pendulum on the surface of moon, if its time period on the surface of earth is 3.5 s? (g on the surface of earth is 9.8 m/s^2.) **NCERT [3 M]**

35. The length of a second pendulum on the surface of earth is 1 m. What will be the length of a second pendulum on the moon? **NCERT Exemplar [3 M]**

36. You are riding in an automobile of mass 3000 kg. Assuming that you are examining the oscillation characteristics of its suspension system. The suspension sags 15 cm when the entire automobile is placed on it. Also, the amplitude of oscillation decreases by 50% during one complete oscillation. Estimate the value of (i) the spring constant k and (ii) the damping constant b for the spring and shock absorber system of one wheel, assuming that each wheel supports 750 kg. **NCERT [3 M]**

37. A body weighing 10 g has a velocity of 6 cm s^{-1} after one second of its starting from mean position. If the time period is 6 s, then find the kinetic energy, potential energy and the total energy. **[3 M]**

38. A person normally weighing 50 kg stands on a massless platform which oscillates up and down harmonically at a frequency of 2.0 s^{-1} and an amplitude 5.0 cm. A weighing machine on the platform gives the persons weight against time.
(i) Will there be any change in weight of the body, during the oscillation?
(ii) If answer to part (i) is yes, then what will be the maximum and minimum reading in the machine and at which position? **NCERT Exemplar [5 M]**

Hints & Solutions

1. (*b*) When, $\frac{1}{2}kx^2 = \frac{1}{2}mv^2 = \frac{1}{2}$ (Total mechanical energy)

$$\frac{1}{2}kx^2 = \frac{1}{2}\left[\frac{1}{2}kA^2\right] \Rightarrow x = A/\sqrt{2}$$

2. (*d*) $x\left(\frac{T}{4}\right) = A\cos\left(\frac{2\pi}{T}\times\frac{T}{4}\right) = 0$, as $\omega = \frac{2\pi}{T}$

At $x = 0$, PE $= \frac{1}{2}kx^2 = 0$

3. (*a*) $KE(x) = \frac{1}{2}m\omega^2(A^2 - x^2)$

So, KE at $x = 0$, $KE(0) = \frac{1}{2}m\omega^2A^2 = (KE)_{max}$

4. (*c*)

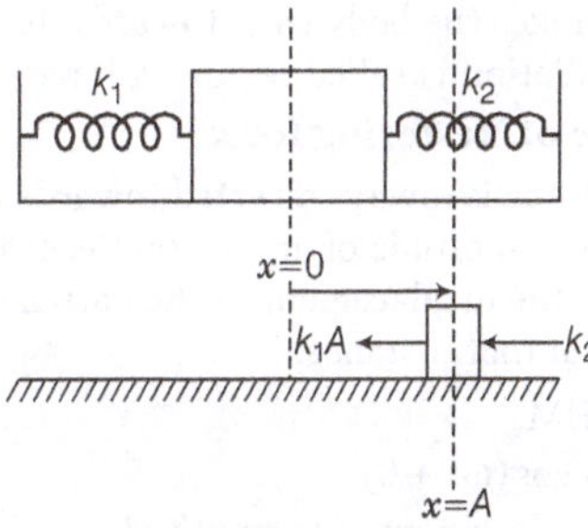

From FBD, $\mathbf{F}_{net} = -(k_1 + k_2)A$

$\Rightarrow \quad |\mathbf{F}_{net}| = (k_1 + k_2)A$

5. According to force equation of SHM, $F = -kx$, where k is a constant known as force constant.

6. When the displacement amplitude of the pendulum is extremely small as compared to its length.

7. Sine and/or cosine functions of time or their combinations may represent analytically periodic/oscillatory motions.

8. Total distance travelled by an oscillator in one time period, from its mean position to one extreme position, then to other extreme position and finally back to mean position is 4 A, where A is the amplitude of oscillation.

Hence, the ratio $= \frac{4A}{A} = 4$

9. As value of g on moon is less than that on earth, in accordance with the relation $T = 2\pi\sqrt{l/g}$, the time period of oscillations of a simple pendulum on moon will be greater.

10. The time period of a simple pendulum depends upon
(i) string must have length but no weight.
(ii) bob must have weight and must be point sized.

11. The kinetic energy is maximum at mean position and potential energy is zero. The potential energy is maximum at the extreme position, where kinetic energy is zero. In between it is partly kinetic and partly potential. Total energy remains constant during each oscillation. [2]

12. The direction of acceleration of the bob at its mean position is radial, i.e. towards the point of suspension. [1]
At extreme points, however, the acceleration is tangential towards the mean position. [1]

13. (i) The motion of an artificial satellite around the earth is periodic as it repeats after a regular interval of time. But it cannot be taken as SHM because it is not a to and fro motion about any fixed point that is, mean position. [1]

(ii) Time period of simple pendulum,

$$T = 2\pi\sqrt{\frac{l}{g}}, \quad \text{i.e.} \quad T \propto \sqrt{l}$$

Clearly, if the length is increased four times, the time period gets doubles. [1]

14. A force which takes the body back towards the mean position in oscillation is called restoring force.

Characteristic of Restoring force

The restoring force is always directed towards the mean position and its magnitude of any instant is directly proportional to the displacement of the particle from its mean position of that instance. [2]

15. We have for SHM

$$x = A\cos(\omega t + \theta) \quad \text{...(i)}$$

where, x = displacement, A = amplitude
θ = phase constant, we get

On differentiating with respect to t,

$$\frac{dx}{dt} = -A\omega\sin(\omega t + \theta)$$

$$\Rightarrow \quad v = -A\omega\sin(\omega t + \theta) \quad \text{...(ii)[1]}$$

where, v = instantaneous velocity of the particle at t.
Now, at $t = 0$, $x = x_0$
From Eq. (i),

$$\Rightarrow \quad x_0 = A\cos\theta \quad \text{...(iii)}$$

Again at $t = 0$, $v = -v_0$
From Eq. (ii),

$$-v_0 = -A\omega\sin\theta \quad \text{or} \quad \frac{v_0}{\omega} = A\sin\theta \quad \text{...(iv) [1]}$$

On squaring and adding Eqs. (iii) and (iv), we get

$$A^2(\cos^2\theta + \sin^2\theta) = x_0^2 + \left(\frac{v_0}{\omega}\right)^2$$

$$\Rightarrow A^2 = x_0^2 + \left(\frac{v_0}{\omega}\right)^2 \quad \text{or} \quad A = \sqrt{x_0^2 + \left(\frac{v_0}{\omega}\right)^2}$$ [1]

16. Refer to text on page 447 (Expression for time period of a simple pendulum).

17. (i) For a simple pendulum, k is proportional to m the mass of the particle, hence $\frac{m}{k}$ becomes constant and does not affect the time period. [1/2]

(ii) If we replace $\sin\theta \approx \theta$ for large angles, then actually $\sin\theta < \theta$. Now, since this factor is multiplied to the restoring force $mg\sin\theta$ is replaced by $mg\theta$ which means an effective reduction in g for large angles. Hence, there is an increase in time period T over that given by the formula $T = 2\pi\sqrt{\frac{l}{g}}$ as compared to the case which it is assumed $\sin\theta \simeq \theta$. [1]

(iii) Yes, since the motion of hands of a wristwatch to indicate time depends on action of the spring and has nothing to do with acceleration due to gravity. [1/2]

(iv) In a free fall the effective $g = 0$, i.e. gravity disappears (also called **weightlessness**)

$$\therefore \quad \text{Time period } T = 2\pi\sqrt{\frac{l}{g}} = 2\pi\sqrt{\frac{l}{0}} = \infty$$

$$\text{Frequency, } \nu = \frac{1}{T} = 0$$

i.e. frequency of oscillation is zero. [1]

18. The bob is subjected to two simultaneous, accelerations perpendicular to each other *viz*, acceleration due to gravity g and radial acceleration, $a_R = \frac{v^2}{R}$ towards the centre of the circular path.

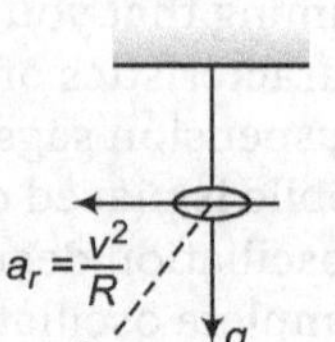

$\therefore$ Effective acceleration, $g_{\text{eff}} = \sqrt{g^2 + \left(\frac{v^2}{R}\right)^2}$ [1½]

$\therefore$ Time period of the simple pendulum

$$T = 2\pi\sqrt{\frac{l}{g_{\text{eff}}}} = 2\pi\sqrt{\frac{l}{\left(g^2 + \left(\frac{v^2}{R}\right)^2\right)^{1/2}}}$$

$$= 2\pi\sqrt{\frac{l}{\left(g^2 + \frac{v^4}{R^2}\right)^{1/2}}}$$ [1½]

19. Before pressing the ball, the pressure inside the chamber = pressure outside the chamber = atmospheric pressure. [1/2]

Let now the ball is depressed by x units. As a result, the volume will decrease and this would increase the pressure inside.

Decrease in the volume of air, $\Delta V = ax$

where, a = cross-sectional area of the neck

$$\text{Volume strain} = \frac{\text{Change in volume}}{\text{Original volume}} = \frac{\Delta V}{V} = \frac{ax}{V}$$ [1/2]

Volume stress = Bulk stress = p

As, $B = \frac{-p}{\left(\frac{ax}{V}\right)}$ where, negative sign shows the decrease in volume.

$\therefore$ Increases in the pressure, $p = -\frac{Bax}{V}$ [1/2]

The restoring force on the ball

$$F = pa = -\frac{Bax}{V}\cdot a = \frac{-Ba^2x}{V} \quad \left[\because \frac{Ba^2}{V} = \text{constant}\right]$$

$F \propto -$ displacement (x) [1]

Hence, motion is SHM.

$$\therefore \quad T = 2\pi\sqrt{\frac{m}{k}} = 2\pi\sqrt{\frac{mV}{Ba^2}}$$ [1/2]

20. Let area of cross-section of each arm of the U-tube be A. When a small pressure difference be maintained between two columns then liquid column falls through height h in one arm.

Now, difference in liquid column in two arms = $2h$

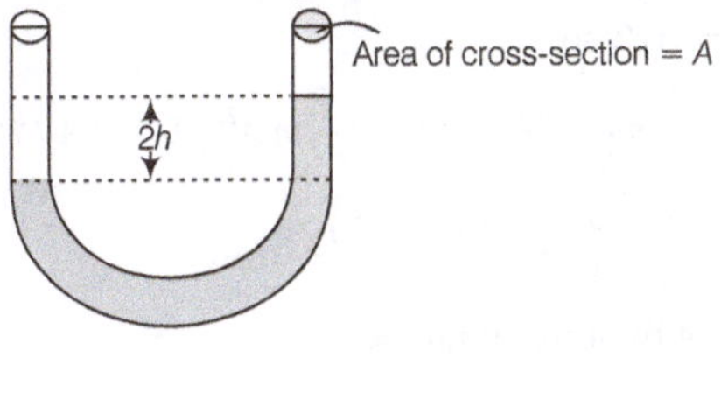

[1]

Density of mercury column = ρ

Acceleration due to gravity = g

Restoring force

$F = -$ Weight of mercury column in excess of one arm

$= -(\text{Volume} \times \text{Density} \times g) = -(A \times 2h \times \rho \times g)$

$= -2A\rho gh = -k \times$ Displacement in one arm (h)

Clearly, $2A\rho g$ = constant = k (say) [as $F = -kx$]

$F \propto -h$ [1]

Hence, motion is SHM and $k = 2A\rho g$

$$\therefore \text{Time period, } T = 2\pi\sqrt{\frac{m}{k}} = 2\pi\sqrt{\frac{m}{2A\rho g}}$$

where, m = mass of the mercury column of length l

If ρ is density of mercury,

Then, $m = Al\rho \Rightarrow T = 2\pi\sqrt{\frac{Al\rho}{2A\rho g}} = 2\pi\sqrt{\frac{l}{2g}}$ [1]

21. Suppose a particle of mass m executes SHM of period T. The displacement of the particle at any instant t is given by

$$y = A\sin\omega t$$

$\therefore$ Velocity, $v = \frac{dy}{dt} = \omega A\cos\omega t$

Kinetic energy, $E_k = \frac{1}{2}mv^2 = \frac{1}{2}m\omega^2A^2\cos^2\omega t$

Potential energy, $E_p = \frac{1}{2}m\omega^2y^2 = \frac{1}{2}m\omega^2A^2\sin^2\omega t$

$\therefore$ Average KE over a period of oscillation,

$$E_{k_{av}} = \frac{1}{T}\int_0^T E_k\,dt = \frac{1}{T}\int_0^T \frac{1}{2}m\omega^2A^2\cos^2\omega t\,dt$$

$$= \frac{1}{2T}m\omega^2A^2\int_0^T \frac{(1+\cos 2\omega t)}{2}dt$$

$$= \frac{1}{4T}m\omega^2A^2\left[t + \frac{\sin 2\omega t}{2\omega}\right]_0^T$$

$$= \frac{1}{4T}m\omega^2A^2(T) = \frac{1}{4}m\omega^2A^2 \quad [\because \sin 2\omega T = 0] \quad \text{...(i)}$$

Average PE over a period of oscillation, [1½]

$$E_{p_{av}} = \frac{1}{T}\int_0^T E_p\,dt = \frac{1}{T}\int_0^T \frac{1}{2}m\omega^2A^2\sin^2\omega t\,dt$$

$$= \frac{1}{2T}m\omega^2A^2\int_0^T \frac{(1-\cos 2\omega t)}{2}dt$$

$$= \frac{1}{4T}m\omega^2A^2\left[t - \frac{\sin 2\omega t}{2\omega}\right]_0^T$$

$$= \frac{1}{4T}m\omega^2A^2(T) = \frac{1}{4}m\omega^2A^2 \quad \text{...(ii)}$$

Clearly, from Eqs. (i) and (ii), $E_{k_{av}} = E_{p_{av}}$. [1½]

22. Refer to text on pages 443 and 444 (Total energy of a particle in simple harmonic motion).

23. Consider a cylinder of mass m, length L, density of material ρ and uniform area of cross-section A.

Therefore, $m = AL\rho$ ...(i)

Let the cylinder be floated in the liquid of density ρ_L.

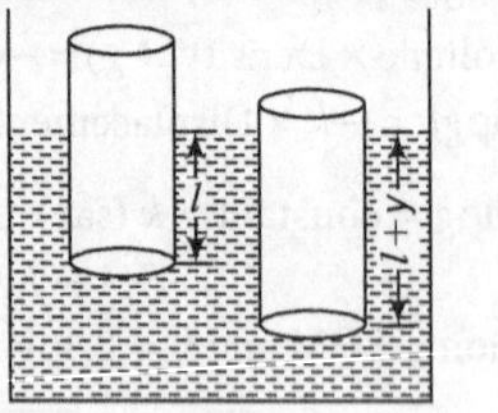

[1]

In equilibrium, let l be the length of cylinder dipping in liquid.

In equilibrium, weight of cylinder = Weight of liquid displaced $mg = Al\rho_L g$

$$m = Al\rho_L \quad \text{...(ii)} \quad [1]$$

Let the cylinder be pushed down by y, then

Total upward thrust, $F_2 = A(l + y)\rho_L g$

Restoring force, $F = -(F_2 - mg)$

$$F = -[A(l+y)\rho_L g - Al\rho_L g] = -A\rho_L gy \quad \text{...(iii)}$$

In SHM, $F \propto -y$

$$F = -ky \quad \text{...(iv)} \quad [1]$$

From Eq. (iii) and Eq. (iv),

Spring factor, $k = A\rho_L g$

Inertia factor, $m = AL\rho$

Time period, $T = 2\pi\sqrt{\dfrac{\text{Inertia factor}}{\text{Spring factor}}}$

$$T = 2\pi\sqrt{\frac{AL\rho}{A\rho_L g}} = 2\pi\sqrt{\frac{L\rho}{\rho_L g}} \quad \text{...(v)} \quad [1]$$

Using, $m = Al\rho_L = AL\rho$

So, $l\rho_L = L\rho$

So, another form of time period

$$T = 2\pi\sqrt{\frac{l\rho_L}{g\rho_L}} = 2\pi\sqrt{\frac{l}{g}}$$

[1]

24. (i) For **Case** (a), as we know that, $F = -kx \Rightarrow |F| = kx$

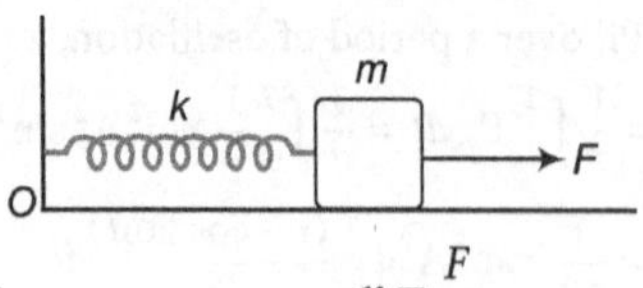

$\therefore$ So, $x = \dfrac{F}{k}$ [1]

Case (b)

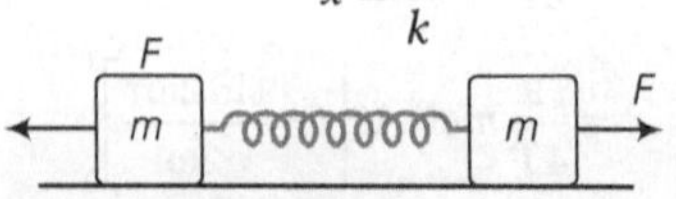

If x' is the extension in the spring, then drawing free body diagram of either mass (as the system under applied force is under equilibrium).

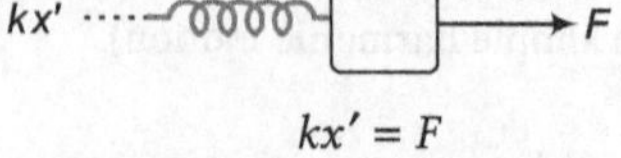

$$kx' = F$$

$$\therefore \quad x' = \frac{F}{k}$$

In both the cases, extension is the same $\left(\dfrac{F}{k}\right)$. [1]

(ii) The period of oscillation in case (a),

As, $F = -kx$

where, x = given extension

But $F = ma$

$$\therefore \quad ma = -kx \Rightarrow a = -\left(\frac{k}{m}\right)x \quad \text{...(i)}$$

$$a \propto -x \quad \left[\text{as, } \frac{k}{m} \text{ is a constant}\right]$$

On comparing Eq. (i) with $a = -\omega^2 x$, we get

$$\therefore \quad \omega = \sqrt{\frac{k}{m}}$$

Period of oscillation, $T = \dfrac{2\pi}{\omega} = 2\pi\sqrt{\dfrac{m}{k}}$ [1½]

Case (b)

The system is divided into two similar systems with spring divided in two equal halves. $k' = 2k$

Hence, $F = -k'x$

$k' = 2k$ (on cutting a spring in two halves, its k doubles)

$\Rightarrow \quad F = -2kx$

But $\quad F = ma$

$\therefore \quad ma = -2kx$

$$\Rightarrow \quad a = -\left(\frac{2k}{m}\right)x \quad \text{...(ii)}$$

$$\Rightarrow \quad a \propto -\text{displacement} \quad \left[\text{as } \frac{2k}{m} \text{ is a constant}\right]$$

On comparing Eq. (ii) with $a = -\omega^2 x$, we get

$$\omega = \sqrt{\frac{2k}{m}}$$

Period of oscillation, $T = \dfrac{2\pi}{\omega} = 2\pi\sqrt{\dfrac{m}{2k}}$ [1½]

25. Refer to text on pages 445 and 446 (Restoring force and simple pendulum).

26. $\because$ Time period, $T = 2\pi\sqrt{\dfrac{l}{g}}$ or $T \propto \sqrt{l}$ [1/2]

$\therefore$ % increase in time period,

$$\frac{\Delta T}{T} \times 100 = \frac{1}{2} \cdot \frac{\Delta l}{l} \times 100 = \frac{1}{2} \times 25 = 12.5\%$$

[1/2]

27. $\because x = A/2$, so

$$\text{KE} = \frac{1}{2}m\omega^2(A^2 - x^2) = \frac{1}{2}m\omega^2[A^2 - (A/2)^2]$$ [1/2]

$$= \frac{1}{2} \times \frac{3}{4}[m\omega^2 A^2] = \frac{3}{4}(\text{KE})_{\text{max}}$$

It is 3/4 th of maximum KE. [1/2]

28. Given, $m = 12$ kg, original length $l = 50$ cm,

$$k = 2.0 \times 10^3 \text{ Nm}^{-1}$$

As, $F = ky$

$$\therefore \quad y = \frac{F}{k} = \frac{mg}{k} = \frac{12 \times 9.8}{2 \times 10^3}$$

$$= 5.9 \times 10^{-2} \text{ m} = 5.9 \text{ cm}$$

$\therefore$ Stretched length of the spring $= l + y = 50 + 55.9$ cm $= 105.9$cm [1]

Frequency of oscillations,

$$\nu = \frac{1}{T} = \frac{1}{2\pi}\sqrt{\frac{k}{m}}$$

$$= \frac{1}{2 \times 3.14}\sqrt{\frac{2 \times 10^3}{12}} = 2.06 \text{ s}^{-1}$$ [1]

29. Here, $F = 10$ N, $\Delta l = 0.1$ m, $m = 4$ kg

(i) $k = \frac{F}{\Delta l} = \frac{10}{0.1} = 100 \text{ Nm}^{-1}$ [1/2]

(ii) $y = \frac{mg}{k} = \frac{4 \times 10}{100} = 0.4$ m [1/2]

(iii) $T = 2\pi\sqrt{\frac{m}{k}} = 2 \times \frac{22}{7}\sqrt{\frac{4}{100}} = 1.26$ s [1/2]

(iv) Frequency, $\nu = \frac{1}{T} = \frac{1}{1.26} = 0.8$ Hz [1/2]

30. Given, mass of the disc, $m = 10$ kg

Radius of the disc, $r = 15$ cm $= 0.15$ m

$T = 1.5$ s

I is the moment of inertia of the disc about the axis of rotation which is perpendicular to the plane of the disc and passing through its centre.

$$\therefore \quad I = \frac{1}{2}mr^2 = \frac{1}{2} \times (10) \times (0.15)^2$$

$$= 0.1125 \text{ kg-m}^2$$ [1]

Time period, $T = 2\pi\sqrt{\frac{I}{\alpha}}$

$$\alpha = \frac{4\pi^2 I}{T^2} = \frac{4 \times (3.14)^2 \times 0.1125}{(1.5)^2} = 1.972 \text{ N-m/rad}$$ [1]

31. The length of the scale 20 cm reads upto 50 kg.

So, $F = mg = 50 \times 9.8$ N and $y = 20$ cm $= 0.20$ m

Now, force constant, $k = \frac{F}{y} = \frac{50 \times 9.8}{0.20} = 2450 \text{ Nm}^{-1}$ [1]

Suppose the spring oscillates with time period of 0.60 s when loaded with a mass of M kg.

Then, $T = 2\pi\sqrt{\frac{M}{k}}$ or $T^2 = 4\pi^2\frac{M}{k}$

$$M = \frac{T^2 k}{4\pi^2} = \frac{(0.60)^2 \times 2450}{4 \times (3.14)^2} = 22.36 \text{ kg}$$ [1 ½]

$\therefore$ Weight $= Mg = 22.36 \times 9.8 = 219.13$ N [1/2]

32. Here, $k = 1200 \text{ Nm}^{-1}$, $m = 3.0$ kg

and $A = 2.0$ cm $= 2.0 \times 10^{-2}$ m

(i) Frequency of oscillation of the mass,

$$\nu = \frac{1}{2\pi}\sqrt{\frac{k}{m}} = \frac{1}{2 \times 3.14}\sqrt{\frac{1200}{3.0}} = \frac{1}{2 \times 3.14} \times 20$$

$$= 3.18 s^{-1} \approx 3.2 s^{-1}$$ [1]

(ii) Angular frequency,

$$\omega = \sqrt{\frac{k}{m}} = \sqrt{\frac{1200}{3.0}} = 20 s^{-1}$$

$\therefore$ Maximum acceleration of the mass

$$= \omega^2 A = (20)^2 \times 2.0 \times 10^{-2} = 8.0 \text{ ms}^{-2}$$ [1]

(iii) Maximum speed of the mass

$$= \omega \cdot A = 20 \times 2.0 \times 10^{-2} = 0.40 \text{ ms}^{-1}$$ [1]

33. Assuming the standard equation

$$x(t) = A\sin(\omega t + \phi)$$

(i) When $t = 0$, $x = 0$ [mean position]

$\Rightarrow \quad 0 = A\sin(\omega \times 0 + \phi)$

$A\sin\phi = 0$ [as $A \neq 0$]

or $\sin\phi = 0 \quad \therefore \quad \phi = 0$

$\therefore$ Required function is

$$x(t) = A\sin(\omega t + 0) \text{ or } x(t) = A\sin\omega t$$

where, $\omega = \sqrt{\frac{k}{m}} = \sqrt{\frac{1200}{3.0}} = 20$ rad/s

$\therefore \quad x(t) = A\sin 20t$

or $\quad x(t) = 2\sin 20t$ [1]

(ii) When $t = 0$, $x = +A$ (maximum stretched position)

$x(t) = A\sin(\omega t + \phi)$ at $t = 0$ and $x = +A$

$+A = A\sin(\omega \times 0 + \phi)$

or $\quad 1 = \sin\phi \Rightarrow \phi = \frac{\pi}{2}$

$$\therefore \quad x(t) = A\sin\left(\omega t + \frac{\pi}{2}\right)$$

$$= A\cos\omega t = A\cos 20t = 2\cos 20t$$ [1]

(iii) When the spring is at maximum compressed position.

At $t = 0$, $x(t) = -A$

$\Rightarrow \quad -A = A\sin(\omega \times 0 + \phi)$

or $-1 = \sin\phi$ or $\phi = \frac{3\pi}{2}$

$$\therefore \quad x(t) = A\sin\left(\omega t + \frac{3\pi}{2}\right) = -A\cos\omega t = -2\cos 20t$$

So, the equations only differ in initial phase and in no other factors. [1]

34. Given, acceleration due to gravity on the moon $(g_m) = 1.7 \text{ m/s}^2$

Acceleration due to gravity on the earth, $(g_e) = 9.8 \text{ m/s}^2$

Time period on the earth, $T_e = 3.5$ s

Time period on the moon, $T_m = ?$

On the surface of the earth, time period $= T_e$

$\therefore \quad T_e = 2\pi\sqrt{\frac{l}{g_e}}$ ...(i)

On the surface of the moon, time period = T_m

$\therefore \quad T_m = 2\pi\sqrt{\frac{l}{g_m}}$ ...(ii) [1]

Suppose g_e, g_m are accelerations due to gravity on the earth and the moon surface, respectively. [1/2]

On dividing Eq. (i) by Eq. (ii), we get

$$\frac{T_e}{T_m} = \frac{2\pi}{2\pi}\sqrt{\frac{l}{l} \times \frac{g_m}{g_e}} \Rightarrow \frac{T_e}{T_m} = \sqrt{\frac{g_m}{g_e}}$$

$$\Rightarrow \quad T_m = \left(\sqrt{\frac{g_e}{g_m}}\right) T_e$$

Putting the values, we get $T_m = \sqrt{\frac{9.8}{1.7}} \times 3.5$

$= 8.4$ s [1½]

35. A second pendulum means a simple pendulum having time period, $T = 2$ s

For a simple pendulum, $T = 2\pi\sqrt{\frac{l}{g}}$

where, l = length of the pendulum and g = acceleration due to gravity on surface of the earth.

$T_s = 2\pi\sqrt{\frac{l_e}{g_e}}$ ...(i) [1 / 2]

On the surface of the moon,

$T_m = 2\pi\sqrt{\frac{l_m}{g_m}}$ ...(ii)

Dividing Eq. (i) by Eq. (ii), we get

$$\therefore \quad \frac{T_s}{T_m} = \frac{2\pi}{2\pi}\sqrt{\frac{l_e}{g_e}} \times \sqrt{\frac{g_m}{l_m}}$$

$T_s = T_m$ to maintain the second pendulum time period.

$\therefore \quad 1 = \sqrt{\frac{l_e}{l_m} \times \frac{g_m}{g_e}}$ ...(iii) [1]

But the acceleration due to gravity at moon is 1/6 of the acceleration due to gravity at earth, i.e. $g_m = \frac{g_e}{6}$

Squaring Eq. (iii) and putting this value,

$$1 = \frac{l_e}{l_m} \times \frac{g_e/6}{g_e} = \frac{l_e}{l_m} \times \frac{1}{6} \Rightarrow \frac{l_e}{6l_m} = 1$$

or $\quad l_m = \frac{1}{6} l_e = \frac{1}{6} \times 1 = \frac{1}{6}$ m [1½]

36. (i) Mass of the automobile, $m = 3000$ kg

Displacement in the suspension system, $x = 15$ cm $= 0.15$ m

There are 4 springs in parallel to the support of the mass of the automobile. The equation for the restoring force of the system

$F = -4kx = mg$ [1/2]

Here, k = spring constant.

$$\therefore \quad k = \frac{mg}{4x} = \frac{3000 \times 9.8}{4 \times 0.15}$$

(neglecting negative sign, which is only for direction)

$= 500 \times 98 = 4.9 \times 10^4$ N/m

$\simeq 5 \times 10^4$ N/m [1]

(ii) Mass supported by each wheel = 750 kg

For damping factor b, the equation of displacement is

$x = x_0 e^{-bt/2m}$

As $\quad x = x_0/2$

We have, $\quad \frac{x_0}{2} = x_0 e^{-bt/2m}$

$\Rightarrow \quad \log_e 2 = \frac{bt}{2m}$ or $b = \frac{2m \log_e 2}{t}$ ...(i)

The time taken in 50% damping

= One time period = T

$$T = 2\pi\sqrt{\frac{m}{4k}} = 2\pi\sqrt{\frac{3000}{4 \times 5 \times 10^4}} = 0.769 \text{ s}$$

$\therefore$ Substituting value in Eq. (i), we get

$$b = \frac{2 \times 750 \times 0.693}{0.7691} = 1351.58 \text{ kg/s}$$ [1½]

37. Here, $m = 10$ g, $T = 6$ s

$$\omega = \frac{2\pi}{T} = \frac{2\pi}{6} = \frac{\pi}{3} \text{ rad s}^{-1}$$

When $t = 1$ s, $v = 6$ cm s^{-1}

As $v = A\omega\cos\omega t$

$$6 = A \times \frac{\pi}{3}\cos\frac{\pi}{3} \times 1 = A \times \frac{\pi}{3}\cos 60°$$

$$= A \times \frac{\pi}{3} \times \frac{1}{2} = \frac{\pi A}{6} \text{ or } A = \frac{36}{\pi} \text{ cm}$$ [1]

Total energy, $E = \frac{1}{2} mA^2\omega^2$

$$= \frac{1}{2} \times 10 \times \left(\frac{36}{\pi}\right)^2 \times \left(\frac{\pi}{3}\right)^2 = 720 \text{ erg}$$ [1/2]

Kinetic energy $= \frac{1}{2}mv^2 = \frac{1}{2} \times 10 \times 6^2 = 180$ erg [1/2]

$\therefore$ Potential energy = Total energy − Kinetic energy

$= 720 - 180 = 540$ erg [1]

38. (i) This is a case of variable acceleration. In accelerated motion, weight of body depends on the magnitude and direction of acceleration for upward or downward motion.

Hence, the weight of body changes. [1]

(ii) Considering the situation in two extreme positions, as their acceleration is maximum in magnitude.

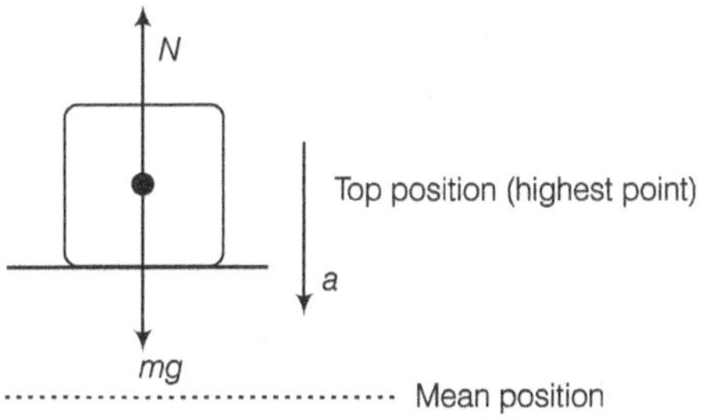

[1]

We have, $mg - N = ma$

Note, at the highest point, the platform is accelerating downward.

$\Rightarrow \quad N = mg - ma$

But $\quad a = \omega^2 A$ (in magnitude)

$\therefore \quad N = mg - m\omega^2 A$ [1/2]

where, A = amplitude of motion.

Given, $m = 50$ kg, frequency $\nu = 2\ s^{-1}$

$\therefore \quad \omega = 2\pi\nu = 4\pi$ rad/s

$A = 5\text{ cm} = 5 \times 10^{-2}$ m

$\therefore \quad N = 50 \times 9.8 - 50 \times (4\pi)^2 \times 5 \times 10^{-2}$

$= 50[9.8 - 16\pi^2 \times 5 \times 10^{-2}] = 50[9.8 - 7.89]$

$= 50 \times 1.91 = 95.5$ N [1/2]

When the platform is at the lowest position of its oscillation,

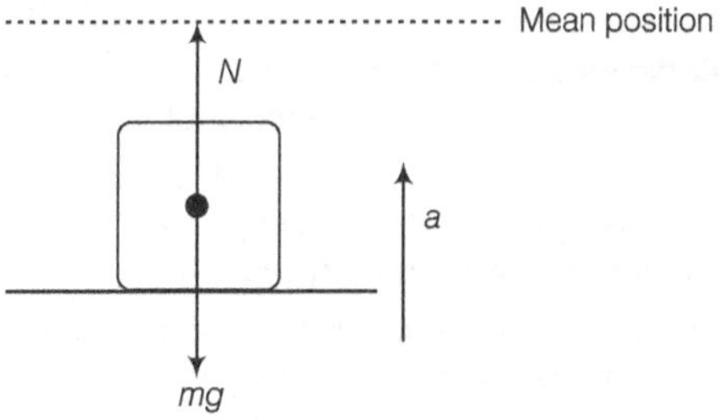

It is accelerating towards mean position that is vertically upwards. [1]

Writing equation of motion

$N - mg = ma = m\omega^2 A$

or $\quad N = mg + m\omega^2 A$

$= m[g + \omega^2 A]$ [1/2]

Putting the data, $N = 50[9.8 + (4\pi)^2 \times 5 \times 10^{-2}]$

$= 50[9.8 + (12.56)^2 \times 5 \times 10^{-2}]$

$= 50[9.8 + 7.88] = 50 \times 17.68 = 884.4$ N

Now, the machine reads the normal reaction. It is clear that

maximum weight = 884.4 N (at lowest point)

minimum weight = 95.5 N (at top point) [1/2]

SUMMARY

- **Periodic motion** A motion which repeats itself after a regular interval of time is called a **periodic motion**.
- **Oscillatory motion** A motion in which a body moves to and fro repeatedly about a fixed point (called mean position) is called **oscillatory** or **vibratory motion**.
- **Simple harmonic motion** It is a special type of periodic motion in which the body moves to and fro repeatedly about a mean position under the influence of a restoring force is known as simple harmonic motion (SHM). The restoring force is directly proportional to its displacement from the mean position.

  $$F \propto x \quad \text{or} \quad F = -kx$$

  where, k is the force constant or spring constant.

  Differential equation of SHM, $\frac{d^2x}{dt^2} + \omega^2 x = 0$

  Since, ω is the angular frequency $\left[\omega = \sqrt{\frac{k}{m}}\right]$.

- **Displacement in SHM** The displacement of a particle executing SHM is expressed as,

  $$y = A\sin(\omega t + \phi)$$

  where, A is amplitude of SHM, ω is the angular frequency $\left(\text{where, } \omega = \frac{2\pi}{T} = 2\pi\nu\right)$ and ϕ is the initial phase of SHM.

- **Frequency** It is the number of oscillations completed per second by a particle about its mean position. It is denoted by ν and is equal to the reciprocal of time period. Thus, $\nu = \frac{1}{T}$.

  Frequency is measured in hertz.

  $$1 \text{ hertz} = 1 \text{ Hz} = 1 \text{ oscillation per second} = 1 \text{ s}^{-1}.$$

- **Angular frequency** It is the quantity obtained by multiplying frequency ν by a factor of 2π. It is denoted by ω.

  Thus, $\omega = 2\pi\nu = \frac{2\pi}{T}$. SI unit of $\omega = \text{rad s}^{-1}$.

- **Phase** The phase of vibrating particle at any instant gives the state of the particle as regards its position and the direction of motion at that instant. It is denoted by ϕ.
- **Velocity in SHM** The velocity of particle executing SHM is defined as the time rate of change of its displacement at particular instant.

  $$\text{Velocity, } v = \omega\sqrt{A^2 - y^2}$$

  At mean position ($y = 0$) during its motion, $v = A\omega = v_{max}$ and at extreme positions ($y = \pm A$), $v = 0$.

  where, v_{max} velocity amplitude $= A\omega$ or velocity, $v(t) = -\omega A\sin(\omega t + \phi)$

- **Acceleration in SHM** The acceleration of a SHM at an instant is defined as the time rate of change of velocity at that instant.

  $$\text{Acceleration, } a = -\omega^2 y$$

- The acceleration is also variable. At mean position ($y = 0$), acceleration, $a = 0$ and at extreme position ($y = \pm A$), acceleration is $a_{max} = \mp A\omega^2$.

  where, a_{max}, acceleration amplitude $= A\omega^2$ or acceleration, $a(t) = \omega^2 A\cos(\omega t + \phi)$

  Time Period in SHM It is the time taken by a particle to complete one oscillation about its mean position. It is denoted by T.

  $$\text{Time period of SHM, } T = \frac{2\pi}{\omega} 2\pi\sqrt{\frac{|y|}{|a|}}$$

  $$= 2\pi\sqrt{\frac{\text{Displacement}}{\text{Acceleration}}}$$

- **Energy in SHM** If a particle of mass m executes SHM, then at a displacement x from mean position, the particle possesses potential and kinetic energy.

  At any displacement x,

  (i) Potential energy, $U = \frac{1}{2}m\omega^2x^2 = \frac{1}{2}kx^2$

  (ii) Kinetic energy, $K = \frac{1}{2}m\omega^2(A^2 - x^2) = \frac{1}{2}k(A^2 - x^2)$

  (iii) Total energy, $E = U + K = \frac{1}{2}m\omega^2A^2 = 2\pi^2 m\nu^2 A^2$

- **Simple pendulum** A simple pendulum in practice, consist of a heavy but small sized metallic bob suspended by a light, inextensible and flexible string. The motion of a simple pendulum is simple harmonic whose time period and frequency are given by

  $$T = 2\pi\sqrt{\frac{l}{g}} \quad \text{and} \quad \nu = \frac{1}{2\pi}\sqrt{\frac{g}{l}}$$

Chapter Practice

Multiple Choice Questions

1 Mark

1 The periodic function $f(t) = A\sin(\omega t)$ repeats itself

(a) 2π (b) 3π
(c) π (d) $\pi/2$

2 The x-t graph of a particle undergoing simple harmonic motion is shown below.

The acceleration of the particle at $t = \frac{4}{3}$ s is

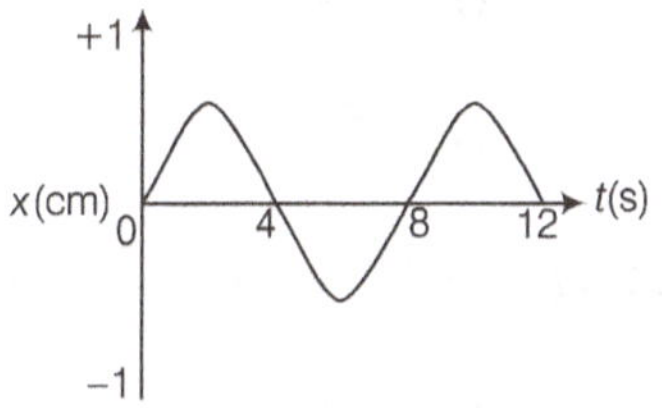

(a) $\frac{\sqrt{3}}{32}\pi^2\text{cms}^{-2}$ (b) $-\frac{\pi^2}{32}\text{cms}^{-2}$
(c) $\frac{\pi^2}{32}\text{cms}^{-2}$ (d) $-\frac{\sqrt{3}}{32}\pi^2\text{cms}^{-2}$

3 The block is maximum stretched. The expression for force acting on block in SHM is

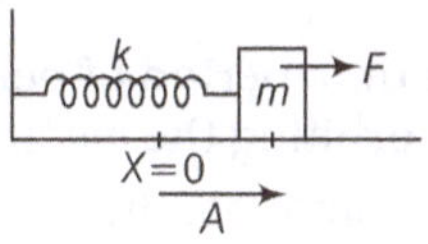

(a) $-kA$ (b) $-m\omega^2 A$
(c) $-kA/2$ (d) kA

Assertion and Reason

Directions (Q. Nos. 4-8) *In the following questions, two statements are given- one labelled Assertion (A) and the other labelled Reason (R). Select the correct answer to these questions from the codes (a), (b), (c) and (d) as given below*

(a) Both Assertion and Reason are true and Reason is the correct explanation of Assertion.
(b) Both Assertion and Reason are true but Reason is not the correct explanation of Assertion.
(c) Assertion is true but Reason is false.
(d) Assertion is false but Reason is true.

4 **Assertion (A)** The periodic time of a hard spring is less as compared to that of a soft spring.

Reason (R) The periodic time depends upon the spring contant, which is large for hard spring.

5 **Assertion (A)** In SHM, acceleration is always directed towards the mean position.

Reason (R) In SHM, the body has to stop momentarily at the extreme position and move back to mean position.

6 **Assertion (A)** The spring constant of a spring is K. When it is divided into n equal parts, then spring constant of one piece is nk.

Reason (R) The spring constant is independent of material used for spring.

7 **Assertion (A)** Vibrations and oscillations are two different types of motion.

Reason (R) For vibration, frequency is more and for oscillation, the frequency is less.

8 **Assertion (A)** $x(t) = A\sin(\omega t)$ is periodic but cannot represent an oscillatory motion.

Reason (R) $\sin\theta$ is a sinusoidal periodic function.

Very Short Answer Type Questions

1 Mark

9 When are the displacement and velocity in the same direction of SHM?

10 Can we use a pendulum watch in an artificial satellite?

11 Write the relation between time period T, displacement x and acceleration a of a particle in SHM.

12 Write the relation between acceleration, displacement and frequency of a particle executing SHM.

Short Answer Type I Questions

2 Marks

13 What is meant by phase of an oscillating particle?

14 On what factors does the energy of a harmonic oscillator depend?

15 What would be the time period of a simple pendulum at the centre of the earth?

Short Answer Type II Questions

3 Marks

16 Obtain an expression for the velocity of a particle executing SHM, when is this velocity
(i) maximum and (ii) minimum.

17 Write down the differential equation for SHM. Give its solution. Hence, obtain an expression for the time period of SHM.

Long Answer Type Questions

5 Marks

18 Explain the relation in phase between displacement, velocity and acceleration in SHM, graphically as well as theoretically.

19 Draw the graphical representation of simple harmonic motion showing the
(i) displacement-time curve
(ii) velocity-time curve and
(iii) acceleration-time curve

20 Explain the total energy in simple harmonic motion and show the graphical representation of energy in SHM.

21 Explain the time period of a simple pendulum.

Case Based Questions

Directions (Q. No. 22) *These questions are case study based questions. Read the following paragraph and answer the questions.*

22 Consider a pendulum of length l with a mass m suspended at the end displaces through an angle θ from the vertical. The restoring force F is the component of the weight of the bob, therefore

$$F = -mg\sin\theta \Rightarrow ma = -mg\sin\theta$$

or $\quad a = -g\sin\theta$

As for small angles, $\sin\theta \simeq \theta$

$\therefore \quad a = -g\theta = \frac{-gx}{l} \qquad \left(\because \theta = \frac{x}{l}\right)$

$$a = \frac{-gx}{l}$$

where, x is the distance of the bob from the mid-point of the oscillation.

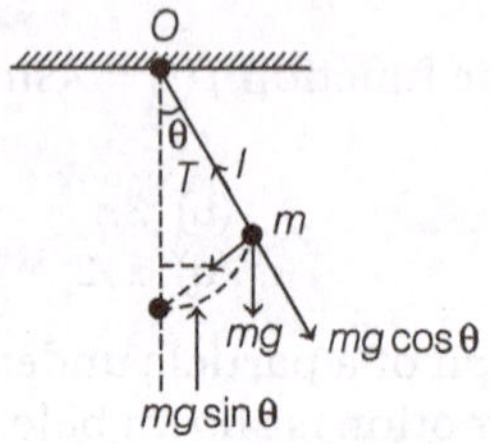

As, $\quad a = -\omega^2 x$

$\therefore \quad \omega^2 = \frac{-a}{x}$

or $\quad \omega^2 = \frac{g}{l} \qquad \left(\text{using } a = \frac{gx}{l}\right)$

Substituting $\omega = \frac{2\pi}{T}$, we get

$$T = 2\pi\sqrt{\frac{l}{g}}$$

This is the time period of simple pendulum.

(i) A simple pendulum of length L has mass M and its oscillates freely with amplitude A. What will be the potential energy at extreme position? (g = acceleration due to gravity)

(ii) Find the time period of pendulum, on a satellite orbiting the earth.

(iii) When a simple pendulum is moved from the earth's surface to deep mine, what will be the period of oscillation?

(iv) Two simple pendulums of lengths in the ratio 4 : 1 start oscillating at $t = 0$. They will again be in phase after the shorter pendulum has made n oscillations. Find the value of n.

Numerical Problems

23 What will be the period of oscillation, if the length of a second's pendulum is halved? **[1 M]**

24 The maximum velocity of a particle executing a simple harmonic motion with an amplitude of 7 mm, is 4.4 ms^{-1}. What is the period of oscillation? **[2 M]**

25 The following figures depict two circular motions. The radius of the circle, the period of revolution, the initial position and the sense of revolution are indicated on the figures.

Obtain the simple harmonic motion of the x-projection of the radius vector of the rotating particle P in each case. **[NCERT, 3 M]**

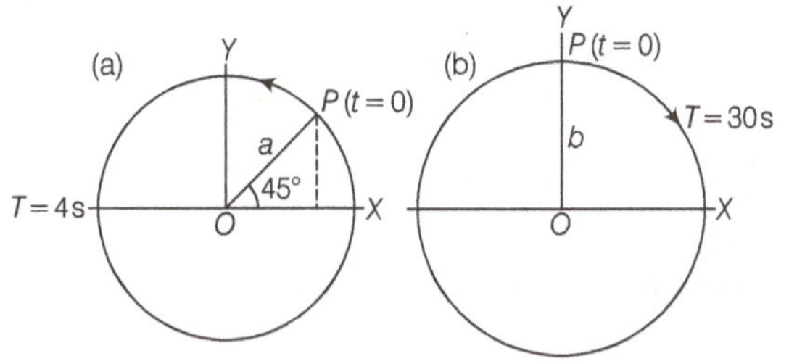

Answers

1 (*a*) A periodic function repeats itself after a time period T.

and; $$f(t) = f(t + T)$$

As, $\sin(\omega t) = \sin(\omega t + 2\pi)$

$\therefore$ period of function is 2π.

2 (*d*) Given, $T = 8\text{s}, \omega = \frac{2\pi}{T} = \left(\frac{\pi}{4}\right)\text{rads}^{-1}$

$$x = A\sin\omega t$$

$$\therefore \quad a = -\omega^2 x = -\left(\frac{\pi^2}{16}\right)\sin\left(\frac{\pi}{4}t\right)$$

On substituting $t = \frac{4}{3}$ s, we get

$$a = -\left(\frac{\sqrt{3}}{32}\pi^2\right)\text{cms}^{-2}$$

3 (*a*) The expression for SHM is

$$F = -m\omega^2 x$$

As, $$x = A$$

$$\Rightarrow \quad F = -m\omega^2 A = -kA = \text{restoring force}$$

4 (*a*) Time period of a hard spring is given by

$$T = 2\pi\sqrt{\left(\frac{m}{k}\right)}, \text{ i.e. } T \propto \frac{1}{\sqrt{k}}$$

Since spring constant is more for hard spring, hence hard spring has a less periodic time as compared to soft spring.

5 (*b*) Acceleration and displacement are in opposite phase.

6 (*c*) When a spring is cut into n equal parts, then spring constant k' of each part is given by $k' = nk$

Also, spring constant depends on the properties of the material of the spring.

7 (*d*) The basic nature of vibration and oscillation is same, it is just that in vibration, frequency is more and in oscillation, frequency is less.

8 (*d*) $x(t) = A\sin(\omega t)$ is a sinusoidal periodic function that can represent an oscillatory motion. Motion of a particle in SHM can be represented by this function.

9 When a particle moves from mean position to extreme position, its displacement and velocity are in the same direction.

10 No, in an artificial satellite, a body is in a state of weightlessness, i.e. $g = 0$.

$$\therefore \quad T = 2\pi\sqrt{\frac{l}{g}} = \infty$$

Inside the satellite, the pendulum does not oscillate. Hence, a pendulum watch cannot be used in an artificial satellite.

11 Refer to text on pages 433 and 434 (Characteristics of simple harmonic motion).

12 Refer to text on pages 433 and 434 (Characteristics of simple harmonic motion).

13 Refer to text on page 433 (Phase).

14 Refer to text on page 444 (Total energy).

15 Refer to text on page 447 (Expression for time period of a simple pendulum).

16 Refer to text on page 434 (Velocity).

17 Refer to text on pages 434 and 435 (Differential equation of SHM and time period and time period).

18 Refer to text on pages 433 and 434 (Characteristics of simple harmonic motion).

19 Refer to text on page 436 (Graphical representation of displacement, velocity and acceleration).

20 Refer to text on pages 443 and 444 (Total energy of a particle in simple harmonic motion).

21 Refer to text on page 447 (Expression for time period of a simple pendulum).

22 (i) The potential energy $= \frac{1}{2}M\omega^2 A^2$

$$= \frac{1}{2}M\frac{g}{l}\cdot A^2 = \frac{MgA^2}{2l} \qquad \left(\because \omega = \sqrt{\frac{g}{l}}\right)$$

(ii) On an artificial satellite orbiting the earth, the acceleration is given by $\frac{GM}{R^2}$ towards the centre of the earth. Now for a body of mass m on the satellite, the gravitational force due to earth is $\frac{GMm}{R^2}$ towards the centre of the earth. Let the reaction force on the surface of the satellite be N, then

$$\frac{GMm}{R^2} - N = m\left(\frac{GM}{R^2}\right)$$

$$\Rightarrow \quad N = 0$$

i.e. On the satellite, there is a state of weightlessness or g = 0.

∴ The time period of the simple pendulum,

$$T = 2\pi\sqrt{\frac{l}{g}} = \infty$$

(iii) As we move from earth's surface to deep mine, the acceleration due to gravity decreases and hence the time period of oscillation of a simple pendulum increases.

Since, $T = 2\pi\sqrt{\frac{l}{g}}$

∴ As g decreases, T increases.

(iv) Let the lengths of pendulums be 4l and l, therefore, time periods of pendulums will be $2\pi\sqrt{\frac{4l}{g}}$ and $2\pi\sqrt{\frac{l}{g}}$, respectively.

Consider the two pendulums are in phase again after t seconds and longer pendulum has made N oscillations in t seconds.

$$\therefore \quad N2\pi\sqrt{\frac{4l}{g}} = n2\pi\sqrt{\frac{l}{g}} \text{ or } n = 2N.$$

∴ N = 1, n = 2 ; N = 2, n = 4; etc

23 $\therefore \frac{l_1}{l_2} = \frac{T_1^2}{T_2^2}$

$$\Rightarrow \frac{l}{l/2} = \frac{2 \times 2}{T_2^2}$$

$$\Rightarrow T_2^2 = 2$$

$$\Rightarrow T_2 = \sqrt{2}\text{s}$$

24 $\therefore v_{max} = \omega A = \frac{2\pi}{T}A$ [1]

$$\Rightarrow T = \frac{2\pi A}{v_{max}} = \frac{2 \times 22 \times 7 \times 10^{-3}}{7 \times 4.4} = 0.01 \text{ s}$$ [1]

25

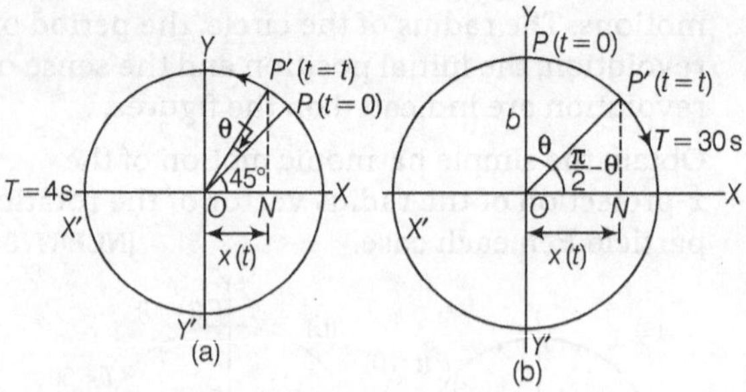

(a) (b) [1/2]

In figure, suppose the particle moves in the anti-clockwise sense from P to P′ in time t as shown in Fig.(a).

Angle swept by the radius vector,

$$\theta = \omega t = \frac{2\pi}{T}t = \frac{2\pi}{4}t \quad [\because T = 4 \text{ s}]$$ [1/2]

N is the foot of perpendicular drawn from P′ on the XOX′-axis.

Displacement, $ON = OP' \cos(\theta + \pi/4)$

or $x(t) = a\cos\left(\frac{2\pi}{4}t + \frac{\pi}{4}\right)$ [1/2]

This equation represents SHM of amplitude a, period 4 s and an initial phase of $\frac{\pi}{4}$ rad.

Now, in Fig. (b), suppose the particle moves in the clockwise sense from P to P′ in time t.

Angle swept by the radius vector,

$$\theta = \omega t = \frac{2\pi}{T}t = \frac{2\pi}{30}t \quad [\because T = 30 \text{ s}]$$ [1/2]

Displacement, $ON = OP'\cos\left(\frac{\pi}{2} - \theta\right)$ [1/2]

or $x(t) = b\cos\left(\frac{\pi}{2} - \frac{2\pi}{30}t\right)$

or $x(t) = b\cos\left(\frac{2\pi}{30}t - \frac{\pi}{2}\right)$

$[\because \cos(-\theta) = \cos\theta]$

This equation represents SHM of amplitude b period 30 s and an initial phase of $-\frac{\pi}{2}$ rad. [1/2]

CHAPTER

14

Waves

A wave is a periodic disturbance that travels through a medium (or vacuum). In general, a wave transports energy and momentum from one part of the medium (or vacuum) to the other part of it, without any bulk motion of the material of medium. All our communications essentially depend on transmission of signals through waves.

- Waves and Their Properties
- Superposition of Waves and Beats
- Stationary or Standing Wave

TOPIC 01 Waves and Their Properties

Waves occur when a system is disturbed from its equilibrium position and this disturbance travels or propagates from one region of the system to other. In a wave, both information and energy propagate (in the form of signals) from one point to another but there is no motion of matter as a whole through a medium.

Types of Waves

According to the direction of oscillation of the particles, waves are classified into two types as given below

Transverse Wave

Transverse wave motion is that wave motion in which the individual particles of the medium execute simple harmonic motion about their mean positions in a direction perpendicular to the direction of propagation of the wave. The wave itself is known as **transverse wave.**

e.g. Waves in string, ripples on the surface of water. Movement of string of stringed musical instruments like sitar, guitar, etc.

In a transverse wave, the position of maximum displacement in the upward direction is called **crest** and the position of maximum in the downward direction is called **trough.** The distance between two successive crests or between two successive troughs, is called the wavelength of the **transverse wave.**

Longitudinal Wave

The waves in which the individual particles of the medium execute simple harmonic motion about their mean positions along the direction of propagation of the wave are called **longitudinal waves.**

e.g. Waves in spring, sound waves, vibration of air column in organ pipes, etc.

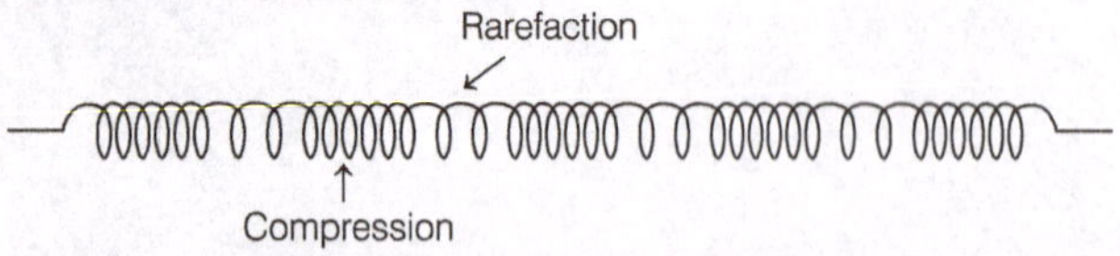

The places, where the turn are closer are said to be in the state of **compression**, while the places, where the turns are farther are said to be in the state of **rarefaction.** These state of compression and rarefaction continue to advance along the direction of the length of the spring. The distance between the centres of two successive compressions or between the centres of two successive rarefactions are called the wavelength of the longitudinal waves.

Example 1 Given below are some examples of wave motion. State in each case if the wave motion is transverse, longitudinal or a combination of both.

(i) Motion of a kink in a longitudinal spring produced by displacing one end of the spring side ways.

(ii) Waves produced in a cylinder containing a liquid by moving its piston back and forth.

(iii) Waves produced by a motorboat sailing in water.

(iv) Ultrasonic waves in air produced by a vibrating quartz crystal. **NCERT**

Sol. (i) Transverse and longitudinal (ii) Longitudinal
(iii) Transverse and longitudinal (iv) Longitudinal

Wave Motion

A wave motion is a disturbance produce in a physical medium which advances in the medium with a definite speed without changing its speed.

Characteristics of Wave Motion

(i) In a wave motion, the disturbance travels through the medium due to repeated periodic oscillations of the particles of the medium about their mean positions.

(ii) The energy is transferred from one place to another without any actual transfer of the particles of the medium.

(iii) There is a continuous phase difference between two successive particles because each particle receives disturbance a little later than its preceding particle.

(iv) The velocity with which a wave travels is different from the velocity of the particles with which they vibrate simple harmonically about their mean positions.

(v) In a given medium, the wave velocity remains constant, while the particle velocity changes continuously during its vibration about the mean position.
The particle's velocity is maximum at the mean position and zero at the extreme position.

(vi) For the propagation of a mechanical wave, the medium must possess the properties of inertia, elasticity as well as friction.

Some Definitions Regarding Waves

Amplitude and Phase

The magnitude of the maximum displacement of the particles of medium from their equilibrium position, as a wave passes through them is known as **amplitude** of the particle.

Let a wave motion with the displacement $y(x, t)$ varies between a and $-a$. Here, a represents the maximum displacement of the constituents of the medium from their mean position.

The displacement y may be positive or negative but a is positive. It is called the **amplitude** of the particle. The quantity $(kx - \omega t + \phi)$ is called the **phase** of the wave which appears as the argument of the sine or cosine function.

Wavelength and Angular Wave Number

The distance travelled by a wave during the time in which any particle of the medium completes one vibration about its mean position is known as **wavelength** of the wave.

As, $y(x, t) = a \sin(kx - \omega t + \phi)$

Taking $\phi = 0$ in the displacement at $t = 0$,

$y(x, 0) = a \sin kx$

Because, the sine function is having period 2π.

$$\therefore \quad \sin kx = \sin(kx + 2n\pi) = \sin k\left(x + \frac{2n\pi}{k}\right)$$

The displacement will be same at points x and $x+\frac{2n\pi}{k}$ with $n = 1, 2, 3, \ldots$. The least distance between two points with same phase will be

$$\lambda = \frac{2\pi}{k} + x - x \qquad \text{(for } n = 1\text{)}$$

$$\boxed{\text{Wavelength, } \lambda = \frac{2\pi}{k}}$$

$\Rightarrow$ Angular wave number, $k = \frac{2\pi}{\lambda}$ rad m^{-1}

where, k is called **angular wave number**. Hence, the angular wave number also known as **propagation constant** is 2π times the number of waves that can be accommodated per unit length.

Period, Angular Frequency and Frequency

Figure below shows a sinusoidal plot. It describes the shape as well as displacement. We are monitoring the motion of the element by putting $\phi = 0$ and $x = 0$ in equation given as

$$y(x, t) = a\sin(kx - \omega t + \phi)$$

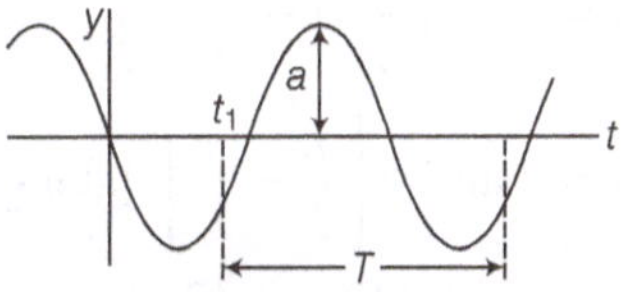

Graph for displacement time period, amplitude and frequency

We will get, $y(0, t) = a\sin(-\omega t) = -a\sin\omega t$

Time Period and Angular Frequency

The time taken by a wave to travel a distance equal to one wavelength is known as the **time period** of wave.

If period of sine function is T measured from an arbitrary time t_1, then

$\Rightarrow \quad -a\sin\omega t_1 = -a\sin\omega(t_1 + T) = -a\sin(\omega t_1 + \omega T)$

Because, sine function repeats after every 2π.

$\therefore \qquad \omega T = 2\pi$

$\Rightarrow \quad \boxed{\text{Angular frequency, } \omega = \frac{2\pi}{T}}$

where, ω is called the **angular frequency** and its SI unit is rad s^{-1}.

Frequency

The number of complete vibrations or oscillations produced by a wave in one second is known as the **frequency** of the wave. The frequency ν of a wave is defined as $\frac{1}{T}$ and is related to the angular frequency ω by

$$\boxed{\text{Frequency, } \nu = \frac{1}{T} = \frac{\omega}{2\pi}}$$

where, $\nu =$ frequency of the wave

ν is usually measured in hertz (Hz).

Relation Between Frequency, Wave Velocity and Wavelength

Let the frequency and time period of an oscillating body are n and T, respectively. Thus,

distance travel in T second $= \lambda$ and

distance travel in 1 second $= \frac{\lambda}{T}$.

But the distance travelled by a body in one second is equivalent to the speed or velocity.

Therefore, $v = \frac{\lambda}{T}$

But $\qquad n = \frac{1}{T}$

$$\boxed{v = n\lambda}$$

Note The frequency of a wave will remain unchanged during any type of interaction that the wave suffers because it depends only on the frequency of the source.

Example 2 If a progressive wave travelling in positive x-direction having the amplitude of 6 cm, frequency 200 Hz and velocity is 400 m/s, then write the equation of that progressive wave.

Sol. Given, $A = 6\,\text{cm} = 0.06\,\text{m}$

$$\nu = 200\,\text{Hz}$$

$$k = \frac{2\pi}{\lambda} = \frac{2\pi}{v/\nu} \qquad \left[\because \lambda = \frac{v}{\nu}\right]$$

$$k = \frac{2\pi\nu}{v} = \frac{2\pi \times 200}{400} = \pi\,\text{m}^{-1}$$

$$\omega = 2\pi\nu = 2\pi \times 200 = 400\pi \text{ rad/s}$$

The standard equation of the progressive wave is

$$y(x, t) = A\sin(kx - \omega t)$$

put the values to get the equation

$$y(x, t) = 0.06\sin(\pi x - 400\pi t)\,\text{m}$$

Example 3 A wave travelling along a string is described by $y(x,t) = 0.005\sin(80.0x - 3.0t)$ in which the numerical constants are in SI units (0.005 m, 80.0 rad m^{-1} and 3.0 rad s^{-1}). Calculate

(i) the amplitude of particle,

(ii) the wavelength and

(iii) the period and frequency of the wave. Also, calculate displacement y of the particle at a distance $x = 30.0$ cm and time $t = 20$ s ? **NCERT**

Sol. Given, $y(x,t) = 0.005 \sin(80.0x - 3.0t)$

Then, $y(x,t) = a\sin(kx - \omega t)$

Now, compare the given equation with standard equation to find out all the physical quantities.

$a = 0.005$ m

$k = 80.0$ rad/m

$\omega = 3.0$ rad/s

The physical quantities by using the given fundamental physical quantities.

(i) Amplitude, $a = 0.005$ m $= 5$ mm

(ii) Wavelength, $\lambda = \frac{2\pi}{k} = \frac{2\pi}{80} = 7.85\,\text{cm}$

(iii) Time period, $T = 2\pi/\omega = \frac{2\pi}{3} = 2.09$ s

and frequency, $\nu = \frac{1}{T} = \frac{1}{2.09}$

$= 0.478 \simeq 0.48\,\text{Hz}$

Now, the displacement y of the particle at a distance.

$x = 30.0$ cm $= 0.3$ m and time $t = 20$ s

$y(0.3, 20) = 0.005 \sin(80 \times 0.3 - 3.0 \times 20)$

$y(0.3, 20) = 0.005 \sin(24 - 60) = 0.00495\text{ m} \simeq 5\text{ mm}$

Expression for Displacement in Wave Motion

A wave that travels from one point of the medium to another, is called a progressive wave. It can be transverse or longitudinal.

During the propagation of a wave through a medium, if the particles of the medium vibrate simple harmonically about their mean positions, then the wave is said to be **plane progressive harmonic wave.**

The displacement curve of this wave is shown below

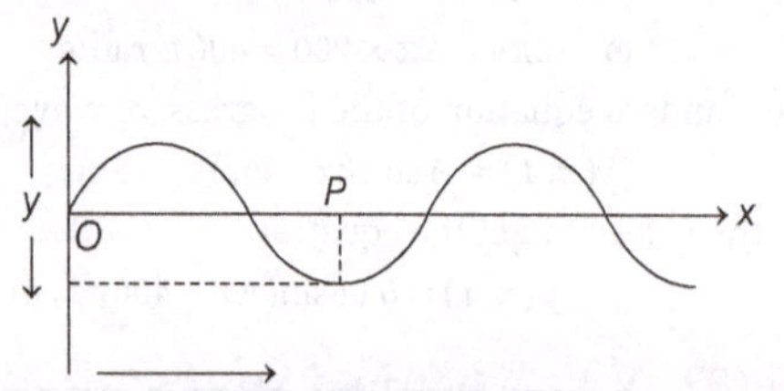

The displacement of particle at point O is given by the following equation

$$y = a\sin\omega t$$

where, a is the amplitude and ω is the angular frequency of particle.

Alternative Forms of Wave Equation

If ϕ is the phase lag of a particle P distant x from the origin as shown in the above figure, then the displacement equation of particle P at instant time t is given by

$$y = a\sin(\omega t - \phi) \quad \text{...(i)}$$

Since, $$\phi = \frac{2\pi}{\lambda}x = kx \quad \text{...(ii)}$$

Substituting the value of Eq. (ii) in Eq (i), we get

$$y = a\sin(\omega t - kx) \quad [\text{along} + x\text{-direction}]\text{...(iii)}$$

$$y = a\sin(\omega t + kx) \quad [\text{along} - x\text{-direction}]\text{...(iv)}$$

These equations can also be written as

$$y = a\cos(\omega t - kx) \quad \text{...(v)}$$

$$y = a\cos(\omega t + kx) \quad \text{...(vi)}$$

From Eq. (iii), we get

$$y = a\sin\left(\frac{2\pi}{T}t - \frac{2\pi}{\lambda}x\right)$$

$$y = a\sin 2\pi\left[\frac{t}{T} - \frac{x}{\lambda}\right] \quad [\text{along} + x\text{-direction}]$$

$$y = a\sin 2\pi\left[\frac{t}{T} + \frac{x}{\lambda}\right] \quad [\text{along} - x\text{-direction}]$$

$$y = a\sin\frac{2\pi}{\lambda}(vt - x) \quad \left[\because \nu = \frac{v}{\lambda} \text{ or } \frac{1}{T} = \frac{v}{\lambda}\right]$$

Along $-x$-direction,

$$y = a\sin\frac{2\pi}{\lambda}(vt + x)$$

If ϕ be the phase difference between the wave travelling along $+x$-direction and the another wave is travelling along same direction, then the equation of wave is given by

$$y = A\sin\left[2\pi\left(\frac{t}{T} - \frac{x}{\lambda}\right) \pm \phi\right]$$

and displacement relation for a wave travelling in $-x$-direction is given by

$$y = A\sin\left[2\pi\left(\frac{t}{T} + \frac{x}{\lambda}\right) \pm \phi\right]$$

Graphical Representation of Simple Harmonic Wave

The equation of simple harmonic wave is given by the following equation

$$y = a \sin 2\pi\left(\frac{t}{T} - \frac{x}{\lambda}\right) \quad \text{...(i)}$$

where, y is the displacement of particle, x is the position of particle and t is the time. We shall study how displacement y varies with time t at a particular position x, and how displacement y varies with position x at particular time t.

Displacement-Time Graph of Particle

If the value of x for a particle is zero, then the equation of simple harmonic wave is given by

$$y = \sin 2\pi \frac{t}{T}$$

The above equation shows that the displacement y of the particle depends on t. The displacement y of a particle at different instants of time is given in the table as below

t	0	$\frac{T}{4}$	$\frac{T}{2}$	$\frac{3T}{4}$	T	$\frac{5T}{4}$	$\frac{3T}{4}$	$\frac{7T}{4}$	$2T$
y	0	$+a$	0	$-a$	0	$+a$	0	$-a$	0

The graphical representation of y-t is given below

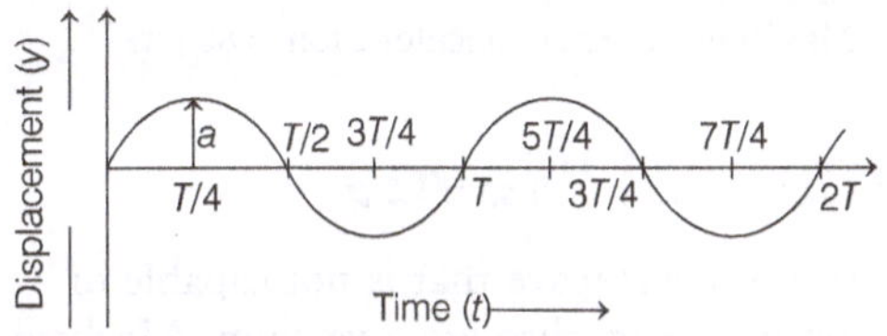

Distance-Displacement Graph of Particle

At $t = \frac{3T}{2}$ in Eq. (i), we get

$$y = a \sin 2\pi\left(\frac{3}{2} - \frac{x}{\lambda}\right)$$

In the different position x of the particles, the displacement are given in the table as below

x	0	$\frac{\lambda}{4}$	$\frac{\lambda}{2}$	$\frac{3\lambda}{4}$	λ	$\frac{5\lambda}{4}$	$\frac{3\lambda}{2}$	$\frac{7\lambda}{4}$	2λ
y	0	$+a$	0	$-a$	0	$+a$	0	$-a$	0

On the basis of table value, the graph between distance and displacement is drawn in the figure.

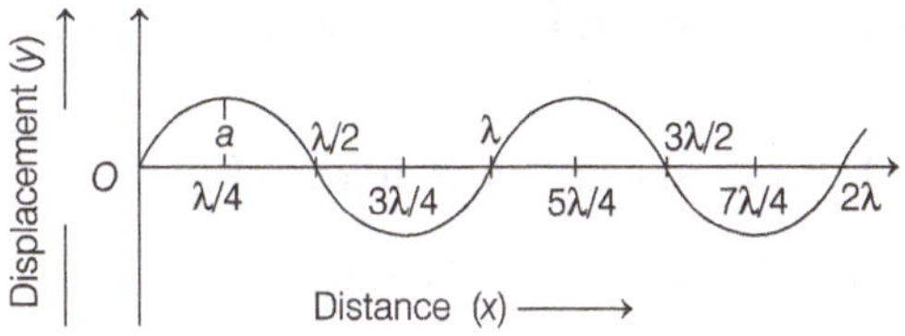

Phase, and Time Difference

Relation Between the Phase Difference and Path Difference of a Plane Progressive Wave

At any instant t, if ϕ_1 and ϕ_2 are the phases of two particles whose distances from the origin are x_1 and x_2 respectively, then

$$\phi_1 = (\omega t - kx_1)$$

and $$\phi_2 = (\omega t - kx_2) \Rightarrow \phi_1 - \phi_2 = k(x_2 - x_1)$$

$$\boxed{\text{Phase difference } (\Delta\phi) = \frac{2\pi}{\lambda} \text{ Path difference } (\Delta x)}$$

Example 4 If the phase difference between two waves is 60°, then find the value of path difference between the two.

Sol. $\Delta\phi = 60° = \frac{\pi}{3}$

As we know, $\Delta\phi = \frac{2\pi}{\lambda} \times \Delta x$

$$\therefore \quad \Delta x = \frac{\Delta\phi}{2\pi} \times \lambda = \frac{\lambda \times \pi}{3 \times 2\pi} \Rightarrow \Delta x = \frac{\lambda}{6}$$

Relation Between Phase Difference and Time Difference of a Plane Progressive Wave

If the phases of a particle distance x from the origin is ϕ_1 at time t_1 and ϕ_2 at time t_2, then $\phi_1 = (\omega t_1 - kx)$ and

$$\phi_2 = (\omega t_2 - kx) \Rightarrow \phi_1 - \phi_2 = \omega(t_1 - t_2)$$

$$\boxed{\text{Phase difference } (\Delta\phi) = \frac{2\pi}{T} \text{ Time difference } (\Delta t)}$$

Example 5 The frequency of a progressive wave travelling in a medium is 40 Hz. Calculate the change in phase at a given place at 0.02 s.

Sol. $\Delta t = 0.02$ s

$$T = \frac{1}{\nu} = \frac{1}{40}$$

$$\Delta\phi = \frac{2\pi}{T} \times \Delta t = \frac{2\pi}{\left(\frac{1}{40}\right)} \times 0.02 = 2\pi \times 40 \times \frac{2}{100} = \frac{8\pi}{5}$$

Relation Between Particle Velocity and Wave Velocity

As particle displacement, $y = A\sin(\omega t - kx)$

$\therefore$ Particle velocity, $u = \dfrac{dy}{dt} = A\omega\cos(\omega t - kx)$

Again differentiating the above equation, we get

$$a = \frac{d^2y}{dt^2} = -A\omega^2\sin(\omega t - kx) = -\omega^2 y$$

Consider a motion of a string along X-axis. Its one end is connected to a source executing SHM of amplitude A, time period $T = 2\pi/\omega$ and frequency of oscillation $f = 1/T$. The wave produced by such a vibrating source is sine wave as shown in figure.

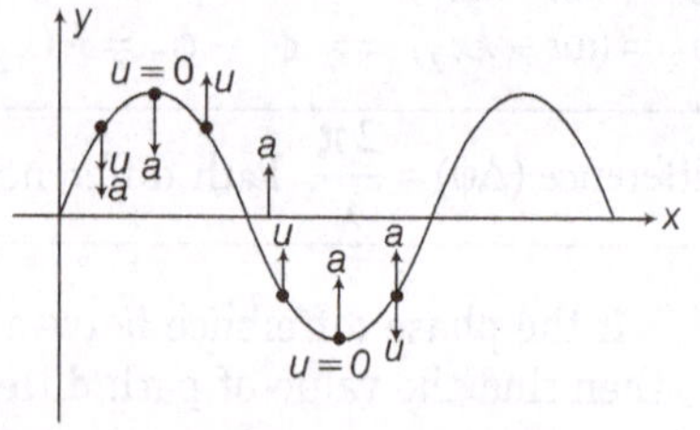

Now, slope of string, $\dfrac{dy}{dx} = -Ak\cos(\omega t - kx)$

$$\therefore \quad \frac{dy/dt}{dy/dx} = -\frac{\omega}{K} \Rightarrow \frac{dy}{dt} = -v\frac{dy}{dx}$$

$\Rightarrow$ **Particle velocity = − Wave velocity × Slope**

$$\text{Similarly,} \quad \frac{d^2y}{dt^2} \times \frac{dx^2}{d^2y} = \frac{\omega^2}{k^2} = v^2$$

$$\Rightarrow \quad \boxed{\frac{d^2y}{dt^2} = v^2\frac{d^2y}{dx^2}} \quad \text{(wave equation)}$$

The direction of particle velocity and acceleration at various position along the motion of the string is shown in the graph with the help of upward and downward arrows.

- If the slope of the curve is positive, while displacement is positive. Hence, u is negative (downward) and a will also be negative (downward).
- If the slope of the curve is negative, while displacement is positive. Hence, u is positive (upward) and a will also be negative (downward).

Example 6 Equation of a transverse wave travelling in a rope is given by $y = 5\sin(4.0t - 0.02x)$, where y and x are expressed in cm and time in second.

Calculate

(i) the amplitude, frequency, velocity and wavelength of the wave.

(ii) the maximum transverse speed and acceleration of a particle in the rope.

Sol. (i) Comparing the given equation with the standard equation of wave motion $y = A\sin\left(2\pi ft - \dfrac{2\pi}{\lambda}x\right)$

where A, f and λ are amplitude, frequency and wavelength, respectively.

Thus, amplitude $A = 5$ cm, $2\pi f = 4$

$\Rightarrow$ Frequency, $f = \dfrac{4}{2\pi} = 0.637$ Hz

Again, $\dfrac{2\pi}{\lambda} = 0.02$

or Wavelength, $\lambda = \dfrac{2\pi}{0.02} = 100\pi$ cm

Velocity of the wave,

$$v = f\lambda = \frac{4}{2\pi}\,\frac{2\pi}{0.02} = 200\text{ cms}^{-1}$$

(ii) Transverse velocity of the particle,

$$u = \frac{dy}{dt} = 5 \times 4\cos(4.0t - 0.02x)$$
$$= 20\cos(4.0t - 0.02x)$$

Maximum velocity of the particle = 20 cms^{-1}

Particle acceleration,

$$a = \frac{d^2y}{dt^2} = -20 \times 4\sin(4.0t - 0.02x)$$

Maximum particle acceleration = 80 cms^{-2}.

Mechanical Waves

A mechanical wave is wave that is not capable of transmitting its energy through a vacuum. Mechanical waves require a medium in order to transport their energy from one position to another. A sound wave is an example of mechanical wave. Sound waves are incapable of travelling through a vacuum.

Slinky waves, water waves, stadium waves and jump rope waves are other examples of mechanical waves. Each requires some medium in order to exist, like a slinky wave requires the coils of the slinky, a water wave requires water, a stadium wave requires fans in a stadium and jump rope wave requires a jump rope.

Speed of Wave Motion

The nature of mechanical wave can be transverse or longitudinal. The speed of transverse and longitudinal waves are different in the solid.

Speed of Transverse Waves

The expression for speed of transverse waves in a solid can be obtained theoretically and verified experimentally.

(a) If medium is solid, then

$$v = \sqrt{\frac{\eta}{\rho}}$$

where, η is modulus of rigidity and ρ is density of solid materials.

(b) In a stretched string,

$$v = \sqrt{\frac{T}{\mu}}$$

where, T is tension and μ is linear mass density of the string.

$$\mu = \text{Volume per unit length} \times \text{Density}$$
$$= \pi r^2 \times 1 \times \rho = \pi r^2 \rho$$

$$v = \sqrt{\frac{T}{\pi r^2 \rho}}$$

$$\frac{T}{\pi r^2} = \frac{\text{Tension in the string}}{\text{Cross - section area of string}} = \text{Stress}$$

$$\therefore \quad v = \sqrt{\frac{\text{Stress}}{\text{Density}}}$$

Example 7 A wave moves with speed 300 m/s on a wire which is under tension of 400 N. Find how much tension must be changed to increase the speed to 315 m/s?

Sol. We know, speed, $v = \sqrt{\frac{T}{\mu}}$

$$\Rightarrow \quad \frac{dv}{dT} = \frac{1}{2\sqrt{\mu T}}$$

$$\Rightarrow \quad \frac{dv}{v} = \frac{1}{2}\frac{dT}{T} \qquad \left[\text{putting } \sqrt{\mu} = \frac{\sqrt{T}}{V}\right]$$

$$\Rightarrow \quad dT = (2T)\frac{dv}{v}$$

$$= 2 \times 400 \times \left(\frac{315-300}{300}\right)$$

$$= \frac{2\times 4}{3} \times 15 = 2 \times 4 \times 5 = 40 \text{ N}$$

Hence, tension should be increased by 40 N.

or

Alternate Method

As speed $v = \sqrt{\frac{T}{\mu}}$

$$\Rightarrow \quad \frac{v_2}{v_1} = \sqrt{\frac{T_2}{T_1}} \qquad [\mu \text{ is same}]$$

$$\frac{T_2}{T_1} = \left(\frac{v_2}{v_1}\right)^2 = \left(\frac{315}{300}\right)^2 = \left(\frac{300+15}{300}\right)^2$$

$$\frac{T_2}{T_1} = \left(1+\frac{15}{300}\right)^2 = \left(1+\frac{1}{20}\right)^2$$

$$\frac{T_2}{T_1} = 1 + 2 \times \frac{1}{20} \qquad [\text{use Binomial theorem}]$$

$$\frac{T_2}{T_1} = 1 + \frac{1}{10}$$

$$\frac{T_2}{T_1} - 1 = \frac{1}{10} \Rightarrow \frac{T_2 - T_1}{T_1} = \frac{1}{10}$$

$$\Delta T = \frac{1}{10} \times T_1 = \frac{1}{10} \times 400 = 40 \text{ N}$$

Hence, tension should be increased by 40 N.

(Previous method is not familiar for the student, so the given solution gives more comfort to the student).

Example 8 A uniform cord have a mass 0.2 kg and length 6 m. If tension is maintained in the cord by suspending a mass of 3 kg from one end, then find out the speed of a pulse on this cord. Also find the time, it takes the pulse to travel from the wall to the pulley.

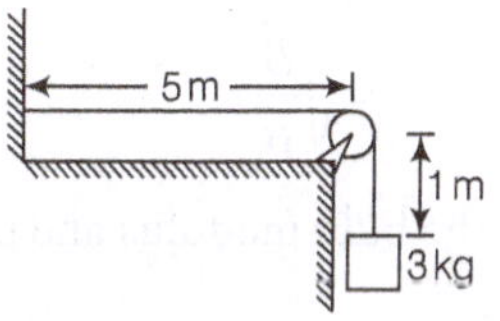

Sol. Given, Mass of a suspended block, $m = 3$ kg

Mass of the cord = 0.2 kg

Length of the cord = 6 m

Speed of the cord = ?

Tension, T = weight of mass of 3 kg = $m \times g$

$= 3 \times 9.8 = 29.4$ N

$$\mu = \frac{m}{l} = \frac{0.2}{6} = 0.033 \text{ kg/m}$$

As we know the wave speed or speed of a pulse on the cord is given by

$$v = \sqrt{\frac{T}{\mu}}$$

Put the values to get the speed of the pulse,

$$v = \sqrt{\frac{T}{\mu}} = \sqrt{\frac{29.4}{0.033}} \simeq 29.85 \text{ m/s}$$

Thus, the time for this speed to travel from the wall to pulley, i.e. a distance of 5 m.

$$\text{Time} = \frac{5}{29.85} = 0.168 \text{ s}$$

Speed of Longitudinal Waves (Sound)

Following are the expressions for the speed of longitudinal waves in the different types of media

(a) If the medium is solid,

$$v=\sqrt{\frac{B+\frac{4}{3}\eta}{\rho}}$$

where B, η and ρ are values of bulk modulus, modulus of rigidity and density of the solid respectively.

If the solid is in the form of a long rod, then

$$v=\sqrt{\frac{Y}{\rho}}$$

where, Y is the Young's modulus of the solid material.

(b) If the medium is liquid,

$$v=\sqrt{\frac{B}{\rho}}$$

where, B is the bulk modulus and ρ is density of liquid.

(c) If the medium is gas,

$$v=\sqrt{\frac{B}{\rho}}$$

where, B is the bulk modulus and ρ is the density of gas.

Example 9 An aluminium rod of length 90 cm and of mass is clamped at its mid-point and is set into longitudinal vibrations by stroking it with resined cloth. Assume that the rod vibrates in its fundamental mode of vibration. The density of aluminium is 2.6 g/cm^3 and its Young's modulus is 7.80×10^{10} N/m^2. Find the speed of the sound in aluminium. If the wavelength is 180 m then, find frequency of vibration.

Sol. Given, Young's modulus, $Y = 7.80\times10^{10}$ N/m^2

Density of aluminium, $\rho = 2.6 \text{ g/cm}^3 = \frac{2.6\times(100)^3}{1000} \text{ kg/m}^3$

$$\rho = 2600 \text{ kg/m}^3$$

Wavelength, $\lambda = 180$ m

Speed of the sound in aluminium, $v=\sqrt{\frac{Y}{\rho}}$

$$=\sqrt{\frac{7.80\times10^{10}\text{ N/m}^2}{2600\text{ kg/m}^3}}$$

$$v = 5477 \text{ m/s}$$

As, $\lambda=\frac{v}{\nu} \Rightarrow \nu=\frac{v}{\lambda}=\frac{5477\text{ m/s}}{180\text{ m}}=30.42$ Hz

Liquids and solids generally have higher speeds of sound than in gases.

Newton's Formula for Speed of Sound in Gases

For an ideal gas, we know that

$$pV = Nk_BT$$

where, p is pressure, V is volume, N is molecular density, k_B is Boltzmann constant and T is the temperature on absolute scale (Kelvin).

For isothermal change, $\Delta T = 0$

$$\Rightarrow \quad V\Delta p + p\Delta V = 0 \Rightarrow -\frac{\Delta p}{\Delta V/V}=p$$

As, $$B=-\frac{\Delta p}{\Delta V/V}$$

$\therefore$ $$B=p$$

Hence, $$v=\sqrt{\frac{p}{\rho}}$$

or **Speed of longitudinal waves in an ideal gas, $v=\sqrt{\frac{p}{\rho}}$**

This is known as **Newton's formula.**

As we know, standard atmosphere pressure is 1.01×10^5 Nm^{-2} and the density of air at STP is 1.29 kg m^{-3}.

Speed of sound in air at STP,

$$v=\sqrt{\frac{1.01\times10^5\text{ Nm}^{-2}}{1.29\text{ kgm}^{-3}}}=280\text{ ms}^{-1}$$

By experimentally, the value of speed of sound in air at 0° C was found to be nearly 332 ms^{-1}.

Example 10 Estimate the speed of sound in air at STP. The mass of 1 mole of air is 29.0×10^{-3} kg. **NCERT**

Sol. We know that volume of any gas at STP is 22.4 litre.

Density of air at STP is

$$\rho_0=\left(\frac{\text{mass}}{\text{volume at STP}}\right)_{\text{for one mole of air}}$$

$$=\frac{29.0\times10^{-3}\text{ kg}}{22.4\times10^{-3}}=1.29\text{ kgm}^{-3}$$

According to Newton's formula,

Speed of sound, $v=\left[\frac{1.01\times10^5\text{ Nm}^{-2}}{1.29\text{ kgm}^{-3}}\right]^{1/2}=280\text{ ms}^{-1}$

Laplace Correction

The result obtained as the speed of sound in air at STP is 280 ms^{-1}, which is about 15% smaller as compared to the experimental value of 331 ms^{-1}. The mistake in the formula (Newton's formula) was pointed out by Laplace and he told that the changes in pressure and volume of a gas, when sound waves are propagated through it, are not isothermal, but adiabatic.

Hence, we will apply pV^{γ} = constant

$$\Rightarrow \quad p\gamma V^{\gamma-1}\Delta V + V^{\gamma}\Delta p = 0$$

The adiabatic bulk modulus, $B_{ad} = -\dfrac{\Delta p}{\Delta V/V} = \gamma p$

where, γ is the ratio of two specific heats C_p/C_V. The speed of sound is therefore, given by

$$\boxed{\text{Speed of sound, } v = \sqrt{\frac{\gamma p}{\rho}}}$$

This modification of Newton's formula is referred to as the **Laplace correction**. For air, $\gamma = 7/5$.

By this formula, we will get a value of 331.3 ms^{-1}, which agree with the practical value.

Note

According to the standard gas equation,

$$pV = RT$$

$$\Rightarrow \quad p = \frac{RT}{V} \quad \text{...(i)}$$

$$\therefore \text{ Speed of sound, } v = \sqrt{\frac{\gamma p}{\rho}} = \sqrt{\frac{\gamma RT}{\rho \times V}} = \sqrt{\frac{\gamma RT}{M}}$$

Substituting value of ρ, where $\rho \times V = M$.
where, T is temperature of the gas
and M is molar mass of the gas.

Effect of Pressure, Temperature, Humidity and Frequency on the Speed of Longitudinal Wave

Given below are the factors which affects the speed of sound in air (or gas).

1. Effect of Temperature

Since, from the equation,

$$v = \sqrt{\frac{\gamma p}{\rho}}$$

We can write

$$v = \sqrt{\frac{\gamma RT}{M}} \quad (\because pV = RT)$$

where, M is molecular mass of gas, T is absolute temperature and R is gas constant.
We can see that,

$$v \propto \sqrt{T}$$

or

$$\boxed{\frac{v_1}{v_2} = \sqrt{\frac{T_1}{T_2}}}$$

At STP, the temperature is 0°C or 273 K. If the speed of sound at 0°C is v_0, its value at t°C will satisfy

$$\frac{v_t}{v_0} = \sqrt{\frac{273+T}{273}} = \left(1+\frac{T}{273}\right)^{1/2} \simeq 1+\frac{T}{546}$$

$$\therefore \quad \boxed{v_t = v_0\left(1+\frac{T}{546}\right)} \quad \text{(For smaller value of } T\text{)}$$

If the speed of sound in air at 0°C (v_0) be taken as 332 ms^{-1}, then

$$v_t = 332\left(1+\frac{T}{546}\right)$$

or

$$\boxed{v_t = 332 + 0.61T}$$

Thus, the velocity of sound in air increases roughly by 0.61 ms^{-1} with per degree centigrade rise in temperature. It means sound travels faster in warm air.

Example 11 The density of air at NTP is 1.29 kgm^{-3}. Assume air to be diatomic with $\gamma = 1.4$. What will be the velocity of sound at 127° C?

Sol. Since, according to Laplace formula, speed of sound in air at NTP is

$$v = \sqrt{\frac{\gamma p}{\rho}} = \sqrt{\frac{1.4 \times 1.013 \times 10^5}{1.29}} = 331.6 \text{ ms}^{-1}$$

The velocity of sound is proportional to the square root of absolute temperature.

$$\Rightarrow \quad \frac{v_2}{v_1} = \sqrt{\frac{T_2}{T_1}}$$

$$\Rightarrow \quad v_2 = v_1\sqrt{\frac{T_2}{T_1}} = 331.6\sqrt{\frac{273+127}{273+27}}$$

$$v_2 = 382.8 \text{ ms}^{-1}$$

2. Effect of Pressure

From the formula for the speed of sound in a gas $v = \sqrt{\dfrac{\gamma p}{\rho}}$, it appears that $v \propto \sqrt{p}$. But actually it is not so.

Because $\frac{p}{\rho} = \frac{RT}{M}$ = constant at constant temperature.

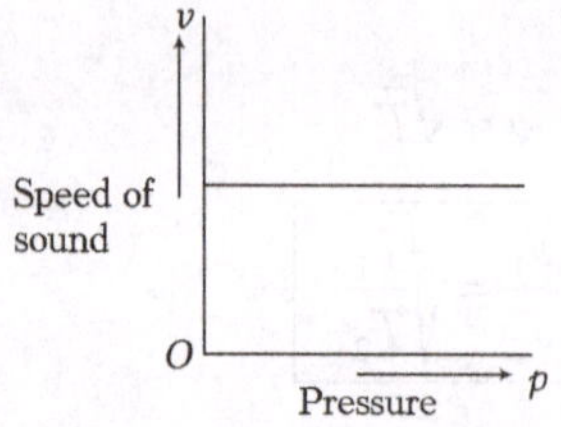

Variation of pressure and speed of sound

From this it is clear that, if the temperature of the gas remains constant, then there is no effect of the pressure change on the speed of sound.

Example 12 A sample of oxygen at NTP has volume V and a sample of hydrogen at NTP has volume $4V$. Both the gases are mixed and the mixture is maintained at NTP, if the speed of sound in hydrogen at NTP is 1270 ms^{-1}, then calculate the speed of sound in mixture.

Sol. $p_{mix} = \frac{p_{O_2}V_{O_2} + p_{H_2}V_{H_2}}{V_{O_2} + V_{H_2}} = \frac{1 \times V + 1 \times 4V}{V + 4V} = 1 \text{ atm}$

As temperature remains same, therefore pressure remains constant.

$$\therefore \quad \frac{v_{mix}}{v_{H_2}} = \sqrt{\frac{p_{mix}}{p_{H_2}}} = \sqrt{\frac{1}{1}} = 1$$

$$v_{mix} = v_{H_2} = 1270 \text{ ms}^{-1}$$

3. Effect of Humidity

The density of moist air (i.e. air mixed with water-vapour) is less than the density of dry air. It is clear from the formula, $v = \sqrt{\gamma p/\rho}$ that the speed of sound in moist air is slightly greater than in dry air. So, speed of sound increases with increase in humidity.

4. Effect of Frequency

The speed of sound in air is independent of its frequency. Sound waves of different frequency travels with the same speed in air but their wavelengths in air are different.

Speed of Sound in Different Gases

Consider two gases which have same value of γ. At the same temperature and pressure, the speed of sound in the gases are v_1 and v_2, respectively.

Now, $v_1 = \sqrt{\frac{\gamma p}{\rho_1}}$ and $v_2 = \sqrt{\frac{\gamma p}{\rho_2}}$

where, ρ_1 and ρ_2 are the densities of the gases.

$$\therefore \quad \frac{v_1}{v_2} = \sqrt{\frac{\rho_2}{\rho_1}} \quad \text{...(i)}$$

If the molecular masses of gases be M_1 and M_2, respectively. Then,

$$v_1 = \sqrt{\frac{\gamma RT}{M_1}} \text{ and } v_2 = \sqrt{\frac{\gamma RT}{M_2}}$$

$$\therefore \quad \frac{v_1}{v_2} = \sqrt{\frac{M_2}{M_1}} \quad \text{...(ii)}$$

From the Eqs. (i) and (ii), it is clear that the speed of sound in a gas is inversely proportional to square root of the density or the molecular mass of gas.

Relation Between Speed of Sound in Gas and Root-Mean-Square Speed of the Molecules of that Gas

If sound travels in a gaseous medium, then velocity of sound in gas will be

$$v_{sound} = \sqrt{\frac{\gamma p}{\rho}} \text{ or } v_{sound} = \sqrt{\frac{\gamma RT}{M}}$$

where, M is the molecular mass of the gas.

rms velocity of gas is given by

$$v_{rms} = \sqrt{\frac{3RT}{M}} \text{ or } \sqrt{\frac{3p}{\rho}}$$

So, $\frac{v_{rms}}{v_{sound}} = \sqrt{\frac{3}{\gamma}}$ or $v_{sound} = [\gamma / 3]^{1/2} v_{rms}$

$$\Rightarrow \quad \sqrt{\frac{\gamma}{3}} < 1$$

$$\therefore \quad v < v_{rms}$$

Hence, speed of sound in a gas is less than its rms speed.

Example 13 Compute the ratio of speed of sound in hydrogen gas to the rms speed of hydrogen molecules.

Sol. As hydrogen is a diatomic gas

$$\gamma = \frac{7}{5}$$

Speed of sound in hydrogen, $v_H = \sqrt{\frac{\gamma p}{\rho}}$

rms speed of hydrogen molecules, $v_{rms} = \sqrt{\frac{3p}{d}}$

$$\therefore \quad \frac{v_H}{(v_{rms})_H} = \sqrt{\frac{\gamma}{3}} = \sqrt{\frac{7/5}{3}} = \sqrt{\frac{7}{15}}$$

Concept of Supersonic and Ultrasonic Waves

Supersonic Waves

The term supersonic is used to define a speed that is over the speed of sound. At a typical temperature like 21°C, the threshold value required for an object to be travelling at a supersonic speed is approximately 344 m/s. Speeds greater than 5 times the speed of sound are often referred to as hypersonic.

Ultrasonic Waves

Ultrasonic is the study and application of high frequency sound waves usually in excess of 20 kHz, beyond the range of human hearing. Ultrasonic is intimately related to the electronics industry. One reason is of course, because ultrasonic waves are generated, detected and interpreted by electronic devices. Also, ultrasonic technology is used extensively for the testing, cleaning and soldering of electronic components. Ultrasonic whistles, which cannot be heard by human beings are audible to dogs and are used to summons them.

Topic Practice 1

Multiple Choice Questions

(1 Mark)

1. Water waves produced by a motorboat sailing in water are
(a) Neither longitudinal nor transverse
(b) Both longitudinal and transverse
(c) only longitudinal
(d) only transverse **NCERT Exemplar**

2. Sound waves of wavelength λ travelling in a medium with a speed of v m/s enter into another medium where its speed in $2v$ m/s. Wavelength of sound waves in the second medium is
(a) λ (b) $\frac{\lambda}{2}$
(c) 2λ (d) 4λ **NCERT Exemplar**

3. Equation of a plane progressive wave is given by $y = 0.6 \sin 2\pi\left(t - \frac{x}{2}\right)$. On reflection from a denser medium its amplitude becomes $\frac{2}{3}$ of the amplitude of the incident wave. The equation of the reflected wave is
(a) $y = 0.6 \sin 2\pi\left(t + \frac{x}{2}\right)$ (b) $y = -0.4 \sin 2\pi\left(t + \frac{x}{2}\right)$
(c) $y = 0.4 \sin 2\pi\left(t + \frac{x}{2}\right)$ (d) $y = -0.4 \sin 2\pi\left(t - \frac{x}{2}\right)$
NCERT Exemplar

4. A sound wave is passing through air column in the form of compression and rarefaction. In consecutive compressions and rarefactions,
(a) density remains constant
(b) Boyle's law is obeyed
(c) bulk modulus of air oscillates
(d) there is no transfer of heat

5. Speed of sound wave in air
(a) is independent of temperature
(b) increases with pressure
(c) increases with increase in humidity
(d) decreases with increase in humidity

Very Short Answer Type Questions

(1 Mark)

6. What is the quantity transmitted with propagation of longitudinal waves through a medium? **NCERT Exemplar**

7. What is the nature of water waves produced by a motorboat sailing in water?

8. What do you mean by the time period of wave?

9. What is the relation between frequency, wave velocity and wavelength?

10. Is Newton's law of motion applicable for material waves? Is this applicable for electromagnetic waves?

11. Does a vibrating source always produce sound?

12. How speed of sound waves in air varies with humidity?

13. Sound waves of wavelength λ travelling in a medium with a speed of v m/s enter into another medium where, its speed is $2v$ m/s. Wavelength of sound waves in the second medium is **NCERT Exemplar**

Short Answer Type I Questions

(2 Marks)

14. What do you mean by transverse wave? Write its example.

15. Write down the two characteristics of wave motion.

16. Define the following terms of wave.
 (i) Time period
 (ii) Angular frequency

17. Derive the relation between phase difference and path difference of a plane progressive wave.

18. Prove that the speed of longitudinal wave in a gas is, $v = \sqrt{\frac{p}{\rho}}$.

19. What is the effect of humidity on the speed of longitudinal wave?

20. Prove that the speed of sound in a gas is less than its rms speed.

21. You have learnt that a travelling wave in one dimension is represented by a function $y = f(x,t)$ where, x and t must appear in the combination $x - vt$ or $x + vt$, i.e. $y = f(x \pm vt)$. Is the converse true? Examine if the following functions for y can possibly represent a travelling wave
 (i) $(x - vt)^2$ (ii) $\log[(x + vt)/x_0]$
 (iii) $1/(x + vt)$ **NCERT Exemplar**

Short Answer Type II Questions

3 Marks

22. What do you mean by the wave? Explain its types.

23. What is the wave motion? Write its characteristics.

24. Define the following terms of wave.
 (i) Wavelength (ii) Angular wave number
 (iii) Time period

25. Explain the distance-displacement graph of simple harmonic wave.

26. Prove that $\frac{d^2y}{dt^2} = v^2 \frac{d^2y}{dx^2}$

 where, y is displacement, x is position and v is the velocity.

27. Why mechanical wave requires a medium? Explain with an example.

Long Answer Type Questions

5 Marks

28. Derive an expression for displacement in wave motion. Also, explain the alternative forms of wave equation.

29. Explain the graphical representation of simple harmonic wave.

30. What is the Laplace correction? Explain it with derivation.

31. What is the effect of temperature and pressure on the speed of longitudinal wave? Explain.

Numerical Problems

32. A steel wire 0.72 m long has a mass of 5.0×10^{-3} kg. If the wire is under a tension of 60 N, what is the speed of transverse waves on the wire? **NCERT [1 M]**

33. A steel wire has a length of 12 m and a mass of 2.10 kg. What will be the speed of a transverse wave on this wire when a tension of 2.06×10^4 N is applied? **NCERT Exemplar [2 M]**

34. A steel wire has a length of 12.0 m and a mass of 2.10 kg. What should be the tension in the wire so that speed of a transverse wave on the wire equals the speed of sound in dry air at $20°C = 343 \text{ ms}^{-1}$? **NCERT [2 M]**

35. A string of mass 2.5 kg is under a tension of 200 N. The length of the stretched string is 20.0 m. If the transverse jerk is struck at one end of the string, the disturbance will reach the other end in ... **[2 M]**

36. Equation of a plane progressive wave is given by $y = 0.6 \sin 2\pi \left(t - \frac{x}{2}\right)$. On reflection from a denser medium, its amplitude becomes 2/3 of the amplitude of incident wave. What will be equation of reflected wave? **NCERT Exemplar [2 M]**

37. At what temperature (in °C) will the speed of sound in air be 3 times its value at 0°C? **[2 M]**

38. Earthquakes generate sound waves inside the earth. Unlike a gas, the earth can experience both transverse S and longitudinal P sound waves. Typically the speed of S wave is about 4.0 kms^{-1} and that of P wave is 8.0 kms^{-1}.

A seismograph records P and S waves from an earthquake. The first P wave arrives 4 min before the first S wave. Assuming the waves travel in straight line, at what distance does the earthquake occur? **NCERT [3 M]**

39. A stone dropped from the top of a tower of height 300 m in high splashes into the water of a pond near the base of the tower. When is the splash heard at the top, given that the speed of sound in air is 340 ms^{-1}? ($g = 9.8 \text{ m s}^{-2}$) **[3 M]**

40. If c is rms speed of molecules in a gas and v is the speed of sound waves in the gas, show that c/v is constant and independent of temperature for all diatomic gases. **[3 M]**

41. For the wave $y(x,t) = 3.0 \sin(36t + 0.018x + \pi/4)$, plot the displacement (y) *versus* (t) graph for $x = 0$, 2 and 4 cm. What are the shapes of these graphs? In which aspects does the oscillatory motion in travelling wave differ from one point to another amplitude, frequency or phase? **NCERT [3 M]**

42. A transverse harmonic wave on a string is described by $y(x, t) = 3.0 \sin(36t + 0.018x + \pi/4)$ Where, x and y are in cm and t in seconds. The positive direction of x is from left to right.

(i) Is this a travelling wave or a stationary wave? If it is travelling, what are the speed and direction of its propagation?
(ii) What are its amplitude and frequency?
(iii) What is the initial phase at the origin?
(iv) What is the least distance between two successive crests in the wave? **[3 M]**

43. A source of frequency 250Hz produces sound waves of wavelength 1.32 m in a gas at STP. Calculate the change in the wavelength, when temperature of the gas is 40°C. **[3 M]**

44. The earth has a radius of 6400 km. The inner core of 1000 km radius is solid. Outside it, there is a region from 1000 km to a radius of 3500 km which is in molten state. Then, again from 3500 km to 6400 km the earth is solid. Only longitudinal P waves can travel inside a liquid. Assume that the P wave has a speed of 8 kms^{-1} in solid parts and of 5 kms^{-1} in liquid parts of the earth. An earthquake occurs at some place close to the surface of the earth. Calculate the time after which it will be recorded in a seismometer at a diametrically opposite point on the earth if wave travels along diameter? **NCERT Exemplar [5 M]**

45. In the given progressive wave,

$$y = 5 \sin(100\pi t - 0.4\pi x)$$

where, y and x are in m, t is in second. What is the

(i) amplitude,
(ii) wavelength,
(iii) frequency,
(iv) wave velocity and
(v) particle velocity amplitude? **NCERT Exemplar [5 M]**

46. Use the formula, $v = \sqrt{\frac{\gamma p}{\rho}}$ to explain, why the speed of sound in air

(i) is independent on pressure?
(ii) increases with temperature?
(iii) increases with humidity? **NCERT [5 M]**

47. For the harmonic travelling wave

$$y = 2\cos 2\pi(10t - 0.0080x + 3.5)$$

where, x and y are in cm and t is in second. What is the phase difference between the oscillatory motion at two points separated by a distance of

(i) 4 m (ii) 0.5 m (iii) $\frac{\lambda}{2}$
(iv) $\frac{3\lambda}{4}$ (at a given instant in time)?
(v) What is the phase difference between the oscillation of a particle located at $x = 100$ cm, at $t = T$ s and $t = 5$ s? **[5 M]**

48. The equation of a wave is,

$$y(x, t) = 0.05 \sin\left[\frac{\pi}{2}(10x - 40t) - \frac{\pi}{4}\right] \text{m}$$

Find

(i) the wavelength, the frequency and the wave velocity,
(ii) the particle velocity and acceleration at $x = 0.5$ m and $t = 0.05$ s. **[5 M]**

49. For the wave shown in figure, write the equation of this wave, if its position is shown at $t = 0$. Speed of wave is $v = 300 \text{ ms}^{-1}$.

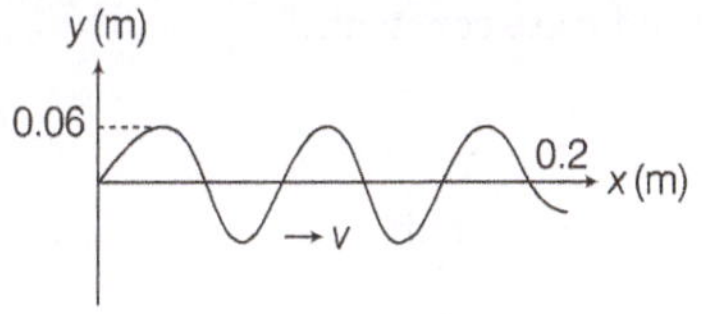

[5 M]

Hints & Solutions

1. (*b*) Water waves produced by a motorboat sailing in water are both longitudinal and transverse, because the waves, produce transverse as well as lateral vibrations in the particles of the medium.

2. (*c*) Let the frequency in the first medium is ν and in the second medium is ν.′

Frequency remains same in both the medium

So, $\nu = \nu' \Rightarrow \frac{v}{\lambda} = \frac{v'}{\lambda'}$

$\Rightarrow \lambda' = \left(\frac{v'}{v}\right)\lambda$

λ and λ′, *v* and *v*′ are wavelengths and speeds in first and second medium, respectively.

So, $\lambda' = \left(\frac{2v}{v}\right)\lambda = 2\lambda$

3. (*b*) Amplitude of reflected wave,

$$A_r = \frac{2}{3} \times A_i = \frac{2}{3} \times 0.6 = 0.4 \text{ units}$$

Given equation of incident wave,

$$y_i = 0.6 \sin 2\pi \left(t - \frac{x}{2}\right)$$

Equation of reflected wave,

$$y_r = A_r \sin 2\pi \left(t + \frac{x}{2} + \pi\right)$$

[∵ At denser medium, phase changes by π]

The positive sign is due to reversal of direction of propagation.

So, $y_r = -0.4 \sin 2\pi \left(t + \frac{x}{2}\right)$ [$\because \sin(\pi + \theta) = -\sin\theta$]

4. (*d*)
   (a) Due to compression and rarefactions density of the medium (air) changes. At compressed regions density is maximum and at rarefactions density is minimum.
   (b) As density is changing, so Boyle's law is not obeyed.
   (c) Bulk modulus remains same.
   (d) The time of compression and rarefaction is too small, i.e. we can assume adiabatic process and hence no transfer of heat.

5. (*c*) Due to presence of moisture density of air decreases.

We know that, speed of sound in air is given by $v = \sqrt{\frac{\gamma p}{\rho}}$

For air γ and *p* are constants.

$$v \propto \frac{1}{\sqrt{\rho}}$$

where, ρ is density of air.

$$\frac{v_2}{v_1} = \sqrt{\frac{\rho_2}{\rho_1}}$$

where, ρ_1 is density of dry air and ρ_2 is density of moist air.

As, $\rho_2 < \rho_1 = \frac{v_2}{v_1} > 1 \Rightarrow v_2 > v_1$

Hence, speed of sound wave in air increases with increase in humidity.

6. Propagation of longitudinal waves through a medium leads to transmission of energy through the medium.
7. Water waves produced by a motorboat sailing in water are both longitudinal and transverse.
8. The time taken by wave to travel a distance equal to one wavelength is called time period.
9. $v = n\lambda$

   where, *v* = velocity, *f* = frequency and λ = wavelength.
10. Newton's laws of motion are applicable for material waves but not applicable for electromagnetic waves.
11. A vibrating source produces sound when it vibrates in a medium and frequency of vibration lies within the audible range (20 Hz to 20 kHz).
12. Speed of sound waves in air increases with increase in humidity. This is because, presence of moisture decreases the density of air.
13. Frequency in the first medium, $\nu = \frac{v}{\lambda}$

    Frequency will remain same in the second medium, as the source.

    $\Rightarrow \nu' = \nu \Rightarrow \frac{2v}{\lambda'} = \frac{v}{\lambda} \Rightarrow \lambda' = 2\lambda$
14. Refer to text on page 463 (Transverse wave).
15. Refer to text on page 464 (Characteristics of wave motion).
16. Refer to text on page 465 (Time period and angular frequency).
17. Refer to text on page 467 (Relation between the phase difference and path difference of a plane progressive wave).
18. Refer to text on page 470 (Newton's formula for speed of sound in gases).
19. Refer to text on page 472 (Effect of humidity).
20. Refer to text on page 472 (Relation between speed of sound in gas and root mean square speed of the molecules of that gas).
21. Conceptual question based on fundamentals of characteristics of a travelling wave.

    The converse is not true means if the function can be represented in the form $y = f(x \pm vt)$, it does not necessarily express a travelling wave. As the essential condition for a travelling wave is that the vibrating particle must have finite displacement value for all *x* and *t*.

    (i) For $x = 0$,

    If $t \to 0$, then $(x - vt)^2 \to 0$ which is finite, hence, it is a wave as it passes the two tests.

(ii) $\log\left(\frac{x+vt}{x_0}\right)$

At $x=0$ and $t=0$,

$$f(x,t)=\log\left(\frac{0+0}{x_0}\right)=\log 0 \rightarrow \text{ not defined}$$

Hence, it is not a wave.

(iii) $\frac{1}{x+vt}$

For $x=0, t=0,\ f(x)\rightarrow\infty$

Though the function is of $(x\pm vt)$ type still at $x=0$, it is infinite, hence, it is not a wave. [2]

22. Refer to text on pages 463 and 464 (Wave and types of waves).

23. Refer to text on page 464 (Wave motion and characteristics of wave motion).

24. Refer to text on pages 464 and 465 (Wavelength and angular wave number, time period).

25. Refer to text on page 467 (Distance-displacement graph of particle).

26. Refer to text on page 468 (Relation between particle velocity and wave velocity).

27. Refer to text on page 468 (Mechanical waves).

28. Refer to text on page 466 (Expression for displacement in wave motion and alternative forms of wave equation).

29. Refer to text on page 467 (Graphical representation of simple harmonic wave).

30. Refer to text on page 471 (Laplace correction).

31. Refer to text on pages 471 and 472 (Effect of temperature and effect of pressure).

32. Mass per unit length of the wire,

$$\mu=\frac{5.0\times10^{-3}\text{ kg}}{0.72\text{ m}}=6.9\times10^{-3}\text{ kgm}^{-1}$$ [1/2]

Tension, $T=60$ N

Speed, $v=\sqrt{\frac{T}{\mu}}=\sqrt{\frac{60}{6.9\times10^{-3}}}=93\text{ ms}^{-1}$ [1/2]

33. Given, $l=12$ m, $M=2.10$ kg, $T=2.06\times10^4$ N, $v=?$

$$\mu=\frac{M}{l}=\frac{2.10}{12}\text{ kg/m}$$ [1]

$$v=\sqrt{\frac{T}{\mu}}=\sqrt{\frac{2.06\times10^4}{2.10/12}}=3.43\times10^2\text{ m/s}$$ [1]

34. Given, $l=12.0$ m, $M=2.10$ kg, $T=?$, $v=343$ m/s

μ = mass per unit length

$$=\frac{M}{l}=\frac{2.10}{12}=0.175\text{ kgm}^{-1}$$ [1]

As we know that, $v=\sqrt{\frac{T}{\mu}}$

$\Rightarrow\quad T=v^2\mu=(343)^2\times(0.175)$

$\Rightarrow\quad T=2.06\times10^4$ N [1]

35. Here, $\mu=\frac{2.5}{20}$ kg/m, $T=200$ N [1]

$$v=\sqrt{\frac{T}{\mu}}=\sqrt{\frac{200}{2.5/20}}=\sqrt{\frac{200\times20}{2.5}}$$

$$=\sqrt{\frac{4\times10^4}{25}}=\frac{2\times10^2}{5}=\frac{20\times10}{5}=40\text{ m/s}$$

So, $t=\frac{l}{v}=\frac{20}{40}=0.50$ s [1]

36. On reflection from the denser medium, there will be a phase change of 180°.

Net amplitude $=\frac{2}{3}\times0.6=0.4$ [1]

Hence, equation of reflected wave will be

$$y=0.4\sin2\pi\left[t+\frac{x}{2}+\pi\right]$$

$$=-0.4\sin2\pi(t+x/2)$$ [1]

37. We know that, speed, $v\propto\sqrt{T}$

By formula $v=\frac{\chi RT}{\rho}$

where, T is in kelvin.

$$\frac{v_t}{v_0}=\sqrt{\frac{273+t}{273+0}}=3\Rightarrow\frac{273+t}{273}=9$$ [1]

$\Rightarrow\quad t=9\times273-273=2184°\text{C}$ [1]

38. Let v_1, v_2 be the velocities of S wave and P wave and t_1, t_2 be the time taken by these waves to reach the seismograph.

l = distance of occurrence of earthquake from the seismograph

$v_1t_1=v_2t_2$ [1]

$\Rightarrow\quad v_1=4\text{ km s}^{-1}, v_2=8\text{ km s}^{-1}$

$\Rightarrow\quad 4t_1=8t_2$

$\Rightarrow\quad t_1=2t_2$ ...(i)

$t_1-t_2=4$ min $\quad[\because t_1=2t_2]$ [1]

$\Rightarrow\quad 2t_2-t_2=4$ min

$t_2=240$ s

Putting the value of t_2 in Eq. (i), we get

$\Rightarrow\quad t_1=2t_2=2\times240=480$s

$\Rightarrow\quad l=v_1t_1=4\times480=1920$km [1]

39. Given, $h=300$ m, $g=9.8\text{ m/s}^2$, $v=340\text{ ms}^{-1}$

t_1 = time taken by stone to strike the water surface

$$t_1=\sqrt{\frac{2h}{g}}=\sqrt{\frac{300}{4.9}}=7.82\text{ s}\left(\text{As } h=0+\frac{1}{2}gt_1^2\right)$$ [1]

t_2 = time taken by the splash's sound to reach top of the tower

$$t_2=\frac{h}{v}=\frac{300}{340}=0.882\quad\left[\because v=\frac{h}{t_2}\right]$$ [1]

Total time, t = time to hear splash of sound

$$=t_1+t_2=7.82+0.882=8.702$$ [1]

40. From kinetic theory of gases,

$p = \frac{1}{3}\rho c^2$, where c is rms speed of molecules of gas. [1/2]

$$\Rightarrow \quad c = \sqrt{\frac{3p}{\rho}} \quad \text{...(i)}$$ [1/2]

$$v = \text{speed of sound in the gas} = \sqrt{\frac{\gamma p}{\rho}} \quad \text{...(ii)}$$ [1/2]

From Eqs. (i) and (ii), we get

$$\frac{c}{v} = \sqrt{\frac{3p}{\rho} \times \frac{\rho}{\gamma p}} = \sqrt{\frac{3}{\gamma}}$$ [1]

For diatomic gases, $\gamma = 1.4$ = constant

$$\Rightarrow \quad \frac{c}{v} = \sqrt{\frac{3}{1.4}} = 1.46 = \text{constant}$$ [1/2]

41. The transverse harmonic wave is

$$y(x,t) = 3.0 \sin\left[36t + 0.018x + \frac{\pi}{4}\right]$$

It is the equation of travelling wave along negative direction of x. [1]

For $x = 0$, ...(i)

$$y(x,t) = 3.0\sin[36t + \pi/4]$$

Here, $\omega = \frac{2\pi}{T} = 36, \; T = \frac{2\pi}{36} = \frac{\pi}{18}$ s

For different values of t, we calculate y using Eq. (i). These values are tabulated below [1]

t	0	$T/8$	$2T/8$	$3T/8$	$4T/8$	$5T/8$	$6T/8$	$7T/8$	T
y	$3/\sqrt{2}$	3	$3/\sqrt{2}$	0	$-3/\sqrt{2}$	-3	$-3/\sqrt{2}$	0	$3/\sqrt{2}$

On plotting y *versus* t graph, we obtain a sinusoidal curve as shown in figure below.

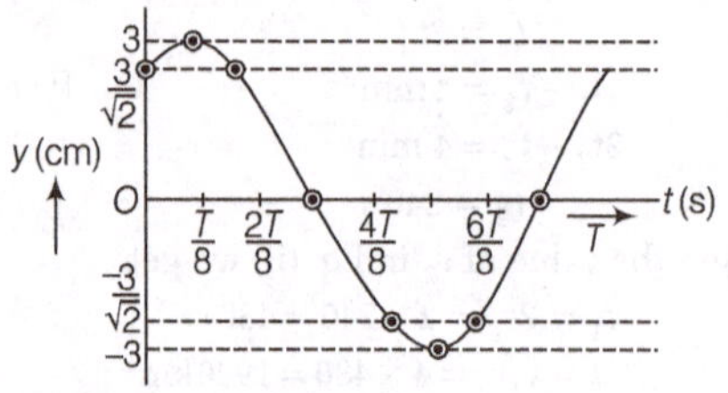

Similar graphs are obtained for x = 2 cm and x = 4 cm. The oscillatory motion in travelling wave differs from one point to another only in terms of phase. Amplitude and frequency of oscillatory motion remain the same in all the three cases. [1]

42. Given equation is $y(x, t) = 3.0\sin(36t + 0.018x + \pi/4)$

Comparing with standard equation [1/2]

$$y(x, t) = a\sin(\omega t + kx + \phi)$$

(i) The given equation represents a transverse harmonic wave travelling from right to left (i.e. along negative X-axis). It is not a stationary wave. [1/2]

By comparing, we get ω = 36 rad/s, k = 0.018/cm

$\therefore$ Speed of wave, $v = \frac{\omega}{k} = \frac{36}{0.018} = 2000$ cm/s

(ii) By comparing amplitude, a = 3 cm

$$\Rightarrow \quad 2\pi v = 36$$

$$\Rightarrow \quad v = \frac{36}{2\pi} = 5.73\text{Hz}$$ [1/2]

(iii) Initial phase, $\phi = \frac{\pi}{4}$ [1/2]

(iv) $\omega = 36, \; k = \frac{2\pi}{\lambda} = 0.018$

$\Rightarrow \lambda$ = least distance $= \frac{2\pi}{k} = \frac{2\pi}{0.018}$ cm = 349.1 cm [1]

43. We have, v_0 = 250 Hz, T_0 = 273 K

$T_1 = 273 + 40 = 313$K; $\lambda_0 = 1.32$ m

$\therefore$ Speed of sound, $v_0 = v_0 \cdot \lambda_0 = 250 \times 1.32 = 330$ m/s

As we know that,

Speed of sound, $v \propto \sqrt{T}$ [1]

Thus, $\frac{v_1}{v_0} = \sqrt{\frac{T_1}{T_0}}$

$$v_1 = v_0\sqrt{\frac{T_1}{T_0}} = 330\sqrt{\frac{313}{273}} = 353.34 \text{ m/s}$$

$\because \quad v_1 = v_0 \lambda_1$

$$\lambda_1 = \frac{353.34}{250} = 1.41 \text{ m}$$ [1]

$\therefore$ Change in the wavelength,

$$\Delta\lambda = \lambda_1 - \lambda_0 = 1.41 - 1.32 = 0.09 \text{ m}$$ [1]

44. Consider the diagram shown below

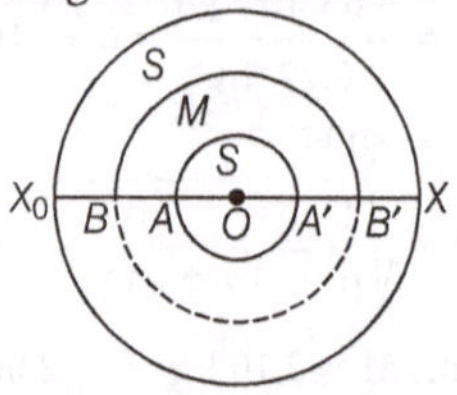

The wave is travelling along the diameter X_0X. [1]

(i) x_1 = distance through solid portion

$= X_0B + AA' + B'X$

$= (2900 + 2 \times 1000 + 2900)$ km = 7800 km [2]

(ii) x_2 = distance through molten portion

$= BA + A'B' = (2500 + 2500)$ km = 5000 km

Now, v_1 = 8 km/s, v_2 = 5 km/s, t = total time

$$\left[\text{Time} = \frac{\text{Distance}}{\text{Speed}} \quad t = \frac{x}{v}\right]$$

$$= t_1 + t_2 = \frac{x_1}{v_1} + \frac{x_2}{v_2} = \frac{7800}{8} + \frac{5000}{5}$$

$t = 975 + 1000 = 1975$ s = 32 minutes 55 seconds [2]

45. Comparing with the standard form of equation

$y = a\sin[\omega t - kx]$

(i) Amplitude, $a = 5$ m [1]

(ii) $\omega = \frac{2\pi}{T} = 100\pi$

$k = \frac{2\pi}{\lambda} = 0.4\,\pi \Rightarrow \lambda = \frac{2}{0.4} = \frac{20}{4} = 5$ m [1]

(iii) $\omega = 2\pi\nu = 100\pi \Rightarrow \nu = 50$ Hz [1]

(iv) Wave velocity, $v = \nu\lambda = 50 \times 5 = 250$ m/s [1]

(v) Particle velocity $= \frac{dy}{dt} = a\omega\cos(\omega t - kx)$

$\left(\frac{dy}{dt}\right)_{max} = a\omega = 5 \times 100\pi = 500\pi$ m/s [1]

46. (i) Effect of pressure

v = speed of sound in a gas $= \sqrt{\frac{\gamma p}{\rho}}$

p = pressure, ρ = density, $\frac{M}{V} \Rightarrow v = \sqrt{\frac{\gamma pV}{M}}$

When T is constant,

pV = constant $\Rightarrow v$ = constant

Hence, velocity of sound is independent of the change in pressure of the gas provided temperature remains constant. [2]

(ii) Formula for velocity, $v = \sqrt{\frac{\gamma p}{\rho}}$

According to standard gas equation,

$pV = RT \Rightarrow p = \frac{RT}{V} \Rightarrow v = \sqrt{\frac{\gamma \times RT}{pV}} = \sqrt{\frac{\gamma RT}{M}}$

where, $M = pV$ = molecular weight of the gas

$\Rightarrow \quad v \propto \sqrt{T}$

Hence, v increases with temperature. [1½]

(iii) Due to presence of water vapours in air density changes. Hence, velocity of sound changes with humidity.

Let ρ_m = density of moist, ρ_d = density of dry air

v_m = velocity of sound in moist air

v_d = velocity of sound in dry air

$v_m = \sqrt{\frac{\gamma p}{\rho_m}}, v_d = \sqrt{\frac{\gamma p}{\rho_d}}$

$\frac{v_m}{v_d} = \sqrt{\frac{\rho_d}{\rho_m}}$ as $\rho_d > \rho_m \Rightarrow v_m > v_d$ [1½]

47. Given equation is $y = 2\cos 2\pi(10t - 0.008x + 3.5)$

Comparing with standard equation,

$y = a\cos(\omega t - kx + \phi)$

$a = 2$ cm, $\omega = \frac{2\pi}{T} = 20\pi,\ T = 0.1$ s

$k = \frac{2\pi}{\lambda} = 0.008 \times 2\pi \Rightarrow \lambda = \frac{2\pi}{2\pi \times 0.008} = 1.25$ m

$\phi = 2\pi \times 3.5 = 7\pi$ rad

(i) $\phi_1 = \frac{2\pi}{\lambda} \times 4 = \frac{2\pi}{1.25} \times 4 = 6.4\pi$ rad [1]

(ii) $\phi_2 = \frac{2\pi}{\lambda} \times x = \frac{2\pi}{1.25} \times 0.5 = 0.8\pi$ rad [1]

(iii) When $x = \lambda/2$

$\phi_3 = \frac{2\pi}{\lambda} \times \lambda/2 = \pi$ rad [1]

(iv) When $x = \frac{3\lambda}{4}$; $\phi_4 = \frac{2\pi}{\lambda} \times \frac{3\lambda}{4} = \frac{3\pi}{2}$ rad [1]

(v) At $t = T$; $\phi = \frac{2\pi}{T} = \frac{2\pi}{0.1} = 20\pi$ rad

and at $t = 5$s; $\phi' = \frac{2\pi}{0.1} \times 5.100\pi$ rad

$\therefore$ Phase difference $\phi' - \phi = 100\pi - 20\pi = 80\pi$ rad [1]

48. (i) The equation may be rewritten as

$y(x, t) = 0.05\sin\left(5\pi x - 20\pi t - \frac{\pi}{4}\right)$ m

Comparing this with equation of plane progressive harmonic wave,

$y(x, t) = A\sin(kx - \omega t + \phi)$

we have, wave number, $k = \frac{2\pi}{\lambda} = 5\pi$ rad m^{-1}

$\therefore \quad \lambda = 0.4$ m

The angular frequency is

$\omega = 2\pi f = 20\pi$ rad s^{-1} $\Rightarrow f = 10$ Hz

The wave velocity is

$v = f\lambda = \frac{\omega}{k} = 4$ ms^{-1} in + x-direction [3]

(ii) The particle velocity and acceleration are

$\frac{\partial y}{\partial t} = -(20\pi)(0.05)\cos\left(\frac{5\pi}{2} - \pi - \frac{\pi}{4}\right) = 2.22$ ms^{-1}

$\frac{\partial^2 y}{\partial t^2} = -(20\pi)^2(0.05)\sin\left(\frac{5\pi}{2} - \pi - \frac{\pi}{4}\right) = 140$ ms^{-2} [2]

49. The wavelength, $\frac{5}{2}\lambda = 0.2$ m

$\therefore \quad \lambda = 0.08$ m $\Rightarrow f = \frac{v}{\lambda} = \frac{300}{0.08} = 3750$ Hz

$k = \frac{2\pi}{\lambda} = 78.5$ m^{-1} and $\omega = 2\pi f = 23562$ rad^{-1}

At $\quad t = 0,\ x = 0, \frac{dy}{dx}$ = positive

and the given curve is a sine curve. [3]

Hence, equation of wave travelling in positive x-direction should have the form,

$y(x, t) = A\sin(kx - \omega t)$

Substituting the values, we have

$y(x, t) = (0.06\text{ m})\sin[(78.5\text{ m}^{-1})x - (23562\text{ s}^{-1})t]$ m

[2]

TOPIC 02 Superposition of Waves and Beats

Principle of Superposition of Waves

This principle states that when two or more pulses overlap, the resultant displacement is the algebraic sum of the displacements due to each pulse.

Consider the two waves travelling together along the same stretched string in opposite directions.

They meet and pass through each other, and move on independently as shown in figure.

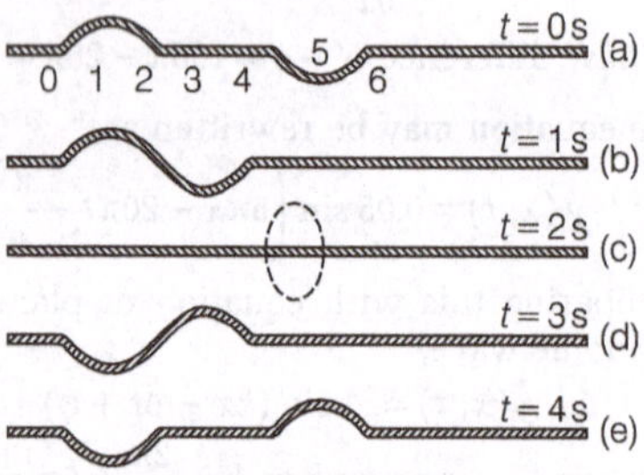

Superposition of two waves

In the graph (c), the displacement due to the two pulses have exactly cancelled each other and there is zero displacement throughout.

Three important applications of superposition principle are:

1. Stationary waves
2. Beats
3. Interference of waves

Interference of Two Waves

Wave interference is the phenomenon that occurs when the two or more waves pass through the same medium. The interference of waves causes the medium to take on a shape that results from the net effect of the two individual waves upon the particles of the medium.

To illustrate the principle, we will consider two harmonic travelling waves having the same angular frequency ω and wave number $k = 2\pi/\lambda$. Let us assume that their amplitudes are identical.

If the two waves are out of phase by a phase constant ϕ, then the two waves are represented as

$$y_1(x, t) = a_1 \sin(\omega t - kx) \quad \text{...(i)}$$

and

$$y_2(x, t) = a_2 \sin(\omega t - kx + \phi) \quad \text{...(ii)}$$

By the principle of superposition, the net displacement of the resultant wave

$$\begin{aligned} y(x, t) &= y_1(x, t) + y_2(x, t) \\ &= a_1 \sin(\omega t - kx) + a_2 \sin(\omega t - kx + \phi) \\ &= a_1 \sin(\omega t - kx) + a_2 \sin(\omega t - kx)\cos\phi \\ &\quad + a_2 \cos(\omega t - kx)\sin\phi \\ &= \sin(\omega t - kx)(a_1 + a_2\cos\phi) \\ &\quad + \cos(\omega t - kx)\, a_2 \sin\phi \end{aligned}$$

Let $a_1 + a_2 \cos\phi = R\cos\theta$ ...(iii)

$a_2 \sin\phi = R\sin\theta$ ...(iv)

Now, $y = R\sin(\omega t - kx)\cos\theta + R\cos(\omega t - kx)\sin\theta$

$$y = R\sin(\omega t - kx + \theta) \quad \text{...(v)}$$

After squaring Eqs. (iii) and (iv), we get

$$(R\cos\theta)^2 + (R\sin\theta)^2 = (a_1 + a_2\cos\phi)^2 + (a_2\sin\phi)^2$$

$$R^2 = a_1^2 + a_2^2 + 2a_1a_2\cos\phi$$

$$[\because \cos^2\phi + \sin^2\phi = 1] \quad \text{...(vi)}$$

Intensity is directly proportional to the square of amplitude,

$$I \propto R^2$$

$$I = kR^2$$

From Eq. (vi), we get

$$I = k(a_1^2 + a_2^2 + 2a_1a_2\cos\phi)$$

$$I = ka_1^2 + ka_2^2 + k \cdot 2a_1a_2\cos\phi$$

$$\boxed{I = I_1 + I_2 + 2\sqrt{I_1 I_2}\cos\phi} \quad [\because I \propto a^2]$$

Constructive Interference

If the resultant wave has maximum amplitude then the interference is called **constructive interference.**

For maximum amplitude, $\cos\phi = +1$ or $\phi = 0, 2\pi, \dots 2n\pi$

Resultant amplitude, $A = A_{\max} = A_1 + A_2$

or

$$\boxed{I = I_{\max} = (\sqrt{I_1} + \sqrt{I_2})^2}$$

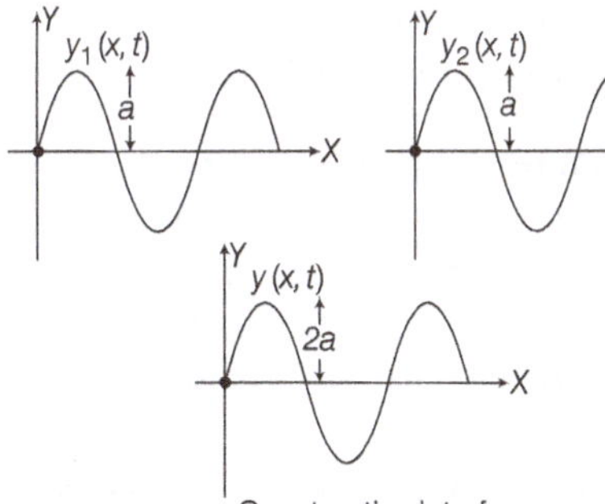

Constructive interference

Destructive Interference

If the resultant wave has minimum amplitude then the interference is called **destructive interference.**

For minimum amplitude, $\cos\phi = -1$

or $\phi = \pi, 3\pi, \ldots 2(n+1)\pi$

Resultant amplitude $A = A_{\min} = A_1 - A_2$

or $$\boxed{I = I_{\min} = (\sqrt{I_1} - \sqrt{I_2})^2}$$

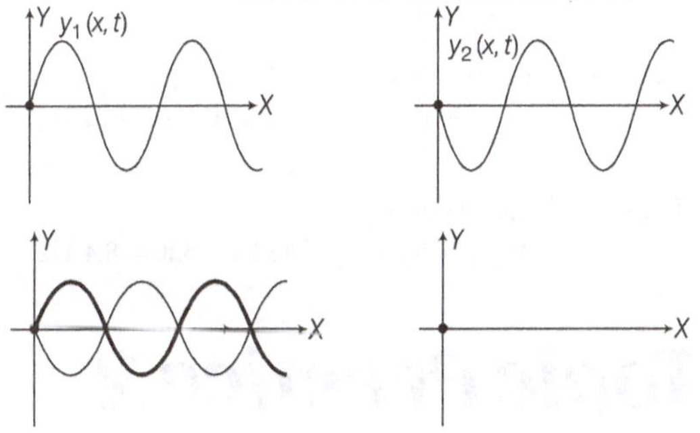

Destructive interference

The graph given below shows the variation of resultant intensity, I with $(I_1 + I_2)$.

i.e. sum of individual intensities

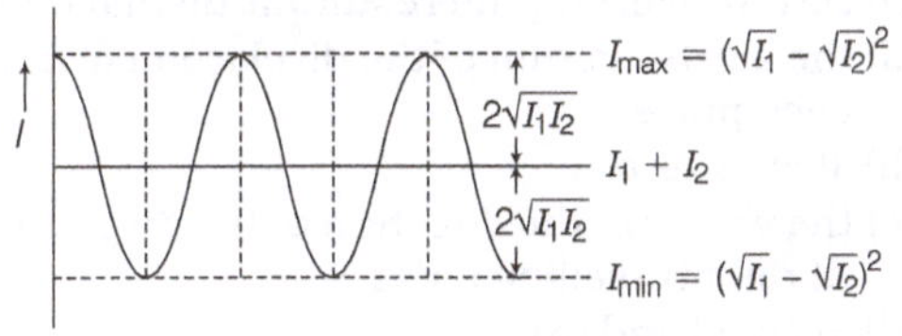

From the graph it is clear that $I_{\max}$ exceeds the sum of individual intensities $(I_1 + I_2)$ by $2\sqrt{I_1 I_2}$, while $I_{\min}$ lacks $(I_1 + I_2)$ by $2\sqrt{I_1 I_2}$, i.e. in interference energy is neither created nor destroyed, but is redistributed.

Example 1 **Let us Mix with Each Other**

Two waves of equal frequencies have their amplitudes in the ratio of 3 : 5. They are superimposed on each other. Calculate the ratio of $I_{\max}/I_{\min}$.

Sol. $\dfrac{A_1}{A_2} = \dfrac{3}{5} \Rightarrow \sqrt{\dfrac{I_1}{I_2}} = \dfrac{3}{5}$

Now, $$\frac{I_{\max}}{I_{\min}} = \left(\frac{\sqrt{I_1} + \sqrt{I_2}}{\sqrt{I_1} - \sqrt{I_2}}\right)^2 = \left(\frac{\sqrt{I_1/I_2} + 1}{\sqrt{I_1/I_2} - 1}\right)^2$$

$$= \left(\frac{3/5 + 1}{3/5 - 1}\right)^2 = \frac{64}{4} = \frac{16}{1}$$

Beats

This phenomenon arises from interference of waves having nearly same frequencies. The periodic variation in the intensity of sound wave caused by the superposition of two sound waves of nearly same frequencies and amplitude travelling in the same direction are called **beats.**

One rise and one fall in the intensity of sound constitutes **one beat** and the number of beats per second is called **beat frequency.**

The frequency of two sources or two waves should not differ by more than 10 Hz because, if it is more than 10 Hz, then it becomes difficult to distinguish between rise and fall in intensity of sound due to persistence of hearing.

Artists use the phenomenon of beat, while tuning their instruments with each other. They go on tuning until their sensitive ears do not detect any beats. In this way, they match the frequencies of different instruments of the band.

Analytical Method of Beats

Let us consider two harmonic sound waves of nearly equal angular frequency ω_1 and ω_2 and suppose we are concerned with $y = 0$ only. Then, we can write the equations of waves as

$$y_1 = a\cos\omega_1 t \text{ and } y_2 = a\cos\omega_2 t$$

Here, we are considering sound wave, hence waves are represented by y_1, y_2 to show longitudinal displacement.

Now, by principle of superposition, the resultant displacement (y) is

$$y = y_1 + y_2$$
$$= a[\cos\omega_1 t + \cos\omega_2 t]$$
$$= 2a\cos\frac{(\omega_1 - \omega_2)t}{2}\cos\frac{(\omega_1 + \omega_2)t}{2}$$
$$= 2a\cos\omega_b t\cos\omega_a t$$

where, $\omega_b = \dfrac{\omega_1 - \omega_2}{2}$ and $\omega_a = \dfrac{\omega_1 + \omega_2}{2}$

Now, if we assume $|\omega_1 - \omega_2| << \omega_1, \omega_2$ which means $\omega_a >> \omega_b$. This can be interpreted as the resultant wave is oscillating with the average angular frequency ω_a. The amplitude will be maximum when $|\cos \omega_b t|$ is 1.

Hence, the resultant wave, waxes and wanes with a frequency which is $2\omega_b = \omega_1 - \omega_2$.

Hence, beat frequency,

$$\text{Beat frequency, } \nu_{beat} = \nu_1 - \nu_2.$$

The figures below illustrate the phenomenon of beats for two harmonic waves of frequencies 11 Hz and 9 Hz. The amplitude of the resultant wave shows beats at a frequency of 2 Hz.

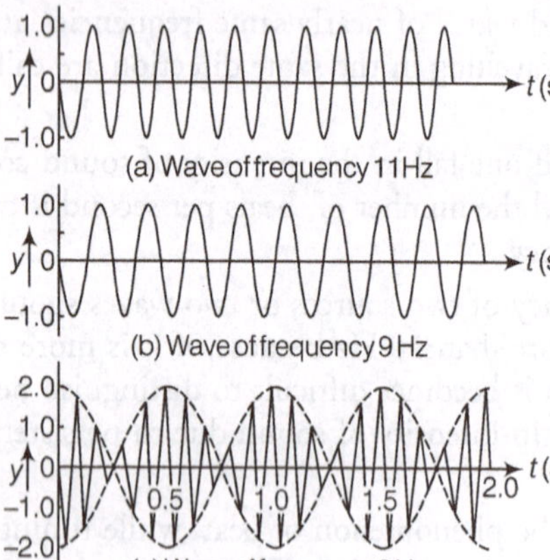

(a) Wave of frequency 11 Hz
(b) Wave of frequency 9 Hz
(c) Wave of frequency 2 Hz

Musical Pillars

Temples often have some pillars. The rock used produces basic notes.

Musical pillars are categorised into three types.

Shruti pillar It can produce the basic note 'swaras'.

Ganga Thoongal It produces the basic tunes which make up the 'ragas'.

Laya Thoongal It produces 'taal' (beats) when tapped.

Example 2 Two sitar strings A and B playing the note 'Dha' are slightly out of tune and produce beats of frequency 5 Hz. The tension of string B is slightly increased and the beat frequency is found to decrease to 3 Hz. What is the original frequency of B, if the frequency of A is 427 Hz? **NCERT**

Sol. Here, frequency of $A = 427$ Hz

As number of beats/sec $(m) = 5$ Hz

$\therefore$ Possible frequencies of B are (427 ± 5) Hz $= 432$ Hz or 422 Hz.

When tension of B is increased, its frequency increases. Number of beats/s decreases to 3.

Therefore, m is negative.

Hence, original frequency of $B = 427 - 5 = 422$ Hz.

Example 3 Consider the two identical piano strings, each tuned exactly to the 420 Hz. The tension in any one of the strings is increased by 2.0%. If they are now struck, what is the beat frequency between the fundamentals of the two strings? (Take, length of the strings $= 65$ cm).

Sol. If ν_1, v_1, T_1 and ν_2, v_2, T_2 are the frequencies, velocity and tension in the first and second strings respectively, then

$$\frac{\nu_2}{\nu_1} = \frac{v_2/2L}{v_1/2L} = \frac{v_2}{v_1} \Rightarrow \frac{\nu_2}{\nu_1} = \frac{\sqrt{T_2/\mu}}{\sqrt{T_1/\mu}} = \sqrt{\frac{T_2}{T_1}}$$

Given that the tension in one string is 2.0% larger than the other,

i.e. $T_2 = T_1 + \frac{2}{100} T_1 = 1.02\, T_1$

The ratio of frequencies,

$$\frac{\nu_2}{\nu_1} = \sqrt{\frac{1.02\, T_1}{T_1}} = 1.02 \text{ Hz}$$

Now, solve for the frequency of the tightened string.

$$\nu_2 = 1.02\, \nu_1 = 1.02 \times 420 = 428.4 \text{ Hz}$$

[given, $\nu_1 = 420$ Hz]

Thus, the beat frequency,

$$\nu_{beat} = \nu_2 - \nu_1 = 428.4 - 420 = 8.4 \text{ Hz}$$

Topic Practice 2

Multiple Choice Questions

(1 Mark)

1. When two wave pulses travelling in opposite direction overlap, the resultant displacement is
(a) the algebraic sum of the displacement due to each pulse
(b) always zero
(c) the vector in the direction of the displacement of right travelling pulse
(d) Both (a) and (b)

2. Two pulses having equal and opposite displacements moving in opposite directions overlap at $t = t_1$ second. The resultant displacement of the wave at $t = t_1$ second is
(a) twice the displacement of each pulse
(b) half the displacement of each pulse
(c) zero
(d) Either (a) or (c)

3. Two sine waves travel in the same direction in a medium. The amplitude of each wave is A and the phase difference between the two waves is 120°. The resultant amplitude will be
(a) A (b) $2A$ (c) $4A$ (d) $\sqrt{2}A$

4. A source of unknown frequency gives 4 beat/s when sounded with a source of known frequency 250 Hz. The second harmonic of the source of unknown frequency gives 5 beat/s when sounded with a source of frequency 513 Hz. The unknown frequency is
(a) 254 Hz (b) 246 Hz (c) 240 Hz (d) 260 Hz

5. When two tuning forks (fork 1 and fork 2) are sounded simultaneously, 4 beats/s are heard. Now, some tape is attached on the prong of the fork 2. When the tuning forks are sounded again, 6 beats/s are heard. If frequency of fork 1 is 200 Hz, then what was the original frequency of fork 2?
(a) 200 Hz (b) 202 Hz
(c) 196 Hz (d) 204 Hz

Very Short Answer Type Questions
1 Mark

6. Why is interference not possible in the sound produced by two violins.

7. In what multiplies of $\frac{\lambda}{2}$ will be the path difference between two destructive interference waves having the same wavelength, phase and amplitude.

8. Why should the difference between the frequencies be less than 10 to produce beats?

9. What do you mean by the beat frequency?

10. When two waves of almost equal frequencies n_1 and n_2 reach at a point, simultaneously. What is the time interval between successive maxima? **NCERT Exemplar**

Short Answer Type I Questions
2 Marks

11. State the necessary conditions for the interference of two sound waves.

12. State the necessary conditions for the constructive and destructive interference.

13. As in sound, can beats be observed by two light sources? Explain.

Short Answer Type II Questions
3 Marks

14. Two waves of the same frequency and amplitudes a and $3a$ are superimposed on each other.
(i) For what values of the phase difference ϕ, the amplitude A of the resultant wave will be maximum and for what values minimum?
(ii) Calculate the maximum intensities of the resultant wave.

15. Explain the principle of superposition of waves.

16. Derive an expression of beat frequency by analytical method.

Long Answer Type Questions
5 Marks

17. What do you understand by superposition of sound waves? Use this principle in interference of waves and obtain the relation
$$I_{max} = (a_1 + a_2)^2$$
where, a_1 and a_2 are amplitude.

18. What do you mean by interference of waves? Explain, constructive, destructive interference and write the phase relationship, respectively.

19. What are beats? Prove that the number of beats per second produced by two sources of sound is equal to the difference in the frequencies of two sources $(\nu_1 - \nu_2)$.

Numerical Problems

20. Write the amplitude of resultant wave produced by the superposition of two waves of the same frequency and amplitude A_1 and A_2, when the phase difference between the waves is
(i) 90° (ii) 180° **[2 M]**

21. The number of beats produced per second by the vibrations.
If $y_1 = 10\sin(100\pi t)$ and $y_2 = 10\sin(104\pi t)$ **[2 M]**

22. A tuning fork A, marked 512 Hz, produces 5 beats per second, where sounded with another unmarked tuning fork B. If B is loaded with wax, the number of beats is again 5 per second. What is the frequency of the tuning fork B when not loaded? **NCERT Exemplar [2 M]**

23. Two sitar strings *A* and *B* playing the note 'Ga' are slightly out of tune and produce beats of frequency 6 Hz. The tension in the string *A* is slightly reduced and the beat frequency is found to reduce to 3 Hz. If the original frequency of *A* is 324 Hz, then what is the frequency of *B*? **NCERT [2 M]**

24. The ratio of intensities of two waves is 16 : 9. What is the ratio of amplitudes? If these two waves produces interference, then find the ratio of maximum and minimum intensities. **[3 M]**

25. *X*, *Y* and *Z* are three tuning forks. The frequency of *A* is 350 Hz, *X* and *Y* produce 5 beats per second, while *Y* and *Z* produce 4 beats per second. When *X* is loaded with some iron flux, it produces 2 beats per second with *Y* and 6 beats per second with *Z*. What are the frequencies of *Y* and *Z*? **[5 M]**

Hints & Solutions

1. (*a*) When the pulses overlap, the resultant displacement is the algebraic sum of the displacement due to each pulse.

2. (*c*) The displacement due to two pulses will exactly cancel out each other and there is no displacement throughout.

3. (*a*) Amplitude of the resultant of the two waves

$$= A(\phi) = 2A\cos\left(\frac{\phi}{2}\right)$$

Given, $\phi = 120° \Rightarrow A(\phi) = 2A\cos\left(\frac{120°}{2}\right) = 2A\cos 60°$

or $A(\phi) = (2A) \times \frac{1}{2} = A$

4. (*a*) Given

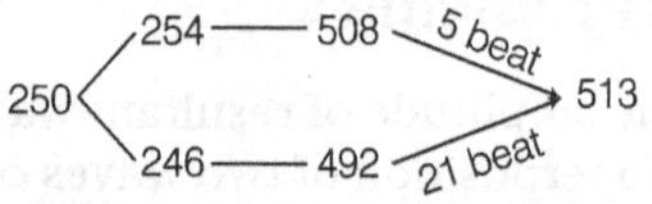

Hence, unknown frequency is 254 Hz.

5. (*c*) The frequency of fork 2 = 200 ± 4 = 196 or 204 Hz.

Since, on attaching the tape on the prong of fork 2, its frequency decreases, but now the number of beats per second is 6, i.e. the frequency difference now increases. It is possible only when before attaching the tape, the frequency of fork 2 is less than the frequency of tuning fork 1. Hence, the original frequency of fork 2 was 196 Hz.

6. For interference, the phase difference between the waves must remain constant. Each violin produces wave train of sound discontinuously, hence the phase arriving at a point varies with time.

7. Odd multiples.

8. Human ear cannot identify any change in intensity is less than $\left(\frac{1}{10}\right)$th of a second. So, difference should be less than 10.

9. The number of beats per second is called beat frequency.

10. Number of beats/second = $(n_1 - n_2)$

Hence, time interval between two successive beats = time interval between two successive maxima = $\frac{1}{n_1 - n_2}$

11. Refer to text on pages 480 and 481 (Interference of two waves).

12. Refer to text on pages 480 and 481 (Constructive interference and destructive interference).

13. No. To observe beats by two light sources, the phase difference between the source should change regularly. In light source consists of enumerative atoms and each atom emits independently. [2]

14. (i) $\phi_{max} = 0, 2\pi, 4\pi......$ and $\phi_{min} = \pi, 3\pi, 5\pi.......$ [1½]

(ii) As we know,

$$I = A_1^2 + A_2^2 + 2A_1A_2$$

$$= a^2 + 9a^2 + 2 \times a \times 3a = 16a^2$$ [1½]

15. Refer to text on page 480 (Principle of superposition of waves).

16. Refer to text on pages 481 and 482 (Analytical method of beats).

17. Refer to text on pages 480 and 481 (Principle of superposition of waves and interference of two waves).

18. Refer to text on pages 480 and 481 (Interference of two waves and constructive and destructive interference).

19. Refer to text on pages 481 and 482 (Beats and analytical method of beats).

20. Given, amplitude = A_1 and A_2

and phase differences = 90° and 180°

So, for maxima,

$$R = \sqrt{a_1^2 + a_2^2 + 2a_1a_2\cos\phi}$$

$$R_{90°} = \sqrt{A_1^2 + A_2^2 + 2A_1A_2\cos 90°} = \sqrt{A_1^2 + A_2^2}$$ [1]

Similarly,

$$R_{180°} = \sqrt{A_1^2 + A_2^2 + 2A_1A_2\cos 180°} = A_1 - A_2$$ [1]

21. As we know, general equation of wave,

$$Y = A\sin\omega t = A\sin(2\pi ft) \quad (\because \omega = 2\pi f)$$ [1]

So, by comparing the wave equations,

$$f_1 = 50\text{ Hz and } f_2 = 52\text{ Hz}$$

$$\text{Beats} = f_2 - f_1 = 52 - 50 = 2\text{ Hz}$$ [1]

22. Frequency of *A*, $\nu_0 = 512$ Hz

Number of beats/second = 5

Frequency of $B = 512 \pm 5 = 517$ or 517 Hz [1]

On loading its frequency decreases from 517 to 507, so that number of beats/second remain 5.

Hence, frequency of *B* when not loaded = 517 Hz. [1]

23. Given, frequency of A, $f_A = 324$ Hz

Now, frequency of B, $f_B = f_A \pm$ beat frequency

$$= 324 \pm 6$$

or $f_B = 330$ or 318 Hz [1]

Now, if tension in the string is slightly reduced, its frequency will also reduce from 324 Hz.

Now, if $f_B = 330$ and f_A reduces, then beat frequency should increase which is not the case, but if $f_B = 318$ Hz and f_A decreases, the beat frequency should decrease, which is the case and hence $f_B = 318$ Hz. [1]

24. Given, $I_1 : I_2 = 16 : 9$

We know, $\frac{I_1}{I_2} = \frac{a_1^2}{a_2^2} = \frac{16}{9}$

$$\Rightarrow \quad \frac{a_1}{a_2} = \frac{4}{3} \Rightarrow a_1 = \frac{4}{3} a_2 \quad \text{...(i)}$$ [1]

So, $$\frac{I_{max}}{I_{min}} = \frac{k(a_1 + a_2)^2}{k(a_1 - a_2)^2}$$ [1]

From Eq. (i), we get

$$\frac{I_{max}}{I_{min}} = \frac{\left(\frac{4}{3}a_2 + a_2\right)}{\left(\frac{4}{3}a_2 - a_2\right)} = \frac{49}{1}$$ [1]

25. Possible frequencies for fork Y,

$350 \pm 5 = 355$ and 345 Hz [1]

X is loaded with iron flux, so its frequency decrease from 350 Hz.

Now, frequency = 345 ($\because$ produce 2 beats) [1]

The frequency of X decrease from 350 to 347 Hz.

The fork X, loads with iron flux, produces 6 beats/s with Z.

$347 \pm 6 = 353$ or 341 Hz [1]

But X (frequency 345) and Z produces 4 beats/s. [1]

Hence, the frequency of Z cannot be 353 Hz.

$\therefore$ Frequency of $Z = 341$ Hz [1]

TOPIC 03 Stationary or Standing Wave

Reflection of Waves

If a pulse or wave meets a rigid boundary, they get reflected, e.g. Echo. If the boundary is not completely rigid, a part of the incident wave is reflected and a part is transmitted into the second medium.

If a wave is incident obliquely on the boundary between two different media, the transmitted wave is called the **refracted wave.** The incident and refracted waves obey Snell's law of refraction and incident and reflected waves obey usual laws of reflection.

Reflection of a pulse meeting a rigid boundary is shown in the figure below

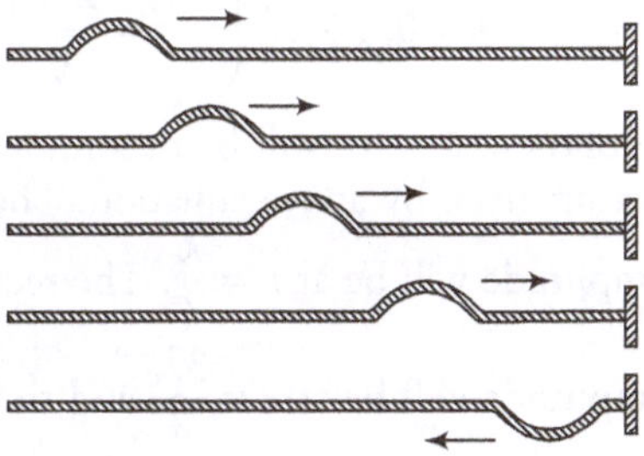

Reflection of pulse meeting a rigid boundary

In the above diagram, the travelling pulse is moving towards the non-absorptive wall (i.e. there is no absorption of energy at the boundary). As the displacement of connecting point at the boundary must be zero, hence by the principle of superposition, the reflected wave must have equal amplitude as well as phase difference of π.

If boundary point is completely free to move, the reflected pulse has the same phase and amplitude as the incident pulse. The net maximum displacement at the boundary will be twice of amplitude of each pulse.

Let the incident travelling wave is

$$y(x, t) = a \sin(kx - \omega t)$$

At the rigid boundary, the reflected wave is given by

$$y_r(x, t) = a \sin(kx - \omega t + \pi)$$
$$= -a \sin(kx - \omega t)$$

At an open boundary, the reflected wave is given by

$$y_r(x, t) = a \sin(kx - \omega t + 0)$$
$$= a \sin(kx - \omega t)$$

At the rigid boundary, $y' = y + y_r = 0$ at all times.

Standing Waves and Normal Modes

Standing Waves

A new set of waves formed when two sets of progressive wave trains of the same type, i.e. both transverse or both longitudinal having the same amplitude and same time period/frequency/wavelength and travelling with same speed along the same straight line in opposite directions superimpose are called **standing waves or stationary waves.**

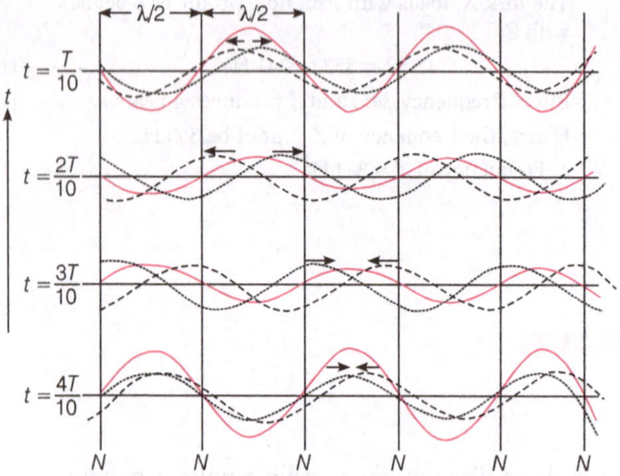

Stationary waves arising from superposition of two harmonic waves travelling in opposite directions

The resultant waves do not propagate in any direction, there is no transfer of energy in the medium.

When we are considering reflections at two or more boundaries (a string fixed at both ends or an air column in a pipe with both ends closed), here due to interference between incident and reflected wave, a steady wave pattern will set up on the string. Such wave patterns are called **standing waves** or **stationary waves.**

Now, consider wave equations

$y_1(x, t) = a \sin(kx - \omega t)$ (for wave along +ve X-axis)

$y_2(x, t) = a \sin(kx + \omega t)$ (for wave along –ve X-axis)

Resultant wave, $y(x, t) = y_1(x, t) + y_2(x, t)$

$$= a[\sin(kx - \omega t) + \sin(kx + \omega t)]$$

$$\boxed{\text{Net resultant wave, } y(t) = 2a \sin kx \cos \omega t}$$

Here, the amplitude of the standing/stationary wave is $2a \sin kx$.

Thus, in this wave pattern, the amplitude varies from point-to-point, but each element of the string oscillates with the same angular frequency ω or time period and there is no phase difference.

As the wave pattern remains stationary, the amplitude is fixed at a given location, but different at different locations.

Normal Modes

Points having zero amplitude (i.e. where, there is no motion are called **nodes** and the points having largest amplitude are known as **antinodes.**

The significant feature of stationary waves is that the system cannot oscillate with any arbitrary frequency, but is characterised by a set of natural frequencies or **normal modes** of oscillation.

Now, let us determine these normal modes for a stretched string fixed at both ends.

From above equation for **nodes,** the amplitude is zero for values of kx that give $\sin kx = 0$

$\sin kx = 0 \Rightarrow kx = n\pi$; where, $n = 0, 1, 2, 3, 4, \ldots$

$$\Rightarrow \boxed{\text{For nodes, } x = \frac{n\pi}{k}}$$

$$x = \frac{n\pi}{2\pi/\lambda} = \frac{n\lambda}{2}; \text{ where, } n = 0, 1, 2, 3, \ldots$$

So, the first node is formed at $x = 0$. The second node is formed at $x = \frac{\lambda}{2}$ and so on.

Hence, distance between two successive nodes is $\frac{\lambda}{2}$.

For **antinodes,** the maximum value of amplitude is $2a$ which occurs for values of kx that give $|\sin kx| = 1$

$$\Rightarrow \quad kx = \left(n + \frac{1}{2}\right)\pi; \text{ where, } n = 0, 1, 2, 3, \ldots$$

$$\Rightarrow \boxed{\text{For antinodes, } x = (2n + 1)\frac{\lambda}{4}}$$

$$n = 0, 1, 2, \ldots \left(\because k = \frac{2\pi}{\lambda}\right) \quad \ldots\text{(i)}$$

Thus, the amplitude of wave will be maximum at the position of string given by above equation. The first maximum amplitude will be at $x = \frac{\lambda}{4}$. The second maximum amplitude will be at $x = \frac{3\lambda}{4}$ and so on.

Hence, distance between two consecutive antinodes is $\frac{\lambda}{2}$.

Example 1 The two individual wave functions are $y_1 = (5 \text{ cm}) \sin (4x - t)$ and $y_2 = (5 \text{ cm}) \sin (4x + t)$ where, x and y are in centimetres. Find out the maximum displacement of the motion at $x = 2.0$ cm. Also, find the positions of nodes and antinodes.

Sol. Given, $y_1 = (5 \text{ cm}) \sin (4x - t)$

$y_2 = (5 \text{ cm}) \sin (4x + t)$

The resulting wave,

$$y = (2A \sin kx) \cos \omega t$$

Now, compare the given equation,

$y_1 = (5 \text{ cm}) \sin (4x - t)$ with $y_1 = A \sin (kx - \omega t)$.

$A = 5$ cm, $k = 4$ and $\omega = 1$ rad/s

$$y = (2A \sin kx) \cos \omega t$$

$$y = (10 \sin 4x) \cos t$$

The maximum displacement of the motion at position $x = 2.0$ cm

$$y_{max} = 10 \sin 4x |_{x = 2.0}$$

$$= 10 \sin (4 \times 2) = 10 \sin (8 \text{ rad})$$

$$y_{max} = 9.89 \text{ cm}$$

The wavelength by using the relation between wavelength and wave number,

$$k = \frac{2\pi}{\lambda} = 4$$

$$\Rightarrow \quad \lambda = \frac{2\pi}{4} = \frac{\pi}{2} \text{ cm}$$

The nodes and antinodes can be given as

Nodes at $x = \frac{n\lambda}{2} = n \times \left(\frac{\pi}{4}\right)$ cm

where, $n = 0, 1, 2, \ldots$

Antinodes at $x = (2n+1)\frac{\lambda}{4} = (2n+1) \times \left(\frac{\pi}{8}\right)$ cm

where, $n = 0, 1, 2, \ldots$

Comparison between Progressive and Standing Waves

Progressive Waves	Standing Waves
These waves advance in a medium with definite velocity.	These waves remain stationary between two boundaries in the medium.
In these waves, all particles of the medium oscillate with same frequency and amplitude.	In these waves, all particles except nodes oscillate with same frequency, but different amplitude. It is zero at nodes and maximum at antinodes.
At any instant, the phase of vibration varies continuously from one particle to the other, i.e. phase difference between two particles can have any value between zero and 2π.	At any instant, the phase of all particles between two successive nodes is the same, but phase of particles on one side of a node is opposite to the phase of particles on the other side of the node, i.e. phase difference between any two particles can be either zero or π.
In these waves, at no instant, all particles of the medium pass through their mean positions simultaneously.	In these waves, all particles of the medium pass through their mean positions simultaneously twice in each time period.

Vibrations of Stretched String

In an unbounded continuous medium, there is no restriction on the frequencies or wavelengths of the standing waves. However, if the waves are confined in space, (e.g. when a string is tied at both ends) standing waves can be setup for a discrete set of frequencies or wavelengths.

Consider a string of definite length l, rigidly held at both ends. When we setup a sinusoidal wave on such a string, it gets reflected from the fixed ends. By the superposition of two identical waves travelling in opposite directions standing waves are established on the string. The only requirement we have to satisfy is that the end points should be nodes as these points cannot oscillate.

The nodes are permanently at rest. There may be any number of nodes in between or none at all, so that the wavelength associated with the standing waves can take on many different values. The distance between adjacent nodes is $\lambda/2$, so that in a string of length l, there must be exactly an integral number n of half wavelengths $\lambda/2$. i.e.

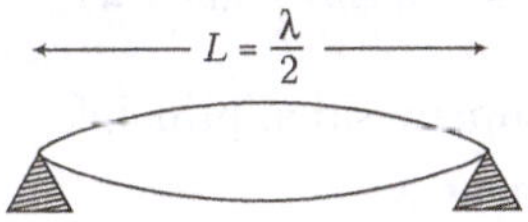

$$\frac{n\lambda}{2} = l \text{ or } \lambda = \frac{2l}{n} \quad \text{(where, } n = 1, 2, 3, \ldots)$$

$$n = \frac{v}{\lambda} = \frac{v}{2l}$$

Since, speed of wave, $v = \sqrt{\frac{T}{\mu}}$

$$n = \frac{1}{2l}\sqrt{\frac{T}{\mu}}$$

Laws of Transverse Vibration of a Stretched String

(i) **Law of Length** For a given string under a tension (T), the frequency of the vibrating string is inversely proportional to the vibrating length (L) of the string.

i.e. $f \propto \frac{1}{L} \Rightarrow fL = \text{constant} \Rightarrow f_1L_1 = f_2L_2$

(ii) **Law of Tension** The frequency of the uniform string of given length is proportional to the square root of the tension (T) in the string.

i.e. $f \propto \sqrt{T} \Rightarrow \dfrac{f}{\sqrt{T}} = \text{constant} \Rightarrow \dfrac{f_1}{f_2} = \sqrt{\dfrac{T_1}{T_2}}$

(iii) **Law of Mass** For a given vibrating length and tension of the string, the frequency of the vibrating string is inversely proportional to the square root of the mass per unit length of the string.

i.e. $f \propto \dfrac{1}{\sqrt{\mu}}$

Standing Waves in String Fixed at Both Ends

Consider a stretched string having length L fixed at both ends. The one end be at $x = 0$ fixed, while the other one at $x = L$ and at $x = L$, a node will be obtained as this end is fixed.

The wave motion is represented by

$$y_1 = a \sin \frac{2\pi}{\lambda}(vt - x) \quad \text{[along X-axis]} \quad \text{...(i)}$$

After reflection, phase change by π,

$$y_2 = a \sin\left[\frac{2\pi}{\lambda}(vt + x) + \pi\right]$$

$$= -a \sin \frac{2\pi}{\lambda}(vt + x) \quad \text{...(ii)}$$

According to the superposition principle, resultant displacement,

$$y = y_1 + y_2$$

$$y = a \sin \frac{2\pi}{\lambda}(vt - x) - a \sin \frac{2\pi}{\lambda}(vt + x)$$

$$y = -a\left[\sin \frac{2\pi}{\lambda}(vt + x) - \sin \frac{2\pi}{\lambda}(vt - x)\right]$$

$$y = -2a \cos\left(\frac{2\pi vt}{\lambda}\right) \sin\left(\frac{2\pi x}{\lambda}\right) \quad \text{...(iii)}$$

At the boundary condition ($x = 0$ and $x = l$),

$y = 0$ at $x = 0$

$y = 0$ at $x = l$

Applying the second condition in Eq. (iii), we get

$$0 = -2a \cos\left(\frac{2\pi vt}{\lambda}\right) \sin\left(\frac{2\pi l}{\lambda}\right)$$

$$\sin\left(\frac{2\pi l}{\lambda}\right) = 0 \Rightarrow \frac{2\pi l}{\lambda} = n\pi \Rightarrow \lambda = \frac{2l}{n}$$

Here, $n = 1, 2, 3, \ldots$

Modes of Vibration

The manner in which the string vibrates and give rise to a standing wave is known as **mode of vibration** of the string.

First Mode of Vibration

The mode of vibration in which string will vibrate in one segment or the lowest possible natural frequency (as shown in figure) is called **fundamental mode** or **first harmonic.**

As, $l = \dfrac{n\lambda}{2}$ for first harmonic, put $n = 1$, then

$$l = \frac{\lambda_1}{2} \quad \text{and} \quad \nu = \frac{v}{2l}$$

Second Mode of Vibration

The mode of vibration in which string will vibrate in two segments (as shown in figure) is called **second harmonic** or **first overtone.** For the second harmonic, put $n = 2$ in $l = \dfrac{n\lambda}{2}$

For this, $l = \lambda_2$ and $\nu_2 = \dfrac{2v}{2l}$ or $2\nu_1$

As, $\nu = \dfrac{nv}{2l}$

Third Mode of Vibration

If $n = 3$, the frequency $\nu = \dfrac{3v}{2L}$ or $\nu = 3\nu_1$ is called **third harmonic** and so on.

Figure below shows the first four harmonics of a stretched string fixed at both ends.

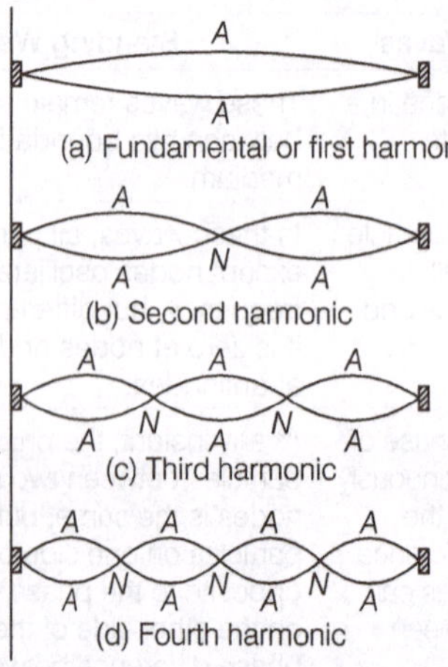

The vibration of a string will be a superposition of different modes. Some modes may be strongly excited and some less.

Note Musical instruments like sitar or violin are based on this principle. Where the string is plucked or bowed, determines which modes are more prominent than others.

Example 2 A guitar string is 100 cm long and has a fundamental frequency of 125 Hz. Where should it be pressed to produce a fundamental frequency of 200 Hz ?

Sol. Fundamental frequency of a string fixed at both end is

$$\nu = \frac{v}{2L}$$

$$\nu = \frac{1}{2L}\sqrt{\frac{T}{\mu}} \qquad \left[\because v = \sqrt{\frac{T}{\mu}}\right]$$

As T and μ are fixed, so

$$\frac{\nu_1}{\nu_2} = \frac{L_2}{L_1} \Rightarrow L_2 = \frac{\nu_1}{\nu_2} L_1$$

$$\Rightarrow \quad L_2 = \frac{125 \text{ Hz}}{200 \text{ Hz}} \times 100$$

$$= \frac{125}{2} = 62.5 \text{ cm}$$

Vibration of a String Fixed at one End

Standing waves can also be produced on a string which is fixed at one end and whose other end is free to move in a transverse direction. Here, in this case, we will have antinode at the free end and node at the fixed end.

Now, consider the equation of standing wave,

$$y(x, t) = 2a \sin kx \cos \omega t$$

As we are having antinode at the end, $x = L$

$$\Rightarrow \quad \sin kL = \pm 1 \quad \Rightarrow \quad kL = (2n+1)\frac{\pi}{2}$$

where, $n = 0, 1, 2, \ldots$

$$\Rightarrow \quad \frac{2\pi}{\lambda} \times L = (2n+1)\frac{\pi}{2}$$

$$\Rightarrow \quad \frac{2L}{\lambda} = (2n+1) \times \frac{1}{2}$$

$$\Rightarrow \quad \frac{2Lv}{v} = (2n+1)\frac{1}{2}$$

$$\boxed{\text{Frequency of the vibration, } \nu = \frac{(2n+1)}{4L} v}$$

where, $n = 0, 1, 2, \ldots$

where, ν is frequency and v is the speed of the wave.

The above frequencies are the normal frequencies of vibration. The fundamental frequency is obtained when $n = 0$.

$$\nu_0 = \frac{v}{4L} \qquad \text{[first harmonic]}$$

The overtone frequencies are

$$\nu_1 = \frac{3v}{4L} = 3\nu_0 \qquad \text{[third harmonic]}$$

$$\nu_2 = \frac{5v}{4L} = 5\nu_0 \qquad \text{[fifth harmonic]}$$

$$\nu_3 = \frac{7v}{4L} = 7\nu_0 \qquad \text{[seventh harmonic]}$$

$\nu_0 : \nu_1 : \nu_2 : \nu_3 \ldots = 1:3:5:7:\ldots$

Here, we see that only odd harmonics are present. (i.e. contains odd multiples of the fundamental frequency)

The figure below shows shapes of the string.

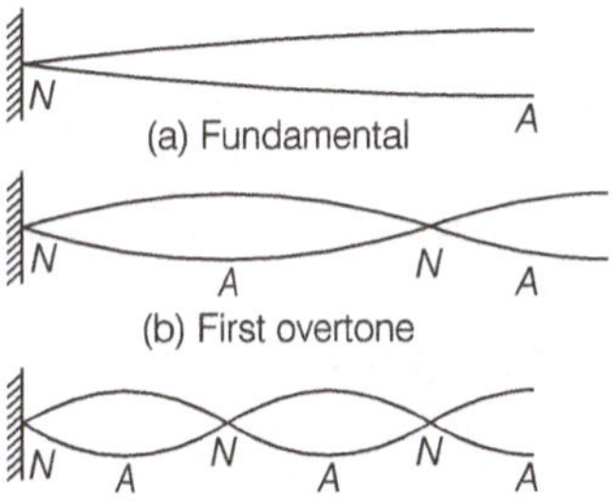

(a) Fundamental

(b) First overtone

(c) Second overtone

Example 3 A 50 cm long wire of mass 20 g supports a mass of 1.6 kg as shown in figure. Find the fundamental frequency of the portion of the string between the wall and the pulley. (Take $g = 10 \text{ m/s}^2$)

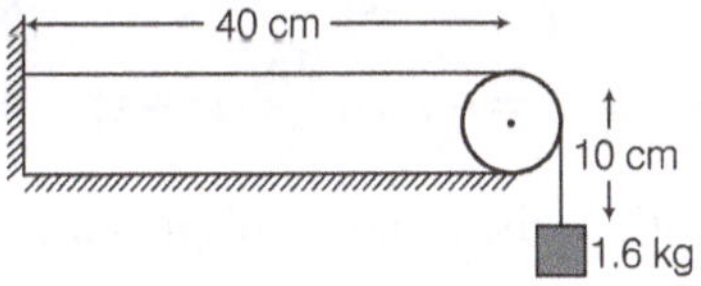

Sol. Here, mass/length, $\mu = \frac{20 \times 10^{-3}}{50/100} = 0.04$ kg/m

$$T = 1.6 \text{ kg} = 1.6 \times 10 \text{ N} = 16 \text{ N}$$

Length that vibrates, $L = 50 - 10 = 40$ cm $= 0.4$ m

$$\therefore \quad \nu = \frac{1}{2L}\sqrt{\frac{T}{\mu}} = \frac{1}{2 \times 0.04}\sqrt{\frac{16}{0.04}} = \frac{20}{0.8} = 25 \text{ Hz}$$

Example 4 Two identical wires of length L and $2L$ vibrate with fundamental frequencies 100 Hz and 150 Hz, respectively. What is the ratio of their tensions?

Sol. Let $\quad \mu_1 = \mu_2 = \mu$

$$\nu_1 = 100 = \frac{1}{2L}\sqrt{\frac{T_1}{\mu}}$$

$$\nu_2 = 150 = \frac{1}{2(2L)}\sqrt{\frac{T_2}{\mu}}$$

$$\frac{v_1}{v_2} = \frac{100}{150} = 2\sqrt{\frac{T_1}{T_2}}$$

$$\frac{T_1}{T_2} = \left(\frac{1}{3}\right)^2 = \frac{1}{9}$$

$$\therefore \quad T_2 = 9\,T_1$$

Vibrations of Air Column in Organ Pipe

(i) Closed Organ Pipe

Closed organ pipes are those which are closed at one end and open to the other. A glass tube partially filled with water is an example of such a system. A node formed at closed end and an antinode is formed at open end. If the length of air column is L, then the closed end can be denoted by $x = 0$, while the open end can be taken as $x = L$.

Incident wave along negative X-axis is given by

$$y_1 = a \sin \frac{2\pi}{\lambda}(vt + x) \quad \text{...(i)}$$

The wave reflected at the closed end of pipe, suffers a phase change of π. The wave equation of reflected wave is given by

$$y_2 = a \sin\left[\frac{2\pi}{\lambda}(vt - x) + \pi\right]$$

$$= -a \sin \frac{2\pi}{\lambda}(vt - x) \quad \text{...(ii)}$$

After superposition, the resultant displacement at time t is given by

$$y = y_1 + y_2 = a\left[\sin \frac{2\pi}{\lambda}(vt + x) - \sin \frac{2\pi}{\lambda}(vt - x)\right]$$

After solving, we get

$$y = 2a \cos\left(\frac{2\pi vt}{\lambda}\right) \sin\left(\frac{2\pi x}{\lambda}\right)$$

At the closed end $(x = 0)$,

$$y = 0$$

At the open end $(x = l)$,

$$y = 2a \cos\left(\frac{2\pi vt}{x}\right) \sin\left(\frac{2\pi l}{\lambda}\right)$$

For the maximum value of y, $\sin\left(\dfrac{2\pi l}{\lambda}\right)$ is maximum $= \pm 1$

$$\frac{2\pi l}{\lambda} = (2n - 1)\frac{\pi}{2}$$

$$\therefore \quad \lambda = \frac{4l}{2n - 1}; \text{ where, } n = 1, 2, 3, 4, \ldots$$

Position of Nodes

Nodes are the points of zero oscillation

$$\therefore \quad \sin kx = 0 \Rightarrow kx = n\pi$$

$$\frac{2\pi}{\lambda} x = n\pi \quad \text{or} \quad x = \frac{n\lambda}{2} \quad \text{...(i)}$$

where, $n = 0, 1, 2, \ldots$

Position of Antinodes

Antinodes are the points of maximum displacement.

$$\therefore \quad \sin kx = \pm 1 \Rightarrow kx = (2n - 1)\frac{\pi}{2}$$

$$\text{or} \quad x = (2n - 1)\frac{\lambda}{4} \quad \left[\because k = 2\frac{\pi}{\lambda}\right] \quad \text{...(ii)}$$

where, $n = 1, 2, \ldots$

Modes of Vibration of Air Columns in Closed Organ Pipe

At the open end $x = L$, an antinode is formed

$$\therefore \quad L = (2n - 1)\frac{\lambda}{4} \Rightarrow \lambda = \frac{4L}{(2n - 1)}$$

where, $n = 1, 2, \ldots$

The corresponding frequencies are given by

$$f = \frac{v}{\lambda} \Rightarrow f = \frac{(2n - 1)v}{4L}$$

(i) **First Mode**

For $n = 1 \Rightarrow \lambda = 4L$ or $L = \dfrac{\lambda}{4}$ and $f_1 = \dfrac{v}{4L}$

where, f_1 = fundamental frequency,

v = speed of sound in air

and L = length of pipe.

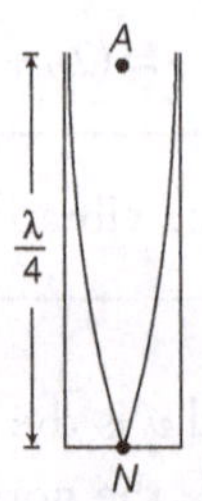

This mode is called **fundamental mode or 1st harmonic.**

(ii) **Second Mode**

For $n=2 \Rightarrow L=\frac{3\lambda}{4} \Rightarrow f_2=\frac{3v}{4L}$ or $f_2=3f_1$

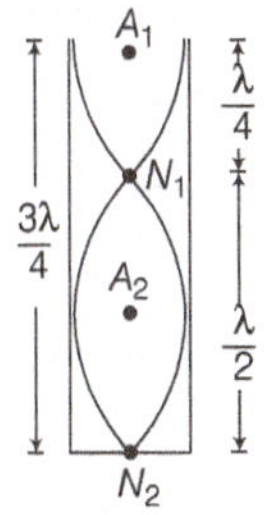

This mode is called **3rd harmonic** or **1st overtone.**

(iii) **Third Mode**

For $n=3 \Rightarrow L=\frac{5\lambda}{4}, f_3=\frac{5v}{4L}$ or $f_3=5f_1$

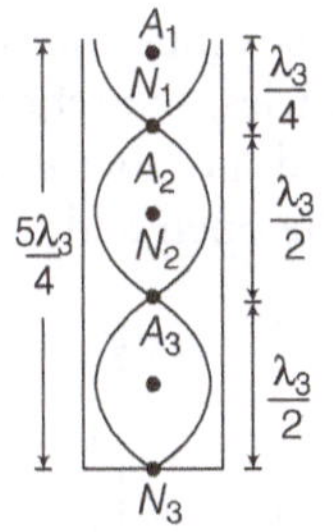

This mode is called **5th harmonic** or **2nd overtone.**

From the above discussion, we can say that in a closed organ pipe, only odd harmonics are present. Ratio of harmonic is $f_1 : f_2 : f_3 \ldots = 1:3:5 \ldots$

Ratio of overtones $= 3:5:7$.

Also, $f_n=(2n-1)f_1$ and frequency of nth overtone $f_n=(2n+1)f_1$

(ii) Open Organ Pipe

Open organ pipes are those which are open at both ends. Therefore, a displacement antinode or pressure node is formed at each end.

Let us consider a pipe of length l, which is open at both ends, lying along the X-axis. The incident and reflected waves are given by the following equation

$$y_1 = a\sin\frac{2\pi}{\lambda}(vt+x) \quad \ldots\text{(i)}$$

$$y_2 = a\sin\frac{2\pi}{\lambda}(vt-x) \quad \ldots\text{(ii)}$$

Resultant displacement,

$$y = y_1 + y_2$$

$$= a\left[\sin\frac{2\pi}{\lambda}(vt+x)+\sin\frac{2\pi}{\lambda}(vt-x)\right]$$

$$= 2a\sin\left(\frac{2\pi vt}{\lambda}\right)\cos\left(\frac{2\pi x}{\lambda}\right)$$

At both ends of the pipe, the resultant displacement should always be maximum.

$$y = 2a\sin\left(\frac{2\pi vt}{\lambda}\right)\cos\left(\frac{2\pi l}{\lambda}\right)$$

y will always is maximum, if

$\cos\left(\frac{2\pi l}{\lambda}\right)$ is maximum $=\pm 1$

$$\frac{2\pi l}{\lambda} = n\pi$$

$$\Rightarrow \quad \lambda = \frac{2l}{n}$$

Position of Antinodes

For position of antinodes,

$$\cos kx = \pm 1 \quad \Rightarrow \quad kx = n\pi$$

where, $n = 0, 1, 2, 3, \ldots$

$$\frac{2\pi}{\lambda}x = n\pi \quad \Rightarrow \quad x = \frac{n\lambda}{2}$$

Further at $x = L$, an antinode is formed

$$\Rightarrow \quad L = \frac{n\lambda}{2}$$

$$\Rightarrow \quad \lambda = \frac{2L}{n}$$

Modes of Vibrations of Air Column in Open Organ Pipe

The corresponding frequencies are given by

$$f = \frac{v}{\lambda} \text{ or } f = \frac{nv}{2L}$$

where, $n = 1, 2, 3, \ldots$

(i) **First mode**

For $n=1$, $\lambda_1 = 2L \Rightarrow L=\frac{\lambda_1}{2} \Rightarrow f_1=\frac{v}{2L}$

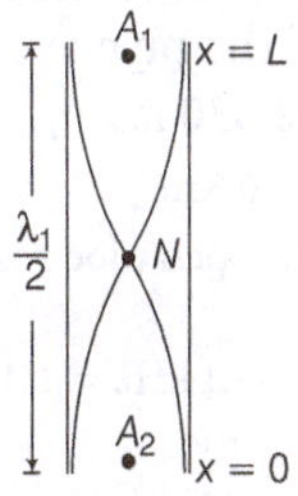

This mode is called **fundamental mode** or **1st harmonic.** Variation of excess pressure and displacement of an open organ pipe is shown in above figure.

(ii) **Second mode**

For $n=2 \Rightarrow \lambda_2 = \frac{2L}{2}$ or $L = \frac{2\lambda_2}{2}$

$f_2 = \frac{2v}{2L}$ or $f_2 = 2f_1$

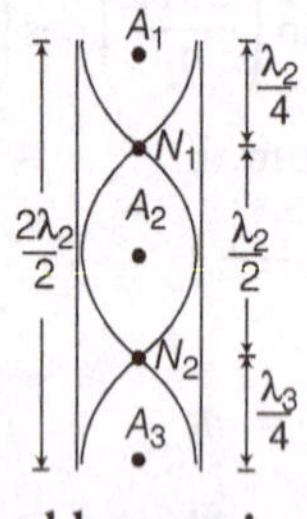

This is called **2nd harmonic** or **1st overtone.**

(iii) **Third mode**

For $n=3$, $\lambda_3 = \frac{2L}{3}$ or $L = \frac{3\lambda_3}{2}$

$\Rightarrow f_3 = \frac{3v}{2L}$ or $f_3 = 3f_1$

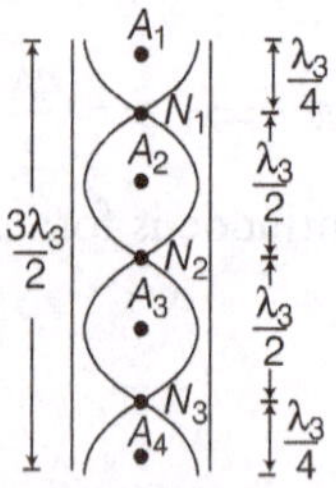

This is called **3rd harmonic** or **2nd overtone.**

Therefore, in general $f_n = nf_1$.

From the above discussion, we can say that in open organ pipe all (even and odd) harmonic are present. Ratio of harmonics is $f_1 : f_2 : f_3 \ldots = 1:2:3\ldots$ and ratio of overtones $= 2:3:4:5$.

Frequency of nth overtone is $(n+1)f_1 = f_n$

Example 5 A pipe 30.0 cm long is opened at both ends. Which harmonic mode of the pipe resonates with a 1.1 kHz source? Will resonance with the same source be observed, if one end of the pipe is closed? (Take, the speed of sound in air as 330 ms^{-1}). **NCERT**

Sol. Here, $L = 30.0 \text{ cm} = 0.3 \text{ m}$

Let nth harmonic of open pipe resonate with 1.1 kHz source, i.e.

$$\nu_n = 1.1 \text{ kHz} = 1100 \text{ Hz}$$

As, $$\nu_n = \frac{nv}{2L}$$

$$\therefore \quad n = \frac{2L\nu_n}{v} = \frac{2 \times 0.30 \times 1100}{330} = 2$$

i.e. **2nd harmonic** resonates with open pipe.

If one end of pipe is closed, its fundamental frequency put $n=0$ in $\nu = (2n+1)\frac{v}{4L}$

$$\nu_1 = \frac{v}{4L} = \frac{330}{4 \times 0.3} = 275 \text{ Hz}$$

As odd harmonics alone are produced in a closed organ pipe, therefore possible frequencies are $3\nu_1 = 3 \times 275 = 825$ Hz, $5\nu_1 = 5 \times 275 = 1375$ Hz and so on. As the source frequency is 1100 Hz, therefore **no resonance** can occur when the pipe is closed at one end.

End Correction

It was found that the antinode is not formed exactly at the open end of the **organ pipe**, but due to finite momentum of the particles, the reflection takes place a little above the open end, i.e. that is why the antinode is formed a little above the open end.

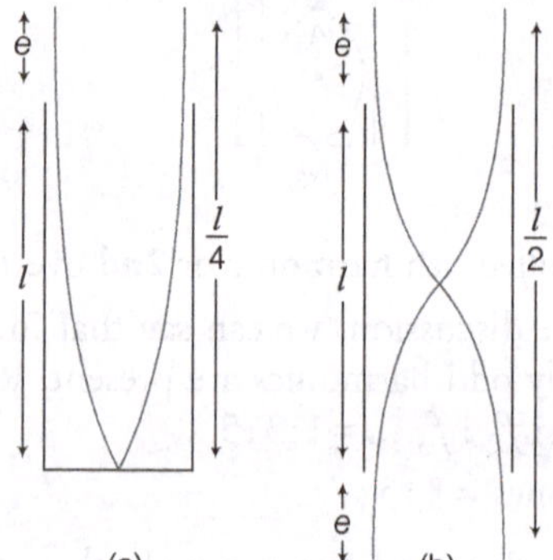

(a) For closed organ pipe (b) For open organ pipe

For obtaining true frequency, an end correction must be applied which takes account of this additional length. This is denoted by e. If length of organ pipe is l and end correction is e, then length of air column in closed pipe will be $(l+e)$ and in **open pipe** $(l+2e)$.

Thus, for a closed organ pipe replace L by $L+e$,

$$f_1 = \frac{v}{4(L+e)}$$

and for an open organ pipe replace L by $L+2e$,

$$f_2 = \frac{v}{2(L+2e)}$$

Topic Practice 3

Multiple Choice Questions

1 Mark

1. A standing wave is generated on a string. Which of the following statement(s) is/are correct for the standing waves?
   (a) The amplitude of standing wave varies from point-to-point, but each element of the string oscillates with the same angular frequency ω or time period
   (b) The string as a whole vibrates in phase with differing amplitudes at different points
   (c) The wave pattern in neither moving to the right nor to the left
   (d) All of the above

2. A wire under tension vibrates with a fundamental frequency of 600 Hz. If the length of the wire is doubled, the radius is halved and the wire is made to vibrate under one-ninth the tension, then the fundamental frequency will become
   (a) 400 Hz (b) 600 Hz
   (c) 300 Hz (d) 200 Hz

3. An air column, closed at one end and open at the other, resonates with a tunning fork when the smallest length of the column is 50 cm. The next larger length of the column resonating with the same tunning fork is
   (a) 100 cm (b) 150 cm
   (c) 200 cm (d) 66.7 cm

Very Short Answer Type Questions

1 Mark

4. What is the law of length for stretched string?

5. What do you mean by mode of vibration of the string?

6. Show that when a string fixed at its two ends vibrates in 1 loop, 2 loops, 3 loops and 4 loops, the frequencies are in the ratio 1 : 2 : 3 : 4. **NCERT Exemplar**

7. In a hot summer day, pitch of an organ pipe will be higher or lower?

Short Answer Type I Questions

2 Marks

8. What do you mean by the reflection of wave?

9. What is the stationary wave? Write down the expression of stationary wave.

10. Explain (i) nodes and (ii) antinodes.

11. What is an organ pipe? Explain its types.

12. A narrow sound pulse (e.g. A short pip by a whistle) is sent across a medium.
    (i) Does the pulse have a definite (a) frequency? (b) wavelength? (c) speed of propagation?
    (ii) If the pulse rate is 1 after every 20 s, (i.e. the whistle is blown for a split of second after every 20 s), is the frequency of the note produced by the whistle equal to 1/20 or 0.05 Hz? **NCERT**

Short Answer Type II Questions

3 Marks

13. Write the comparison between progressive and standing wave.

14. Derive an expression of frequency of vibration of stretched string.

15. Write the law of transverse vibration of a stretched string.

16. Derive an expression of standing waves in string which is fixed at both ends.

17. What is the position of node and antinode in closed organ pipe? Explain it.

Long Answer Type Questions

5 Marks

18. Explain the mode of vibration of standing wave in string which is fixed at both ends.

19. Explain the mode of vibrations of air column in open organ pipe.

20. Explain why (or how)
    (i) in a sound wave, a displacement node is a pressure antinode and *vice-versa*?

(ii) bats can ascertain distances, directions, nature and sizes of the obstacles without any eyes?

(iii) a violin note and sitar note may have the same frequency, yet we can distinguish between the two notes?

(iv) solids can support both longitudinal and transverse waves, but only longitudinal waves can propagate in gases?

(v) the shape of a pulse gets distorted during propagation in a dispersive medium?

Numerical Problems

21. A hospital uses an ultrasonic scanner to locate tumours in a tissue. What is the wavelength of sound in the tissue in which the speed of sound is 1.7 kms^{-1}? The operating frequency of the scanner is 4.2 MHz. **NCERT [1 M]**

22. A steel rod 100 cm long is clamped at its middle. The fundamental frequency of longitudinal vibrations of the rod are given to be 2.53 kHz. What is the speed of sound in steel? **[2 M]**

23. A pipe 20 cm long is closed at one end. Which harmonic mode of the pipe is resonantly excited by a source of 1237.5 Hz? (Take, sound velocity in air = 330 ms^{-1}) **NCERT Exemplar [2 M]**

24. (i) For the wave on a string described by $Y = 0.06 \sin 2\pi/3x \cos(120\pi t)$, do all the points on the string oscillate with the same (a) frequency, (b) phase and (c) amplitude?
Explain your answers.

(ii) What is the amplitude of a point 0.375 m away from one end? **[2 M]**

25. A sitar wire is replaced by another wire of same length and material, but of three times the earlier radius. If the tension in the wire remains the same, then by what factor will the frequency change? **[2 M]**

26. A wire stretched between two rigid supports vibrates in its fundamental mode with a frequency of 45 Hz. The mass of the wire is 3.5×10^{-2} kg and its linear mass density is 4.0×10^{-2} kgm^{-1}. What is

(i) the speed of a transverse wave on the string?

(ii) the tension in the string? **NCERT [2 M]**

27. The pattern of standing waves formed on a stretched string at two instants of time are shown in figure. The velocity of two waves superimposing to form stationary waves is 360 m/s and their frequencies are 256 Hz.

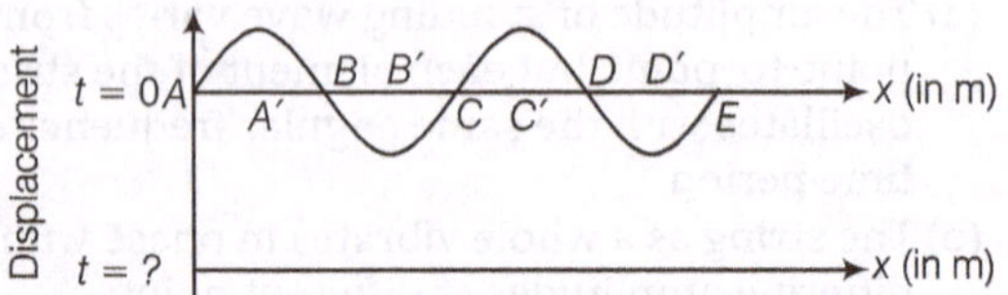

(i) Calculate the time at which the second curve is plotted.

(ii) Mark nodes and antinodes on the curve.

(iii) Calculate the distance between A' and C'. **NCERT Exemplar [3 M]**

28. The wave pattern on a stretched string is shown in figure. Interpret what kind of wave this is and find its wavelength?

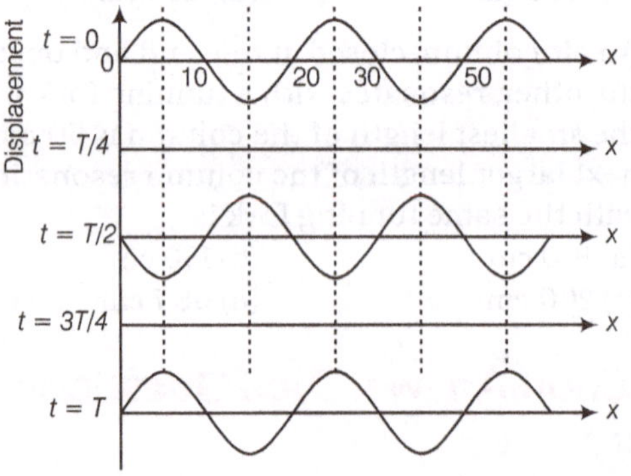

NCERT Exemplar [3 M]

29. A tuning fork vibrating with a frequency of 512 Hz is kept close to the open end of a tube filled with water shown in figure. The water level in the tube is gradually lowered. When the water level is 17 cm below the open end, maximum intensity of sound is heard.
If the room temperature is 20°C, then calculate

(i) speed of sound in air at room temperature.

(ii) speed of sound in air at 0°C.

(iii) if the water in the tube is replaced with mercury, will there be any difference in your observations.

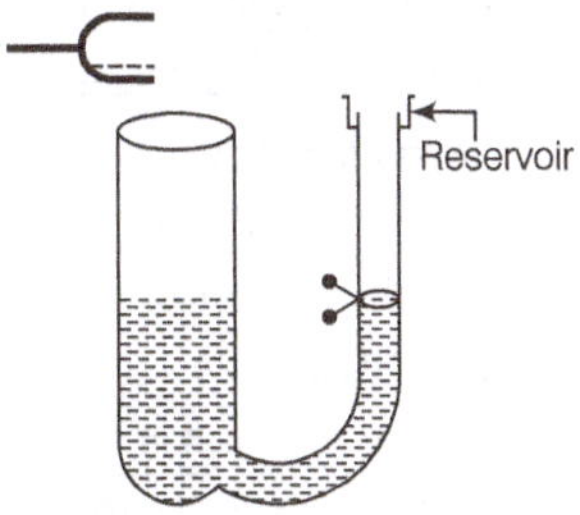

[3 M]

30. A pipe 20 cm long is closed at one end. Which harmonic mode of the pipe is resonantly excited by a 430 Hz source? Will the same source be in resonance with the pipe, if both ends are open? (Take, speed of sound in air is 340 ms^{-1}). NCERT [3 M]

31. An organ pipe of length L open at both ends is found to vibrate in its first harmonic when sounded with a tuning fork of 480 Hz. What should be the length of a pipe closed at one end, so that it also vibrates in its first harmonic with the same tuning fork? [5 M]

Hints & Solutions

1. (*d*) There is no phase difference between oscillations of different elements of the wave. The string as a whole vibrates in phase with different amplitudes at different points. The wave pattern is neither moving to the right nor to the left. Hence, they are called standing or stationary waves.

2. (*d*) Fundamental frequency, $\nu_0 = \frac{nv}{2L}; n = 1 = \frac{v}{2L}$ ...(i)

Wave velocity, $v = \sqrt{\frac{T}{\mu}} = \sqrt{\frac{T}{(m/L)}}$ ...(ii)

$\because$ Mass of the string, m = Volume × Density

$$= (\pi r^2 \times L) \times \rho \Rightarrow \mu = \frac{m}{L} = \pi r^2 \rho$$

On substituting the value of μ in Eq. (ii), we get

$$\Rightarrow \quad v = \sqrt{\frac{T}{\pi r^2 \rho}} = \frac{1}{r}\sqrt{\frac{T}{\pi\rho}}$$

From Eq. (i), we get

$$\nu_0 = \frac{1}{2rL}\sqrt{\frac{T}{\pi\rho}}$$

$$\Rightarrow \quad \frac{\nu_{01}}{\nu_{02}} = \frac{L_2}{L_1} \times \frac{r_2}{r_1}\sqrt{\frac{T_1}{T_2}}$$

$$\Rightarrow \quad \frac{600}{\nu_{02}} = \frac{2}{1} \times \frac{1}{2} \times \sqrt{\frac{T}{T/9}} = 3$$

$$\therefore \quad \nu_{02} = \frac{600}{3} = 200 \text{ Hz}$$

3. (*b*) The smallest length of the air column is associated with fundamental mode of vibration of the air column as shown in the figure.

$$\because \quad L_{min} = \frac{\lambda}{4} \Rightarrow 50 \text{ cm} = \frac{\lambda}{4}$$

$$\Rightarrow \quad \lambda = 200 \text{ cm}$$

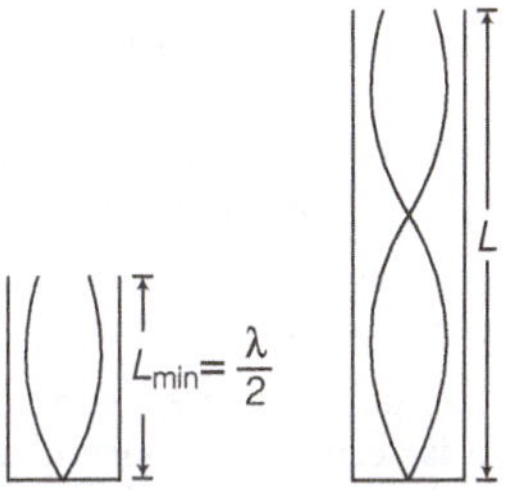

The next higher length of the air column is

$$L = \frac{\lambda}{4} + \frac{\lambda}{2} = \frac{\lambda + 2\lambda}{4} = \frac{3\lambda}{4}$$

$$= \frac{3}{4} \times 200 = 150 \text{ cm}$$

4. String under a tension (T), the frequency of vibrating string is inversely proportional to vibrating length (L),

i.e. $f = \frac{1}{L}$

5. The manner in which the string vibrates and give rise to a standing wave is known as mode of vibration of string.

6. In case of a string fixed at two ends, when the string vibrates in n loops,

$$\nu_n = \frac{n}{2l}\sqrt{\frac{T}{\mu}}$$

$$\Rightarrow \quad \nu_n \propto n$$

Hence, when the string vibrates in 1 loop, 2 loops, 3 loops and 4 loops, the frequencies are in the ratio 1 : 2 : 3 : 4.

7. The speed of sound in air is more at higher temperature, as $\nu \propto \sqrt{T}$. As we know, frequency $\nu = \frac{v}{\lambda}$ as v is more, hence ν will be more and accordingly pitch will be more.

8. Refer to text on page 485 (Reflection of waves).

9. Refer to text on page 486 (Standing waves).

10. Refer to text on page 486 (Normal modes).

11. Refer to text on pages 490 and 491 (Closed organ pipe) and pages 491 and 492 (Open organ pipe).

12. (i) A short pip by a whistle

(a) will not have a fixed frequency.

(b) will not have fixed wavelength.

(c) will have definite speed that will be equal to speed of sound in air. [1]

(ii) 0.05 Hz will be the frequency of repetition of the short pip. [1]

13. Refer to text on page 487 (Comparison between progressive and standing waves).

14. Refer to text on page 487 (Vibrations of stretched string).

15. Refer to text on pages 487 and 488 (Law of transverse vibration of a stretched string).

16. Refer to text on page 488 (Standing waves in string fixed at both ends).

17. Refer to text on page 490 (Position of nodes and antinodes).

18. Refer to text on page 488 (Standing waves in string fixed at both ends and modes of vibration).

19. Refer to text on pages 491 and 492 (Modes of vibrations of air column in open organ pipe).

20. (i) **Node** It is a point, where the amplitude of oscillation is zero, i.e. displacement is minimum. As pressure is inversely related with displacement, i.e. when displacement will be minimum, pressure will be maximum. [1/2]

Antinode At this point, displacement is maximum, i.e. amplitude of oscillation will be maximum and hence pressure will be minimum as it is inversely related. [1/2]

(ii) Bats emit ultrasonic waves of large frequencies. These waves will be reflected by the obstacles in their path. The reflected rays received by the bat will give idea about the obstacle, i.e. distance, direction, size and nature. [1]

(iii) As overtones produced and relative strengths of notes are different in two notes of violin and sitar.
Although frequencies are same, we will distinguish by their strengths. [1]

(iv) The reason behind is that solids have both the elasticity of volume as well as shape, whereas gases have only the volume elasticity. [1]

(v) As in the dispersive medium wavelengths are different, hence the velocities, therefore the shape of the pulse gets distorted. [1]

21. Given, $v = 1.7$ km/s $= 1700$ m/s

and $\nu = 4.2$ MHz $= 4.2 \times 10^6$ Hz

$$\therefore \quad \lambda = \frac{v}{\nu} = \frac{1700}{4.2 \times 10^6}$$

$$= 0.405 \times 10^{-3} \text{ m}$$

$$= 0.405 \text{ mm}$$

$$\approx 4.1 \times 10^{-4} \text{ m}$$

22. Given, $L = 100$ cm $= 1$ m,

$\nu = 2.53$ kHz $= 2.53 \times 10^3$ Hz

As the given rod is clamped at middle, hence there will be a node at the middle.. [1]

Hence, length, $L = \frac{\lambda}{4} + \frac{\lambda}{4} = \frac{\lambda}{2}$

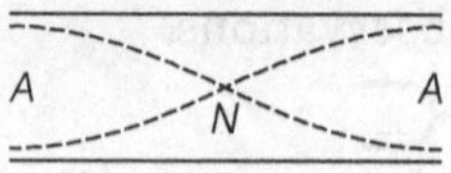

$$\Rightarrow \quad \lambda = 2L = 2 \text{ m}$$

Speed, $v = \nu\lambda = 2.53 \times 10^3 \times 2$

$= 5.06 \times 10^3$ ms^{-1} [1]

23. Length of pipe (l) $= 20$ cm $= 20 \times 10^{-2}$ m

$$\therefore \quad \nu_{funda} = \frac{v}{4L} = \frac{330}{4 \times 20 \times 10^{-2}}$$

$$\nu_{funda} = \frac{330 \times 100}{80} = 412.5 \text{ Hz}$$ [1]

$$\frac{\nu_{given}}{\nu_{funda}} = \frac{1237.5}{412.5} = 3$$

Hence, 3rd harmonic mode of the pipe is resonantly excited by the source of given frequency. [1]

24. (i) All the points except the nodes on the string have the same frequency and phase, but not the same amplitude. [1]

(ii) Given, $Y = 0.06 \sin \frac{2\pi}{3} x \cos (120\pi t)$

Putting $x = 0.375$ m

Amplitude, $Y = 0.06 \sin \frac{2\pi}{3} \times (0.375)$

$$= 0.06 \sin \frac{\pi}{4} = \frac{0.06}{\sqrt{2}} = 0.042 \text{ m}$$ [1]

25. $\nu_1 = \frac{1}{l_1 D_1} \sqrt{\frac{T_1}{\pi\rho_1}}$

where, D = diameter of wire.

$$\nu_2 = \frac{1}{l_2 D_2} \sqrt{\frac{T_2}{\pi\rho_2}}$$ [1]

$$l_1 = l_2, \rho_2 = \rho_1$$

$$T_2 = T_1, D_2 = 3D_1 \Rightarrow \nu_2 = \frac{\nu_1}{3}$$

New frequency is $\frac{1}{3}$ rd of the original frequency. [1]

26. Here given, $\nu = 45$ Hz, $M = 3.5 \times 10^{-2}$ kg

$$\mu = \frac{\text{Mass}}{\text{Length}} = 4.0 \times 10^{-2} \text{ kgm}^{-1}$$

$$l = \frac{M}{\mu} = \frac{3.5 \times 10^{-2}}{4 \times 10^{-2}} = \frac{7}{8} \text{ m}$$

$$l = \frac{\lambda}{2} = \frac{7}{8} \Rightarrow \lambda = \frac{7}{4} \text{ m} = 1.75 \text{ m}$$

(i) Speed, $v = \nu \times \lambda = 45 \times 1.75 = 78.75$ m/s [1]

(ii) As $v = \sqrt{\frac{T}{\mu}} \Rightarrow T = v^2 \times \mu$

$$\Rightarrow T = (78.75)^2 \times 4 \times 10^{-2} \Rightarrow T = 248.06 \text{ N}$$ [1]

27. Here, $v = 360$ m/s, $\nu = 256$ Hz

(i) In the figure, second curve represents all the particles passing simultaneously through mean position. This happens at $t = \frac{T}{4}\left(T = \frac{1}{256}\text{s}\right)$.

$$= \frac{1}{4 \times 256}\text{ s} = 9.8 \times 10^{-4}\text{ s}$$ [1]

(ii) Nodes are at points A, B, C, D, E and antinodes are at A', B', C', D' [1]

(iii) Distance between A' and C'

$$= \frac{2\lambda}{2} = \lambda = \frac{v}{\nu} = \frac{360}{256} = 1.41\text{ m}$$ [1]

28. The wave pattern shown represent stationary wave.

t	x (cm)
0	0
$\frac{T}{2}$	10
T	20

At the above time and position and similarly for next interval and position. These points are at rest and called nodes. [2]

Distance between successive nodes $= \frac{\lambda}{2} = 10$ cm

$\Rightarrow \quad \lambda = 20$ cm [1]

29. (i) $\nu = \frac{v}{4l} \Rightarrow v = (\nu)(4l) = (512)\left(\frac{4 \times 17}{100}\right)$ m/s

$= 348.16$ m/s [1]

(ii) $v_0 = v_t\sqrt{\frac{T_0}{T}} = 348.16\sqrt{\frac{273}{273 + 20}}$

$= 336.1$ m/s [1]

(iii) There will not be any change in resonance length, as frequency will remain same. As mercury acts as reflector intensity may change to some extent. [1]

30. Given, $L = 20\text{ cm} = 0.2\text{ m}$, $\nu_n = 430$ Hz, $v = 340$ m/s

It will behave as closed organ pipe,

$$\nu_n = (2n-1)\frac{v}{4L}\text{, where } n = 1, 2, 3, \ldots$$ [1]

$$\Rightarrow \quad 430 = (2n-1)\frac{v}{4L} = (2n-1) \times \frac{340}{4 \times 0.2}$$

$$\Rightarrow (2n-1) = \frac{430 \times (0.8)}{340} \Rightarrow 2n = \frac{(430)(0.8)}{340} + 1$$

$$\Rightarrow \quad n = \frac{43 \times 4}{340} + \frac{1}{2} = \frac{2 \times 172 + 340}{340 \times 2} = \frac{684}{680} = 1.006$$

Hence, it will be the 1st normal mode or harmonic mode of vibration. [1]

In a pipe open at both ends,

$$\nu_n = n \times \frac{v}{2l} = \frac{n \times 340}{2 \times 0.2} = 430$$

$$\Rightarrow \quad n = \frac{430 \times 2 \times 0.2}{340} = \frac{43 \times 2 \times 2}{340} = 0.5$$

As n is not integer, hence open organ pipe cannot be in resonance with the source. [1]

31. Consider the situation shown in the figure.

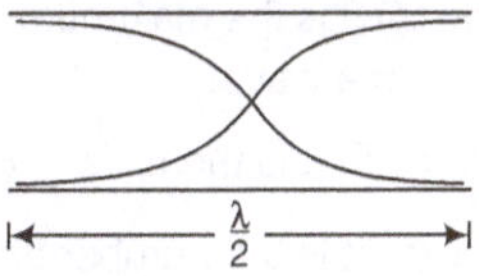

[1]

As the organ pipe is open at both ends, hence for first harmonic,

$$l = \frac{\lambda}{2} \Rightarrow \lambda = 2l \Rightarrow \frac{c}{\nu} = 2l \Rightarrow \nu = \frac{c}{2l}$$

where, c is speed of the sound wave in air. [1]

For pipe closed at one end, $\nu' = \frac{c}{4L'}$ [1]

c for first harmonic

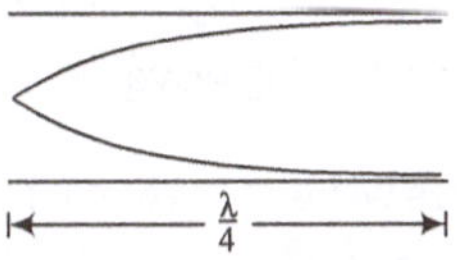

[1]

Hence, $\nu = \nu'$ [for resonance with same tuning fork]

$$\Rightarrow \quad \frac{c}{2L} = \frac{c}{4L'} \quad [\because \text{ speed remains constant}]$$

$$\Rightarrow \quad \frac{L'}{L} = \frac{2}{4} = \frac{1}{2} \Rightarrow L' = \frac{L}{2}$$ [1]

Summary

- **Transverse waves** These are the waves in which particles of the medium vibrate about their mean positions in a direction perpendicular to the direction of propagation of the disturbance. These waves can propagate in those media which have a shear modulus of elasticity. e.g. Solids.
- **Longitudinal waves** These are the waves in which particles of the medium vibrate about their mean positions along the direction of propagation of the disturbance. These waves can propagate in those media having a bulk modulus of elasticity and are therefore possible in all media: solids, liquids and gases.
- **Wave motion** It is a kind of disturbance which travels through a medium due to the repeated vibrations of the particles of the medium about their mean positions, the disturbance being handed over from one particle to the next.
- **Amplitude** (A) It is the maximum displacement suffered by the particles of the medium from the mean position during the propagation of a wave.
- **Time period** (T) It is the time in which a particle of the medium completes one vibration about its mean position.
- **Frequency (ν)** It is the number of waves produced per second in a given medium.
- **Wavelength (λ)** It is the distance covered by a wave during the time a particle of the medium completes one vibration about its mean position. It is the distance between two nearest particles of the medium which are vibrating in the same phase.
- **Characteristics of waves** Wavelength and angular wave number,

$$\lambda = \frac{2\pi}{k}$$

- Period, angular frequency and frequency, $\omega = \frac{2\pi}{T}, \nu = \frac{1}{T}$
- Speed of a travelling wave, $v = \nu\lambda = \frac{\lambda}{T}$
- **Progressive wave** A wave that moves from one point of medium to another is called a progressive wave.
- **Expression for displacement in wave motion** $Y = a\sin\omega t$ or $Y = a\sin(\omega t - kx \pm \phi)$.
- **Relation between phase difference, path difference and time difference** Relation between phase difference, path difference and time difference is given by

$$\text{Phase difference } (\phi) = \frac{2\pi}{\lambda} \times \text{Path difference } (x)$$

$$\Rightarrow \qquad \phi = \frac{2\pi x}{\lambda} \Rightarrow x = \frac{\phi\lambda}{2\pi}$$

- **Relation between particle velocity and wave velocity,** $u = -v \times \frac{dy}{dx}$

  Particle velocity = Wave velocity × Slope of displacement
- **Speed of a transverse wave on stretched string**

$$\nu = \sqrt{\frac{T}{m}}$$

where, T = tension in the string and m = linear mass density.

- Solid medium, $v = \sqrt{\frac{Y}{\rho}}$ where, Y is the Young's modulus of elasticity and ρ is its density.
- **Liquid medium** $v = \sqrt{\frac{B}{\rho}}$

  where, B is the bulk modulus of liquid and ρ is its density.
- **Gas medium** $v = \sqrt{\frac{p}{\rho}}$, where p is the pressure of gas and ρ is its density.

$$v_{solid} > v_{liquid} > v_{gaseous}$$

- **Laplace's correction** He pointed out that the propagation of sound in gaseous medium is not an isothermal process, but an adiabatic process. Thus, $v = \sqrt{\frac{\gamma p}{\rho}}$

  where, γ is the ratio of specific heat of the gas at constant pressure p to that at constant volume.
- **Supersonic waves** The term supersonic is used to define a speed, i.e. over the speed of sound.
- **Ultrasonic waves** Ultrasonic waves are generated, detected and integrated by electronic devices.
- **Principle of superposition of waves** When two or more pulses overlap, the resultant displacement is the algebraic sum of the displacements due to each pulse $y'(x, t) = y_1(x, t) + y_2(x, t)$.
- **Interference of waves** The phenomenon that occurs when the two waves meet, while travelling along the same medium.

$$y(x, t) = 2a\cos\frac{\phi}{2}\sin\left(kx - \omega t + \frac{\phi}{2}\right)$$

- If $f = 0$, two waves are in phase $y(x, t) = 2a\sin(kx - \omega t)$.
- If $\phi = \pi$, two waves are out of phase by 180° $y(x, t) = 0$.
- **Constructive interference** When waves interfere in phase

$$\phi = 2n\pi, \Delta x = n\lambda$$

- **Destructive interference** When waves interfere in phase opposition

$$\phi = (2n+1)\pi, \Delta x = \frac{(2n+1)\lambda}{2}$$

- **Vibrations of air column** Closed organ pipe, $v = (2n+1)\frac{v}{4L}$

  Open organ pipe, $v = \frac{nv}{2L}$
- Transverse wave on stretched spring $v = \sqrt{T/\mu}$
- **Beats** It is the difference of nearly same frequencies and amplitudes.

  Beat frequency, $v_{beat} = v_1 - v_2$

Chapter Practice

Multiple Choice Questions

1 Mark

1 Two sine waves travel in the same direction in a medium. The amplitude of each wave is A and the phase difference between the two waves is 120°. The resultant amplitude will be
(a) A (b) $2A$ (c) $4A$ (d) $\sqrt{2}A$

2 Two solid bars having Young's modulus Y_1 and Y_2 in the ratio $Y_1/Y_2 = 4$. If the bars are made up of materials with same density, then the ratio of the speed of longitudinal waves in the solid bars, i.e. v_1/v_2 is
(a) 2 (b) 1
(c) 3 (d) 4

3 Steel rod 100 cm long is clamped at its middle. The fundamental frequency of longitudinal vibrations of the rod is given to be 2.53 kHz. What is the speed of sound in steel?
(a) 7.08 kms^{-1} (b) 25.3 kms^{-1}
(c) 5.06 kms^{-1} (d) 10.74 kms^{-1}

4 The density of air at NTP is 1.29 kgm^{-3}. Assume air to be diatomic with $\gamma = 1.4$. The velocity of sound at 127°C is
(a) 382.8 ms^{-1} (b) 350 ms^{-1}
(c) 350.6 ms^{-1} (d) 348.6 ms^{-1}

5 A bullet passes past a person at a speed 220 ms^{-1}. The fractional change in the frequency of the whistling sound heard by the person as the bullet crosses the person is (Take, speed of sound = 330 ms^{-1})
(a) 0.67 (b) 0.8
(c) 1.2 (d) 3.0

Assertion and Reason

Directions (Q. Nos. 6-10) *In the following questions, two statements are given- one labelled Assertion (A) and the other labelled Reason (R). Select the correct answer to these questions from the codes (a), (b), (c) and (d) as given below*

(a) Both Assertion and Reason are true and Reason is the correct explanation of Assertion.
(b) Both Assertion and Reason are true but Reason is not the correct explanation of Assertion.
(c) Assertion is true but Reason is false.
(d) Assertion is false but Reason is true.

6 **Assertion (A)** The light emitted by stars, which are hundreds of light years away, reaches us through inter-stellar spaces even though the inter-stellar spaces are practically vacuum.

Reason (R) Light is an electromagnetic wave and do not necessarily require a medium for propagation, they can even travel in vacuum.

7 **Assertion (A)** Sound waves cannot propagate through vacuum but light waves can.

Reason (R) Sound waves cannot be polarised but light waves can be polarised.

8 **Assertion (A)** Transverse waves are possible in solids and strings (under tension) but not in fluids.

Reason (R) Solids and strings have no zero shear modulus, i.e. they can sustain shearing stress but fluids yield to shearing stress and hence they do not have shape of their own.

9 **Assertion (A)** Longitudinal waves can be propagated through solids and fluids both.

Reason (R) Solids as well as fluids have non-zero bulk modulus, i.e. they can sustain compressive stress and longitudinal waves involve compressive stress (pressure).

10 **Assertion (A)** Speed of sound is more in liquids and solids than gases.

Reason (R) Liquids and solids have higher densities than gases.

Very Short Answer Type Questions

1 Mark

11 Is there transfer of energy or momentum or mass or particle in a wave motion?

12 Is an oscillation, a wave, why?

13 Give two examples of each of longitudinal and transverse waves.

14 At which point, the wave having zero amplitude?

Short Answer Type I Questions

(2 Marks)

15 What is the direction of oscillations of the particles of a medium through which (i) transverse, (ii) longitudinal wave is propagating?

16 Establish the relation $v = n\lambda$ for a wave motion.

17 What do you mean by progressive harmonic wave? Write down its equation.

Short Answer Type II Questions

(3 Marks)

18 State what are important characteristics of a wave motion.

19 What are stationary waves? Explain their formation analytically in case of a string fixed at both of its ends.

Long Answer Type Questions

(5 Marks)

20 State Newton's formula for velocity of sound in air. Point out the error and hence, discuss Laplace's correction and calculate the temperature at which the speed of sound will be two times of its value at 0°C.

21 How are standing waves set up in air columns? Explain it.

22 Explain the formation of beat graphically.

Case Based Questions

Directions (Q. No. 23) *These questions are case study based questions. Read the following paragraph and answer the questions.*

23 A stone is dropped in a liquid at rest in a tank. The Fig. (a) below shows circular wavefronts. The waves produced at the centre of a circular ripple tank. Two corks A and B, floats on the water and moves up & down on the surface as the wave passes. The wavelength of the wave is 8.0 cm.

The Fig. (b) shows how the displacement of A varies with time.

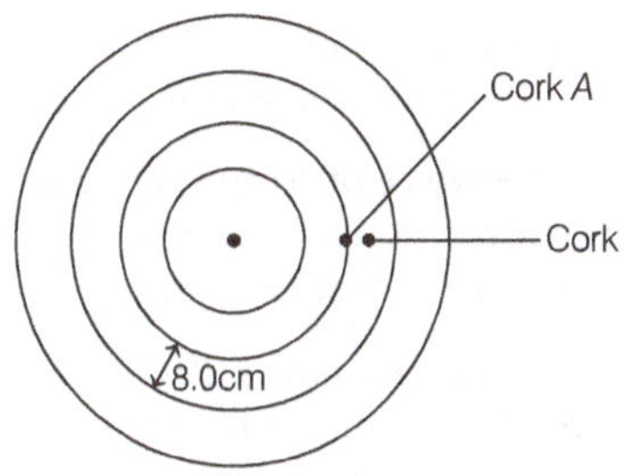

(a)

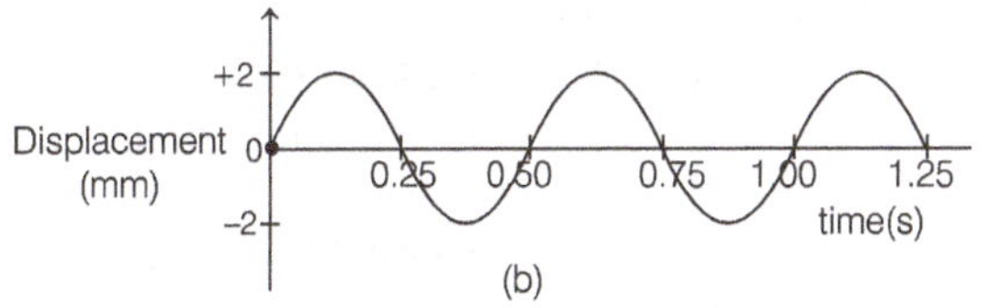

(b)

(i) Which type of waves is produced on water surface?
(a) Longitudinal wave
(b) Transverse wave
(c) Sound wave
(d) EM wave

(ii) What is the amplitude of the vibrations of A as wave passes?
(a) 2 mm (b) 0.25 mm
(c) 0.50 mm (d) 8 mm

(iii) The horizontal distance between A and B is half the wavelength of the wave, then the displacement of B with time is
(a) same as that of A with equal magnitude
(b) opposite to that of A with equal magnitude
(c) double in magnitude as that of A
(d) half in magnitude as that of A

(iv) What is the frequency of the wave?
(a) 4 Hz (b) 0.4 Hz
(c) 2 Hz (d) 0.2 Hz

(v) If the distance between the centre of the ripple tank and its edge is 40 cm, then the time taken by the wave to travel from the centre of the tank to the edge is
(a) 5 s (b) 2.5 s
(c) 3 s (d) 4.5 s

Numerical Problems

24 What is the audible range of sound frequencies? **[1 M]**

25 Two sound waves produce 12 beats in 4 s. By how much do their frequencies differ? **[1 M]**

26 A progressive wave of frequency 500 Hz is travelling with a velocity of 360 m/s. How far particles are two points 60° out of phase? **[2 M]**

27 A tuning fork of frequency 200 Hz is in resonance with a sonometer wire. How many beats will be heard if tension in the wire is increased by 2%? **[3 M]**

28 Two tuning forks A and B give 5 beats/s. A resounds with a closed column of air 15 cm long and B with an open column of air 30.5 cm long. Calculate their frequencies. Neglect and correction. **[5 M]**

29 Stationary waves are set up by the superposition of two waves given by $y_1 = 0.05\sin(5\pi t - x)$ and $y_2 = 0.05\sin(5\pi t + x)$, where x and y are in metre and t in second. Calculate the amplitude of a particle at a distance of $x = 1$ m. **[5 M]**

Answers

1 (*a*) Amplitude of the resultant of the two waves

$$= A(\phi) = 2A\cos\left(\frac{\phi}{2}\right)$$

Given, $\phi = 120°$

$$\Rightarrow A(\phi) = 2A\cos\left(\frac{120°}{2}\right) = 2A\cos 60°$$

$$\text{or}\quad A(\phi) = (2A) \times \frac{1}{2} = A$$

2 (*a*) $v = \sqrt{\dfrac{Y}{\rho}}$

where, Y = Young's modulus, ρ = mass density

Since, solid bars are made up of the materials with same density, $\rho_1 = \rho_2$

$$\Rightarrow \frac{v_1}{v_2} = \sqrt{\frac{Y_1}{Y_2}} = \sqrt{4} = 2$$

3 (*c*) For the fundamental mode of vibration,

$$\lambda = 2L = 2 \times 100 = 200 \text{ cm} = 2 \text{ m}$$

Frequency, $\nu = 2.53$ kHz $= 2530$ Hz

$\therefore$ Speed of sound,

$$v = \nu\lambda = 2530 \times 2 = 5060 \text{ ms}^{-1} = 5.06 \text{ km s}^{-1}$$

4 (*a*) Velocity of sound in air at NTP

$$= \sqrt{\frac{\gamma p}{\rho}} = \sqrt{\frac{1.4 \times 1.013 \times 10^5 \text{ Nm}^{-2}}{1.29 \text{ kgm}^{-3}}} = 331.6 \text{ ms}^{-1}$$

The velocity of sound is proportional to the square root of absolute temperature

$$\Rightarrow \frac{v_2}{v_1} = \sqrt{\frac{T_2}{T_1}} \Rightarrow v_2 = v_1\sqrt{\frac{T_2}{T_1}} = 331.6\sqrt{\frac{273+127}{273+27}}$$

$$= 382.8 \text{ ms}^{-1}$$

5 (*b*) Limiting cases when it is just at the verge of crossing and when it has just crossed are taken. From Doppler's effect, we have

$$f_1 = \left(\frac{v}{v + v_S}\right) f = 0.6f$$

$$f_2 = \frac{v}{v - v_S} f = 3f$$

$$f_{\text{net}} = \frac{f_1 + f_2}{2} = \frac{3.6f}{2} = 1.8f$$

$$\Delta f = 0.8f \text{ or } \frac{\Delta f}{f} = 0.8$$

6 (*a*) **7** (*b*) **8** (*a*)

9 (*a*) **10** (*a*)

11 Energy transfer.

12 Wave is an oscillation accompained by energy transfer through a medium.

13 **Longitudinal wave** Wave in spring, sound wave. **Transverse wave** Wave in string, ripple on water surface.

14 Node

15 Refer to text on pages 463 and 464 (Transverse and longitudinal waves).

16 Refer to text on page 465 (Relation between frequency, wave velocity and wavelength).

17 Refer to text on page 466 (Expression for displacement in wave motion).

18 Refer to text on page 464 (Characteristics of wave motion).

19 Refer to text on pages 486 and 488 (Standing waves and standing waves in string fixed at both ends and laplace correction).

20 Refer to text on pages 470 and 471 (Newton's formula for speed of sound in gases and laplace).

21 Refer to text on pages 486 (Standing waves).

22 Refer to text on pages 481 and 482 (Analytical method of beats).

23 (i) (*d*) (ii) (*d*) (iii) (*d*) (iv) (*c*) (*b*)

24 Audible range, 20-20 kHz

25 Frequencies differ by $\Delta f = \dfrac{12}{4} = 3$ Hz

26 360 m **27** 4 beats

28 $f_A = 305$ and $f_B = 300$

29 0.054 m

All in One

COMPLETE STUDY | COMPLETE PRACTICE | COMPLETE ASSESSMENT

3 Sample Question Papers

SAMPLE QUESTION PAPER 1

A Highly Simulated Sample Question Paper for ISC Class XI

PHYSICS (Fully Solved)

Time : 3 hours **Max. Marks : 70**

General Instructions

1. This paper is divided into four **sections A, B, C** and **D.** Answer all questions.
2. **Section A** consists of one question having sub-parts of one mark each.
3. **Section B** consists of seven questions of two marks each.
4. **Section C** consists of nine questions of three marks each.
5. **Section D** consists of three questions of five marks each.
6. Internal choices have been provided in two questions each in Section B, Section C and Section D.

FULLY SOLVED

Section–A

[14 Marks]

1. A. Choose the correct alternative (a), (b), (c) or (d) for each of the following questions given below. [7 × 1]

(i) If the gravitation force on body 1 due to 2 is given by $\mathbf{F}_{12}$ and on body 2 due to 1 is given as $\mathbf{F}_{21}$, then • ***Recall***

(a) $\mathbf{F}_{12} = \mathbf{F}_{21}$ (b) $\mathbf{F}_{12} = -\mathbf{F}_{21}$

(c) $\mathbf{F}_{12} = \dfrac{\mathbf{F}_{21}}{4}$ (d) None of these

(ii) If a person can throw a stone to maximum height of h metre vertically, then the maximum distance through which it can be thrown horizontally by the same person is • ***Application***

(a) $\dfrac{h}{2}$ (b) h (c) $2h$ (d) $3h$

(iii) Which of the following pairs of physical quantities does not have same dimensional formula? • ***Understanding***

(a) Work and torque

(b) Angular momentum and Planck constant

(c) Tension and surface tension

(d) Impulse and linear momentum

(iv) A uniform rod of length L and density ρ is being pulled along a smooth floor with a horizontal acceleration α. The magnitude of the stress at the transverse cross-section through the mid-point of the rod is • ***Application***

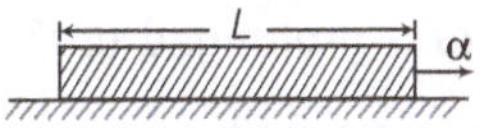

(a) $L\rho\alpha$ (b) $\dfrac{L\rho\alpha}{2}$ (c) $\dfrac{2}{3}L\rho\alpha$ (d) None of these

(v) A system is provided with 200 cal of heat and the work done by the system on the surroundings is 40 J. Then, its internal energy • *Understanding*

(a) increases by 600 J

(b) decreases by 800 J

(c) increases by 800 J

(d) decreases by 50 J

(vi) **Assertion** Stopping distance $= \dfrac{\text{Kinetic energy}}{\text{Stopping force}}$ • *Understanding*

Reason Work done in stopping a body is equal to change in kinetic energy of the body.

(a) Both Assertion and Reason are correct and Reason is the correct explanation of the Assertion.

(b) Both Assertion and Reason are correct but Reason is not the correct explanation of the Assertion.

(c) Assertion is correct and Reason is incorrect.

(d) Assertion is incorrect and Reason is correct.

(vii) **Assertion** If the temperature of two systems is not same, it means that they must not be in thermodynamic equilibrium.

Reason If the temperature of two systems is same, it means that they must not be in thermal equilibrium. • *Applicaiton*

(a) Both Assertion and Reason are correct and Reason is the correct explanation of the Assertion.

(b) Both Assertion and Reason are correct but Reason is not the correct explanation of the Assertion.

(c) Assertion is correct and Reason is incorrect.

(d) Assertion is incorrect and Reason is correct.

B. Answer the following questions briefly. [7 × 1]

(i) Find the dimensional formula for coefficient of viscosity (η). • *Recall*

(ii) Rahul tied a stone at the end of the string, then whirled it in a circle. When the string breaks, the stone flies tangentially. Why? • *Application*

(iii) If pressure is made 16 times, what will be the effect on the velocity of sound? • *Application*

(iv) Given that for two vectors **A** and **B**, $|\mathbf{A} \times \mathbf{B}| = |\mathbf{A} \cdot \mathbf{B}|$. Find the acute angle between **A** and **B**. • *Application*

(v) A body of mass m is oscillating harmonically suspended from a massless spring of spring constant k. What is the time period? • *Application*

(vi) Can a body move on a curved path without having acceleration? Why ? • *Application*

(vii) Define the angle of repose. • *Recall*

Section–B

[14 Marks]

2. (i) Why do springs become slack after a prolonged use? • *Recall*

(ii) What is the work done in streching a wire? • *Recall* [2]

Or

Figure shows the strain-stress curve for a given material. What are (i) Young's modulus and (ii) approximate yield strength for this material? • *Analysis* [2]

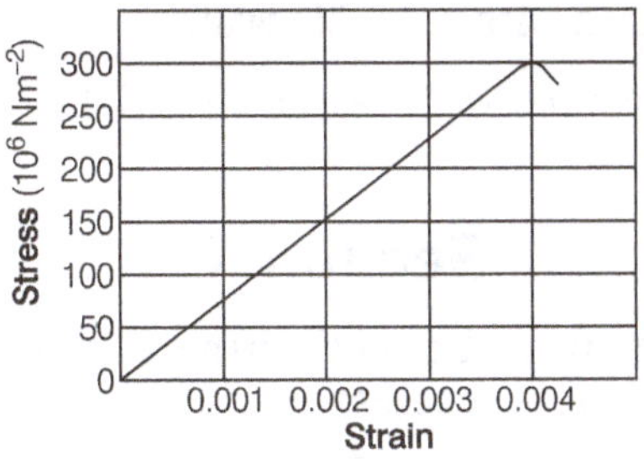

3. A monoatomic ideal gas of two moles is taken through a cyclic process starting from A as shown in figure.

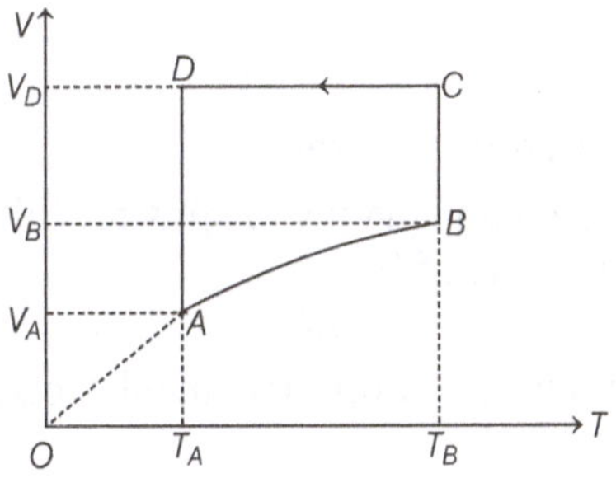

The volume ratios are $\frac{V_B}{V_A} = 2$ and $\frac{V_D}{V_A} = 4$. If the temperature T_A at A is 27°C, calculate

(i) the temperature of the gas at point B.

(ii) heat absorbed or released by the gas in each process. • *Analysis* [2]

4. The pattern of standing waves formed on a stretched string at two instants of time are shown in figure. The velocity of two waves superimposing to form stationary waves is 360 m/s and their frequencies are 256 Hz.

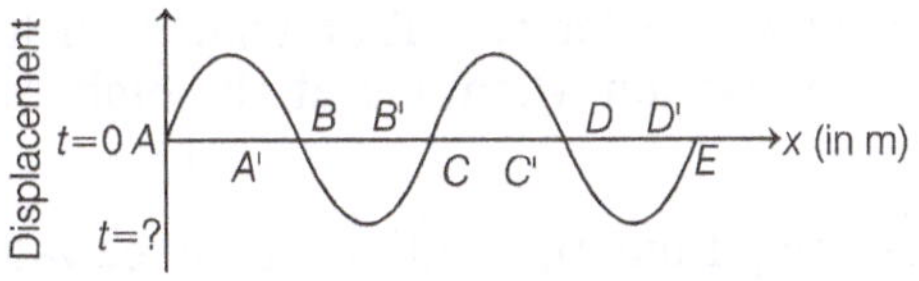

(i) Calculate the time at which the second curve is plotted. • *Analysis* [2]

(ii) Mark nodes and antinodes on the curve. • *Analysis*

5. Resultant of two vectors of equal amplitude is equal in magnitude with one of the vectors, calculate the angle between them. • *Analysis* [2]

Or

A woman throws an object of mass 500g with a speed of 25m/s .

(i) What is the impulse imparted to the object? • *Understanding*

(ii) If the object hits a wall and rebounds with half the original speed, what is the change in momentum of the object? [2]

6. (i) A capillary of radius 0.05 cm is immersed in water. Find the value of rise of water in capillary if value for the surface tension is 0.073 N/m and angle of contact is 0°. • *Understanding* [1]

(ii) It becomes easier to spray the water in which some soap is dissolved, explain it. • *Analysis* [1]

FULLY SOLVED

7. Rooms are provided with the ventilators near the roof. Why? • *Recall* [2]

8. (i) Why an ice box is constructed with a double wall? • *Recall*

(ii) Why birds are often seen to swell their feathers in winter? • *Recall* [2]

Section–C

[27 Marks]

9. Two blocks are placed over a horizontal smooth plane as shown in the figure. Find the minimum value of μ_2, so that block could move together. • *Analysis* [3]

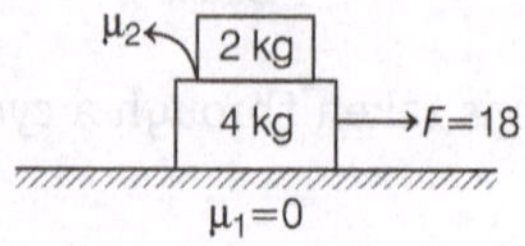

10. (i) What gives the measure of inertia? • *Recall* [1/2]

(ii) What is the principle of working of a rocket? • *Recall* [1/2]

(iii) A body placed on a rough inclined plane just begins to slide, when the slope of the plane equal to 1 in 4. Calculate the coefficient of friction. • *Understanding* [2]

Or

A uniform square plate S (side c) and a uniform rectangular plate R (sides b, a) have identical areas and masses (figure). • *Analysis* [2]

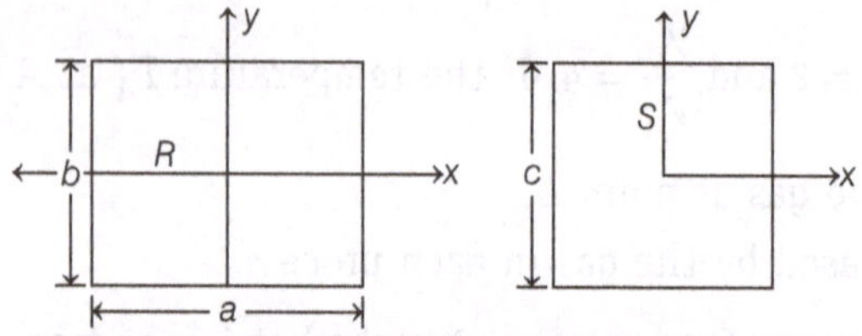

Show that (i) $I_{xR}/I_{xS} < 1$ (ii) $I_{yR}/I_{yS} > 1$ and (iii) $I_{zR}/I_{zS} > 1$ [1]

11. A particle of mass m is projected with velocity u at an angle θ with the horizontal. Find its angular momentum about the point of projection when it is at the highest point of its trajectory. • *Analysis* [3]

12. A spring mass system is hanging from the ceiling of an elevator in equilibrium. The elevator suddenly starts accelerating upwards with acceleration a.

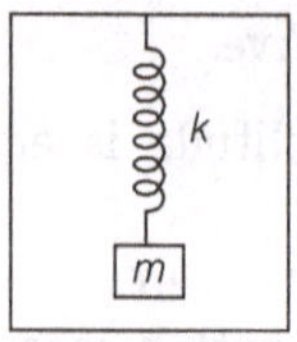

Find

(i) the frequency.

(ii) the amplitude of the resulting SHM. • *Analysis* [3]

Or

A body oscillates with SHM according to the equation

$$x(t) = 10\cos\left(2\pi t + \frac{\pi}{6}\right)$$

where, x is in metre and t is in second.
Calculate
(i) displacement at time $t = 0$.
(ii) magnitude of maximum velocity.
(iii) angular frequency. • *Understanding* [3]

13. Find the expression for variation of acceleration due to gravity g, with height above the surface of the earth. • *Recall* [3]

14. (i) Two isothermal curves do not intersect each other, why? • *Application*

(ii) What is an isothermal process? Derive an expression for work done during an isothermal expansion of a gas. • *Recall and Analysis* [3]

15. (i) What is capillarity? • *Recall* [1]

(ii) Water rises in a capillary tube to a height of 4.0 cm. In another capillary tube whose radius is one third of it, how much the water will rise? • *Application* [2]

16. Compute the fractional change in volume of a glass slab, when subjected to a hydraulic pressure of 10 atm. • *Understanding* [3]

17. A student records the amplitude A of a sound wave at different distances x from a point source. The data is as follows

Distance x	Amplitude A
$x = a$	A_0
$x = 2a$	$\frac{A_0}{2}$
$x = 3a$	$\frac{A_0}{3}$

Does this follow the expected relation for amplitude variation with distance ?
Explain why amplitude decreases with distance. • *Analysis*

FULLY SOLVED

Section–D

[15 Marks]

18. A helicopter lifts a 72 kg astronaut 15 m vertically from the ocean by means of a cable. The acceleration of the astronaut is $\frac{g}{10}$. How much work is done on the astronaut by

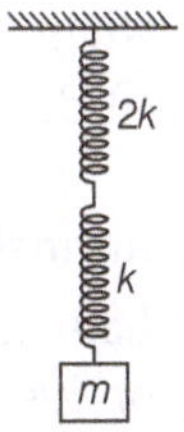

(i) the force from the helicopter and • *Analysis*
(ii) the gravitational force on him?
(iii) what are the kinetic energy and

(iv) the speed of the astronaut just before he reaches the helicopter? (Take, $g = 10\ ms^{-2}$) [5]

Or (i) An object of mass 5 kg falls from rest through a vertical distance of 20 m and attains a velocity of $10\ ms^{-1}$. How much work is done by the resistance of the air on the object? (Take, $g = 10\ ms^{-2}$) • *Understanding*

(ii) A vehicle of mass 10 kg is moving in x-direction with a constant speed of $10\ ms^{-1}$. It is subjected to a retarding force $F = -\ 0.1x\ Jm^{-1}$ during its travel from $x = 20$ m to $x = 30$ m. Evaluate its final kinetic energy. • *Understanding* [5]

19. Plot the corresponding reference circle for each of the following simple harmonic motions. Indicate the initial ($t = 0$) position of the particle, the radius of the circle and the angular speed of the rotating particle. For simplicity, the sense of rotation may be fixed to be anti-clockwise in every case (x is in cm and t is in second).

(i) $x = -2\sin\left(3t + \frac{\pi}{3}\right)$ (ii) $x = \cos\left(\frac{\pi}{6} - t\right)$

(iii) $x = 3\sin\left(2\pi t + \frac{\pi}{4}\right)$ (iv) $x = 2\cos \pi t$

• *Understanding* [5]

Or

For the harmonic travelling wave $y = 2\cos 2\pi\,(10t - 0.0080x + 3.5)$, where x and y are in cm and t in second. What is the phase difference between the oscillatory motion at two points separated by a distance of • *Understanding*

(i) 4 m (ii) 0.5 m

(iii) $\frac{\lambda}{2}$ (iv) $\frac{3\lambda}{4}$ (at a given instant of time)?

(v) What is the phase difference between the oscillation of a particle located at $x = 100\,\text{cm}$, at $t = T$ s and $t = 5$ s? [5]

Read the passage given below and answer the questions that follow.

20. A collision is an isolated event in which or more colliding bodies exert strong forces on each other for a relatively short time. For a collision to take place, the actual physical contact is not necessary. Collision between two bodies have been divided into two types.

(i) Elastic collision (ii) Inelastic collision

Force involved during elastic collision must be conserved in nature. While some or all forces involved during inelastic collision may be non-conservative in nature.

Answer carefully with reasons [5]

(i) In an elastic collision of two billiard balls, is the total kinetic energy conserved during the short time of collision of the balls i.e. when they are in contact? • *Application*

(ii) Is the total linear momentum conserved during the short time of an elastic collision of two balls? • *Application*

(iii) What are the answer to (i) and (ii) for an inelastic collision? • *Application*

(iv) If the potential energy of two billiard balls depends only on the separation distance between their centres, is the collision elastic or inelastic? (Note : We are talking here of potential energy corresponding to the force during collision, not gravitational potential energy.) • *Understanding*

FULLY SOLVED

Hints & Solutions

1. A. (i) (*b*) Since, gravitational forces are attractive $\mathbf{F}_{12}$ is directed opposite to $\mathbf{F}_{21}$ and they are also equal in magnitude.

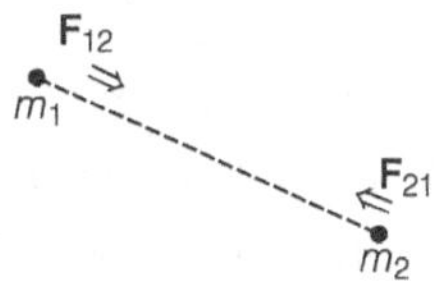

Hence, $\mathbf{F}_{21} = -\mathbf{F}_{12}$ or $\mathbf{F}_{12} = -\mathbf{F}_{21}$

(ii) (*c*) $h = \dfrac{u^2}{2g}$

$\Rightarrow u^2 = 2gh$

[stone is thrown vertically upward]

Maximum horizontal distance,

$$R_{max} = \frac{u^2}{g} \text{ (when } \theta = 45°\text{)}, \quad R_{max} = 2h$$

(iii) (*c*) (a) Work = Force × Distance

$= [MLT^{-2}][L] = [ML^2T^{-2}]$

Torque = Force × Distance = $[ML^2T^{-2}]$

(b) Angular momentum = mvr

$= [M][LT^{-1}][L] = [ML^2T^{-1}]$

Planck constant $= \dfrac{E}{\nu} = \dfrac{[ML^2T^{-2}]}{[T^{-1}]} = [ML^2T^{-1}]$

(c) Tension = Force = $[MLT^{-2}]$

Surface tension $= \dfrac{\text{Force}}{\text{Length}} = \dfrac{[MLT^{-2}]}{[L]}$

$= [ML^0T^{-2}]$

(d) Impulse = Force × Time

$= [MLT^{-2}][T] = [MLT^{-1}]$

Momentum = Mass × Velocity

$= [M][LT^{-1}] = [MLT^{-1}]$

(iv) (*b*) The force at the cross-section through the mid-point of the rod is

$$F = \frac{L}{2} A\rho\alpha$$

$\therefore$ Stress $= \dfrac{F}{A} = \dfrac{1}{2} L\rho\alpha$

(v) (*c*) Given,

$dQ = +200$ Cal

$= 200 \times 4.2$

$= 840$ J

$dW = +40$ J

From first law of thermodynamics,

$dQ = dU + dW$

$dU = dQ - dW$

$= 840 - 40 = 800$ J

(vi) (*a*) Work done = Force × Distance

Work done in stopping a body is equal to change in kinetic energy of the body,

so, kinetic energy = force × distance

Kinetic energy = Stopping force × Stopping distance

(vii) (d) In thermodynamic equilibrium, the state variables of the system do not change with time.

Two systems can be in thermodynamic equilibrium even if, they have unequal temperatures. In thermal equilibrium, the temperature of two systems must be same.

B. (i) We know that, $F = 6\pi\eta rv$

$\Rightarrow \quad [F] = [6\pi][\eta][r][v]$

$\Rightarrow \quad [\eta] = \dfrac{[F]}{[r][v]}$

$= \dfrac{[MLT^{-2}]}{[L][LT^{-1}]} = [ML^{-1}T^{-1}]$

(ii) When a stone is going around a circular path, the instantaneous velocity of stone is acting as tangent to the circle. When the string breaks, the centripetal force stops to act. Due to inertia, the stone continues to move along the tangent to circular path. So, the stone flies off tangentially to the circular path.

(iii) At constant temperature, $\dfrac{p}{\rho} = \dfrac{1}{3}c^2$ will remain constant. Hence, speed will not be affected with the variation of sound.

(iv) $AB \sin\theta = AB \cos\theta$

$\Rightarrow \tan\theta = 1 \Rightarrow \theta = \dfrac{\pi}{4}$

(v) Angular frequency,

$$\omega = \sqrt{\frac{k}{m}},$$

$$T = \frac{2\pi}{\omega} = 2\pi\sqrt{\frac{m}{k}}$$

(vi) No, a body cannot move on a curved path without acceleration because while moving on a curved path the velocity of the body changes with time as the direction changes at each point.

(vii) The minimum angle that an inclined plane makes with the horizontal when a body placed on it just begins to slide down.

2. (i) The elasticity of the material decreases due to repeated deformation in the long run. The elastic limit also decreases and springs become deformed permanently. **[1]**

(ii) Work done in stretching a wire is

$= \dfrac{1}{2} \times \text{stress} \times \text{strain} \times \text{volume}$

or $= \dfrac{1}{2} \times Y \times (\text{strain})^2 \times \text{volume}$ **[1]**

Or

(i) Young's modulus of the given material (Y)

= Slope of strain-stress curve **[1/2]**

$$Y = \frac{150 \times 10^6}{0.002}$$

$= 75 \times 10^9$ N/m^2 **[1/2]**

$= 7.5 \times 10^{10}$ N/m^2

(ii) Yield strength of the given material

= Maximum stress, the material can sustain **[1/2]**

$= 300 \times 10^6$ N/m^2

$= 3 \times 10^8$ N/m^2 **[1/2]**

3. (i) The process $A \rightarrow B$ is isobaric.

$$\therefore \quad \frac{V}{T} = \text{Constant}$$

Hence, $\frac{V_A}{T_A} = \frac{V_B}{T_B}$

Or, $T_B = \frac{V_B}{V_A} \cdot T_A$

$= 2 \times 300$

$= 600\,K = 327°C$

(ii) The heat absorbed in the process $A \rightarrow B$ is given by,

$$Q_1 + nC_p dT = (5R)(600 - 300)$$

$$= 1500\,R$$

4. Here, $v = 360$ m/s, $\nu = 256$ Hz

(i) In the figure, second curve represents all the particles passing simultaneously through mean position. This happens at $t = \frac{T}{4}\left(T = \frac{1}{256}\text{ s}\right)$

$$= \frac{1}{4 \times 256}\text{ s} = 9.8 \times 10^{-4}\text{ s}$$

(ii) Nodes are at points A, B, C, D, E and antinodes are at A', B', C', D'.

(iii) Distance between A' and C'

$$= \frac{2\lambda}{2} = \lambda = \frac{v}{\nu} = \frac{360}{256} = 1.41\text{ m}$$

5. Let $A = B = A$

Resultant $= \sqrt{A^2 + B^2 + 2AB\cos\theta}$

$$= \sqrt{2A^2(1 + \cos\theta)} = \sqrt{2}A\sqrt{2\cos^2\frac{\theta}{2}}$$

$$= 2A\cos\frac{\theta}{2}$$

$$\Rightarrow \quad 2A\cos\frac{\theta}{2} = A \Rightarrow \cos\frac{\theta}{2} = \frac{1}{2}$$

$$\Rightarrow \quad \frac{\theta}{2} = 60° \Rightarrow \theta = 120°$$ **[2]**

Or

Mass of the object, $m = 500$ g $= 0.5$ kg

Speed of the object, $v = 25$ m/s

(i) Impulse imparted to the object = Change in momentum $= mv - mu = m(v - u)$

$= 0.5(25 - 0) = 12.5$ N-s **[1]**

(ii) Velocity of the object after rebounding

$$= -\frac{25}{2}\text{ m/s}$$

$$v' = -12.5\text{ m/s}$$

$\therefore$ Change in momentum $= m(v' - v)$ **[1]**

$= 0.5(-12.5 - 25) = -18.75$ N-s

6. (i) Given, $S = 0.073$ N/m,

$R = 0.05\text{ cm} = 5 \times 10^{-4}$ m

$\theta = 0°, h = ?$

From the formula,

$$h = \frac{2S\cos\theta}{\rho g R} = \frac{2 \times 0.073 \times \cos 0°}{10^3 \times 9.8 \times 5 \times 10^{-4}}$$

$= 0.02979$ m **[1]**

(ii) When some soap is dissolved in water, the surface tension of water decreases. Thus, the less energy required to spray water. **[1]**

7. It is done so to remove the harmful impure air and to replace it by the cool fresh air. The air we breath out is warm and so it is lighter. It rises upwards and can go out through the ventilator provided near the roof. The cold fresh air from outside enters the room through the doors and windows. Thus, the convection current is set up in the air. **[2]**

8. (i) An ice box is made of double wall and the space in between the walls is filled with some non-conducting material to provide heat insulation, so that the loss of heat can be minimised. **[1]**

(ii) When the birds swell their feathers, they are able to enclose air in the feathers. Air, being a poor conductor of heat, so it prevents the loss of heat from the bodies of the birds to the surroundings and as such they do not feel cold in winter. **[1]**

9. Let us draw the given figure.

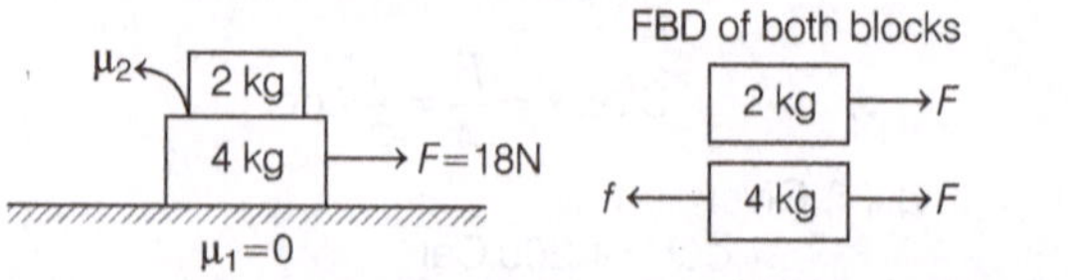

From the above figure,

$$f = \mu_2 N$$

$$f = \mu_2 \times 20$$

For blocks to move together, both of them must have same acceleration. So,

$$F - f = 4a$$

$$\Rightarrow \quad 180 - 20\mu_2 = 4a$$

$$\Rightarrow \quad F = ma$$

$\Rightarrow \quad F = 2a$

$\Rightarrow \quad 20\mu_2 = 2a$

$a = 10\mu_2$

Putting the value of $a = 10\mu_2$ in Eq. (ii), we have

$18 - 20\mu_2 = 40\mu_2$

$\Rightarrow \quad 18 = 60\mu_2$

$\Rightarrow \quad \mu_2 = \frac{18}{60}$

$\Rightarrow \quad \mu_2 = 0.3$

10. (i) Mass of a body gives the measure of its inertia. [1/2]

(ii) Law of conservation of linear momentum. [1/2]

(iii) The slope of the plane equal to 1 in 4 implies that if $BC = 4$ and $AB = 1$. Suppose that the plane is inclined at angle θ with the horizontal AC. From the relation between the coefficient of friction and angle of repose, we have [1]

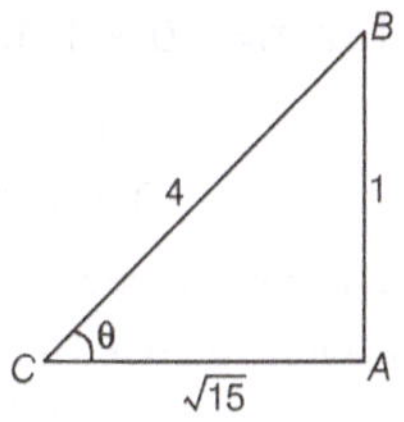

$\mu = \tan\theta$ [here, θ is angle of repose]

or $\mu = \frac{AB}{AC} = \frac{AB}{\sqrt{BC^2 - AB^2}}$

$= \frac{1}{\sqrt{4^2 - 1^2}} = \frac{1}{\sqrt{16-1}}$

Coefficient of the friction,

$\mu = \frac{1}{\sqrt{15}}$ or $\mu = 0.258$ [1]

Or

By given question

Area of square = Area of rectangular plate

$\Rightarrow \quad c^2 = a \times b \Rightarrow c^2 = ab$

Now, by definition,

(i) $\frac{I_{xR}}{I_{xS}} = \frac{b^2}{c^2}$ [$\because I \propto$ area]

From the diagram $b < c$,

$\Rightarrow \quad \frac{I_{xR}}{I_{xS}} = \left(\frac{b}{c}\right)^2 < 1$

$\Rightarrow \quad I_{xR} < I_{xS}$ [1]

(ii) $\frac{I_{yR}}{I_{yS}} = \frac{a^2}{c^2}$

as $a > c$

$\frac{I_{yR}}{I_{yS}} = \left(\frac{a}{c}\right)^2 > 1$ [1]

(iii) $I_{zR} - I_{zS} \propto (a^2 + b^2 - 2c^2)$

$= a^2 + b^2 - 2ab = (a-b)^2$

[$\because c^2 = ab$]

$\Rightarrow (I_{zR} - I_{zS}) > 0 \Rightarrow \frac{I_{zR}}{I_{zS}} > 1$ [1]

11. Consider the diagram in the below diagram.

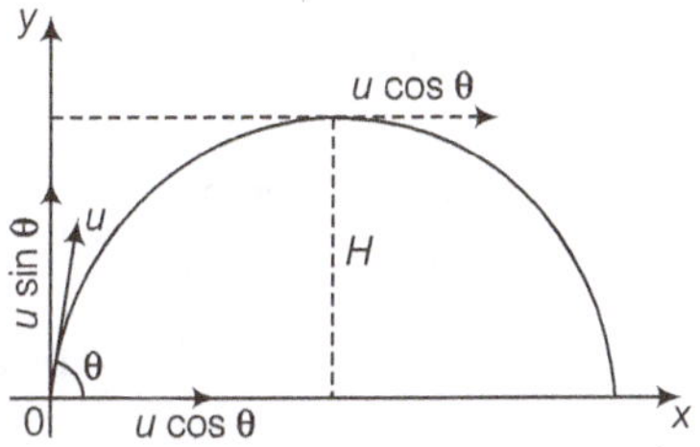

We know that time of flight, $T = \frac{2u\sin\theta}{g}$

At maximum height, $v_y = 0$

$\Rightarrow \quad v_y^2 = u_y^2 - 2gH = 0$

$\Rightarrow \quad H = \frac{u_y^2}{2g} = \frac{u^2\sin^2\theta}{2g}$

Angular momentum $= (mu\cos\theta)\, H$

$= (mu\cos\theta)\left(\frac{u^2\sin^2\theta}{2g}\right) = \frac{mu^3\sin^2\theta\cos\theta}{2g}$ [3]

12. (i) The time period of oscillation,

$T = 2\pi\sqrt{\frac{m}{k}}$

We know that, frequency $= \frac{1}{\text{Time period}}$

Then, $\nu = \frac{1}{2\pi}\sqrt{\frac{k}{m}}$

(ii) When spring was in equilibrium, then

Initial extension, $x_0 = \frac{mg}{k}$

As, the lift is going upward the pseudo force will be downward.

Hence, extension in equilibrium in accelerating lift $= \frac{m(g+a)}{k}$

Amplitude $= \frac{m(g+a)}{k} - \frac{mg}{k} = \frac{ma}{k}$ [3]

Or

Given equation is $x(t) = 10\cos\left(2\pi t + \frac{\pi}{6}\right)$

Compare with the standard equation,

$$x(t) = A\cos(\omega t + \phi)$$

where, A = amplitude = 10 m, $\omega = 2\pi\ s^{-1}$

and ϕ = phase difference = $\frac{\pi}{6}$.

(i) Put $t = 0$

$$\Rightarrow x(0) = A\cos\phi = A\cos\frac{\pi}{6}$$

$$= 10 \times \frac{\sqrt{3}}{2} = 5\sqrt{3}\ \text{m}$$

(ii) $v = \frac{dx}{dt} = -10\sin\left(2\pi t + \frac{\pi}{6}\right)2\pi$

$$\Rightarrow |v_{max}| = 10 \times 2\pi = 20\pi\ \text{m/s}$$

(iii) Angular frequency, $\omega = 2\pi\ \text{rad s}^{-1}$ [3]

13. Consider the diagram shown in the below figure. The mass m is at height h, then force of gravity on the object,

$$F = \frac{GMm}{(R+h)^2}$$

Acceleration due to gravity,

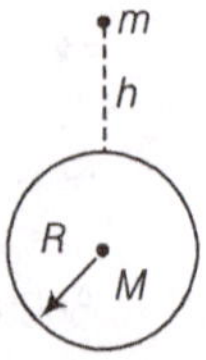

$$g' = \frac{F}{m} = \frac{GM}{(R+h)^2} = \frac{GM}{R^2\left(1+\frac{h}{R}\right)^2}$$

$$g' = \frac{g}{\left(1+\frac{h}{R}\right)^2}$$

(as $g = \frac{GM}{R^2}$ = acceleration due to gravity on the surface of the earth)

$$= g\left(1+\frac{h}{R}\right)^{-2}$$

$$\simeq g\left(1-\frac{2h}{R}\right) \quad (\because h << R)$$

$$\Rightarrow \quad g' \simeq g\left(1-\frac{2h}{R}\right)$$ [3]

14. (i) If two isothermal curves intersect, this implies that the pressure and volume of a gas are the same at two different temperatures, that's impossible.

(ii) In an isothermal process, the temperature of the system remains constant.

Let there is a small expansion of volume (dV), then work done by the gas

$$dW = p\,dV$$

Work done in expansion of volume from V_1 to V_2

$$W = \int_{V_1}^{V_2} p\,dV = \int_{V_1}^{V_2} \frac{nRT}{V}dV$$

$$= nRT(\ln V)_{V_1}^{V_2} = nRT\ln\frac{V_2}{V_1}$$

$$\Rightarrow \quad W = nRT\ln\left(\frac{V_2}{V_1}\right)$$

$$= 2.303\,nRT\log_{10}\left(\frac{V_2}{V_1}\right)$$ [3]

15. (i) Capillarity is the phenomenon of rise (or fall) of a liquid in a capillary tube as compared to the surroundings. [1]

(ii) We know that, $h = \frac{2T\cos\theta}{r\rho g}$

$$\Rightarrow \quad hr = \frac{2T\cos\theta}{\rho g} = \text{constant}$$

$$\Rightarrow \quad h_1r_1 = h_2r_2 \Rightarrow h_2 = \frac{h_1r_1}{r_2}$$

$$\Rightarrow \quad h_2 = (4)(3) = 12\ \text{cm}$$ [2]

16. Pressure, $p = 10$ atm $= 10 \times 1.013 \times 10^5$ Pa

($\because$ 1 atm $= 1.013 \times 10^5$ Pa)

$= 1.013 \times 10^6$ Pa

Bulk modulus for glass, $K = 37 \times 10^9\ \text{N/m}^2$

(Using value from table given in book)

Fractional change in volume $\left(\frac{\Delta V}{V}\right) = ?$

Bulk modulus, $K = \frac{p}{\Delta V/V} = \frac{pV}{\Delta V}$

$$\therefore \quad \frac{\Delta V}{V} = \frac{p}{K}$$

$$= \frac{1.013 \times 10^6}{37 \times 10^9}$$

$$= \frac{101.3}{37} \times 10^{-5}$$

$$= 2.74 \times 10^{-5}$$

$\therefore$ Fractional change in volume $\left(\frac{\Delta V}{V}\right) = 2.74 \times 10^{-5}$ [3]

17. Yes, the data follows the expected relation. The amplitude of a sound wave from a point source decreases as $A \propto \frac{1}{x}$. This means that when the distance doubles, the amplitude becomes half, and when the distance triples, the amplitude becomes one-third.

The amplitude decreases with distance because the wave spreads out in all directions, causing the energy to distribute over a larger area.

Since, energy is related to the square of amplitude, the amplitude reduces as distance increases.

FULLY SOLVED

18. Here, mass of astronaut $m = 72$ kg, vertical distance $h = 15$ m and acceleration of astronaut $a = \frac{g}{10}$.

(i) Force from the helicopter

$$F = mg + ma$$
$$= mg + \frac{mg}{10} = \frac{11mg}{10}$$ [1]

$\therefore$ Work done by force from the helicopter

$$W = F \times h = \frac{11mg}{10} \times h$$
$$W = \frac{11 \times 72 \times 10 \times 15}{10} = 11880 \text{ J}$$ [1]

(ii) Work done by gravitational force

$$W' = (mg)(h)(\cos 180°)$$
$$W' = -mgh$$
$$= -72 \times 10 \times 15 = -10800 \text{ J}$$ [1]

(iii) KE of astronaut K = network done on him

$$= W + W' = (11880 - 10800) \text{ J}$$
$$= +1080 \text{ J}$$ [1]

(iv) As $\text{KE} = \frac{1}{2}mv^2$, hence

Speed of the astronaut,

$$v = \sqrt{\frac{2K}{m}} = \sqrt{\frac{2 \times 1080}{72}} = 5.48 \text{ ms}^{-1}$$ [1]

Or

(i) Applying work-energy theorem,
work done by all the forces = change in kinetic energy

or $$W_{mg} + W_{\text{air}} = \frac{1}{2}mv^2$$ [1]

$$\therefore \quad W_{\text{air}} = \frac{1}{2}mv^2 - W_{mg} = \frac{1}{2}mv^2 - mgh$$
$$= \frac{1}{2} \times 5 \times (10)^2 - (5) \times (10) \times (20)$$
$$= -750 \text{ J}$$ [1]

(ii) According to work-energy theorem,
work done = change in kinetic energy of the vehicle

$$\therefore \quad W = K_f - K_i \text{ or } F \cdot dx = K_f - \frac{1}{2}mv_i^2$$ [1]

or $$F \cdot dx = K_f - \frac{1}{2} \times 10 \times (10)^2$$

or $$F \cdot dx = K_f - 500$$

or $$\int_{x=20}^{x=30} (-0.1)x\, dx = K_f - 500$$

or $$-0.1\left[\frac{x^2}{2}\right]_{x=20}^{x=30} = K_f - 500$$ [1]

or $$-0.1\left[\frac{(30)^2}{2} - \frac{(20)^2}{2}\right] = K_f - 500$$

or $$K_f - 500 = -0.1(450 - 200)$$

or $$K_f - 500 = -25$$

$$\therefore \quad K_f = 500 - 25 = 475 \text{ J}$$ [1]

19. (i) Given, $x = -2\sin\left(3t + \frac{\pi}{3}\right)$

$$= 2\cos\left(3t + \frac{\pi}{3} + \frac{\pi}{2}\right) = 2\cos\left(3t + \frac{5\pi}{6}\right)$$

On comparing with standard equation for SHM, $x = A\cos\left[\frac{2\pi}{T}t + \phi\right]$, we get amplitude

$A = 2$ cm (radius of the circle)

Phase angle, $\phi = \frac{5\pi}{6} = 150°$

Angular velocity, $\omega = \frac{2\pi}{T} = 3$ rad/s

This corresponding reference circle is plotted as below

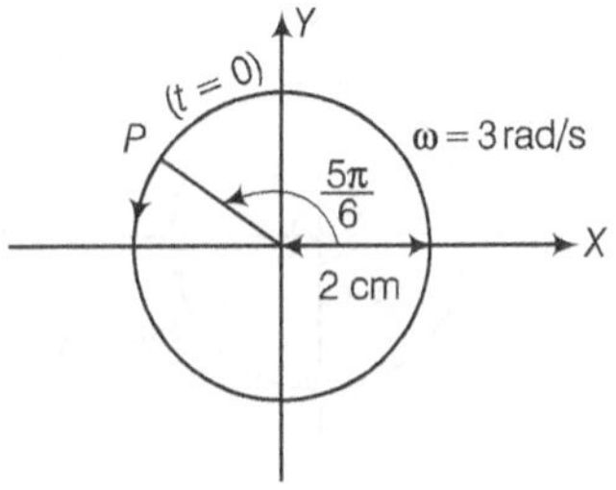

[1]

(ii) $x = A\cos\left(\frac{2\pi}{T}t + \phi\right)$ is the standard SHM equation.

The given equation, $x = \cos\left(\frac{\pi}{6} - t\right)$

$$x = \cos\left(t - \frac{\pi}{6}\right) [\text{as } \cos(-\theta) = \cos\theta]$$

On comparison, amplitude $A = 1$ cm (radius of the circle)

Phase angle, $\phi = -\frac{\pi}{6} = -30°$

Angular velocity, $\omega = \frac{2\pi}{T} = 1$ rad/s

The reference circle is plotted below.

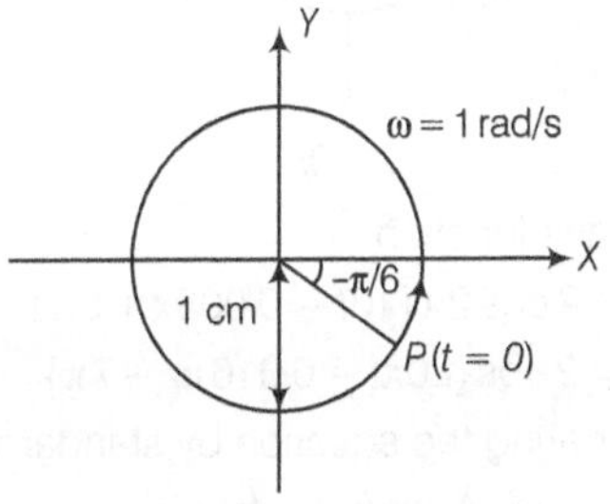

[1]

(iii) Given equation,

$$x = 3\sin\left(2\pi t + \frac{\pi}{4}\right)$$
$$= -3\cos\left[\left(2\pi t + \frac{\pi}{4}\right) + \frac{\pi}{2}\right]$$

FULLY SOLVED

$$\left[\because \cos\left(\frac{\pi}{2}+\theta\right) = -\sin\theta\right]$$

or $x = 3\cos\left(2\pi t + \dfrac{3\pi}{4}\right)$

On comparing with standard SHM equation

$$x = A\cos\left(\frac{2\pi}{T}t + \phi\right)$$

We get, $A = 3$ cm (radius of the circle)

Phase angle, $\phi = \dfrac{3\pi}{4} = 135°$

and $\omega = \dfrac{2\pi}{T} = 2\pi$ rad/s

The reference circle of the motion of the particle is plotted below.

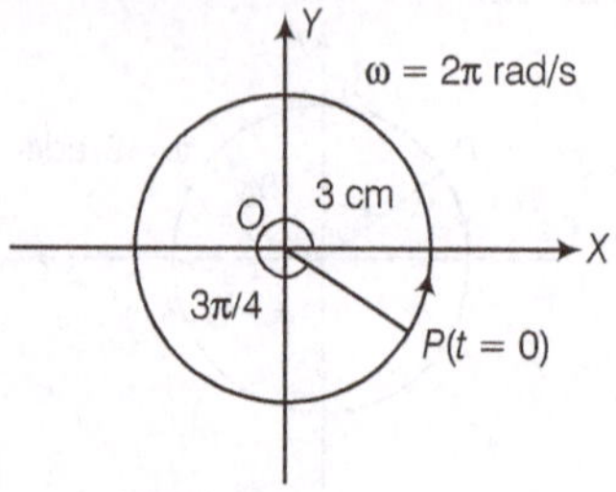

[1]

(iv) Given, $x = 2\cos \pi t$

Standard SHM equation, $x = A\cos\left(\dfrac{2\pi}{T}t + \phi\right)$

Then, we get amplitude, $A = 2$ cm (radius of circle)

Phase angle, $\phi = 0$

Angular velocity, $\omega = \pi$ rad/s

The reference circle of the motion is plotted below.

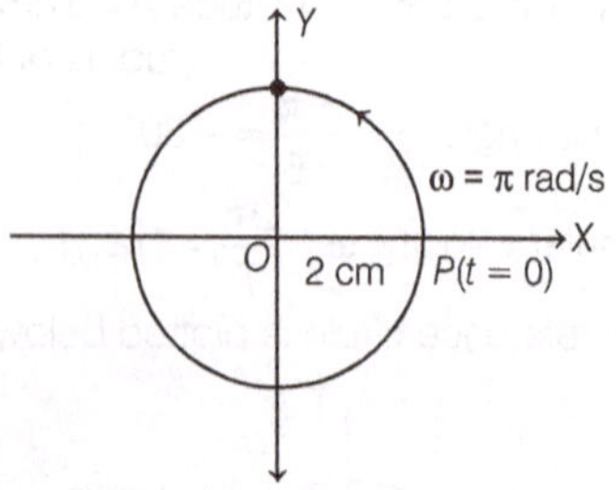

[2]

Or

Given wave function

$$y = 2\cos 2\pi\{10t - 0.008x + 3.5\}$$
$$y = 2\cos\{20\pi t - 0.016\pi x + 7\pi\}$$

On comparing the equation by standard equation

$$y = A\cos(\omega t - kx + \phi)$$

We get $A = 2$ cm

$\omega = 20\,\pi$ rad/s

$k = 0.016\,\pi$

(i) Phase difference,

$$\Delta\phi = \frac{2\pi}{\lambda} \times \text{Path difference}$$

$\therefore \quad \Delta\phi = 0.016\pi \times 4 \times 100 \quad \left[\because \dfrac{2\pi}{\lambda} = k\right]$ [1]

$= 6.4\pi$ rad

(ii) $\Delta\phi = \dfrac{2\pi}{\lambda} \times (0.5 \times 100)$

$= 0.016\pi \times 0.5 \times 100 = 0.8\pi$ rad [1]

(iii) $\Delta\phi = \dfrac{2\pi}{\lambda} \times \left(\dfrac{\lambda}{2}\right) = \pi$ rad [1]

(iv) $\Delta\phi = \dfrac{2\pi}{\lambda} \times \dfrac{3\lambda}{4} = \dfrac{3\pi}{2}$ rad [1]

(v) $T = \dfrac{2\pi}{\omega} = \dfrac{2\pi}{20\pi} = \dfrac{1}{10}$ s

$\therefore$ At $x = 100$ cm, $t = T$

$$\phi_1 = 20\pi T - 0.016\pi(100) + 7\pi$$
$$= 20\pi\left(\frac{1}{10}\right) - 1.6\pi + 7\pi$$
$$= 2\pi - 1.6\pi + 7\pi \quad \ldots(i)$$

Again at $x = 100$ cm, $t = 5$ s

$$\phi_2 = 20\pi(5) - 0.016\pi(100) + 7\pi$$
$$= 100\pi - (0.016 \times 100)\pi + 7\pi]$$
$$= 100\pi - 1.6\pi + 7\pi \quad \ldots(ii)$$

$\therefore$ From Eqs. (i) and (ii), we get

$$\Delta\phi = \phi_2 - \phi_1$$
$$= (100\pi - 1.6\pi + 7\pi) - (2\pi - 1.6\pi + 7\pi)$$
$$= 98\pi \text{ rad}$$ [1]

20. (i) No, the total kinetic energy, does not remain conserved during the short time when two billiard balls are in contact. At that time, balls are at rest and their KE is zero. In fact, all this KE has been transformed into elastic potential energy of balls. [1]

(ii) Yes, total linear momentum remains conserved during the short time of an elastic collision of two balls. The balls exert forces on one another due to which individual momenta of two balls change but total linear momentum remains conserved. [1]

(iii) For an inelastic, collision kinetic energy is not conserved but total linear momentum is conserved even now. [1]

(iv) As the potential energy depends only on the separation distance between the centres of balls, it means that conservative forces are in action (because PE changes due to conservative forces only). Hence, collision is surely inelastic collision. [2]

SAMPLE QUESTION PAPER 2

A Highly Simulated Sample Question Paper for ISC Class XI

PHYSICS (Unsolved)

Time : 3 hours **Max. Marks : 70**

General Instructions

1. This paper is divided into four **sections A, B, C** and **D.** Answer all questions.
2. **Section A** consists of one question having sub-parts of one mark each.
3. **Section B** consists of seven questions of two marks each.
4. **Section C** consists of nine questions of three marks each.
5. **Section D** consists of three questions of five marks each.
6. Internal choices have been provided in two questions each in Section B, Section C and Section D.

UNSOLVED

Section–A

[14 Marks]

1. A. Choose the correct alternative (a), (b), (c) or (d) for each of the following questions given below. [7 × 1]

(i) A thin rod of mass m elongates by l when a body of mass m is suspended from it. The work done is • *Recall*

(a) mgl (b) $\frac{1}{2}mgl$ (c) $2\ mgl$ (d) zero

(ii) Pressure is applied to an enclosed fluid, it is • *Understanding*

(a) increased and applied to every part of the fluid

(b) diminished and transmitted to the walls of the container

(c) increased in proportion to the walls of the fluid and then transmitted

(d) transmitted unchanged to every portion of the fluid and the walls of container

(iii) The ratio of frequencies of two pendulums are 2 : 3, then their lengths are in ratio • *Analysis*

(a) $\sqrt{2/3}$ (b) $\sqrt{3/2}$

(c) 4/9 (d) 9/4

(iv) Which of the following is incorrect regarding the first law of thermodynamics? • *Understanding*

(a) It is not applicable to any cyclic process

(b) It is a restatement of the principle of conservation of energy

(c) It introduces the concept of the internal energy

(d) Both (a) and (c)

(v) A one kilowatt motor is used to pump water from a well 10 m deep. The quantity of water pumped out per second is nearly • *Application*

(a) 1kg (b) 10 kg

(c) 100 kg (d) 1000 kg

(vi) **Assertion** Earth has atmosphere, whereas moon doesn't have any atmosphere. • *Understanding*

Reason The escape velocity on moon is very small as compared to that on earth.

In the light of the above statements, choose the correct answer from the options given below

(a) Both Assertion and Reason are correct and Reason is the correct explanation of the Assertion.

(b) Both Assertion and Reason are correct but Reason is not the correct explanation of the Assertion.

(c) Assertion is correct but Reason is incorrect.

(d) Assertion is incorrect but Reason is correct.

(vii) **Assertion** Speed of sound is more in liquids.

Reason Liquids and solids have higher densities than gases. • *Understanding*

(a) Both Assertion and Reason are correct and Reason is the correct explanation of the Assertion.

(b) Both Assertion and Reason are correct but Reason is not the correct explanation of the Assertion.

(c) Assertion is correct but Reason is incorrect.

(d) Assertion is incorrect but Reason is correct.

B. Answer the following questions briefly. [7×1]

(i) If the radius of the earth were increased by a factor of 3, then by what factor would its density have to be changed to keep g the same? • *Understanding*

(ii) What is the value of bulk modulus for an incompressible liquid? • *Recall*

(iii) All constants are dimensionless. Comment. • *Recall*

(iv) Shopkeepers suggests Rahul that, while using the sprayer (which has water in it) dissolve some soap in it, as it becomes easy to spray water. Why? • *Application*

(v) A particle is moving in a straight line. Is it possible for it to maintain the motion in the same direction while the acceleration is in the reverse direction? • *Analysis*

(vi) On what factors does the value of angle of contact depend? • *Understanding*

(vii) Plot a graph showing the variation of specific heat of water with temperature. • *Application*

Section–B

[14 Marks]

2. Indicate the forces acting on a block of mass m resting on a plane inclined at an angle θ.

• *Recall and Analysis* [2]

Or

The below figure is the part of a horizontal stretched net. Section AB is stretched with a force of 10 N, then determine the forces in the sections BC and BF. • *Recall and Analysis* [2]

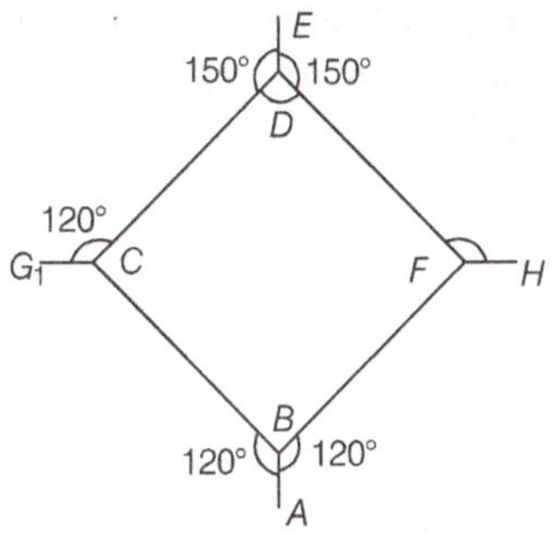

3. You drive your car along a curving road at constant speed.

(i) Does your kinetic energy change, why?

(ii) Is the work done by the force accelerating your car positive, negative or zero?

• *Understanding and Analysis* [2]

4. Courier companies always wrap porcelian objects in paper or straw before packing for transportation. Why? • *Application* [2]

5. State what happens when a wave suffers reflection at the • *Understanding*

(i) closed end or rigid boundary

(ii) an open boundary? [2]

Or

Two particles of same amplitude A and frequency ν are in SHM and meet each other at point $x = \frac{A}{2}$ from the mean position but in mutually opposite directions. What is the phase difference between these motions? • *Analysis* [2]

6. What is the significance of • *Application*

(i) wetting agents used by dyers?

(ii) water proofing agents? [2]

7. The speed-time graph for a car is shown in figure below • *Analysis*

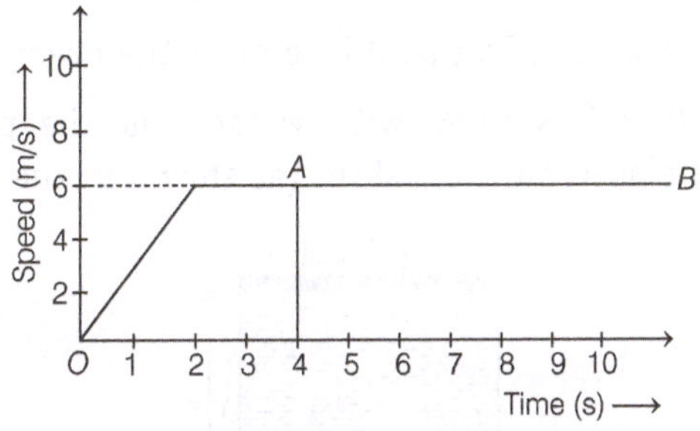

(i) Find how far does the car travel in the first 4 s. Shade the area on the graph that represents the distance travelled by the car during the period.

(ii) Which part of the graph represents uniform motion of the car? [2]

8. Each side of a cube is measured to be 7.203 m. What is the total surface area of the cube to appropriate significant figures? • *Understanding* [2]

UNSOLVED

Section–C

[27 Marks]

9. The block A of weight 100 N rests on a frictionless inclined plane of slope angle 30° as shown in the figure. A flexible cord attached to A passes over a frictionless pulley and is connected to block B of weight w. Find the weight w for which the system is in equilibrium. • *Recall and Understanding* [3]

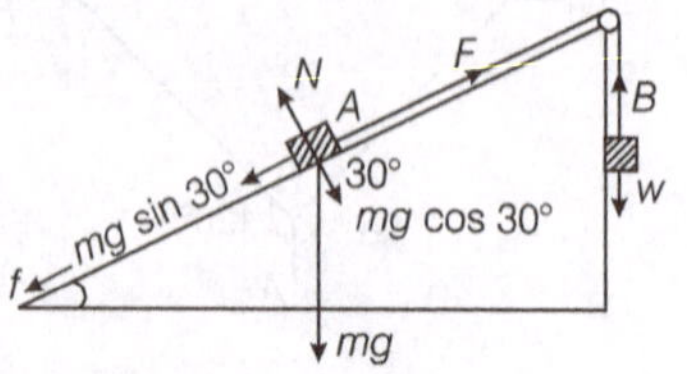

10. (i) Why does a gas have two molar specific heats? • *Understanding*

(ii) Which one is greater and why? • *Understanding*

(iii) What is the difference between the two molar specific heats and what is their ratio? • *Recall* [3]

Or The electrical resistance in ohm of a certain thermometer varies with temperature according to the approximate law $R = R_0 [1 + \alpha (T - T_0)]$.

The resistance is 101.6 Ω at the triple point of water 273.16 K and 165.5 Ω at the normal melting point of lead (600.5 K). What is the temperature when the resistance is 123.4 Ω? • *Application* [3]

11. A lift pump of 5 HP pumps water in an overhead tank of 4 m × 3 m × 2 m size and situated at a height of 15 m from the ground level. The efficiency of the pump is 75%. What is the time required to completely fill the overhead tank? • *Application* [3]

12. What do you mean by centre of mass of a rigid body? How will you specify the location of the centre of mass of the body? • *Understanding* [3]

Or

Explain the concept of torque. Obtain an expression for torque in polar coordinates. • *Understanding* [3]

13. Using the expression for pressure exerted by a gas, deduce Avogadro's law and Graham's law of diffusion. • *Recall and Analysis* [3]

14. (i) What is the cause of rolling friction? • *Analysis* [1]

(ii) Establish the relation between linear velocity and angular velocity. • *Recall* [2]

15. (i) Will a ship ride higher in water of an land lake or in the ocean, why? • *Understanding* [1]

(ii) A container of area 0.02 m^2 is filled with water. Find the pressure at the bottom of the container if a weight is placed on the piston. (as shown in the figure). • *Application*

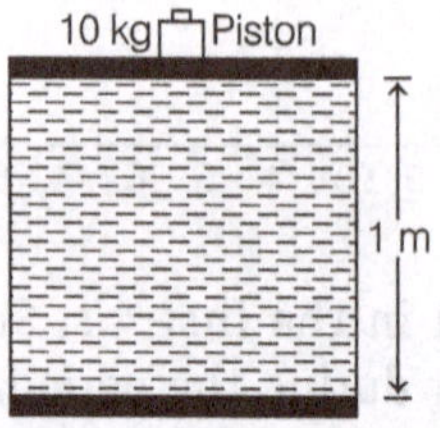

[2]

16. Find the displacement of a simple harmonic oscillator at which its PE is half of the maximum energy of the oscillator. • *Application* [3]

UNSOLVED

17. A student records the following data for the work done (W) by a constant force on an object as it moves along a straight path. The object starts from rest, and its displacement (x) is measured at different points. Verify (for any two) that these observations match the expected theoretical values of W. • *Analysis* [3]

x	Work done (W)
$x = 0$	0
$x = a$	$\frac{W_0}{2}$
$x = 2a$	W_0
$x = 3a$	$\frac{3W_0}{2}$

Section–D

[15 Marks]

18. (i) Is the centrifugal force a reaction of the centripetal force? Give reason for your answer. • *Understanding*

(ii) What is the effect of reversing the sense of revolution on the centripetal force? • *Understanding*

(iii) What provide the centripetal force to a car taking a turn on level road? • *Recall*

(iv) What is the angle of banking? • *Recall*

(v) What is the advantage of banking? • *Understanding* [5]

Or

The bob A of a pendulum released from horizontal to the vertical hits another bob B of the same mass at rest on a table as shown in figure. • *Understanding* [5]

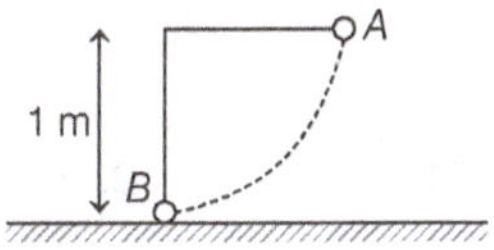

If the length of the pendulum is 1 m, calculate

(a) the height to which bob A will rise after collision.

(b) the speed with which bob B starts moving.

Neglect the size of the bobs and assume the collision to be elastic.

19. A player throws a ball upwards with an initial speed of 29.4 ms^{-1}.

(i) What is the direction of acceleration during the upward motion of the ball? • *Understanding*

(ii) What are the velocity and acceleration of the ball at the highest point of its motion? • *Recall*

(iii) Choose $x = 0$ and $t = 0$ be the location and time at its highest point, vertically downward direction to be the positive direction of x-axis and give the signs of position, velocity and acceleration of the ball during its upward and downward motion. • *Analysis*

(iv) To what height does the ball rise and after how long does the ball return to the player's hands? (Take $g = 9.8$ ms^{-2} and neglect air resistance) • *Application* [5]

Or It is a common observation that rain clouds can be at about a kilometre altitude above the ground.

(i) If a rain drop falls from such a height freely under gravity, what will be its speed? Also, calculate in km/h ($g = 10$ m/s^2). • *Application*

UNSOLVED

(ii) A typical rain drop is about 4 mm diameter. Momentum is mass × speed in magnitude. Estimate its momentum when it hits ground. • *Application*

(iii) Estimate time required to flatten the drop. • *Understanding*

(iv) Rate of change of momentum is force. Estimate how much force such a drop would exert on you? • *Application*

(v) Estimate the order of magnitude of force on umbrella. Typical lateral separation between two rain drops is 5 cm. • *Application*

(Assume that umbrella is circular and has a diameter of 1 m and cloth is not pierced through it). [5]

Read the passage given below and answer the questions that follow.

20. Bernoulli's principle is passed on the law of conservation of energy and applied to ideal fluids. It states that the same of pressure energy per unit valume, kinetic energy per unit volume and potential energy per unit volume of an incompressible, non-viscous fluid in a streamlined irrotational flow remains constant at every cross-section through out the liquid flow.

Bernoulli's theorem ideally applies to fluids with zero viscosity or non-viscous fluids and it is applicable only to streamline flow of a fluid. It is not valid for non-steady viscosity or turbulent flow.

(i) Can Bernoulli's equation be used to describe the flow of water through a rapid in a river? Explain. • *Understanding* [1]

(ii) To keep a piece of a paper horizontal; you should blow over, not under it. • *Application* [1]

(iii) A spinning cricket ball in air does not follow a parabolic trajectory. • *Analysis* [3]

UNSOLVED

Answers

1. A. (i)-b, (ii)-d, (iii)-d, (iv)-d, (v)-b, (vi)-a, (vii)-a

B. (i) $\rho' = \frac{\rho}{3}$

2. *Or* 10 N **5.** *Or* $\phi_1 - \phi_2 = \frac{2\pi}{3}$ **8.** $A = 311.3\ m^2$ **9.** $w = 50$ N **10.** *Or* $T_2 = 384.3$ K

11. $t = 22$ min 45 s **15.** (ii) 14700 N **16.** $\frac{A}{\sqrt{2}}$

19. (iv) 44.1 m, 6 s

Or (i) 510 km/h (ii) 4.7×10^{-3} kg m/s (iii) 2×10^{-5} s (iv) 168 N (v) 53760 N

SAMPLE QUESTION PAPER 3

A Highly Simulated Sample Question Paper for ISC Class XI

PHYSICS (Unsolved)

Time : 3 hours **Max. Marks : 70**

General Instructions

1. This paper is divided into four **sections A, B, C** and **D**. Answer all questions.
2. **Section A** consists of one question having sub-parts of one mark each.
3. **Section B** consists of seven questions of two marks each.
4. **Section C** consists of nine questions of three marks each.
5. **Section D** consists of three questions of five marks each.
6. Internal choices have been provided in two questions each in Section B, Section C and Section D.

UNSOLVED

Section–A

[14 Marks]

1. A. Choose the correct alternative (a), (b), (c) or (d) for each of the following questions given below. [7 × 1]

(i) In the formula $x = 3yz^2$, x and z have dimensions of capacitance and magnetic induction, respectively. The dimension of y in MKS system are • *Understanding*

(a) $[M^{-2}L^{-2}T^4A^4]$ (b) $[M^{-3}L^{-3}T^4A^5]$ (c) $[M^{-3}L^{-2}T^8A^4]$ (d) $[M^{-1}L^{-4}T^2A^4]$

(ii) The kinematic equations of rectilinear motion for constant acceleration is • *Recall*

(a) $v = v_0 + at$ (b) $x = v_0 t + \frac{1}{2}at^2$

(c) $v^2 = v_0^2 + 2ax$ (d) All of these

(iii) A particle of man 2 kg is moving on a circular path of radius 10 m with a speed of 5 ms^{-1} and its speed is increasing at rate of 3 ms^{-1}. Find the force acting on the particle. • *Understanding*

(a) 5 N (b) 10 N (c) 12 N (d) 14 N

(iv) **Assertion** If three forces F_1, F_2 and F_3 are represented by three sides of a triangle and $F_1 + F_2 = -F_3$, then these three forces are concurrent forces and satisfy the condition for equilibrium.

Reason A triangle made up of three forces F_1, F_2 and F_3 as its sides taken in the same order, satisfy the condition for translatory equilibrium.

In the light of the above statements, choose the most appropriate answer from the options given below. • *Understanding*

(a) Both Assertion and Reason are correct and Reason is the correct explanation of the Assertion.

(b) Both Assertion and Reason are correct but Reason is not the correct explanation of the Assertion.

(c) Assertion is correct but Reason is incorrect.
(d) Assertion is incorrect but Reason is correct.

(v) In figure, pressure inside a spherical drop is more than pressure outside. (S = surface tension and r = radius of bubble).

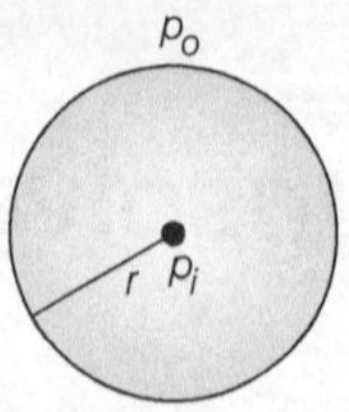

The extra surface energy, if radius of bubble is increased by Δr, is • *Application*

(a) $4\pi r\ \Delta rS$
(b) $8\pi r\ \Delta rS$
(c) $2\pi r\ \Delta rS$
(d) $10\pi r\ \Delta rS$

(vi) In the given figure, if the dimensions of the wire are the same and materials are different, Young's modulus is more for • *Analysis*

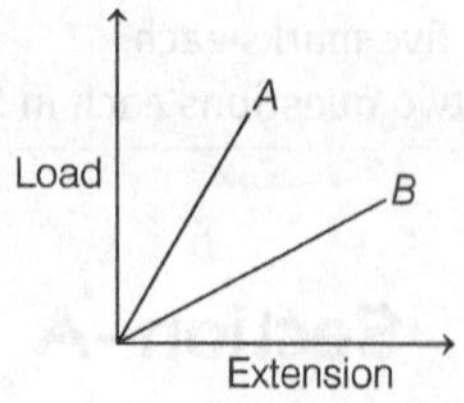

(a) A
(b) B
(c) Both
(d) None of these

(vii) **Assertion** In gases, the molecules move faster and move long distance without colliding.
Reason In gases, the interatomic forces are negligible.

(a) Both Assertion and Reason are correct and Reason is the correct explanation of the Assertion.
(b) Both Assertion and Reason are correct but Reason is not the correct explanation of the Assertion.
(c) Assertion is correct but Reason is incorrect.
(d) Assertion is incorrect but Reason is correct.

B. Answer the following questions briefly. [7 × 1]

(i) Write the dimensional formula of torque. • *Recall*

(ii) While driving a car around a curve, an observer sees a road sign. Is the road sign moving with respect to the car? Is it accelerated with respect to the car? • *Application*

(iii) Under what condition is the relation $s = vt$, constant? • *Application*

(iv) The linear speed of a planet around the sun is not constant in its orbit. Why? • *Application*

(v) Is it possible to cool a closed room with a fan that circulates air within that room? • *Application*

(vi) Calculate the impulse necessary to step 1500 kg car travelling at 90 km/h. • *Understanding*

(vii) Is it possible for a body to be accelerated without speeding up or slowing down? If it is so, give example. • *Application*

UNSOLVED

Section–B

[14 Marks]

2. (i) The density of air is 1.293 kg/m^3. Express it in CGS units. • *Recall* [1]

(ii) Why pressure is a scalar quantity? • *Recall* [1]

Or

Torricelli's barometer used mercury. Pascal duplicated it using French wine of density 948 kg/m^3. Determine the height of the wine column for normal atmospheric pressure. • *Understanding* [2]

The pressure exerted by a liquid column

where, $p = h\rho g$, h = height of liquid column

ρ = density of liquid

g = acceleration due to gravity.

3. (i) Why fruits fall down from a tree, when its branches are shaken? • *Recall*

(ii) A 30 kg shell is flying at 48 m/s. When it explodes, one part of it of mass 18 kg stops, while the remaining part flies off. Find the velocity of the later. • *Understanding* [2]

4. Explain perfectly inelastic collision in one dimension. • *Recall* [2]

5. A bullet fired at an angle of 30° with the horizontal hits the ground 3 km away. By adjusting its angle of projection, can one hope to hit a target 5 km away? Assume the muzzle speed to be fixed, and neglect air resistance. • *Understanding* [2]

Or

What will be the effect on maximum height of a projectile when its angle of projection is changed from 30° to 60°, keeping the same initial velocity of projection? • *Application* [2]

6. Answer the following questions.

(i) The frequency of oscillation of a simple pendulum mounted in a cabin that is falling freely under gravity is zero. Why? • *Application*

(ii) The motion of an artificial satellite around the earth cannot be taken as SHM. Why? • *Recall* [2]

7. A block of marble whose weight is 2.0×10^4 N is suspended from a cable supported crane as shown in figure. The cable's weight is 4.0×10^2 N. Find the tension in the top and bottom of the cable, when the block is accelerating downward at the rate of 2.5 m/s^2. • *Understanding*

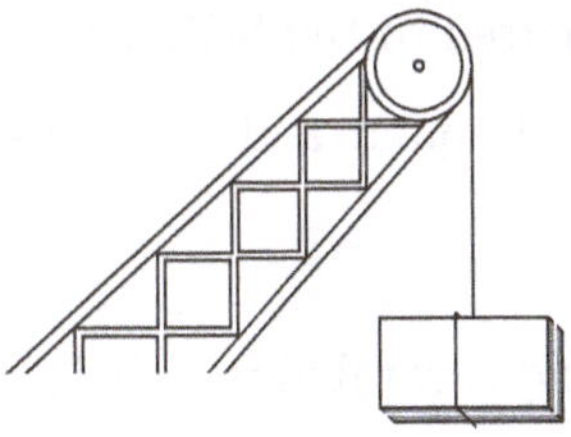

[2]

8. Figure shows plot of $\frac{pV}{T}$ versus p for 1.00×10^{-3} kg of oxygen gas at two different temperatures. • *Understanding and Analysis*

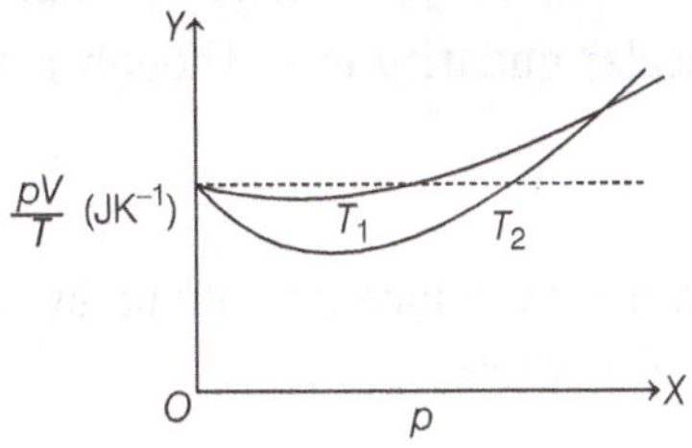

UNSOLVED

(i) What does the dotted plot signify?

(ii) Which is true, $T_1 > T_2$ or $T_1 < T_2$?

(iii) What is the value of $\frac{pV}{T}$, where the curves meet on the Y-axis? [2]

Section–C [27 Marks]

9. The bob A of a pendulum released from horizontal to the vertical hits another bob B of the same mass at rest on a table as shown below in the figure. • *Analysis*

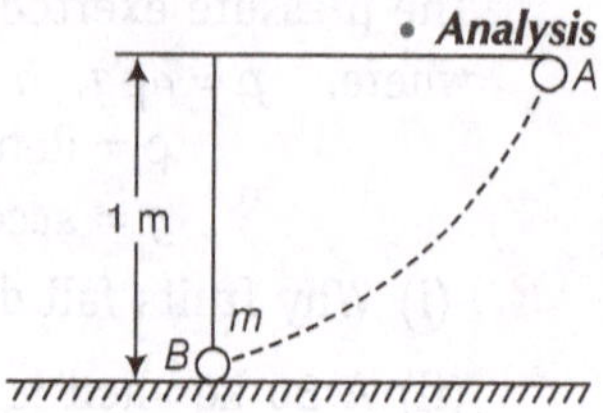

If the length of the pendulum is 1 m. Calculate

(i) the height to which bob A will rise after collision.

(ii) the speed with which bob B starts moving.

Neglect the size of the bobs and assume the collision to be elastic. [3]

10. (i) The length of a wire is cut to half.

(a) What will be the effect on the increase in its length under a given load?

(b) What will be the effect on the maximum load which it can bear?

(ii) Within elastic limit, what is the slope of stress-strain curve? • *Analaysis* [3]

Or

The relative velocity between two parallel layers of water is 8 cms^{-1} and the perpendicular distance between them is 0.1 cm. Calculate the velocity gradient. • *Understanding* [3]

11. Show that the velocity with which an object is to be projected from the surface of the earth so that it may just overcome the gravitational pull of the earth is $\sqrt{\frac{2Gm}{R}}$. • *Understanding* [3]

12. Two cars A and B are travelling in the same direction with the velocities v_a and v_b, respectively. When the car A is at a distance d and behind the car B, the brakes are applied on A, causing a deceleration at the rate a. Show that to prevent a collision between A and B, it is necessary that $v_a - v_b < \sqrt{2ad}$. • *Understanding* [3]

Or A batsman deflects a ball by an angle of 45° without changing its initial speed, which is equal to 54 km/h. What is the impulse imparted to the ball? Mass of the ball is 0.15 kg. • *Understanding* [3]

13. Obtain a relation between speed of sound and rms speed of gas molecules in a given gaseous medium. • *Analysis* [3]

14. Explain why?

(i) A stone tied at the end of string is whirled is a circle. If the string breaks, the stone flies away tangentially. Why? • *Recall*

(ii) Atmospheric pressure at a height of about 6 km decreases to nearly half its value at the sea level though the height of the atmosphere is more than 100 km. • *Analysis*

(iii) Hydrostatic pressure is a scalar quantity even though pressure is force divided by area. • *Analysis* [3]

15. Explain, why?

(i) 500 J of work is done on a gas to reduce its volume by compression adiabatically. What is the change in internal energy of the gas? • *Understanding*

UNSOLVED

(ii) The coolant in a chemical or a nuclear plant, i.e. the liquid used to prevent the different parts of a plant from getting too hot should have high specific heat. • *Application*

(iii) Air pressure in a car tyres increases during driving. • *Application*

(iv) The climate of a harbour town is more temperate than that of a town in a desert at the same latitude. • *Application* [3]

16. When the load of a wire is increased from 3 kg-wt to 5 kg-wt, the length of that wire changes from 0.61 mm to 1.02 mm. Calculate the change in the elastic potential energy of the wire. • *Understanding* [3]

17. A student records the following data for the displacement (x) of a simple harmonic oscillator at different time intervals (t). The motion follows the equation $x = A\cos(\omega t)$. Verify (for any two) that these observations are in good agreement with the expected theoretical values of x. • *Application* [3]

Time (t)	Displacement (x)
$t = 0$	A
$t = \frac{T}{4}$	$\frac{A}{\sqrt{2}}$
$t = \frac{T}{2}$	0
$t = \frac{3T}{4}$	$-\frac{A}{\sqrt{2}}$

Section–D

[15 Marks]

18. Consider a block of mass 700 g is fastened to a spring having spring constant of 70 N/m. Find out the following parameters, if block is pulled a distance of 14 cm from its mean position on a frictionless surface and released from rest at $t = 0$. • *Analysis*

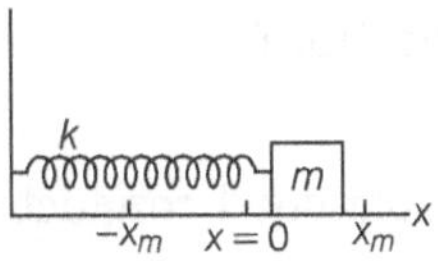

(i) The angular frequency, the frequency and the period of the resulting motion.

(ii) The amplitude of the oscillation.

(iii) The maximum speed of the oscillating block.

(iv) The maximum acceleration of the block.

(v) The phase constant and hence the displacement function $x(t)$. [5]

Or (a) A spring of force constant 1200 Nm^{-1} is mounted on a horizontal table. A mass of 3.0 kg is attached to the free end of the spring, pulled sideways to a distance of 2.0 cm and then released. • *Analysis*

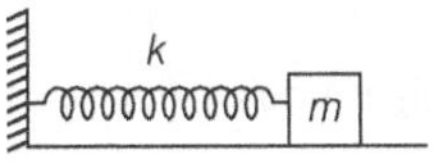

(i) What is the frequency of oscillation of the mass?

(ii) What is the maximum acceleration of the mass?

UNSOLVED

(iii) What is the maximum speed of the mass?

(b) A spring compressed by 0.1 m develops a restoring force 10 N. A body of mass 4 kg placed on it. Deduce • *Understanding*

(i) the force constant of the spring.

(ii) the depression of the spring under the weight of the body (take $g = 10$ N/kg)

(iii) the period of oscillation, the body is distributed and

(iv) frequency of oscillation [5]

19. (a) Magnitude of force F experienced by a certain object moving with speed v is given by $F = kv^2$, where k is constant. Find the dimensions of k. • *Understanding*

(b) The wavelength λ associated with a moving particle depends upon its mass m, its velocity v and Planck's constant h. Show dimensional relation between them. • *Understanding*

(c) A laser signal is beamed towards a planet from earth and its echo is received 680 s later. If distance of planet be 1.02×10^{11} m, what is the speed of laser light? [5]

Or

(a) (i) How many metric tons are there in teragram? • *Understanding*

(ii) What is common between bar and torr? • *Understanding*

(b) Distinguish between fundamental and derived units. • *Recall*

(c) The radius of atom is of the order of 2 Å and radius of a nucleus is of the order of fermi. How many magnitudes higher is the volume of atom as compared to the volume of nucleus?

• *Understanding* [5]

UNSOLVED

Read the passage given below and answer the questions that follow

20. Heat is the form of energy which can flow from one body to another due to their temperature difference in the form of radiations, molecular vibrations, molecular displacement etc. These process of heat flow are collectively known as heat transfer.
There are three modes of heat transfer namely (i) conduction (ii) convection (iii) radiation. Generally in solids, heat is transferred by the process of conduction and the heat from the sun reaches to the earth by radiation. [5]

(i) What do you understand by convection? • *Recall*

(ii) What is the thermal radiation? • *Recall*

(iii) Why are cooking utensils made from good conductors of heat? • *Recall*

(iv) Can we boil water inside in the earth's satellite? • *Recall*

(v) Write the two difference between the conduction and radiation. • *Recall*

Answers

1. A. (i)-c, (ii)-d, (iii)-a, (iv)-c, (v)-b, (vi)-a, (vii)-a **B.** (vi) Impulse = 37500 kg ms^{-1}

2. (i) $\rho = 0.001293$ g/cm^3 *Or* 10.5 m **3.** (ii) $v_2 = 120$ m/s

7. $T_1 = 1.52 \times 10^4$ N, $T_2 = 1.49 \times 10^4$ N **9.** (i) Ball *A* does not rise at all (ii) $v = 4.42$ m/s

10. *Or* velocity gradient = 80 s^{-1} **12.** *Or* Impulse = 4.16 kg ms^{-1}

16. 16.03×10^{-3} J

18. (i) 10 rad/s, 1.59 Hz, 630 ms (ii) 0.14 m (iii) 1.4 m/s (iv) 14 m/s (v) 0.14 cos10t

Or (a) (i) 3.2 s^{-1} (ii) 8.0 ms^{-2} (iii) 0.4 m/s (b) (i) 100 N/m (ii) 0.4 m (iii) 1.26 s (iv) 0.8 Hz

19. (a) [M^{-1}L^{-1}] (b) $\lambda = \dfrac{kh}{mv}$ 3×10^8 m/s *Or* (a) (i)10^6 (ii) 760 torr (c) 8×10^{15}